CRICKET
RECORD FILE

BRUCE SMITH
SALIM PARVEZ

First published in Great Britain in 2000 by
Virgin Books
an imprint of Virgin Publishing Ltd
Thames Wharf Studios
Rainville Road
London W6 9HA

A catalogue record for this book is available from the British Library.

ISBN 0 7535 0466 9

Designed by Roger Kohn
Typeset by Mark Webb
Printed and bound by Mackays of Chatham plc, Chatham, Kent

CONTENTS

TEST MATCH RECORDS

TEST MATCH SCORECARDS 1946–2000

ONE-DAY INTERNATIONAL RECORDS

ONE-DAY
INTERNATIONAL SCORECARDS

CRICKET RECORD FILE

English cricket has had its ups and downs during the last fifty years. The heyday of the fifties threw up names like Hutton, Cowdrey and May when the title of 'top dog' was more often than not a tight battle between the English and the Aussies. Now we've had the disappointment of the nineties as English cricket hit rock bottom as the unofficial worst team on Planet Earth. But was England really that bad in the last decade of the millennium? The stats suggest that in fact the eighties, when England won less than one-fifth of its Test games, was its worst period. In the nineties the international team won just less than a quarter of its Test games. Is this the start of a recovery of English cricket at the top-most level?

Was Mike Brearley the best England captain ever? Did Ian Botham's undoubted talent swing results in England's favour? Was David Gower's greatest moment in a biplane? Which players forged the best wicket stands down the years and, more importantly, which innings were actually responsible for winning games? Did certain players build their reputations against the lesser nations? Lots of questions but you will find all the answers to this sort of query within these pages, plus many more points of discussion and interest.

Built around detailed scorecards for every England Test Match and One-Day International since 1950, the *Virgin Cricket Record File* provides a unique analysis of every aspect of English cricket on a decade-by-decade basis. You can thumb through the precise records of what occurred in any given match but you can equally see trends in the team performances over different decades as groups of players come and go. English team performances also depend on the strength of opposition and the statistics show how England has coped with the West Indian fast bowlers in Test cricket and with the Sri Lankan pinch hitters in One-Day Internationals.

I hope you will find this to be one of the most comprehensive cricket books covering this period of time. Its 50-year scope offers an insight into long-term trends which are undetectable in an annual publication. One thing is for sure: at under a tenner, it is the most cost-effective analysis and I hope that it will accompany you to matches or to the arm of your favourite chair when you are settling in to watch the next big series.

The information herein is taken from the extensive computer database I have developed down the years, which I believe to be about as error-free as possible. However, I am a realist and would appreciate hearing from anyone who spots any errors that have crept into this book; anyone doing so will receive a credit in the next edition.

CONTACT DETAILS

email: SmithBruce@Hotmail.com
Address: PO Box 382, St Albans, Herts, AL2 3JD

ONE-DAY INTERNATIONAL SCORECARDS

Because of space it hasn't been possible to provide individual headings to each of the scorecards – so what follows is a description of how each one is laid out.

Each scorecard begins with the name of England's international opponent, followed by an information panel containing the game number and tournament title, venue, date, outcome of the toss and result summary. Each innings contains individual batsmen details – their name followed by 'how out' and their score. The extras show byes (b), leg byes (lb), wides (w) and no balls (nb). The last two items are the number of overs completed and a total score for the innings. This is followed by FoW (Fall of each Wicket), showing at which score in the innings each wicket went down.

Next comes a table showing the fielding side's bowling figures. The four columns which follow the bowler's name represent overs, maidens (overs without score), runs conceded and wickets taken. In the Test Match scorecards, the second innings details are shown in the right-hand column.

THANK YOU

Many thanks to both Salim Parvez and Mark Webb for their invaluable help in producing this book. Salim helped produce many of the unique statistics for the Test and ODI matches, while Mark helped format all the scorecards for inclusion in the *Record File*.

TEST MATCH RECORDS OF THE LAST FIVE DECADES
SUMMARY OF ALL MATCHES SERIES BY SERIES

YEAR	CAPTAIN	VS	V	P	W	L	D
1950	NWD Yardley (3)	West Indies	H	4	1	3	–
	FR Brown (1)						
1950-51	FR Brown	Australia	A	5	1	4	–
1950-51	FR Brown	New Zealand	A	2	1	–	1
1951	FR Brown	South Africa	H	5	3	1	1
1951-52	ND Howard (4)	India	A	5	1	1	3
	DB Carr (1)						
1952	L Hutton	India	H	4	3	–	1
1953	L Hutton	Australia	H	5	1	–	4
1953-54	L Hutton	West Indies	A	5	2	2	1
1954	L Hutton (2)	Pakistan	H	4	1	1	2
	DS Sheppard (2)						
1954-55	L Hutton	Australia	A	5	3	1	1
1954-55	L Hutton	New Zealand	A	2	2	–	–
1955	PBH May	South Africa	H	5	3	2	–
1956	PBH May	Australia	H	5	2	1	2
1956-57	PBH May	South Africa	A	5	2	2	1
1957	PBH May	West Indies	H	5	3	–	2
1958	PBH May	New Zealand	H	5	4	–	1
1958-59	PBH May	Australia	A	5	–	4	1
1958-59	PBH May	New Zealand	A	2	1	–	1
1959	PBH May (3)	India	H	5	5	–	–
	MC Cowdrey (2)						
1959-60	PBH May (3)	West Indies	A	5	1	–	4
	MC Cowdrey (2)						
1950s Total Decade				**88**	**40**	**22**	**26**
Success Ratio in the 50s		**45.45%**					

YEAR	CAPTAIN	VS	V	P	W	L	D
1960	MC Cowdrey	South Africa	H	5	–	3	2
1961	MC Cowdrey (2)	Australia	H	5	1	2	2
	PBH May (3)						
1961-62	ER Dexter	Pakistan	A	3	1	–	2
1961-62	ER Dexter	India	A	5	–	2	3
1962	ER Dexter (4)	Pakistan	H	5	4	–	1
	MC Cowdrey (1)						
1962-63	ER Dexter	Australia	A	5	1	1	3
1962-63	ER Dexter	New Zealand	A	3	3	–	–
1963	ER Dexter	West Indies	H	5	1	3	1
1963-64	MJK Smith	India	A	5	–	–	5
1964	ER Dexter	Australia	H	5	–	1	4
1964-65	MJK Smith	South Africa	A	5	1	–	4
1965	MJK Smith	New Zealand	H	3	3	–	–
1965	MJK Smith	South Africa	H	3	–	1	2
1965-66	MJK Smith	Australia	A	5	1	1	3
1965-66	MJK Smith	New Zealand	A	3	–	–	3
1966	MJK Smith (1)	West Indies	H	5	1	3	1
	MC Cowdrey (3)						
	DB Close (1)						

YEAR	CAPTAIN	VS	V	P	W	L	D
1967	DB Close	India	H	3	3	–	–
1967	DB Close	Pakistan	H	3	2	–	1
1967-68	MC Cowdrey	West Indies	A	5	1	–	4
1968	MC Cowdrey (4)	Australia	H	5	1	1	3
	TW Graveney (1)						
1968-69	MC Cowdrey	Pakistan	A	3	–	–	3
1969	R Illingworth	New Zealand	H	3	2	–	1
1969	R Illingworth	West Indies	H	3	2	–	1
1960s Total Decade				**95**	**31**	**15**	**49**
Success Ratio in the 60s		**32.63%**					

YEAR	CAPTAIN	VS	V	P	W	L	D
1970-71	R Illingworth	Australia	A	6	2	–	4
1970-71	R Illingworth	New Zealand	A	2	1	–	1
1971	R Illingworth	India	H	3	–	1	2
1971	R Illingworth	Pakistan	H	3	1	–	2
1972	R Illingworth	Australia	H	5	2	2	1
1972-73	AR Lewis	India	A	5	1	2	2
1972-73	AR Lewis	Pakistan	A	3	–	–	3
1973	R Illingworth	New Zealand	H	3	2	–	1
1973	R Illingworth	West Indies	H	3	–	2	1
1973-74	MH Denness	West Indies	A	5	1	1	3
1974	MH Denness	India	H	3	3	–	–
1974	MH Denness	Pakistan	H	3	–	–	3
1974-75	MH Denness	Australia	A	6	1	4	1
1974-75	MH Denness	New Zealand	A	2	1	–	1
1975	MH Denness (1)	England	H	4	–	1	3
	AW Greig (3)						
1976	AW Greig	West Indies	H	5	–	3	2
1976-77	AW Greig	India	A	5	3	1	1
1976-77	AW Greig	Australia	A	1	–	1	–
1977	JM Brearley	Australia	H	5	3	–	2
1977-78	JM Brearley (2)	Pakistan	A	3	–	–	3
	G Boycott (1)						
1977-78	G Boycott	New Zealand	A	3	1	1	1
1978	JM Brearley	Pakistan	H	3	2	–	1
1978	JM Brearley	New Zealand	H	3	3	–	–
1978-79	JM Brearley	Australia	A	6	5	1	–
1979	JM Brearley	India	H	4	1	–	3
1979-80	JM Brearley	Australia	A	3	–	3	–
1979-80	JM Brearley	India	A	1	1	–	–
1970s Total Decade				**98**	**34**	**23**	**41**
Success Ratio in the 80s		**34.69%**					

YEAR	CAPTAIN	VS	V	P	W	L	D
1980	IT Botham	West Indies	H	5	–	1	4
1980	IT Botham	Australia	H	1	–	–	1
1980-81	IT Botham	West Indies	A	4	2	–	2
1981	IT Botham (2)	Australia	H	6	3	1	2
	JM Brearley (4)						
1981-82	KWR Fletcher	India	A	6	–	1	5

YEAR	CAPTAIN	VS	V	P	W	L	D
1981-82	KWR Fletcher	Sri Lanka	A	1	1	–	–
1982	RGD Willis	India	H	3	1	–	2
1982	RGD Willis (2)	Pakistan	H	3	2	1	–
	DI Gower (1)						
1982-83	RGD Willis	Australia	A	5	1	2	2
1983	RGD Willis	New Zealand	H	4	3	1	–
1983-84	RGD Willis	New Zealand	A	3	–	1	2
1983-84	RGD Willis (1)	Pakistan	A	3	–	1	2
	DI Gower (2)						
1984	DI Gower	West Indies	H	5	–	5	–
1984	DI Gower	Sri Lanka	H	1	–	–	1
1984-85	DI Gower	India	A	5	2	1	2
1985	DI Gower	Australia	H	6	3	1	2
1985-86	DI Gower	West Indies	A	5	–	5	–
1986	DI Gower (1)	India	H	3	–	2	1
	MW Gatting (2)						
1986	MW Gatting	New Zealand	H	3	–	1	2
1986-87	MW Gatting	Australia	A	5	2	1	2
1987	MW Gatting	Pakistan	H	5	–	1	4
1987-88	MW Gatting	Pakistan	A	3	–	1	2
1987-88	MW Gatting	Australia	A	1	–	–	1
1987-88	MW Gatting	New Zealand	A	3	–	–	3
1988	MW Gatting (1)	West Indies	H	5	–	4	1
	JE Emburey (2)						
	CS Cowdrey (1)						
	GA Gooch (1)						
1988	GA Gooch	Sri Lanka	H	1	1	–	–
1989	DI Gower	Australia	H	6	–	4	2
1989-90	GA Gooch (2)	West Indies	A	4	1	2	1
	AJ Lamb (2)						
1980s Total Decade				**105**	**20**	**39**	**46**
Success Ratio in the 80s		**19.04%**					

YEAR	CAPTAIN	VS	V	P	W	L	D
1990	GA Gooch	New Zealand	H	3	1	–	2
1990	GA Gooch	India	H	3	1	–	2
1990-91	AJ Lamb (1)	Australia	A	5	–	3	2
	GA Gooch (4)						
1991	GA Gooch	West Indies	H	5	2	2	1
1991	GA Gooch	Sri Lanka	H	1	1	–	–
1991-92	GA Gooch	New Zealand	A	3	2	–	1
1992	GA Gooch	Pakistan	H	5	1	2	2
1992-93	GA Gooch (2)	India	A	3	–	3	–
	AJ Stewart (1)						
1992-93	AJ Stewart	Sri Lanka	A	1	–	1	–
1993	GA Gooch (4)	Australia	H	6	1	4	1
	MA Atherton (2)						
1993-94	MA Atherton	West Indies	A	5	1	3	1
1994	MA Atherton	New Zealand	H	3	1	–	2
1994	MA Atherton	South Africa	H	3	1	–	2
1994-95	MA Atherton	Australia	A	5	1	3	1

YEAR	CAPTAIN	VS	V	P	W	L	D
1995	MA Atherton	West Indies	H	6	2	2	2
1995-96	MA Atherton	South Africa	A	5	–	1	4
1996	MA Atherton	India	H	3	1	–	2
1996	MA Atherton	Pakistan	H	3	–	2	1
1996-97	MA Atherton	Zimbabwe	A	2	–	–	1
1996-97	MA Atherton	New Zealand	A	3	2	–	1
1997	MA Atherton	Australia	H	6	2	3	1
1997-98	MA Atherton	West Indies	A	6	1	3	2
1998	AJ Stewart	South Africa	H	5	2	1	2
1998	AJ Stewart	Sri Lanka	H	1	–	1	–
1998-99	AJ Stewart	Australia	A	5	1	3	1
1999	N Hussain (3)	New Zealand	H	4	1	2	1
	MA Butcher (1)						
1999-00	N Hussain	South Africa	A	5	1	2	2
1990s Total Decade				**105**	**26**	**42**	**37**
Success Ratio in the 90s		**24.76%**					

HOME & AWAY AGAINST EACH OPPOSITION

PERIOD	VS	P	W	L	D	SR
1950 to 1997-98	West Indies	100	20	46	34	20.00%
1950-51 to 1998-99	Australia	143	38	53	52	26.57%
1950-51 to 1999	New Zealand	65	34	6	25	52.30%
1951 to 1998	South Africa	46	16	11	19	34.78%
1951-52 to 1996	India	74	26	14	34	35.13%
1954 to 1996	Pakistan	55	14	9	32	25.45%
1981-82 to 1998	Sri Lanka	6	3	2	1	50.00%
1997-98	Zimbabwe	2	–	–	2	
	Total	**491**	**151**	**141**	**199**	**30.75%**

FIVE DECADES SUCCESS AND FAILURE AT A GLANCE

DECADE	P	W	L	D	SR	FR
1950 to 1959-60	88	40	22	26	45.45%	25.00%
1960 to 1969	95	31	15	49	32.63%	15.78%
1970-71 to 1979-80	98	34	23	41	34.69%	23.46%
1980 to 1989-90	105	20	39	46	19.04%	37.14%
1990 to 1999-00	105	26	42	37	24.76%	40.00%

HOME RECORD 1950 TO 1999

VS	P	W	L	D	SR
Australia	70	19	21	30	
South Africa	26	12	6	8	
West Indies	56	12	28	16	
New Zealand	34	20	4	10	
India	34	18	3	13	
Pakistan	37	13	7	17	
Sri Lanka	4	2	1	1	
Total	**261**	**96**	**70**	**95**	**36.78%**

AWAY 1950-51 TO 1998-99

VS	P	W	L	D	SR
Australia	73	19	32	22	
South Africa	20	4	5	11	
West Indies	44	8	18	18	
New Zealand	31	14	2	15	
India	40	8	11	21	
Pakistan	18	1	2	15	
Sri Lanka	2	1	1	–	
Zimbabwe	2	–	–	2	
Total	**230**	**55**	**71**	**104**	**23.91%**

HOME 1950 TO 1959

VS	P	W	L	D	SR
Australia	10	3	1	6	
South Africa	10	6	3	1	
West Indies	9	4	3	2	
New Zealand	5	4	–	1	
India	9	8	–	1	
Pakistan	4	1	1	2	
Total	**47**	**26**	**8**	**13**	**55.31%**

HOME 1960 TO 1969

VS	P	W	L	D	SR
Australia	15	2	4	9	
South Africa	8	3	1	4	
West Indies	13	4	6	3	
New Zealand	6	5	–	1	
India	3	3	–	–	
Pakistan	8	6	–	2	
Total	**53**	**23**	**11**	**19**	**43.39%**

HOME 1971 TO 1979

VS	P	W	L	D	SR
Australia	14	5	3	6	
West Indies	8	–	5	3	
New Zealand	6	5	–	1	
India	10	4	1	5	
Pakistan	9	3	–	6	
Total	**47**	**17**	**9**	**21**	**36.17%**

HOME 1980 TO 1989

VS	P	W	L	D	SR
Australia	19	6	6	7	
West Indies	15	–	10	5	
New Zealand	7	3	2	2	
India	6	1	2	3	
Pakistan	8	2	2	4	
Sri Lanka	2	1	–	1	
Total	**57**	**13**	**22**	**22**	**22.80%**

HOME 1990 TO 1999

VS	P	W	L	D	SR
Australia	12	3	7	2	
South Africa	8	3	2	3	
West Indies	11	4	4	3	
New Zealand	10	3	2	5	
India	6	2	–	4	
Pakistan	8	1	4	3	
Sri Lanka	2	1	1	–	
Total	**57**	**17**	**20**	**20**	**29.82%**

AWAY 1950-51 TO 1959-60

VS	P	W	L	D	SR
Australia	15	4	9	2	
South Africa	5	2	2	1	
West Indies	10	3	2	5	
New Zealand	6	4	–	2	
India	5	1	1	3	
Total	**41**	**14**	**14**	**13**	**34.14%**

AWAY 1961-62 TO 1968-69

VS	P	W	L	D	SR
Australia	10	2	2	6	
South Africa	5	1	–	4	
West Indies	5	1	–	4	
New Zealand	6	3	–	3	
India	10	–	2	8	
Pakistan	6	1	–	5	
Total	**42**	**8**	**4**	**30**	**19.04%**

AWAY 1970-71 TO 1979-80

VS	P	W	L	D	SR
Australia	22	8	9	5	
West Indies	5	1	1	3	
New Zealand	7	3	1	3	
India	11	5	3	3	
Pakistan	6	–	–	6	
Total	**51**	**17**	**14**	**20**	**33.33%**

AWAY 1980-81 TO 1989-90

VS	P	W	L	D	SR
Australia	11	3	3	5	
West Indies	13	1	9	3	
New Zealand	6	–	1	5	
India	11	2	2	7	
Pakistan	6	–	2	4	
Sri Lanka	1	1	–	–	
Total	**48**	**9**	**22**	**17**	**18.75%**

AWAY 1990-91 TO 1999-00

VS	P	W	L	D	SR
Australia	15	2	9	4	
South Africa	10	1	3	6	
West Indies	11	2	6	3	
New Zealand	6	4	–	2	
India	3	–	3	–	
Sri Lanka	1	–	1	–	
Zimbabwe	2	–	–	2	
Total	**43**	**8**	**20**	**15**	**18.60%**

MAJOR SUCCESSES OVERSEAS SERIES VICTORIES

VS	YEAR	TESTS	RESULT	CAPTAIN
New Zealand	1950-51	2	1-0	FR Brown
Australia	1954-55	5	3-1	L Hutton
New Zealand	1954-55	2	2-0	L Hutton
New Zealand	1958-59	2	1-0	PBH May
West Indies	1959-60	5	1-0	PBH May (3), MC Cowdrey (2)
Pakistan	1961-62	3	1-0	ER Dexter
New Zealand	1962-63	3	3-0	ER Dexter
South Africa	1964-65	5	1-0	MJK Smith
West Indies	1967-68	5	1-0	MC Cowdrey
Australia	1970-71	6	2-0	R Illingworth
New Zealand	1970-71	2	1-0	R Illingworth
New Zealand	1974-75	2	1-0	MH Denness
India	1976-77	5	3-1	AW Greig
Australia	1978-79	6	5-1	JM Brearley
India	1979-80	1	1-0	JM Brearley
Sri Lanka	1981-82	1	1-0	KWR Fletcher
India	1984-85	5	2-1	DI Gower
Australia	1986-87	5	2-1	MW Gatting
New Zealand	1991-92	3	2-0	GA Gooch
New Zealand	1996-97	3	2-0	MA Atherton

SERIES DEFEATS AT HOME

VS	YEAR	TESTS	RESULT	CAPTAIN
West Indies	1950	4	1-3	NWD Yardley (3), FR Brown (1)
Australia	1961	5	1-2	MC Cowdrey (2), PBH May (3)
West Indies	1963	5	1-3	ER Dexter
Australia	1964	5	0-1	ER Dexter
South Africa	1965	3	0-1	MJK Smith
West lindies	1966	5	1-3	MJK Smith (1), MC Cowdrey (3), DB Close (1)

VS	YEAR	TESTS	RESULT	CAPTAIN
India	1971	3	0-1	R Illingworth
West Indies	1973	3	0-2	R Illingworth
Australia	1975	4	0-1	MH Denness (1), AW Greig (3)
West Indies	1976	5	0-3	AW Greig
West Indies	1980	5	0-1	IT Botham
West Indies	1984	5	0-5	DI Gower
India	1986	3	0-2	DI Gower (1), MW Gatting
New Zealand	1986	3	0-1	MW Gatting
Pakistan	1987	5	0-1	MW Gatting
West Indies	1988	5	0-4	MW Gatting (1) JE Emburey (2), S Cowdrey (1), GA Gooch (1)
Australia	1989	6	0-4	DI Gower
Pakistan	1992	5	1-2	GA Gooch
Australia	1993	6	1-4	GA Gooch (4), MA Atherton (2)
Pakistan	1996	3	0-2	MA Atherton
Australia	1997	6	2-3	MA Atherton
New Zealand	1999	4	1-2	N Hussain (3), MA Butcher (1)

ENGLISH CAPTAINS (MINIMUM TEST MATCHES: 10)

CAPTAIN	FROM	TO	P	W	L	D	SR%
JM Brearley	1977	1981	31	18	4	9	58.06
PBH May	1955	1961	41	20	10	11	48.78
L Hutton	1952	1954-55	23	11	4	8	47.82
RGD Willis	1982	1983-84	18	7	5	6	38.88
R Illingworth	1969	1973	31	12	5	14	38.70
FR Brown	1950	1951	13	5	6	2	38.46
MH Denness	1973-74	1975	19	6	5	8	31.57
ER Dexter	1961-62	1964	30	9	7	14	30.00
MC Cowdrey	1959	1968-69	27	8	4	15	29.62
GA Gooch	1988	1993	34	10	12	12	29.41
AJ Stewart	1998	1998-99	11	3	5	3	27.27
MA Atherton	1993	1997-98	52	13	19	20	25.00
AW Greig	1975	1976-77	14	3	5	6	21.42
MJK Smith	1963-64	1966	25	5	3	17	20.00
DI Gower	1982	1989	32	5	18	9	15.62
MW Gatting	1986	1988	23	2	5	16	8.69
IT Botham	1980	1981	12	–	4	8	–

The above table is headed by Mike Brearley, perhaps the most astute brain to captain his country. The fact remains that 10 of his Test wins between June 1978 to February 1979 were achieved against Australia and Pakistan without their star players in the Kerry Packer era and a pretty ordinary New Zealand side. His only series against a top-class opposition at full strength, i.e. Australia 1979-80, ended in a three-nil drubbing. Later he returned to

inspire Ian Botham for that memorable summer in 1981.
Remember that the great all-rounder's twelve-match reign included nine games against the mighty West Indians.

HIGHEST INNINGS TOTALS
1950S

SCORE	TEAM	VENUE	YEAR
619-6d	West Indies	Nottingham	1957
583-4d	West Indies	Birmingham	1957
558-6d	Pakistan	Nottingham	1954
550	New Zealand	Christchurch	1950-51
546-4d	New Zealand	Leeds	1965
537	India	Lord's	1952
537	West Indies	Port-Of-Spain	1953-54
505	South Africa	Leeds	1951

1960S

SCORE	TEAM	VENUE	YEAR
611	Australia	Manchester	1964
568	West Indies	Port-Of-Spain	1967-68
562-7d	New Zealand	Auckland	1962-63
559-8d	India	Kanpur	1963-64
558	Australia	Melbourne	1965-66
550-4d	India	Leeds	1967
544-5d	Pakistan	Birmingham	1962
531	South Africa	Johannesburg	1964-65
527	West Indies	The Oval	1966
507	Pakistan	Karachi	1961-62
502-7	Pakistan	Lahore	1968-69
500-8d	India	Bombay	1961-62

1970S

SCORE	TEAM	VENUE	YEAR
633-5d	India	Birmingham	1979
629	India	Lord's	1974
545	Pakistan	The Oval	1974
538	Australia	The Oval	1975
529	Australia	Melbourne	1974-75

1980S

SCORE	TEAM	VENUE	YEAR
652-7d	India	Madras	1984-85
595-5d	Australia	Birmingham	1985
594	India	The Oval	1982
592-8d	Australia	Perth	1986-87
546-8d	Pakistan	Faisalabad	1983-84
533	Australia	Leeds	1985
521	Pakistan	Birmingham	1987

1990S

SCORE	TEAM	VENUE	YEAR
653-4d	India	Lord's	1990
593	West Indies	Antigua	1993-94
580-9d	New Zealand	Christchurch	1991-92
567-8d	New Zealand	Nottingham	1994
564	India	Nottingham	1996
521	New Zealand	Auckland	1996-97
519	India	Manchester	1990
501	Pakistan	Leeds	1996

HIGHEST INNINGS TOTALS – AGAINST
1950S

SCORE	TEAM	VENUE	YEAR
681-8d	West Indies	Port-of-Spain	1953-54
601-8d	Australia	Brisbane	1954-55
563-8d	West Indies	Bridgetown	1959-60
558	West Indies	Nottingham	1950
538	South Africa	Leeds	1951
521-8d	South Africa	Manchester	1955
503	West Indies	The Oval	1950
500	South Africa	Leeds	1955

1960S

SCORE	TEAM	VENUE	YEAR
656-8d	Australia	Manchester	1964
543-8d	Australia	Melbourne	1965-66
526-7d	West Indies	Port-of-Spain	1967-68
516-9d	Australia	Birmingham	1961
516	Australia	Adelaide	1965-66
510	India	Leeds	1967
502	South Africa	Port Elizabeth	1964-65
501-6d	West Indies	Manchester	1963
501-7d	South Africa	Cape Town	1964-65
500-9d	West Indies	Leeds	1966

1970S

SCORE	TEAM	VENUE	YEAR
687-8d	West Indies	The Oval	1976
652-8d	West Indies	Lord's	1973
608-7d	Pakistan	Birmingham	1971
600-7d	Pakistan	The Oval	1974
596-8d	West Indies	Bridgetown	1973-74
583-9d	West Indies	Kingston	1973-74
569-9d	Pakistan	Hyderabad	1972-73
551-9d	New Zealand	Lord's	1973
532-9d	Australia	The Oval	1975

TEAM STATS

1980S

SCORE	TEAM	VENUE	YEAR
708	Pakistan	The Oval	1987
606	West Indies	Birmingham	1984
602-6d	Australia	Nottingham	1989
601-7d	Australia	Leeds	1989
553-8d	India	Kanpur	1984-85
539	Australia	Nottingham	1985
537	New Zealand	Wellington	1983-84
528	Australia	Lord's	1989
518	West Indies	Lord's	1980
514-5d	Australia	Adelaide	1986-87
512-6d	New Zealand	Wellington	1987-88
500	West Indies	Manchester	1984

1990S

SCORE	TEAM	VENUE	YEAR
692-8d	West Indies	The Oval	1995
653-4d	Australia	Leeds	1993
632-4d	Australia	Lord's	1993
606-9d	India	The Oval	1990
593-5d	West Indies	Antigua	1993-94
591	India	Bombay	1992-93
591	Sri Lanka	The Oval	1998
560-6d	India	Madras	1992-93
556	West Indies	Georgetown	1993-94
552-5d	South Africa	Manchester	1998
521-8d	Pakistan	The Oval	1996
521	India	Nottingham	1996
518	Australia	Sydney	1990-91
505-9d	Pakistan	Manchester	1992
501	Australia	Leeds	1997
500-7d	West Indies	Antigua	1997-98

LOWEST INNINGS TOTAL – FOR

1950S

SCORE	TEAM	VENUE	YEAR
87	Australia	Melbourne	1958-59
103	West Indies	The Oval	1950
110	South Africa	Port Elizabeth	1956-57
114	South Africa	Leeds	1951
122	Australia	Brisbane	1950-51
123	Australia	Sydney	1950-51

1960S

SCORE	TEAM	VENUE	YEAR
104	Australia	Melbourne	1962-63

1970S

SCORE	TEAM	VENUE	YEAR
64	New Zealand	Wellington	1977-78
71	West Indies	Manchester	1976
95	Australia	Melbourne	1976-77
101	India	The Oval	1971
101	Australia	Birmingham	1975
116	Australia	Lord's	1972
123	Australia	Sydney	1979-80

1980S

SCORE	TEAM	VENUE	YEAR
82	New Zealand	Christchurch	1983-84
93	New Zealand	Christchurch	1983-84
93	West Indies	Manchester	1988
102	India	Bombay	1981-82
102	India	Leeds	1986
122	West Indies	Bridgetown	1980-81

1990S

SCORE	TEAM	VENUE	YEAR
46	West Indies	Port-of-Spain	1993-94
77	Australia	Lord's	1997
89	West Indies	Birmingham	1995
92	Australia	Melbourne	1994-95
99	South Africa	Lord's	1994
110	South Africa	Lord's	1998
112	Australia	Perth	1998-99
114	Australia	Brisbane	1990-91
123	Australia	Perth	1994-95

LOWEST INNINGS TOTAL – AGAINST

1950S

SCORE	TEAM	VENUE	YEAR
26	New Zealand	Auckland	1954-55
47	New Zealand	Lord's	1958
58	India	Manchester	1952
67	New Zealand	Leeds	1958
72	South Africa	Johannesburg	1956-57
72	South Africa	Cape Town	1956-57
74	New Zealand	Lord's	1958
82	India	Manchester	1952
84	Australia	Manchester	1956
85	New Zealand	Leeds	1958
86	West Indies	The Oval	1957
87	Pakistan	Lord's	1954
89	West Indies	The Oval	1957
90	Pakistan	Manchester	1954
94	New Zealand	Birmingham	1958
98	India	The Oval	1952
111	Australia	Melbourne	1954-55
111	Australia	Adelaide	1954-55
111	South Africa	Lord's	1955

SCORE	TEAM	VENUE	YEAR
112	South Africa	The Oval	1955
112	West Indies	Port-of-Spain	1959-60
121	South Africa	Nottingham	1951
121	India	Kanpur	1951-52
123	Australia	Nottingham	1953

1960S

SCORE	TEAM	VENUE	YEAR
78	Australia	Lord's	1968
88	South Africa	Nottingham	1960
89	New Zealand	Auckland	1962-63
91	West Indies	Birmingham	1963
92	India	Birmingham	1967
100	Pakistan	Lord's	1962
110	India	Lord's	1967
114	Pakistan	Nottingham	1967
116	New Zealand	Birmingham	1965
120	Australia	Leeds	1961

1970S

SCORE	TEAM	VENUE	YEAR
42	India	Lord's	1974
65	New Zealand	Christchurch	1970-71
67	New Zealand	Lord's	1978
83	India	Madras	1976-77
96	India	Lord's	1979
97	New Zealand	Nottingham	1973
103	Australia	Leeds	1977
105	New Zealand	Christchurch	1977-78
105	Pakistan	Lord's	1978
111	Australia	Sydney	1978-79
116	Australia	Sydney	1970-71
116	Australia	Brisbane	1978-79
120	New Zealand	Nottingham	1978
122	India	Delhi	1976-77
123	New Zealand	Wellington	1977-78

1980S

SCORE	TEAM	VENUE	YEAR
111	Australia	Leeds	1981
121	Australia	Birmingham	1981

1990S

SCORE	TEAM	VENUE	YEAR
104	Australia	The Oval	1997
107	New Zealand	Birmingham	1999
116	Australia	Sydney	1994-95
118	Australia	Birmingham	1997
124	New Zealand	Wellington	1996-97

INDIVIDUAL BATTING FREQUENCY OF HUNDREDS

	INNINGS	100S	INNINGS/100S
KF Barrington	131	20	6.55
DL Amiss	88	11	8.00
PBH May	106	13	8.15
L Hutton	66	8	8.25
MC Cowdrey	188	22	8.55
G Boycott	193	22	8.77
GA Gooch	215	20	10.75
JH Edrich	127	12	10.58
AJ Lamb	149	14	10.64
TW Graveney	123	11	11.18
ER Dexter	102	9	11.33
DI Gower	204	18	11.33
IT Botham	161	14	11.50
AW Greig	93	8	11.62
RA Smith	112	9	12.44
MA Atherton	175	13	13.46
KWR Fletcher	96	7	13.71
MW Gatting	138	10	13.80
AJ Stewart	172	12	14.33
GP Thorpe	105	6	17.50
GA Hick	94	5	18.80
APE Knott	149	5	29.80

CLEAN SWEEPS

OPPOSITION	YEAR	T	CAPTAIN
New Zealand	1954-55	2	L Hutton
India	1959	5	PBH May (3), MC Cowdrey (2)
New Zealand	1962-63	3	ER Dexter
New Zealand	1965	3	MJK Smith
India	1967	3	DB Close
India	1974	3	MH Denness
New Zealand	1978	3	JM Brearley
India	1979-80	1	JM Brearley
Sri Lanka	1981-82	1	KWR Fletcher
Sri Lanka	1988	1	GA Gooch
Sri Lanka	1991	1	GA Gooch

CLEAN SWEEPS – AGAINST ENGLAND

OPPOSITION	YEAR	T	CAPTAIN
Australia	1976-77	1	AW Greig
Australia	1979-80	1	JM Brearley
West Indies	1984	5	DI Gower
West Indies	1985-86	5	DI Gower
India	1992-93	3	GA Gooch (2), AJ Stewart (1)
Sri Lanka	1992-93	1	AJ Stewart
Sri Lanka	1998	1	AJ Stewart

TEAM STATS

OTHER SIGNIFICANT WINS FOR ENGLAND

OPPOSITION	YEAR	RESULT	T	CAPTAIN
India	1952	3-0	4	L Hutton
West Indies	1957	3-0	5	PBH May
New Zealand	1958	4-0	5	PBH May
South Africa	1960	3-0	5	MC Cowdrey
Pakistan	1962	4-0	5	ER Dexter (4),
				MC Cowdrey (1)
Australia	1977	3-0	5	JM Brearley
Australia	1978-79	5-1	6	JM Brearley

OTHER SIGNIFICANT DEFEATS FOR ENGLAND

OPPOSITION	YEAR	RESULT	T	CAPTAIN
Australia	1950-51	1-4	5	FR Brown
Australia	1958-59	0-4	5	PBH May
Australia	1974-75	1-4	6	MH Denness
West Indies	1976	0-3	5	AW Greig
West Indies	1988	0-4	5	MW Gatting,
				JE Emburey (2), CS Cowdrey, GA Gooch
Australia	1989	0-4	6	DI Gower
Australia	1990-91	0-3	5	AJ Lamb (2),
				GA Gooch (3)
Australia	1993	1-4	6	GA Gooch (4),
				MA Atherton (2)

INNINGS-WINS RECORDED BY ENGLAND (42)

MARGIN	OPPOSITION	VENUE	YEAR
5	South Africa	Nottingham	1951
207	India	Manchester	1952
129	Pakistan	Nottingham	1954
20	New Zealand	Auckland	1954-55
42	Australia	Leeds	1956
170	Australia	Manchester	1956
36	West Indies	Lord's	1957
5	West Indies	Leeds	1957
237	West Indies	The Oval	1957
148	New Zealand	Lord's	1958
71	New Zealand	Leeds	1958
13	New Zealand	Manchester	1958
99	New Zealand	Christchurch	1958-59
59	India	Nottingham	1959
173	India	Leeds	1959
27	India	The Oval	1959
73	South Africa	Lord's	1960
24	Pakistan	Birmingham	1962
117	Pakistan	Leeds	1962
215	New Zealand	Auckland	1962-63
47	New Zealand	Wellington	1962-63
104	South Africa	Durban	1964-65
187	New Zealand	Leeds	1965
93	Australia	Sydney	1965-66
34	West Indies	The Oval	1966
124	India	Lord's	1967

MARGIN	OPPOSITION	VENUE	YEAR
1	New Zealand	Leeds	1973
285	India	Lord's	1974
78	India	Birmingham	1974
4	Australia	Melbourne	1974-75
83	New Zealand	Auckland	1974-75
25	India	Delhi	1976-77
85	Australia	Leeds	1977
57	Pakistan	Birmingham	1978
120	Pakistan	Lord's	1978
83	India	Birmingham	1979
118	Australia	Birmingham	1985
94	Australia	The Oval	1985
14	Australia	Melbourne	1986-87
4	New Zealand	Christchurch	1991-92
90	New Zealand	Nottingham	1994
68	New Zealand	Wellington	1996-97

The higher number of innings wins (16) in the 1950s indicates England's glory days. But an interesting equation is the 87.5% heavy wins in home conditions.

INNINGS-WINS RECORDED AGAINST ENGLAND (28)

MARGIN	OPPOSITION	VENUE	YEAR
56	West Indies	The Oval	1950
13	Australia	Sydney	1950-51
8	India	Madras	1951-52
154	Australia	Brisbane	1954-55
9	Australia	Adelaide	1965-66
40	West Indies	Manchester	1966
55	West Indies	Leeds	1966
226	West Indies	Lord's	1973
85	Australia	Birmingham	1975
79	West Indies	Port-of-Spain	1980-81
132	New Zealand	Christchurch	1983-84
180	West Indies	Birmingham	1984
64	West Indies	Manchester	1984
18	Pakistan	Leeds	1987
87	Pakistan	Lahore	1987-88
156	West Indies	Manchester	1988
180	Australia	Nottingham	1989
32	West Indies	Antigua	1989-90
22	India	Madras	1992-93
15	India	Bombay	1992-93
62	Australia	Lord's	1993
148	Australia	Leeds	1993
44	West Indies	Georgetown	1993-94
64	West Indies	Birmingham	1995
61	Australia	Leeds	1997
42	West Indies	Antigua	1997-98
21	South Africa	Johannesburg	1999-00
37	South Africa	Cape Town	1999-00

The dramatic rise in heavy defeats in the last decade illustrates decline again.

VICTORY BY HUGE MARGIN IN RUNS

MARGIN	TARGET	VS	VENUE	YEAR
312	385	South Africa	Cape Town	1956-57
299	416	Australia	Sydney	1970-71
256	501	West Indies	Port-of-Spain	1959-60
247	472	India	Lord's	1990
230	362	New Zealand	Lord's	1969
226	352	Australia	The Oval	1968
217	309	West Indies	Birmingham	1963
208	446	West Indies	Bridgetown	1993-94
205	343	New Zealand	Birmingham	1958
205	366	Australia	Adelaide	1978-79
202	386	West Indies	Manchester	1950
200	284	India	Madras	1976-77

DEFEAT BY HUGE MARGIN IN RUNS

MARGIN	TARGET	VS	VENUE	YEAR
425	552	West Indies	Manchester	1976
356	456	South Africa	Lord's	1994
329	453	Australia	Perth	1994-95
326	601	West Indies	Lord's	1950
298	523	West Indies	Bridgetown	1980-81
295	388	Australia	Melbourne	1994-95
279	408	India	Leeds	1986
274	503	Australia	Adelaide	1950-51
268	469	Australia	Manchester	1997
264	451	Australia	Nottingham	1997
242	380	West Indies	Georgetown	1997-98
231	435	West Indies	The Oval	1976
224	481	South Africa	Leeds	1955
221	453	West Indies	Leeds	1963
210	402	Australia	Leeds	1989
205	443	Australia	Adelaide	1998-99

CLOSE AFFAIR – IN ENGLAND'S FAVOUR IN RUNS

MARGIN	TARGET	VS	VENUE	YEAR
3	292	Australia	Melbourne	1982-83
12	175	Australia	Melbourne	1998-99
18	130	Australia	Leeds	1981
19	124	Australia	The Oval	1997
23	219	South Africa	Leeds	1998
25	231	Pakistan	Leeds	1971
26	226	West Indies	Port-of-Spain	1973-74
29	151	Australia	Birmingham	1981
30	303	West Indies	Leeds	1969

CLOSE AFFAIR – IN OPPOSITION'S FAVOUR IN RUNS

MARGIN	TARGET	VS	VENUE	YEAR
17	232	South Africa	Johannesburg	1956-57
24	168	Pakistan	The Oval	1954
28	192	India	Calcutta	1972-73

HIGHEST TOTAL IN FOURTH INNINGS TO WIN – FOR

RUNS	R/O	VS	VENUE	YEAR
307-6	2.09	New Zealand	Christchurch	1996-97
247-2	2.83	South Africa	Nottingham	1998
237-3	3.68	Australia	Melbourne	1962-63
225-7	2.08	West Indies	Port-of-Sapin	1997-98
219-7	2.72	Pakistan	Leeds	1982
218-3	3.58	New Zealand	Lord's	1965
215-3	4.08	West Indies	Port-of-Spain	1967-68
211-3	4.83	New Zealand	Birmingham	1999
209-5	3.54	Pakistan	Lahore	1961-62
208-4	2.34	India	Delhi	1972-73
205-2	5.77	South Africa	The Oval	1994

HIGHEST TOTAL IN FOURTH INNINGS TO WIN – AGAINST

RUNS	R/O	VS	VENUE	YEAR
344-1	5.19	West Indies	Lord's	1984
282-7	2.86	West Indies	Port-of-Spain	1997-98
255-2	2.68	West Indies	The Oval	1963
242-5	2.62	Australia	The Oval	1972
226-2	2.48	West Indies	The Oval	1988
219-4	2.56	Australia	Sydney	1979-80
209-8	3.03	West Indies	Nottingham	1980

MESSED UP RUN CHASES FOR ENGLAND

TARGET	ALL OUT	RESULT	VS	VENUE	YEAR
137	64	L 72 runs	NZ	Wellington	1977-78
168	143	L 24 runs	P	The Oval	1954
179	150	L 28 runs	A	Melbourne	1950-51
186	114	L 71 runs	SA	Nottingham	1951
192	163	L 28 runs	I	Calcutta	1972-73
193	122	L 70 runs	A	Brisbane	1950-51
194	46	L 147 runs	WI	Port-of-Spain	1993-94
232	214	L 14 runs	SA	Johannesburg	1956-57
241	102	L 138runs	I	Bombay	1981-82

MESSED UP RUN CHASES AGAINST ENGLAND

TARGET	ALL OUT	RESULT	VS	VENUE	YEAR
124	104	W 19 runs	A	The Oval	1997
130	111	W 18runs	A	Leeds	1981
151	121	W 29runs	A	Manchester	1981
175	162	W 12 runs	A	Melbourne	1998-99
183	111	W 71runs	SA	Lord's	1955
189	130	W 38 runs	SA	Port Elizabeth	1956-57
204	72	W 131runs	SA	Johannesburg	1956-57
205	111	W 93 runs	A	Sydney	1978-79
219	195	W 23 runs	SA	Leeds	1998
223	184	W 38runs	A	Sydney	1954-55
223	160	W 62 runs	A	Sydney	1970-71
226	199	W 26 runs	WI	Port-of-Spain	1973-74
231	205	W 25 runs	P	Leeds	1971
244	151	W 92 runs	SA	The Oval	1955
250	111	W 128runs	A	Melbourne	1954-55

BATTING STATS

LEADING BATSMEN OF THE FIVE DECADES (1950-1999/2000) AGGREGATE TABLE

	T	I	NO	RUNS	HS	AVE.	100	50	0	1-9
GA Gooch	118	215	6	8900	333	42.58	20	46	13	39
DI Gower	117	204	18	8231	215	44.25	18	39	7	36
G Boycott	108	193	23	8114	*246	47.72	22	42	10	35
MC Cowdrey	114	188	15	7624	182	44.06	22	38	9	38
KF Barrington	82	131	15	6806	256	58.67	20	35	5	21
AJ Stewart	95	172	12	6525	190	40.78	12	35	7	36
MA Atherton	95	175	6	6403	*185	37.88	13	39	19	37
IT Botham	102	161	6	5200	208	33.12	14	22	14	36
H Edrich	77	127	9	5138	*310	43.54	12	24	6	29
TW Graveney	79	123	13	4882	258	44.38	11	20	8	16
AJ Lamb	79	149	10	4656	142	33.49	14	18	9	34
PBH May	66	106	9	4537	*285	46.77	13	22	8	19
ER Dexter	62	102	8	4502	205	47.89	9	27	6	13
MW Gatting	79	138	14	4409	207	35.55	10	20	16	27
APE Knott	95	149	15	4389	135	32.75	5	30	8	44
RA Smith	62	112	15	4236	175	43.67	9	28	8	19
DL Amiss	50	88	10	3612	*262	46.30	11	11	10	19
AW Greig	58	93	4	3599	148	40.43	8	20	5	17
GP Thorpe	57	105	13	3599	138	39.11	6	24	9	20
KWR Fletcher	59	96	14	3272	216	39.90	7	19	6	25
L Hutton	38	66	10	3183	205	56.83	8	16	2	8
GA Hick	54	94	6	3005	178	34.14	5	17	6	27

PERFORMANCE IN HOME CONDITIONS (1950-1999/2000) AVERAGE TABLE

	T	I	NO	RUNS	HS	AVE.	100	50	0	1-9
PBH May	39	57	7	2865	*285	57.30	9	14	5	7
L Hutton	19	33	5	1572	*202	56.14	5	6	2	3
KF Barrington	46	73	7	3347	256	50.71	6	21	3	15
RA Smith	36	66	11	2716	*148	49.38	7	17	5	8
G Boycott	57	100	10	4356	*246	48.80	14	15	6	16
TW Graveney	48	70	5	3115	258	47.92	7	15	3	11
KWR Fletcher	20	32	7	1156	178	46.24	3	7	2	10
GA Gooch	74	131	3	5917	333	46.23	15	26	11	20
JH Edrich	45	77	5	3155	*310	43.82	7	14	5	16
MC Cowdrey	55	88	6	3537	182	43.13	9	18	4	18
ER Dexter	32	54	3	2195	180	43.03	3	15	3	5
DI Gower	65	113	9	4454	215	42.83	10	19	4	23
AJ Stewart	46	83	7	3196	190	42.05	5	16	1	16
DL Amiss	26	45	6	1610	203	41.28	4	6	5	10
MA Atherton	53	99	3	3861	160	40.21	7	26	8	21
GP Thorpe	30	57	7	1990	138	39.80	2	15	6	8
MW Gatting	39	71	8	2453	*183	38.93	6	12	3	16
AJ Lamb	43	76	8	2550	139	37.50	11	6	6	20
IT Botham	59	89	4	2969	208	34.93	8	13	8	24
AW Greig	31	49	2	1628	139	34.63	3	10	5	11
GA Hick	30	50	3	1440	*118	30.63	3	8	3	15
APE Knott	56	87	5	2191	135	26.71	3	13	8	29

BATTING STATS

PERFORMANCE IN OVERSEAS CONDITIONS (1950-1999/2000) AVERAGE TABLE

	T	I	NO	RUNS	HS	AVE.	100	50	0	1-9
KF Barrington	36	58	8	3459	172	69.18	14	14	2	6
L Hutton	19	33	5	1611	205	57.53	3	10	–	5
ER Dexter	30	48	5	2307	205	53.65	6	12	3	8
DL Amiss	24	43	4	2002	*262	51.33	7	5	5	9
G Boycott	51	93	13	3758	*142	46.98	8	27	4	19
AW Greig	27	44	2	1971	148	46.92	5	10	–	6
DI Gower	52	91	9	3777	*173	46.06	8	20	3	13
MC Cowdrey	59	100	9	4087	151	44.91	13	20	5	20
JH Edrich	32	50	4	1983	146	43.11	5	10	1	13
APE Knott	39	62	10	2198	*106	42.26	2	17	–	15
AJ Stewart	49	89	5	3329	173	39.63	7	19	6	20
TW Graveney	31	53	8	1767	175	39.26	4	5	5	5
GP Thorpe	27	48	6	1609	123	38.30	4	9	2	12
GA Hick	24	44	3	1565	178	38.17	2	9	3	12
KWR Fletcher	39	64	7	2116	216	37.12	4	12	4	15
GA Gooch	44	84	3	2983	153	36.82	5	20	2	19
RA Smith	26	46	4	1520	175	36.19	2	11	3	11
PBH May	27	49	2	1672	135	35.57	4	8	3	12
MA Atherton	42	76	3	2542	*185	34.82	6	13	11	16
AJ Lamb	36	63	2	2106	142	34.52	3	12	3	14
MW Gatting	40	67	6	1956	207	32.06	4	8	13	11
IT Botham	43	72	2	2231	142	31.87	6	9	6	12

WINNING CONTRIBUTION (1950-1999/2000) AVERAGE TABLE

	T	I	NO	RUNS	HS	AVE.	100	50	0	1-9
KF Barrington	31	42	6	2319	163	64.42	8	10	2	8
L Hutton	17	30	4	1563	205	60.11	4	7	–	2
GA Gooch	32	56	4	2950	333	56.73	9	9	2	13
JH Edrich	22	35	3	1771	*310	55.34	5	8	–	5
MC Cowdrey	43	63	7	3087	182	55.13	10	17	3	13
G Boycott	35	62	8	2950	*246	54.63	10	10	3	10
ER Dexter	22	32	4	1502	172	53.64	2	13	3	2
AW Greig	17	22	2	1064	139	53.20	3	8	2	2
DI Gower	32	53	8	2302	215	51.16	6	9	1	9
DL Amiss	18	28	4	1206	188	50.25	3	3	1	4
GP Thorpe	13	24	3	1050	138	50.00	2	7	1	3
AJ Stewart	21	38	5	1529	148	46.33	5	5	1	8
RA Smith	14	25	4	970	109	46.19	2	7	3	1
TW Graveney	36	49	4	2014	165	44.75	4	9	4	5
AJ Lamb	21	36	5	1379	139	44.48	4	6	2	10
IT Botham	33	48	3	1951	*149	43.36	8	7	3	7
MA Atherton	21	40	4	1556	118	43.22	2	13	2	10
KWR Fletcher	16	24	3	874	216	41.61	3	2	1	10
MW Gatting	15	27	3	984	207	41.00	3	3	1	3
PBH May	33	51	5	1845	*113	40.10	6	8	6	9
GA Hick	12	19	1	545	*81	30.27	–	4	–	8
APE Knott	29	40	4	1029	135	28.58	1	4	4	9

BATTING STATS

CAREER RECORDS AGAINST TOP OPPOSITION – AUSTRALIA, SOUTH AFRICA, WEST INDIES AND PAKSITAN (1950-1999/2000) AVERAGE TABLE

	T	I	NO	RUNS	HS	AVE.	100	50	0	1-9
L Hutton	30	54	9	2603	205	57.84	6	13	2	7
KF Barrington	63	104	12	4857	256	52.79	14	25	5	19
G Boycott	80	146	19	6114	191	48.14	16	34	8	22
ER Dexter	47	80	4	3558	205	46.81	7	20	5	8
PBH May	50	85	6	3578	*285	45.29	9	18	8	15
DL Amiss	31	57	7	2214	*262	44.28	7	6	8	11
TW Graveney	60	95	9	3784	258	44.00	9	17	8	14
DI Gower	78	142	10	5603	215	42.44	12	27	4	25
RA Smith	44	80	9	2975	175	41.90	6	18	6	13
JH Edrich	56	98	7	3804	175	41.80	8	19	4	23
GP Thorpe	45	84	9	2942	138	39.22	4	22	8	14
AJ Stewart	69	127	9	4601	190	38.99	6	25	4	29
KWR Fletcher	31	53	6	1775	146	37.76	3	11	4	12
GA Gooch	81	152	2	5651	196	37.67	10	34	8	26
AW Greig	40	69	2	2449	148	36.55	4	13	4	13
GA Hick	39	70	6	2175	141	33.98	3	14	4	22
MA Atherton	74	139	4	4577	*185	33.90	7	29	17	32
APE Knott	72	114	13	3352	135	33.18	4	24	5	36
MW Gatting	51	92	6	2772	160	32.23	6	16	11	22
AJ Lamb	50	91	5	2660	132	30.93	7	9	7	23
IT Botham	70	118	4	3112	149*	27.29	6	13	12	29

CAREER RECORDS AGAINST NOT-SO-FORMIDABLE – NEW ZEALAND, INDIA, SRI LANKA AND ZIMBABWE (1950-1999/2000) AVERAGE TABLE

	T	I	NO	RUNS	HS	AVE.	100	50	0	1-9
KF Barrington	19	27	3	1949	172	81.20	6	10	-	2
MC Cowdrey	26	35	7	1786	160	63.78	5	10	1	4
GA Gooch	37	63	4	3249	333	55.06	10	12	5	13
MA Atherton	21	36	2	1826	160	53.70	6	10	2	5
IT Botham	32	43	2	2088	208	53.53	8	9	2	7
PBH May	16	21	3	959	*124	53.27	4	4	–	4
L Hutton	8	12	1	580	150	52.72	2	3	-	1
ER Dexter	15	22	4	944	141	52.44	2	7	1	5
AW Greig	18	24	2	1150	148	52.27	4	7	1	4
DL Amiss	19	31	3	1398	188	49.92	4	5	2	8
JH Edrich	21	29	2	1334	310*	49.40	4	5	2	6
DI Gower	39	62	8	2628	200*	48.66	6	12	3	11
RA Smith	18	32	6	1261	128	48.50	3	10	2	6
G Boycott	28	47	4	2000	246*	46.51	6	8	2	13
AJ Lamb	29	48	5	1996	142	46.41	7	9	2	11
AJ Stewart	26	45	3	1924	173	45.80	6	10	3	7
TW Graveney	19	28	4	1098	175	45.75	2	3	-	13
KWR Fletcher	28	42	8	1497	216	44.02	4	8	2	13
MW Gatting	28	46	8	1637	207	43.07	4	4	5	5
GP Thorpe	12	21	4	657	119	38.64	2	2	-	6
GA Hick	15	24	–	830	178	34.58	2	3	2	6
APE Knott	25	35	2	1037	101	31.42	1	6	3	8

BATTING STATS

AGAINST AUSTRALIA (1950/51- 1998/99) AVERAGE TABLE

	T	I	NO	RUNS	HS	AVE.	100	50	0	1-9
KF Barrington	23	39	6	2111	256	63.97	5	13	1	5
L Hutton	15	28	5	1196	*156	52.00	2	8	1	5
JH Edrich	32	57	3	2644	175	48.96	7	13	–	14
GP Thorpe	15	29	4	1213	138	48.52	3	8	2	5
G Boycott	38	71	9	2945	191	47.50	7	14	3	10
PBH May	21	37	3	1566	113	46.05	3	10	2	6
DI Gower	42	77	4	3269	215	44.78	9	12	3	12
RA Smith	15	30	3	1074	143	39.77	2	7	1	6
ER Dexter	19	35	–	1358	180	38.80	2	8	2	5
MW Gatting	27	48	4	1661	160	37.75	4	12	6	6
AW Greig	21	37	1	1303	110	36.19	1	10	2	7
GA Hick	10	20	1	669	*98	35.21	–	6	2	5
AJ Lamb	20	35	2	1138	125	34.48	1	7	3	8
MC Cowdrey	43	75	4	2433	113	34.27	5	11	5	15
GA Gooch	42	79	–	2632	196	33.31	4	16	5	16
APE Knott	34	57	6	1682	135	32.98	2	11	2	15
TW Graveney	22	38	4	1075	111	31.61	1	6	2	9
MA Atherton	28	56	2	1679	105	31.09	1	13	6	13
IT Botham	36	59	2	1673	*149	29.35	4	6	10	10
AJ Stewart	24	48	3	1259	107	27.97	1	8	2	17
KWR Fletcher	15	27	1	661	146	25.42	1	3	3	8
DL Amiss	11	21	1	305	90	15.25	–	2	7	6

AGAINST SOUTH AFRICA (1951-1999/2000) AVERAGE TABLE

	T	I	NO	RUNS	HS	AVE.	100	50	0	1-9
L Hutton	5	9	2	378	100	54.00	1	2	–	–
KF Barrington	14	23	3	989	*148	49.45	2	6	1	3
MA Atherton	18	32	2	1315	*185	43.83	3	8	5	7
AJ Stewart	18	31	2	1268	164	43.72	1	7	1	4
GA Hick	10	17	3	606	141	43.28	2	2	–	6
PBH May	12	22	1	906	138	43.14	3	4	3	5
MC Cowdrey	14	27	1	1021	155	39.27	3	7	1	8
ER Dexter	10	16	1	585	172	39.00	1	3	2	1
G Boycott	7	12	2	373	117	37.30	1	2	1	3
RA Smith	5	7	–	254	66	36.28	–	2	–	1
GP Thorpe	10	18	2	486	79	30.37	–	4	3	1
TW Graveney	6	10	–	234	64	23.40	–	1	1	1
GA Gooch	3	6	–	139	33	23.17	–	–	–	1
JH Edrich	1	2	1	7	*7	7.00	–	–	1	–

AGAINST THE WEST INDIES (1950-1997/98) AVERAGE TABLE

	T	I	NO	RUNS	HS	AVE.	100	50	0	1-9
L Hutton	8	14	2	1010	205	84.16	3	3	–	1
DL Amiss	10	18	2	1130	*262	70.62	4	2	–	2
TW Graveney	19	31	5	1532	258	58.92	5	5	4	3
KWR Fletcher	7	13	3	528	*129	52.80	1	3	1	3
PBH May	13	21	2	986	*285	51.89	3	3	2	4
MC Cowdrey	21	36	2	1751	154	51.50	6	10	2	8
ER Dexter	10	19	1	866	*136	48.11	2	5	1	2
G Boycott	29	53	5	2205	128	45.94	5	15	4	9

BATTING STATS

	T	I	NO	RUNS	HS	AVE.	100	50	0	1-9
GA Gooch	26	51	2	2197	*154	44.84	5	13	3	8
RA Smith	19	35	5	1333	175	44.43	3	8	4	4
AJ Stewart	19	35	3	1281	143	40.03	2	6	1	5
GP Thorpe	17	32	3	1084	103	37.37	1	8	3	6
AW Greig	13	23	1	795	148	36.13	3	1	2	5
KF Barrington	17	30	–	1042	143	34.73	3	4	2	8
JH Edrich	14	25	2	792	146	34.43	1	4	2	6
AJ Lamb	22	42	3	1342	132	34.41	6	2	2	10
GA Hick	14	26	2	794	*118	33.08	1	5	2	8
DI Gower	19	38	3	1149	*154	32.83	1	6	–	9
MA Atherton	22	41	–	1276	144	31.12	3	5	5	10
APE Knott	22	38	4	994	116	29.23	1	8	2	16
IT Botham	20	38	1	792	81	21.41	–	4	1	12
MW Gatting	9	17	–	258	56	15.17	–	1	2	7

AGAINST NEW ZEALAND (1950/51-1999) AVERAGE TABLE

	T	I	NO	RUNS	HS	AVE.	100	50	0	1-9
KF Barrington	5	6	–	594	163	99.00	3	1	–	–
DL Amiss	5	7	2	433	*164	86.60	2	1	–	2
MA Atherton	11	17	1	1088	118	68.00	4	6	1	–
PBH May	9	11	2	603	124	67.00	3	2	–	1
JH Edrich	11	15	1	840	*310	60.00	3	2	–	4
MC Cowdrey	18	24	5	1133	*128	59.63	2	8	1	1
ER Dexter	8	10	2	477	141	59.62	1	4	–	2
KWR Fletcher	8	11	–	578	216	52.54	2	1	–	5
GA Gooch	15	24	2	1148	210	52.18	4	3	4	3
DI Gower	13	22	1	1051	131	50.05	4	4	–	4
AJ Lamb	14	23	3	941	142	47.05	3	4	2	4
AJ Stewart	16	26	1	1145	173	45.80	4	5	1	5
AW Greig	5	6	–	267	139	44.50	1	2	1	1
IT Botham	15	23	2	846	138	40.29	3	4	1	5
GP Thorpe	7	12	2	394	119	39.40	2	–	–	4
G Boycott	15	25	1	916	131	38.17	2	6	2	8
RA Smith	9	14	–	485	96	34.64	–	5	2	2
TW Graveney	8	10	1	293	46	32.55	–	–	–	1
APE Knott	9	12	1	352	101	32.00	1	1	2	2
L Hutton	4	6	–	181	57	30.16	–	2	–	1
MW Gatting	11	17	2	435	121	29.00	1	1	2	3
GA Hick	7	10	–	279	58	27.90	–	1	–	1

AGAINST INDIA (1951/52-1996) AVERAGE TABLE

	T	I	NO	RUNS	HS	AVE.	100	50	0	1-9
L Hutton	4	6	1	399	150	79.80	2	1	–	–
KF Barrington	14	21	3	1355	172	75.28	3	9	–	2
MC Cowdrey	8	11	2	653	160	72.56	3	2	–	3
IT Botham	14	17	–	1201	208	70.65	5	5	1	1
RA Smith	6	12	4	507	*121	63.37	2	4	–	3
MA Atherton	7	13	1	689	160	57.41	2	4	1	2
G Boycott	13	22	3	1084	*246	57.05	4	2	–	5
GA Gooch	19	33	2	1725	333	55.65	5	8	1	10
AW Greig	13	18	2	883	148	55.18	3	5	–	3

BATTING STATS

	T	I	NO	RUNS	HS	AVE.	100	50	0	1-9
MW Gatting	16	27	6	1155	207	55.00	3	3	3	2
TW Graveney	11	18	3	805	175	53.66	2	3	–	1
GP Thorpe	3	5	1	193	89	48.25	–	1	–	–
ER Dexter	7	12	2	467	*126	46.70	1	3	1	3
DI Gower	24	37	6	1391	*200	44.87	2	6	3	7
AJ Lamb	13	22	2	877	139	43.85	3	4	–	6
DL Amiss	14	24	1	965	188	41.95	2	4	2	6
KWR Fletcher	19	29	7	874	*123	39.72	2	7	2	8
PBH May	7	10	1	356	106	39.55	1	2	–	3
JH Edrich	10	14	1	494	*100	38.00	1	3	2	2
GA Hick	6	10	–	350	178	35.00	1	1	1	4
AJ Stewart	5	9	–	282	74	31.33	–	3	2	–
APE Knott	16	23	1	685	90	31.13	–	5	1	6

AGAINST PAKISTAN (1954-1996) AVERAGE TABLE

	T	I	NO	RUNS	HS	AVE.	100	50	0	1-9
ER Dexter	8	10	2	749	205	93.62	2	4	–	–
G Boycott	6	10	3	591	*121	84.43	3	3	–	–
KF Barrington	9	12	3	715	148	79.44	4	2	1	3
AJ Stewart	8	13	1	793	190	66.08	2	4	–	3
TW Graveney	13	16	–	943	153	58.93	3	5	1	1
DL Amiss	10	18	4	779	183	55.64	3	2	1	3
DI Gower	17	27	3	1185	*173	49.38	2	9	1	4
KWR Fletcher	9	14	2	586	122	48.83	1	5	–	1
MC Cowdrey	10	15	1	633	182	45.21	3	–	–	3
RA Smith	5	8	1	314	127	44.85	1	1	1	2
GA Gooch	10	16	–	683	135	42.69	1	5	–	1
APE Knott	14	19	3	676	116	42.25	1	5	1	5
AW Greig	6	9	–	351	72	39.00	–	2	–	1
MW Gatting	15	27	2	853	*150	34.12	2	3	3	9
IT Botham	14	21	1	647	108	32.35	2	3	1	7
GP Thorpe	3	5	–	159	77	31.80	–	2	–	2
MA Atherton	6	10	–	307	76	30.70	–	3	1	2
JH Edrich	9	14	1	361	70	27.77	–	2	1	3
PBH May	4	5	–	120	53	24.00	–	1	1	–
GA Hick	5	7	–	106	51	15.14	–	1	–	3
AJ Lamb	8	14	–	180	33	12.85	–	–	2	5
L Hutton	2	3	–	19	14	6.33	–	–	1	1

AGAINST SRI LANKA (1981/82-1998) AVERAGE TABLE

	T	I	NO	RUNS	HS	AVE.	100	50	0	1-9
DI Gower	2	3	1	186	89	93.00	–	2	–	–
RA Smith	3	6	2	269	128	67.25	1	1	–	1
GA Gooch	3	6	–	376	174	62.57	1	1	–	–
AJ Lamb	2	3	–	178	107	59.33	1	1	–	1
AJ Stewart	3	6	1	256	*113	51.20	1	1	–	2
GA Hick	2	4	–	201	107	50.25	1	1	1	–
KWR Fletcher	1	2	1	45	45	45.00	–	–	–	–
MW Gatting	1	2	–	47	29	23.50	–	–	–	–
IT Botham	3	3	–	41	22	13.67	–	–	–	1
MA Atherton	1	2	–	15	13	7.50	–	–	–	1

BATTING STATS

AGAINST ZIMBABWE (1996/97) AVERAGE TABLE

	T	I	NO	RUNS	HS	AVE.	100	50	0	1-9
AJ Stewart	2	4	1	241	*101	80.33	1	1	–	–
GP Thorpe	2	4	1	70	*50	23.33	–	1	–	2
MA Atherton	2	4	–	34	16	8.50	–	–	–	2

HIGHEST AGGREGATE IN A SERIES FOR ENGLAND

	VS	YEAR	T	I	NO	RUNS	HS	AVE.	100	50
GA Gooch	I	1990	3	6	–	752	333	125.33	3	2
DI Gower	A	1985	6	9	–	732	215	81.33	3	1
L Hutton	WI	1953-54	5	8	1	677	205	96.71	2	3
GA Gooch	A	1993	6	12	–	673	133	56.08	2	4
DL Amiss	WI	1973-74	5	9	1	663	*262	82.87	3	–
G Boycott	A	1970-71	5	10	3	657	*142	93.85	2	5
JH Edrich	A	1970-71	6	11	2	648	130	72.00	2	4

HIGHEST AGGREGATE IN A SERIES AGAINST ENGLAND

	FOR	YEAR	T	I	NO	RUNS	HS	AVE.	100	50
MA Taylor	A	1989	6	11	1	839	219	83.90	2	5
IVA Richards	WI	1976	4	7	–	829	291	118.42	3	2
BC Lara	WI	1993-94	5	8	–	798	375	99.75	2	2
BC Lara	WI	1995	6	10	1	765	179	85.00	3	3
GstA Sobers	WI	1966	5	8	1	722	174	103.14	3	2
GstA Sobers	WI	1959-60	5	8	1	709	226	101.28	3	1
CL Walcott	WI	1953-54	5	10	2	698	220	87.25	3	3
KR Stackpole	A	1970-71	6	12	–	627	207	52.25	2	2
MJ Slater	A	1994-95	5	10	–	623	176	62.30	3	1
LG Rowe	WI	1973-74	5	7	–	616	302	88.00	3	–
GS Chappell	A	1974-75	6	11	–	608	144	55.27	2	5

BATTING STATS

TOP TEN INNINGS FOR EACH BATTING POSITION

OPENERS

RUNS	PLAYER	VS	VENUE	YEAR
333	GA Gooch	India	Lord's	1990
310 no	JH Edrich	New Zealand	Leeds	1965
262 no	DL Amiss	West Indies	Kingston	1973-74
246 no	G Boycott	India	Leeds	1967
214 no	D Lloyd	India	Birmingham	1974
205	L Hutton	West Indies	Kingston	1953-54
203	DL Amiss	West Indies	The Oval	1976
202 no	L Hutton	West Indies	The Oval	1950
201	G Fowler	India	Madras	1984-85
196	GA Gooch	Australia	The Oval	1985

NO.3

RUNS	PLAYER	VS	VENUE	YEAR
258	TW Graveney	West Indies	Nottingham	1957
215	DI Gower	Australia	Birmingham	1985
210	GA Gooch	New Zealand	Nottingham	1994
207	MW Gatting	India	Madras	1984-85
205	ER Dexter	Pakistan	Karachi	1961-62
180	ER Dexter	Australia	Birmingham	1961
175	TW Graveney	India	Bombay	1951-52
174	ER Dexter	Australia	Manchester	1964
174	DW Randall	Australia	Melbourne	1976-77
173	AJ Stewart	New Zealand	Auckland	1996-97

NO.4

RUNS	PLAYER	VS	VENUE	YEAR
285 no	PBH May	West Indies	Birmingham	1957
278	DCS Compton	Pakistan	Nottingham	1954
256	KF Barrington	Australia	Manchester	1964
207	N Hussain	Australia	Birmingham	1997
188	MH Denness	Australia	Sydney	1974-75
181	MH Denness	New Zealand	Auckland	1974-75
178	KWR Fletcher	New Zealand	Lord's	1973
175	RA Smith	West Indies	Antigua	1993-94
173 no	DI Gower	Pakistan	Lahore	1983-84
165	TW Graveney	West Indies	The Oval	1966

NO.5

RUNS	PLAYER	VS	VENUE	YEAR
216	KWR Fletcher	New Zealand	Auckland	1974-75
208	IT Botham	India	The Oval	1982
200 no	DI Gower	India	Birmingham	1979
183 no	MW Gatting	India	Birmingham	1986
154	MC Cowdrey	West Indies	Birmingham	1957
152	MC Cowdrey	West Indies	Lord's	1957
152	DI Gower	Pakistan	Faisalabad	1983-84
150 no	MW Gatting	Pakistan	The Oval	1987
149	RA Woolmer	Australia	The Oval	1975
146	KWR Fletcher	Australia	Sydney	1974-75

NO.6

RUNS	PLAYER	VS	VENUE	YEAR
178	GA Hick	India	Bombay	1992-93
158	BL D'Oliveira	Australia	The Oval	1968
154	MR Ramprakash	West Indies	Bridgetown	1997-98
151	MC Cowdrey	India	Delhi	1963-64
148 no	RA Smith	West Indies	Lord's	1991
148	AW Greig	India	Bombay	1972-73
148	AW Greig	West Indies	Bridgetown	1973-74
141	ER Dexter	New Zealand	Christchurch	1958-59
139	AW Greig	New Zealand	Nottingham	1973
138	IT Botham	New Zealand	Wellington	1983-84
	IT Botham	Australia	Brisbane	1986-87

NO.7

RUNS	PLAYER	VS	VENUE	YEAR
164	DW Randall	New Zealand	Wellington	1983-84
149 no	IT Botham	Australia	Leeds	1981
135	APE Knott	Australia	Nottingham	1977
133	CJ Richards	Australia	Perth	1986-87
128 no	RC Russell	Australia	Manchester	1989
126	DW Randall	India	Lord's	1982
125	BR Knight	New Zealand	Auckland	1962-63
124	RC Russell	India	Lord's	1996
119 no	IT Botham	Australia	Sydney	1979-80
118	IT Botham	Australia	Manchester	1981

NO.8

RUNS	PLAYER	VS	VENUE	YEAR
104	TG Evans	West Indies	Manchester	1950
10 no	JM Parks	West Indies	Port-of-Spain	1959-60
128 no	MC Cowdrey	New Zealand	Wellington	1962-63
113	R Illingworth	West Indies	Lord's	1969
100 no	P Willey	West Indies	The Oval	1980
97	RW Taylor	Australia	Adelaide	1978-79
92	APE Knott	Australia	The Oval	1972
88	DA Allen	New Zealand	Christchurch	1965-66
88	PAJ DeFreitas	Australia	Adelaide	1994-95
85	IT Botham	Australia	Lord's	1985

NO.9

RUNS	PLAYER	VS	VENUE	YEAR
104	TG Evans	West Indies	Manchester	1950
112	JT Murray	West Indies	The Oval	1966
89	GAR Lock	West Indies	Georgetown	1967-68
88 no	P Lever	India	Manchester	1971
73	JA Snow	India	Lord's	1971
65	CM Old	Pakistan	The Oval	1974
65	D Gough	New Zealand	Manchester	1994
64	RW Taylor	India	Lord's	1979
62	DA Allen	Pakistan	Leeds	1962
59	GG Arnold	Pakistan	Oval	1967
59	GC Small	Australia	Oval	1989

BATTING STATS

NO. 10

RUNS		PLAYER	VS	VENUE	YEAR
59		GC Small	Australia	Oval	1989
69	no	AC Smith	New Zealand	Wellington	1962-63
65		CC Lewis	West Indies	Birmingham	1991
63		K Higgs	West Indies	The Oval	1966
56		GAR Lock	West Indies	Birmingham	1963
54		RW Taylor	Pakistan	Birmingham	1982
53		GAR Lock	West Indies	Leeds	1963
52	no	PJW Allott	Australia	Manchester	1981
50	no	DA Allen	Australia	Sydney	1965-66
50		PH Edmonds	New Zealand	Christchurch	1977-78
49		GAR Lock	India	Kanpur	1961-62

NO.11

RUNS		PLAYER	VS	VENUE	YEAR
45	no	DL Underwood	Australia	Leeds	1968
36	no	JB Statham	Australia	Adelaide	1958-59
36		TG Evans	South Africa	Manchester	1955
36		NG Cowans	Australia	Perth	1982-83
34		DR Smith	India	Madras	1961-62
34		DV Lawrence	West Indies	Nottingham	1991
33		PI Pocock	Pakistan	Hyderabad	1972-73
32		ARC Fraser	Sri Lanka	The Oval	1998
31	no	JG Thomas	West Indies	Port-of-Spain	1985-86

SUMMARY OF INDIVIDUAL HUNDREDS FOR ENGLAND

	1950S	1960S	1970S	1980S	1990S	TOTAL
Openers	23	24	30	27	32	136
3	15	24	9	13	11	72
4	16	16	8	12	11	63
5	7	9	11	15	11	53
6	3	8	10	4	7	32
7	1	2	10	7	3	23
8	2	2	–	1	–	5
9	–	1	–	–	–	1
10	–	–	–	–	–	–
11	–	–	–	–	–	–
	67	86	78	79	75	385

HIGHEST INDIVIDUAL INNINGS AGAINST ENGLAND
DOUBLE HUNDREDS (31)

RUNS	PLAYER	VS	VENUE	YEAR
375	BC Lara	West Indies	Antigua	1993-94
311	RB Simpson	Australia	Manchester	1964
307	RM Cowper	Australia	Melbourne	1965-66
302	LG Rowe	West Indies	Bridgetown	1973-74
291	IVA Richards	West Indies	The Oval	1976
275	G Kirsten	South Africa	Durban	1999-00
274	Zaheer Abbas	Pakistan	Birmingham	1971
261	FM Worrell	West Indies	Nottingham	1950
260	Javed Miandad	Pakistan	The Oval	1987

240	Zaheer Abbas	Pakistan	The Oval	1974
236	EAB Rowan	South Africa	Leeds	1951
232	IVA Richards	West Indies	Nottingham	1976
226	GS Sobers	West Indies	Bridgetown	1959-60
225	RB Simpson	Australia	Adelaide	1965-66
224	VG Kambli	India	Bombay	1992-93
223	CG Greenidge	West Indies	Manchester	1984
222	GR Vishwanath	India	Madras	1981-82
221	SM Gavaskar	India	The Oval	1979
220	CL Walcott	West Indies	Bridgetown	1953-54
219	MA Taylor	Australia	Nottingham	1989
214*	CG Greenidge	West Indies	Lord's	1984
213	ST Jayasuriya	Sri Lanka	The Oval	1998
210	G Kirsten	South Africa	Manchester	1998
209*	BF Butcher	West Indies	Nottingham	1966
208	AD Nourse	South Africa	Nottingham	1951
207	KR Stackpole	Australia	Brisbane	1970-71
206	AR Morris	Australia	Adelaide	1950-51
206	ED Weekes	West Indies	Port-of-Spain	1953-54
205	Aamir Sohail	Paksitan	Manchester	1992
203*	MAK Pataudi	India	Delhi	1963-64
200*	AR Border	Australia	Leeds	1993
200	Mohin Khan	Pakistan	Lord's	1982

PARTNERSHIP RECORDS – TOP TEN FOR EACH WICKET
1ST WICKET STAND

RUNS	PLAYERS	VS	VENUE	YEAR
290	G Pullar (175), MC Cowdrey (155)	SA	The Oval	1955
234	G Boycott (84), RW Barber (185)	A	Sydney	1965-66
225	GA Gooch (116), MA Atherton (131)	I	Manchester	1990
223	G Fowler (105), CJ Tavare (109)	NZ	The Oval	1983
223	BC Broad (162), CWJ Athey (96)	A	Perth	1986-87
212	C Washbrook (102), RT Simpson (94)	WI	Nottingham	1950
209	G Boycott (99), DL Amiss (174)	WI	Port-of-Sp.	73-74
204	GA Gooch (123), MA Atherton (72)	I	Lord's	1990
203	GA Gooch (117), MA Atherton (87)	A	Adelaide	1990-91
198	G Pullar (165), RW Barber (86)	P	Dacca	1961-62

2ND WICKET STAND

RUNS	PLAYERS	VS	VENUE	YEAR
369	JH Edrich (310*), KF Barrington (163)	NZ	Leeds	1965
351	GA Gooch (196), DI Gower (157)	A	The Oval	1985
351	RT Robinson (148), DI Gower (215)	A	Birmingham	1985
266	PE Richardson (126), TW Graveney (258)	WI	Nottingham	1957
263	MA Atherton (101), GA Gooch (210)	NZ	Nottingham	1994
249	JH Edrich (155), PJ Sharpe (111)	NZ	Nottingham	1969
248	MC Cowdrey (182), ER Dexter (172)	P	The Oval	1962
241	G Fowler (201), MW Gatting (207)	I	Madras	1984-85
221	DL Amiss (188), JH Edrich (96)	I	Lord's	1974
211	D Lloyd (214*), MH Denness (100)	I	Birmingham	1974

BATTING STATS

3RD WICKET STAND

RUNS	PLAYERS	VS	VENUE	YEAR
308	GA Gooch (333), AJ Lamb (139)	I	Lord's	1990
303	MA Atherton (135), RA Smith (175)	WI	Antigua	1993-94
246	E R Dexter (174), KF Barrington (256)	A	Manchester	1964
227	AJ Stewart (190), RA Smith (127)	P	Birmingham	1992
207	TW Graveney (258), PBH May (104)	WI	Nottingham	1957
201	KF Barrington (148), TW Garveney (81)			
		P	Lord's	1967
194*	CA Milton (104*), PBH May (113*)	NZ	Leeds	1958
192	KF Barrington (139), MJK Smith (99)	P	Lahore	1961-62
191	ER Dexter (172), KF Barrington (121)	SA	Johann.	1964-65
187	DI Gower (166), MW Gatting (74)	A	Nottingham	1985

4TH WICKET STAND

RUNS	PLAYERS	VS	VENUE	YEAR
411	PBH May (285*), MC Cowdrey (154)	WI	Birmingham	1957
266	MH Denness (181), KWR Fletcher (216)			
		NZ	Auckland	1974-75
252	G Boycott (246*), BL D'Oliveira (109)	I	Leeds	1967
223	DI Gower (131), MW Gatting (121)	NZ	The Oval	1986
206	KF Barrington (172), ER Dexter (126)	I	Kanpur	1961-62
193	MC Cowdrey (160), KF Barrington (80)	I	Leeds	1959
193	AJ Lamb (119), RA Smith (62)	WI	Bridgetn	1989-90
192	MH Denness (188), KWR Fletcher (146)			
		A	Sydney	1974-75
192	GA Gooch (333), RA Smith (100*)	I	Lord's	1990
191	BR Knight (127), PH Parfitt (121)	I	Kanpur	1963-64

5TH WICKET STAND

RUNS	PLAYERS	VS	VENUE	YEAR
254	KWR Fletcher (113), AW Greig (148)	I	Bombay	1972-73
210	DL Amiss (138*), AW Greig (139)	NZ	Nottingham	1973
202	MH Denness (118), AW Greig (106)	I	Lord's	1974
192	DCS Compton (278), TE Bailey (36*)	P	Nottingham	1954
176*	MW Gatting (150*), IT Botham (51*)	P	The Oval	1987
172	R Subba Row (137), KF Barrington (83)			
		A	The Oval	1961
163	W Watson (109), TE Bailey (71)	I	Lord's	1953
151	IT Botham (208), DW Randall (95)	I	The Oval	1982
150	AJ Stewart (143), GP Thorpe (84)	WI	Bridgetown	93-94
148	TW Graveney (175), AJ Watkins (80)	I	Bombay	1951-52

6TH WICKET STAND

RUNS	PLAYERS	VS	VENUE	YEAR
240	PH Parfitt (131*), BR Knight (125)	NZ	Auckland	1962-63
232	IT Botham (138), DW Randall (164)	NZ	Wellington	83-84
215	G Boycott (107), APE Knott (135)	A	Leeds	1977
207	DI Gower (136), CJ Richards (133)	A	Perth	1986-87
206*	KF Barrington (148*), JM Parks (108*)			
		SA	Durban	1964-65
186	IT Botham (103), DW Randall (83)	NZ	Nottingham	1983
171	IT Botham (114), RW Taylor (43)	I	Bombay	1979-80

169	IT Botham (208), G Miller (98)	I	Manchester	1982
165*	DI Gower (200*), G Miller (63*)	I	Birmingham	1979
163	AW Greig (148), APE Knott (87)	WI	Bridgetn	1973-74

7TH WICKET STAND

RUNS	PLAYERS	VS	VENUE	YEAR
197	MJK Smith (96), JM Parks (101*)	WI	Port-of-Spain	59-60
174	MC Cowdrey (152), TG Evans (82)	WI	Lord's	1957
167	DI Gower (152), VJ Marks (83)	P	Faisalabad	83-84
159	APE Knott (116), P Lever (47)	P	Birmingham	1971
149	APE Knott (104), P Lever (64)	NZ	Auckland	1970-71
143	MW Gatting (123), JE Emburey (58)	P	Birmingham	1987
142	RC Russell (128*), JE Emburey (64)	A	Manchester	1989
135	G Miller (64), RW Taylor (97)	A	Adelaide	1978-79
131	MW Gatting (75*), IT Botham (85)	A	Lord's	1985
130	KWR Fletcher (122), CM Old (65)	P	The Oval	1974

8TH WICKET STAND

RUNS	PLAYERS	VS	VENUE	YEAR
217	TW Graveney (165), JT Murray (112)	WI	The Oval	1966
168	R Illingworth (107), P Lever (88*)	I	Manchester	1971
130	PAJ DeFreitas (69), D Gough (65)	NZ	Manchester	1994
117	IT Botham (149*), GR Dilley (56)	A	Leeds	1981
107	DA Allen (88), DJ Brown (44)	NZ	Christchurch	65-66
104	R Illingworth (57), JA Snow (48)	A	Leeds	1972
103	G Miller (62), RW Taylor (64)	I	Lord's	1979
99	PH Parfitt (119), DA Allen (62)	P	Leeds	1962
96	J Birkenshaw (64), GG Arnold (45)	I	Kanpur	1972-73
94	APE Knott (75), JK Lever (53)	I	Delhi	1976-77

9TH WICKET STAND

RUNS	PLAYERS	VS	VENUE	YEAR
163*	MC Cowdrey (128*), AC Smith (69*)	NZ	Wellington	62-63
117	TE Bailey (134*), DVP Wright (45)	NZ	Christchurch	50-51
109	GAR Lock (89), PI Pocock (13)	WI	Georgetn	1967-68
92	KWR Fletcher (178), GG Arnold (23*)	NZ	Lord's	1973
89	PJ Sharpe (85*), GAR Lock (56)	WI	Birmingham	1963
	IT Botham (119*), JK Lever (12)	A	Melbourne	79-80
83	KWR Fletcher (97*), N Gifford (19)	I	Madras	1972-73
81	RW Barber (69*), GAR Lock (49)	I	Kanpur	1961-62
	APE Knott (92), GG Arnold (22)	A	The Oval	1972
79	FJ Titmus (33), GAR Lock (53)	WI	Leeds	1963

10TH WICKET STAND

RUNS	PLAYERS	VS	VENUE	YEAR
128	K Higgs (63), JA Snow (59*)	WI	The Oval	1966
117*	P Willey (100*), RGD Wiilis (24*)	WI	The Oval	1980
83	R Illingworth (113), JA Snow (9*)	WI	Lord's	1969
79	RW Taylor (54), RGD Willis (28*)	P	Birmingham	1982
74	RT Simpson (156*), R Tattersall (10)	A	Melbourne	
				50-51
70	PJW Allott (41*), RGD Willis (28)	I	Lord's	1982
66	DW Randall (115), NG Cowans (36)	A	Brisbane	1982-83

65	BL D'Oliveira (76), DL Underwood (12*)		
		WI	Nottingham	1966
61	DJ Brown (14), DL Underwood (45*)	A	Leeds	1968
60	TE Bailey (95), MJ Hilton (9*)	SA	Leeds	1951

SUMMARY OF HUNDRED-WICKET STANDS FOR ENGLAND

	1950S	1960S	1970S	1980S	1990S	TOTAL
1st	10	13	20	17	20	80
2nd	14	21	17	16	17	85
3rd	14	17	15	13	13	72
4th	17	20	15	18	20	90
5th	8	13	7	12	8	48
6th	4	11	16	9	5	45
7th	5	–	5	8	4	22
8th	–	2	3	1	1	7
9th	1	2	–	–	–	3
10th	–	1	–	1	–	2
Total	73	100	98	95	88	453

MOST RUNS SCORED BY WICKET-KEEPERS OVER THE FIVE DECADES

	T	RUNS	AVE.	100	50
APE Knott	95	4389	32.75	5	30
AJ Stewart	44	2602	34.23	3	12
RC Russell	54	1897	27.10	2	6
JM Parks	43	1876	32.34	2	9
TG Evans	64	1693	19.68	2	6
RW Taylor	57	1156	16.28	–	3
PR Downton	30	785	19.62	–	4
JR Murray	21	506	22.00	1	2

PRODUCTIVE TEST SERIES BY WICKET-KEEPERS

	T	RUNS	AVE.	VS	YEAR
AJ Stewart	5	465	51.66	SA	1998
AJ Stewart	6	378	31.50	A	1993
APE Knott	5	365	45.62	WI	1973-74
APE Knott	6	364	36.40	A	1974-75
AJ Stewart	5	342	42.75	SA	1999-00
RC Russell	6	314	39.25	A	1989
JM Parks	5	290	48.33	A	1965-66
APE Knott	5	270	30.00	WI	1976
APE Knott	6	268	38.28	I	1976-77
AJ Stewart	6	268	24.36	A	1997
CJ Richards	5	264	37.71	A	1986-87
APE Knott	4	261	37.28	A	1975
AJ Stewart	3	257	64.25	NZ	1996-97
APE Knott	5	255	36.42	A	1977

BOWLING RECORDS

EIGHT WICKETS IN AN INNINGS FOR ENGLAND (12)

ANALYSIS	BOWLER	VS	VENUE	YEAR
10-53	JC Laker	A	Manchester	1956
9-37	JC Laker	A	Manchester	1956
9-57	DE Malcolm	SA	The Oval	1994
8-31	FS Trueman	I	Manchester	1952
8-34	IT Botham	P	Lord's	1978
8-43	RGD Willis	A	Leeds	1981
8-51	DL Underwood	P	Lord's	1974
8-53	ARC Fraser	WI	Port-of-Spain	1997-98
8-75	ARC Fraser	WI	Bridgetown	1993-94
8-86	AW Greig	WI	Port-of Spain	1973-74
8-103	IT Botham	WI	Lord's	1984
8-107	NE Foster	P	Leeds	1987

EIGHT WICKETS IN AN INNINGS AGAINST ENGLAND (16)

ANALYSIS	BOWLER	VS	VENUE	YEAR
9-56	Abdul Qadir	P	Lahore	1987-88
9-65	M Muralitharan	SL	The Oval	1998
9-113	HJ Tayfield	SA	Johannesburg	1956-57
8-38	GD Mc Grath	A	Lord's	1997
8-45	CEL Ambrose	WI	Bridgetown	1989-90
8-53	RAL Massie	A	Lord's	1972
8-55	VMH Mankad	I	Madras	1951-52
8-69	HJ Tayfield	SA	Durban	1956-57
8-71	SK Warne	A	Brisbane	1994-95
8-79	BS Chandrasekhar	I	Delhi	1972-73
8-84	RAL Massie	A	Lord's	1972
8-92	MA Holding	WI	The Oval	1976
8-97	CJ McDermott	A	Perth	1990-91
8-104	AL Valentine	WI	Manchester	1950
8-141	CJ McDermott	A	Manchester	1985
8-143	MHN Walker	A	Sydney	1974-75

TWELVE WICKETS IN A MATCH FOR ENGLAND (11)

ANALYSIS	BOWLER	VS	VENUE	YEAR
19-90	JC Laker	A	Manchester	1956
14-99	AV Bedser	A	Nottingham	1953
13-71	DL Underwood	P	Lord's	1974
13-106	IT Botham	I	Bombay	1979-80
13-156	AW Greig	WI	Port-of-Spain	1973-74
12-89	JH Wardle	SA	Cape Town	1956-57
12-97	DL Underwood	NZ	Christchurch	1970-71
12-101	R Tattersall	SA	Lord's	1951
12-101	DL Underwood	NZ	The Oval	1969
12-112	AV Bedser	SA	Manchester	1951
12-119	FS Trueman	WI	Birmingham	1963

TWELVE WICKETS IN A MATCH AGAINST ENGLAND (10)

ANALYSIS	BOWLER	VS	VENUE	YEAR
16-137	RAL Massie	A	Lord's	1972
16-220	M Muralitharan	SL	The Oval	1998
14-149	MA Holding	WI	The Oval	1976
13-101	Abdul Qadir	P	Lahore	1987-88
13-148	BA Reid	A	Melbourne	1990-91
13-192	HJ Tayfield	SA	Johannesburg	1956-57
12-99	Fazal Mahmood	P	The Oval	1954
12-107	SCG MacGill	A	Sydney	1998-99
12-108	VMH Mankad	I	Madras	1951-52
12-181	L Sivaramakrishnan	I	Bombay	1984-85

MOST WICKETS IN A SERIES FOR ENGLAND

	T	RUNS	WKTS	AVE.	VS	YEAR
JC Laker	5	442	46	9.60	A	1956
AV Bedser	5	682	39	17.48	A	1953
GAR Lock	5	254	34	7.47	NZ	1958
FS Trueman	5	594	34	17.47	WI	1963
IT Botham	6	700	34	20.58	A	1981
JA Snow	6	708	31	22.83	A	1970-71
IT Botham	6	855	31	27.58	A	1985
AV Bedser	5	482	30	16.06	A	1950-51
AV Bedser	5	517	30	17.23	SA	1951
FS Trueman	4	386	29	13.31	I	1952
DLUnderw'd	5	509	29	17.55	I	1976-77
RGD Willis	6	666	29	22.96	A	1981
FH Tyson	5	583	28	20.82	A	1954-55

MOST WICKETS IN A SERIES AGAINST ENGLAND

	T	RUNS	WKTS	AVE.	VS	YEAR
TM Alderman	6	893	42	21.26	A	1981
RM Hogg	6	527	41	12.85	A	1978-79
TM Alderman	6	712	41	17.36	A	1989
DK Lillee	6	870	39	22.30	A	1981
HJ Tayfield	6	636	37	17.18	SA	1956-57
GD McGrath	6	701	36	19.47	A	1997
BS Chandr'r	5	662	35	18.91	I	1972-73
MD Marshall	5	443	35	12.65	WI	1988
VMH Mankad	5	571	34	16.79	I	1951-52
GF Lawson	5	687	34	20.20	A	1982-83
SK Warne	6	877	34	25.79	A	1993
AL Valentine	4	674	33	22.46	WI	1950
JR Thomson	5	592	33	17.93	A	1974-75
AA Donald	5	653	33	19.78	SA	1998
CC Griffith	5	519	32	16.21	WI	1963
CJ McDer't	5	675	32	21.09	A	1994-95
R Benaud	5	584	31	18.83	A	1958-59
DK Lillee	5	548	31	17.67	A	1972
MG Hughes	6	845	31	27.25	A	1993
CJ McDer't	6	901	30	30.03	A	1985
Abdul Qadir	3	437	30	14.56	P	1987-88
CEL Ambr.	6	428	30	14.26	WI	1997-98
GD McKen.	5	654	29	22.55	A	1964
J Garner	5	540	29	18.62	WI	1984
GF Lawson	6	791	29	27.27	A	1989
MA Holding	4	356	28	12.71	WI	1976
AME Roberts	5	537	28	19.17	WI	1976
CEL Ambrose	5	560	28	20.00	WI	1991

LEADING BOWLERS OF THE FIVE DECADES – MINIMUM 100 WICKETS

	T	BALLS	RUNS	WKTS	AVE.	BB	5	10
IT Botham	102	21815	10878	383	28.40	8-34	27	4
RGD Willis	90	17357	8190	325	25.20	8-43	16	–
FS Trueman	67	15178	6625	307	21.57	8-31	17	3
DL Underw'd	86	21862	7674	297	25.83	8-51	17	6
JB Statham	70	16056	6261	252	24.84	7-39	9	1
JA Snow	49	12021	5387	202	26.66	7-40	8	1
ARC Fraser	46	10876	4836	177	27.32	8-53	13	2
GAR Lock	49	13147	4451	174	25.58	7-35	9	3
JC Laker	38	9493	2992	162	18.46	10-53	8	3
FJ Titmus	53	15118	4931	153	32.22	7-79	7	–
AV Bedser	28	8370	2917	147	19.84	7-44	13	3
JE Emburey	64	15391	5646	147	38.80	7-78	6	–
CM Old	46	8858	4020	143	28.11	7-50	4	–
AW Greig	58	9802	4541	141	32.20	8-86	6	2
PAJ De Frei.	44	9838	4700	140	33.57	7-70	4	–
D Gough	36	7722	4105	139	29.53	6-42	6	–
GR Dilley	41	8192	4107	138	29.76	6-38	6	–
DE Malcolm	40	8480	4748	128	37.09	9-57	5	2
PH Edmonds	51	12028	4273	125	34.18	7-66	2	–
DA Allen	39	11297	3779	122	30.97	5-30	4	–
R Illingworth	61	11934	3807	122	31.20	6-29	3	–
PCR Tufnell	41	11053	4387	120	36.55	7-47	5	2
TE Bailey	57	8764	3257	116	28.07	7-34	3	1
GG Arnold	34	7650	3254	115	28.29	6-45	6	–
AR Caddick	30	6765	3274	110	29.76	7-46	7	–
JH Wardle	27	6579	2071	102	20.30	7-36	5	1

HOME CONDITIONS (1950–99) AVERAGE TABLE

	T	BALLS	RUNS	WKTS	AVE.	BB	5	10
JC Laker	25	6273	1881	122	15.41	10-53	7	3
AV Bedser	20	6010	2166	114	19.00	7-44	11	2
GAR Lock	28	6450	2030	104	19.51	7-35	6	2
FS Trueman	47	10295	4590	229	20.04	8-31	14	3
JH Wardle	15	3935	1180	57	20.70	7-56	1	–
JB Statham	37	8760	3370	148	22.77	7-39	7	1
RGD Willis	41	8121	4137	176	23.50	8-43	10	–
GG Arnold	18	4361	1792	75	23.89	5-27	4	–
DL Underw'd	42	9973	3515	145	24.24	8-51	10	4
PCR Tufnell	11	2850	1220	47	25.95	7-66	3	1
GR Dilley	21	4239	2097	78	26.88	6-154	3	–
CM Old	24	5046	2303	85	27.09	7-50	3	–
R Illingworth	43	8778	2769	102	27.14	6-29	3	–

IT Botham	59	12243	6226	226	27.54	8-34	17	2
ARC Fraser	23	5865	2624	90	29.15	5-42	7	1
JA Snow	37	9004	4090	140	29.21	5-57	3	–
PAJ De Freit.	23	5106	2481	84	29.53	7-70	3	–
FJ Titmus	24	5123	1605	54	29.72	5-19	2	–
D Gough	16	3259	1822	58	31.41	6-42	2	–
DA Allen	14	2947	1111	35	31.74	4-58	–	–
PH Edmonds	32	6654	2427	74	32.79	5-28	1	–
DE Malcolm	21	4060	2350	68	34.55	9-57	4	1
TE Bailey	29	4212	1629	46	35.41	7-44	1	1
AW Greig	31	4587	2237	59	37.91	4-33	–	–
JE Emburey	33	6857	2549	63	40.46	5-82	1	–

DL Underwood	29	8000	2770	105	26.38	7-50	4	2
IT Botham	36	8479	4093	148	27.65	6-78	9	2
D Gough	12	2978	1623	57	28.47	6-49	3	–
GG Arnold	8	1992	898	30	29.93	5-86	1	–
ARC Fraser	12	3192	1383	46	30.06	6-82	3	–
CM Old	12	2789	1232	40	30.80	4-104	–	–
JB Statham	22	5405	2138	69	30.98	7-57	3	–
DA Allen	10	2492	892	28	31.85	4-47	–	–
R Illingworth	18	3337	1094	34	32.17	6-87	1	–
TE Bailey	23	3300	1373	42	32.69	4-22	–	–
GR Dilley	12	2666	1349	41	32.90	5-68	1	–
PCR Tufnell	11	2996	1199	35	34.25	7-66	2	1
JE Emburey	25	7650	2698	78	34.58	7-78	3	–
GAR Lock	13	3442	1128	31	36.38	5-45	1	–
PH Edmonds	13	3516	1338	36	37.16	5-28	1	–
AW Greig	21	3472	1663	44	37.79	4-53	–	–
FJ Titmus	19	5765	1794	47	38.17	7-79	2	–
AR Caddick	9	1997	1122	29	38.68	5-42	2	–
PAJ DeFreitas	13	3298	1664	37	44.97	4-56	–	–
DE Malcolm	15	3528	1896	42	45.14	4-39	–	–

OVERSEAS PERFORMANCES
(1950-51 – 1999-2000) AVERAGE TABLE

	T	BALLS	RUNS	WKTS	AVE.	BB	5	10
JH Wardle	12	2644	891	45	19.80	7-36	4	1
JA Snow	12	3017	1297	62	20.91	7-40	5	1
AV Bedser	8	2360	751	33	22.75	5-46	2	1
TE Bailey	28	4552	1628	70	23.25	7-34	2	–
ARC Fraser	23	5011	2212	87	25.42	8-53	6	1
FS Trueman	20	4883	2035	78	26.08	7-75	3	–
RGD Willis	49	9236	4053	149	27.20	6-53	6	–
DL Underwood	44	11889	4159	152	27.36	7-113	7	2
JC Laker	13	3220	1111	40	27.77	5-107	1	–
JB Statham	33	7296	2891	104	27.79	7-57	2	–
AW Greig	27	5215	2304	82	28.09	8-86	6	2
D Gough	20	4463	2283	81	28.18	6-49	4	–
AR Caddick	16	3379	1575	55	28.63	7-46	4	–
CM Old	22	3812	1717	58	29.60	6-54	1	–
IT Botham	43	9572	4652	157	29.63	7-48	10	2
DA Allen	25	8350	2668	87	30.66	5-30	4	–
GR Dilley	20	3953	2010	60	33.50	6-38	3	–
FJ Titmus	29	9995	3326	99	33.59	7-79	5	–
GAR Lock	21	6697	2421	70	34.58	6-53	3	1
PH Edmonds	19	5374	1846	51	36.19	7-66	1	–
GG Arnold	16	3289	1462	40	36.55	6-45	2	–
JE Emburey	31	8534	3097	84	36.86	7-78	5	–
PAJ DeFreitas	21	4732	2219	56	39.62	5-86	1	–
DE Malcolm	19	4420	2398	60	39.96	6-77	1	1
PCR Tufnell	30	8203	3167	73	43.38	7-47	2	1
R Illingworth	18	3156	1038	20	51.90	4-34	–	–

AGAINST AUSTRALIA
(1950-51 – 1998-99) AVERAGE TABLE

	T	BALLS	RUNS	WKTS	AVE.	BB	5	10
JC Laker	12	3078	972	70	13.88	10-53	5	2
AV Bedser	11	3447	1295	70	18.50	7-44	7	2
FS Trueman	19	4361	1999	79	25.30	6-30	5	1
JA Snow	20	5073	2126	83	25.61	7-40	4	–
RGD Willis	35	7294	3346	128	26.14	8-43	7	–
JH Wardle	8	1661	632	24	26.33	5-79	1	–

AGAINST SOUTH AFRICA
(1951 – 1999-2000) AVERAGE TABLE

	T	BALLS	RUNS	WKTS	AVE.	BB	5	10
JH Wardle	9	2687	803	46	17.45	7-36	3	1
JC Laker	8	1901	616	32	19.25	6-55	2	1
AV Bedser	6	1901	670	34	19.70	7-58	3	1
JB Statham	16	3930	1426	69	20.66	7-39	4	1
DE Malcolm	3	591	333	16	20.81	9-57	1	1
FS Trueman	6	1293	620	27	22.96	5-27	1	–
R Illingworth	4	462	146	6	24.33	3-15	–	–
TE Bailey	12	2386	728	28	26.00	5-20	1	–
GAR Lock	4	1252	391	15	26.06	4-39	–	–
ARC Fraser	10	2132	924	35	26.40	5-42	3	1
DA Allen	6	1876	559	21	26.61	5-41	1	–
AR Caddick	5	1110	468	16	29.25	7-46	1	–
D Gough	14	2708	1441	42	34.80	6-42	1	–
JA Snow	1	330	146	4	36.50	3-83	–	–
PAJ DeFreitas	3	681	358	9	39.77	4-89	–	–
FJ Titmus	10	2951	1111	27	41.14	5-66	1	–
PCR Tufnell	4	1360	545	10	54.50	4-124	–	–

AGAINST THE WEST INDIES
(1950 – 1997-98) AVERAGE TABLE

	T	BALLS	RUNS	WKTS	AVE.	BB	5	10
FS Trueman	18	4584	2018	86	23.46	7-44	6	2
ARC Fraser	17	3691	1659	70	23.70	8-53	5	1
JA Snow	14	3594	1917	72	26.62	7-49	4	1
GR Dilley	11	2039	1036	36	28.77	5-55	1	–
TE Bailey	11	2078	857	29	29.55	7-34	2	1
AR Caddick	9	1742	933	31	30.09	6-65	3	–
JC Laker	9	2991	1003	33	30.39	4-71	–	–

BOWLING STATS

	T	BALLS	RUNS	WKTS	AVE.	BB	5	10
GG Arnold	6	1192	538	17	31.64	5-113	1	–
PAJ DeFreitas	11	2302	1067	33	32.33	4-34	–	–
JB Statham	12	3138	1422	42	33.85	5-118	1	–
GAR Lock	13	3432	1323	39	33.92	6-20	2	1
AV Bedser	3	1086	377	11	34.27	5-127	1	–
IT Botham	20	3609	2146	61	35.18	8-103	3	–
AW Greig	13	2462	1281	36	35.58	8-86	3	1
RGD Willis	13	2164	1381	38	36.34	5-42	2	–
DE Malcolm	9	1696	1109	30	36.96	6-77	1	1
FJ Titmus	9	1500	611	15	40.73	5-83	1	–
JE Emburey	15	2817	1260	30	42.00	5-78	2	–
D Gough	3	420	255	6	42.50	3-79	–	–
DL Underwood	17	3877	1656	38	43.57	5-39	1	–
CM Old	9	1470	825	18	45.83	3-80	–	–
DA Allen	8	1898	729	15	48.60	3-57	–	–
JH Wardle	4	915	344	7	49.14	3-24	–	–
PCR Tufnell	9	2317	905	18	50.27	6-25	1	–
R Illingworth	13	2884	1077	19	56.68	3-50	–	–
PH Edmonds	3	555	260	3	86.66	2-98	–	–

AGAINST NEW ZEALAND
(1950-51 – 1999) AVERAGE TABLE

	T	BALLS	RUNS	WKTS	AVE.	BB	5	10
GAR Lock	7	1505	367	47	7.80	7-35	5	2
JC Laker	4	786	173	17	10.17	5-17	1	–
DL Underwood	8	2118	586	48	12.20	7-32	6	3
JB Statham	5	898	268	20	13.40	4-24	–	–
FJ Titmus	6	1812	461	28	16.46	5-19	1	–
TE Bailey	8	928	267	16	16.68	3-43	–	–
AW Greig	5	849	361	20	18.05	5-51	2	1
GR Dilley	6	1196	441	24	18.37	6-38	2	–
RGD Willis	14	3018	1132	60	18.86	5-32	3	–
FS Trueman	11	2167	762	40	19.05	7-75	2	–
D Gough	4	1052	513	25	20.52	5-40	1	–
DE Malcolm	4	878	353	17	20.76	5-46	2	–
AR Caddick	6	1572	586	28	20.92	5-32	1	–
CM Old	6	1141	448	21	21.33	6-54	2	–
JH Wardle	2	459	116	5	23.20	2-41	–	–
IT Botham	15	3284	1500	64	23.43	6-34	6	1
PCR Tufnell	10	2703	926	37	25.02	7-47	1	1
PH Edmonds	11	2593	779	31	25.12	4-20	–	–
PAJ DeFreitas	10	2406	1036	39	26.56	5-53	2	–
R Illingworth	13	2101	597	22	27.13	4-34	–	–
DA Allen	3	1146	359	13	27.61	5-123	1	–
JA Snow	6	1387	554	20	27.70	3-21	–	–
GG Arnold	6	1482	561	20	28.05	5-27	2	–
ARC Fraser	3	756	296	7	42.28	2-40	–	–
JE Emburey	6	1457	417	9	46.33	2-39	–	–
AV Bedser	2	504	138	2	69.00	1-34	–	

AGAINST INDIA
(1951-52 – 1996) AVERAGE TABLE

	T	BALLS	RUNS	WKTS	AVE.	BB	5	10
AV Bedser	4	983	279	20	13.95	5-27	2	–
FS Trueman	9	1784	787	53	14.84	8-31	2	–
GG Arnold	6	1220	504	27	18.66	6-45	1	–
R Illingworth	8	2148	592	31	19.09	6-29	2	–
CM Old	11	1879	821	43	19.09	5-21	1	–
JB Statham	8	1430	516	25	20.64	5-31	1	–
RGD Willis	17	2941	1441	62	23.24	6-53	3	–
JC Laker	4	543	189	8	23.62	4-39	–	–
GAR Lock	7	1932	665	26	25.57	6-65	1	–
IT Botham	14	3371	1558	59	26.40	7-48	6	1
JA Snow	5	1120	433	16	27.06	3-49	–	–
DL Underwood	20	4995	1699	62	27.40	5-84	1	–
FJ Titmus	5	2393	747	27	27.66	6-73	2	–
DA Allen	5	1811	583	21	27.76	5-67	1	–
AW Greig	13	2070	759	27	28.11	5-24	1	–
ARC Fraser	3	955	460	16	28.75	5-104	2	–
GR Dilley	6	1142	649	17	38.17	4-47	–	–
PH Edmonds	14	3747	1346	33	40.78	4-31	–	–
JE Emburey	8	1409	507	12	42.25	2-35	–	–
DE Malcolm	5	1002	606	10	60.60	3-67	–	–
PCR Tufnell	2	483	274	4	68.50	4-142	–	–
PAJ DeFreitas	1	120	75	0	–	–	–	–

AGAINST PAKISTAN
(1954 – 1996) AVERAGE TABLE

	T	BALLS	RUNS	WKTS	AVE.	BB	5	10
JH Wardle	4	857	176	20	8.80	7-56	1	–
AV Bedser	2	449	158	10	15.80	3-9	–	–
JB Statham	7	1255	491	27	18.18	4-18	–	–
JC Laker	1	194	39	2	19.50	1-17	–	–
FS Trueman	4	989	439	22	19.95	6-31	1	–
FJ Titmus	4	697	207	9	23.00	2-3	–	–
RGD Willis	10	1772	820	34	24.11	5-47	1	–
DL Underwood	11	2537	868	36	24.11	8-51	4	1
PH Edmonds	10	1617	550	22	25.00	7-66	1	–
DA Allen	7	2074	657	24	27.37	5-30	1	–
PAJ DeFreitas	5	743	385	14	27.50	5-86	1	–
AR Caddick	1	344	165	6	27.50	3-52	–	–
DE Malcolm	3	617	380	13	29.23	5-94	1	–
R Illingworth	5	1002	301	10	30.10	3-58	–	–
JA Snow	3	517	211	7	30.14	4-70	–	–
GR Dilley	6	1149	632	20	31.60	6-154	2	–
IT Botham	14	2491	1271	40	31.77	8-34	2	–
TE Bailey	3	72	32	1	32.00	1-13	–	–
CM Old	8	1579	694	21	33.04	7-50	1	–
AW Greig	6	949	477	14	34.07	4-86	–	–
GG Arnold	6	1764	753	21	35.85	5-58	1	–
GAR Lock	5	1584	577	16	36.06	4-70	–	–
JE Emburey	7	1386	473	7	67.57	3-49	–	–
PCR Tufnell	1	204	87	1	87.00	1-87	–	–

AGAINST SRI LANKA
(1981-82 – 1998) AVERAGE TABLE

	T	BALLS	RUNS	WKTS	AVE.	BB	5	10
DL Underwood	1	335	95	8	11.87	5-28	1	–
PAJ DeFreitas	1	288	115	8	14.37	7-70	1	–
RGD Willis	1	168	70	3	23.33	2-46	–	–
JE Emburey	3	672	291	11	26.45	6-33	1	–
IT Botham	3	581	310	11	28.18	6-90	1	–
PCR Tufnell	2	493	259	8	32.37	5-94	1	–
ARC Fraser	1	150	114	3	38.00	3-95	–	–
D Gough	1	180	102	2	51.00	2-102	–	–
DE Malcolm	1	168	71	0	–	–	–	–

AGAINST ZIMBABWE
(1996 – 1997) AVERAGE TABLE

	T	BALLS	RUNS	WKTS	AVE.	BB	5	10
D Gough	2	384	171	7	24.42	4-40	–	–
PCR Tufnell	2	497	192	7	27.42	4-61	–	–

AGAINST TOP GUNS – AUSTRALIA, SOUTH AFRICA, WEST INDIES AND PAKISTAN
(1950 – 1999-2000) AVERAGE TABLE

	T	BALLS	RUNS	WKTS	AVE.	BB	5	10
JC Laker	30	8164	2630	137	19.19	10-53	7	3
AV Bedser	22	6883	2500	125	20.00	7-44	11	3
JH Wardle	25	6120	1955	97	20.15	7-56	5	1
FS Trueman	47	11227	5076	214	23.71	7-44	13	3
ARC Fraser	39	9015	3966	151	26.26	8-53	11	2
JB Statham	57	13728	5477	207	26.45	7-39	8	1
JA Snow	38	9514	4400	166	26.50	7-40	8	1
RGD Willis	58	11230	5547	200	27.73	8-43	10	–
DL Underwood	57	14414	5294	179	29.57	8-51	9	3
TE Bailey	49	7836	2990	100	29.90	7-34	3	1
IT Botham	70	14579	7510	249	30.16	8-34	14	2
D Gough	24	5080	2792	91	30.68	6-42	4	–
GR Dilley	29	5854	3-17	97	31.10	6-154	4	–
GG Arnold	22	4948	2189	68	32.19	5-58	3	–
DA Allen	31	8340	2837	88	32.23	5-30	2	–
AR Caddick	24	5193	2688	82	32.78	7-46	6	–
GAR Lock	35	9710	3419	101	33.85	6-20	3	1
CM Old	29	5838	2751	79	34.82	7-50	1	–
PH Edmonds	26	5688	2148	61	35.21	7-66	2	–
AW Greig	40	6883	3421	94	36.39	8-86	3	1
DE Malcolm	30	6432	3718	101	36.81	9-57	3	2
PAJ DeFreitas	32	7024	3474	93	37.35	5-86	1	–
R Illingworth	40	7685	2618	69	37.94	6-87	1	–
FJ Titmus	32	10913	3723	98	37.98	7-79	4	–
JE Emburey	47	11853	4431	115	38.53	7-78	5	–
PCR Tufnell	22	5847	2303	58	39.70	7-66	3	1

AGAINST NOT SO FORMIDABLE – NEW ZEALAND, INDIA, SRI LANKA AND ZIMBABWE
(1950/51 – 1999) AVERAGE TABLE

	T	BALLS	RUNS	WKTS	AVE.	BB	5	10
GAR Lock	14	3437	1032	73	14.13	7-35	6	2
JC Laker	8	1329	362	25	14.48	5-17	1	–
FS Trueman	20	3951	1549	93	16.65	8-31	4	–
TE Bailey	8	928	267	16	16.68	3-43	–	–
JB Statham	13	2328	784	45	17.42	5-31	1	–
AV Bedser	6	1487	417	22	18.95	5-27	2	–
CM Old	17	3020	1269	64	19.82	6-54	3	–
DL Underwood	29	7448	2380	118	20.16	7-32	8	3
AR Caddick	6	1572	586	28	20.92	5-32	1	–
RGD Willis	32	6127	2643	125	21.14	6-53	6	–
FJ Titmus	21	4205	1208	55	21.96	6-73	3	–
R Illingworth	21	4249	1189	53	22.43	6-29	2	–
GG Arnold	12	2702	1065	47	22.65	6-45	3	–
D Gough	7	1616	786	34	23.11	5-40	1	–
JH Wardle	2	459	116	5	23.20	2-41	–	–
AW Greig	18	2919	1120	47	23.82	5-24	3	1
IT Botham	32	7236	3368	134	25.13	7-48	13	2
PAJ DeFreitas	12	2814	1226	47	26.08	7-70	3	–
GR Dilley	12	2338	1090	41	26.58	6-38	2	–
JA Snow	11	2507	987	36	27.41	3-21	–	–
DA Allen	8	2957	942	34	27.70	5-67	2	–
PCR Tufnell	16	4176	1651	56	29.48	7-47	2	1
PH Edmonds	25	6340	2125	64	33.20	4-20	–	–
ARC Fraser	7	1861	870	26	33.46	5-104	2	–
JE Emburey	17	3538	1215	32	37.96	6-33	1	–
DE Malcolm	10	2048	1030	27	38.14	5-46	2	–

MATCH-WINNING CONTRIBUTION (1950 – 1999-2000) AVERAGE TABLE

	T	BALLS	RUNS	WKTS	AVE.	BB	5	10
JC Laker	19	4858	1379	101	13.65	10-53	7	3
GAR Lock	19	4317	1365	93	14.67	7-35	8	3
DL Underwood	27	6384	1868	123	15.18	7-32	10	4
ARC Fraser	12	3238	1289	78	16.52	8-75	9	1
JH Wardle	12	2474	710	42	16.90	7-36	2	1
FS Trueman	31	6956	2936	171	17.16	8-31	11	3
AV Bedser	10	2806	863	50	17.26	5-27	5	2
FJ Titmus	14	3369	901	52	17.32	5-19	2	–
JB Statham	27	6230	2242	127	17.65	7-39	5	1
TE Bailey	24	2936	983	55	17.87	7-34	3	1
RGD Willis	32	6285	2760	141	19.57	8-43	7	–
PCR Tufnell	11	2802	1012	51	19.84	7-47	4	2
IT Botham	32	7319	3390	169	20.05	8-34	15	2
GG Arnold	13	2783	1128	56	20.14	6-45	4	–
AW Greig	17	3069	1230	59	20.84	8-86	4	2
D Gough	7	1818	955	45	21.22	6-42	3	–
CM Old	17	3068	1254	58	21.62	5-21	2	–
AR Caddick	7	1570	762	35	21.77	5-42	4	–

PAJ DeFreitas	10	2332	1063	48	22.14	7-70	2	–
JA Snow	16	3612	1444	65	22.21	7-40	1	–
R Illingworth	29	5789	1636	71	23.04	6-29	1	–
JE Emburey	15	3379	1085	47	23.08	6-33	3	–
DA Allen	8	2265	744	32	23.25	5-41	1	–
PH Edmonds	16	3454	1076	46	23.39	4-6	–	–
DE Malcolm	10	2071	1135	45	25.22	9-57	2	1
GR Dilley	2	442	204	8	25.50	5-68	1	–

CAREER STRIKE RATES – MEDIUM TO FAST CATEGORY

	BALLS	WKTS	BALLS/WKT
FS Trueman	15178	307	49.43
RGD Willis	17357	325	53.40
D Gough	7722	139	55.55
AV Bedser	8370	147	56.93
IT Botham	21815	383	56.95
GR Dilley	8192	138	59.36
JA Snow	12021	202	59.50
ARC Fraser	10876	177	61.44
AR Caddick	6765	110	61.50
CM Old	8858	143	61.94
JB Statham	16056	252	63.71
DE Malcolm	8480	128	66.25
GG Arnold	7650	115	66.52
AW Greig	9802	141	69.51
PAJ DeFreitas	9838	140	70.27
TE Bailey	8764	116	75.55

CAREER SRIKE RATES – SLOW BOWLERS

	BALLS	WKTS	BALLS/WKT
JC Laker	9493	162	58.59
JH Wardle	6579	102	64.50
DL Underwood	21862	297	73.60
GAR Lock	13147	174	75.55
PCR Tufnell	11053	120	92.10
DA Allen	11297	122	92.59
PH Edmonds	12028	125	96.22
R Illingworth	11934	122	97.81
FJ Titmus	15118	153	98.81
J E Emburey	15391	147	104.70

WICKET-KEEPERS
ENGLISH WICKET-KEEPERS OF THE LAST FIVE DECADES

	FROM	TO	TESTS
TG Evans	1950	1959	64
AJW McIntyre	1950	1955	2
DV Brennan	1951		2
RT Spooner	1951-52	1955	7
KV Andrew	1954-55	1963	2
R Swetman	1958-59	1959-60	11
JM Parks	1959-60	1967-68	43
JT Murray	1961	1967	20
G Millman	1961-62	1962	6
AC Smith	1962-63		6
JG Binks	1963-64		2
APE Knott	1967	1981	95
RW Taylor	1970-71	1983-84	57
DL Bairstow	1979	1980-81	4
PR Downton	1980-81	1988	30
BN French	1986	1987-88	16
CJ Richards	1986-87	1988	8
RC Russell	1988	1997-98	54
AJ Stewart	1990-91	1999-00	43
RJ Blakey	1992-93		2
SJ Rhodes	1994	1994-95	11
WK Hegg	1998-99		2
CMW Read	1999		3

LEADING WICKET-KEEPERS OF THE LAST FIVE DECADES – MINIMUM 50 DISMISSALS

	T	CT.	ST.	TOTAL
APE Knott	95	250	19	269
RW Taylor	57	167	7	174
RC Russell	54	153	12	165
TG Evans	64	125	28	153
AJ Stewart	44	136	8	144
JM Parks	43	101	11	112
PR Downton	30	70	5	75
JT Murray	21	52	3	55

MOST DISMISSALS IN A TEST SERIES

DIS	TEST	KEEPER	VS	YEAR
27 (25c.2s)	5	RC Russell	SA	1995-96
24 (21c.3s)	6	APE Knott	A	1970-71
23 (22c.1s)	6	APE Knott	A	1974-75
23 (all ct)	6	AJ Stewart	A	1997
23 (all ct)	5	AJ Stewart	SA	1998
21 (20c.1s)	5	SJ Rhodes	A	1994-95
20 (18c.2s)	5	TG Evans	SA	1956-57
20 (18c.2s)	6	RW Taylor	A	1978-79
20 (19c.1s)	6	PR Downton	A	1985

FIELDING STATS

MOST DISMISSALS IN A MATCH

DIS		KEEPER	VS	VEN	YEAR
11	(all ct)	RC Russell	SA	Johannesburg	1995-96
10	(all ct)	RW Taylor	I	Bombay	1979-80
9	(7c.2s)	RC Russell	SA	Port Elizabeth	1995-96
8	(all ct)	JM Parks	NZ	Christchurch	1965-66
8	(all ct)	AJ Stewart	A	Manchester	1997
8	(all ct)	AJ Stewart	SA	Nottingham	1998
8	(7c.1s)	WW Read	NZ	Birmingham	1999

MOST DISMISSALS IN AN INNINGS

DIS		KEEPER	VS	VEN	YEAR
7	(all ct)	RW Taylor	I	Bombay	1979-80
6	(all ct)	JT Murray	I	Lord's	1967
6	(all ct)	RC Russell	A	Melbourne	1990-91
6	(all ct)	RC Russell	SA	Johannesburg	1995-96
6	(all ct)	AJ Stewart	A	Manchester	1997
6	(5c.1s)	WW Read	NZ	Birmingham	1999
5	(all ct)	JG Binks	I	Calcutta	1963-64
5	(3c.2s)	JM Parks	A	Sydney	1965-66
5	(all ct)	JM Parks	NZ	Christchurch	1965-66
5	(4c.1s)	APE Knott	I	Manchester	1974
5	(all ct)	RW Taylor	NZ	Nottingham	1978
5	(all ct)	RW Taylor	A	Brisbane	1978-79
5	(all ct)	CJ Richards	A	Melbourne	1986-87
5	(all ct)	RC Russell	WI	Bridgetown	1989-90
5	(all ct)	RC Russell	SA	Johannesburg	1995-96
5	(4c.1s)	RC Russell	SA	Port Elizabeth	1995-96
5	(all ct)	AJ Stewart	SA	Lord's	1998
5	(all ct)	AJ Stewart	SA	Nottingham	1998

LEADING FIELDERS OF THE LAST FIVE DECADES

	TESTS	CATCHES
IT Botham	120	102
MC Cowdrey	120	114
GA Gooch	103	118
AW Greig	58	87
TW Graveney	79	80
GA Hick	54	76
AJ Lamb	79	75
DI Gower	117	74
FS Trueman	67	64
GAR Lock	49	59
MW Gatting	79	59
MA Atherton	95	62
KF Barrington	82	58
KWR Fletcher	59	54
MJK Smith	50	53
GP Thorpe	57	53
JM Brearley	39	52

MOST CATCHES IN A TEST SERIES

CATCHES	PLAYER	TESTS	VS	YEAR
12	JT Ikin	3	SA	1951
12	AW Greig	6	A	1974-75
12	IT Botham	6	A	1981
11	AW Greig	3	P	1974
11	IT Botham	6	A	1978-79
11	GA Hick	4	A	1998-99
10	MC Cowdrey	5	SA	1956-57
10	MJK Smith	5	SA	1964-65
10	IT Botham	4	I	1979
10	AJ Lamb	4	NZ	1983
10	IT Botham	4	A	1986-87
10	GA Hick	4	P	1992

MOST CATCHES IN A TEST

CATCHES	PLAYER	VS	VENUE	YEAR
6	MC Cowdrey	WI	Lord's	1963
6	AW Greig	P	Leeds	1974
6	AJ Lamb	NZ	Lord's	1983
6	GA Hick	P	Leeds	1992

MOST CATCHES IN AN INNINGS

CATCHES	PLAYER	VS	VENUE	YEAR
4	JE McConnon	P	Manchester	1954
4	PBH May	A	Adelaide	1954-55
4	PH Parfitt	A	Nottingham	1972
4	AW Greig	P	Leeds	1974
4	PH Edmonds	NZ	Christchurch	1977-78
4	AJ Lamb	NZ	Lord's	1983
4	GA Hick	P	Leeds	1992
4	GA Hick	I	Calcutta	1992-93
4	GA Hick	NZ	Nottingham	1994
4	NV Knight	NZ	Christchurch	1996-97

1000 RUNS AND 100 WICKETS

	T	RUNS	WKTS	TEST FOR DOUBLE
TE Bailey	57	2071	116	46
IT Botham	102	5200	383	21
JE Emburey	64	1713	147	46
AW Greig	58	3599	141	37
R Illingworth	61	1836	122	47
FJ Titmus	53	1449	153	40

A HUNDRED RUNS AND FOUR WICKETS IN AN INNINGS IN THE SAME MATCH

	BAT	BALL	VS	AT	YEAR
AW Greig	139	4-33	NZ	Nottingham	1973
AW Greig	148	6-64	WI	Bridgetown	1973-74
IT Botham	103	5-73	NZ	Christchurch	1977-78
IT Botham	108	8-34	P	Lord's	1978
IT Botham	114	6-58 7-48	I	Bombay	1979-80
IT Botham	*149	6-95	A	Leeds	1981
IT Botham	138	5-59	NZ	Wellington	1983-84

MOST TEST APPEARANCES

	TOTAL	A	SA	WI	NZ	I	P	SL	Z
GA Gooch	118	42	3	26	15	19	10	3	–
DI Gower	117	42	–	19	13	24	17	2	–
MC Cowdrey	114	43	14	21	18	8	10	–	–
G Boycott	108	38	7	29	15	13	6	–	–
IT Botham	102	36	–	20	15	14	14	3	–
APE Knott	95	34	–	22	9	16	14	–	–
RGD Willis	90	35	–	13	14	17	10	1	–
MA Atherton	95	28	18	22	11	7	6	1	2
AJ Stewart	95	24	18	19	16	5	8	3	2
DL Underwood	86	29	–	17	8	20	11	1	–
KF Barrington	82	23	14	17	5	14	9	–	–
TW Graveney	79	22	6	19	8	11	13	–	–
MW Gatting	79	27	–	9	11	16	15	1	–
AJ Lamb	79	20	–	22	14	13	8	2	–
JH Edrich	77	32	1	14	11	10	9	–	–
JB Statham	70	22	16	12	5	8	7	–	–
FS Trueman	67	19	6	18	11	9	4	–	–
PBH May	66	21	12	13	9	7	4	–	–
TG Evans	64	22	11	12	9	6	4	–	–
JE Emburey	64	25	–	15	6	8	7	3	–
ER Dexter	62	19	10	10	8	7	8	–	–
RA Smith	62	15	5	19	9	6	5	3	–
R Illingworth	61	18	4	13	13	8	5		
KWR Fletcher	59	15	–	7	8	19	9	1	–
AW Greig	58	21	–	13	5	13	6	–	–
TE Bailey	57	23	12	11	8	–	3	–	–
RW Taylor	57	17	–	–	14	13	12	1	–
GP Thorpe	57	15	10	17	7	3	3	–	2
RC Russell	54	9	5	21	6	6	5	–	–

GA Hick	54	10	10	14	7	6	5	2	–
FJ Titmus	53	19	10	9	6	5	4	–	–
PH Edmonds	51	13	–	3	11	14	10	–	–
MJK Smith	50	9	12	6	9	11	3	–	–
DL Amiss	50	11	–	10	5	14	10	–	–

THE BOTHAM FACTOR

It's worth having a look at the effect of Ian Botham, hailed as the greatest English all-rounder, on his side's fortunes over the fifteen years he was an international player.

	P	W	L	D	SR%
Pre Botham era (1950 to 1977)	252	90	55	107	35.71
Ian Botham era (1977 to 1992)	156	42	50	64	26.92
Post Botham era (1992 to 1999-00)	83	19	36	28	22.89
Total	491	151	141	199	30.75

The above figures suggest even the mercurial all-rounder could not alter the downward trend of England's international standing over the fifteen years.

THE VERY BOTHAM PRESENCE (1977 TO 1992)

	P	W	L	D	SR%
Botham in the line-up	102	33	32	37	32.35
Botham not in the line-up	54	9	18	27	16.66
Total	156	42	50	64	26.92

A further breakdown would indicate that, during the fifteen years he was on the scene, England relied heavily on his match-winning contribution for elusive Test wins.

PLAYERS STATS

COMPLETE TEST CAREER RECORDS OF ENGLISH PLAYERS (1950 – 1999-00)

From vs W I (8-12 June 1950) at Old Trafford to vs SA (14-18 January 2000) at Centurion Park.

NB : * indicates the players who began their careers prior to 1950 and continued into the above period, i.e. 1950 to 1999-00, do not have their full career figures in the following set of statistics. In the HS column it indicates not-out.

	T	I	NO	RUNS	HS	AVE.	100	50	CT/ST	BALLS	RUNS	WKTS	AVE.	BB	5WI	10WM
CJ Adams	5	8	–	104	31	13.00	–	–	6	120	59	1	59.00	1-42	–	–
JP Agnew	3	4	3	5	10	10.00	–	–	–	552	373	4	93.25	2-51	–	–
DA Allen	39	51	15	918	88	25.50	–	5	10	11297	3779	122	30.97	5-30	4	–
PJW Allott	13	18	3	213	*52	14.20	–	1	4	2225	1084	26	41.69	6-61	1	–
DL Amiss	50	88	10	3612	*262	46.30	11	11	24							
KV Andrew	2	4	1	29	15	9.66	–	–	1							
R Appleyard	9	9	6	51	*19	17.00	–	–	4	1596	554	31	17.87	5-51	1	–
GG Arnold	34	46	11	421	59	12.02	–	1	9	7650	3254	115	28.29	6-45	6	–
MA Atherton	95	175	6	6403	*185	37.88	13	39	62	408	302	2	151.00	1-20	–	–
CWJ Athey	23	41	1	919	123	22.97	1	4	13							
RJ Bailey	4	8	–	119	43	14.87	–	–	–							
*TE Bailey	57	86	12	2071	93	27.98	1	8	32	8764	3257	116	28.07	7-34	3	1
DL Bairstow	4	7	1	125	59	20.83	–	1	12/1							
JC Balderstone	2	4	–	39	35	9.75	–	1	1	96	80	1	80.00	1-80	–	–
RW Barber	28	45	3	1495	185	35.59	1	9	21	3426	1806	42	43.00	4-132	–	–
GD Barlow	3	5	1	17	*7	4.25	–	–	–							
KJ Barnett	4	7	–	207	80	29.57	–	2	1	36	32	0	–	–	–	–
KF Barrington	82	131	15	6806	256	58.67	20	35	58	2715	1300	29	44.82	3-4	–	–
* AV Bedser	28	36	9	263	*30	9.74	–	–	9	8370	2917	147	19.84	7-44	13	3
JE Benjamin	1	1	–	0	0	–	–	–	–	168	80	4	20.00	4-42	–	–
MR Benson	1	2	–	51	30	25.50	–	–	–							
R Berry	2	4	2	6	*4	3.00	–	–	2	653	228	9	25.33	5-63	1	–
MP Bicknell	2	4	–	26	14	6.50	–	–	–	522	263	4	65.75	3-99	–	–
JG Binks	2	4	–	91	55	22.75	–	1	8							
J Birkenshaw	5	7	–	148	64	21.14	–	1	3	1017	469	13	36.07	5-57	1	–
RJ Blakey	2	4	–	7	6	1.75	–	–	2							
JB Bolus	7	12	–	496	88	41.33	–	4	2	18	16	0	–	–	–	–'
IT Botham	102	161	6	5200	208	33.54	14	22	120	21815	10878	383	28.40	8-34	27	4
G Boycott	108	193	23	8114	*246	47.72	22	42	33	944	382	7	54.57	3-47	–	–
JM Brearley	39	66	3	1442	91	22.88	–	9	52							
DV Brennan	2	2	–	16	16	8.00	–	–	–/1							
BC Broad	25	44	2	1661	162	39.54	6	6	10	6	4	0	–	–	–	–
A Brown	2	1	1	3	*3	–	–	–	1	323	150	3	50.00	3-27	–	–
DJ Brown	26	34	5	342	*44	11.79	–	–	7	5098	2237	79	28.31	5-42	2	–
* FR Brown	14	22	1	516	79	24.57	–	3	15	2140	901	32	28.15	5-49	1	–
SJE Brown	1	2	1	11	*10	11.00	–	–	1	198	138	2	69.00	1-60	–	–
AR Butcher	1	2	–	34	20	17.00	–	–	–	12	9	0	–	–	–	–
MA Butcher	27	51	1	1253	116	25.06	2	4	21	332	169	3	56.33	2-32	–	–
RO Butcher	3	5	–	71	32	14.20	–	–	3							
AR Caddick	30	47	5	522	48	12.42	–	–	14	6765	3274	110	29.76	7-46	7	–
DJ Capel	15	25	1	374	98	15.58	–	2	6	2000	1064	21	50.66	3-88	–	–
DB Carr	2	4	–	135	76	33.75	–	1	–	210	140	2	70.00	2-84	–	–
TW Cartwright	5	7	2	26	9	5.20	–	–	2	1611	544	15	36.26	6-94	1	–

PLAYERS STATS

	T	I	NO	RUNS	HS	AVE.	100	50	CT/ST	BALLS	RUNS	WKTS	AVE.	BB	5WI	10WM
JH Childs	2	4	4	2	*2	–	–	–	1	516	183	3	61.00	1-13	–	–
DB Close	22	37	2	887	70	25.34	–	4	24	1212	532	18	29.55	4-35	–	–
LJ Coldwell	7	7	5	9	*6	4.50	–	–	1	1668	610	22	27.72	6-85	1	–
*DCS Compton	42	71	7	2675	278	41.79	4	16	22	572	369	5	73.80	2-40	–	–
G Cook	7	13	–	203	66	15.61	–	2	9	42	27	0	–	–	–	–
NGB Cook	15	25	4	179	31	8.52	–	–	5	4174	1689	52	32.48	6-65	4	1
GA Cope	3	3	–	40	22	13.33	–	–	1	864	277	8	34.62	3-102	–	–
WH Copson	3	1	–	6	6	6.00	–	–	1	762	297	15	19.80	5-85	1	–
DG Cork	27	42	6	634	59	17.61	–	2	13	5963	3118	98	31.81	7-43	5	–
RMH Cottom	4	5	1	27	13	6.75	–	–	2	903	327	14	23.35	4-50	–	–
NG Cowans	19	29	7	175	36	7.95	–	–	9	3452	2003	51	39.27	6-77	2	–
CS Cowdrey	6	8	1	101	38	14.42	–	–	5	399	309	4	77.25	2-65	–	–
MC Cowdrey	114	188	15	7624	182	44.06	22	38	120	119	104	0	–	–	–	–
JF Crapp	7	13	2	319	56	29.00	–	3	7							
JP Crawley	29	47	5	1329	*156	31.64	3	7	26							
RDB Croft	15	24	6	295	*37	16.38	–	–	8	3479	1380	36	38.33	5-95	1	–
TS Curtis	5	9	–	140	41	15.55	–	–	3	18	7	0	–	–	–	–
PAJ DeFreitas	44	68	5	934	88	14.82	–	4	14	9838	4700	140	33.57	7-70	4	–
MH Denness	28	45	3	1667	188	39.69	4	7	28							
* JG Dewes	4	8	–	110	67	13.75	–	1	–							
ER Dexter	62	102	8	4502	205	47.89	9	27	29	5317	2306	66	34.93	4-10	–	–
GR Dilley	41	58	19	521	56	13.35	–	2	10	8192	4107	138	29.76	6-38	6	–
GHG Doggart	2	4	–	76	29	19.00	–	–	3							
BL D'Oliveira	44	70	8	2484	158	40.06	5	15	29	5706	1859	47	39.55	3-46	–	–
* HE Dollery	1	2	–	8	8	4.00	–	–	1							
PR Downton	30	48	8	785	74	19.62	–	4	70/5							
MA Ealham	8	13	3	210	53*	21.00	–	2	4	1060	488	17	28.70	4-21	–	–
PH Edmonds	51	65	15	875	64	17.50	–	2	42	12028	4273	125	34.18	7-66	2	–
JH Edrich	77	127	9	5138	*310	43.54	12	24	43	30	23	0	–	–	–	–
* WJ Edrich	10	18	1	434	88	25.52	–	4	11	228	109	0	–	–	–	–
RM Ellison	11	16	1	202	41	13.46	–	–	2	2264	1048	35	29.94	6-77	3	1
JE Emburey	64	96	20	1713	75	22.53	–	10	34	15391	5646	147	38.80	7-78	6	–
* TG Evans	64	93	7	1693	104	19.68	2	6	125/28							
NH Fairbrother	10	15	1	219	83	15.64	–	1	4	12	9	0	–	–	–	–
JA Flavell	4	6	2	31	14	7.75	–	–	–	792	367	7	52.42	2-65	–	–
KWR Fletcher	59	96	14	3272	216	39.90	7	19	54	285	193	2	96.50	1-6	–	–
A Flintoff	6	9	–	172	42	19.11	–	–	3	611	302	6	50.33	2-31	–	–
NA Foster	29	45	7	446	39	11.73	–	–	7	6261	2891	88	32.85	8-107	5	1
G Fowler	21	37	–	1307	201	35.32	3	8	10	18	11	0	–	–	–	–
ARC Fraser	46	67	15	388	32	7.46	–	–	9	10876	4836	177	27.32	8-53	13	2
BN French	16	21	4	308	59	18.11	–	1	38/1							
JER Gallian	3	6	–	74	28	12.33	–	–	1	84	62	0	–	–	–	–
MW Gatting	79	138	14	4409	207	35.55	10	21	59	752	317	4	79.25	1-14	–	–
N Gifford	15	20	9	179	*25	16.27	–	–	8	3084	1026	33	31.09	5-55	1	–
ESH Giddins	1	2	1	0	*0	–	–	–	–	156	79	4	19.75	3-38	–	–
AF Giles	1	2	1	17	*16	17.00	–	–	–	216	106	1	106.00	1-106	–	–
GA Gooch	118	215	6	8900	333	42.58	20	46	103	2655	1069	23	46.47	3-39	–	–

	T	I	NO	RUNS	HS	AVE.	100	50	CT/ST	BALLS	RUNS	WKTS	AVE.	BB	5WI	10WM
D Gough	36	54	9	532	65	11.82	–	2	9	7722	4105	139	29.53	6-42	6	–
DI Gower	117	204	18	8231	215	44.25	18	39	74	36	20	1	20.00	1-1	–	–
TW Graveney	79	123	13	4882	258	44.38	11	20	80	260	167	1	167.00	1-34	–	–
T Greenhough	4	4	1	4	2	1.33	–	–	1	1129	357	16	22.31	5-35	1	–
AW Greig	58	93	4	3599	148	40.43	8	20	87	9802	4541	141	32.20	8-86	6	2
IA Greig	2	4	–	26	14	6.50	–	–	–	188	114	4	28.50	4-53	–	–
A Habib	2	3	–	26	19	8.66	–	–	–							
GM Hamilton	1	2	–	0	0	–	–	–	–	90	63	0	–	–	–	–
JH Hampshire	8	16	1	403	107	26.86	1	2	9							
FC Hayes	9	17	1	244	*106	15.25	1	–	7							
DW Headley	15	26	4	186	31	8.45	–	–	7	3026	1671	60	27.85	6-60	1	–
WK Hegg	2	4	–	30	15	7.50	–	–	8							
EE Hemmings	16	21	44	383	95	22.52	–	2	5	4437	1825	43	42.44	6-58	1	–
M Hendrick	30	35	15	128	15	6.40	–	–	25	6208	2248	87	25.83	4-28	–	–
GA Hick	54	94	6	3005	178	34.14	5	17	76	2985	1256	22	57.09	4-126	–	–
K Higgs	15	19	3	185	63	11.56	–	1	4	4112	1473	71	20.74	6-91	2	–
MJ Hilton	4	6	1	37	15	7.40	–	–	1	1244	477	14	34.07	5-61	1	–
RNS Hobbs	7	8	3	34	*15	6.80	–	–	8	1291	481	12	40.08	3-25	–	–
*WE Hollies	2	4	1	5	3	1.66	–	–	–	714	268	10	26.80	5-63	1	–
AJ Hollioake	4	6	–	65	45	10.83	–	–	4	144	67	2	33.50	2-31	–	–
BC Holliioake	2	4	–	44	28	11.00	–	–	2	252	199	4	49.75	2-105	–	–
MJ Horton	2	2	–	60	58	30.00	–	1	2	238	59	2	29.50	2-24	–	–
ND Howard	4	6	1	86	23	17.20	–	–	4							
N Hussain	47	84	8	2974	207	39.13	8	13	36	42	25	0	–	–	–	–
* L Hutton	38	66	10	3183	205	56.83	8	16	30	54	50	0	–	–	–	–
RA Hutton	5	8	2	219	81	36.50	–	2	9	738	257	9	28.55	3-72	–	–
AP Igglesden	3	5	3	6	*3	3.00	–	–	1	555	329	6	54.83	2-91	–	–
*JT Ikin	6	10	1	248	53	27.55	–	2	17							
R Illingworth	61	90	11	1836	113	23.24	2	5	45	11934	3807	122	31.20	6-29	3	–
RK Illingworth	9	14	7	128	28	18.28	–	–	5	1485	615	19	32.36	4-96	–	–
MC Ilott	5	6	2	28	15	7.00	–	–	–	1042	542	12	45.16	3-48	–	–
DJ Insole	9	17	2	408	*110	27.20	1	1	8							
RC Irani	3	5	–	86	41	17.20	–	–	2	192	112	3	38.00	1-22	–	–
RD Jackman	4	6	–	42	17	7.00	–	–	–	1070	445	14	31.78	4-110	–	–
*HL Jackson	1	1	–	8	8	8.00	–	–	1	264	83	4	20.75	2-26	–	–
SP James	2	4	–	71	36	17.75	–	–	–							
JA Jameson	4	8	–	214	82	26.75	–	1	–	42	17	1	17.00	1-17	–	–
PW Jarvis	9	15	2	132	*29	10.15	–	–	2	1912	965	21	45.95	4-107	–	–
*RO Jenkins	4	6	1	112	39	22.40	–	–	2	1055	603	16	37.68	5-116	1	–
IJ Jones	9	12	1	198	39	18.00	–	–	4	2118	1098	32	34.31	5-116	1	–
D Kenyon	8	15	–	192	87	12.80	–	1	5							
BR Knight	29	38	7	812	127	26.19	2	–	14	5377	2223	70	31.75	4-38	–	–
NV Knight	12	21	–	585	113	27.85	1	4	21							
APE Knott	95	149	15	4389	135	32.75	5	30	250/19							
*JC Laker	38	49	13	453	48	12.58	–	–	11	9493	2992	162	18.46	10-53	8	3
AJ Lamb	79	139	10	4656	142	36.09	14	18	75	30	23	1	23.00	1-6	–	–
W Larkins	13	25	1	493	64	20.54	–	3	8							

	T	I	NO	RUNS	HS	AVE.	100	50	CT/ST	BALLS	RUNS	WKTS	AVE.	BB	5WI	10WM
JDF Larter	10	7	2	16	10	3.20	–	–	5	2172	941	37	25.43	5-57	2	–
MN Lathwell	2	4	–	78	33	19.50	–	–	–							
DV Lawrence	5	6	–	60	34	10.00	–	–	–	1089	676	18	37.55	5-106	1	–
E Leabeater	2	2	–	40	38	20.00	–	–	3	289	218	2	109.00	1-38	–	–
JK Lever	21	31	5	306	53	11.76	–	1	11	4433	1951	73	26.72	7-46	3	1
P Lever	17	18	2	350	*88	21.87	–	2	11	3571	1509	41	36.80	6-38	2	–
AR Lewis	9	16	2	457	125	32.64	1	3	–							
CC Lewis	32	51	3	1105	117	23.02	1	4	25	6852	3490	93	37.52	6-111	3	–
D Lloyd	9	15	2	552	*214	42.46	1	–	11	24	17	0	–	–	–	–
TA Lloyd	1	1	1	10	*10	–	–	–	–							
PJ Loader	13	19	6	76	17	5.84	–	–	2	2662	878	39	22.51	6-36	1	–
GAR Lock	49	63	9	742	89	13.74	–	3	59	13147	4451	174	25.58	7-35	9	3
FA Lowson	7	13	–	245	68	18.84	–	2	5							
BW Luckhurst	21	41	5	1298	131	36.05	4	5	14	57	32	1	32.00	1-9	–	–
MJ McCague	3	5	–	21	11	4.20	–	–	1	593	390	6	65.00	4-121	–	–
JE McConnon	2	3	1	18	11	9.00	–	–	4	216	74	4	18.50	3-19	–	–
AJW McIntyre	3	6	–	19	7	3.16	–	–	8							
DL Maddy	3	4	–	46	24	11.50	–	–	4	84	40	0	–	–	–	–
DE Malcolm	40	58	19	236	29	6.05	–	–	7	8480	4748	128	37.09	9-57	5	2
NA Mallender	2	3	–	8	4	2.66	–	–	–	449	215	10	21.50	5-50	1	–
VJ Marks	6	10	1	249	83	27.66	–	3	–	1082	484	11	44.00	3-78	–	–
PJ Martin	8	13	–	115	29	8.84	–	–	6	1452	580	17	34.11	4-60	–	–
PBH May	66	106	9	4537	*285	46.77	13	22	42							
MP Maynard	4	8	–	87	35	10.87	–	–	3							
C Milburn	9	16	2	654	139	46.71	2	2	7							
G Miller	34	51	4	1213	98	25.80	–	7	17	5149	1859	60	30.98	5-44	1	–
G Millman	6	7	2	60	32*	12.00	–	–	13/2							
CA Milton	6	9	1	204	104*	25.50	1	–	5	24	12	0	–	–	–	–
H Morris	3	6	–	115	44	19.16	–	–	3							
JE Morris	3	5	2	71	32	23.66	–	–	3							
JB Mortimore	9	12	2	243	73*	24.30	–	1	3	2162	733	13	56.38	3-36	–	–
AE Moss	9	7	1	61	26	10.16	–	–	1	1657	626	21	29.80	4-35	–	–
MD Moxon	10	17	1	455	99	28.43	–	3	10	48	30	0	–	–	–	–
AD Mullally	18	26	4	127	24	5.77	–	–	6	4342	1713	56	30.58	5-105	1	–
TA Munton	2	2	1	25	25*	25.00	–	–	–	405	200	4	50.00	2-22	–	–
JT Murray	21	28	5	506	112	22.00	1	2	52/3							
PJ Newport	3	5	1	110	40*	27.50	–	–	1	669	417	10	41.70	4-87	–	–
ASM Oakman	2	2	–	14	10	5.00	–	–	7	48	21	0	–	–	–	–
CM Old	46	66	9	845	*65	14.82	–	2	22	8858	4020	143	28.11	7-50	4	–
DEV Padgett	2	4	–	51	31	12.75	–	–	–	12	8	0	–	–	–	–
CH Palmer	1	2	–	22	22	11.00	–	–	–	30	15	0	–	–	–	–
KE Palmer	1	1	–	10	10	10.00	–	–	–	378	189	1	189.00	1-113	–	–
PH Parfitt	37	52	6	1882	*131	40.91	7	6	42	1326	574	12	47.83	2-5	–	–
PWG Parker	1	2	–	13	13	6.50	–	–	–							
WGA Parkhouse	7	13	–	373	78	28.69	–	2	3							
JM Parks	46	68	7	1962	*108	32.16	2	9	103/11	54	51	1	51.00	1-43	–	–
MM Patel	2	2	–	45	27	22.50	–	–	2	276	180	1	180.00	1-101	–	–

	T	I	NO	RUNS	HS	AVE.	100	50	CT/ST	BALLS	RUNS	WKTS	AVE.	BB	5WI	10WM
ACS Pigott	1	2	1	12	*8	12.00	–	–	–	102	75	2	37.50	2-75	–	–
PI Pocock	25	37	4	206	33	6.24	–	–	15	6650	2976	67	44.41	6-79	3	–
CJ Poole	3	5	1	161	*69	40.25	–	2	1	30	9	0	–	–	–	–
JSE Price	15	15	6	66	32	7.33	–	–	7	2724	1401	40	35.02	5-73	1	–
RM Prideaux	3	6	1	102	64	20.40	–	1	–	12	0	0	–	–	–	–
DR Pringle	30	50	4	695	63	15.10	–	1	10	5287	2518	70	35.97	5-95	3	–
G Pullar	28	49	4	1974	175	43.86	4	12	2	66	37	1	37.00	1-1	–	–
NV Radford	3	4	1	21	*12	7.00	–	–	–	678	351	4	87.75	2-131	–	–
CT Radley	8	10	–	481	158	48.10	2	2	4							
MR Ramprakash	38	67	6	1701	154	27.88	1	10	28	841	445	4	111.25	1-2	–	–
DW Randall	47	79	5	2470	174	33.37	7	12	31	16	3	0	–	–	–	–
CMW Read	3	4	–	38	37	9.50	–	–	10/1							
DA Reeve	3	5	–	124	59	24.80	–	1	1	149	60	2	30.00	1-4	–	–
HJ Rhodes	2	1	1	0	*0	–	–	–	–	449	244	9	27.11	4-50	–	–
SJ Rhodes	11	17	5	294	*65	24.50	–	1	46/3							
CJ Richards	8	13	–	285	133	21.92	1	–	20/1							
DW Richardson	1	1	–	33	33	33.00	–	–	1							
PE Richardson	34	56	1	2061	126	37.47	5	9	6	120	48	3	16.00	2-10	–	–
F Ridgway	5	6	–	49	24	8.16	–	–	3	793	379	7	54.14	4-83	–	–
*JDB Robertson	5	9	1	310	77	34.44	–	3	2	138	58	2	29.00	2-17	–	–
RT Robinson	29	49	5	1601	175	36.38	4	6	8	6	0	0	–	–	–	–
GRJ Roope	21	32	4	860	77	30.71	–	7	35	172	76	0	–	–	–	–
BC Rose	9	16	2	358	70	25.57	–	2	4							
FE Rumsey	5	5	3	30	*21	15.00	–	–	–	1145	461	17	27.11	4-25	–	–
RC Russell	54	86	16	1897	*128	27.10	2	6	153/12							
WE Russell	10	18	1	362	70	21.29	–	2	4	144	44	0	–	–	–	–
IDK Salisbury	12	22	2	284	50	14.20	–	1	5	2078	1346	19	70.84	4-163	–	–
MWW Selvey	3	5	3	15	*5	7.50	–	–	1	492	343	6	57.16	4-41	–	–
D Shackleton	7	13	7	113	42	18.83	–	–	1	2078	768	18	42.66	4-72	–	–
PJ Sharpe	12	21	4	786	111	46.23	1	4	17							
DS Sheppard	22	33	2	1172	119	37.80	3	6	12							
K Shuttleworth	5	6	–	46	21	7.66	–	–	1	1071	427	12	35.58	5-47	1	–
A Sidebottom	1	1	–	2	2	2.00	–	–	–	112	65	1	65.00	1-65	–	–
CEW Silverwood	5	6	3	19	*7	6.33	–	–	2	804	415	11	37.72	5-91	1	–
*RT Simpson	24	41	3	1225	*156	32.23	3	5	5	33	13	2	6.50	2-4	–	–
WN Slack	3	6	–	81	52	13.50	–	1	3							
GC Small	17	24	7	263	59	15.47	–	1	9	3927	1871	55	34.01	5-48	2	–
AM Smith	1	2	1	4	*4	4.00	–	–	–	138	89	0	–	–	–	–
AC Smith	6	7	3	118	*69	29.50	–	1	20							
CL Smith	8	14	1	392	91	30.15	–	2	5	102	39	3	13.00	2-31	–	–
DM Smith	2	4	–	80	47	20.00	–	–	–							
DR Smith	5	5	1	38	34	9.50	–	–	2	972	359	6	59.83	2-60	–	–
DV Smith	3	4	1	25	*16	8.33	–	–	–	270	97	1	97.00	1-12	–	–
MJK Smith	50	78	6	2278	121	31.63	3	11	53	214	128	1	128.00	1-10	–	–
RA Smith	62	112	15	4236	175	43.67	9	28	39	24	6	0	–	–	–	–
JA Snow	49	71	14	772	73	13.54	–	2	16	12021	5387	202	26.66	7-40	8	1
RT Spooner	7	14	1	354	92	27.23	–	3	10/2							

	T	I	NO	RUNS	HS	AVE.	100	50	CT/ST	BALLS	RUNS	WKTS	AVE.	BB	5WI	10WM
JB Statham	70	87	28	675	38	11.44	–	–	28	16056	6261	252	24.84	7-39	9	1
DS Steele	8	16	–	673	106	42.06	1	5	7	88	39	2	19.50	1-1	–	–
JP Stephenson	1	2	–	36	25	18.00	–	–	–							
GB Stevenson	2	2	1	28	*27	28.00	–	–	–	312	183	5	36.60	3-111	–	–
AJ Stewart	95	172	12	6525	190	40.78	12	35	172/8	20	13	0	–	–	–	–
MJ Stewart	8	12	1	385	87	35.00	–	2	6							
R Subba Row	13	22	1	984	137	46.85	3	4	5	6	2	0	–	–	–	–
PM Such	11	16	5	67	*14	6.09	–	–	4	3124	1242	37	33.56	6-67	2	–
R Swetman	11	17	2	254	65	16.93	–	1	24/2							
R Tattersall	16	17	7	50	*10	5.00	–	–	8	4228	1513	58	26.08	7-52	4	1
CJ Tavare	31	56	2	1755	149	32.50	2	12	20	30	11	0	–	–	–	–
JP Taylor	2	4	2	34	*17	17.00	–	–	–	288	156	3	52.00	1-18	–	–
K Taylor	3	5	–	57	24	11.40	–	–	1	12	6	0	–	–	–	–
LB Taylor	2	1	1	1	*1	–	–	–	1	381	178	4	44.50	2-34	–	–
RW Taylor	57	83	12	1156	97	16.28	–	3	167/7	12	6	0	–	–	–	–
VP Terry	2	3	–	16	8	5.33	–	–	2							
JG Thomas	5	10	4	83	*31	13.83	–	–	–	774	504	10	50.40	4-70	–	–
NI Thomson	5	4	1	69	39	23.00	–	–	3	1488	568	9	63.11	2-55	–	–
GP Thorpe	57	105	13	3599	138	39.11	6	24	53	138	37	0	–	–	–	–
FJ Titmus	53	76	11	1449	*84	22.29	–	10	35	15118	4931	153	32.22	7-79	7	–
RW Tolchard	4	7	2	129	67	25.80	–	1	5							
FS Trueman	67	85	14	981	*39	13.81	–	–	64	15178	6625	307	21.57	8-31	17	3
AJ Tudor	3	6	3	166	*99	55.33	–	1	–	350	239	8	29.87	4-89	–	–
PCR Tufnell	41	57	28	146	*22	5.03	–	–	12							
FH Tyson	17	24	3	230	*37	10.95	–	–	4	3452	1411	76	18.56	7-27	4	1
DL Underwood	86	116	35	937	*45	11.56	–	–	44	21862	7674	297	25.83	8-51	17	6
MP Vaughan	4	7	–	204	69	29.14	–	1	6	96	64	0	–	–	–	–
PM Walker	3	4	–	128	52	32.00	–	1	5	78	34	0	–	–	–	–
Alan Ward	5	6	1	40	21	8.00	–	–	3	761	453	14	32.35	4-61	–	–
*JH Wardle	27	39	7	647	66	20.21	–	2	12	6579	2071	102	20.30	7-36	5	1
JJ Warr	2	4	–	4	4	1.00	–	–	–	584	281	1	281.00	1-76	–	–
*C Washbrook	11	18	–	590	114	32.77	2	2	3	24	25	1	25.00	1-25	–	–
SL Watkin	3	5	–	25	13	5.00	–	–	1	534	305	11	27.72	4-65	–	–
*AJ Watkins	8	11	1	502	*137	50.20	1	3	10	1002	375	7	53.57	3-20	–	–
M Watkinson	4	6	1	167	*82	33.40	–	1	1	672	348	10	34.80	3-64	–	–
W Watson	23	37	3	879	116	25.85	2	3	8							
AP Wells	1	2	1	3	*3	3.00	–	–	–							
JJ Whitaker	1	1	–	11	11	11.00	–	–	1							
C White	8	12	–	166	51	13.83	–	1	3	811	452	11	41.09	3-18	–	–
DW White	2	2	–	0	0	–	–	–	–	220	119	4	29.75	3-65	–	–
P Willey	26	50	6	1184	*102	26.90	2	5	3	1091	456	7	65.14	2-73	–	–
NF Williams	1	1	–	38	38	38.00	–	–	–	246	148	2	74.00	2-148	–	–
RGD Willis	90	128	55	840	*28	11.50	–	–	39	17357	8190	325	25.20	8-43	16	–
D Wilson	6	7	1	75	42	12.50	–	–	1	1472	466	11	42.36	2-17	–	–
B Wood	12	21	–	454	90	21.61	–	2	6	98	50	0	–	–	–	–
RA Woolmer	19	34	2	1059	149	33.09	3	2	10	546	299	4	74.75	1-8	–	–
*DVP Wright	8	11	3	87	45	10.87	–	–	1	1490	820	23	35.65	5-48	2	–
*NWD Yardley	3	6	–	108	41	18.00	–	–	3	186	94	1	94.00	1-82	–	–

No	Date	Test	Match	Venue	Winner	Result
1	15th Mar 1877	1	Aus v Eng	MCG	Aus	45 runs
2	31st Mar 1877	2	Aus v Eng	MCG	Eng	4 wickets
3	2nd Jan 1879	1	Aus v Eng	MCG	Aus	10 wickets
4	6th Sep 1880	1	Eng v Aus	The Oval	Eng	5 wickets
5	31st Dec 1881	1	Aus v Eng	MCG	drawn	
6	17th Feb 1882	2	Aus v Eng	Sydney (SCG)	Aus	5 wickets
7	3rd Mar 1882	3	Aus v Eng	Sydney (SCG)	Aus	6 wickets
8	10th Mar 1882	4	Aus v Eng	MCG	drawn	
9	28th Aug 1882	1	Eng v Aus	The Oval	Aus	7 runs
10	30th Dec 1882	1	Aus v Eng	MCG	Aus	9 wickets
11	19th Jan 1883	2	Aus v Eng	MCG	Eng	Innings and 27 runs
12	26th Jan 1883	3	Aus v Eng	Sydney (SCG)	Eng	69 runs
13	17th Feb 1883	4	Aus v Eng	Sydney (SCG)	Aus	4 wickets
14	10th Jul 1884	1	Eng v Aus	Old Trafford	drawn	
15	21st Jul 1884	2	Eng v Aus	Lord's	Eng	Innings and 5 runs
16	11th Aug 1884	3	Eng v Aus	The Oval	drawn	
17	12th Dec 1884	1	Aus v Eng	Adelaide	Eng	8 wickets
18	1st Jan 1885	2	Aus v Eng	MCG	Eng	10 wickets
19	20th Feb 1885	3	Aus v Eng	Sydney (SCG)	Aus	6 runs
20	14th Mar 1885	4	Aus v Eng	Sydney (SCG)	Aus	8 wickets
21	21st Mar 1885	5	Aus v Eng	MCG	Eng	Innings and 98
22	5th Jul 1886	1	Eng v Aus	Old Trafford	Eng	4 wickets
23	19th Jul 1886	2	Eng v Aus	Lord's	Eng	Innings and 106 runs
24	12th Aug 1886	3	Eng v Aus	The Oval	Eng	Innings and 217 runs
25	28th Jan 1887	1	Aus v Eng	Sydney (SCG)	Eng	13 runs
26	25th Feb 1887	2	Aus v Eng	Sydney (SCG)	Eng	71 runs
27	10th Feb 1888	1	Aus v Eng	Sydney (SCG)	Eng	126 runs
28	16th Jul 1888	1	Eng v Aus	Lord's	Aus	61 runs
29	13th Aug 1888	2	Eng v Aus	The Oval	Eng	Innings and 137 runs
30	30th Aug 1888	3	Eng v Aus	Old Trafford	Eng	Innings and 21 runs
31	12th Mar 1889	1	SA v Eng	Port Elizabeth	Eng	8 wickets
32	25th Mar 1889	2	SA v Eng	Cape Town	Eng	Innings and 202 runs
33	21st Jul 1890	1	Eng v Aus	Lord's	Eng	7 wickets
34	11th Aug 1890	2	Eng v Aus	The Oval	Eng	2 wickets
35	1st Jan 1892	1	Aus v Eng	MCG	Aus	54 runs
36	29th Jan 1892	2	Aus v Eng	Sydney (SCG)	Aus	72 runs
37	19th Mar 1892	1	SA v Eng	Cape Town	Eng	Innings and 189 runs
38	24th Mar 1892	3	Aus v Eng	Adelaide	Eng	Innings and 230 runs
39	17th Jul 1893	1	Eng v Aus	Lord's	drawn	
40	14th Aug 1893	2	Eng v Aus	The Oval	Eng	Innings and 43 runs
41	24th Aug 1893	3	Eng v Aus	Old Trafford	drawn	
42	14th Dec 1894	1	Aus v Eng	Sydney (SCG)	Eng	10 runs
43	29th Dec 1894	2	Aus v Eng	MCG	Eng	94 runs
44	11th Jan 1895	3	Aus v Eng	Adelaide	Aus	382 runs
45	1st Feb 1895	4	Aus v Eng	Sydney (SCG)	Aus	Innings and 147 runs
46	1st Mar 1895	5	Aus v Eng	MCG	Eng	6 wickets
47	13th Feb 1896	1	SA v Eng	Port Elizabeth	Eng	288 runs
48	2nd Mar 1896	2	SA v Eng	Old Wanderers	Eng	Innings and 197 runs

ALL-TIME TEST MATCH SUMMARY

No	Date	Test	Match	Venue	Winner	Result
49	21st Mar 1896	3	SA v Eng	Cape Town	Eng	Innings and 33 runs
50	22nd Jun 1896	1	Eng v Aus	Lord's	Eng	6 wickets
51	16th Jul 1896	2	Eng v Aus	Old Trafford	Aus	3 wickets
52	10th Aug 1896	3	Eng v Aus	The Oval	Eng	66 runs
53	13th Dec 1897	1	Aus v Eng	Sydney (SCG)	Eng	9 wickets
54	1st Jan 1898	2	Aus v Eng	MCG	Aus	Innings and 55 runs
55	14th Jan 1898	3	Aus v Eng	Adelaide	Aus	Innings and 13 runs
56	29th Jan 1898	4	Aus v Eng	MCG	Aus	8 wickets
57	26th Feb 1898	5	Aus v Eng	Sydney (SCG)	Aus	6 wickets
58	14th Feb 1899	1	SA v Eng	Old Wanderers	Eng	32 runs
59	1st Apr 1899	2	SA v Eng	Cape Town	Eng	210 runs
60	1st Jun 1899	1	Eng v Aus	Trent Bridge	drawn	
61	15th Jun 1899	2	Eng v Aus	Lord's	Aus	10 wickets
62	29th Jun 1899	3	Eng v Aus	Headingley	drawn	
63	17th Jul 1899	4	Eng v Aus	Old Trafford	drawn	
64	14th Aug 1899	5	Eng v Aus	The Oval	drawn	
65	13th Dec 1901	1	Aus v Eng	Sydney (SCG)	Eng	Innings and 124 runs
66	1st Jan 1902	2	Aus v Eng	MCG	Aus	229 runs
67	17th Jan 1902	3	Aus v Eng	Adelaide	Aus	4 wickets
68	14th Feb 1902	4	Aus v Eng	Sydney (SCG)	Aus	7 wickets
69	28th Feb 1902	5	Aus v Eng	MCG	Aus	32 runs
70	29th May 1902	1	Eng v Aus	Edgbaston	drawn	
71	12th Jun 1902	2	Eng v Aus	Lord's	drawn	
72	3rd Jul 1902	3	Eng v Aus	Bramall Lane	Aus	143 runs
73	24th Jul 1902	4	Eng v Aus	Old Trafford	Aus	3 runs
74	11th Aug 1902	5	Eng v Aus	The Oval	Eng	1 wicket
75	11th Dec 1903	1	Aus v Eng	Sydney (SCG)	Eng	5 wickets
76	1st Jan 1904	2	Aus v Eng	MCG	Eng	185 runs
77	15th Jan 1904	3	Aus v Eng	Adelaide	Aus	216 runs
78	26th Feb 1904	4	Aus v Eng	Sydney (SCG)	Eng	157 runs
79	5th Mar 1904	5	Aus v Eng	MCG	Aus	218 runs
80	29th May 1905	1	Eng v Aus	Trent Bridge	Eng	213 runs
81	15th Jun 1905	2	Eng v Aus	Lord's	drawn	
82	3rd Jul 1905	3	Eng v Aus	Headingley	drawn	
83	24th Jul 1905	4	Eng v Aus	Old Trafford	Eng	Innings and 80 runs
84	14th Aug 1905	5	Eng v Aus	The Oval	drawn	
85	2nd Jan 1906	1	SA v Eng	Old Wanderers	SA	1 wicket
86	6th Mar 1906	2	SA v Eng	Old Wanderers	SA	9 wickets
87	10th Mar 1906	3	SA v Eng	Old Wanderers	SA	243 runs
88	24th Mar 1906	4	SA v Eng	Cape Town	Eng	4 wickets
89	30th Mar 1906	5	SA v Eng	Cape Town	SA	Innings and 16 runs
90	1st Jul 1907	1	Eng v SA	Lord's	drawn	
91	29th Jul 1907	2	Eng v SA	Headingley	Eng	53 runs
92	19th Aug 1907	3	Eng v SA	The Oval	drawn	
93	13th Dec 1907	1	Aus v Eng	Sydney (SCG)	Aus	2 wickets
94	1st Jan 1908	2	Aus v Eng	MCG	Eng	1 wicket
95	10th Jan 1908	3	Aus v Eng	Adelaide	Aus	245 runs
96	7th Feb 1908	4	Aus v Eng	MCG	Aus	308 runs

No	Date	Test	Match	Venue	Winner	Result
97	21st Feb 1908	5	Aus v Eng	Sydney (SCG)	Aus	49 runs
98	27th May 1909	1	Eng v Aus	Edgbaston	Eng	10 wickets
99	14th Jun 1909	2	Eng v Aus	Lord's	Aus	9 wickets
100	1st Jul 1909	3	Eng v Aus	Headingley	Aus	126 runs
101	26th Jul 1909	4	Eng v Aus	Old Trafford	drawn	
102	9th Aug 1909	5	Eng v Aus	The Oval	drawn	
103	1st Jan 1910	1	SA v Eng	Old Wanderers	SA	19 runs
104	21st Jan 1910	2	SA v Eng	Durban Lord's	SA	95 runs
105	26th Feb 1910	3	SA v Eng	Old Wanderers	Eng	3 wickets
106	7th Mar 1910	4	SA v Eng	Cape Town	SA	4 wickets
107	11th Mar 1910	5	SA v Eng	Cape Town	Eng	9 wickets
108	15th Dec 1911	1	Aus v Eng	Sydney (SCG)	Aus	146 runs
109	30th Dec 1911	2	Aus v Eng	MCG	Eng	8 wickets
110	12th Jan 1912	3	Aus v Eng	Adelaide	Eng	7 wickets
111	9th Feb 1912	4	Aus v Eng	MCG	Eng	Innings and 225 runs
112	23rd Feb 1912	5	Aus v Eng	Sydney (SCG)	Eng	70 runs
113	10th Jun 1912	1	Eng v SA	Lord's	Eng	Innings and 62 runs
114	24th Jun 1912	1	Eng v Aus	Lord's	drawn	
115	8th Jul 1912	2	Eng v SA	Headingley	Eng	174 runs
116	29th Jul 1912	2	Eng v Aus	Old Trafford	drawn	
117	12th Aug 1912	3	Eng v SA	The Oval	Eng	10 wickets
118	19th Aug 1912	3	Eng v Aus	The Oval	Eng	244 runs
119	13th Dec 1913	1	SA v Eng	Durban Lord's	Eng	Innings and 157 runs
120	26th Dec 1913	2	SA v Eng	Old Wanderers	Eng	Innings and 12 runs
121	1st Jan 1914	3	SA v Eng	Old Wanderers	Eng	91 runs
122	14th Feb 1914	4	SA v Eng	Durban Lord's	drawn	
123	27th Feb 1914	5	SA v Eng	Port Elizabeth	Eng	10 wicket
124	17th Dec 1920	1	Aus v Eng	Sydney (SCG)	Aus	373 runs
125	31st Dec 1920	2	Aus v Eng	MCG	Aus	Innings and 91 runs
126	14th Jan 1921	3	Aus v Eng	Adelaide	Aus	119 runs
127	11th Feb 1921	4	Aus v Eng	MCG	Aus	8 wickets
128	25th Feb 1921	5	Aus v Eng	Sydney (SCG)	Aus	9 wickets
129	28th May 1921	1	Eng v Aus	Trent Bridge	Aus	10 wickets
130	11th Jun 1921	2	Eng v Aus	Lord's	Aus	8 wickets
131	2nd Jul 1921	3	Eng v Aus	Headingley	Aus	219 runs
132	23rd Jul 1921	4	Eng v Aus	Old Trafford	drawn	
133	13th Aug 1921	5	Eng v Aus	The Oval	drawn	
134	23rd Dec 1922	1	SA v Eng	Old Wanderers	SA	168 runs
135	1st Jan 1923	2	SA v Eng	Cape Town	Eng	1 wicket
136	18th Jan 1923	3	SA v Eng	Kingsmead	drawn	
137	9th Feb 1923	4	SA v Eng	Old Wanderers	drawn	
138	16th Feb 1923	5	SA v Eng	Kingsmead	Eng	109 runs
139	14th Jun 1924	1	Eng v SA	Edgbaston	Eng	Innings and 18 runs
140	28th Jun 1924	2	Eng v SA	Lord's	Eng	Innings and 18 runs
141	12th Jul 1924	3	Eng v SA	Headingley	Eng	9 wickets
142	26th Jul 1924	4	Eng v SA	Old Trafford	drawn	
143	16th Aug 1924	5	Eng v SA	The Oval	drawn	
144	19th Dec 1924	1	Aus v Eng	Sydney (SCG)	Aus	193 runs

ALL-TIME TEST MATCH SUMMARY

No	Date	Test	Match	Venue	Winner	Result
145	1st Jan 1925	2	Aus v Eng	MCG	Aus	81 runs
146	16th Jan 1925	3	Aus v Eng	Adelaide	Aus	11 runs
147	13th Feb 1925	4	Aus v Eng	MCG	Eng	Innings and 29 runs
148	27th Feb 1925	5	Aus v Eng	Sydney (SCG)	Aus	307 runs
149	12th Jun 1926	1	Eng v Aus	Trent Bridge	drawn	
150	26th Jun 1926	2	Eng v Aus	Lord's	drawn	
151	10th Jul 1926	3	Eng v Aus	Headingley	drawn	
152	24th Jul 1926	4	Eng v Aus	Old Trafford	drawn	
153	14th Aug 1926	5	Eng v Aus	The Oval	Eng	289 runs
154	24th Dec 1927	1	SA v Eng	Old Wanderers	Eng	10 wickets
155	31st Dec 1927	2	SA v Eng	Cape Town	Eng	87 runs
156	21st Jan 1928	3	SA v Eng	Kingsmead	drawn	
157	28th Jan 1928	4	SA v Eng	Old Wanderers	SA	4 wickets
158	4th Feb 1928	5	SA v Eng	Kingsmead	SA	8 wickets
159	23rd Jun 1928	1	Eng v WI	Lord's	Eng	Innings and 58 runs
160	21st Jul 1928	2	Eng v WI	Old Trafford	Eng	Innings and 30 runs
161	11th Aug 1928	3	Eng v WI	The Oval	Eng	Innings and 71 runs
162	30th Nov 1928	1	Aus v Eng	Brisbane (Ex)	Eng	675 runs
163	14th Dec 1928	2	Aus v Eng	Sydney (SCG)	Eng	8 wickets
164	29th Dec 1928	3	Aus v Eng	MCG	Eng	3 wickets
165	1st Feb 1929	4	Aus v Eng	Adelaide	Eng	12 runs
166	8th Mar 1929	5	Aus v Eng	MCG	Aus	5 wickets
167	15th Jun 1929	1	Eng v SA	Edgbaston	drawn	
168	29th Jun 1929	2	Eng v SA	Lord's	drawn	
169	13th Jul 1929	3	Eng v SA	Headingley	Eng	5 wickets
170	27th Jul 1929	4	Eng v SA	Old Trafford	Eng	Innings and 32 runs
171	17th Aug 1929	5	Eng v SA	The Oval	drawn	
172	10th Jan 1930	1	NZ v Eng	Christchurch	Eng	8 wickets
173	11th Jan 1930	1	WI v Eng	Bridgetown	drawn	
174	24th Jan 1930	2	NZ v Eng	Wellington	drawn	
175	1st Feb 1930	2	WI v Eng	Port-of-Spain	Eng	167 runs
176	14th Feb 1930	3	NZ v Eng	Auckland	drawn	
177	21st Feb 1930	4	NZ v Eng	Auckland	drawn	
178	21st Feb 1930	3	WI v Eng	Georgetown	WI	289 runs
179	3rd Apr 1930	4	WI v Eng	Kingston	drawn	
180	13th Jun 1930	1	Eng v Aus	Trent Bridge	Eng	93 runs
181	27th Jun 1930	2	Eng v Aus	Lord's	Aus	7 wickets
182	11th Jul 1930	3	Eng v Aus	Headingley	drawn	
183	25th Jul 1930	4	Eng v Aus	Old Trafford	drawn	
184	16th Aug 1930	5	Eng v Aus	The Oval	Aus	Innings and 39 runs
185	24th Dec 1930	1	SA v Eng	Old Wanderers	SA	28 runs
186	1st Jan 1931	2	SA v Eng	Cape Town	drawn	
187	16th Jan 1931	3	SA v Eng	Kingsmead	drawn	
188	13th Feb 1931	4	SA v Eng	Old Wanderers	drawn	
189	21st Feb 1931	5	SA v Eng	Kingsmead	drawn	
190	27th Jun 1931	1	Eng v NZ	Lord's	drawn	
191	29th Jul 1931	2	Eng v NZ	The Oval	Eng	Innings and 26 runs
192	15th Aug 1931	3	Eng v NZ	Old Trafford	drawn	

ALL-TIME TEST MATCH SUMMARY

No	Date	Test	Match	Venue	Winner	Result
193	25th Jun 1932	1	Eng v Ind	Lord's	Eng	158 runs
194	2nd Dec 1932	1	Aus v Eng	Sydney (SCG)	Eng	10 wickets
195	30th Dec 1932	2	Aus v Eng	MCG	Aus	111 runs
196	13th Jan 1933	3	Aus v Eng	Adelaide	Eng	338 runs
197	10th Feb 1933	4	Aus v Eng	The Gabba	Eng	6 wickets
198	23rd Feb 1933	5	Aus v Eng	Sydney (SCG)	Eng	8 wickets
199	24th Mar 1933	1	NZ v Eng	Christchurch	drawn	
200	31st Mar 1933	2	NZ v Eng	Auckland	drawn	
201	24th Jun 1933	1	Eng v WI	Lord's	Eng	Innings and 27 runs
202	22nd Jul 1933	2	Eng v WI	Old Trafford	drawn	
203	12th Aug 1933	3	Eng v WI	The Oval	Eng	Innings and 17 runs
204	15th Dec 1933	1	Ind v Eng	Bombay (Gym.)	Eng	9 wickets
205	5th Jan 1934	2	Ind v Eng	Calcutta	drawn	
206	10th Feb 1934	3	Ind v Eng	Chepauk	Eng	202 runs
207	8th Jun 1934	1	Eng v Aus	Trent Bridge	Aus	238 runs
208	22nd Jun 1934	2	Eng v Aus	Lord's	Eng	Innings and 38 runs
209	6th Jul 1934	3	Eng v Aus	Old Trafford	drawn	
210	20th Jul 1934	4	Eng v Aus	Headingley	drawn	
211	18th Aug 1934	5	Eng v Aus	The Oval	Aus	562 runs
212	8th Jan 1935	1	WI v Eng	Bridgetown	Eng	4 wickets
213	24th Jan 1935	2	WI v Eng	Port-of-Spain	WI	217 runs
214	14th Feb 1935	3	WI v Eng	Georgetown	drawn	
215	14th Mar 1935	4	WI v Eng	Kingston	WI	Innings and 161 runs
216	15th Jun 1935	1	Eng v SA	Trent Bridge	drawn	
217	29th Jun 1935	2	Eng v SA	Lord's	SA	157 runs
218	13th Jul 1935	3	Eng v SA	Headingley	drawn	
219	27th Jul 1935	4	Eng v SA	Old Trafford	drawn	
220	17th Aug 1935	5	Eng v SA	The Oval	drawn	
221	27th Jun 1936	1	Eng v Ind	Lord's	Eng	9 wickets
222	25th Jul 1936	2	Eng v Ind	Old Trafford	drawn	
223	15th Aug 1936	3	Eng v Ind	The Oval	Eng	9 wickets
224	4th Dec 1936	1	Aus v Eng	The Gabba	Eng	322 runs
225	18th Dec 1936	2	Aus v Eng	Sydney (SCG)	Eng	Innings and 22 runs
226	1st Jan 1937	3	Aus v Eng	MCG	Aus	365 runs
227	1st Feb 1937	4	Aus v Eng	Adelaide	Aus	148 runs
228	26th Feb 1937	5	Aus v Eng	MCG	Aus	Innings and 200 runs
229	26th Jun 1937	1	Eng v NZ	Lord's	drawn	
230	24th Jul 1937	2	Eng v NZ	Old Trafford	Eng	130 runs
231	14th Aug 1937	3	Eng v NZ	The Oval	drawn	
232	10th Jun 1938	1	Eng v Aus	Trent Bridge	drawn	
233	24th Jun 1938	2	Eng v Aus	Lord's	drawn	
234	22nd Jul 1938	4	Eng v Aus	Headingley	Aus	5 wickets
235	20th Aug 1938	5	Eng v Aus	The Oval	Eng	Innings and 579 runs
236	24th Dec 1938	1	SA v Eng	Old Wanderers	drawn	
237	31st Dec 1938	2	SA v Eng	Cape Town	drawn	
238	20th Jan 1939	3	SA v Eng	Kingsmead	Eng	Innings and 13 runs
239	18th Feb 1939	4	SA v Eng	Old Wanderers	drawn	
240	3rd Mar 1939	5	SA v Eng	Kingsmead	drawn	

ALL-TIME TEST MATCH SUMMARY

No	Date	Test	Match	Venue	Winner	Result
241	24th Jun 1939	1	Eng v WI	Lord's	Eng	8 wickets
242	22nd Jul 1939	2	Eng v WI	Old Trafford	drawn	
243	19th Aug 1939	3	Eng v WI	The Oval	drawn	
244	22nd Jun 1946	1	Eng v Ind	Lord's	Eng	10 wickets
245	20th Jul 1946	2	Eng v Ind	Old Trafford	drawn	
246	17th Aug 1946	3	Eng v Ind	The Oval	drawn	
247	29th Nov 1946	1	Aus v Eng	The Gabba	Aus	Innings and 332 runs
248	13th Dec 1946	2	Aus v Eng	Sydney (SCG)	Aus	Innings and 33 runs
249	1st Jan 1947	3	Aus v Eng	MCG	drawn	
250	31st Jan 1947	4	Aus v Eng	Adelaide	drawn	
251	28th Feb 1947	5	Aus v Eng	Sydney (SCG)	Aus	5 wickets
252	21st Mar 1947	1	NZ v Eng	Christchurch	drawn	
253	7th Jun 1947	1	Eng v SA	Trent Bridge	drawn	
254	21st Jun 1947	2	Eng v SA	Lord's	Eng	10 wickets
255	5th Jul 1947	3	Eng v SA	Old Trafford	Eng	7 wickets
256	26th Jul 1947	4	Eng v SA	Headingley	Eng	10 wickets
257	16th Aug 1947	5	Eng v SA	The Oval	drawn	
258	21st Jan 1948	1	WI v Eng	Bridgetown	drawn	
259	11th Feb 1948	2	WI v Eng	Port-of-Spain	drawn	
260	3rd Mar 1948	3	WI v Eng	Georgetown	WI	7 wickets
261	27th Mar 1948	4	WI v Eng	Kingston	WI	10 wickets
262	10th Jun 1948	1	Eng v Aus	Trent Bridge	Aus	8 wickets
263	24th Jun 1948	2	Eng v Aus	Lord's	Aus	409 runs
264	8th Jul 1948	3	Eng v Aus	Old Trafford	drawn	
265	22nd Jul 1948	4	Eng v Aus	Headingley	Aus	7 wickets
266	14th Aug 1948	5	Eng v Aus	The Oval	Aus	Innings and 149 runs
267	16th Dec 1948	1	SA v Eng	Kingsmead	Eng	2 wickets
268	27th Dec 1948	2	SA v Eng	Ellis Park	drawn	
269	1st Jan 1949	3	SA v Eng	Cape Town	drawn	
270	12th Feb 1949	4	SA v Eng	Ellis Park	drawn	
271	5th Mar 1949	5	SA v Eng	Port Elizabeth	Eng	3 wickets
272	11th Jun 1949	1	Eng v NZ	Headingley	drawn	
273	25th Jun 1949	2	Eng v NZ	Lord's	drawn	
274	23rd Jul 1949	3	Eng v NZ	Old Trafford	drawn	
275	13th Aug 1949	4	Eng v NZ	The Oval	drawn	
276	8th Jun 1950	1	Eng v WI	Old Trafford	Eng	202 runs
277	24th Jun 1950	2	Eng v WI	Lord's	WI	326 runs
278	20th Jul 1950	3	Eng v WI	Trent Bridge	WI	10 wickets
279	12th Aug 1950	4	Eng v WI	The Oval	WI	Innings and 56 runs
280	1st Dec 1950	1	Aus v Eng	The Gabba	Aus	70 runs
281	22nd Dec 1950	2	Aus v Eng	MCG	Aus	28 runs
282	5th Jan 1951	3	Aus v Eng	Sydney (SCG)	Aus	Innings and 13 runs
283	2nd Feb 1951	4	Aus v Eng	Adelaide	Aus	274 runs
284	23rd Feb 1951	5	Aus v Eng	MCG	Eng	8 wickets
285	17th Mar 1951	1	NZ v Eng	Christchurch	drawn	
286	24th Mar 1951	2	NZ v Eng	Wellington	Eng	6 wickets
287	7th Jun 1951	1	Eng v SA	Trent Bridge	SA	71 runs
288	21st Jun 1951	2	Eng v SA	Lord's	Eng	10 wickets

No	Date	Test	Match	Venue	Winner	Result
289	5th Jul 1951	3	Eng v SA	Old Trafford	Eng	9 wickets
290	26th Jul 1951	4	Eng v SA	Headingley	drawn	
291	16th Aug 1951	5	Eng v SA	The Oval	Eng	4 wickets
292	2nd Nov 1951	1	Ind v Eng	Delhi	drawn	
293	14th Dec 1951	2	Ind v Eng	Bombay (Bra.)	drawn	
294	30th Dec 1951	3	Ind v Eng	Calcutta	drawn	
295	12th Jan 1952	4	Ind v Eng	Kanpur	Eng	8 wickets
296	6th Feb 1952	5	Ind v Eng	Chepauk	Ind	Innings and 8 runs
297	5th Jun 1952	1	Eng v Ind	Headingley	Eng	7 wickets
298	19th Jun 1952	2	Eng v Ind	Lord's	Eng	8 wickets
299	17th Jul 1952	3	Eng v Ind	Old Trafford	Eng	Innings and 207 runs
300	14th Aug 1952	4	Eng v Ind	The Oval	drawn	
301	11th Jun 1953	1	Eng v Aus	Trent Bridge	drawn	
302	25th Jun 1953	2	Eng v Aus	Lord's	drawn	
303	9th Jul 1953	3	Eng v Aus	Old Trafford	drawn	
304	23rd Jul 1953	4	Eng v Aus	Headingley	drawn	
305	15th Aug 1953	5	Eng v Aus	The Oval	Eng	8 wickets
306	15th Jan 1954	1	WI v Eng	Kingston	WI	140 runs
307	6th Feb 1954	2	WI v Eng	Bridgetown	WI	181 runs
308	24th Feb 1954	3	WI v Eng	Georgetown	Eng	9 wickets
309	17th Mar 1954	4	WI v Eng	Port-of-Spain	drawn	
310	30th Mar 1954	5	WI v Eng	Kingston	Eng	9 wickets
311	10th Jun 1954	1	Eng v Pak	Lord's	drawn	
312	1st Jul 1954	2	Eng v Pak	Trent Bridge	Eng	Innings and 129 runs
313	22nd Jul 1954	3	Eng v Pak	Old Trafford	drawn	
314	12th Aug 1954	4	Eng v Pak	The Oval	Pak	24 runs
315	26th Nov 1954	1	Aus v Eng	The Gabba	Aus	Innings and 154 runs
316	17th Dec 1954	2	Aus v Eng	Sydney (SCG)	Eng	38 runs
317	31st Dec 1954	3	Aus v Eng	MCG	Eng	128 runs
318	28th Jan 1955	4	Aus v Eng	Adelaide	Eng	5 wickets
319	25th Feb 1955	5	Aus v Eng	Sydney (SCG)	drawn	
320	11th Mar 1955	1	NZ v Eng	Dunedin	Eng	8 wickets
321	25th Mar 1955	2	NZ v Eng	Auckland	Eng	Innings and 20 runs
322	9th Jun 1955	1	Eng v SA	Trent Bridge	Eng	Innings and 5 runs
323	23rd Jun 1955	2	Eng v SA	Lord's	Eng	71 runs
324	7th Jul 1955	3	Eng v SA	Old Trafford	SA	3 wickets
325	21st Jul 1955	4	Eng v SA	Headingley	SA	224 runs
326	13th Aug 1955	5	Eng v SA	The Oval	Eng	92 runs
327	7th Jun 1956	1	Eng v Aus	Trent Bridge	drawn	
328	21st Jun 1956	2	Eng v Aus	Lord's	Aus	185 runs
329	12th Jul 1956	3	Eng v Aus	Headingley	Eng	Innings and 42 runs
330	26th Jul 1956	4	Eng v Aus	Old Trafford	Eng	Innings and 170 runs
331	23rd Aug 1956	5	Eng v Aus	The Oval	drawn	
332	24th Dec 1956	1	SA v Eng	Wanderers	Eng	131 runs
333	1st Jan 1957	2	SA v Eng	Cape Town	Eng	312 runs
334	25th Jan 1957	3	SA v Eng	Kingsmead	drawn	
335	15th Feb 1957	4	SA v Eng	Wanderers	SA	17 runs
336	1st Mar 1957	5	SA v Eng	Port Elizabeth	SA	58 runs

ALL-TIME TEST MATCH SUMMARY

No	Date	Test	Match	Venue	Winner	Result
337	30th May 1957	1	Eng v WI	Edgbaston	drawn	
338	20th Jun 1957	2	Eng v WI	Lord's	Eng	Innings and 36 runs
339	4th Jul 1957	3	Eng v WI	Trent Bridge	drawn	
340	25th Jul 1957	4	Eng v WI	Headingley	Eng	Innings and 5 runs
341	22nd Aug 1957	5	Eng v WI	The Oval	Eng	Innings and 237 runs
342	5th Jun 1958	1	Eng v NZ	Edgbaston	Eng	205 runs
343	19th Jun 1958	2	Eng v NZ	Lord's	Eng	Innings and 148 runs
344	3rd Jul 1958	3	Eng v NZ	Headingley	Eng	Innings and 71 runs
345	24th Jul 1958	4	Eng v NZ	Old Trafford	Eng	Innings and 13 runs
346	21st Aug 1958	5	Eng v NZ	The Oval	drawn	
347	5th Dec 1958	1	Aus v Eng	The Gabba	Aus	8 wickets
348	31st Dec 1958	2	Aus v Eng	MCG	Aus	8 wickets
349	9th Jan 1959	3	Aus v Eng	Sydney (SCG)	drawn	
350	30th Jan 1959	4	Aus v Eng	Adelaide	Aus	10 wickets
351	13th Feb 1959	5	Aus v Eng	MCG	Aus	9 wickets
352	27th Feb 1959	1	NZ v Eng	Christchurch	Eng	Innings and 99 runs
353	14th Mar 1959	2	NZ v Eng	Auckland	drawn	
354	4th Jun 1959	1	Eng v Ind	Trent Bridge	Eng	Innings and 59 runs
355	18th Jun 1959	2	Eng v Ind	Lord's	Eng	8 wickets
356	2nd Jul 1959	3	Eng v Ind	Headingley	Eng	Innings and 173 runs
357	23rd Jul 1959	4	Eng v Ind	Old Trafford	Eng	171 runs
358	20th Aug 1959	5	Eng v Ind	The Oval	Eng	Innings and 27 runs
359	6th Jan 1960	1	WI v Eng	Bridgetown	drawn	
360	28th Jan 1960	2	WI v Eng	Port-of-Spain	Eng	256 runs
361	17th Feb 1960	3	WI v Eng	Kingston	drawn	
362	9th Mar 1960	4	WI v Eng	Georgetown	drawn	
363	25th Mar 1960	5	WI v Eng	Port-of-Spain	drawn	
364	9th Jun 1960	1	Eng v SA	Edgbaston	Eng	100 runs
365	23rd Jun 1960	2	Eng v SA	Lord's	Eng	Innings and 73 runs
366	7th Jul 1960	3	Eng v SA	Trent Bridge	Eng	8 wickets
367	21st Jul 1960	4	Eng v SA	Old Trafford	drawn	
368	18th Aug 1960	5	Eng v SA	The Oval	drawn	
369	8th Jun 1961	1	Eng v Aus	Edgbaston	drawn	
370	22nd Jun 1961	2	Eng v Aus	Lord's	Aus	5 wickets
371	6th Jul 1961	3	Eng v Aus	Headingley	Eng	8 wickets
372	27th Jul 1961	4	Eng v Aus	Old Trafford	Aus	54 runs
373	17th Aug 1961	5	Eng v Aus	The Oval	drawn	
374	21st Oct 1961	1	Pak v Eng	Lahore (Gd.)	Eng	5 wickets
375	11th Nov 1961	1	Ind v Eng	Bombay (Bra.)	drawn	
376	1st Dec 1961	2	Ind v Eng	Kanpur	drawn	
377	13th Dec 1961	3	Ind v Eng	Delhi	drawn	
378	30th Dec 1961	4	Ind v Eng	Calcutta	Ind	187 runs
379	10th Jan 1962	5	Ind v Eng	Madras (Nehru)	Ind	128 runs
380	19th Jan 1962	2	Pak v Eng	Dhaka (Dacca)	drawn	
381	2nd Feb 1962	3	Pak v Eng	Karachi (Nat.)	drawn	
382	31st May 1962	1	Eng v Pak	Edgbaston	Eng	Innings and 24 runs
383	21st Jun 1962	2	Eng v Pak	Lord's	Eng	9 wickets
384	5th Jul 1962	3	Eng v Pak	Headingley	Eng	Innings and 117 runs

No	Date	Test	Match	Venue	Winner	Result
385	26th Jul 1962	4	Eng v Pak	Trent Bridge	drawn	
386	16th Aug 1962	5	Eng v Pak	The Oval	Eng	10 wickets
387	30th Nov 1962	1	Aus v Eng	The Gabba	drawn	
388	29th Dec 1962	2	Aus v Eng	MCG	Eng	7 wickets
389	11th Jan 1963	3	Aus v Eng	Sydney (SCG)	Aus	8 wickets
390	25th Jan 1963	4	Aus v Eng	Adelaide	drawn	
391	15th Feb 1963	5	Aus v Eng	Sydney (SCG)	drawn	
392	23rd Feb 1963	1	NZ v Eng	Auckland	Eng	Innings and 215 runs
393	1st Mar 1963	2	NZ v Eng	Wellington	Eng	Innings and 47 runs
394	15th Mar 1963	3	NZ v Eng	Christchurch	Eng	7 wickets
395	6th Jun 1963	1	Eng v WI	Old Trafford	WI	10 wickets
396	20th Jun 1963	2	Eng v WI	Lord's	drawn	
397	4th Jul 1963	3	Eng v WI	Edgbaston	Eng	217 runs
398	25th Jul 1963	4	Eng v WI	Headingley	WI	221 runs
399	22nd Aug 1963	5	Eng v WI	The Oval	WI	8 wickets
400	10th Jan 1964	1	Ind v Eng	Madras (Nehru)	drawn	
401	21st Jan 1964	2	Ind v Eng	Bombay (Bra.)	drawn	
402	29th Jan 1964	3	Ind v Eng	Calcutta	drawn	
403	8th Feb 1964	4	Ind v Eng	Delhi	drawn	
404	15th Feb 1964	5	Ind v Eng	Kanpur	drawn	
405	4th Jun 1964	1	Eng v Aus	Trent Bridge	drawn	
406	18th Jun 1964	2	Eng v Aus	Lord's	drawn	
407	2nd Jul 1964	3	Eng v Aus	Headingley	Aus	7 wickets
408	23rd Jul 1964	4	Eng v Aus	Old Trafford	drawn	
409	13th Aug 1964	5	Eng v Aus	The Oval	drawn	
410	4th Dec 1964	1	SA v Eng	Kingsmead	Eng	Innings and 104 runs
411	23rd Dec 1964	2	SA v Eng	Wanderers	drawn	
412	1st Jan 1965	3	SA v Eng	Cape Town	drawn	
413	22nd Jan 1965	4	SA v Eng	Wanderers	drawn	
414	12th Feb 1965	5	SA v Eng	Port Elizabeth	drawn	
415	27th May 1965	1	Eng v NZ	Edgbaston	Eng	9 wickets
416	17th Jun 1965	2	Eng v NZ	Lord's	Eng	7 wickets
417	8th Jul 1965	3	Eng v NZ	Headingley	Eng	Innings and 187 runs
418	22nd Jul 1965	1	Eng v SA	Lord's	drawn	
419	5th Aug 1965	2	Eng v SA	Trent Bridge	SA	94 runs
420	26th Aug 1965	3	Eng v SA	The Oval	drawn	
421	10th Dec 1965	1	Aus v Eng	The Gabba	drawn	
422	30th Dec 1965	2	Aus v Eng	MCG	drawn	
423	7th Jan 1966	3	Aus v Eng	Sydney (SCG)	Eng	Innings and 93 runs
424	28th Jan 1966	4	Aus v Eng	Adelaide	Aus	Innings and 9 runs
425	11th Feb 1966	5	Aus v Eng	MCG	drawn	
426	25th Feb 1966	1	NZ v Eng	Christchurch	drawn	
427	4th Mar 1966	2	NZ v Eng	Dunedin	drawn	
428	11th Mar 1966	3	NZ v Eng	Auckland	drawn	
429	2nd Jun 1966	1	Eng v WI	Old Trafford	WI	Innings and 40 runs
430	16th Jun 1966	2	Eng v WI	Lord's	drawn	
431	30th Jun 1966	3	Eng v WI	Trent Bridge	WI	139 runs
432	4th Aug 1966	4	Eng v WI	Headingley	WI	Innings and 55 runs

ALL-TIME TEST MATCH SUMMARY

No	Date	Test	Match	Venue	Winner	Result
433	18th Aug 1966	5	Eng v WI	The Oval	Eng	Innings and 34 runs
434	8th Jun 1967	1	Eng v Ind	Headingley	Eng	6 wickets
435	22nd Jun 1967	2	Eng v Ind	Lord's	Eng	Innings and 124 runs
436	13th Jul 1967	3	Eng v Ind	Edgbaston	Eng	132 runs
437	27th Jul 1967	1	Eng v Pak	Lord's	drawn	
438	10th Aug 1967	2	Eng v Pak	Trent Bridge	Eng	10 wickets
439	24th Aug 1967	3	Eng v Pak	The Oval	Eng	8 wickets
440	19th Jan 1968	1	WI v Eng	Port-of-Spain	drawn	
441	8th Feb 1968	2	WI v Eng	Kingston	drawn	
442	29th Feb 1968	3	WI v Eng	Bridgetown	drawn	
443	14th Mar 1968	4	WI v Eng	Port-of-Spain	Eng	7 wickets
444	28th Mar 1968	5	WI v Eng	Georgetown	drawn	
445	6th Jun 1968	1	Eng v Aus	Old Trafford	Aus	159 runs
446	20th Jun 1968	2	Eng v Aus	Lord's	drawn	
447	11th Jul 1968	3	Eng v Aus	Edgbaston	drawn	
448	25th Jul 1968	4	Eng v Aus	Headingley	drawn	
449	22nd Aug 1968	5	Eng v Aus	The Oval	Eng	226 runs
450	21st Feb 1969	1	Pak v Eng	Lahore (Gd.)	drawn	
451	28th Feb 1969	2	Pak v Eng	Dhaka (Dacca)	drawn	
452	6th Mar 1969	3	Pak v Eng	Karachi (Nat.)	drawn	
453	12th Jun 1969	1	Eng v WI	Old Trafford	Eng	10 wickets
454	26th Jun 1969	2	Eng v WI	Lord's	drawn	
455	10th Jul 1969	3	Eng v WI	Headingley	Eng	30 runs
456	24th Jul 1969	1	Eng v NZ	Lord's	Eng	230 runs
457	7th Aug 1969	2	Eng v NZ	Trent Bridge	drawn	
458	21st Aug 1969	3	Eng v NZ	The Oval	Eng	8 wickets
459	27th Nov 1970	1	Aus v Eng	The Gabba	drawn	
460	11th Dec 1970	2	Aus v Eng	Perth (WACA)	drawn	
461	9th Jan 1971	4	Aus v Eng	Sydney (SCG)	Eng	299 runs
462	21st Jan 1971	5	Aus v Eng	MCG	drawn	
463	29th Jan 1971	6	Aus v Eng	Adelaide	drawn	
464	12th Feb 1971	7	Aus v Eng	Sydney (SCG)	Eng	62 runs
465	25th Feb 1971	1	NZ v Eng	Christchurch	Eng	8 wickets
466	5th Mar 1971	2	NZ v Eng	Auckland	drawn	
467	3rd Jun 1971	1	Eng v Pak	Edgbaston	drawn	
468	17th Jun 1971	2	Eng v Pak	Lord's	drawn	
469	8th Jul 1971	3	Eng v Pak	Headingley	Eng	25 runs
470	22nd Jul 1971	1	Eng v Ind	Lord's	drawn	
471	5th Aug 1971	2	Eng v Ind	Old Trafford	drawn	
472	19th Aug 1971	3	Eng v Ind	The Oval	Ind	4 wickets
473	8th Jun 1972	1	Eng v Aus	Old Trafford	Eng	89 runs
474	22nd Jun 1972	2	Eng v Aus	Lord's	Aus	8 wickets
475	13th Jul 1972	3	Eng v Aus	Trent Bridge	drawn	
476	27th Jul 1972	4	Eng v Aus	Headingley	Eng	9 wickets
477	10th Aug 1972	5	Eng v Aus	The Oval	Aus	5 wickets
478	20th Dec 1972	1	Ind v Eng	Delhi	Eng	6 wickets
479	30th Dec 1972	2	Ind v Eng	Calcutta	Ind	28 runs
480	12th Jan 1973	3	Ind v Eng	Chepauk	Ind	4 wickets

No	Date	Test	Match	Venue	Winner	Result
481	25th Jan 1973	4	Ind v Eng	Kanpur	drawn	
482	6th Feb 1973	5	Ind v Eng	Bombay (Bra.)	drawn	
483	2nd Mar 1973	1	Pak v Eng	Lahore (Gd.)	drawn	
484	16th Mar 1973	2	Pak v Eng	Hyderabad (P)	drawn	
485	24th Mar 1973	3	Pak v Eng	Karachi (Nat.)	drawn	
486	7th Jun 1973	1	Eng v NZ	Trent Bridge	Eng	38 runs
487	21st Jun 1973	2	Eng v NZ	Lord's	drawn	
488	5th Jul 1973	3	Eng v NZ	Headingley	Eng	Innings and 1 run
489	26th Jul 1973	1	Eng v WI	The Oval	WI	158 runs
490	9th Aug 1973	2	Eng v WI	Edgbaston	drawn	
491	23rd Aug 1973	3	Eng v WI	Lord's	WI	Innings and 226 runs
492	2nd Feb 1974	1	WI v Eng	Port-of-Spain	WI	7 wickets
493	16th Feb 1974	2	WI v Eng	Kingston	drawn	
494	6th Mar 1974	3	WI v Eng	Bridgetown	drawn	
495	22nd Mar 1974	4	WI v Eng	Georgetown	drawn	
496	30th Mar 1974	5	WI v Eng	Port-of-Spain	Eng	26 runs
497	6th Jun 1974	1	Eng v Ind	Old Trafford	Eng	113 runs
498	20th Jun 1974	2	Eng v Ind	Lord's	Eng	Innings and 285 runs
499	4th Jul 1974	3	Eng v Ind	Edgbaston	Eng	Innings and 78 runs
500	25th Jul 1974	1	Eng v Pak	Headingley	drawn	
501	8th Aug 1974	2	Eng v Pak	Lord's	drawn	
502	22nd Aug 1974	3	Eng v Pak	The Oval	drawn	
503	29th Nov 1974	1	Aus v Eng	The Gabba	Aus	166 runs
504	13th Dec 1974	2	Aus v Eng	Perth (WACA)	Aus	9 wickets
505	26th Dec 1974	3	Aus v Eng	MCG	drawn	
506	4th Jan 1975	4	Aus v Eng	Sydney (SCG)	Aus	171 runs
507	25th Jan 1975	5	Aus v Eng	Adelaide	Aus	163 runs
508	8th Feb 1975	6	Aus v Eng	MCG	Eng	Innings and 4 runs
509	20th Feb 1975	1	NZ v Eng	Auckland	Eng	Innings and 83 runs
510	28th Feb 1975	2	NZ v Eng	Christchurch	drawn	
511	10th Jul 1975	1	Eng v Aus	Edgbaston	Aus	Innings and 85 runs
512	31st Jul 1975	2	Eng v Aus	Lord's	drawn	
513	14th Aug 1975	3	Eng v Aus	Headingley	drawn	
514	28th Aug 1975	4	Eng v Aus	The Oval	drawn	
515	3rd Jun 1976	1	Eng v WI	Trent Bridge	drawn	
516	17th Jun 1976	2	Eng v WI	Lord's	drawn	
517	8th Jul 1976	3	Eng v WI	Old Trafford	WI	425 runs
518	22nd Jul 1976	4	Eng v WI	Headingley	WI	55 runs
519	12th Aug 1976	5	Eng v WI	The Oval	WI	231 runs
520	17th Dec 1976	1	Ind v Eng	Delhi	Eng	Innings and 25 runs
521	1st Jan 1977	2	Ind v Eng	Calcutta	Eng	10 wickets
522	14th Jan 1977	3	Ind v Eng	Chepauk	Eng	200 runs
523	28th Jan 1977	4	Ind v Eng	Bangalore	Ind	140 runs
524	11th Feb 1977	5	Ind v Eng	Wankhede	drawn	
525	12th Mar 1977	1	Aus v Eng	MCG	Aus	45 runs
526	16th Jun 1977	1	Eng v Aus	Lord's	drawn	
527	7th Jul 1977	2	Eng v Aus	Old Trafford	Eng	9 wickets
528	28th Jul 1977	3	Eng v Aus	Trent Bridge	Eng	7 wickets

No	Date	Test	Match	Venue	Winner	Result
529	11th Aug 1977	4	Eng v Aus	Headingley	Eng	Innings and 85 runs
530	25th Aug 1977	5	Eng v Aus	The Oval	drawn	
531	14th Dec 1977	1	Pak v Eng	Lahore (Gd.)	drawn	
532	2nd Jan 1978	2	Pak v Eng	Hyderabad (P)	drawn	
533	18th Jan 1978	3	Pak v Eng	Karachi (Nat.)	drawn	
534	10th Feb 1978	1	NZ v Eng	Wellington	NZ	72 runs
535	24th Feb 1978	2	NZ v Eng	Christchurch	Eng	174 runs
536	4th Mar 1978	3	NZ v Eng	Auckland	drawn	
537	1st Jun 1978	1	Eng v Pak	Edgbaston	Eng	Innings and 57 runs
538	15th Jun 1978	2	Eng v Pak	Lord's	Eng	Innings and 120 runs
539	29th Jun 1978	3	Eng v Pak	Headingley	drawn	
540	27th Jul 1978	1	Eng v NZ	The Oval	Eng	7 wickets
541	10th Aug 1978	2	Eng v NZ	Trent Bridge	Eng	Innings and 119 runs
542	24th Aug 1978	3	Eng v NZ	Lord's	Eng	7 wickets
543	1st Dec 1978	1	Aus v Eng	The Gabba	Eng	7 wickets
544	15th Dec 1978	2	Aus v Eng	Perth (WACA)	Eng	166 runs
545	29th Dec 1978	3	Aus v Eng	MCG	Aus	103 runs
546	6th Jan 1979	4	Aus v Eng	Sydney (SCG)	Eng	93 runs
547	27th Jan 1979	5	Aus v Eng	Adelaide	Eng	205 runs
548	10th Feb 1979	6	Aus v Eng	Sydney (SCG)	Eng	9 wickets
549	12th Jul 1979	1	Eng v Ind	Edgbaston	Eng	Innings and 83 runs
550	2nd Aug 1979	2	Eng v Ind	Lord's	drawn	
551	16th Aug 1979	3	Eng v Ind	Headingley	drawn	
552	30th Aug 1979	4	Eng v Ind	The Oval	drawn	
553	14th Dec 1979	1	Aus v Eng	Perth (WACA)	Aus	138 runs
554	4th Jan 1980	2	Aus v Eng	Sydney (SCG)	Aus	6 wickets
555	1st Feb 1980	3	Aus v Eng	MCG	Aus	8 wickets
556	15th Feb 1980	1	Ind v Eng	Wankhede	Eng	10 wickets
557	5th Jun 1980	1	Eng v WI	Trent Bridge	WI	2 wickets
558	19th Jun 1980	2	Eng v WI	Lord's	drawn	
559	10th Jul 1980	3	Eng v WI	Old Trafford	drawn	
560	24th Jul 1980	4	Eng v WI	The Oval	drawn	
561	7th Aug 1980	5	Eng v WI	Headingley	drawn	
562	28th Aug 1980	1	Eng v Aus	Lord's	drawn	
563	13th Feb 1981	1	WI v Eng	Port-of-Spain	WI	Innings and 79 runs
564	13th Mar 1981	3	WI v Eng	Bridgetown	WI	298 runs
565	27th Mar 1981	4	WI v Eng	St. John's	drawn	
566	10th Apr 1981	5	WI v Eng	Kingston	drawn	
567	18th Jun 1981	1	Eng v Aus	Trent Bridge	Aus	4 wickets
568	2nd Jul 1981	2	Eng v Aus	Lord's	drawn	
569	16th Jul 1981	3	Eng v Aus	Headingley	Eng	18 runs
570	30th Jul 1981	4	Eng v Aus	Edgbaston	Eng	29 runs
571	13th Aug 1981	5	Eng v Aus	Old Trafford	Eng	103 runs
572	27th Aug 1981	6	Eng v Aus	The Oval	drawn	
573	27th Nov 1981	1	Ind v Eng	Wankhede	Ind	138 runs
574	9th Dec 1981	2	Ind v Eng	Bangalore	drawn	
575	23rd Dec 1981	3	Ind v Eng	Delhi	drawn	
576	1st Jan 1982	4	Ind v Eng	Calcutta	drawn	

No	Date	Test	Match	Venue	Winner	Result
577	13th Jan 1982	5	Ind v Eng	Chepauk	drawn	
578	30th Jan 1982	6	Ind v Eng	Kanpur	drawn	
579	17th Feb 1982	1	SL v Eng	Saravanamuttu	Eng	7 wickets
580	10th Jun 1982	1	Eng v Ind	Lord's	Eng	7 wickets
581	24th Jun 1982	2	Eng v Ind	Old Trafford	drawn	
582	8th Jul 1982	3	Eng v Ind	The Oval	drawn	
583	29th Jul 1982	1	Eng v Pak	Edgbaston	Eng	113 runs
584	12th Aug 1982	2	Eng v Pak	Lord's	Pak	10 wickets
585	26th Aug 1982	3	Eng v Pak	Headingley	Eng	3 wickets
586	12th Nov 1982	1	Aus v Eng	Perth (WACA)	drawn	
587	26th Nov 1982	2	Aus v Eng	The Gabba	Aus	7 wickets
588	10th Dec 1982	3	Aus v Eng	Adelaide	Aus	8 wickets
589	26th Dec 1982	4	Aus v Eng	MCG	Eng	3 runs
590	2nd Jan 1983	5	Aus v Eng	Sydney (SCG)	drawn	
591	14th Jul 1983	1	Eng v NZ	The Oval	Eng	189 runs
592	28th Jul 1983	2	Eng v NZ	Headingley	NZ	5 wickets
593	11th Aug 1983	3	Eng v NZ	Lord's	Eng	127 runs
594	25th Aug 1983	4	Eng v NZ	Trent Bridge	Eng	165 runs
595	20th Jan 1984	1	NZ v Eng	Wellington	drawn	
596	3rd Feb 1984	2	NZ v Eng	Christchurch	NZ	Innings and 132 runs
597	10th Feb 1984	3	NZ v Eng	Auckland	drawn	
598	2nd Mar 1984	1	Pak v Eng	Karachi (Nat.)	Pak	3 wickets
599	12th Mar 1984	2	Pak v Eng	Faisalabad	drawn	
600	19th Mar 1984	3	Pak v Eng	Lahore (Gd.)	drawn	
601	14th Jun 1984	1	Eng v WI	Edgbaston	WI	Innings and 180 runs
602	28th Jun 1984	2	Eng v WI	Lord's	WI	9 wickets
603	12th Jul 1984	3	Eng v WI	Headingley	WI	8 wickets
604	26th Jul 1984	4	Eng v WI	Old Trafford	WI	Innings and 64 runs
605	9th Aug 1984	5	Eng v WI	The Oval	WI	172 runs
606	23rd Aug 1984	1	Eng v SL	Lord's	drawn	
607	28th Nov 1984	1	Ind v Eng	Wankhede	Ind	8 wickets
608	12th Dec 1984	2	Ind v Eng	Delhi	Eng	8 wickets
609	31st Dec 1984	3	Ind v Eng	Calcutta	drawn	
610	13th Jan 1985	4	Ind v Eng	Chepauk	Eng	9 wickets
611	31st Jan 1985	5	Ind v Eng	Kanpur	drawn	
612	13th Jun 1985	1	Eng v Aus	Headingley	Eng	5 wickets
613	27th Jun 1985	2	Eng v Aus	Lord's	Aus	4 wickets
614	11th Jul 1985	3	Eng v Aus	Trent Bridge	drawn	
615	1st Aug 1985	4	Eng v Aus	Old Trafford	drawn	
616	15th Aug 1985	5	Eng v Aus	Edgbaston	Eng	Innings and 118 runs
617	29th Aug 1985	6	Eng v Aus	The Oval	Eng	Innings and 94 runs
618	21st Feb 1986	1	WI v Eng	Kingston	WI	10 wickets
619	7th Mar 1986	2	WI v Eng	Port-of-Spain	WI	7 wickets
620	21st Mar 1986	3	WI v Eng	Bridgetown	WI	Innings and 30 runs
621	3rd Apr 1986	4	WI v Eng	Port-of-Spain	WI	10 wickets
622	11th Apr 1986	5	WI v Eng	St. John's	WI	240 runs
623	5th Jun 1986	1	Eng v Ind	Lord's	Ind	5 wickets
624	19th Jun 1986	2	Eng v Ind	Headingley	Ind	279 runs

ALL-TIME TEST MATCH SUMMARY

No	Date	Test	Match	Venue	Winner	Result
625	3rd Jul 1986	3	Eng v Ind	Edgbaston	drawn	
626	24th Jul 1986	1	Eng v NZ	Lord's	drawn	
627	7th Aug 1986	2	Eng v NZ	Trent Bridge	NZ	8 wickets
628	21st Aug 1986	3	Eng v NZ	The Oval	drawn	
629	14th Nov 1986	1	Aus v Eng	The Gabba	Eng	7 wickets
630	28th Nov 1986	2	Aus v Eng	Perth (WACA)	drawn	
631	12th Dec 1986	3	Aus v Eng	Adelaide	drawn	
632	26th Dec 1986	4	Aus v Eng	MCG	Eng	Innings and 14 runs
633	10th Jan 1987	5	Aus v Eng	Sydney (SCG)	Aus	55 runs
634	4th Jun 1987	1	Eng v Pak	Old Trafford	drawn	
635	18th Jun 1987	2	Eng v Pak	Lord's	drawn	
636	2nd Jul 1987	3	Eng v Pak	Headingley	Pak	Innings and 18 runs
637	23rd Jul 1987	4	Eng v Pak	Edgbaston	drawn	
638	6th Aug 1987	5	Eng v Pak	The Oval	drawn	
639	25th Nov 1987	1	Pak v Eng	Lahore (Gd.)	Pak	Innings and 87 runs
640	7th Dec 1987	2	Pak v Eng	Faisalabad	drawn	
641	16th Dec 1987	3	Pak v Eng	Karachi (Nat.)	drawn	
642	29th Jan 1988	1	Aus v Eng	Sydney (SCG)	drawn	
643	12th Feb 1988	1	NZ v Eng	Christchurch	drawn	
644	25th Feb 1988	2	NZ v Eng	Auckland	drawn	
645	3rd Mar 1988	3	NZ v Eng	Wellington	drawn	
646	2nd Jun 1988	1	Eng v WI	Trent Bridge	drawn	
647	16th Jun 1988	2	Eng v WI	Lord's	WI	134 runs
648	30th Jun 1988	3	Eng v WI	Old Trafford	WI	Innings and 156 runs
649	21st Jul 1988	4	Eng v WI	Headingley	WI	10 wickets
650	4th Aug 1988	5	Eng v WI	The Oval	WI	8 wickets
651	25th Aug 1988	1	Eng v SL	Lord's	Eng	7 wickets
652	8th Jun 1989	1	Eng v Aus	Headingley	Aus	210 runs
653	22nd Jun 1989	2	Eng v Aus	Lord's	Aus	6 wickets
654	6th Jul 1989	3	Eng v Aus	Edgbaston	drawn	
655	27th Jul 1989	4	Eng v Aus	Old Trafford	Aus	9 wickets
656	10th Aug 1989	5	Eng v Aus	Trent Bridge	Aus	Innings and 180 runs
657	24th Aug 1989	6	Eng v Aus	The Oval	drawn	
658	24th Feb 1990	1	WI v Eng	Kingston	Eng	9 wickets
659	23rd Mar 1990	3	WI v Eng	Port-of-Spain	drawn	
660	5th Apr 1990	4	WI v Eng	Bridgetown	WI	164 runs
661	12th Apr 1990	5	WI v Eng	St. John's	WI	Innings and 32 runs
662	7th Jun 1990	1	Eng v NZ	Trent Bridge	drawn	
663	21st Jun 1990	2	Eng v NZ	Lord's	drawn	
664	5th Jul 1990	3	Eng v NZ	Edgbaston	Eng	114 runs
665	26th Jul 1990	1	Eng v Ind	Lord's	Eng	247 runs
666	9th Aug 1990	2	Eng v Ind	Old Trafford	drawn	
667	23rd Aug 1990	3	Eng v Ind	The Oval	drawn	
668	23rd Nov 1990	1	Aus v Eng	The Gabba	Aus	10 wickets
669	26th Dec 1990	2	Aus v Eng	MCG	Aus	8 wickets
670	4th Jan 1991	3	Aus v Eng	Sydney (SCG)	drawn	
671	25th Jan 1991	4	Aus v Eng	Adelaide	drawn	
672	1st Feb 1991	5	Aus v Eng	Perth (WACA)	Aus	9 wickets

No	Date	Test	Match	Venue	Winner	Result
673	6th Jun 1991	1	Eng v WI	Headingley	Eng	115 runs
674	20th Jun 1991	2	Eng v WI	Lord's	drawn	
675	4th Jul 1991	3	Eng v WI	Trent Bridge	WI	9 wickets
676	25th Jul 1991	4	Eng v WI	Edgbaston	WI	7 wickets
677	8th Aug 1991	5	Eng v WI	The Oval	Eng	5 wickets
678	22nd Aug 1991	1	Eng v SL	Lord's	Eng	137 runs
679	18th Jan 1992	1	NZ v Eng	Christchurch	Eng	Innings and 4 runs
680	30th Jan 1992	2	NZ v Eng	Auckland	Eng	168 runs
681	6th Feb 1992	3	NZ v Eng	Wellington	drawn	
682	4th Jun 1992	1	Eng v Pak	Edgbaston	drawn	
683	18th Jun 1992	2	Eng v Pak	Lord's	Pak	2 wickets
684	2nd Jul 1992	3	Eng v Pak	Old Trafford	drawn	
685	23rd Jul 1992	4	Eng v Pak	Headingley	Eng	6 wickets
686	6th Aug 1992	5	Eng v Pak	The Oval	Pak	10 wickets
687	29th Jan 1993	1	Ind v Eng	Calcutta	Ind	8 wickets
688	11th Feb 1993	2	Ind v Eng	Chepauk	Ind	Innings and 22 runs
689	19th Feb 1993	3	Ind v Eng	Wankhede	Ind	Innings and 15 runs
690	13th Mar 1993	1	SL v Eng	Colombo (SSC)	SL	5 wickets
691	3rd Jun 1993	1	Eng v Aus	Old Trafford	Aus	179 runs
692	17th Jun 1993	2	Eng v Aus	Lord's	Aus	Innings and 62 runs
693	1st Jul 1993	3	Eng v Aus	Trent Bridge	drawn	
694	22nd Jul 1993	4	Eng v Aus	Headingley	Aus	Innings and 148 runs
695	5th Aug 1993	5	Eng v Aus	Edgbaston	Aus	8 wickets
696	19th Aug 1993	6	Eng v Aus	The Oval	Eng	161 runs
697	19th Feb 1994	1	WI v Eng	Kingston	WI	8 wickets
698	17th Mar 1994	2	WI v Eng	Georgetown	WI	Innings and 44 runs
699	25th Mar 1994	3	WI v Eng	Port-of-Spain	WI	147 runs
700	8th Apr 1994	4	WI v Eng	Bridgetown	Eng	208 runs
701	16th Apr 1994	5	WI v Eng	St. John's	drawn	
702	2nd Jun 1994	1	Eng v NZ	Trent Bridge	Eng	Innings and 90 runs
703	16th Jun 1994	2	Eng v NZ	Lord's	drawn	
704	30th Jun 1994	3	Eng v NZ	Old Trafford	drawn	
705	21st Jul 1994	1	Eng v SA	Lord's	SA	356 runs
706	4th Aug 1994	2	Eng v SA	Headingley	drawn	
707	18th Aug 1994	3	Eng v SA	The Oval	Eng	8 wickets
708	25th Nov 1994	1	Aus v Eng	The Gabba	Aus	184 runs
709	24th Dec 1994	2	Aus v Eng	MCG	Aus	295 runs
710	1st Jan 1995	3	Aus v Eng	Sydney (SCG)	drawn	
711	26th Jan 1995	4	Aus v Eng	Adelaide	Eng	106 runs
712	3rd Feb 1995	5	Aus v Eng	Perth (WACA)	Aus	329 runs
713	8th Jun 1995	1	Eng v WI	Headingley	WI	9 wickets
714	22nd Jun 1995	2	Eng v WI	Lord's	Eng	72 runs
715	6th Jul 1995	3	Eng v WI	Edgbaston	WI	Innings and 64 runs
716	27th Jul 1995	4	Eng v WI	Old Trafford	Eng	6 wickets
717	10th Aug 1995	5	Eng v WI	Trent Bridge	drawn	
718	24th Aug 1995	6	Eng v WI	The Oval	drawn	
719	16th Nov 1995	1	SA v Eng	Centurion	drawn	
720	30th Nov 1995	2	SA v Eng	Wanderers	drawn	

No	Date	Test	Match	Venue	Winner	Result
721	14th Dec 1995	3	SA v Eng	Kingsmead	drawn	
722	26th Dec 1995	4	SA v Eng	Port Elizabeth	drawn	
723	2nd Jan 1996	5	SA v Eng	Cape Town	SA	10 wickets
724	6th Jun 1996	1	Eng v Ind	Edgbaston	Eng	8 wickets
725	20th Jun 1996	2	Eng v Ind	Lord's	drawn	
726	4th Jul 1996	3	Eng v Ind	Trent Bridge	drawn	
727	25th Jul 1996	1	Eng v Pak	Lord's	Pak	164 runs
728	8th Aug 1996	2	Eng v Pak	Headingley	drawn	
729	22nd Aug 1996	3	Eng v Pak	The Oval	Pak	9 wickets
730	18th Dec 1996	1	Zim v Eng	Bulawayo Q.C.	drawn	
731	26th Dec 1996	2	Zim v Eng	Harare	drawn	
732	24th Jan 1997	1	NZ v Eng	Auckland	drawn	
733	6th Feb 1997	2	NZ v Eng	Wellington	Eng	Innings and 68 runs
734	14th Feb 1997	3	NZ v Eng	Christchurch	Eng	4 wickets
735	5th Jun 1997	1	Eng v Aus	Edgbaston	Eng	9 wickets
736	19th Jun 1997	2	Eng v Aus	Lord's	drawn	
737	3rd Jul 1997	3	Eng v Aus	Old Trafford	Aus	268 runs
738	24th Jul 1997	4	Eng v Aus	Headingley	Aus	Innings and 61 runs
739	7th Aug 1997	5	Eng v Aus	Trent Bridge	Aus	264 runs
740	21st Aug 1997	6	Eng v Aus	The Oval	Eng	19 runs
741	29th Jan 1998	1	WI v Eng	Kingston	drawn	
742	5th Feb 1998	2	WI v Eng	Port-of-Spain	WI	3 wickets
743	13th Feb 1998	3	WI v Eng	Port-of-Spain	Eng	3 wickets
744	27th Feb 1998	4	WI v Eng	Georgetown	WI	242 runs
745	12th Mar 1998	5	WI v Eng	Bridgetown	drawn	
746	20th Mar 1998	6	WI v Eng	St. John's	WI	Innings and 52 runs
747	4th Jun 1998	1	Eng v SA	Edgbaston	drawn	
748	18th Jun 1998	2	Eng v SA	Lord's	SA	10 wickets
749	2nd Jul 1998	3	Eng v SA	Old Trafford	drawn	
750	23rd Jul 1998	4	Eng v SA	Trent Bridge	Eng	8 wickets
751	6th Aug 1998	5	Eng v SA	Headingley	Eng	23 runs
752	27th Aug 1998	1	Eng v SL	The Oval	SL	10 wickets
753	20th Nov 1998	1	Aus v Eng	The Gabba	drawn	
754	28th Nov 1998	2	Aus v Eng	Perth (WACA)	Aus	7 wickets
755	11th Dec 1998	3	Aus v Eng	Adelaide	Aus	205 runs
756	26th Dec 1998	4	Aus v Eng	MCG	Eng	12 runs
757	2nd Jan 1999	5	Aus v Eng	Sydney (SCG)	Aus	98 runs
758	1st Jul 1999	1	Eng v NZ	Edgbaston	Eng	7 wickets
759	22-Jul-99	2	Eng v NZ	Lord's	NZ	9 wickets
760	0Aug-99	3	Eng v NZ	Old Trafford	drawn	
761	1Aug-99	4	Eng v NZ	Oval	NZ	83 runs
762	2Nov-99	1	SA v Eng	Johannesburg	SA	Innings and 21 runs
763	0Dec-99	2	SA v Eng	Crusaders	drawn	
764	2Dec-99	3	SA v Eng	Durban	drawn	
765	0Jan-00	4	SA v Eng	Cape Town	SA	Innings and 37 runs
766	1Jan-00	5	SA v Eng	Centurion	Eng	2 wickets

No. 244: 1st Test		
VENUE: Lord's		
DATE: 22nd-25th June 1946		
TOSS WON BY: India		
RESULT: England won by 10 wickets		

No: 245 2nd Test		
VENUE: Old Trafford		
DATE: 20th-23rd July 1946		
TOSS WON BY: India		
RESULT: Match drawn		

INDIA 1st innings / 2nd innings

INDIA	1st innings		2nd innings	
VM Merchant	c Gibb b Bedser	12	lbw b Ikin	27
MH Mankad	b Wright	14	c Hammond b Smailes	63
L Amarnath	lbw b Bedser	0	lbw b Smailes	21
VS Hazare	b Bedser	31	c Hammond b Bedser	34
RS Modi	not out	57	b Bedser	0
Pataudi	c Ikin b Bedser	9	b Wright	22
Gul Mahomed	b Wright	1	lbw b Wright	9
AH Kardar	b Bowes	43	b Smailes	50
DD Hindlekar+	lbw b Bedser	3	c Ikin b Bedser	17
CS Nayudu	st Gibb b Bedser	4	b Bedser	13
SG Shinde	b Bedser	10	not out	4
Extras	(10b, 6lb, 0w, 0nb)	16	(10b, 2lb, 0w, 3nb)	15
	76.1 overs		81.1 overs	
Total		**200**		**275**

1st innings FoW: 15, 15, 44, 74, 86, 87, 144, 147, 157, 200
2nd innings FoW: 67, 117, 126, 129, 174, 185, 190, 249, 263, 275

WE Bowes	25	7	64	1		4	1	9	0
AV Bedser	29.1	11	49	7		32.1	3	96	4
TF Smailes	5	1	18	0		15	2	44	3
DVP Wright	17	4	53	2		20	3	68	2
JT Ikin						10	1	43	1

ENGLAND	1st innings		2nd innings	
L Hutton	c Nayudu b Amarnath	7	not out	22
C Washbrook	c Mankad b Amarnath	27	not out	24
DCS Compton	b Amarnath	0		
J Hardstaff jr	not out	205		
Hammond*	b Amarnath	33		
PA Gibb+	c Hazare b Mankad	60		
JT Ikin	c Hindlekar b Shinde	16		
TF Smailes	c Mankad b Amarnath	25		
AV Bedser	b Hazare	30		
DVP Wright	b Mankad	3		
WE Bowes	lbw b Hazare	2		
Extras	(11b, 8lb, 0w, 1nb)	20	(0b, 1lb, 1w, 0nb)	2
	169.4 overs		16.5 overs	
Total		**428**		**48**

1st innings FoW: 16, 16, 61, 70, 252, 284, 34,4 416, 421, 428

VS Hazare	34.4	4	100	2		4	2	7	0
L Amarnath	57	18	118	5		4	0	15	0
Gul Mahomed	2	0	2	0					
MH Mankad	48	11	107	2					
SG Shinde	23	2	66	1		4.5	1	11	0
CS Nayudu	5	1	15	0					

ENGLAND	1st innings		2nd innings	
L Hutton	c Mushtaq b Mankad	67	c Hindlekar b Amarnath	2
C Washbrook	c Hindlekar b Mankad	52	lbw b Mankad	26
DCS Compton	lbw b Amarnath	51	not out	71
Hammond*	b Amarnath	69	c Kardar b Mankad	8
J Hardstaff jr	c Merchant b Amarnath	5	b Amarnath	0
PA Gibb+	b Mankad	24	c Modi b Amarnath	0
JT Ikin	c Mankad b Amarnath	2	not out	29
W Voce	b Mankad	0		
R Pollard	not out	10		
AV Bedser	lbw b Amarnath	8		
DVP Wright	lbw b Mankad	0		
Extras	(2b, 4lb, 0w, 0nb)	6	(6b, 10lb, 1w, 0nb)	17
	129 overs		61 overs	
Total		**294**		**153**

1st innings FoW: 81, 156, 186, 193, 250, 265, 270, 274, 287, 294
2nd innings FoW: 7, 48, 68, 68, 84

SW Sohoni	11	1	31	0					
L Amarnath	51	17	96	5		30	9	71	3
VS Hazare	14	2	48	0		10	3	20	0
MH Mankad	46	15	101	5		21	6	45	2
CT Sarwate	7	0	12	0					

INDIA	1st innings		2nd innings	
VM Merchant	c Bedser b Pollard	78	c Ikin b Pollard	0
Mushtaq Ali	b Pollard	46	b Pollard	1
AH Kardar	c & b Pollard	1	b Bedser	4
MH Mankad	b Pollard	0	b Bedser	30
VS Hazare	b Voce	3	b Bedser	44
RS Modi	c Ikin b Bedser	2	b Bedser	3
Pataudi	b Pollard	11	c & b Bedser	35
L Amarnath	b Bedser	8	c Pollard b Bedser	5
SW Sohoni	c & b Bedser	3	not out	11
CT Sarwate	c Ikin b Bedser	0	c Gibb b Bedser	2
DD Hindlekar+	not out	1	not out	4
Extras	(10b, 5lb, 0w, 2nb)	17	(5b, 8lb, 0w, 0nb)	13
	82 overs		61 overs	
Total		**170**		**152**

1st innings FoW: 124, 130, 130, 141, 141, 146, 156, 168, 169, 170
2nd innings FoW: 0, 3, 5, 79, 84, 87, 113, 132, 138

W Voce	20	3	44	1		6	5	2	0
AV Bedser	26	9	41	4		25	4	52	7
R Pollard	27	16	24	5		25	10	63	2
DVP Wright	2	0	12	0		2	0	17	0
DCS Compton	4	0	18	0		3	1	5	0
JT Ikin	2	0	11	0					
WR Hammond	1	0	3	0					

India		Australia	

No. 246: 3rd Test
VENUE: The Oval
DATE: 17th-20th August 1946
TOSS WON BY: India
RESULT: Match drawn

No. 247: 1st Test
VENUE: Brisbane (Gabba)
DATE: 29th Nov-4th December 1946
TOSS WON BY: Australia
RESULT: Aus won by an innings and 332 runs

INDIA 1st innings — 2nd innings

INDIA	1st innings		2nd innings
VM Merchant	run out	128	
Mushtaq Ali	run out	59	
Pataudi	b Edrich	9	
L Amarnath	b Edrich	8	
VS Hazare	c Compton b Gover	11	
RS Modi	b Smith	27	
AH Kardar	b Edrich	1	
MH Mankad	b Bedser	42	
SW Sohoni	not out	29	
CS Nayudu	c Washbrook b Bedser	4	
DD Hindlekar+	lbw b Edrich	3	
Extras	(1b, 5lb, 0w, 4nb)	10	
	127.2 overs		
Total		331	

1st innings FoW: 94, 124, 142, 162, 225, 226, 272, 313, 325, 331

AR Gover	21	3	56	1
AV Bedser	32	6	60	2
TPB Smith	21	4	58	1
WJ Edrich	19.2	4	68	4
J Langridge	29	9	64	0
DCS Compton	5	0	15	0

ENGLAND 1st innings — 2nd innings

ENGLAND	1st innings		2nd innings
L Hutton	lbw b Mankad	25	
C Washbrook	c Mushtaq b Mankad	17	
LB Fishlock	c Merchant b Nayudu	8	
DCS Compton	not out	24	
Hammond*	not out	9	
WJ Edrich			
J Langridge			
TPB Smith			
TG Evans+			
AV Bedser			
AR Gover			
Extras	(11b, 1lb, 0w, 0nb)	12	
	50 overs		
Total		95	

1st innings FoW: 48, 55, 67

L Amarnath	15	6	30	0
SW Sohoni	4	3	2	0
VS Hazare	2	1	4	0
MH Mankad	20	7	28	2
CS Nayudu	9	2	19	1

AUSTRALIA 1st innings — 2nd innings

AUSTRALIA	1st innings		2nd innings
SG Barnes	c Bedser b Wright	31	
AR Morris	c Hammond b Bedser	2	
DG Bradman*	b Edrich	187	
AL Hassett	c Yardley b Bedser	128	
KR Miller	lbw b Wright	79	
CL McCool	lbw b Wright	95	
IW Johnson	lbw b Wright	47	
D Tallon+	lbw b Edrich	14	
RR Lindwall	c Voce b Wright	31	
GE Tribe	c Gibb b Edrich	1	
ERH Toshack	not out	1	
Extras	(5b, 11lb, 2w, 11nb)	29	
	158.6 overs		
Total		645	

1st innings FoW: 9, 46, 322, 428, 465, 596, 599, 629, 643, 645

W Voce	28	9	92	0
AV Bedser	41	5	159	2
DVP Wright	43.6	4	167	5
WJ Edrich	25	2	107	3
NWD Yardley	13	1	47	0
JT Ikin	2	0	24	0
DCS Compton	6	0	20	0

ENGLAND 1st innings — 2nd innings

ENGLAND	1st innings		2nd innings	
L Hutton	b Miller	7	c Barnes b Miller	0
C Washbrook	c Barnes b Miller	6	c Barnes b Miller	13
WJ Edrich	c McCool b Miller	16	lbw b Toshack	7
DCS Compton	lbw b Miller	17	c Barnes b Toshack	15
Hammond*	lbw b Toshack	32	b Toshack	23
JT Ikin	c Tallon b Miller	0	b Tribe	32
NWD Yardley	c Tallon b Toshack	29	c Hassett b Toshack	0
PA Gibb+	b Miller	13	lbw b Toshack	11
W Voce	not out	1	c Hassett b Tribe	18
AV Bedser	lbw b Miller	0	c & b Toshack	18
DVP Wright	c Tallon b Toshack	4	not out	10
Extras	(8b, 3lb, 2w, 3nb)	16	(15b, 7lb, 1w, 2nb)	25
	61.5 overs		43.7 overs	
Total		141		172

1st innings FoW: 10, 25, 49, 56, 56, 121, 134, 136, 136, 141
2nd innings FoW: 0, 13, 33, 62, 65, 65, 112, 114, 143, 172

RR Lindwall	12	4	23	0				
KR Miller	22	4	60	7	11	3	17	2
ERH Toshack	16.5	11	17	3	20.7	2	82	6
GE Tribe	9	2	19	0	12	2	48	2
CL McCool	1	0	5	0				
SG Barnes	1	0	1	0				

Australia

No. 248: 2nd Test
VENUE: Sydney (SCG)
DATE: 13th-19th December 1946
TOSS WON BY: England
RESULT: Aus won by an innings and 33 runs

ENGLAND 1st innings / 2nd innings

Batsman	1st innings		2nd innings	
L Hutton	c Tallon b Johnson	39	hit wkt b Miller	37
C Washbrook	b Freer	1	c McCool b Johnson	41
WJ Edrich	lbw b McCool	71	b McCool	119
DCS Compton	c Tallon b McCool	5	c Bradman b Freer	54
Hammond*	c Tallon b McCool	1	c Toshack b McCool	37
JT Ikin	c Hassett b Johnson	60	b Freer	17
NWD Yardley	c Tallon b Johnson	25	b McCool	35
TPB Smith	lbw b Johnson	4	c Hassett b Johnson	2
TG Evans+	b Johnson	5	st Tallon b McCool	9
AV Bedser	b Johnson	14	not out	3
DVP Wright	not out	15	c Tallon b McCool	0
Extras	(4b, 11lb, 0w, 0nb)	15	(8b, 6lb, 1w, 2nb)	17
Total	96.1 overs	**255**	106.4 overs	**371**

1st innings FoW: 10, 88, 97, 99, 148, 187, 197, 205, 234, 255
2nd innings FOW: 49, 118, 220, 280, 309, 327, 346, 366, 369, 371

Bowler	O	M	R	W	O	M	R	W
KR Miller	9	2	24	0	11	3	37	1
FW Freer	7	1	25	1	13	2	49	2
ERH Toshack	7	2	6	0	6	1	16	0
GE Tribe	20	3	70	0	12	0	40	0
IW Johnson	30.1	12	42	6	29	7	92	2
CL McCool	23	2	73	3	32.4	4	109	5
SG Barnes					3	0	11	0

AUSTRALIA 1st innings / 2nd innings

Batsman	1st innings		2nd innings
SG Barnes	c Ikin b Bedser	234	
AR Morris	b Edrich	5	
IW Johnson	c Washbrook b Edrich	7	
AL Hassett	c Compton b Edrich	34	
KR Miller	c Evans b Smith	40	
DG Bradman*	lbw b Yardley	234	
CL McCool	c Hammond b Smith	12	
D Tallon+	c & b Wright	30	
FW Freer	not out	28	
GE Tribe	not out	25	
ERH Toshack			
Extras	(0b, 7lb, 1w, 2nb)	10	
Total	173 overs	**659**	

1st innings FOW: 24, 37, 96, 159, 564, 564, 595, 617

Bowler	O	M	R	W
AV Bedser	46	7	153	1
WJ Edrich	26	3	79	3
DVP Wright	46	8	169	1
TPB Smith	37	1	172	2
JT Ikin	3	0	15	0
DCS Compton	6	0	38	0
NWD Yardley	9	0	23	1

Australia '47

No. 249: 3rd Test
VENUE: Melbourne (MCG)
DATE: 1st-7th January 1947
TOSS WON BY: Australia
RESULT: Match drawn

AUSTRALIA 1st innings / 2nd innings

Batsman	1st innings		2nd innings	
SG Barnes	lbw b Bedser	45	c Evans b Yardley	32
AR Morris	lbw b Bedser	21	b Bedser	155
DG Bradman*	b Yardley	79	c & b Yardley	49
AL Hassett	c Hammond b Wright	12	b Wright	9
KR Miller	c Evans b Wright	33	c Hammond b Yardley	34
IW Johnson	lbw b Yardley	0	run out	0
CL McCool	not out	104	c Evans b Bedser	43
D Tallon+	c Evans b Edrich	35	c & b Wright	92
RR Lindwall	b Bedser	9	c Washbrook b Bedser	100
B Dooland	c Hammond b Edrich	19	c Compton b Wright	1
ERH Toshack	c Hutton b Edrich	6	not out	2
Extras	(0b, 0lb, 0w, 2nb)	2	(14b, 2lb, 0w, 3nb)	19
Total	97.3 overs	**365**	113.3 overs	**536**

1st innings FoW: 32, 108, 143, 188, 188,192, 255, 272, 355, 365
2nd innings FoW: 68, 159, 177, 242, 333, 335, 341, 495, 511, 536

Bowler	O	M	R	W	O	M	R	W
W Voce	10	2	40	0	6	1	29	0
AV Bedser	31	4	99	3	34.3	4	176	3
DVP Wright	26	2	124	2	32	3	131	3
NWD Yardley	20	4	50	2	20	0	67	3
WJ Edrich	10.3	2	50	3	18	1	86	0
L Hutton					3	0	28	0

ENGLAND 1st innings / 2nd innings

Batsman	1st innings		2nd innings	
L Hutton	c McCool b Lindwall	2	c Bradman b Toshack	40
C Washbrook	c Tallon b Dooland	62	b Dooland	112
WJ Edrich	lbw b Lindwall	89	lbw b McCool	13
DCS Compton	lbw b Toshack	11	run out	14
WR Hammond*	c & b Dooland	9	b Lindwall	26
JT Ikin	c Miller b Dooland	48	c Hassett b Miller	5
NWD Yardley	b McCool	61	not out	53
TG Evans+	b McCool	17	not out	0
W Voce	lbw b Dooland	0		
AV Bedser	not out	27	lbw b Miller	25
DVP Wright	b Johnson	10		
Extras	(1b, 12lb, 0w, 2nb)	15	(15b, 6lb, 1w, 0nb)	22
Total	108.5 overs	**351**	100 overs	**310**

1st innings FoW: 8, 155, 167, 176, 179, 292, 298, 298, 324, 351
2nd innings FoW: 138, 163, 186, 197, 221, 249, 294

Bowler	O	M	R	W	O	M	R	W
RR Lindwall	20	1	64	2	16	2	59	1
KR Miller	10	0	34	0	11	0	41	2
ERH Toshack	26	5	88	1	16	5	39	1
CL McCool	19	3	53	2	24	9	41	1
B Dooland	27	5	69	4	21	1	84	1
IW Johnson	6.5	1	28	1	12	4	24	0

No. 250: 4th Test	No. 251: 5th Test
VENUE: Adelaide	VENUE: Sydney (SCG)
DATE: 31st January-6th Feb 1947	DATE: 28th Feb-5th March 1947
TOSS WON BY: England	TOSS WON BY: England
RESULT: Match drawn	RESULT: Australia won by 5 wickets

Match 250 — Adelaide

ENGLAND 1st innings

Batsman	Dismissal	Runs	2nd innings	Runs
L Hutton	lbw b McCool	94	b Johnson	76
C Washbrook	c Tallon b Dooland	65	c Tallon b Lindwall	39
WJ Edrich	c & b Dooland	17	c Bradman b Toshack	46
Hammond*	b Toshack	18	c Lindwall b Toshack	22
DCS Compton	c & b Lindwall	147	not out	103
J Hardstaff jr	b Miller	67	b Toshack	9
JT Ikin	c Toshack b Dooland	21	lbw b Toshack	1
NWD Yardley	not out	18	c Tallon b Lindwall	18
AV Bedser	b Lindwall	2	c Tallon b Miller	3
TG Evans+	b Lindwall	0	not out	10
DVP Wright	b Lindwall	0		
Extras	(4b, 5lb, 2w, 0nb)	11	(5b, 3lb, 2w, 3nb)	13
Total	153 overs	**460**	125.1 overs	**340**

1st innings FoW: 137, 173, 196, 202, 320, 381, 455, 460, 460, 460
2nd innings FoW: 100, 137, 178, 188, 207, 215, 250, 255

Bowler	O	M	R	W	O	M	R	W
RR Lindwall	23	5	52	4	17.1	4	60	2
KR Miller	16	0	45	1	11	0	34	1
ERH Toshack	30	13	59	1	36	6	76	4
CL McCool	29	1	91	1	19	3	41	0
IW Johnson	22	3	69	0	25	8	51	1
B Dooland	33	1	133	3	17	2	65	0

AUSTRALIA 1st innings

Batsman	Dismissal	Runs	2nd innings	Runs
MR Harvey	b Bedser	12	b Yardley	31
AR Morris	c Evans b Bedser	122	not out	124
DG Bradman*	b Bedser	0	not out	56
AL Hassett	c Hammond b Wright	78		
KR Miller	not out	141		
IW Johnson	lbw b Wright	52		
CL McCool	c Bedser b Yardley	2		
D Tallon+	b Wright	3		
RR Lindwall	c Evans b Yardley	20		
B Dooland	c Bedser b Yardley	29		
ERH Toshack	run out	0		
Extras	(16b, 6lb, 2w, 4nb)	28	(0b, 2lb, 0w, 2nb)	4
Total	118.4 overs	**487**	44 overs	**215**

1st innings FoW: 18, 18, 207, 222, 372, 389, 396, 423, 486, 487
2nd innings FoW: 116

Bowler	O	M	R	W	O	M	R	W
AV Bedser	30	6	97	3	15	1	68	0
WJ Edrich	20	3	88	0	7	2	25	0
DVP Wright	32.4	1	152	3	9	0	49	0
NWD Yardley	31	7	101	3	13	0	69	1
JT Ikin	2	0	9	0				
DCS Compton	3	0	12	0				

Match 251 — Sydney (SCG)

ENGLAND 1st innings

Batsman	Dismissal	Runs	2nd innings	Runs
L Hutton	retired ill	122		
LB Fishlock	lbw b Lindwall	0		
C Washbrook	b Lindwall	0	b McCool	24
WJ Edrich	c Tallon b Lindwall	60	st Tallon b McCool	24
LB Fishlock	b McCool	14		
DCS Compton	c Miller b Toshack	76	hit wkt b Lindwall	17
JT Ikin	st Tallon b McCool	0	b Lindwall	0
NWD Yardley*	c Miller b Lindwall	2	b McCool	11
TG Evans+	c Tallon b Lindwall	20	b Lindwall	29
TPB Smith	c Tallon b Lindwall	24	b Lindwall	2
AV Bedser	st Tallon b McCool	4	not out	10
Extras	(1b, 1lb, 0w, 0nb)	2	(7b, 8lb, 1w, 1nb)	17
Total	60.4 overs	**186**	94.3 overs	**280**

1st innings FoW: 1, 151, 188, 215, 225, 225, 244, 269, 280
2nd innings FoW: 0, 42, 65, 65, 85, 120, 157, 184, 186

Bowler	O	M	R	W	O	M	R	W
RR Lindwall	22	3	63	7	12	1	46	2
KR Miller	15.3	2	31	1	6	1	11	1
GE Tribe	28	2	95	0	14	0	58	0
ERH Toshack	16	4	40	0	4	1	14	1
CL McCool	13	0	34	1	21.4	5	44	5
SG Barnes					3	0	11	0

AUSTRALIA 1st innings

Batsman	Dismissal	Runs	2nd innings	Runs
SG Barnes	c Evans b Bedser	71	c Evans b Bedser	30
AR Morris	lbw b Bedser	57	run out	17
DG Bradman*	b Wright	12	c Compton b Bedser	63
AL Hassett	c Ikin b Wright	24	c Ikin b Wright	47
KR Miller	c Ikin b Wright	23	not out	34
RA Hamence	not out	30	c Edrich b Wright	1
CL McCool	c Yardley b Wright	3	not out	13
D Tallon+	c Compton b Wright	0		
RR Lindwall	c Smith b Wright	0		
GE Tribe	c Fishlock b Wright	9		
ERH Toshack	run out	5		
Extras	(7b, 6lb, 0w, 6nb)	19	(4b, 1lb, 0w, 4nb)	9
Total	76 overs	**253**	52.2 overs	**214**

1st innings FoW: 126, 146, 146, 187, 218, 230, 230, 233, 245, 253
2nd innings FoW: 45, 51, 149, 173, 180

Bowler	O	M	R	W	O	M	R	W
AV Bedser	27	7	49	2	22	4	75	2
WJ Edrich	7	0	34	0	2	0	14	0
TPB Smith	8	0	38	0	2	0	8	0
DVP Wright	29	4	105	7	22	1	93	2
NWD Yardley	5	2	8	0	3	1	7	0
DCS Compton					1.2	0	8	0

No. 252:	2nd Test
VENUE:	Christchurch
DATE:	21st-25th March 1947
TOSS WON BY:	England
RESULT:	Match drawn

No. 253:	1st Test
VENUE:	Trent Bridge
DATE:	7th-11th June 1947
TOSS WON BY:	South Africa
RESULT:	Match drawn

NEW ZEALAND 1st innings   2nd innings

WA Hadlee*	c Bedser b Yardley	116
B Sutcliffe	c Evans b Bedser	58
VJ Scott	c Hammond b Pollard	18
WM Wallace	c Evans b Bedser	9
DD Taylor	lbw b Bedser	12
FB Smith	b Bedser	18
EWT Tindill+	b Pollard	1
RH Scott	b Edrich	18
J Cowie	b Pollard	45
TB Burtt	not out	24
CA Snedden		
Extras	(10b, 11lb, 0w, 5nb)	26
	102.4 overs	
Total		**345**

1st innings FoW: 133, 195, 212, 212, 234, 238, 258, 281, 345

AV Bedser	39	5	95	4
R Pollard	29.4	8	73	3
WJ Edrich	11	2	35	1
DVP Wright	13	1	61	0
TPB Smith	6	0	43	0
NWD Yardley	4	0	12	1

ENGLAND 1st innings   2nd innings

C Washbrook	c Smith b Cowie	2
NWD Yardley	b Cowie	22
WJ Edrich	c Taylor b RH Scott	42
DCS Compton	b Cowie	38
Hammond*	c Sutcliffe b Cowie	79
JT Ikin	c Tindill b Cowie	45
TG Evans+	not out	21
TPB Smith	c (sub) b Cowie	1
AV Bedser	not out	8
DVP Wright		
R Pollard		
Extras	(5b, 1lb, 0w, 1nb)	7
	83 overs	
Total		**265**

1st innings FoW: 2, 46, 79, 125, 222, 241, 249

J Cowie	30	4	83	6
RH Scott	23	3	74	1
TB Burtt	14	1	55	0
CA Snedden	16	5	46	0

SOUTH AFRICA 1st innings   2nd innings

B Mitchell	b Bedser	14	c Evans b Bedser	4
A Melville*	b Martin	189	not out	104
KG Viljoen	lbw b Edrich	10	not out	51
AD Nourse	b Hollies	149		
OC Dawson	st Evans b Hollies	48		
TA Harris	c Hutton b Hollies	60		
AMB Rowan	not out	34		
L Tuckett	lbw b Hollies	0		
NBF Mann	b Bedser	8		
JD Lindsay+	b Bedser	0		
VI Smith	c Yardley b Hollies	1		
Extras	(7b, 12lb, 1w, 0nb)	20	(1b, 0lb, 5w, 1nb)	7
	196.3 overs		51 overs	
Total		**533**		**166**

1st innings FoW: 23, 44, 363, 384, 450, 505, 505, 528, 530, 533
2nd innings FoW: 21

JW Martin	36	4	111	1		9	2	18	0
AV Bedser	57.1	14	106	3		14	3	31	1
WJ Edrich	20	8	56	1		4	0	8	0
WE Hollies	55.2	16	123	5		9	1	33	0
C Cook	21	4	87	0		9	0	40	0
NWD Yardley	5	0	24	0					
DCS Compton	2	1	6	0		4	0	14	0
L Hutton	2	0	15	0					

ENGLAND 1st innings   2nd innings

L Hutton	lbw b Rowan	17	b Tuckett	9
C Washbrook	lbw b Tuckett	25	c Lindsay b Rowan	59
WJ Edrich	b Smith	57	b Smith	50
DCS Compton	c Mitchell b Tuckett	65	c Mitchell b Mann	163
HE Dollery	b Dawson	9	c & b Dawson	17
NWD Yardley*	lbw b Tuckett	22	c Tuckett b Dawson	99
TG Evans+	st Lindsay b Smith	2	c & b Smith	74
AV Bedser	c Melville b Smith	7	c Harris b Smith	2
C Cook	b Tuckett	0	c Dawson b Smith	4
JW Martin	c Lindsay b Tuckett	0	not out	18
WE Hollies	not out	0	b Rowan	26
Extras	(1b, 2lb, 1w, 0nb)	4	(15b, 13lb, 2w, 0nb)	30
	113.1 overs		226.2 overs	
Total		**208**		**551**

1st innings FoW: 40, 48, 154, 165, 198, 198, 207, 208, 208, 208
2nd innings FoW: 20, 116, 133, 170, 407, 434, 472, 499, 500, 551

L Tuckett	37	9	68	5		47	12	127	1
OC Dawson	13	2	35	1		25	7	57	2
AMB Rowan	16	6	45	1		43.2	8	100	2
NBF Mann	20	13	10	0		60	22	94	1
VI Smith	27.1	10	46	3		51	15	143	4

South Africa	South Africa

No. 254: 2nd Test		No. 255: 3rd Test	
VENUE: Lord's		VENUE: Old Trafford	
DATE: 21st-25th June 1947		DATE: 5th-9th July 1947	
TOSS WON BY: England		TOSS WON BY: South Africa	
RESULT: England won by 10 wickets		RESULT: England won by 7 wickets	

ENGLAND 1st innings / 2nd innings

Batsman	1st innings		2nd innings	
L Hutton	b Rowan	18	not out	13
C Washbrook	c Tuckett b Dawson	65	not out	13
WJ Edrich	b Mann	189		
DCS Compton	c Rowan b Tuckett	208		
CJ Barnett	b Tuckett	33		
NWD Yardley*	c Rowan b Tuckett	5		
TG Evans+	b Tuckett	16		
GH Pope	not out	8		
AV Bedser	b Tuckett	0		
DVP Wright				
WE Hollies				
Extras	(2b, 10lb, 0w, 0nb)	12	(0b, 0lb, 0w, 0nb)	0
Total	215 overs	**554**	12.1 overs	**26**

1st innings FoW: 75, 96, 466, 515, 526, 541, 554, 554

L Tuckett	47	8	115	5		3	0	4	0
OC Dawson	33	11	81	1		6	2	6	0
NBF Mann	53	16	99	1		3.1	1	16	0
AMB Rowan	65	11	174	1					
VI Smith	17	2	73	0					

SOUTH AFRICA 1st innings / 2nd innings

Batsman	1st innings		2nd innings	
B Mitchell	st Evans b Compton	46	c Edrich b Wright	80
A Melville*	c Bedser b Hollies	117	b Edrich	8
KG Viljoen	b Wright	1	b Edrich	6
AD Nourse	lbw b Wright	61	b Edrich	58
OC Dawson	c Barnett b Hollies	36	c Edrich b Compton	33
TA Harris	st Evans b Compton	30	c Yardley b Compton	3
AMB Rowan	b Wright	8	not out	38
L Tuckett	b Wright	5	lbw b Wright	9
NBF Mann	b Wright	4	b Wright	5
JD Lindsay+	not out	7	c Yardley b Wright	5
VI Smith	c Edrich b Pope	11	c Edrich b Wright	0
Extras	(0b, 1lb, 0w, 0nb)	1	(3b, 4lb, 0w, 0nb)	7
Total	142.2 overs	**327**	128.2 overs	**252**

1st innings FoW: 95, 104, 222, 230, 290, 300, 302, 308, 309, 327
2nd innings FoW: 16, 28, 120, 192, 192, 201, 224, 236, 252, 252

WJ Edrich	9	1	22	0		13	5	31	3
AV Bedser	26	1	76	0		14	6	20	0
GH Pope	19.2	5	49	1		17	7	36	0
DVP Wright	39	10	95	5		32.2	6	80	5
WE Hollies	28	10	52	2		20	7	32	0
DCS Compton	21	11	32	2		32	10	46	2

SOUTH AFRICA 1st innings / 2nd innings

Batsman	1st innings		2nd innings	
A Melville*	c Hutton b Gladwin	17	b Edrich	59
DV Dyer	b Edrich	62	b Gladwin	1
B Mitchell	run out	80	c Hutton b Compton	6
AD Nourse	c Yardley b Cranston	23	b Edrich	115
KG Viljoen	c Compton b Edrich	93	c Hutton b Wright	32
OC Dawson	b Cranston	1	b Edrich	9
AMB Rowan	lbw b Hollies	13	c Evans b Wright	0
L Tuckett	b Edrich	13	lbw b Wright	17
NBF Mann	c Hollies b Gladwin	8	c Barnett b Wright	9
JD Lindsay+	not out	9	b Hollies	0
JB Plimsoll	c Evans b Edrich	8	not out	8
Extras	(3b, 9lb, 0w, 0nb)	12	(5b, 5lb, 0w, 1nb)	11
Total	166.1 overs	**339**	84.4 overs	**267**

1st innings FoW: 32, 125, 163, 214, 215, 260, 287, 298, 327, 339
2nd innings FoW: 12, 42, 96, 217, 225, 228, 232, 244, 244, 267

WJ Edrich	35.1	9	95	4		22.4	4	77	4
C Gladwin	50	24	58	2		16	6	28	1
K Cranston	34	12	64	2					
CJ Barnett	8	3	11	0		5	1	12	0
DVP Wright	9	1	30	0		10	2	32	3
WE Hollies	23	8	42	1		14	4	49	1
DCS Compton	7	1	27	0		17	2	58	1

ENGLAND 1st innings / 2nd innings

Batsman	1st innings		2nd innings	
L Hutton	c Lindsay b Plimsoll	12	c Dawson b Mann	24
C Washbrook	c Nourse b Tuckett	29	c Lindsay b Dawson	40
WJ Edrich	b Tuckett	191	not out	22
DCS Compton	c Tuckett b Dawson	115	hit wkt b Mann	6
CJ Barnett	c (sub) b Mann	5	not out	19
NWD Yardley*	c Melville b Plimsoll	41		
K Cranston	c Dawson b Rowan	23		
TG Evans+	b Tuckett	27		
C Gladwin	b Tuckett	16		
DVP Wright	not out	4		
WE Hollies	c Nourse b Plimsoll	5		
Extras	(2b, 7lb, 0w, 1nb)	10	(9b, 8lb, 0w, 2nb)	19
Total	151.3 overs	**478**	36.5 overs	**130**

1st innings FoW: 40, 48, 276, 289, 363, 415, 439, 466, 471, 478
2nd innings FoW: 63, 80, 103

L Tuckett	50	5	148	4		5	0	26	0
JB Plimsoll	35.3	9	128	3		4	0	15	0
AMB Rowan	17	1	63	1		4	0	13	0
NBF Mann	35	12	85	1		14	8	19	2
OC Dawson	14	2	44	1		9.5	2	38	1

No. 256: 4th Test	No. 257: 5th Test
VENUE: Headingley	VENUE: The Oval
DATE: 26th-29th July 1947	DATE: 16th-20th August 1947
TOSS WON BY: South Africa	TOSS WON BY: England
RESULT: England won by 10 wickets	RESULT: Match drawn

SOUTH AFRICA 1st innings / 2nd innings

Batsman	1st innings		2nd innings	
A Melville*	b Edrich	0	c Compton b Young	30
DV Dyer	c Evans b Wright	9	c Yardley b Edrich	2
B Mitchell	b Butler	53	b Young	5
AD Nourse	b Butler	51	lbw b Butler	57
KG Viljoen	b Wright	5	lbw b Butler	29
OC Dawson	c Young b Butler	5	b Butler	17
GM Fullerton+	c Cranston b Edrich	13	lbw b Cranston	13
AMB Rowan	c Yardley b Edrich	0	not out	21
NBF Mann	c Edrich b Cranston	29	c Evans b Cranston	0
L Tuckett	c Evans b Butler	3	b Cranston	0
VI Smith	not out	0	b Cranston	0
Extras	(0b, 5lb, 0w, 2nb)	7	(4b, 6lb, 0w, 0nb)	10
	97.1 overs		80 overs	
Total		**175**		**184**

1st innings FoW: 1, 23, 113, 121, 125, 130, 131, 158, 175, 175
2nd innings FoW: 6, 16, 59, 130, 139, 156, 184, 184, 184, 184

Bowler								
HJ Butler	28	15	34	4	24	9	32	3
WJ Edrich	17	4	46	3	14	2	35	1
JA Young	17	5	31	0	19	7	54	2
DVP Wright	20	9	24	2	14	7	31	0
K Cranston	11.1	3	24	1	7	3	12	4
DCS Compton	4	0	9	0	2	0	10	0

ENGLAND 1st innings / 2nd innings

Batsman	1st innings		2nd innings	
L Hutton	run out	100	not out	32
C Washbrook	b Mann	75	not out	15
WJ Edrich	c Melville b Mann	43		
DCS Compton	c Mitchell b Mann	30		
CJ Barnett	c Tuckett b Rowan	6		
NWD Yardley*	c Nourse b Smith	36		
K Cranston	c Melville b Mann	3		
TG Evans+	not out	6		
JA Young	not out	0		
DVP Wright				
HJ Butler				
Extras	(8b, 8lb, 0w, 2nb)	18	(0b, 0lb, 0w, 0nb)	0
	154 overs		15.4 overs	
Total		**317**		**47**

1st innings FoW: 141, 218, 241, 253, 289, 306, 316

Bowler								
L Tuckett	18	4	48	0	6	1	12	0
OC Dawson	4	0	12	0	4	1	13	0
NBF Mann	50	20	68	4	3.4	0	17	0
VI Smith	36	9	82	1				
AMB Rowan	46	12	89	1				
B Mitchell					2	1	5	0

ENGLAND 1st innings / 2nd innings

Batsman	1st innings		2nd innings	
L Hutton	b Mann	83	c Tuckett b Mann	36
C Washbrook	lbw b Mann	32	c Fullerton b Rowan	43
JDB Robertson	c Melville b Smith	4	b Rowan	30
DCS Compton	c Tuckett b Rowan	53	c Nourse b Dawson	113
NWD Yardley*	b Mann	59	c (sub) b Mann	11
K Cranston	st Fullerton b Rowan	45	c Mitchell b Rowan	0
R Howorth	c Fullerton b Rowan	23	not out	45
TG Evans+	run out	45	not out	39
C Gladwin	not out	51		
DVP Wright	b Mann	14		
WH Copson	b Dawson	6		
Extras	(4b, 7lb, 0w, 1nb)	12	(6b, 0lb, 2w, 0nb)	8
	190 overs		77 overs	
Total		**427**		**325**

1st innings FoW: 63, 80, 178, 178, 271, 290, 322, 358, 408, 427
2nd innings FoW: 73, 89, 158, 179, 180, 267

Bowler								
L Tuckett	32	6	82	0	7	0	34	0
OC Dawson	35	5	80	1	15	1	59	1
NBF Mann	64	28	93	4	27	7	102	2
AMB Rowan	38	9	92	3	25	1	95	3
VI Smith	21	0	68	1	3	0	27	0

SOUTH AFRICA 1st innings / 2nd innings

Batsman	1st innings		2nd innings	
B Mitchell	c Evans b Copson	120	not out	189
DV Dyer	c Gladwin b Howorth	18	lbw b Wright	4
KG Viljoen	c Evans b Wright	10	st Evans b Howorth	33
AD Nourse	c Yardley b Howorth	10	b Howorth	97
A Melville*	lbw b Cranston	39	c Evans b Cranston	6
OC Dawson	lbw b Wright	55	c Howorth b Cranston	0
GM Fullerton+	c Howorth b Cranston	6	c Evans b Howorth	14
AMB Rowan	b Howorth	0	c Hutton b Wright	10
NBF Mann	b Copson	36	not out	40
L Tuckett	not out	0		
VI Smith	lbw b Copson	0		
Extras	(3b, 2lb, 1w, 2nb)	8	(12b, 14lb, 4w, 0nb)	30
	131 overs		141 overs	
Total		**302**		**423**

1st innings FoW: 47, 62, 78, 164, 243, 253, 254, 292, 302, 302
2nd innings FoW: 8, 48, 232, 247, 249, 266, 314

Bowler								
WH Copson	27	13	46	3	30	11	66	0
C Gladwin	16	2	39	0	16	5	33	0
DVP Wright	29	7	89	2	30	8	103	2
R Howorth	39	16	64	3	37	12	85	3
DCS Compton	11	4	31	0	4	0	30	0
K Cranston	9	2	25	2	21	3	61	2
L Hutton					2	0	14	0
NWD Yardley					1	0	1	0

West Indies | West Indies

No. 258:	1st Test
VENUE:	Bridgetown (Barbados)
DATE:	21st-26th January 1948
TOSS WON BY:	West Indies
RESULT:	Match drawn

No. 259:	2nd Test
VENUE:	Port-of-Spain (Trinidad)
DATE:	11th-16th February 1948
TOSS WON BY:	England
RESULT:	Match drawn

WEST INDIES 1st innings / 2nd innings

Batsman	1st innings		2nd innings	
JB Stollmeyer	c Robertson b Ikin	78	c Evans b Howorth	31
CL Walcott+	b Laker	8	c Ikin b Howorth	16
EdeC Weekes	c Evans b Tremlett	35	b Laker	25
GE Gomez	b Laker	86	st Evans b Howorth	0
GA Headley*	b Laker	29	c Ikin b Laker	18
RJ Christiani	lbw b Laker	1	lbw b Cranston	99
JDC Goddard	b Howorth	28	c Evans b Howorth	72
EAV Williams	c Ikin b Laker	2	c Robertson b Howorth	7
W Ferguson	b Laker	5	not out	56
PE Jones	not out	10	c Brookes b Howorth	7
BBM Gaskin	c Ikin b Laker	10	not out	7
Extras	(0b, 4lb, 2w, 3nb)	9	(6b, 4lb, 1w, 2nb)	13
Total	124 overs	**296**	106 overs	**351**

1st innings FoW: 18, 81, 185, 245, 246, 271, 273, 273, 279, 296
2nd innings FoW: 46, 69, 71, 87, 144, 240, 252, 301, 328

Bowler	O	M	R	W		O	M	R	W
MF Tremlett	26	8	49	1		10	0	40	0
K Cranston	15	4	29	0		13	3	31	1
JC Laker	37	9	103	7		30	12	95	2
JT Ikin	16	3	38	1		12	1	48	0
R Howorth	30	8	68	1		41	8	124	6

ENGLAND 1st innings / 2nd innings

Batsman	1st innings		2nd innings	
JDB Robertson	lbw b Williams	80	not out	51
W Place	c Gomez b Goddard	12	c Walcott b Goddard	7
D Brookes	b Jones	10	b Ferguson	16
J Hardstaff jr	b Williams	98	lbw b Gaskin	8
JT Ikin	c Walcott b Williams	3	c Gomez b Goddard	4
GA Smithson	c Gomez b Jones	0	not out	1
K Cranston*	run out	2		
R Howorth	c Goddard b Ferguson	14		
TG Evans+	b Jones	26		
JC Laker	c Walcott b Jones	2		
MF Tremlett	not out	0		
Extras	(2b, 2lb, 1w, 1nb)	6	(0b, 3lb, 0w, 0nb)	3
Total	110.2 overs	**253**	45.4 overs	**86**

1st innings FoW: 32, 67, 130, 153, 156, 176, 197, 250, 252, 253
2nd innings FoW: 33, 55, 70, 71

Bowler	O	M	R	W		O	M	R	W
PE Jones	25.2	6	54	4		9	1	29	0
BBM Gaskin	11	0	30	0		10	4	15	1
EAV Williams	33	15	51	3		9	3	17	0
JDC Goddard	21	6	49	1		14	4	18	2
W Ferguson	14	1	52	1		3.4	1	4	1
GA Headley	6	1	11	0					

ENGLAND 1st innings / 2nd innings

Batsman	1st innings		2nd innings	
JDB Robertson	run out	2	c Christiani b Ferguson	133
SC Griffith	lbw b Worrell	140	c Ferguson b Gomez	4
JT Ikin	b Ferguson	21	lbw b Ferguson	19
K Cranston	c & b Ferguson	7	c Christiani b Williams	6
GOB Allen*	c Walcott b Gaskin	36	c Carew b Williams	24
R Howorth	b Ferguson	14	c Walcott b Williams	2
TG Evans+	c Walcott b Williams	30	b Ferguson	14
GA Smithson	c Goddard b Ferguson	35	st Walcott b Ferguson	21
JC Laker	c Gaskin b Goddard	55	b Ferguson	35
JH Wardle	c Worrell b Ferguson	4	not out	2
HJ Butler	not out	15	b Ferguson	0
Extras	(0b, 1lb, 0w, 2nb)	3	(5b, 3lb, 0w, 7nb)	15
Total	143.3 overs	**362**	113.2 overs	**275**

1st innings FoW: 5, 42, 54, 126, 158, 201, 288, 296, 306, 362
2nd innings FoW: 18, 53, 62, 97, 122, 149, 196, 270, 275, 275

Bowler	O	M	R	W		O	M	R	W
BBM Gaskin	37	14	72	1		21	6	41	0
EAV Williams	21	8	31	1		27	7	64	3
W Ferguson	39	5	137	5		34.2	4	92	6
JDC Goddard	23.3	6	64	1		9	4	11	0
FMM Worrell	23	4	55	1		14	2	30	0
GE Gomez						8	2	22	1

WEST INDIES 1st innings / 2nd innings

Batsman	1st innings		2nd innings	
GM Carew	lbw b Laker	107	c Evans b Butler	20
AG Ganteaume	Ikin b Howorth	112	lbw b Allen	2
EdeC Weekes	b Butler	36	b Butler	0
FMM Worrell	c Evans b Cranston	97	not out	28
CL Walcott+	c Butler b Howorth	20	not out	18
GE Gomez*	lbw b Laker	62		
RJ Christiani	c Robertson b Allen	7		
JDC Goddard	not out	9		
EAV Williams	c & b Allen	31		
W Ferguson	b Butler	5		
BBM Gaskin	b Butler	0		
Extras	(2b, 4lb, 1w, 4nb)	11	(0b, 2lb, 1w, 1nb)	4
Total	146 overs	**497**	16.2 overs	**72**

1st innings FoW: 173, 226, 306, 341, 440, 447, 454, 488, 497, 497
2nd innings FoW: 3, 8, 41

Bowler	O	M	R	W		O	M	R	W
HJ Butler	32	4	122	3		8	2	27	2
GOB Allen	16	0	82	2		4.2	0	21	1
JC Laker	36	10	108	2					
K Cranston	7	1	29	1		3	0	18	0
JT Ikin	20	5	60	0					
R Howorth	32	3	76	2		1	0	2	0
JH Wardle	3	0	9	0					

No. 260: 3rd Test	No. 261: 4th Test
VENUE: Georgetown (Guyana)	VENUE: Kingston (Jamaica)
DATE: 3rd-6th March 1948	DATE: 27th March-1st April 1948
TOSS WON BY: West Indies	TOSS WON BY: England
RESULT: West Indies won by 7 wickets	RESULT: West Indies won by 10 wickets

WEST INDIES 1st innings / 2nd innings (No. 260)

Batsman	1st innings		2nd innings	
GM Carew	b Cranston	17	c Allen b Laker	8
JDC Goddard*	b Allen	1	lbw b Laker	3
CL Walcott+	lbw b Cranston	11	not out	31
RJ Christiani	c Hardstaff jr b Tremlett	51	lbw b Howorth	3
FMM Worrell	not out	131	not out	25
GE Gomez	c Evans b Cranston	36		
EdeC Weekes	b Cranston	36		
EAV Williams	b Laker	7		
W Ferguson	c Allen b Laker	2		
J Trim				
LR Pierre				
Extras	(0b, 1lb, 3w, 1nb)	5	(0b, 7lb, 0w, 1nb)	8
	105.4 overs		20 overs	
Total		**297**		**78**

1st innings FoW: 7, 26, 48, 127, 224, 284, 295, 297
2nd innings FoW: 10, 23, 26

Bowler								
GOB Allen	2.4	0	5	1				
MF Tremlett	14	4	35	1				
K Cranston	25	5	78	4	2	0	11	0
JC Laker	36	11	94	2	9	1	34	2
R Howorth	23	4	58	0	9	0	25	1
JT Ikin	5	2	22	0				

ENGLAND 1st innings / 2nd innings (No. 260)

Batsman	1st innings		2nd innings	
L Hutton	c Williams b Goddard	31	b Ferguson	24
JDB Robertson	c Ferguson b Goddard	23	lbw b Ferguson	9
W Place	c Christiani b Goddard	1	b Ferguson	15
J Hardstaff jr	b Ferguson	3	c Christiani b Trim	63
JT Ikin	c Ferguson b Goddard	7	lbw b Ferguson	20
K Cranston	st Walcott b Ferguson	24	c Christiani b Goddard	32
R Howorth	c Ferguson b Goddard	4	c Goddard b Williams	37
JC Laker	c Walcott b Ferguson	10	run out	24
TG Evans+	b Trim	1	lbw b Ferguson	2
MF Tremlett	c Christiani b Trim	0	c Goddard b Williams	6
GOB Allen*	not out	0	not out	18
Extras	(4b, 1lb, 0w, 2nb)	7	(4b, 5lb, 1w, 3nb)	13
	50.2 overs		106.4 overs	
Total		**111**		**263**

1st innings FoW: 59, 61, 64, 64, 94, 96, 109, 110, 110, 111
2nd innings FoW: 21, 51, 52, 137, 145, 185, 226, 233, 241, 263

Bowler								
J Trim	10	6	6	2	13	2	38	1
LR Pierre	2	0	9	0	5	0	19	0
EAV Williams	6	0	21	0	24.4	12	34	2
JDC Goddard	14.2	5	31	5	24	8	43	1
FMM Worrell	2	0	5	0	40	6	116	5
W Ferguson	15	5	23	3				
GE Gomez	1	0	9	0				

ENGLAND 1st innings / 2nd innings (No. 261)

Batsman	1st innings		2nd innings	
L Hutton	b Johnson	56	c (sub) b Goddard	60
JDB Robertson	lbw b Johnson	64	b Johnson	28
W Place	st Walcott b Ferguson	8	st Walcott b Stollmeyer	107
J Hardstaff jr	c Gomez b Ferguson	9	b Johnson	64
K Cranston	c Walcott b Johnson	13	b Kentish	36
GOB Allen*	c Walcott b Kentish	23	lbw b Johnson	13
JT Ikin	run out	5	c Worrell b Stollmeyer	3
TG Evans+	c Weekes b Kentish	9	b Johnson	4
R Howorth	not out	12	st Walcott b Stollmeyer	1
JC Laker	c Walcott b Johnson	6	not out	6
MF Tremlett	b Johnson	0	c Walcott b Johnson	2
Extras	(12b, 8lb, 0w, 2nb)	22	(8b, 2lb, 0w, 2nb)	12
	128.5 overs		153 overs	
Total		**227**		**336**

1st innings FoW: 129, 132, 147, 150, 173, 185, 200, 205, 221, 227
2nd innings FoW: 69, 101, 214, 291, 316, 316, 327, 327, 329, 336

Bowler								
HHH Johnson	34.5	13	41	5	31	11	55	5
ESM Kentish	21	8	38	2	26	7	68	1
JDC Goddard	19	7	33	0	25	9	38	1
W Ferguson	38	14	53	2	32	7	90	0
FMM Worrell	11	1	25	0	20	3	41	0
JB Stollmeyer	5	1	15	0	19	7	32	3

WEST INDIES 1st innings / 2nd innings (No. 261)

Batsman	1st innings		2nd innings	
JDC Goddard*	c Hutton b Howorth	17	not out	46
JB Stollmeyer	lbw b Howorth	30	not out	25
EdeC Weekes	c Hutton b Ikin	141		
FMM Worrell	lbw b Allen	38		
GE Gomez	b Tremlett	23		
KR Rickards	b Laker	67		
RJ Christiani	c & b Laker	14		
CL Walcott+	c Hutton b Tremlett	45		
W Ferguson	c Hardstaff jr b Laker	75		
HHH Johnson	b Howorth	8		
ESM Kentish	not out	1		
Extras	(11b, 17lb, 0w, 3nb)	31	(0b, 4lb, 1w, 0nb)	5
	146.4 overs		11 overs	
Total		**490**		**76**

1st innings FoW: 39, 62, 144, 204, 320, 351, 358, 455, 482, 490

Bowler								
GOB Allen	20	1	83	1	2	0	14	0
MF Tremlett	31	1	98	2	1	0	4	0
R Howorth	40	10	106	3	4	0	27	0
JC Laker	36.4	5	103	3	2	0	11	0
JT Ikin	19	0	69	1	2	0	15	0

Australia

No. 262: 1st Test
VENUE: Trent Bridge
DATE: 10th-15th June 1948
TOSS WON BY: England
RESULT: Australia won by 8 wickets

ENGLAND	1st innings		2nd innings	
L Hutton	b Miller	3	b Miller	74
C Washbrook	c Brown b Lindwall	6	c Tallon b Miller	1
WJ Edrich	b Johnston	18	c Tallon b Johnson	13
DCS Compton	b Miller	19	hit wkt b Miller	184
J Hardstaff jr	c Miller b Johnston	0	c Hassett b Toshack	43
CJ Barnett	b Johnston	8	c Miller b Johnston	6
NWD Yardley*	lbw b Toshack	3	c & b Johnston	22
TG Evans+	c Morris b Johnston	12	c Tallon b Johnston	50
JC Laker	c Tallon b Miller	63	b Miller	4
AV Bedser	c Brown b Johnston	22	not out	3
JA Young	not out	1	b Johnston	9
Extras	(5b, 5lb, 0w, 0nb)	10	(12b, 17lb, 0w, 3nb)	32
Total	79 overs	165	183 overs	441

1st innings FoW: 9, 15, 46, 46, 48, 60, 74, 74, 163, 165
2nd innings FoW: 5, 39, 150, 243, 264, 321, 405, 413, 423, 441

RR Lindwall	13	5	30	1					
KR Miller	19	8	38	3	44	10	125	4
WA Johnston	25	11	36	5	59	12	147	4
ERH Toshack	14	8	28	1	33	14	60	1
IW Johnson	5	1	19	0	42	15	66	1
AR Morris	3	1	4	0				
SG Barnes					5	2	11	0

AUSTRALIA	1st innings		2nd innings	
SG Barnes	c Evans b Laker	62	not out	64
AR Morris	b Laker	31	b Bedser	9
DG Bradman*	c Hutton b Bedser	138	c Hutton b Bedser	0
KR Miller	c Edrich b Laker	0	not out	21
WA Brown	lbw b Yardley	17		
AL Hassett	b Bedser	137		
IW Johnson	b Laker	21		
D Tallon+	c & b Young	10		
RR Lindwall	c Evans b Yardley	42		
WA Johnston	not out	17		
ERH Toshack	lbw b Bedser	19		
Extras	(9b, 4lb, 1w, 1nb)	15	(0b, 2lb, 1w, 1nb)	4
Total	216.2 overs	509	28.3 overs	98

1st innings FoW: 73, 121, 121, 185, 305, 338, 365, 472, 476, 509
2nd innings FoW: 38, 48

WJ Edrich	18	1	72	0	4	0	20	0
AV Bedser	44.2	12	113	3	14.3	4	46	2
CJ Barnett	17	5	36	0				
JA Young	60	28	79	1	10	3	28	0
JC Laker	55	14	138	4				
DCS Compton	5	0	24	0				
NWD Yardley	17	6	32	2				

Australia

No. 263: 2nd Test
VENUE: Lord's
DATE: 24th-29th June 1948
TOSS WON BY: Australia
RESULT: Australia won by 409 runs

AUSTRALIA	1st innings		2nd innings	
SG Barnes	c Hutton b Coxon	0	c Washbrook b Yardley	141
AR Morris	c Hutton b Coxon	105	b Wright	62
DG Bradman*	c Hutton b Bedser	38	c Edrich b Bedser	89
AL Hassett	b Yardley	47	b Yardley	0
KR Miller	lbw b Bedser	4	c Bedser b Laker	74
WA Brown	lbw b Yardley	24	c Evans b Coxon	32
IW Johnson	c Evans b Edrich	4	st Evans b Laker	25
D Tallon+	c Yardley b Bedser	53	not out	9
RR Lindwall	b Bedser	15		
WA Johnston	st Evans b Wright	29		
ERH Toshack	not out	20		
Extras	(3b, 7lb, 0w, 1nb)	11	(22b, 5lb, 0w, 1nb)	28
Total	129.3 overs	350	130.2 overs	460

1st innings FoW: 3, 87, 166, 173, 216, 225, 246, 275, 320, 350
2nd innings FoW: 122, 296, 296, 329, 416, 445, 460

AV Bedser	43	14	100	4	34	6	112	1
A Coxon	35	10	90	2	28	3	82	1
WJ Edrich	8	0	43	1	2	0	11	0
DVP Wright	21.3	8	54	1	19	4	69	1
JC Laker	7	3	17	0	31.2	6	111	2
NWD Yardley	15	4	35	2	13	4	36	2

ENGLAND	1st innings		2nd innings	
L Hutton	b Johnson	20	c Johnson b Lindwall	13
C Washbrook	c Tallon b Lindwall	8	c Tallon b Toshack	37
WJ Edrich	b Lindwall	5	c Johnson b Toshack	2
DCS Compton	c Miller b Johnston	53	c Miller b Johnston	29
HE Dollery	b Lindwall	0	b Lindwall	37
NWD Yardley*	b Lindwall	44	b Toshack	11
A Coxon	c & b Johnston	19	lbw b Toshack	0
TG Evans+	c Miller b Johnston	9	not out	24
JC Laker	c Tallon b Johnson	28	b Lindwall	0
AV Bedser	b Lindwall	9	c Hassett b Johnston	9
DVP Wright	not out	13	c Lindwall b Toshack	4
Extras	(0b, 3lb, 0w, 4nb)	7	(16b, 4lb, 0w, 0nb)	20
Total	102.4 overs	215	78.1 overs	186

1st innings FoW: 17, 32, 46, 46, 133, 134, 145, 186, 197, 215
2nd innings FoW: 42, 52, 65, 106, 133, 133, 141, 141, 158, 186

RR Lindwall	27.4	7	70	5	23	9	61	3
WA Johnston	22	4	43	2	33	15	62	2
IW Johnson	35	13	72	3	2	1	3	0
ERH Toshack	18	11	23	0	20.1	6	40	5

No. 264: 3rd Test	No. 265: 4th Test
VENUE: Old Trafford	VENUE: Headingley
DATE: 8th-13th July 1948	DATE: 22nd-27th July 1948
TOSS WON BY: England	TOSS WON BY: England
RESULT: Match drawn	RESULT: Australia won by 7 wickets

Match 264 — Old Trafford

ENGLAND 1st innings		2nd innings	
C Washbrook b Johnston	11	not out	85
GM Emmett c Barnes b Lindwall	10	c Tallon b Lindwall	0
WJ Edrich c Tallon b Lindwall	32	run out	53
DCS Compton not out	145	c Miller b Toshack	0
JF Crapp lbw b Lindwall	37	not out	19
HE Dollery b Johnston	1		
NWD Yardley* c Johnson b Toshack	22		
TG Evans+ c Johnston b Lindwall	34		
AV Bedser run out	37		
R Pollard b Toshack	3		
JA Young c Bradman b Johnston	4		
Extras (7b, 17lb, 0w, 3nb)	27	(9b, 7lb, 1w, 0nb)	17
171.5 overs		69 overs	
Total	**363**		**174**

1st innings FoW: 22, 28, 96, 97, 119, 141, 216, 337, 352, 363
2nd innings FoW: 1, 125, 129

RR Lindwall	40	8	99	4	14	4	37	1
WA Johnston	45.5	13	67	3	14	3	34	0
SJE Loxton	7	0	18	0	8	2	29	0
ERH Toshack	41	20	75	2	12	5	26	1
IW Johnson	38	16	77	0	7	3	16	0
KR Miller					14	7	15	0

AUSTRALIA 1st innings		2nd innings	
AR Morris c Compton b Bedser	51	not out	54
IW Johnson c Evans b Bedser	1	c Crapp b Young	6
DG Bradman* lbw b Pollard	7	not out	30
AL Hassett c Washbrook b Young	38		
KR Miller lbw b Pollard	31		
SG Barnes retired hurt	1		
SJE Loxton b Pollard	36		
D Tallon+ c Evans b Edrich	18		
RR Lindwall c Washbrook b Bedser	23		
WA Johnston c Crapp b Bedser	3		
ERH Toshack not out	0		
Extras (5b, 4lb, 0w, 3nb)	12	(0b, 0lb, 0w, 2nb)	2
93 overs		61 overs	
Total	**221**		**92**

1st innings FoW: 3, 13, 82, 135, 139, 172, 208, 219, 221
2nd innings FoW: 10

AV Bedser	36	12	81	4	19	12	27	0
R Pollard	32	9	53	3	10	8	6	0
WJ Edrich	7	3	27	1	2	0	8	0
NWD Yardley	4	0	12	0				
JA Young	14	5	36	1				
JA Young					21	12	31	1
DCS Compton					9	3	18	0

Match 265 — Headingley

ENGLAND 1st innings		2nd innings	
L Hutton b Lindwall	81	c Bradman b Johnson	57
C Washbrook c Lindwall b Johnston	143	c Harvey b Johnston	65
WJ Edrich c Morris b Johnson	111	lbw b Lindwall	54
AV Bedser c & b Johnson	79	c Miller b Johnston	66
DCS Compton c Saggers b Lindwall	23	b Lindwall	18
JF Crapp b Toshack	5	c Harvey b Johnston	7
NWD Yardley* b Miller	25	c Saggers b Johnston	0
K Cranston b Loxton	10	not out	47
TG Evans+ c Hassett b Loxton	3	c Hassett b Miller	17
JC Laker c Saggers b Loxton	4	not out	15
R Pollard not out	0		
Extras (2b, 8lb, 1w, 1nb)	12	(4b, 12lb, 0w, 3nb)	19
192.1 overs		107 overs	
Total	**496**		**365**

1st innings FoW: 168, 268, 423, 426, 447, 473, 486, 490, 496, 496
2nd innings FoW: 129, 129, 232, 260, 277, 278, 293, 330

RR Lindwall	38	10	79	2	26	6	84	2
KR Miller	17.1	2	43	1	21	5	53	1
WA Johnston	38	12	86	1	29	5	95	4
ERH Toshack	35	6	112	1				
SJE Loxton	26	4	55	3	10	2	29	0
IW Johnson	33	9	89	2	21	2	85	1
AR Morris	5	0	20	0				

AUSTRALIA 1st innings		2nd innings	
AR Morris c Cranston b Bedser	6	c Pollard b Yardley	182
AL Hassett c Crapp b Pollard	13	c & b Compton	17
DG Bradman* b Pollard	33	not out	173
KR Miller c Edrich b Yardley	58	lbw b Cranston	12
RN Harvey b Laker	112	not out	4
SJE Loxton b Yardley	93		
IW Johnson c Cranston b Laker	10		
RR Lindwall c Crapp b Bedser	77		
RA Saggers+ st Evans b Laker	5		
WA Johnston c Edrich b Bedser	13		
ERH Toshack not out	12		
Extras (9b, 14lb, 0w, 3nb)	26	(6b, 9lb, 0w, 1nb)	16
136.2 overs		114.1 overs	
Total	**458**		**404**

1st innings FoW: 13, 65, 68, 189, 294, 329, 344, 355, 403, 458
2nd innings FoW: 57, 358, 396

AV Bedser	31.2	4	92	3	21	2	56	0
R Pollard	38	6	104	2	22	6	55	0
K Cranston	14	1	51	0	7.1	0	28	1
WJ Edrich	3	0	19	0	32	11	93	0
JC Laker	30	8	113	3	13	1	44	1
NWD Yardley	17	6	38	2	15	3	82	1
DCS Compton	3	0	15	0	4	1	30	0

Australia		**South Africa**	

No. 266: 5th Test		No. 267: 1st Test	
VENUE: The Oval		VENUE: Durban (Kingsmead)	
DATE: 14th-18th August 1948		DATE: 16th-20th December 1948	
TOSS WON BY: England		TOSS WON BY: South Africa	
RESULT: Aus won by an innings and 149 runs		RESULT: England won by 2 wickets	

ENGLAND 1st innings / 2nd innings

ENGLAND	1st innings		2nd innings	
L Hutton	c Tallon b Lindwall	30	c Tallon b Miller	64
JG Dewes	b Miller	1	b Lindwall	10
WJ Edrich	c Hassett b Johnston	3	b Lindwall	28
DCS Compton	c Morris b Lindwall	4	c Lindwall b Johnston	39
JF Crapp	c Tallon b Miller	0	b Miller	9
NWD Yardley*	b Lindwall	7	c Miller b Johnston	9
AJ Watkins	lbw b Johnston	0	c Hassett b Ring	2
TG Evans+	b Lindwall	1	b Lindwall	8
AV Bedser	b Lindwall	0	b Johnston	0
JA Young	b Lindwall	0	not out	3
WE Hollies	not out	0	c Morris b Johnston	0
Extras	(6b, 0lb, 0w, 0nb)	6	(9b, 4lb, 0w, 3nb)	16
	42.1 overs		105.3 overs	
Total		**52**		**188**

1st innings FoW: 2, 10, 17, 23, 35, 42, 45, 45, 47, 52
2nd innings FoW: 20, 64, 125, 153, 164, 167, 178, 181, 188, 188

RR Lindwall	16.1	5	20	6		25	3	50	3
KR Miller	8	5	5	2		15	6	22	2
WA Johnston	16	4	20	2		27.3	12	40	4
SJE Loxton	2	1	1	0		10	2	16	0
DT Ring						28	13	44	1

AUSTRALIA 1st innings

AUSTRALIA	1st innings		2nd innings	
SG Barnes	c Evans b Hollies	61		
AR Morris	run out	196		
DG Bradman*	b Hollies	0		
AL Hassett	lbw b Young	37		
KR Miller	st Evans b Hollies	5		
RN Harvey	c Young b Hollies	17		
SJE Loxton	c Evans b Edrich	15		
RR Lindwall	c Edrich b Young	9		
D Tallon+	c Crapp b Hollies	31		
DT Ring	c Crapp b Bedser	9		
WA Johnston	not out	0		
Extras	(4b, 2lb, 0w, 3nb)	9		
	158.2 overs			
Total		**389**		

1st innings FoW: 117, 117, 226, 243, 265, 304, 332, 359, 389, 389

AV Bedser	31.2	9	61	1					
AJ Watkins	4	1	19	0					
JA Young	51	16	118	2					
WE Hollies	56	14	131	5					
DCS Compton	2	0	6	0					
WJ Edrich	9	1	38	1					
NWD Yardley	5	1	7	0					

SOUTH AFRICA 1st innings

SOUTH AFRICA	1st innings		2nd innings	
EAB Rowan	c Evans b Jenkins	7	c Compton b Jenkins	16
OE Wynne	c Compton b Bedser	5	c Watkins b Wright	4
B Mitchell	c Evans b Bedser	27	b Wright	19
AD Nourse*	c Watkins b Wright	37	c & b Bedser	32
WW Wade+	run out	0	b Jenkins	63
DW Begbie	c Compton b Bedser	37	c Mann b Bedser	48
OC Dawson	b Gladwin	24	c Compton b Wright	3
AMB Rowan	not out	5	b Wright	15
L Tuckett	lbw b Gladwin	1	not out	3
NBF Mann	c Evans b Gladwin	4	c Mann b Compton	10
CN McCarthy	b Bedser	0	b Jenkins	0
Extras	(3b, 2lb, 0w, 1nb)	6	(1b, 5lb, 0w, 0nb)	6
	53.5 overs		89.3 overs	
Total		**161**		**219**

1st innings FoW: 9, 18, 69, 80, 99, 148, 150, 152, 160, 161
2nd innings FoW: 22, 22, 67, 89, 174, 179, 197, 208, 219, 219

AV Bedser	13.5	2	39	4		18	5	51	2
C Gladwin	12	3	21	3		7	3	15	0
RO Jenkins	14	3	50	1		22.3	6	64	3
DVP Wright	9	3	29	1		26	3	72	4
DCS Compton	2	0	5	0		16	11	11	1
AJ Watkins	3	0	11	0					

ENGLAND 1st innings

ENGLAND	1st innings		2nd innings	
L Hutton	c McCarthy b Rowan	83	c Dawson b Tuckett	5
C Washbrook	c Wade b Mann	35	lbw b Mann	25
RT Simpson	c Begbie b Mann	5	c Mitchell b McCarthy	13
DCS Compton	c Wade b Mann	72	b McCarthy	28
AJ Watkins	c Nourse b AMB Rowan	9	b McCarthy	4
FG Mann*	c E Rowan b A Rowan	19	c EAB Rowan b McCarthy	0
TG Evans+	c Wynne b AMB Rowan	0	b McCarthy	4
RO Jenkins	c Mitchell b Mann	5	c Wade b McCarthy	22
AV Bedser	c Tuckett b Mann	11	not out	1
C Gladwin	not out	0	not out	7
DVP Wright	c Tuckett b Mann	0		
Extras	(2b, 12lb, 0w, 0nb)	14	(9b, 10lb, 0w, 0nb)	19
	99.4 overs		28 overs	
Total		**253**		**128**

1st innings FoW: 84, 104, 146, 172, 212, 212, 221, 247, 253, 253
2nd innings FoW: 25, 49, 52, 6,4, 64, 70, 115, 116

CN McCarthy	9	2	20	0		12	2	43	6
OC Dawson	3	0	16	0					
L Tuckett	6	0	36	0		10	0	38	1
AMB Rowan	44	8	108	4		4	0	15	0
NBF Mann	37.4	14	59	6		2	0	13	1

No. 268: 2nd Test	No. 269: 3rd Test
VENUE: Johannesburg (Ellis Park)	VENUE: Cape Town
DATE: 27th-30th December 1948	DATE: 1st-5th January 1949
TOSS WON BY: England	TOSS WON BY: England
RESULT: Match drawn	RESULT: Match drawn

2nd Test — Johannesburg

ENGLAND — 1st innings / 2nd innings

Batsman	1st innings		2nd innings	
L Hutton	c Wade b McCarthy	158		
C Washbrook	c Begbie b McCarthy	195		
JF Crapp	c & b Mitchell	56		
DCS Compton	c Mitchell b Mann	114		
AJ Watkins	c Wade b Mann	7		
FG Mann*	c McCarthy b Mann	7		
TG Evans+	run out	18		
RO Jenkins	c Wade b AMB Rowan	4		
AV Bedser	b McCarthy	12		
C Gladwin	lbw b Dawson	23		
DVP Wright	not out	1		
Extras	(3b, 10lb, 0w, 0nb)	13		
Total		**608**		
	149.5 overs			

1st innings FoW: 359, 366, 516, 540, 549, 550, 570, 576, 602, 608

Bowler	O	M	R	W				
CN McCarthy	26	1	102	3				
OC Dawson	16.5	3	59	1				
AMB Rowan	41	4	155	1				
L Tuckett	12	0	55	0				
NBF Mann	30	2	107	3				
DW Begbie	6	0	38	0				
B Mitchell	18	1	79	1				

SOUTH AFRICA 1st innings / 2nd innings

Batsman	1st innings		2nd innings	
EAB Rowan	lbw b Bedser	8	not out	156
OE Wynne	lbw b Wright	4	lbw b Bedser	4
B Mitchell	b Gladwin	86	c Hutton b Wright	40
AD Nourse*	lbw b Wright	32	not out	56
WW Wade+	c Evans b Compton	85		
DW Begbie	c Watkins b Jenkins	5		
OC Dawson	c Watkins b Jenkins	12		
AMB Rowan	b Wright	8		
L Tuckett	st Evans b Watkins	38		
NBF Mann	st Evans b Jenkins	23		
CN McCarthy	not out	1		
Extras	(4b, 7lb, 0w, 2nb)	13	(9b, 4lb, 0w, 1nb)	14
Total		**315**		**270**
	104.4 overs		91 overs	

1st innings FoW: 12, 17, 96, 191, 204, 220, 235, 273, 313, 315
2nd innings FoW: 15, 108

Bowler	O	M	R	W	O	M	R	W
AV Bedser	22	6	42	1	17	4	51	1
C Gladwin	20	6	29	1	16	5	37	0
RO Jenkins	21.4	3	88	3	19	3	54	0
DVP Wright	26	2	104	3	14	3	35	1
DCS Compton	10	0	34	1	13	3	31	0
AJ Watkins	5	2	5	1	12	2	48	0

3rd Test — Cape Town

ENGLAND — 1st innings / 2nd innings

Batsman	1st innings		2nd innings	
L Hutton	run out	41	b Rowan	87
C Washbrook	b Rowan	74	c Mitchell b McCarthy	9
JF Crapp	c Wynne b Mitchell	35	c Wade b McCarthy	54
DCS Compton	b Rowan	1	not out	51
AJ Watkins	c Melville b Dawson	27	not out	64
FG Mann*	c Mitchell b Hanley	44		
TG Evans+	b Rowan	27		
RO Jenkins	c Wynne b Rowan	1		
AV Bedser	b McCarthy	16		
C Gladwin	not out	17		
DVP Wright	c Dawson b Rowan	11		
Extras	(7b, 7lb, 0w, 0nb)	14	(8b, 3lb, 0w, 0nb)	11
Total		**308**		**276**
	91.2 overs		96 overs	

1st innings FoW: 88, 149, 151, 152, 203, 249, 251, 263, 281, 308
2nd innings FoW: 11, 145, 165

Bowler	O	M	R	W	O	M	R	W
CN McCarthy	26	2	95	1	20	2	75	2
OC Dawson	7	2	35	1	13	3	33	0
AMB Rowan	31.2	3	80	5	30	5	65	1
NBF Mann	3	0	18	0	15	5	27	0
MA Hanley	18	4	57	1	11	3	31	0
B Mitchell	6	0	9	1	7	1	34	0

SOUTH AFRICA 1st innings / 2nd innings

Batsman	1st innings		2nd innings	
OE Wynne	c Crapp b Watkins	50	c Bedser b Jenkins	46
A Melville	b Jenkins	15	st Evans b Jenkins	24
B Mitchell	b Compton	120	c Evans b Jenkins	11
AD Nourse*	c & b Compton	112	st Evans b Jenkins	34
WW Wade+	c Watkins b Compton	0	not out	20
DW Begbie	run out	18	not out	5
OC Dawson	c Mann b Compton	25		
AMB Rowan	c Hutton b Gladwin	2		
NBF Mann	not out	10		
MA Hanley	run out	0		
CN McCarthy	st Evans b Compton	1		
Extras	(1b, 0lb, 0w, 2nb)	3	(0b, 1lb, 0w, 1nb)	2
Total		**356**		**142**
	119.2 overs		31 overs	

1st innings FoW: 30, 108, 298, 298, 303, 342, 344, 349, 349, 356
2nd innings FoW: 58, 83, 83, 132

Bowler	O	M	R	W	O	M	R	W
AV Bedser	34	5	92	0	7	0	40	0
C Gladwin	30	7	51	1	10	2	27	0
DVP Wright	9	0	58	0	2	0	18	0
RO Jenkins	11	1	46	1	9	0	48	4
AJ Watkins	10	0	36	1				
DCS Compton	25.2	3	70	5	3	1	7	0

South Africa

No. 270:	4th Test
VENUE:	Johannesburg (Ellis Park)
DATE:	12th-16th February 1949
TOSS WON BY:	England
RESULT:	Match drawn

ENGLAND	1st innings		2nd innings	
L Hutton	b Tuckett	2	b AMB Rowan	123
C Washbrook	c EAB Rowan b McCarthy	97	lbw b AMB Rowan	31
JF Crapp	b AMB Rowan	51	b Markham	25
DCS Compton	c AMB Rowan b Tuckett	24	lbw b AMB Rowan	16
AJ Watkins	hit wkt b McCarthy	111	hit wkt b McCarthy	5
FG Mann*	c Wade b McCarthy	17	b AMB Rowan	10
RO Jenkins	lbw b Mitchell	25	b McCarthy	19
AV Bedser	lbw b Tuckett	1	not out	7
C Gladwin	b McCarthy	19		
SC Griffith+	c Mitchell b McCarthy	8		
JA Young	not out	10		
Extras	(2b, 12lb, 0w, 0nb)	14	(5b, 11lb, 0w, 1nb)	17
Total	105.7 overs	379	78.2 overs	253

1st innings FoW: 3, 123, 172, 180, 213, 282, 287, 316, 346, 379
2nd innings FoW: 77, 151, 186, 204, 222, 237, 253

CN McCarthy	35.7	3	114	5	12.2	2	50	2
L Tuckett	29	2	109	3	10	0	43	0
AMB Rowan	23	1	70	1	34	10	69	4
LA Markham	5	1	38	0	8	0	34	1
NBF Mann	10	3	26	0	7	0	20	0
B Mitchell	3	0	8	1	7	1	20	0

SOUTH AFRICA	1st innings		2nd innings	
B Mitchell	c Griffith b Bedser	2	c Compton b Gladwin	6
EAB Rowan	run out	6	not out	86
KG Viljoen	run out	0	b Watkins	63
AD Nourse*	not out	129	b Watkins	
WW Wade+	lbw b Young	54	lbw b Bedser	27
TA Harris	b Bedser	6	not out	1
AMB Rowan	b Gladwin	12		
L Tuckett	b Young	0		
LA Markham	c Griffith b Jenkins	20		
NBF Mann	c Griffith b Gladwin	14		
CN McCarthy	not out	0		
Extras	(4b, 10lb, 0w, 0nb)	14	(7b, 1lb, 0w, 2nb)	10
Total	85 overs	257	65 overs	194

1st innings FoW: 4, 4, 19, 125, 137, 156, 161, 192, 236
2nd innings FoW: 23, 136, 140, 182

AV Bedser	24	3	81	2	17	0	54	1
C Gladwin	24	7	43	2	16	6	39	1
RO Jenkins	8	1	39	1	9	2	26	0
JA Young	23	6	52	2	11	6	14	0
AJ Watkins	2	0	9	0	3	0	16	2
DCS Compton	4	0	19	0	9	2	35	0

South Africa

No. 271:	5th Test
VENUE:	Port Elizabeth
DATE:	5th-9th March 1949
TOSS WON BY:	South Africa
RESULT:	England won by 3 wickets

SOUTH AFRICA	1st innings		2nd innings	
B Mitchell	c Griffith b Bedser	99	c Griffith b Bedser	56
EAB Rowan	c Watkins b Gladwin	3	c Jenkins b Young	37
KG Viljoen	b Bedser	2	c Compton b Young	18
AD Nourse*	b Bedser	73	not out	30
WW Wade+	c Compton b Jenkins	125	not out	34
JE Cheetham	c & b Bedser	2		
OC Dawson	c Gladwin b Jenkins	20		
AMB Rowan	not out	29		
L Tuckett	b Jenkins	2		
NBF Mann	c Compton b Gladwin	11		
CN McCarthy	b Gladwin	3		
Extras	(2b, 5lb, 0w, 3nb)	10	(6b, 5lb, 0w, 1nb)	12
Total	143.5 overs	379	58 overs	187

2nd innings FoW: 10, 13, 114, 264, 282, 330, 336, 338, 375, 379
2nd innings FoW: 101, 101, 127

AV Bedser	38	9	61	4	16	3	43	1
C Gladwin	30.5	6	70	3	6	2	14	0
RO Jenkins	15	2	53	3	4	0	27	0
AJ Watkins	5	0	24	0				
JA Young	48	9	122	0	23	9	34	2
DCS Compton	7	0	39	0	9	0	57	0

ENGLAND	1st innings		2nd innings	
L Hutton	c Dawson b AMB Rowan	46	st Wade b AMB Rowan	32
C Washbrook	c Dawson b AMB Rowan	36	c AMB Rowan b Mann	40
JF Crapp	b McCarthy	4	c Cheetham b AMB Rowan	42
DCS Compton	c Wade b Mann	49	c Dawson b Mann	2
AJ Watkins	c AMB Rowan b Mann	14	c Nourse b AMB Rowan	1
FG Mann*	not out	136	not out	26
RO Jenkins	lbw b Mann	29	c Tuckett b Mann	15
AV Bedser	c Mitchell b AMB Rowan	33	b Mann	0
C Gladwin	c Dawson b AMB Rowan	10	not out	5
SC Griffith+	c EAB Rowan b A Rowan	5		
JA Young	c Wade b McCarthy	0		
Extras	(11b, 18lb, 4w, 0nb)	33	(3b, 8lb, 0w, 0nb)	11
Total	141.4 overs	395	23.7 overs	174

1st innings FoW: 78, 82, 96, 149, 168, 268, 341, 362, 390, 395
2nd innings FoW: 58, 104, 124, 125, 125, 152, 153

CN McCarthy	17.4	1	42	2	2	0	20	0
OC Dawson	3	0	10	0				
L Tuckett	5	0	22	0	2	0	13	0
AMB Rowan	60	9	167	5	10	0	65	3
NBF Mann	51	18	95	3	9.7	0	65	4
B Mitchell	5	0	26	0				

No. 272 1st Test	No. 273: 2nd Test
VENUE: Headingley	VENUE: Lord's
DATE: 11th-14th June 1949	DATE: 25th-28th June 1949
TOSS WON BY: England	TOSS WON BY: England
RESULT: Match drawn	RESULT: Match drawn

ENGLAND 1st innings / 2nd innings

	1st innings		2nd innings	
L Hutton	c Sutcliffe b Cowie	101	c Mooney b Cave	0
C Washbrook	c Sutcliffe b Cowie	10	not out	103
WJ Edrich	c Donnelly b Cowie	36	b Cave	70
DCS Compton	st Mooney b Burtt	114	c Mooney b Cave	26
A Wharton	lbw b Cowie	7	b Sutcliffe	13
FG Mann*	c Scott b Burtt	38	not out	49
TE Bailey	c Scott b Cowie	12		
TG Evans+	c Mooney b Burtt	27		
AV Bedser	c Donnelly b Burtt	20		
JA Young	st Mooney b Burtt	0		
WE Hollies	not out	0		
Extras	(3b, 4lb, 0w, 0nb)	7	(4b, 2lb, 0w, 0nb)	6
	127.3 overs		68 overs	
Total		**372**		**267**

1st innings FoW: 17, 92, 194, 214, 273, 322, 330, 353, 367, 372
2nd innings FoW: 0, 118, 162, 201

J Cowie	43	6	127	5	26	3	103	3
HB Cave	27	5	85	0				
GO Rabone	18	7	56	0	17	4	56	0
TB Burtt	39.3	16	97	5	15	2	56	0
MP Donnelly					5	0	20	0
B Sutcliffe					4	1	17	1
VJ Scott					1	0	9	0

NEW ZEALAND 1st innings / 2nd innings

	1st innings		2nd innings	
B Sutcliffe	c Evans b Young	32	c Bedser b Young	82
VJ Scott	c Washbrook b Bailey	1	c Bedser b Young	43
WA Hadlee*	c Edrich b Bailey	34	not out	54
WM Wallace	c Evans b Bailey	3	not out	13
MP Donnelly	c Young b Bailey	64		
FB Smith	c Compton b Edrich	96		
GO Rabone	c Evans b Edrich	13		
FLH Mooney+	c Edrich b Bailey	46		
TB Burtt	c Bedser b Compton	7		
HB Cave	c Edrich b Bailey	2		
J Cowie	not out	26		
Extras	(2b, 8lb, 0w, 7nb)	17	(1b, 2lb, 0w, 0nb)	3
	118.3 overs		49 overs	
Total		**341**		**195**

1st innings FoW: 4, 64, 69, 80, 200, 251, 254, 273, 284, 341
2nd innings FoW: 112, 147

TE Bailey	32.3	6	118	6	9	0	51	0
AV Bedser	22	8	56	0	9	1	26	0
WJ Edrich	9	2	18	2	2	0	13	0
JA Young	22	6	52	1	14	3	41	2
WE Hollies	25	6	57	0	11	3	33	0
DCS Compton	8	2	23	1	1	0	5	0
L Hutton					3	0	23	0

ENGLAND 1st innings / 2nd innings

	1st innings		2nd innings	
L Hutton	b Burtt	23	c Cave b Rabone	66
JDB Robertson	c Mooney b Cowie	26	c Cave b Rabone	121
WJ Edrich	c Donnelly b Cowie	9	c Hadlee b Burtt	31
DCS Compton	c Sutcliffe b Burtt	116	b Burtt	6
AJ Watkins	c Wallace b Burtt	6	not out	49
FG Mann*	b Cave	18	c Donnelly b Rabone	17
TE Bailey	c Sutcliffe b Rabone	93	not out	6
TG Evans+	b Burtt	5		
C Gladwin	run out	5		
JA Young	not out	1		
WE Hollies				
Extras	(9b, 2lb, 0w, 0nb)	11	(9b, 1lb, 0w, 0nb)	10
	103.1 overs		103 overs	
Total		**313**		**306**

1st innings FoW: 48, 59, 72, 83, 112, 301, 307, 307, 313
2nd innings FoW: 143, 216, 226, 226, 252

J Cowie	26.1	5	64	2	14	3	39	0
HB Cave	27	2	79	1	7	1	23	0
GO Rabone	14	5	56	1	28	6	116	3
TB Burtt	35	7	102	4	37	12	58	2
B Sutcliffe	1	0	1	0	16	1	55	0
WM Wallace					1	0	5	0

NEW ZEALAND 1st innings / 2nd innings

	1st innings		2nd innings
B Sutcliffe	c Compton b Gladwin	57	
VJ Scott	c Edrich b Compton	42	
WA Hadlee*	c Robertson b Hollies	43	
WM Wallace	c Evans b Hollies	2	
MP Donnelly	c Hutton b Young	206	
FB Smith	b Hollies	23	
GO Rabone	b Hollies	25	
FLH Mooney+	c Watkins b Young	33	
TB Burtt	c Edrich b Hollies	23	
HB Cave	c & b Young	6	
J Cowie	not out	1	
Extras	(16b, 3lb, 3w, 1nb)	23	
	159.4 overs		
Total		**484**	

1st innings FoW: 89, 124, 137, 160, 197, 273, 351, 436, 464, 484

TE Bailey	33	3	136	0
C Gladwin	28	5	67	1
WJ Edrich	4	0	16	0
WE Hollies	58	18	133	5
DCS Compton	7	0	33	1
JA Young	26.4	4	65	3
AJ Watkins	3	1	11	0

No. 274: 3rd Test	No. 275: 4th Test
VENUE: Old Trafford	VENUE: The Oval
DATE: 23rd-26th July 1949	DATE: 13th-16th August 1949
TOSS WON BY: England	TOSS WON BY: New Zealand
RESULT: Match drawn	RESULT: Match drawn

Left — No. 274: 3rd Test

NEW ZEALAND 1st innings / **2nd innings**

Batsman	1st innings		2nd innings	
B Sutcliffe	b Bailey	9	lbw b Compton	101
VJ Scott	b Bailey	13	b Jackson	13
WA Hadlee*	b Bailey	34	c Brown b Hollies	22
WM Wallace	c Washbrook b Close	12	lbw b Hollies	14
MP Donnelly	lbw b Bailey	75	st Evans b Brown	80
JR Reid	lbw b Jackson	50	b Bailey	25
GO Rabone	c Brown b Bailey	33	not out	39
FLH Mooney+	b Jackson	5	st Evans b Brown	15
TB Burtt	st Evans b Compton	32	not out	27
HB Cave	b Bailey	12		
J Cowie	not out	3		
Extras	(3b, 9lb, 0w, 3nb)	15	(2b, 4lb, 0w, 6nb)	12
Total	128.2 overs	**293**	110 overs	**348**

1st innings FoW: 22, 23, 62, 82, 198, 205, 217, 269,, 288, 293
2nd innings FoW: 24, 58, 109, 187, 235, 295, 313

Bowler	O	M	R	W		O	M	R	W
TE Bailey	30.2	5	84	6		16	0	71	1
HL Jackson	27	11	47	2		12	3	25	1
DB Close	25	12	39	1		17	2	46	0
WE Hollies	18	8	29	0		26	6	52	2
FR Brown	18	4	43	0		21	3	71	2
DCS Compton	6	0	28	1		8	0	28	1
WJ Edrich	4	1	8	0		5	0	26	0
RT Simpson						2	1	9	0
C Washbrook						2	0	8	0
L Hutton						1	1	0	0

ENGLAND 1st innings / **2nd innings**

Batsman	1st innings		2nd innings
L Hutton	st Mooney b Burtt	73	
C Washbrook	c Mooney b Cowie	44	
WJ Edrich	c Rabone b Burtt	78	
DCS Compton	b Cowie	25	
RT Simpson	c Donnelly b Burtt	103	
TE Bailey	not out	72	
FR Brown*	c Wallace b Burtt	22	
TG Evans+	b Mooney b Burtt	12	
DB Close	c Rabone b Burtt	0	
WE Hollies	c Mooney b Cowie	0	
HL Jackson	not out	7	
Extras	(2b, 2lb, 0w, 0nb)	4	
Total	128 overs	**440**	

1st innings FoW: 103, 127, 172, 258, 363, 404, 419, 419, 419

Bowler	O	M	R	W
J Cowie	36	8	98	3
HB Cave	30	4	97	0
TB Burtt	45	11	162	6
GO Rabone	10	0	43	0
B Sutcliffe	5	0	22	0
JR Reid	2	0	14	0

Right — No. 275: 4th Test

NEW ZEALAND 1st innings / **2nd innings**

Batsman	1st innings		2nd innings	
B Sutcliffe	c Bedser b Hollies	88	c Brown b Bedser	54
VJ Scott	c Edrich b Bedser	60	c Evans b Bedser	6
JR Reid+	lbw b Wright	5	c Edrich b Hollies	22
WM Wallace	c Edrich b Bedser	55	st Evans b Hollies	58
MP Donnelly	c Edrich b Bailey	27	c Brown b Bedser	10
WA Hadlee*	c Evans b Bedser	25	c Wright b Laker	93
GO Rabone	c Evans b Bailey	18	lbw b Laker	20
TB Burtt	c Evans b Bailey	36	c Compton b Laker	6
HB Cave	b Compton	10	not out	14
J Cowie	c Hutton b Bedser	1	c Wright b Laker	4
GF Cresswell	not out	12	not out	0
Extras	(0b, 1lb, 1w, 6nb)	8	(10b, 5lb, 0w, 6nb)	21
Total	112.1 overs	**345**	97 overs	**308**

1st innings FoW: 121, 134, 170, 239, 239, 272, 287, 311, 320, 345
2nd innings FoW: 24, 68, 115, 131, 188, 276, 283, 299, 308

Bowler	O	M	R	W		O	M	R	W
TE Bailey	26.1	7	72	3		11	1	67	0
AV Bedser	31	6	74	4		23	4	59	3
WJ Edrich	3	0	16	0					
DVP Wright	22	1	93	1		6	0	21	0
JC Laker	3	0	11	0		29	6	78	4
WE Hollies	20	7	51	1		17	6	30	2
FR Brown	5	1	14	0		10	0	29	0
DCS Compton	2	0	6	1		1	0	3	0

ENGLAND 1st innings / **2nd innings**

Batsman	1st innings		2nd innings
L Hutton	c Rabone b Cresswell	206	
RT Simpson	c Donnelly b Cresswell	68	
WJ Edrich	c Cave b Cresswell	100	
DCS Compton	c Scott b Cresswell	13	
TE Bailey	c Reid b Cowie	36	
FR Brown*	c Hadlee b Cresswell	21	
TG Evans+	c Donnelly b Cowie	17	
JC Laker	c Scott b Cowie	0	
AV Bedser	c Reid b Cowie	0	
WE Hollies	not out	1	
DVP Wright	lbw b Cresswell	0	
Extras	(6b, 11lb, 0w, 3nb)	20	
Total	117.2 overs	**482**	

1st innings FoW: 147, 365, 396, 401, 436, 469, 470, 472, 481, 482

Bowler	O	M	R	W
J Cowie	28	1	123	4
GF Cresswell	41.2	6	168	6
HB Cave	24	4	78	0
TB Burtt	24	2	93	0

	No. 276: 1st Test		No. 277: 2nd Test
VENUE:	Old Trafford	VENUE:	Lord's
DATE:	8th-12th June 1950	DATE:	24th-29th June 1950
TOSS WON BY:	England	TOSS WON BY:	West Indies
RESULT:	England won by 202 runs	RESULT:	West Indies won by 326 runs

ENGLAND 1st innings / 2nd innings

Batsman	1st innings		2nd innings	
L Hutton	b Valentine	39	c Weekes b Gomez	0
RT Simpson	c Goddart b Valentine	27	c Weekes b Ramadhin	71
WJ Edrich	c Gomez b Valentine	7	c Goddard b Valentine	22
GHG Doggart	c Rae b Valentine	29	c Gomez b Valentine	0
HE Dollery	c Gomez b Valentine	8	lbw b Gomez	25
NWD Yardley*	c Gomez b Valentine	0	run out	33
TE Bailey	not out	82	c Worrell b Ramadhin	15
TG Evans+	c & b Valentine	104	c & b Worrell	45
JC Laker	b Valentine	4	c Stollmeyer b Valentine	40
WE Hollies	c Weekes b Ramadhin	0	c Walcott b Worrell	3
R Berry	b Ramadhin	0	not out	4
Extras	(8b, 3lb, 0w, 1nb)	12	(17b, 12lb, 0w, 1nb)	30
	128.3 overs		141.5 overs	
Total		**312**		**288**

1st innings FoW: 31, 74, 79, 83, 88, 249, 293, 301, 308, 312
2nd innings FoW: 0, 31, 43, 106, 131, 151, 200, 266, 284, 288

Bowler	O	M	R	W	O	M	R	W
HHH Johnson	10	3	18	0				
GE Gomez	10	1	29	0	25	12	47	2
AL Valentine	50	14	104	8	56	22	100	3
S Ramadhin	39.3	12	90	2	42	17	77	2
JDC Goddard	15	1	46	0	9	3	12	0
FMM Worrell	4	1	13	0	5.5	1	10	2
CL Walcott					4	1	12	0

WEST INDIES 1st innings / 2nd innings

Batsman	1st innings		2nd innings	
AF Rae	c Doggart b Berry	14	c Doggart b Hollies	10
JB Stollmeyer	lbw b Hollies	43	c (sub) b Laker	78
FMM Worrell	st Evans b Berry	15	st Evans b Hollies	28
EdeC Weekes	c (sub) b Bailey	52	lbw b Hollies	9
CL Walcott+	c Evans b Berry	13	b Berry	9
RJ Christiani	lbw b Berry	17	c Yardley b Hollies	6
GE Gomez	c Berry b Hollies	35	st Evans b Berry	8
JDC Goddard*	run out	7	not out	16
HHH Johnson	c Dollery b Hollies	8	b Berry	22
S Ramadhin	not out	4	b Berry	0
AL Valentine	c & b Berry	0	c Bailey b Hollies	0
Extras	(0b, 6lb, 0w, 1nb)	7	(4b, 0lb, 1w, 0nb)	5
	93.5 overs		81.2 overs	
Total		**215**		**183**

1st innings FoW: 52, 74, 74, 94, 146, 178, 201, 211, 211, 215
2nd innings FoW: 32, 68, 80, 113, 126, 141, 146, 178, 178, 183

Bowler	O	M	R	W	O	M	R	W
TE Bailey	10	2	28	1	3	1	9	0
WJ Edrich	2	1	4	0	3	1	10	0
WE Hollies	33	13	70	3	35.2	11	63	5
JC Laker	17	5	43	0	14	4	43	1
R Berry	31.5	13	63	5	26	12	53	4

WEST INDIES 1st innings / 2nd innings

Batsman	1st innings		2nd innings	
AF Rae	c & b Jenkins	106	b Jenkins	24
JB Stollmeyer	lbw b Wardle	20	b Jenkins	30
FMM Worrell	b Bedser	52	c Doggatt b Jenkins	45
EdeC Weekes	b Bedser	63	run out	63
CL Walcott+	st Evans b Jenkins	14	c Evans b Jenkins	11
GE Gomez	st Evans b Jenkins	1	not out	168
RJ Christiani	b Bedser	33	c Edrich b Bedser	70
JDC Goddard*	b Wardle	14	not out	5
PE Jones	c Evans b Jenkins	0		
S Ramadhin	not out	1		
AL Valentine	c Hutton b Jenkins	5		
Extras	(10b, 5lb, 1w, 1nb)	17	(0b, 8lb, 0w, 1nb)	9
	131.2 overs		178 overs	
Total		**326**		**425**

1st innings FoW: 37, 128, 233, 262, 273, 274, 320, 320, 320, 326
2nd innings FoW: 48, 75, 108, 146, 199, 410

Bowler	O	M	R	W	O	M	R	W
AV Bedser	40	14	60	3	44	16	80	1
WJ Edrich	16	4	30	0	13	2	37	0
RO Jenkins	35.2	6	116	5	59	13	174	4
JH Wardle	17	6	46	2	30	10	58	0
R Berry	19	7	45	0	32	15	67	0
NWD Yardley	4	1	12	0				

ENGLAND 1st innings / 2nd innings

Batsman	1st innings		2nd innings	
L Hutton	st Walcott b Valentine	35	b Valentine	10
C Washbrook	st Walcott b Ramadhin	36	b Ramadhin	114
WJ Edrich	c Walcott b Ramadhin	8	c Jones b Ramadhin	8
GHG Doggart	lbw b Ramadhin	0	b Ramadhin	25
W Parkhouse	b Valentine	0	c Goddard b Valentine	48
NWD Yardley*	b Valentine	16	c Weekes b Valentine	19
TG Evans+	b Ramadhin	8	c Rae b Ramadhin	2
RO Jenkins	c Walcott b Valentine	4	b Ramadhin	4
JH Wardle	not out	33	lbw b Worrell	21
AV Bedser	b Ramadhin	5	b Ramadhin	0
R Berry	c Goddard b Jones	2	not out	0
Extras	(2b, 1lb, 1w, 0nb)	4	(16b, 7lb, 0w, 0nb)	23
	106.4 overs		191.3 overs	
Total		**151**		**274**

1st innings FoW: 62, 74, 74,7 5, 86, 102, 110, 113, 122, 151
2nd innings FoW: 28, 57, 140, 218, 228, 238, 245, 248, 258, 274

Bowler	O	M	R	W	O	M	R	W
PE Jones	8.4	2	13	1	7	1	22	0
FMM Worrell	10	4	20	0	22.3	9	39	1
AL Valentine	45	28	48	4	71	47	79	3
S Ramadhin	43	27	66	5	72	43	86	6
GE Gomez					13	1	25	0
JDC Goddard					6	6	0	0

No. 278:	3rd Test
VENUE:	Trent Bridge
DATE:	20th-25th July 1950
TOSS WON BY:	England
RESULT:	West Indies won by 10 wickets

No. 279:	4th Test
VENUE:	The Oval
DATE:	12th-16th August 1950
TOSS WON BY:	West Indies
RESULT:	WI won by an innings and 56 runs

ENGLAND 1st innings / 2nd innings

	1st innings		2nd innings	
RT Simpson	c Walcott b Johnson	4	run out	94
C Washbrook	c Stollmeyer b Worrell	3	c Worrell b Valentine	102
W Parkhouse	c Weekes b Johnson	13	lbw b Goddard	69
JG Dewes	c Gomez b Worrell	0	lbw b Valentine	67
NWD Yardley*	c Goddard b Valentine	41	b Ramadhin	7
DJ Insole	lbw b Ramadhin	21	st Walcott b Ramadhin	0
TG Evans+	b Ramadhin	32	c Stollmeyer b Ramadhin	63
D Shackleton	b Worrell	42	c Weekes b Valentine	1
RO Jenkins	b Johnson	39	not out	6
AV Bedser	c Stollmeyer b Valentine	13	b Ramadhin	2
WE Hollies	not out	2	lbw b Ramadhin	0
Extras	(0b, 12lb, 0w, 1nb)	13	(11b, 10lb, 2w, 2nb)	25
	98.4 overs		245.2 overs	
Total		**223**		**436**

1st innings FoW: 6, 18, 23, 25, 75, 105, 147, 174, 191, 223
2nd innings FoW: 212, 220, 326, 346, 350, 408, 410, 434, 436, 436

HHH Johnson	25.4	5	59	3	30	5	65	0
FMM Worrell	17	4	40	3	19	8	30	0
GE Gomez	3	1	9	0	11	3	23	0
JDC Goddard	6	3	10	0	12	6	18	1
S Ramadhin	29	12	49	2	81.2	25	135	5
AL Valentine	18	6	43	2	92	49	140	3

WEST INDIES 1st innings / 2nd innings

	1st innings		2nd innings	
AF Rae	st Evans b Yardley	68	not out	46
JB Stollmeyer	c & b Jenkins	46	not out	52
RJ Christiani	lbw b Shackleton	10		
FMM Worrell	c Yardley b Bedser	261		
EdeC Weekes	c & b Hollies	129		
CL Walcott+	b Bedser	8		
GE Gomez	not out	19		
JDC Goddard*	c Yardley b Bedser	0		
HHH Johnson	c Insole b Bedser	0		
S Ramadhin	b Bedser	2		
AL Valentine	b Hollies	1		
Extras	(2b, 10lb, 0w, 2nb)	14	(0b, 0lb, 0w, 5nb)	5
	174.4 overs		36.3 overs	
Total		**558**		**103**

1st innings FoW: 77, 95, 238, 521, 535, 537, 538, 539, 551, 558

AV Bedser	48	9	127	5	11	1	35	0
D Shackleton	43	7	128	1	6	2	7	0
NWD Yardley	27	3	82	1				
RO Jenkins	13	0	73	1	11	1	46	0
WE Hollies	43.4	8	134	2	7	6	1	0
RT Simpson					1.3	0	9	0

WEST INDIES 1st innings / 2nd innings

	1st innings		2nd innings	
AF Rae	b Bedser	109		
JB Stollmeyer	lbw b Bailey	36		
FMM Worrell	lbw b Wright	138		
EdeC Weekes	c Hutton b Wright	30		
CL Walcott+	b Wright	17		
GE Gomez	c McIntyre b Brown	74		
RJ Christiani	c McIntyre b Bedser	11		
JDC Goddard*	not out	58		
PE Jones	b Wright	1		
S Ramadhin	c McIntyre b Wright	3		
AL Valentine	b Bailey	9		
Extras	(5b, 11lb, 0w, 1nb)	17		
	194.2 overs			
Total		**503**		

1st innings FoW: 72, 244, 295, 318, 337, 446, 480, 482, 490, 503

TE Bailey	34.2	9	84	2	
AV Bedser	38	9	75	2	
FR Brown	21	4	74	1	
DVP Wright	53	16	141	5	
MJ Hilton	41	12	91	0	
DCS Compton	7	2	21	0	

ENGLAND 1st innings / 2nd innings

	1st innings		2nd innings	
L Hutton	not out	202	c Christiani b Goddard	2
RT Simpson	c Jones b Valentine	30	b Ramadhin	16
DS Sheppard	b Ramadhin	11	c Weekes b Valentine	29
DCS Compton	run out	44	c Weekes b Valentine	11
JG Dewes	c Worrell b Valentine	17	c Christiani b Valentine	3
TE Bailey	c Weekes b Goddard	18	lbw b Ramadhin	12
FR Brown*	c Weekes b Valentine	0	c Stollmeyer b Valentine	15
AJ McIntyre+	c & b Valentine	4	c (sub) b Ramadhin	0
AV Bedser	lbw b Goddard	0	c Weekes b Valentine	0
MJ Hilton	b Goddard	3	c (sub) b Valentine	0
DVP Wright	lbw b Goddard	4	not out	6
Extras	(5b, 6lb, 0w, 0nb)	11	(6b, 3lb, 0w, 0nb)	9
	179.4 overs		69.3 overs	
Total		**344**		**103**

2nd innings FoW: 73, 120, 229, 259, 310, 315, 321, 322, 326, 344
2nd innings FoW: 2, 39, 50, 56, 79, 83, 83, 83, 85, 103

PE Jones	23	4	70	0				
FMM Worrell	20	9	30	0				
S Ramadhin	23	23	63	1	26	11	38	3
AL Valentine	64	21	121	4	26.3	10	39	6
GE Gomez	10	3	24	0	8	4	6	0
JDC Goddard	17.4	6	25	4	9	4	11	1

No. 280: 1st Test	
VENUE: Brisbane (Gabba)	
DATE: 1st-5th December 1950	
TOSS WON BY: Australia	
RESULT: Australia won by 70 runs	

No. 281: 2nd Test	
VENUE: Melbourne (MCG)	
DATE: 22nd-27th December 1950	
TOSS WON BY: Australia	
RESULT: Australia won by 28 runs	

AUSTRALIA 1st innings / 2nd innings

Batsman	1st innings		2nd innings	
J Moroney	c Hutton b Bailey	0	lbw b Bailey	0
AR Morris	lbw b Bedser	25	c Bailey b Bedser	0
RN Harvey	c Evans b Bedser	74	lbw b Bailey	8
KR Miller	c McIntyre b Wright	15	c Bailey b Bedser	0
AL Hassett*	b Bedser	8	lbw b Bailey	3
SJE Loxton	c Evans b Brown	24	c Simpson b Bedser	12
RR Lindwall	c Bedser b Bailey	41	c Simpson b Bailey	8
D Tallon+	c Simpson b Brown	5	not out	0
IW Johnson	c Simpson b Bailey	23		
WA Johnston	c Hutton b Bedser	1		
JB Iverson	not out	1		
Extras	(5b, 3lb, 0w, 3nb)	11	(0b, 0lb, 0w, 1nb)	1
Total	55.5 overs	**228**	13.5 overs	**32**

1st innings FoW: 0, 69, 116, 118, 129, 156, 172, 219, 226, 228
2nd innings FoW: 0, 0, 0, 12, 19, 31, 32

Bowler	O	M	R	W		O	M	R	W
TE Bailey	12	4	28	3		7	2	22	4
AV Bedser	16.5	4	45	4		6.5	2	9	3
DVP Wright	16	0	81	1					
FR Brown	11	0	63	2					

AUSTRALIA 1st innings / 2nd innings

Batsman	1st innings		2nd innings	
KA Archer	c Bedser b Bailey	26	c Bailey b Bedser	46
AR Morris	c Hutton b Bedser	2	lbw b Wright	18
RN Harvey	c Evans b Bedser	42	run out	31
KR Miller	lbw b Brown	18	b Bailey	14
AL Hassett*	b Bailey	52	c Bailey b Brown	19
SJE Loxton	c Evans b Close	32	c Evans b Brown	2
RR Lindwall	lbw b Bailey	8	c Evans b Brown	7
D Tallon+	not out	7	lbw b Brown	0
IW Johnson	c Parkhouse b Bedser	0	c Close b Brown	23
WA Johnston	c Hutton b Bedser	0	b Bailey	6
JB Iverson	b Bailey	1	not out	0
Extras	(4b, 2lb, 0w, 0nb)	6	(10b, 5lb, 0w, 0nb)	15
Total	59.1 overs	**194**	53.3 overs	**181**

1st innings FoW: 6, 67, 89, 93, 177, 177, 192, 193, 193, 194
2nd innings FoW: 43, 99, 100, 126, 131, 151, 151, 156, 181, 181

Bowler	O	M	R	W		O	M	R	W
TE Bailey	17.1	5	40	4		15	3	47	2
AV Bedser	19	3	37	4		16.3	2	43	2
DVP Wright	8	0	63	0		9	0	42	1
FR Brown	9	0	28	1		12	2	26	4
DB Close	6	1	20	1		1	0	8	0

ENGLAND 1st innings / 2nd innings

Batsman	1st innings		2nd innings	
RT Simpson	b Johnston	12	b Lindwall	0
C Washbrook	c Hassett b Johnston	19	c Loxton b Lindwall	6
TG Evans+	c Iverson b Johnston	16	b Miller	9
DCS Compton	c Lindwall b Johnston	5	c Johnston b Iverson	7
JG Dewes	c Loxton b Miller	1	c Harvey b Iverson	0
L Hutton	not out	8	c Loxton b Johnston	5
AJW McIntyre	b Johnston		run out	7
FR Brown*	c Tallon b Miller	4	not out	62
TE Bailey	not out	1	c Loxton b Johnston	0
AV Bedser			c Loxton b Iverson	17
DVP Wright			c Lindwall b Iverson	2
Extras	(0b, 2lb, 0w, 1nb)	3	(6b, 0lb, 0w, 1nb)	7
Total	22 overs	**68**	38 overs	**122**

1st innings FoW: 28, 49, 52, 52, 56, 57, 67
2nd innings FoW: 0, 16, 22, 23, 23, 30, 46, 46, 77, 122

Bowler	O	M	R	W		O	M	R	W
RR Lindwall	1	0	1	0		7	3	21	2
WA Johnston	11	2	35	5		11	2	30	2
KR Miller	10	1	29	2		7	3	21	1
JB Iverson						13	3	43	4

ENGLAND 1st innings / 2nd innings

Batsman	1st innings		2nd innings	
RT Simpson	c Johnson b Miller	4	b Lindwall	23
C Washbrook	lbw b Lindwall	21	b Iverson	8
JG Dewes	c Miller b Johnston	8	b Johnson	0
L Hutton	c Tallon b Iverson	12	c Lindwall b Johnston	40
W Parkhouse	c Hassett b Miller	9	c Harvey b Iverson	5
DB Close	c Loxton b Iverson	0	lbw b Johnston	28
FR Brown*	c Johnson b Iverson	62	lbw b Johnston	1
TE Bailey	b Lindwall	12	b Lindwall	8
TG Evans+	c Johnson b Iverson	49	b Lindwall	2
AV Bedser	not out	4	not out	14
DVP Wright	lbw b Johnston	2	lbw b Johnston	2
Extras	(8b, 6lb, 0w, 0nb)	14	(17b, 2lb, 0w, 0nb)	19
Total	62 overs	**197**	63.7 overs	**150**

1st innings FoW: 11, 33, 37, 54, 54, 61, 126, 153, 194, 197
2nd innings FoW: 21, 52, 52, 82, 92, 95, 122, 124, 134, 150

Bowler	O	M	R	W		O	M	R	W
RR Lindwall	13	2	46	2		12	1	29	3
KR Miller	13	0	39	2		5	2	16	0
WA Johnston	9	1	28	2		13.7	1	26	4
JB Iverson	18	3	37	4		20	4	36	2
IW Johnson	5	1	19	0		13	3	24	1
SJE Loxton	4	1	14	0					

No. 282: 3rd Test		No. 283: 4th Test	
VENUE: Sydney (SCG)		VENUE: Adelaide	
DATE: 5th-9th January 1951		DATE: 2nd-8th February 1951	
TOSS WON BY: England		TOSS WON BY: Australia	
RESULT: Aus won by an innings and 13 runs		RESULT: Australia won by 274 runs	

ENGLAND 1st innings and **2nd innings**

ENGLAND	1st innings		2nd innings	
L Hutton	lbw b Miller	62	c Tallon b Iverson	9
C Washbrook	c Miller b Johnson	18	b Iverson	34
RT Simpson	c Loxton b Miller	49	c Tallon b Iverson	0
DCS Compton	b Miller	0	c Johnson b Johnston	23
W Parkhouse	c Morris b Johnson	25	run out	15
FR Brown*	b Lindwall	79	b Iverson	18
TE Bailey	c Tallon b Johnson	15	b Johnson	14
TG Evans+	not out	23	not out	0
AV Bedser	b Lindwall	3	b Iverson	4
JJ Warr	b Miller	4	b Iverson	0
DVP Wright	run out	0	absent hurt	0
Extras	(0b, 10lb, 0w, 2nb)	12	(1b, 5lb, 0w, 0nb)	6
Total	98.7 overs	**290**	52.4 overs	**123**

1st innings FoW: 34, 128, 128, 137, 187, 258, 267, 281, 286, 290
2nd innings FoW: 32, 40, 45, 74, 91, 119, 119, 123,123

RR Lindwall	16	0	60	2		4	1	12	0
KR Miller	15.7	4	37	4		6	2	15	0
IW Johnson	31	8	94	3		10	2	32	1
WA Johnston	21	5	50	0		13	6	31	1
JB Iverson	10	1	25	0		19.4	8	27	6
SJE Loxton	5	0	12	0					

AUSTRALIA 1st innings   **2nd innings**

AUSTRALIA	1st innings		2nd innings
KA Archer	c Evans b Bedser	48	
AR Morris	b Bedser	0	
AL Hassett*	c Bedser b Brown	70	
RN Harvey	b Bedser	39	
KR Miller	not out	145	
SJE Loxton	c Bedser b Brown	17	
D Tallon+	lbw b Bedser	18	
IW Johnson	b Brown	77	
RR Lindwall	lbw b Brown	1	
WA Johnston	run out	0	
JB Iverson	run out	1	
Extras	(3b, 7lb, 0w, 0nb)	10	
Total	129 overs	**426**	

1st innings FoW: 1, 122, 122, 190, 223, 252, 402, 406, 418, 426

AV Bedser	43	4	107	4	
JJ Warr	36	4	142	0	
FR Brown	44	4	153	4	
DCS Compton	6	1	14	0	

AUSTRALIA 1st innings and **2nd innings**

AUSTRALIA	1st innings		2nd innings	
KA Archer	c Compton b Bedser	0	c Bedser b Tattersall	32
AR Morris	b Tattersall	206	run out	16
AL Hassett*	c Evans b Wright	43	lbw b Wright	31
RN Harvey	b Bedser	43	b Brown	68
KR Miller	c Brown b Wright	44	b Wright	99
JW Burke	b Tattersall	12	not out	101
IW Johnson	c Evans b Bedser	16	c Evans b Warr	3
RR Lindwall	lbw b Wright	1	run out	31
D Tallon+	b Tattersall	1	c Hutton b Compton	5
WA Johnston	c Hutton b Wright	0	not out	9
JB Iverson	not out	0		
Extras	(2b, 1lb, 1w, 1nb)	5	(7b, 1lb, 0w, 0nb)	8
Total	96.5 overs	**371**	101.6 overs	**403**

1st innings FoW: 0, 95, 205, 281, 310, 357, 363, 366, 367, 371
2nd innings FoW: 26, 79, 95, 194, 281, 297, 367, 378

AV Bedser	26	4	74	3		25	6	62	0
JJ Warr	16	2	63	0		21	0	76	1
DVP Wright	25	1	99	4		21	2	109	2
R Tattersall	25.5	5	95	3		27	2	116	1
FR Brown	3	0	24	0		3	1	14	1
DCS Compton	1	0	11	0		4.6	1	18	1

ENGLAND 1st innings and **2nd innings**

ENGLAND	1st innings		2nd innings	
L Hutton	not out	156	c (sub) b Johnston	45
C Washbrook	c Iverson b Lindwall	2	lbw b Johnston	31
RT Simpson	b Johnston	29	c Burke b Johnston	61
DCS Compton	c Tallon b Lindwall	5	c (sub) b Johnston	0
DS Sheppard	b Iverson	9	lbw b Miller	41
FR Brown*	b Miller	16	c Johnson b Miller	21
TG Evans+	c Burke b Johnston	13	c Morris b Miller	0
AV Bedser	lbw b Iverson	7	c Morris b Johnson	6
R Tattersall	c Harvey b Iverson	0	b Johnson	0
JJ Warr	b Johnston	0	not out	0
DVP Wright	lbw b Lindwall	14		
Extras	(15b, 5lb, 0w, 1nb)	21	(15b, 3lb, 2w, 3nb)	23
Total	92.3 overs	**272**	78.6 overs	**228**

1st innings FoW: 7, 80, 96, 132, 161, 195, 206, 214, 219, 272
2nd innings FoW: 74, 90, 90, 181, 221, 221, 228, 228, 228

RR Lindwall	13.3	0	51	3		10	2	35	0
KR Miller	13	2	36	1		13	4	27	3
IW Johnson	15	2	38	0		25.6	6	63	2
JB Iverson	26	4	68	3					
WA Johnston	25	4	58	3		27	4	73	4
JW Burke						3	1	7	0

No. 284: 5th Test	No. 285: 1st Test
VENUE: Melbourne (MCG)	VENUE: Christchurch
DATE: 23rd - 28th February1951	DATE: 17th-21st March 1951
TOSS WON BY:	TOSS WON BY: New Zealand
RESULT: England won by 8 wickets	RESULT: Match drawn

Australia 1st innings / 2nd innings

Batsman	1st innings		2nd innings	
JW Burke	c Tattersall b Bedser	11	c Hutton b Bedser	1
AR Morris	lbw b Brown	50	lbw b Bedser	4
AL Hassett*	c Hutton b Brown	92	b Wright	48
RN Harvey	c Evans b Brown	1	lbw b Wright	52
KR Miller	c & b Brown	7	c & b Brown	0
GB Hole	b Bedser	18	b Bailey	63
IW Johnson	lbw b Bedser	1	c Brown b Wright	0
RR Lindwall	c Compton b Bedser	21	b Bedser	14
D Tallon+	c Hutton b Bedser	1	not out	2
WA Johnston	not out	12	b Bedser	1
JB Iverson	c Washbrook b Brown	0	c Compton b Bedser	0
Extras	(2b, 1lb, 0w, 0nb)	3	(2b, 8lb, 1w, 1nb)	12
	69 overs			
Total		**217**		**197**

1st innings FoW: 23, 111, 115, 123, 156, 166, 184, 187, 216, 217
2nd innings FoW: 5, 6, 87, 89, 142, 142, 192, 196, 197, 197

Bowler	O	M	R	W	O	M	R	W
AV Bedser	22	5	46	5	20.3	4	59	5
TE Bailey	9	1	29	0	15	3	32	1
FR Brown	18	4	49	5	9	1	32	1
DVP Wright	9	1	50	0	15	2	56	3
R Tattersall	11	3	40	0	5	2	6	0

NEW ZEALAND 1st innings / 2nd innings

Batsman	1st innings		2nd innings	
B Sutcliffe	b Statham	116	c Evans b Simpson	8
VJ Scott	b Bailey	16	lbw b Washbrook	19
JR Reid	b Wright	50	c Evans b Simpson	2
WM Wallace	c Brown b Bedser	66	not out	7
WA Hadlee*	c Brown b Bailey	50	not out	10
A MacGibbon	lbw b Wright	4		
FLH Mooney+	st Evans b Tattersall	39		
TB Burtt	b Brown	42		
AM Moir	not out	0		
JA Hayes				
GF Cresswell				
Extras	(16b, 16lb, 1w, 1nb)	34	(0b, 0lb, 0w, 0nb)	0
	157.2 overs		13 overs	
Total		**417**		**46**

1st innings FoW: 37, 168, 203, 297, 307, 335, 415, 417
2nd innings FoW: 9, 29, 29

Bowler	O	M	R	W	O	M	R	W
AV Bedser	41	10	83	1				
TE Bailey	30	9	51	2				
JB Statham	24	6	47	1				
R Tattersall	16	3	48	1				
DVP Wright	27	2	99	2				
FR Brown	15.2	3	34	1				
DCS Compton	4	0	21	0	2	0	10	0
C Washbrook					4	0	25	1
RT Simpson					4	1	4	2
L Hutton					3	1	7	0

ENGLAND 1st innings

Batsman	1st innings		2nd innings	
L Hutton	b Hole	79	not out	60
C Washbrook	c Tallon b Miller	27	c Lindwall b Johnston	7
RT Simpson	not out	156	run out	15
DCS Compton	c Miller b Lindwall	11	not out	11
DS Sheppard	c Tallon b Miller	1		
FR Brown*	b Lindwall	6		
TG Evans+	b Miller	1		
AV Bedser	b Lindwall	11		
TE Bailey	c Johnson b Iverson	5		
DVP Wright	lbw b Iverson	3		
R Tattersall	b Miller	10		
Extras	(9b, 1lb, 0w, 0nb)	10	(0b, 2lb, 0w, 0nb)	2
	90.7 overs		29.6 overs	
Total		**320**		**95**

1st innings FoW: 40, 171, 204, 205, 212, 213, 228, 236, 246, 320
2nd innings FoW: 32, 62

Bowler	O	M	R	W	O	M	R	W
RR Lindwall	21	1	77	3	2	0	12	0
KR Miller	21.7	5	76	4	2	0	5	0
WA Johnston	12	1	55	0	11	3	36	1
JB Iverson	20	4	52	2	12	2	32	0
IW Johnson	11	1	40	0	1	0	1	0
GB Hole	5	0	10	1	1	0	3	0
AL Hassett					0.6	0	4	0

ENGLAND 1st innings / 2nd innings

Batsman	1st innings	
L Hutton	b Moir	28
C Washbrook	c Mooney b Hayes	58
RT Simpson	c Wallace b Moir	81
DCS Compton	b Burtt	79
TE Bailey	not out	134
FR Brown*	c Scott b Cresswell	62
TG Evans+	c Hayes b Moir	19
AV Bedser	c Hayes b Moir	5
R Tattersall	b Moir	2
DVP Wright	c MacGibbon b Cresswell	45
JB Statham	b Moir	9
Extras	(20b, 8lb, 0w, 0nb)	28
	221.3 overs	
Total		**550**

1st innings FoW: 57, 108, 237, 264, 356, 388, 398, 406, 523, 550

Bowler	O	M	R	W
JA Hayes	43	11	85	1
JR Reid	10	2	29	0
AR MacGibbon	27	6	74	0
GF Cresswell	34	10	75	2
AM Moir	56.3	16	155	6
TB Burtt	49	23	99	1
VJ Scott	2	0	5	0

New Zealand

No. 286: 2nd Test
VENUE: Wellington
DATE: 24th-28th March 1951
TOSS WON BY: New Zealand
RESULT: England won by 6 wickets

NEW ZEALAND

1st innings			2nd innings	
B Sutcliffe	c & b Wright	20	b Tattersall	11
VJ Scott	lbw b Bailey	0	b Tattersall	31
JR Reid	b Brown	11	b Tattersall	11
WM Wallace	b Wright	15	c Bailey b Tattersall	9
WA Hadlee*	lbw b Wright	15	c Brown b Bailey	1
A MacGibbon	c Brown b Wright	20	lbw b Tattersall	0
FLH Mooney+	c Compton b Bailey	3	c Sheppard b Bedser	60
TB Burtt	c Parkhouse b Wright	3	b Tattersall	0
AM Moir	not out	26	c Bedser b Bailey	26
JA Hayes	b Tattersall	0	b Bailey	5
GF Cresswell	run out	0	not out	0
Extras	(3b, 5lb, 0w, 4nb)	12	(30b, 2lb, 0w, 3nb)	35
	70 overs		72.2 overs	
Total		**125**		**189**

1st innings FoW: 1, 25, 37, 68, 69, 83, 94, 102, 105, 125
2nd innings FoW: 25, 62, 76, 82, 82, 98, 105, 156, 187, 189

TE Bailey	11	2	18	2	14.2	1	43	3
AV Bedser	19	6	21	0	24	10	34	1
FR Brown	6	1	10	1	1	0	1	0
R Tattersall	15	9	16	1	21	6	44	6
DVP Wright	19	3	48	5	12	2	32	0

ENGLAND

1st innings			2nd innings	
L Hutton	c Reid b Moir	57	c Hadlee b Cresswell	29
RT Simpson	b Moir	6	b Burtt	5
W Parkhouse	b Burtt	2	c & b Burtt	20
DS Sheppard	b Hayes	3	b Cresswell	18
DCS Compton	b Burtt	10	not out	4
FR Brown*	b Hayes	47	not out	10
TE Bailey	st Mooney b Burtt	29		
TG Evans+	b Cresswell	13		
AV Bedser	b Cresswell	28		
DVP Wright	not out	9		
R Tattersall	b Cresswell	1		
Extras	(11b, 8lb, 0w, 3nb)	22	(1b, 4lb, 0w, 0nb)	5
	97 overs		45.2 overs	
Total		**227**		**91**

1st innings FoW: 10, 31, 40, 69, 140, 144, 173, 216, 218, 227
2nd innings FoW: 16, 56, 60, 80

JA Hayes	20	2	44	2				
GF Cresswell	15	6	18	3	18	8	31	2
AM Moir	28	5	65	2	6	0	19	0
TB Burtt	27	14	46	3	21.2	10	36	2
AR MacGibbon	7	0	32	0				

South Africa

No. 287: 1st Test
VENUE: Trent Bridge
DATE: 7th-12th June 1951
TOSS WON BY: South Africa
RESULT: South Africa won by 71 runs

SOUTH AFRICA

1st innings			2nd innings	
EAB Rowan	c Evans b Brown	17	c Ikin b Bedser	11
JHB Waite+	run out	76	c Ikin b Tattersall	5
DJ McGlew	b Brown	40	st Evans b Bedser	5
AD Nourse*	run out	208	c Brown b Tattersall	13
JE Cheetham	c Ikin b Bedser	31	b Bedser	28
GM Fullerton	c Compton b Tattersall	54	c Hutton b Bedser	22
Van Ryneveld	lbw b Bedser	32	c Evans b Bedser	5
AMB Rowan	b Bedser	2	b Tattersall	2
NBF Mann	c Tattersall b Wardle	1	not out	11
GWA Chubb	not out	0	b Bedser	5
CN McCarthy	not out	1		
Extras	(3b, 17lb, 0w, 1nb)	21	(4b, 9lb, 0w, 1nb)	14
	240 overs		51.4 overs	
Total		**483**		**121**

1st innings FoW: 31, 107, 189, 273, 394, 465, 467, 476, 482
2nd innings FoW: 12, 20, 24, 52, 87, 98, 103, 106, 121

AV Bedser	63	18	122	3	22.4	8	37	6
TE Bailey	45	13	102	0	2	0	10	0
FR Brown	34	11	74	2				
R Tattersall	47	20	80	1	23	6	56	3
JH Wardle	49	21	77	1	4	3	4	0
DCS Compton	2	0	7	0				

ENGLAND

1st innings			2nd innings	
L Hutton	c Waite b AMB Rowan	63	c & b AMB Rowan	11
JT Ikin	c McCarthy b Chubb	1	b Mann	33
RT Simpson	c Waite b McCarthy	137	c & b AMB Rowan	7
DCS Compton	c Waite b McCarthy	112	lbw b AMB Rowan	5
W Watson	lbw b McCarthy	57	lbw b Mann	5
FR Brown*	c Fullerton b Chubb	29	c Waite b Mann	11
TG Evans+	c (sub) b Chubb	5	c McCarthy b AMB Rowan	7
JH Wardle	c Fullerton b Chubb	5	c Van Ryneveld b Mann	0
TE Bailey	c Fullerton b McCarthy	3	c (sub) b AMB Rowan	30
AV Bedser	not out	0	b McCarthy	0
R Tattersall			not out	0
Extras	(4b, 3lb, 0w, 0nb)	7	(0b, 5lb, 0w, 0nb)	5
	163.2 overs		65.2 overs	
Total		**419**		**114**

1st innings FoW: 4, 148, 234, 375, 385, 395, 410, 419, 419
2nd innings FoW: 23, 41, 57, 63, 67, 80, 83, 84, 110, 114

CN McCarthy	48	10	104	4	8	1	8	1
GWA Chubb	46.2	12	146	4	6	2	9	0
AMB Rowan	46	10	101	1	27.2	4	68	5
NBF Mann	20	5	51	0	24	16	24	4
CB Van Ryneveld	3	0	10	0				

No. 288: 2nd Test	
VENUE:	Lord's
DATE:	21st-23rd June 1951
TOSS WON BY:	England
RESULT:	England won by 10 wickets

No: 289 3rd Test	
VENUE:	Old Trafford
DATE:	5th-10th July 1951
TOSS WON BY:	South Africa
RESULT:	England won by 9 wickets

ENGLAND 1st innings / 2nd innings

Batsman	1st innings		2nd innings	
L Hutton	lbw b McCarthy	12	not out	12
JT Ikin	b Mann	51	not out	4
RT Simpson	lbw b McCarthy	26		
DCS Compton	lbw b McCarthy	79		
W Watson	c McCarthy b Chubb	79		
FR Brown*	b Chubb	1		
TG Evans+	c Fullerton b McCarthy	0		
JH Wardle	lbw b Chubb	18		
AV Bedser	not out	26		
JB Statham	b Chubb	1		
R Tattersall	b Chubb	1		
Extras	(8b, 9lb, 0w, 0nb)	17	(0b, 0lb, 0w, 0nb)	0
	107.4 overs		3.5 overs	
Total		**311**		**16**

1st innings FoW: 20, 89, 103, 225, 226, 231, 265, 299, 301, 311

CN McCarthy	23	2	76	4					
GWA Chubb	34.4	9	77	5					
AMB Rowan	13	1	63	0					
NBF Mann	32	12	51	1					
CB Van Ryneveld	5	0	27	0					
AD Nourse	2	0	9	0					
EAB Rowan	1.5	0	7	0					

SOUTH AFRICA 1st innings / 2nd innings

Batsman	1st innings		2nd innings	
EAB Rowan	c Ikin b Tattersall	24	c Ikin b Statham	10
JHB Waite+	c Hutton b Wardle	15	c Compton b Tattersall	17
DJ McGlew	c Evans b Tattersall	3	b Tattersall	2
AD Nourse*	c Watson b Tattersall	20	lbw b Wardle	3
JE Cheetham	c Hutton b Tattersall	15	b Statham	54
GM Fullerton	b Tattersall	12	lbw b Bedser	60
Van Ryneveld	lbw b Wardle	0	c Ikin b Tattersall	18
AMB Rowan	c Ikin b Tattersall	3	c Brown b Bedser	10
NBF Mann	c Brown b Tattersall	14	c Brown b Tattersall	13
GWA Chubb	c Tattersall b Wardle	5	b Tattersall	3
CN McCarthy	not out	1	not out	2
Extras	(0b, 3lb, 0w, 0nb)	3	(11b, 8lb, 0w, 0nb)	19
	64.5 overs		96.2 overs	
Total		**115**		**211**

1st innings FoW: 25, 38, 47, 72, 88, 91, 91, 103, 112, 115
2nd innings FoW: 21, 29, 32, 58, 152, 160, 178, 196, 200, 211

AV Bedser	8	5	7	0		24	8	53	2
JB Statham	6	3	7	0		18	6	33	2
R Tattersall	28	10	52	7		32.2	14	49	5
JH Wardle	22.5	10	46	3		20	5	44	1
DCS Compton						2	0	13	0

SOUTH AFRICA 1st innings / 2nd innings

Batsman	1st innings		2nd innings	
EAB Rowan	c Brown b Bedser	0	c Ikin b Laker	57
JHB Waite+	c Ikin b Bedser	1	b Statham	0
Van Ryneveld	lbw b Tattersall	40	b Laker	7
AD Nourse*	c Ikin b Bedser	29	c Evans b Tattersall	20
JE Cheetham	c Hutton b Bedser	20	b Bedser	46
GM Fullerton	c Hutton b Bedser	0	c Tattersall b Laker	10
RA McLean	b Laker	20	c Ikin b Bedser	19
AMB Rowan	b Statham	17	lbw b Bedser	3
NBF Mann	b Bedser	0	b Bedser	4
GWA Chubb	not out	15	b Bedser	1
CN McCarthy	c Ikin b Bedser	0	not out	0
Extras	(0b, 14lb, 0w, 2nb)	16	(13b, 10lb, 0w, 1nb)	24
	84.3 overs		78.2 overs	
Total		**158**		**191**

1st innings FOW: 0, 12, 66, 87, 88, 105, 129, 132, 143, 158
2nd innings FOW: 4, 19, 60, 145, 155, 168, 181, 185, 190, 191

AV Bedser	32.3	10	58	7		24.2	8	54	5
JB Statham	7	2	8	1		17	3	30	1
JC Laker	27	7	47	1		19	3	42	3
R Tattersall	18	6	29	1		18	3	41	1

ENGLAND 1st innings / 2nd innings

Batsman	1st innings		2nd innings	
L Hutton	c Van Ry'lld b A Rowan	27	not out	98
JT Ikin	c Cheetham b Chubb	22	b Mann	38
RT Simpson	st Waite b Mann	11	not out	4
TW Graveney	b AMB Rowan	15		
W Watson	b Chubb	21		
FR Brown*	c Ryneveld b AMB Rowan	42		
TG Evans+	c Waite b Chubb	2		
JC Laker	c Nourse b Chubb	27		
AV Bedser	not out	30		
R Tattersall	c Cheetham b Chubb	1		
JB Statham	c Cheetham b Chubb	1		
Extras	(4b, 8lb, 0w, 0nb)	12	(0b, 1lb, 0w, 1nb)	2
	85.3 overs		51.3 overs	
Total		**211**		**142**

1st innings FOW: 30, 58, 70,91, 127, 143, 147, 200, 207, 211
2nd innings FOW: 121

CN McCarthy	14	4	36	0		19	4	46	0
GWA Chubb	26.3	7	51	6		23	6	72	0
AMB Rowan	29	4	75	3		7	1	17	0
NBF Mann	16	5	37	1		2.3	1	5	1

South Africa

No. 290:	4th Test
VENUE:	Headingley
DATE:	26th-31st July 1951
TOSS WON BY:	South Africa
RESULT:	Match drawn

SOUTH AFRICA 1st innings / 2nd innings

			2nd innings	
EAB Rowan	c Bedser b Brown	236	not out	60
JHB Waite+	lbw b Bedser	13	not out	25
Van Ryneveld	c & b Hilton	83		
AD Nourse*	lbw b Brown	13		
JE Cheetham	b Bedser	7		
RA McLean	run out	67		
PNF Mansell	c Tattersall b Hilton	90		
AMB Rowan	b Brown	9		
NBF Mann	b Tattersall	2		
GWA Chubb	c Lowson b Hilton	11		
CN McCarthy	not out	0		
Extras	(1b, 6lb, 0w, 0nb)	7	(0b, 2lb, 0w, 0nb)	2
	235.3 overs		49 overs	
Total		**538**		**87**

1st innings FoW: 40, 238, 267, 286, 394, 480, 489, 505, 538, 538

AV Bedser	58	14	113	2	4	1	5	0
TE Bailey	17	4	48	0	1	0	8	0
FR Brown	38	10	107	3	11	2	26	0
R Tattersall	60	23	83	1	16	9	13	0
MJ Hilton	61.3	18	176	3	10	5	17	0
DCS Compton	1	0	4	0	7	1	16	0

ENGLAND 1st innings / 2nd innings

			2nd innings
L Hutton	b Van Ryneveld	100	
FA Lowson	c Mansell b AMB Rowan	58	
PBH May	b AMB Rowan	138	
DCS Compton	lbw b AMB Rowan	25	
W Watson	b Chubb	32	
TE Bailey	b Mann	95	
FR Brown*	c EAB b AMB Rowan	2	
AV Bedser	b Mann	8	
DV Brennan+	b Mann	16	
R Tattersall	c EAB b AMB Rowan	4	
MJ Hilton	not out	9	
Extras	(10b, 7lb, 0w, 1nb)	18	
	224.5 overs		
Total		**505**	

1st innings FoW: 99, 228, 266, 345, 387, 391, 400, 432, 445, 505

CN McCarthy	41	10	81	0
GWA Chubb	43	12	99	1
AMB Rowan	68	17	174	5
NBF Mann	60.5	23	96	3
PNF Mansell	4	0	11	0
CB Van Ryneveld	8	0	26	1

South Africa

No. 291:	5th Test
VENUE:	The Oval
DATE:	16th-18th August 1951
TOSS WON BY:	South Africa
RESULT:	England won by 4 wickets

SOUTH AFRICA 1st innings / 2nd innings

			2nd innings	
EAB Rowan	c Hutton b Brown	55	lbw b Laker	45
WR Endean+	c Brown b Laker	31	lbw b Bedser	7
Van Ryneveld	st Brennan b Laker	10	lbw b Laker	5
AD Nourse*	lbw b Brown	4	b Laker	0
JE Cheetham	lbw b Laker	0	c Hutton b Tattersall	18
RA McLean	c May b Laker	14	c Lowson b Laker	18
PNF Mansell	b Tattersall	8	lbw b Laker	0
AMB Rowan	c Laker b Bedser	41	not out	15
GWA Chubb	b Bedser	10	c Hutton b Bedser	7
MG Melle	b Shackleton	5	b Laker	17
CN McCarthy	not out	4	b Bedser	0
Extras	(11b, 8lb, 0w, 1nb)	20	(11b, 7lb, 0w, 0nb)	18
	106.3 overs		75.5 overs	
Total		**202**		**154**

1st innings FoW: 66, 106, 106, 106, 126, 131, 146, 175, 186, 202
2nd innings FoW: 15, 35, 57, 84, 106, 111, 116, 130, 153, 154

AV Bedser	19.3	6	36	2	19.5	6	32	3
D Shackleton	15	5	20	1	10	2	19	0
R Tattersall	14	7	26	1	5	1	10	1
JC Laker	37	12	64	4	28	8	55	6
FR Brown	20	10	31	2	13	5	20	0
DCS Compton	1	0	5	0				

ENGLAND 1st innings / 2nd innings

			2nd innings	
L Hutton	lbw b AMB Rowan	28	obstructing field	27
FA Lowson	c Endean b Melle	0	c Ry'ld b A Rowan	37
PBH May	b Chubb	33	c EAB b AMB Rowan	0
DCS Compton	b McCarthy	73	c Van Ryneveld b Chubb	18
W Watson	run out	31	c Endean b Chubb	15
FR Brown*	c Van Ry'ld b AMB Rowan	1	lbw b Chubb	40
JC Laker	b Chubb	6	not out	13
D Shackleton	c Van Ryneveld b Melle	14	not out	5
AV Bedser	c Endean b Melle	2		
DV Brennan+	lbw b Melle	0		
R Tattersall	not out	0		
Extras	(0b, 4lb, 0w, 2nb)	6	(5b, 3lb, 0w, 1nb)	9
	87 overs		62.1 overs	
Total		**194**		**164**

1st innings FoW: 2, 51, 79, 128, 134, 145, 173, 189, 190, 194
2nd innings FoW: 53, 53, 84, 90, 132, 151

CN McCarthy	17	0	45	1	7	0	17	0
MG Melle	10	6	9	4	3	0	8	0
AMB Rowan	27	9	44	2	24.1	2	77	2
GWA Chubb	30	5	70	2	28	10	53	3
CB Van Ryneveld	3	0	20	0				

No. 292: 1st Test
VENUE:	Delhi
DATE:	2nd-7th November 1951
TOSS WON BY:	England
RESULT:	Match drawn

No. 293: 2nd Test
VENUE:	Bombay (Brabourne)
DATE:	14th-19th December 1951
TOSS WON BY:	India
RESULT:	Match drawn

ENGLAND 1st innings

Batsman			2nd innings	
JDB Robertson	lbw b Shinde	50	c Phadkar b Mankad	22
FA Lowson	lbw b Phadkar	4	c Phadkar b Mankad	68
D Kenyon	b Shinde	35	c Roy b Shinde	6
DB Carr	c Joshi b Shinde	14	not out	137
AJ Watkins	c Joshi b Mankad	40	c Umrigar b Shinde	76
RT Spooner+	hit wkt b Shinde	11	b Mankad	1
ND Howard*	st Joshi b Mankad	13	lbw b Mankad	9
D Shackleton	st Joshi b Mankad	10	not out	21
JB Statham	b Shinde	4		
R Tattersall	not out	4		
F Ridgway	b Shinde	15		
Extras	(0b, 3lb, 0w, 0nb)	3	(18b, 7lb, 1w, 2nb)	28
	102.3 overs		221 overs	
Total		**203**		**368**

1st innings FoW: 9, 79, 102, 111, 153, 161, 175, 184, 184, 203
2nd innings FoW: 61, 78, 116, 274, 275, 309

DG Phadkar	11	4	26	1	14	3	28	0
NR Chowdhury	18	4	30	0	31	11	45	0
VS Hazare	5	5	0	0	12	4	24	0
MH Mankad	33	15	53	3	76	47	58	4
SG Shinde	35.3	9	91	6	73	26	162	2
PR Umrigar					6	1	8	0
RS Modi					5	1	14	0
Pank Roy					4	3	1	0

INDIA 1st innings   **2nd innings**

VM Merchant	b Statham	154
Pank Roy	lbw b Shackleton	12
PR Umrigar	run out	21
VS Hazare*	not out	164
DG Phadkar	run out	3
MH Mankad	c Spooner b Tattersall	4
RS Modi	lbw b Tattersall	7
HR Adhikari	not out	38
SG Shinde		
PG Joshi+		
NR Chowdhury		
Extras	(12b, 2lb, 0w, 1nb)	15
	175 overs	
Total		**418**

1st innings FoW: 18, 64, 275, 278, 292, 328

JB Statham	21	4	49	1
F Ridgway	20	1	55	0
AJ Watkins	31	7	60	0
D Shackleton	29	7	76	1
R Tattersall	53	17	95	2
DB Carr	16	4	56	0
JDB Robertson	5	1	12	0

INDIA 1st innings

Batsman			2nd innings	
Pank Roy	c Kenyon b Statham	140	lbw b Ridgway	0
MK Mantri+	c Spooner b Statham	39	c Spooner b Ridgway	7
PR Umrigar	lbw b Leadbeater	8	c Watkins b Statham	38
VS Hazare*	run out	155	c (sub) b Watkins	6
L Amarnath	c Howard b Tattersall	32	c Howard b Watkins	4
CT Sarwate	b Tattersall	18	run out	16
HR Adhikari	c Spooner b Tattersall	25	c Howard b Tattersall	15
CD Gopinath	not out	50	c Leadbeater b Tattersall	42
SW Sohoni	c Robertson b Statham	6	b Watkins	41
MH Mankad	b Statham	0	run out	28
SG Shinde	not out	8	not out	3
Extras	(0b, 4lb, 0w, 0nb)	4	(6b, 2lb, 0w, 0nb)	8
	139 overs		83.1 overs	
Total		**485**		**208**

1st innings FoW: 75, 99, 286, 368, 388, 397, 460, 471, 471
2nd innings FoW: 2, 13, 24, 34, 72, 77, 88, 159, 177, 208

JB Statham	29	5	96	4	20	11	30	1
F Ridgway	32	5	137	0	16	3	33	2
AJ Watkins	32	2	97	0	13	4	20	3
E Leadbeater	11	2	38	1	14.1	4	62	0
R Tattersall	34	8	112	3	20	6	55	2
JDB Robertson	1	0	1	0				

ENGLAND 1st innings

Batsman			2nd innings	
FA Lowson	c Mantri b Sohoni	5	c Sohoni b Gopinath	22
JDB Robertson	c Amarnath b Mankad	44	lbw b Sohoni	2
TW Graveney	c Adhikari b Shinde	175	not out	25
RT Spooner+	lbw b Hazare	46	not out	5
D Kenyon	lbw b Amarnath	21		
AJ Watkins	c & b Mankad	80		
ND Howard*	c Umrigar b Mankad	20		
E Leadbeater	lbw b Mankad	2		
JB Statham	c Mankad b Amarnath	27		
R Tattersall	not out	10		
F Ridgway	c & b Amarnath	5		
Extras	(10b, 11lb, 0w, 0nb)	21	(0b, 1lb, 0w, 0nb)	1
	207.1 overs		36 overs	
Total		**456**		**55**

1st innings FoW: 18, 79, 166, 233, 381, 389, 407, 408, 448, 456
2nd innings FoW: 3, 43

SW Sohoni	30	7	72	1	13	5	16	1
L Amarnath	34.1	9	61	3	5	1	6	0
SG Shinde	53	13	151	1	5	0	11	0
MH Mankad	57	22	91	4	5	1	10	0
CT Sarwate	13	2	27	0				
VS Hazare	17	5	30	1				
PR Umrigar	3	1	3	0				
CD Gopinath					8	2	11	1

	No. 294: 3rd Test		No. 295: 4th Test
	VENUE: Calcutta		VENUE: Kanpur
	DATE: 30th Dec 1951-4th Jan 1952		DATE: 12th-14th Jan 1952
	TOSS WON BY: England		TOSS WON BY: India
	RESULT: Match drawn		RESULT: England won by 8 wickets

ENGLAND 1st innings / 2nd innings

	1st innings		2nd innings	
JDB Robertson	c Phadkar b Divecha	13	st Sen b Mankad	22
RT Spooner+	c Sen b Mankad	71	b Mankad	92
TW Graveney	c Amarnath b Divecha	24	c Sen b Divecha	21
AJ Watkins	c Sen b Phadkar	68	b Divecha	2
D Kenyon	c Manjrekar b Mankad	3	b Phadkar	0
CJ Poole	c Divecha b Phadkar	55	not out	69
ND Howard*	c Amarnath b Mankad	23	not out	20
JB Statham	b Phadkar	1		
E Leadbeater	run out	38		
F Ridgway	st Sen b Mankad	24		
R Tattersall	not out	5		
Extras	(4b, 1lb, 1w, 11nb)	17	(13b, 6lb, 2w, 5nb)	26
Total	159.5 overs	342	120 overs	252

1st innings FoW: 22, 76, 133, 139, 246, 247, 259, 290, 332, 342

DG Phadkar	38	11	89	3	20	7	27	1
RV Divecha	33	9	60	2	25	7	55	2
L Amarnath	20	5	35	0	22	5	43	0
MH Mankad	52.5	16	89	4	35	13	64	2
SP Gupte	13	0	43	0	5	0	14	0
VS Hazare	3	0	9	0	9	4	11	0
PR Umrigar					4	1	12	0

INDIA 1st innings / 2nd innings

	1st innings		2nd innings	
Pank Roy	c Spooner b Ridgway	42	not out	31
MH Mankad	c Tattersall b Leadbeater	59	not out	71
PR Umrigar	c Howard b Ridgway	10		
VS Hazare*	b Tattersall	2		
L Amarnath	b Tattersall	0		
DG Phadkar	c Leadbeater b Ridgway	115		
VL Manjrekar	b Tattersall	48		
CD Gopinath	c Robertson b Ridgway	19		
RV Divecha	c Watkins b Tattersall	26		
SP Gupte	c Leadbeater b Statham	0		
P Sen+	not out	7		
Extras	(3b, 10lb, 1w, 2nb)	16	(1b, 0lb, 0w, 0nb)	1
Total	149.1 overs	344	29 overs	103

1st innings FoW: 72, 90, 93, 93, 144, 220, 272, 320, 327, 344
2nd innings FoW: 52, 93, 99, 102, 184

JB Statham	27	10	46	1	4	0	8	0
F Ridgway	38.1	10	83	4	2	1	8	0
R Tattersall	48	13	104	4	4	2	4	0
E Leadbeater	15	2	64	1	8	0	54	0
AJ Watkins	21	9	31	0				
CJ Poole					5	1	9	0
JDB Robertson					5	1	10	0
TW Graveney					1	0	9	0

INDIA 1st innings / 2nd innings

	1st innings		2nd innings	
Pank Roy	b Tattersall	37	c Ridgway b Hilton	14
MH Mankad	b Tattersall	19	c Statham b Hilton	7
PR Umrigar	b Tattersall	0	c Ridgway b Hilton	20
VS Hazare*	c Ridgway b Tattersall	0	b Hilton	9
DG Phadkar	b Tattersall	8	c Spooner b Robertson	36
HR Adhikari	b Hilton	6	lbw b Hilton	2
VL Manjrekar	c Graveney b Hilton	6	c Lowson b Tattersall	60
CS Nayudu	st Spooner b Hilton	21	b Robertson	0
PG Joshi+	b Tattersall	4	c Lowson b Tattersall	14
SG Shinde	not out	5	run out	0
Ghulam Ah'd	c Poole b Hilton	6	not out	2
Extras	(8b, 1lb, 0w, 0nb)	9	(2b, 0lb, 0w, 0nb)	2
Total	61.5 overs	121	66.5 overs	157

2nd innings FoW: 39, 39, 39, 49, 66, 76, 101, 106, 110, 121
2nd innings FoW: 7, 37, 37, 42, 44, 102, 102, 142, 143, 157

JB Statham	6	3	10	0				
F Ridgway	7	1	16	0				
AJ Watkins	5	3	6	0				
MJ Hilton	22.5	10	32	4	32	11	61	5
R Tattersall	21	3	48	6	27.5	7	77	2
JDB Robertson					7	1	17	2

ENGLAND 1st innings / 2nd innings

	1st innings		2nd innings	
FA Lowson	hit wkt b Mankad	26	c Adhikari b Ghulam	12
RT Spooner+	b Shinde	21	b Mankad	0
TW Graveney	b Mankad	6	not out	48
JDB Robertson	lbw b Mankad	21	not out	5
AJ Watkins	c Joshi b Ghulam	66		
MJ Hilton	st Joshi b Ghulam	10		
CJ Poole	b Ghulam	19		
ND Howard*	b Mankad	1		
JB Statham	not out	12		
F Ridgway	b Ghulam	5		
R Tattersall	st Joshi b Ghulam	2		
Extras	(13b, 1lb, 0w, 0nb)	14	(11b, 0lb, 0w, 0nb)	11
Total	95.1 overs	203	19.2 overs	76

1st innings FoW: 46, 57, 60, 103, 114, 175, 181, 181, 197, 203
2nd innings FoW: 1, 57

DG Phadkar	2	2	0	0	2	0	11	0
VS Hazare	2	0	5	0				
Ghulam Ahmed	37.1	14	70	5	10	1	10	1
MH Mankad	35	13	54	4	7.2	0	44	1
SG Shinde	17	4	46	1				
CS Nayudu	2	0	14	0				

No. 296: 5th Test	No. 297: 1st Test
VENUE: Madras (Chepauk)	VENUE: Headingley
DATE: 6th-10th February 1952	DATE: 5th-9th June 1952
TOSS WON BY: England	TOSS WON BY: India
RESULT: India won by an innings and 8 runs	RESULT: England won by 7 wickets

ENGLAND 1st innings / 2nd innings

Batsman	1st innings		2nd innings	
FA Lowson	b Phadkar	1	c Mankad b Phadkar	7
RT Spooner+	c Phadkar b Hazare	66	lbw b Divecha	6
TW Graveney	st Sen b Mankad	39	c Divecha b Ghulam	25
JDB Robertson	c & b Mankad	77	lbw b Ghulam	56
AJ Watkins	c Gopinath b Mankad	9	c & b Mankad	48
CJ Poole	b Mankad	15	c Divecha b Ghulam	3
DB Carr*	st Sen b Mankad	40	c Mankad b Ghulam	5
MJ Hilton	st Sen b Mankad	0	st Sen b Mankad	15
JB Statham	st Sen b Mankad	6	c Gopinath b Mankad	9
F Ridgway	lbw b Mankad	0	b Mankad	0
R Tattersall	not out	2	not out	0
Extras	(4b, 4lb, 0w, 3nb)	11	(7b, 2lb, 0w, 0nb)	9
Total	121.5 overs	**266**	75.5 overs	**183**

1st innings FoW: 3, 71, 131, 174, 197, 244, 252, 261, 261, 266
2nd innings FoW: 12, 15, 68, 117, 135, 159, 159, 178, 178, 183

Bowler									
DG Phadkar	16	2	49	1	9	2	17	1
RV Divecha	12	2	27	0	7	1	21	1
L Amarnath	27	6	56	0	3	0	6	0
Ghulam Ahmed	18	5	53	0	26	6	77	4
MH Mankad	38.5	15	55	8	30.5	9	53	4
VS Hazare	10	5	15	1				

INDIA 1st innings / 2nd innings

Batsman	1st innings		2nd innings
Mushtaq Ali	st Spooner b Carr	22	
Pank Roy	c Watkins b Tattersall	111	
VS Hazare*	b Hilton	20	
MH Mankad	c Watkins b Carr	22	
L Amarnath	c Spooner b Statham	31	
DG Phadkar	b Hilton	61	
PR Umrigar	not out	130	
CD Gopinath	b Tattersall	35	
RV Divecha	c Spooner b Ridgway	12	
P Sen+	b Watkins	2	
Ghulam Ah'd	not out	1	
Extras	(8b, 2lb, 0w, 0nb)	10	
Total	153 overs	**457**	

1st innings FoW: 53, 97, 157, 191, 216, 320, 413, 430, 448

Bowler				
JB Statham	19	3	54	1
F Ridgway	17	2	47	1
R Tattersall	39	13	94	2
MJ Hilton	40	9	100	2
DB Carr	19	2	84	2
AJ Watkins	14	1	50	1
JDB Robertson	5	1	18	0

INDIA 1st innings / 2nd innings

Batsman	1st innings		2nd innings	
Pank Roy	st Evans b Jenkins	19	c Compton b Trueman	0
DK Gaekwad	b Bedser	9	c Laker b Bedser	0
PR Umrigar	c Evans b Trueman	8	b Trueman	0
VS Hazare*	c Evans b Bedser	89	c & b Jenkins	9
VL Manjrekar	c Watkins b Trueman	133	b Trueman	0
DG Phadkar	c Watkins b Laker	12	b Trueman	56
CD Gopinath	b Trueman	0	b Bedser	64
MK Mantri+	not out	13	lbw b Jenkins	8
GS Ramchand	c Watkins b Laker	0	st Evans b Jenkins	0
SG Shinde	c May b Laker	2	not out	7
Ghulam Ah'd	b Laker	0	st Evans b Jenkins	14
Extras	(1b, 7lb, 0w, 0nb)	8	(0b, 5lb, 1w, 1nb)	7
Total	126.3 overs	**293**	67 overs	**165**

1st innings FoW: 18, 40, 42, 264, 264, 264, 291, 291, 293, 293
2nd innings FoW: 0, 0, 0, 0, 26, 131, 143, 143, 143, 165

Bowler									
AV Bedser	33	13	38	2	21	9	32	2
FS Trueman	26	6	89	3	9	1	27	4
JC Laker	22.3	9	39	4	13	4	17	0
AJ Watkins	11	1	21	0	11	2	32	0
RO Jenkins	27	6	78	1	13	2	50	4
DCS Compton	7	1	20	0				

ENGLAND 1st innings / 2nd innings

Batsman	1st innings		2nd innings	
L Hutton*	c Ramchand b Ghulam	10	b Phadkar	10
RT Simpson	c Ramchand b Ghulam	23	c Mantri b Ghulam	51
PBH May	b Shinde	16	c Phadkar b Ghulam	4
DCS Compton	c Ramchand b Ghulam	14	not out	35
TW Graveney	b Ghulam	71	not out	20
AJ Watkins	lbw b Ghulam	48	
TG Evans+	lbw b Hazare	66	
RO Jenkins	c Mantri b Ramchand	38	
JC Laker	b Phadkar	15	
AV Bedser	b Ramchand	7	
FS Trueman	not out	0	
Extras	(15b, 11lb, 0w, 0nb)	26	(4b, 3lb, 0w, 1nb)	8
Total	165.2 overs	**334**	55 overs	**128**

1st innings FoW: 21, 48, 62, 92, 182, 211, 290, 325, 329, 334
2nd innings FoW: 16, 42, 89

Bowler									
DG Phadkar	24	7	54	1	11	2	21	1
GS Ramchand	36.2	11	61	2	17	3	43	0
Ghulam Ahmed	63	24	100	5	22	8	37	2
VS Hazare	20	9	22	1	3	0	11	0
SG Shinde	22	5	71	1	2	0	8	0

India	India

No. 298: 2nd Test	No. 299: 3rd Test
VENUE: Lord's	VENUE: Old Trafford
DATE: 19th-24th June 1952	DATE: 17th-19th July 1952
TOSS WON BY: India	TOSS WON BY: England
RESULT: England won by 8 wickets	RESULT: Eng won by an innings and 207 runs

Left — No. 298: 2nd Test

INDIA 1st innings / 2nd innings

INDIA 1st innings			2nd innings	
MH Mankad	c Watkins b Trueman	72	b Laker	184
Pank Roy	c & b Bedser	35	b Bedser	0
PR Umrigar	b Trueman	5	b Trueman	16
VS Hazare*	not out	69	c Laker b Bedser	49
VL Manjrekar	lbw b Bedser	5	b Laker	1
DG Phadkar	b Watkins	8	b Laker	16
HR Adhikari	lbw b Watkins	0	b Trueman	14
GS Ramchand	b Trueman	18	c Compton b Laker	5
MK Mantri+	b Trueman	1	b Trueman	42
SG Shinde	st Evans b Watkins	5	c Hutton b Trueman	14
Ghulam Ah'd	b Jenkins	0	not out	1
Extras	(7b, 0lb, 0w, 10nb)	17	(29b, 3lb, 0w, 4nb)	36
	94.3 overs		122 overs	
Total		**235**		**378**

1st innings FoW: 106, 116, 118, 126, 135, 139,167, 180, 221, 235
2nd innings FoW: 7, 59, 270, 272, 289, 312, 314, 323, 377, 378

AV Bedser	33	8	62	2	36	13	60	2
FS Trueman	25	3	72	4	27	4	110	4
RO Jenkins	7.3	1	26	1	10	1	40	0
JC Laker	12	5	21	0	39	15	102	4
AJ Watkins	17	7	37	3	8	0	20	0
DCS Compton					2	0	10	0

ENGLAND 1st innings / 2nd innings

ENGLAND 1st innings			2nd innings	
L Hutton*	c Mantri b Hazare	150	not out	39
RT Simpson	b Mankad	53	run out	2
PBH May	c Mantri b Mankad	74	c Roy b Ghulam	26
DCS Compton	lbw b Hazare	6	not out	4
TW Graveney	c Mantri b Ghulam	73		
AJ Watkins	b Mankad	0		
TG Evans+	c & b Ghulam	104		
RO Jenkins	st Mantri b Mankad	21		
JC Laker	not out	23		
AV Bedser	c Ramchand b Mankad	3		
FS Trueman	b Ghulam	17		
Extras	(8b, 5lb, 0w, 0nb)	13	(4b, 4lb, 0w, 0nb)	8
	206.4 overs		49.2 overs	
Total		**537**		**79**

1st innings FoW: 106, 264, 272, 292, 292, 451, 468, 506, 514, 537
2nd innings FoW: 8, 71

DG Phadkar	27	8	44	0				
GS Ramchand	29	8	67	0	1	0	5	0
VS Hazare	24	4	53	2	1	1	0	0
MH Mankad	73	24	196	5	24	12	35	0
Ghulam Ahmed	43.4	12	106	3	23.2	9	31	1
SG Shinde	6	0	43	0				
PR Umrigar	4	0	15	0				

Right — No. 299: 3rd Test

ENGLAND 1st innings / 2nd innings

ENGLAND 1st innings			2nd innings
L Hutton*	c Sen b Divecha	104	
DS Sheppard	lbw b Ramchand	34	
JT Ikin	c Divecha b Ghulam	29	
PBH May	c Sen b Mankad	69	
TW Graveney	lbw b Divecha	14	
AJ Watkins	c Phadkar b Mankad	4	
TG Evans+	c & b Ghulam	71	
JC Laker	c Sen b Divecha	0	
AV Bedser	c Phadkar b Ghulam	17	
GAR Lock	not out	1	
FS Trueman			
Extras	(2b, 2lb, 0w, 0nb)	4	
	144 overs		
Total		**347**	

1st innings FoW: 78, 133, 214, 248, 252, 284, 292, 336, 347
2nd innings FoW: 7, 7, 55, 59, 66, 66, 66, 67, 77, 82

DG Phadkar	22	10	30	0
RV Divecha	45	12	102	3
GS Ramchand	33	7	78	1
MH Mankad	28	9	67	2
Ghulam Ahmed	9	3	43	3
VS Hazare	7	3	23	0

INDIA 1st innings / 2nd innings

INDIA 1st innings			2nd innings	
MH Mankad	c Lock b Bedser	4	lbw b Bedser	6
Pank Roy	c Hutton b Trueman	0	c Laker b Trueman	0
HR Adhikari	c Graveney b Trueman	0	c May b Lock	27
VS Hazare*	b Bedser	16	c Ikin b Lock	16
PR Umrigar	b Trueman	4	c Watkins b Bedser	3
DG Phadkar	c Sheppard b Trueman	0	b Bedser	5
VL Manjrekar	c Ikin b Trueman	22	c Evans b Bedser	0
RV Divecha	b Trueman	4	b Bedser	2
GS Ramchand	c Graveney b Trueman	2	c Watkins b Lock	1
P Sen+	c Lock b Trueman	4	not out	13
Ghulam Ah'd	not out	1	c Ikin b Lock	0
Extras	(0b, 1lb, 0w, 0nb)	1	(8b, 0lb, 0w, 1nb)	9
	21.4 overs		36.3 overs	
Total		**58**		**82**

1st innings FoW: 4, 4, 5, 17, 17, 45, 51, 53, 53, 58

AV Bedser	11	4	19	2	15	6	27	5
FS Trueman	8.4	2	31	8	8	5	9	1
JC Laker	2	0	7	0	4	3	1	0
GAR Lock					9.3	2	36	4

No. 300: 4th Test	No. 301: 1st Test
VENUE: The Oval	VENUE: Trent Bridge
DATE: 14th-19th August 1952	DATE: 11th-16th June 1953
TOSS WON BY: England	TOSS WON BY: Australia
RESULT: Match drawn	RESULT: Match drawn

ENGLAND	1st innings		2nd innings
L Hutton*	c Phadkar b Ramchand	86	
DS Sheppard	lbw b Divecha	119	
JT Ikin	c Sen b Phadkar	53	
PBH May	c Manjrekar b Mankad	17	
TW Graveney	c Divecha b Ghulam	13	
W Watson	not out	18	
TG Evans+	c Phadkar b Mankad	1	
JC Laker	not out	6	
AV Bedser			
GAR Lock			
FS Trueman			
Extras	(10b, 2lb, 0w, 1nb)	13	
	154 overs		
Total		**326**	

1st innings FoW: 143, 261, 273, 293, 304, 307

RV Divecha	33	9	60	1
DG Phadkar	32	8	61	1
GS Ramchand	14	2	50	1
MH Mankad	48	23	88	2
Ghulam Ahmed	24	1	54	1
VS Hazare	3	3	0	0

INDIA	1st innings		2nd innings
MH Mankad	c Evans b Trueman	5	
Pank Roy	c Lock b Trueman	0	
HR Adhikari	c Trueman b Bedser	0	
VS Hazare*	c May b Trueman	38	
VL Manjrekar	c Ikin b Bedser	1	
PR Umrigar	b Bedser	0	
DG Phadkar	b Trueman	17	
RV Divecha	b Bedser	16	
GS Ramchand	c Hutton b Bedser	5	
P Sen+	b Trueman	9	
Ghulam Ah'd	not out	2	
Extras	(0b, 3lb, 0w, 2nb)	5	
	38.5 overs		
Total		**98**	

1st innings FoW: 0, 5, 5, 6, 6, 64, 71, 78, 94, 98

AV Bedser	14.5	4	41	5
FS Trueman	16	4	48	5
GAR Lock	6	5	1	0
JC Laker	2	0	3	0

Australia	1st innings		2nd innings	
GB Hole	b Bedser	0	b Bedser	5
AR Morris	lbw b Bedser	67	b Tattersall	60
AL Hassett*	b Bedser	115	c Hutton b Bedser	5
RN Harvey	c Compton b Bedser	0	c Graveney b Bedser	2
KR Miller	c Bailey b Wardle	55	c Kenyon b Bedser	5
R Benaud	c Evans b Bailey	3	b Bedser	0
AK Davidson	b Bedser	4	c Graveney b Tattersall	6
D Tallon+	b Bedser	0	c Simpson b Tattersall	15
RR Lindwall	c Evans b Bailey	0	c Tattersall b Bedser	12
JC Hill	b Bedser	0	c Tattersall b Bedser	4
WA Johnston	not out	0	not out	4
Extras	(2b, 2lb, 0w, 1nb)	5	(0b, 5lb, 0w, 0nb)	5
	140.3 overs		39.2 overs	
Total		**249**		**123**

1st innings FoW: 2, 124, 128, 237, 244, 244, 246, 247, 248, 249
2nd innings FoW: 28, 44, 50, 64, 68, 81, 92, 106, 115, 123

AV Bedser	38.3	16	55	7	17.2	7	44	7
TE Bailey	44	14	75	2	5	1	28	0
JH Wardle	35	16	55	1	12	3	24	0
R Tattersall	23	5	59	0	5	0	22	3

ENGLAND	1st innings		2nd innings	
L Hutton*	c Benaud b Davidson	43	not out	60
D Kenyon	c Hill b Lindwall	8	c Hassett b Hill	16
RT Simpson	lbw b Lindwall	0	not out	28
DCS Compton	c Morris b Lindwall	0		
TW Graveney	c Benaud b Hill	22		
PBH May	c Tallon b Hill	9		
TE Bailey	lbw b Hill	13		
TG Evans+	c Tallon b Davidson	8		
JH Wardle	not out	29		
AV Bedser	lbw b Lindwall	2		
R Tattersall	b Lindwall	2		
Extras	(5b, 3lb, 0w, 0nb)	8	(8b, 4lb, 2w, 2nb)	16
	72.4 overs		58 overs	
Total		**144**		**120**

1st innings FoW: 17, 17, 17, 76, 82, 92, 107, 121, 136, 144
2nd innings FoW: 26

RR Lindwall	20.4	2	57	5	16	4	37	0
WA Johnston	18	7	22	0	18	9	14	0
JC Hill	19	8	35	3	12	3	26	1
AK Davidson	15	7	22	2	5	1	7	0
R Benaud					5	0	15	0
AR Morris					2	0	5	0

No. 302: 2nd Test	No. 303: 3rd Test
VENUE: Lord's	VENUE: Old Trafford
DATE: 25th-30th June 1953	DATE: 9th-14th July 1953
TOSS WON BY: Australia	TOSS WON BY: Australia
RESULT: Match drawn	RESULT: Match drawn

No. 302

Australia	1st innings		2nd innings	
AL Hassett*	c Bailey b Bedser	104	c Evans b Statham	3
AR Morris	st Evans b Bedser	30	c Statham b Compton	89
RN Harvey	lbw b Bedser	59	b Wardle	109
KR Miller	lbw b Wardle	25	b Bedser	21
GB Hole	c Compton b Wardle	13	lbw b Brown	47
R Benaud	lbw b Wardle	0	c Graveney b Bedser	5
AK Davidson	c Statham b Bedser	76	c & b Brown	15
DT Ring	b Wardle	18	lbw b Brown	7
RR Lindwall	b Statham	9	b Bedser	50
GRA Langley+	c Watson b Bedser	1	b Brown	9
WA Johnston	not out	3	not out	0
Extras	(4b, 4lb, 0w, 0nb)	8	(8b, 5lb, 0w, 0nb)	13
Total	140.4 overs	**346**	132.5 overs	**368**

1st innings FoW: 65, 190, 225, 229, 240, 280, 291, 330, 331, 346
2nd innings FoW: 3, 168, 227, 235, 248, 296, 305, 308, 362, 368

AV Bedser	42.4	8	105	5	31.5	8	77	3
JB Statham	28	7	48	1	15	3	40	1
FR Brown	25	7	53	0	27	4	82	4
TE Bailey	16	2	55	0	10	4	24	0
JH Wardle	29	8	77	4	46	18	111	1
DCS Compton					3	0	21	1

ENGLAND	1st innings		2nd innings	
L Hutton*	c Hole b Johnston	145	c Hole b Lindwall	5
D Kenyon	c Davidson b Lindwall	3	c Hassett b Lindwall	2
TW Graveney	b Lindwall	78	c Langley b Johnston	2
DCS Compton	c Hole b Benaud	57	lbw b Johnston	33
W Watson	st Langley b Johnston	4	c Hole b Ring	109
TE Bailey	c & b Miller	2	c Benaud b Ring	71
FR Brown	c Langley b Lindwall	22	c Hole b Benaud	28
TG Evans+	b Lindwall	0	not out	11
JH Wardle	b Davidson	23	not out	0
AV Bedser	b Lindwall	1		
JB Statham	not out	17		
Extras	(11b, 1lb, 1w, 7nb)	20	(7b, 6lb, 2w, 6nb)	21
Total	126.5 overs	**372**	126 overs	**282**

1st innings FoW: 9, 177, 279, 291, 301, 328, 328, 332, 341, 372
2nd innings FoW: 6, 10, 12, 73, 236, 246, 282

RR Lindwall	23	4	66	5	19	3	26	2
KR Miller	25	6	57	1	17	8	17	0
WA Johnston	35	11	91	2	29	10	70	2
DT Ring	14	2	43	0	29	5	84	2
R Benaud	19	4	70	1	17	6	51	1
AK Davidson	10.5	2	25	1	14	5	13	0
GB Hole					1	1	0	0

No. 303

Australia	1st innings		2nd innings	
AL Hassett*	b Bailey	26	c Bailey b Bedser	8
AR Morris	b Bedser	1	c Hutton b Laker	0
KR Miller	b Bedser	17	st Evans b Laker	6
RN Harvey	c Evans b Bedser	122	c Evans b Bedser	2
GB Hole	c Evans b Bedser	66	st Evans b Wardle	8
JH De Courcy	lbw b Wardle	41	not out	4
AK Davidson	st Evans b Laker	15	b Wardle	0
RG Archer	c Compton b Bedser	5	lbw b Wardle	0
RR Lindwall	c Edrich b Wardle	1	b Wardle	4
JC Hill	not out	8	not out	0
GRA Langley+	c Edrich b Wardle	8		
Extras	(6b, 1lb, 0w, 1nb)	8	(0b, 3lb, 0w, 0nb)	3
Total	116.3 overs	**318**	18 overs	**35**

1st innings FoW: 15, 48, 48, 221, 256, 285, 290, 291, 302, 318
2nd innings FoW: 8, 12, 18, 18, 31, 31, 31, 35

AV Bedser	45	10	115	5	4	1	14	2
TE Bailey	26	4	83	1				
JH Wardle	28.3	10	70	3	5	2	7	4
JC Laker	17	3	42	1	9	5	11	2

ENGLAND	1st innings		2nd innings
L Hutton*	lbw b Lindwall	66	
WJ Edrich	c Hole b Hill	6	
TW Graveney	c De Courcy b Miller	5	
DCS Compton	c Langley b Archer	45	
JH Wardle	b Lindwall	5	
W Watson	b Davidson	16	
RT Simpson	c Langley b Davidson	31	
TE Bailey	c Hole b Hill	27	
TG Evans+	not out	44	
JC Laker	lbw b Hill	5	
AV Bedser	b Morris	10	
Extras	(8b, 8lb, 0w, 0nb)	16	
Total	120 overs	**276**	

1st innings FoW: 19, 32, 126, 126, 149, 149, 209, 231, 243, 276

RR Lindwall	20	8	30	2
RG Archer	15	8	12	1
JC Hill	35	7	97	3
KR Miller	24	11	38	1
AK Davidson	20	4	60	2
RN Harvey	3	2	2	0
GB Hole	2	0	16	0
AR Morris	1	0	5	1

No. 304: 4th Test

VENUE:	Headingley
DATE:	23rd-28th July 1953
TOSS WON BY:	Australia
RESULT:	Match drawn

ENGLAND

1st innings			2nd innings	
L Hutton*	b Lindwall	0	c Langley b Archer	25
WJ Edrich	lbw b Miller	10	c De Courcy b Lindwall	64
TW Graveney	c Benaud b Miller	55	b Lindwall	3
DCS Compton	c Davidson b Lindwall	0	lbw b Lindwall	61
W Watson	b Lindwall	24	c Davidson b Miller	15
RT Simpson	c Langley b Lindwall	15	c De Courcy b Miller	0
TE Bailey	run out	7	c Hole b Davidson	38
TG Evans+	lbw b Lindwall	25	c Lindwall b Miller	1
JC Laker	c Lindwall b Archer	10	c Benaud b Davidson	48
GAR Lock	b Davidson	9	c Morris b Miller	8
AV Bedser	not out	0	not out	3
Extras	(8b, 4lb, 0w, 0nb)	12	(1b, 8lb, 0w, 0nb)	9
	109.4 overs		177.3 overs	
Total		**167**		**275**

1st innings FoW: 0, 33, 36, 98, 108, 110, 133, 149, 167, 167
2nd innings FoW: 57, 62, 139, 167, 171, 182, 239, 244, 258, 275

RR Lindwall	35	10	54	5	54	19	104	3
KR Miller	28	13	39	2	47	19	63	4
AK Davidson	20.4	7	23	1	29.3	15	36	2
RG Archer	18	4	27	1	25	12	31	1
R Benaud	8	1	12	0	19	8	26	0
GB Hole					3	1	6	0

Australia

1st innings			2nd innings	
AL Hassett*	c Lock b Bedser	37		
AR Morris	c Lock b Bedser	10	b Lock	4
RN Harvey	lbw b Bailey	71	st Evans b Laker	38
KR Miller	c Edrich b Bailey	5	c Graveney b Bailey	33
GB Hole	c Lock b Bedser	53	lbw b Bedser	34
JH De Courcy	lbw b Lock	10	not out	17
R Benaud	b Bailey	7	not out	13
AK Davidson	c Evans b Bedser	2		
RG Archer	not out	31		
RR Lindwall	b Bedser	9		
GRA Langley+	c Hutton b Bedser	17		
Extras	(4b, 8lb, 2w, 0nb)	14	(3b, 4lb, 1w, 0nb)	8
	82.5 overs		33 overs	
Total		**266**		**147**

1st innings FoW: 27, 70, 84, 168, 183, 203, 203, 208, 218, 266
2nd innings FoW: 27, 54, 111, 117

AV Bedser	28.5	2	95	6	17	1	65	1
TE Bailey	22	4	71	3	6	1	9	1
GAR Lock	23	9	53	1	8	1	48	1
JC Laker	9	1	33	0	2	0	17	1

No. 305: 5th Test

VENUE:	The Oval
DATE:	15th-19th August 1953
TOSS WON BY:	Australia
RESULT:	England won by 8 wickets

Australia

1st innings			2nd innings	
AL Hassett*	c Evans b Bedser	53	lbw b Laker	10
AR Morris	lbw b Bedser	16	lbw b Lock	26
KR Miller	lbw b Bailey	1	lbw b Laker	17
RN Harvey	c Hutton b Trueman	36	b Lock	1
GB Hole	c Evans b Trueman	37	c Trueman b Laker	0
JH De Courcy	c Evans b Trueman	5	run out	4
RG Archer	c & b Bedser	10	c Edrich b Lock	49
AK Davidson	c Edrich b Bedser	22	b Lock	21
RR Lindwall	c Evans b Trueman	62	c Compton b Laker	12
GRA Langley+	c Edrich b Lock	18	c Trueman b Lock	2
WA Johnston	not out	9	not out	6
Extras	(4b, 0lb, 0w, 2nb)	6	(11b, 3lb, 0w, 0nb)	14
	81.3 overs		50.5 overs	
Total		**275**		**162**

1st innings FoW: 38, 41, 107, 107, 118, 160, 160, 207, 245, 275
2nd innings FoW: 23, 59, 60, 61, 61, 85, 135, 140, 144, 162

AV Bedser	29	3	88	3	11	2	24	0
FS Trueman	24.3	3	86	4	2	1	4	0
TE Bailey	14	3	42	1				
GAR Lock	9	2	19	1	21	9	45	5
JC Laker	5	0	34	1	16.5	2	75	4

ENGLAND

1st innings			2nd innings	
L Hutton*	b Johnston	82	run out	17
WJ Edrich	lbw b Lindwall	21	not out	55
PBH May	c Archer b Johnston	39	c Davidson b Miller	37
DCS Compton	c Langley b Lindwall	16	not out	22
TW Graveney	c Miller b Lindwall	4		
TE Bailey	b Archer	64		
TG Evans+	run out	28		
JC Laker	c Langley b Miller	1		
GAR Lock	c Davidson b Lindwall	4		
FS Trueman	b Johnston	10		
AV Bedser	not out	22		
Extras	(9b, 5lb, 1w, 0nb)	15	(0b, 1lb, 0w, 0nb)	1
	142.3 overs		63.5 overs	
Total		**306**		**132**

1st innings FoW: 37, 137, 154, 167, 170, 210, 225, 237, 262, 306
2nd innings FoW: 24, 88

RR Lindwall	32	7	70	4	21	5	46	0
KR Miller	34	12	65	1	11	3	24	0
WA Johnston	45	16	94	3	29	14	52	0
AK Davidson	10	1	26	0				
RG Archer	10.3	2	25	1	1	1	0	0
GB Hole	11	6	11	0				
AL Hassett					1	0	4	0
AR Morris					0.5	0	5	0

No. 306: 1st Test
VENUE: Kingston (Jamaica)
DATE: 15th-21st January 1954
TOSS WON BY: West Indies
RESULT: West Indies won by 140 runs

No. 307: 2nd Test
VENUE: Bridgetown (Barbados)
DATE: 6th-12th February 1954
TOSS WON BY: West Indies
RESULT: West Indies won by 181 runs

WEST INDIES 1st innings **2nd innings**

MC Frederick	c Graveney b Statham	0	lbw b Statham		30
Stollmeyer*	lbw b Statham	60	c Evans b Bailey		8
JK Holt	lbw b Statham	94	lbw b Moss		1
EdeC Weekes	b Moss	55	not out		90
CL Walcott	b Lock	65	c Bailey b Lock		25
GA Headley	c Graveney b Lock	16	b Lock		1
GE Gomez	not out	47	lbw b Statham		3
CA McWatt+	b Lock	54	not out		36
S Ramadhin	lbw b Trueman	7			
ESM Kentish	b Statham	0			
AL Valentine	b Trueman	0			
Extras	(9b, 4lb, 1w, 5nb)	19	(10b, 4lb, 0w, 1nb)		15
	155.4 overs		67 overs		
Total		**417**			**209**

1st innings FoW: 6, 140, 216, 234, 286, 316, 404, 415, 416, 417
2nd innings FoW: 28, 31, 46, 92, 94, 119

JB Statham	36	6	90	4	17	2	50	2
FS Trueman	34.4	8	107	2	6	0	32	0
AE Moss	26	5	84	1	10	0	30	1
TE Bailey	16	4	36	0	20	4	46	1
GAR Lock	41	14	76	3	14	2	36	2
DCS Compton	2	1	5	0				

ENGLAND 1st innings **2nd innings**

W Watson	b Gomez	3	c & b Stollmeyer		116
L Hutton*	b Valentine	24	lbw b Gomez		56
PBH May	c Headley b Ramadhin	31	c McWatt b Kentish		69
DCS Compton	lbw b Valentine	12	c Weekes b Kentish		34
TW Graveney	lbw b Ramadhin	16	b Ramadhin		2
TE Bailey	not out	28	not out		15
TG Evans+	c Kentish b Valentine	10	b Kentish		0
GAR Lock	b Ramadhin	4	b Kentish		0
JB Statham	b Ramadhin	8	lbw b Ramadhin		1
FS Trueman	c McWatt b Gomez	18	b Kentish		1
AE Moss	b Gomez	0	run out		16
Extras	(9b, 2lb, 1w, 4nb)	16	(4b, 1lb, 0w, 1nb)		6
	89.2 overs		129.3 overs		
Total		**170**			**316**

1st innings FoW: 4, 49, 73, 79, 94, 105, 117, 135, 165, 170
2nd innings FoW: 130, 220, 277, 282, 282, 282, 282, 283, 285, 316

ESM Kentish	14	5	23	0	29	11	49	5
GE Gomez	9.2	3	16	3	30	9	63	1
S Ramadhin	35	14	65	4	35.3	12	88	2
AL Valentine	31	10	50	3	25	6	71	0
GA Headley					5	0	23	0
CL Walcott					2	1	4	0
JB Stollmeyer					3	0	12	1

WEST INDIES 1st innings **2nd innings**

JK Holt	c Graveney b Bailey	11	c & b Statham		166
Stollmeyer*	run out	0	run out		28
FMM Worrell	b Statham	0	not out		76
CL Walcott	st Evans b Laker	220	not out		17
BH Pairaudeau	c Hutton b Laker	71			
GE Gomez	lbw b Statham	7			
DStE Atkinson	c Evans b Laker	53			
CA McWatt+	lbw b Lock	11			
S Ramadhin	b Statham	1			
FM King	b Laker	5			
AL Valentine	not out	0			
Extras	(0b, 2lb, 0w, 2nb)	4	(4b, 0lb, 0w, 1nb)		5
	125.1 overs		96 overs		
Total		**383**			**292**

1st innings FoW: 11, 11, 25, 190, 226, 319, 352, 372, 378, 383
2nd innings FoW: 51, 273

JB Statham	27	6	90	3	15	1	49	1
TE Bailey	22	6	63	1	12	1	48	0
GAR Lock	41	9	116	1	33	7	100	0
JC Laker	30.1	6	81	4	30	13	62	0
DCS Compton	5	0	29	0	1	0	13	0
CH Palmer					5	1	15	0

ENGLAND 1st innings **2nd innings**

L Hutton*	c Ramadhin b Valentine	72	c Worrell b Ramadhin		77
W Watson	st McWatt b Ramadhin	6	c McWatt b King		0
PBH May	c King b Ramadhin	7	c Walcott b Gomez		62
DCS Compton	c King b Valentine	13	lbw b Stollmeyer		93
TW Graveney	c & b Ramadhin	15	not out		64
CH Palmer	c Walcott b Ramadhin	22	c Gomez b Atkinson		0
TE Bailey	c McWatt b Atkinson	28	c (sub) b Stollmeyer		4
TG Evans+	b Gomez	10	b Ramadhin		5
JC Laker	c Gomez b Atkinson	1	lbw b Ramadhin		0
GAR Lock	not out	0	b King		0
JB Statham	c Holt b Valentine	3	b Gomez		0
Extras	(2b, 1lb, 0w, 1nb)	4	(6b, 1lb, 1w, 0nb)		8
	150.5 overs		139.4 overs		
Total		**181**			**313**

1st innings FoW: 35, 45, 70, 107, 119, 158, 176, 176, 177, 181
2nd innings FoW: 1, 108, 181, 258, 259, 264, 281, 281, 300, 313

FM King	14	6	28	0	18	6	56	2
GE Gomez	13	8	10	1	13.4	3	28	2
FMM Worrell	9	2	21	0	1	0	10	0
DStE Atkinson	9	7	5	2	23	10	35	1
S Ramadhin	53	30	50	4	37	17	71	3
AL Valentine	51.5	30	61	3	39	18	87	0
JB Stollmeyer	1	0	2	0	6	1	14	2
CL Walcott					2	0	4	0

No. 308: 3rd Test
VENUE: Georgetown (Guyana)
DATE: 24th Feb-2nd March 1954
TOSS WON BY: England
RESULT: England won by 9 wickets

ENGLAND	1st innings		2nd innings	
W Watson	b Ramadhin	12	not out	27
L Hutton*	c Worrell b Ramadhin	169		
PBH May	lbw b Atkinson	12	b Atkinson	12
DCS Compton	c Stollmeyer b Atkinson	64		
TW Graveney	b Ramadhin	0	not out	33
JH Wardle	b Ramadhin	38		
TE Bailey	c Weekes b Ramadhin	49		
TG Evans+	lbw b Atkinson	19		
JC Laker	b Valentine	27		
GAR Lock	b Ramadhin	13		
JB Statham	not out	10		
Extras	(20b, 0lb, 0w, 2nb)	22	(3b, 0lb, 0w, 0nb)	3
	220 overs		20.1 overs	
Total		**435**		**75**

1st innings FoW: 33, 76, 226, 227, 306, 321, 350, 390, 412, 435
2nd innings FoW: 18

GE Gomez	32	6	75	0	5	1	15	0	
FMM Worrell	15	4	33	0					
S Ramadhin	67	34	113	6	4	0	7	0	
AL Valentine	44	18	109	1					
DStE Atkinson	58	27	78	3	7	0	34	1	
JB Stollmeyer	2	1	3	0					
CL Walcott	2	0	2	0	2	0	6	0	
EdeC Weekes					1.1	0	8	0	
RJ Christiani					1	0	2	0	

WEST INDIES	1st innings		2nd innings	
FMM Worrell	c Evans b Statham	0	b Lock	64
Stollmeyer*	b Statham	2	c Compton b Laker	44
EdeC Weekes	b Lock	94	c Evans b Statham	2
CL Walcott	b Statham	4	c Graveney b Bailey	38
RJ Christiani	c Watson b Laker	25	lbw b Laker	26
GE Gomez	b Statham	8	b Bailey	11
DStE Atkinson	c & b Lock	0	c Graveney b Wardle	35
CA McWatt+	run out	54	b Wardle	18
JK Holt	not out	48	not out	9
S Ramadhin	b Laker	0	b Statham	1
AL Valentine	run out	0	b Wardle	0
Extras	(8b, 7lb, 1w, 0nb)	16	(2b, 4lb, 0w, 2nb)	8
	105.5 overs		117.3 overs	
Total		**251**		**256**

1st innings FoW: 1, 12, 16, 78, 132, 134, 139, 238, 240, 251
2nd innings FoW: 79, 96, 120, 168, 186, 200, 245, 246, 251, 256

JB Statham	27	6	64	4	22	3	86	2	
TE Bailey	5	0	13	0	22	9	41	2	
JC Laker	21	11	32	2	36	18	56	2	
JH Wardle	22	4	60	0	12.3	4	24	3	
DCS Compton	3	1	6	0					
GAR Lock	27.5	7	60	2	25	11	41	1	

No. 309: 4th Test
VENUE: Port-of-Spain (Trinidad)
DATE: 17th-23rd March 1954
TOSS WON BY: West Indies
RESULT: Match drawn

WEST INDIES	1st innings		2nd innings	
JK Holt	c Compton b Trueman	40	hit wkt b Bailey	5
JB Stollmeyer*	c & b Compton	41	b Bailey	44
EdeC Weekes	c Bailey b Lock	206	c (sub) b Trueman	1
FMM Worrell	b Lock	167	c (sub) b Lock	56
CL Walcott	c & b Laker	124	not out	51
BH Pairaudeau	run out	0	not out	53
DStE Atkinson	c Graveney b Compton	74		
CA McWatt+	b Laker	4		
W Ferguson	not out	8		
S Ramadhin				
FM King				
Extras	(6b, 4lb, 4w, 3nb)	17	(0b, 2lb, 0w, 0nb)	2
	198.4 overs		55 overs	
Total		**681**		**212**

1st innings FoW: 78, 92, 430, 517, 540, 627, 641, 681
2nd innings FoW: 19, 20, 72, 111

JB Statham	9	0	31	0					
FS Trueman	33	3	131	1	15	5	23	1	
TE Bailey	32	7	104	1	12	2	20	2	
JC Laker	50	8	154	2					
GAR Lock	63	14	178	2	10	2	40	1	
DCS Compton	8.4	1	40	2	7	0	51	0	
TW Graveney	3	0	26	0	5	0	33	0	
L Hutton					6	0	43	0	

ENGLAND	1st innings		2nd innings	
L Hutton*	c Ferguson b King	44	c Ferguson b Worrell	32
TE Bailey	c Weekes b Ferguson	46	c Ferguson b Ramadhin	16
PBH May	c Pairaudeau b King	135	c Worrell b McWatt	16
DCS Compton	c & b Ramadhin	133	not out	30
W Watson	c Atkinson b Walcott	4	not out	0
TW Graveney	c & b Walcott	92		
RT Spooner+	b Walcott	19		
JC Laker	retired hurt	7		
GAR Lock	lbw b Worrell	10		
FS Trueman	lbw b King	19		
JB Statham	not out	6		
Extras	(10b, 5lb, 7w, 0nb)	22	(0b, 4lb, 0w, 0nb)	4
	221.2 overs		30 overs	
Total		**537**		**98**

1st innings FoW: 73, 135, 301, 314, 424, 493, 496, 510, 537
2nd innings FoW: 52, 52, 83

FM King	48.2	16	97	3					
FMM Worrell	20	2	58	1	9	1	29	1	
S Ramadhin	34	13	74	1	7	4	6	1	
DStE Atkinson	32	12	60	0	4	0	12	0	
W Ferguson	47	7	155	1					
JB Stollmeyer	6	2	19	0					
CL Walcott	34	18	52	3					
EdeC Weekes					5	1	28	0	
CA McWatt					4	2	16	1	
BH Pairaudeau					1	0	3	0	

West Indies

No. 310:	5th Test
VENUE:	Kingston (Jamaica)
DATE:	30th March-3rd April 1954
TOSS WON BY:	West Indies
RESULT:	England won by 9 wickets

Pakistan

No. 311	1st Test
VENUE:	Lord's
DATE:	10th-15th June 1954
TOSS WON BY:	England
RESULT:	Match drawn

WEST INDIES 1st innings

		1st		2nd	
JK Holt	c Lock b Bailey	0	c Lock b Trueman	8
Stollmeyer*	c Evans b Bailey	9	lbw b Trueman	64
EdeC Weekes	b Bailey	0	b Wardle	3
FMM Worrell	c Wardle b Trueman	4	c Graveney b Trueman	29
CL Walcott	c Laker b Lock	50	c Graveney b Laker	116
DStE Atkinson	lbw b Bailey	21	lbw b Laker	22
GE Gomez	c Watson b Bailey	4	c Watson b Bailey	40
CA McWatt+	c Lock b Bailey	22	c Wardle b Laker	8
GStA Sobers	not out	14	c Compton b Lock	26
FM King	b Bailey	9	c & b Laker	10
S Ramadhin	lbw b Trueman	4	not out	10
Extras	(0b, 1lb, 0w, 1nb)	2	(4b, 3lb, 1w, 2nb)	10
Total	60.4 overs	**139**	170 overs	**346**

1st innings FoW: 0, 2, 13, 13, 65, 75, 110, 115, 133, 139
2nd innings FoW: 26, 38, 102, 123, 191, 273, 293, 306, 326, 346

TE Bailey	16	7	34	7	25	11	54	1
FS Trueman	15.4	4	39	2	29	7	88	3
JH Wardle	10	1	20	0	39	14	83	1
GAR Lock	15	6	31	1	27	16	40	1
JC Laker	4	1	13	0	50	27	71	4

ENGLAND 1st innings / 2nd innings

		1st		2nd
L Hutton*	c McWatt b Walcott	205		
TE Bailey	c McWatt b Sobers	23		
PBH May	c (sub) b Ramadhin	30	not out	40
DCS Compton	hit wkt b King	31		
W Watson	c McWatt b King	4	not out	20
TW Graveney	lbw b Atkinson	11	b King	0
TG Evans+	c Worrell b Ramadhin	28		
JH Wardle	c Holt b Sobers	66		
GAR Lock	b Sobers	4		
JC Laker	b Sobers	9		
FS Trueman	not out	0		
Extras	(0b, 3lb, 0w, 0nb)	3	(12b, 0lb, 0w, 0nb)	12
Total	176.5 overs	**414**	15.5 overs	**72**

1st innings FoW: 43, 104, 152, 160, 179, 287, 392, 401, 406, 414
2nd innings FoW: 0

FM King	26	12	45	2	4	1	21	1
GE Gomez	25	8	56	0	3	0	8	0
DStE Atkinson	41	15	82	1	3	0	14	0
S Ramadhin	29	9	71	2	1	0	6	0
GStA Sobers	28.5	9	75	4				
CL Walcott	11	5	26	1				
FMM Worrell	11	0	34	0	4	0	8	0
JB Stollmeyer	5	0	22	0				
EdeC Weekes					0.5	0	3	0

Pakistan 1st innings / 2nd innings

		1st		2nd
Hanif Moh'd	b Tattersall	20	lbw b Laker	39
Alimuddin	c Edrich b Wardle	19	b Bailey	0
Waqar Hassan	c Compton b Wardle	9	c Statham b Compton	53
Maqsood Ahd'd	st Evans b Wardle	0	not out	29
Imtiaz Ah'd+	b Laker	12		
AH Kardar*	b Statham	2		
Fazal Mah'd	b Wardle	5		
Khalid Wazir	b Statham	3		
Khan Moh'd	b Statham	0		
Zulfiqar Ah'd	b Statham	11		
Shujauddin	not out	0		
Extras	(4b, 1lb, 0w, 1nb)	6	(0b, 0lb, 0w, 0nb)	0
Total	83.5 overs	**87**	52.2 overs	**121**

1st innings FoW: 24, 42, 43, 57, 67, 67, 71, 71, 87, 87
2nd innings FoW: 0, 71, 121

JB Statham	13	6	18	4	5	2	17	0
TE Bailey	3	2	1	0	6	2	13	1
JH Wardle	30.5	22	33	4	8	6	6	0
R Tattersall	15	8	12	1	10	1	27	0
JC Laker	22	12	17	1	10.2	5	22	1
DCS Compton					13	2	36	1

ENGLAND 1st innings / 2nd innings

		1st	2nd
L Hutton*	b Khan Mohammad	0	
RT Simpson	lbw b Fazal	40	
PBH May	b Khan Mohammad	27	
DCS Compton	b Fazal	0	
WJ Edrich	b Khan Mohammad	4	
JH Wardle	c Maqsood Ah'd b Fazal	3	
TG Evans+	b Khan Mohammad	25	
TE Bailey	b Khan Mohammad	3	
JC Laker	not out	13	
JB Statham	b Fazal	0	
R Tattersall			
Extras	(2b, 0lb, 0w, 0nb)	2	
Total	31 overs	**117**	

1st innings FoW: 9, 55, 59, 72, 75, 79, 85, 110, 117

Fazal Mahmood	16	2	54	4
Khan Mohammad	15	3	61	5

No. 312:	2nd Test
VENUE:	Trent Bridge
DATE:	1st-5th July 1954
TOSS WON BY:	Pakistan
RESULT:	Eng won by an innings and 129 runs

No. 313:	3rd Test
VENUE:	Old Trafford
DATE:	22nd-27th July 1954
TOSS WON BY:	England
RESULT:	Match drawn

Pakistan 1st innings / 2nd innings

Batsman	1st innings		2nd innings	
Hanif Moh'd	lbw b Appleyard	19	c Evans b Bedser	51
Alimuddin	b Statham	4	b Statham	18
Waqar Hassan	b Appleyard	7	c Evans b Statham	7
Maqsood Ah'd	c Evans b Appleyard	6	c Statham b Appleyard	69
Imtiaz Ah'd+	b Appleyard	11	lbw b Wardle	33
AH Kardar*	c Compton b Bedser	28	c Graveney b Wardle	4
Fazal Mah'd	c Sheppard b Bedser	14	b Statham	36
MEZ Ghazali	b Statham	18	c Statham b Bedser	14
Moh'd Aslam	b Wardle	16	c Sheppard b Appleyard	18
Khalid Hassan	c May b Appleyard	10	c Compton b Wardle	8
Khan Moh'd	not out	13	not out	7
Extras	(9b, 1lb, 0w, 1nb)	11	(4b, 3lb, 0w, 0nb)	7
	65 overs		112.4 overs	
Total		**157**		**272**

1st innings FoW: 26, 37, 43, 50, 55, 86, 111, 121, 138, 157
2nd innings FoW: 69, 70, 95, 164, 168, 189, 216, 242, 254, 272

Bowler	O	M	R	W		O	M	R	W
AV Bedser	21	8	30	2		30	11	83	2
JB Statham	18	3	38	2		20	3	66	3
R Appleyard	17	5	51	5		30.4	8	72	2
TE Bailey	3	0	18	0					
JH Wardle	6	3	9	1		32	17	44	3

ENGLAND 1st innings / 2nd innings

Batsman	1st innings		2nd innings
DS Sheppard*	c Imtiaz Ahmed b Khan	37	
RT Simpson	b Khalid Hassan	101	
PBH May	b Khan Mohammad	0	
DCS Compton	b Khalid Hassan	278	
TW Graveney	c Maqsood b Kardar	84	
TE Bailey	not out	36	
TG Evans+	b Khan Mohammad	4	
JH Wardle	not out	14	
AV Bedser			
JB Statham			
R Appleyard			
Extras	(2b, 1lb, 0w, 1nb)	4	
	139 overs		
Total		**558**	

1st innings FoW: 98, 102, 185, 339, 531, 536

Bowler	O	M	R	W
Fazal Mahmood	47	§7	148	0
Khan Mohammad	40	3	155	3
AH Kardar	28	4	110	1
Khalid Hassan	21	1	116	2
Maqsood Ahmed	3	0	25	0

ENGLAND 1st innings / 2nd innings

Batsman	1st innings		2nd innings
DS Sheppard*	b Fazal Mahmood	13	
TE Bailey	run out	42	
PBH May	c Imtiaz b Shujauddin	14	
DCS Compton	c Imtiaz b Shujauddin	93	
TW Graveney	st Imtiaz b Shujauddin	65	
JM Parks	b Fazal Mahmood	15	
TG Evans+	c Hanif b Fazal	31	
JH Wardle	c Waqar b Fazal	54	
AV Bedser	not out	22	
JE McConnon	not out	5	
JB Statham			
Extras	(1b, 4lb, 0w, 0nb)	5	
	129 overs		
Total		**359**	

1st innings FoW: 20, 57, 97, 190, 217, 261, 293, 348

Bowler	O	M	R	W
Fazal Mahmood	42	14	107	4
Mahmood Hussain	27	5	88	0
Shujauddin	42	12	127	3
MEZ Ghazali	8	1	18	0
Maqsood Ahmed	4	0	14	0

Pakistan 1st innings / 2nd innings

Batsman	1st innings		2nd innings	
Hanif	c Wardle b McConnon	32	c Sheppard b Wardle	1
Imtiaz Ahmed+	c McConnon b Wardle	13	c Graveney b Bedser	1
Waqar Hassan	c & b McConnon	11	c Parks b Bedser	7
Maqsood	c Wardle b McConnon	4	not out	0
AH Kardar*	b Wardle	9	c Wardle b Bedser	0
MEZ Ghazali	c Sheppard b Wardle	0	not out	9
Wazir	c McConnon b Bedser	5		
Fazal Mahm'd	c Compton b Bedser	9		
Khalid Wazir	c McConnon b Wardle	2		
Shujauddin	not out	0		
M Hussain	b Bedser	0		
Extras	(4b, 0lb, 0w, 1nb)	5	(2b, 4lb, 0w, 1nb)	7
	56.5 overs		15 overs	
Total		**90**		**25**

1st innings FoW: 26, 58, 63, 66, 66, 77,80, 87, 89, 90
2nd innings FoW: 1, 8, 10, 10

Bowler	O	M	R	W		O	M	R	W
JB Statham	4	0	11	0					
AV Bedser	15.5	4	36	3		8	5	9	3
JH Wardle	24	16	19	4		7	2	9	1
JE McConnon	13	5	19	3					

Pakistan

No. 314:	4th Test
VENUE:	The Oval
DATE:	12th-17th August 1954
TOSS WON BY:	Pakistan
RESULT:	Pakistan won by 24 runs

Pakistan	1st innings		2nd innings	
Hanif Moh'd	lbw b Statham	0	c Graveney b Wardle	19
Alimuddin	b Tyson	10	c May b Wardle	12
Waqar Hassan	b Loader	7	run out	9
Maqsood Ah'd	b Tyson	0	c Wardle b McConnon	4
Imtiaz Ah'd+	c Evans b Tyson	23	c Wardle b Tyson	12
AH Kardar*	c Evans b Statham	36	c & b Wardle	17
Wazir Moh'd	run out	0	lbw b Wardle	0
Fazal Mah'd	c Evans b Loader	16	not out	42
Shujauddin	not out	16	b Wardle	6
Zulfiqar Ah'd	c Compton b Loader	16	c May b Wardle	34
M Hussain	b Tyson	23	c Statham b Wardle	6
Extras	(0b, 0lb, 0w, 2nb)	2	(3b, 0lb, 0w, 0nb)	3
Total	51.4 overs	**133**	92 overs	**164**

1st innings FoW: 0, 10, 10, 26, 51, 51, 51, 77, 106, 133
2nd innings FoW: 19, 38, 43, 54, 63, 73, 76, 82, 140, 164

JB Statham	11	5	26	2	18	7	37	0
FH Tyson	13.4	3	35	4	9	2	22	1
PJ Loader	18	5	35	3	16	6	26	0
JE McConnon	9	2	35	0	14	5	20	1
JH Wardle					35	16	56	7

ENGLAND	1st innings		2nd innings	
L Hutton*	c Imtiaz Ahmed b Fazal	14	c Imtiaz Ahmed b Fazal	5
RT Simpson	c Kardar b Hussain	2	c & b Zulfiqar Ahmed	27
PBH May	c Kardar b Fazal	26	c Kardar b Fazal	53
DCS Compton	c Imtiaz Ahmed b Fazal	53	c Imtiaz Ahmed b Fazal	29
TW Graveney	c Hanif b Fazal	1	b Fazal Mahmood	3
TG Evans+	c Maqsood b Hussain	0	lbw b Shujauddin	0
JH Wardle	c Imtiaz b Fazal Mah'd	8	c Shujauddin b Fazal	8
FH Tyson	c Imtiaz Ahmed b Fazal	3	c Imtiaz Ahmed b Fazal	3
JE McConnon	c Fazal b Hussain	11	c Waqar b Hussain	0
JB Statham	c Shujauddin b Hussain	1	run out	2
PJ Loader	not out	8	not out	2
Extras	(0b, 1lb, 1w, 1nb)	3	(0b, 2lb, 0w, 3nb)	5
Total	59.3 overs	**130**	68 overs	**143**

1st innings FoW: 6, 26, 56, 63, 69, 92, 106, 115, 115, 130
2nd innings FoW: 15, 66, 109, 115, 116, 121, 131, 138, 138, 143

Fazal Mahmood	30	16	53	6	30	11	46	6
Mahmood Hussain	21.3	6	58	4	14	4	32	1
Zulfiqar Ahmed	5	2	8	0	14	2	35	1
Shujauddin	3	0	8	0	10	1	25	1

Australia

No. 315:	1st Test
VENUE:	Brisbane (Gabba)
DATE:	26th Nov-1st December 1954
TOSS WON BY:	England
RESULT:	Aus won by an innings and 154 runs

Australia	1st innings		2nd innings
LE Favell	c Cowdrey b Statham	23	
AR Morris	c Cowdrey b Bailey	153	
KR Miller	b Bailey	49	
RN Harvey	c Bailey b Bedser	162	
GB Hole	run out	57	
R Benaud	c May b Tyson	34	
RG Archer	c Bedser b Statham	0	
RR Lindwall	not out	64	
GRA Langley+	b Bailey	16	
IW Johnson*	not out	24	
WA Johnston			
Extras	(11b, 7lb, 0w, 1nb)	19	
Total	129 overs	**601**	

1st innings FoW: 51, 123, 325, 456, 463, 464, 545, 572

AV Bedser	37	4	131	1
JB Statham	34	2	123	2
FH Tyson	29	1	160	1
TE Bailey	26	1	140	3
WJ Edrich	3	0	28	0

ENGLAND	1st innings		2nd innings	
L Hutton*	c Langley b Lindwall	4	lbw b Miller	13
RT Simpson	b Miller	2	run out	9
WJ Edrich	c Langley b Archer	15	b Johnston	88
PBH May	b Lindwall	1	lbw b Lindwall	44
MC Cowdrey	c Hole b Johnston	40	b Benaud	10
TE Bailey	b Johnston	88	c Langley b Lindwall	23
FH Tyson	b Johnson	7	not out	37
AV Bedser	b Johnson	5	c Archer b Johnson	5
KV Andrew+	b Lindwall	6	b Johnson	5
JB Statham	b Johnson	11	c Langley b Benaud	0
DCS Compton	not out	2	c Harvey b Benaud	14
Extras	(3b, 6lb, 0w, 0nb)	9	(7b, 2lb, 0w, 0nb)	9
Total	76.1 overs	**190**	90.1 overs	**257**

1st innings FoW: 4, 10, 11, 25, 107, 132, 141, 156, 181, 190
2nd innings FoW: 22, 23, 147, 163, 181, 220, 231, 242, 243, 257

RR Lindwall	14	4	27	3	17	3	50	2
KR Miller	11	5	19	1	12	2	30	1
RG Archer	4	1	14	1	15	4	28	0
IW Johnson	19	5	46	3	17	5	38	2
R Benaud	12	5	28	0	8.1	1	43	3
WA Johnston	16.1	5	47	2	21	8	59	1

Australia		'55

Left match:

No. 316: 2nd Test
VENUE: Sydney (SCG)
DATE: 17th-22nd December 1954
TOSS WON BY: Australia
RESULT: England won by 38 runs

ENGLAND — 1st innings / 2nd innings

Batsman	1st innings		2nd innings	
L Hutton*	c Davidson b Johnston	30	c Benaud b Johnston	28
TE Bailey	b Lindwall	0	c Langley b Archer	6
PBH May	c Johnston b Archer	5	b Lindwall	104
TW Graveney	c Favell b Johnston	21	c Langley b Johnston	0
MC Cowdrey	c Langley b Davidson	23	c Archer b Benaud	54
WJ Edrich	c Benaud b Archer	10	b Archer	29
FH Tyson	b Lindwall	0	b Lindwall	9
TG Evans+	c Langley b Archer	3	c Lindwall b Archer	4
JH Wardle	c Burke b Johnston	35	lbw b Lindwall	8
R Appleyard	c Hole b Davidson	8	not out	19
JB Statham	not out	14	c Langley b Johnston	25
Extras	(0b, 5lb, 0w, 0nb)	5	(0b, 6lb, 0w, 4nb)	10
	54.3 overs		104.3 overs	
Total		**154**		**296**

1st innings FoW: 14, 19, 58, 63, 84, 85, 88, 99, 111, 154
2nd innings FoW: 18, 55, 55, 171, 222, 232, 239, 249, 250, 296

Bowler	O	M	R	W	O	M	R	W
RR Lindwall	17	3	47	2	31	10	69	3
RG Archer	12	7	12	3	22	9	53	3
AK Davidson	12	3	34	2	13	2	52	0
WA Johnston	13.3	1	56	3	19.3	2	70	3
R Benaud					19	3	42	1

Australia — 1st innings / 2nd innings

Batsman	1st innings		2nd innings	
LE Favell	c Graveney b Bailey	26	c Edrich b Tyson	16
AR Morris*	c Hutton b Bailey	12	lbw b Statham	10
JW Burke	c Graveney b Bailey	44	b Tyson	14
RN Harvey	c Cowdrey b Tyson	12	not out	92
GB Hole	b Tyson	12	b Tyson	0
R Benaud	lbw b Statham	20	c Tyson b Appleyard	12
RG Archer	c Hutton b Tyson	49	b Tyson	6
AK Davidson	b Statham	20	c Evans b Statham	5
RR Lindwall	c Evans b Tyson	19	b Tyson	8
GRA Langley+	b Bailey	5	b Statham	0
WA Johnston	not out	0	c Evans b Tyson	11
Extras	(5b, 2lb, 0w, 2nb)	9	(0b, 7lb, 0w, 3nb)	10
	55.4 overs		53.4 overs	
Total		**228**		**184**

1st innings FoW: 18, 65, 100, 104, 122, 141, 193, 213, 224, 228
2nd innings FoW: 27, 34, 77, 77,102, 122, 127, 136, 145, 184

Bowler	O	M	R	W	O	M	R	W
JB Statham	18	1	83	2	19	6	45	3
TE Bailey	17.4	3	59	4	6	0	21	0
FH Tyson	13	2	45	4	18.4	1	85	6
R Appleyard	7	1	32	0	6	1	12	1
JH Wardle					4	2	11	0

Right match:

No. 317: 3rd Test
VENUE: Melbourne (MCG)
DATE: 31st Dec 1954-5th Jan 1955
TOSS WON BY: England
RESULT: England won by 128 runs

ENGLAND — 1st innings / 2nd innings

Batsman	1st innings		2nd innings	
L Hutton*	c Hole b Miller	12	lbw b Archer	42
WJ Edrich	c Lindwall b Miller	4	b Johnston	13
PBH May	c Benaud b Lindwall	0	b Johnston	91
MC Cowdrey	b Johnson	102	b Benaud	7
DCS Compton	c Harvey b Miller	4	c Maddocks b Archer	23
TE Bailey	c Maddocks b Johnston	30	not out	24
TG Evans+	lbw b Archer	20	c Maddocks b Miller	22
JH Wardle	b Archer	0	b Johnson	38
FH Tyson	b Archer	6	c Harvey b Johnston	6
JB Statham	b Archer	3	c Favell b Johnston	0
R Appleyard	not out	1	b Johnston	0
Extras	(9b, 0lb, 0w, 0nb)	9	(2b, 4lb, 1w, 0nb)	7
	67.6 overs		100.5 overs	
Total		**191**		**279**

1st innings FoW: 14, 21, 29, 41, 115, 169, 181, 181, 190, 191
2nd innings FoW: 40, 96, 128, 173, 185, 211, 257, 273, 273, 279

Bowler	O	M	R	W	O	M	R	W
RR Lindwall	13	0	59	1	18	3	52	0
KR Miller	11	8	14	3	18	6	35	1
RG Archer	13.6	4	33	4	24	7	50	2
R Benaud	7	0	30	0	8	2	25	1
WA Johnston	12	6	26	1	24.5	2	85	5
IW Johnson	11	3	20	1	8	2	25	1

Australia — 1st innings / 2nd innings

Batsman	1st innings		2nd innings	
LE Favell	lbw b Statham	25	b Appleyard	30
AR Morris	lbw b Tyson	3	c Cowdrey b Tyson	4
KR Miller	c Evans b Statham	7	b Tyson	22
RN Harvey	b Appleyard	31	c Evans b Tyson	11
GB Hole	b Tyson	11	c Edrich b Tyson	6
R Benaud	c (sub) b Appleyard	15	c Evans b Statham	5
RG Archer	b Wardle	23	b Statham	15
LV Maddocks+	c Evans b Statham	47	b Tyson	0
RR Lindwall	b Statham	13	lbw b Tyson	0
IW Johnson*	not out	33	not out	4
WA Johnston	b Statham	11	c Evans b Tyson	0
Extras	(7b, 3lb, 0w, 2nb)	12	(1b, 13lb, 0w, 0nb)	14
	63.3 overs		31.3 overs	
Total		**231**		**111**

1st innings FoW: 15, 38, 43, 65, 92, 115, 134, 151, 205, 231
2nd innings FoW: 23, 57, 77, 86, 87, 97, 98, 98, 110, 111

Bowler	O	M	R	W	O	M	R	W
FH Tyson	21	2	68	2	12.3	1	27	7
JB Statham	16.3	0	60	5	11	1	38	2
TE Bailey	9	1	33	0	3	0	14	0
R Appleyard	11	3	38	2	4	1	17	1
JH Wardle	6	0	20	1	1	0	1	0

Australia

	No. 318:	4th Test	
	VENUE:	Adelaide	
	DATE:	28th January-2nd Feb 1955	
	TOSS WON BY:	Australia	
	RESULT:	England won by 5 wickets	

Australia	1st innings		2nd innings	
CC McDonald	c May b Appleyard	48	b Statham	29
AR Morris	c Evans b Tyson	25	c & b Appleyard	16
JW Burke	c May b Tyson	18	b Appleyard	5
RN Harvey	c Edrich b Bailey	25	b Appleyard	7
KR Miller	c Bailey b Appleyard	44	b Statham	14
R Benaud	c May b Appleyard	15	lbw b Statham	2
LV Maddocks+	run out	69	lbw b Tyson	1
RG Archer	c May b Tyson	21	c Evans b Tyson	3
AK Davidson	c Evans b Bailey	5	lbw b Wardle	23
IW Johnson*	c Statham b Bailey	41	c Appleyard b Tyson	3
WA Johnston	not out	0	not out	3
Extras	(3b, 7lb, 0w, 2nb)	12	(4b, 1lb, 0w, 0nb)	5
	99.1 overs		43.2 overs	
Total		**323**		**111**

1st innings FoW: 59, 86, 115, 129, 175, 182, 212, 229, 321, 323
2nd innings FoW: 24, 40, 54, 69, 76, 77, 79, 83, 101, 111

FH Tyson	26.1	4	85	3	15	2	47	3
JB Statham	19	4	70	0	12	1	38	3
TE Bailey	12	3	39	3				
R Appleyard	23	7	58	3	12	7	13	3
JH Wardle	19	5	59	0	4.2	1	8	1

ENGLAND	1st innings		2nd innings	
L Hutton*	c Davidson b Johnston	80	c Davidson b Miller	5
WJ Edrich	b Johnson	21	b Miller	0
PBH May	c Archer b Benaud	1	c Miller b Johnston	26
MC Cowdrey	c Maddocks b Davidson	79	c Archer b Miller	4
DCS Compton	lbw b Miller	44	not out	34
TE Bailey	c Davidson b Johnston	38	lbw b Johnston	15
TG Evans+	c Maddocks b Benaud	37	not out	6
JH Wardle	c & b Johnson	23		
FH Tyson	c Burke b Benaud	1		
R Appleyard	not out	10		
JB Statham	c Maddocks b Benaud	0		
Extras	(1b, 2lb, 0w, 4nb)	7	(3b, 4lb, 0w, 0nb)	7
	140.6 overs		30.4 overs	
Total		**341**		**97**

1st innings FoW: 60, 63, 162, 232, 232, 283, 321, 323, 336, 341
2nd innings FoW: 3, 10, 18, 49, 90

KR Miller	11	4	34	1	10.4	2	40	3
RG Archer	3	0	12	0	4	0	13	0
IW Johnson	36	17	46	2				
AK Davidson	25	8	55	1	2	0	7	0
WA Johnston	27	11	60	2	8	2	20	2
R Benaud	36.6	6	120	4	6	2	10	0
JW Burke	2	0	7	0				

Australia

	No. 319:	5th Test	
	VENUE:	Sydney (SCG)	
	DATE:	25th Feb-3rd March 1955	
	TOSS WON BY:	Australia	
	RESULT:	Match drawn	

ENGLAND	1st innings		2nd innings	
L Hutton*	c Burge b Lindwall	6		
TW Graveney	c & b Johnson	111		
PBH May	c Davidson b Benaud	79		
MC Cowdrey	c Maddocks b Johnson	0		
DCS Compton	c & b Johnson	84		
TE Bailey	b Lindwall	72		
TG Evans+	c McDonald b Lindwall	10		
JH Wardle	not out	5		
FH Tyson				
R Appleyard				
JB Statham				
Extras	(1b, 3lb, 0w, 0nb)	4		
	94.6 overs			
Total		**371**		

1st innings FoW: 6, 188, 188, 196, 330, 359, 371

RR Lindwall	20.6	5	77	3
KR Miller	15	1	71	0
AK Davidson	19	3	72	0
IW Johnson	20	5	68	3
R Benaud	20	4	79	1

Australia	1st innings		2nd innings	
WJ Watson	b Wardle	18	c Graveney b Statham	3
CC McDonald	c May b Appleyard	72	c Evans b Graveney	37
LE Favell	b Tyson	1	c Graveney b Wardle	9
RN Harvey	c & b Tyson	13	c & b Wardle	8
KR Miller	run out	19	b Wardle	28
PJP Burge	c Appleyard b Wardle	17	not out	18
R Benaud	b Wardle	7	b Hutton	22
LV Maddocks+	c Appleyard b Wardle	32		
AK Davidson	c Evans b Wardle	18		
IW Johnson*	run out	11		
RR Lindwall	not out	2		
Extras	(10b, 1lb, 0w, 0nb)	11	(0b, 0lb, 0w, 0nb)	0
	60.4 overs		28.6 overs	
Total		**221**		**118**

1st innings FoW: 52, 53, 58, 129, 138, 147, 157, 202, 217, 221
2nd innings FoW: 14, 27, 29, 67, 87, 118

FH Tyson	11	1	46	2	5	2	20	0
JB Statham	9	1	31	0	5	0	11	1
R Appleyard	16	2	54	1				
JH Wardle	24.4	6	79	5	12	1	51	3
TW Graveney					6	0	34	1
L Hutton					0.6	0	2	1

No. 320: 1st Test

VENUE:	Dunedin
DATE:	11th-16th March 1955
TOSS WON BY:	England
RESULT:	England won by 8 wickets

NEW ZEALAND 1st innings

	1st innings		2nd innings	
GO Rabone*	st Evans b Wardle	18	lbw b Wardle	7
ME Chapple	b Statham	0	run out	35
B Sutcliffe	c Statham b Bailey	74	b Statham	20
JR Reid	b Statham	4	b Tyson	28
SN McGregor	b Tyson	2	c Cowdrey b Appleyard	8
L Watt	b Tyson	0	b Appleyard	2
HB Cave	b Tyson	1	b Tyson	1
AM Moir	b Statham	7	b Tyson	0
RW Blair	b Statham	0	lbw b Tyson	10
A MacGibbon	c Evans b Bailey	7	b Wardle	3
IA Colquhoun+	not out	0	not out	1
Extras	(5b, 4lb, 0w, 3nb)	12	(7b, 10lb, 0w, 0nb)	17
	81.2 overs		56.3 overs	
Total		**125**		**132**

1st innings FoW: 3, 63, 68, 72, 76, 86, 103, 113, 122, 125
2nd innings FoW: 24, 68, 75, 96, 98, 103, 103, 123, 126, 132

FH Tyson	19	7	23	3	12	6	16	4
JB Statham	17	9	24	4	15	5	30	1
TE Bailey	12.2	6	19	2	8	4	9	0
JH Wardle	26	15	31	1	14.3	4	41	2
R Appleyard	7	3	16	0	7	2	19	2

ENGLAND 1st innings

	1st innings		2nd innings	
L Hutton*	c Colquhoun b Reid	11	c Colquhoun b Blair	3
TW Graveney	b Cave	41	not out	32
PBH May	b MacGibbon	10	b MacGibbon	13
MC Cowdrey	lbw b Reid	42	not out	0
RT Simpson	b Cave	21		
TE Bailey	lbw b Reid	0		
TG Evans+	b Reid	0		
JH Wardle	not out	32		
FH Tyson	c McGregor b MacGibbon	16		
R Appleyard	not out	0		
JB Statham				
Extras	(13b, 17lb, 0w, 6nb)	36	(0b, 1lb, 0w, 0nb)	1
	92.5 overs		15.2 overs	
Total		**209**		**49**

1st innings FoW: 60, 71, 101, 150, 152, 152, 156, 208
2nd innings FoW: 22, 47

RW Blair	8	1	29	0	4	0	20	1
AR MacGibbon	24.5	11	39	2	7.2	2	16	1
JR Reid	27	11	36	4	4	2	12	0
HB Cave	24	15	27	2				
AM Moir	9	1	42	0				

No. 321: 2nd Test

VENUE:	Auckland
DATE:	25th-28th March 1955
TOSS WON BY:	New Zealand
RESULT:	Eng won by an innings and 20 runs

NEW ZEALAND 1st innings

	1st innings		2nd innings	
B Sutcliffe	c Bailey b Statham	49	b Wardle	11
JG Leggat	lbw b Tyson	4	c Hutton b Tyson	1
MB Poore	c Evans b Tyson	0	b Tyson	0
JR Reid	c Statham b Wardle	73	b Statham	1
GO Rabone*	c Evans b Statham	29	c May b Appleyard	1
SN McGregor	not out	15	lbw b Statham	7
HB Cave	c Bailey b Appleyard	6	c Graveney b Appleyard	5
A MacGibbon	b Appleyard	9	lbw b Appleyard	0
IA Colquhoun+	c (sub) b Appleyard	0	c Graveney b Appleyard	0
AM Moir	lbw b Statham	0	not out	0
JA Hayes	b Statham	0	b Statham	0
Extras	(3b, 6lb, 4w, 2nb)	15	(0b, 0lb, 0w, 0nb)	0
	88.4 overs		27 overs	
Total		**200**		**26**

1st innings FoW: 13, 13, 76, 154, 171, 189, 199, 199, 200, 200
2nd innings FoW: 6, 8, 9, 14, 14, 22, 22, 22, 26, 26

FH Tyson	11	2	41	2	7	2	10	2
JB Statham	17.4	7	28	4	9	3	9	3
TE Bailey	13	2	34	0				
R Appleyard	16	4	38	3	6	3	7	4
JH Wardle	31	19	44	1	5	5	0	1

ENGLAND 1st innings

	1st innings		2nd innings
RT Simpson	c & b Moir	23	
TW Graveney	c Rabone b Hayes	13	
PBH May	b Hayes	48	
MC Cowdrey	b Moir	22	
L Hutton*	b MacGibbon	53	
TE Bailey	c Colquhoun b Cave	18	
TG Evans+	c Reid b Moir	0	
JH Wardle	c Reid b Moir	0	
FH Tyson	not out	27	
R Appleyard	c Colquhoun b Hayes	6	
JB Statham	c Reid b Moir	13	
Extras	(12b, 3lb, 0w, 8nb)	23	
	119.1 overs		
Total		**246**	

1st innings FoW: 21, 56, 112, 112, 163, 164, 164, 201, 218, 246

JA Hayes	23	7	71	3
AR MacGibbon	20	7	33	1
JR Reid	25	15	28	0
HB Cave	24	10	25	1
AM Moir	25.1	3	62	5
GO Rabone	2	0	4	0

	No. 322: 1st Test	No. 323: 2nd Test
VENUE:	Trent Bridge	Lord's
DATE:	9th-13th June 1955	23rd-27th June 1955
TOSS WON BY:	England	England
RESULT:	Eng won by an innings and 5 runs	England won by 71 runs

1st Test — Trent Bridge

ENGLAND

Batsman	1st innings		2nd innings
D Kenyon	lbw b Goddard	87	
TW Graveney	c Waite b Adcock	42	
PBH May*	c McGlew b Smith	83	
DCS Compton	lbw b Adcock	27	
KF Barrington	c Waite b Fuller	0	
TE Bailey	lbw b Goddard	49	
TG Evans+	c Goddard b Fuller	12	
JH Wardle	lbw b Tayfield	2	
FH Tyson	c McLean b Tayfield	0	
JB Statham	c Waite b Fuller	20	
R Appleyard	not out	0	
Extras	(6b, 6lb, 0w, 0nb)	12	
	168.4 overs		
Total		**334**	

2nd innings FoW: 91, 166, 228, 233, 252, 285, 294, 298, 334, 334

NAT Adcock	36	9	74	2
TL Goddard	36.4	18	61	2
ERH Fuller	29	5	59	3
HJ Tayfield	37	11	66	2
VI Smith	30	9	62	1

SOUTH AFRICA

Batsman	1st innings		2nd innings	
DJ McGlew	c Evans b Wardle	68	c May b Bailey	51
TL Goddard	lbw b Statham	12	run out	32
JHB Waite+	run out	0	c Compton b Tyson	3
WR Endean	lbw b Tyson	0	c Graveney b Bailey	6
RA McLean	b Tyson	13	c Graveney b Tyson	16
PL Winslow	c May b Appleyard	2	b Tyson	5
JE Cheetham*	c Graveney b Wardle	54	b Tyson	3
HJ Tayfield	c Bailey b Appleyard	11	b Tyson	0
ERH Fuller	b Wardle	15	c Evans b Wardle	6
VI Smith	c May b Wardle	0	not out	2
NAT Adcock	not out	1	b Tyson	6
Extras	(1b, 2lb, 0w, 2nb)	5	(8b, 4lb, 4w, 2nb)	18
	114 overs		96.3 overs	
Total		**181**		**148**

1st innings FoW: 15, 17, 19, 35, 55, 149, 156, 174, 180, 181
2nd innings FoW: 73, 83, 101, 108, 131, 132, 132, 135, 141, 148

JB Statham	25	5	47	1	10	4	16	0
FH Tyson	24	5	51	2	21.3	7	28	6
TE Bailey	5	2	8	0	17	8	21	2
R Appleyard	28	9	46	2	19	4	32	0
JH Wardle	32	23	24	4	29	17	33	1

2nd Test — Lord's

ENGLAND

Batsman	1st innings		2nd innings	
D Kenyon	b Adcock	1	lbw b Goddard	2
TW Graveney	c Waite b Heine	15	c Heine b Goddard	60
PBH May*	c Tayfield b Heine	0	hit wkt b Heine	112
DCS Compton	c Keith b Heine	20	c Mansell b Goddard	69
KF Barrington	b Heine	34	c McLean b Tayfield	18
TE Bailey	lbw b Goddard	13	c Adcock b Tayfield	22
TG Evans+	c Waite b Heine	20	c & b Tayfield	14
FJ Titmus	lbw b Goddard	4	c Heine b Tayfield	4
JH Wardle	c Tayfield b Goddard	20	c Waite b Adcock	16
JB Statham	c McLean b Goddard	0	b Tayfield	11
FS Trueman	not out	2	not out	6
Extras	(2b, 2lb, 0w, 0nb)	4	(15b, 2lb, 0w, 2nb)	19
	54.2 overs		149.5 overs	
Total		**133**		**353**

1st innings FoW: 7, 8, 30, 45, 82, 98, 111, 111, 111, 133
2nd innings FoW: 9, 141, 237, 277, 285, 302, 306, 336, 336, 353

PS Heine	25	7	60	5	29	5	87	1
NAT Adcock	8	3	10	1	25	5	64	1
TL Goddard	21.2	8	59	4	55	23	96	3
HJ Tayfield					38.5	12	80	5
PNF Mansell					2	0	7	0

SOUTH AFRICA

Batsman	1st innings		2nd innings	
DJ McGlew	c Evans b Statham	0	lbw b Statham	0
TL Goddard	c Evans b Trueman	0	c Evans b Statham	10
JE Cheetham*	lbw b Bailey	13	retired hurt	3
WR Endean	lbw b Wardle	48	c Evans b Statham	3
RA McLean	b Statham	142	c Evans b Statham	28
JHB Waite+	c Evans b Trueman	8	b Statham	8
HJ Keith	c Titmus b Wardle	57	c Graveney b Statham	5
PNF Mansell	c Graveney b Wardle	2	lbw b Statham	9
HJ Tayfield	b Titmus	21	c Kenyon b Wardle	16
PS Heine	st Evans b Wardle	2	c Kenyon b Wardle	14
NAT Adcock	not out	0	not out	0
Extras	(6b, 1lb, 0w, 4nb)	11	(11b, 3lb, 0w, 1nb)	15
	102 overs		57.4 overs	
Total		**304**		**111**

2nd innings FoW: 0, 7, 51, 101, 138, 247, 259, 302, 304, 304
2nd innings FoW: 0, 17, 40, 54, 63, 75, 78, 111, 111

JB Statham	27	9	49	2	29	12	39	7
FS Trueman	16	2	73	2	19	2	39	0
TE Bailey	16	2	56	1				
JH Wardle	29	10	65	4	9.4	4	18	2
FJ Titmus	14	3	50	1				

No. 324: 3rd Test	No. 325: 4th Test
VENUE: Old Trafford	VENUE: Headingley
DATE: 7th-12th July 1955	DATE: 21st-26th July 1955
TOSS WON BY: England	TOSS WON BY: South Africa
RESULT: South Africa won by 3 wickets	RESULT: South Africa won by 224 runs

ENGLAND 1st innings / 2nd innings

Batsman	1st innings		2nd innings	
D Kenyon	c Waite b Heine	5	c Waite b Heine	1
TW Graveney	c Tayfield b Adcock	0	b Adcock	1
PBH May*	c Mansell b Goddard	34	b Mansell	117
DCS Compton	c Waite b Adcock	158	c Mansell b Heine	71
MC Cowdrey	c Mansell b Tayfield	1	c Goddard b Heine	50
TE Bailey	c Waite b Adcock	44	c McGlew b Adcock	17
FJ Titmus	lbw b Heine	0	not out	38
TG Evans+	c Keith b Heine	0	c Mansell b Adcock	19
GAR Lock	not out	19	b Heine	4
FH Tyson	b Goddard	2	c Waite b Heine	3
AV Bedser	lbw b Goddard	1	c McLean b Tayfield	36
Extras	(13b, 6lb, 1w, 0nb)	20	(13b, 5lb, 2w, 0nb)	20
Total	126 overs	**284**	173.5 overs	**381**

1st innings FoW: 2, 22, 70, 75, 219, 234, 242, 271, 280, 284
2nd innings FoW: 2, 2, 126, 234, 270, 274, 304, 325, 333, 381

Bowler									
PS Heine	24	4	71	3		32	8	86	5
NAT Adcock	28	5	52	3		28	12	48	3
HJ Tayfield	35	15	57	1		51.5	21	102	1
TL Goddard	27	10	52	3		47	21	92	0
PNF Mansell	6	2	13	0		15	3	33	1
HJ Keith	6	2	19	0					

SOUTH AFRICA 1st innings / 2nd innings

Batsman	1st innings		2nd innings	
DJ McGlew*	not out	104	b Tyson	48
TL Goddard	c Graveney b Tyson	62	c May b Bedser	8
HJ Keith	c Graveney b Bailey	38	b Bedser	0
PNF Mansell	lbw b Lock	7	run out	50
WR Endean	c Evans b Lock	5	b Tyson	16
RA McLean	b Tyson	3	lbw b Tyson	4
JHB Waite+	c Kenyon b Bedser	113	not out	10
PL Winslow	lbw b Bedser	108	c Titmus b Lock	2
HJ Tayfield	b Tyson	28	not out	1
PS Heine	not out	22		
NAT Adcock				
Extras	(15b, 12lb, 1w, 3nb)	31	(2b, 2lb, 1w, 1nb)	6
Total	195 overs	**521**	30.3 overs	**145**

1st innings FoW: 147, 171, 179, 182, 245, 416, 457, 494
2nd innings FoW: 18, 23, 95, 112, 129, 132, 135

Bowler									
AV Bedser	31	2	92	2		10	1	61	2
FH Tyson	44	5	124	3		13.3	2	55	3
TE Bailey	37	8	102	1					
GAR Lock	64	24	121	2		7	2	23	1
FJ Titmus	19	7	51	0					

SOUTH AFRICA 1st innings / 2nd innings

Batsman	1st innings		2nd innings	
DJ McGlew*	c McIntyre b Loader	23	c May b Wardle	133
TL Goddard	b Loader	9	c McIntyre b Wardle	74
HJ Keith	c McIntyre b Loader	0	b Wardle	73
PNF Mansell	b Bailey	0	c Lowson b Wardle	3
RA McLean	c May b Loader	41	c Lock b Statham	19
JHB Waite+	run out	2	not out	116
PL Winslow	b Statham	8	c McIntyre b Lock	32
WR Endean	b Statham	41	lbw b Bailey	1
HJ Tayfield	not out	25	lbw b Statham	14
PS Heine	b Lock	14	b Bailey	10
NAT Adcock	lbw b Statham	0	b Bailey	6
Extras	(0b, 4lb, 0w, 4nb)	8	(8b, 6lb, 1w, 4nb)	19
Total	70.2 overs	**171**	208.5 overs	**500**

1st innings FoW: 33, 33, 34, 34, 38, 63, 98, 154, 170, 171
2nd innings FoW: 176, 265, 269, 303, 311, 387, 400, 439, 468, 500

Bowler									
JB Statham	20.2	7	35	3		40	10	129	2
PJ Loader	19	7	52	4		29	9	67	0
TE Bailey	16	7	23	1		40.5	11	97	3
JH Wardle	9	1	33	0		57	22	100	4
GAR Lock	6	1	20	1		42	13	88	1

ENGLAND 1st innings / 2nd innings

Batsman	1st innings		2nd innings	
TE Bailey	lbw b Heine	9	c McLean b Tayfield	36
FA Lowson	lbw b Goddard	5	b Goddard	0
PBH May*	b Tayfield	47	lbw b Tayfield	97
GAR Lock	lbw b Goddard	17	c Keith b Goddard	47
DCS Compton	c Mansell b Tayfield	61	c Waite b Goddard	26
TW Graveney	lbw b Heine	10	c & b Tayfield	8
DJ Insole	lbw b Heine	3	c Heine b Tayfield	4
AJW McIntyre+	lbw b Heine	3	c Mansell b Goddard	21
JH Wardle	c Goddard b Tayfield	24	c Mansell b Goddard	7
JB Statham	b Tayfield	4	hit wkt b Goddard	3
PJ Loader	not out	0	not out	0
Extras □	(5b, 2lb, 1w, 0nb)	8	(1b, 6lb, 0w, 0nb)	7
Total	89.5 overs	**191**	142.1 overs	**256**

1st innings FoW: 15, 23, 53, 117, 152, 152, 161, 186, 191, 191
2nd innings FoW: 3, 59, 160, 204, 210, 215, 239, 246, 256, 256

Bowler									
PS Heine	29.5	11	70	4		14	2	33	0
NAT Adcock	4	3	4	0					
TL Goddard	25	12	39	2		62	37	69	5
HJ Tayfield	31	14	70	4		47.1	15	94	5
PNF Mansell						19	2	53	0

South Africa

No. 326:	5th Test	
VENUE:	The Oval	
DATE:	13th-17th August 1955	
TOSS WON BY:	England	
RESULT:	England won by 92 runs	

ENGLAND	1st innings		2nd innings	
JT Ikin	c Waite b Heine	17	c Goddard b Heine	0
DB Close	c Mansell b Goddard	32	b Goddard	15
PBH May*	c Goddard b Fuller	3	b Tayfield	42
DCS Compton	c Waite b Goddard	30	not out	89
W Watson	c Mansell b Tayfield	25	c Waite b Fuller	30
TW Graveney	c Fuller b Goddard	13	b Fuller	3
TE Bailey	c Heine b Tayfield	0	lbw b Tayfield	1
RT Spooner+	b Tayfield	0	b Tayfield	0
JC Laker	c & b Goddard	2	b Tayfield	12
GAR Lock	c McLean b Goddard	18	lbw b Heine	1
JB Statham	not out	4	lbw b Tayfield	0
Extras	(2b, 5lb, 0w, 0nb)	7	(4b, 6lb, 0w, 1nb)	11
Total	89.4 overs	151	123.4 overs	204

1st innings FoW: 51, 59, 69, 105, 117, 117, 118, 123, 130, 151
2nd innings FoW: 5, 30, 95, 157, 165, 166, 170, 188, 197, 204

PS Heine	21	3	43	1		25	6	44	2
TL Goddard	22.4	9	31	5		19	10	29	1
ERH Fuller	27	11	31	1		20	3	36	2
HJ Tayfield	19	7	39	3		53.4	29	60	5
PNF Mansell						6	0	24	0

SOUTH AFRICA	1st innings		2nd innings	
DJ McGlew	c Spooner b Statham	30	lbw b Lock	19
TL Goddard	lbw b Bailey	8	c Graveney b Lock	20
HJ Keith	b Lock	5	c May b Lock	0
WR Endean	c Ikin b Lock	0	lbw b Laker	0
RA McLean	b Lock	1	lbw b Laker	0
JHB Waite+	c Lock b Laker	28	b Laker	60
JE Cheetham*	not out	12	lbw b Laker	9
PNF Mansell	lbw b Laker	6	c Watson b Lock	9
HJ Tayfield	b Statham	]4	not out	10
ERH Fuller	c Spooner b Lock	5	run out	16
PS Heine	run out	5	c Graveney b Laker	7
Extras	(0b, 7lb, 0w, 1nb)	8	(0b, 1lb, 0w, 0nb)	1
Total	65 overs	112	87.4 overs	151

1st innings FoW: 22, 29, 31, 33, 77, 77, 86, 91, 98, 112
2nd innings FoW: 28, 28, 29, 33, 59, 88, 118, 118, 144, 151

JB Statham	15	3	31	2		11	4	17	0
TE Bailey	5	1	6	1		6	1	15	0
GAR Lock	22	11	39	4		33	14	62	4
JC Laker	23	13	28	2		37.4	18	56	5

Australia

No. 327:	1st Test	
VENUE:	Trent Bridge	
DATE:	7th-12th June 1956	
TOSS WON BY:	England	
RESULT:	Match drawn	

ENGLAND	1st innings		2nd innings	
PE Richardson	c Langley b Miller	81	c Langley b Archer	73
MC Cowdrey	c Miller b Davidson	25	c Langley b Miller	81
TW Graveney	c Archer b Johnson	8	c Langley b Miller	8
PBH May*	c Langley b Miller	73	not out	10
W Watson	lbw b Archer	0	not out	8
TE Bailey	c Miller b Archer	14		
TG Evans+	c Langley b Miller	0		
JC Laker	not out	9		
GAR Lock	lbw b Miller	0		
R Appleyard	not out	1		
AE Moss				
Extras	(5b, 1lb, 0w, 0nb)	6	(4b, 1lb, 2w, 1nb)	8
Total	103.4 overs	217	61 overs	188

1st innings FoW: 53, 72, 180, 181, 201, 203, 213, 214
2nd innings FoW: 151, 163, 178

RR Lindwall	15	4	43	0					
KR Miller	33	5	69	4		19	2	58	2
AK Davidson	9.4	1	22	1					
RG Archer	31	10	51	2		9	0	46	1
IW Johnson	14	7	26	1		12	2	29	0
JW Burke	1	1	0	0		3	1	6	0
R Benaud						18	4	41	0

AUSTRALIA	1st innings		2nd innings	
CC McDonald	lbw b Lock	1	c Lock b Laker	6
JW Burke	c Lock b Laker	11	not out	58
RN Harvey	lbw b Lock	64	b Lock	3
PJP Burge	c (sub) b Lock	7	lbw b Laker	4
KR Miller	lbw b Laker	0	not out	35
RG Archer	c Lock b Appleyard	33		
R Benaud	b Appleyard	17		
IW Johnson*	c Bailey b Laker	12		
RR Lindwall	c Bailey b Laker	0		
GRA Langley+	not out	0		
AK Davidson	absent hurt	0		
Extras	(0b, 3lb, 0w, 0nb)	3	(10b, 3lb, 0w, 1nb)	14
Total	83.1 overs	148	86 overs	120

1st innings FoW: 10, 12, 33, 36, 90, 110, 148, 148, 148
2nd innings FoW: 13, 18, 41

AE Moss	4	3	1	0					
TE Bailey	3	1	8	0		9	3	16	0
JC Laker	29.1	11	58	4		30	19	29	2
GAR Lock	36	16	61	3		22	11	23	1
R Appleyard	11	4	17	2		19	6	32	0
TW Graveney						6	3	6	0

No. 328: 2nd Test		No. 329: 3rd Test
VENUE: Lord's		VENUE: Headingley
DATE: 21st-26th June 1956		DATE: 12th-17th July 1956
TOSS WON BY: Australia		TOSS WON BY: England
RESULT: Australia won by 185 runs		RESULT: Eng won by an innings and 42 runs

AUSTRALIA 1st innings / 2nd innings

AUSTRALIA 1st innings			2nd innings	
CC McDonald	c Trueman b Bailey	78	c Cowdrey b Bailey	26
JW Burke	st Evans b Laker	65	c Graveney b Trueman	16
RN Harvey	c Evans b Bailey	0	c Bailey b Trueman	10
PJP Burge	b Statham	21	b Trueman	14
KR Miller	b Trueman	28	c Evans b Statham	31
KD Mackay	c Bailey b Laker	38	c Evans b Bailey	1
RG Archer	b Wardle	28	c Evans b Trueman	30
R Benaud	b Statham	5	c Evans b Trueman	97
IW Johnson*	c Evans b Trueman	6	lbw b Bailey	17
GRA Langley+	c Bailey b Laker	14	not out	7
WPA Crawford	not out	0	lbw b Bailey	0
Extras	(0b, 2lb, 0w, 0nb)	2	(2b, 2lb, 0w, 4nb)	8
Total	146.1 overs	**285**	92.5 overs	**257**

1st innings FoW: 137, 137, 151, 185, 196, 249, 255, 265, 285, 285
2nd innings FoW: 36, 47, 69, 70, 79, 112, 229, 243, 257, 257

JB Statham	35	9	70	2	26	5	59	1
FS Trueman	28	6	54	2	28	2	90	5
TE Bailey	34	12	72	2	24.5	8	64	4
JC Laker	29.1	10	47	3	7	3	17	0
JH Wardle	20	7	40	1	7	2	19	0

ENGLAND 1st innings / 2nd innings

ENGLAND 1st innings			2nd innings	
PE Richardson	c Langley b Miller	9	c Langley b Archer	21
MC Cowdrey	c Benaud b Mackay	23	lbw b Benaud	27
TW Graveney	b Miller	5	c Langley b Miller	18
PBH May*	b Benaud	63	b Miller	18
W Watson	c Benaud b Miller	6	c Langley b Miller	53
TE Bailey	b Miller	32	c Harvey b Archer	18
TG Evans+	st Langley b Benaud	0	c Langley b Miller	20
JC Laker	b Archer	12	c Langley b Archer	4
JH Wardle	c Langley b Archer	0	b Miller	0
FS Trueman	c Langley b Miller	7	b Archer	2
JB Statham	not out	0	not out	0
Extras	(0b, 14lb, 0w, 0nb)	14	(0b, 5lb, 0w, 0nb)	5
Total	82 overs	**171**	99.2 overs	**186**

1st innings FoW: 22, 32, 60, 87, 128, 128, 161, 161, 170, 171
2nd innings FoW: 35, 59, 89, 91, 142, 175, 180, 184, 184, 186

KR Miller	34.1	9	72	5	36	12	80	5
WPA Crawford	4.5	2	4	0				
RG Archer	23	9	47	2	31.2	8	71	4
KD Mackay	11	3	15	1				
R Benaud	9	2	19	2	28	14	27	1
IW Johnson					4	2	3	0

ENGLAND 1st innings / 2nd innings

ENGLAND 1st innings			2nd innings	
PE Richardson	c Maddocks b Archer	5		
MC Cowdrey	c Maddocks b Archer	0		
ASM Oakman	b Archer	4		
PBH May*	c Lindwall b Johnson	101		
C Washbrook	lbw b Benaud	98		
GAR Lock	c Miller b Benaud	21		
DJ Insole	c Mackay b Benaud	5		
TE Bailey	not out	33		
TG Evans+	b Lindwall	40		
JC Laker	b Lindwall	5		
FS Trueman	c & b Lindwall	0		
Extras	(4b, 9lb, 0w, 0nb)	13		
Total	167.4 overs	**325**		

1st innings FoW: 2, 8, 17, 204, 226, 243, 248, 301, 321, 325

RR Lindwall	33.4	11	67	3
RG Archer	50	24	68	3
KD Mackay	13	3	29	0
R Benaud	42	9	89	3
IW Johnson	29	8	59	1

AUSTRALIA 1st innings / 2nd innings

AUSTRALIA 1st innings			2nd innings	
CC McDonald	c Evans b Trueman	2	b Trueman	6
JW Burke	lbw b Lock	41	b Laker	16
RN Harvey	c Trueman b Lock	11	c & b Lock	69
PJP Burge	lbw b Laker	2	c Trueman b Laker	26
KD Mackay	c Bailey b Laker	2	lbw b Laker	5
KR Miller	b Laker	41	b Laker	1
RG Archer	b Laker	4	c Oakman b Laker	3
R Benaud	c Oakman b Laker	30	b Laker	2
LV Maddocks+	c Trueman b Lock	0	c Washbrook b Lock	1
IW Johnson*	c Richardson b Lock	0	lbw b Lock	0
RR Lindwall	not out	0	not out	0
Extras	(4b, 6lb, 0w, 0nb)	10	(7b, 4lb, 0w, 0nb)	11
Total	71.1 overs	**143**	99.3 overs	**140**

1st innings FoW: 2, 40, 59, 59, 63, 69, 142, 143, 143, 143
2nd innings FoW: 10, 45, 108, 120, 128, 136, 138, 140, 140, 140

FS Trueman	8	2	19	1	11	3	21	1
TE Bailey	7	2	15	0	7	2	13	0
JC Laker	29	10	58	5	41.3	21	55	6
GAR Lock	27.1	11	41	4	40	23	40	3

Australia

No. 330: 4th Test	
VENUE: Old Trafford	
DATE: 26th-31st July 1956	
TOSS WON BY: England	
RESULT: Eng won by an innings and 170 runs	

ENGLAND	1st innings		2nd innings
PE Richardson	c Maddocks b Benaud	104	
MC Cowdrey	c Maddocks b Lindwall	80	
DS Sheppard	b Archer	113	
PBH May*	c Archer b Benaud	43	
TE Bailey	b Johnson	20	
C Washbrook	lbw b Johnson	6	
ASM Oakman	c Archer b Johnson	10	
TG Evans+	st Maddocks b Johnson	47	
JC Laker	run out	3	
GAR Lock	not out	25	
JB Statham	c Maddocks b Lindwall	0	
Extras	(2b, 5lb, 1w, 0nb)	8	
	158.3 overs		
Total		**459**	

1st innings FoW: 174, 195, 288, 321, 327, 339, 401, 417, 458, 459

RR Lindwall	21.3	6	63	2					
KR Miller	21	6	41	0					
RG Archer	22	6	73	1					
IW Johnson	47	10	151	4					
R Benaud	47	17	123	2					

AUSTRALIA 1st innings			2nd innings	
CC McDonald	c Lock b Laker	32	c Oakman b Laker	89
JW Burke	c Cowdrey b Lock	22	c Lock b Laker	33
RN Harvey	b Laker	0	c Cowdrey b Laker	0
ID Craig	lbw b Laker	8	lbw b Laker	38
KR Miller	c Oakman b Laker	6	c Oakman b Laker	0
KD Mackay	c Oakman b Laker	0	b Laker	0
RG Archer	st Evans b Laker	6	c Oakman b Laker	0
R Benaud	c Statham b Laker	0	b Laker	18
RR Lindwall	not out	6	c Lock b Laker	8
LV Maddocks+	b Laker	4	not out	1
IW Johnson*	b Laker	0	lbw b Laker	2
Extras	(0b, 0lb, 0w, 0nb)	0	(12b, 4lb, 0w, 0nb)	16
	40.4 overs		150.2 overs	
Total		**84**		**205**

1st innings FoW: 48, 48, 62, 62, 62, 73, 73, 78, 84, 84
2nd innings FoW: 28, 55, 114, 124, 130, 130, 181, 198, 203, 205

JB Statham	6	3	6	0		16	10	15	0
TE Bailey	4	3	4	0		20	8	31	0
JC Laker	16.4	4	37	9		51.2	23	53	10
GAR Lock	14	3	37	1		55	30	69	0
ASM Oakman						8	3	21	0

Australia

No. 331: 5th Test	
VENUE: The Oval	
DATE: 23rd-28th August 1956	
TOSS WON BY: England	
RESULT: Match drawn	

ENGLAND	1st innings		2nd innings	
PE Richardson	c Langley b Miller	37	c Langley b Lindwall	34
MC Cowdrey	c Langley b Lindwall	0	c Benaud b Davidson	8
DS Sheppard	c Archer b Miller	24	c Archer b Miller	62
PBH May*	not out	83	not out	37
DCS Compton	c Davidson b Archer	94	not out	35
GAR Lock	c Langley b Archer	0		
C Washbrook	lbw b Archer	0		
TG Evans+	b Miller	0		
JC Laker	c Archer b Miller	4		
FH Tyson	c Davidson b Archer	3		
JB Statham	b Archer	0		
Extras	(0b, 0lb, 2w, 0nb)	2	(3b, 3lb, 0w, 0nb)	6
	109.2 overs		61 overs	
Total		**247**		**182**

1st innings FoW: 1, 53, 66, 222, 222, 222, 223, 231, 243, 247
2nd innings FoW: 17, 100, 108

RR Lindwall	18	5	36	1		12	3	29	1
KR Miller	40	7	91	4		22	3	56	1
AK Davidson	5	1	16	0		5	0	18	1
RG Archer	28.2	7	53	5		13	3	42	0
IW Johnson	9	2	28	0		4	1	7	0
R Benaud	9	2	21	0		1	0	10	0
JW Burke						4	2	14	0

AUSTRALIA 1st innings			2nd innings	
CC McDonald	c Lock b Tyson	3	lbw b Statham	0
JW Burke	b Laker	8	lbw b Laker	1
RN Harvey	c May b Lock	39	c May b Lock	1
ID Craig	c Statham b Lock	2	c Lock b Laker	7
IW Johnson*	b Laker	12	not out	7
AK Davidson	c May b Laker	8	c Lock b Laker	10
KR Miller	c Washbrook b Statham	61	not out	0
RG Archer	c Tyson b Laker	9		
R Benaud	b Statham	32		
RR Lindwall	not out	22		
GRA Langley+	lbw b Statham	0		
Extras	(6b, 0lb, 0w, 0nb)	6	(1b, 0lb, 0w, 0nb)	1
	92 overs		38.1 overs	
Total		**202**		**27**

1st innings FoW: 3, 17, 20, 35, 47, 90, 111, 154, 202, 202
2nd innings FoW: 0, 1, 5, 10, 27

JB Statham	21	8	33	3		2	1	1	1
FH Tyson	14	5	34	1					
JC Laker	32	12	80	4		18	14	8	3
GAR Lock	25	10	49	2		18.1	11	17	1

No. 332: 1st Test
VENUE: Johannesburg (Wanderers)
DATE: 24th–29th December 1956
TOSS WON BY: England
RESULT: England won by 131 runs

No. 333: 2nd Test
VENUE: Cape Town
DATE: 1st-5th January 1957
TOSS WON BY: England
RESULT: England won by 312 runs

ENGLAND 1st innings / 2nd innings (1st Test)

Batsman	1st innings		2nd innings	
PE Richardson	lbw b Goddard	117	lbw b Adcock	10
TE Bailey	c Waite b Heine	16	c Endean b Heine	10
DCS Compton	c Keith b Goddard	5	c & b Tayfield	32
PBH May*	c Goddard b Adcock	6	lbw b Heine	0
MC Cowdrey	c Goddard b Heine	59	c Waite b Goddard	29
DJ Insole	c Waite b Van Ryneveld	1	c Endean b Heine	14
TG Evans+	c Keith b Adcock	20	c Goddard b Adcock	6
FH Tyson	b Adcock	22	c Heine b Tayfield	30
JH Wardle	not out	6	c Watkins b Adcock	4
JC Laker	c Goddard b Adcock	0	not out	3
JB Statham	c Waite b Goddard	0	lbw b Tayfield	2
Extras	(4b, 9lb, 0w, 3nb)	16	(8b, 1lb, 0w, 3nb)	12
Total	118.5 overs	268	66.6 overs	150

1st innings FoW: 28, 37, 48, 169, 170, 205, 259, 263, 263, 268
2nd innings FoW: 11, 37, 37, 84, 100,1 07, 126, 145, 147, 150

Bowler								
PS Heine	31	5	89	2	19	7	41	3
NAT Adcock	20	6	36	4	13	1	33	3
TL Goddard	28.5	9	51	3	14	7	14	1
JC Watkins	11	3	23	0	3	0	10	0
HJ Tayfield	20	4	30	0	17.6	5	40	3
CB Van Ryneveld	8	2	23	1				

SOUTH AFRICA 1st innings / 2nd innings (1st Test)

Batsman	1st innings		2nd innings	
Al Taylor	st Evans b Wardle	12	c Insole b Bailey	6
TL Goddard	c Cowdrey b Statham	49	c Insole b Bailey	5
HJ Keith	c Cowdrey b Bailey	42	c Evans b Bailey	2
WR Endean	c Cowdrey b Laker	18	b Statham	0
RA McLean	lbw b Bailey	0	b Statham	3
JC Watkins	c Insole b Wardle	9	c Insole b Bailey	6
Van Ryneveld*	c Bailey b Statham	10	b Laker	8
JHB Waite+	c Evans b Bailey	17	run out	16
HJ Tayfield	b Wardle	24	c Evans b Bailey	2
PS Heine	not out	13	run out	17
NAT Adcock	b Statham	17	not out	0
Extras	(1b, 3lb, 0w, 0nb)	4	(2b, 3lb, 0w, 2nb)	7
Total	89.1 overs	215	33.4 overs	72

1st innings FoW: 54, 92, 112, 112, 126, 141, 141, 176, 194, 215
2nd innings FoW: 6, 10, 11, 20, 25, 36, 40, 44, 71, 72

Bowler								
JB Statham	24.1	4	71	3	13	4	22	2
FH Tyson	9	1	22	0				
JH Wardle	20	4	52	3	3	0	18	0
JC Laker	21	10	33	1	2	1	5	1
TE Bailey	15	5	33	3	15.4	6	20	5

ENGLAND 1st innings / 2nd innings (2nd Test)

Batsman	1st innings		2nd innings	
PE Richardson	lbw b Heine	45	c Endean b Goddard	44
TE Bailey	c Waite b Tayfield	34	b Heine	28
DCS Compton	c McLean b Tayfield	58	c & b Goddard	64
PBH May*	c Waite b Tayfield	8	c Waite b Heine	15
MC Cowdrey	lbw b Adcock	101	c Waite b Tayfield	61
DJ Insole	c Goddard b Adcock	29	not out	3
TG Evans+	c McGlew b Goddard	62	c Endean b Goddard	1
JH Wardle	st Waite b Tayfield	3		
JC Laker	b Adcock	0		
PJ Loader	c Keith b Tayfield	10		
JB Statham	not out	2		
Extras	(6b, 6lb, 0w, 5nb)	17	(0b, 2lb, 0w, 2nb)	4
Total	135.2 overs	369	63.5 overs	220

1st innings FoW: 76, 88, 116, 183, 233, 326, 334, 335, 346, 369
2nd innings FoW: 74, 74, 109, 196, 208, 220

Bowler								
PS Heine	19	0	78	1	21	1	67	2
NAT Adcock	22.2	2	54	3	3	0	8	0
HJ Tayfield	53	21	130	5	12	4	33	1
TL Goddard	38	12	74	1	17.5	1	62	3
CB Van Ryneveld	3	0	16	0				
JC Watkins					10	2	46	0

SOUTH AFRICA 1st innings / 2nd innings (2nd Test)

Batsman	1st innings		2nd innings	
DJ McGlew*	c Cowdrey b Laker	14	b Wardle	7
TL Goddard	c Evans b Loader	18	c Bailey b Wardle	26
HJ Keith	c Evans b Loader	14	c May b Wardle	4
Van Ryneveld	b Wardle	25	handled ball	0
HJ Tayfield	run out	5	lbw b Laker	22
RA McLean	c May b Statham	42	c Cowdrey b Wardle	2
JHB Waite+	c Evans b Wardle	49	not out	0
WR Endean	b Wardle	17	c & b Wardle	0
JC Watkins	not out	7	b Wardle	0
PS Heine	b Wardle	0	c Evans b Wardle	4
NAT Adcock	c Evans b Wardle	11	b Laker	1
Extras	(1b, 1lb, 0w, 1nb)	3	(0b, 2lb, 0w, 1nb)	3
Total	99.6 overs	205	50.1 overs	72

1st innings FoW: 23, 39, 48, 63, 110, 126, 178, 191, 191, 205
2nd innings FoW: 21, 28, 42, 56, 67, 67, 67, 67, 71, 72

Bowler								
JB Statham	16	0	38	1	8	2	12	0
PJ Loader	21	5	33	2	7	2	11	0
JC Laker	28	8	65	1	14.1	9	7	2
TE Bailey	11	5	13	0				
JH Wardle	23.6	9	53	5	19	3	36	7
DCS Compton					2	1	3	0

No. 334: 3rd Test	No. 335: 4th Test
VENUE: Durban (Kingsmead)	VENUE: Johannesburg (Wanderers)
DATE: 25th-30th January 1957	DATE: 15th-20th February 1957
TOSS WON BY: England	TOSS WON BY: South Africa
RESULT: Match drawn	RESULT: South Africa won by 17 runs

ENGLAND 1st innings / 2nd innings

Batsman	1st innings		2nd innings	
PE Richardson	lbw b Adcock	68	b Van Ryneveld	32
TE Bailey	c Keith b Adcock	80	c Ryneveld b Tayfield	18
DCS Compton	b Heine	16	c Keith b Tayfield	19
PBH May*	c Goddard b Tayfield	2	not out	110
MC Cowdrey	lbw b Goddard	6	lbw b Tayfield	2
DJ Insole	b Van Ryneveld	13	lbw b Heine	24
TG Evans+	st Waite b Van Ryneveld	0	c Waite b Tayfield	10
JH Wardle	b Heine	13	c Waite b Tayfield	8
JC Laker	not out	0	c Goddard b Tayfield	6
PJ Loader	c Waite b Adcock	1	lbw b Tayfield	3
JB Statham	b Adcock	6	c Van Ry'd b Tayfield	9
Extras	(2b, 4lb, 5w, 2nb)	13	(8b, 4lb, 0w, 1nb)	13
	94.3 overs		107.7 overs	
Total		**218**		**254**

1st innings FoW: 115, 148, 151, 163, 186, 186, 202, 210, 212, 218
2nd innings FoW: 45, 77, 79, 144, 167, 192, 203, 220, 230, 254

Bowler	O	M	R	W	O	M	R	W
PS Heine	16	2	65	2	22	3	58	1
NAT Adcock	15.3	3	39	4	21	8	39	0
TL Goddard	25	11	42	1	13	5	26	0
HJ Tayfield	24	17	21	1	37.7	14	69	8
CB Van Ryneveld	14	4	38	2	14	2	49	1

SOUTH AFRICA 1st innings / 2nd innings

Batsman	1st innings		2nd innings	
AJ Pithey	st Evans b Wardle	25	b Statham	0
TL Goddard	lbw b Statham	69	c Cowdrey b Wardle	18
HJ Keith	c Evans b Loader	6	c (sub) b Laker	22
WR Endean	c (sub) b Wardle	5	c & b Laker	26
RA McLean	c Insole b Bailey	100	b Wardle	4
KJ Funston	b Wardle	19	b Loader	44
JHB Waite+	b Statham	12	not out	14
CB Van Ryneveld*	c Cowdrey b Loader	16	not out	1
HJ Tayfield	not out	20		
PS Heine	b Wardle	6		
NAT Adcock	lbw b Wardle	3		
Extras	(0b, 2lb, 0w, 0nb)	2	(5b, 6lb, 0w, 2nb)	13
	96.2 overs		58 overs	
Total		**283**		**142**

1st innings FoW: 65, 76, 81, 145, 199, 225, 241, 264, 279, 283
2nd innings FoW: 0, 39, 45, 49, 124, 124

Bowler	O	M	R	W	O	M	R	W
JB Statham	22	4	56	2	11	0	32	1
PJ Loader	25	6	79	2	8	2	21	1
TE Bailey	17	3	38	1				
JH Wardle	20.2	6	61	5	20	7	42	2
JC Laker	12	1	47	0	18	7	29	2
DCS Compton					1	0	5	0

SOUTH AFRICA 1st innings / 2nd innings

Batsman	1st innings		2nd innings	
AJ Pithey	c Wardle b Bailey	10	b Laker	18
TL Goddard	b Bailey	67	c Evans b Bailey	49
JHB Waite+	c Evans b Statham	61	run out	23
KJ Funston	c Evans b Bailey	20	c Cowdrey b Statham	0
RA McLean	run out	93	c Insole b Bailey	2
C Duckworth	c Wardle b Loader	13	b Wardle	3
WR Endean	b Statham	13	c Cowdrey b Statham	17
Van Ryneveld	c Cowdrey b Laker	36	c & b Statham	12
HJ Tayfield	c Bailey b Wardle	10	run out	12
PS Heine	not out	1	c Insole b Wardle	0
NAT Adcock	lbw b Wardle	6	run out	1
Extras	(0b, 8lb, 1w, 1nb)	10	(4b, 1lb, 0w, 0nb)	5
	101.6 overs		60 overs	
Total		**340**		**142**

1st innings FoW: 22, 134, 151, 172, 238, 251, 309, 328, 333, 340
2nd innings FoW: 62, 91, 94, 95, 97, 104, 129, 130, 131, 142

Bowler	O	M	R	W	O	M	R	W
JB Statham	23	5	81	2	13	1	37	3
PJ Loader	23	3	78	1	13	3	33	0
TE Bailey	21	3	54	3	13	4	12	2
JH Wardle	19.6	4	68	2	14	4	29	2
JC Laker	15	3	49	1	7	1	26	1

ENGLAND 1st innings / 2nd innings

Batsman	1st innings		2nd innings	
PE Richardson	c Tayfield b Heine	11	b Tayfield	39
TE Bailey	c Waite b Adcock	13	c Endean b Tayfield	1
DJ Insole	run out	47	c Tayfield b Goddard	68
PBH May*	b Adcock	61	c & b Tayfield	55
DCS Compton	c Pithey b Heine	42	c Endean b Tayfield	0
MC Cowdrey	c Goddard b Tayfield	8	c Goddard b Tayfield	1
TG Evans+	c Endean b Tayfield	7	c Waite b Tayfield	22
JH Wardle	c Goddard b Tayfield	16	b Tayfield	8
JC Laker	lbw b Tayfield	17	c Duckworth b Tayfield	5
PJ Loader	c Endean b Goddard	13	c (sub) b Tayfield	7
JB Statham	not out	12	not out	4
Extras	(0b, 1lb, 0w, 3nb)	4	(1b, 3lb, 0w, 0nb)	4
	114.2 overs		78 overs	
Total		**251**		**214**

1st innings FoW: 25, 40, 131, 135, 152, 160, 176, 213, 227, 251
2nd innings FoW: 10, 65, 147, 148, 156, 186, 196, 199, 208, 214

Bowler	O	M	R	W	O	M	R	W
NAT Adcock	21	5	52	2	8	1	22	0
PS Heine	23	6	54	2	8	1	21	0
TL Goddard	25.2	15	22	1	25	5	54	1
HJ Tayfield	37	15	79	4	37	11	113	9
CB Van Ryneveld	8	0	40	0				

No. 336: 5th Test	No. 337: 1st Test
VENUE: Port Elizabeth	VENUE: Edgbaston
DATE: 1st-5th March 1957	DATE: 30th May-4th June 1957
TOSS WON BY: South Africa	TOSS WON BY: England
RESULT: South Africa won by 58 runs	RESULT: Match drawn

SOUTH AFRICA 1st innings / 2nd innings

Batsman	1st innings		2nd innings	
AJ Pithey	c Evans b Bailey	15	b Laker	6
TL Goddard	lbw b Bailey	2	c Evans b Tyson	30
JHB Waite+	c Evans b Loader	3	b Tyson	1
KJ Funston	b Bailey	3	b Lock	24
WR Endean	lbw b Tyson	70	lbw b Tyson	13
RA McLean	c Evans b Lock	23	b Bailey	19
Van Ryneveld*	c Tyson b Loader	24	b Tyson	6
CAR Duckworth	lbw b Laker	6	c Evans b Tyson	10
HJ Tayfield	b Loader	4	not out	7
PS Heine	b Tyson	4	c Evans b Tyson	4
NAT Adcock	not out	0	b Bailey	3
Extras	(0b, 1lb, 0w, 9nb)	10	(1b, 7lb, 0w, 3nb)	11
Total	87 overs	**164**	80.7 overs	**134**

1st innings FoW: 4, 15, 21, 41, 78, 143, 155, 155, 163, 164
2nd innings FoW: 20, 21, 65, 98, 99, 105, 111, 123, 129, 134

Bowler	O	M	R	W	O	M	R	W
PJ Loader	20	3	35	3	4	3	1	0
TE Bailey	25	12	23	3	24.7	5	39	2
FH Tyson	17	6	38	2	23	7	40	6
JC Laker	14	1	37	1	14	5	26	1
GAR Lock	11	5	21	1	15	6	17	1

ENGLAND 1st innings / 2nd innings

Batsman	1st innings		2nd innings	
PE Richardson	lbw b Adcock	0	b Adcock	3
TE Bailey	b Heine	41	c McLean b Tayfield	18
DCS Compton	b Adcock	0	lbw b Goddard	21
PBH May*	c Duckworth b Goddard	24	c Van Ry'ld b Tayfield	8
DJ Insole	lbw b Heine	4	b Duckworth b Tayfield	8
MC Cowdrey	c Waite b Adcock	3	c Endean b Tayfield	5
TG Evans+	b Heine	5	c Endean b Heine	21
GAR Lock	b Adcock	14	c Goddard b Tayfield	12
FH Tyson	c & b Heine	1	c Tayfield b Goddard	23
JC Laker	b Goddard	6	not out	4
PJ Loader	not out	0	c McLean b Tayfield	0
Extras	(8b, 4lb, 0w, 0nb)	12	(5b, 3lb, 0w, 0nb)	8
Total	61.3 overs	**110**	58.3 overs	**130**

1st innings FoW: 1, 1, 55, 77, 78, 86, 89, 97, 110, 110
2nd innings FoW: 15, 41, 53, 57, 71, 72, 99, 127, 129, 130

Bowler	O	M	R	W	O	M	R	W
PS Heine	15	6	22	4	11	3	22	1
NAT Adcock	11.3	4	20	4	7	2	10	1
HJ Tayfield	22	8	43	0	24.3	6	78	6
TL Goddard	13	8	13	2	16	8	12	2

ENGLAND 1st innings / 2nd innings

Batsman	1st innings		2nd innings	
PE Richardson	c Walcott b Ramadhin	47	c (sub) b Ramadhin	34
DB Close	c Kanhai b Gilchrist	15	c Weekes b Gilchrist	42
DJ Insole	b Ramadhin	20	b Ramadhin	0
PBH May*	c Weekes b Ramadhin	30	not out	285
MC Cowdrey	c Gilchrist b Ramadhin	4	c (sub) b Smith	154
TE Bailey	b Ramadhin	1	not out	29
GAR Lock	b Ramadhin	0		
TG Evans+	b Gilchrist	14		
JC Laker	b Ramadhin	7		
FS Trueman	not out	29		
JB Statham	b Atkinson	13		
Extras	(3b, 3lb, 0w, 0nb)	6	(23b, 16lb, 0w, 0nb)	39
Total	79.4 overs	**186**	258 overs	**583**

1st innings FoW: 32, 61, 104, 115, 116, 118, 121, 130, 150, 186
2nd innings FoW: 63, 65, 113, 524

Bowler	O	M	R	W	O	M	R	W
FMM Worrell	9	1	27	0				
R Gilchrist	27	4	74	2	26	2	67	1
S Ramadhin	31	16	49	7	98	35	179	2
DStE Atkinson	12.4	3	30	1	72	29	137	0
GStA Sobers					30	4	77	0
OG Smith					26	4	72	1
JDC Goddard					6	2	12	0

WEST INDIES 1st innings / 2nd innings

Batsman	1st innings		2nd innings	
BH Pairaudeau	b Trueman	1	b Trueman	7
RB Kanhai+	lbw b Statham	42	c Close b Trueman	1
CL Walcott	c Evans b Laker	90	c Cowdrey b Lock	14
EdeC Weekes	b Trueman	9	c Trueman b Lock	33
GStA Sobers	c Bailey b Statham	53	c May b Lock	42
OG Smith	lbw b Laker	161	c Lock b Laker	1
FMM Worrell	b Statham	81	lbw b Laker	5
JDC Goddard*	c Lock b Laker	24	not out	0
DStE Atkinson	c Statham b Laker	1	not out	4
S Ramadhin	not out	5		
R Gilchrist	run out	0		
Extras	(1b, 6lb, 0w, 0nb)	7	(7b, 0lb, 0w, 0nb)	7
Total	191.4 overs	**474**	60 overs	**72**

1st innings FoW: 4, 83, 120, 183, 197, 387, 466, 469, 474, 474
2nd innings FoW: 1, 9, 25, 27, 43, 66, 68

Bowler	O	M	R	W	O	M	R	W
JB Statham	39	4	114	3	2	0	6	0
FS Trueman	30	4	99	2	5	3	7	2
TE Bailey	34	11	80	0	24	20	13	2
JC Laker	54	17	119	4	27	19	31	3
GAR Lock	34.4	15	55	0	2	1	8	0

West Indies	**West Indies**

No. 338: 2nd Test	No. 339: 3rd Test
VENUE: Lord's	VENUE: Trent Bridge
DATE: 20th-22nd June 1957	DATE: 4th-9th July 1957
TOSS WON BY: West Indies	TOSS WON BY: England
RESULT: Eng won by an innings and 36 runs	RESULT: Match drawn

Left: WEST INDIES

WEST INDIES 1st innings / **2nd innings**

	1st innings		2nd innings	
NS Asgarali	lbw b Trueman	0	c Bailey b Statham	0
RB Kanhai+	c Cowdrey b Bailey	34	lbw b Statham	5
CL Walcott	lbw b Bailey	14	c Trueman b Bailey	21
GStA Sobers	c May b Statham	17	c Trueman b Wardle	26
EdeC Weekes	c Evans b Bailey	13	c May b Bailey	66
FMM Worrell	c Close b Bailey	12	c Evans b Bailey	90
OG Smith	c Graveney b Bailey	25	c Evans b Trueman	10
JDC Goddard*	c Cowdrey b Bailey	1	c Evans b Trueman	21
S Ramadhin	b Trueman	0	c Statham b Bailey	0
R Gilchrist	c & b Bailey	4	not out	11
AL Valentine	not out	0	b Statham	1
Extras	(2b, 1lb, 4w, 0nb)	7	(4b, 6lb, 0w, 0nb)	10
	51.3 overs		96.1 overs	
Total		**127**		**261**

1st innings FoW: 7, 34, 55, 79, 85, 118, 120, 123, 127, 127
2nd innings FoW: 0, 17, 32, 80, 180, 203, 233, 241, 256, 261

JB Statham	18	3	46	1	29.1	9	71	3
FS Trueman	12.3	2	30	2	23	5	73	2
TE Bailey	21	8	44	7	22	6	54	4
JH Wardle					22	5	53	1

Right: ENGLAND

ENGLAND 1st innings / **2nd innings**

	1st innings		2nd innings	
PE Richardson	c Walcott b Atkinson	126	c Kanhai b Gilchrist	11
DV Smith	c Kanhai b Worrell	1	not out	16
TW Graveney	b Smith	258	not out	28
PBH May*	lbw b Smith	104		
MC Cowdrey	run out	55		
DW Richardson	b Sobers	33		
TG Evans+	not out	26		
TE Bailey	not out	3		
JC Laker				
FS Trueman				
JB Statham				
Extras	(1b, 10lb, 1w, 1nb)	13	(7b, 2lb, 0w, 0nb)	9
	212 overs		17 overs	
Total		**619**		**64**

1st innings FoW: 14, 280, 487, 510, 573, 609
2nd innings FoW: 13

FMM Worrell	21	4	79	1	7	1	27	0
R Gilchrist	29	3	118	0	7	0	21	1
DStE Atkinson	40	7	99	1	1	0	1	0
S Ramadhin	38	5	95	0				
AL Valentine	23	4	68	0				
GStA Sobers	21	6	60	1				
JDC Goddard	15	5	26	0	1	0	2	0
OG Smith	25	5	61	2				
CL Walcott					1	0	4	0

Left lower: ENGLAND

ENGLAND 1st innings / **2nd innings**

	1st innings		2nd innings
PE Richardson	b Gilchrist	76	
DV Smith	lbw b Worrell	8	
TW Graveney	lbw b Gilchrist	0	
PBH May*	c Kanhai b Gilchrist	0	
MC Cowdrey	c Walcott b Sobers	152	
TE Bailey	b Worrell	1	
DB Close	c Kanhai b Goddard	32	
TG Evans+	b Sobers	82	
JH Wardle	c Sobers b Ramadhin	11	
FS Trueman	not out	36	
JB Statham	b Gilchrist	7	
Extras	(7b, 11lb, 1w, 0nb)	19	
	123.3 overs		
Total		**424**	

1st innings FoW: 25, 34, 34, 129, 134, 192, 366, 379, 387, 424

FMM Worrell	42	7	114	2
R Gilchrist	36.3	7	115	4
S Ramadhin	22	5	83	1
AL Valentine	3	0	20	0
JDC Goddard	13	1	45	1
GStA Sobers	7	0	28	2

Right lower: WEST INDIES

WEST INDIES 1st innings / **2nd innings**

	1st innings		2nd innings	
FMM Worrell	not out	191	b Statham	16
GStA Sobers	b Laker	47	lbw b Trueman	9
CL Walcott	c & b Laker	17	c Evans b Laker	7
RB Kanhai+	c Evans b Bailey	42	c Evans b Trueman	28
EdeC Weekes	b Trueman	33	b Statham	3
OG Smith	c Evans b Trueman	2	b Trueman	168
DStE Atkinson	c Evans b Trueman	4	c Evans b Statham	46
JDC Goddard*	c May b Trueman	0	c Evans b Statham	61
R Gilchrist	c DW Richardson b Laker	1	b Trueman	15
AL Valentine	b Trueman	1	b Trueman	0
S Ramadhin	b Statham	19	not out	2
Extras	(5b, 10lb, 0w, 0nb)	15	(2b, 10lb, 0w, 0nb)	12
	160.4 overs		148.2 overs	
Total		**372**		**367**

1st innings FoW: 87, 120, 229, 295, 297, 305, 305, 314, 317, 372
2nd innings FoW: 22, 30, 39, 56, 89, 194, 348, 352, 365, 367

JB Statham	28.4	9	78	1	41.2	12	118	5
FS Trueman	30	8	63	5	35	5	80	4
JC Laker	62	27	101	3	43	14	98	1
TE Bailey	28	9	77	1	12	3	22	0
DV Smith	12	1	38	0	12	5	23	0
TW Graveney					5	2	14	0

No. 340: 4th Test

VENUE:	Headingley
DATE:	25th-27th July 1957
TOSS WON BY:	West Indies
RESULT:	Eng won by an innings and 5 runs

WEST INDIES 1st innings / 2nd innings

	1st innings		2nd innings	
FMM Worrell	b Loader	29	c Cowdrey b Trueman	7
GStA Sobers	c Lock b Loader	4	run out	29
RB Kanhai	lbw b Laker	47	lbw b Loader	0
EdeC Weekes	b Loader	0	c Cowdrey b Trueman	14
CL Walcott	c Cowdrey b Laker	38	c Sheppard b Loader	35
OG Smith	b Trueman	15	c Evans b Smith	8
BH Pairaudeau	b Trueman	6	c Trueman b Loader	6
JDC Goddard*	b Loader	1	c Loader b Lock	4
F Alexander+	not out	0	b Laker	11
S Ramadhin	c Trueman b Loader	0	run out	6
R Gilchrist	b Loader	0	not out	6
Extras	(0b, 2lb, 0w, 0nb)	2	(0b, 5lb, 0w, 1nb)	6
	85.3 overs		36.2 overs	
Total		**142**		**132**

1st innings FoW: 16, 42, 42, 112, 125, 139, 142, 142, 142, 142
2nd innings FoW: 40, 40, 49, 56, 71, 92, 103, 113, 123, 132

FS Trueman	17	4	33	2		11	0	42	2
PJ Loader	20.3	9	36	6		14	2	50	3
DV Smith	17	6	24	0		4	1	12	1
JC Laker	17	4	24	2		6.2	1	16	1
GAR Lock	14	6	23	0		1	0	6	1

ENGLAND 1st innings / 2nd innings

	1st innings		2nd innings
PE Richardson	c Alexander b Worrell	10	
DV Smith	b Worrell	0	
TW Graveney	b Gilchrist	22	
PBH May*	c Alexander b Sobers	69	
MC Cowdrey	c Weekes b Worrell	68	
DS Sheppard	c Walcott b Worrell	68	
TG Evans+	b Worrell	10	
GAR Lock	b Gilchrist	20	
JC Laker	c Alexander b Worrell	1	
FS Trueman	not out	2	
PJ Loader	c Pairaudeau b Worrell	1	
Extras	(2b, 5lb, 1w, 0nb)	8	
	124.2 overs		
Total		**279**	

1st innings FoW: 1, 12, 42,1 36, 227, 239, 264, 272, 278, 279

FMM Worrell	38.2	9	70	7
R Gilchrist	27	3	71	2
GStA Sobers	32	9	79	1
S Ramadhin	19	5	34	0
OG Smith	8	1	17	0

No. 341: 5th Test

VENUE:	The Oval
DATE:	22nd-24th August 1957
TOSS WON BY:	England
RESULT:	Eng won by an innings and 237 runs

ENGLAND 1st innings / 2nd innings

	1st innings		2nd innings
PE Richardson	b Smith	107	
DS Sheppard	c & b Goddard	40	
TW Graveney	b Ramadhin	164	
PBH May*	c Worrell b Smith	1	
MC Cowdrey	b Ramadhin	2	
TE Bailey	run out	0	
TG Evans+	c Weekes b Dewdney	40	
GAR Lock	c Alexander b Sobers	17	
FS Trueman	b Ramadhin	22	
JC Laker	not out	10	
PJ Loader	lbw b Ramadhin	0	
Extras	(1b, 8lb, 0w, 0nb)	9	
	176.3 overs		
Total		**412**	

1st innings FoW: 92, 238, 242, 255, 256, 322, 366, 399, 412, 412

FMM Worrell	11	3	26	0
DT Dewdney	15	2	43	1
S Ramadhin	53.3	12	107	4
GStA Sobers	44	6	111	1
JDC Goddard	23	10	43	1
OG Smith	30	4	73	2

WEST INDIES 1st innings / 2nd innings

	1st innings		2nd innings	
FMM Worrell	c Lock b Loader	4	c Evans b Trueman	8
NS Asgarali	c Cowdrey b Lock	29	b Lock	7
GStA Sobers	b Lock	39	b Lock	42
CL Walcott	b Laker	5	c Cowdrey b Lock	0
EdeC Weekes	c Trueman b Laker	9	not out	19
OG Smith	c May b Laker	7	b Lock	0
RB Kanhai	not out	4	c Sheppard b Lock	0
F Alexander+	b Lock	0	b Laker	0
DT Dewdney	b Lock	0	st Evans b Lock	1
S Ramadhin	c Trueman b Lock	0	b Laker	2
JDC Goddard*	absent hurt	0	absent hurt	0
Extras	(0b, 0lb, 0w, 1nb)	1	(4b, 2lb, 0w, 1nb)	7
	56.4 overs		41 overs	
Total		**89**		**86**

1st innings FoW: 7, 68, 73, 73, 85, 89, 89, 89, 89
2nd innings FoW: 10, 39, 43, 69, 69, 69, 70, 75, 86

FS Trueman	5	1	9	0		5	2	19	1
PJ Loader	7	4	12	1		3	2	2	0
JC Laker	23	12	39	3		17	4	38	2
GAR Lock	21.4	12	28	5		16	7	20	6

No. 342: 1st Test

VENUE: Edgbaston
DATE: 5th-9th June 1958
TOSS WON BY: England
RESULT: England won by 205 runs

ENGLAND	1st innings		2nd innings	
PE Richardson	lbw b MacGibbon	4	c Cave b MacGibbon	100
MJK Smith	lbw b MacGibbon	0	c Petrie b MacGibbon	7
TW Graveney	c Alabaster b Hayes	7	c Petrie b Cave	19
PBH May*	c Petrie b MacGibbon	84	c Petrie b MacGibbon	11
MC Cowdrey	b MacGibbon	81	c Reid b Hayes	70
TE Bailey	c Petrie b Alabaster	2	not out	6
TG Evans+	c Petrie b MacGibbon	2	c Reid b Cave	0
GAR Lock	lbw b Alabaster	4		
FS Trueman	b Alabaster	0		
JC Laker	not out	11		
PJ Loader	b Alabaster	17		
Extras	(0b, 3lb, 4w, 2nb)	9	(1b, 1lb, 0w, 0nb)	2
	75.5 overs		96.2 overs	
Total		221		215

1st innings FoW: 4, 11, 29, 150, 153, 172, 185,191, 191, 221
2nd innings FoW: 24, 71, 94, 198, 214, 215

JA Hayes	15	2	57	1	20	3	51	1
AR MacGibbon	27	11	64	5	24	8	41	3
HB Cave	12	2	29	0	28.2	9	70	2
JR Reid	6	3	16	0	9	2	18	0
JC Alabaster	15.5	4	46	4	15	7	33	0

NEW ZEALAND	1st innings		2nd innings	
LSM Miller	lbw b Trueman	7	b Trueman	8
JW D'Arcy	c Evans b Trueman	19	c Trueman b Loader	25
NS Harford	b Bailey	9	c Bailey b Loader	8
JR Reid*	b Bailey	7	c Graveney b Loader	23
WR Playle	b Trueman	4	c Smith b Lock	10
T Meale	lbw b Trueman	7	b Bailey	13
MacGibbon	c Evans b Laker	5	b Bailey	1
EC Petrie+	lbw b Loader	1	c Cowdrey b Laker	26
JC Alabaster	b Trueman	9	c Laker b Lock	11
HB Cave	not out	12	not out	5
JA Hayes	run out	14	c Bailey b Lock	5
Extras	(0b, 0lb, 0w, 0nb)	0	(0b, 1lb, 1w, 0nb)	2
	69.3 overs		77.3 overs	
Total		94		137

1st innings FoW: 12, 21, 39, 43, 46, 54, 59, 67, 68, 94
2nd innings FoW: 19, 42, 49, 64, 93, 94, 95, 123, 131, 137

FS Trueman	21	8	31	5	17	5	33	1
PJ Loader	21.3	6	37	1	23	11	40	3
TE Bailey	20	9	17	2	20	9	23	2
GAR Lock	2	2	0	0	8.3	3	25	3
JC Laker	5	2	9	1	9	4	14	1

No. 343: 2nd Test

VENUE: Lord's
DATE: 19th-21st June 1958
TOSS WON BY: England
RESULT: Eng won by an innings and 148 runs

ENGLAND	1st innings		2nd innings
PE Richardson	c Petrie b Hayes	36	
MJK Smith	c Petrie b Hayes	47	
TW Graveney	c Petrie b Alabaster	37	
PBH May*	c Alabaster b MacGibbon	19	
MC Cowdrey	b Hayes	65	
TE Bailey	c Petrie b Reid	17	
TG Evans+	c Hayes b MacGibbon	11	
GAR Lock	not out	23	
FS Trueman	b Hayes	8	
JC Laker	c Blair b MacGibbon	1	
PJ Loader	c Playle b MacGibbon	4	
Extras	(0b, 1lb, 0w, 0nb)	1	
	123.4 overs		
Total		269	

1st innings FoW: 54, 113, 139, 141, 201, 222, 237, 259, 260, 269

AR MacGibbon	36.4	11	86	4
RW Blair	25	6	57	0
JR Reid	24	12	41	1
JC Alabaster	16	6	48	1

NEW ZEALAND	1st innings		2nd innings	
LSM Miller	lbw b Trueman	4	c Trueman b Loader	0
JW D'Arcy	c Trueman b Laker	14	c Bailey b Trueman	33
WR Playle	c Graveney b Laker	1	b Loader	3
NS Harford	c & b Laker	0	c May b Lock	3
JR Reid*	c Loader b Lock	6	c Cowdrey b Trueman	5
B Sutcliffe	b Lock	18	b Bailey	0
MacGibbon	c May b Lock	2	c May b Lock	7
JC Alabaster	c & b Lock	0	b Laker	5
EC Petrie+	c Trueman b Laker	0	not out	4
RW Blair	not out	0	b Lock	0
JA Hayes	c Cowdrey b Lock	1	c & b Lock	14
Extras	(0b, 1lb, 0w, 0nb)	1	(0b, 0lb, 0w, 0nb)	0
	32.3 overs		50.3 overs	
Total		47		74

1st innings FoW: 4, 12, 12, 19, 25, 31, 34, 46, 46, 47
2nd innings FoW: 11, 21, 34, 41, 44, 44, 56, 56, 56, 74

FS Trueman	4	1	6	1	11	6	24	2
PJ Loader	4	2	6	0	9	6	7	2
JC Laker	12	6	13	4	13	8	24	1
GAR Lock	11.3	7	17	5	12.3	8	12	4
TE Bailey	1	0	4	0	5	1	7	1

No. 344: 3rd Test	
VENUE: Headingley	
DATE: 3rd-8th July 1958	
TOSS WON BY: New Zealand	
RESULT: Eng won by an innings and 71 runs	

No. 345: 4th Test	
VENUE: Old Trafford	
DATE: 24th-29th July 1958	
TOSS WON BY: New Zealand	
RESULT: Eng won by an innings and 13 runs	

NEW ZEALAND 1st innings / 2nd innings

Batsman	1st innings		2nd innings	
LSM Miller	c Smith b Laker	26	lbw b Lock	18
JW D'Arcy	c Smith b Trueman	11	b Lock	6
NS Harford	c Cowdrey b Laker	0	lbw b Lock	0
B Sutcliffe	b Laker	6	lbw b Lock	0
JR Reid*	b Lock	3	c Trueman b Laker	13
WR Playle	c Milton b Lock	0	b Laker	18
MacGibbon	b Laker	3	lbw b Lock	39
JT Sparling	not out	9	c May b Lock	18
EC Petrie+	c Cowdrey b Lock	5	b Lock	3
HB Cave	c Milton b Laker	2	c Cowdrey b Laker	2
JA Hayes	c Evans b Lock	1	not out	0
Extras	(0b, 1lb, 0w, 0nb)	1	12	
	59.1 overs		101.2 overs	
Total		**67**		**129**

1st innings FoW: 37, 37, 37, 40, 46, 46, 49, 59, 66, 67
2nd innings FoW: 23, 23, 24, 32, 42, 88, 121, 124, 129, 129

Bowler	O	M	R	W		O	M	R	W
FS Trueman	11	5	18	1		14	6	22	0
PJ Loader	5	2	10	0		13	7	14	0
TE Bailey	3	0	7	0		3	2	3	0
JC Laker	22	11	17	5		36	23	27	3
GAR Lock	18.1	13	14	4		35.2	20	51	7

NEW ZEALAND 1st innings / 2nd innings

Batsman	1st innings		2nd innings	
B Sutcliffe	b Statham	41	b Statham	28
JW D'Arcy	lbw b Trueman	1	c Subba Row b Lock	8
NS Harford	lbw b Statham	2	b Illingworth	4
JR Reid*	c Trueman b Lock	14	c Watson b Lock	8
WR Playle	lbw b Illingworth	15	lbw b Lock	1
MacGibbon	c Evans b Statham	66	lbw b Lock	1
JT Sparling	c Evans b Statham	50	c & b Lock	2
EC Petrie+	retired hurt	45	c Statham b Illingworth	9
AM Moir	not out	21	c Evans b Lock	12
JA Hayes	b Trueman	4	not out	5
RW Blair	b Trueman	2	b Lock	0
Extras	(4b, 2lb, 0w, 0nb)	6	(5b, 2lb, 0w, 0nb)	7
	128.5 overs		52 overs	
Total		**267**		**85**

1st innings FoW: 15, 22, 62, 62, 117, 166, 227, 257, 267
2nd innings FoW: 36, 36, 46, 49, 49, 51, 60, 78, 80, 85

Bowler	O	M	R	W		O	M	R	W
FS Trueman	29.5	4	67	3		2	1	11	0
JB Statham	33	10	71	4		9	4	12	1
ER Dexter	5	0	23	0					
GAR Lock	33	12	61	1		24	11	35	7
R Illingworth	28	9	39	1		17	9	20	2

ENGLAND 1st innings / 2nd innings

Batsman	1st innings		2nd innings
MJK Smith	c Reid b MacGibbon	3	
CA Milton	not out	104	
TW Graveney	c & b Sparling	31	
PBH May*	not out	113	
MC Cowdrey			
TE Bailey			
TG Evans+			
GAR Lock			
FS Trueman			
JC Laker			
PJ Loader			
Extras	(5b, 8lb, 1w, 2nb)	16	
	102 overs		
Total		**267**	

1st innings FoW: 7, 73

Bowler	O	M	R	W
JA Hayes	13	4	30	0
AR MacGibbon	27	8	47	1
JR Reid	26	7	54	0
JT Sparling	23	2	78	1
HB Cave	13	4	42	0

ENGLAND 1st innings / 2nd innings

Batsman	1st innings		2nd innings
PE Richardson	st Reid b Sparling	74	
W Watson	c MacGibbon b Moir	66	
TW Graveney	c (sub) b MacGibbon	25	
PBH May*	c Playle b MacGibbon	101	
R Subba Row	c Petrie b Blair	9	
ER Dexter	lbw b Reid	52	
TG Evans+	c Blair b Reid	3	
R Illingworth	not out	3	
GAR Lock	lbw b MacGibbon	7	
FS Trueman	b Reid	5	
JB Statham			
Extras	(13b, 4lb, 1w, 2nb)	20	
	129.3 overs		
Total		**365**	

1st innings FoW: 126, 180, 193, 248, 330, 337, 351, 360, 365

Bowler	O	M	R	W
JA Hayes	19	4	51	0
AR MacGibbon	34	8	86	3
RW Blair	27	5	68	1
AM Moir	17	3	47	1
JT Sparling	21	7	46	1
JR Reid	11.3	2	47	3

New Zealand

No. 346: 5th Test		
VENUE: The Oval		
DATE: 21st-26th August 1958		
TOSS WON BY: New Zealand		
RESULT: Match drawn		

NEW ZEALAND 1st innings   **2nd innings**

LSM Miller	c Lock b Laker	25	c Evans b Statham	4
JW D'Arcy	c Milton b Bailey	9	c & b Lock	10
T Meale	c Lock b Trueman	1	c Cowdrey b Laker	3
B Sutcliffe	c Watson b Trueman	11	not out	18
JR Reid*	b Lock	27	not out	51
WR Playle	b Statham	6		
MacGibbon	b Bailey	26		
JT Sparling	retired hurt	0		
EC Petrie+	c Milton b Lock	8		
AM Moir	not out	41		
RW Blair	run out	3		
Extras	(0b, 4lb, 0w, 0nb)	4	(2b, 3lb, 0w, 0nb)	5
Total	75 overs	**161**	55 overs	**91**

1st innings FoW: 19, 24, 40, 46, 55, 93, 105, 132, 161
2nd innings FoW: 9, 17, 21

FS Trueman	16	3	41	2	6	5	3	0	
JB Statham	18	6	21	1	7	0	26	1	
TE Bailey	14	3	32	2					
JC Laker	14	3	44	1	20	10	25	1	
GAR Lock	13	6	19	2	18	11	20	1	
CA Milton					4	2	12	0	

ENGLAND 1st innings   **2nd innings**

PE Richardson	b Blair	28
CA Milton	lbw b MacGibbon	36
W Watson	b MacGibbon	10
PBH May*	c Petrie b Blair	9
MC Cowdrey	c Playle b Reid	25
TE Bailey	c Petrie b MacGibbon	14
TG Evans+	c Petrie b MacGibbon	12
GAR Lock	c Reid b Moir	25
JC Laker	c Blair b Reid	15
FS Trueman	not out	39
JB Statham		
Extras	(2b, 4lb, 0w, 0nb)	6
Total	68.5 overs	**219**

1st innings FoW: 39, 62, 85, 87, 109, 125, 162,1 62, 219

RW Blair	26	5	85	2
AR MacGibbon	27	4	65	4
JR Reid	7.5	2	11	2
AM Moir	8	1	52	1

Australia

No. 347: 1st Test		
VENUE: Brisbane (Gabba)		
DATE: 5th-10th December 1958		
TOSS WON BY: England		
RESULT: Australia won by 8 wickets		

ENGLAND 1st innings   **2nd innings**

PE Richardson	c Mackay b Davidson	11	c & b Benaud	8
CA Milton	b Meckiff	5	c Grout b Davidson	17
TW Graveney	c Grout b Davidson	19	b Mackay	68
PBH May*	c Grout b Meckiff	26	run out	36
MC Cowdrey	c Kline b Meckiff	13	lbw b Benaud	4
TE Bailey	st Grout b Benaud	27	c Kline b Meckiff	28
TG Evans+	c Burge b Davidson	4	lbw b Davidson	4
GAR Lock	c Davidson b Benaud	5	b Meckiff	1
JC Laker	c Burke b Benaud	13	b Benaud	15
JB Statham	c Grout b Mackay	2	c McDonald b Benaud	3
PJ Loader	not out	6	not out	0
Extras	(0b, 1lb, 1w, 1nb)	3	(10b, 4lb, 0w, 0nb)	14
Total	59.4 overs	**134**	119.2 overs	**198**

1st innings FoW: 16, 16, 62, 75, 79, 83, 92, 112, 116, 134
2nd innings FoW: 28, 34, 96, 102, 153, 161, 169, 190, 198, 198

AK Davidson	16	4	36	3	28	12	30	2	
I Meckiff	17	5	33	3	19	7	30	2	
KD Mackay	8	1	16	1	9	6	7	1	
R Benaud	18.4	9	46	3	39.2	10	66	4	
LF Kline					14	4	34	0	
JW Burke					10	5	17	0	

AUSTRALIA 1st innings   **2nd innings**

CC McDonald	c Graveney b Bailey	42	c Statham b Laker	15
JW Burke	c Evans b Loader	20	not out	28
RN Harvey	lbw b Loader	14	c Milton b Lock	23
NC O'Neill	c Graveney b Bailey	34	not out	71
PJP Burge	c Cowdrey b Bailey	2		
KD Mackay	c Evans b Laker	16		
R Benaud*	lbw b Loader	16		
AK Davidson	lbw b Laker	25		
ATW Grout+	b Statham	2		
I Meckiff	b Loader	5		
LF Kline	not out	4		
Extras	(4b, 1lb, 0w, 1nb)	6	(2b, 3lb, 0w, 5nb)	10
Total	72.1 overs	**186**	51.7 overs	**147**

1st innings FoW: 55, 65, 88, 94, 122, 136, 162, 165, 178, 186
2nd innings FoW: 20, 58

JB Statham	20	2	57	1	6	1	13	0	
PJ Loader	19	4	56	4	9	1	27	0	
TE Bailey	13	2	35	3	5	1	21	0	
JC Laker	10.1	3	15	2	17	3	39	1	
GAR Lock	10	4	17	0	14.7	5	37	1	

No. 348:	2nd Test
VENUE:	Melbourne (MCG)
DATE:	31st Dec 1958-5th Jan 1959
TOSS WON BY:	England
RESULT:	Australia won by 8 wickets

ENGLAND	**1st innings**		**2nd innings**	
PE Richardson	c Grout b Davidson	3	c Harvey b Meckiff	2
TE Bailey	c Benaud b Meckiff	48	c Burke b Meckiff	14
W Watson	b Davidson	0	b Davidson	7
TW Graveney	lbw b Davidson	0	c Davidson b Meckiff	3
PBH May*	b Meckiff	113	c Davidson b Meckiff	17
MC Cowdrey	c Grout b Davidson	44	c Grout b Meckiff	12
TG Evans+	c Davidson b Meckiff	4	run out	11
GAR Lock	st Grout b Benaud	5	c & b Davidson	6
JC Laker	not out	22	c Harvey b Davidson	3
JB Statham	b Davidson	13	not out	8
PJ Loader	b Davidson	0	b Meckiff	0
Extras	(1b, 2lb, 3w, 0nb)	6	(1b, 1lb, 0w, 2nb)	4
Total	98.5 overs	**259**	31.2 overs	**87**

1st innings FoW: 7, 7, 7, 92, 210, 218, 218, 233, 253, 259
2nd innings FoW: 3, 14, 21, 27, 44, 57, 71, 75, 80, 87

AK Davidson	25.5	7	64	6		15	2	41	3
I Meckiff	24	4	69	3		15.2	3	38	6
KD Mackay	9	2	16	0					
R Benaud	29	7	61	1		1	0	4	0
LF Kline	11	2	43	0					

AUSTRALIA 1st innings			**2nd innings**	
CC McDonald	c Graveney b Statham	47	lbw b Statham	5
JW Burke	b Statham	3	not out	18
RN Harvey	b Loader	167	st Evans b Laker	12
NC O'Neill	c Evans b Statham	37	not out	7
KD Mackay	c Evans b Statham	18		
RB Simpson	lbw b Loader	0		
R Benaud*	lbw b Statham	0		
AK Davidson	b Statham	24		
ATW Grout+	c May b Loader	8		
I Meckiff	b Statham	0		
LF Kline	not out	1		
Extras	(0b, 3lb, 0w, 0nb)	3	(0b, 0lb, 0w, 0nb)	0
Total	100.2 overs	**308**	17.1 overs	**42**

1st innings FoW: 11, 137, 255, 257, 261, 262, 295, 300, 300, 308
2nd innings FoW: 6, 26

JB Statham	28	6	57	7		5	1	11	1
PJ Loader	27.2	4	97	3		5	1	13	0
TE Bailey	16	0	50	0		4	1	7	1
JC Laker	12	1	47	0		3.1	1	11	0
GAR Lock	17	2	54	0					

No. 349:	3rd Test
VENUE:	Sydney (SCG)
DATE:	9th-15th January 1959
TOSS WON BY:	England
RESULT:	Match drawn

ENGLAND	**1st innings**		**2nd innings**	
TE Bailey	lbw b Meckiff	8	c (sub) b Benaud	25
CA Milton	c Meckiff b Davidson	8	c Davidson b Benaud	8
TW Graveney	c Harvey b Benaud	33	lbw b Davidson	22
PBH May*	c Mackay b Slater	42	b Burke	92
MC Cowdrey	c Harvey b Benaud	34	not out	100
ER Dexter	lbw b Slater	1	c Grout b Benaud	11
R Swetman+	c Mackay b Benaud	41	lbw b Burke	5
GAR Lock	lbw b Mackay	21	st Grout b Benaud	0
FS Trueman	c Burke b Benaud	18	not out	11
JC Laker	c Harvey b Benaud	2		
JB Statham	not out	0		
Extras	(4b, 5lb, 2w, 0nb)	11	(11b, 1lb, 1w, 0nb)	13
Total	82.4 overs	**219**	109 overs	**287**

1st innings FoW: 19, 23, 91, 97, 98, 155, 194, 200, 202, 219
2nd innings FoW: 30, 37, 64, 246, 262, 269, 270

AK Davidson	12	3	21	1		33	–	11	65	1
I Meckiff	15	2	45	1		3	1	7	0
R Benaud	33.4	10	83	5		33	7	94	4
KN Slater	14	4	40	2		18	5	61	0
KD Mackay	8	3	19	1		11	2	21	0
JW Burke						11	3	26	2

AUSTRALIA 1st innings			**2nd innings**	
CC McDonald	c Graveney b Lock	40	b Laker	16
JW Burke	c Lock b Laker	12	b Laker	7
RN Harvey	b Laker	7	not out	18
NC O'Neill	c Swetman b Laker	77	not out	7
LE Favell	c Cowdrey b Lock	54		
KD Mackay	b Trueman	57		
R Benaud*	b Laker	6		
AK Davidson	lbw b Lock	71		
ATW Grout+	c Statham b Laker	14		
KN Slater	not out	1		
I Meckiff	b Lock	2		
Extras	(5b, 10lb, 0w, 1nb)	16	(6b, 0lb, 0w, 0nb)	6
Total	128.2 overs	**357**	25 overs	**54**

1st innings FoW: 26, 52, 87, 197, 199, 208, 323, 353, 355, 357
2nd innings FoW: 22, 33

JB Statham	16	2	48	0		2	0	6	0
FS Trueman	18	3	37	1		4	1	9	0
GAR Lock	43.2	9	130	4		11	4	23	0
JC Laker	46	19	107	5		8	3	10	2
TE Bailey	5	0	19	0					

Australia | Australia

No. 350: 4th Test	No. 351: 5th Test
VENUE: Adelaide	VENUE: Melbourne (MCG)
DATE: 30th January-5th Feb 1959	DATE: 13th-18th February 1959
TOSS WON BY: England	TOSS WON BY: Australia
RESULT: Australia won by 10 wickets	RESULT: Australia won by 9 wickets

AUSTRALIA 1st innings / **2nd innings**

Batsman	1st innings		2nd innings	
CC McDonald	b Trueman	170	not out	15
JW Burke	c Cowdrey b Bailey	66	not out	16
RN Harvey	run out	41		
NC O'Neill	b Statham	56		
LE Favell	b Statham	4		
KD Mackay	c Evans b Statham	4		
R Benaud*	b Trueman	46		
AK Davidson	c Bailey b Tyson	43		
ATW Grout+	lbw b Trueman	9		
RR Lindwall	b Trueman	19		
GF Rorke	not out	2		
Extras	(2b, 8lb, 4w, 2nb)	16	(4b, 1lb, 0w, 0nb)	5
	128.1 overs		10.3 overs	
Total		**476**		**36**

1st innings FoW: 171, 276, 286, 294, 369, 388, 407, 445, 473, 476

Bowler	O	M	R	W	O	M	R	W
JB Statham	23	0	83	3	4	0	11	0
FS Trueman	30.1	6	90	4	3	1	3	0
FH Tyson	28	1	100	1				
TE Bailey	22	2	91	1				
GAR Lock	25	0	96	0	2	0	8	0
MC Cowdrey					1.3	0	9	0

ENGLAND 1st innings / **2nd innings**

Batsman	1st innings		2nd innings	
PE Richardson	lbw b Lindwall	4	lbw b Benaud	43
TE Bailey	b Davidson	4	c Favell b Benaud	40
PBH May*	b Benaud	37	lbw b Rorke	59
MC Cowdrey	b Rorke	84	b Lindwall	8
TW Graveney	c Benaud b Rorke	41	not out	53
W Watson	b Rorke	25	c Grout b Lindwall	6
FS Trueman	c Grout b Benaud	0	c Grout b Davidson	0
GAR Lock	c Grout b Benaud	2	b Rorke	9
FH Tyson	c & b Benaud	0	c Grout b Benaud	33
TG Evans+	c Burke b Benaud	4	c O'Neill b Benaud	2
JB Statham	not out	36	c Benaud b Davidson	0
Extras	(0b, 2lb, 0w, 1nb)	3	(5b, 5lb, 3w, 4nb)	17
	74.1 overs		101.3 overs	
Total		**240**		**270**

1st innings FoW: 7, 11, 74, 170, 173, 180, 184,184, 188, 240
2nd innings FoW: 89, 110, 125, 177, 198, 199, 222, 268, 270, 270

Bowler	O	M	R	W	O	M	R	W
AK Davidson	12	0	49	1	8.3	3	17	2
RR Lindwall	15	0	66	1	26	6	70	2
GF Rorke	18.1	7	23	3	34	7	78	2
R Benaud	27	6	91	5	29	10	82	4
NC O'Neill	2	1	8	0				
JW Burke					4	2	6	0

ENGLAND 1st innings / **2nd innings**

Batsman	1st innings		2nd innings	
PE Richardson	c & b Benaud	68	lbw b Benaud	23
TE Bailey	c Davidson b Lindwall	0	b Lindwall	0
PBH May*	c Benaud b Meckiff	11	c Harvey b Lindwall	4
MC Cowdrey	c Lindwall b Davidson	22	run out	46
TW Graveney	c McDonald b Benaud	19	c Harvey b Davidson	54
ER Dexter	c Lindwall b Meckiff	0	c Grout b Davidson	6
R Swetman+	c Grout b Davidson	1	lbw b Lindwall	9
JB Mortimore	not out	44	b Rorke	11
FS Trueman	c & b Benaud	21	b Rorke	36
FH Tyson	c Grout b Benaud	9	c Grout b Rorke	6
JC Laker	c Harvey b Davidson	2	not out	5
Extras	(4b, 0lb, 4w, 0nb)	8	(9b, 3lb, 2w, 0nb)	14
	64.5 overs		54.4 overs	
Total		**205**		**214**

1st innings FoW: 0, 13, 61, 109, 112, 124, 128,191, 203, 205
2nd innings FoW: 0, 12, 78, 105, 131, 142, 158, 172, 182, 214

Bowler	O	M	R	W	O	M	R	W
AK Davidson	12.5	2	38	3	21	1	95	2
RR Lindwall	14	2	36	1	11	2	37	3
I Meckiff	15	2	57	2	4	0	13	0
GF Rorke	6	1	23	0	12.4	2	41	3
R Benaud	17	5	43	4	6	1	14	1

AUSTRALIA 1st innings / **2nd innings**

Batsman	1st innings		2nd innings	
CC McDonald	c Cowdrey b Laker	133	not out	51
JW Burke	c Trueman b Tyson	16	lbw b Tyson	13
RN Harvey	c Swetman b Trueman	13	not out	1
NC O'Neill	c Cowdrey b Trueman	0		
KD Mackay	c Graveney b Laker	23		
AK Davidson	b Mortimore	17		
R Benaud*	c Swetman b Laker	64		
ATW Grout+	c Trueman b Laker	74		
RR Lindwall	c Cowdrey b Trueman	0		
I Meckiff	c & b Trueman	2		
GF Rorke	not out	0		
Extras	(5b, 4lb, 0w, 0nb)	9	(0b, 4lb, 0w, 0nb)	4
	100.5 overs		12.7 overs	
Total		**351**		**69**

1st innings FoW: 41, 83, 83, 154, 207, 209, 324, 327, 329, 351

Bowler	O	M	R	W	O	M	R	W
FS Trueman	25	0	92	4	6.7	0	45	0
FH Tyson	20	1	73	1	6	0	20	1
TE Bailey	14	2	43	0				
JC Laker	30.5	4	93	4				
JB Mortimore	11	1	41	1				

No. 352: 1st Test	
VENUE:	Christchurch
DATE:	27th Feb-2nd March 1959
TOSS WON BY:	England
RESULT:	Eng won by an innings and 99 runs

No. 353: 2nd Test	
VENUE:	Auckland
DATE:	14th-18th March 1959
TOSS WON BY:	New Zealand
RESULT:	Match drawn

ENGLAND 1st innings / **2nd innings**

Batsman	1st innings		2nd innings	
PE Richardson	c Petrie b Blair	8	c May b Mortimore	26
W Watson	c Petrie b Blair	10	b Trueman	13
TW Graveney	lbw b Hough	42	c Lock b Tyson	56
PBH May*	c Hough b Moir	71	c Cowdrey b Lock	1
MC Cowdrey	b Hough	15	c Trueman b Lock	12
ER Dexter	b Reid	141	lbw b Lock	6
JB Mortimore	c & b Moir	11	b Tyson	0
R Swetman+	b Hough	9	c Swetman b Lock	1
FS Trueman	lbw b Reid	21	not out	2
GAR Lock	b Reid	15	c Trueman b Lock	2
FH Tyson	not out	6	b Lock	7
Extras	(12b, 13lb, 0w, 0nb)	25	(1b, 5lb, 0w, 1nb)	7
	142.1 overs		72.2 overs	
Total		**374**		**133**

1st innings FoW: 13, 30, 98, 126, 171, 197, 224, 305, 367, 374
2nd innings FoW: 37, 68, 79, 10, 117, 119, 120, 121, 123, 133

	O	M	R	W
RW Blair	31	5	89	2
KW Hough	39	11	96	3
AM Moir	36	9	83	2
JR Reid	18.1	9	34	3
JT Sparling	16	7	38	0
B Sutcliffe	2	0	9	0

NEW ZEALAND 1st innings / **2nd innings**

Batsman	1st innings	
BA Bolton	c Swetman b Lock	33
RM Harris	c Lock b Tyson	6
JW Guy	c Trueman b Lock	3
JR Reid*	b Tyson	40
B Sutcliffe	c Lock b Tyson	0
SN McGregor	c Lock b Mortimore	0
JT Sparling	st Swetman b Lock	12
AM Moir	c Graveney b Lock	0
EC Petrie+	lbw b Trueman	8
RW Blair	lbw b Lock	0
KW Hough	not out	31
Extras	(5b, 4lb, 0w, 0nb)	9
	72.5 overs	
Total		**142**

1st innings FoW: 22, 33, 83, 83, 86, 101, 101, 102, 102, 142

	O	M	R	W	O	M	R	W
FS Trueman	10.5	3	39	1	8	2	20	1
FH Tyson	14	4	23	3	14	6	23	2
GAR Lock	26	15	31	5	28.2	13	53	6
JB Mortimore	22	8	40	1	21	10	27	1
ER Dexter					1	0	3	0

NEW ZEALAND 1st innings / **2nd innings**

Batsman	1st innings	
BA Bolton	run out	0
RM Harris	c Swetman b Dexter	12
SN McGregor	hit wkt b Trueman	1
JW Guy	b Dexter	1
B Sutcliffe	b Lock	61
JR Reid*	b Dexter	3
JT Sparling	c Swetman b Trueman	25
AM Moir	c Graveney b Trueman	10
EC Petrie+	c Trueman b Lock	13
RW Blair	c Cowdrey b Tyson	22
KW Hough	not out	24
Extras	(7b, 1lb, 0w, 1nb)	9
	89.3 overs	
Total		**181**

1st innings FoW: 3, 6, 11, 16, 41, 98, 116, 125, 157, 181

	O	M	R	W
FS Trueman	26	12	46	3
FH Tyson	20	9	50	1
ER Dexter	19	8	23	3
GAR Lock	20.3	12	29	2
JB Mortimore	4	1	24	0

ENGLAND 1st innings / **2nd innings**

Batsman	1st innings	
PE Richardson	c Bolton b Moir	67
W Watson	b Hough	11
TW Graveney	b Moir	46
PBH May*	not out	124
MC Cowdrey	b Hough	5
ER Dexter	c Petrie b Moir	1
JB Mortimore	b Hough	9
R Swetman+	run out	17
FS Trueman	not out	21
GAR Lock		
FH Tyson		
Extras	(4b, 6lb, 0w, 0nb)	10
	118 overs	
Total		**311**

1st innings FoW: 26, 94, 165, 182, 183, 223, 261

	O	M	R	W
RW Blair	27	6	69	0
KW Hough	38	12	79	3
JR Reid	4	1	19	0
JT Sparling	20	7	48	0
AM Moir	28	4	84	3
B Sutcliffe	1	0	2	0

No. 354: 1st Test
VENUE: Trent Bridge
DATE: 4th-8th June 1959
TOSS WON BY: England
RESULT: Eng won by an innings and 59 runs

ENGLAND	1st innings		2nd innings
CA Milton	b Surendranath	9	
K Taylor	lbw b Gupte	24	
MC Cowdrey	c Borde b Surendranath	5	
PBH May*	c Joshi b Gupte	106	
KF Barrington	b Nadkarni	56	
MJ Horton	c Nadkarni b Desai	58	
TG Evans+	c Umrigar b Nadkarni	73	
JB Statham	not out	29	
T Greenhough	c Gaekwad b Gupte	0	
AE Moss	c Roy b Gupte	11	
Extras	(15b, 7lb, 1w, 0nb)	23	
Total	143.2 overs	422	

1st innings FoW: 17, 29, 60, 185, 221, 327, 358, 389, 390, 422

RB Desai	33	7	127	1				
Surendranath	24	8	59	2				
SP Gupte	38.1	11	102	4				
RG Nadkarni	28.1	15	48	2				
CG Borde	20	4	63	1				

INDIA	1st innings		2nd innings	
Pank Roy	b Trueman	54	c Trueman b Greenh'gh	49
NJ Contractor	c Barrington b Greenh'gh	15	c Cowdrey b Statham	0
PR Umrigar	b Trueman	21	b Statham	20
VL Manjrekar	lbw b Trueman	17	lbw b Greenhough	44
CG Borde	retired hurt	15	c Horton b Statham	31
DK Gaekwad*	c Evans b Statham	33	b Statham	1
RG Nadkarni	lbw b Trueman	15	lbw b Trueman	1
PG Joshi+	lbw b Moss	21	c May b Statham	8
SP Gupte	c Taylor b Moss	2	not out	1
Surendranath	not out	4	c May b Trueman	1
RB Desai	b Statham	0	(0b, 0lb, 0w, 1nb)	1
Extras	(5b, 0lb, 0w, 4nb)	9	97.3 overs	
Total	102.5 overs	206		157

1st innings FoW: 34, 85, 95, 126, 158, 190, 198, 206, 206
2nd innings FoW: 8, 52 , 85 , 124, 140, 143, 147, 156, 157

JB Statham	23.5	11	46	2	21	10	31	5
FS Trueman	24	9	45	4	22.3	10	44	2
AE Moss	24	11	33	2	12	7	13	0
T Greenhough	26	7	58	1	23	5	48	2
MJ Horton	5	0	15	0	19	11	20	0

No. 355: 2nd Test
VENUE: Lord's
DATE: 18th-20th June 1959
TOSS WON BY: India
RESULT: England won by 8 wickets

INDIA	1st innings		2nd innings	
Pank Roy*	c Evans b Statham	15	c May b Trueman	0
NJ Contractor	b Greenhough	81	lbw b Moss	8
PR Umrigar	b Statham	1	c Horton b Trueman	0
VL Manjrekar	lbw b Trueman	12	c Evans b Statham	22
JM Ghorpade	lbw b Greenhough	41	lbw b Statham	61
Kripal Singh	b Greenhough	0	b Statham	41
ML Jaisimha	lbw b Greenhough	14	b Moss	6
PG Joshi+	b Horton	4	not out	11
Surendranath	b Greenhough	0	run out	0
SP Gupte	c May b Horton	0	st Evans b Greenhough	7
RB Desai	not out	2	b Greenhough	5
Extras	(0b, 11lb, 0w, 0nb)	11	(0b, 4lb, 0w, 0nb)	4
Total	77.4 overs	168	79.1 overs	165

1st innings FoW: 32, 40, 61, 144, 152, 158, 163, 163, 164, 168
2nd innings FoW: 0 , 0, 22, 42, 131, 140, 147, 147, 159, 165

FS Trueman	16	4	40	1	21	3	55	2
JB Statham	16	6	27	2	17	7	45	3
AE Moss	14	5	31	0	23	10	30	2
T Greenhough	16	4	35	5	18.1	8	31	2
MJ Horton	15.4	7	24	2				

ENGLAND	1st innings		2nd innings	
CA Milton	c Surendranath b Desai	14	c Joshi b Desai	3
K Taylor	c Gupte b Desai	6	lbw b Surendranath	3
MC Cowdrey	c Joshi b Desai	34	not out	63
PBH May*	b Surendranath	9	not out	33
KF Barrington	c (sub) b Desai	80		
MJ Horton	b Desai	2		
TG Evans+	b Surendranath	0		
FS Trueman	lbw b Gupte	7		
JB Statham	c Surendranath b Gupte	38		
AE Moss	b Surendranath	26		
T Greenhough	not out	0		
Extras	(5b, 4lb, 1w, 0nb)	10	(5b, 1lb, 0w, 0nb)	6
Total	84.4 overs	226	27.2 overs	108

1st innings FoW: 9, 26, 35, 69, 79, 80, 100, 184, 226, 226
2nd innings FoW: 8 , 12

RB Desai	31.4	8	89	5	7	1	29	1
Surendranath	30	17	46	3	11	2	32	1
PR Umrigar	1	1	0	0	1	0	8	0
SP Gupte	19	2	62	2	6	2	21	0
AG Kripal Singh	3	0	19	0	1	1	0	0
ML Jaisimha					1	0	8	0
Pank Roy					0.2	0	4	0

	No. 356: 3rd Test
	VENUE: Headingley
	DATE: 2nd-4th July 1959
	TOSS WON BY: India
	RESULT: Eng won by an innings and 173 runs

	No. 357: 4th Test
	VENUE: Old Trafford
	DATE: 23rd-28th July 1959
	TOSS WON BY: England
	RESULT: England won by 171 runs

INDIA 1st innings / 2nd innings

Batsman	1st innings		2nd innings	
Pank Roy	c Swetman b Rhodes	2	c Swetman b Trueman	20
AL Apte	b Moss	8	c Close b Moss	7
JM Ghorpade	c Swetman b Trueman	8	lbw b Trueman	0
CG Borde	c Swetman b Rhodes	0	c May b Close	41
PR Umrigar	c Trueman b Moss	29	c Trueman b Mortimore	39
DK Gaekwad*	c Cowdrey b Rhodes	25	c & b Close	8
RG Nadkarni	c Parkhouse b Rhodes	27	c Barrington b Close	11
NS Tamhane+	c Moss b Trueman	20	not out	9
Surendranath	c Close b Rhodes	4	c Cowdrey b Mortimore	1
SP Gupte	c Swetman b Close	21	c & b Close	1
RB Desai	not out	7	c Cowdrey b Mortimore	8
Extras	(0b, 4lb, 0w, 5nb)	9	(0b, 4lb, 0w, 0nb)	4
	68.5 overs		55.4 overs	
Total		**161**		**149**

1st innings FoW: 10, 10, 11, 23, 75, 75, 103, 112, 141, 161
2nd innings FoW: 16, 19, 38, 107, 115, 121, 138, 139, 140, 149

Bowler	O	M	R	W		O	M	R	W
FS Trueman	15	6	30	3		10	1	29	2
AE Moss	22	11	30	2		6	3	10	1
HJ Rhodes	18.5	3	50	4		10	2	35	0
JB Mortimore	8	3	24	0		18.4	6	36	3
DB Close	5	1	18	1		11	0	35	4

ENGLAND 1st innings / 2nd innings

Batsman	1st innings		2nd innings
W Parkhouse	c Tamhane b Desai	78	
G Pullar	c Borde b Nadkarni	75	
MC Cowdrey	c Ghorpade b Gupte	160	
PBH May*	b Desai	2	
KF Barrington	c Tamhane b Nadkarni	80	
DB Close	b Gupte	27	
JB Mortimore	b Gupte	7	
R Swetman+	not out	19	
FS Trueman	c Desai b Gupte	17	
AE Moss			
HJ Rhodes			
Extras	(13b, 5lb, 0w, 0nb)	18	
	174.3 overs		
Total		**483**	

1st innings FoW: 146, 180, 186, 379, 432, 439, 453, 483

Bowler	O	M	R	W
RB Desai	38	10	111	2
Surendranath	32	11	84	0
SP Gupte	44.3	13	111	4
PR Umrigar	24	8	44	0
CG Borde	14	1	51	0
RG Nadkarni	22	2	64	2

ENGLAND 1st innings / 2nd innings

Batsman	1st innings		2nd innings	
W Parkhouse	c Roy b Surendranath	17	c Contractor b Nadkarni	49
G Pullar	c Joshi b Surendranath	131	c Joshi b Gupte	14
MC Cowdrey*	c Joshi b Nadkarni	67	c Umrigar b Gupte	45
MJK Smith	c Desai b Borde	100	c Desai b Gupte	9
KF Barrington	lbw b Surendranath	87	c Borde b Gupte	9
ER Dexter	c Roy b Surendranath	13	lbw b Nadkarni	46
R Illingworth	c Gaekwad b Desai	21	not out	47
JB Mortimore	c Contractor b Gupte	29	c Baig b Borde	8
R Swetman+	c Joshi b Gupte	9	c Nadkarni b Borde	7
FS Trueman	b Surendranath	0	not out	21
HJ Rhodes	not out	0		
Extras	(7b, 7lb, 2w, 0nb)	16	(9b, 1lb, 0w, 0nb)	10
	174.1 overs		90 overs	
Total		**490**		**265**

1st innings FoW: 33, 164, 262, 371, 417, 440, 454, 490, 490, 490
2nd innings FoW: 44, 100, 117, 132, 136, 196, 209, 219

Bowler	O	M	R	W		O	M	R	W
RB Desai	39	7	129	1		8	2	14	0
Surendranath	47.1	17	115	5		8	5	15	0
PR Umrigar	19	3	47	0		7	3	4	0
SP Gupte	28	8	98	2		26	6	76	4
RG Nadkarni	28	14	47	1		30	6	93	2
CG Borde	13	1	38	1		11	1	53	2

INDIA 1st innings / 2nd innings

Batsman	1st innings		2nd innings	
Pank Roy	c Smith b Rhodes	15	c Illingworth b Dexter	21
NJ Contractor	c Swetman b Rhodes	23	c Barrington b Rhodes	56
AA Baig	c Cowdrey b Illingworth	26	run out	112
DK Gaekwad*	lbw b Trueman	5	c Illingworth b Rhodes	0
PR Umrigar	b Rhodes	2	c Illingw'th b Barri'ton	118
CG Borde	c & b Barrington	75	c Swetman b Mortimore	3
RG Nadkarni	b Barrington	31	lbw b Trueman	28
PG Joshi+	run out	5	b Illingworth	5
Surendranath	b Illingworth	11	c Trueman b Barrington	4
SP Gupte	not out	4	b Trueman	8
RB Desai	b Barrington	5	not out	7
Extras	(0b, 1lb, 4w, 1nb)	6	(8b, 5lb, 0w, 1nb)	14
	79 overs		145.1 overs	
Total		**208**		**376**

1st innings FoW: 23, 54, 70, 72, 78, 124, 154, 199, 199, 208
2nd innings FoW: 35, 144, 146, 180, 243, 321, 334, 358, 361, 376

Bowler	O	M	R	W		O	M	R	W
FS Trueman	15	4	29	1		23.1	6	75	2
HJ Rhodes	18	3	72	3		28	2	87	2
ER Dexter	3	0	3	0		12	2	33	1
R Illingworth	16	10	16	2		39	13	63	1
JB Mortimore	13	6	46	0		16	6	29	1
KF Barrington	14	3	36	3		27	4	75	2

India

West Indies

No. 358: 5th Test	
VENUE: The Oval	
DATE: 20th-24th August 1959	
TOSS WON BY: India	
RESULT: Eng won by an innings and 27 runs	

No. 359: 1st Test	
VENUE: Bridgetown (Barbados)	
DATE: 6th-12th January 1960	
TOSS WON BY: England	
RESULT: Match drawn	

INDIA 1st innings / 2nd innings

Batsman	1st innings		2nd innings	
Pank Roy	b Statham	3	lbw b Statham	0
NJ Contractor	c Illingworth b Dexter	22	c Trueman b Statham	25
AA Baig	c Cowdrey b Trueman	23	c Cowdrey b Statham	4
RG Nadkarni	c Swetman b Trueman	6	lbw b Illingworth	76
CG Borde	b Greenhough	0	run out	6
DK Gaekwad*	c Barrington b Dexter	11	c Swetman b Greenh'gh	15
JM Ghorpade	b Greenhough	5	b Greenhough	24
NS Tamhane+	c Swetman b Statham	32	b Trueman	9
Surendranath	c Illingworth b Trueman	27	not out	17
SP Gupte	b Trueman	2	c Greenh'gh b Trueman	5
RB Desai	not out	3	c Swetman b Trueman	0
Extras	(1b, 4lb, 0w, 1nb)	6	(4b, 6lb, 0w, 3nb)	13
	85.3 overs		95 overs	
Total		**140**		**194**

1st innings FoW: 12, 43, 49, 50, 67, 72, 74, 132, 134, 140
2nd innings FoW: 5, 17, 44, 70, 106, 159, 163, 173, 188, 194

Bowler	O	M	R	W		O	M	R	W
FS Trueman	17	6	24	4		14	4	30	3
JB Statham	16.3	6	24	2		18	4	50	3
ER Dexter	16	7	24	2		7	1	11	0
T Greenhough	29	11	36	2		27	12	47	2
R Illingworth	1	0	2	0		29	10	43	1
KF Barrington	6	0	24	0					

ENGLAND 1st innings / 2nd innings

Batsman	1st innings		2nd innings
G Pullar	c Tamhane b Surendr'ath	22	
R Subba Row	c Tamhane b Desai	94	
MC Cowdrey*	c Borde b Surendranath	6	
MJK Smith	b Desai	98	
KF Barrington	c (sub) b Gupte	8	
ER Dexter	c Tamhane b Surendr'ath	0	
R Illingworth	c Gaekwad b Nadkarni	50	
R Swetman+	c Baig b Surendranath	65	
FS Trueman	st Tamhane b Nadkarni	1	
JB Statham	not out	3	
T Greenhough	c Contractor b Surendr'ath	2	
Extras	(3b, 8lb, 1w, 0nb)	12	
	147.3 overs		
Total		**361**	

1st innings FoW: 38, 52, 221, 232, 233, 235, 337, 347, 358, 361

Bowler	O	M	R	W
RB Desai	33	5	103	2
Surendranath	51.3	25	75	5
SP Gupte	38	9	119	1
RG Nadkarni	25	11	52	2

ENGLAND 1st innings / 2nd innings

Batsman	1st innings		2nd innings	
G Pullar	run out	65	not out	46
MC Cowdrey	c Sobers b Watson	30	not out	16
KF Barrington	c Alexander b Ramadhin	128		
PBH May*	c Alexander b Hall	4		
MJK Smith	c Alexander b Scarlett	39		
ER Dexter	not out	136		
R Illingworth	b Ramadhin	5		
R Swetman+	c Alexander b Worrell	45		
FS Trueman	c Alexander b Ramadhin	3		
DA Allen	lbw b Watson	10		
AE Moss	b Watson	4		
Extras	(4b, 6lb, 0w, 6nb)	16	(7b, 1lb, 1w, 0nb)	9
	188.4 overs		42 overs	
Total		**482**		**71**

1st innings FoW: 50, 153, 162, 251, 291, 303, 426, 439, 478, 482

Bowler	O	M	R	W		O	M	R	W
WW Hall	40	9	98	1		6	2	9	0
CD Watson	32.4	6	121	3		8	1	19	0
FMM Worrell	15	2	39	1					
S Ramadhin	54	22	109	3		7	2	11	0
RO Scarlett	26	9	46	1		10	4	12	0
GStA Sobers	21	3	53	0					
CC Hunte						7	2	9	0
RB Kanhai						4	3	2	0

WEST INDIES 1st innings / 2nd innings

Batsman	1st innings		2nd innings
CC Hunte	c Swetman b Barrington	42	
EDAS McMorris	run out	0	
RB Kanhai	b Trueman	40	
GStA Sobers	b Trueman	226	
FMM Worrell	not out	197	
BF Butcher	c Trueman b Dexter	13	
WW Hall	lbw b Trueman	14	
FCM Alexander+	c Smith b Trueman	3	
RO Scarlett	lbw b Dexter	7	
CD Watson			
S Ramadhin			
Extras	(8b, 7lb, 1w, 5nb)	21	
	239.4 overs		
Total		**563**	

1st innings FoW: 6, 68, 102, 501, 521, 544, 556, 563

Bowler	O	M	R	W
FS Trueman	47	15	93	4
AE Moss	47	14	116	0
ER Dexter	37.4	11	85	2
R Illingworth	47	9	106	0
DA Allen	43	12	82	0
KF Barrington	18	3	60	1

No. 360: 2nd Test
VENUE: Port-of-Spain (Trinidad)
DATE: 28th January-3rd Feb 1960
TOSS WON BY: England
RESULT: England won by 256 runs

No. 361: 3rd Test
VENUE: Kingston (Jamaica)
DATE: 17th-23rd February 1960
TOSS WON BY: England
RESULT: Match drawn

ENGLAND

Batsman	1st innings		2nd innings	
G Pullar	c Alexander b Watson	17	c Worrell b Ramadhin	28
MC Cowdrey	b Hall	18	c Alexander b Watson	5
KF Barrington	c Alexander b Hall	121	c Alexander b Hall	49
PBH May*	c Kanhai b Watson	0	c & b Singh	28
ER Dexter	c & b Singh	77	b Hall	0
MJK Smith	c Worrell b Ramadhin	108	lbw b Watson	12
R Illingworth	b Ramadhin	10	not out	41
R Swetman+	lbw b Watson	1	lbw b Singh	1
FS Trueman	lbw b Ramadhin	7	c Alexander b Watson	37
DA Allen	not out	10	c Alexander b Hall	16
JB Statham	b Worrell	1		
Extras	(0b, 3lb, 1w, 8nb)	12	(6b, 2lb, 4w, 2nb)	14
	143.5 overs		90.4 overs	
Total		**382**		**230**

1st innings FoW: 37, 42, 57, 199, 276, 307, 308, 343, 378, 382
2nd innings FoW: 18, 79, 97, 101, 122, 133, 133, 201, 230

Bowler	O	M	R	W	O	M	R	W
WW Hall	33	9	92	2	23.4	4	50	3
CD Watson	31	5	100	3	19	6	57	3
FMM Worrell	11.5	3	23	1	12	5	27	0
CK Singh	23	6	59	1	8	3	28	2
S Ramadhin	35	12	61	3	28	8	54	1
GStA Sobers	3	0	16	0				
JS Solomon	7	0	19	0				

WEST INDIES

Batsman	1st innings		2nd innings	
CC Hunte	c Trueman b Statham	8	c Swetman b Allen	47
JS Solomon	run out	23	c Swetman b Allen	9
RB Kanhai	lbw b Trueman	5	c Smith b Dexter	110
GStA Sobers	c Barrington b Trueman	0	lbw b Trueman	31
FMM Worrell	c Swetman b Trueman	9	lbw b Statham	0
BF Butcher	lbw b Statham	9	lbw b Statham	9
F Alexander*+	lbw b Trueman	28	c Trueman b Allen	7
S Ramadhin	b Trueman	23	lbw b Dexter	0
CK Singh	run out	0	c & b Barrington	11
WW Hall	b Statham	4	not out	0
CD Watson	not out	0	c Allen b Barrington	0
Extras	(0b, 2lb, 1w, 0nb)	3	(11b, 6lb, 2w, 1nb)	20
	68.3 overs		134.5 overs	
Total		**112**		**244**

1st innings FoW: 22, 31, 31, 45, 45, 73, 94, 98, 108, 112
2nd innings FoW: 29, 107, 158, 159, 188, 222, 222, 244, 244, 244

Bowler	O	M	R	W	O	M	R	W
FS Trueman	21	11	35	5	19	9	44	1
JB Statham	19.3	8	42	3	25	12	44	2
DA Allen	5	0	9	0	31	13	57	3
KF Barrington	16	10	15	0	25.5	13	34	2
R Illingworth	7	3	8	0	28	14	38	0
ER Dexter					6	3	7	2

ENGLAND

Batsman	1st innings		2nd innings	
G Pullar	c Sobers b Hall	19	lbw b Ramadhin	66
MC Cowdrey	c Scarlett b Ramadhin	114	c Alexander b Scarlett	97
KF Barrington	c Alexander b Watson	16	lbw b Solomon	4
PBH May*	c Hunte b Hall	9	b Hall	45
ER Dexter	c Alexander b Hall	25	b Watson	16
MJK Smith	b Hall	0	lbw b Watson	10
R Illingworth	c Alexander b Hall	17	b Ramadhin	6
R Swetman+	b Hall	0	lbw b Watson	5
FS Trueman	c Solomon b Ramadhin	17	lbw b Watson	4
DA Allen	not out	30	not out	17
JB Statham	b Hall	13	lbw b Ramadhin	12
Extras	(0b, 4lb, 10w, 3nb)	17	(8b, 10lb, 3w, 2nb)	23
	104.2 overs		123.3 overs	
Total		**277**		**305**

1st innings FoW: 28, 54, 68, 113, 113, 165, 170, 215, 245, 277
2nd innings FoW: 177, 177, 190, 211, 239, 258, 269, 269, 280, 305

Bowler	O	M	R	W	O	M	R	W
WW Hall	31.2	8	69	7	26	5	93	1
CD Watson	29	7	74	1	27	8	62	4
S Ramadhin	28	3	78	2	28.3	14	38	3
RO Scarlett	10	4	13	0	28	12	51	1
GStA Sobers	2	0	14	0	8	2	18	0
JS Solomon	4	1	12	0	6	1	20	1

WEST INDIES

Batsman	1st innings		2nd innings	
CC Hunte	c Illingworth b Statham	7	b Trueman	40
McMorris	b Barrington	73	b Trueman	1
RB Kanhai	run out	18	b Trueman	57
GStA Sobers	lbw b Trueman	147	run out	19
SM Nurse	c Smith b Illingworth	70	b Trueman	11
JS Solomon	c Swetman b Allen	8	lbw b Statham	12
RO Scarlett	c Statham b Illingworth	6	not out	7
F Alexander*+	b Trueman	0	not out	10
S Ramadhin	b Statham	5		
CD Watson	b Statham	3		
WW Hall	not out	0		
Extras	(6b, 7lb, 1w, 2nb)	16	(9b, 3lb, 6w, 0nb)	18
	156.1 overs		63 overs	
Total		**353**		**175**

1st innings FoW: 12, 56, 299, 329, 329, 329, 341, 347, 350, 353
2nd innings FoW: 11, 48, 86, 111, 140, 152

Bowler	O	M	R	W	O	M	R	W
JB Statham	32.1	8	76	3	18	6	45	1
FS Trueman	33	10	82	2	18	4	54	4
ER Dexter	12	3	38	0				
DA Allen	28	10	57	1	9	4	19	0
KF Barrington	21	7	38	1	4	4	0	0
R Illingworth	30	13	46	2	13	4	35	0
MC Cowdrey					1	0	4	0

No. 362: 4th Test
VENUE: Georgetown (Guyana)
DATE: 9th-15th March 1960
TOSS WON BY: England
RESULT: Match drawn

No. 363: 5th Test
VENUE: Port-of-Spain (Trinidad)
DATE: 25th-31st March 1960
TOSS WON BY: England
RESULT: Match drawn

ENGLAND 1st innings / 2nd innings (No. 362)

Batsman	1st innings		2nd innings	
G Pullar	c Alexander b Hall	33	lbw b Worrell	47
MC Cowdrey*	c Alexander b Hall	65	st Alexander b Singh	27
R Subba Row	c Alexander b Sobers	27	c Worrell b Walcott	110
KF Barrington	c Walcott b Sobers	27	lbw b Worrell	100
ER Dexter	c Hunte b Hall	39	c Scarlett b Sobers	23
MJK Smith	b Hall	0	c Kanhai b Worrell	9
R Illingworth	b Sobers	4	c Walcott b Worrell	0
R Swetman+	lbw b Watson	4	not out	1
DA Allen	c Alexander b Hall	55	c Hall b Singh	3
FS Trueman	b Hall	6		
JB Statham	not out	20		
Extras	(5b, 2lb, 2w, 6nb)	15	(6b, 4lb, 0w, 4nb)	14
	119.2 overs		149.2 overs	
Total		**295**		**334**

1st innings FoW: 73, 121, 152, 161, 169, 175, 219, 258, 268, 295
2nd innings FoW: 40, 110, 258, 320, 322, 322, 331, 334

Bowler	O	M	R	W	O	M	R	W
WW Hall	30.2	8	90	6	18	1	79	0
CD Watson	20	2	56	1				
FMM Worrell	16	9	22	0	31	12	49	4
RO Scarlett	22	11	24	0	38	13	63	0
CK Singh	12	4	29	0	41.2	22	50	2
GStA Sobers	19	1	59	3	12	1	36	1
CL Walcott					9	0	43	1

WEST INDIES 1st innings / 2nd innings (No. 362)

Batsman	1st innings	
CC Hunte	c Trueman b Allen	39
McMorris	c Swetman b Statham	35
RB Kanhai	c Dexter b Trueman	55
GStA Sobers	st Swetman b Allen	145
CL Walcott	b Trueman	9
FMM Worrell	b Allen	38
F Alexander*+	run out	33
RO Scarlett	not out	29
CK Singh	b Trueman	0
WW Hall	not out	1
CD Watson		
Extras	(4b, 12lb, 0w, 2nb)	18
	172 overs	
Total		**402**

1st innings FoW: 67, 77, 192, 21, 333, 338, 393, 398

Bowler	O	M	R	W
FS Trueman	40	6	116	3
JB Statham	36	8	79	1
R Illingworth	43	11	72	0
KF Barrington	6	2	22	0
DA Allen	42	11	75	3
ER Dexter	5	0	20	0

ENGLAND 1st innings / 2nd innings (No. 363)

Batsman	1st innings		2nd innings	
G Pullar	c Sobers b Griffith	10	c & b Sobers	54
MC Cowdrey*	c Alexander b Sobers	119	c Worrell b Hall	0
ER Dexter	c & b Sobers	76	run out	25
R Subba Row	c Hunte b Hall	22	run out	47
KF Barrington	c Alexander b Ramadhin	69	lbw b Ramadhin	13
MJK Smith	b Ramadhin	20	c McMorris b Sobers	6
JM Parks+	c & b Sobers	43	c Alexander b Hunte	96
R Illingworth	c Sobers b Ramadhin	0	not out	101
DA Allen	c (sub) b Ramadhin	7	not out	2
FS Trueman	not out	10		
AE Moss	b Watson	1		
Extras	(7b, 0lb, 0w, 9nb)	16	(2b, 3lb, 0w, 1nb)	6
	123.2 overs		124 overs	
Total		**393**		**350**

1st innings FoW: 19, 210, 215, 268, 317, 350, 350, 374, 388, 393
2nd innings FoW: 3, 69, 102, 136, 145, 148, 345

Bowler	O	M	R	W	O	M	R	W
WW Hall	24	3	83	1	4	0	16	1
CC Griffith	15	2	62	1	9	1	40	0
CD Watson	18.2	3	52	1	14	1	52	0
S Ramadhin	34	13	73	4	34	9	67	1
FMM Worrell	8	1	29	0	22	5	44	0
GStA Sobers	20	1	75	3	29	6	84	2
CL Walcott	4	2	3	0	7	2	24	0
CC Hunte					5	1	17	1

WEST INDIES 1st innings / 2nd innings (No. 363)

Batsman	1st innings		2nd innings	
CC Hunte	not out	72	st Parks b Illingworth	36
McMorris	run out	13	lbw b Moss	2
F Alexander*+	b Allen	26	c Trueman b Illingworth	34
GStA Sobers	b Moss	92	c Parks b Barrington	22
CL Walcott	st Parks b Allen	53	c Trueman b Pullar	61
FMM Worrell	b Trueman	15	not out	49
RB Kanhai	b Moss	6	not out	4
S Ramadhin	c Cowdrey b Dexter	13		
WW Hall	b Trueman	29		
CC Griffith	not out	5		
CD Watson				
Extras	(6b, 4lb, 0w, 4nb)	14	(0b, 1lb, 0w, 0nb)	1
	119.3 overs		52 overs	
Total		**338**		**209**

1st innings FoW: 26, 103, 190, 216, 227, 230, 263, 328
2nd innings FoW: 11, 72, 75, 107, 194

Bowler	O	M	R	W	O	M	R	W
FS Trueman	37.3	6	103	2	5	1	22	0
AE Moss	34	3	94	2	4	0	16	1
DA Allen	24	1	61	2	15	2	57	0
R Illingworth	12	4	25	0	16	3	53	2
ER Dexter	4	1	20	1				
KF Barrington	8	0	21	0	8	2	27	1
R Subba Row					1	0	2	0
MJK Smith					1	0	15	0
G Pullar					1	0	1	1
MC Cowdrey					1	0	15	0

No. 364: 1st Test
VENUE: Edgbaston
DATE: 9th-14th June 1960
TOSS WON BY: England
RESULT: England won by 100 runs

No. 365: 2nd Test
VENUE: Lord's
DATE: 23rd-27th June 1960
TOSS WON BY: England
RESULT: Eng won by an innings and 73 runs

ENGLAND 1st innings / 2nd innings

Batsman	1st innings		2nd innings	
G Pullar	c McLean b Goddard	37	b Adcock	0
MC Cowdrey*	c Waite b Adcock	3	c Waite b Tayfield	32
ER Dexter	b Tayfield	52	b Adcock	26
R Subba Row	c Waite b Griffin	56	c O'Linn b Tayfield	28
MJK Smith	c Waite b Adcock	54	b Griffin	4
JM Parks+	c Waite b Adcock	35	c Waite b Adcock	16
R Illingworth	b Tayfield	1	c McLean b Tayfield	4
RW Barber	lbw b Adcock	5	c Goddard b Griffin	37
PM Walker	c Goddard b Adcock	9	b Tayfield	25
FS Trueman	b Tayfield	11	c McLean b Griffin	22
JB Statham	not out	14	not out	1
Extras	(4b, 9lb, 0w, 2nb)	15	(2b, 4lb, 0w, 2nb)	8
	150.5 overs		86 overs	
Total		**292**		**203**

1st innings FoW: 19, 80, 100, 196, 225, 234, 255, 262, 275, 292
2nd innings FoW: 0, 42, 69, 74, 112, 112, 118, 163, 202, 203

Bowler	O	M	R	W	O	M	R	W
NAT Adcock	41.5	14	62	5	28	8	57	3
GM Griffin	21	3	61	1	21	4	44	3
TL Goddard	33	17	47	1	10	5	32	0
HJ Tayfield	50	19	93	3	27	12	62	4
JP Fellows-Smith	5	1	14	0				

SOUTH AFRICA 1st innings / 2nd innings

Batsman	1st innings		2nd innings	
DJ McGlew*	c Parks b Trueman	11	c Parks b Statham	5
TL Goddard	c Smith b Statham	10	c Walker b Statham	0
AJ Pithey	lbw b Statham	6	b Illingworth	17
RA McLean	c Statham b Trueman	21	lbw b Trueman	68
JHB Waite+	b Illingworth	58	not out	56
PR Carlstein	lbw b Trueman	4	b Trueman	10
S O'Linn	c Cowdrey b Illingworth	42	lbw b Barber	12
Fellows-Smith	lbw b Illingworth	18	lbw b Illingworth	5
GM Griffin	b Trueman	6	b Illingworth	3
HJ Tayfield	run out	6	c Walker b Trueman	14
NAT Adcock	not out	1	b Statham	7
Extras	(2b, 0lb, 0w, 1nb)	3	(7b, 5lb, 0w, 0nb)	12
	82.5 overs		84 overs	
Total		**186**		**209**

1st innings FoW: 11, 21, 40, 52, 61, 146, 168, 179, 179, 186
2nd innings FoW: 4, 5, 58, 120, 132, 156, 161, 167, 200, 209

Bowler	O	M	R	W	O	M	R	W
JB Statham	28	8	67	2	18	5	41	3
FS Trueman	24.5	4	58	4	22	4	58	3
ER Dexter	1	0	4	0	6	4	4	0
RW Barber	6	0	26	0	10	2	29	1
R Illingworth	17	11	15	3	24	6	57	3
PM Walker	6	1	13	0	4	2	8	0

ENGLAND 1st innings / 2nd innings

Batsman	1st innings		2nd innings
MC Cowdrey*	c McLean b Griffin	4	
R Subba Row	lbw b Adcock	90	
ER Dexter	c McLean b Adcock	56	
KF Barrington	lbw b Goddard	24	
MJK Smith	c Waite b Griffin	99	
JM Parks+	c Smith b Adcock	3	
PM Walker	b Griffin	52	
R Illingworth	not out	0	
FS Trueman	b Griffin	0	
JB Statham	not out	2	
AE Moss			
Extras	(6b, 14lb, 1w, 11nb)	32	
	129 overs		
Total		**362**	

1st innings FoW: 7, 103, 165, 220, 227, 347, 360, 360

Bowler	O	M	R	W
NAT Adcock	36	11	70	3
GM Griffin	30	7	87	4
TL Goddard	31	6	96	1
HJ Tayfield	27	9	64	0
JP Fellows-Smith	5	0	13	0

SOUTH AFRICA 1st innings / 2nd innings

Batsman	1st innings		2nd innings	
DJ McGlew*	lbw b Statham	15	b Statham	17
TL Goddard	b Statham	19	c Parks b Statham	24
S O'Linn	c Walker b Moss	18	lbw b Trueman	8
RA McLean	c Cowdrey b Statham	15	c Parks b Trueman	13
JHB Waite+	c Parks b Statham	3	lbw b Statham	0
PR Carlstein	c Cowdrey b Moss	12	c Parks b Moss	6
C Wesley	c Parks b Statham	11	b Dexter	35
Fellows-Smith	c Parks b Moss	29	not out	27
HJ Tayfield	c Smith b Moss	12	b Dexter	4
GM Griffin	b Statham	5	b Statham	0
NAT Adcock	not out	8	b Statham	2
Extras	(0b, 4lb, 0w, 1nb)	5	(0b, 0lb, 0w, 1nb)	1
	43.3 overs		57 overs	
Total		**152**		**137**

1st innings FoW: 33, 48, 56, 69, 78, 88, 112, 132, 138, 152
2nd innings FoW: 26, 49, 49, 50, 63, 72, 126, 132, 133, 137

Bowler	O	M	R	W	O	M	R	W
JB Statham	20	5	63	6	21	6	34	5
FS Trueman	13	2	49	0	17	5	44	2
AE Moss	10.3	0	35	4	14	1	41	1
R Illingworth					1	1	0	0
ER Dexter					4	0	17	2

South Africa | South Africa

	No. 366: 3rd Test		No. 367: 4th Test
VENUE:	Trent Bridge	VENUE:	Old Trafford
DATE:	7th-11th July 1960	DATE:	21st-26th July 1960
TOSS WON BY:	England	TOSS WON BY:	England
RESULT:	England won by 8 wickets	RESULT:	Match drawn

ENGLAND 1st innings / 2nd innings (No. 366)

ENGLAND	1st innings		2nd innings	
R Subba Row	b Tayfield	30	not out	16
MC Cowdrey*	c Fellows b Godd'd	67	lbw b Goddard	27
ER Dexter	b Adcock	3	c Adcock b Goddard	0
KF Barrington	c O'Linn b Goddard	80	not out	1
MJK Smith	lbw b Goddard	0		
JM Parks+	run out	16		
R Illingworth	c & b Tayfield	37		
PM Walker	c O'Linn b Tayfield	30		
FS Trueman	b Goddard	15		
JB Statham	b Goddard	2		
AE Moss	not out	3		
Extras	(2b, 2lb, 0w, 0nb)	4	(4b, 1lb, 0w, 0nb)	5
	125.3 overs		14.4 overs	
Total		**287**		**49**

1st innings FoW: 57, 82, 129, 129, 154, 229, 241, 261, 267, 287
2nd innings FoW: 48, 48

NAT Adcock	30	2	86	1	7.4	2	16	0
JE Pothecary	20	5	42	0	2	0	15	0
JP Fellows-Smith	5	0	17	0	5	1	13	2
TL Goddard	42	17	80	5				
HJ Tayfield	28.3	11	58	3				

SOUTH AFRICA 1st innings / 2nd innings (No. 366)

SOUTH AFRICA	1st innings		2nd innings	
DJ McGlew*	c Parks b Trueman	0	run out	45
TL Goddard	run out	16	b Trueman	0
S O'Linn	c Walker b Trueman	1	c Illingworth b Trueman	15
RA McLean	b Statham	11	c Parks b Trueman	0
PR Carlstein	c Walker b Statham	2	c Cowdrey b Moss	98
C Wesley	c Subba Row b Statham	0	c Cowdrey b Statham	19
Fellows-Smith	not out	31	c Parks b Statham	0
JHB Waite+	c Trueman b Moss	1	lbw b Moss	60
HJ Tayfield	b Trueman	11	c Parks b Moss	6
JE Pothecary	b Trueman	7	c Parks b Trueman	3
NAT Adcock	b Trueman	0	not out	1
Extras	(4b, 4lb, 0w, 0nb)	8	(0b, 0lb, 0w, 0nb)	0
	38.3 overs		94.4 overs	
Total		**88**		**247**

1st innings FoW: 0, 12, 31, 33, 33, 44, 49, 68, 82, 88
2nd innings FoW: 1, 23, 23, 91, 122, 122, 231, 242, 245, 247

FS Trueman	14.3	6	27	5	22	3	77	4
JB Statham	14	5	27	3	26	3	71	2
AE Moss	10	3	26	1	15.4	3	36	3
R Illingworth					19	9	33	0
KF Barrington					3	1	5	0
ER Dexter					6	2	12	0
PM Walker					3	0	13	0

ENGLAND 1st innings / 2nd innings (No. 367)

ENGLAND	1st innings		2nd innings	
G Pullar	b Pothecary	12	c & b Pothecary	9
R Subba Row	lbw b Adcock	27	b Adcock	25
ER Dexter	b Pothecary	38	c McLean b Pothecary	22
MC Cowdrey*	c Waite b Adcock	20	c McLean b Adcock	5
KF Barrington	b Goddard	76	c Waite b Adcock	2
DEV Padgett	c Wesley b Pothecary	5	c & b Goddard	20
JM Parks+	lbw b Goddard	36	c Waite b Goddard	35
R Illingworth	not out	22	not out	14
DA Allen	lbw b Goddard	0	not out	14
FS Trueman	c Tayfield b Adcock	10	(1b, 5lb, 0w, 1nb)	7
JB Statham	b Adcock	0	75 overs	
Extras	(8b, 6lb, 0w, 0nb)	14		
	93 overs			
Total		**260**		**153**

1st innings FoW: 27, 85, 108, 113, 134, 197, 239, 239, 260, 260
2nd innings FoW: 23, 41, 63, 65, 71, 101, 134

NAT Adcock	23	5	66	4	27	9	59	3
JE Pothecary	28	3	85	3	32	10	61	2
TL Goddard	24	16	26	3	16	5	26	2
HJ Tayfield	18	3	69	0				

SOUTH AFRICA 1st innings / 2nd innings (No. 367)

SOUTH AFRICA	1st innings		2nd innings	
DJ McGlew*	c Subba Row b Trueman	32	not out	26
TL Goddard	c Parks b Statham	8	not out	16
AJ Pithey	c Parks b Statham	7		
PR Carlstein	b Trueman	11		
RA McLean	b Allen	109		
JHB Waite+	b Statham	11		
S O'Linn	c (sub) b Allen	27		
C Wesley	c Trueman b Allen	3		
HJ Tayfield	c Trueman b Allen	4		
JE Pothecary	b Trueman	12		
NAT Adcock	not out	0		
Extras	(1b, 4lb, 0w, 0nb)	5	(3b, 0lb, 0w, 1nb)	4
	89.5 overs		26 overs	
Total		**229**		**46**

1st innings FoW: 25, 33, 57, 62, 92, 194, 198, 202, 225, 229

JB Statham	22	11	32	3	4	2	3	0
FS Trueman	20	2	58	3	6	1	10	0
ER Dexter	17	5	41	0				
DA Allen	19.5	6	58	4	7	4	5	0
R Illingworth	11	2	35	0	5	3	6	0
G Pullar					1	0	6	0
DEV Padgett					2	0	8	0
MC Cowdrey					1	0	4	0

No. 368: 5th Test	No. 369: 1st Test
VENUE: The Oval	VENUE: Edgbaston
DATE: 18th-23rd August 1960	DATE: 8th-13th June 1961
TOSS WON BY: England	TOSS WON BY: England
RESULT: Match drawn	RESULT: Match drawn

South Africa match — ENGLAND

ENGLAND	1st innings		2nd innings	
G Pullar	c Goddard b Pothecary	59	st Waite b McKinnon	175
MC Cowdrey*	b Adcock	11	lbw b Goddard	155
ER Dexter	b Adcock	28	b Tayfield	16
KF Barrington	lbw b Pothecary	1	lbw b McKinnon	10
MJK Smith	b Adcock	0	c Waite b Adcock	17
DEV Padgett	c Waite b Pothecary	13	c Goddard b Tayfield	11
JM Parks+	c Waite b Pothecary	23	run out	31
DA Allen	lbw b Adcock	0	not out	12
FS Trueman	lbw b Adcock	0	b Goddard	24
JB Statham	not out	13	c Pothecary b Goddard	4
T Greenhough	b Adcock	2		
Extras	(3b, 2lb, 0w, 0nb)	5	(14b, 9lb, 1w, 0nb)	24
	76.3 overs		157 overs	
Total		**155**		**479**

1st innings FoW: 27, 89, 90, 95, 107, 125, 130, 130, 142, 155
2nd innings FoW: 290, 339, 362, 373, 387, 412, 447, 475, 479

NAT Adcock	31.3	10	65	6	38	8	106	1
JE Pothecary	29	9	58	4	27	5	93	0
TL Goddard	14	6	25	0	27	6	69	3
AH McKinnon	2	1	2	0	24	7	62	2
HJ Tayfield					37	14	108	2
JP Fellows-Smith					4	0	17	0

SOUTH AFRICA	1st innings		2nd innings	
DJ McGlew*	c Smith b Greenhough	22	c Allen b Statham	16
TL Goddard	c Cowdrey b Statham	99	c Cowdrey b Statham	28
Fellows-Smith	c Smith b Dexter	35	c Parks b Trueman	6
RA McLean	lbw b Dexter	0	lbw b Trueman	13
JHB Waite+	c Trueman b Dexter	77	not out	32
S O'Linn	b Trueman	55	not out	1
PR Carlstein	b Greenhough	42		
JE Pothecary	run out	4		
HJ Tayfield	not out	46		
AH McKinnon	run out	22		
NAT Adcock	b Trueman	1		
Extras	(6b, 7lb, 0w, 3nb)	16	(0b, 0lb, 1w, 0nb)	1
	171.1 overs		29.2 overs	
Total		**419**		**97**

1st innings FoW: 44, 107, 107, 222, 252, 326, 330, 374, 412, 419
2nd innings FoW: 21, 30, 52, 89

FS Trueman	31.1	4	93	2	10	0	34	2
JB Statham	38	8	96	1	12	1	57	2
ER Dexter	30	5	79	3	0.2	0	0	0
T Greenhough	44	17	99	2	5	2	3	0
DA Allen	28	15	36	0	2	1	2	0

Australia match — ENGLAND

ENGLAND	1st innings		2nd innings	
G Pullar	b Davidson	17	c Grout b Misson	28
R Subba Row	c Simpson b Mackay	59	b Misson	112
ER Dexter	c Davidson b Mackay	10	st Grout b Simpson	180
MC Cowdrey*	b Misson	13	b Mackay	14
KF Barrington	c Misson b Mackay	21	not out	48
MJK Smith	c Lawry b Mackay	0	not out	1
R Illingworth	c Grout b Benaud	15		
JT Murray+	c Davidson b Benaud	16		
DA Allen	run out	11		
FS Trueman	c Burge b Benaud	20		
JB Statham	not out	7		
Extras	(3b, 3lb, 0w, 0nb)	6	(0b, 18lb, 0w, 0nb)	18
	84.3 overs		154 overs	
Total		**195**		**401**

1st innings FoW: 36, 53, 88, 121, 121, 122, 153, 156, 181, 195
2nd innings FoW: 93, 202, 239, 400

AK Davidson	26	6	70	1	31	10	60	0
FM Misson	15	6	47	1	28	6	82	2
KD Mackay	29	10	57	4	41	13	87	1
R Benaud	14.3	8	15	3	20	4	67	0
RB Simpson					34	12	87	1

AUSTRALIA	1st innings		2nd innings
WM Lawry	c Murray b Illingworth	57	
CC McDonald	c Illingworth b Statham	22	
RN Harvey	lbw b Allen	114	
NC O'Neill	b Statham	82	
PJP Burge	lbw b Allen	25	
RB Simpson	c & b Trueman	76	
AK Davidson	c & b Illingworth	22	
KD Mackay	c Barrington b Statham	64	
R Benaud*	not out	36	
ATW Grout+	c Dexter b Trueman	5	
FM Misson			
Extras	(8b, 4lb, 0w, 1nb)	13	
	152.5 overs		
Total		**516**	

1st innings FoW: 47, 106, 252, 299, 322, 381, 469, 501, 516

FS Trueman	36.5	1	136	2
JB Statham	43	6	147	3
R Illingworth	44	12	110	2
DA Allen	24	4	88	2
ER Dexter	5	1	22	0

Australia

No. 370: 2nd Test
VENUE: Lord's
DATE: 22nd-26th June 1961
TOSS WON BY: England
RESULT: Australia won by 5 wickets

ENGLAND 1st innings / 2nd innings

Batsman	1st innings		2nd innings	
G Pullar	b Davidson	11	c Grout b Misson	42
R Subba Row	lbw b Mackay	48	c Grout b Davidson	8
ER Dexter	c McKenzie b Misson	27	b McKenzie	17
MC Cowdrey*	c Grout b McKenzie	16	c Mackay b Misson	7
PBH May	c Grout b Davidson	17	c Grout b McKenzie	22
KF Barrington	c Mackay b Davidson	4	lbw b Davidson	66
R Illingworth	b Misson	13	c Harvey b Simpson	0
JT Murray+	lbw b Mackay	18	c Grout b McKenzie	25
GAR Lock	c Grout b Davidson	5	b McKenzie	1
FS Trueman	b Davidson	25	c Grout b McKenzie	0
JB Statham	not out	11	not out	2
Extras	(0b, 9lb, 2w, 0nb)	11	(1b, 10lb, 1w, 0nb)	12
Total	78.3 overs	**206**	97 overs	**202**

1st innings FoW: 26, 87, 87, 111, 115, 127, 156, 164, 167, 206
2nd innings FoW: 33, 63, 67, 80, 127, 144, 191, 199, 199, 202

Bowler	O	M	R	W		O	M	R	W
AK Davidson	24.3	6	42	5		24	8	50	2
GD McKenzie	26	7	81	1		29	13	37	5
FM Misson	16	4	48	2		17	2	66	2
KD Mackay	12	3	24	2		8	6	5	0
RB Simpson						19	10	32	1

AUSTRALIA 1st innings / 2nd innings

Batsman	1st innings		2nd innings	
WM Lawry	c Murray b Dexter	130	c Murray b Statham	1
CC McDonald	b Statham	4	c Illingworth b Trueman	14
RB Simpson	c Illingworth b Trueman	0	c Illingworth b Statham	15
RN Harvey*	c Barrington b Trueman	27	c Murray b Trueman	4
NC O'Neill	b Dexter	1	b Statham	0
PJP Burge	c Murray b Statham	46	not out	37
AK Davidson	lbw b Trueman	6	not out	0
KD Mackay	c Barrington b Illingworth	54		
ATW Grout+	lbw b Dexter	0		
GD McKenzie	b Trueman	34		
FM Misson	not out	25		
Extras	(1b, 12lb, 0w, 0nb)	13	(0b, 0lb, 0w, 0nb)	0
Total	139.3 overs	**340**	20.5 overs	**71**

1st innings FoW: 5, 6, 81, 88, 183, 194, 238, 238, 291, 340
2nd innings FoW: 15, 15, 19, 19, 58

Bowler	O	M	R	W		O	M	R	W
JB Statham	44	10	89	2		10.5	3	31	3
FS Trueman	34	3	118	4		10	0	40	2
ER Dexter	24	7	56	3					
GAR Lock	26	13	48	0					
R Illingworth	11.3	5	16	1					

Australia

No. 371: 3rd Test
VENUE: Headingley
DATE: 6th-8th July 1961
TOSS WON BY: Australia
RESULT: England won by 8 wickets

AUSTRALIA 1st innings / 2nd innings

Batsman	1st innings		2nd innings	
CC McDonald	st Murray b Lock	54	b Jackson	1
WM Lawry	lbw b Lock	28	c Murray b Allen	28
RN Harvey	c Lock b Trueman	73	c Dexter b Trueman	53
NC O'Neill	c Cowdrey b Trueman	27	c Cowdrey b Trueman	19
PJP Burge	c Cowdrey b Jackson	5	lbw b Allen	0
KD Mackay	lbw b Jackson	6	b Trueman	3
RB Simpson	lbw b Trueman	2	c Cowdrey b Trueman	7
AK Davidson	not out	22	b Trueman	0
R Benaud*	b Trueman	0	c Murray b Trueman	0
ATW Grout+	c Murray b Trueman	3	c & b Jackson	7
GD McKenzie	b Allen	8	not out	0
Extras	(7b, 2lb, 0w, 0nb)	9	(0b, 2lb, 0w, 0nb)	2
Total	110 overs	**237**	52.5 overs	**120**

1st innings FoW: 65, 113, 187, 192, 196, 203, 203, 204, 208, 237
2nd innings FoW: 4, 49, 99, 102, 102, 105, 109, 109, 120, 120

Bowler	O	M	R	W		O	M	R	W
FS Trueman	22	5	58	5		15.5	5	30	6
HL Jackson	31	11	57	2		13	5	26	2
DA Allen	28	12	45	1		14	6	30	2
GAR Lock	29	5	68	2		10	1	32	0

ENGLAND 1st innings / 2nd innings

Batsman	1st innings		2nd innings	
G Pullar	b Benaud	53	not out	26
R Subba Row	lbw b Davidson	35	b Davidson	6
MC Cowdrey	c Grout b McKenzie	93	c Grout b Benaud	22
PBH May*	c & b Davidson	26	not out	8
ER Dexter	b Davidson	28		
KF Barrington	c Simpson b Davidson	6		
JT Murray+	b McKenzie	6		
FS Trueman	c Burge b Davidson	4		
GAR Lock	lbw b McKenzie	30		
DA Allen	not out	5		
HL Jackson	run out	8		
Extras	(0b, 5lb, 0w, 0nb)	5	(0b, 0lb, 0w, 0nb)	0
Total	149 overs	**299**	23 overs	**62**

1st innings FoW: 59, 145, 190, 223, 239, 248, 252, 286, 291, 299
2nd innings FoW: 14, 45

Bowler	O	M	R	W		O	M	R	W
AK Davidson	47	23	63	5		11	6	17	1
GD McKenzie	27	4	64	3		5	0	15	0
KD Mackay	22	4	34	0		1	0	8	0
R Benaud	39	15	86	1		6	1	22	1

No. 372: 4th Test	No. 373: 5th Test
VENUE: Old Trafford	VENUE: The Oval
DATE: 27th July-1st August 1961	DATE: 17th-22nd August 1961
TOSS WON BY: Australia	TOSS WON BY: England
RESULT: Australia won by 54 runs	RESULT: Match drawn

Left match — No. 372: 4th Test

AUSTRALIA 1st innings

			2nd innings	
WM Lawry	lbw b Statham	74	c Trueman b Allen	102
RB Simpson	c Murray b Statham	4	c Murray b Flavell	51
RN Harvey	c Subba Row b Statham	19	c Murray b Dexter	35
NC O'Neill	hit wkt b Trueman	11	c Murray b Statham	67
PJP Burge	b Flavell	15	c Murray b Dexter	23
BC Booth	c Close b Statham	46	lbw b Dexter	9
KD Mackay	c Murray b Statham	11	c Close b Allen	18
AK Davidson	c Barrington b Dexter	0	not out	77
R Benaud*	b Dexter	2	lbw b Allen	1
ATW Grout+	c Murray b Dexter	2	c Statham b Allen	0
GD McKenzie	not out	1	b Flavell	32
Extras	(4b, 1lb, 0w, 0nb)	5	(6b, 9lb, 2w, 0nb)	17
Total	63.4 overs	**190**	171.4 overs	**432**

1st innings FoW: 8, 51, 89, 106, 150, 174, 185, 185 , 189, 190
2nd innings FoW: 113, 175, 210, 274, 290, 296, 332, 334, 334, 432

FS Trueman	14	1	55	1	32	6	92	0
JB Statham	21	3	53	5	44	9	106	1
JA Flavell	22	8	61	1	29.4	4	65	2
ER Dexter	6.4	2	16	3	20	4	61	3
DA Allen					38	25	58	4
DB Close					8	1	33	0

ENGLAND 1st innings

			2nd innings	
G Pullar	b Davidson	63	c O'Neill b Davidson	26
R Subba Row	c Simpson b Davidson	2	b Benaud	49
ER Dexter	c Davidson b McKenzie	16	c Grout b Benaud	76
PBH May*	c Simpson b Davidson	95	b Benaud	0
DB Close	lbw b McKenzie	33	c O'Neill b Benaud	8
KF Barrington	c O'Neill b Simpson	78	lbw b Mackay	5
JT Murray+	c Grout b Mackay	24	c Simpson b Benaud	4
DA Allen	c Booth b Simpson	42	c Simpson b Benaud	10
FS Trueman	c Harvey b Simpson	3	c Benaud b Simpson	8
JB Statham	c Mackay b Simpson	4	b Davidson	8
JA Flavell	not out	0	not out	0
Extras	(2b, 4lb, 1w, 0nb)	7	(5b, 0lb, 2w, 0nb)	7
Total	163.4 overs	**367**	71.4 overs	**201**

1st innings FoW: 3, 43, 154, 212, 212, 272, 358, 362, 367, 367
2nd innings FoW: 40, 150, 150, 158, 163, 171, 171, 189, 193, 201

AK Davidson	39	11	70	3	14.4	1	50	2
GD McKenzie	38	11	106	2	4	1	20	0
KD Mackay	40	9	81	1	13	7	33	1
R Benaud	35	15	80	0	32	11	70	6
RB Simpson	11.4	4	23	4	8	4	21	1

Right match — No. 373: 5th Test

ENGLAND 1st innings

			2nd innings	
G Pullar	b Davidson	8	c Grout b Mackay	13
R Subba Row	lbw b Gaunt	12	c & b Benaud	137
MC Cowdrey	c Grout b Davidson	0	c Gaunt b Mackay	0
PBH May*	c Lawry b Benaud	71	c O'Neill b Mackay	33
ER Dexter	c Grout b Gaunt	24	c Benaud b Mackay	3
KF Barrington	c Grout b Gaunt	53	c O'Neill b Benaud	83
JT Murray+	c O'Neill b Mackay	27	c Grout b Benaud	40
GAR Lock	c Grout b Mackay	3	c Benaud b Mackay	0
DA Allen	not out	22	not out	42
JB Statham	b Davidson	18	not out	9
JA Flavell	c Simpson b Davidson	14		
Extras	(1b, 2lb, 1w, 0nb)	4	(6b, 3lb, 1w, 0nb)	10
Total	118.1 overs	**256**	177 overs	**370**

1st innings FoW: 18, 20, 20, 67, 147, 193, 199, 202, 238, 256
2nd innings FoW: 33, 33, 83, 90, 262, 283, 283, 355

AK Davidson	34.1	8	83	4	29	7	67	0
RA Gaunt	24	3	53	3	22	7	33	0
R Benaud	17	4	35	1	51	18	113	3
KD Mackay	39	14	75	2	68	21	121	5
RB Simpson	4	2	6	0	2	0	13	0
NC O'Neill					4	1	13	0
RN Harvey					1	1	0	0

AUSTRALIA 1st innings

			2nd innings
WM Lawry	c Murray b Statham	0	
RB Simpson	b Allen	40	
RN Harvey	lbw b Flavell	13	
NC O'Neill	c (sub) b Allen	117	
PJP Burge	b Allen	181	
BC Booth	c Subba Row b Lock	71	
KD Mackay	c Murray b Flavell	5	
AK Davidson	lbw b Statham	17	
R Benaud*	b Allen	6	
ATW Grout+	not out	30	
RA Gaunt	b Statham	3	
Extras	(10b, 1lb, 0w, 0nb)	11	
Total	165.5 overs	**494**	

1st innings FoW: 0, 15, 88, 211, 396, 401, 441, 455, 472, 494

JB Statham	38.5	10	75	3
JA Flavell	31	5	105	2
ER Dexter	24	2	68	0
DA Allen	30	6	133	4
GAR Lock	42	14	102	1

Pakistan

No. 374: 1st Test
VENUE: Lahore (Gaddafi)
DATE: 21st-26th October 1961
TOSS WON BY: Pakistan
RESULT: England won by 5 wickets

PAKISTAN

1st innings			2nd innings	
Hanif Moh'd	b White	19	c Murray b Brown	17
Imtiaz Ah'd*+	c Murray b White	4	b Dexter	12
Saeed Ahmed	c Murray b Barber	74	c Murray b Brown	0
Javed Burki	c Murray b Allen	138	c Allen b Barber	15
Mushtaq	run out	76	c Pullar b Allen	23
W Mathias	c Smith b Barber	3	lbw b Allen	32
Intikhab Alam	b Barber	24	b Barber	17
Mohammad	b Allen	7	c Dexter b Brown	12
M'ad Hussain	b White	14	b Allen	7
Afaq Hussain	not out	10	not out	35
Haseeb Ahsan	not out	7	c Smith b Barber	14
Extras	(4b, 3lb, 0w, 4nb)	11	(9b, 2lb, 0w, 5nb)	16
	142.5 overs		75.5 overs	
Total		**387**		**200**

1st innings FoW: 17, 24, 162, 315, 324, 324, 327, 365, 369
2nd innings FoW: 33, 33, 33, 69, 93, 113, 138, 146, 148, 200

DW White	22	3	65	3	12	2	42	0
A Brown	15.5	3	44	0	14	4	27	3
ER Dexter	7	1	26	0	7	2	10	1
RW Barber	40	4	124	3	20.5	6	54	3
DA Allen	33	14	67	2	22	13	51	3
WE Russell	19	9	25	0				
KF Barrington	6	0	25	0				

ENGLAND

1st innings			2nd innings	
PE Richardson	c Afaq Hussain b Munaf	4	c Imtiaz Ahmed b Intikhab	48
G Pullar	c Hussain b Munaf	0	b Mohammad Munaf	0
KF Barrington	run out	139	lbw b Mahmood Hussain	6
MJK Smith	run out	99	c Afaq Hussain b Has'b	34
ER Dexter*	hit wkt b Afaq Hussain	20	not out	66
WE Russell	b Intikhab	34	b Intikhab	
RW Barber	st Imtiaz Ahmed b Haseeb	6	not out	39
JT Murray+	b Mohammad Munaf	4		
DA Allen	lbw b Mohammad Munaf	40		
DW White	b Saeed Ahmed	0		
A Brown	not out	3		
Extras	(21b, 1lb, 0w, 9nb)	31	(10b, 4lb, 0w, 2nb)	16
	174.1 overs		59 overs	
Total		**380**		**209**

1st innings FoW: 2, 21, 213, 275, 294, 306, 322, 361, 362, 380
2nd innings FoW: 1, 17, 86, 108, 108

Mah'd Hussain	25	8	35	0	12	3	30	1
Moh'd Munaf	31.1	15	42	4	15	1	54	1
Intikhab Alam	48	6	118	1	16	3	37	2
Afaq Hussain	23	6	40	1	5	0	21	0
Haseeb Ahsan	36	7	95	1	9	0	42	1
Saeed Ahmed	11	3	19	1	2	0	9	0

India

No. 375: 1st Test
VENUE: Bombay (Brabourne)
DATE: 11th-16th November 1961
TOSS WON BY: England
RESULT: Match drawn

ENGLAND

1st innings			2nd innings	
PE Richardson	c Kunderan b Borde	71	c Kripal Singh b Durani	43
G Pullar	st Kunderan b Borde	83	run out	31
KF Barrington	not out	151	not out	52
MJK Smith	c Kunderan b Ranjane	36	b Durani	0
ER Dexter*	b Durani	85	c (sub) b Ranjane	27
RW Barber	st Kunderan b Borde	19	b Desai	2
JT Murray+	c (sub) b Ranjane	8	not out	22
DA Allen	c Kunderan b Ranjane	0		
GAR Lock	b Ranjane	23		
DR Smith				
A Brown				
Extras	(7b, 15lb, 0w, 2nb)	24	(3b, 4lb, 0w, 0nb)	7
	173 overs		58 overs	
Total		**500**		**184**

1st innings FoW: 159, 164, 228, 389, 434, 458, 458, 500
2nd innings FoW: 74, 93, 93, 144, 147

RB Desai	32	4	85	0	13	2	39	1
VB Ranjane	21	2	76	4	13	1	53	1
AG Kripal Singh	33	9	64	0	14	3	33	0
VV Kumar	27	8	70	0	11	1	28	2
SA Durani	30	5	91	1	7	1	24	0
CG Borde	30	5	90	3				

INDIA

1st innings			2nd innings	
NJ Contractor*	b Allen	19	c Allen b DR Smith	1
ML Jaisimha	c Barrington b Dexter	56	c Barber b MJK Smith	51
VL Manjrekar	c Lock b Barber	68	lbw b Lock	84
Milkha Singh	c Brown b Allen	2	c Allen b Richardson	12
CG Borde	b DR Smith	69	not out	12
SA Durani	c Barber b Allen	71	c & b Richardson	0
Kripal Singh	not out	38	not out	13
BK Kunderan+	lbw b Lock	5		
RB Desai	c Richardson b Lock	1		
VB Ranjane	c Barber b Lock	16		
VV Kumar	b Lock	0		
Extras	(33b, 4lb, 0w, 8nb)	45	(4b, 2lb, 0w, 1nb)	7
	168 overs		73 overs	
Total		**390**		**180**

1st innings FoW: 80, 121, 140, 173, 315, 341, 356, 358, 383, 390
2nd innings FoW: 5, 136, 140, 162, 162

DR Smith	31	12	54	1	7	2	18	1
A Brown	19	2	64	0	5	0	15	0
ER Dexter	12	4	25	1	4	0	15	0
RW Barber	22	5	74	1	13	2	42	0
GAR Lock	45	22	74	4	16	9	33	1
DA Allen	39	21	54	3	11	5	12	0
KF Barrington					3	0	18	0
MJK Smith					8	3	10	1
PE Richardson					6	3	10	2

No. 376:	2nd Test
VENUE:	Kanpur
DATE:	1st-6th December 1961
TOSS WON BY:	India
RESULT:	Match drawn

No. 377:	3rd Test
VENUE:	Delhi
DATE:	13th-18th December 1961
TOSS WON BY:	India
RESULT:	Match drawn

INDIA 1st innings　　　　**2nd innings**

ML Jaisimha	c Richardson b Lock	70
NJ Contractor*	b Knight	17
VL Manjrekar	c Knight b Allen	96
SA Durani	c Lock b Dexter	37
PR Umrigar	not out	147
CG Borde	b Dexter	21
DN Sardesai	hit wkt b Lock	28
Kripal Singh	b Knight	7
FM Engineer+	st Murray b Lock	33
VB Ranjane		
SP Gupte		
Extras	(2b, 7lb, 0w, 2nb)	11
	198 overs	
Total		**467**

1st innings FoW: 41, 150, 193, 261, 293, 368, 414, 467

DR Smith	44	11	111	0
BR Knight	36	11	80	2
ER Dexter	31	5	84	2
GAR Lock	44	15	93	3
DA Allen	43	17	88	1

ENGLAND 1st innings　　　　**2nd innings**

PE Richardson	c Engineer b Gupte	22	c Umrigar b Borde	48
G Pullar	c Sardesai b Gupte	46	c Contractor b Durani	119
KF Barrington	b Gupte	21	run out	172
MJK Smith	c & b Gupte	0	lbw b Gupte	0
ER Dexter*	c Kripal Singh b Gupte	2	not out	126
RW Barber	not out	69	run out	10
JT Murray+	b Borde	2	not out	9
BR Knight	c & b Borde	12		
DA Allen	c Engineer b Borde	12		
GAR Lock	c & b Durani	49		
DR Smith	lbw b Ranjane	0		
Extras	(6b, 2lb, 0w, 1nb)	9	(4b, 7lb, 0w, 2nb)	13
	106.3 overs		184 overs	
Total		**244**		**497**

1st innings FoW: 29, 87, 87, 95, 100, 104, 128, 162, 243, 244
2nd innings FoW: 94, 233, 234, 440, 459

VB Ranjane	21.3	9	38	1		18	1	61	0
PR Umrigar	6	1	11	0		19	6	53	0
SP Gupte	40	12	90	5		33	8	89	1
AG Kripal Singh	1	0	5	0		36	7	78	0
SA Durani	16	6	36	1		53	15	139	1
CG Borde	22	6	55	3		16	4	44	1
ML Jaisimha						6	1	8	0
NJ Contractor						2	0	9	0
DN Sardesai						1	0	3	0

INDIA 1st innings　　　　**2nd innings**

ML Jaisimha	c & b DR Smith	127
NJ Contractor*	c Pullar b Lock	39
VL Manjrekar	not out	189
Pataudi jr	c Richardson b Allen	13
PR Umrigar	lbw b Allen	22
CG Borde	b Barber	45
SA Durani	b Allen	18
FM Engineer+	lbw b Allen	1
Kripal Singh	run out	2
RB Desai	lbw b Knight	5
SP Gupte	b Knight	0
Extras	(2b, 2lb, 0w, 1nb)	5
	177.3 overs	
Total		**466**

1st innings FoW: 121, 199, 244, 276, 408, 443, 451, 455, 462, 466

DR Smith	30	11	66	1
BR Knight	24.3	5	72	2
DA Allen	47	18	87	4
RW Barber	25	3	103	1
ER Dexter	2	0	11	0
GAR Lock	40	15	83	1
KF Barrington	9	1	39	0

ENGLAND 1st innings　　　　**2nd innings**

PE Richardson	lbw b Desai	1
G Pullar	c Manjrekar b Kripal	89
KF Barrington	not out	113
MJK Smith	b Gupte	2
ER Dexter*	not out	45
RW Barber		
JT Murray+		
BR Knight		
DA Allen		
GAR Lock		
DR Smith		
Extras	(5b, 0lb, 0w, 1nb)	6
	114 overs	
Total		**256**

1st innings FoW: 2, 166, 177

RB Desai	28	5	57	1
ML Jaisimha	11	2	28	0
SP Gupte	36	14	78	1
SA Durani	13	3	38	0
AG Kripal Singh	12	4	27	1
CG Borde	10	4	19	0
PR Umrigar	4	1	3	0

No. 378: 4th Test	No. 379: 5th Test
VENUE: Calcutta	VENUE: Madras (Nehru)
DATE: 30th Dec 1961-4th Jan 1962	DATE: 10th-15th January 1962
TOSS WON BY: India	TOSS WON BY: India
RESULT: India won by 187 runs	RESULT: India won by 128 runs

Match 378 — Calcutta

INDIA 1st innings / 2nd innings

Batsman	1st innings		2nd innings	
N Contractor*	b Smith	4	st Millman b Allen	11
VL Mehra	c Parfitt b Lock	62	b Lock	36
VL Manjrekar	b Allen	24	st Millman b Lock	27
Pataudi	c Lock b Allen	64	c Millman b Allen	32
PR Umrigar	c Smith b Allen	36	c Millman b Allen	9
ML Jaisimha	c Millman b Smith	37	b Allen	36
CG Borde	run out	68	c Parfitt b Lock	0
SA Durani	b Allen	43	c Barrington b Allen	61
FM Engineer+	c Parfitt b Lock	12	c Parfitt b Knight	29
RB Desai	not out	13	c Lock b Knight	0
VB Ranjane	c Barber b Allen	7	not out	7
Extras	(2b, 6lb, 0w, 2nb)	10	(0b, 3lb, 0w, 1nb)	4
	156 overs		101.2 overs	
Total		**380**		**252**

1st innings FoW: 6, 50, 145, 185, 194, 259, 314, 355, 357, 380
2nd innings FoW: 39, 55, 102, 119, 119, 119, 192, 233, 233, 252

Bowler								
DR Smith	31	10	60	2	3	0	15	0
BR Knight	18	3	61	0	7	2	18	2
ER Dexter	29	7	83	0				
DA Allen	34	13	67	5	43.2	16	95	4
GAR Lock	36	19	63	2	46	15	111	4
RW Barber	3	0	17	0	2	0	9	0
WE Russell	5	0	19	0				

ENGLAND 1st innings / 2nd innings

Batsman	1st innings		2nd innings	
PE Richardson	c Contractor b Borde	62	b Umrigar	42
WE Russell	b Ranjane	10	b Ranjane	9
KF Barrington	b Durani	14	c Durani b Desai	3
PH Parfitt	c (sub) b Borde	21	lbw b Durani	62
ER Dexter*	b Borde	57	c Jaisimha b Durani	6
RW Barber	b Borde	12	lbw b Umrigar	46
BR Knight	st Engineer b Durani	12	not out	39
DA Allen	b Durani	15	c Manjrekar b Desai	7
G Millman+	c Engineer b Durani	0	b Ranjane	4
GAR Lock	not out	2	run out	1
DR Smith	b Durani	0	c Manjrekar b Durani	2
Extras	(1b, 2lb, 0w, 4nb)	7	(1b, 11lb, 0w, 0nb)	12
	79.2 overs		116.2 overs	
Total		**212**		**233**

1st innings FoW: 26, 69, 91, 130, 155, 181, 208, 209, 212, 212
2nd innings FoW: 20, 27, 92, 101, 129, 195, 208, 217, 224, 233

Bowler								
RB Desai	10	1	34	0	17	4	32	2
VB Ranjane	21	3	59	1	14	3	31	2
SA Durani	23.2	8	47	5	33.2	12	66	3
CG Borde	25	8	65	4	22	10	46	0
PR Umrigar					30	10	46	2

Match 379 — Madras

INDIA 1st innings / 2nd innings

Batsman	1st innings		2nd innings	
ML Jaisimha	b Knight	12	c Millman b Lock	10
NJ Contractor*	b Barber	86	c Parfitt b DR Smith	3
VL Manjrekar	c Lock b Parfitt	13	run out	85
Pataudi	c Lock b Knight	103	c MJK Smith b Lock	10
PR Umrigar	c Millman b Allen	2	c & b Allen	11
CG Borde	b Lock	31	c Parfitt b Lock	12
SA Durani	b Allen	21	c Dexter b Parfitt	7
RG Nadkarni	b Allen	63	c Millman b Lock	9
FM Engineer+	b Dexter	65	c Parfitt b Lock	1
RB Desai	lbw b Barber	13	not out	15
EAS Prasanna	not out	9	c Dexter b Lock	17
Extras	(4b, 6lb, 0w, 0nb)	10	(6b, 4lb, 0w, 0nb)	10
	144.3 overs		94.3 overs	
Total		**428**		**190**

1st innings FoW: 27, 74, 178, 193, 245, 273, 277, 378, 398, 428
2nd innings FoW: 15, 30, 50, 80, 99, 122, 146, 150, 158, 190

Bowler								
DR Smith	9	1	20	0	7	0	15	1
BR Knight	14	2	62	2	4	0	12	0
GAR Lock	40	13	106	1	39.3	16	65	6
DA Allen	51.3	20	116	3	33	11	64	1
PH Parfitt	11	2	22	1	11	3	24	1
RW Barber	14	0	70	2				
ER Dexter	5	0	22	1				

ENGLAND 1st innings / 2nd innings

Batsman	1st innings		2nd innings	
PE Richardson	c Contractor b Desai	13	c Jaisimha b Desai	2
RW Barber	lbw b Borde	16	b Durani	21
KF Barrington	c Manjrekar b Durani	20	lbw b Nadkarni	48
ER Dexter*	b Borde	2	c Nadkarni b Borde	3
MJK Smith	c Umrigar b Durani	73	c Borde b Durani	15
PH Parfitt	c Prasanna b Durani	25	c Contractor b Durani	33
BR Knight	c Nadkarni b Durani	19	c Engineer b Durani	33
DA Allen	b Durani	34	c Umrigar b Borde	21
G Millman+	not out	32	c Contractor b Prasanna	14
GAR Lock	c Borde b Durani	0	c Nadkarni b Borde	11
DR Smith	b Nadkarni	34	not out	2
Extras	(1b, 12lb, 0w, 0nb)	13	(2b, 4lb, 0w, 0nb)	6
	110.1 overs		92.3 overs	
Total		**281**		**209**

1st innings FoW: 18, 41, 45, 54, 134, 180, 189, 226, 226, 281
2nd innings FoW: 2, 32, 41, 86, 90, 155, 164, 194, 202, 209

Bowler								
RB Desai	12	1	56	1	4	0	16	1
ML Jaisimha	5	0	18	0				
SA Durani	36	9	105	6	34	12	72	4
CG Borde	30	9	58	2	25.3	8	59	3
EAS Prasanna	9	2	20	0	11	3	19	1
PR Umrigar	12	6	11	0	6	1	12	0
RG Nadkarni	6.1	6	0	1	12	3	25	1

No. 380: 1st Test

VENUE:	Dhaka (Dacca)
DATE:	19th-24th January 1962
TOSS WON BY:	Pakistan
RESULT:	Match drawn

PAKISTAN 1st innings / 2nd innings

Batsman	1st innings		2nd innings	
Hanif Moh'd	c Lock b Allen	111	b Allen	104
Alimuddin	c Smith b Lock	7	c Dexter b Richardson	50
Saeed Ahmed	b Knight	69	c Parfitt b Lock	13
Javed Burki	c & b Lock	140	c Knight b Lock	0
Intikhab Alam	c Barrington b Lock	18	c & b Allen	6
Mushtaq	b Allen	26	hit wkt b Allen	0
Imtiaz Ah'd*+	b Lock	0	b Lock	0
Ul-Ghani	not out	15	c Richardson b Allen	12
Shujauddin	b Lock	5		
Moh'd Munaf	b Allen	12		
A D'Souza	not out	7		
Extras	(4b, 3lb, 0w, 0nb)	7	(5b, 1lb, 0w, 1nb)	7
	192.3 overs		134.1 overs	
Total		**393**		**216**

1st innings FoW: 14, 127, 283, 344, 361, 365, 393
2nd innings FoW: 122, 137, 137, 158, 158, 159, 184, 191, 201, 216

Bowler	O	M	R	W	O	M	R	W
BR Knight	29	13	52	1	14	6	19	0
ER Dexter	28	12	34	0	5	4	1	0
GAR Lock	73	24	155	4	42	23	70	4
DA Allen	40.3	13	94	2	23.1	11	30	5
KF Barrington	11	1	39	0	21	13	17	0
RW Barber	11	8	12	0				
PH Parfitt					8	3	14	0
PE Richardson					12	5	28	1
G Pullar					9	3	30	0

ENGLAND 1st innings / 2nd innings

Batsman	1st innings		2nd innings	
G Pullar	c & b D'Souza	165	not out	8
RW Barber	lbw b Nasim-Ul-Ghani	86	not out	21
KF Barrington	b D'Souza	84		
MJK Smith	lbw b D'Souza	10		
ER Dexter*	c Mohammad Munaf	12		
PE Richardson	c D'Souza b Nasim	19		
PH Parfitt	c & b Shujauddin	9		
BR Knight	b D'Souza	10		
DA Allen	b Shujauddin	0		
G Millman+	not out	3		
GAR Lock	c Hanif b Shujauddin	4		
Extras	(16b, 15lb, 0w, 6nb)	37	(2b, 6lb, 0w, 1nb)	9
	181 overs		16 overs	
Total		**439**		**38**

1st innings FoW: 198, 345, 358, 373, 386, 414, 418, 422, 432, 439

Bowler	O	M	R	W	O	M	R	W
Moh'd Munaf	30	5	55	1				
A D'Souza	46	13	94	4				
Shujauddin	34	10	73	3				
Nasim-Ul-Ghani	50	19	119	2	3	3	0	0
Intikhab Alam	9	0	43	0	5	0	16	0
Saeed Ahmed	12	3	18	0	4	2	2	0
Javed Burki					2	1	3	0
Hanif Moh'd					2	0	8	0

No. 381: 2nd Test

VENUE:	Karachi (National Stadium)
DATE:	2nd-7th February 1962
TOSS WON BY:	Pakistan
RESULT:	Match drawn

PAKISTAN 1st innings / 2nd innings

Batsman	1st innings		2nd innings	
Hanif Moh'd	c Dexter b Lock	67	c Dexter b Knight	89
Imtiaz Ah'd*+	b White	0	c Parfitt b Barber	53
Saeed Ahmed	c Millman b Knight	16	c & b Barber	19
Javed Burki	c Millman b Dexter	3	c Millman b Dexter	44
Mushtaq	lbw b Knight	14	c Smith b Dexter	86
Alimuddin	c Lock b Knight	109	c Lock b Barber	5
Shujauddin	c Parfitt b Allen	15	b Lock	41
Ul-Ghani	b Barber	3	not out	41
Fazal Mah'd	b Knight	12	b Dexter	0
A D'Souza	b Dexter	3	not out	10
Haseeb Ahsan	not out	4		
Extras	(2b, 1lb, 0w, 4nb)	7	(8b, 2lb, 0w, 6nb)	16
	95 overs		167 overs	
Total		**253**		**404**

1st innings FoW: 2, 25, 36, 56, 148, 183, 196, 245, 248, 253
2nd innings FoW: 91, 129, 211, 227, 256, 337, 373, 383

Bowler	O	M	R	W	O	M	R	W
BR Knight	19	4	66	4	17	3	43	1
DW White	2.4	0	12	1				
ER Dexter	18.2	4	48	2	32	9	86	3
DA Allen	27	14	51	1	35	19	42	0
RW Barber	14	1	44	1	41	7	117	3
GAR Lock	14	8	25	1	37	16	86	1
PH Parfitt					3	2	4	0
PE Richardson					2	1	10	0

ENGLAND 1st innings / 2nd innings

Batsman	1st innings		2nd innings
PE Richardson	c Alimuddin b Nasim	26	
G Pullar	c Alimuddin b Nasim	60	
ER Dexter*	c Saeed b D'Souza	205	
MJK Smith	c Imtiaz b Nasim'Ghani	56	
PH Parfitt	c Saeed b D'Souza	111	
RW Barber	st Imtiaz b Haseeb	23	
BR Knight	c Imtiaz b D'Souza	6	
DA Allen	c Imtiaz b D'Souza	1	
G Millman+	c Nasim'Ghani b Haseeb	0	
GAR Lock	not out	0	
DW White	b D'Souza	0	
Extras	(7b, 11lb, 0w, 1nb)	19	
	233.5 overs		
Total		**507**	

1st innings FoW: 77, 107, 250, 438, 493, 497, 502, 503, 507, 507

Bowler	O	M	R	W
Fazal Mahmood	63	23	98	0
A D'Souza	57.5	16	112	5
Nasim-Ul-Ghani	45	10	125	3
Haseeb Ahsan	36	7	68	2
Shujauddin	27	5	63	0
Saeed Ahmed	3	0	12	0
Mushtaq Moh'd	2	0	10	0

No. 382: 1st Test
VENUE: Edgbaston
DATE: 31st May-4th June 1962
TOSS WON BY: England
RESULT: Eng won by an innings and 24 runs

ENGLAND	1st innings		2nd innings
G Pullar	b D'Souza	22	
MC Cowdrey	c Imtiaz b Intikhab	159	
ER Dexter*	c Javed b Intikhab	72	
TW Graveney	c Ijaz b M Hussain	97	
KF Barrington	lbw b M Hussain	9	
PH Parfitt	not out	101	
DA Allen	not out	79	
G Millman+			
GAR Lock			
FS Trueman			
JB Statham			
Extras	(0b, 5lb, 0w, 0nb)	5	
	146 overs		
Total		**544**	

1st innings FoW: 31, 197, 304, 330, 391

M Hussain	43	14	130	2
A D'Souza	46	9	161	1
Intikhab Alam	25	2	117	2
Nasim-Ul-Ghani	30	7	109	0
Saeed Ahmed	2	0	22	0

PAKISTAN	1st innings		2nd innings	
Hanif Moh'd	c Millman b Allen	47	c Cowdrey b Allen	31
Ijaz Butt	c Lock b Statham	10	c Trueman b Allen	33
Saeed Ahmed	c Graveney b Trueman	5	c Graveney b Lock	46
Mushtaq	c Cowdrey b Lock	63	c Millman b Allen	8
Javed Burki*	c Barrington b Allen	13	c Parfitt b Lock	65
Imtiaz Ah'd+	b Trueman	39	b Statham	19
W Mathias	b Statham	21	b Statham	4
Ul-Ghani	b Statham	0	c Parfitt b Trueman	35
Intikhab Alam	b Lock	16	c Cowdrey b Lock	0
M Hussain	b Statham	0	c Graveney b Trueman	22
A D'Souza	not out	23	not out	9
Extras	(8b, 1lb, 0w, 0nb)	9	(1b, 1lb, 0w, 0nb)	2
	101 overs		123 overs	
Total		**246**		**274**

1st innings FoW: 11, 30, 108, 144, 146, 202, 206, 206, 206, 246
2nd innings FoW: 60, 77, 119, 127, 187, 199, 207, 207, 257, 274

JB Statham	21	9	54	4	19	6	32	2
FS Trueman	13	3	59	2	24	5	70	2
ER Dexter	12	6	23	0	7	2	16	0
DA Allen	32	16	62	2	36	16	73	3
GAR Lock	19	8	37	2	36	14	80	3
PH Parfitt	2	1	2	0				
KF Barrington	2	2	0	0				
MC Cowdrey					1	0	1	0

No. 383: 2nd Test
VENUE: Lord's
DATE: 21st-23rd June 1962
TOSS WON BY: Pakistan
RESULT: England won by 9 wickets

PAKISTAN	1st innings		2nd innings	
Hanif Moh'd	c Cowdy b Trueman	13	lbw b Coldwell	24
Imtiaz Ah'd+	b Coldwell	1	c Graveney b Allen	10
Saeed Ahmed	b Dexter	10	b Coldwell	20
Javed Burki*	c Dexter b Trueman	5	c Millman b Trueman	18
Mushtaq	c Cowdy b Trueman	7	lbw b Coldwell	101
Alimuddin	b Coldwell	9	c Graveney b Coldwell	101
W Mathias	b Trueman	15	c Trueman b Coldwell	33
Ul-Ghani	c Millman b Trueman	17	c Graveney b Trueman	1
M Hussain	c Cowdy b Coldwell	1	b Coldwell	20
A D'Souza	not out	6	not out	12
Moh'd Farooq	c Stewart b Trueman	13	b Trueman	1
Extras	(1b, 2lb, 0w, 0nb)	3	(6b, 4lb, 4w, 0nb)	14
	43.4 overs		119.3 overs	
Total		**100**		**355**

1st innings FoW: 2, 23, 25, 31, 36, 51, 77, 78, 78, 100
2nd innings FoW: 36, 36, 57, 77, 274, 299, 300, 333, 354, 355

FS Trueman	17.4	6	31	6	33.3	6	85	3
LJ Coldwell	14	2	25	3	41	13	85	6
ER Dexter	12	3	41	1	15	4	44	0
DA Allen					15	6	41	0
GAR Lock					14	1	78	0
KF Barrington					1	0	8	0

ENGLAND	1st innings		2nd innings	
MJ Stewart	c Imtiaz b D'Souza	39	not out	34
MC Cowdrey	c D'Souza b Farooq	41	c Imtiaz b D'Souza	20
ER Dexter*	c Imtiaz b Farooq	65	not out	32
TW Graveney	b D'Souza	153		
KF Barrington	c Imtiaz Ahmed b Farooq	0		
DA Allen	lbw b Moh'd Farooq	2		
PH Parfitt	b Mahmood	16		
G Millman+	c Hanif b Mahmood	7		
GAR Lock	c Mathias b Ahmed	7		
FS Trueman	lbw b Saeed Ahmed	29		
LJ Coldwell	not out	0		
Extras	(1b, 5lb, 0w, 5nb)	11	(0b, 0lb, 0w, 0nb)	0
	101.4 overs		17 overs	
Total		**370**		**86**

1st innings FoW: 59, 137, 168, 168, 184, 221, 247, 290, 366, 370
2nd innings FoW: 36

M Hussain	40	9	106	2				
Moh'd Farooq	19	4	70	4	7	1	37	0
A D'Souza	35.4	3	147	2	7	0	29	1
Nasim-Ul-Ghani	2	0	15	0				
Saeed Ahmed	5	1	21	2	2	0	12	0
Mushtaq Moh'd					1	0	8	0

No. 384: 3rd Test

VENUE:	Leeds (Headingley)
DATE:	5th-7th July 1962
TOSS WON BY:	Pakistan
RESULT:	Eng won by an innings and 117 runs

ENGLAND 1st innings / 2nd innings

MJ Stewart	lbw b Munir	86
MC Cowdrey*	c Saeed b M Hussain	7
ER Dexter	b Mahmood	20
TW Graveney	c Ijaz b Munir	37
KF Barrington	c Mushtaq b Farooq	1
PH Parfitt	c & b Nasim-Ul-Ghani	119
FJ Titmus	c & b Munir	2
JT Murray+	c & b Nasim-Ul-Ghani	29
DA Allen	c Ijaz b Munir	62
FS Trueman	lbw b Munir	20
JB Statham	not out	26
Extras	(6b, 9lb, 1w, 3nb)	19
	132 overs	
Total		**428**

1st innings FoW: 7, 43, 108, 117, 177, 180, 247, 346, 377, 428

Bowler	O	M	R	W
Mohammad Farooq	28	8	74	1
Mahmood Hussain	25	5	87	2
Munir Malik	49	11	128	5
Javed Akhtar	16	5	52	0
Nasim-Ul-Ghani	14	2	68	2

PAKISTAN 1st innings / 2nd innings

Batsman	1st innings	Runs	2nd innings	Runs
Alimuddin	c Barrington b Titmus	50	c Titmus b Allen	60
Ijaz Butt+	b Trueman	1	b Trueman	6
Saeed Ahmed	c Trueman b Statham	16	lbw b Statham	19
Mushtaq	c Murray b Dexter	27	c Trueman b Allen	8
Hanif Moh'd	b Statham	9	c Cowdrey b Statham	54
Javed Burki*	b Trueman	1	c Barrington b Allen	4
Ul-Ghani	c Graveney b Titmus	5	c Murray b Statham	21
M Hussain	not out	0	c & b Dexter	0
Munir Malik	b Dexter	3	b Statham	4
Javed Akhtar	b Dexter	2	not out	2
Farooq	c Statham b Dexter	8	c Statham b Trueman	0
Extras	(8b, 0lb, 0w, 1nb)	9	(0b, 2lb, 0w, 0nb)	2
	65.1 overs		74.4 overs	
Total		**131**		**180**

1st innings FoW: 13, 51, 72, 88, 118, 118, 118, 121, 123, 131
2nd innings FoW: 10, 40, 57, 130, 136, 163, 178, 179, 179, 180

Bowler	O	M	R	W	O	M	R	W
FS Trueman	23	6	55	2	10.4	3	33	2
JB Statham	20	9	40	2	20	3	50	4
ER Dexter	9.1	3	10	4	8	1	24	1
DA Allen	9	6	14	0	24	11	47	3
FJ Titmus	4	1	3	2	11	2	20	0
KF Barrington					1	0	4	0

No. 385: 4th Test

VENUE:	Trent Bridge
DATE:	26th-31st July 1962
TOSS WON BY:	Pakistan
RESULT:	Match drawn

ENGLAND 1st innings / 2nd innings

G Pullar	lbw b Munir	5
DS Sheppard	c Imtiaz b Intikhab	83
ER Dexter*	c Javed b Fazal	85
TW Graveney	c Intikhab b Fazal	114
PH Parfitt	not out	101
BR Knight	c Saeed Ahmed b Fazal	14
FJ Titmus	not out	11
JT Murray+		
FS Trueman		
GAR Lock		
JB Statham		
Extras	(0b, 13lb, 0w, 2nb)	15
	136.2 overs	
Total		**428**

1st innings FoW: 11, 172, 185, 369, 388

Bowler	O	M	R	W
Fazal Mahmood	60	15	130	3
Munir Malik	34	4	130	1
Ul-Ghani	20.2	1	76	0
Intikhab Alam	14	3	49	1
Shahid Mahmood	6	1	23	0
Saeed Ahmed	2	0	5	0

PAKISTAN 1st innings / 2nd innings

Batsman	1st innings	Runs	2nd innings	Runs
Hanif	c Titmus b Trueman	0	c & b Trueman	3
Shahid Moh'd	c Graveney b Trueman	16	c Murray b Statham	11
Mushtaq	c Lock b Knight	55	not out	100
Javed Burki*	c Murray b Knight	19	c (sub) b Titmus	28
Saeed Ahmed	c Murray b Knight	43	c Trueman b Lock	64
Imtiaz Ah'd+	lbw b Trueman	15	lbw b Statham	1
Alimuddin	b Trueman	0	c Statham b Dexter	9
Ul-Ghani	c Murray b Knight	41	not out	0
Intikhab Alam	c Murray b Knight	14	(0b, 0lb, 0w, 0nb)	0
Fazal Mahm'd	lbw b Knight	2	101 overs	
Munir Malik	not out	0		216
Extras	(2b, 10lb, 0w, 2nb)	14		
	86.1 overs			
Total		**219**		

1st innings FoW: 0, 39, 95, 98, 120, 120, 171, 213, 217, 219
2nd innings FoW: 4, 22, 78, 185, 187, 216

Bowler	O	M	R	W	O	M	R	W
FS Trueman	24	3	71	4	19	5	35	1
JB Statham	18.1	5	55	2	22	8	47	2
BR Knight	17	1	38	4	21	6	48	0
GAR Lock	14	5	19	0	15	4	27	1
FJ Titmus	13	2	22	0	16	7	29	1
ER Dexter					7	0	25	1
PH Parfitt					1	0	5	0

Pakistan

No. 386: 5th Test
VENUE: The Oval
DATE: 16th-20th August 1962
TOSS WON BY: England
RESULT: England won by 10 wickets

ENGLAND	1st innings		2nd innings	
DS Sheppard	c Fazal b Ul-Ghani	57	not out	9
MC Cowdrey	c Hanif Moh'd b Fazal	182	not out	14
ER Dexter*	b Fazal	172		
KF Barrington	not out	50		
PH Parfitt	c Imtiaz Ah'd b D'Souza	3		
BR Knight	b D'Souza	3		
R Illingworth	not out	2		
JT Murray+				
DA Allen				
LJ Coldwell				
JDF Larter				
Extras	(4b, 5lb, 0w, 2nb)	11	(4b, 0lb, 0w, 0nb)	4
	140 overs		8.3 overs	
Total		**480**		**27**

2nd innings FoW: 117, 365, 441, 444, 452

Fazal Mahmood	49	9	192	2	4	1	10	0
A D'Souza	42	9	116	2	3	1	8	0
Intikhab Alam	38	5	109	0				
Javed Burki	1	0	12	0	1	0	2	0
Nasim-Ul-Ghani	9	1	39	1				
Saeed Ahmed	1	0	1	0				
Mushtaq Moh'd					0.3	0	3	0

PAKISTAN	1st innings		2nd innings	
Ijaz Butt	c Cowdrey b Larter	10	run out	6
Imtiaz Ah'd+	c Murray b Knight	49	c Cowdrey b Larter	98
Mushtaq	lbw b Larter	43	b Illingworth	72
Javed Burki*	b Larter	3	c Dexter b Larter	0
Saeed Ahmed	c Parfitt b Allen	21	c Knight b Allen	4
Hanif Moh'd	b Larter	46	c Parfitt b Knight	42
W Mathias	c Murray b Larter	0	run out	48
A D'Souza	c Parfitt b Coldwell	5	b Coldwell	24
Ul-Ghani	c Murray b Coldwell	1	b Larter	12
Intikhab Alam	not out	3	not out	2
Fazal Mah'd	b Coldwell	0	b Larter	5
Extras	(0b, 0lb, 0w, 2nb)	2	(4b, 5lb, 0w, 1nb)	10
	97 overs		111.1 overs	
Total		**183**		**323**

2nd innings FoW: 11, 93, 102, 115, 165, 168, 175, 179, 183, 183
2nd innings FoW: 34, 171, 171, 180, 186, 250, 294, 316, 316, 323

LJ Coldwell	28	11	53	3	23	4	60	1
JDF Larter	25	4	57	5	21.1	0	88	4
DA Allen	22	9	33	1	27	14	52	1
BR Knight	9	5	11	1	11	3	33	1
R Illingworth	13	5	27	0	21	9	54	1
ER Dexter					6	1	16	0
KF Barrington					2	0	10	0

Australia

No. 387: 1st Test
VENUE: Brisbane (Gabba)
DATE: 30th Nov-5th December 1962
TOSS WON BY: Australia
RESULT: Match drawn

AUSTRALIA	1st innings		2nd innings	
WM Lawry	c Smith b Trueman	5	c Sheppard b Titmus	98
RB Simpson	c Trueman b Dexter	50	c Smith b Dexter	71
NC O'Neill	c Statham b Trueman	19	lbw b Statham	56
RN Harvey	b Statham	39	c Statham b Dexter	57
PJP Burge	c Dexter b Trueman	6	not out	47
BC Booth	c Dexter b Titmus	112	not out	19
AK Davidson	c Trueman b Barrington	23		
KD Mackay	not out	86		
R Benaud*	c Smith b Knight	51		
GD McKenzie	c & b Knight	4		
BN Jarman+	c Barrington b Knight	2		
Extras	(5b, 1lb, 0w, 1nb)	7	(4b, 10lb, 0w, 0nb)	14
	106.5 overs		87 overs	
Total		**404**		**362**

1st innings FoW: 5, 46, 92, 101, 140, 194, 297, 388, 392, 404
2nd innings FoW: 136, 216, 241, 325

JB Statham	16	1	75	1	16	1	67	1
FS Trueman	18	0	76	3	15	0	59	0
BR Knight	17.5	2	65	3	14	1	63	0
FJ Titmus	33	8	91	1	26	3	81	1
ER Dexter	10	0	46	1	16	0	78	2
KF Barrington	12	3	44	1				

ENGLAND	1st innings		2nd innings	
G Pullar	c & b Benaud	33	c & b Davidson	56
DS Sheppard	c McKenzie b Benaud	31	c Benaud b Davidson	53
ER Dexter*	b Benaud	70	b McKenzie	99
MC Cowdrey	c Lawry b Simpson	21	c & b Benaud	9
KF Barrington	c Burge b Benaud	78	c McKenzie b Davidson	23
AC Smith+	c Jarman b McKenzie	21	c Jarman b McKenzie	4
PH Parfitt	c Davidson b Benaud	80	not out	3
FJ Titmus	c Simpson b Benaud	21	not out	4
BR Knight	c Davidson b McKenzie	0		
FS Trueman	c Jarman b McKenzie	19		
JB Statham	not out	8		
Extras	(4b, 2lb, 1w, 0nb)	7	(15b, 10lb, 0w, 2nb)	27
	135.3 overs		83 overs	
Total		**389**		**278**

1st innings FoW: 62, 65, 145, 169, 220, 297, 361, 362, 362, 389
2nd innings FoW: 114, 135, 191, 257, 257, 261

AK Davidson	21	4	77	0	20	6	43	3
GD McKenzie	25.3	2	78	3	20	4	61	2
KD Mackay	28	7	55	0	7	0	28	0
R Benaud	42	12	115	6	27	7	71	1
RB Simpson	18	6	52	1	7	0	48	0
NC O'Neill	1	0	5	0	2	2	0	0

No. 388: 2nd Test
VENUE: Melbourne (MCG)
DATE: 29th Dec 1962-3rd Jan 1963
TOSS WON BY: Australia
RESULT: England won by 7 wickets

No. 389: 3rd Test
VENUE: Sydney (SCG)
DATE: 11th-15th January 1963
TOSS WON BY: England
RESULT: Australia won by 8 wickets

AUSTRALIA 1st innings / 2nd innings

Batsman	1st innings		2nd innings	
WM Lawry	b Trueman	52	b Dexter	57
RB Simpson	c Smith b Coldwell	38	b Trueman	14
NC O'Neill	c Graveney b Statham	19	c Cowdrey b Trueman	0
RN Harvey	b Coldwell	0	run out	10
PJP Burge	lbw b Titmus	23	b Statham	14
BC Booth	c Barrington b Titmus	27	c Trueman b Statham	103
AK Davidson	c Smith b Trueman	40	c Smith b Titmus	17
KD Mackay	lbw b Titmus	49	lbw b Trueman	9
R Benaud*	c Barrington b Titmus	36	c Cowdrey b Trueman	4
GD McKenzie	b Trueman	16	b Trueman	0
BN Jarman+	not out	10	not out	11
Extras	(2b, 4lb, 0w, 0nb)		(4b, 5lb, 0w, 0nb)	9
Total	92 overs	316	96 overs	248

1st innings FoW: 62, 111, 112, 112, 155, 164, 237, 289, 294, 316
2nd innings FoW: 30, 30, 46, 69, 161, 193, 212, 228, 228, 248

Bowler	O	M	R	W		O	M	R	W
FS Trueman	23	1	83	3		20	1	62	5
JB Statham	22	2	83	1		23	1	52	2
LJ Coldwell	17	2	58	2		25	2	60	0
KF Barrington	6	0	23	0		5	0	22	0
ER Dexter	6	1	10	0		9	2	18	1
FJ Titmus	15	2	43	4		14	4	25	1
TW Graveney	3	1	10	0					

ENGLAND 1st innings / 2nd innings

Batsman	1st innings		2nd innings	
DS Sheppard	lbw b Davidson	0	run out	113
G Pullar	b Davidson	11	c Jarman b McKenzie	5
ER Dexter*	c Simpson b Benaud	93	run out	52
MC Cowdrey	c Burge b McKenzie	113	not out	58
KF Barrington	lbw b McKenzie	35	not out	0
TW Graveney	run out	41		
FJ Titmus	c Jarman b Davidson	15		
AC Smith+	not out	6		
FS Trueman	c O'Neill b Davidson	6		
JB Statham	b Davidson	1		
LJ Coldwell	c Benaud b Davidson	1		
Extras	(4b, 4lb, 0w, 1nb)	9	(5b, 3lb, 0w, 1nb)	9
Total	88.1 overs	331	64.2 overs	237

1st innings FoW: 0, 19, 194, 254, 255, 292, 315, 324, 327, 331
2nd innings FoW: 5, 129, 233

Bowler	O	M	R	W		O	M	R	W
AK Davidson	23.1	4	75	6		19	2	53	0
GD McKenzie	29	3	95	2		20	3	58	1
KD Mackay	6	2	17	0		9	0	34	0
R Benaud	18	3	82	1		14	1	69	0
RB Simpson	7	1	34	0		2	0	10	0
NC O'Neill	5	1	19	0					
BC Booth						0.2	0	4	0

ENGLAND 1st innings / 2nd innings

Batsman	1st innings		2nd innings	
G Pullar	c Benaud b Simpson	53	b Davidson	0
DS Sheppard	c McKenzie b Davidson	3	c Simpson b Davidson	12
ER Dexter*	c Lawry b Benaud	32	c Simpson b Davidson	11
MC Cowdrey	c Jarman b Simpson	85	c Simpson b Benaud	8
KF Barrington	lbw b Davidson	35	b McKenzie	21
PH Parfitt	c Lawry b Simpson	0	c O'Neill b McKenzie	28
FJ Titmus	b Davidson	32	c Booth b O'Neill	6
JT Murray+	lbw b Davidson	0	not out	3
FS Trueman	b Simpson	32	c Jarman b McKenzie	9
JB Statham	c Benaud b Simpson	0	b Davidson	2
LJ Coldwell	not out	2	c Shepherd b Davidson	0
Extras	(0b, 3lb, 2w, 0nb)	5	(2b, 2lb, 0w, 0nb)	4
Total	86.5 overs	279	56.6 overs	104

1st innings FoW: 4, 65, 132, 201, 203, 221, 221, 272, 272, 279
2nd innings FoW: 0, 20, 25, 37, 53, 71, 90, 100, 104, 104

Bowler	O	M	R	W		O	M	R	W
AK Davidson	24.5	7	54	4		10.6	2	25	5
GD McKenzie	15	3	52	0		14	3	26	3
CEJ Guest	16	0	51	0		2	0	8	0
R Benaud	16	2	60	1		19	10	29	1
RB Simpson	15	3	57	5		4	2	5	0
NC O'Neill						7	5	7	1

AUSTRALIA 1st innings / 2nd innings

Batsman	1st innings		2nd innings	
WM Lawry	c Murray b Coldwell	8	b Trueman	8
RB Simpson	b Titmus	91	not out	34
RN Harvey	c Barrington b Titmus	64	lbw b Trueman	15
BC Booth	c Trueman b Titmus	16	not out	5
NC O'Neill	b Titmus	3		
BK Shepherd	not out	71		
BN Jarman+	run out	0		
AK Davidson	c Trueman b Titmus	15		
R Benaud*	c & b Titmus	15		
GD McKenzie	lbw b Titmus	4		
CEJ Guest	b Statham	11		
Extras	(10b, 11lb, 0w, 0nb)	21	(5b, 0lb, 0w, 0nb)	5
Total	101.2 overs	319	12.2 overs	67

1st innings FoW: 14, 174, 177, 187, 212, 216, 242, 274, 280, 319
2nd innings FoW: 28, 54

Bowler	O	M	R	W		O	M	R	W
FS Trueman	20	2	68	0		6	1	20	2
JB Statham	21.2	2	67	1		3	0	15	0
LJ Coldwell	15	1	41	1					
FJ Titmus	37	14	79	7					
KF Barrington	8	0	43	0					
ER Dexter						3.2	0	27	0

131

Australia

No. 390:	4th Test
VENUE:	Adelaide
DATE:	25th-30th January 1963
TOSS WON BY:	Australia
RESULT:	Match drawn

AUSTRALIA

1st innings			2nd innings	
WM Lawry	b Illingworth	10	c Graveney b Trueman	16
RB Simpson	c Smith b Statham	0	c Smith b Dexter	71
RN Harvey	c Statham b Dexter	154	c Barrington b Statham	6
BC Booth	c Cowdrey b Titmus	34	c Smith b Dexter	77
NC O'Neill	c Cowdrey b Dexter	100	c Cowdrey b Trueman	23
AK Davidson	b Statham	46	c Titmus b Dexter	13
BK Shepherd	b Trueman b Statham	10	c Graveney b Trueman	3
KD Mackay	c Smith b Trueman	1	c Barrington b Trueman	48
R Benaud*	b Dexter	16	c Smith b Statham	13
GD McKenzie	c Sheppard b Titmus	15	b Statham	2
ATW Grout+	not out	1	not out	16
Extras	(0b, 5lb, 1w, 0nb)	6	(1b, 4lb, 0w, 0nb)	5
Total	103.1 overs	**393**	90.3 overs	**293**

1st innings FoW: 2, 16, 101, 295, 302, 331, 336, 366, 383, 393
2nd innings FoW: 27, 37, 170, 175, 199, 205, 228, 254, 258, 293

FS Trueman	19	1	54	1	23.3	3	60	4
JB Statham	21	5	66	3	21	2	71	3
R Illingworth	20	3	85	1	5	1	23	0
ER Dexter	23	1	94	3	17	0	65	3
FJ Titmus	20.1	2	88	2	24	5	69	0

ENGLAND

1st innings			2nd innings	
G Pullar	b McKenzie	9	c Simpson b McKenzie	3
DS Sheppard	st Grout b Benaud	30	c Grout b Mackay	1
KF Barrington	b Simpson	63	not out	132
MC Cowdrey	c Grout b McKenzie	13	run out	32
ER Dexter*	c Grout b McKenzie	61	c Simpson b Benaud	10
TW Graveney	c Booth b McKenzie	22	not out	36
FJ Titmus	not out	59		
R Illingworth	c Grout b McKenzie	12		
AC Smith+	c Lawry b Mackay	13		
FS Trueman	c Benaud b Mackay	38		
JB Statham	b Mackay	1		
Extras	(5b, 5lb, 0w, 0nb)	10	(4b, 0lb, 5w, 0nb)	9
Total	90.2 overs	**331**	57 overs	**223**

1st innings FoW: 17, 84, 117, 119, 165, 226, 246, 275, 327, 331
2nd innings FoW: 2, 4, 98, 122

AK Davidson	3.4	0	30	0				
GD McKenzie	33	3	89	5	14	0	64	1
KD Mackay	27.6	8	80	3	8	2	13	1
R Benaud	18	3	82	1	15	3	38	1
RB Simpson	8	1	40	1	10	1	50	0
NC O'Neill					8	0	49	0
WM Lawry					1	1	0	0
RN Harvey					1	1	0	0

Australia

No. 391:	5th Test
VENUE:	Sydney (SCG)
DATE:	15th-20th February 1963
TOSS WON BY:	England
RESULT:	Match drawn

ENGLAND

1st innings			2nd innings	
DS Sheppard	c & b Hawke	19	c Harvey b Benaud	68
MC Cowdrey	c Harvey b Davidson	2	c Hawke b Benaud	18
KF Barrington	c Harvey b Benaud	101	c Grout b McKenzie	94
ER Dexter*	c Simpson b O'Neill	47	st Grout b Benaud	6
TW Graveney	c Harvey b McKenzie	14	c Benaud b Davidson	53
R Illingworth	c Grout b Davidson	27	c & b Davidson	3
FJ Titmus	c Grout b Hawke	34	not out	12
FS Trueman	c Harvey b Benaud	30	c Harvey b McKenzie	8
AC Smith+	b Simpson	6	c Simpson b Davidson	1
DA Allen	c Benaud b Davidson	14		
JB Statham	not out	17		
Extras	(4b, 6lb, 0w, 0nb)	10	(1b, 4lb, 0w, 0nb)	5
Total	134.6 overs	**321**	82 overs	**268**

1st innings FoW: 5, 39, 129, 177, 189, 224, 276, 286, 293, 321
2nd innings FoW: 40, 137, 145, 239, 247, 249, 257, 268

AK Davidson	25.6	4	43	3	28	1	80	3
GD McKenzie	27	4	57	1	8	0	39	2
NJN Hawke	20	1	51	2	9	0	38	0
R Benaud	34	9	71	2	30	8	71	3
RB Simpson	18	4	51	1	4	0	22	0
NC O'Neill	10	0	38	1				
RN Harvey					3	0	13	0

AUSTRALIA

1st innings			2nd innings	
WM Lawry	c Smith b Trueman	11	not out	45
RB Simpson	c Trueman b Titmus	32	b Trueman	0
BC Booth	b Titmus	11	b Allen	28
NC O'Neill	c Graveney b Allen	73	c Smith b Allen	17
PJP Burge	lbw b Titmus	103	b Allen	0
RN Harvey	c (sub) b Statham	22	not out	52
AK Davidson	c Allen b Dexter	15		
R Benaud*	c Graveney b Allen	57		
GD McKenzie	c & b Titmus	0		
NJN Hawke	c Graveney b Titmus	14		
ATW Grout+	not out	0		
Extras	(6b, 5lb, 0w, 0nb)	11	(4b, 6lb, 0w, 0nb)	10
Total	131.2 overs	**349**	72 overs	**152**

1st innings FoW: 28, 50, 71, 180, 231, 271, 299, 303, 347, 349
2nd innings FoW: 0, 39, 70, 70

FS Trueman	11	0	33	1	3	0	6	1
JB Statham	18	1	76	1	4	1	8	0
ER Dexter	7	1	24	1	4	1	11	0
FJ Titmus	47.2	9	103	5	20	7	37	0
DA Allen	43	15	87	2	19	11	26	3
R Illingworth	5	1	15	0	10	5	8	0
KF Barrington					8	3	22	0
TW Graveney					4	0	24	0

No. 392:	1st Test
VENUE:	Auckland
DATE:	23rd-27th February 1963
TOSS WON BY:	England
RESULT:	Eng won by an innings and 215 runs

No. 393:	2nd Test
VENUE	Wellington
DATE:	1st-4th March 1963
TOSS WON BY:	England
RESULT:	Eng won by an innings and 47 runs

ENGLAND 1st innings / 2nd innings

Batsman	Dismissal	Runs	2nd innings
DS Sheppard	c Dick b Cameron	12	
R Illingworth	c Reid b Cameron	20	
KF Barrington	c Playle b Cameron	126	
ER Dexter*	c Barton b Yuile	7	
MC Cowdrey	c Barton b Cameron	86	
PH Parfitt	not out	131	
BR Knight	b Alabaster	125	
FJ Titmus	st Dick b Sparling	26	
JT Murray+	not out	9	
JDF Larter			
LJ Coldwell			
Extras	(18b, 1lb, 0w, 1nb)	20	
Total	186 overs	**562**	

1st innings FoW: 24, 45, 63, 229, 258, 498, 535

RC Motz	42	12	98	0
FJ Cameron	43	7	118	4
JC Alabaster	40	6	130	1
BW Yuile	21	4	77	1
JR Reid	28	8	67	0
JT Sparling	12	2	52	1

NEW ZEALAND 1st innings / 2nd innings

Batsman	Dismissal	Runs	2nd innings	Runs
GT Dowling	b Coldwell	3	b Illingworth	14
WR Playle	c Dexter b Larter	0	c Dexter b Coldwell	4
PT Barton	c Sheppard b Larter	3	lbw b Titmus	16
JR Reid*	b Titmus	59	c Barrington b Illing'rth	0
BW Sinclair	c Coldwell b Titmus	24	b Larter	2
JT Sparling	c Murray b Larter	3	not out	21
AE Dick+	run out	29	c Illingworth b Larter	0
BW Yuile	run out	64	lbw b Larter	1
RC Motz	c Murray b Knight	60	c & b Illingworth	20
JC Alabaster	b Knight	2	c Titmus b Illingworth	0
FJ Cameron	not out	0	b Larter	1
Extras	(5b, 3lb, 1w, 2nb)	11	(2b, 8lb, 0w, 0nb)	10
Total	110.4 overs	**258**	53.1 overs	**89**

1st innings FoW: 0, 7, 7, 62, 71, 109, 161, 256, 256, 258
2nd innings FoW: 15, 42, 42, 42, 46, 46, 56, 83, 83, 89

LJ Coldwell	27	9	66	1	5	2	4	1
JDF Larter	26	12	51	3	14.1	3	26	4
BR Knight	10.4	2	23	2	10	2	13	0
FJ Titmus	25	9	44	2	6	5	2	1
KF Barrington	12	4	38	0				
ER Dexter	9	4	20	0				
R Illingworth	1	0	5	0	18	7	34	4

NEW ZEALAND 1st innings / 2nd innings

Batsman	Dismissal	Runs	2nd innings	Runs
GT Dowling	c Smith b Trueman	12	c Knight b Trueman	2
WR Playle	c Smith b Knight	23	c & b Illingworth	65
PT Barton	c Cowdrey b Trueman	0	c Barrington b Knight	3
JR Reid*	c Smith b Knight	0	c Barrington b Titmus	9
BW Sinclair	b Trueman	4	c & b Barrington	36
M Shrimpton	lbw b Knight	28	c Parfitt b Barrington	10
AE Dick+	c Sheppard b Trueman	7	not out	38
BW Yuile	c Illingworth b Titmus	13	b Titmus	0
RW Blair	not out	64	c Larter b Titmus	5
BD Morrison	run out	10	c Larter b Titmus	0
FJ Cameron	lbw b Barrington	12	lbw b Barrington	0
Extras	(13b, 5lb, 0w, 3nb)	21	(13b, 4lb, 0w, 2nb)	19
Total	76.3 overs	**194**	98 overs	**187**

1st innings FoW: 32, 32, 35, 40, 61, 74, 96, 129, 150, 194
2nd innings FoW: 15, 18, 41, 122, 126, 158, 159, 171, 179, 187

FS Trueman	20	5	46	4	18	7	27	1
JDF Larter	14	2	52	0	7	1	18	0
BR Knight	21	8	32	3	4	1	7	1
FJ Titmus	18	3	40	1	31	15	50	4
KF Barrington	2.3	1	1	1	11	3	32	3
ER Dexter	1	0	2	0				
R Illingworth					27	14	34	1

ENGLAND 1st innings / 2nd innings

Batsman	Dismissal	Runs	2nd innings
DS Sheppard	b Blair	0	
R Illingworth	c Morrison b Blair	46	
KF Barrington	c Dick b Reid	76	
ER Dexter*	b Morrison	31	
PH Parfitt	c Dick b Morrison	0	
BR Knight	c Dick b Cameron	31	
FJ Titmus	run out	33	
MC Cowdrey	not out	128	
FS Trueman	b Cameron	3	
AC Smith+	not out	69	
JDF Larter			
Extras	(3b, 6lb, 0w, 2nb)	11	
Total	149 overs	**428**	

1st innings FoW: 0, 77, 125, 125, 173, 197, 258, 265

RW Blair	33	11	81	2
BD Morrison	31	5	129	2
FJ Cameron	43	16	98	2
JR Reid	32	8	73	1
BW Yuile	10	1	36	0

New Zealand	**West Indies**

No. 394: 3rd Test	No. 395: 1st Test
VENUE: Christchurch	VENUE: Old Trafford
DATE: 15th-19th March 1963	DATE: 6th-10th June 1963
TOSS WON BY: New Zealand	TOSS WON BY: West Indies
RESULT: England won by 7 wickets	RESULT: West Indies won by 10 wickets

NEW ZEALAND 1st innings

Batsman			2nd innings	
GT Dowling	c Dexter b Titmus	40	c Smith b Larter	22
WR Playle	c Barrington b Trueman	0	c Smith b Trueman	3
BW Sinclair	hit wkt b Trueman	44	lbw b Larter	0
JR Reid*	c Parfitt b Knight	74	b Titmus	100
PT Barton	c Smith b Knight	11	lbw b Knight	12
M Shrimpton	c Knight b Trueman	31	b Titmus	8
AE Dick+	b Trueman	16	c Parfitt b Titmus	1
RC Motz	c Parfitt b Trueman	7	b Larter	3
RW Blair	c Parfitt b Trueman	0	b Titmus	0
JC Alabaster	not out	20	c Parfitt b Trueman	1
FJ Cameron	c Smith b Trueman	1	not out	0
Extras	(1b, 9lb, 3w, 9nb)	22	(0b, 7lb, 0w, 2nb)	9
Total	118.2 overs	**266**	83.4 overs	**159**

1st innings FoW: 3, 83, 98, 128, 195, 234, 235, 235, 251, 266
2nd innings FoW: 16, 17, 66, 91, 129, 133, 151, 154, 159, 159

FS Trueman	30.2	9	75	7	19.4	8	16	2
JDF Larter	21	5	59	0	23	8	32	3
BR Knight	23	5	39	2	10	3	38	1
FJ Titmus	30	13	45	1	21	8	46	4
ER Dexter	9	3	8	0	10	2	18	0
KF Barrington	5	0	18	0				

ENGLAND 1st innings

Batsman			2nd innings	
DS Sheppard	b Cameron	42	b Alabaster	31
R Illingworth	c Dick b Cameron	2		
KF Barrington	lbw b Motz	47	c Reid b Blair	45
ER Dexter*	b Alabaster	46		
MC Cowdrey	c Motz b Blair	43	not out	35
PH Parfitt	lbw b Reid	4	c Shrimpton b Alabaster	31
BR Knight	b Blair	32	not out	20
FJ Titmus	c Dick b Motz	4		
FS Trueman	c Reid b Alabaster	11		
AC Smith+	not out	2		
JDF Larter	b Motz	2		
Extras	(4b, 6lb, 5w, 3nb)	18	(9b, 0lb, 0w, 2nb)	11
Total	95.5 overs	**253**	59.3 overs	**173**

1st innings FoW: 11, 87, 103, 186, 188, 210, 225, 244, 250, 253
2nd innings FoW: 70, 96, 149

RC Motz	19.5	3	68	3	20	6	33	0
FJ Cameron	24	6	47	2	12	3	38	0
RW Blair	24	12	42	2	12	3	34	1
JC Alabaster	20	6	47	2	15.3	5	57	2
JR Reid	8	1	31	1				

WEST INDIES 1st innings

Batsman			2nd innings	
CC Hunte	c Titmus b Allen	182	not out	1
MC Carew	c Andrew b Trueman	16	not out	1
RB Kanhai	run out	90		
BF Butcher	lbw b Trueman	22		
GStA Sobers	c Edrich b Allen	64		
JS Solomon	lbw b Titmus	35		
FMM Worrell*	not out	74		
DL Murray+	not out	7		
WW Hall				
CC Griffith				
LR Gibbs				
Extras	(3b, 7lb, 0w, 1nb)	11	(0b, 0lb, 0w, 0nb)	0
Total	196 overs	**501**	0.1 overs	**0**

1st innings FoW: 37, 188, 239, 359, 398, 479

FS Trueman	40	7	95	2				
JB Statham	37	6	121	0				
FJ Titmus	40	13	105	1				
DB Close	10	2	31	0				
DA Allen	57	22	122	2	0.1	0	1	0
ER Dexter	12	4	16	0				

ENGLAND 1st innings

Batsman			2nd innings	
MJ Stewart	c Murray b Gibbs	37	c Murray b Gibbs	87
JH Edrich	c Murray b Hall	20	c Hunte b Worrell	38
KF Barrington	c Murray b Hall	16	c Murray b Sobers	15
MC Cowdrey	b Hall	4	b Gibbs	4
ER Dexter*	c Worrell b Sobers	73	c Hunte b Gibbs	8
DB Close	c Hunte b Gibbs	30	c Murray b Gibbs	35
FJ Titmus	c Sobers b Gibbs	0	c Sobers b Gibbs	32
DA Allen	c Sobers b Gibbs	5	b Sobers	17
FS Trueman	c Worrell b Sobers	5	b Gibbs	1
KV Andrew+	not out	3	not out	29
JB Statham	b Gibbs	0	b Griffith	7
Extras	(2b, 7lb, 0w, 3nb)	12	(10b, 4lb, 0w, 1nb)	15
Total	90.3 overs	**205**	109.5 overs	**296**

1st innings FoW: 34, 61, 67, 108, 181, 190, 192, 202, 202, 205
2nd innings FoW: 93, 131, 160, 165, 186, 231, 254, 256, 268, 296

WW Hall	17	4	51	3	14	0	39	0
CC Griffith	21	4	37	0	8.5	4	11	1
LR Gibbs	29.3	9	59	5	46	16	98	6
GStA Sobers	22	11	34	2	37	4	122	2
FMM Worrell	1	0	12	0	4	2	11	1

No. 396: 2nd Test
VENUE: Lord's
DATE: 20th-25th June 1963
TOSS WON BY: West Indies
RESULT: Match drawn

No. 397: 3rd Test
VENUE: Edgbaston
DATE: 4th-9th July 1963
TOSS WON BY: England
RESULT: England won by 217 runs

WEST INDIES 1st innings / 2nd innings

Batsman	1st innings		2nd innings	
CC Hunte	c Close b Trueman	44	c Cowdrey b Shackleton	7
McMorris	lbw b Trueman	16	c Cowdrey b Trueman	8
GStA Sobers	c Cowdrey b Allen	42	c Cowdrey b Shackleton	21
RB Kanhai	c Edrich b Trueman	73	lbw b Shackleton	133
BF Butcher	c Barrington b Trueman	14	c Parks b Trueman	8
JS Solomon	lbw b Shackleton	56	c Stewart b Allen	5
FMM Worrell*	b Trueman	0	c Stewart b Trueman	33
DL Murray+	c Cowdrey b Trueman	20	c Parks b Trueman	2
WW Hall	not out	25	c Parks b Trueman	2
CC Griffith	c Cowdrey b Shackleton	0	b Shackleton	1
LR Gibbs	c Stewart b Shackleton	0	not out	1
Extras	(10b, 1lb, 0w, 0nb)	11	(5b, 2lb, 0w, 1nb)	8
Total	133.2 overs	**301**	98 overs	**229**

1st innings FoW: 51, 64, 127, 145, 219, 219, 263, 297, 297, 301
2nd innings FoW: 15, 15, 64, 84, 104, 214, 224, 226, 228, 229

Bowler	O	M	R	W		O	M	R	W
FS Trueman	44	16	100	6		26	9	52	5
D Shackleton	50.2	22	93	3		34	14	72	4
ER Dexter	20	6	41	0					
DB Close	9	3	21	0					
DA Allen	10	3	35	1		21	7	50	1
FJ Titmus						17	3	47	0

ENGLAND 1st innings / 2nd innings

Batsman	1st innings		2nd innings	
MJ Stewart	c Kanhai b Griffith	2	c Solomon b Hall	17
JH Edrich	c Murray b Griffith	0	c Murray b Hall	8
ER Dexter*	lbw b Sobers	70	b Gibbs	2
KF Barrington	c Sobers b Worrell	80	c Murray b Griffith	60
MC Cowdrey	b Gibbs	4	not out	19
DB Close	c Murray b Griffith	9	c Murray b Griffith	70
JM Parks+	b Worrell	35	lbw b Griffith	17
FJ Titmus	not out	52	c McMorris b Hall	11
FS Trueman	b Hall	10	c Murray b Hall	0
DA Allen	lbw b Griffith	2	not out	4
D Shackleton	b Griffith	8	run out	4
Extras	(8b, 8lb, 0w, 9nb)	25	(5b, 8lb, 0w, 3nb)	16
Total	102 overs	**297**	91 overs	**228**

1st innings FoW: 2, 20, 102, 115, 151, 206, 235, 271, 274, 297
2nd innings FoW: 15, 27, 31, 130, 158, 203, 203, 219, 228

Bowler	O	M	R	W		O	M	R	W
WW Hall	18	2	65	1		40	9	93	4
CC Griffith	26	6	91	5		30	7	59	3
GStA Sobers	18	4	45	1		4	1	4	0
LR Gibbs	27	9	59	1		17	7	56	1
FMM Worrell	13	6	12	2					

ENGLAND 1st innings / 2nd innings

Batsman	1st innings		2nd innings	
PE Richardson	b Hall	2	c Murray b Griffith	14
MJ Stewart	lbw b Sobers	39	c Murray b Griffith	27
ER Dexter*	b Sobers	29	b Sobers	13
KF Barrington	b Sobers	9	c Sobers b Griffith	13
DB Close	lbw b Sobers	55	st Murray b Gibbs	57
PJ Sharpe	c Kanhai b Gibbs	23	not out	85
JM Parks+	c Murray b Sobers	12	c Sobers b Gibbs	5
FJ Titmus	c Griffith b Hall	27	b Gibbs	0
FS Trueman	b Griffith	4	c Gibbs b Sobers	1
GAR Lock	b Griffith	1	b Gibbs	56
D Shackleton	not out	6		
Extras	(0b, 6lb, 0w, 3nb)	9	(9b, 9lb, 0w, 1nb)	19
Total	98.4 overs	**216**	105.2 overs	**278**

1st innings FoW: 2, 50, 72, 89, 129, 172, 187, 194, 200, 216
2nd innings FoW: 30, 31, 60, 69, 170, 184, 184, 189, 278

Bowler	O	M	R	W		O	M	R	W
WW Hall	16.4	2	56	2		16	1	47	0
CC Griffith	21	5	48	2		28	7	55	3
GStA Sobers	31	10	60	5		27	4	80	2
FMM Worrell	14	5	15	0		8	3	28	0
LR Gibbs	16	7	28	1		26.2	4	49	4

WEST INDIES 1st innings / 2nd innings

Batsman	1st innings		2nd innings	
CC Hunte	b Trueman	18	c Barrington b Trueman	5
MC Carew	c & b Trueman	40	lbw b Shackleton	1
RB Kanhai	c Lock b Shackleton	32	c Lock b Trueman	38
BF Butcher	lbw b Dexter	15	b Dexter	14
JS Solomon	lbw b Dexter	0	c Sharpe b Shackleton	9
GStA Sobers	b Trueman	19	c Parks b Trueman	14
FMM Worrell*	b Dexter	1	c Parks b Trueman	0
DL Murray+	not out	20	c Parks b Trueman	3
WW Hall	c Sharpe b Dexter	28	b Trueman	0
CC Griffith	lbw b Trueman	5	lbw b Trueman	0
LR Gibbs	b Trueman	0	not out	4
Extras	(0b, 7lb, 1w, 0nb)	8	(0b, 2lb, 1w, 0nb)	3
Total	69 overs	**186**	34.3 overs	**91**

1st innings FoW: 42, 79, 108, 109, 128, 130, 130, 178, 186, 186
2nd innings FoW: 2, 10, 38, 64, 78, 80, 86, 86, 86, 91

Bowler	O	M	R	W		O	M	R	W
FS Trueman	26	5	75	5		14.3	2	44	7
D Shackleton	21	9	60	1		17	4	37	2
GAR Lock	2	1	5	0					
ER Dexter	20	5	38	4		3	1	7	1

No. 398: 4th Test
VENUE: Headingley
DATE: 25th-29th July 1963
TOSS WON BY: West Indies
RESULT: West Indies won by 221 runs

No. 399: 5th Test
VENUE: The Oval
DATE: 22nd-26th August 1963
TOSS WON BY: England
RESULT: West Indies won by 8 wickets

WEST INDIES 1st innings / 2nd innings

Batsman	1st innings		2nd innings	
CC Hunte	c Parks b Trueman	22	b Trueman	4
McMorris	c Bar'on b Shackleton	11	lbw b Trueman	1
RB Kanhai	b Lock	92	lbw b Shackleton	44
BF Butcher	c Parks b Dexter	23	c Dexter b Shackleton	78
GStA Sobers	c & b Lock	102	c Sharpe b Titmus	52
JS Solomon	c Stewart b Trueman	62	c Titmus b Shackleton	16
DL Murray+	lbw b Titmus	34	c Parks b Titmus	0
FMM Worrell*	c Close b Lock	25	c Lock b Titmus	2
WW Hall	c Shackleton b Trueman	15	c Trueman b Titmus	7
CC Griffith	c Stewart b Trueman	1	not out	12
LR Gibbs	not out	0	c Sharpe b Lock	6
Extras	(4b, 5lb, 1w, 0nb)	10	(0b, 7lb, 0w, 0nb)	7
Total	164.4 overs	**397**	67.1 overs	**229**

1st innings FoW: 28, 42, 71, 214, 287, 348, 355, 379, 389, 397
2nd innings FoW: 1, 20, 85, 181, 186, 188, 196, 206, 212, 229

Bowler	O	M	R	W		O	M	R	W
FS Trueman	46	10	117	4		13	1	46	2
D Shackleton	42	10	88	1		26	2	63	3
ER Dexter	23	4	68	1		2	0	15	0
FJ Titmus	25	5	60	1		19	2	44	4
GAR Lock	28.4	9	54	3		7.1	0	54	1

ENGLAND 1st innings / 2nd innings

Batsman	1st innings		2nd innings	
MJ Stewart	c Gibbs b Griffith	2	b Sobers	0
JB Bolus	c Hunte b Hall	14	c Gibbs b Sobers	43
ER Dexter*	b Griffith	8	lbw b Griffith	10
KF Barrington	c Worrell b Gibbs	25	lbw b Sobers	32
DB Close	b Griffith	0	c Solomon b Griffith	56
PJ Sharpe	c Kanhai b Griffith	0	c Kanhai b Gibbs	13
JM Parks+	c Gibbs b Griffith	22	lbw b Gibbs	57
FJ Titmus	lbw b Gibbs	33	st Murray b Gibbs	5
FS Trueman	c Hall b Gibbs	4	c Griffith b Gibbs	5
GAR Lock	b Griffith	53	c Murray b Griffith	1
D Shackleton	not out	1	not out	1
Extras	(4b, 6lb, 0w, 2nb)	12	(3b, 5lb, 0w, 0nb)	8
Total	54 overs	**174**	92.4 overs	**231**

1st innings FoW: 13, 19, 32, 32, 34, 69, 87, 93, 172, 174
2nd innings FoW: 0, 23, 82, 95, 130, 199, 221, 224, 225, 231

Bowler	O	M	R	W		O	M	R	W
WW Hall	13	2	61	1		5	1	12	0
CC Griffith	21	5	36	6		18	5	45	3
LR Gibbs	14	2	50	3		37.4	12	76	4
GStA Sobers	6	1	15	0		32	5	90	3

ENGLAND 1st innings / 2nd innings

Batsman	1st innings		2nd innings	
JB Bolus	c Murray b Sobers	33	c Gibbs b Sobers	15
JH Edrich	c Murray b Sobers	25	c Murray b Griffith	12
ER Dexter*	c & b Griffith	29	c Murray b Sobers	27
KF Barrington	c Sobers b Gibbs	16	b Griffith	28
DB Close	b Griffith	46	lbw b Sobers	4
PJ Sharpe	c Murray b Griffith	63	c Murray b Hall	83
JM Parks+	c Kanhai b Griffith	19	lbw b Griffith	23
FS Trueman	b Griffith	19	c Sobers b Hall	5
GAR Lock	hit wkt b Griffith	4	b Hall	0
JB Statham	b Hall	8	b Hall	14
D Shackleton	not out	0	not out	0
Extras	(4b, 2lb, 0w, 7nb)	13	(5b, 3lb, 0w, 4nb)	12
Total	102.2 overs	**275**	81 overs	**223**

1st innings FoW: 59, 64, 103, 115, 216, 224, 254, 258, 275, 275
2nd innings FoW: 29, 31, 64, 69, 121, 173, 196, 196, 218, 223

Bowler	O	M	R	W		O	M	R	W
WW Hall	22.2	2	71	1		16	3	39	4
CC Griffith	27	4	71	6		23	7	66	3
GStA Sobers	21	4	44	2		33	6	77	3
LR Gibbs	27	7	50	1		9	1	29	0
FMM Worrell	5	0	26	0					

WEST INDIES 1st innings / 2nd innings

Batsman	1st innings		2nd innings	
CC Hunte	c Parks b Shackleton	80	not out	108
WV Rodriguez	c Lock b Statham	5	c Lock b Dexter	28
RB Kanhai	b Lock	30	c Bolus b Lock	77
BF Butcher	run out	53	not out	31
GStA Sobers	run out	26		
JS Solomon	c Trueman b Statham	16		
FMM Worrell*	b Statham	9		
DL Murray+	c Lock b Trueman	5		
WW Hall	b Trueman	2		
CC Griffith	not out	13		
LR Gibbs	b Trueman	4		
Extras	(0b, 3lb, 0w, 0nb)	3	(4b, 7lb, 0w, 0nb)	11
Total	104.1 overs	**246**	95 overs	**255**

1st innings FoW: 10, 72, 152, 185, 198, 214, 221, 225, 233, 246
2nd innings FoW: 78, 191

Bowler	O	M	R	W		O	M	R	W
FS Trueman	26.1	2	65	3		1	1	0	0
JB Statham	22	3	68	3		22	2	54	0
D Shackleton	21	5	37	1		32	7	68	0
GAR Lock	29	6	65	1		25	8	52	1
ER Dexter	6	1	8	0		9	1	34	1
DB Close						6	0	36	0

No. 400: 1st Test

VENUE:	Madras (Nehru)
DATE:	10th-15th January 1964
TOSS WON BY:	India
RESULT:	Match drawn

INDIA 1st innings

			2nd innings	
VL Mehra	c Parks b Titmus	17	run out	26
BK Kunderan+	b Titmus	192	lbw b Titmus	38
DN Sardesai	b Titmus	65	b Titmus	35
VL Manjrekar	c Smith b Knight	108	st Parks b Mortimore	2
Pataudi *	lbw b Titmus	0	c Parks b Mortimore	3
SA Durani	lbw b Titmus	8	c Bolus b Titmus	18
ML Jaisimha	lbw b Wilson	51	run out	0
Kripal Singh	not out	2	b Wilson	10
CG Borde	not out	8	not out	11
RG Nadkarni			c Parks b Titmus	7
VB Ranjane				
Extras	(1b, 5lb, 0w, 0nb)	6	(0b, 2lb, 0w, 0nb)	2
	162 overs		58.5 overs	
Total		**457**		**152**

1st innings FoW: 85, 228, 323, 323, 343, 431, 447
2nd innings FoW: 59, 77, 82, 100, 104, 106, 125, 135, 152

JDF Larter	19	2	62	0	11	3	33	0
BR Knight	27	7	73	1	7	1	22	0
D Wilson	24	6	67	1	4	2	2	1
FJ Titmus	50	14	116	5	19.5	4	46	4
JB Mortimore	38	7	110	0	15	3	41	2
KF Barrington	4	0	23	0	2	0	6	0

ENGLAND 1st innings

			2nd innings	
JB Bolus	lbw b Durani	88	st Kunderan b Borde	22
MJK Smith*	c Kunderan b Ranjane	3	c Kunderan b Nadkarni	57
PJ Sharpe	lbw b Borde	27	c Kunderan b Nadkarni	57
D Wilson	c Manjrekar b Durani	42	c Kund'n b Kripal Singh	7
KF Barrington	c & b Borde	80	not out	73
BR Knight	b Durani	6	b Kripal Singh	10
JM Parks+	b Borde	27	not out	31
FJ Titmus	c Pataudi b Kripal Singh	14		
JB Mortimore	c & b Borde	0		
MJ Stewart	st Kunderan b Borde	15		
JDF Larter	not out	2		
Extras	(6b, 5lb, 0w, 2nb)	13	(6b, 2lb, 0w, 3nb)	11
	190.4 overs		87 overs	
Total		**317**		**241**

1st innings FoW: 12, 49, 116, 235, 251, 263, 287, 287, 314, 317
2nd innings FoW: 67, 105, 120, 123, 155

VB Ranjane	16	2	46	1	2	0	14	0
ML Jaisimha	7	3	16	0	4	2	8	0
CG Borde	67.4	30	88	5	22	7	44	1
SA Durani	43	13	97	3	21	8	64	0
RG Nadkarni	32	27	5	0	6	4	6	2
AG Kripal Singh	25	10	52	1	26	7	66	2
VL Manjrekar					3	0	3	0
VL Mehra					1	0	2	0

No. 401: 2nd Test

VENUE:	Bombay (Brabourne)
DATE:	21st-26th January 1964
TOSS WON BY:	India
RESULT:	Match drawn

INDIA 1st innings

			2nd innings	
VL Mehra	lbw b Knight	9	lbw b Titmus	35
BK Kunderan+	c Wilson b Price	29	c Titmus b Price	16
DN Sardesai	b Price	12	run out	66
VL Manjrekar	c Binks b Titmus	0	b Price	0
Pataudi	c Titmus b Knight	10	c Larter b Knight	66
ML Jaisimha	c Price b Titmus	23	c Knight b Titmus	3
CG Borde	c Binks b Wilson	84	c Smith b Titmus	7
SA Durani	c Binks b Price	90	not out	43
RG Nadkarni	not out	26	lbw b Knight	0
Rajinder Pal	lbw b Larter	3	not out	3
BS Chan'har	b Larter	0		
Extras	(2b, 9lb, 0w, 3nb)	14	(0b, 4lb, 1w, 5nb)	10
	113.3 overs		115 overs	
Total		**300**		**249**

1st innings FoW: 20, 55, 56, 58, 75, 99, 252, 284, 300, 300
2nd innings FoW: 23, 104, 107, 140, 152, 180, 231, 231

BR Knight	20	3	53	2	13	2	28	2
JDF Larter	10.3	2	35	2	5	0	13	0
IJ Jones	13	0	48	0	11	1	31	0
JSE Price	19	2	66	3	17	1	47	2
FJ Titmus	36	17	56	2	46	18	79	3
D Wilson	15	5	28	1	23	10	41	0

ENGLAND 1st innings

			2nd innings	
JB Bolus	c Chan'har b Durani	25	c Pataudi b Durani	57
MJK Smith*	c Borde b Chan'har	46	c Borde b Jaisimha	55
JM Parks	run out	1	c Pataudi b Chan'har	2
BR Knight	b Chandrasekhar	12	not out	31
FJ Titmus	not out	84	not out	40
D Wilson	c & b Durani	1		
JG Binks+	b Chandrasekhar	10		
JSE Price	b Chandrasekhar	32		
JDF Larter	c Borde b Durani	0		
IJ Jones	run out	5		
MJ Stewart	absent hurt			
Extras	(4b, 7lb, 0w, 6nb)	17	(12b, 7lb, 1w, 1nb)	21
	130 overs		134 overs	
Total		**233**		**206**

1st innings FoW: 42, 48, 82, 91, 98, 116, 184, 185, 233
2nd innings FoW: 125, 127, 134

Rajinder Pal	11	4	19	0	2	0	3	0
ML Jaisimha	3	1	9	0	22	9	36	1
SA Durani	38	15	59	3	29	12	35	1
CG Borde	34	12	54	0	37	12	38	0
BS Chan'har	40	16	67	4	22	5	40	1
RG Nadkarni	4	2	8	0	14	11	3	0
DN Sardesai					3	2	6	0
VL Mehra					2	1	1	0

No. 402: 3rd Test

VENUE: Calcutta
DATE: 29th January-3rd Feb 1964
TOSS WON BY: India
RESULT: Match drawn

INDIA

Batsman	1st innings		2nd innings	
ML Jaisimha	c Binks b Price	33	c Larter b Titmus	129
BK Kunderan+	c Binks b Price	23	lbw b Wilson	27
DN Sardesai	c Binks b Larter	54	c & b Parfitt	36
VL Manjrekar	c & b Price	25	b Parfitt	16
RF Surti	b Price	0	c Smith b Larter	31
CG Borde	c Cowdrey b Wilson	21	c Parks b Titmus	8
Pataudi*	c Binks b Wilson	2	c Cowdrey b Larter	25
SA Durani	c Binks b Larter	8	not out	10
RG Nadkarni	not out	43	not out	2
RB Desai	lbw b Titmus	11		
BS Chan'har	c Cowdrey b Knight	16		
Extras	(0b, 1lb, 0w, 4nb)	5	(7b, 5lb, 0w, 4nb)	16
	85.2 overs		120 overs	
Total		**241**		**300**

1st innings FoW: 47, 61, 103, 103, 150, 158, 169, 169, 190, 241
2nd innings FoW: 80, 161, 217, 218, 237, 272, 289

Bowler	O	M	R	W	O	M	R	W
BR Knight	13.2	5	39	1	4	0	33	0
JSE Price	23	4	73	5	7	0	31	0
JDF Larter	18	4	61	1	8	0	27	2
FJ Titmus	15	4	46	1	46	23	67	2
D Wilson	16	10	17	2	21	7	55	1
PH Parfitt					34	16	71	2

ENGLAND

Batsman	1st innings		2nd innings	
JB Bolus	c & b Durani	39	c Jaisimha b Borde	35
JG Binks+	c Desai b Durani	13	b Durani	13
MJK Smith*	c Jaisimha b Borde	19	not out	75
MC Cowdrey	c Pataudi b Desai	107	not out	13
JM Parks	lbw b Nadkarni	30		
PH Parfitt	c & b Desai	4		
D Wilson	st Kunderan b Chan'har	1		
BR Knight	c Manjrekar b Nadkarni	13		
FJ Titmus	b Desai	26		
JSE Price	not out	1		
JDF Larter	c Manjrekar b Desai	0		
Extras	(6b, 5lb, 0w, 3nb)	14	(9b, 0lb, 0w, 0nb)	9
	148.5 overs		55 overs	
Total		**267**		**145**

1st innings FoW: 40, 74, 77, 158, 175, 193, 214, 258, 267, 267
2nd innings FoW: 30, 87

Bowler	O	M	R	W	O	M	R	W
RB Desai	22.5	3	62	4	5	0	12	0
RF Surti	6	2	8	0				
ML Jaisimha	4	1	10	0	13	5	32	0
SA Durani	22	7	59	2	8	3	15	1
CG Borde	31	14	40	1	15	5	39	1
BS Chan'har	21	5	36	1	8	2	20	0
RG Nadkarni	42	24	38	2				
Pataudi jr				3	1	8	0	
DN Sardesai					3	0	10	0

No. 403: 4th Test

VENUE: Delhi
DATE: 8th-13th February 1964
TOSS WON BY: India
RESULT: Match drawn

INDIA

Batsman	1st innings		2nd innings	
ML Jaisimha	b Titmus	47	st Parks b Parfitt	50
BK Kunderan+	b Titmus	40	lbw b Price	100
DN Sardesai	c Parks b Mortimore	44	b Wilson	4
Pataudi*	b Titmus	13	not out	203
Hanumant S'h	c & b Mortimore	105	c Mortimore b Wilson	23
CG Borde	b Price	26	not out	67
SA Durani	c Smith b Wilson	16		
Kripal Singh	b Mortimore	0		
RG Nadkarni	run out	34		
RB Desai	not out	14		
BS Chan'har	run out	0		
Extras	(0b, 3lb, 0w, 2nb)	5	(5b, 9lb, 0w, 2nb)	16
	148 overs		165 overs	
Total		**344**		**463**

1st innings FoW: 81, 90, 116, 201, 267, 283, 283, 307, 344, 344
2nd innings FoW: 74, 101, 226, 273

Bowler	O	M	R	W	O	M	R	W
JSE Price	23	3	71	1	9	1	36	1
BR Knight	11	0	46	0	8	1	47	0
D Wilson	22	9	41	1	41	17	74	2
FJ Titmus	49	15	100	3	43	12	105	0
JB Mortimore	38	13	74	3	32	11	52	0
PH Parfitt	5	2	7	0	19	3	81	1
MJK Smith					13	0	52	0

ENGLAND

Batsman	1st innings		2nd innings
JB Bolus	lbw b Kripal Singh	58	
JH Edrich	c & b Kripal Singh	41	
MJK Smith*	c Pataudi b Kripal Singh	37	
D Wilson	c Pataudi b Chan'har	6	
PH Parfitt	c Kunderan b Durani	67	
MC Cowdrey	lbw b Nadkarni	151	
JM Parks+	c (sub) b Chan'har	32	
BR Knight	c Desai b Nadkarni	21	
JB Mortimore	c Hanumant b Nadkarni	21	
FJ Titmus	not out	4	
JSE Price	b Chandrasekhar	0	
Extras	(8b, 3lb, 0w, 2nb)	13	
	185.3 overs		
Total		**451**	

1st innings FoW: 101, 114, 134, 153, 268, 354, 397, 438, 451, 451

Bowler	O	M	R	W
RB Desai	9	2	23	0
ML Jaisimha	4	0	14	0
AG Kripal Singh	36	13	90	3
BS Chan'har	34.3	11	79	3
CG Borde	12	2	42	0
SA Durani	33	5	93	1
RG Nadkarni	57	30	97	3

India

No. 404: 5th Test	No. 405: 1st Test
VENUE: Kanpur	VENUE: Trent Bridge
DATE: 15th-20th February 1964	DATE: 4th-9th June 1964
TOSS WON BY: India	TOSS WON BY: England
RESULT: Match drawn	RESULT: Match drawn

ENGLAND 1st innings / 2nd innings (Kanpur)

Batsman	1st innings		2nd innings	
JB Bolus	c Hanumant b Nadkarni	67		
JH Edrich	c Pataudi b Borde	35		
MJK Smith*	c Borde b Gupte	38		
BR Knight	c Manjrekar b Jaisimha	127		
PH Parfitt	lbw b Jaisimha	121		
MC Cowdrey	lbw b Pataudi	38		
JM Parks+	not out	51		
JB Mortimore	b Chandrasekhar	19		
FJ Titmus	c & b Nadkarni	5		
D Wilson	not out	18		
JSE Price				
Extras	(29b, 9lb, 0w, 2nb)	40		
	203 overs			
Total		**559**		

1st innings FoW: 63, 134, 174, 365, 458, 474, 520, 531

	O	M	R	W				
ML Jaisimha	19	4	54	2				
SA Durani	25	8	49	0				
BS Chan'har	36	7	97	1				
BP Gupte	40	9	115	1				
CG Borde	23	4	73	1				
RG Nadkarni	57	22	121	2				
Pataudi jr	3	1	10	1				

INDIA 1st innings / 2nd innings

Batsman	1st innings		2nd innings	
ML Jaisimha	c Parks b Titmus	5	c Cowdrey b Titmus	5
BK Kunderan+	b Price	5	lbw b Parfitt	55
VL Manjrekar	c & b Titmus	33	not out	122
DN Sardesai	c Mortimore b Parfitt	79	c Edrich b Parks	87
Hanumant S'h	c Parks b Titmus	24	not out	61
Pataudi*	b Titmus	31		
CG Borde	b Titmus	0		
SA Durani	b Mortimore	16		
RG Nadkarni	not out	52		
BP Gupte	c & b Titmus	8		
BS Chan'har	b Price	3		
Extras	(5b, 1lb, 0w, 4nb)	10	(5b, 11lb, 0w, 1nb)	17
	182.1 overs		133 overs	
Total		**266**		**347**

1st innings FoW: 9, 17, 96, 135, 182, 182, 188, 229, 245, 266
2nd innings FoW: 17, 126, 270

	O	M	R	W	O	M	R	W
JSE Price	16.1	5	32	2	10	2	27	0
BR Knight	1	0	4	0	2	0	12	0
FJ Titmus	60	37	73	6	34	12	59	1
JB Mortimore	48	31	39	1	23	14	28	0
D Wilson	27	9	47	0	19	10	26	0
PH Parfitt	30	12	61	1	27	7	68	1
JH Edrich					4	1	17	0
JB Bolus					3	0	16	0
JM Parks					6	0	43	1
MC Cowdrey					5	0	34	0

Australia

ENGLAND 1st innings / 2nd innings (Trent Bridge)

Batsman	1st innings		2nd innings	
G Boycott	c Simpson b Corling	48	c O'Neill b McKenzie	68
FJ Titmus	c Redpath b Hawke	16	lbw b McKenzie	17
ER Dexter*	c Grout b Hawke	9	b McKenzie	33
MC Cowdrey	b Hawke	32	b Corling	33
KF Barrington	c Lawry b Veivers	22	c Hawke b Veivers	19
PJ Sharpe	not out	35	c & b Veivers	1
JM Parks+	c Booth b Veivers	15	c Grout b McKenzie	4
FS Trueman	c Simpson b Veivers	0	lbw b McKenzie	3
DA Allen	c Grout b McKenzie	21	c Booth b Corling	7
LJ Coldwell	not out	0	not out	0
JA Flavell				
Extras	(5b, 11lb, 0w, 2nb)	18	(2b, 2lb, 1w, 3nb)	8
	102 overs		66.5 overs	
Total		**216**		**193**

1st innings FoW: 38, 70, 90, 135, 141, 164, 165, 212
2nd innings FoW: 90, 95, 147, 174, 179, 180, 186, 187, 193

	O	M	R	W	O	M	R	W
GD McKenzie	28	7	53	1	24	5	53	5
GE Corling	23	7	38	1	15.5	4	54	2
NJN Hawke	35	15	68	3	19	5	53	0
TR Veivers	16	2	39	3	8	0	25	2

AUSTRALIA 1st innings / 2nd innings

Batsman	1st innings		2nd innings	
WM Lawry	c Barrington b Coldwell	11	run out	3
IR Redpath	b Trueman	6	c Parks b Flavell	2
NC O'Neill	b Allen	26	retired hurt	24
PJP Burge	lbw b Trueman	31	not out	4
BC Booth	run out	0	not out	6
RB Simpson*	c Barrington b Titmus	50		
TR Veivers	c Trueman b Flavell	8		
GD McKenzie	c Parks b Coldwell	4		
NJN Hawke	not out	10		
ATW Grout+	c Parks b Coldwell	13		
GE Corling	b Trueman	3		
Extras	(0b, 1lb, 0w, 5nb)	6	(0b, 0lb, 0w, 1nb)	1
	78.3 overs		9.2 overs	
Total		**168**		**40**

1st innings FoW: 8, 37, 57, 61, 91, 118, 137, 141, 165, 168
2nd innings FoW: 3, 25

	O	M	R	W	O	M	R	W
FS Trueman	20.3	3	58	3	5	0	28	0
LJ Coldwell	22	3	48	3				
DA Allen	16	8	22	1				
JA Flavell	16	3	28	1	4.2	0	11	1
FJ Titmus	4	1	6	1				

	No. 406: 2nd Test		No. 407: 3rd Test
VENUE:	Lord's	VENUE:	Headingley
DATE:	18th-23rd June 1964	DATE:	2nd-6th July 1964
TOSS WON BY:	England	TOSS WON BY:	England
RESULT:	Match drawn	RESULT:	Australia won by 7 wickets

AUSTRALIA 1st innings / 2nd innings

Batsman	1st innings		2nd innings	
WM Lawry	b Trueman	4	c Dexter b Gifford	20
IR Redpath	c Parfitt b Coldwell	30	lbw b Titmus	36
NC O'Neill	c Titmus b Dexter	26	c Parfitt b Trueman	22
PJP Burge	lbw b Dexter	1	c Parfitt b Titmus	59
BC Booth	lbw b Trueman	14	not out	2
RB Simpson*	c Parfitt b Trueman	0	not out	15
TR Veivers	b Gifford	54		
GD McKenzie	b Trueman	10		
ATW Grout+	c Dexter b Gifford	14		
NJN Hawke	not out	5		
GE Corling	b Trueman	0		
Extras	(8b, 5lb, 0w, 5nb)	18	(8b, 4lb, 0w, 2nb)	14
	84 overs		74 overs	
Total		**176**		**168**

1st innings FoW: 8, 46, 58, 84, 84, 88, 132, 163, 167, 176
2nd innings FoW: 35, 76, 143, 148

Bowler	O	M	R	W	O	M	R	W
FS Trueman	25	8	48	5	18	6	52	1
LJ Coldwell	23	7	51	1	19	4	59	0
N Gifford	12	6	14	2	17	9	17	1
ER Dexter	7	1	16	2	3	0	5	0
FJ Titmus	17	6	29	0	17	7	21	2

ENGLAND 1st innings / 2nd innings

Batsman	1st innings		2nd innings
ER Dexter*	b McKenzie	2	
JH Edrich	c Redpath b McKenzie	120	
MC Cowdrey	c Burge b Hawke	10	
KF Barrington	lbw b McKenzie	5	
PH Parfitt	lbw b Corling	20	
PJ Sharpe	lbw b Hawke	35	
JM Parks+	c Simpson b Hawke	12	
FJ Titmus	b Corling	15	
FS Trueman	b Corling	8	
N Gifford	c Hawke b Corling	5	
LJ Coldwell	not out	6	
Extras	(0b, 7lb, 0w, 1nb)	8	
	99.3 overs		
Total		**246**	

1st innings FoW: 2, 33, 42, 83, 138, 170, 227, 229, 235, 246

Bowler	O	M	R	W
GD McKenzie	26	8	69	3
GE Corling	27.3	9	60	4
NJN Hawke	16	4	41	3
TR Veivers	9	4	17	0
RB Simpson	21	8	51	0

ENGLAND 1st innings / 2nd innings

Batsman	1st innings		2nd innings	
G Boycott	c Simpson b Corling	38	c Simpson b Corling	4
JH Edrich	c Veivers b McKenzie	3	c Grout b McKenzie	32
ER Dexter*	c Grout b McKenzie	66	c Redpath b Hawke	6
KF Barrington	b McKenzie	29	lbw b Veivers	85
PH Parfitt	b Hawke	32	c Redpath b Veivers	17
K Taylor	c Grout b Hawke	9	c Booth b McKenzie	23
JM Parks+	c Redpath b Hawke	68	b McKenzie	1
FJ Titmus	c Burge b McKenzie	3	b Veivers	15
FS Trueman	c Cowper b Hawke	4	c Cowper b Corling	14
N Gifford	not out	1	not out	12
JA Flavell	c Redpath b Hawke	5	c Simpson b Corling	5
Extras	(0b, 9lb, 0w, 1nb)	10	(6b, 6lb, 1w, 2nb)	15
	103.3 overs		89.5 overs	
Total		**268**		**229**

1st innings FoW: 17, 74, 129, 138, 163, 215, 232, 260, 263, 268
2nd innings FoW: 13, 88, 145, 156, 169, 184, 192, 199, 212, 229

Bowler	O	M	R	W	O	M	R	W
GD McKenzie	26	7	74	4	28	8	53	3
NJN Hawke	31.3	11	75	5	13	1	28	1
GE Corling	24	7	50	1	17.5	6	52	3
TR Veivers	17	3	35	0	30	12	70	3
RB Simpson	5	0	24	0	1	0	11	0

AUSTRALIA 1st innings / 2nd innings

Batsman	1st innings		2nd innings	
WM Lawry	run out	78	c Gifford b Trueman	1
RB Simpson*	b Gifford	24	c Barrington b Titmus	30
IR Redpath	b Gifford	20	not out	58
PJP Burge	c (sub) b Trueman	160	b Titmus	8
BC Booth	st Parks b Titmus	4	not out	12
RM Cowper	b Trueman	2		
TR Veivers	c Parks b Titmus	8		
GD McKenzie	b Titmus	0		
NJN Hawke	c Parfitt b Trueman	37		
ATW Grout+	lbw b Titmus	37		
GE Corling	not out	0		
Extras	(1b, 8lb, 2w, 6nb)	17	(1b, 1lb, 0w, 0nb)	2
	158.3 overs		57 overs	
Total		**389**		**111**

1st innings FoW: 50, 124, 129, 154, 157, 178, 178, 283, 372, 389
2nd innings FoW: 3, 45, 64

Bowler	O	M	R	W	O	M	R	W
FS Trueman	24.3	2	98	3	7	0	28	1
JA Flavell	29	5	97	0				
N Gifford	34	15	62	2	20	5	47	0
ER Dexter	19	5	40	0	3	0	9	0
FJ Titmus	50	24	69	4	27	19	25	2
K Taylor	2	0	6	0				

No. 408: 4th Test
VENUE: Old Trafford
DATE: 23rd-28th July 1964
TOSS WON BY: Australia
RESULT: Match drawn

No. 409: 5th Test
VENUE: The Oval
DATE: 13th-18th August 1964
TOSS WON BY: England
RESULT: Match drawn

AUSTRALIA 1st innings / 2nd innings

Batsman	1st innings		2nd innings	
WM Lawry	run out	106	not out	0
RB Simpson*	c Parks b Price	311	not out	4
IR Redpath	lbw b Cartwright	19		
NC O'Neill	b Price	47		
PJP Burge	c Price b Cartwright	34		
BC Booth	c & b Price	98		
TR Veivers	c Edrich b Rumsey	22		
ATW Grout+	c Dexter b Rumsey	0		
GD McKenzie	not out	0		
NJN Hawke				
GE Corling				
Extras	(1b, 9lb, 0w, 9nb)	19	(0b, 0lb, 0w, 0nb)	0
Total	255.5 overs	**656**	2 overs	**4**

1st innings FoW: 201, 233, 318, 382, 601, 646, 652, 656

Bowler	O	M	R	W		O	M	R	W
FE Rumsey	35.5	4	99	2					
JSE Price	45	4	183	3					
TW Cartwright	77	32	118	2					
FJ Titmus	44	14	100	0		1	1	0	0
ER Dexter	4	0	12	0					
JB Mortimore	49	13	122	0					
G Boycott	1	0	3	0					
KF Barrington						1	0	4	0

ENGLAND 1st innings

Batsman	1st innings		2nd innings
G Boycott	b McKenzie	58	
JH Edrich	c Redpath b McKenzie	6	
ER Dexter*	b Veivers	174	
KF Barrington	lbw b McKenzie	256	
PH Parfitt	c Grout b McKenzie	12	
JM Parks+	c Hawke b Veivers	60	
FJ Titmus	c Simpson b McKenzie	9	
JB Mortimore	c Burge b McKenzie	12	
TW Cartwright	b McKenzie	4	
JSE Price	b Veivers	1	
FE Rumsey	not out	3	
Extras	(5b, 11lb, 0w, 0nb)	16	
Total	293.1 overs	**611**	

1st innings FoW: 15, 126, 372, 417, 560, 589, 594, 602, 607, 611

Bowler	O	M	R	W
GD McKenzie	60	15	153	7
GE Corling	46	11	96	0
NJN Hawke	63	28	95	0
RB Simpson	19	4	59	0
TR Veivers	95.1	36	155	3
NC O'Neill	10	0	37	0

ENGLAND 1st innings / 2nd innings

Batsman	1st innings		2nd innings	
G Boycott	b Hawke	30	c Redpath b Simpson	113
RW Barber	b Hawke	24	lbw b McKenzie	29
ER Dexter*	c Booth b Hawke	23	c Simpson b McKenzie	25
MC Cowdrey	c Grout b McKenzie	20	b McKenzie	56
KF Barrington	c Simpson b Hawke	47	not out	93
PH Parfitt	b McKenzie	3	not out	54
JM Parks+	c Simpson b Corling	10		
FJ Titmus	c Grout b Hawke	8		
FS Trueman	c Redpath b Hawke	14		
TW Cartwright	c Grout b McKenzie	0		
JSE Price	not out	0		
Extras	(0b, 3lb, 0w, 0nb)	3	(6b, 4lb, 0w, 1nb)	11
Total	71.4 overs	**182**	163 overs	**381**

1st innings FoW: 44, 61, 82, 111, 117, 141, 160, 173, 174, 182
2nd innings FoW: 80, 120, 200, 255

Bowler	O	M	R	W		O	M	R	W
GD McKenzie	26	6	87	3		38	5	112	3
GE Corling	14	2	32	1		25	4	65	0
NJN Hawke	25.4	8	47	6		39	8	89	0
TR Veivers	6	1	13	0		47	15	90	0
RB Simpson						14	7	14	1

AUSTRALIA 1st innings

Batsman	1st innings		2nd innings
RB Simpson*	c Dexter b Cartwright	24	
WM Lawry	c Trueman b Dexter	94	
NC O'Neill	c Parfitt b Cartwright	11	
PJP Burge	lbw b Titmus	25	
BC Booth	c Trueman b Price	74	
IR Redpath	b Trueman	45	
ATW Grout+	b Cartwright	20	
TR Veivers	not out	67	
GD McKenzie	c Cowdrey b Trueman	0	
NJN Hawke	c Cowdrey b Trueman	14	
GE Corling	c Parfitt b Trueman	0	
Extras	(4b, 1lb, 0w, 0nb)	5	
Total	177.3 overs	**379**	

1st innings FoW: 45, 57, 96, 202, 245, 279, 343, 343, 367, 379

Bowler	O	M	R	W
FS Trueman	33.3	6	87	4
JSE Price	21	2	67	1
TW Cartwright	62	23	110	3
FJ Titmus	42	20	51	1
RW Barber	6	1	23	0
ER Dexter	13	1	36	1

	No. 410: 1st Test
	VENUE: Durban (Kingsmead)
	DATE: 4th-8th December 1964
	TOSS WON BY: England
	RESULT: Eng won by an innings and 104 runs

ENGLAND 1st innings / 2nd innings

ENGLAND	1st innings		2nd innings
G Boycott	lbw b Partridge	73	
RW Barber	b Goddard	74	
ER Dexter	c & b Seymour	28	
KF Barrington	not out	148	
PH Parfitt	c Goddard b Partridge	0	
MJK Smith*	c Lindsay b Partridge	35	
JM Parks+	not out	108	
FJ Titmus			
DA Allen			
NI Thomson			
JSE Price			
Extras	(2b, 1lb, 0w, 16nb)	19	
	190 overs		
Total		**485**	**226**

1st innings FoW: 120, 169, 205, 206, 279

	O	M	R	W
PM Pollock	33	11	80	0
JT Partridge	45	14	85	3
EJ Barlow	20	5	36	0
MA Seymour	46	4	144	1
TL Goddard	32	8	79	1
RG Pollock	10	1	32	0
KC Bland	4	1	10	0

SOUTH AFRICA 1st innings / 2nd innings

SOUTH AFRICA	1st innings		2nd innings	
TL Goddard*	c Smith b Price	8	c Thomson b Titmus	15
EJ Barlow	b Thomson	2	c Barrington b Price	0
AJ Pithey	b Allen	15	c Dexter b Allen	43
RG Pollock	b Titmus	5	c Smith b Titmus	0
KC Bland	c Barber b Allen	26	c Barber b Titmus	68
DT Lindsay+	c Price b Barber	38	c Dexter b Titmus	10
RA McLean	c Smith b Allen	30	c Smith b Allen	9
GD Varnals	b Allen	3	c Parks b Thomson	11
MA Seymour	not out	15	b Titmus	36
PM Pollock	c Dexter b Barber	3	not out	18
JT Partridge	b Allen	6	run out	1
Extras	(4b, 0lb, 0w, 0nb)	4	(9b, 6lb, 0w, 0nb)	15
	74.5 overs		122.5 overs	
Total		**155**		**226**

1st innings FoW: 10, 10, 19, 54, 67, 120, 130, 131, 142, 155
2nd innings FoW: 4, 28, 28, 123, 142, 145, 157, 178, 225, 226

	O	M	R	W	O	M	R	W
JSE Price	6	2	19	1	9	7	7	1
NI Thomson	15	5	23	1	13	6	25	1
FJ Titmus	20	9	20	1	45.5	19	66	5
DA Allen	19.5	5	41	5	47	15	99	2
RW Barber	14	1	48	2	6	2	8	0
PH Parfitt					2	0	6	0

	No. 411: 2nd Test
	VENUE: Johannesburg (Wanderers)
	DATE: 23rd-29th December 1964
	TOSS WON BY: England
	RESULT: Match drawn

ENGLAND 1st innings / 2nd innings

ENGLAND	1st innings		2nd innings
G Boycott	c Lindsay b PM Pollock	4	
RW Barber	b Seymour	97	
ER Dexter	c Lindsay b R Pollock	172	
KF Barrington	c R Pollock b P Pollock	121	
PH Parfitt	c Goddard b Partridge	52	
MJK Smith*	c McLean b Goddard	25	
JM Parks+	lbw b RG Pollock	26	
FJ Titmus	b PM Pollock	2	
DA Allen	lbw b PM Pollock	2	
NI Thomson	not out	27	
JSE Price	b PM Pollock	0	
Extras	(0b, 3lb, 0w, 0nb)	3	
	166.3 overs		
Total		**531**	

1st innings FoW: 10, 146, 337, 419, 467, 477, 484, 490, 526, 531

	O	M	R	W
PM Pollock	38.3	10	129	5
JT Partridge	40	10	106	1
TL Goddard	31	8	90	1
MA Seymour	35	10	109	1
EJ Barlow	8	2	33	0
RG Pollock	11	1	50	2
KC Bland	3	0	11	0

SOUTH AFRICA 1st innings / 2nd innings

SOUTH AFRICA	1st innings		2nd innings	
TL Goddard*	b Titmus	40	c Smith b Allen	50
EJ Barlow	c Price b Titmus	71	c Smith b Allen	15
AJ Pithey	b Allen	85	c Dexter b Allen	6
RG Pollock	c Smith b Titmus	12	b Titmus	24
KC Bland	c Thomson b Price	29	b Allen	55
RA McLean	lbw b Barber	12	not out	144
GD Varnals	b Price	21	c Parks b Dexter	23
DT Lindsay+	b Thomson	10	not out	4
MA Seymour	run out	2		
PM Pollock	c Smith b Titmus	20		
JT Partridge	not out	13		
Extras	(0b, 2lb, 0w, 0nb)	2	(4b, 8lb, 0w, 3nb)	15
	159.5 overs		140 overs	
Total		**317**		**336**

1st innings FoW: 78, 139, 153, 211, 231, 271, 271, 282, 285, 317
2nd innings FoW: 50, 74, 75, 109, 196, 320

	O	M	R	W	O	M	R	W
JSE Price	32	11	66	2	15	3	49	0
NI Thomson	23	8	47	1	16	5	36	0
FJ Titmus	39.5	15	73	4	45	18	101	1
ER Dexter	4	0	16	0	8	0	33	1
DA Allen	39	19	45	1	49	17	87	4
KF Barrington	4	0	29	0	2	0	12	0
RW Barber	14	1	33	1				
PH Parfitt	4	2	6	0				
G Boycott					5	3	3	0

South Africa

No. 412:	3rd Test
VENUE:	Cape Town
DATE:	1st-6th January 1965
TOSS WON BY:	South Africa
RESULT:	Match drawn

SOUTH AFRICA 1st innings / **2nd innings**

Batsman	1st innings		2nd innings	
TL Goddard*	b Titmus	40	c Parfitt b Price	6
EJ Barlow	c Parks b Thomson	138	c Parks b Dexter	78
AJ Pithey	c Barber b Allen	154	c Parks b Thomson	2
RG Pollock	c Parks b Allen	31	c Smith b Parfitt	20
KC Bland	run out	78	b Boycott	73
DT Lindsay+	lbw b Thomson	2	b Boycott	64
GD Varnals	c Smith b Titmus	19	b Barrington	50
SF Burke	not out	10	c Barber b Boycott	20
PM Pollock			lbw b Barrington	7
HD Bromfield			not out	12
GG Hall			b Barrington	0
Extras	(5b, 11lb, 1w, 12nb)	29	(1b, 9lb, 1w, 3nb)	14
	179.2 overs		119.1 overs	
Total		**501**		**346**

1st innings FoW: 80, 252, 313, 430, 439, 470, 501
2nd innings FoW: 10, 13, 86, 144, 231, 256, 310, 331, 334, 346

Bowler									
JSE Price	34	6	133	0	11	4	19	1
NI Thomson	45	19	89	2	14	4	31	1
FJ Titmus	50.2	11	133	2	6	2	21	0
ER Dexter	2	0	10	0	17	3	64	1
DA Allen	40	14	79	2	17	6	27	0
PH Parfitt	8	0	28	0	19	4	74	1
RW Barber					1	0	2	0
G Boycott					20	5	47	3
MJK Smith					11	1	43	0
KF Barrington					3.1	1	4	3

ENGLAND 1st innings / **2nd innings**

Batsman	1st innings		2nd innings	
G Boycott	c Barlow b Bromfield	15	not out	1
RW Barber	lbw b Goddard	58	not out	14
ER Dexter	c & b Bromfield	61		
KF Barrington	c Lindsay b PM Pollock	49		
PH Parfitt	b Hall	44		
MJK Smith*	c Goddard b Bromfield	121		
JM Parks+	c Lindsay b Barlow	59		
FJ Titmus	c Lindsay b PM Pollock	4		
DA Allen	c Barlow b Bromfield	22		
NI Thomson	c RG Pollock b Bromfield	0		
JSE Price	not out	0		
Extras	(2b, 5lb, 0w, 2nb)	9	(0b, 0lb, 0w, 0nb)	0
	205.2 overs		8 overs	
Total		**442**		**15**

1st innings FoW: 72, 80 , 170, 206, 243, 360, 368, 438, 440, 442

Bowler									
PM Pollock	39	14	89	2				
SF Burke	29	8	61	0				
HD Bromfield	57.2	26	88	5				
GG Hall	31	7	94	1				
TL Goddard	37	13	64	1				
EJ Barlow	12	3	37	1				
KC Bland					2	0	3	0
RG Pollock					2	1	5	0
AJ Pithey					2	0	5	0
GD Varnals					2	1	2	0

South Africa '65

No. 413:	4th Test
VENUE:	Johannesburg (Wanderers)
DATE:	22nd-27th January 1965
TOSS WON BY:	England
RESULT:	Match drawn

SOUTH AFRICA 1st innings / **2nd innings**

Batsman	1st innings		2nd innings	
TL Goddard*	run out	60	c Barber b Price	112
EJ Barlow	c & b Cartwright	96	c Barber b Titmus	42
KC Bland	c Parks b Price	55	b Cartwright	39
AJ Pithey	c Cartwright b Titmus	95	not out	65
RG Pollock	c Parks b Price	4	not out	38
JHB Waite+	run out	64		
V der Merwe	not out	5		
PM Pollock	not out	0		
HD Bromfield				
AH McKinnon				
JT Partridge				
Extras	(0b, 7lb, 0w, 4nb)	11	(0b, 7lb, 0w, 4nb)	11
	146 overs		88 overs	
Total		**390**		**307**

1st innings FoW: 134, 189, 222, 226, 383, 389
2nd innings FoW: 65, 180, 211

Bowler									
JSE Price	17	1	68	2	14	1	56	1
NI Thomson	31	3	91	0	19	4	43	0
TW Cartwright	55	18	97	1	24	6	99	1
ER Dexter	6	0	30	0	31	4	98	1
FJ Titmus	29	2	68	1				
G Boycott	8	1	25	0				

ENGLAND 1st innings / **2nd innings**

Batsman	1st innings		2nd innings	
G Boycott	c Barlow b Partridge	5	not out	76
RW Barber	lbw b McKinnon	61	c Merwe b PM Pollock	13
ER Dexter	c Waite b Goddard	38	c R Pollock b P Pollock	0
KF Barrington	c Waite b Barlow	93	c Bromf'd b McKinnon	11
PH Parfitt	not out	122	c Barlow b McKinnon	22
MJK Smith*	c R Pollock b McKinnon	42	b Bromfield	8
JM Parks+	c Barlow b Partridge	0	c RG Poll'k b McKinnon	10
FJ Titmus	lbw b McKinnon	1	not out	8
TW Cartwright	b McKinnon	9		
NI Thomson	c Barlow b PM Pollock	3		
JSE Price	c Bromfield b P Pollock	0		
Extras	(1b, 5lb, 1w, 3nb)	10	(0b, 5lb, 0w, 0nb)	5
	147.2 overs		87 overs	
Total		**384**		**153**

1st innings FoW: 7, 78, 144, 244, 333, 333, 338, 350, 374, 384
2nd innings FoW: 21, 21, 33, 80, 107, 124

Bowler									
PM Pollock	15.2	4	42	2	11	3	27	2
JT Partridge	30	6	92	2	7	4	10	0
EJ Barlow	18	5	34	1				
TL Goddard	16	4	35	1	6	4	5	0
AH McKinnon	51	13	128	4	35	17	44	3
RG Pollock	4	0	12	0	11	2	35	0
HD Bromfield	13	4	31	0	17	8	27	1

South Africa

No. 414:	5th Test
VENUE:	Port Elizabeth
DATE:	12th-17th February 1965
TOSS WON BY:	South Africa
RESULT:	Match drawn

SOUTH AFRICA 1st innings / 2nd innings

Batsman	1st innings		2nd innings	
TL Goddard*	c Boycott b Allen	61	c Boycott b Thomson	13
EJ Barlow	c Parfitt b Boycott	69	b Titmus	47
KC Bland	c Parfitt b Titmus	48	c & b Thomson	22
RG Pollock	c & b Allen	137	not out	77
AJ Pithey	c Barrington b Allen	23	c Titmus b Boycott	12
JHB Waite+	run out	6	not out	0
V Der Merwe	c Barrington b Palmer	66		
PM Pollock	c Titmus b Thomson	18		
MJ Macaulay	b Titmus	21		
AH McKinnon	run out	27		
HD Bromfield	not out	1		
Extras	(10b, 11lb, 0w, 4nb)	25	(1b, 4lb, 0w, 2nb)	7
Total	**189.1 overs**	**502**	**60 overs**	**178**

1st innings FoW: 114, 171, 185, 268, 276, 389, 447, 455, 498, 502
2nd innings FoW: 30, 69, 124, 171

Bowler	O	M	R	W	O	M	R	W
NI Thomson	47	7	128	1	25	7	55	2
KE Palmer	35	6	113	1	28	1	76	0
G Boycott	26	7	69	1	2	0	13	1
FJ Titmus	37.1	7	87	2	5	0	27	1
DA Allen	44	13	80	3				

ENGLAND 1st innings / 2nd innings

Batsman	1st innings		2nd innings	
G Boycott	c V der Merwe b Brom'd	117	c Waite b Macaulay	7
JT Murray	lbw b Macaulay	4	not out	8
FJ Titmus	b PM Pollock	12	not out	5
ER Dexter	run out	40		
KF Barrington	c Vd Merwe b Goddard	72		
NI Thomson	c Barlow b McKinnon	39		
MJK Smith*	c Waite b Barlow	26		
PH Parfitt	lbw b Barlow	0		
JM Parks+	c Waite b Barlow	35		
DA Allen	not out	38		
KE Palmer	lbw b Goddard	10		
Extras	(7b, 14lb, 2w, 19nb)	42	(7b, 2lb, 0w, 0nb)	9
Total	**207.5 overs**	**435**	**19.2 overs**	**29**

1st innings FoW: 28, 52, 115, 272, 277, 346, 346, 346, 410, 435
2nd innings FoW: 17

Bowler	O	M	R	W	O	M	R	W
PM Pollock	27	8	71	1	5.2	1	7	0
MJ Macaulay	37	13	63	1	9	4	10	1
TL Goddard	35.5	18	34	2	5	3	3	0
AH McKinnon	46	17	99	1				
EJ Barlow	22	2	55	3				
HD Bromfield	33	14	57	1				
RG Pollock	7	3	14	0				

New Zealand

No. 415:	1st Test
VENUE:	Edgbaston
DATE:	27th May-1st June 1965
TOSS WON BY:	England
RESULT:	England won by 9 wickets

ENGLAND 1st innings / 2nd innings

Batsman	1st innings		2nd innings	
G Boycott	c Dick b Motz	23	not out	44
RW Barber	b Motz	31	c (sub) b Morgan	51
ER Dexter	c Dick b Motz	57	not out	0
KF Barrington	c Dick b Collinge	137		
MC Cowdrey	b Collinge	85		
MJK Smith*	lbw b Collinge	0		
JM Parks+	c Cameron b Reid	34		
FJ Titmus	c Congdon b Motz	13		
TW Cartwright	b Motz	4		
FS Trueman	c Pollard b Cameron	3		
FE Rumsey	not out	21		
Extras	(10b, 6lb, 0w, 11nb)	27	(0b, 0lb, 0w, 1nb)	1
Total	**156.4 overs**	**435**	**30.5 overs**	**96**

1st innings FoW: 54, 76, 164, 300, 300, 335, 368, 391, 394, 435
2nd innings FoW: 92

Bowler	O	M	R	W	O	M	R	W
RO Collinge	29.4	8	63	3	5	1	14	0
FJ Cameron	43	10	117	1	3	0	11	0
RC Motz	43	14	108	5	13	3	34	0
V Pollard	18	4	60	0	1	0	5	0
BE Congdon	7	2	17	0	2	1	6	0
JR Reid	16	5	43	1	5	2	7	0
RW Morgan					1.5	0	18	1

NEW ZEALAND 1st innings / 2nd innings

Batsman	1st innings		2nd innings	
GT Dowling	b Titmus	32	b Barber	41
BE Congdon	c Smith b Titmus	24	b Titmus	47
BW Sinclair	b Titmus	14	st Parks b Barber	2
JR Reid*	b Trueman	2	c Barrington b Titmus	44
B Sutcliffe	retired hurt	4	lbw b Trueman	43
RW Morgan	c Parks b Barber	22	b Barber	42
AE Dick+	c Titmus b Cartwright	0	c Titmus b Dexter	53
V Pollard	lbw b Titmus	4	not out	81
RC Motz	c Trueman b Cartwright	0	c & b Barber	21
RO Collinge	c Dexter b Barber	4	c Parks b Trueman	9
FJ Cameron	not out	4	b Trueman	0
Extras	(1b, 1lb, 0w, 4nb)	6	(17b, 11lb, 0w, 2nb)	30
Total	**63 overs**	**116**	**175.4 overs**	**413**

1st innings FoW: 54, 63, 67, 86, 97, 104, 105, 108, 115
2nd innings FoW: 72, 105, 131, 145, 220, 249, 353, 386, 413, 413

Bowler	O	M	R	W	O	M	R	W
FE Rumsey	9	2	22	0	17	5	32	0
FS Trueman	18	3	49	1	32.4	8	79	3
FJ Titmus	26	17	18	4	59	30	85	2
TW Cartwright	7	3	14	2	12	6	12	0
RW Barber	3	2	7	2	45	15	132	4
KF Barrington					5	0	25	0
ER Dexter					5	1	18	1

No. 416: 2nd Test
VENUE: Lord's
DATE: 17th-22nd June 1965
TOSS WON BY: New Zealand
RESULT: England won by 7 wickets

No. 417: 3rd Test
VENUE: Headingley
DATE: 8th-13th July 1965
TOSS WON BY: England
RESULT: Eng won by an innings and 187 runs

NEW ZEALAND 1st innings / 2nd innings

Batsman	1st innings		2nd innings	
BE Congdon	lbw b Rumsey	0	lbw b Titmus	26
GT Dowling	lbw b Rumsey	12	b Parfitt	66
BW Sinclair	b Rumsey	1	c Parks b Barber	72
JR Reid*	c Parks b Snow	21	b Titmus	22
RW Morgan	c Parfitt b Rumsey	0	lbw b Rumsey	35
V Pollard	c & b Titmus	55	run out	55
AE Dick+	b Snow	7	c Parks b Snow	3
BR Taylor	b Trueman	51	c Smith b Snow	0
RC Motz	c Parks b Titmus	11	c Parks b Barber	21
RO Collinge	b Trueman	7	c Snow b Barber	8
FJ Cameron	not out	3	not out	9
Extras	(3b, 2lb, 0w, 2nb)	7	(8b, 12lb, 0w, 10nb)	30
	74.5 overs		149 overs	
Total		**175**		**347**

1st innings FoW: 0, 4, 24, 28, 49, 62, 154, 160, 171, 175
2nd innings FoW: 59, 149, 196, 206, 253, 258, 259, 293, 303, 347

Bowler	O	M	R	W	O	M	R	W
FE Rumsey	13	4	25	4	26	10	42	1
FS Trueman	19.5	8	40	2	26	4	69	0
ER Dexter	8	2	27	0				
JA Snow	11	2	27	2	24	4	53	2
FJ Titmus	15	7	25	2	39	12	71	2
RW Barber	8	2	24	0	28	10	57	3
PH Parfitt					6	2	25	1

ENGLAND 1st innings / 2nd innings

Batsman	1st innings		2nd innings	
G Boycott	c Dick b Motz	14	lbw b Motz	76
RW Barber	c Dick b Motz	13	b Motz	34
ER Dexter	c Dick b Taylor	62	c Dick b Motz	1
MC Cowdrey	c (sub) b Collinge	119	not out	80
PH Parfitt	c Dick b Cameron	11	not out	4
MJK Smith*	c (sub) b Taylor	44		
JM Parks+	b Collinge	2		
FJ Titmus	run out	13		
FS Trueman	b Collinge	3		
FE Rumsey	b Collinge	3		
JA Snow	not out	2		
Extras	(1b, 7lb, 1w, 12nb)	21	(9b, 5lb, 0w, 9nb)	23
	100.2 overs		60.5 overs	
Total		**307**		**218**

1st innings FoW: 18, 38, 131, 166, 271, 285, 292, 300, 302, 307
2nd innings FoW: 64, 70, 196

Bowler	O	M	R	W	O	M	R	W
RO Collinge	28.2	4	85	4	15	1	43	0
RC Motz	20	1	62	2	19	5	45	3
BR Taylor	25	4	66	2	10	0	53	0
FJ Cameron	19	6	40	1	13	0	39	0
RW Morgan	8	1	33	0	3	0	11	0
JR Reid					0.5	0	4	0

ENGLAND 1st innings / 2nd innings

Batsman	1st innings		2nd innings	
RW Barber	c Ward b Taylor	13		
JH Edrich	not out	310		
KF Barrington	c Ward b Motz	163		
MC Cowdrey	b Taylor	13		
PH Parfitt	b Collinge	32		
MJK Smith*	not out	2		
JM Parks+				
R Illingworth				
FJ Titmus				
FE Rumsey				
JDF Larter				
Extras	(4b, 8lb, 0w, 1nb)	13		
	151 overs			
Total		**546**		

1st innings FoW: 13, 382, 407, 516

Bowler	O	M	R	W
RC Motz	41	8	140	1
BR Taylor	40	8	140	2
RO Collinge	32	7	87	1
BW Yuile	17	5	80	0
RW Morgan	6	0	28	0
V Pollard	11	2	46	0
BE Congdon	4	0	12	0

NEW ZEALAND 1st innings / 2nd innings

Batsman	1st innings		2nd innings	
GT Dowling	c Parks b Larter	5	b Rumsey	41
BE Congdon	c Parks b Rumsey	13	b Rumsey	1
BW Sinclair	c Smith b Larter	13	lbw b Larter	29
JR Reid*	lbw b Illingworth	54	c Barrington b Rumsey	5
RW Morgan	b Illingworth	1	c Cowdrey b Larter	53
V Pollard	run out	33	b Titmus	21
BW Yuile	b Larter	46	c Cowdrey b Titmus	12
BR Taylor	c Parks b Illingworth	9	c & b Titmus	0
RC Motz	c Barber b Illingworth	9	c Barrington b Titmus	0
JT Ward+	not out	0	b Titmus	0
RO Collinge	b Larter	8	not out	2
Extras	(5b, 1lb, 2w, 0nb)	8	(0b, 0lb, 0w, 2nb)	2
	88.1 overs		84 overs	
Total		**193**		**166**

1st innings FoW: 15, 19, 53, 61, 100, 153, 165, 173, 181, 193
2nd innings FoW: 4, 67, 75, 86, 111, 158, 158, 158, 158, 166

Bowler	O	M	R	W	O	M	R	W
FE Rumsey	24	6	59	1	15	5	49	3
JDF Larter	28.1	6	66	4	22	10	54	2
R Illingworth	28	14	42	4	7	0	28	0
FJ Titmus	6	2	16	0	26	17	19	5
RW Barber	2	0	2	0	14	7	14	0

South Africa | South Africa

	No. 418: 1st Test			No. 419: 2nd Test	
	VENUE: Lord's			VENUE: Trent Bridge	
	DATE: 22nd-27th July 1965			DATE: 5th-9th August 1965	
	TOSS WON BY: South Africa			TOSS WON BY: South Africa	
	RESULT: Match drawn			RESULT: South Africa won by 94 runs	

SOUTH AFRICA 1st innings / 2nd innings (No. 418)

Batsman	1st innings		2nd innings	
EJ Barlow	c Barber b Rumsey	1	c Parks b Brown	52
HR Lance	c & b Brown	28	c Titmus b Brown	9
DT Lindsay+	c Titmus b Rumsey	40	c Parks b Larter	22
RG Pollock	c Barrington b Titmus	56	b Brown	5
KC Bland	b Brown	39	c Edrich b Barber	70
A Bacher	lbw b Titmus	4	b Titmus	37
V Der Merwe*	c Barrington b Rumsey	17	c Barrington b Rumsey	31
R Dumbrill	b Barber	3	c Cowdrey b Rumsey	2
JT Botten	b Brown	33	b Rumsey	0
PM Pollock	st Parks b Barber	34	not out	14
HD Bromfield	not out	9	run out	0
Extras	(0b, 14lb, 0w, 2nb)	16	(4b, 2lb, 0w, 0nb)	6
	119.3 overs		110 overs	
Total		**280**		**248**

2nd innings FoW: 1, 60, 75, 155, 170, 170, 178, 212, 241, 280
2nd innings FoW: 55, 62, 68, 120, 170, 216, 230, 230, 247, 248

Bowler	O	M	R	W	O	M	R	W
JDF Larter	26	10	47	0	17	2	67	1
FE Rumsey	30	9	84	3	21	8	49	3
DJ Brown	24	9	44	3	21	11	30	3
FJ Titmus	29	10	59	2	26	13	36	1
RW Barber	10.3	3	30	2	25	5	60	1

SOUTH AFRICA 1st innings / 2nd innings (No. 419)

Batsman	1st innings		2nd innings	
EJ Barlow	c Cowdrey b Cartwright	19	c Cowdrey b Larter	9
HR Lance	lbw b Cartwright	7	c Barber b Snow	0
DT Lindsay+	c Parks b Cartwright	0	lbw b Larter	67
RG Pollock	c Cowdrey b Cartwright	125	b Titmus	76
KC Bland	st Parks b Titmus	1	c Titmus b Larter	59
A Bacher	b Snow	12	b Snow	10
V der Merwe*	run out	38	c Parfitt b Larter	4
R Dumbrill	c Parfitt b Cartwright	30	b Snow	13
JT Botten	c Parks b Larter	10	b Larter	18
PM Pollock	c Larter b Cartwright	15	not out	12
AH McKinnon	not out	8	b Titmus	9
Extras	(0b, 4lb, 0w, 0nb)	4	(4b, 5lb, 0w, 3nb)	12
	101.3 overs		110.4 overs	
Total		**269**		**289**

1st innings FoW: 16, 16, 42, 43, 80, 178, 221, 242, 252, 269
2nd innings FoW: 2, 35, 134, 193, 228, 232, 243, 265, 269, 289

Bowler	O	M	R	W	O	M	R	W
JDF Larter	17	6	25	1	29	7	68	5
JA Snow	22	6	63	1	33	6	83	3
TW Cartwright	31.3	9	94	6				
FJ Titmus	22	8	44	1	19.4	5	46	2
RW Barber	9	3	39	0	3	0	20	0
G Boycott					26	10	60	0

ENGLAND 1st innings / 2nd innings (No. 418)

Batsman	1st innings		2nd innings	
G Boycott	c Barlow b Botten	31	c & b Dumbrill	28
RW Barber	b Bromfield	56	c Lindsay b PM Pollock	12
JH Edrich	lbw b PM Pollock	0	retired hurt	7
KF Barrington	run out	91	lbw b Dumbrill	18
MC Cowdrey	b Dumbrill	29	lbw b PM Pollock	37
MJK Smith*	c Lindsay b Botten	26	c Lindsay b Dumbrill	13
JM Parks+	run out	32	c Merwe b Dumbrill	7
FJ Titmus	c P Pollock b Bromfield	59	not out	9
DJ Brown	b Bromfield b Dumbrill	1	c Barlow b RG Pollock	5
FE Rumsey	b Dumbrill	4	not out	0
JDF Larter	not out	0		
Extras	(1b, 4lb, 1w, 4nb)	10	(0b, 7lb, 1w, 1nb)	9
	150.2 overs		68 overs	
Total		**338**		**145**

1st innings FoW: 82, 88, 88, 144, 240, 240, 294, 314, 338, 338
2nd innings FoW: 23, 70, 79, 113, 121, 135, 140

Bowler	O	M	R	W	O	M	R	W
PM Pollock	39	12	91	1	20	6	52	2
JT Botten	33	11	65	2	12	6	25	0
EJ Barlow	19	6	31	0	9	1	25	0
HD Bromfield	25.2	5	71	2	5	4	4	0
R Dumbrill	24	11	31	3	18	8	30	4
HR Lance	5	0	18	0				
RG Pollock	5	1	21	0				
RG Pollock					4	4	0	1

ENGLAND 1st innings / 2nd innings (No. 419)

Batsman	1st innings		2nd innings	
G Boycott	c Lance b PM Pollock	0	b McKinnon	16
RW Barber	c Bacher b Dumbrill	41	c Lindsay b PM Pollock	1
KF Barrington	b PM Pollock	1	c Lindsay b McKinnon	4
FJ Titmus	c R Pollock b McKinnon	20	b Botten	0
MC Cowdrey	c Lindsay b Botten	105	c Lindsay b PM Pollock	1
PH Parfitt	c Dumbrill b P Pollock	18	st Lindsay b McKinnon	20
MJK Smith*	b PM Pollock	32	b PM Pollock	86
JM Parks+	c & b Botten	6	lbw b RG Pollock	24
JA Snow	run out	3	not out	44
JDF Larter	b PM Pollock	2	lbw b PM Pollock	0
TW Cartwright	not out	1	c Vd Merwe b P Poll'k	10
Extras	(1b, 3lb, 1w, 6nb)	11	(0b, 5lb, 2w, 11nb)	18
	93.5 overs		98 overs	
Total		**240**		**224**

1st innings FoW: 0, 8, 63, 67, 133, 225, 229, 236, 238, 240
2nd innings FoW: 1, 10, 10, 13, 41, 59, 114, 207, 207, 224

Bowler	O	M	R	W	O	M	R	W
PM Pollock	23.5	8	53	5	24	15	34	5
JT Botten	23	5	60	2	19	5	58	1
AH McKinnon	28	11	54	1	27	12	50	3
R Dumbrill	18	3	60	1	16	4	40	0
RG Pollock	1	0	2	0	5	2	4	1
EJ Barlow					7	1	20	0

No. 420: 3rd Test
VENUE: The Oval
DATE: 26th-31st August 1965
TOSS WON BY: England
RESULT: Match drawn

No. 421: 1st Test
VENUE: Brisbane (Gabba)
DATE: 10th-15th December 1965
TOSS WON BY: Australia
RESULT: Match drawn

SOUTH AFRICA 1st innings

	1st innings		2nd innings	
EJ Barlow	lbw b Statham	18	b Statham	18
DT Lindsay+	lbw b Higgs	4	b Brown	17
A Bacher	lbw b Higgs	28	c Smith b Statham	70
RG Pollock	b Titmus	12	run out	34
KC Bland	lbw b Statham	39	c Titmus b Higgs	127
HR Lance	lbw b Statham	69	b Higgs	53
V der Merwe*	c Bar'ton b Higgs	20	b Higgs	0
R Dumbrill	c Smith b Higgs	14	c Barrington b Brown	36
JT Botten	c Cowdrey b Statham	0	b Titmus	4
PM Pollock	b Statham	3	not out	9
AH McKinnon	not out	0	b Higgs	14
Extras	(0b, 0lb, 0w, 1nb)	1	(1b, 7lb, 0w, 2nb)	10
	96.2 overs		133.1 overs	
Total		**208**		**392**

1st innings FoW: 21, 23, 60, 86, 109, 156, 196, 197, 207, 208
2nd innings FoW: 28, 61, 123, 164, 260, 260, 343, 367, 371, 392

JB Statham	24.2	11	40	5		29	1	105	2
DJ Brown	22	4	63	0		23	3	63	2
K Higgs	24	4	47	4		41.1	10	96	4
FJ Titmus	26	12	57	1		27	3	74	1
RW Barber						13	1	44	0

ENGLAND 1st innings

	1st innings		2nd innings	
RW Barber	st Lindsay b McKinnon	40	c & b PM Pollock	22
WE Russell	lbw b PM Pollock	0	c Bacher b McKinnon	70
KF Barrington	b Botten	18	lbw b Botten	46
MC Cowdrey	c Barlow b PM Pollock	58	lbw b PM Pollock	73
PH Parfitt	c & b McKinnon	24	not out	78
MJK Smith*	lbw b PM Pollock	7	not out	10
DJ Brown	c Dumbrill b McKinnon	0		
JM Parks+	c Bland b Botten	42		
FJ Titmus	not out	2		
K Higgs	b PM Pollock	2		
JB Statham	b PM Pollock	0		
Extras	(0b, 6lb, 3w, 0nb)	9	(0b, 6lb, 0w, 3nb)	9
	98.1 overs		104.2 overs	
Total		**202**		**308**

1st innings FoW: 1, 42 , 76, 125, 141, 142, 198, 198, 200, 202
2nd innings FoW: 39, 138, 144, 279

PM Pollock	25.1	7	43	5		32.2	7	93	2
JT Botten	27	6	56	2		24	4	73	1
EJ Barlow	11	1	27	0		6	1	22	0
R Dumbrill	6	2	11	0		9	1	30	0
AH McKinnon	27	11	50	3		31	7	70	1
HR Lance	2	0	6	0		2	0	11	0

AUSTRALIA 1st innings

	1st innings		2nd innings
WM Lawry	c Parks b Higgs	166	
IR Redpath	b Brown	17	
RM Cowper	c Barrington b Brown	22	
PJP Burge	b Brown	0	
BC Booth*	c & b Titmus	16	
KD Walters	c Parks b Higgs	155	
TR Veivers	not out	56	
NJN Hawke	not out	6	
PI Philpott			
ATW Grout+			
PJ Allan			
Extras	(0b, 2lb, 0w, 3nb)	5	
	137 overs		
Total		**443**	

1st innings FoW: 51, 90, 90, 125, 312, 431

DJ Brown	21	4	71	3
K Higgs	30	6	102	2
FJ Titmus	38	9	99	1
DA Allen	39	12	108	0
RW Barber	5	0	42	0
G Boycott	4	0	16	0

ENGLAND 1st innings

	1st innings		2nd innings	
RW Barber	c Walters b Hawke	5	c Veivers b Walters	34
G Boycott	b Philpott	45	not out	63
JH Edrich	c Lawry b Philpott	32	c Veivers b Philpott	37
KF Barrington	b Hawke	53	c Booth b Cowper	38
MJK Smith*	b Allan	16	not out	10
JM Parks+	c Redpath b Philpott	52		
FJ Titmus	st Grout b Philpott	60		
DA Allen	c Cowper b Walters	3		
DJ Brown	b Philpott	3		
K Higgs	lbw b Allan	4		
WE Russell	not out	0		
Extras	(4b, 0lb, 0w, 3nb)	7	(2b, 2lb, 0w, 0nb)	4
	93.1 overs		50 overs	
Total		**280**		**186**

1st innings FoW: 5, 75, 86, 115, 191, 221, 232, 253, 272, 280
2nd innings FoW: 46, 114, 168

PJ Allan	21	6	58	2		3	0	25	0
NJN Hawke	16	7	44	2		10	2	16	0
KD Walters	10	1	25	1		5	1	22	1
PI Philpott	28.1	3	90	5		14	1	62	1
RM Cowper	7	4	7	0		6	0	20	1
TR Veivers	11	1	49	0		12	0	37	0

No. 422: 2nd Test
VENUE: Melbourne (MCG)
DATE: 30th Dec 1965-4th Jan 1966
TOSS WON BY: Australia
RESULT: Match drawn

No. 423: 3rd Test
VENUE: Sydney (SCG)
DATE: 7th-11th January 1966
TOSS WON BY: England
RESULT: Eng won by an innings and 93 runs

AUSTRALIA 1st innings / 2nd innings

Batsman	1st innings		2nd innings	
RB Simpson*	c Edrich b Allen	59	c Barrington b Knight	67
WM Lawry	c Cowdrey b Allen	88	c Smith b Barber	78
PJP Burge	b Jones	5	lbw b Jones	5
RM Cowper	c Titmus b Jones	99	c Edrich b Boycott	120
BC Booth	lbw b Jones	23	b Allen	10
KD Walters	c Parks b Knight	22	c & b Barrington	115
TR Veivers	run out	19	st Parks b Boycott	3
PI Philpott	b Knight	10	b Knight	2
ATW Grout+	c Barber b Knight	11	c Allen b Barrington	16
GD McKenzie	not out	12	run out	2
AN Connolly	c Parks b Knight	0	not out	0
Extras	(2b, 7lb, 0w, 1nb)	10	(1b, 3lb, 1w, 3nb)	8
Total	107.5 overs	**358**	116.4 overs	**426**

1st innings FoW: 93, 109, 203, 262, 297, 318, 330, 342, 352, 358
2nd innings FoW: 120, 141, 163, 176, 374, 382, 385, 417, 426, 426

Bowler	O	M	R	W	O	M	R	W
IJ Jones	24	4	92	3	20	1	92	1
BR Knight	26.5	2	84	4	21	4	61	2
FJ Titmus	31	7	93	0	22	6	43	0
DA Allen	20	4	55	2	18	3	48	1
RW Barber	6	1	24	0	17	0	87	1
KF Barrington					7.4	0	47	2
G Boycott					9	0	32	2
MJK Smith					2	0	8	0

ENGLAND 1st innings / 2nd innings

Batsman	1st innings		2nd innings	
G Boycott	c McKenzie b Walters	51	not out	5
RW Barber	c Grout b McKenzie	48	not out	0
JH Edrich	c & b Veivers	109		
KF Barrington	c Burge b Veivers	63		
MC Cowdrey	c Connolly b Cowper	104		
MJK Smith*	c Grout b McKenzie	41		
JM Parks+	c Cowper b McKenzie	71		
BR Knight	c Simpson b McKenzie	1		
FJ Titmus	not out	56		
DA Allen	c Grout b Connolly	2		
IJ Jones	b McKenzie	1		
Extras	(4b, 5lb, 2w, 0nb)	11	(0b, 0lb, 0w, 0nb)	
Total	143.2 overs	**558**	2 overs	**5**

1st innings FoW: 98, 110, 228, 333, 409, 443, 447, 540, 551, 558

Bowler	O	M	R	W	O	M	R	W
GD McKenzie	35.2	3	134	5	1	0	2	0
AN Connolly	37	5	125	1	1	0	3	0
PI Philpott	30	2	133	0				
KD Walters	10	2	32	1				
RB Simpson	16	4	61	0				
TR Veivers	12	3	46	2				
RM Cowper	3	0	16	1				

ENGLAND 1st innings / 2nd innings

Batsman	1st innings		2nd innings
G Boycott	c & b Philpott	84	
RW Barber	b Hawke	185	
JH Edrich	c & b Philpott	103	
KF Barrington	c McKenzie b Hawke	1	
MC Cowdrey	c Grout b Hawke	0	
MJK Smith*	c Grout b Hawke	6	
DJ Brown	c Grout b Hawke	1	
JM Parks+	c Grout b Hawke	13	
FJ Titmus	c Grout b Walters	14	
DA Allen	not out	50	
IJ Jones	b Hawke	16	
Extras	(3b, 8lb, 2w, 2nb)	15	
Total	122.7 overs	**488**	

1st innings FoW: 234, 303, 309, 309, 317, 328, 358, 395, 433, 488

Bowler	O	M	R	W
GD McKenzie	25	2	113	0
NJN Hawke	33.7	6	105	7
KD Walters	10	1	38	1
PI Philpott	28	3	86	2
DJ Sincock	20	1	98	0
RM Cowper	6	1	33	0

AUSTRALIA 1st innings / 2nd innings

Batsman	1st innings		2nd innings	
WM Lawry	c Parks b Jones	0	c Cowdrey b Brown	33
G Thomas	c Titmus b Brown	51	c Cowdrey b Titmus	25
RM Cowper	st Parks b Allen	60	c Boycott b Titmus	0
PJP Burge	c Parks b Brown	6	run out	4
BC Booth*	c Cowdrey b Jones	8	b Allen	27
DJ Sincock	c Parks b Brown	29	not out	27
KD Walters	st Parks b Allen	23	c Smith b Allen	27
NJN Hawke	c Barber b Brown	0	lbw b Allen	5
ATW Grout+	b Brown	0	c Smith b Titmus	2
GD McKenzie	c Cowdrey b Barber	24	c Smith b Allen	3
PI Philpott	not out	5	c Barber b Titmus	12
Extras	(7b, 8lb, 0w, 0nb)	15	(3b, 1lb, 0w, 0nb)	4
Total	84.1 overs	**221**	60.3 overs	**174**

1st innings FoW: 0, 81, 91, 105, 155, 174, 174, 174, 203, 221
2nd innings FoW: 46, 50, 51, 86, 86, 119, 131, 135, 140, 174

Bowler	O	M	R	W	O	M	R	W
IJ Jones	20	6	51	2	7	0	35	0
DJ Brown	17	1	63	5	11	2	32	1
G Boycott	3	1	8	0	17.3	4	40	4
FJ Titmus	23	8	40	0	5	0	16	0
RW Barber	2.1	1	2	1	20	8	47	4
DA Allen	19	5	42	2				

No. 424: 4th Test	No. 425: 5th Test
VENUE: Adelaide	VENUE: Melbourne (MCG)
DATE: 28th January-1st Feb 1966	DATE: 11th-16th February 1966
TOSS WON BY: England	TOSS WON BY: England
RESULT: Aus won by an innings and 9 runs	RESULT: Match drawn

ENGLAND 1st innings / 2nd innings (No. 424)

Batsman	1st innings		2nd innings	
G Boycott	c Chappell b Hawke	22	lbw b McKenzie	12
RW Barber	b McKenzie	0	c Grout b Hawke	19
JH Edrich	c Simpson b McKenzie	5	c Simpson b Hawke	1
KF Barrington	lbw b Walters	60	c Chappell b Hawke	102
MC Cowdrey	run out	38	c Grout b Stackpole	35
MJK Smith*	b Veivers	29	c McKenzie b Stackpole	5
JM Parks+	c Stackpole b McKenzie	49	run out	16
FJ Titmus	lbw b McKenzie	33	c Grout b Hawke	53
DA Allen	c Simpson b McKenzie	2	not out	5
DJ Brown	c Thomas b McKenzie	1	c & b Hawke	0
IJ Jones	not out	0	c Lawry b Veivers	8
Extras	(0b, 2lb, 0w, 0nb)	2	(0b, 2lb, 0w, 8nb)	10
Total	80.7 overs	241	87.7 overs	266

1st innings FoW: 7, 25, 33, 105, 150, 178, 210, 212, 222, 241
2nd innings FoW: 23, 31, 32, 114, 123, 163, 244, 253, 257, 266

Bowler	O	M	R	W		O	M	R	W
GD McKenzie	21.7	4	48	6		18	4	53	1
NJN Hawke	23	2	69	1		21	6	54	5
KD Walters	14	0	50	1		9	0	47	0
KR Stackpole	5	0	30	0		14	3	33	2
IM Chappell	4	1	18	0		22	4	53	0
TR Veivers	13	3	24	1		3.7	0	16	1

ENGLAND 1st innings / 2nd innings (No. 425)

Batsman	1st innings		2nd innings	
G Boycott	c Stackpole b McKenzie	17	lbw b McKenzie	1
RW Barber	run out	17	b McKenzie	20
JH Edrich	c McKenzie b Walters	85	b McKenzie	3
KF Barrington	c Grout b Walters	115	not out	32
MC Cowdrey	c Grout b Walters	79	not out	11
MJK Smith*	c Grout b Walters	0		
JM Parks+	run out	89		
FJ Titmus	not out	42		
BR Knight	c Grout b Hawke	13		
DJ Brown	c & b Chappell	12		
IJ Jones	not out	4		
Extras	(9b, 2lb, 0w, 1nb)	12	(0b, 2lb, 0w, 0nb)	2
Total	127 overs	485	17 overs	69

1st innings FoW: 36, 41, 219, 254, 254, 392, 419, 449, 474
2nd innings FoW: 6, 21, 34

Bowler	O	M	R	W		O	M	R	W
GD McKenzie	26	5	100	1		6	2	17	3
NJN Hawke	35	5	109	1		4	1	22	0
KD Walters	19	3	53	4		2	0	16	0
RB Simpson	5	1	20	0		3	0	10	0
KR Stackpole	10	2	43	0					
TR Veivers	15	3	78	0					
IM Chappell	17	4	70	1		2	0	2	0

AUSTRALIA 1st innings (No. 424)

Batsman	1st innings		2nd innings
RB Simpson*	c Titmus b Jones	225	
WM Lawry	b Titmus	119	
G Thomas	b Jones	52	
TR Veivers	c Parks b Jones	1	
PJP Burge	c Parks b Jones	27	
KD Walters	c Parks b Brown	0	
IM Chappell	c Edrich b Jones	17	
KR Stackpole	c Parks b Jones	43	
NJN Hawke	not out	20	
ATW Grout+	b Titmus	4	
GD McKenzie	lbw b Titmus	1	
Extras	(4b, 3lb, 0w, 0nb)	7	
Total	126 overs	516	

1st innings FoW: 244, 331, 333, 379, 383, 415, 480, 501, 506, 516

Bowler	O	M	R	W
IJ Jones	29	3	118	6
DJ Brown	28	4	109	1
G Boycott	7	3	33	0
FJ Titmus	37	6	116	3
DA Allen	21	1	103	0
RW Barber	4	0	30	0

AUSTRALIA 1st innings (No. 425)

Batsman	1st innings		2nd innings
WM Lawry	c Edrich b Jones	108	
RB Simpson*	b Brown	4	
G Thomas	c Titmus b Jones	19	
RM Cowper	b Knight	307	
KD Walters	c & b Barber	60	
IM Chappell	c Parks b Jones	19	
KR Stackpole	b Knight	9	
TR Veivers	b Titmus	4	
NJN Hawke	not out	0	
ATW Grout+			
GD McKenzie			
Extras	(6b, 5lb, 0w, 2nb)	13	
Total	154.2 overs	543	

1st innings FoW: 15, 36, 248, 420, 481, 532, 543, 543

Bowler	O	M	R	W
DJ Brown	31	3	134	1
IJ Jones	29	1	145	3
BR Knight	36.2	4	105	2
FJ Titmus	42	12	86	1
RW Barber	16	0	60	1

	No. 426: 1st Test		No. 427: 2nd Test
VENUE:	Christchurch	VENUE:	Dunedin
DATE:	25th Feb-1st March 1966	DATE:	4th-8th March 1966
TOSS WON BY:	England	TOSS WON BY:	New Zealand
RESULT:	Match drawn	RESULT:	Match drawn

Left: No. 426 1st Test — Christchurch

ENGLAND	1st innings		2nd innings	
G Boycott	c Petrie b Motz	4	run out	4
WE Russell	b Motz	30	b Bartlett	25
JH Edrich	c Bartlett b Motz	2	lbw b Cunis	2
MC Cowdrey	c Bilby b Cunis	0	c Pollard b Motz	21
MJK Smith*	c Puna b Pollard	54	c Bilby b Puna	87
PH Parfitt	c Congdon b Bartlett	54	not out	46
JM Parks+	c Petrie b Chapple	30	not out	4
DA Allen	c Chapple b Bartlett	88		
DJ Brown	b Cunis	44		
K Higgs	not out	8		
IJ Jones	b Bartlett	0		
Extras	(6b, 6lb, 0w, 16nb)	28	(4b, 1lb, 0w, 7nb)	12
Total	127.2 overs	**342**	67 overs	**201**

1st innings FoW: 19, 28, 47, 47, 160, 160, 209, 316, 342, 342
2nd innings FoW: 18, 32, 48, 68, 193

RC Motz	31	9	83	3	20	6	38	1
GA Bartlett	33.2	6	63	3	14	2	44	1
RS Cunis	31	9	63	2	19	3	58	1
N Puna	18	6	54	0	14	6	49	1
ME Chapple	9	3	24	1				
V Pollard	5	1	27	1				

NEW ZEALAND	1st innings		2nd innings	
GP Bilby	c Parks b Higgs	28	c Parks b Brown	3
M Shrimpton	c Parks b Brown	11	c Smith b Allen	13
BE Congdon	c Smith b Jones	104	c Cowdrey b Higgs	4
BW Sinclair	c & b Higgs	23	c Parks b Higgs	0
V Pollard	lbw b Higgs	23	not out	6
ME Chapple*	c Cowdrey b Jones	15	lbw b Higgs	1
GA Bartlett	c Parks b Brown	0	c Parks b Higgs	0
EC Petrie+	c Parks b Brown	55	c Brown b Parfitt	0
RC Motz	c Parks b Jones	58	c Russell b Parfitt	2
RS Cunis	not out	8	not out	16
N Puna	c Smith b Jones	1		
Extras	(7b, 13lb, 0w, 1nb)	21	(2b, 1lb, 0w, 0nb)	3
Total	143.4 overs	**347**	48 overs	**48**

1st innings FoW: 39, 41, 112, 181, 202, 203, 237, 326, 344, 347
2nd innings FoW: 5, 19, 21, 21, 22, 22, 22, 32

DJ Brown	30	3	80	3	4	2	6	1
IJ Jones	28.4	9	71	4	7	3	13	0
K Higgs	30	6	51	3	9	7	5	4
DA Allen	40	14	80	0	19	15	8	1
G Boycott	12	6	30	0				
PH Parfitt	3	0	14	0	6	3	5	2
JM Parks					3	1	8	0

Right: No. 427 2nd Test — Dunedin

NEW ZEALAND	1st innings		2nd innings	
GP Bilby	c Murray b Jones	3	c Parfitt b Higgs	21
M Shrimpton	c Boycott b Higgs	38	b Higgs	2
BE Congdon	c Murray b Jones	0	b Parfitt	19
BW Sinclair*	b Knight	33	c Knight b Jones	39
V Pollard	c Murray b Higgs	8	c Smith b Allen	3
RW Morgan	c Murray b Higgs	0	b Allen	0
GA Bartlett	c Parfitt b Allen	6	c Knight b Allen	4
EC Petrie+	c Smith b Jones	28	not out	13
RC Motz	c Higgs b Knight	57	b Jones	1
RS Cunis	c Boycott b Allen	8	lbw b Allen	9
N Puna	not out	3	not out	18
Extras	(4b, 4lb, 0w, 0nb)	8	(10b, 6lb, 0w, 2nb)	18
Total	105.4 overs	**192**	82 overs	**147**

1st innings FoW: 4, 6, 66, 83, 83, 92, 100, 179, 181, 192
2nd innings FoW: 8, 27, 66, 75, 75, 79, 100, 102, 111

IJ Jones	26	11	46	3	15	4	32	2
K Higgs	20	6	29	3	13	7	12	2
BR Knight	32	14	41	2	3	1	3	0
DA Allen	27.4	9	68	2	33	17	46	4
PH Parfitt					17	6	30	1
JH Edrich					1	0	6	0

ENGLAND	1st innings		2nd innings	
G Boycott	b Bartlett	5		
WE Russell	b Motz	11		
JH Edrich	c Bilby b Cunis	36		
MC Cowdrey	not out	89		
MJK Smith*	c Pollard b Bartlett	20		
PH Parfitt	c Pollard b Puna	4		
JT Murray+	c Sinclair b Puna	50		
BR Knight	c Bartlett b Motz	12		
DA Allen	b Cunis	9		
K Higgs	not out	0		
IJ Jones				
Extras	(4b, 6lb, 0w, 8nb)	18		
Total	104 overs	**254**		

1st innings FoW: 9, 32, 72, 103, 119, 200, 213, 241

RC Motz	32	7	76	2
GA Bartlett	29	4	70	2
RS Cunis	28	7	49	2
N Puna	14	2	40	2
V Pollard	1	0	1	0

No. 428: 3rd Test	No. 429: 1st Test
VENUE: Auckland	VENUE: Old Trafford
DATE: 11th-15th March 1966	DATE: 2nd-4th June 1966
TOSS WON BY: New Zealand	TOSS WON BY: West Indies
RESULT: Match drawn	RESULT: WI won by an innings and 40 runs

NEW ZEALAND 1st innings / 2nd innings

Batsman	1st innings		2nd innings	
TW Jarvis	c Parks b Jones	39	c Parks b Jones	0
M Shrimpton	b Brown	6	lbw b Brown	0
BE Congdon	lbw b Higgs	64	run out	23
BW Sinclair*	c Russell b Jones	114	b Higgs	9
RW Morgan	c Smith b Allen	5	lbw b Knight	25
V Pollard	c Knight b Allen	2	c Parks b Jones	25
EC Petrie+	c Smith b Higgs	12	c Smith b Jones	14
RC Motz	c Jones b Allen	16	b Higgs	6
BR Taylor	b Allen	18	b Higgs	6
RS Cunis	not out	6	c (sub) b Allen	8
N Puna	c Russell b Allen	7	not out	2
Extras	(1b, 4lb, 0w, 2nb)	7	(2b, 7lb, 0w, 2nb)	11
	132.5 overs		102.4 overs	
Total		**296**		**129**

1st innings FoW: 22, 99, 142, 153, 189, 237, 262, 264, 288, 296
2nd innings FoW: 0, 0, 20, 48, 68, 88, 109, 118, 121, 129

Bowler								
DJ Brown	18	6	32	1	8.1	3	8	1
IJ Jones	21	4	52	2	25	9	28	3
K Higgs	28	13	33	2	28	11	27	3
DA Allen	47.5	12	123	5	23.3	7	34	1
BR Knight	16	7	40	0	18	9	21	1
PH Parfitt	2	0	9	0				

WEST INDIES 1st innings / 2nd innings

Batsman	1st innings		2nd innings
CC Hunte	c Smith b Higgs	135	
McMorris	c Russell b Higgs	11	
RB Kanhai	b Higgs	0	
BF Butcher	c Parks b Titmus	44	
SM Nurse	b Titmus	49	
GStA Sobers*	c Cowdrey b Titmus	161	
DAJ Holford	c Smith b Allen	32	
DW Allan+	lbw b Titmus	1	
CC Griffith	lbw b Titmus	30	
WW Hall	b Allen	1	
LR Gibbs	not out	1	
Extras	(8b, 10lb, 0w, 1nb)	19	
	153.1 overs		
Total		**484**	

1st innings FoW: 38, 42, 116, 215, 283, 410, 411, 471, 482, 484

Bowler				
IJ Jones	28	6	100	0
DJ Brown	28	4	84	0
K Higgs	31	5	94	3
DA Allen	31.1	8	104	2
FJ Titmus	35	10	83	5

ENGLAND 1st innings / 2nd innings (vs New Zealand)

Batsman	1st innings		2nd innings	
PH Parfitt	b Taylor	3	b Taylor	30
WE Russell	lbw b Motz	56	c Petrie b Taylor	1
MC Cowdrey	run out	59	lbw b Puna	27
MJK Smith*	b Taylor	18	lbw b Cunis	30
JM Parks+	lbw b Taylor	38	not out	45
BR Knight	c Taylor b Pollard	25	not out	13
DA Allen	not out	7		
DJ Brown	b Pollard	0		
K Higgs	c Petrie b Pollard	0		
IJ Jones	b Cunis	0		
JH Edrich	absent hurt			
Extras	(11b, 3lb, 0w, 2nb)	16	(4b, 4lb, 0w, 5nb)	13
	88.5 overs		75 overs	
Total		**222**		**159**

1st innings FoW: 3, 121, 128, 175, 195, 215, 215, 219, 222
2nd innings FoW: 2, 50, 79, 112

Bowler								
RC Motz	15	4	42	1	16	1	32	0
BR Taylor	21	6	46	3	12	4	20	2
RS Cunis	25.5	8	45	1	18	5	33	1
N Puna	22	2	70	0	12	4	27	1
V Pollard	5	2	3	3	14	3	30	0
MJF Shrimpton					2	1	1	0
TW Jarvis					1	0	3	0

ENGLAND 1st innings / 2nd innings (vs West Indies)

Batsman	1st innings		2nd innings	
C Milburn	run out	0	b Gibbs	94
WE Russell	c Sobers b Gibbs	26	b Griffith	20
KF Barrington	c & b Griffith	5	c Nurse b Holford	13
MC Cowdrey	c & b Gibbs	12	c Butcher b Sobers	69
MJK Smith*	c Butcher b Gibbs	5	b Gibbs	6
JM Parks+	c Nurse b Holford	43	c & b Sobers	11
FJ Titmus	b Holford	15	c Butcher b Sobers	12
DA Allen	c Sobers b Gibbs	37	c Allan b Gibbs	1
DJ Brown	b Gibbs	14	c Sobers b Gibbs	10
K Higgs	c Sobers b Holford	1	st Allan b Gibbs	5
IJ Jones	not out	0	not out	0
Extras	(1b, 4lb, 0w, 4nb)	9	(11b, 1lb, 0w, 7nb)	19
	74.1 overs		108 overs	
Total		**167**		**277**

1st innings FoW: 11, 24, 42, 48, 65, 85, 143, 153, 163, 167
2nd innings FoW: 53, 142, 166, 184, 203, 217, 218, 268, 276, 277

Bowler								
WW Hall	14	6	43	0	5	0	28	0
CC Griffith	10	3	28	1	6	1	25	1
GStA Sobers	7	1	16	0	42	11	87	3
LR Gibbs	28.1	13	37	5	41	16	69	5
DAJ Holford	15	4	34	3	14	2	49	1

West Indies | West Indies

No. 430: 2nd Test
VENUE: Lord's
DATE: 16th-21st June 1966
TOSS WON BY: West Indies
RESULT: Match drawn

No. 431: 3rd Test
VENUE: Trent Bridge
DATE: 30th June-5th July 1966
TOSS WON BY: West Indies
RESULT: West Indies won by 139 runs

No. 430: 2nd Test — Lord's

WEST INDIES 1st innings

Batsman	How out	Runs	2nd innings	Runs
CC Hunte	c Parks b Higgs	18	c Milburn b Knight	13
MC Carew	c Parks b Higgs	2	c Knight b Higgs	0
RB Kanhai	c Titmus b Higgs	25	c Parks b Knight	40
BF Butcher	c Milburn b Knight	49	lbw b Higgs	3
SM Nurse	b D'Oliveira	64	c Parks b D'Oliveira	35
GStA Sobers*	lbw b Knight	46	not out	163
DAJ Holford	b Jones	26	not out	105
DW Allan+	c Titmus b Higgs	13		
CC Griffith	lbw b Higgs	5		
WW Hall	not out	8		
LR Gibbs	c Parks b Higgs	4		
Extras	(2b, 7lb, 0w, 0nb)	9	(0b, 8lb, 0w, 2nb)	10
Total	94 overs	**269**	133 overs	**369**

1st innings FoW: 8, 42, 53, 119, 205, 213, 252. 252, 261, 269
2nd innings FoW: 2, 22, 25, 91, 95

Bowler	O	M	R	W	O	M	R	W
IJ Jones	21	3	64	1	25	2	95	0
K Higgs	33	9	91	6	34	5	82	2
BR Knight	21	0	63	2	30	3	106	2
FJ Titmus	5	0	18	0	19	3	30	0
BL D'Oliveira	14	5	24	1	25	7	46	1

ENGLAND 1st innings

Batsman	How out	Runs	2nd innings	Runs
G Boycott	c Griffith b Gibbs	60	c Allan b Griffith	25
C Milburn	lbw b Hall	6	not out	126
TW Graveney	c Allan b Hall	96	b Griffith	5
KF Barrington	b Sobers	19	c Allan b Hall	5
MC Cowdrey*	c Gibbs b Hall	9	b Hall	0
JM Parks+	lbw b Carew	91	not out	30
BL D'Oliveira	run out	27		
BR Knight	b Griffith	6		
FJ Titmus	c Allan b Hall	6		
K Higgs	c Holford b Gibbs	13		
IJ Jones	not out	0		
Extras	(7b, 10lb, 0w, 5nb)	22	(4b, 2lb, 0w, 0nb)	6
Total	143.3 overs	**355**	55 overs	**197**

1st innings FoW: 8, 123, 164, 198, 203, 251, 266, 296, 355, 355
2nd innings FoW: 37, 43, 67, 67

Bowler	O	M	R	W	O	M	R	W
GStA Sobers	39	12	89	1	8	4	8	0
WW Hall	36	2	106	4	14	1	65	2
CC Griffith	28	4	79	1	11	2	43	2
LR Gibbs	37.3	18	48	2	13	4	40	0
MC Carew	3	0	11	1				
DAJ Holford					9	1	35	0

No. 431: 3rd Test — Trent Bridge

WEST INDIES 1st innings

Batsman	How out	Runs	2nd innings	Runs
CC Hunte	lbw b Higgs	9	c Graveney b D'Oliveira	12
PD Lashley	c Parks b Snow	49	lbw b D'Oliveira	23
RB Kanhai	c Underwood b Higgs	32	c Cowdrey b Higgs	63
BF Butcher	b Snow	5	not out	209
SM Nurse	c Illingworth b Snow	93	lbw b Higgs	53
GStA Sobers*	c Parks b Snow	3	c Underwood b Higgs	94
DAJ Holford	lbw b D'Oliveira	11	not out	17
JL Hendriks+	b D'Oliveira	2		
CC Griffith	c Cowdrey b Higgs	14		
WW Hall	b Higgs	12		
LR Gibbs	not out	0		
Extras	(3b, 2lb, 0w, 0nb)	5	(0b, 6lb, 5w, 0nb)	11
Total	90.4 overs	**235**	178 overs	**482**

1st innings FoW: 19, 68, 80, 140, 144, 180, 190, 215, 228, 235
2nd innings FoW: 29, 65, 175, 282, 455

Bowler	O	M	R	W	O	M	R	W
JA Snow	25	7	82	4	38	10	117	0
K Higgs	25.4	3	71	4	38	6	109	3
BL D'Oliveira	30	14	51	2	34	8	77	2
DL Underwood	2	1	5	0	43	15	86	0
R Illingworth	8	1	21	0	25	7	82	0

ENGLAND 1st innings

Batsman	How out	Runs	2nd innings	Runs
G Boycott	lbw b Sobers	0	c Sobers b Griffith	71
C Milburn	c Sobers b Hall	7	c Griffith b Hall	12
WE Russell	b Hall	4	c Sobers b Gibbs	13
TW Graveney	b Holford b Sobers	109	c Hendriks b Griffith	32
MC Cowdrey*	c Hendriks b Griffith	96	c Sobers b Gibbs	32
JM Parks+	c Butcher b Sobers	11	c Lashley b Hall	7
BL D'Oliveira	b Hall	76	lbw b Griffith	54
R Illingworth	c Lashley b Griffith	0	c Lashley b Sobers	4
K Higgs	c Lashley b Sobers	5	c Sobers b Gibbs	4
JA Snow	b Hall	0	b Griffith	3
DL Underw'd	not out	12	not out	10
Extras	(0b, 2lb, 0w, 3nb)	5	(8b, 2lb, 0w, 3nb)	13
Total	134.3 overs	**325**	108.3 overs	**253**

1st innings FoW: 0, 10, 13, 182, 221, 238, 247, 255, 260, 325
2nd innings FoW: 32, 71, 125, 132, 142, 176, 181, 222, 240, 253

Bowler	O	M	R	W	O	M	R	W
GStA Sobers	49	12	90	4	31	6	71	1
WW Hall	34.3	8	105	4	16	3	52	2
CC Griffith	20	5	62	2	13.3	3	34	4
LR Gibbs	23	9	40	0	48	16	83	3
DAJ Holford	8	2	23	0				

No. 432:	4th Test
VENUE:	Headingley
DATE:	4th-8th August 1966
TOSS WON BY:	West Indies
RESULT:	WI won by an innings and 55 runs

WEST INDIES 1st innings   **2nd innings**

CC Hunte	b Snow	48	
PD Lashley	b Higgs	9	
RB Kanhai	c Graveney b Underw'd	45	
BF Butcher	c Parks b Higgs	38	
SM Nurse	c Titmus b Snow	137	
GStA Sobers*	b Barber	174	
DAJ Holford	b Higgs	24	
CC Griffith	b Higgs	0	
JL Hendriks+	not out	9	
WW Hall	b Snow	1	
LR Gibbs	not out	2	
Extras	(1b, 12lb, 0w, 0nb)	13	
	164 overs		
Total		**500**	

1st innings FoW: 37, 102, 122, 154, 419, 467, 467, 489, 491

JA Snow	42	6	146	3
K Higgs	43	11	94	4
BL D'Oliveira	19	3	52	0
FJ Titmus	22	7	59	0
DL Underwood	24	9	81	1
RW Barber	14	2	55	1

ENGLAND   1st innings   **2nd innings**

G Boycott	c Holford b Hall	12	c Hendriks b Lashley	14
RW Barber	c Hendriks b Griffith	6	b Sobers	55
C Milburn	not out	29	c Butcher b Sobers	7
TW Graveney	b Hall	8	b Gibbs	19
MC Cowdrey*	b Hall	17	lbw b Gibbs	12
BL D'Oliveira	c Hall b Griffith	88	c Nurse b Gibbs	16
JM Parks+	lbw b Sobers	2	b Gibbs	42
FJ Titmus	c Hendriks b Sobers	6	b Gibbs	22
K Higgs	c Nurse b Sobers	49	c Hunte b Sobers	7
DL Underw'd	c Gibbs b Sobers	0	c Kanhai b Gibbs	0
JA Snow	c Holford b Sobers	0	not out	0
Extras	(12b, 11lb, 0w, 0nb)	23	(8b, 1lb, 0w, 2nb)	11
	78.3 overs		71.1 overs	
Total		**240**		**205**

1st innings FoW: 10, 18, 42, 49, 63, 83, 179, 238, 240, 240
2nd innings FoW: 28, 70 , 84, 109, 128, 133, 184, 205, 205, 205

WW Hall	17	5	47	3		8	2	24	0
CC Griffith	12	2	37	2		12	0	52	0
GStA Sobers	19.3	4	41	5		20.1	5	39	3
LR Gibbs	20	5	49	0		19	6	39	6
DAJ Holford	10	3	43	0		9	0	39	0
PD Lashley						3	2	1	1

No. 433:	5th Test
VENUE:	The Oval
DATE:	18th-22nd August 1966
TOSS WON BY:	West Indies
RESULT:	Eng won by an innings and 34 runs

WEST INDIES 1st innings   **2nd innings**

CC Hunte	b Higgs	1	c Murray b Snow	7
McMorris	b Snow	14	c Murray b Snow	1
RB Kanhai	c Graveney b Illingworth	104	b D'Oliveira	15
BF Butcher	c Illingworth b Close	12	c Barber b Illingworth	60
SM Nurse	c Graveney b D'Oliveira	0	c Edrich b Barber	70
GStA Sobers*	c Graveney b Barber	81	run out	7
DAJ Holford	c D'Oliveira b Illingworth	5	c Close b Snow	0
JL Hendriks+	b Barber	0	b Higgs	0
CC Griffith	c Higgs b Barber	4	not out	29
WW Hall	not out	30	c D'Oliveira b Illing'th	17
LR Gibbs	c Murray b Snow	12	c & b Barber	3
Extras	(1b, 3lb, 0w, 1nb)	5	(1b, 14lb, 0w, 1nb)	16
	97.5 overs		85.1 overs	
Total		**268**		**225**

1st innings FoW: 1, 56, 73, 74, 196, 218, 218, 223, 223, 268
2nd innings FoW: 5, 12, 50, 107, 137, 137, 142, 168, 204, 225

JA Snow	20.5	1	66	2		13	5	40	3
K Higgs	17	4	52	1		15	6	18	1
BL D'Oliveira	21	7	35	1		17	4	44	1
DB Close	9	2	21	1		3	1	7	0
RW Barber	15	3	49	3		22.1	2	78	2
R Illingworth	15	7	40	2		15	9	22	2

ENGLAND   1st innings   **2nd innings**

G Boycott	b Hall	4	
RW Barber	c Nurse b Sobers	36	
JH Edrich	c Hendriks b Sobers	35	
TW Graveney	run out	165	
DL Amiss	lbw b Hall	17	
BL D'Oliveira	b Hall	4	
DB Close*	run out	4	
R Illingworth	c Hendriks b Griffith	3	
JT Murray+	lbw b Sobers	112	
K Higgs	c & b Holford	63	
JA Snow	not out	59	
Extras	(8b, 14lb, 0w, 3nb)	25	
	199.5 overs		
Total		**527**	

1st innings FoW: 6, 72, 85, 126, 130, 150, 166, 383, 399, 527

WW Hall	31	8	85	3
CC Griffith	32	7	78	1
GStA Sobers	54	23	104	3
DAJ Holford	25.5	1	79	1
LR Gibbs	44	16	115	0
CC Hunte	13	2	41	0

India

ENGLAND	1st innings		2nd innings	
JH Edrich	c Engineer b Surti	1	c Wadekar b Chan'har	22
G Boycott	not out	246	c Engineer b Chan'har	46
KF Barrington	run out	93	b Chandrasekhar	14
TW Graveney	c (sub) b Chan'har	59	not out	24
BL D'Oliveira	c (sub) b Chan'har	109	c (sub) b Prasanna	4
DB Close*	not out	22	not out	12
JT Murray+				
R Illingworth				
K Higgs				
JA Snow				
RNS Hobbs				
Extras	(8b, 12lb, 0w, 0nb)	20	(3b, 1lb, 0w, 0nb)	4
	183 overs		47.3 overs	
Total		**550**		**126**

1st innings FoW: 7, 146, 253, 505
2nd innings FoW: 58, 78, 87, 92

S Guha	43	10	105	0		5	0	10	0
RF Surti	11	2	25	1					
BS Chan'har	45	9	121	2		19	8	50	3
BS Bedi	15	8	32	0					
EAS Prasanna	59	8	187	0		21.3	5	54	1
Pataudi jr	4	1	13	0					
AL Wadekar	1	0	9	0		2	0	8	0
Hanumant Singh	3	0	27	0					
RC Saxena	2	0	11	0					

INDIA	1st innings		2nd innings	
FM Engineer+	c & b Illingworth	42	c & b Close	87
RC Saxena	b D'Oliveira	9	c Murray b Snow	5
AL Wadekar	run out	0	c Close b Illingworth	91
CG Borde	b Snow	8	b Illingworth	33
Hanumant S'h	c D'Oliveira b Illing'th	9	c D'Oliveira b Illing'th	73
Pataudi	c Barrington b Hobbs	64	b Illingworth	148
EAS Prasanna	c Murray b Illingworth	0	b Snow	16
S Guha	b Snow	4	lbw b Close	19
RF Surti	c & b Hobbs	22	b Higgs	1
BS Bedi	lbw b Hobbs	0	c Snow b Hobbs	14
BS Chan'har	not out	0	not out	0
Extras	(0b, 6lb, 0w, 0nb)	6	(10b, 13lb, 0w, 0nb)	23
	87.2 overs		209.2 overs	
Total		**164**		**510**

1st innings FoW: 39, 40, 59, 59, 81, 81, 92, 151, 151, 164
2nd innings FoW: 5, 173, 217, 228, 362, 388, 448, 469, 506, 510

JA Snow	17	7	34	2		41	11	108	2
K Higgs	14	8	19	0		24	3	71	1
BL D'Oliveira	9	4	29	1		11	5	22	0
RNS Hobbs	22.2	9	45	3		45.2	13	100	1
R Illingworth	22	11	31	3		58	26	100	4
DB Close	3	3	0	0		21	5	48	2
KF Barrington						9	1	38	0

India

INDIA	1st innings		2nd innings	
DN Sardesai	c Murray b Illingworth	28	c Amiss b Snow	8
FM Engineer+	c Murray b Brown	8	lbw b Illingworth	47
AL Wadekar	c Illing'th b D'Oliveira	57	b Illingworth	19
CG Borde	b Snow	0	c Snow b Close	1
Pataudi	c Murray b Brown	5	c Graveney b Close	5
RF Surti	c Murray b D'Oliveira	6	c D'Oliveira b Illing'th	0
V Subramanya	c Murray b Brown	0	c Edrich b Illing'th	1
BK Kunderan	c Murray b Snow	20	c D'Oliveira b Illing'th	0
EAS Prasanna	run out	17	b Illingworth	11
BS Bedi	c Amiss b Snow	5	not out	3
BS Chan'har	not out	2	absent hurt	0
Extras	(2b, 2lb, 0w, 0nb)	4	(11b, 4lb, 0w, 0nb)	15
	55.4 overs		56.3 overs	
Total		**152**		**110**

1st innings FoW: 12, 24, 29, 45, 58, 102, 112, 144, 145, 152
2nd innings FoW: 8, 60, 67, 79, 80, 86, 90, 101, 110

JA Snow	20.4	5	49	3		8	4	12	1
DJ Brown	18	3	61	3		5	2	10	0
BL D'Oliveira	15	6	38	2					
R Illingworth	2	2	0	1		22.3	12	29	6
RNS Hobbs						6	1	16	0
DB Close						15	5	28	2

ENGLAND	1st innings		2nd innings	
JH Edrich	c & b Surti	12		
KF Barrington	b Chandrasekhar	97		
DL Amiss	b Chandrasekhar	29		
TW Graveney	st Engineer b Bedi	151		
BL D'Oliveira	c & b Chandrasekhar	33		
DB Close*	c Borde b Prasanna	7		
JT Murray+	b Chandrasekhar	7		
R Illingworth	lbw b Chandrasekhar	4		
RNS Hobbs	b Bedi	7		
DJ Brown	c Pataudi b Bedi	5		
JA Snow	not out	8		
Extras	(5b, 18lb, 1w, 2nb)	26		
	154.2 overs			
Total		**386**		

1st innings FoW: 46, 107, 185, 307, 334, 359, 365, 372, 372, 386

RF Surti	31	10	67	1
V Subramanya	7	1	20	0
BS Chandrasekhar	53	9	127	5
BS Bedi	31.2	13	68	3
EAS Prasanna	32	5	78	1

	India		Pakistan
No. 436:	3rd Test	No. 437:	1st Test
VENUE:	Edgbaston	VENUE:	Lord's
DATE:	13th-15th July 1967	DATE:	27th July-1st August 1967
TOSS WON BY:	England	TOSS WON BY:	England
RESULT:	England won by 132 runs	RESULT:	Match drawn

India match

ENGLAND	1st innings		2nd innings	
G Boycott	st Engineer b Bedi	25	b Subramanya	6
C Milburn	c Wadekar b Chan'har	40	b Bedi	15
KF Barrington	c Wadekar b Prasanna	75	c Kunderan b Chan'har	13
TW Graveney	c Venk'van b Chan'har	10	c Subra'ya b Prasanna	17
DL Amiss	c Wadekar b Venk'van	5	c Wadekar b Prasanna	45
DB Close*	c Subra'ya b Prasanna	26	c Chan'har b Prasanna	47
JT Murray+	c Subra'ya b Chan'har	77	b Bedi	4
R Illingworth	c Wadekar b Prasanna	2	c Pataudi b Prasanna	10
DJ Brown	run out	3	not out	29
JA Snow	c Engineer b Bedi	10	c Borde b Chan'har	9
RNS Hobbs	not out	15	c Prasanna b Chan'har	2
Extras	(5b, 5lb, 0w, 0nb)	10	(4b, 2lb, 0w, 0nb)	6
Total		298		203
	106 overs		76.5 overs	

1st innings FoW: 63, 67, 89, 112, 182, 183, 186, 191, 241, 298
2nd innings FoW: 6, 32, 34, 66, 144, 149, 149, 179, 193, 203

V Subramanya	10	2	28	0		4	0	22	1
BK Kunderan	4	0	13	0					
BS Bedi	27	6	76	2		24	9	60	2
BS Chan'har	32	8	94	3		20.5	6	43	3
S Venk'van	13	3	26	1		2	1	4	0
EAS Prasanna	20	5	51	3		24	9	60	4
Pataudi jr						2	0	8	0

INDIA	1st innings		2nd innings	
FM Engineer+	c Graveney b Brown	23	c Barrington b Hobbs	28
BK Kunderan	b Brown	2	c Murray b Close	33
AL Wadekar	c Amiss b Snow	5	c Boycott b Illingworth	70
CG Borde	b Snow	8	b Illingworth	10
Pataudi*	b Brown	0	c Hobbs b Close	47
Hanumant S'h	c Amiss b Illingworth	15	c Milburn b Illingworth	6
V Subramanya	b Hobbs	10	c Milburn b Illingworth	4
S Venk'van	not out	19	c Hobbs b Close	17
EAS Prasanna	b Illingworth	1	b Hobbs	15
BS Bedi	c & b Hobbs	1	not out	15
BS Chan'har	st Murray b Hobbs	0	c Boycott b Close	22
Extras	(4b, 2lb, 0w, 2nb)	8	(5b, 5lb, 0w, 0nb)	10
Total		92		277
	36.3 overs		112.4 overs	

1st innings FoW: 9, 18, 35, 35, 41, 66, 72, 73, 82, 92
2nd innings FoW: 48, 91, 102, 185, 201, 203, 207, 226, 240, 277

JA Snow	12	3	28	2		14	0	33	0
DJ Brown	11	6	17	3		2	1	1	0
R Illingworth	7	4	14	2		43	13	92	4
RNS Hobbs	6.3	1	25	3		32	10	73	2
DB Close						21.4	7	68	4

Pakistan match

ENGLAND	1st innings		2nd innings	
C Milburn	c Wasim b Asif	3	c Asif b Majid	32
WE Russell	b Intikhab	43	b Majid	12
KF Barrington	c Wasim b Asif	148	b Intikhab	14
TW Graveney	b Salim	81	c Khalid b Asif	30
BL D'Oliveira	c Intikhab b Mushtaq	59	not out	81
DB Close*	c (sub) b Salim	4	st Wasim b Ul-Ghani	36
JT Murray+	b Salim	0	c & b Nasim-Ul-Ghani	0
R Illingworth	b Asif	4	c & b Nasim-Ul-Ghani	9
K Higgs	lbw b Mushtaq	14	c Hanif b Intikhab	1
JA Snow	b Mushtaq	0	c Hanif b Mushtaq	7
RNS Hobbs	not out	1	not out	1
Extras	(0b, 5lb, 0w, 7nb)	12	(12b, 5lb, 0w, 1nb)	18
Total		369		241
	138.3 overs		90.3 overs	

1st innings FoW: 5, 82, 283, 283, 287, 287, 292, 352, 354, 369
2nd innings FoW: 33, 48, 76, 95, 199, 201, 215, 220, 239

Salim Altaf	33	6	74	3		0.3	0	4	0
Asif Iqbal	28	10	76	3		21	5	50	1
Khalid Ibadulla	3	0	5	0					
Majid Khan	11	2	28	0		10	1	32	2
Nasim-Ul-Ghani	12	1	36	0		13	3	32	3
Intikhab Alam	29	3	86	1		30	7	70	2
Mushtaq	11.3	3	23	3		16	4	35	1
Saeed Ahmed	11	3	29	0					

PAKISTAN	1st innings		2nd innings	
Khalid Ibadulla	b Higgs	8	c Close b Illingworth	32
Javed Burki	lbw b Higgs	31	c & b Barrington	13
Mushtaq	c Murray b Higgs	4	c Close b Barrington	5
Hanif	not out	187	not out	30
Majid Khan	c & b Hobbs	5	not out	6
Ul-Ghani	c D'Oliveira b Snow	2		
Saeed Ahmed	c Graveney b Snow	6		
Intikhab Alam	lbw b Illingworth	17		
Asif Iqbal	c Barrington b Illing'th	76		
Wasim Bari+	c Close b Barrington	13		
Salim Altaf	c Milburn b Snow	2		
Extras	(1b, 2lb, 0w, 0nb)	3	(1b, 1lb, 0w, 0nb)	2
Total		354		88
	182.1 overs		62 overs	

1st innings FoW: 19, 25, 67, 76, 91, 99, 139, 269, 310, 354
2nd innings FoW: 27, 39, 77

JA Snow	45.1	11	120	3		4	2	6	0
K Higgs	39	12	81	3		6	3	6	0
BL D'Oliveira	15	7	17	0		15	11	10	1
R Illingworth	31	14	48	2		16	9	28	0
RNS Hobbs	35	16	46	1		13	2	23	2
KF Barrington	11	1	29	1		8	5	13	0
DB Close	6	3	10	0					

No. 438: 2nd Test	No. 439: 3rd Test
VENUE: Trent Bridge	VENUE: The Oval
DATE: 10th-15th August 1967	DATE: 24th-28th August 1967
TOSS WON BY: Pakistan	TOSS WON BY: England
RESULT: England won by 10 wickets	RESULT: England won by 8 wickets

PAKISTAN 1st innings / 2nd innings (No. 438)

Batsman	1st innings		2nd innings	
Khalid Ibadullac	Knott b Higgs	2	c Knott b Close	5
Javed Burki	lbw b Arnold	1	c Knott b Higgs	3
Saeed Ahmed	c Knott b Arnold	44	c Arnold b Underwood	68
Mushtaq	b Higgs	29	c Close b Titmus	6
Hanif Moh'd	c Titmus b Underwood	16	c Knott b Higgs	4
Majid Khan	lbw b D'Oliveira	17	lbw b Underwood	0
Asif Iqbal	b Higgs	18	c Close b Underwood	5
Ul-Ghani	run out	11	c (sub) b Titmus	1
Intikhab Alam	c Knott b Arnold	0	c Knott b Underwood	16
Wasim Bari+	b Higgs	0	c Barrington b Underw'd	3
Niaz Ahmed	not out	0	not out	1
Extras	(0b, 1lb, 0w, 1nb)	2	(0b, 1lb, 0w, 1nb)	2
	69 overs		64 overs	
Total		**140**		**114**

1st innings FoW: 3, 21, 65, 82, 104, 116, 140, 140, 140, 140
2nd innings FoW: 4, 35, 60, 71, 76, 89, 93, 99, 113, 114

Bowler	O	M	R	W	O	M	R	W
GG Arnold	17	5	35	3	5	3	5	0
K Higgs	19	12	35	4	6	1	8	2
BL D'Oliveira	18	9	27	1	4	1	11	1
DB Close	3	0	12	0	23	11	36	2
FJ Titmus	7	3	12	0	26	8	52	5
DL Underwood	5	2	17	1				

ENGLAND 1st innings / 2nd innings (No. 438)

Batsman	1st innings		2nd innings	
G Boycott	b Asif	15	not out	1
MC Cowdrey	c Majid b Ul-Ghani	14	not out	2
KF Barrington	not out	109		
TW Graveney	c Niaz Ahmed b Khalid	28		
BL D'Oliveira	run out	7		
DB Close*	c Wasim b Niaz Ahmed	41		
FJ Titmus	lbw b Asif	13		
APE Knott+	c Hanif b Mushtaq	0		
GG Arnold	lbw b Niaz Ahmed	14		
K Higgs	not out	0		
DL Underw'd				
Extras	(3b, 3lb, 1w, 4nb)	11	(0b, 0lb, 0w, 0nb)	0
	134.3 overs		2.1 overs	
Total		**252**		**3**

1st innings FoW: 21, 31, 75, 92, 187, 213, 214, 251

Bowler	O	M	R	W	O	M	R	W
Asif Iqbal	39	10	72	2				
Niaz Ahmed	37	10	72	2				
Nasim-Ul-Ghani	8	2	20	1				
Saeed Ahmed	2	2	0	0	1	1	0	0
Intikhab Alam	7	2	19	0				
Khalid Ibadulla	32	13	42	1				
Mushtaq	9.3	3	16	1	1.1	0	3	0

PAKISTAN 1st innings / 2nd innings (No. 439)

Batsman	1st innings		2nd innings	
Hanif Moh'd*	b Higgs	3	b Titmus	12
Moh'd Ilyas	b Arnold	2	c Cowdrey b Higgs	1
Saeed Ahmed	b Arnold	38	c Knott b Higgs	0
Majid Khan	c Knott b Arnold	6	b Higgs	0
Mushtaq	lbw b Higgs	66	c Knott b Higgs	18
Javed Burki	c D'Oliveira b Titmus	27	c Knott b Higgs	0
Ghulam Abbas	c Underwood b Titmus	12	c D'Oliveira b Underw'd	17
Asif Iqbal	c Close b Arnold	26	b Underwood	7
Intikhab Alam	b Higgs	20	st Knott b Close	146
Wasim Bari+	c Knott b Arnold	1	b Titmus	51
Salim Altaf	not out	7	not out	0
Extras	(5b, 2lb, 0w, 1nb)	8	(1b, 1lb, 0w, 1nb)	3
	102 overs		101.1 overs	
Total		**216**		**255**

1st innings FoW: 3, 5, 17, 74, 138, 155, 182, 188, 194, 216
2nd innings FoW: 1, 5, 5, 26, 26, 41, 53, 65, 255, 255

Bowler	O	M	R	W	O	M	R	W
GG Arnold	29	9	58	5	17	5	49	0
K Higgs	29	10	61	3	20	7	58	5
BL D'Oliveira	17	6	41	0				
DB Close	5	1	15	0	1	0	4	1
FJ Titmus	13	6	21	2	29.1	8	64	2
DL Underwood	9	5	12	0	26	12	48	2
KF Barrington					8	2	29	0

ENGLAND 1st innings / 2nd innings (No. 439)

Batsman	1st innings		2nd innings	
MC Cowdrey	c Mushtaq b Majid	16	c Intikhab b Asif	9
DB Close*	c Wasim b Asif	6	b Asif	8
KF Barrington	c Wasim b Salim	142	not out	13
TW Graveney	c Majid b Intikhab	77	not out	3
DL Amiss	c Saeed b Asif	26		
BL D'Oliveira	c Mushtaq b Asif	3		
FJ Titmus	c (sub) b Mushtaq	65		
APE Knott+	c Ilyas b Mushtaq	28		
GG Arnold	c Majid b Mushtaq	59		
K Higgs	b Mushtaq Mohammad	7		
DL Underw'd	not out	2		
Extras	(0b, 4lb, 0w, 5nb)	9	(0b, 0lb, 0w, 1nb)	1
	167.4 overs		8.2 overs	
Total		**440**		**34**

1st innings FoW: 16, 35, 176, 270, 276, 276, 323, 416, 437, 440
2nd innings FoW: 17, 20

Bowler	O	M	R	W	O	M	R	W
Salim Altaf	40	14	94	1	2	1	8	0
Asif Iqbal	42	19	66	3	4	1	14	2
Majid Khan	10	0	29	1				
Mushtaq	26.4	7	80	4				
Saeed Ahmed	21	5	69	0	2	0	7	0
Intikhab Alam	28	3	93	1				
Hanif Mohammad					0.2	0	4	0

No. 440: 1st Test
VENUE: Port-of-Spain (Trinidad)
DATE: 19th-24th January 1968
TOSS WON BY: England
RESULT: Match drawn

ENGLAND	1st innings		2nd innings
G Boycott	lbw b Holford	68	
JH Edrich	c Murray b Gibbs	25	
MC Cowdrey*	c Murray b Griffith	72	
KF Barrington	c Griffith b Gibbs	143	
TW Graveney	b Gibbs	118	
JM Parks+	lbw b Sobers	42	
BL D'Oliveira	b Griffith	32	
FJ Titmus	lbw b Griffith	15	
DJ Brown	not out	22	
RNS Hobbs	c Butcher b Griffith	2	
IJ Jones	c Murray b Griffith	2	
Extras	(8b, 11lb, 1w, 7nb)	27	
	200.5 overs		
Total		**568**	

1st innings FoW: 80, 110, 244, 432, 471, 511, 527, 554, 566, 568

WW Hall	28	5	92	0
GStA Sobers	26	5	83	1
CC Griffith	29.5	13	69	5
LR Gibbs	63	15	147	3
DAJ Holford	43	1	121	1
CH Lloyd	8	3	17	0
GS Camacho	3	1	12	0

WEST INDIES	1st innings		2nd innings	
SM Nurse	c Graveney b Titmus	41	b Titmus	42
GS Camacho	c Graveney b Brown	22	c Graveney b Bar'ton	43
RB Kanhai	c Cowdrey b D'Oliveira	85	lbw b Brown	52
BF Butcher	lbw b Brown	14	c & b Hobbs	37
CH Lloyd	b Jones	118	c Titmus b Jones	2
GStA Sobers*	c Graveney b Barrington	17	b Titmus	1
DAJ Holford	run out	4	not out	33
DL Murray+	c D'Oliveira b Hobbs	16	lbw b Brown	0
CC Griffith	c Parks b Jones	18	b Brown	0
WW Hall	not out	10	not out	26
LR Gibbs	b Jones	1		
Extras	(4b, 6lb, 0w, 7nb)	17	(0b, 5lb, 0w, 2nb)	7
	135 overs		90 overs	
Total		**363**		**243**

1st innings FoW: 50, 102, 124, 240, 290, 294, 329, 352, 357, 363
2nd innings FoW: 70, 100, 164, 167, 178, 180, 180, 180

DJ Brown	22	3	65	2	14	4	27	3
IJ Jones	19	5	63	3	15	3	32	1
BL D'Oliveira	27	13	49	1	5	2	21	0
FJ Titmus	34	9	91	1	27	13	42	2
RNS Hobbs	15	1	34	1	13	2	44	1
KF Barrington	18	6	44	1	15	0	69	1
MC Cowdrey					1	0	1	0

No. 441: 2nd Test
VENUE: Kingston (Jamaica)
DATE: 8th-14th February 1968
TOSS WON BY: England
RESULT: Match drawn

ENGLAND	1st innings		2nd innings	
G Boycott	b Hall	17	b Sobers	0
JH Edrich	c Kanhai b Sobers	96	b Hall	6
MC Cowdrey*	c Murray b Gibbs	101	lbw b Sobers	0
KF Barrington	c & b Holford	63	lbw b Griffith	13
TW Graveney	b Hall	30	c Griffith b Gibbs	21
JM Parks+	c Sobers b Holford	3	lbw b Gibbs	3
BL D'Oliveira	st Murray b Holford	0	not out	13
FJ Titmus	lbw b Hall	19	c Camacho b Gibbs	4
DJ Brown	c Murray b Hall	14	b Sobers	0
JA Snow	b Griffith	10		
IJ Jones	not out	0		
Extras	(12b, 7lb, 0w, 4nb)	23	(8b, 0lb, 0w, 0nb)	8
	169.2 overs		38.5 overs	
Total		**376**		**68**

1st innings FoW: 49, 178, 279, 310, 318, 318, 351, 352, 376, 376
2nd innings FoW: 0, 0, 19, 19, 38, 51, 61, 68

WW Hall	27	5	63	4	3	2	3	1
CC Griffith	31.2	7	72	1	5	2	13	1
GStA Sobers	31	11	56	1	16.5	7	33	3
LR Gibbs	47	18	91	1	14	11	11	3
DAJ Holford	33	10	71	3				

WEST INDIES	1st innings		2nd innings	
GS Camacho	b Snow	5	b D'Oliveira	25
DL Murray+	c D'Oliveira b Brown	0	b Snow	73
RB Kanhai	c Graveney b Snow	26	c Edrich b Jones	36
SM Nurse	b Jones	22	c Parks b D'Oliveira	25
CH Lloyd	not out	34	b Brown	7
GStA Sobers*	lbw b Snow	0	not out	113
BF Butcher	c Parks b Snow	21	lbw b Titmus	35
DAJ Holford	c Parks b Snow	6	lbw b Brown	14
CC Griffith	c D'Oliveira b Snow	8	lbw b Jones	14
WW Hall	b Snow	0	c Parks b Jones	0
LR Gibbs	c Parks b Jones	0	not out	1
Extras	(12b, 5lb, 1w, 3nb)	21	(33b, 10lb, 0w, 5nb)	48
	48.1 overs		135 overs	
Total		**143**		**391**

1st innings FoW: 5, 5, 51, 80, 80, 120, 126, 142, 142, 143
2nd innings FoW: 102, 122, 164, 174, 204, 314, 351, 388, 388

DJ Brown	13	1	34	1	33	9	65	2
JA Snow	21	7	49	7	27	4	91	1
IJ Jones	14.1	4	39	2	30	4	90	3
BL D'Oliveira					32	12	51	2
FJ Titmus					7	2	32	1
KF Barrington					6	1	14	0

No. 442: 3rd Test
VENUE: Bridgetown (Barbados)
DATE: 29th Feb-5th March 1968
TOSS WON BY: West Indies
RESULT: Match drawn

No. 443: 4th Test
VENUE: Port-of-Spain (Trinidad)
DATE: 14th-19th March 1968
TOSS WON BY: West Indies
RESULT: England won by 7 wickets

WEST INDIES 1st innings / 2nd innings (3rd Test)

Batsman	1st innings		2nd innings	
SM Nurse	c Cowdrey b Brown	26	c Parks b Snow	19
GS Camacho	c Graveney b Bar'ton	57	lbw b Snow	18
RB Kanhai	c Parks b Snow	12	lbw b Snow	12
BF Butcher	lbw b Snow	86	run out	60
CH Lloyd	c & b Pocock	20	not out	113
GStA Sobers*	c Jones b Snow	68	b Brown	19
DAJ Holford	c Graveney b Snow	0	c Snow b Pocock	18
DL Murray+	c Parks b Brown	27	not out	8
CC Griffith	not out	16		
WW Hall	c Barrington b Snow	2		
LR Gibbs	b Jones	14		
Extras	(1b, 14lb, 0w, 6nb)	21	(8b, 3lb, 0w, 6nb)	17
Total	143.1 overs	**349**	53 overs	**284**

1st innings FoW: 54, 67, 163, 198, 252, 252, 315, 315, 319, 349
2nd innings FoW: 38, 49, 79, 180, 217, 274

Bowler	O	M	R	W		O	M	R	W
DJ Brown	32	10	66	2		11	0	61	1
JA Snow	35	11	86	5		10	2	39	3
BL D'Oliveira	19	5	36	0		4	0	19	0
PI Pocock	28	11	55	1		13	0	78	1
IJ Jones	21.1	3	56	1		11	3	53	0
KF Barrington	8	1	29	1		4	0	17	0

WEST INDIES 1st innings / 2nd innings (4th Test)

Batsman	1st innings		2nd innings	
GS Camacho	c Knott b Brown	87	c Graveney b Snow	31
MC Carew	c Lock b Brown	36	not out	40
SM Nurse	c Edrich b Barrington	136	run out	9
RB Kanhai	c Barrington b Lock	153	not out	2
CH Lloyd	b Jones	43		
GStA Sobers*	c Jones b Brown	48		
BF Butcher	not out	7		
WV Rodriguez	b Jones	0		
DL Murray+	not out	5		
CC Griffith				
LR Gibbs				
Extras	(0b, 6lb, 0w, 5nb)	11	(1b, 7lb, 0w, 2nb)	10
Total	133 overs	**526**	30 overs	**92**

1st innings FoW: 119, 142, 415, 421, 506, 513, 514
2nd innings FoW: 66, 88

Bowler	O	M	R	W		O	M	R	W
DJ Brown	27	2	107	3		10	2	33	0
JA Snow	20	3	68	0		9	0	29	1
IJ Jones	29	1	108	2		11	2	20	0
BL D'Oliveira	15	2	62	0					
GAR Lock	32	3	129	1					
KF Barrington	10	2	41	1					

ENGLAND 1st innings (3rd Test)

Batsman	1st innings		2nd innings
JH Edrich	c Murray b Griffith	146	
G Boycott	lbw b Sobers	90	
MC Cowdrey*	c Sobers b Griffith	1	
KF Barrington	c Butcher b Hall	17	
TW Graveney	c Sobers b Gibbs	55	
JM Parks+	lbw b Gibbs	0	
BL D'Oliveira	b Hall	51	
DJ Brown	b Griffith	1	
JA Snow	c Nurse b Gibbs	37	
PI Pocock	b Sobers	6	
IJ Jones	not out	1	
Extras	(16b, 9lb, 0w, 19nb)	44	
Total	180.5 overs	**449**	

1st innings FoW: 172, 174, 210, 319, 319, 349, 354, 411, 439, 449

Bowler	O	M	R	W
GStA Sobers	41	10	76	2
WW Hall	32	8	98	2
CC Griffith	24	6	71	3
LR Gibbs	47.5	16	98	3
DAJ Holford	32	9	52	0
CH Lloyd	3	0	10	0
SM Nurse	1	1	0	0

ENGLAND 1st innings / 2nd innings (4th Test)

Batsman	1st innings		2nd innings	
JH Edrich	c Lloyd b Carew	32	b Rodriguez	29
G Boycott	c Nurse b Rodriguez	62	not out	80
MC Cowdrey*	c Murray b Butcher	148	c Sobers b Gibbs	71
KF Barrington	lbw b Gibbs	48	b Gibbs	2
TW Graveney	c Murray b Rodriguez	30	not out	12
BL D'Oliveira	b Rodriguez	0		
APE Knott+	not out	69		
JA Snow	b Butcher	0		
DJ Brown	c Murray b Butcher	0		
GAR Lock	lbw b Butcher	3		
IJ Jones	b Butcher	1		
Extras	(13b, 11lb, 2w, 7nb)	33	(11b, 6lb, 0w, 4nb)	21
Total	175.4 overs	**404**	52.4 overs	**215**

1st innings FoW: 86, 112, 245, 260, 260, 373, 377, 377, 381, 404
2nd innings FoW: 55, 173, 182

Bowler	O	M	R	W		O	M	R	W
CC Griffith	3	1	7	0					
LR Gibbs	57	24	68	1		16.4	1	76	2
WV Rodriguez	35	4	145	3		10	1	34	1
MC Carew	25	18	23	1		7	2	19	0
BF Butcher	13.4	2	34	5		5	1	17	0
CH Lloyd	4	2	7	0					
SM Nurse	2	2	0	0					
GStA Sobers						14	0	48	0

	West Indies		Australia	
No.	444: 5th Test		445: 1st Test	
VENUE:	Georgetown (Guyana)		Old Trafford	
DATE:	28th March-3rd April 1968		6th-11th June 1968	
TOSS WON BY:	West Indies		Australia	
RESULT:	Match drawn		Australia won by 159 runs	

WEST INDIES 1st innings / 2nd innings

Batsman	1st innings		2nd innings	
SM Nurse	c Knott b Snow	17	lbw b Snow	49
GS Camacho	c & b Jones	14	c Graveney b Snow	26
RB Kanhai	c Edrich b Pocock	150	c Edrich b Jones	22
BF Butcher	run out	18	c Knott b Snow	1
GStA Sobers*	c Cowdrey b Bar'ton	152	not out	95
CH Lloyd	b Lock	31	c Lock b Pocock	18
DAJ Holford	lbw b Snow	1	c Boycott b Pocock	16
DL Murray+	c Knott b Lock	8	b Lock	3
LA King	b Snow	8	b Snow	20
WW Hall	not out	5	b Snow	7
LR Gibbs	b Snow	1	b Snow	0
Extras	(0b, 3lb, 2w, 4nb)	9	(1b, 2lb, 1w, 3nb)	7
Total	150.4 overs	414	66.2 overs	264

1st innings FoW: 29, 35, 72, 322, 385, 387, 399, 400, 412, 414
2nd innings FoW: 78, 84, 86, 133, 171, 201, 216, 252, 264, 264

JA Snow	27.4	2	82	4	15.2	0	60	6
IJ Jones	31	5	114	1	17	1	81	1
BL D'Oliveira	8	1	27	0	8	0	28	0
PI Pocock	38	11	78	1	17	1	66	2
GAR Lock	28	7	61	2	9	1	22	1
KF Barrington	18	4	43	1				

ENGLAND 1st innings / 2nd innings

Batsman	1st innings		2nd innings	
JH Edrich	c Murray b Sobers	0	c Gibbs b Sobers	6
G Boycott	c Murray b Hall	116	b Gibbs	30
MC Cowdrey*	lbw b Sobers	59	lbw b Gibbs	82
TW Graveney	c Murray b Hall	27	c Murray b Gibbs	0
KF Barrington	c Kanhai b Sobers	4	c Lloyd b Gibbs	0
BL D'Oliveira	c Nurse b Holford	27	c & b Gibbs	2
APE Knott+	lbw b Holford	7	not out	73
JA Snow	b Gibbs	0	lbw b Sobers	1
GAR Lock	b King	89	c King b Sobers	2
PI Pocock	c & b King	13	c Lloyd b Gibbs	0
IJ Jones	not out	0	not out	0
Extras	(12b, 14lb, 0w, 3nb)	29	(9b, 0lb, 1w, 0nb)	10
Total	163.2 overs	371	120 overs	206

1st innings FoW: 13, 185, 185, 194, 240, 252, 257, 259, 368, 371
2nd innings FoW: 33, 37, 37, 39, 41, 168, 198, 200, 206

GStA Sobers	37	15	72	3	31	16	53	3
WW Hall	19	3	71	2	13	6	26	0
LA King	38.2	11	79	2	9	1	11	0
DAJ Holford	31	10	54	2	17	9	37	0
LR Gibbs	33	9	59	1	40	20	60	6
BF Butcher	5	3	7	0	10	7	9	0

AUSTRALIA 1st innings / 2nd innings

Batsman	1st innings		2nd innings	
WM Lawry*	c Boycott b Barber	81	c Pocock b D'Oliveira	16
IR Redpath	lbw b Snow	8	lbw b Snow	8
RM Cowper	b Snow	0	c & b Pocock	37
KD Walters	lbw b Barber	81	lbw b Pocock	86
AP Sheahan	c D'Oliveira b Snow	88	c Graveney b Pocock	8
IM Chappell	run out	73	c Knott b Pocock	9
BN Jarman+	c & b Higgs	12	b Pocock	41
NJN Hawke	c Knott b Snow	5	c Edrich b Pocock	0
GD McKenzie	c Cowdrey b D'Oliveira	0	c Snow b Barber	0
JW Gleeson	c Knott b Higgs	0	run out	2
AN Connolly	not out	0	not out	2
Extras	(0b, 7lb, 0w, 2nb)	9	(2b, 9lb, 0w, 0nb)	11
Total	130.3 overs	357	88 overs	220

1st innings FoW: 29, 29, 173, 174, 326, 341, 351, 353, 357, 357
2nd innings FoW: 24 , 24, 106, 122, 140, 211, 211, 214, 214, 220

JA Snow	34	5	97	4	17	2	51	1
K Higgs	35.3	11	80	2	23	8	41	0
BL D'Oliveira	25	11	38	1	5	3	7	1
PI Pocock	25	5	77	0	33	10	79	6
RW Barber	11	0	56	2	10	1	31	1

ENGLAND 1st innings / 2nd innings

Batsman	1st innings		2nd innings	
JH Edrich	run out	49	c Jarman b Cowper	38
G Boycott	c Jarman b Cowper	35	c Redpath b McKenzie	11
MC Cowdrey*	c Lawry b McKenzie	4	c Jarman b McKenzie	11
TW Graveney	c McKenzie b Cowper	2	c Jarman b Gleeson	33
DL Amiss	c Cowper b McKenzie	0	b Cowper	0
RW Barber	c Sheahan b McKenzie	20	c Cowper b Hawke	46
BL D'Oliveira	b Connolly	9	not out	87
APE Knott+	c McKenzie b Cowper	5	lbw b Connolly	4
JA Snow	not out	18	c Lawry b Connolly	2
K Higgs	lbw b Cowper	2	c Jarman b Gleeson	0
PI Pocock	c Redpath b Gleeson	6	lbw b Gleeson	10
Extras	(9b, 3lb, 3w, 0nb)	15	(5b, 6lb, 0w, 0nb)	11
Total	104.3 overs	165	110 overs	253

1st innings FoW: 86, 87, 89, 90, 97, 120, 137, 137, 144, 165
2nd innings FoW: 13, 25, 91, 91, 106, 185, 214, 218, 219, 253

GD McKenzie	28	11	33	3	18	3	52	2
NJN Hawke	15	7	18	0	8	4	15	1
AN Connolly	28	15	26	1	13	4	35	2
JW Gleeson	6.3	2	21	1	30	14	44	3
RM Cowper	26	11	48	4	39	12	82	2
IM Chappell	1	0	4	0	2	0	14	0

Australia | Australia

No. 446: 2nd Test	No. 447: 3rd Test
VENUE: Lord's	VENUE: Edgbaston
DATE: 20th-25th June 1968	DATE: 11th-16th July 1968
TOSS WON BY: England	TOSS WON BY: England
RESULT: Match drawn	RESULT: Match drawn

ENGLAND 1st innings / 2nd innings (2nd Test)

Batsman	1st innings		2nd innings	
JH Edrich	c Cowper b McKenzie	7	c Brown b Snow	28
G Boycott	c Sheahan b McKenzie	49	b Underwood	53
C Milburn	c Walters b Gleeson	83	c Underw'd b Bar'ton	32
MC Cowdrey*	c Cowper b McKenzie	45	b Underwood	0
KF Barrington	c Jarman b Connolly	75	not out	0
TW Graveney	c Jarman b Connolly	14	not out	12
BR Knight	not out	27		
APE Knott+	run out	33		
JA Snow	not out	0		
DJ Brown				
DL Underw'd				
Extras	(7b, 5lb, 1w, 5nb)	18	(0b, 0lb, 0w, 2nb)	2
Total	144.3 overs	**351**	67 overs	**127**

1st innings FoW: 10, 142, 147, 244, 271, 330, 351
2nd innings FoW: 66, 93, 97, 115

Bowler	O	M	R	W		O	M	R	W
GD McKenzie	45	18	111	3					
NJN Hawke	35	7	82	0					
AN Connolly	26.3	8	55	2					
KD Walters	3	2	2	0					
RM Cowper	8	2	40	0					
JW Gleeson	27	11	43	1					

AUSTRALIA 1st innings / 2nd innings (2nd Test)

Batsman	1st innings		2nd innings
WM Lawry*	c Knott b Brown	0	
IR Redpath	c Cowdrey b Brown	4	
RM Cowper	c Graveney b Snow	8	
KD Walters	c Knight b Brown	26	
AP Sheahan	c Knott b Knight	6	
IM Chappell	lbw b Knight	7	
NJN Hawke	c Cowdrey b Knight	2	
GD McKenzie	b Brown	5	
JW Gleeson	c Cowdrey b Brown	14	
BN Jarman+	retired hurt	0	
AN Connolly	not out	0	
Extras	(0b, 2lb, 0w, 4nb)	6	
Total	33.4 overs	**78**	

1st innings FoW: 1, 12, 23, 46, 52, 58, 63, 78, 78

Bowler	O	M	R	W		O	M	R	W
JA Snow	9	5	14	1		12	5	30	1
DJ Brown	14	5	42	5		19	9	40	0
BR Knight	10.4	5	16	3		16	9	35	0
DL Underwood						18	15	8	2
KF Barrington						2	0	12	1

ENGLAND 1st innings / 2nd innings (3rd Test)

Batsman	1st innings		2nd innings	
JH Edrich	c Taber b Freeman	88	c Cowper b Freeman	64
G Boycott	lbw b Gleeson	36	c Taber b Connolly	31
MC Cowdrey*	b Freeman	104	not out	39
KF Barrington	lbw b Freeman	0	b Connolly	1
TW Graveney	b Connolly	96	not out	4
BR Knight	c Chappell b Connolly	6		
APE Knott+	b McKenzie	4		
R Illingworth	lbw b Gleeson	27		
DJ Brown	b Connolly	0		
JA Snow	c Connolly b Freeman	19		
DL Underw'd	not out	14		
Extras	(4b, 6lb, 1w, 4nb)	15	(0b, 2lb, 0w, 1nb)	3
Total	172.5 overs	**409**	42 overs	**142**

1st innings FoW: 80, 188, 189, 282, 293, 323, 374, 374, 376, 409
2nd innings FoW: 57, 131, 134

Bowler	O	M	R	W		O	M	R	W
GD McKenzie	47	14	115	1		18	1	57	0
EW Freeman	30.5	8	78	4		9	2	23	1
AN Connolly	35	8	84	3		15	3	59	2
JW Gleeson	46	19	84	2					
RM Cowper	7	1	25	0					
KD Walters	7	3	8	0					

AUSTRALIA 1st innings / 2nd innings (3rd Test)

Batsman	1st innings		2nd innings	
WM Lawry*	retired hurt	6	not out	25
IR Redpath	b Brown	0	lbw b Snow	22
RM Cowper	b Snow	57	not out	18
IM Chappell	b Knight	71		
KD Walters	c & b Underwood	46		
AP Sheahan	b Underwood	4		
HB Taber+	c Barrington b Illingworth	16		
EW Freeman	b Illingworth	6		
GD McKenzie	not out	0		
JW Gleeson	c Illingworth b Underwood	3		
AN Connolly	b Illingworth	0		
Extras	(1b, 10lb, 0w, 2nb)	13	(0b, 1lb, 0w, 2nb)	3
Total	91 overs	**222**	28.2 overs	**68**

1st innings FoW: 10, 121, 165, 176, 213, 213, 219, 222, 222
2nd innings FoW: 44

Bowler	O	M	R	W		O	M	R	W
JA Snow	17	3	46	1		9	1	32	1
DJ Brown	13	2	44	1		6	1	15	0
BR Knight	14	2	34	1					
DL Underwood	25	9	48	3		8	4	14	0
R Illingworth	22	10	37	3		5.2	2	4	0

No. 448: 4th Test

VENUE:	Headingley
DATE:	25th-30th July 1968
TOSS WON BY:	Australia
RESULT:	Match drawn

AUSTRALIA	1st innings		2nd innings	
RJ Inverarity	b Snow	8	lbw b Illingworth	34
RM Cowper	b Snow	27	st Knott b Illingworth	5
IR Redpath	b Illingworth	92	c Edrich b Snow	48
KD Walters	c Bar'ton b Underw'd	42	c Graveney b Snow	56
IM Chappell	b Brown	65	c Bar'ton b Underw'd	81
AP Sheahan	c Knott b Snow	38	st Knott b Illingworth	31
BN Jarman*+	c Dexter b Brown	10	st Knott b Illingworth	4
EW Freeman	b Underwood	21	b Illingworth	10
GD McKenzie	lbw b Underwood	5	c Snow b Illingworth	10
JW Gleeson	not out	2	c Knott b Underwood	7
AN Connolly	c Graveney b Underw'd	0	not out	0
Extras	(0b, 4lb, 0w, 1nb)	5	(13b, 8lb, 0w, 5nb)	26
Total	133.4 overs	315	154.1 overs	312

1st innings FoW: 10, 104, 152, 188, 248, 267, 307, 309, 315, 315
2nd innings FoW: 28, 81, 119, 198, 273, 281, 283, 296, 311, 312

JA Snow	35	3	98	3	24	3	51	2
DJ Brown	35	4	99	2	27	5	79	0
R Illingworth	29	15	47	1	51	22	87	6
DL Underwood	27.4	13	41	4	45.1	22	52	2
ER Dexter	7	0	25	0	1	0	3	0
KF Barrington					6	1	14	0

ENGLAND	1st innings		2nd innings	
JH Edrich	c Jarman b McKenzie	62	c Jarman b Connolly	65
RM Prideaux	c Freeman b Gleeson	64	b McKenzie	2
ER Dexter	b McKenzie	10	b Connolly	38
TW Graveney*	c Cowper b Connolly	37	c & b Cowper	41
KF Barrington	b Connolly	49	not out	46
KWR Fletcher	c Jarman b Connolly	0	not out	23
APE Knott+	lbw b Freeman	4		
R Illingworth	c Gleeson b Connolly	6		
JA Snow	b Connolly	0		
DJ Brown	b Cowper	14		
DL Underw'd	not out	45		
Extras	(1b, 7lb, 0w, 3nb)	11	(0b, 7lb, 0w, 8nb)	15
Total	147 overs	302	84 overs	230

1st innings FoW: 123, 136, 141, 209, 215, 235, 237, 241, 241, 302
2nd innings FoW: 4, 81, 134, 168

GD McKenzie	39	20	61	2	25	2	65	1
EW Freeman	22	6	60	1	6	1	25	0
JW Gleeson	25	5	68	1	11	4	26	0
AN Connolly	39	13	72	5	31	10	68	2
RM Cowper	18	10	24	1	5	0	22	1
IM Chappell	4	1	6	0	5	3	6	0
RJ Inverarity					1	0	3	0

No. 449: 5th Test

VENUE:	The Oval
DATE:	22nd-27th August 1968
TOSS WON BY:	England
RESULT:	England won by 226 runs

ENGLAND	1st innings		2nd innings	
JH Edrich	b Chappell	164	c Lawry b Mallett	17
C Milburn	b Connolly	8	c Lawry b Connolly	18
ER Dexter	b Gleeson	21	b Connolly	28
MC Cowdrey*	lbw b Mallett	16	b Mallett	35
TW Graveney	c Redpath b McKenzie	63	run out	12
BL D'Oliveira	c Inverarity b Mallett	158	c Gleeson b Connolly	9
APE Knott+	c Jarman b Mallett	28	run out	34
R Illingworth	lbw b Connolly	8	b Gleeson	10
JA Snow	run out	4	c Sheahan b Gleeson	13
DL Underw'd	not out	9	not out	1
DJ Brown	c Sheahan b Gleeson	2	b Connolly	1
Extras	(1b, 11lb, 1w, 0nb)	13	(0b, 3lb, 0w, 0nb)	3
Total	201.2 overs	494	58.4 overs	181

1st innings FoW: 28, 84, 113, 238, 359, 421, 458, 468, 489, 494
2nd innings FoW: 23, 53, 67, 90, 114, 126, 149, 179, 179, 181

GD McKenzie	40	8	87	1	4	0	14	0
AN Connolly	57	12	127	2	22.4	2	65	4
KD Walters	6	2	17	0				
JW Gleeson	41.2	8	109	2	7	2	22	2
AA Mallett	36	11	87	3	25	4	77	2
IM Chappell	21	5	54	1				

AUSTRALIA	1st innings		2nd innings	
WM Lawry*	c Knott b Snow	135	c Milburn b Brown	4
RJ Inverarity	c Milburn b Snow	1	lbw b Underwood	56
IR Redpath	c Cowdrey b Snow	67	lbw b Underwood	8
IM Chappell	c Knott b Brown	10	lbw b Underwood	2
KD Walters	c Knott b Brown	5	c Knott b Underwood	1
AP Sheahan	b Illingworth	14	c Snow b Illingworth	24
BN Jarman+	st Knott b Illingworth	0	b D'Oliveira	21
GD McKenzie	b Brown	12	c Brown b Underwood	0
AA Mallett	not out	43	c Brown b Underwood	0
JW Gleeson	c Dexter b Underwood	19	b Underwood	5
AN Connolly	b Underwood	3	not out	0
Extras	(4b, 7lb, 0w, 4nb)	15	(0b, 4lb, 0w, 0nb)	4
Total	163.3 overs	324	83.3 overs	125

1st innings FoW: 7, 136, 151, 161, 185, 188, 237, 269, 302, 324
2nd innings FoW: 4, 13, 19, 29, 65, 110, 110, 110, 120, 125

JA Snow	35	12	67	3	11	5	22	0
DJ Brown	22	5	63	3	8	3	19	1
R Illingworth	48	15	87	2	28	18	29	1
DL Underwood	54.3	21	89	2	31.3	19	50	7
BL D'Oliveira	4	2	3	0	5	4	1	1

No. 450: 1st Test
VENUE: Lahore (Gaddafi)
DATE: 21st-24th February 1969
TOSS WON BY: England
RESULT: Match drawn

No. 451: 2nd Test
VENUE: Dhaka (Dacca)
DATE: 28th Feb-3rd March 1969
TOSS WON BY: Pakistan
RESULT: Match drawn

England/Pakistan 1st Test

ENGLAND	1st innings		2nd innings	
JH Edrich	c Asif Masood b Intikhab	54	c Majid b Asif Masood	8
RM Prideaux	c Shafqat b Asif Masood	9	b Majid	5
MC Cowdrey*	c Wasim b Majid	100	c Wasim b Asif Masood	12
TW Graveney	c Asif Iqbal b Intikhab	13	run out	12
KWR Fletcher	c Intikhab b Saeed	20	b Majid	83
BL D'Oliveira	c Ilyas b Intikhab	26	c Mushtaq b Saeed	5
APE Knott+	lbw b Saeed	52	b Asif Masood	30
DL Underw'd	c Intikhab b Saeed	0	c Aftab b Mushtaq	6
DJ Brown	b Saeed	7	not out	44
PI Pocock	b Intikhab	12	b Saeed	1
RMH Cottam	not out	4		
Extras	(4b, 2lb, 0w, 3nb)	9	(6b, 9lb, 0w, 4nb)	19
	119.1 overs		84.5 overs	
Total		**306**		**225**

1st innings FoW: 41, 92, 113, 182, 219, 246, 257, 287, 294, 306
2nd innings FoW: 8, 25, 41, 46, 68, 136, 151, 201, 225

Asif Masood	21	5	59	1	25	4	68	3
Asif Iqbal	4	2	11	0				
Majid Khan	18	8	25	1	20	5	41	2
Intikhab Alam	40.1	8	117	4	15	5	29	0
Saeed Ahmed	20	5	64	4	15.5	3	44	2
Mushtaq	14	6	15	0	9	1	24	1
Shafqat Rana	2	0	6	0				

PAKISTAN	1st innings		2nd innings	
Moh'd Ilyas	lbw b Brown	0	c Fletcher b Brown	1
Aftab Gul	c D'Oliveira b Brown	12	c Pocock b Underwood	29
Saeed Ah'd*	c Knott b D'Oliveira	18	b Cottam	39
Asif Iqbal	c D'Oliveira b Cottam	70	c & b Cottam	0
Mushtaq Mo'd	c Fletcher b Cottam	4	not out	34
Hanif Moh'd	b Brown	7	c Pocock b Brown	68
Majid Khan	c Pocock b Underwood	18	not out	23
Shafqat Rana	c Knott b Cottam	30		
Intikhab Alam	c D'Oliveira b Pocock	12		
Wasim Bari+	not out	14		
Asif Masood	b Cottam	11		
Extras	(8b, 4lb, 0w, 1nb)	13	(3b, 5lb, 0w, 1nb)	9
	70.2 overs		79 overs	
Total		**209**		**203**

1st innings FoW: 0, 32, 32, 52, 72, 119, 145, 176, 187, 209
2nd innings FoW: 6, 71, 71, 71, 156

DJ Brown	14	0	43	3	15	4	47	2
RMH Cottam	22.2	5	50	4	13	1	35	2
BL D'Oliveira	8	2	28	1	19	8	29	1
DL Underwood	16	4	36	1	16	4	41	0
PI Pocock	10	3	39	1	8	2	31	0
KWR Fletcher					6	0	11	0
TW Graveney					2	2	0	0

2nd Test

PAKISTAN	1st innings		2nd innings	
Moh'd Ilyas	c Knott b Snow	20	c Snow b Cottam	21
Salahuddin	c Brown b Snow	6	lbw b Underwood	5
Saeed Ahmed*	b Brown	19	b Underwood	16
Asif Iqbal	b Brown	44	c D'Oliveira b Underw'd	31
Mushtaq	c Cottam b Snow	52	c Knott b Underwood	33
Majid Khan	c Knott b Brown	27	not out	49
Hanif Moh'd	lbw b Snow	8	lbw b Underwood	8
Intikhab Alam	lbw b Underwood	25	not out	19
Wasim Bari+	c Knott b Cottam	14		
Niaz Ahmed	not out	16		
Pervez Sajjad	b Cottam	2		
Extras	(4b, 4lb, 0w, 5nb)	13	(0b, 5lb, 0w, 8nb)	13
	110.1 overs		101 overs	
Total		**246**		**195**

1st innings FoW: 16, 39, 55, 123, 168, 184, 186, 211, 237, 246
2nd innings FoW: 8, 48, 50, 97, 129, 147

JA Snow	25	5	70	4	12	7	15	0
DJ Brown	23	8	51	3	6	1	18	0
DL Underwood	27	13	45	1	44	15	94	5
RMH Cottam	27.1	6	52	2	30	17	43	1
BL D'Oliveira	8	1	15	0	9	2	12	0

ENGLAND	1st innings		2nd innings	
JH Edrich	c Mushtaq b Intikhab	24	not out	12
RM Prideaux	c Hanif b Pervez	4	not out	18
TW Graveney	b Pervez	46		
KWR Fletcher	c Hanif b Saeed Ahmed	16		
MC Cowdrey*	lbw b Pervez	7		
BL D'Oliveira	not out	114		
APE Knott+	c & b Pervez	2		
DJ Brown	c Hanif b Saeed Ahmed	4		
JA Snow	c Majid b Niaz Ahmed	9		
DL Underw'd	c Ilyas b Mushtaq	22		
RMH Cottam	c Hanif b Saeed Ahmed	4		
Extras	(14b, 8lb, 0w, 0nb)	22	(2b, 0lb, 0w, 1nb)	3
	132.4 overs		20 overs	
Total		**274**		**33**

1st innings FoW: 17, 61, 96, 100, 113, 117, 130, 170, 236, 274

Niaz Ahmed	10	4	20	1	2	0	2	0
Majid Khan	11	4	15	0				
Pervez Sajjad	37	8	75	4	3	2	1	0
Saeed Ahmed	37.4	15	59	3	3	2	4	0
Intikhab Alam	26	7	65	1	4	0	19	0
Mushtaq Mohammad	11	3	18		1			
Asif Iqbal					4	2	2	0
Hanif Mohammad					3	2	1	0

Pakistan

No. 452: 3rd Test	
VENUE: Karachi (National Stadium)	
DATE: 6th–8th March 1969	
TOSS WON BY: England	
RESULT: Match drawn	

ENGLAND	1st innings		2nd innings
C Milburn	c Wasim b Asif Masood	139	
JH Edrich	c Saeed b Intikhab	32	
TW Graveney	c Asif Iqbal b Intikhab	105	
MC Cowdrey*	c Hanif b Intikhab	14	
KWR Fletcher	b Mushtaq Mohammad	38	
BL D'Oliveira	c Aftab b Mushtaq	16	
APE Knott+	not out	96	
JA Snow	b Asif Masood	9	
DJ Brown	not out	25	
DL Underw'd			
RNS Hobbs			
Extras	(5b, 12lb, 0w, 11nb)	28	
Total	175.1 overs	**502**	

1st innings FoW: 78, 234, 286, 309, 360, 374, 427

Asif Masood	28	2	94	2
Majid Khan	20	5	51	0
Sarfraz Nawaz	34	6	78	0
Intikhab Alam	48	4	129	3
Saeed Ahmed	22	5	53	0
Mushtaq	23.1	5	69	2

PAKISTAN 1st innings	2nd innings
Aftab Gul	
Hanif Mohammad	
Mushtaq Mohammad	
Asif Iqbal	
Saeed Ahmed*	
Majid Khan	
Shafqat Rana	
Intikhab Alam	
Wasim Bari+	
Asif Masood	
Sarfraz Nawaz	

West Indies

No. 453: 1st Test	
VENUE: Old Trafford	
DATE: 12th–17th June 1969	
TOSS WON BY: England	
RESULT: England won by 10 wickets	

ENGLAND	1st innings		2nd innings	
G Boycott	lbw b Shepherd	128	not out	1
JH Edrich	run out	58	not out	9
PJ Sharpe	b Gibbs	2		
TW Graveney	b Holder	75		
BL D'Oliveira	c Hendriks b Shepherd	57		
APE Knott+	c Gibbs b Shepherd	0		
R Illingworth*	c & b Gibbs	21		
BR Knight	lbw b Shepherd	31		
DJ Brown	b Sobers	15		
DL Underw'd	not out	11		
JA Snow	b Shepherd	0		
Extras	(5b, 9lb, 1w, 0nb)	15	(0b, 1lb, 0w, 1nb)	2
Total	197.5 overs	**413**	4.5 overs	**12**

1st innings FoW: 112, 121, 249, 307, 314, 343, 365, 390, 411, 413

GStA Sobers	27	7	78	1	2	1	1	0
VA Holder	38	11	93	1	2.5	1	9	0
JN Shepherd	58.5	19	104	5				
LR Gibbs	60	22	96	2				
CA Davis	1	0	1	0				
MC Carew	11	3	19	0				
MLC Foster	2	0	7	0				

WEST INDIES 1st innings			2nd innings	
RC Fredericks	c Graveney b Snow	0	c Illing'rth b Underw'd	64
MC Carew	b Brown	1	c Sharpe b D'Oliveira	44
BF Butcher	lbw b Snow	31	lbw b Knight	48
CA Davis	c D'Oliveira b Brown	34	c Underw'd b Illing'th	24
GStA Sobers*	c Edrich b Brown	10	c Sharpe b Knight	48
CH Lloyd	b Snow	32	c Knott b Brown	13
MLC Foster	st Knott b Underwood	4	lbw b Brown	3
JN Shepherd	c Illingworth b Snow	9	lbw b Snow	13
JL Hendriks+	c Edrich b Brown	1	not out	5
VA Holder	run out	19	lbw b Brown	0
LR Gibbs	not out	1	b Snow	0
Extras	(0b, 3lb, 0w, 2nb)	5	(4b, 8lb, 0w, 1nb)	13
Total	48 overs	**147**	114.3 overs	**275**

1st innings FoW: 0, 5, 58, 72, 83, 92, 119, 126, 139, 147
2nd innings FoW: 92, 138, 180, 202, 234, 256, 258, 273, 274, 275

JA Snow	15	2	54	4	22.3	4	76	2
DJ Brown	13	1	39	4	22	3	59	3
BR Knight	2	0	11	0	12	3	15	2
R Illingworth	6	2	23	0	30	12	52	1
DL Underwood	12	6	15	1	19	11	31	1
BL D'Oliveira					9	2	29	1

West Indies | West Indies

No. 454: 2nd Test	No. 455: 3rd Test
VENUE: Lord's	VENUE: Headingley
DATE: 26th June-1st July 1969	DATE: 10th-15th July 1969
TOSS WON BY: West Indies	TOSS WON BY: England
RESULT: Match drawn	RESULT: England won by 30 runs

WEST INDIES 1st innings / 2nd innings

Batsman	1st innings		2nd innings	
RC Fredericks	c Hampshire b Knight	63	c Hampshire b Illing'th	60
GS Camacho	c Sharpe b Snow	67	b D'Oliveira	45
CA Davis	c Knott b Brown	103	c Illingworth b D'Oliveira	0
BF Butcher	c Hampshire b Brown	9	b Illingworth	24
GStA Sobers*	run out	29	not out	50
CH Lloyd	c Illingworth b Brown	18	c Knott b Snow	70
JN Shepherd	c Edrich b Snow	32	c Sharpe b Illingworth	11
TM Findlay+	b Snow	23	c Sharpe b Knight	11
VA Holder	lbw b Snow	6	run out	7
LR Gibbs	not out	18	b Knight	5
GC Shill'ford	c Knott b Snow	3	(4b, 7lb, 0w, 1nb)	12
Extras	(5b, 4lb, 0w, 0nb)	9	100.5 overs	
Total	158 overs	**380**		**295**

1st innings FoW: 106, 151, 167, 217, 247, 324, 336, 343, 376, 380
2nd innings FoW: 73, 73, 128, 135, 191, 232, 263, 280, 295

Bowler	O	M	R	W		O	M	R	W
JA Snow	39	5	114	5		22	4	69	1
DJ Brown	38	8	99	3		9	3	25	0
BR Knight	38	11	65	1		27.5	6	78	2
BL D'Oliveira	26	10	46	0		15	2	45	2
R Illingworth	16	4	39	0		27	9	66	3
PH Parfitt	1	0	8	0					

ENGLAND 1st innings / 2nd innings

Batsman	1st innings		2nd innings	
G Boycott	c Findlay b Shepherd	23	c Butcher b Shillingford	106
JH Edrich	c Fredericks b Holder	7	c Camacho b Holder	1
PH Parfitt	c Davis b Sobers	4	c Findlay b Shepherd	39
BL D'Oliveira	c Shepherd b Sobers	0	c Fredericks b Gibbs	18
PJ Sharpe	b Holder	11	c Davis b Sobers	86
JH Hampshire	lbw b Shepherd	107	run out	5
APE Knott+	b Shillingford	53	not out	9
R Illingworth*	c & b Gibbs	113	b Shillingford	11
BR Knight	lbw b Shillingford	0	not out	1
DJ Brown	c Findlay b Shepherd	1		
JA Snow	not out	9	(9b, 5lb, 0w, 5nb)	19
Extras	(1b, 5lb, 0w, 10nb)	16	106 overs	
Total	157.4 overs	**344**		**295**

1st innings FoW: 19, 37, 37, 37, 61, 189, 249, 250, 261, 344
2nd innings FoW: 1, 94, 137, 263, 271, 272, 292

Bowler	O	M	R	W		O	M	R	W
VA Holder	38	16	83	2		11	4	36	1
GC Shillingford	19	4	53	2		13	4	30	2
JN Shepherd	43	14	74	3		12	3	45	1
LR Gibbs	27.4	9	53	1		41	14	93	1
CA Davis	1	0	2	0					
BF Butcher	3	1	6	0					
GStA Sobers						29	8	72	1

ENGLAND 1st innings / 2nd innings

Batsman	1st innings		2nd innings	
G Boycott	lbw b Sobers	12	c Findlay b Sobers	0
JH Edrich	lbw b Shepherd	79	lbw b Sobers	15
PJ Sharpe	c Findlay b Holder	6	lbw b Sobers	15
JH Hampshire	c Findlay b Holder	1	lbw b Shillingford	22
BL D'Oliveira	c Sobers b Shepherd	48	c Sobers b Davis	39
APE Knott+	c Findlay b Sobers	44	c Findlay b Sobers	31
R Illingworth*	b Shepherd	1	c Lloyd b Holder	19
BR Knight	c Fredericks b Gibbs	7	c Holder b Gibbs	27
DL Underw'd	c Findlay b Holder	4	b Sobers	10
DJ Brown	b Holder	12	b Shillingford	34
JA Snow	not out	1	not out	15
Extras	(4b, 3lb, 0w, 1nb)	8	(0b, 5lb, 1w, 1nb)	7
Total	98 overs	**223**	131.4 overs	**240**

1st innings FoW: 30, 52, 64, 140, 165, 167, 182, 199, 217, 223
2nd innings FoW: 0, 23, 42, 58, 102, 147, 147, 171, 203, 240

Bowler	O	M	R	W		O	M	R	W
GStA Sobers	21	1	68	2		40	18	42	5
VA Holder	26	7	48	4		33	13	66	1
GC Shillingford	7	0	21	0		20.4	4	56	2
LR Gibbs	19	6	33	1		21	6	42	1
JN Shepherd	24	8	43	3					
CA Davis	1	0	2	0		17	8	27	1

WEST INDIES 1st innings / 2nd innings

Batsman	1st innings		2nd innings	
RC Fredericks	lbw b Knight	11	c Sharpe b Snow	6
GS Camacho	c Knott b Knight	4	c H'pshire b Underw'd	71
CA Davis	c Underwood b Knight	18	c & b Underwood	29
BF Butcher	b Snow	35	c Knott b Underwood	91
GStA Sobers*	c Sharpe b Knight	13	c Knott b Illingworth	23
CH Lloyd	c Snow b Brown	27	b Knight	0
TM Findlay+	lbw b D'Oliveira	1	lbw b Knight	16
VA Holder	b Snow	35	c Knott b Underwood	0
LR Gibbs	not out	6	c Sharpe b Brown	13
GC Shil'ford	c Knott b Brown	3	c Knott b Brown	4
JN Shepherd	absent hurt	0	not out	5
Extras	(0b, 7lb, 0w, 1nb)	8	(0b, 11lb, 0w, 3nb)	14
Total	64.3 overs	**161**	106.2 overs	**272**

1st innings FoW: 17, 37, 46, 80, 88, 91, 151, 153, 161
2nd innings FoW: 8, 69, 177, 219, 224, 228, 228, 251, 255, 272

Bowler	O	M	R	W		O	M	R	W
JA Snow						21	7	43	1
DJ Brown	7.3	2	13	2		21	8	53	2
BR Knight	22	5	63	4		18.2	4	47	2
BL D'Oliveira	15	8	27	1		10	3	22	0
R Illingworth						14	5	38	1
DL Underwood						22	12	55	4

No. 456: 1st Test	
VENUE: Lord's	
DATE: 24th-28th July 1969	
TOSS WON BY: England	
RESULT: England won by 230 runs	

No. 457: 2nd Test	
VENUE: Trent Bridge	
DATE: 7th-12th August 1969	
TOSS WON BY: New Zealand	
RESULT: Match drawn	

ENGLAND 1st innings / **2nd innings**

	1st innings		2nd innings	
G Boycott	c Congdon b Motz	0	c Turner b Pollard	47
JH Edrich	c Motz b Taylor	16	c Wadsworth b Hadlee	115
PJ Sharpe	c Turner b Taylor	20	c Congdon b Howarth	46
KWR Fletcher	b Motz	9	b Howarth	7
BL D'Oliveira	run out	37	c Wadsworth b Taylor	12
APE Knott+	c & b Hadlee	8	lbw b Howarth	10
R Illingworth*	c Wadsworth b Howarth	53	c Wadsworth b Taylor	0
BR Knight	c Hadlee b Pollard	29	b Motz	49
DJ Brown	not out	11	c Wadsworth b Taylor	7
DL Underw'd	c Pollard b Howarth	1	b Motz	4
Alan Ward	b Taylor	0	not out	19
Extras	(1b, 3lb, 1w, 1nb)	6	(4b, 15lb, 0w, 5nb)	24
Total	74.5 overs	**190**	140.4 overs	**340**

1st innings FoW: 0, 27, 47, 47, 63, 113, 158, 186, 188, 190
2nd innings FoW: 125, 199, 234, 243, 259, 259, 259, 284, 300, 340

RC Motz	19	5	46	2	39.4	17	78	2
DR Hadlee	14	2	48	1	16	5	43	1
BR Taylor	13.5	4	35	3	25	4	62	3
HJ Howarth	19	9	24	2	49	20	102	3
V Pollard	9	1	31	1	8	2	20	1
MG Burgess					3	0	11	0

NEW ZEALAND 1st innings / **2nd innings**

	1st innings		2nd innings	
GT Dowling*	c Illingworth b Underw'd	41	c Knott b Ward	4
GM Turner	c Knott b Ward	5	not out	43
BE Congdon	c Sharpe b Ward	41	c Fletcher b Underwood	17
BF Hastings	c Ward b Illingworth	23	c Knott b Underwood	0
V Pollard	c Ward b Underwood	8	lbw b Underwood	0
MG Burgess	lbw b Illingworth	10	lbw b Underwood	6
KJ Wadsworth+	lbw b Illingworth	14	b Underwood	0
BR Taylor	c Brown b Illingworth	3	b Underwood	5
RC Motz	b Underwood	15	c Knott b Underwood	23
DR Hadlee	c Illingworth b Underw'd	1	c Sharpe b D'Oliveira	19
HJ Howarth	not out	0	b Ward	4
Extras	(4b, 4lb, 0w, 0nb)	8	(5b, 4lb, 0w, 1nb)	10
Total	87.3 overs	**169**	75.5 overs	**131**

1st innings FoW: 14, 76, 92, 101, 126, 137, 146, 150, 168, 169
2nd innings FoW: 5, 27, 45, 45, 67, 67, 73, 101, 126, 131

DJ Brown	12	5	17	0	5	3	6	0
Alan Ward	14	2	49	2	10.5	0	48	2
DL Underwood	29.3	16	38	4	31	18	32	7
BR Knight	10	3	20	0	3	1	5	0
R Illingworth	22	8	37	4	18	9	24	0
BL D'Oliveira					8	3	6	1

NEW ZEALAND 1st innings / **2nd innings**

	1st innings		2nd innings	
GT Dowling*	b Ward	18		
BAG Murray	c Knight b D'Oliveira	23	b Illingworth	22
BE Congdon	c Knott b Illingworth	66	not out	40
BF Hastings	c Sharpe b Illingworth	83	not out	1
V Pollard	c Fletcher b Underwood	8		
MG Burgess	c Knight b Ward	2		
KJ Wadsworth+	c D'Oliveira b Ward	21		
DR Hadlee	not out	35		
RO Collinge	c Knott b Knight	19		
RC Motz	b Ward	1		
HJ Howarth	b Knight	3		
Extras	(1b, 12lb, 0w, 2nb)	15	(0b, 1lb, 0w, 2nb)	3
Total	127.5 overs	**294**	23 overs	**66**

1st innings FoW: 47, 53, 203, 206, 212, 229, 244, 280, 285, 294
2nd innings FoW: 61

JA Snow	24	4	61	0	6	2	19	0
Alan Ward	23	3	61	4	3	0	14	0
BR Knight	18.5	4	44	2	4	0	14	0
BL D'Oliveira	25	9	40	1	5	0	8	0
DL Underwood	22	8	44	1	3	1	5	0
R Illingworth	12	4	15	2	2	0	3	1
KWR Fletcher	3	1	14	0				

ENGLAND 1st innings / **2nd innings**

	1st innings		2nd innings
G Boycott	b Motz	0	
JH Edrich	b Hadlee	155	
PJ Sharpe	c & b Howarth	111	
KWR Fletcher	b Hadlee	31	
BL D'Oliveira	c & b Hadlee	45	
APE Knott+	c Burgess b Motz	15	
R Illingworth*	lbw b Collinge	33	
BR Knight	not out	18	
DL Underw'd	c Collinge b Hadlee	16	
JA Snow	not out	4	
Alan Ward			
Extras	(6b, 12lb, 1w, 4nb)	23	
Total	155 overs	**451**	

1st innings FoW: 2, 251, 301, 314, 344, 408, 408, 441

RC Motz	36	5	97	2
RO Collinge	29	6	88	1
DR Hadlee	25	3	88	4
HJ Howarth	41	14	89	1
V Pollard	10	2	26	0
MG Burgess	14	4	40	0

New Zealand	Australia

NEW ZEALAND 1st innings / 2nd innings

Batsman	1st innings		2nd innings	
BAG Murray	b Snow	2	c & b Underwood	5
GM Turner	c Sharpe b Underwood	53	b Underwood	25
BE Congdon	c Sharpe b Underwood	24	b Underwood	30
GT Dowling*	c Edrich b Illingworth	14	lbw b Snow	30
BF Hastings	b Illingworth	21	c Knott b Ward	61
V Pollard	st Knott b Illingworth	13	c Denness b Underwood	9
BR Taylor	c Denness b Underwood	0	st Knott b Underwood	4
KJ Wadsworth+	c Arnold b Underwood	2	c Knott b Snow	10
RC Motz	c Arnold b Underwood	16	c Denness b Underw'd	11
RS Cunis	c Illingworth b Underwood	0	lbw b Underwood	7
HJ Howarth	not out	0	not out	4
Extras	(0b, 0lb, 0w, 5nb)	5	(3b, 11lb, 0w, 19nb)	33
Total	82.3 overs	**150**	116.3 overs	**229**

1st innings FoW: 3, 77, 90, 96, 118, 119, 123, 150, 150, 150
2nd innings FoW: 22, 39, 88, 124, 153, 159, 200, 206, 224, 229

Bowler	O	M	R	W		O	M	R	W
GG Arnold	8	2	13	0		10	3	17	0
JA Snow	10	4	22	1		21	4	52	2
Alan Ward	5	0	10	0		18	10	28	2
R Illingworth	32.3	13	55	3		15	9	20	0
DL Underw'd	26	12	41	6		38.3	15	60	6
BL D'Oliveira	1	0	4	0		14	9	19	0

AUSTRALIA 1st innings / 2nd innings

Batsman	1st innings		2nd innings	
WM Lawry*	c Knott b Snow	4	c Snow b Fletcher	84
KR Stackpole	c Knott b Snow	207	c Knott b Shuttleworth	8
IM Chappell	run out	59	st Knott b Illingworth	10
KD Walters	b Underwood	112	c Luckhurst b Snow	7
IR Redpath	c Illingworth b Underw'd	22	c & b Underwood	28
AP Sheahan	c Knott b Underwood	0	c Shuttleworth b Snow	36
RW Marsh+	b Snow	9	b Shuttleworth	14
TJ Jenner	c Cowdrey b Snow	0	c Boycott b Shuttleworth	2
GD McKenzie	not out	3	b Underwood	1
JW Gleeson	c Cowdrey b Snow	0	b Shuttleworth	6
AL Thomson	b Snow	0	not out	4
Extras	(7b, 4lb, 0w, 6nb)	17	(4b, 3lb, 0w, 7nb)	14
Total	115.3 overs	**433**	93.5 overs	**214**

1st innings FoW: 12, 163, 372, 418, 418, 421, 422, 433, 433, 433
2nd innings FoW: 30, 47, 64, 137, 152, 193, 199, 201, 208, 214

Bowler	O	M	R	W		O	M	R	W
JA Snow	32.3	6	114	6		20	3	48	2
K Shuttleworth	27	6	81	0		17.5	2	47	5
BL D'Oliveira	16	2	63	0		7	5	7	0
R Illingworth	11	1	47	0		18	11	19	1
DL Underwood	28	6	101	3		20	10	23	1
MC Cowdrey	1	0	10	0		2	0	8	0
KWR Fletcher						9	1	48	1

ENGLAND 1st innings / 2nd innings

Batsman	1st innings		2nd innings	
JH Edrich	b Howarth	68	c Wadsworth b Cunis	22
G Boycott	b Cunis	46	b Cunis	8
MH Denness	c Wadsworth b Cunis	2	not out	55
PJ Sharpe	lbw b Motz	48	not out	45
BL D'Oliveira	c Cunis b Howarth	1		
APE Knott+	c Murray b Taylor	21		
R Illingworth*	c Wadsworth b Taylor	4		
GG Arnold	b Taylor	1		
DL Underwood	lbw b Taylor	3		
JA Snow	not out	21		
Alan Ward	c Turner b Cunis	21		
Extras	(0b, 5lb, 0w, 1nb)	6	(2b, 4lb, 0w, 2nb)	8
Total	98 overs	**242**	52.3 overs	**138**

1st innings FoW: 88, 118, 118, 131, 174, 180, 188, 192, 202, 242
2nd innings FoW: 19, 56

Bowler	O	M	R	W		O	M	R	W
RC Motz	19	6	54	1		9.3	1	35	0
BR Taylor	21	9	47	4		4	0	11	0
RS Cunis	19	3	49	3		11	3	36	2
HJ Howarth	34	14	66	2		23	10	32	0
V Pollard	5	1	20	0		5	1	16	0

ENGLAND 1st innings / 2nd innings

Batsman	1st innings		2nd innings	
G Boycott	c Marsh b Gleeson	37	c & b Jenner	16
BW Luckhurst	run out	74	not out	20
APE Knott+	c Lawry b Walters	73		
JH Edrich	c Chappell b Jenner	79		
MC Cowdrey	c Chappell b Gleeson	28		
KWR Fletcher	c Marsh b McKenzie	34		
BL D'Oliveira	c Sheahan b McKenzie	57		
R Illingworth*	b Marsh b Thomson	8		
JA Snow	c Marsh b Walters	34		
DL Underw'd	not out	2		
K Shuttleworth	c Lawry b Walters	7		
Extras	(2b, 7lb, 0w, 22nb)	31	(0b, 3lb, 0w, 0nb)	3
Total	146.5 overs	**464**	15.6 overs	**39**

1st innings FoW: 92, 136, 245, 284, 336, 346, 371, 449, 456, 464
2nd innings FoW: 39

Bowler	O	M	R	W		O	M	R	W
GD McKenzie	28	5	90	2		3	0	6	0
AL Thomson	43	8	136	1		4	0	20	0
JW Gleeson	42	15	97	2					
TJ Jenner	24	5	86	1		4.6	2	9	1
KR Stackpole	4	0	12	0		4	3	1	0
KD Walters	5.5	0	12	3					

No. 460: 2nd Test	No. 461: 4th Test
VENUE: Perth (WACA)	VENUE: Sydney (SCG)
DATE: 11th-16th December 1970	DATE: 9th-14th January 1971
TOSS WON BY: Australia	TOSS WON BY: England
RESULT: Match drawn	RESULT: England won by 299 runs

Left match (No. 460)

ENGLAND 1st innings / 2nd innings

Batsman	1st innings		2nd innings	
G Boycott	c McKenzie b Gleeson	70	st Marsh b Gleeson	50
BW Luckhurst	b McKenzie	131	c Stackpole b Walters	19
JH Edrich	run out	47	not out	115
APE Knott+	c Stackpole b Thomson	24	lbw b Gleeson	0
KWR Fletcher	b Walters	22	c Marsh b Thomson	1
MC Cowdrey	c & b GS Chappell	40	b Gleeson	31
BL D'Oliveira	c Stackpole b Thomson	8	c Marsh b Stackpole	29
R Illingworth*	b McKenzie	34	not out	30
JA Snow	not out	4		
K Shuttleworth	b McKenzie	2		
P Lever	b McKenzie	2		
Extras	(0b, 8lb, 1w, 4nb)	13	(2b, 3lb, 0w, 7nb)	12
	133.4 overs		101 overs	
Total		**397**		**287**

1st innings FoW: 171, 243, 281, 291, 310, 327, 389, 389, 393, 397
2nd innings FoW: 60, 98, 98, 101, 152, 209

Bowler	O	M	R	W	O	M	R	W
GD McKenzie	31.4	4	66	4	18	2	50	0
AL Thomson	24	4	118	2	25	3	71	1
GS Chappell	24	4	54	1	4	1	17	0
JW Gleeson	32	10	78	1	32	11	68	3
KD Walters	11	1	35	1	7	1	26	1
KR Stackpole	11	2	33	0	15	3	43	1

AUSTRALIA 1st innings / 2nd innings

Batsman	1st innings		2nd innings	
WM Lawry*	c Illingworth b Snow	0	not out	38
KR Stackpole	c Lever b Snow	5	c (sub) b Snow	0
IM Chappell	c Knott b Snow	50	c (sub) b Snow	17
KD Walters	c Knott b Lever	7	b Lever	8
IR Redpath	c & b Illingworth	171	not out	26
AP Sheahan	run out	2		
GS Chappell	c Luckhurst b Shuttlew'th	108		
RW Marsh+	c D'Oliveira b Shuttlew'th	44		
GD McKenzie	c Lever b D'Oliveira	7		
JW Gleeson	c Knott b Snow	15		
AL Thomson	not out	12		
Extras	(5b, 4lb, 0w, 10nb)	19	(4b, 4lb, 0w, 3nb)	11
	114.5 overs		32 overs	
Total		**440**		**100**

1st innings FoW: 5, 8, 17, 105, 107, 326, 393, 408, 426, 440
2nd innings FoW: 0, 20, 40

Bowler	O	M	R	W	O	M	R	W
JA Snow	33.5	3	143	4	9	4	17	2
K Shuttleworth	28	4	105	2	3	1	9	0
P Lever	21	3	78	1	5	2	10	1
BL D'Oliveira	17	1	41	1	4	2	5	0
R Illingworth	13	2	43	1	4	2	12	0
G Boycott	1	0	7	0				
KWR Fletcher	1	0	4	0	4	0	18	0
MC Cowdrey					3	0	18	0

Right match (No. 461)

ENGLAND 1st innings / 2nd innings

Batsman	1st innings		2nd innings	
G Boycott	c Gleeson b Connolly	77	not out	142
BW Luckhurst	lbw b Gleeson	38	c I Chappell b McKenzie	5
JH Edrich	c Gleeson b G Chappell	55	run out	12
KWR Fletcher	c Walters b Mallett	23	c Stackpole b Mallett	8
BL D'Oliveira	c Connolly b Mallett	0	c IM Ch'll b GS Ch'll	56
R Illingworth*	b Gleeson	25	st Marsh b Mallett	53
APE Knott+	st Marsh b Mallett	6	not out	21
JA Snow	c Lawry b Gleeson	37		
P Lever	c Connolly b Mallett	36		
DL Underw'd	c G Chappell b Gleeson	0		
RGD Willis	not out	15		
Extras	(5b, 2lb, 1w, 12nb)	20	(9b, 4lb, 0w, 9nb)	22
	94.7 overs		94 overs	
Total		**332**		**319**

1st innings FoW: 116, 130, 201, 205, 208, 219, 262, 291, 291, 332
2nd innings FoW: 7, 35, 48, 181, 276

Bowler	O	M	R	W	O	M	R	W
GD McKenzie	15	3	74	0	15	0	65	1
AN Connolly	13	2	43	1	14	1	38	0
JW Gleeson	29	7	83	4	23	4	54	0
GS Chappell	11	4	30	1	15	5	24	1
AA Mallett	16.7	5	40	4	19	1	85	2
KD Walters	3	1	11	0	2	0	14	0
KR Stackpole	7	2	31	0	6	1	17	0

AUSTRALIA 1st innings / 2nd innings

Batsman	1st innings		2nd innings	
WM Lawry*	c Edrich b Lever	9	not out	60
IM Chappell	c Underwood b Snow	12	c D'Oliveira b Snow	0
IR Redpath	c Fletcher b D'Oliveira	64	c Edrich b Snow	0
KD Walters	c Luckhurst b Illing'th	55	c Knott b Lever	3
GS Chappell	c & b Underwood	15	b Snow	2
KR Stackpole	c Boycott b Underwood	33	c Lever b Snow	30
RW Marsh+	c D'Oliveira b Underw'd	4	c Willis b Snow	0
AA Mallett	b Underwood	4	c Knott b Willis	6
GD McKenzie	not out	11	retired hurt	6
JW Gleeson	c Fletcher b D'Oliveira	0	b Snow	0
AN Connolly	b Lever	14	c Knott b Snow	0
Extras	(0b, 0lb, 0w, 11nb)	11	(2b, 0lb, 0w, 1nb)	3
	76.6 overs		56.5 overs	
Total		**236**		**116**

1st innings FoW: 14, 38, 137, 160, 189, 199, 208, 208, 219, 236
2nd innings FoW: 1, 11, 14, 21, 66, 66, 86, 116, 116

Bowler	O	M	R	W	O	M	R	W
JA Snow	14	6	23	1	17.5	5	40	7
RGD Willis	9	2	26	0	3	2	1	1
P Lever	8.6	1	31	2	11	1	24	1
DL Underwood	22	7	66	4	8	2	17	0
R Illingworth	14	3	59	1	9	5	9	0
BL D'Oliveira	9	2	20	2	7	3	16	0
KWR Fletcher					1	0	6	0

Australia | Australia

No. 462: 5th Test	
VENUE: Melbourne (MCG)	
DATE: 21st-26th January 1971	
TOSS WON BY: Australia	
RESULT: Match drawn	

AUSTRALIA 1st innings / 2nd innings

Batsman	1st innings		2nd innings	
KR Stackpole	c Lever b D'Oliveira	30	c Knott b Willis	18
WM Lawry*	c Snow b Willis	56	c (sub) b Snow	42
IM Chappell	c Luckhurst b Snow	111	b Underwood	30
IR Redpath	b Snow	72	c Knott b Snow	5
KD Walters	b Underwood	55	not out	39
GS Chappell	c Edrich b Willis	3	not out	20
RW Marsh+	not out	92		
KJ O'Keeffe	c Luckhurst b Illingworth	27		
JW Gleeson	c Cowdrey b Willis	5		
JRF Duncan	c Edrich b Illingworth	3		
AL Thomson	not out	0		
Extras	(10b, 17lb, 0w, 12nb)	39	(8b, 3lb, 0w, 4nb)	15
	128 overs		46 overs	
Total		**493**		**169**

1st innings FoW: 64, 266, 269, 310, 314, 374, 471, 477, 480
2nd innings FoW: 51, 84, 91, 132

Bowler	O	M	R	W		O	M	R	W
JA Snow	29	6	94	2		12	4	21	2
P Lever	25	6	79	0		12	1	53	0
BL D'Oliveira	22	6	71	1					
RGD Willis	20	5	73	3		10	1	42	1
DL Underwood	19	4	78	1		12	0	38	1
R Illingworth	13	0	59	2					

ENGLAND 1st innings / 2nd innings

Batsman	1st innings		2nd innings	
G Boycott	c Redpath b Thomson	12	not out	76
BW Luckhurst	b Walters	109	not out	74
JH Edrich	c Marsh b Thomson	9		
MC Cowdrey	c & b Gleeson	13		
BL D'Oliveira	c Marsh b Thomson	117		
R Illingworth*	c Redpath b Gleeson	41		
APE Knott+	lbw b Stackpole	19		
JA Snow	b IM Chappell	1		
P Lever	run out	19		
DL Underwood	c & b Gleeson	5		
RGD Willis	not out	5		
Extras	(17b, 14lb, 0w, 11nb)	42	(1b, 8lb, 0w, 2nb)	11
	137.5 overs		58 overs	
Total		**392**		**161**

1st innings FoW: 40, 64, 88, 228, 306, 340, 354, 362, 379, 392

Bowler	O	M	R	W		O	M	R	W
AL Thomson	34	5	110	3		11	5	26	0
JRF Duncan	14	4	30	0					
GS Chappell	8	0	21	0		5	0	19	0
KJ O'Keeffe	31	11	71	0		19	3	45	0
JW Gleeson	25	7	60	3		3	1	18	0
KR Stackpole	17.5	4	41	1		13	2	28	0
KD Walters	5	2	7	1		7	1	14	0
IM Chappell	3	0	10	1					

No. 463: 6th Test	
VENUE: Adelaide	
DATE: 29th January-3rd Feb 1971	
TOSS WON BY: England	
RESULT: Match drawn	

ENGLAND 1st innings / 2nd innings

Batsman	1st innings		2nd innings	
G Boycott	run out	58	not out	119
JH Edrich	c Stackpole b Lillee	130	b Thomson	40
KWR Fletcher	b Thomson	80	b Gleeson	5
APE Knott+	c Redpath b Lillee	7	c Walters b Thomson	21
BL D'Oliveira	c Marsh b GS Chappell	47	lbw b Thomson	3
JH Hampshire	c Lillee b GS Chappell	55	not out	48
R Illingworth*	b Lillee	24		
JA Snow	b Lillee	38		
P Lever	b Thomson	5		
DL Underwood	not out	1		
RGD Willis	c Walters b Lillee	4		
Extras	(1b, 5lb, 4w, 11nb)	21	(0b, 4lb, 1w, 8nb)	13
	136.2 overs		51 overs	
Total		**470**		**233**

1st innings FoW: 107, 276, 289, 289, 385, 402, 458, 465, 465, 470
2nd innings FoW: 10, 128, 143, 151

Bowler	O	M	R	W		O	M	R	W
AL Thomson	29.7	6	94	2		19	2	79	3
DK Lillee	28.3	0	84	5		7	0	40	0
KD Walters	9	2	29	0		3	0	5	0
GS Chappell	18	1	54	2		5	0	27	0
JW Gleeson	19	1	78	0		16	1	69	1
AA Mallett	20	1	63	0		1	1	0	0
KR Stackpole	12	2	47	0					

AUSTRALIA 1st innings / 2nd innings

Batsman	1st innings		2nd innings	
KR Stackpole	b Underwood	87	b Snow	136
WM Lawry*	c Knott b Snow	10	c Knott b Willis	21
IM Chappell	c Knott b Lever	28	c Willis b Underwood	104
IR Redpath	c Lever b Illingworth	9	not out	21
KD Walters	c Knott b Lever	55	not out	36
GS Chappell	c Edrich b Lever	0		
RW Marsh+	c Knott b Willis	28		
AA Mallett	c Illingworth b Snow	28		
JW Gleeson	c Boycott b Willis	16		
DK Lillee	c Boycott b Lever	10		
AL Thomson	not out	6		
Extras	(0b, 2lb, 0w, 3nb)	5	(2b, 3lb, 0w, 5nb)	10
	76.1 overs		115 overs	
Total		**235**		**328**

1st innings FoW: 61, 117, 131, 141, 145, 163, 180, 219, 221, 235
2nd innings FoW: 65, 267, 271

Bowler	O	M	R	W		O	M	R	W
JA Snow	21	4	73	2		17	3	60	1
P Lever	17.1	2	49	4		17	4	49	0
DL Underwood	21	6	45	1		35	7	85	1
RGD Willis	12	3	49	2		13	1	48	1
R Illingworth	5	2	14	1		14	7	32	0
BL D'Oliveira						15	4	28	0
KWR Fletcher						4	0	16	0

	Australia	New Zealand
	No. 464: 7th Test	No. 465: 1st Test
VENUE:	Sydney (SCG)	Christchurch
DATE:	12th-17th February 1971	25th Feb-1st March 1971
TOSS WON BY:	Australia	New Zealand
RESULT:	England won by 62 runs	England won by 8 wickets

ENGLAND

1st innings		2nd innings	
JH Edrich	c GS Chappell b Dell	30	c IM Ch'll b O'Keeffe	57
BW Luckhurst	c Redpath b Walters	0	b Lillee b O'Keeffe	59
KWR Fletcher	c Stackpole b O'Keeffe	33	c Stackpole b Eastwood	20
JH Hampshire	c Marsh b Lillee	10	c IM Ch'll b O'Keeffe	24
BL D'Oliveira	b Dell	1	c IM Chappell b Lillee	47
R Illingworth*	b Jenner	42	lbw b Lillee	29
APE Knott+	c Stackpole b O'Keeffe	27	b Dell	15
JA Snow	b Jenner	7	c Stackpole b Dell	24
P Lever	c Jenner b O'Keeffe	4	c Redpath b Jenner	17
DL Underwood	not out	8	c Marsh b Dell	0
RGD Willis	b Jenner	11	not out	2
Extras	(4b, 4lb, 1w, 2nb)	11	(3b, 3lb, 0w, 6nb)	12
	76 overs		100.7 overs	
Total		**184**		**302**

1st innings FoW: 5, 60, 68, 69, 98, 145, 156, 165, 165, 184
2nd innings FoW: 94, 130, 158, 165, 234, 251, 276, 298, 299, 302

DK Lillee	13	5	32	1	14	0	43	2
AR Dell	16	8	32	2	26.7	3	65	3
KD Walters	4	0	10	1	5	0	18	0
GS Chappell	3	0	9	0				
TJ Jenner	16	3	42	3	21	5	39	1
KJ O'Keeffe	24	8	48	3	26	8	96	3
KH Eastwood					5	0	21	1
KR Stackpole					3	1	8	0

AUSTRALIA 1st innings

1st innings		2nd innings	
KH Eastwood	c Knott b Lever	5	b Snow	0
KR Stackpole	b Snow	6	b Illingworth	67
RW Marsh+	c Willis b Lever	4	c Knott b Lever	6
IM Chappell*	b Willis	25	c H'shire b Illingworth	14
IR Redpath	c & b Underwood	59	c D'Oliveira b Willis	1
KD Walters	st Knott b Underwood	42	st Knott b Illingworth	30
GS Chappell	b Willis	65	b Underwood	16
KJ O'Keeffe	c Knott b Illingworth	3	c (sub) b D'Oliveira	12
TJ Jenner	b Lever	30	c Fletcher b Underwood	4
DK Lillee	c Knott b Willis	6	c Hampshire b D'Oliveira	0
AR Dell	not out	3	not out	3
Extras	(0b, 5lb, 1w, 10nb)	16	(2b, 0lb, 0w, 5nb)	7
	83.6 overs		62.6 overs	
Total		**264**		**160**

1st innings FoW: 11, 13, 32, 66, 147, 162, 178, 235, 239, 264
2nd innings FoW: 0 , 22, 71, 82, 96, 131, 142, 154, 154, 160

JA Snow					2	1	7	1
P Lever	14.6	3	43	3	12	2	23	1
BL D'Oliveira	12	2	24	0	5	1	15	2
RGD Willis	12	1	58	3	9	1	32	1
DL Underwood	16	3	39	2	13.6	5	28	2
R Illingworth	11	3	16	1	20	7	39	3
KWR Fletcher					1	0	9	0

NEW ZEALAND 1st innings

1st innings		2nd innings	
GT Dowling*	c Edrich b Underwood	13	c Luckhurst b Lever	1
BAG Murray	c Taylor b Shuttleworth	1	b Shuttleworth	1
BE Congdon	c Taylor b Shuttleworth	1	b Underwood	55
RW Morgan	c Luckhurst b Shuttlew'th	6	b Underwood	76
MJF Shrimpton	c Fletcher b Underw'd	0	b Underwood	0
GM Turner	b Underwood	11	c Illingworth b Underw'd	8
V Pollard	b Wilson	18	lbw b Underwood	34
KJ Wadsworth+	c Fletcher b Underwood	0	c Fletcher b Wilson	1
RS Cunis	b Underwood	0	b Shuttleworth	35
HJ Howarth	st Taylor b Underwood	0	c Illingworth b Underw'd	25
RO Collinge	not out	3	not out	7
Extras	(9b, 1lb, 1w, 1nb)	12	(6b, 3lb, 1w, 1nb)	11
	37.6 overs		97.3 overs	
Total		**65**		**254**

1st innings FoW: 4, 7, 19, 28, 33, 54, 54, 62, 62, 65
2nd innings FoW: 1, 6 , 83, 83, 99, 151, 152, 209, 231, 254

P Lever					15	3	30	1
K Shuttleworth	8	1	14	3	12	1	27	2
BL D'Oliveira	3	1	2	0				
DL Underwood	11.6	7	12	6	32.3	7	85	6
R Illingworth	6	3	12	0	17	5	45	0
D Wilson	4	2	12	1	21	6	56	1

ENGLAND 1st innings

1st innings		2nd innings	
BW Luckhurst	c Wadsworth b Collinge	10	not out	29
JH Edrich	lbw b Cunis	12	c Wadsworth b Collinge	2
KWR Fletcher	b Collinge	4	c Howarth b Collinge	2
JH Hampshire	c Turner b Howarth	40	not out	51
BL D'Oliveira	b Shrimpton	100		
R Illingworth*	b Shrimpton	36		
RW Taylor+	st Wadsworth b Howarth	4		
D Wilson	c Murray b Howarth	5		
P Lever	b Howarth	4		
K Shuttleworth	b Shrimpton	5		
DL Underwood	not out	0		
Extras	(1b, 9lb, 0w, 1nb)	11	(1b, 4lb, 0w, 0nb)	5
	67.5 overs		25 overs	
Total		**231**		**89**

1st innings FoW: 20, 26, 31, 95, 188, 213, 220, 224, 231, 231
2nd innings FoW: 3, 11

RO Collinge	12	2	39	2	7	2	20	2
RS Cunis	13	2	44	1	8	0	17	0
HJ Howarth	19	7	46	4	4	0	17	0
V Pollard	9	3	45	0	3	1	9	0
MJF Shrimpton	11.5	0	35	3	3	0	21	0
BE Congdon	3	0	11	0				

New Zealand

No. 466: 2nd Test
VENUE: Auckland
DATE: 5th-8th March 1971
TOSS WON BY: New Zealand
RESULT: Match drawn

Pakistan

No. 467: 1st Test
VENUE: Edgbaston
DATE: 3rd-8th June 1971
TOSS WON BY: Pakistan
RESULT: Match drawn

ENGLAND 1st innings / 2nd innings

Batsman	1st innings		2nd innings	
JH Edrich	c Morgan b Webb	1	c Burgess b Collinge	24
BW Luckhurst	c Dowling b Cunis	14	c Wadsworth b Webb	15
MC Cowdrey	c Congdon b Cunis	54	c Wadsworth b Cunis	0
JH Hampshire	c Turner b Cunis	9	c Turner b Collinge	22
BL D'Oliveira	c Morgan b Congdon	58	b Cunis	96
R Illingworth*	c Wadsworth b Cunis	0	b Collinge	45
APE Knott+	b Collinge	101	lbw b Howarth	0
P Lever	c Wadsworth b Cunis	64	c Wadsworth b Morgan	11
K Shuttleworth	c Wadsworth b Cunis	0	b Collinge	5
RGD Willis	c Burgess b Collinge	7	lbw b Cunis	3
DL Underwood	not out	1	not out	8
Extras	(1b, 4lb, 0w, 7nb)	12	(5b, 3lb, 0w, 0nb)	8
	72.6 overs		84.7 overs	
Total		**321**		**237**

1st innings FoW: 8, 38, 59, 111, 111, 145, 294, 297, 317, 321
2nd innings FoW: 26, 27, 62, 67, 143, 152, 177, 199, 218, 237

Bowler	O	M	R	W		O	M	R	W
MG Webb	18	0	94	1		11	0	50	1
RO Collinge	18.6	5	51	2		19	6	41	4
RS Cunis	24	4	76	6		21.7	5	52	3
HJ Howarth	7	0	41	0		21	8	37	1
BE Congdon	2	0	18	1					
MJF Shrimpton	3	0	29	0		6	0	33	0
RW Morgan						6	0	16	1

NEW ZEALAND 1st innings / 2nd innings

Batsman	1st innings		2nd innings	
GM Turner	c & b Underwood	65	not out	8
GT Dowling*	c & b Underwood	53	not out	31
BE Congdon	b Underwood	0		
RW Morgan	c & b Underwood	8		
MG Burgess	c Edrich b Willis	104		
MJF Shrimpton	lbw b Underwood	46		
KJ Wadsworth+	c Hampshire b Willis	16		
RS Cunis	not out	5		
HJ Howarth	not out	2		
RO Collinge				
MG Webb				
Extras	(7b, 4lb, 0w, 3nb)	14	(0b, 1lb, 0w, 0nb)	1
	106 overs		16 overs	
Total		**313**		**40**

1st innings FoW: 91, 91, 121, 142, 283, 302, 307

Bowler	O	M	R	W		O	M	R	W
P Lever	19	3	43	0		2	0	6	0
K Shuttleworth	17	3	49	0		4	0	12	0
RGD Willis	14	2	54	2		6	1	15	0
DL Underwood	38	12	108	5		2	2	0	0
R Illingworth	18	4	45	0		2	0	6	0

PAKISTAN 1st innings / 2nd innings

Batsman	1st innings		2nd innings
Aftab Gul	b D'Oliveira	28	
Sadiq Mohammad	c & b Lever	17	
Zaheer Abbas	c Luckhurst b Illingw'th	274	
Mushtaq	c Cowdrey b Illingw'th	100	
Majid Khan	c Lever b Illingworth	35	
Asif Iqbal	not out	104	
Intikhab Alam*	c Underw'd b D'Oliveira	9	
Imran Khan	run out	5	
Wasim Bari+	not out	4	
Asif Masood			
Pervez Sajjad			
Extras	(6b, 14lb, 0w, 12nb)	32	
	195 overs		
Total		**608**	

1st innings FoW: 68, 359, 441, 456, 469, 567, 581

Bowler	O	M	R	W
Alan Ward	29	3	115	0
P Lever	38	7	126	1
K Shuttleworth	23	2	83	0
BL D'Oliveira	38	17	78	2
DL Underwood	41	13	102	0
R Illingworth	26	5	72	3

ENGLAND 1st innings / 2nd innings

Batsman	1st innings		2nd innings	
JH Edrich	c Zaheer b Asif Masood	0	c Wasim b Asif Masood	15
BW Luckhurst	c Sadiq b Pervez	35	not out	108
MC Cowdrey	b Asif Masood	16	b Asif Masood	34
DL Amiss	b Asif Masood	4	c Pervez b Asif Masood	22
BL D'Oliveira	c Mushtaq b Intikhab	73	c Mushtaq b Asif Iqbal	22
R Illingworth*	b Intikhab	1	c Wasim b Asif Masood	1
APE Knott+	b Asif Masood	116	not out	4
P Lever	c Pervez b Asif Masood	47		
K Shuttleworth	c Imran Khan b Pervez	21		
DL Underwood	not out	9		
Alan Ward	c Mushtaq b Pervez	0		
Extras	(16b, 6lb, 3w, 6nb)	31	(4b, 5lb, 6w, 8nb)	23
	120.5 overs		90.5 overs	
Total		**353**		**229**

1st innings FoW: 0, 29, 46, 112, 127, 148, 307, 324, 351, 353
2nd innings FoW: 34, 114, 169, 218, 221

Bowler	O	M	R	W		O	M	R	W
Asif Masood	34	6	111	5		23.5	7	49	4
Imran Khan	23	9	36	0		5	0	19	0
Majid Khan	4	1	8	0					
Intikhab Alam	31	13	82	2		20	8	52	0
Pervez Sajjad	15.5	6	46	3		14	4	27	0
Mushtaq	13	3	39	0		8	2	23	0
Asif Iqbal						20	6	36	1

No. 468: 2nd Test
VENUE:	Lord's
DATE:	17th–22nd June 1971
TOSS WON BY:	England
RESULT:	Match drawn

ENGLAND 1st innings / 2nd innings

Batsman	1st innings		2nd innings	
G Boycott	not out	121		
BW Luckhurst	c Wasim b Salim	46	not out	53
JH Edrich	c Asif Masood b Pervez	37		
DL Amiss	not out	19	not out	58
RA Hutton				
BL D'Oliveira				
R Illingworth*				
APE Knott+				
P Lever				
N Gifford				
JSE Price				
Extras	(6b, 2lb, 5w, 5nb)	18	(1b, 1lb, 0w, 4nb)	6
	83 overs		45 overs	
Total		**241**		**117**

1st innings FoW: 124, 205

Bowler	O	M	R	W	O	M	R	W
Asif Masood	21	3	60	0	3	1	3	0
Salim Altaf	19	5	42	1	5	2	11	0
Asif Iqbal	13	2	24	0	4	1	11	0
Majid Khan	4	0	16	0	6	2	7	0
Intikhab Alam	20	2	64	0	9	1	26	0
Pervez Sajjad	6	2	17	1				
Mushtaq Moh'd					11	3	31	0
Sadiq Mohammad					5	1	17	0
Aftab Gul					1	0	4	0
Zaheer Abbas					1	0	1	0

PAKISTAN 1st innings / 2nd innings

Aftab Gul	c Knott b Hutton	33
Sadiq	c Knott b D'Oliveira	28
Zaheer Abbas	c Hutton b Lever	40
Mushtaq	c Amiss b Hutton	2
Asif Iqbal	c Knott b Gifford	9
Majid Khan	c Edrich b Price	9
Intikhab Alam*	c Gifford b Lever	18
Wasim Bari+	c Knott b Price	0
Salim Altaf	not out	0
Asif Masood	b Price	0
Pervez Sajjad	absent hurt	0
Extras	(0b, 5lb, 1w, 3nb)	9
	72.4 overs	
Total		**148**

1st innings FoW: 57, 66, 97, 117, 119, 146, 148, 148, 148

Bowler	O	M	R	W
JSE Price	11.4	5	29	3
P Lever	16	3	38	2
N Gifford	12	6	13	1
R Illingworth	7	6	1	0
RA Hutton	16	5	36	2
BL D'Oliveira	10	5	22	1

No. 469: 3rd Test
VENUE:	Headingley
DATE:	8th–13th July 1971
TOSS WON BY:	England
RESULT:	England won by 25 runs

ENGLAND 1st innings / 2nd innings

Batsman	1st innings		2nd innings	
G Boycott	c Wasim b Intikhab	112	c Mushtaq b Asif Mas'd	13
BW Luckhurst	c Wasim b Salim	0	c Wasim b Asif Masood	0
JH Edrich	c Wasim b Asif Masood	2	c Mushtaq b Intikhab	33
DL Amiss	c Wasim b Pervez	23	c & b Saeed	56
BL D'Oliveira	b Intikhab	74	c Wasim b Salim	72
APE Knott+	b Asif Masood	10	c Zaheer b Intikhab	7
R Illingworth*	b Asif Iqbal	20	c Wasim b Salim	45
RA Hutton	c Sadiq b Asif Iqbal	28	c Zaheer b Intikhab	4
RNS Hobbs	c Wasim b Asif Iqbal	6	b Salim	0
P Lever	c Salim b Intikhab	19	b Salim	8
N Gifford	not out	3	not out	2
Extras	(5b, 5lb, 0w, 9nb)	19	(6b, 11lb, 2w, 5nb)	24
	105.2 overs		107.3 overs	
Total		**316**		**264**

1st innings FoW: 4, 10, 74, 209, 234, 234, 283, 286, 294, 316
2nd innings FoW: 0, 21, 112, 120, 142, 248, 252, 252, 262, 264

Bowler	O	M	R	W	O	M	R	W
Asif Masood	18	2	75	2	20	7	46	2
Salim Altaf	20.1	4	46	1	14.3	9	11	4
Asif Iqbal	13	2	37	3				
Pervez Sajjad	20	2	65	1	16	3	46	0
Intikhab Alam	27.1	12	51	3	36	10	91	3
Saeed Ahmed	4	0	13	0	15	4	30	1
Mushtaq Moh'd	3	1	10	0	6	1	16	0

PAKISTAN 1st innings / 2nd innings

Batsman	1st innings		2nd innings	
Aftab Gul	b Gifford	27	c Hobbs b Illingworth	18
Sadiq Mohammad	c Knott b Gifford	28	c & b D'Oliveira	91
Zaheer Abbas	c Edrich b Lever	72	c Luckhurst b Illingworth	0
Mushtaq	c Knott b Hutton	57	c Edrich b Illingworth	0
Saeed Ahmed	c Knott b D'Oliveira	22	c D'Oliveira b Gifford	5
Asif Iqbal	c Hutton b D'Oliveira	14	st Knott b Gifford	33
Intikhab Alam*	c Hobbs b D'Oliveira	17	c Hutton b D'Oliveira	4
Wasim Bari+	c Edrich b Gifford	63	c Knott b Lever	10
Salim Altaf	c Knott b Hutton	22	not out	8
Asif Masood	c & b Hutton	0	c Knott b Lever	1
Pervez Sajjad	not out	9	lbw b Lever	0
Extras	(6b, 11lb, 1w, 1nb)	19	(17b, 9lb, 1w, 3nb)	30
	209.4 overs		88.3 overs	
Total		**350**		**205**

1st innings FoW: 54, 69, 198, 198, 223, 249, 256, 313, 313, 350
2nd innings FoW: 25, 25, 54, 65, 160, 184, 187, 203, 205, 205

Bowler	O	M	R	W	O	M	R	W
P Lever	31	9	65	1	3.3	1	10	3
RA Hutton	41	8	72	3	6	0	18	0
N Gifford	53.4	26	69	3	34	14	51	2
R Illingworth	28	14	31	0	26	11	58	3
RNS Hobbs	20	5	48	0	4	0	22	0
BL D'Oliveira	36	18	46	3	15	7	16	2

India

ENGLAND	1st innings		2nd innings	
G Boycott	c Engineer b Abid Ali	3	c Wadekar b Venkat'n	33
BW Luckhurst	c Solkar b Chan'har	30	b Solkar	1
JH Edrich	c Venk'van b Bedi	18	c Engineer b Bedi	62
DL Amiss	c Engineer b Bedi	9	run out	0
BL D'Oliveira	c Solkar b Chan'har	4	b Bedi	30
APE Knott+	c Wadekar b Venkat'n	67	c Wadekar b Chandra'r	24
R Illingworth*	c Engineer b Bedi	33	c Wadekar b Venkat'n	20
RA Hutton	b Venk'van	20	b Chandrasekhar	0
JA Snow	c Abid Ali b Chandr'r	73	c Chandra'r b Venkat'n	9
N Gifford	b Bedi	17	not out	7
JSE Price	not out	5	c Abid Ali b Venkat'n	0
Extras	(8b, 12lb, 0w, 5nb)	25	(0b, 5lb, 0w, 0nb)	5
Total	139.3 overs	**304**	98.5 overs	**191**

1st innings FoW: 18, 46, 56, 61, 71, 161, 183, 223, 294, 304
2nd innings FoW: 4, 65, 70, 117, 145, 153, 153, 174, 189, 191

S Abid Ali	15	3	38	1		9	1	20	0
ED Solkar	8	3	17	0		6	3	13	1
S Venk'van	28	8	44	2		30.5	11	52	4
BS Chan'har	49	10	110	3		23	7	60	2
BS Bedi	39.3	18	70	4		30	13	41	2

INDIA	1st innings		2nd innings	
AV Mankad	c Gifford b Snow	1	c Knott b Snow	5
SM Gavaskar	c Amiss b Price	4	c Edrich b Gifford	53
AL Wadekar*	c Illingworth b Gifford	85	c Boycott b Price	5
DN Sardesai	c Illingworth b Gifford	25	st Knott b Gifford	35
GR Viswanath	c Knott b Hutton	68	c Amiss b Gifford	9
FM Engineer+	c Illingworth b Hutton	28	b Illingworth	1
ED Solkar	c Knott b Gifford	67	not out	6
S Abid Ali	c Luckhurst b Snow	4	c Snow b Illingworth	14
S Venk'van	c Hutton b Price	11	c Hutton b Gifford	7
BS Bedi	c Price b Gifford	0	not out	2
BS Chandrasekhar	not out	0		
Extras	(7b, 9lb, 0w, 2nb)	18	(0b, 7lb, 0w, 1nb)	8
Total	165.3 overs	**313**	50 overs	**145**

1st innings FoW: 1, 29, 108, 125, 175, 267, 279, 302, 311, 313
2nd innings FoW: 8, 21, 87, 101, 108, 114, 135,142

JSE Price	25	9	46	2		4	0	26	1
JA Snow	31	9	64	2		8	0	23	1
RA Hutton	24	8	38	2		3	0	12	0
N Gifford	45.3	14	84	4		19	4	43	4
BL D'Oliveira	15	7	20	0		16	2	33	2
R Illingworth	25	12	43	0					

India

ENGLAND	1st innings		2nd innings	
BW Luckhurst	c Viswanath b Bedi	78	st Engineer b Solkar	101
JA Jameson	c Gavaskar b Abid Ali	15	run out	28
JH Edrich	c Engineer b Abid Ali	0	b Bedi	59
KWR Fletcher	lbw b Abid Ali	1	not out	28
BL D'Oliveira	c Gavaskar b Abid Ali	12	not out	23
APE Knott+	b Venk'van	41		
R Illingworth*	c Gavaskar b Venkat'n	107		
RA Hutton	c & b Venk'van	15		
P Lever	not out	88		
N Gifford	c Engineer b Solkar	8		
JSE Price	run out	0		
Extras	(6b, 12lb, 1w, 2nb)	21	(0b, 5lb, 0w, 1nb)	6
Total	160.4 overs	**386**	66 overs	**245**

1st innings FoW: 21, 21, 25, 41, 116, 168, 187, 355, 384, 386
2nd innings FoW: 44, 167, 212

S Abid Ali	32.4	5	64	4		26	2	95	0
ED Solkar	21	5	46	1		5	0	23	1
BS Chan'har	30	6	90	0		2	0	5	0
BS Bedi	40	10	72	1		5	0	21	1
S Venk'van	35	9	89	3		16	3	58	0
SM Gavaskar	2	0	4	0		12	3	37	0

INDIA	1st innings		2nd innings	
AV Mankad	c Knott b Lever	8	b Price	7
SM Gavaskar	c Knott b Price	57	c Knott b Hutton	24
AL Wadekar*	c Knott b Hutton	12	b Price	9
DN Sardesai	c Knott b Lever	14	not out	13
GR Viswanath	b Lever	10	not out	8
FM Engineer+	c Edrich b Lever	22		
ED Solkar	c Hutton b D'Oliveira	50		
S Abid Ali	b D'Oliveira	0		
S Venk'van	c Knott b Lever	20		
BS Bedi	b Price	8		
BS Chandrasekhar	not out	4		
Extras	(1b, 4lb, 0w, 2nb)	7	(0b, 2lb, 0w, 2nb)	4
Total	93 overs	**212**	27 overs	**65**

1st innings FoW: 19, 52, 90, 103, 104, 163, 164, 194, 200, 212
2nd innings FoW: 9, 22, 50

JSE Price	22	7	44	2		10	3	30	2
P Lever	26	4	70	5		7	3	14	0
BL D'Oliveira	24	11	40	2		3	2	1	0
RA Hutton	14	3	35	1		7	1	16	1
R Illingworth	7	2	16	0					

India   Australia   '71

India		Australia	
No. 472: 3rd Test		No. 473: 1st Test	
VENUE: The Oval		VENUE: Old Trafford	
DATE: 19th-24th August 1971		DATE: 8th-13th June 1972	
TOSS WON BY: England		TOSS WON BY: England	
RESULT: India won by 4 wickets		RESULT: England won by 89 runs	

India (No. 472)

ENGLAND

	1st innings		2nd innings	
BW Luckhurst	c Gavaskar b Solkar	1	c Venkat'n b Chandr'r	33
JA Jameson	run out	82	run out	16
JH Edrich	c Engineer b Bedi	41	b Chandrasekhar	0
KWR Fletcher	c Gavaskar b Bedi	1	c Solkar b Chandra'ar	0
BL D'Oliveira	c Mankad b Chandr'ar	2	c (sub) b Venk'van	17
APE Knott+	c & b Solkar	90	c Solkar b Venk'van	1
R Illingworth*	b Chandrasekhar	11	c & b Chandrasekhar	4
RA Hutton	b Venk'van	81	not out	13
JA Snow	c Engineer b Solkar	0	c & b Chandrasekhar	0
DL Underwood	c Wadekar b Venk'van	22	c Mankad b Bedi	11
JSE Price	not out	1	lbw b Chandrasekhar	3
Extras	(4b, 15lb, 1w, 0nb)	20	(0b, 3lb, 0w, 0nb)	3
	108.4 overs		45.1 overs	
Total		**355**		**101**

1st innings FoW: 5, 111, 135, 139, 143, 175, 278, 284, 352, 355
2nd innings FoW: 23, 24, 24, 49, 54, 65, 72, 72, 96, 101

S Abid Ali	12	2	47	0	3	1	5	0
ED Solkar	15	4	28	3	3	1	10	0
SM Gavaskar	1	0	1	0				
BS Bedi	36	5	120	2	1	0	1	1
BS Chan'har	24	6	76	2	18.1	3	38	6
S Venk'van	20.4	3	63	2	20	4	44	2

INDIA

	1st innings		2nd innings	
SM Gavaskar	b Snow	6	lbw b Snow	0
AV Mankad	b Price	10	c Hutton b Underwood	11
AL Wadekar*	c Hutton b Illingworth	48	run out	45
DN Sardesai	b Illingworth	54	c Knott b Underwood	40
GR Viswanath	b Illingworth	0	c Knott b Luckhurst	33
ED Solkar	c Fletcher b D'Oliveira	44	c & b Underwood	1
FM Engineer+	c Illingworth b Snow	59	not out	28
S Abid Ali	b Illingworth	26	not out	4
S Venk'van	lbw b Underwood	24	(6b, 5lb, 0w, 1nb)	12
BS Bedi	c D'Oliveira b Illingworth	2	101 overs	
BS Chandrasekhar	not out	0		174
Extras	(6b, 4lb, 0w, 1nb)	11		
	117.3 overs			
Total		**284**		

1st innings FoW: 17, 21, 114, 118, 125, 222, 230, 278, 284, 284
2nd innings FoW: 2, 37, 76, 124, 134, 170

JA Snow	24	5	68	2	11	7	14	1
JSE Price	15	2	51	1	5	0	10	0
RA Hutton	12	2	30	0				
BL D'Oliveira	7	5	5	1	9	3	17	0
R Illingworth	34.3	12	70	5	36	15	40	0
DL Underwood	25	6	49	1	38	14	72	3
BW Luckhurst					2	0	9	1

Australia (No. 473)

ENGLAND

	1st innings		2nd innings	
G Boycott	c Stackpole b Gleeson	8	lbw b Gleeson	47
JH Edrich	run out	49	c Marsh b Watson	26
BW Luckhurst	b Colley	14	c Marsh b Colley	0
MJK Smith	lbw b Lillee	10	c Marsh b Lillee	34
BL D'Oliveira	b GS Chappell	23	c Watson b Lillee	37
AW Greig	lbw b Colley	57	b GS Chappell	62
APE Knott+	c Marsh b Lillee	18	c Marsh b Lillee	1
R Illingworth*	not out	26	c IM Chappell b Lillee	14
JA Snow	b Colley	3	lbw b Lillee	0
N Gifford	run out	15	c Marsh b Lillee	0
GG Arnold	c Francis b Gleeson	1	not out	0
Extras	(10b, 9lb, 2w, 4nb)	25	(4b, 8lb, 1w, 0nb)	13
	120.4 overs		86.2 overs	
Total		**249**		**234**

1st innings FoW: 50, 86, 99, 118, 127, 190, 200, 209, 243, 249
2nd innings FoW: 60, 65, 81, 140, 182, 192, 234, 234, 234, 234

DK Lillee	29	14	40	2	30	8	66	6
DJ Colley	33	3	83	3	23	3	68	1
GS Chappell	16	6	28	1	21.2	6	42	1
KD Walters	5	1	7	0	5	0	29	1
GD Watson	4	2	8	0	7	3	16	1
JW Gleeson	24.4	10	45	2				
RJ Inverarity	9	3	13	0				

AUSTRALIA

	1st innings		2nd innings	
KR Stackpole	lbw b Arnold	53	b Greig	67
BC Francis	lbw b D'Oliveira	27	lbw b Snow	6
IM Chappell*	c Smith b Greig	0	c Knott b Snow	7
GS Chappell	c Greig b Snow	24	c D'Oliveira b Arnold	23
GD Watson	c Knott b Arnold	2	c & b Snow	0
KD Walters	c Illingworth b Snow	17	b Greig	20
RJ Inverarity	c Knott b Arnold	4	c Luckhurst b D'Oliveira	3
RW Marsh+	c Edrich b Arnold	8	c Knott b Greig	91
DJ Colley	b Snow	1	c Greig b Snow	4
JW Gleeson	b Snow	0	b Greig	30
DK Lillee	not out	1	not out	0
Extras	(1b, 4lb, 0w, 0nb)	5	(0b, 0lb, 1w, 0nb)	1
	58 overs		85.2 overs	
Total		**142**		**252**

1st innings FoW: 68, 69, 91, 99, 119, 124, 134, 137, 137, 142
2nd innings FoW: 9, 31, 77, 78, 115, 120, 136, 147, 251, 252

JA Snow	20	7	41	4	27	2	87	4
GG Arnold	25	4	62	4	20	2	59	1
AW Greig	7	1	21	1	19.2	7	53	4
BL D'Oliveira	6	1	13	1	16	4	23	1
N Gifford					3	0	29	0

Australia | Australia

No. 474: 2nd Test
VENUE: Lord's
DATE: 22nd-26th June 1972
TOSS WON BY: England
RESULT: Australia won by 8 wickets

ENGLAND	1st innings		2nd innings	
G Boycott	b Massie	11	b Lillee	6
JH Edrich	lbw b Lillee	10	c Marsh b Massie	6
BW Luckhurst	b Lillee	1	c Marsh b Lillee	4
MJK Smith	b Massie	34	c Edwards b Massie	30
BL D'Oliveira	lbw b Massie	32	c GS Chappell b Massie	3
AW Greig	c Marsh b Massie	54	c IM Chappell b Massie	3
APE Knott+	c Colley b Massie	43	c GS Chappell b Massie	12
R Illingworth*	lbw b Massie	30	c Stackpole b Massie	12
JA Snow	b Massie	37	c Marsh b Massie	0
N Gifford	c Marsh b Massie	3	not out	16
JSE Price	not out	4	c GS Chappell b Massie	19
Extras	(0b, 6lb, 1w, 6nb)	13	(0b, 0lb, 1w, 4nb)	5
	91.5 overs		55.2 overs	
Total		**272**		**116**

1st innings FoW: 22, 23, 28, 84, 97, 193, 200, 260, 265, 272
2nd innings FoW: 12, 16, 18, 25, 31, 52, 74, 74, 81, 116

DK Lillee	28	3	90	2		21	6	50	2
RAL Massie	32.5	7	84	8		27.2	9	53	8
DJ Colley	16	2	42	0		7	1	8	0
GS Chappell	6	1	18	0					
JW Gleeson	9	1	25	0					

AUSTRALIA	1st innings		2nd innings	
KR Stackpole	c Gifford b Price	5	not out	57
BC Francis	b Snow	0	c Knott b Price	9
IM Chappell*	c Smith b Snow	56	c Luckhurst b D'Oliveira	6
GS Chappell	b D'Oliveira	131	not out	7
KD Walters	c Illingworth b Snow	1		
R Edwards	c Smith b Illingworth	28		
JW Gleeson	c Knott b Greig	1		
RW Marsh+	c Greig b Snow	50		
DJ Colley	c Greig b Price	25		
RAL Massie	c Knott b Snow	0		
DK Lillee	not out	2		
Extras	(0b, 7lb, 0w, 2nb)	9	(0b, 2lb, 0w, 0nb)	2
	122.1 overs		26.5 overs	
Total		**308**		**81**

1st innings FoW: 1, 7, 82, 84, 190, 212, 250, 290, 290, 308
2nd innings FoW: 20, 51

JA Snow	32	13	57	5		8	2	15	0
JSE Price	26.1	5	87	2		7	0	28	1
AW Greig	29	6	74	1		3	0	17	0
BL D'Oliveira	17	5	48	1		8	3	14	1
N Gifford	11	4	20	0					
R Illingworth	7	2	13	1					
BW Luckhurst						0.5	0	5	0

No. 475: 3rd Test
VENUE: Trent Bridge
DATE: 13th-18th July 1972
TOSS WON BY: England
RESULT: Match drawn

AUSTRALIA	1st innings		2nd innings	
KR Stackpole	c Parfitt b Greig	114	c Luckhurst b Snow	12
BC Francis	c Smith b Lever	10	not out	170
IM Chappell*	c Knott b Snow	34	lbw b Illingworth	50
GS Chappell	c Parfitt b Snow	26	b Snow	72
KD Walters	c Parfitt b Snow	2	c Gifford b Snow	7
R Edwards	c Knott b Snow	13	not out	7
RW Marsh+	c D'Oliveira b Gifford	41		
DJ Colley	c Greig b D'Oliveira	54		
RAL Massie	c Parfitt b Snow	0		
JW Gleeson	not out	6		
DK Lillee	c Knott b Greig	0		
Extras	(4b, 6lb, 0w, 5nb)	15	(0b, 4lb, 1w, 1nb)	6
	118.4 overs		92 overs	
Total		**315**		**324**

1st innings FoW: 16, 98, 157, 165, 189, 227, 289, 298, 315, 315
2nd innings FoW: 15, 139, 285, 295

JA Snow	31	8	92	5		24	1	94	3
P Lever	26	8	61	1		19	3	76	0
AW Greig	38.4	9	88	2		12	1	46	0
BL D'Oliveira	18	5	41	1		7	0	12	0
N Gifford	5	1	18	1		15	1	49	0
R Illingworth						15	4	41	1

ENGLAND	1st innings		2nd innings	
BW Luckhurst	lbw b Lillee	23	c GS Chap'l b IM Chap'l	96
JH Edrich	c Marsh b Colley	37	b Massie	15
PH Parfitt	b Massie	0	b Lillee	46
MJK Smith	b Lillee	17	lbw b Lillee	15
BL D'Oliveira	lbw b Lillee	29	not out	50
N Gifford	c Marsh b Massie	16	not out	36
AW Greig	c Marsh b Massie	7		
APE Knott+	c Marsh b Massie	0		
R Illingworth*	not out	24		
JA Snow	c Marsh b Lillee	6		
P Lever	c Walters b Colley	9		
Extras	(5b, 2lb, 1w, 13nb)	21	(17b, 9lb, 4w, 2nb)	32
	88.3 overs		148 overs	
Total		**189**		**290**

1st innings FoW: 55, 60, 74, 111, 133, 145, 145, 155, 166, 189
2nd innings FoW: 50, 167, 200, 201

DK Lillee	29	15	35	4		25	10	40	2
RAL Massie	30	10	43	4		36	13	49	1
DJ Colley	23.3	5	68	2		19	6	43	0
JW Gleeson	6	1	22	0		30	13	49	0
IM Chappell						12	5	26	1
GS Chappell						9	4	16	0
KR Stackpole						17	7	35	0

No. 476: 4th Test
VENUE: Headingley
DATE: 27th-29th July 1972
TOSS WON BY: Australia
RESULT: England won by 9 wickets

No. 477: 5th Test
VENUE: The Oval
DATE: 10th-16th August 1972
TOSS WON BY: England
RESULT: Australia won by 5 wickets

AUSTRALIA 1st innings / 2nd innings

Batsman	1st innings		2nd innings	
KR Stackpole	c Knott b Underwood	52	lbw b Underwood	28
R Edwards	c Knott b Snow	0	c Knott b Arnold	0
IM Chappell*	c & b Illingworth	26	c Knott b Arnold	0
GS Chappell	lbw b Underwood	12	c D'Oliveira b Underw'd	13
AP Sheahan	c Illingworth b Underwood	0	not out	41
KD Walters	b Illingworth	4	c Parfitt b Underwood	3
RW Marsh+	c Illingworth b Underwood	1	c Knott b Underwood	1
RJ Inverarity	not out	26	c Illingworth b Underwood	0
AA Mallett	lbw b Snow	20	b Illingworth	9
RAL Massie	b Arnold	0	b Underwood	7
DK Lillee	c Greig b Arnold	0	b Illingworth	18
Extras	(0b, 2lb, 0w, 3nb)	5	(0b, 12lb, 0w, 4nb)	16
	86.5 overs		56.1 overs	
Total		**146**		**136**

1st innings FoW: 10, 79, 93, 93, 97, 98, 98, 145, 146, 146
2nd innings FoW: 5, 7, 31, 51, 63, 69, 69, 93, 111, 136

Bowler	O	M	R	W	O	M	R	W
GG Arnold	9.5	2	28	2	6	1	17	2
JA Snow	13	5	11	2	10	2	26	0
AW Greig	10	1	25	0				
R Illingworth	21	11	32	2	19.1	5	32	2
DL Underwood	31	16	37	4	21	6	45	6
BL D'Oliveira	2	1	8	0				

ENGLAND 1st innings / 2nd innings

Batsman	1st innings		2nd innings	
BW Luckhurst	c GS Chappell b Mallett	18	not out	12
JH Edrich	c IM Chappell b Mallett	45	lbw b Lillee	4
PH Parfitt	c Marsh b Lillee	2	not out	0
KWR Fletcher	lbw b Mallett	5		
BL D'Oliveira	b Mallett	12		
AW Greig	c G Chappell b Inverarity	24		
APE Knott+	st Marsh b Mallett	0		
R Illingworth*	lbw b Lillee	57		
JA Snow	st Marsh b Inverarity	48		
DL Underw'd	c IM Chappell b Inverarity	5		
GG Arnold	not out	1		
Extras	(19b, 15lb, 4w, 8nb)	46	(0b, 3lb, 0w, 2nb)	5
	130.1 overs		10 overs	
Total		**263**		**21**

1st innings FoW: 43, 52, 66, 76, 108, 108, 128, 232, 246, 263
2nd innings FoW: 7

Bowler	O	M	R	W	O	M	R	W
DK Lillee	26.1	10	39	2	5	2	7	1
RAL Massie	14	4	34	0				
AA Mallett	52	20	114	5	5	1	9	0
RJ Inverarity	33	19	26	3				
IM Chappell	3	2	1	0				
GS Chappell	2	0	3	0				

ENGLAND 1st innings / 2nd innings

Batsman	1st innings		2nd innings	
B Wood	c Marsh b Watson	26	lbw b Massie	90
JH Edrich	lbw b Lillee	8	b Lillee	18
PH Parfitt	b Lillee	51	b Lillee	18
JH Hampshire	c Inverarity b Mallett	42	c IM Chappell b Watson	20
BL D'Oliveira	c GS Chappell b Mallett	4	c IM Chappell b Massie	43
AW Greig	c Stackpole b Mallett	16	c Marsh b Lillee	29
R Illingworth*	c GS Chappell b Lillee	0	lbw b Lillee	31
APE Knott+	c Marsh b Lillee	92	b Lillee	63
JA Snow	c Marsh b Lillee	3	c Stackpole b Mallett	14
GG Arnold	b Inverarity	22	lbw b Mallett	4
DL Underwood	not out	3	not out	0
Extras	(0b, 8lb, 1w, 8nb)	17	(11b, 8lb, 0w, 7nb)	26
	92.2 overs		121.2 overs	
Total		**284**		**356**

1st innings FoW: 25, 50, 133, 142, 145, 145, 159, 181, 262, 284
2nd innings FoW: 56, 81, 114, 194, 205, 270, 271, 333, 356, 356

Bowler	O	M	R	W	O	M	R	W
DK Lillee	24.2	7	58	5	32.2	8	123	5
RAL Massie	27	5	69	0	32	10	77	2
GD Watson	12	4	23	1	19	8	32	1
AA Mallett	23	4	80	3	23	7	66	2
GS Chappell	2	0	18	0				
RJ Inverarity	4	0	19	1	15	4	32	0

AUSTRALIA 1st innings / 2nd innings

Batsman	1st innings		2nd innings	
GD Watson	c Knott b Arnold	13	lbw b Arnold	6
KR Stackpole	b Snow	18	c Knott b Greig	79
IM Chappell*	c Snow b Arnold	118	c (sub) b Underwood	37
GS Chappell	c Greig b Illingworth	113	lbw b Underwood	16
R Edwards	b Underwood	79	lbw b Greig	1
AP Sheahan	c Hampshire b Underwood	5	not out	44
RW Marsh+	b Underwood	0	not out	43
RJ Inverarity	c Greig b Underwood	28		
AA Mallett	run out	5		
RAL Massie	b Arnold	4		
DK Lillee	not out	0		
Extras	(0b, 8lb, 1w, 7nb)	16	(0b, 6lb, 0w, 10nb)	16
	151.5 overs		92.2 overs	
Total		**399**		**242**

1st innings FoW: 24, 34, 235, 296, 310, 310, 383, 387, 399, 399
2nd innings FoW: 16, 132, 136, 137, 171

Bowler	O	M	R	W	O	M	R	W
GG Arnold	35	11	87	3	15	5	26	1
JA Snow	34.5	5	111	1	6	1	21	0
AW Greig	18	9	25	0	25.3	10	49	2
BL D'Oliveira	9	4	17	0				
DL Underwood	38	16	90	4	35	11	94	2
R Illingworth	17	4	53	1	8.5	2	26	0
PH Parfitt					2	0	10	0

India

No. 478: 1st Test	
VENUE:	Delhi
DATE:	20th-25th December 1972
TOSS WON BY:	India
RESULT:	England won by 6 wickets

No. 479: 2nd Test	
VENUE:	Calcutta
DATE:	30th Dec 1972-4th Jan 1973
TOSS WON BY:	India
RESULT:	India won by 28 runs

INDIA 1st innings / 2nd innings (Delhi)

Batsman	1st innings		2nd innings	
SM Gavaskar	c Greig b Arnold	12	c Greig b Underwood	8
RD Parkar	c Pocock b Arnold	4	lbw b Arnold	35
AL Wadekar*	b Arnold	3	st Knott b Pocock	24
DN Sardesai	b Arnold	12	c Greig b Underwood	10
GR Viswanath	c Knott b Greig	27	b Underwood	3
ED Solkar	c Knott b Greig	20	c (sub) b Arnold	75
FM Engineer+	b Cottam	15	c Knott b Underwood	63
S Abid Ali	c Greig b Cottam	58	c Fletcher b Pocock	0
S Venk'van	c Greig b Arnold	17	b Pocock	0
BS Bedi	not out	4	b Arnold	2
BS Chandrasekhar	b Arnold	0	not out	1
Extras	(0b, 1lb, 0w, 0nb)	1	(8b, 2lb, 0w, 2nb)	12
Total	84.4 overs	**173**	98.4 overs	**233**

1st innings FoW: 7, 15, 20, 43, 59, 80, 123, 169, 169, 173
2nd innings FoW: 26, 59, 82, 86, 103, 206, 207, 211, 215, 233

	O	M	R	W	O	M	R	W
GG Arnold	23.4	7	45	6	20.4	6	46	3
RMH Cottam	23	5	66	2	7	1	18	0
AW Greig	23	8	32	2	6	1	16	0
PI Pocock	6	1	13	0	33	7	72	3
DL Underwood	9	1	16	0	30	13	56	4
B Wood					2	0	13	0

ENGLAND 1st innings / 2nd innings (Delhi)

Batsman	1st innings		2nd innings	
B Wood	c Venk'van b Chan'har	19	c Solkar b Bedi	45
DL Amiss	st Engineer b Bedi	46	c Chandrasekhar b Bedi	9
KWR Fletcher	b Chandrasekhar	2	c Wadekar b Bedi	0
MH Denness	c Engineer b Bedi	16	c Viswanath b Chan'har	35
AR Lewis*	lbw b Chandrasekhar	0	not out	70
AW Greig	not out	68	not out	40
APE Knott+	c Solkar b Chandrasekhar	4		
GG Arnold	c Abid Ali b Chan'har	12		
PI Pocock	lbw b Chandrasekhar	0		
DL Underwood	c Solkar b Chan'har	6		
RMH Cottam	c Abid Ali b Chan'har	3		
Extras	(4b, 17lb, 0w, 3nb)	24	(0b, 9lb, 0w, 0nb)	9
Total	108.5 overs	**200**	88.5 overs	**208**

1st innings FoW: 61, 69, 71, 71, 119, 123, 152, 160, 180, 200
2nd innings FoW: 18, 20, 76, 107

	O	M	R	W	O	M	R	W
S Abid Ali	9	5	13	0	4	2	6	0
ED Solkar	3	0	8	0	3	0	13	0
BS Bedi	47	23	59	2	39	20	50	3
BS Chan'har	41.5	18	79	8	24	7	70	1
S Venk'van	8	2	17	0	16	0	47	0
DN Sardesai					1.5	0	12	0
SM Gavaskar					1	0	1	0

INDIA 1st innings / 2nd innings (Calcutta)

Batsman	1st innings		2nd innings	
SM Gavaskar	c Old b Underwood	18	lbw b Old	2
RD Parkar	c Knott b Old	26	c Fletcher b Old	15
AL Wadekar*	run out	44	c Fletcher b Greig	53
GR Viswanath	c Wood b Cottam	3	c Fletcher b Old	34
SA Durani	b Greig	4	c Knott b Underwood	17
ED Solkar	b Old	19	c Knott b Greig	6
FM Engineer+	b Underwood	75	lbw b Greig	0
S Abid Ali	b Cottam	3	c Amiss b Old	3
EAS Prasanna	lbw b Cottam	6	b Greig	0
BS Bedi	run out	0	not out	9
BS Chandrasekhar	not out	1	b Greig	1
Extras	(0b, 3lb, 0w, 8nb)	11	(8b, 2lb, 0w, 5nb)	15
Total	97.4 overs	**210**	67.5 overs	**155**

1st innings FoW: 29, 68, 78, 99, 100, 163, 176, 192, 192, 210
2nd innings FoW: 2, 33, 104, 112, 133, 133, 135, 135, 147, 155

	O	M	R	W	O	M	R	W
CM Old	26	7	72	2	21	6	43	4
RMH Cottam	23	6	45	3	5	0	18	0
DL Underwood	20.4	11	43	2	14	4	36	1
PI Pocock	19	10	26	0	8	1	19	0
AW Greig	9	1	13	1	19.5	9	24	5

ENGLAND 1st innings / 2nd innings (Calcutta)

Batsman	1st innings		2nd innings	
B Wood	b Bedi	11	b Abid Ali	1
DL Amiss	c Solkar b Chan'har	11	c Engineer b Bedi	1
KWR Fletcher	c Gavaskar b Prasanna	16	lbw b Bedi	5
MH Denness	c Solkar b Chan'har	21	lbw b Chandrasekhar	32
AR Lewis*	lbw b Bedi	4	c Solkar b Bedi	3
AW Greig	c (sub) b Prasanna	29	lbw b Chandrasekhar	67
APE Knott+	st Engineer b Chan'har	35	c Durani b Chan'har	2
CM Old	not out	33	not out	17
PI Pocock	b Prasanna	3	c & b Bedi	5
DL Underwood	c Solkar b Chan'har	0	c Wadekar b Bedi	4
RMH Cottam	lbw b Chandrasekhar	3	lbw b Chandrasekhar	13
Extras	(0b, 4lb, 0w, 4nb)	8	(6b, 5lb, 0w, 2nb)	13
Total	75.2 overs	**174**	91 overs	**163**

1st innings FoW: 18, 37, 47, 56, 84, 117, 144, 153, 154, 174
2nd innings FoW: 3, 8, 11, 17, 114, 119, 123, 130, 138, 163

	O	M	R	W	O	M	R	W
S Abid Ali	4	1	4	0	8	2	12	1
ED Solkar	3	1	5	0	1	1	0	0
BS Bedi	26	7	59	2	40	12	63	5
BS Chan'har	26.2	5	65	5	29	14	42	4
EAS Prasanna	16	4	33	3	9	0	19	0
SA Durani					4	1	14	0

	No. 480: 3rd Test		No. 481: 4th Test
VENUE:	Madras (Chepauk)	VENUE:	Kanpur
DATE:	12th-17th January 1973	DATE:	25th-30th January 1973
TOSS WON BY:	England	TOSS WON BY:	India
RESULT:	India won by 4 wickets	RESULT:	Match drawn

ENGLAND 1st innings / 2nd innings

Batsman	1st innings		2nd innings	
B Wood	c Engineer b Bedi	20	c (sub) b Bedi	5
DL Amiss	c Solkar b Chan'har	15	c Engineer b Chan'har	8
APE Knott+	c Pataudi b Bedi	10	c Chandrasekhar b Bedi	13
MH Denness	b Prasanna	17	c Solkar b Prasanna	76
KWR Fletcher	not out	97	c Chauhan b Bedi	21
AW Greig	lbw b Chandrasekhar	17	c Solkar b Durani	5
AR Lewis*	c Solkar b Chan'har	4	c Chauhan b Bedi	11
CM Old	c Durani b Chan'har	4	c Bedi b Prasanna	9
GG Arnold	c Solkar b Prasanna	17	c Wadekar b Prasanna	17
N Gifford	lbw b Chandrasekhar	19	not out	3
PI Pocock	lbw b Chandrasekhar	2	c Wadekar b Prasanna	0
Extras	(8b, 11lb, 0w, 1nb)	20	(2b, 3lb, 0w, 3nb)	8
	86.5 overs		106 overs	
Total		**242**		**159**

1st innings FoW: 33, 47, 52, 69, 98, 106 / 110, 151, 234, 242
2nd innings FoW: 14, 14, 30, 77, 97, 126, 152, 152, 159, 159

Bowler	O	M	R	W	O	M	R	W
ED Solkar	2	0	13	0	2	2	0	0
SM Gavaskar	1	0	6	0				
BS Bedi	30	9	66	2	43	24	38	4
BS Chan'har	38.5	9	90	6	35	9	69	1
EAS Prasanna	15	3	47	2	10	5	16	4
Pataudi (Nawab of) jr					1	0	4	0
SA Durani					15	5	24	1

INDIA 1st innings / 2nd innings

Batsman	1st innings		2nd innings	
CPS Chauhan	c Knott b Arnold	0	c Knott b Pocock	11
SM Gavaskar	c Greig b Gifford	20	lbw b Old	10
AL Wadekar*	c Wood b Pocock	44	c Greig b Old	0
SA Durani	c & b Gifford	38	lbw b Pocock	38
Pataudi jr	c (sub) b Pocock	73	b Pocock	0
GR Viswanath	c Old b Pocock	37	not out	14
FM Engineer+	c Wood b Gifford	31	c Denness b Pocock	7
ED Solkar	b Pocock	10	not out	0
EAS Prasanna	lbw b Arnold	37		
BS Bedi	b Arnold	5		
BS Chandrasekhar	not out	3		
Extras	(6b, 3lb, 0w, 9nb)	18	(0b, 1lb, 0w, 5nb)	6
	135.1 overs		33.5 overs	
Total		**316**		**86**

1st innings FoW: 4, 28, 89, 155, 220, 224, 247, 288, 303, 316
2nd innings FoW: 11, 11, 44, 51, 67, 78

Bowler	O	M	R	W	O	M	R	W
GG Arnold	23.1	12	34	3	4	1	11	0
CM Old	20	4	51	0	9	3	19	2
N Gifford	34	15	64	3	7.5	2	22	0
AW Greig	12	1	35	0	13	3	28	4
PI Pocock	46	15	114	4				

INDIA 1st innings / 2nd innings

Batsman	1st innings		2nd innings	
CPS Chauhan	c Old b Underwood	22	c Roope b Arnold	1
SM Gavaskar	c Greig b Birkenshaw	69	c (sub) b Underwood	24
AL Wadekar*	c Fletcher b Greig	90	c & b Underwood	9
GR Viswanath	c Denness b Old	25	not out	75
Pataudi (Nawab of) jr	lbw b Arnold	54	c Old b Birkenshaw	2
ED Solkar	b Underwood	10	c Greig b Birkenshaw	26
FM Engineer+	b Underwood	15	b Greig	36
S Abid Ali	b Old	41	not out	2
EAS Prasanna	c Knott b Old	0		
BS Bedi	not out	4		
BS Chandrasekhar	b Old	0		
Extras	(1b, 9lb, 0w, 17nb)	27	(5b, 4lb, 0w, 2nb)	11
	167 overs		84 overs	
Total		**357**		**186**

1st innings FoW: 85, 109, 179, 265, 292, 296, 326, 345, 357, 357
2nd innings FoW: 8, 33, 36, 39, 103, 181

Bowler	O	M	R	W	O	M	R	W
GG Arnold	35	10	72	1	7	3	15	1
CM Old	24	5	69	4	11	3	28	0
DL Underwood	51	20	90	3	26	11	46	2
AW Greig	29	11	40	1	10	7	6	1
N Gifford	8	2	17	0				
J Birkenshaw	20	6	42	1	25	5	66	2
GRJ Roope					5	1	14	0

ENGLAND 1st innings / 2nd innings

Batsman	1st innings		2nd innings
MH Denness	c Abid Ali b Chan'har	31	
GRJ Roope	c Abid Ali b Chan'har	11	
APE Knott+	c Gavaskar b Prasanna	40	
AR Lewis*	b Abid Ali	125	
KWR Fletcher	c Chan'har b Bedi	58	
AW Greig	c Chauhan b Bedi	8	
J Birkenshaw	c Abid Ali b Chan'har	64	
CM Old	lbw b Chandrasekhar	4	
GG Arnold	b Bedi	45	
DL Underwoo	not out	0	
N Gifford	absent hurt	0	
Extras	(1b, 8lb, 1w, 1nb)	11	
	172.5 overs		
Total		**397**	

1st innings FoW: 37, 48, 118, 262, 274, 288, 301, 397, 397

Bowler	O	M	R	W
S Abid Ali	22	3	55	1
ED Solkar	5	0	14	0
BS Bedi	68.5	15	134	3
BS Chan'har	41	12	86	4
EAS Prasanna	34	4	87	1
GR Viswanath	2	0	10	0

India

No. 482: 5th Test
VENUE: Bombay (Brabourne)
DATE: 6th-11th February 1973
TOSS WON BY: India
RESULT: Match drawn

INDIA 1st innings / 2nd innings

Batsman	1st innings		2nd innings	
FM Engineer+	c Roope b Birkenshaw	121	b Underwood	66
SM Gavaskar	b Old	4	c & b Underwood	67
AL Wadekar*	c Old b Birkenshaw	87	c Knott b Pocock	37
SA Durani	c Underwood b Pocock	73	c Knott b Greig	48
Pataudi jr	b Underwood	1	b Pocock	5
GR Viswanath	b Arnold	113	not out	11
ED Solkar	c Denness b Old	6	not out	6
S Abid Ali	c Roope b Arnold	15		
S Venk'van	not out	11		
BS Bedi	b Arnold	0		
BS Chandrasekhar	c Fletcher b Old	3		
Extras	(4b, 4lb, 0w, 6nb)	14	(0b, 4lb, 0w, 0nb)	4
	138.2 overs		96 overs	
Total		**448**		**244**

1st innings FoW: 25, 217, 220, 221, 371, 395, 427, 435, 439, 448
2nd innings FoW: 135, 136, 198, 227, 233

Bowler	O	M	R	W	O	M	R	W
GG Arnold	21	3	64	3	3	0	13	0
CM Old	21.2	2	78	3	3	1	11	0
DL Underwood	26	6	100	1	38	16	70	2
AW Greig	22	7	62	0	13	7	19	1
PI Pocock	25	7	63	1	27	5	75	2
J Birkenshaw	23	2	67	2	12	1	52	0

ENGLAND 1st innings / 2nd innings

Batsman	1st innings		2nd innings	
AR Lewis*	b Abid Ali	0	b Bedi	12
GRJ Roope	c Abid Ali b Chan'har	10	not out	26
APE Knott+	lbw b Chandrasekhar	56	b Chandrasekhar	8
DL Underwood	c Abid Ali b Bedi	9	not out	17
KWR Fletcher	lbw b Bedi	113		
AW Greig	lbw b Chandrasekhar	148		
MH Denness	c Venk'van b Bedi	29		
J Birkenshaw	b Chandrasekhar	36		
CM Old	c & b Venk'van	28		
GG Arnold	lbw b Chandrasekhar	27		
PI Pocock	not out	0		
Extras	(13b, 5lb, 0w, 6nb)	24	(3b, 1lb, 0w, 0nb)	4
	163.1 overs		29 overs	
Total		**480**		**67**

1st innings FoW: 0, 38, 67, 79, 333, 381, 397, 442, 479, 480
2nd innings FoW: 23, 37

Bowler	O	M	R	W	O	M	R	W
S Abid Ali	15	2	60	1				
ED Solkar	4	0	16	0	2	0	4	0
BS Bedi	69	20	138	3	10	4	25	1
BS Chan'har	46.1	8	135	5	9	1	26	1
SA Durani	4	0	21	0				
S Venk'van	25	1	86	1				
S Venk'van					5	1	8	0
SM Gavaskar					2	2	0	0
Pataudi jr					1	1	0	0

Pakistan

No. 483: 1st Test
VENUE: Lahore (Gaddafi)
DATE: 2nd-7th March 1973
TOSS WON BY: England
RESULT: Match drawn

ENGLAND 1st innings / 2nd innings

Batsman	1st innings		2nd innings	
MH Denness	lbw b Salim	50	c Wasim Bari b Intikhab	68
DL Amiss	b Salim	112	c Mushtaq b Intikhab	16
GRJ Roope	c Wasim Bari b Pervez	15	st Wasim Bari b Intikhab	0
AR Lewis*	b Wasim Raja	29	b Salim	74
KWR Fletcher	c Wasim Bari b Pervez	55	b Intikhab	12
AW Greig	c Majid b Sarfraz	41	c Talat b Mushtaq	72
APE Knott+	c Wasim Bari b Mushtaq	29	c Majid b Mushtaq	34
CM Old	b Pervez	0	not out	17
GG Arnold	c Sarfraz b Mushtaq	0	not out	3
DL Underwood	not out	5		
PI Pocock	c Talat b Mushtaq	5		
Extras	(0b, 11lb, 0w, 3nb)	14	(6b, 3lb, 0w, 1nb)	10
	143.3 overs		119 overs	
Total		**355**		**306**

1st innings FoW: 105, 147, 201, 219, 286, 333, 333, 334, 345, 355
2nd innings FoW: 63, 63, 108, 154, 203, 282, 287

Bowler	O	M	R	W	O	M	R	W
Salim Altaf	28	3	80	2	11	2	24	1
Sarfraz Nawaz	31	14	51	1	17	7	41	0
Wasim Raja	21	0	69	1	14	7	36	0
Pervez Sajjad	23	9	58	3	23	9	37	0
Intikhab Alam	32	14	62	0	35	10	80	4
Mushtaq Moh'd	8.3	1	21	3	16	2	66	2
Majid Khan					3	1	12	0

PAKISTAN 1st innings / 2nd innings

Batsman	1st innings		2nd innings	
Sadiq	c Roope b Greig	119	c Roope b Greig	9
Talat Ali	c Greig b Arnold	35	c & b Pocock	57
Majid Khan*	run out	32	c & b Greig	43
Mushtaq	b Underwood	66	not out	5
Asif Iqbal	c Denness b Arnold	102	not out	6
Intikhab Alam	b Underwood	3		
Wasim Raja	c Roope b Greig	23		
Salim Altaf	not out	11		
Wasim Bari+	b Underwood	7		
Sarfraz Nawaz	b Greig	8		
Pervez Sajjad	lbw b Greig	4		
Extras	(1b, 6lb, 0w, 5nb)	12	(0b, 4lb, 0w, 0nb)	4
	158.2 overs		38 overs	
Total		**422**		**124**

1st innings FoW: 99, 155, 222, 294, 310, 383, 391, 404, 413, 422
2nd innings FoW: 9, 102, 114

Bowler	O	M	R	W	O	M	R	W
GG Arnold	43	10	95	2	4	1	12	0
CM Old	27	2	98	0				
DL Underwood	35	15	58	3	13	5	38	0
PI Pocock	24	6	73	0	15	3	42	1
AW Greig	29.2	5	86	4	6	0	28	2

	No. 484: 2nd Test
VENUE:	Hyderabad
DATE:	16th-21st March 1973
TOSS WON BY:	England
RESULT:	Match drawn

	No. 485: 3rd Test
VENUE:	Karachi (National Stadium)
DATE:	24th-29th March 1973
TOSS WON BY:	Pakistan
RESULT:	Match drawn

ENGLAND 1st innings / 2nd innings

Batsman	1st innings		2nd innings	
MH Denness	b Salim	8	c Mushtaq b Salim	0
DL Amiss	st Wasim b Mushtaq	158	c Sadiq b Intikhab	0
KWR Fletcher	c Zaheer b Intikhab	78	c Asif b Intikhab	21
AR Lewis*	c Wasim b Mushtaq	7	c Pervez b Intikhab	21
GRJ Roope	st Wasim b Intikhab	27	b Mushtaq	18
AW Greig	b Mushtaq Mohammad	36	c Wasim b Asif	64
APE Knott+	c Nazir b Mushtaq	71	not out	63
GG Arnold	c Wasim b Intikhab	8	not out	19
N Gifford	b Intikhab	24		
DL Underwood	not out	20		
PI Pocock	b Pervez	33		
Extras	(2b, 11lb, 0w, 4nb)	17	(1b, 5lb, 0w, 6nb)	12
Total	200.2 overs	**487**	85 overs	**218**

1st innings FoW: 22, 190, 250, 259, 319, 343, 364, 428, 432, 487
2nd innings FoW: 0, 0, 34, 52, 77, 189

Bowler	O	M	R	W		O	M	R	W
Salim Altaf	29	10	63	1		10	1	40	1
Asif Iqbal	11	5	31	0		1	0	3	1
Intikhab Alam	65	17	137	4		19	5	44	3
Mohammad Nazir	36	9	84	0		16	3	41	0
Pervez Sajjad	21.2	5	56	1		11	5	11	0
Mushtaq	35	10	93	4		20	5	42	1
Sadiq Mohammad	3	1	6	0		3	0	14	0
Majid Khan						2	0	4	0
Talat Ali						2	1	6	0
Zaheer Abbas						1	0	1	0

PAKISTAN 1st innings / 2nd innings

Batsman	1st innings		2nd innings
Sadiq	c Knott b Pocock	30	
Talat Ali	c Fletcher b Gifford	22	
Majid Khan*	c Knott b Pocock	17	
Mushtaq	lbw b Gifford	157	
Zaheer Abbas	c Roope b Pocock	24	
Asif Iqbal	c Roope b Pocock	68	
Intikhab Alam	b Arnold	138	
Salim Altaf	c Gifford b Pocock	2	
Wasim Bari+	c Pocock b Gifford	48	
Nazir	not out	22	
Pervez Sajjad	not out	10	
Extras	(14b, 10lb, 0w, 7nb)	31	
Total	192 overs	**569**	

1st innings FoW: 53, 66, 77, 139, 292, 437, 449, 514, 553

Bowler	O	M	R	W
GG Arnold	24	2	78	1
AW Greig	13	2	39	0
PI Pocock	52	9	169	5
N Gifford	52	16	111	3
DL Underwood	48	15	119	0
KWR Fletcher	3	0	22	0

PAKISTAN 1st innings / 2nd innings

Batsman	1st innings		2nd innings	
Sadiq	c Denness b Gifford	89	b Gifford	23
Talat Ali	c Amiss b Gifford	33	b Gifford	39
Majid Khan*	c Amiss b Pocock	99	c Knott b Gifford	4
Mushtaq	run out	99	c Fletcher b Gifford	36
Asif Iqbal	c & b Pocock	6	c Denness b Birkenshaw	0
Intikhab Alam	c & b Birkenshaw	61	b Gifford	1
Zaheer Abbas	not out	22	c Greig b Birkenshaw	0
Wasim Bari+	not out	17	c Denness b Birken'w	41
Salim Altaf			c Knott b Birkenshaw	13
Sarfraz Nawaz			not out	33
Asif Masood			c Gifford b Birkenshaw	0
Extras	(4b, 9lb, 0w, 6nb)	19	(0b, 4lb, 0w, 5nb)	9
Total	154 overs	**445**	72.3 overs	**199**

1st innings FoW: 79, 176, 297, 307, 389, 413
2nd innings FoW: 39, 51, 105, 106, 106, 106, 108, 129, 198, 199

Bowler	O	M	R	W		O	M	R	W
GG Arnold						15	2	52	0
AW Greig	20	1	76	0		10	2	26	0
PI Pocock	38	7	93	2					
N Gifford	46	12	99	2		29	9	55	5
J Birkenshaw	31	5	89	1		18.3	5	57	5

ENGLAND 1st innings / 2nd innings

Batsman	1st innings		2nd innings	
B Wood	c Sarfraz b Asif Masood	3	c Asif Masood b Salim	5
DL Amiss	c Sarfraz b Intikhab	99	not out	21
KWR Fletcher	c Talat b Intikhab	54	not out	1
MH Denness	lbw b Asif Masood	47		
AR Lewis*	c Asif Iqbal b Intikhab	88		
PI Pocock	c Sarfraz b Mushtaq	4		
AW Greig	b Majid	48		
APE Knott+	b Majid	2		
J Birkenshaw	c Majid b Mushtaq	21		
GG Arnold	c Mushtaq b Intikhab	2		
N Gifford	not out	4		
Extras	(3b, 3lb, 0w, 8nb)	14	(0b, 0lb, 0w, 3nb)	3
Total	156.3 overs	**386**	10 overs	**30**

1st innings FoW: 13, 143, 182, 220, 323, 331, 370, 373, 381, 386
2nd innings FoW: 27

Bowler	O	M	R	W		O	M	R	W
Salim Altaf	15	3	38	0		5	1	16	1
Asif Masood	21	4	41	2		4	1	11	0
Intikhab Alam	39	8	105	4					
Sarfraz Nawaz	25	3	64	0		1	1	0	0
Mushtaq Moh'd	34.3	9	73	2					
Majid Khan	22	5	51	2					

New Zealand

No. 486:	1st Test
VENUE:	Trent Bridge
DATE:	7th-12th June 1973
TOSS WON BY:	England
RESULT:	England won by 38 runs

ENGLAND	**1st innings**		**2nd innings**	
G Boycott	lbw b Taylor	51	run out	1
DL Amiss	c Wadsworth b Taylor	42	not out	138
GRJ Roope	lbw b DR Hadlee	28	c Wadsworth b Collinge	2
AR Lewis	c Wadsworth b Taylor	2	c Wadsworth b Taylor	2
KWR Fletcher	lbw b DR Hadlee	17	b DR Hadlee	8
AW Greig	c Parker b Collinge	2	lbw b Collinge	139
R Illingworth*	b DR Hadlee	8	c Parker b Pollard	3
APE Knott+	b Congdon	49	c Hastings b Pollard	2
JA Snow	b DR Hadlee	8	b RJ Hadlee	7
GG Arnold	c Wadsworth b Taylor	1	not out	10
N Gifford	not out	25		
Extras	(0b, 10lb, 0w, 7nb)	17	(4b, 6lb, 0w, 3nb)	13
Total	107.4 overs	**250**	97 overs	**325**

1st innings FoW: 92, 106, 108, 140, 147, 161, 162, 184, 191, 250
2nd innings FoW: 2, 8, 11, 24, 234, 241, 263, 311

RO Collinge	27	6	62	1		24	7	43	2
RJ Hadlee	26	5	64	0		19	3	79	1
BR Taylor	29	7	53	4		23	3	87	1
DR Hadlee	19	6	42	4		13	2	51	1
BE Congdon	6.4	1	12	1		9	1	28	0
V Pollard						9	3	24	2

NEW ZEALAND 1st innings			**2nd innings**	
GM Turner	c Roope b Greig	11	c Roope b Arnold	9
JM Parker	c Knott b Greig	2	c Illingworth b Snow	6
BE Congdon*	run out	9	b Arnold	176
BF Hastings	c Roope b Arnold	3	lbw b Arnold	11
MG Burgess	c Knott b Arnold	0	c Knott b Arnold	26
V Pollard	not out	16	lbw b Greig	116
KJ Wadsworth+	c Knott b Greig	0	c Roope b Arnold	46
BR Taylor	c Knott b Snow	19	lbw b Snow	11
DR Hadlee	b Snow	0	hit wkt b Greig	14
RJ Hadlee	b Snow	0	not out	4
RO Collinge	b Greig	17	b Greig	0
Extras	(8b, 6lb, 0w, 6nb)	20	(0b, 13lb, 1w, 7nb)	21
Total	41.4 overs	**97**	188.1 overs	**440**

1st innings FoW: 24, 31, 34, 34, 45, 45, 71, 72, 72, 97
2nd innings FoW: 16, 16, 68, 130, 307, 402, 414, 431, 440, 440

JA Snow	13	5	21	3		43	10	104	2
GG Arnold	18	8	23	2		53	15	131	5
AW Greig	10.4	0	33	4		45.1	10	101	3
GRJ Roope						9	2	17	0
N Gifford						17	7	35	0
R Illingworth						21	7	31	0

New Zealand

No. 487:	2nd Test
VENUE:	Lord's
DATE:	21st-26th June 1973
TOSS WON BY:	New Zealand
RESULT:	Match drawn

ENGLAND	**1st innings**		**2nd innings**	
G Boycott	c Parker b Collinge	61	c & b Howarth	92
DL Amiss	c Howarth b Hadlee	9	c & b Howarth	53
GRJ Roope	lbw b Howarth	56	c Parker b Taylor	51
KWR Fletcher	c Hastings b Howarth	25	c Taylor b Collinge	178
AW Greig	c Howarth b Collinge	63	c Wadsworth b Hadlee	12
R Illingworth*	c Collinge b Hadlee	3	c Turner b Howarth	22
APE Knott+	b Hadlee	0	c Congdon b Howarth	0
CM Old	b Howarth	7	c Congdon b Pollard	7
JA Snow	b Taylor	2	c Hastings b Pollard	0
GG Arnold	not out	8	not out	23
N Gifford	c Wadsworth b Collinge	8	not out	2
Extras	(0b, 1lb, 1w, 9nb)	11	(8b, 3lb, 0w, 12nb)	23
Total	106 overs	**253**	196 overs	**463**

1st innings FoW: 24, 116, 148, 165, 171, 175, 195, 217, 237, 253
2nd innings FoW: 112, 185, 250, 274, 335, 339, 352, 368, 460

RO Collinge	31	8	69	3		19	4	41	1
BR Taylor	19	1	54	1		34	10	90	1
DR Hadlee	26	4	70	3		25	2	79	1
BE Congdon	5	2	7	0		8	3	22	0
HJ Howarth	25	6	42	3		70	24	144	4
V Pollard						39	11	61	2
BF Hastings						1	0	3	0

NEW ZEALAND 1st innings			**2nd innings**
GM Turner	c Greig b Arnold	4	
JM Parker	c Knott b Snow	3	
BE Congdon*	c Knott b Old	175	
BF Hastings	lbw b Snow	86	
HJ Howarth	hit wkt b Old	17	
MG Burgess	b Snow	105	
V Pollard	not out	105	
KJ Wadsworth+	c Knott b Old	27	
BR Taylor	b Old	11	
DR Hadlee	c Fletcher b Old	6	
RO Collinge			
Extras	(0b, 5lb, 0w, 7nb)	12	
Total	204.5 overs	**551**	

1st innings FoW: 5. 10, 200, 249, 330, 447, 523, 535, 551

JA Snow	38	4	109	3
GG Arnold	41	6	108	1
CM Old	41.5	7	113	5
GRJ Roope	6	1	15	0
N Gifford	39	6	107	0
R Illingworth	39	12	87	0

No. 488:	3rd Test
VENUE:	Headingley
DATE:	5th-10th July 1973
TOSS WON BY:	New Zealand
RESULT:	Eng won by an innings and 1 run

No. 489:	1st Test
VENUE:	The Oval
DATE:	26th-31st July 1973
TOSS WON BY:	West Indies
RESULT:	West Indies won by 158 runs

NEW ZEALAND 1st innings / 2nd innings

Batsman	1st innings dismissal	R	2nd innings dismissal	R
GM Turner	lbw b Old	11	lbw b Snow	81
JM Parker	c Knott b Arnold	8	c Knott b Arnold	4
BE Congdon*	c Knott b Arnold	0	c Knott b Arnold	2
BF Hastings	lbw b Arnold	18	b Old	10
MG Burgess	c Roope b Old	87	lbw b Old	18
V Pollard	c Boycott b Old	62	c Roope b Arnold	3
KJ Wadsworth+	b Old	8	b Arnold	5
BR Taylor	c Fletcher b Greig	20	c Roope b Snow	1
DR Hadlee	b Snow	34	lbw b Snow	0
RO Collinge	b Snow	5	b Arnold	0
HJ Howarth	not out	8	not out	15
Extras	(5b, 7lb, 1w, 2nb)	15	(1b, 2lb, 0w, 0nb)	3
Total	98.4 overs	**276**	70.3 overs	**142**

1st innings FoW: 24, 24, 24, 78, 184, 202, 215, 227, 233, 276
2nd innings FoW: 16, 20, 39, 85, 88, 94, 95, 97, 106, 142

Bowler	O	M	R	W	O	M	R	W
JA Snow	21.4	4	52	2	19.3	4	34	3
GG Arnold	27	8	62	3	22	11	27	5
CM Old	20	4	71	4	14	1	41	2
DL Underwood	11	4	27	0	7	2	14	0
AW Greig	13	4	29	1	6	1	22	0
R Illingworth	6	0	20	0	2	1	1	0

ENGLAND 1st innings / 2nd innings

Batsman	1st innings dismissal	R
G Boycott	c Parker b Congdon	115
DL Amiss	lbw b Collinge	8
GRJ Roope	c Turner b Collinge	18
KWR Fletcher	c Howarth b Collinge	81
AW Greig	c Howarth b Congdon	0
R Illingworth*	lbw b Taylor	65
APE Knott+	c Wadsworth b Taylor	21
CM Old	lbw b Collinge	34
JA Snow	c Howarth b Collinge	6
GG Arnold	c Wadsworth b Hadlee	26
DL Underw'd	not out	20
Extras	(5b, 16lb, 1w, 3nb)	25
Total	145.1 overs	**419**

1st innings FoW: 23, 71, 190, 190, 280, 300, 339, 346, 365, 419

Bowler	O	M	R	W
RO Collinge	34	7	74	5
BR Taylor	31	3	111	2
DR Hadlee	23.1	2	98	1
BE Congdon	32	10	54	2
HJ Howarth	18	6	44	0
V Pollard	7	4	13	0

WEST INDIES 1st innings / 2nd innings

Batsman	1st innings dismissal	R	2nd innings dismissal	R
RC Fredericks	lbw b Arnold	35	c Hayes b Arnold	3
RGA Headley	lbw b Greig	8	b Arnold	42
RB Kanhai*	b Greig	10	c Knott b Snow	0
CH Lloyd	lbw b Arnold	132	c Greig b Snow	14
AI Kallicharran	c Knott b Arnold	80	b Illingworth	80
DL Murray+	c Roope b Arnold	28	c Underwood b Snow	51
GStA Sobers	run out	10	c Roope b Underwood	4
BD Julien	lbw b Arnold	11	b Illingworth	23
KD Boyce	b Underwood	72	b Illingworth	9
Inshan Ali	c Boycott b Underwood	15	not out	5
LR Gibbs	not out	1	c Knott b Arnold	3
Extras	(1b, 2lb, 0w, 10nb)	13	(2b, 13lb, 0w, 6nb)	21
Total	145 overs	**415**	87.1 overs	**255**

1st innings FoW: 33, 47, 64, 272, 275, 297, 309, 346, 405, 415
2nd innings FoW: 9, 31, 52, 117, 177, 184, 215, 232, 252, 255

Bowler	O	M	R	W	O	M	R	W
JA Snow	31	8	71	0	18	4	62	3
GG Arnold	39	10	113	5	18.1	7	49	3
AW Greig	30.3	6	81	2	8	1	22	0
GRJ Roope	6	1	26	0				
DL Underwood	23.3	8	68	2	19	5	51	1
R Illingworth	15	3	43	0	24	8	50	3

ENGLAND 1st innings / 2nd innings

Batsman	1st innings dismissal	R	2nd innings dismissal	R
G Boycott	c Murray b Julien	97	c & b Gibbs	30
DL Amiss	b Boyce	29	c Kanhai b Boyce	15
GRJ Roope	b Boyce	9	c & b Gibbs	31
FC Hayes	c Lloyd b Sobers	16	not out	106
KWR Fletcher	c Lloyd b Julien	11	c Kallicharran b Gibbs	5
AW Greig	c Sobers b Boyce	38	c Gibbs b Inshan	0
R Illingworth*	lbw b Sobers	27	lbw b Boyce	7
APE Knott+	not out	4	b Boyce	40
JA Snow	b Boyce	0	lbw b Boyce	5
GG Arnold	c Kallicharran b Boyce	4	c Headley b Boyce	4
DL Underwood	c Headley b Sobers	0	b Boyce	1
Extras	(2b, 7lb, 2w, 11nb)	22	(0b, 5lb, 1w, 5nb)	11
Total	98.1 overs	**257**	105.1 overs	**255**

1st innings FoW: 50, 95, 134, 163, 185, 247, 247, 247, 257, 257
2nd innings FoW: 36, 66, 91, 97, 107, 136, 229, 239, 253, 255

Bowler	O	M	R	W	O	M	R	W
GStA Sobers	22.1	13	27	3	11	3	22	0
KD Boyce	22	4	70	5	21.1	4	77	6
BD Julien	20	6	49	2	17	4	35	0
LR Gibbs	23	8	37	0	33	9	61	3
Inshan Ali	11	3	52	0	23	6	49	1

No. 490: 2nd Test
VENUE: Edgbaston
DATE: 9th-14th August 1973
TOSS WON BY: West Indies
RESULT: Match drawn

No. 491: 3rd Test
VENUE: Lord's
DATE: 23rd-27th August 1973
TOSS WON BY: West Indies
RESULT: WI won by an innings and 226 runs

WEST INDIES 1st innings / 2nd innings (No. 490)

Batsman	1st innings		2nd innings	
RC Fredericks	c Amiss b Underwood	150	c Knott b Arnold	12
RGA Headley	b Old	1	c Knott b Old	11
RB Kanhai*	c Greig b Arnold	2	c Arnold b Illingworth	54
CH Lloyd	lbw b Old	15	c Knott b Underwood	94
AI Kallicharran	c Hayes b Arnold	34	b Underwood	4
GStA Sobers	b Old	21	b Arnold	74
DL Murray+	b Underwood	25	hit wkt b Arnold	15
BD Julien	c Greig b Arnold	54	b Greig	11
KD Boyce	lbw b Illingworth	12	c Knott b Arnold	0
VA Holder	c Boycott b Underwood	6	c Luckhurst b Greig	10
LR Gibbs	not out	1	not out	3
Extras	(0b, 2lb, 1w, 3nb)	6	(0b, 10lb, 0w, 4nb)	14
Total	149.3 overs	**327**	103.4 overs	**302**

1st innings FoW: 14, 17, 39, 93, 128, 242, 280, 302, 325, 327
2nd innings FoW: 24, 42, 136, 152, 197, 247, 283, 283, 293, 302

Bowler	O	M	R	W	O	M	R	W
GG Arnold	37	13	74	3	20	1	43	4
CM Old	30	3	86	3	14	0	65	1
AW Greig	26	3	84	0	7.4	0	35	2
R Illingworth	32	19	37	1	26	6	67	1
DL Underwood	24.3	10	40	3	32	9	66	2
BW Luckhurst					4	2	12	0

WEST INDIES 1st innings / 2nd innings (No. 491)

Batsman	1st innings		2nd innings
RC Fredericks	c Underwood b Willis	51	
DL Murray+	b Willis	4	
RB Kanhai*	c Greig b Willis	157	
CH Lloyd	c & b Willis	63	
AI Kallicharran	c Arnold b Illingworth	14	
GStA Sobers	not out	150	
MLC Foster	c Willis b Greig	9	
BD Julien	c & b Greig	121	
KD Boyce	c Amiss b Greig	36	
VA Holder	not out	23	
LR Gibbs			
Extras	(1b, 14lb, 1w, 8nb)	24	
Total	168.4 overs	**652**	

1st innings FoW: 8, 87, 225, 256, 339, 373, 604, 610

Bowler	O	M	R	W
GG Arnold	35	6	111	0
RGD Willis	35	3	118	4
AW Greig	33	2	180	3
DL Underwood	34	6	105	0
R Illingworth	31.4	3	114	1

ENGLAND 1st innings / 2nd innings (No. 490)

Batsman	1st innings		2nd innings	
G Boycott	not out	56	c Murray b Lloyd	42
DL Amiss	c Murray b Julien	56	not out	86
BW Luckhurst	lbw b Sobers	12	lbw b Lloyd	0
FC Hayes	c Kallicharran b Holder	29	not out	44
AW Greig	c Fredericks b Julien	27		
APE Knott+	b Holder	0		
KWR Fletcher	c Holder b Sobers	52		
R Illingworth*	lbw b Holder	27		
CM Old	run out	0		
GG Arnold	c Kallicharran b Sobers	24		
DL Underwood	c Murray b Gibbs	2		
Extras	(4b, 1lb, 0w, 15nb)	20	(8b, 0lb, 0w, 2nb)	10
Total	156.4 overs	**305**	67 overs	**182**

1st innings FoW: 119, 139, 191, 191, 197, 249, 249, 299, 302, 305
2nd innings FoW: 96, 100

Bowler	O	M	R	W	O	M	R	W
VA Holder	44	16	83	3	7	1	17	0
GStA Sobers	30	6	62	3	7	1	21	0
KD Boyce	19	2	48	0				
BD Julien	26	8	55	2	18	3	32	0
LR Gibbs	35.4	21	32	1	12	2	32	0
CH Lloyd	2	0	5	0	12	3	26	2
RC Fredericks					4	0	23	0
RB Kanhai					7	1	21	0

ENGLAND 1st innings / 2nd innings (No. 491)

Batsman	1st innings		2nd innings	
G Boycott	c Kanhai b Holder	4	c Kallicharran b Boyce	15
DL Amiss	c Sobers b Holder	35	c Sobers b Boyce	10
BW Luckhurst	c Murray b Boyce	1	c Murray b Boyce	5
FC Hayes	c Fredericks b Holder	8	c Sobers b Julien	12
KWR Fletcher	c Sobers b Gibbs	68	c Holder b Boyce	0
AW Greig	c Sobers b Boyce	44	not out	86
R Illingworth*	c Sobers b Gibbs	0	lbw b Julien	13
APE Knott+	c Murray b Boyce	21	c Kanhai b Gibbs	13
GG Arnold	c Murray b Boyce	5	c Fredericks b Gibbs	1
RGD Willis	not out	5	c Fredericks b Julien	0
DL Underwood	c Gibbs b Holder	12	b Gibbs	14
Extras	(6b, 4lb, 3w, 17nb)	30	(9b, 1lb, 0w, 14nb)	24
Total	73 overs	**233**	65.3 overs	**193**

1st innings FoW: 5, 7, 29, 97, 176, 176, 187, 205, 213, 233
2nd innings FoW: 32, 38, 42, 49, 63, 87, 132, 143, 146, 193

Bowler	O	M	R	W	O	M	R	W
VA Holder	15	3	56	4	14	4	18	0
KD Boyce	20	7	50	4	16	5	49	4
BD Julien	11	4	26	0	18	2	69	3
LR Gibbs	18	3	39	2	13.3	3	26	3
GStA Sobers	8	0	30	0	4	1	7	0
MLC Foster	1	0	2	0				

No. 492: 1st Test
VENUE: Port-of-Spain (Trinidad)
DATE: 2nd-7th February 1974
TOSS WON BY: West Indies
RESULT: West Indies won by 7 wickets

No. 493: 2nd Test
VENUE: Kingston (Jamaica)
DATE: 16th-21st February 1974
TOSS WON BY: England
RESULT: Match drawn

First Test

ENGLAND	1st innings		2nd innings	
G Boycott	c Julien b Boyce	6	c Fredericks b Gibbs	93
DL Amiss	c Murray b Sobers	6	lbw b Sobers	174
MH Denness*	b Julien	9	run out	44
FC Hayes	c Fredericks b Sobers	12	b Sobers	8
KWR Fletcher	b Julien	4	c Rowe b Sobers	0
AW Greig	c Murray b Boyce	37	b Gibbs	20
APE Knott+	b Boyce	7	c Rowe b Gibbs	21
CM Old	c Fredericks b Inshan	11	c & b Gibbs	3
PI Pocock	b Boyce	2	c Fredericks b Gibbs	0
DL Underwood	not out	10	c Kanhai b Gibbs	9
RGD Willis	b Gibbs	6	not out	0
Extras	(1b, 8lb, 0w, 12nb)	21	(5b, 5lb, 0w, 10nb)	20
	55 overs		166.2 overs	
Total		**131**		**392**

1st innings FoW: 6, 22, 23, 30, 71, 90, 100, 108, 116, 131
2nd innings FoW: 209, 328, 338, 338, 349, 366, 378, 378, 391, 392

KD Boyce	19	4	42	4	10	1	36	0	
BD Julien	12	5	14	2	15	2	48	0	
GStA Sobers	14	3	37	2	34	15	54	3	
LR Gibbs	3	1	5	1	57.2	15	108	6	
Inshan Ali	7	5	12	1	37	5	99	0	
					10	2	24	0	
					3	1	3	0	

WEST INDIES	1st innings		2nd innings	
RC Fredericks	c Knott b Old	5	not out	65
LG Rowe	c Knott b Willis	13	c Hayes b Pocock	5
AI Kallicharran	c Underwood b Pocock	158	c Greig b Underwood	21
CH Lloyd	c Denness b Old	18	c Hayes b Underwood	0
RB Kanhai*	b Pocock	8	not out	39
GStA Sobers	c Denness b Underwood	23		
DL Murray+	c Fletcher b Pocock	19		
BD Julien	not out	86		
KD Boyce	c Boycott b Pocock	26		
Inshan Ali	c Knott b Pocock	9		
LR Gibbs	b Old	2		
Extras	(3b, 6lb, 0w, 16nb)	25	(0b, 1lb, 0w, 1nb)	2
	122.4 overs		37.5 overs	
Total		**392**		**132**

1st innings FoW: 14, 27, 63, 106, 147, 196, 296, 324, 373, 392
2nd innings FoW: 15, 77, 77

RGD Willis	19	5	52	1	4	1	6	0	
CM Old	20.4	2	89	3	3	0	18	0	
AW Greig	17	3	60	0	2	1	4	0	
PI Pocock	43	12	110	5	16	6	49	1	
DL Underwood	23	8	56	1	12	2	48	2	
KWR Fletcher					0.5	0	5	0	

Second Test

ENGLAND	1st innings		2nd innings	
G Boycott	c Kanhai b Sobers	68	c Murray b Boyce	5
DL Amiss	c Kanhai b Barrett	27	not out	262
JA Jameson	st Murray b Gibbs	23	c Rowe b Barrett	38
FC Hayes	c Boyce b Sobers	10	run out	0
MH Denness*	c Fredericks b Boyce	67	c Rowe b Barrett	28
AW Greig	c Fredericks b Barrett	45	b Gibbs	14
APE Knott+	c Murray b Barrett	39	c Murray b Sobers	12
CM Old	c Murray b Julien	2	run out	6
DL Underwood	c Fredericks b Sobers	24	b Barrett	19
PI Pocock	c Gibbs b Julien	23	c (sub) b Boyce	4
RGD Willis	not out	6	not out	3
Extras	(0b, 7lb, 0w, 12nb)	19	(10b, 11lb, 1w, 19nb)	41
	157 overs		183 overs	
Total		**353**		**432**

1st innings FoW: 68, 104, 133, 134, 224, 278, 286, 32, 333, 353
2nd innings FoW: 32, 102, 107, 176, 217, 258, 271, 343, 392

KD Boyce	19	2	52	1	21	4	70	2	
BD Julien	18	3	40	2	13	3	36	0	
GStA Sobers	33	11	65	3	34	13	73	1	
AG Barrett	39	16	86	3	54	24	87	3	
LR Gibbs	40	16	78	1	44	15	82	1	
RC Fredericks	4	0	11	0	6	1	17	0	
CH Lloyd	4	2	2	0	3	1	5	0	
RB Kanhai					3	1	8	0	
LG Rowe					2	1	1	0	
AI Kallicharran					3	0	12	0	

WEST INDIES	1st innings	
RC Fredericks	b Old	94
LG Rowe	lbw b Willis	120
AI Kallicharran	c Denness b Old	93
CH Lloyd	b Jameson	49
RB Kanhai*	c Willis b Greig	39
GStA Sobers	c Willis b Greig	57
BD Julien	c Denness b Greig	66
KD Boyce	c Greig b Willis	8
DL Murray+	not out	6
AG Barrett	lbw b Willis	0
LR Gibbs	not out	6
Extras	(16b, 18lb, 0w, 11nb)	45
	196 overs	
Total		**583**

1st innings FoW: 206, 226, 338, 401, 439, 551, 563, 567, 574

RGD Willis	24	5	97	3
CM Old	23	6	72	2
PI Pocock	57	14	152	0
DL Underwood	36	12	98	0
AW Greig	49	14	102	3
JA Jameson	7	2	17	1

West Indies

No. 494: 3rd Test
VENUE: Bridgetown (Barbados)
DATE: 6th–11th March 1974
TOSS WON BY: West Indies
RESULT: Match drawn

West Indies

No. 495: 4th Test
VENUE: Georgetown (Guyana)
DATE: 22nd–27th March 1974
TOSS WON BY: England
RESULT: Match drawn

ENGLAND 1st innings / 2nd innings

	1st innings		2nd innings	
MH Denness*	c Murray b Sobers	24	lbw b Holder	0
DL Amiss	b Julien	12	c Julien b Roberts	4
JA Jameson	c Fredericks b Julien	3	lbw b Roberts	9
G Boycott	c Murray b Julien	10	c Kanhai b Sobers	13
KWR Fletcher	c Murray b Julien	37	not out	129
AW Greig	c Sobers b Julien	148	c Roberts b Gibbs	25
APE Knott+	b Gibbs	87	lbw b Lloyd	67
CM Old	c Murray b Roberts	1	b Lloyd	0
GG Arnold	b Holder	12	not out	2
PI Pocock	c Lloyd b Gibbs	18		
RGD Willis	not out	10		
Extras	(0b, 5lb, 0w, 28nb)	33	(7b, 5lb, 0w, 16nb)	28
Total	144.4 overs	**395**	126.3 overs	**277**

1st innings FoW: 28, 34, 53, 68, 130, 293, 306, 344, 371, 395
2nd innings FoW: 4, 8, 29, 40, 106, 248, 248

VA Holder	27	6	68	1	15	6	37	1
AME Roberts	33	8	75	1	17	4	49	2
BD Julien	26	9	57	5	11	4	21	0
GStA Sobers	18	4	57	1	35	21	55	1
LR Gibbs	33.4	10	91	2	28.3	15	40	1
CH Lloyd	4	2	9	0	12	4	13	2
RC Fredericks	3	0	5	0	6	2	24	0
LG Rowe					1	0	5	0
AI Kallicharran					1	0	5	0

ENGLAND 1st innings / 2nd innings

	1st innings		2nd innings
G Boycott	b Julien	15	
DL Amiss	c Murray b Boyce	118	
MH Denness*	b Barrett	42	
KWR Fletcher	c Murray b Julien	41	
AW Greig	b Boyce	121	
FC Hayes	c & b Gibbs	6	
APE Knott+	c Julien b Gibbs	61	
J Birkenshaw	c Murray b Fredericks	0	
CM Old	c Kanhai b Boyce	14	
GG Arnold	run out	1	
DL Underwood	not out	7	
Extras	(1b, 13lb, 0w, 8nb)	22	
Total	171.4 overs	**448**	

1st innings FoW: 41, 128, 228, 244, 257, 376, 377, 410, 428, 448

KD Boyce	27.4	6	70	3
BD Julien	36	10	96	2
CH Lloyd	19	5	27	0
MLC Foster	16	5	32	0
LR Gibbs	37	5	102	2
AG Barrett	31	6	87	1
RC Fredericks	5	2	12	1

WEST INDIES 1st innings / 2nd innings

	1st innings		2nd innings
RC Fredericks	b Greig	32	
LG Rowe	c Arnold b Greig	302	
AI Kallicharran	b Greig	119	
CH Lloyd	c Fletcher b Greig	8	
VA Holder	c & b Greig	8	
RB Kanhai*	b Arnold	18	
GStA Sobers	c Greig b Willis	0	
DL Murray+	not out	53	
BD Julien	c Willis b Greig	1	
AME Roberts	not out	9	
LR Gibbs			
Extras	(3b, 8lb, 0w, 35nb)	46	
Total	154 overs	**596**	

1st innings FoW: 126, 375, 390, 420, 465, 466, 551, 556

GG Arnold	26	5	91	1
RGD Willis	26	4	100	1
AW Greig	46	2	164	6
CM Old	28	4	102	0
PI Pocock	28	4	93	0

WEST INDIES 1st innings / 2nd innings

	1st innings		2nd innings
RC Fredericks	c & b Greig	98	
LG Rowe	b Greig	28	
AI Kallicharran	b Birkenshaw	6	
RB Kanhai*	b Underwood	44	
CH Lloyd	not out	7	
MLC Foster			
DL Murray+			
BD Julien			
KD Boyce			
AG Barrett			
LR Gibbs			
Extras	(6b, 4lb, 0w, 5nb)	15	
Total	86.5 overs	**198**	

1st innings FoW: 73, 90, 179, 198

GG Arnold	10	5	17	0
CM Old	13	3	32	0
DL Underwood	17.5	4	36	1
AW Greig	24	8	57	2
J Birkenshaw	22	7	41	1

No. 496: 5th Test	No. 497: 1st Test
VENUE: Port-of-Spain (Trinidad)	VENUE: Old Trafford
DATE: 30th March-5th April 1974	DATE: 6th-11th June 1974
TOSS WON BY: England	TOSS WON BY: England
RESULT: England won by 26 runs	RESULT: England won by 113 runs

ENGLAND 1st innings / 2nd innings

Batsman	1st innings		2nd innings	
G Boycott	c Murray b Julien	99	b Gibbs	112
DL Amiss	c Kanhai b Sobers	44	b Lloyd	16
MH Denness*	c Fredericks b Inshan	13	run out	4
KWR Fletcher	c Kanhai b Gibbs	6	b Julien	45
AW Greig	lbw b Gibbs	19	c Kallicharran b Boyce	5
FC Hayes	c Rowe b Inshan	24	c Fredericks b Julien	1
APE Knott+	not out	33	lbw b Julien	0
J Birkenshaw	c Lloyd b Julien	8	lbw b Sobers	44
GG Arnold	run out	0	c Gibbs b Inshan	7
PI Pocock	c Lloyd b Inshan	6	b Sobers	13
DL Underwood	b Gibbs	4	not out	1
Extras	(2b, 3lb, 0w, 6nb)	11	(0b, 4lb, 0w, 11nb)	15
	135.3 overs		149.2 overs	
Total		**267**		**263**

1st innings FoW: 83, 114, 133, 165, 204, 212, 244, 257, 260, 267
2nd innings FoW: 39, 44, 145, 169, 174, 176, 213, 226, 258, 263

Bowler	O	M	R	W	O	M	R	W
KD Boyce	10	3	14	0	12	3	40	1
BD Julien	21	8	35	2	22	7	31	3
GStA Sobers	31	16	44	1	24.2	9	36	2
Inshan Ali	35	12	86	3	34	12	51	1
LR Gibbs	34.3	10	70	3	50	15	85	1
CH Lloyd	4	2	7	0	7	4	5	1

WEST INDIES 1st innings / 2nd innings

Batsman	1st innings		2nd innings	
RC Fredericks	c Fletcher b Pocock	67	run out	36
LG Rowe	c Boycott b Greig	123	lbw b Birkenshaw	25
AI Kallicharran	c & b Pocock	0	c Fletcher b Greig	0
CH Lloyd	c Knott b Greig	52	c & b Greig	13
GStA Sobers	c Birkenshaw b Greig	0	c Fletcher b Greig	7
RB Kanhai*	c & b Greig	2	b Underwood	20
DL Murray+	c Pocock b Greig	2	c Fletcher b Greig	33
BD Julien	c Birkenshaw b Greig	17	c Denness b Pocock	2
KD Boyce	c Pocock b Greig	19	not out	34
Inshan Ali	lbw b Greig	5	c Underwood b Greig	15
LR Gibbs	not out	0	b Arnold	1
Extras	(11b, 4lb, 0w, 3nb)	18	(9b, 2lb, 0w, 2nb)	13
	117.1 overs		88.3 overs	
Total		**305**		**199**

1st innings FoW: 110, 122, 224, 224, 226, 232, 270, 300, 300, 305
2nd innings FoW: 63, 64, 65, 84, 85, 135, 138, 166, 197, 199

Bowler	O	M	R	W	O	M	R	W
GG Arnold	8	0	27	0	5.3	1	13	1
AW Greig	36.1	10	86	8	33	7	70	5
PI Pocock	31	7	86	2	25	7	60	1
DL Underwood	34	12	57	0	15	7	19	1
J Birkenshaw	8	1	31	0	10	1	24	1

ENGLAND 1st innings / 2nd innings

Batsman	1st innings		2nd innings	
G Boycott	lbw b Abid Ali	10	c Engineer b Solkar	6
DL Amiss	c Madan Lal b Chan'har	56	c Gavaskar b Bedi	47
JH Edrich	b Abid Ali	7	c Engineer b Abid Ali	100
MH Denness*	b Bedi	26	not out	45
KWR Fletcher	not out	123	not out	
DL Underwood	c Solkar b Bedi	7		9
AW Greig	c Engineer b Madan Lal	53		
APE Knott+	lbw b Madan Lal	0		
CM Old	c Engineer b Chan'har	12		
RGD Willis	lbw b Abid Ali	24		
M Hendrick				
Extras	(1b, 7lb, 1w, 1nb)	10	(4b, 2lb, 0w, 0nb)	6
	143.3 overs		70 overs	
Total		**328**		**213**

1st innings FoW: 18, 28, 90, 104, 127, 231, 231, 265, 328
2nd innings FoW: 13, 30, 104

Bowler	O	M	R	W	O	M	R	W
S Abid Ali	30.3	6	79	3	11	2	31	1
ED Solkar	13	4	33	0	7	0	24	1
S Madan Lal	31	11	56	2	12	2	39	0
S Venk'van	5	1	8	0	9	1	17	0
BS Bedi	43	14	87	2	20	2	58	1
BS Chan'har	21	4	55	2	11	2	38	0

INDIA 1st innings / 2nd innings

Batsman	1st innings		2nd innings	
SM Gavaskar	run out	101	c Hendrick b Old	58
ED Solkar	c Willis b Hendrick	7	c Hendrick b Underw'd	19
S Venk'van	b Willis	3	c Knott b Greig	5
AL Wadekar*	c Hendrick b Old	6	c Knott b Old	14
GR Viswanath	b Underwood	40	c Knott b Old	50
BP Patel	c Knott b Willis	5	c Knott b Hendrick	3
FM Engineer+	b Willis	0	hit wkt b Willis	12
S Madan Lal	b Hendrick	2	c Boycott b Greig	7
S Abid Ali	c Knott b Hendrick	71	not out	4
BS Bedi	b Willis	0	b Old	0
BS Chan'har	not out	0	st Knott b Greig	0
Extras	(3b, 3lb, 0w, 5nb)	11	(1b, 2lb, 0w, 7nb)	10
	84 overs		85.1 overs	
Total		**246**		**182**

1st innings FoW: 22, 25, 32, 105, 129, 135, 143, 228, 228, 246
2nd innings FoW: 32, 68, 103, 111, 139, 157, 165, 180, 180, 182

Bowler	O	M	R	W	O	M	R	W
RGD Willis	24	3	64	4	12	5	33	1
CM Old	16	0	46	1	16	7	20	4
M Hendrick	20	4	57	3	17	1	39	1
DL Underwood	19	7	50	1	15	4	45	1
AW Greig	5	1	18	0	25.1	8	35	3

India

No. 498: 2nd Test
VENUE: Lord's
DATE: 20th-24th June 1974
TOSS WON BY: England
RESULT: Eng won by an innings and 285 runs

ENGLAND	1st innings		2nd innings
DL Amiss	lbw b Prasanna	188	
D Lloyd	c Solkar b Prasanna	46	
JH Edrich	lbw b Bedi	96	
MH Denness*	c (sub) b Bedi	118	
KWR Fletcher	c Solkar b Bedi	15	
AW Greig	c & b Abid Ali	106	
APE Knott+	c & b Bedi	26	
CM Old	b Abid Ali	3	
GG Arnold	b Bedi	5	
DL Underwood	c Solkar b Bedi	9	
M Hendrick	not out	1	
Extras	(8b, 4lb, 2w, 2nb)	16	
	182.5 overs		
Total		**629**	

1st innings FoW: 116, 337, 339, 369, 571, 591, 604, 611, 624, 629

S Abid Ali	22	2	79	2				
ED Solkar	6	2	16	0				
S Madan Lal	30	6	93	0				
BS Bedi	64.2	8	226	6				
BS Chan'har	9.3	1	33	0				
EAS Prasanna	51	6	166	2				

INDIA	1st innings		2nd innings	
SM Gavaskar	c Knott b Old	49	lbw b Arnold	5
FM Engineer+	c Denness b Old	86	lbw b Arnold	0
AL Wadekar*	c Underwood b Hendrick	18	b Old	3
GR Viswanath	b Underwood	52	c Knott b Arnold	5
BP Patel	c Fletcher b Greig	1	c Knott b Arnold	1
ED Solkar	c Underwood b Hendrick	43	not out	18
S Abid Ali	c Arnold b Old	14	c Knott b Old	3
S Madan Lal	c Knott b Old	0	c Hendrick b Old	2
EAS Prasanna	c Denness b Hendrick	0	b Old	5
BS Bedi	b Arnold	14	b Old	0
BS Chan'har	not out	2	absent hurt	0
Extras	(4b, 7lb, 0w, 12nb)	23	(0b, 0lb, 0w, 0nb)	0
	101.5 overs		17 overs	
Total		**302**		**42**

1st innings FoW: 131, 149, 183, 188, 250, 280, 281, 286, 286, 302
2nd innings FoW: 2, 5, 12, 14, 25, 28, 30, 42, 42

GG Arnold	24.5	6	81	1	8	1	19	4
CM Old	21	6	67	4	8	3	21	5
M Hendrick	18	4	46	3	1	0	2	0
AW Greig	21	4	63	1				
DL Underwood	15	10	18	1				
D Lloyd	2	0	4	0				

India

No. 499: 3rd Test
VENUE: Edgbaston
DATE: 4th-8th July 1974
TOSS WON BY: India
RESULT: Eng won by an innings and 78 runs

INDIA	1st innings		2nd innings	
SM Gavaskar	c Knott b Arnold	0	c Knott b Old	4
SS Naik	b Arnold	4	lbw b Greig	77
AL Wadekar*	c Knott b Hendrick	36	b Arnold	3
GR Viswanath	b Hendrick	28	lbw b Old	5
AV Mankad	c Knott b Arnold	14	c Greig b Hendrick	25
FM Engineer+	not out	64	hit wkt b Old	43
ED Solkar	lbw b Old	3	lbw b Hendrick	33
S Abid Ali	run out	6	c Edrich b Arnold	8
S Venk'van	b Underwood	0	c Lloyd b Greig	5
EAS Prasanna	c Greig b Hendrick	0	b Hendrick	4
BS Bedi	c Old b Hendrick	0	not out	1
Extras	(1b, 1lb, 0w, 8nb)	10	(0b, 3lb, 0w, 5nb)	8
	59.2 overs		67.4 overs	
Total		**165**		**216**

1st innings FoW: 0, 12, 62, 81, 115, 129, 153, 156, 165, 165
2nd innings FoW: 6, 12, 21, 59, 146, 172, 183, 196, 211, 216

GG Arnold	14	3	43	3	19	3	61	2
CM Old	13	0	43	1	15	3	52	3
M Hendrick	14.2	1	28	4	14.4	4	43	3
AW Greig	3	0	11	0	16	3	49	2
DL Underwood	15	3	30	1	3	1	3	0

ENGLAND	1st innings		2nd innings
DL Amiss	c Mankad b Prasanna	79	
D Lloyd	not out	214	
MH Denness*	c & b Bedi	100	
KWR Fletcher	not out	51	
JH Edrich			
AW Greig			
APE Knott+			
CM Old			
GG Arnold			
DL Underwood			
M Hendrick			
Extras	(4b, 5lb, 1w, 5nb)	15	
	140 overs		
Total		**459**	

1st innings FoW: 157, 368

S Abid Ali	18	2	63	0
ED Solkar	18	5	52	0
BS Bedi	45	4	152	1
S Venk'van	23	1	71	0
EAS Prasanna	35	4	101	1
SM Gavaskar	1	0	5	0

No. 500: 1st Test
VENUE: Headingley
DATE: 25th-30th July 1974
TOSS WON BY: Pakistan
RESULT: Match drawn

PAKISTAN 1st innings / 2nd innings

Batsman	1st innings		2nd innings	
Sadiq Mohammad	c Lloyd b Hendrick	28	c Greig b Old	12
Shafiq Ahmed	b Old	7	c Greig b Arnold	18
Majid Khan	c & b Greig	75	c Knott b Arnold	4
Mushtaq	c Fletcher b Underwood	6	c Greig b Hendrick	43
Zaheer Abbas	c Knott b Hendrick	48	c Knott b Greig	19
Asif Iqbal	c Knott b Arnold	14	b Old	8
Intikhab Alam*	c Knott b Arnold	3	lbw b Old	10
Imran Khan	c Greig b Old	23	c Greig b Hendrick	31
Wasim Bari+	c Denness b Old	2	b Hendrick	4
Sarfraz Nawaz	b Arnold	53	c Fletcher b Arnold	3
Asif Masood	not out	4	not out	2
Extras	(0b, 5lb, 2w, 15nb)	22	(0b, 14lb, 1w, 12nb)	27
Total	101.5 overs	285	68.1 overs	179

1st innings FoW: 12, 60, 70, 170, 182, 189, 198, 209, 223, 285
2nd innings FoW: 24, 35, 38, 83, 97, 115, 154, 168, 177, 179

Bowler	O	M	R	W	O	M	R	W
GG Arnold	31.5	8	67	3	23.1	11	36	3
CM Old	21	4	65	3	17	0	54	3
M Hendrick	26	4	91	2	18	6	39	3
DL Underwood	12	6	26	1	1	1	0	0
AW Greig	11	4	14	1	9	3	23	1

ENGLAND 1st innings / 2nd innings

Batsman	1st innings		2nd innings	
DL Amiss	c Sadiq b Sarfraz	13	lbw b Sarfraz	8
D Lloyd	c Sadiq b Asif Masood	48	c Wasim b Sarfraz	9
JH Edrich	c Asif Iqbal b Asif Masood	9	c Sadiq b Imran Khan	70
MH Denness*	b Asif Masood	9	c Sarfraz b Intikhab	44
KWR Fletcher	lbw b Sarfraz	11	not out	67
AW Greig	c Wasim b Imran Khan	37	c Majid Khan b Sarfraz	12
APE Knott+	c Wasim b Asif Iqbal	35	c Majid Khan b Sarfraz	5
CM Old	c Asif Masood b Imran Khan	0	not out	10
GG Arnold	c Intikhab b Sarfraz	1		
DL Underwood	run out	9		
M Hendrick	not out	1		
Extras	(1b, 3lb, 4w, 2nb)	10	(4b, 3lb, 1w, 5nb)	13
Total	72 overs	183	107 overs	238

1st innings FoW: 25, 69, 79, 84, 100, 172, 172, 172, 182, 183
2nd innings FoW: 17, 22, 94, 174, 198, 213

Bowler	O	M	R	W	O	M	R	W
Asif Masood	16	3	50	3	19	2	63	0
Sarfraz Nawaz	22	4	51	3	36	14	56	4
Imran Khan	21	1	55	2	29	7	55	1
Mushtaq	1	1	0	0	4	1	8	0
Intikhab Alam	6	2	14	0	14	4	25	1
Asif Iqbal	6	3	3	1	5	1	18	0

No. 501: 2nd Test
VENUE: Lord's
DATE: 8th-13th August 1974
TOSS WON BY: Pakistan
RESULT: Match drawn

PAKISTAN 1st innings / 2nd innings

Batsman	1st innings		2nd innings	
Sadiq	lbw b Hendrick	40	lbw b Arnold	43
Majid Khan	c Old b Greig	48	lbw b Underwood	19
Zaheer Abbas	c Hendrick b Underwood	1	c Greig b Underwood	4
Mushtaq	c Greig b Underwood	0	c Denness b Greig	76
Wasim Raja	c Greig b Underwood	24	c Lloyd b Underwood	53
Asif Iqbal	c Amiss b Underwood	2	c Greig b Underwood	0
Intikhab Alam*	b Underwood	5	c Lloyd b Underwood	0
Imran Khan	c Hendrick b Greig	4	b Underwood	0
Wasim Bari+	lbw b Greig	4	c Lloyd b Underwood	1
Sarfraz Nawaz	not out	0	lbw b Underwood	0
Asif Masood			not out	17
Extras	(0b, 0lb, 0w, 2nb)	2	(0b, 8lb, 0w, 7nb)	15
Total	44.5 overs	130	97.5 overs	226

1st innings FoW: 71, 91, 91, 91, 103, 111, 116, 130, 130
2nd innings FoW: 55, 61, 77, 192, 192, 200, 200, 206, 208, 226

Bowler	O	M	R	W	O	M	R	W
GG Arnold	8	1	32	0	15	3	37	1
CM Old	5	0	17	0	14	1	39	0
M Hendrick	9	2	36	1	15	4	29	0
DL Underwood	14	8	20	5	34.5	17	51	8
AW Greig	8.5	4	23	3	19	6	55	1

ENGLAND 1st innings / 2nd innings

Batsman	1st innings		2nd innings	
DL Amiss	c Sadiq b Asif Masood	2	not out	14
D Lloyd	c Zaheer b Sarfraz	23	not out	12
JH Edrich	c Sadiq b Intikhab	40		
MH Denness*	b Imran Khan	20		
KWR Fletcher	lbw b Imran Khan	8		
AW Greig	run out	9		
A Knott+	c Wasim Bari b Asif Masood	83		
CM Old	c Wasim Bari b Mushtaq	41		
G Arnold	c Wasim Bari b Asif Masood	10		
DL Underwood	not out	12		
M Hendrick	c Imran Khan b Intikhab	6		
Extras	(0b, 14lb, 1w, 1nb)	16	(0b, 0lb, 0w, 1nb)	1
Total	105 overs	270	10 overs	27

1st innings FoW: 2, 52, 90, 94, 100, 118, 187, 231, 254, 270

Bowler	O	M	R	W	O	M	R	W
Asif Masood	25	10	47	3	4	0	9	0
Sarfraz Nawaz	22	8	42	1	3	0	7	0
Intikhab Alam	26	4	80	2	1	1	0	0
Wasim Raja	2	0	8	0				
Mushtaq	7	3	16	1				
Imran Khan	18	2	48	2				
Asif Iqbal	5	0	13	0				
Majid Khan					2	0	10	0

Pakistan

No. 502: 3rd Test
VENUE: The Oval
DATE: 22nd-27th August 1974
TOSS WON BY: Pakistan
RESULT: Match drawn

Australia

No. 503: 1st Test
VENUE: Brisbane (Gabba)
DATE: 29th Nov to 4th Dec 1974
TOSS WON BY: Australia
RESULT: Australia won by 166 runs

PAKISTAN 1st innings / 2nd innings

Batsman	1st innings		2nd innings	
Sadiq Mohammad	c Old b Willis	21	c & b Arnold	4
Majid Khan	b Underwood	98	c Denness b Old	18
Zaheer Abbas	b Underwood	240	c Knott b Arnold	15
Mushtaq Mohammad	b Arnold	76	b Underwood	8
Asif Iqbal	c & b Greig	29	not out	30
Wasim Raja	c Denness b Greig	28	not out	10
Imran Khan	c Knott b Willis	24		
Intikhab Alam*	not out	32		
Sarfraz Nawaz	not out	14		
Wasim Bari+				
Asif Masood				
Extras	(6b, 18lb, 0w, 14nb)	38	(5b, 0lb, 0w, 4nb)	9
Total	165.3 overs	600	30 overs	94

1st innings FoW: 66, 166, 338, 431, 503, 550, 550
2nd innings FoW: 8, 33, 41, 68

Bowler	O	M	R	W		O	M	R	W
GG Arnold	37	5	106	1		6	0	22	2
RGD Willis	28	3	102	2		7	1	27	0
CM Old	29.3	3	143	0		2	0	6	1
DL Underwood	44	14	106	2		8	2	15	1
AW Greig	25	5	92	2		7	1	15	0
D Lloyd	2	0	13	0					

AUSTRALIA 1st innings / 2nd innings

Batsman	1st innings		2nd innings	
IR Redpath	b Willis	5	b Willis	25
WJ Edwards	c Amiss b Hendrick	4	c Knott b Willis	5
IM Chappell*	c Greig b Willis	90	c Fletcher b Underwood	11
GS Chappell	c Fletcher b Underwood	58	b Underwood	71
R Edwards	c Knott b Underwood	32	c Knott b Willis	53
KD Walters	c Lever b Willis	3	not out	62
RW Marsh+	c Denness b Hendrick	14	not out	46
TJ Jenner	c Lever b Willis	12	(1b, 7lb, 1w, 6nb)	15
DK Lillee	c Knott b Greig	15	85 overs	
MHN Walker	not out	41		
JR Thomson	run out	23		
Extras	(0b, 4lb, 0w, 8nb)	12		
Total	92.5 overs	309		288

1st innings FoW: 7, 10, 110, 197, 202, 205, 228, 229, 257, 309
2nd innings FoW: 15, 39, 59, 173, 190

Bowler	O	M	R	W		O	M	R	W
RGD Willis	21.5	3	56	4		15	3	45	3
P Lever	16	1	53	0		18	4	58	0
M Hendrick	19	3	64	2		13	2	47	0
AW Greig	16	2	70	1		13	2	60	0
DL Underwood	20	6	54	2		26	6	63	2

ENGLAND 1st innings / 2nd innings

Batsman	1st innings		2nd innings
DL Amiss	c Majid Khan b Intikhab	183	
D Lloyd	c Sadiq b Sarfraz	4	
DL Underwood	lbw b Wasim Raja	43	
JH Edrich	c Wasim Bari b Intikhab	25	
M Denness*	c Imran Khan b Asif	18	
KWR Fletcher	run out	122	
AW Greig	b Intikhab	32	
APE Knott+	b Intikhab	9	
CM Old	lbw b Intikhab	65	
GG Arnold	c Wasim Bari b Mushtaq	2	
RGD Willis	not out	1	
Extras	(8b, 13lb, 0w, 20nb)	41	
Total	225.4 overs	545	

1st innings FoW: 14, 143, 209, 244, 383, 401, 531, 539, 539, 545

Bowler	O	M	R	W
Asif Masood	40	13	66	1
Sarfraz Nawaz	38	8	103	1
Intikhab Alam	51.4	14	116	5
Imran Khan	44	16	100	0
Mushtaq	29	12	51	1
Wasim Raja	23	6	68	1

ENGLAND 1st innings / 2nd innings

Batsman	1st innings		2nd innings	
DL Amiss	c Jenner b Thomson	7	c Walters b Thomson	25
BW Luckhurst	c Marsh b Thomson	1	c IM Chappell b Lillee	3
JH Edrich	c I Chappell b Thomson	48	b Thomson	6
MH Denness*	lbw b Walker	6	c Walters b Thomson	27
KWR Fletcher	b Lillee	17	c GS Chappell b Jenner	19
AW Greig	c Marsh b Lillee	110	b Thomson	2
APE Knott+	c Jenner b Walker	12	b Thomson	19
P Lever	c IM Chappell b Walker	4	c Redpath b Lillee	14
DL Underwood	c Redpath b Walters	25	c Walker b Jenner	30
RGD Willis	not out	13	not out	3
M Hendrick	c Redpath b Walker	4	b Thomson	0
Extras	(5b, 2lb, 3w, 8nb)	18	(8b, 3lb, 2w, 5nb)	18
Total	80.5 overs	265	56.5 overs	166

1st innings FoW: 9, 10, 33, 57, 130, 162, 168, 226, 248, 265
2nd innings FoW: 18, 40, 44, 92, 94, 94, 115, 162, 163, 166

Bowler	O	M	R	W		O	M	R	W
DK Lillee	23	6	73	2		12	2	25	2
JR Thomson	21	5	59	3		17.5	3	46	6
MHN Walker	24.5	2	73	4		9	4	32	0
KD Walters	6	1	18	1		2	2	0	0
TJ Jenner	6	1	24	0		16	5	45	2

No. 504: 2nd Test	No: 505 3rd Test
VENUE: Perth (WACA)	VENUE: Melbourne (MCG)
DATE: 13th-17th December 1974	DATE: 26th-31st December 1974
TOSS WON BY: Australia	TOSS WON BY: Australia
RESULT: Australia won by 9 wickets	RESULT: Match drawn

ENGLAND 1st innings / 2nd innings

Batsman	1st innings		2nd innings	
D Lloyd	c G Chappell b Thomson	49	c G Chappell b Walker	35
BW Luckhurst	c Mallett b Walker	27	lbw b Thomson	41
MC Cowdrey	b Thomson	22	c Redpath b Thomson	20
AW Greig	c Mallett b Walker	23	c GS Ch'l b Thomson	32
KWR Fletcher	c Redpath b Lillee	4	c Marsh b Thomson	0
MH Denness*	c GS Chappell b Lillee	2	c GS Chappell b Lillee	18
APE Knott+	c Redpath b Walters	51	c Mallett b Lillee	23
FJ Titmus	c Redpath b Walters	10	c GS Chap'l b Mallett	61
CM Old	c G Chappell b I Chappell	7	c Thomson b Mallett	43
GG Arnold	run out	1	c Mallett b Thomson	4
RGD Willis	not out	4	not out	0
Extras	(0b, 0lb, 3w, 5nb)	8	(0b, 4lb, 1w, 11nb)	16
Total	65.3 overs	**208**	91.1 overs	**293**

1st innings FoW: 44, 99, 119, 128, 132, 132, 194, 201, 202, 208
2nd innings FoW: 62, 106, 124, 124, 154, 156, 219, 285, 293, 293

Bowler	O	M	R	W		O	M	R	W
DK Lillee	16	4	48	2		22	5	59	2
JR Thomson	15	6	45	2		25	4	93	5
MHN Walker	20	5	49	2		24	7	76	1
AA Mallett	10	3	35	0		11.1	4	32	2
KD Walters	2.3	0	13	2		9	4	17	0
IM Chappell	2	0	10	1					

AUSTRALIA 1st innings / 2nd innings

Batsman	1st innings		2nd innings	
IR Redpath	st Knott b Titmus	41	not out	12
WJ Edwards	c Lloyd b Greig	30	lbw b Arnold	0
IM Chappell*	c Knott b Arnold	25	not out	11
GS Chappell	c Greig b Willis	62		
R Edwards	b Arnold	115		
KD Walters	c Fletcher b Willis	103		
RW Marsh+	c Lloyd b Titmus	41		
MHN Walker	c Knott b Old	19		
DK Lillee	b Old	11		
AA Mallett	c Knott b Old	0		
JR Thomson	not out	11		
Extras	(7b, 14lb, 0w, 2nb)	23	(0b, 0lb, 0w, 0nb)	0
Total	108.6 overs	**481**	3.7 overs	**23**

1st innings FoW: 64, 101, 113, 192, 362, 416, 449, 462, 462, 481
2nd innings FoW: 4

Bowler	O	M	R	W		O	M	R	W
RGD Willis	22	0	91	2		2	0	8	0
GG Arnold	27	1	129	2		1.7	0	15	1
CM Old	22.6	3	85	3					
AW Greig	9	0	69	1					
FJ Titmus	28	3	84	2					

ENGLAND 1st innings / 2nd innings

Batsman	1st innings		2nd innings	
DL Amiss	c Walters b Lillee	4	c IM Chappell b Mallett	90
D Lloyd	c Mallett b Thomson	14	c & b Mallett	44
MC Cowdrey	lbw b Thomson	35	c GS Chappell b Lillee	8
JH Edrich	c Marsh b Mallett	49	c Marsh b Thomson	4
MH Denness*	c Marsh b Mallett	8	c IM Ch'l b Thomson	2
AW Greig	run out	28	c GS Chappell b Lillee	60
APE Knott+	b Thomson	52	c Marsh b Thomson	4
FJ Titmus	c Mallett b Lillee	10	b Mallett	0
DL Underw'd	c Marsh b Walker	9	c IM Chappell b Mallett	4
RGD Willis	c Walters b Thomson	13	b Thomson	15
M Hendrick	not out	8	not out	0
Extras	(0b, 2lb, 1w, 9nb)	12	(2b, 9lb, 2w, 0nb)	13
Total	88.4 overs	**242**	69 overs	**244**

1st innings FOW: 4, 34, 110, 110, 141, 157, 176, 213, 232, 242
2nd innings FOW: 115, 134, 152, 156, 158, 165, 178, 182, 238, 244

Bowler	O	M	R	W		O	M	R	W
DK Lillee	20	2	70	2		17	3	55	2
JR Thomson	22.4	4	72	4		17	1	71	4
MHN Walker	24	10	36	1		11	0	45	0
KD Walters	7	2	15	0		24	6	60	4
AA Mallett	15	3	37	2					

AUSTRALIA 1st innings / 2nd innings

Batsman	1st innings		2nd innings	
IR Redpath	c Knott b Greig	55	run out	39
WJ Edwards	c Denness b Willis	29	lbw b Greig	0
GS Chappell	c Greig b Willis	2	lbw b Willis	0
R Edwards	c Cowdrey b Titmus	1	lbw b Titmus	61
KD Walters	c Lloyd b Greig	36	c Lloyd b Titmus	10
IM Chappell*	lbw b Willis	36	c Denness b Greig	32
RW Marsh+	c Knott b Titmus	44	c Knott b Greig	40
MHN Walker	c Knott b Willis	30	not out	23
DK Lillee	not out	2	c Denness b Greig	14
AA Mallett	run out	0	not out	0
JR Thomson	b Willis	2		
Extras	(2b, 2lb, 0w, 0nb)	4	(6b, 9lb, 0w, 4nb)	19
Total	92.5 overs	**241**	80 overs	**238**

1st innings FOW: 65, 67, 68, 121, 126, 173, 237, 237, 238, 241
2nd innings FOW: 4, 5, 106, 120, 121, 171, 208, 235

Bowler	O	M	R	W		O	M	R	W
RGD Willis	21.7	4	61	5		14	2	56	1
M Hendrick	2.6	1	8	0					
DL Underwood	22	6	62	0		19	7	43	0
AW Greig	24	2	63	2		18	2	56	4
FJ Titmus	22	11	43	2		29	10	64	2

Australia

AUSTRALIA 1st innings

			2nd innings	
IR Redpath	hit wkt b Titmus	33	c (sub) b Underwood	105
RB McCosker	c Knott b Greig	80		
IM Chappell*	c Knott b Arnold	53	c Lloyd b Willis	5
GS Chappell	c Greig b Arnold	84	c Lloyd b Arnold	144
R Edwards	b Greig	15	b Underwood	17
KD Walters	lbw b Arnold	1	not out	5
RW Marsh+	b Greig	30	not out	7
MHN Walker	c Greig b Arnold	30		
DK Lillee	b Arnold	8		
AA Mallett	lbw b Greig	31		
JR Thomson	not out	24		
Extras	(0b, 4lb, 1w, 11nb)	16	(0b, 2lb, 1w, 3nb)	6
	98.7 overs		64.3 overs	
Total		**405**		**289**

1st innings FoW: 96, 142, 199, 251, 255, 305, 310, 332, 368, 405
2nd innings FoW: 15, 235, 242, 280

RGD Willis	18	2	80	0		11	1	52	1
GG Arnold	29	7	86	5		22	3	78	1
AW Greig	22.7	2	104	4		12	1	64	0
DL Underwood	13	3	54	0		12	1	65	2
FJ Titmus	16	2	65	1		7.3	2	24	0

ENGLAND 1st innings

			2nd innings	
DL Amiss	c Mallett b Walker	12	c Marsh b Lillee	37
D Lloyd	c Thomson b Lillee	19	c GS Cha'l b Thomson	26
MC Cowdrey	c McCosker b Thomson	22	c IM Chappell b Walker	1
JH Edrich*	c Marsh b Walters	50	not out	33
KWR Fletcher	c Redpath b Walker	24	c Redpath b Thomson	11
AW Greig	c G Chappell b Thomson	9	st Marsh b Mallett	54
APE Knott+	b Thomson	82	c Redpath b Mallett	10
FJ Titmus	c Marsh b Walters	22	c Thomson b Mallett	4
DL Underw'd	c Walker b Lillee	27	c & b Walker	5
RGD Willis	b Thomson	2	b Lillee	12
GG Arnold	not out	3	c G Chappell b Mallett	14
Extras	(15b, 7lb, 1w, 0nb)	23	(13b, 3lb, 0w, 5nb)	21
	73.1 overs		79.5 overs	
Total		**295**		**228**

1st innings FoW: 36, 46, 69, 108, 123, 180, 240, 273, 285, 295
2nd innings FoW: 68, 70, 74, 103, 136, 156, 158, 175, 201, 228

DK Lillee	19.1	2	66	2		21	5	65	2
JR Thomson	19	3	74	4		23	7	74	2
MHN Walker	23	2	77	2		16	5	46	2
AA Mallett	1	0	8	0		16.5	9	21	4
KD Walters	7	2	26	2					
IM Chappell	4	0	21	0		3	2	1	0

Australia

AUSTRALIA 1st innings

			2nd innings	
IR Redpath	c Greig b Underw'd	21	b Underwood	52
RB McCosker	c Cowdrey b Underw'd	35	c Knott b Arnold	11
IM Chappell*	c Knott b Underwood	0	c Knott b Underwood	41
GS Chappell	lbw b Underwood	5	c Greig b Underwood	18
KD Walters	c Willis b Underwood	55	not out	71
RW Marsh+	c Greig b Underwood	6	c Greig b Underwood	55
TJ Jenner	b Underwood	74	not out	14
MHN Walker	run out	41		
DK Lillee	b Willis	26		
AA Mallett	not out	23		
JR Thomson	b Arnold	5		
Extras	(4b, 4lb, 0w, 5nb)	13	(0b, 4lb, 0w, 6nb)	10
	68.2 overs		66 overs	
Total		**304**		**272**

1st innings FoW: 52, 52, 58, 77, 84, 164, 241, 259, 295, 304
2nd innings FoW: 16, 92, 128, 133, 245

RGD Willis	10	0	46	1		5	0	27	0
GG Arnold	12.2	3	42	1		20	1	71	1
DL Underwood	29	3	113	7		26	5	102	4
AW Greig	10	0	63	0		2	0	9	0
FJ Titmus	7	1	27	0		13	1	53	0

ENGLAND 1st innings

			2nd innings	
DL Amiss	c IM Chappell b Lillee	0	c Marsh b Lillee	0
D Lloyd	c Marsh b Lillee	4	c Walters b Walker	5
MC Cowdrey	c Walker b Thomson	26	c Mallett b Lillee	3
MH Denness*	c Marsh b Thomson	51	c Jenner b Lillee	14
KWR Fletcher	c IM Ch'l b Thomson	40	lbw b Lillee	63
AW Greig	c Marsh b Lillee	19	lbw b Walker	20
APE Knott+	c Lillee b Mallett	5	not out	106
FJ Titmus	c GS Chappell b Mallett	11	lbw b Jenner	20
DL Underw'd	c Lillee b Mallett	0	c I Chappell b Mallett	0
GG Arnold	b Lillee	0	b Mallett	0
RGD Willis	not out	11	b Walker	3
Extras	(0b, 2lb, 0w, 3nb)	5	(3b, 3lb, 0w, 1nb)	7
	46.5 overs		75 overs	
Total		**172**		**241**

1st innings FoW: 2, 19, 66, 90, 130, 147, 155, 156, 161, 172
2nd innings FoW: 0, 8, 10, 33, 76, 144, 212, 213, 217, 241

DK Lillee	12.5	2	49	4		14	3	69	4
JR Thomson	15	1	58	3					
MHN Walker	5	1	18	0		20	3	89	3
TJ Jenner	5	0	28	0		15	4	39	1
AA Mallett	9	4	14	3		25	10	36	2
IM Chappell						1	0	1	0

No. 508: 6th Test		No. 509: 1st Test
VENUE: Melbourne (MCG)		VENUE: Auckland
DATE: 8th-13th February 1975		DATE: 20th-25th February 1975
TOSS WON BY: Australia		TOSS WON BY: England
RESULT: Eng won by an innings and 4 runs		RESULT: Eng won by an innings and 83 runs

AUSTRALIA 1st innings / 2nd innings

Batsman	1st innings		2nd innings	
IR Redpath	c Greig b Lever	1	c Amiss b Greig	83
RB McCosker	c Greig b Lever	0	c Cowdrey b Arnold	76
IM Chappell*	c Knott b Old	65	c Knott b Greig	50
GS Chappell	c Denness b Lever	1	b Lever	102
R Edwards	c Amiss b Lever	0	c Knott b Arnold	18
KD Walters	c Edrich b Old	12	b Arnold	3
RW Marsh+	b Old	29	c Denness b Lever	1
MHN Walker	not out	20	c & b Greig	17
DK Lillee	c Knott b Lever	12	c Edrich b Greig	0
AA Mallett	b Lever	7	c Knott b Lever	0
G Dymock	c Knott b Greig	0	not out	0
Extras	(2b, 1lb, 0w, 2nb)	5	(9b, 5lb, 4w, 5nb)	231
	36.7 overs		106.7 overs	
Total		**152**		**373**

1st innings FoW: 0, 5, 19, 23, 50, 104, 115, 141, 149, 152
2nd innings FoW: 111, 215, 248, 289, 297, 306, 367, 373, 373, 373

Bowler	O	M	R	W		O	M	R	W
GG Arnold	6	2	24	0		23	6	83	3
P Lever	11	2	38	6		16	1	65	3
CM Old	11	0	50	3		18	1	75	0
AW Greig	8.7	1	35	1		31.7	7	88	4
DL Underwood						18	5	39	0

ENGLAND 1st innings / 2nd innings

Batsman	1st innings		2nd innings
DL Amiss	lbw b Lillee	0	
MC Cowdrey	c Marsh b Walker	7	
JH Edrich	c I Chappell b Walker	70	
MH Denness*	c & b Walker	188	
KWR Fletcher	c Redpath b Walker	146	
AW Greig	c (sub) b Walker	89	
APE Knott+	c Marsh b Walker	5	
CM Old	b Dymock	0	
DL Underw'd	b Walker	11	
GG Arnold	c Marsh b Walker	0	
P Lever	not out	6	
Extras	(4b, 2lb, 0w, 1nb)	7	
	151.2 overs		
Total		**529**	

1st innings FoW: 4, 18, 167, 359, 507, 507, 508, 514, 514, 529

Bowler	O	M	R	W
DK Lillee	6	2	17	1
MHN Walker	42.2	7	143	8
G Dymock	39	6	130	1
KD Walters	23	3	86	0
AA Mallett	29	8	96	0
IM Chappell	12	1	50	0

ENGLAND 1st innings / 2nd innings

Batsman	1st innings		2nd innings
DL Amiss	c Wadsworth b Hadlee	19	
B Wood	c Parker b Hadlee	0	
JH Edrich	c Congdon b Howarth	64	
MH Denness*	c Parker b Congdon	181	
KWR Fletcher	c Hadlee b Congdon	216	
AW Greig	b GP Howarth	51	
APE Knott+	not out	29	
CM Old	not out	9	
DL Underwood			
GG Arnold			
P Lever			
Extras	(2b, 14lb, 0w, 8nb)	24	
	153 overs		
Total		**593**	

1st innings FoW: 4, 36, 153, 419, 497, 578

Bowler	O	M	R	W
RO Collinge	24	6	75	0
DR Hadlee	20	2	102	2
EJ Chatfield	19	2	95	0
BE Congdon	30	3	115	2
HJ Howarth	46	9	135	1
GP Howarth	14	1	47	1

NEW ZEALAND 1st innings / 2nd innings

Batsman	1st innings		2nd innings	
JFM Morrison	c Amiss b Greig	58	c Fletcher b Greig	58
GM Turner	c Amiss b Arnold	8	c Knott b Lever	2
JM Parker	c Knott b Underwood	121	b Underwood	18
BE Congdon*	c Old b Greig	2	c Amiss b Lever	0
BF Hastings	c Knott b Old	13	c Edrich b Greig	13
GP Howarth	c Wood b Greig	6	not out	51
KJ Wad'th+	lbw b Underwood	58	c Fletcher b Underw'd	6
DR Hadlee	c (sub) b Underwood	22	c Edrich b Greig	1
HJ Howarth	c Fletcher b Greig	9	b Greig	4
RO Collinge	not out	0	c Fletcher b Greig	0
EJ Chatfield	c Fletcher b Greig	0	retired hurt	13
Extras	(5b, 4lb, 0w, 20nb)	29	(0b, 6lb, 0w, 12nb)	18
	89 overs		57.5 overs	
Total		**326**		**184**

1st innings FoW: 9, 125, 131, 166, 173, 285, 315, 326, 326, 326
2nd innings FoW: 3, 42, 46, 99, 102, 131, 134, 140, 140

Bowler	O	M	R	W		O	M	R	W
GG Arnold	20	4	69	1		6	1	31	0
P Lever	20	4	75	0		11.5	0	37	2
AW Greig	26	4	98	5		15	3	51	5
DL Underwood	16	6	38	3		25	9	47	2
CM Old	7	3	17	1					

New Zealand

No. 510: 2nd Test	
VENUE: Christchurch	
DATE: 28th February to 5th March 1975	
TOSS WON BY: England	
RESULT: Match drawn	

NEW ZEALAND 1st innings

Batsman	Dismissal	Runs	2nd innings
JFM Morrison	c Hendrick b Arnold	0	
GM Turner	lbw b Arnold	98	
BE Congdon*	c Wood b Hendrick	38	
BF Hastings	c Wood b Lever	0	
JM Parker	c Edrich b Greig	41	
GP Howarth	b Underwood	11	
KJ Wad'rth+	c Lever b Greig	58	
DR Hadlee	c Greig b Arnold	22	
BL Cairns	c & b Hendrick	39	
HJ Howarth	lbw b Underwood	9	
RO Collinge	not out	0	
Extras	(3b, 9lb, 1w, 13nb)	26	
	89.5 overs		
Total		**342**	

1st innings FoW: 0, 64, 66, 181, 208, 212, 267, 318, 338, 342

Bowler	O	M	R	W
GG Arnold	25	5	80	3
P Lever	18	2	66	1
M Hendrick	20	2	89	2
DL Underwood	13.5	3	35	2
AW Greig	9	1	27	2
B Wood	4	0	19	0

ENGLAND 1st innings

Batsman	Dismissal	Runs	2nd innings
DL Amiss	not out	164	
B Wood	c Wadsworth b Hadlee	33	
JH Edrich	c Hadlee b HJ Howarth	11	
MH Denness*	not out	59	
KWR Fletcher			
AW Greig			
APE Knott+			
DL Underwood			
GG Arnold			
P Lever			
M Hendrick			
Extras	(0b, 3lb, 0w, 2nb)	5	
	83 overs		
Total		**272**	

1st innings FoW: 80, 121

Bowler	O	M	R	W
RO Collinge	19	3	63	0
DR Hadlee	19	2	61	1
BL Cairns	13	5	44	0
BE Congdon	7	2	27	0
HJ Howarth	18	5	53	1
GP Howarth	7	0	19	0

Australia

No. 511: 1st Test	
VENUE: Edgbaston	
DATE: 10th-14th July 1975	
TOSS WON BY: England	
RESULT: Aus won by an innings and 85 runs	

AUSTRALIA 1st innings

Batsman	Dismissal	Runs	2nd innings
RB McCosker	b Arnold	59	
A Turner	c Denness b Snow	37	
IM Chappell*	c Fletcher b Snow	52	
GS Chappell	lbw b Old	0	
R Edwards	c Gooch b Old	56	
KD Walters	c Old b Greig	14	
RW Marsh+	c Fletcher b Arnold	61	
MHN Walker	c Knott b Snow	7	
JR Thomson	c Arnold b Underwood	49	
DK Lillee	c Knott b Arnold	3	
AA Mallett	not out	3	
Extras	(1b, 8lb, 0w, 9nb)	18	
	121 overs		
Total		**359**	

1st innings FoW: 80, 126, 135, 161, 186, 265, 286, 332, 343, 359

Bowler	O	M	R	W
GG Arnold	33	3	91	3
JA Snow	33	6	86	3
CM Old	33	7	111	2
AW Greig	15	2	43	1
DL Underwood	7	3	10	1

ENGLAND

	1st innings			2nd innings	
JH Edrich	lbw b Lillee	34	c Marsh b Walker	5
DL Amiss	c Thomson b Lillee	4	c (sub) b Thomson	5
KWR Fletcher	c Mallett b Walker	6	c Walters b Lillee	51
MH Denness*	c GS Chappell b Walker	3	b Thomson	8
GA Gooch	c Marsh b Walker	0	c Marsh b Thomson	0
AW Greig	c Marsh b Walker	8	c Marsh b Walker	7
APE Knott+	b Lillee	14	c McCosker b Th'son	38
DL Underw'd	c Walters b Lillee	10	c Walters b Lillee	7
CM Old	c GS Chappell b Walker	13	c Marsh b Thomson	34
JA Snow	lbw b Lillee	0	b Mallett	3
GG Arnold	not out	0	not out	6
Extras	(0b, 3lb, 5w, 1nb)	9	(0b, 5lb, 2w, 2nb)	9
	45.3 overs		75.2 overs	
Total		**101**		**173**

1st innings FoW: 9, 24, 46, 46, 54, 75, 78, 87, 97, 101
2nd innings FoW: 7, 18, 20, 52, 90, 100, 122, 151, 167, 173

Bowler	O	M	R	W	O	M	R	W
DK Lillee	15	8	15	5	20	8	45	2
JR Thomson	10	3	21	0	18	8	38	5
MHN Walker	17.3	5	48	5	24	9	47	2
AA Mallett	3	1	8	0	13.2	6	34	1

No. 512: 2nd Test	
VENUE: Lord's	
DATE: 31st July to 5th August 1975	
TOSS WON BY: England	
RESULT: Match drawn	

ENGLAND	1st innings		2nd innings	
B Wood	lbw b Lillee	6	c Marsh b Thomson	52
JH Edrich	lbw b Lillee	9	c Thomson b Mallett	175
DS Steele	b Thomson	50	c & b Walters	45
DL Amiss	lbw b Lillee	0	c G Chappell b Lillee	10
GA Gooch	c Marsh b Lillee	6	b Mallett	31
AW Greig*	c IM Chappell b Walker	96	c Walters b I Chappell	41
APE Knott+	lbw b Thomson	69	not out	22
RA Woolmer	c Turner b Mallett	33	b Mallett	31
JA Snow	c Walker b Mallett	11		
DL Underw'd	not out	0		
P Lever	lbw b Walker	4		
Extras	(3b, 1lb, 4w, 23nb)	31	(0b, 18lb, 2w, 9nb)	29
	87.4 overs		147.4 overs	
Total		**315**		**436**

1st innings FoW: 10, 29, 31, 49, 145, 222, 288, 309, 310, 315
2nd innings FoW: 111, 215, 249, 315, 380, 387, 436

DK Lillee	20	4	84	4		33	10	80	1
JR Thomson	24	7	92	2		29	8	73	1
MHN Walker	21.4	7	52	2		37	8	95	0
AA Mallett	22	4	56	2		36.4	10	127	3
IM Chappell						10	2	26	1
KD Walters						2	0	6	1

AUSTRALIA	1st innings		2nd innings	
RB McCosker	c & b Lever	29	lbw b Steele	79
A Turner	lbw b Snow	9	c Gooch b Greig	21
IM Chappell*	c Knott b Snow	2	lbw b Greig	86
GS Chappell	lbw b Snow	4	not out	73
R Edwards	lbw b Woolmer	99	not out	52
KD Walters	c Greig b Lever	2		
RW Marsh+	c Amiss b Greig	3		
MHN Walker	b Snow	5		
JR Thomson	b Underwood	17		
DK Lillee	not out	73		
AA Mallett	lbw b Steele	14		
Extras	(0b, 5lb, 0w, 6nb)	11	(4b, 0lb, 0w, 14nb)	18
	77.4 overs		109 overs	
Total		**268**		**329**

1st innings FoW: 21, 29, 37, 54, 56, 64, 81, 133, 199, 268
2nd innings FoW: 50, 169, 222

JA Snow	21	4	66	4		19	3	82	0
P Lever	15	0	83	2		20	5	55	0
RA Woolmer	13	5	31	1		3	1	3	0
AW Greig	15	5	47	1		26	6	82	2
DL Underwood	13	5	29	1		31	14	64	0
DS Steele	0.4	0	1	1		9	4	19	1
B Wood						1	0	6	0

No. 513: 3rd Test	
VENUE: Headingley	
DATE: 14th-19th August 1975	
TOSS WON BY: England	
RESULT: Match drawn	

ENGLAND	1st innings		2nd innings	
B Wood	lbw b Gilmour	9	lbw b Walker	25
JH Edrich	c Mallett b Thomson	62	b Mallett	35
DS Steele	c Walters b Thomson	73	c GS Ch'l b Gilmour	92
JH Hampshire	lbw b Gilmour	14	c GS Ch'l b Lillee	14
KWR Fletcher	c Mallett b Lillee	8	c & b Mallett	49
AW Greig*	run out	51	st Marsh b Mallett	10
APE Knott+	lbw b Gilmour	14	c GS Ch'l b Thomson	0
PH Edmonds	not out	13	c Thomson b Lillee	31
CM Old	b Gilmour	5	c (sub) b Gilmour	8
JA Snow	c Walters b Gilmour	0	c Marsh b Gilmour	9
D Underw'd	c G Chap'l b Gilmour	0	not out	0
Extras	(4b, 15lb, 11w, 9nb)	39	(5b, 2lb, 2w, 9nb)	18
	101.2 overs		94 overs	
Total		**288**		**291**

1st innings FoW: 25, 137, 159, 189, 213, 268, 269, 284, 284, 288
2nd innings FoW: 55, 70, 103, 197, 209, 210, 272, 276, 285, 291

DK Lillee	28	12	53	1		20	5	48	2
JR Thomson	22	8	53	2		20	6	67	1
GJ Gilmour	31.2	10	85	6		20	5	72	3
MHN Walker	18	4	54	0		15	4	36	1
IM Chappell	2	0	4	0					
AA Mallett						19	4	50	3

AUSTRALIA	1st innings		2nd innings	
RB McCosker	c Hampshire b Old	0	not out	95
RW Marsh+	b Snow	25	b Underwood	12
IM Chappell*	b Edmonds	35	lbw b Old	62
GS Chappell	c Underwood b Edmonds	13	c Steele b Edmonds	12
R Edwards	lbw b Edmonds	0		
KD Walters	lbw b Edmonds	19	not out	25
GJ Gilmour	c Greig b Underwood	6		
MHN Walker	c Old b Edmonds	0		
JR Thomson	c Steele b Snow	16		
DK Lillee	b Snow	11		
AA Mallett	not out	1		
Extras	(0b, 5lb, 1w, 3nb)	9	(4b, 8lb, 0w, 2nb)	14
	76.5 overs		73 overs	
Total		**135**		**220**

1st innings FoW: 8, 53, 78, 78, 81, 96, 104, 107, 128, 135
2nd innings FoW: 55, 161, 174

JA Snow	18.5	7	22	3		15	6	21	0
CM Old	11	3	30	1		17	5	61	1
AW Greig	3	0	14	0		3	3	20	0
B Wood	5	2	10	0		15	4	40	1
DL Underwood	19	12	22	1		17	4	64	1
PH Edmonds	20	7	28	5					

Australia

No. 514: 4th Test	
VENUE:	The Oval
DATE:	28th August to 3rd Sep 1975
TOSS WON BY:	Australia
RESULT:	Match drawn

AUSTRALIA 1st innings

			2nd innings	
RB McCosker	c Roope b Old	127	not out	25
A Turner	c Steele b Old	2	c Woolmer b Greig	8
IM Chappell*	c Greig b Woolmer	192		
GS Chappell	c Knott b Old	0	not out	4
R Edwards	c Edrich b Snow	44	c Old b Underwood	2
KD Walters	b Underwood	65		
RW Marsh+	c & b Greig	32		
MHN Walker	c Steele b Greig	13		
JR Thomson	c Old b Greig	0		
DK Lillee	not out	28		
AA Mallett	not out	5		
Extras	(0b, 5lb, 2w, 17nb)	24	(0b, 1lb, 0w, 0nb)	1
Total	181 overs	532	17.1 overs	40

1st innings FoW: 7, 284, 286, 356, 396, 441, 477, 477, 501
2nd innings FoW: 22, 33

CM Old	28	7	74	3		2	0	7	0		
JA Snow	27	4	74	1		2	1	4	0		
RA Woolmer	18	3	38	1							
PH Edmonds	38	7	118	0		6.1	2	14	0		
DL Underwood	44	13	96	1		2	0	5	1		
AW Greig	24	5	107	3		5	2	9	1		
DS Steele	2	1	1	0							

ENGLAND 1st innings

			2nd innings	
B Wood	b Walker	32	lbw b Thomson	22
JH Edrich	lbw b Walker	12	b Lillee	96
DS Steele	b Lillee	39	c Marsh b Lillee	66
GRJ Roope	c Turner b Walker	0	b Lillee	77
RA Woolmer	c Mallett b Thomson	5	lbw b Walters	149
AW Greig*	c Marsh b Lillee	17	c Marsh b Lillee	15
APE Knott+	lbw b Walker	9	c Marsh b Walters	64
PH Edmonds	b Marsh b Thomson	4	c I Chappell b Walters	0
CM Old	not out	25	run out	7
JA Snow	c GS Ch'l b Thomson	30	c & b Walters	0
D Underw'd	c GS Ch'l b Thomson	0	not out	3
Extras	(0b, 3lb, 3w, 12nb)	18	(2b, 15lb, 5w, 17nb)	39
Total	69.1 overs	191	233.5 overs	538

1st innings FoW: 45, 78, 83, 96, 103, 125, 131, 147, 190, 191
2nd innings FoW: 77, 202, 209, 331, 371, 522, 522, 533, 533, 538

DK Lillee	19	7	44	2		52	18	91	4		
JR Thomson	22.1	7	50	4		30	9	63	1		
MHN Walker	25	7	63	4		46	15	91	0		
AA Mallett	3	1	16	0		64	31	95	0		
IM Chappell						17	6	52	0		
KD Walters						10.5	3	34	4		
GS Chappell						12	2	53	0		
R Edwards						2	0	20	0		

West Indies

No. 515: 1st Test	
VENUE:	Trent Bridge
DATE:	3rd-8th June 1976
TOSS WON BY:	West Indies
RESULT:	Match drawn

WEST INDIES 1st innings

			2nd innings	
RC Fredericks	c Hendrick b Greig	42	b Snow	15
CG Greenidge	c Edrich b Hendrick	22	c & b Old	23
IVA Richards	c Greig b Underwood	232	lbw b Snow	63
AI Kallicharran	c Steele b Underwood	97	not out	29
CH Lloyd*	c Hendrick b Underw'd	16	c Brearley b Snow	21
BD Julien	c Knott b Old	21	c Hendrick b Snow	13
HA Gomes	c Close b Underwood	0		
DL Murray+	c Close b Snow	19		
VA Holder	not out	19		
AME Roberts	b Old	1		
WW Daniel	c Knott b Old	4		
Extras	(0b, 12lb, 1w, 8nb)	21	(0b, 6lb, 2w, 4nb)	12
Total	153.3 overs	494	36 overs	176

1st innings FoW: 36, 105, 408, 423, 432, 432, 458, 481, 488, 494
2nd innings FoW: 33, 77, 109, 124, 176

JA Snow	31	5	123	1		11	2	53	4		
M Hendrick	24	7	59	1		7	2	22	0		
CM Old	34.3	7	80	3		10	0	64	1		
AW Greig	27	4	82	1		1	0	16	0		
RA Woolmer	10	2	47	0							
DL Underwood	27	8	82	4		7	3	9	0		

ENGLAND 1st innings

			2nd innings	
JH Edrich	c Murray b Daniel	37	not out	76
JM Brearley	c Richards b Julien	0	c Murray b Holder	17
DS Steele	c Roberts b Daniel	106	c Julien b Roberts	6
DB Close	c Murray b Daniel	2	not out	36
RA Woolmer	lbw b Julien	82		
AW Greig*	b Roberts	0		
APE Knott+	c (sub) b Holder	9		
CM Old	b Daniel	33		
JA Snow	not out	20		
D Underw'd	c Murray b Holder	0		
M Hendrick	c Daniel b Fredericks	5		
Extras	(5b, 1lb, 3w, 29nb)	38	(9b, 2lb, 0w, 10nb)	21
Total	134.4 overs	332	78 overs	156

1st innings FoW: 0, 98, 105, 226, 229, 255, 278, 279, 318, 332
2nd innings FoW: 38, 55

AME Roberts	34	15	53	1		9	3	20	1		
BD Julien	34	9	75	2		16	8	19	0		
VA Holder	25	5	66	2		12	6	12	1		
WW Daniel	23	8	53	4		10	2	20	0		
RC Fredericks	8.4	2	24	1		9	1	21	0		
IVA Richards	3	1	8	0		3	1	7	0		
HA Gomes	4	1	8	0		9	1	18	0		
CH Lloyd	3	1	7	0							
AI Kallicharran						10	3	18	0		

No. 516: 2nd Test	No. 517: 3rd Test
VENUE: Lord's	VENUE: Old Trafford
DATE: 17th-22nd June 1976	DATE: 8th-13th July 1976
TOSS WON BY: England	TOSS WON BY: West Indies
RESULT: Match drawn	RESULT: West Indies won by 425 runs

Left match (No. 516)

ENGLAND

Batsman	1st innings		2nd innings	
B Wood	c Murray b Roberts	6	c Murray b Holding	30
JM Brearley	b Roberts	40	b Holding	13
DS Steele	lbw b Roberts	7	c Jumadeen b Roberts	3
DB Close	c Holder b Jumadeen	60	c Jumadeen b Roberts	64
RA Woolmer	c Murray b Holding	38	c & b Holder	46
AW Greig*	c Lloyd b Roberts	6	c Murray b Roberts	29
APE Knott+	b Holder	17	c Gomes b Holder	20
CM Old	b Holder	19	lbw b Roberts	4
JA Snow	b Roberts	0	run out	13
D Underw'd	b Holder	31	not out	6
PI Pocock	not out	0	b Roberts	2
Extras	(7b, 5lb, 5w, 9nb)	26	(7b, 7lb, 0w, 10nb)	24
Total	95.4 overs	250	104.5 overs	254

1st innings FoW: 15, 31, 115, 153, 161, 188, 196, 197, 249, 250
2nd innings FoW: 29, 29, 112, 169, 186, 207, 215, 245, 249, 254

Bowler	O	M	R	W	O	M	R	W
AME Roberts	23	6	60	5	29.5	10	63	5
MA Holding	19	4	52	1	27	10	56	2
BD Julien	23	6	54	0	13	5	20	0
VA Holder	18.4	7	35	3	19	2	50	2
RR Jumadeen	12	4	23	1	16	4	41	0

WEST INDIES

Batsman	1st innings		2nd innings	
RC Fredericks	c Snow b Old	0	c Greig b Old	138
CG Greenidge	c Snow b Underwood	84	c Close b Pocock	22
HA Gomes	c Woolmer b Snow	11	b Greig	34
AI Kallicharran	c Old b Snow	0	b Greig	33
CH Lloyd*	c Knott b Underwood	50	b Underwood	1
DL Murray+	b Snow	2	not out	7
BD Julien	lbw b Snow	3	b Underwood	0
MA Holding	b Underwood	0	not out	0
VA Holder	c Woolmer b Underw'd	12		
AME Roberts	b Underwood	16		
RR Jumadeen	not out	0		
Extras	(2b, 0lb, 0w, 2nb)	4	(3b, 2lb, 0w, 1nb)	6
Total	50.4 overs	182	86.3 overs	241

1st innings FoW: 0, 28, 40, 139, 141, 145, 146, 153, 178, 182
2nd innings FoW: 41, 154, 230, 233, 238, 238

Bowler	O	M	R	W	O	M	R	W
CM Old	10	0	58	1	14	4	46	1
JA Snow	19	3	68	4	7	2	22	0
DL Underwood	18.4	7	39	5	24.3	8	73	2
PI Pocock	3	0	13	0	27	9	52	1
AW Greig					14	3	42	2

Right match (No. 517)

WEST INDIES

Batsman	1st innings		2nd innings	
RC Fredericks	c Underwood b Selvey	0	hit wkt b Hendrick	50
CG Greenidge	b Underwood	134	b Selvey	101
IVA Richards	b Selvey	4	lbw b Pocock	135
AI Kallicharran	b Selvey	0	c Underwood b Selvey	43
CH Lloyd*	c Hayes b Hendrick	2	c Close b Pocock	20
CL King	c Greig b Underwood	32	not out	14
DL Murray+	c Greig b Hendrick	1	not out	7
MA Holding	b Selvey	3		
AME Roberts	c Steele b Pocock	6		
AL Padmore	not out	8		
WW Daniel	lbw b Underwood	10		
Extras	(0b, 8lb, 0w, 3nb)	11	(5b, 30lb, 1w, 5nb)	41
Total	70 overs	211	114 overs	411

1st innings FoW: 1, 15, 19, 26, 137, 154, 167, 193, 193, 211
2nd innings FoW: 116, 224, 356, 385, 388

Bowler	O	M	R	W	O	M	R	W
M Hendrick	14	1	48	2	24	4	63	1
MWW Selvey	17	4	41	4	26	3	111	2
AW Greig	8	1	24	0	2	0	8	0
RA Woolmer	3	0	22	0				
DL Underwood	24	5	55	3	35	9	90	0
PI Pocock	4	2	10	1	27	4	98	2

ENGLAND

Batsman	1st innings		2nd innings	
JH Edrich	c Murray b Roberts	8	b Daniel	24
DB Close	lbw b Daniel	2	b Roberts	20
DS Steele	lbw b Roberts	20	c Roberts b Holding	15
PI Pocock	c Kallicharran b Holding	7	lbw b Roberts	3
RA Woolmer	c Murray b Holding	3	c Greenidge b Roberts	18
FC Hayes	c Lloyd b Roberts	0	b Holding	3
AW Greig*	b Daniel	9	c Fredericks b Roberts	14
APE Knott+	c Greenidge b Holding	1	c King b Roberts	0
D Underwood	b Holding	0	c Greenidge b Roberts	4
MWW Selvey	not out	2	c King b Daniel	3
M Hendrick	b Holding	0	not out	0
Extras	(8b, 0lb, 0w, 11nb)	19	(4b, 1lb, 0w, 20nb)	25
Total	32.5 overs	71	63.5 overs	126

1st innings FoW: 9, 36, 46, 48, 48, 65, 66, 67, 71, 71
2nd innings FoW: 54, 60, 60, 80, 94, 112, 118, 124, 126

Bowler	O	M	R	W	O	M	R	W
AME Roberts	12	4	22	3	20.5	8	37	6
MA Holding	14.5	7	17	5	23	15	24	2
WW Daniel	6	2	13	2	17	8	39	2
AL Padmore					3	2	1	0

No. 518: 4th Test		
VENUE: Headingley		
DATE: 22nd-27th July 1976		
TOSS WON BY: West Indies		
RESULT: West Indies won by 55 runs		

WEST INDIES 1st innings / 2nd innings

Batsman	1st innings		2nd innings	
RC Fredericks	b Willis	109	b Snow	6
CG Greenidge	c Ward b Snow	115	lbw b Ward	6
IVA Richards	c Knott b Willis	66	b Willis	38
LG Rowe	c Greig b Woolmer	50	run out	6
CH Lloyd*	c Steele b Ward	18	b Ward	29
CL King	c Hayes b Ward	0	c Greig b Snow	58
DL Murray+	c Willis b Snow	33	b Willis	18
MA Holding	b Snow	2	b Willis	5
VA Holder	c Hayes b Willis	1	lbw b Willis	4
AME Roberts	b Snow	19	b Willis	3
WW Daniel	not out	4	not out	0
Extras	(1b, 15lb, 2w, 15nb)	33	(4b, 6lb, 1w, 12nb)	23
Total	88.4 overs	450	51.3 overs	196

1st innings FoW: 192, 287, 330, 370, 370, 413, 421, 423, 433, 450
2nd innings FoW: 13, 23, 60, 72, 121, 178, 184, 188, 193, 196

	O	M	R	W		O	M	R	W
RGD Willis	20	2	71	3		15.3	6	42	5
JA Snow	18.4	3	77	4		20	1	80	2
DL Underwood	18	2	80	0					
Alan Ward	15	0	103	2		9	2	25	2
AW Greig	10	2	57	0					
RA Woolmer	6	0	25	1		7	0	26	0
P Willey	1	0	4	0					

ENGLAND 1st innings / 2nd innings

Batsman	1st innings		2nd innings	
RA Woolmer	c Greenidge b Holder	18	lbw b Holder	37
DS Steele	b Holding	4	c Murray b Roberts	0
FC Hayes	c Murray b Daniel	7	c Richards b Roberts	0
J Balderstone	c Murray b Roberts	35	c Roberts b Daniel	4
P Willey	lbw b Roberts	36	c Roberts b Holding	45
AW Greig*	c Lloyd b Daniel	116	not out	76
APE Knott+	c Daniel b Holder	116	c Murray b Daniel	0
JA Snow	c Fredericks b Holder	20	c Murray b Daniel	2
D Underw'd	c Lloyd b King	1	c Greenidge b Daniel	8
Alan Ward	lbw b Roberts	0	c Murray b Holding	0
RGD Willis	not out	0	lbw b Holding	0
Extras	(2b, 7lb, 2w, 23nb)	34	(12b, 5lb, 7w, 8nb)	32
Total	133.3 overs	387	56 overs	204

1st innings FoW: 4, 24, 32, 80, 169, 321, 364, 367, 379, 387
2nd innings FoW: 5, 12, 23, 80, 140, 148, 150, 158, 204, 204

	O	M	R	W		O	M	R	W
AME Roberts	35	7	102	3		18	8	41	3
MA Holding	8	2	14	1		14	1	44	3
WW Daniel	29	7	102	2		13	0	60	3
VA Holder	30.3	13	73	3		11	3	27	1
CL King	26	6	56	1					
RC Fredericks	3	1	5	0					
CH Lloyd	2	1	1	0					

No. 519: 5th Test		
VENUE: The Oval		
DATE: 12th-17th August 1976		
TOSS WON BY: West Indies		
RESULT: West Indies won by 231 runs		

WEST INDIES 1st innings / 2nd innings

Batsman	1st innings		2nd innings	
RC Fredericks	c Balderstone b Miller	71	not out	86
CG Greenidge	lbw b Willis	0	not out	85
IVA Richards	b Greig	291		
LG Rowe	st Knott b Underwood	70		
CH Lloyd*	c Knott b Greig	84		
CL King	c Selvey b Balderstone	63		
DL Murray+	c & b Underwood	36		
VA Holder	not out	13		
MA Holding	b Underwood	32		
AME Roberts				
WW Daniel				
Extras	(1b, 17lb, 0w, 9nb)	27	(4b, 1lb, 1w, 5nb)	11
Total	182.5 overs	687	32 overs	182

1st innings FoW: 5, 159, 350, 524, 547, 640, 642, 687

	O	M	R	W		O	M	R	W
RGD Willis	15	3	73	1		7	0	48	0
MWW Selvey	15	0	67	0		9	1	44	0
DL Underwood	60.5	15	165	3		9	2	38	0
RA Woolmer	9	0	44	0		5	0	30	0
G Miller	27	4	106	1					
JC Balderstone	16	0	80	1					
AW Greig	34	5	96	2		2	0	11	0
P Willey	3	0	11	0					
DS Steele	3	0	18	0					

ENGLAND 1st innings / 2nd innings

Batsman	1st innings		2nd innings	
RA Woolmer	lbw b Holding	8	c Murray b Holding	30
DL Amiss	b Holding	203	c Greenidge b Holding	16
DS Steele	lbw b Holding	44	c Murray b Holder	42
JC Balderstone	b Holding	0	b Holding	0
P Willey	c Fredericks b King	33	c Greenidge b Holder	1
AW Greig*	b Holding	12	b Holding	1
D Underw'd	b Holding	4	b Holding	57
APE Knott+	b Holding	50	b Richards	24
G Miller	c (sub) b Holder	36	c Lloyd b Roberts	2
MWW Selvey	b Holding	0	not out	4
RGD Willis	not out	5	lbw b Holding	0
Extras	(8b, 11lb, 0w, 21nb)	40	(15b, 3lb, 8w, 0nb)	26
Total	129.5 overs	435	78.4 overs	203

1st innings FoW: 47, 147, 151, 279, 303, 323, 342, 411, 411, 435
2nd innings FoW: 49, 54, 64, 77, 78, 148, 196, 196, 202, 203

	O	M	R	W		O	M	R	W
AME Roberts	27	4	102	0		13	4	37	1
MA Holding	33	9	92	8		20.4	6	57	6
VA Holder	27.5	7	75	1		14	5	29	2
WW Daniel	10	1	30	0		12	5	33	0
RC Fredericks	11	2	36	0		11	6	11	1
IVA Richards	14	4	30	0		6	2	9	0
CL King	7	3	30	1		2	1	1	0

No. 520: 1st Test
VENUE:	Delhi
DATE:	17th–22nd December 1976
TOSS WON BY:	England
RESULT:	Eng won by an innings and 25 runs

ENGLAND

1st innings			2nd innings	
DL Amiss	c Sharma b Venkat'van	179		
JM Brearley	run out	5		
GD Barlow	c Amarnath b Bedi	0		
RA Woolmer	lbw b Chandrasekhar	4		
KWR Fletcher	b Chandrasekhar	8		
AW Greig*	lbw b Venkataraghavan	25		
APE Knott+	st Kirmani b Bedi	75		
CM Old	c Viswanath b Bedi	15		
JK Lever	c Bedi b Chan'har	53		
RGD Willis	c Venkat'vanb Bedi	1		
DL Underw'd	not out	7		
Extras	(1b, 5lb, 1w, 2nb)	9		
	151.5 overs			
Total		**381**		

1st innings FoW: 34, 34, 51, 65, 125, 226, 263, 357, 363, 381

KD Ghavri	14	3	50	0				
M Amarnath	8	2	12	0				
BS Bedi	59	22	92	4				
BS Chandrasekhar	32.5	6	117	3				
S Venkataraghavan	34	6	94	2				
AD Gaekwad	1	0	1	0				
P Sharma	3	0	6	0				

INDIA

1st innings			2nd innings	
SM Gavaskar	c Willis b Lever	38	c Woolmer b Underw'd	71
AD Gaekwad	lbw b Lever	20	b Willis	11
M Amarnath	lbw b Lever	0	c Fletcher b Underw'd	29
GR Viswanath	lbw b Lever	3	c Knott b Greig	18
S Venk'van	b Lever	0	c & b Underwood	14
BP Patel	c Knott b Lever	33	c (sub) b Underwood	24
P Sharma	c Willis b Underwood	4	c Lever b Greig	10
SMH Kirmani+	b Lever	13	not out	35
KD Ghavri	not out	3	c Knott b Lever	4
BS Bedi*	c Greig b Old	0	b Lever	0
BS Chan'har	b Old	0	b Lever	0
Extras	(0b, 4lb, 1w, 3nb)	8	(3b, 8lb, 0w, 7nb)	18
	51.5 overs		110.4 overs	
Total		**122**		**234**

1st innings FoW: 43, 43, 49, 49, 96, 99, 103, 121, 122, 122
2nd innings FoW: 20, 110, 133, 153, 163, 182, 190, 226, 226, 234

CM Old	12.5	0	28	2	4	2	6	0
RGD Willis	7	3	21	0	9	3	24	1
JK Lever	23	6	46	7	13.4	6	24	3
DL Underwood	9	3	19	1	44	15	78	4
AW Greig					40	11	84	2

No. 521: 2nd Test
VENUE:	Calcutta
DATE:	1st–6th January 1977
TOSS WON BY:	India
RESULT:	England won by 10 wickets

INDIA

1st innings			2nd innings	
SM Gavaskar	c Old b Willis	0	b Underwood	18
AD Gaekwad	b Lever	32	c Tolchard b Greig	8
P Sharma	c Greig b Lever	9	c Knott b Willis	20
GR Viswanath	c Tolchard b Underwood	35	c Lever b Greig	3
BP Patel	hit wkt b Willis	21	lbw b Old	56
ED Solkar	c Greig b Willis	2	c Knott b Willis	3
S Madan Lal	c Knott b Old	17	c Brearley b Old	16
SMH Kirmani+	not out	25	b Old	0
EAS Prasanna	b Willis	2	c Brearley b Underw'd	13
BS Bedi*	c Lever b Old	1	b Underwood	18
BS Chan'har	b Willis	1	not out	4
Extras	(0b, 2lb, 0w, 8nb)	10	(2b, 4lb, 0w, 16nb)	22
	75 overs		70.5 overs	
Total		**155**		**181**

1st innings FoW: 1, 23, 65, 92, 99, 106, 136, 147, 149, 155
2nd innings FoW: 31, 33, 36, 60, 70, 97, 97, 146, 171, 181

RGD Willis	20	3	27	5	13	1	32	2
JK Lever	22	2	57	2	3	0	12	0
DL Underwood	13	5	24	1	32.5	18	50	3
CM Old	20	5	37	2	12	4	38	3
AW Greig					10	0	27	2

ENGLAND

1st innings			2nd innings	
DL Amiss	c Kirmani b Prasanna	35	not out	7
GD Barlow	c Kirmani b Madan Lal	4	not out	7
JM Brearley	c Solkar b Bedi	5		
DW Randall	lbw b Prasanna	37		
RW Tolchard	b Bedi	67		
AW Greig*	lbw b Prasanna	103		
APE Knott+	c Gavaskar b Bedi	2		
CM Old	c Madan Lal b Prasanna	52		
JK Lever	c Gavaskar b Bedi	2		
DL Underw'd	c Gavaskar b Bedi	4		
RGD Willis	not out	0		
Extras	(5b, 5lb, 0w, 0nb)	10	(0b, 1lb, 0w, 1nb)	2
	178.4 overs		3.4 overs	
Total		**321**		**16**

1st innings FoW: 7, 14, 81, 90, 232, 234, 298, 307, 321, 321

S Madan Lal	17	4	25	1	1	0	3	0
ED Solkar	6	1	15	0				
BS Bedi	64	25	110	5	1.4	0	6	0
B Chandrasekhar	33	9	66	0				
EAS Prasanna	57.4	16	93	4	1	0	5	0
P Sharma	1	0	2	0				

India | India

No. 522: 3rd Test
VENUE: Madras (Chepauk)
DATE: 14th–19th January 1977
TOSS WON BY: England
RESULT: England won by 200 runs

No. 523: 4th Test
VENUE: Bangalore
DATE: 28th January to 2nd Feb 1977
TOSS WON BY: India
RESULT: India won by 140 runs

ENGLAND 1st innings / 2nd innings

Batsman	1st innings		2nd innings	
DL Amiss	lbw b Madan Lal	4	c Amarnath b Chan'har	46
RA Woolmer	c Gavaskar b Madan Lal	22	lbw b Prasanna	16
JM Brearley	c & b Prasanna	59	b Chandrasekhar	29
DW Randall	run out	2	c Kirmani b Chan'har	0
RW Tolchard	not out	8	not out	10
AW Greig*	c Viswanath b Bedi	54	lbw b Prasanna	41
APE Knott+	c Viswanath b Bedi	45	c Patel b Prasanna	11
JK Lever	c Kirmani b Bedi	23	c Amarnath b Chan'har	2
CM Old	c Amarnath b Bedi	2	c Chan'har b Prasanna	4
D Underw'd	b Prasanna	23	st Kirmani b Chan'har	8
RGD Willis	run out	7	not out	4
Extras	(5b, 8lb, 0w, 0nb)	13	(14b, 0lb, 0w, 0nb)	14
Total	125.5 overs	**262**	71.5 overs	**185**

1st innings FoW: 14, 29, 31, 142, 162, 201, 209, 228, 253, 262
2nd innings FoW: 39, 54, 83, 83, 124, 135, 141, 169, 180

Bowler	O	M	R	W		O	M	R	W
S Madan Lal	21	5	43	2		9	2	15	0
M Amarnath	14	3	26	0		7	2	18	0
BS Chandrasekhar	25	4	63	0		20.5	4	50	5
BS Bedi	38.5	16	72	4		13	3	33	0
EAS Prasanna	27	11	45	2		22	5	55	4

INDIA 1st innings / 2nd innings

Batsman	1st innings		2nd innings	
SM Gavaskar	c Brearley b Old	39	c Woolmer b Underw'd	24
M Amarnath	b Old	0	c Woolmer b Underw'd	12
GR Viswanath	c Knott b Lever	9	c Brearley b Underwood	6
AV Mankad	b Lever	0	c Old b Lever	4
BP Patel	b Underwood	32	c Old b Willis	4
DB Vengsarkar	c Randall b Lever	8	retired hurt	1
S Madan Lal	c Underwood b Willis	12	c Knott b Willis	6
SMH Kirmani+	c Brearley b Lever	27	c Brearley b Willis	1
EAS Prasanna	c & b Underwood	13	c Brearley b Underwood	0
BS Bedi*	c (sub) b Lever	5	not out	11
BS Chan'har	not out	1	b Lever	6
Extras	(0b, 1lb, 0w, 17nb)	18	(5b, 1lb, 0w, 2nb)	8
Total	73.5 overs	**164**	38.5 overs	**83**

1st innings FoW: 5, 17, 17, 69, 86, 114, 115, 151, 161, 164
2nd innings FoW: 40, 45, 45, 54, 54, 57, 66, 71, 83

Bowler	O	M	R	W		O	M	R	W
RGD Willis	19	5	46	1		13	4	18	3
CM Old	13	4	19	2		5	1	11	0
JK Lever	19.5	2	59	5		6.5	0	18	2
RA Woolmer	1	0	2	0					
AW Greig	4	1	4	0					
DL Underwood	17	9	16	2		14	7	28	4

INDIA 1st innings / 2nd innings

Batsman	1st innings		2nd innings	
SM Gavaskar	c Underwood b Lever	4	c Brearley b Underw'd	50
AD Gaekwad	c Tolchard b Greig	39	b Old	9
S Amarnath	b Greig	63	c Tolchard b Willis	14
GR Viswanath	c Brearley b Underwood	13	c Knott b Underwood	17
BP Patel	c Randall b Willis	23	c Fletcher b Underwood	15
Yaj' Singh	c Knott b Willis	8	c Old b Willis	12
SMH Kirmani+	b Willis	52	not out	79
KD Ghavri	c Knott b Willis	16	c Randall b Underwood	21
EAS Prasanna	c Greig b Willis	6	c Amiss b Lever	12
BS Bedi*	not out	8	run out	15
BS Chan'har	c Knott b Willis	1	not out	0
Extras	(8b, 6lb, 0w, 6nb)	20	(1b, 6lb, 0w, 8nb)	15
Total	85 overs	**253**	91 overs	**259**

1st innings FoW: 9, 102, 124, 134, 153, 170, 236, 240, 249, 253
2nd innings FoW: 31, 80, 82, 104, 124, 154, 189, 223, 257

Bowler	O	M	R	W		O	M	R	W
RGD Willis	17	2	53	6		18	2	47	2
JK Lever	17	4	48	1		9	1	28	1
CM Old	12	0	43	0		10	4	19	1
DL Underwood	21	7	45	1		31	8	76	4
AW Greig	18	5	44	2		23	2	74	0

ENGLAND 1st innings / 2nd innings

Batsman	1st innings		2nd innings	
DL Amiss	c Yaj' b Chan'har	82	c Yajurvindra b Ghavri	0
JM Brearley	c Viswanath b Chan'har	4	c Gaekwad b Bedi	4
KWR Fletcher	c Yaj' b Prasanna	10	c Yajurvindra b Chan'har	1
DW Randall	c Yaj' b Prasanna	10	c Gaekwad b Bedi	0
RW Tolchard	b Chandrasekhar	0	lbw b Chandrasekhar	14
AW Greig*	c Yaj' b Chan'har	2	st Kirmani b Bedi	31
APE Knott+	b Bedi	29	not out	81
CM Old	lbw b Prasanna	5	lbw b Chandrasekhar	13
JK Lever	not out	20	c Ghavri b Bedi	11
DL Underw'd	c Yaj' b Chan'har	12	c Patel b Bedi	10
RGD Willis	lbw b Chandrasekhar	7	st Kirmani b Bedi	0
Extras	(3b, 5lb, 0w, 2nb)	10	(5b, 6lb, 0w, 1nb)	12
Total	96.2 overs	**195**	57.3 overs	**177**

1st innings FoW: 13, 34, 64, 65, 67, 137, 146, 154, 175, 195
2nd innings FoW: 0, 7, 7, 8, 35, 61, 105, 148, 166, 177

Bowler	O	M	R	W		O	M	R	W
KD Ghavri	13	3	31	0		4	1	4	1
Yajurvindra Singh	1	0	2	0					
BS Bedi	23	11	29	1		21.3	4	71	6
BS Chandrasekhar	31.2	7	76	6		15	3	55	3
EAS Prasanna	28	10	47	3		15	5	35	0
SM Gavaskar						2	2	0	0

No. 524: 5th Test	No. 525: 1st Test
VENUE: Bombay (Wankhede)	VENUE: Melbourne (MCG)
DATE: 11th-16th February 1977	DATE: 12th-17th March 1977
TOSS WON BY: India	TOSS WON BY: England
RESULT: Match drawn	RESULT: Australia won by 45 runs

INDIA

1st innings		2nd innings	
SM Gavaskar c & b Underwood	108	c Willis b Underwood	42
AD Gaekwad c Tolchard b Lever	21	st Knott b Underwood	25
S Amarnath b Underwood	40	run out	63
GR Viswanath c & b Lever	4	c Fletcher b Underwood	3
BP Patel st Knott b Greig	83	c Lever b Greig	5
Yaj' Singh b Greig	6	run out	21
SMH Kirmani+ c Knott b Underwood	8	c Greig b Underwood	10
KD Ghavri lbw b Greig	25	c Fletcher b Underwood	8
EAS Prasanna b Underwood	9	not out	0
BS Bedi* not out	20	lbw b Lever	3
BS Chan'har b Lever	3	b Lever	4
Extras (0b, 9lb, 0w, 2nb)	11	(4b, 1lb, 0w, 3nb)	8
105.4 overs		70.4 overs	
Total	**338**		**192**

1st innings FoW: 52, 115, 122, 261, 267, 273, 289, 303, 321, 338
2nd innings FoW: 68, 72, 80, 92, 136, 156, 182, 185, 188, 192

RGD Willis	13	1	52	0		6	1	15	0			
JK Lever	17.4	4	42	3		17.4	6	46	2			
MWW Selvey	15	1	80	0								
DL Underwood	38	13	89	4		33	10	84	5			
AW Greig	22	6	64	3		14	3	39	1			

ENGLAND

1st innings		2nd innings	
DL Amiss c Viswanath b Bedi	50	c Viswanath b Bedi	14
JM Brearley st Kirmani b Prasanna	91	c Yajurvindra b Prasanna	18
DW Randall c Gaekwad b Prasanna	22	c Kirmani b Ghavri	15
KWR Fletcher c Viswanath b Chan'har	14	not out	58
AW Greig* b Prasanna	76	c Bedi b Ghavri	10
APE Knott+ b Chandrasekhar	24	b Ghavri	1
RW Tolchard st Kirmani b Prasanna	4	c Gavaskar b Ghavri	26
JK Lever c Gavaskar b Bedi	7	c Patel b Ghavri	4
DL Underw'd b Bedi	7		
MWW Selvey not out	5		
RGD Willis c Gavaskar b Bedi	0		
Extras (1b, 13lb, 0w, 3nb)	17	(2b, 3lb, 0w, 1nb)	6
154 overs		71 overs	
Total	**317**		**152**

1st innings FoW: 146, 175, 180, 206, 247, 256, 290, 300, 312, 317
2nd innings FoW: 34, 38, 86, 112, 113, 148, 152

KD Ghavri	12	2	31	0		15	6	33	5
SM Gavaskar	2	0	2	0		1	1	0	0
BS Bedi	56	20	109	4		21	5	52	1
BS Chan'har	32	7	85	2		4	0	25	0
EAS Prasanna	52	20	73	4		30	12	36	1

AUSTRALIA

1st innings		2nd innings	
IC Davis lbw b Lever	5	c Knott b Greig	68
RB McCosker b Willis	4	c Willis b Old	14
GJ Cosier c Fletcher b Lever	10	b Old	2
GS Chappell* b Underwood	40	c Knott b Lever	4
DW Hookes c Greig b Old	17	c Knott b Underwood	66
KD Walters c Greig b Willis	4	c Fletcher b Underw'd	56
RW Marsh+ c Knott b Old	28	not out	110
GJ Gilmour c Greig b Old	4	b Lever	16
KJ O'Keeffe c Brearley b Underwood	0	c Amiss b Old	25
DK Lillee not out	10	c Greig b Old	25
MHN Walker b Underwood	2	not out	8
Extras (4b, 2lb, 0w, 8nb)	14	(0b, 10lb, 0w, 15nb)	25
43.6 overs		96.6 overs	
Total	**138**		**419**

1st innings FoW: 11, 13, 23, 45, 51, 102, 114, 117, 136, 138
2nd innings FoW: 33, 40, 53, 132, 187, 244, 277, 353, 407

JK Lever	12	1	36	2		21	1	95	2
RGD Willis	8	0	33	2		22	0	91	0
CM Old	12	4	39	3		27.6	2	104	4
DL Underwood	11.6	2	16	3		12	2	38	1
AW Greig						14	3	66	2

ENGLAND

1st innings		2nd innings	
RA Woolmer c Chappell b Lillee	9	lbw b Walker	12
JM Brearley c Hookes b Lillee	12	lbw b Lillee	43
DL Underw'd c Chappell b Walker	7	c Cosier b O'Keeffe	174
DW Randall c Marsh b Lillee	4	b Chappell	64
DL Amiss c O'Keeffe b Walker	4	c Marsh b Lillee	1
KWR Fletcher c Marsh b Walker	4	c Cosier b O'Keeffe	41
AW Greig* b Walker	18	lbw b Lillee	42
APE Knott+ lbw b Lillee	15	c Chappell b Lillee	2
CM Old c Marsh b Lillee	3	lbw b O'Keeffe	2
JK Lever c Marsh b Lillee	11	b Lillee	4
RGD Willis not out	1	not out	5
Extras (2b, 2lb, 1w, 2nb)	7	(8b, 4lb, 3w, 7nb)	22
34.3 overs		112.4 overs	
Total	**95**		**417**

1st innings FoW: 19, 30, 34, 40, 40, 61, 65. 78, 86, 95
2nd innings FoW: 28, 113, 279, 290, 346, 369, 380, 385, 410, 417

DK Lillee	13.3	2	26	6		34.4	7	139	5
MHN Walker	15	3	54	4		22	4	83	1
KJ O'Keeffe	1	0	4	0		33	6	108	3
GJ Gilmour	5	3	4	0		4	0	29	0
GS Chappell						16	7	29	1
KD Walters						3	2	7	0

Australia | Australia

No. 526: 1st Test	No. 527: 2nd Test
VENUE: Lord's	VENUE: Old Trafford
DATE: 16th-21st June 1977	DATE: 7th-12th July 1977
TOSS WON BY: England	TOSS WON BY: Australia
RESULT: Match drawn	RESULT: Eng won by 9 wickets

ENGLAND

	1st innings		2nd innings	
DL Amiss	b Thomson	4	b Thomson	0
JM Brearley*	c Robinson b Thomson	9	c Robinson b O'Keeffe	49
RA Woolmer	run out	79	c Chappell b Pascoe	120
DW Randall	c Chappell b Walker	53	c McCosker b Thomson	0
AW Greig	b Pascoe	5	c O'Keeffe b Pascoe	91
GD Barlow	c McCosker b Walker	1	lbw b Pascoe	5
APE Knott+	c Walters b Thomson	8	c Walters b Walker	8
CM Old	c Marsh b Walker	9	c Walters b Walker	8
JK Lever	b Pascoe	8	c Marsh b Thomson	3
DL Underw'd	not out	11	not out	12
RGD Willis	b Thomson	17	c Marsh b Thomson	0
Extras	(1b, 3lb, 1w, 7nb)	12	(5b, 9lb, 1w, 2nb)	17
Total	86.5 overs	**216**	112.4 overs	**305**

1st innings FoW: 12, 13, 111, 121, 134, 155, 171, 183, 189, 216
2nd innings FoW: 0, 132, 224, 263, 286, 286, 286, 286, 305, 305

JR Thomson	20.5	5	41	4	24.4	3	86	4
LS Pascoe	23	7	53	2	26	2	96	3
MHN Walker	30	6	66	3	35	13	56	2
KJ O'Keeffe	10	3	32	0	15	7	26	1
GS Chappell	3	0	12	0	12	2	24	0

AUSTRALIA 1st innings

	1st innings		2nd innings	
RD Robinson	b Lever	11	c Woolmer b Old	4
RB McCosker	b Old	23	b Willis	1
GS Chappell*	c Old b Willis	66	c Lever b Old	24
CS Serjeant	c Knott b Willis	81	c & b Willis	50
KD Walters	c Brearley b Willis	53	c (sub) b Underwood	10
DW Hookes	c Brearley b Old	11	c Amiss b Underwood	3
RW Marsh+	lbw b Willis	1	not out	6
KJ O'Keeffe	c (sub) b Willis	12	not out	8
MHN Walker	c Knott b Willis	4		
JR Thomson	b Willis	6		
LS Pascoe	not out	3		
Extras	(0b, 7lb, 1w, 17nb)	25	(0b, 0lb, 0w, 8nb)	8
Total	114.1 overs	**296**	39 overs	**114**

1st innings FoW: 25, 51, 135, 238, 256, 264, 265, 284, 290, 296
2nd innings FoW: 5, 5, 48, 64, 71, 102

RGD Willis	30.1	7	78	7	10	1	40	2
JK Lever	19	5	61	1	5	2	4	0
DL Underwood	25	6	42	0	10	3	16	2
CM Old	35	10	70	2	14	0	46	2
RA Woolmer	5	1	20	0				

AUSTRALIA 1st innings

	1st innings		2nd innings	
RB McCosker	c Old b Willis	2	c Underwood b Willis	0
IC Davis	c Knott b Old	34	c Lever b Willis	12
GS Chappell*	c Knott b Greig	44	b Underwood	112
CS Serjeant	lbw b Lever	14	c Woolmer b Underwood	8
KD Walters	c Greig b Miller	88	lbw b Greig	10
DW Hookes	c Knott b Lever	5	c Brearley b Miller	28
RW Marsh+	c Amiss b Miller	36	c Randall b Underwood	1
RJ Bright	c Greig b Lever	12	c & b Underwood	0
KJ O'Keeffe	c Knott b Willis	12	not out	24
MHN Walker	b Underwood	9	c Greig b Underwood	6
JR Thomson	not out	14	c Randall b Underwood	1
Extras	(0b, 15lb, 0w, 12nb)	27	(0b, 1lb, 1w, 14nb)	16
Total	109.2 overs	**297**		**218**

1st innings FoW: 4, 80, 96, 125, 140, 238, 246, 272, 272, 297
2nd innings FoW: 0, 30, 74, 92, 146, 147, 147, 202, 212, 218

RGD Willis	21	8	45	2	16	2	56	2
JK Lever	25	8	60	3	4	1	11	0
CM Old	20	3	57	1	8	1	26	0
DL Underwood	20.2	7	53	1	32.5	13	66	6
AW Greig	13	4	37	1	12	6	19	1
G Miller	10	3	18	2	9	2	24	1

ENGLAND 1st innings

	1st innings		2nd innings	
DL Amiss	c Chappell b Walker	11	not out	28
JM Brearley*	c Chappell b Thomson	6	c Walters b O'Keeffe	44
RA Woolmer	c Davis b O'Keeffe	137	not out	0
DW Randall	lbw b Bright	79		
AW Greig	c & b Walker	76		
APE Knott+	c O'Keeffe b Thomson	39		
G Miller	c Marsh b Thomson	6		
CM Old	c Marsh b Walker	37		
JK Lever	b Bright	10		
DL Underw'd	b Bright	10		
RGD Willis	not out	1		
Extras	(9b, 9lb, 0w, 7nb)	25	(0b, 3lb, 0w, 7nb)	10
Total	169.1 overs	**437**	29.1 overs	**82**

1st innings FoW: 19, 23, 165, 325, 348, 366, 377, 404, 435, 437

JR Thomson	38	11	73	3	8	2	24	0
MHN Walker	54	15	131	3	7	0	17	0
RJ Bright	35.1	12	69	3	5	2	6	0
KJ O'Keeffe	36	11	114	1	9.1	4	25	1
GS Chappell	6	1	25	0				

No. 528: 3rd Test

VENUE: Trent Bridge
DATE: 28th July to 2nd August 1977
TOSS WON BY: Australia
RESULT: England won by 7 wickets

No. 529: 4th Test

VENUE: Headingley
DATE: 11th-15th August 1977
TOSS WON BY: England
RESULT: Eng won by an innings and 85 runs

AUSTRALIA 1st innings / 2nd innings

Batsman	1st innings		2nd innings	
RB McCosker	c Brearley b Hendrick	51	c Brearley b Willis	107
IC Davis	c Botham b Underwood	33	c Greig b Willis	9
GS Chappell*	b Botham	19	b Hendrick	27
DW Hookes	c Hendrick b Willis	17	lbw b Hendrick	42
KD Walters	c Hendrick b Botham	11	c Randall b Greig	28
RD Robinson	c Brearley b Greig	11	lbw b Underwood	34
RW Marsh+	lbw b Botham	0	c Greig b Willis	0
KJ O'Keeffe	not out	48	not out	21
MHN Walker	c Hendrick b Botham	0	b Willis	17
JR Thomson	c Knott b Botham	21	b Willis	0
LS Pascoe	c Greig b Hendrick	20	c Hendrick b Underw'd	0
Extras	(4b, 2lb, 0w, 6nb)	12	(1b, 5lb, 1w, 17nb)	24
	82.2 overs		127 overs	
Total		**243**		**309**

1st innings FoW: 79, 101, 131, 133, 153, 153, 153, 155, 196, 243
2nd innings FoW: 18, 60, 154, 204, 240, 240, 270, 307, 308, 309

Bowler	O	M	R	W	O	M	R	W
RGD Willis	15	0	58	1	26	6	88	5
M Hendrick	21.2	6	46	2	32	14	56	2
IT Botham	20	5	74	5	25	5	60	0
AW Greig	15	4	35	1	9	2	24	1
DL Underwood	11	5	18	1	27	15	49	2
G Miller					5	2	5	0
RA Woolmer					3	0	3	0

ENGLAND 1st innings / 2nd innings

Batsman	1st innings		2nd innings	
JM Brearley*	c Hookes b Pascoe	15	b Walker	81
G Boycott	c McCosker b Thomson	107	not out	80
RA Woolmer	lbw b Pascoe	0	c O'Keeffe b Walker	2
DW Randall	run out	13	b Walker	0
AW Greig	b Thomson	11	not out	19
G Miller	c Robinson b Pascoe	13		
APE Knott+	c Davis b Thomson	135		
IT Botham	b Walker	25		
DL Underw'd	b Pascoe	7		
M Hendrick	b Walker	1		
RGD Willis	not out	2		
Extras	(9b, 7lb, 3w, 16nb)	35	(2b, 2lb, 1w, 2nb)	7
	124.2 overs		81.2 overs	
Total		**364**		**189**

1st innings FoW: 34, 34, 52, 64, 82, 297, 326, 357, 357, 364
2nd innings FoW: 154, 156, 158

Bowler	O	M	R	W	O	M	R	W
JR Thomson	31	6	103	3	16	6	34	0
LS Pascoe	32	10	80	4	22	6	43	0
MHN Walker	39.2	12	79	2	24	8	40	3
GS Chappell	8	0	19	0				
KJ O'Keeffe	11	4	43	0	19.2	2	65	0
KD Walters	3	0	5	0				

ENGLAND 1st innings / 2nd innings

Batsman	1st innings		2nd innings
JM Brearley*	c Marsh b Thomson	0	
G Boycott	c Chappell b Pascoe	191	
RA Woolmer	c Chappell b Thomson	37	
DW Randall	lbw b Pascoe	20	
AW Greig	b Thomson	43	
GRJ Roope	c Walters b Thomson	34	
APE Knott+	lbw b Bright	57	
IT Botham	b Bright	0	
DL Underw'd	c Bright b Pascoe	6	
M Hendrick	c Robinson b Pascoe	4	
RGD Willis	not out	5	
Extras	(5b, 9lb, 3w, 22nb)	39	
	155.4 overs		
Total		**436**	

1st innings FoW: 0, 82, 105, 201, 275, 398, 398, 412, 422, 436

Bowler	O	M	R	W
JR Thomson	34	7	113	4
MHN Walker	48	21	97	0
LS Pascoe	34.4	10	91	4
KD Walters	3	1	5	0
RJ Bright	26	9	66	2
GS Chappell	10	2	25	0

AUSTRALIA 1st innings / 2nd innings

Batsman	1st innings		2nd innings	
RB McCosker	run out	27	c Knott b Greig	12
IC Davis	lbw b Hendrick	0	c Knott b Greig	19
GS Chappell*	c Brearley b Hendrick	4	c Greig b Willis	36
DW Hookes	lbw b Botham	24	lbw b Hendrick	21
KD Walters	c Hendrick b Botham	4	lbw b Woolmer	15
RD Robinson	c Greig b Hendrick	20	b Hendrick	20
RW Marsh+	c Knott b Botham	2	c Randall b Hendrick	63
RJ Bright	not out	9	c Greig b Hendrick	5
MHN Walker	c Knott b Botham	7	b Willis	30
JR Thomson	b Botham	0	b Willis	0
LS Pascoe	b Hendrick	0	not out	0
Extras	(0b, 3lb, 1w, 2nb)	6	(1b, 4lb, 4w, 18nb)	27
	31.3 overs		89.5 overs	
Total		**103**		**248**

1st innings FoW: 8, 26, 52, 57, 66, 77, 87, 100, 100, 103
2nd innings FoW: 31, 35, 63, 97, 130, 167, 179, 244, 245, 248

Bowler	O	M	R	W	O	M	R	W
RGD Willis	5	0	35	0	14	7	32	3
M Hendrick	15.3	2	41	4	22.5	6	54	4
IT Botham	11	3	21	5	17	3	47	0
AW Greig					20	7	64	2
RA Woolmer					8	4	8	1
DL Underwood					8	3	16	0

Australia

No. 530:	5th Test
VENUE:	The Oval
DATE:	25th-30th August 1977
TOSS WON BY:	Australia
RESULT:	Match drawn

ENGLAND

1st innings			2nd innings	
JM Brearley*	c Marsh b Malone	39	c Serjeant b Thomson	4
G Boycott	c McCosker b Walker	39	not out	25
RA Woolmer	lbw b Thomson	15	c Marsh b Malone	6
DW Randall	c Marsh b Malone	3	not out	20
AW Greig	c Bright b Malone	0		
GRJ Roope	b Thomson	38		
APE Knott+	c McCosker b Malone	6		
JK Lever	lbw b Malone	3		
DL Underw'd	b Thomson	20		
M Hendrick	b Thomson	15		
RGD Willis	not out	24		
Extras	(0b, 6lb, 1w, 5nb)	12	(0b, 0lb, 2w, 0nb)	2
	101.2 overs		26 overs	
Total		**214**		**57**

1st innings FoW: 86, 88, 104, 104, 106, 122, 130, 169, 174, 214
2nd innings FoW: 5, 16

JR Thomson	23.2	3	87	4	5	1	22	1
MF Malone	47	20	63	5	10	4	14	1
MHN Walker	28	11	51	1	8	2	14	0
RJ Bright	3	2	1	0	3	2	5	0

AUSTRALIA 1st innings

1st innings			2nd innings
CS Serjeant	lbw b Willis	0	
RB McCosker	lbw b Willis	32	
GS Chappell*	c & b Underwood	39	
KJ Hughes	c Willis b Hendrick	1	
DW Hookes	c Knott b Greig	85	
KD Walters	b Willis	4	
RW Marsh+	lbw b Hendrick	57	
RJ Bright	lbw b Willis	16	
MHN Walker	not out	78	
MF Malone	b Lever	46	
JR Thomson	b Willis	17	
Extras	(1b, 6lb, 0w, 3nb)	10	
	131.3 overs		
Total		**385**	

1st innings FoW: 0, 54, 67, 84, 104, 184, 236, 252, 352, 385

RGD Willis	29.3	5	102	5
M Hendrick	37	5	93	2
JK Lever	22	6	61	1
DL Underwood	35	9	102	1
AW Greig	8	2	17	1

Pakistan

No. 531:	1st Test
VENUE:	Lahore (Gaddafi)
DATE:	14th-19th December 1977
TOSS WON BY:	Pakistan
RESULT:	Match drawn

PAKISTAN 1st innings

1st innings			2nd innings	
M Nazar	c & b Miller	114	c Taylor b Willis	26
Sadiq Moh'd	lbw b Miller	18	b Lever	1
Shafiq Ahmed	c Rose b Old	0	lbw b Willis	7
Haroon Rashid	c & b Lever	122	not out	45
Javed M'dad	c Taylor b Lever	71	not out	19
Wasim Raja	st Taylor b Cope	24		
Abdul Qadir	lbw b Cope	11		
Wasim Bari*+	c Cope b Miller	17		
Sarfraz Nawaz	b Cope	0		
Iqbal Qasim	not out	8		
Liaquat Ali	not out	0		
Extras	(1b, 4lb, 0w, 17nb)	22	(0b, 0lb, 0w, 8nb)	8
	133 overs		28 overs	
Total		**407**		**106**

1st innings FoW: 48, 49, 229, 329, 356, 378, 387, 387, 403
2nd innings FoW: 15, 40, 45

RGD Willis	17	3	67	0	7	0	34	2
JK Lever	16	1	47	2	3	0	13	1
CM Old	21	7	63	1	4	0	18	0
G Miller	37	10	102	3	10	4	24	0
GA Cope	39	6	102	3	3	0	7	0
G Boycott	3	0	4	0	1	0	2	0

ENGLAND 1st innings

1st innings			2nd innings
G Boycott	b Iqbal	63	
JM Brearley*	run out	23	
BC Rose	lbw b Sarfraz	1	
DW Randall	c Iqbal b Liaquat	19	
GRJ Roope	b Iqbal	19	
G Miller	not out	98	
CM Old	c M Nazar b Iqbal	2	
RW Taylor+	b Sarfraz	32	
GA Cope	lbw b Sarfraz	0	
JK Lever	c Wasim Bari b Sarfraz	0	
RGD Willis	c Iqbal b Abdul	14	
Extras	(2b, 8lb, 0w, 7nb)	17	
	135.7 overs		
Total		**288**	

1st innings FoW: 53, 55, 96, 127, 148, 162, 251, 251, 253, 288

Sarfraz Nawaz	34	11	68	4
Liaquat Ali	27	11	43	1
Abdul Qadir	32.7	7	82	1
Iqbal Qasim	32	12	57	3
Wasim Raja	10	2	21	0

	No. 532: 2nd Test		No. 533: 3rd Test
VENUE:	Hyderabad (P)	VENUE:	Karachi (National Stadium)
DATE:	2nd-7th January 1978	DATE:	18th-23rd January 1978
TOSS WON BY:	Pakistan	TOSS WON BY:	England
RESULT:	Match drawn	RESULT:	Match drawn

PAKISTAN 1st innings / 2nd innings

		1st			2nd
M Nazar	c Edmonds b Cope	27	c Taylor b Willis		66
Sadiq Moh'd	c Taylor b Willis	9	c Edmonds b Cope		22
Shafiq Ahmed	c Miller b Edmonds	13	c Edmonds b Willis		24
Haroon Rashid	c & b Edmonds	108	c Brearley b Cope		35
Javed M'dad	not out	88	not out		61
Wasim Raja	c Brearley b Edmonds	0	not out		27
Abdul Qadir	c Brearley b Cope	4			
Wasim Bari*+	run out	10			
Iqbal Qasim	c Roope b Willis	0			
Liaquat Ali	c Edmonds b Lever	0			
Sikander Bakht	run out	3			
Extras	(4b, 7lb, 0w, 2nb)	13	(13b, 11lb, 0w, 0nb)		24
	79.6 overs		88 overs		
Total		**275**			**259**

1st innings FoW: 14, 40, 101, 213, 213, 222, 247, 248, 249, 275
2nd innings FoW: 55, 116, 117, 189

RGD Willis	16	2	40	2	11	2	26	2
JK Lever	16.6	7	41	1	20	2	62	0
PH Edmonds	24	2	75	3	30	6	95	0
GA Cope	14	6	49	2	24	9	42	2
G Miller	9	0	57	0	2	0	8	0
GRJ Roope					1	0	2	0

ENGLAND 1st innings / 2nd innings

		1st			2nd
G Boycott	run out	79	not out		100
JM Brearley*	c Wasim Bari b Iqbal	17	c (sub) b Wasim Raja		74
BC Rose	b Abdul	27	not out		0
DW Randall	c & b Abdul	7			
GRJ Roope	c & b Abdul	1			
G Miller	c Wasim Bari b Iqbal	5			
RW Taylor+	b Abdul	0			
PH Edmonds	c Wasim Bari b Abdul	4			
GA Cope	c Sadiq b Wasim Raja	22			
JK Lever	b Abdul	4			
RGD Willis	not out	8			
Extras	(10b, 6lb, 1w, 0nb)	17	(4b, 7lb, 0w, 1nb)		12
	86.6 overs		81.4 overs		
Total		**191**			**186**

1st innings FoW: 40, 123, 137, 139, 142, 142, 146, 152, 157, 191
2nd innings FoW: 185

Sikander Bakht	16	4	35	0	10	3	22	0
Liaquat Ali	6	0	18	0	4	1	14	0
Iqbal Qasim	34	11	54	2	24.4	6	42	0
Javed Miandad	5	0	21	0	4	0	10	0
Abdul Qadir	24	8	44	6	27	5	72	0
Wasim Raja	1.6	0	2	1	12	5	14	1

ENGLAND 1st innings / 2nd innings

		1st			2nd
G Boycott*	b Iqbal	31	c Javed b Sikander		56
BC Rose	c Javed b Sarfraz	10	c Haroon b Abdul		18
DW Randall	lbw b Iqbal	23	b Sikander		55
GRJ Roope	lbw b Sikander	56	not out		33
MW Gatting	lbw b Abdul	5	lbw b Iqbal		6
G Miller	c Mudassar b Wasim Raja	11	c Wasim Bari b Iqbal		3
RW Taylor+	lbw b Abdul	36	not out		18
PH Edmonds	lbw b Abdul	6			
GA Cope	b Iqbal	18			
JK Lever	not out	33			
RGD Willis	lbw b Abdul	5			
Extras	(3b, 21lb, 0w, 8nb)	32	(9b, 6lb, 3w, 15nb)		33
	123.1 overs		89 overs		
Total		**266**			**222**

1st innings FoW: 17, 69, 72, 85, 107, 189, 197, 203, 232, 266
2nd innings FoW: 35, 125, 148, 162, 171

Sarfraz Nawaz	15	6	27	1	28	7	57	0
Sikander Bakht	15	4	39	1	17	4	40	2
Iqbal Qasim	40	20	56	3	29	11	51	2
Abdul Qadir	40.1	9	81	4	8	2	26	1
Wasim Raja	13	3	31	1				
Mudassar Nazar					1	0	1	0
Javed Miandad					2	0	5	0
Shafiq Ahmed					1	0	1	0
Wasim Bari					1	0	2	0
Haroon Rashid					1	0	3	0
Mohsin Khan					1	0	3	0

PAKISTAN 1st innings / 2nd innings

		1st
M Nazar	c (sub) b Edmonds	76
Shafiq Ahmed	c (sub) b Willis	10
Mohsin Khan	c Willis b Cope	44
Haroon Rashid	c Taylor b Edmonds	27
Javed M'dad	c Roope b Edmonds	23
Wasim Raja	c Gatting b Edmonds	47
Abdul Qadir	c Roope b Edmonds	21
Wasim Bari*+	lbw b Miller	6
Sarfraz Nawaz	c Gatting b Edmonds	0
Iqbal Qasim	b Edmonds	8
Sikander Bakht	not out	7
Extras	(2b, 3lb, 0w, 7nb)	12
	95 overs	
Total		**281**

1st innings FoW: 33, 121, 167, 170, 230, 243, 263, 263, 269, 281

RGD Willis	8	1	23	1
JK Lever	12	4	32	0
PH Edmonds	33	7	66	7
GA Cope	28	8	77	1
G Miller	14	0	71	1

New Zealand

No. 534: 1st Test
VENUE: Wellington
DATE: 10th–15th February 1978
TOSS WON BY: England
RESULT: New Zealand won by 72 runs

NEW ZEALAND 1st innings			2nd innings	
JG Wright	lbw b Botham	55	c Roope b Willis	19
RW Anderson	c Taylor b Old	28	lbw b Old	26
GP Howarth	c Botham b Old	13	c Edmonds b Willis	21
MG Burgess*	b Willis	9	c Boycott b Botham	6
BE Congdon	c Taylor b Old	44	c Roope b Willis	0
JM Parker	c Rose b Willis	16	c Edmonds b Willis	4
WK Lees+	c Taylor b Old	1	lbw b Hendrick	11
RJ Hadlee	not out	27	c Boycott b Willis	2
DR Hadlee	c Taylor b Old	1	c Roope b Botham	2
RO Collinge	b Old	1	c Edmonds b Hendrick	6
SL Boock	b Botham	4	not out	0
Extras	(12b, 3lb, 1w, 13nb)	29	(2b, 9lb, 2w, 13nb)	26
Total	87.6 overs	228	44.3 overs	123

1st innings FoW: 42, 96, 114, 152, 191, 193, 194, 196, 208, 228
2nd innings FoW: 54, 82, 93, 93, 98, 99, 104, 116, 123, 123

RGD Willis	25	7	65	2		15	2	32	5
M Hendrick	17	2	46	0		10	2	16	2
CM Old	30	11	54	6		9	2	32	1
PH Edmonds	3	1	7	0		1	0	4	0
IT Botham	12.6	2	27	2		9.3	3	13	2

ENGLAND 1st innings			2nd innings	
BC Rose	c Lees b Collinge	21	not out	5
G Boycott*	c Congdon b Collinge	77	b Collinge	1
G Miller	b Boock	24	c Anderson b Collinge	4
RW Taylor+	c & b Collinge	8	lbw b Collinge	9
DW Randall	c Burgess b RJ Hadlee	4	c Lees b RJ Hadlee	0
GRJ Roope	c Lees b RJ Hadlee	37	c Boock b RJ Hadlee	19
IT Botham	c Burgess b RJ Hadlee	7	run out	0
CM Old	b RJ Hadlee	10	lbw b RJ Hadlee	9
PH Edmonds	lbw b Congdon	4	c Parker b RJ Hadlee	11
M Hendrick	lbw b Congdon	0	c Parker b RJ Hadlee	0
RGD Willis	not out	6	c Howarth b RJ Hadlee	3
Extras	(0b, 4lb, 0w, 13nb)	17	(0b, 0lb, 0w, 3nb)	3
Total	94.4 overs	215	27.3 overs	64

1st innings FoW: 39, 89, 108, 126, 183, 188, 203, 205, 206, 215
2nd innings FoW: 2, 8, 18, 18, 38, 38, 53, 53, 63, 64

RJ Hadlee	28	5	74	4		13.3	4	26	6
RO Collinge	18	5	42	3		13	5	35	3
DR Hadlee	21	5	47	0		1	1	0	0
SL Boock	10	5	21	1					
BE Congdon	17.4	11	14	2					

New Zealand

No. 535: 2nd Test
VENUE: Christchurch
DATE: 24th February to 1st March 1978
TOSS WON BY: England
RESULT: England won by 174 runs

ENGLAND 1st innings			2nd innings	
BC Rose	c Howarth b Chatfield	11	c Lees b Collinge	7
G Boycott*	lbw b Collinge	8	run out	26
DW Randall	c Burgess b Hadlee	0	run out	13
GRJ Roope	c Burgess b Hadlee	50	not out	30
G Miller	c Congdon b Collinge	89	b Collinge	1
CT Radley	c Lees b Hadlee	15	not out	9
IT Botham	c Lees b Boock	103		
RW Taylor+	run out	45		
CM Old	b Hadlee	8		
PH Edmonds	c Lees b Collinge	50		
RGD Willis	not out	6		
Extras	(14b, 9lb, 0w, 10nb)	33	(4b, 3lb, 0w, 3nb)	10
Total	145.5 overs	418	22 overs	96

1st innings FoW: 15, 18, 26, 127, 128, 288, 294, 305, 375, 418
2nd innings FoW: 25, 47, 67, 74

RJ Hadlee	43	10	147	4		6	1	17	0
RO Collinge	26.5	6	89	3		9	2	29	2
EJ Chatfield	37	8	94	1		5	0	22	0
BE Congdon	18	11	14	0		2	0	18	0
SL Boock	21	11	41	1					

NEW ZEALAND 1st innings			2nd innings	
JG Wright	c & b Edmonds	4	c Roope b Willis	0
RW Anderson	b Edmonds	62	b Willis	15
GP Howarth	c Edmonds b Willis	5	c Edmonds b Old	1
MG Burgess*	c Roope b Botham	29	not out	6
BE Congdon	lbw b Botham	20	c Botham b Willis	0
JM Parker	not out	53	c Botham b Edmonds	16
WK Lees+	c Miller b Botham	0	b Willis	0
RJ Hadlee	b Edmonds	1	c Botham b Edmonds	39
RO Collinge	c Edmonds b Botham	32	c Miller b Botham	0
SL Boock	c Taylor b Edmonds	2	c Taylor b Botham	0
EJ Chatfield	c Edmonds b Botham	3	lbw b Botham	6
Extras	(4b, 1lb, 0w, 19nb)	24	(0b, 6lb, 0w, 16nb)	22
Total	92.7 overs	235	27 overs	105

1st innings FoW: 37, 52, 82, 119, 148, 151, 153, 211, 216, 235
2nd innings FoW: 2, 14, 19, 25, 25, 59, 81, 90, 95, 105

RGD Willis	20	5	45	1		7	2	14	4
CM Old	14	4	55	0		7	4	9	1
IT Botham	24.7	6	73	5		7	1	38	3
PH Edmonds	34	11	38	4		6	2	22	2

New Zealand

No. 536:	3rd Test
VENUE:	Auckland
DATE:	4th-9th March 1978
TOSS WON BY:	New Zealand
RESULT:	Match drawn

NEW ZEALAND 1st innings / 2nd innings

Batsman	1st innings		2nd innings	
JG Wright	c Taylor b Lever	4	c Taylor b Edmonds	25
RW Anderson	c Gatting b Botham	17	c Botham b Miller	55
GP Howarth	c Roope b Willis	122	b Miller	102
MG Burgess*	c Randall b Botham	50	c Taylor b Edmonds	17
BE Congdon	c Miller b Botham	5	c Roope b Lever	20
JM Parker	lbw b Botham	14	c Randall b Lever	54
GN Edwards+	lbw b Lever	55	not out	47
RJ Hadlee	c Roope b Botham	10	b Miller	10
BL Cairns	b Lever	11	lbw b Edmonds	20
RO Collinge	not out	5	not out	12
SL Boock	c Edmonds b Willis	1		
Extras	(5b, 10lb, 0w, 15nb)	30	(6b, 4lb, 0w, 10nb)	20
	105.6 overs		118 overs	
Total		**315**		**382**

1st innings FoW: 12, 32, 113, 129, 182, 278, 285, 302, 314, 315
2nd innings FoW: 69, 98, 125, 185, 272, 287, 305, 350

Bowler	O	M	R	W	O	M	R	W
RGD Willis	26.6	8	57	2	10	3	42	0
JK Lever	34	5	96	3	17	4	59	2
IT Botham	34	4	109	5	13	1	51	0
PH Edmonds	10	2	23	0	45	15	107	3
G Miller	1	1	0	0	30	10	99	3
MW Gatting					1	0	1	0
GRJ Roope					1	0	2	0
DW Randall					1	0	1	0

ENGLAND 1st innings / 2nd innings

Batsman	1st innings	
G Boycott*	c Burgess b Collinge	54
DW Randall	lbw b Hadlee	30
CT Radley	c Wright b Collinge	158
GRJ Roope	c Burgess b Boock	68
MW Gatting	b Boock	0
IT Botham	c Edwards b Collinge	53
RW Taylor+	b Boock	16
G Miller	lbw b Collinge	15
PH Edmonds	b Boock	8
JK Lever	c & b Boock	1
RGD Willis	not out	0
Extras	(6b, 6lb, 4w, 10nb)	26
	156.3 overs	
Total		**429**

1st innings FoW: 52, 115, 254, 258, 355, 396, 418, 427, 428, 429

Bowler	O	M	R	W
RJ Hadlee	31	6	107	1
RO Collinge	38	9	98	4
BL Cairns	33	9	63	0
BE Congdon	26	8	68	0
SL Boock	28.3	4	67	5

Pakistan

No. 537:	1st Test
VENUE:	Edgbaston
DATE:	1st-5th June 1978
TOSS WON BY:	Pakistan
RESULT:	Eng won by an innings and 57 runs

PAKISTAN 1st innings / 2nd innings

Batsman	1st innings		2nd innings	
M Nazar	c & b Botham	14	b Edmonds	30
Sadiq Moh'd	c Radley b Old	23	b Old	79
Mohsin Khan	b Willis	35	retired hurt	5
Javed M'dad	c Taylor b Old	15	c Old b Miller	38
Haroon Rashid	c Roope b Willis	3	c Brearley b Edmonds	39
Wasim Raja	c Taylor b Old	17	b Willis	4
Sarfraz Nawaz	not out	32	b Edmonds	9
Wasim Bari*+	b Old	0	not out	6
Iqbal Qasim	c Taylor b Old	0	c Miller b Edmonds	3
Sikander Bakht	c Roope b Old	0	c Roope b Miller	2
Liaquat Ali	c Brearley b Old	9	b Willis	3
Extras	(0b, 3lb, 13w, 0nb)	16	(4b, 4lb, 1w, 4nb)	13
	60.4 overs		103.4 overs	
Total		**164**		**231**

1st innings FoW: 20, 56, 91, 94, 103, 125, 125, 126, 126, 164
2nd innings FoW: 94, 123, 176, 193, 214, 220, 224, 227, 231

Bowler	O	M	R	W	O	M	R	W
RGD Willis	16	2	42	2	23.4	3	70	2
CM Old	22.4	6	50	7	25	12	38	1
IT Botham	15	4	52	1	17	3	47	0
B Wood	3	2	2	0				
PH Edmonds	4	2	2	0	26	10	44	4
G Miller					12	4	19	2

ENGLAND 1st innings / 2nd innings

Batsman	1st innings	
JM Brearley*	run out	38
B Wood	lbw b Sikander	14
CT Radley	lbw b Sikander	106
DI Gower	c Javed b Sikander	58
GRJ Roope	b Sikander	32
G Miller	c Wasim Bari b Mud'sar	48
IT Botham	c Iqbal b Liaquat	100
CM Old	c M Nazar b Iqbal	5
PH Edmonds	not out	4
RW Taylor+		
RGD Willis		
Extras	(0b, 26lb, 5w, 16nb)	47
	144 overs	
Total		**452**

1st innings FoW: 36, 101, 190, 275, 276, 399, 448, 452

Bowler	O	M	R	W
Liaquat Ali	42	9	114	1
Sikander Bakht	45	13	132	4
Mudassar Nazar	27	7	59	1
Iqbal Qasim	14	2	56	1
Wasim Raja	10	1	32	0

No. 538: 2nd Test
VENUE: Lord's
DATE: 15th-19th June 1978
TOSS WON BY: England
RESULT: Eng won by an innings and 120 runs

ENGLAND	1st innings		2nd innings	
JM Brearley*	lbw b Liaquat Ali	2		
GA Gooch	lbw b Wasim Raja	54		
CT Radley	c Mohsin b Liaquat Ali	8		
DI Gower	b Iqbal	56		
GRJ Roope	c Mohsin b Iqbal	69		
G Miller	c Javed b Iqbal	0		
IT Botham	b Liaquat Ali	108		
RW Taylor+	c Mudassar b Sikander	10		
CM Old	c Mohsin b Sikander	0		
PH Edmonds	not out	36		
RGD Willis	b Mudassar	18		
Extras	(0b, 2lb, 0w, 1nb)	3		
	91.2 overs			
Total		**364**		

1st innings FoW: 5, 19, 120, 120, 134, 252, 290, 290, 324, 364

Sikander Bakht	27	3	115	2				
Liaquat Ali	18	1	80	3				
Mudassar Nazar	4.2	0	16	1				
Iqbal Qasim	30	5	101	3				
Wasim Raja	12	3	49	1				

PAKISTAN	1st innings		2nd innings	
M Nazar	c Edmonds b Willis	1	c Taylor b Botham	10
Sadiq Moh'd	c Botham b Willis	11	c Taylor b Willis	0
Mohsin Khan	c Willis b Edmonds	31	c Roope b Willis	46
Haroon Rashid	b Old	15	c Roope b Botham	40
Javed M'dad	c Taylor b Willis	0	b Botham	4
Wasim Raja	b Edmonds	28	c Gooch b Botham	22
Talat Ali	c Radley b Edmonds	2	c & b Botham	1
Wasim Bari*+	c Brearley b Willis	0	c Taylor b Botham	2
Iqbal Qasim	b Willis	0	c Roope b Botham	1
Sikander Bakht	c Brearley b Edmonds	4	b Botham	0
Liaquat Ali	not out	4	not out	0
Extras	(0b, 0lb, 0w, 9nb)	9	(1b, 3lb, 5w, 4nb)	13
	36 overs		66.5 overs	
Total		**105**		**139**

1st innings FoW: 11, 22, 40, 41, 84, 96, 97, 97, 97, 105
2nd innings FoW: 1, 45, 100, 108, 114, 119, 121, 130, 130, 139

RGD Willis	13	1	47	5	10	2	26	2
CM Old	10	3	26	1	15	4	36	0
IT Botham	5	2	17	0	20.5	8	34	8
PH Edmonds	8	6	6	4	12	4	21	0
G Miller					9	3	9	0

Pakistan

No. 539: 3rd Test
VENUE: Headingley
DATE: 29th June to 4th July 1978
TOSS WON BY: Pakistan
RESULT: Match drawn

PAKISTAN	1st innings		2nd innings	
M Nazar	c Botham b Old	31		
Sadiq Moh'd	c Brearley b Botham	97		
Mohsin Khan	lbw b Willis	41		
Talat Ali	c Gooch b Willis	0		
Haroon Rashid	c Brearley b Botham	7		
Javed M'dad	b Old	1		
Wasim Raja	lbw b Botham	0		
Sarfraz Nawaz	c Taylor b Botham	4		
Wasim Bari*+	not out	7		
Sikander Bakht	b Old	4		
Iqbal Qasim	lbw b Old	0		
Extras	(0b, 8lb, 0w, 1nb)	9		
	105.4 overs			
Total		**201**		

1st innings FoW: 75, 147, 147, 169, 182, 183, 189, 190, 201, 201

RGD Willis	26	8	48	2				
CM Old	41.4	22	41	4				
IT Botham	18	2	59	4				
PH Edmonds	11	2	22	0				
G Miller	9	3	22	0				

ENGLAND	1st innings		2nd innings	
JM Brearley*	c Wasim Bari b Sarfraz	0		
GA Gooch	lbw b Sarfraz	20		
CT Radley	b Sikander	7		
DI Gower	lbw b Sarfraz	39		
GRJ Roope	c Sadiq b Javed	11		
G Miller	not out	18		
RW Taylor+	c Wasim Bari b Sarfraz	2		
IT Botham	lbw b Sarfraz	4		
PH Edmonds	not out	1		
CM Old				
RGD Willis				
Extras	(1b, 5lb, 1w, 10nb)	17		
	54 overs			
Total		**119**		

1st innings FoW: 0, 24, 51, 77, 102, 110, 116

Sarfraz Nawaz	20	6	39	5				
Sikander Bakht	15	4	26	1				
Mudassar Nazar	5	2	12	0				
Iqbal Qasim	11	8	11	0				
Javed Miandad	3	0	14	1				

	1st Test		2nd Test
No. 540:	1st Test	No. 541:	2nd Test
VENUE:	The Oval	VENUE:	Trent Bridge
DATE:	27th July to 1st August 1978	DATE:	10th-14th August 1978
TOSS WON BY:	New Zealand	TOSS WON BY:	England
RESULT:	England won by 7 wickets	RESULT:	Eng won by an innings and 119 runs

NEW ZEALAND 1st innings / 2nd innings

Batsman	1st innings		2nd innings	
JG Wright	c Radley b Willis	62	lbw b Botham	25
RW Anderson	b Old	4	c Taylor b Botham	2
GP Howarth	c Edmonds b Botham	94	b Willis	0
BA Edgar	c & b Miller	0	b Edmonds	38
MG Burgess*	lbw b Willis	34	lbw b Botham	7
BE Congdon	run out	2	b Edmonds	36
GN Edwards+	b Miller	6	c Brearley b Edmonds	11
RJ Hadlee	c Brearley b Willis	5	b Edmonds	7
BL Cairns	lbw b Willis	5	b Miller	27
BP Bracewell	c Taylor b Willis	0	b Miller	0
SL Boock	not out	3	not out	0
Extras	(1b, 7lb, 0w, 11nb)	19	(8b, 10lb, 0w, 11nb)	29
	104.2 overs		105.1 overs	
Total		**234**		**182**

1st innings FoW: 7, 130, 131, 191, 197, 207, 224, 230, 230, 234
2nd innings FoW: 15, 19, 30, 70, 86, 105, 113, 182, 182, 182

Bowler	O	M	R	W	O	M	R	W
RGD Willis	20.2	9	42	5	13	2	39	1
CM Old	20	7	43	1	5	2	13	0
IT Botham	22	7	58	1	19	2	46	3
G Miller	25	10	31	2	34	19	35	2
PH Edmonds	17	2	41	0	34.1	23	20	4

ENGLAND 1st innings / 2nd innings

Batsman	1st innings		2nd innings	
JM Brearley*	c Edwards b Bracewell	2	lbw b Boock	11
GA Gooch	lbw b Bracewell	0	not out	91
CT Radley	run out	49	lbw b Bracewell	2
DI Gower	run out	111	c Howarth b Cairns	11
GRJ Roope	b Boock	14	not out	10
G Miller	lbw b Cairns	0		
IT Botham	c Bracewell b Boock	22		
RW Taylor+	c Edwards b Hadlee	8		
PH Edmonds	lbw b Hadlee	28		
CM Old	c Edwards b Cairns	16		
RGD Willis	not out	3		
Extras	(15b, 8lb, 0w, 3nb)	26	(2b, 3lb, 0w, 8nb)	13
	134.5 overs		52.3 overs	
Total		**279**		**138**

1st innings FoW: 1, 7, 123, 165, 166, 208, 212, 232, 257, 279
2nd innings FoW: 26, 51, 82

Bowler	O	M	R	W	O	M	R	W
RJ Hadlee	21.5	6	43	2	11.3	3	18	0
BP Bracewell	17	8	46	2	13	3	26	1
BL Cairns	40	16	65	2	7	0	21	1
SL Boock	35	18	61	2	20	6	55	1
BE Congdon	21	6	38	0	1	0	5	0

ENGLAND 1st innings / 2nd innings

Batsman	1st innings		2nd innings	
GA Gooch	c Burgess b Bracewell	55		
G Boycott	c & b Hadlee	131		
CT Radley	lbw b Hadlee	59		
DI Gower	c Cairns b Boock	46		
JM Brearley*	c Parker b Bracewell	50		
IT Botham	c Hadlee b Boock	8		
G Miller	c Howarth b Hadlee	4		
PH Edmonds	b Cairns	6		
RW Taylor+	b Hadlee	22		
M Hendrick	c Edwards b Bracewell	7		
RGD Willis	not out	1		
Extras	(16b, 12lb, 1w, 11nb)	40		
	180.5 overs			
Total		**429**		

1st innings FoW: 111, 240, 301, 342, 350, 364, 374, 419, 427, 429

Bowler	O	M	R	W
RJ Hadlee	42	11	94	4
BP Bracewell	33.5	2	110	3
BL Cairns	38	7	85	1
BE Congdon	39	15	71	0
SL Boock	28	18	29	2

NEW ZEALAND 1st innings / 2nd innings

Batsman	1st innings		2nd innings	
RW Anderson	lbw b Botham	19	run out	0
BA Edgar	c Taylor b Botham	6	c Botham b Edmonds	60
GP Howarth	not out	31	c Botham b Hendrick	34
SL Boock	c Taylor b Willis	8	run out	38
JM Parker	c Taylor b Hendrick	0	c Brearley b Edmonds	7
MG Burgess*	c Taylor b Botham	5	c Brearley b Botham	4
BE Congdon	c Hendrick b Botham	27	c & b Edmonds	18
GN Edwards+	c Taylor b Botham	0	lbw b Botham	0
BL Cairns	b Edmonds	9	c Taylor b Botham	11
RJ Hadlee	c Gooch b Botham	4	b Edmonds	2
BP Bracewell	b Edmonds	0	not out	0
Extras	(0b, 1lb, 1w, 9nb)	11	(0b, 6lb, 1w, 9nb)	16
	69.4 overs		92.1 overs	
Total		**120**		**190**

1st innings FoW: 22, 27, 30, 47, 49, 99, 99, 110, 115, 120
2nd innings FoW: 5, 63, 127, 148, 152, 164, 168, 180, 190, 190

Bowler	O	M	R	W	O	M	R	W
RGD Willis	12	5	22	1	9	0	31	0
M Hendrick	15	9	18	1	20	7	30	1
IT Botham	21	9	34	6	24	7	59	3
PH Edmonds	15.4	5	21	2	33.1	15	44	4
G Miller	6	1	14	0	6	3	10	0

New Zealand

No. 542: 3rd Test	
VENUE: Lord's	
DATE: 24th-28th August 1978	
TOSS WON BY: New Zealand	
RESULT: England won by 7 wickets	

NEW ZEALAND 1st innings / 2nd innings

Batsman	1st innings		2nd innings	
JG Wright	c Edmonds b Botham	17	b Botham	12
BA Edgar+	c Edmonds b Emburey	39	b Botham	4
GP Howarth	c Taylor b Botham	123	c Taylor b Willis	1
JM Parker	lbw b Hendrick	14	c Taylor b Botham	3
MG Burgess*	lbw b Botham	68	c Hendrick b Botham	14
BE Congdon	c Emburey b Botham	2	c Taylor b Willis	3
RW Anderson	b Botham	16	c Radley b Willis	0
RJ Hadlee	c Brearley b Botham	0	c Hendrick b Willis	0
RO Collinge	c Emburey b Willis	19	not out	14
SL Boock	not out	4	run out	5
BP Bracewell	st Taylor b Emburey	4	b Botham	0
Extras	(4b, 18lb, 4w, 7nb)	33	(0b, 3lb, 0w, 8nb)	11
	143.1 overs		37.1 overs	
Total		**339**		**67**

1st innings FoW: 65, 70, 117, 247, 253, 290, 290, 321, 333, 339
2nd innings FoW: 10, 14, 20, 29, 33, 37, 37, 43, 57, 67

Bowler	O	M	R	W		O	M	R	W
RGD Willis	29	9	79	1		16	8	16	4
M Hendrick	28	14	39	1					
IT Botham	38	13	101	6		18.1	4	39	5
PH Edmonds	12	3	19	0					
JE Emburey	26.1	12	39	2		3	2	1	0
GA Gooch	10	0	29	0					

ENGLAND 1st innings / 2nd innings

Batsman	1st innings		2nd innings	
GA Gooch	c Boock b Hadlee	2	not out	42
G Boycott	c Hadlee b Bracewell	24	b Hadlee	4
CT Radley	c Congdon b Hadlee	77	b Hadlee	0
DI Gower	c Wright b Boock	71	c Congdon b Bracewell	46
JM Brearley*	c Edgar b Hadlee	33	not out	8
IT Botham	c Edgar b Collinge	21		
RW Taylor+	lbw b Hadlee	1		
PH Edmonds	c Edgar b Hadlee	5		
JE Emburey	b Collinge	2		
M Hendrick	b Bracewell	12		
RGD Willis	not out	7		
Extras	(7b, 5lb, 0w, 22nb)	34	(0b, 3lb, 4w, 11nb)	18
	112.3 overs		30.5 overs	
Total		**289**		**118**

1st innings FoW: 2, 66, 180, 211, 249, 255, 258, 263, 274, 289
2nd innings FoW: 14, 14, 84

Bowler	O	M	R	W		O	M	R	W
RJ Hadlee	32	9	84	5		13.5	2	31	2
RO Collinge	30	9	58	2		6	1	26	0
BP Bracewell	19.3	1	68	2		6	0	32	1
SL Boock	25	10	33	1		5	1	11	0
BE Congdon	6	1	12	0					

Australia

No. 543: 1st Test	
VENUE: Brisbane (Gabba)	
DATE: 1st-6th December 1978	
TOSS WON BY: Australia	
RESULT: England won by 7 wickets	

AUSTRALIA 1st innings / 2nd innings

Batsman	1st innings		2nd innings	
GM Wood	c Taylor b Old	7	lbw b Old	19
GJ Cosier	run out	1	b Willis	0
PM Toohey	b Willis	1	lbw b Botham	1
GN Yallop*	c Gooch b Willis	7	c & b Willis	102
KJ Hughes	c Taylor b Botham	4	c Edmonds b Willis	129
TJ Laughlin	c (sub) b Willis	2	lbw b Old	5
JA Maclean+	not out	33	lbw b Miller	15
B Yardley	c Taylor b Willis	17	c Brearley b Miller	16
RM Hogg	c Taylor b Botham	36	b Botham	16
AG Hurst	c Taylor b Botham	0	b Botham	17
JD Higgs	b Old	1	not out	0
Extras	(0b, 1lb, 0w, 6nb)	7	(9b, 5lb, 0w, 22nb)	36
	37.7 overs		116.6 overs	
Total		**116**		**339**

1st innings FoW: 2, 5, 14, 22, 24, 26, 53, 113, 113, 116
2nd innings FoW: 0, 2, 49, 219, 228, 261, 310, 339, 339, 339

Bowler	O	M	R	W		O	M	R	W
RGD Willis	14	2	44	4		27.6	3	69	3
CM Old	9.7	1	24	2		17	1	60	2
IT Botham	12	1	40	3		26	5	95	3
GA Gooch	1	0	1	0					
PH Edmonds	1	1	0	0		12	1	27	0
G Miller						34	12	52	2

ENGLAND 1st innings / 2nd innings

Batsman	1st innings		2nd innings	
G Boycott	c Hughes b Hogg	13	run out	16
GA Gooch	c Laughlin b Hogg	2	c Yardley b Hogg	2
DW Randall	c Laughlin b Hurst	75	not out	74
RW Taylor+	lbw b Hurst	20	c Maclean b Yardley	13
JM Brearley*	c Maclean b Hogg	6	not out	48
DI Gower	c Maclean b Hurst	44		
IT Botham	c Maclean b Hogg	49		
G Miller	lbw b Hogg	27		
PH Edmonds	c Maclean b Hogg	1		
CM Old	not out	29		
RGD Willis	c Maclean b Hurst	8		
Extras	(7b, 4lb, 0w, 1nb)	12	(12b, 3lb, 0w, 2nb)	17
	95.4 overs		53.5 overs	
Total		**286**		**170**

1st innings FoW: 2, 38, 111, 120, 120, 215, 219, 226, 266, 286
2nd innings FoW: 16, 37, 74

Bowler	O	M	R	W		O	M	R	W
AG Hurst	27.4	6	93	4		10	4	17	0
RM Hogg	28	8	74	6		12.5	2	35	1
TJ Laughlin	22	6	54	0		3	0	6	0
B Yardley	7	1	34	0		13	1	41	1
GJ Cosier	5	1	10	0		3	0	11	0
JD Higgs	6	2	9	0		12	1	43	0

No. 544: 2nd Test	No. 545: 3rd Test
VENUE: Perth (WACA)	VENUE: Melbourne (MCG)
DATE: 15th-20th December 1978	DATE: 29th Dec 1978 to 3rd Jan 1979
TOSS WON BY: Australia	TOSS WON BY: Australia
RESULT: England won by 166 runs	RESULT: Australia won by 103 runs

Left (No. 544: 2nd Test)

ENGLAND	1st innings		2nd innings	
G Boycott	lbw b Hurst	77	lbw b Hogg	23
GA Gooch	c Maclean b Hogg	1	lbw b Hogg	43
DW Randall	c Wood b Hogg	0	c Cosier b Yardley	45
JM Brearley*	c Maclean b Dymock	17	c Maclean b Hogg	0
DI Gower	b Hogg	102	c Maclean b Hogg	12
IT Botham	lbw b Hurst	11	c Wood b Yardley	30
G Miller	b Hogg	40	c Toohey b Yardley	25
RW Taylor+	c Hurst b Yardley	12	c Maclean b Hurst	10
JK Lever	c Cosier b Hurst	14	c Maclean b Hogg	2
RGD Willis	c Yallop b Hogg	2	not out	3
M Hendrick	not out	7	b Dymock	1
Extras	(6b, 9lb, 3w, 8nb)	26	(0b, 6lb, 0w, 8nb)	14
	117.5 overs		66.3 overs	
Total		**309**		**208**

1st innings FoW: 3, 3, 41, 199, 219, 224, 253, 295, 300, 309
2nd innings FoW: 58, 93, 93, 135, 151, 176, 201, 201, 206, 208

RM Hogg	30.5	9	65	5		17	2	57	5
G Dymock	34	4	72	1		16.3	2	53	1
AG Hurst	26	7	70	3		17	5	43	1
B Yardley	23	1	62	1		16	1	41	3
GJ Cosier	4	2	14	0					

AUSTRALIA	1st innings		2nd innings	
GM Wood	lbw b Lever	5	c Taylor b Lever	64
WM Darling	run out	25	c Boycott b Lever	5
KJ Hughes	b Willis	16	c Gooch b Willis	12
GN Yallop*	b Willis	3	c Taylor b Hendrick	3
PM Toohey	not out	81	c Taylor b Hendrick	0
GJ Cosier	c Gooch b Willis	4	lbw b Miller	47
JA Maclean+	c Gooch b Miller	0	c Brearley b Miller	1
B Yardley	c Taylor b Hendrick	12	c Botham b Lever	7
RM Hogg	c Taylor b Willis	18	b Miller	0
G Dymock	b Hendrick	11	not out	6
AG Hurst	c Taylor b Willis	5	b Lever	5
Extras	(0b, 7lb, 1w, 2nb)	10	(0b, 3lb, 4w, 4nb)	11
	66.5 overs		46.1 overs	
Total		**190**		**161**

1st innings FoW: 8, 34, 38, 60, 78, 79, 100, 128, 185, 190
2nd innings FoW: 8, 36, 58, 58, 141, 143, 143, 147, 151, 161

JK Lever	7	0	20	1		8.1	2	28	4
IT Botham	11	2	46	0		11	1	54	0
RGD Willis	18.5	5	44	5		12	1	36	1
M Hendrick	14	1	39	2		8	3	11	2
G Miller	16	6	31	1		7	4	21	3

Right (No. 545: 3rd Test)

AUSTRALIA	1st innings		2nd innings	
GM Wood	c Emburey b Miller	100	b Botham	34
WM Darling	run out	33	c Randall b Miller	21
KJ Hughes	c Taylor b Botham	0	c Gower b Botham	48
GN Yallop*	c Hendrick b Botham	41	c Taylor b Miller	16
PM Toohey	c Randall b Miller	32	c Botham b Emburey	20
AR Border	c Brearley b Hendrick	29	run out	0
JA Maclean+	b Botham	8	c Hendrick b Emburey	10
RM Hogg	c Randall b Miller	0	b Botham	1
G Dymock	b Hendrick	0	c Brearley b Hendrick	6
AG Hurst	b Hendrick	0	st Taylor b Emburey	0
JD Higgs	not out	1	not out	0
Extras	(0b, 8lb, 0w, 6nb)	14	(4b, 6lb, 0w, 1nb)	11
	89.1 overs		71.2 overs	
Total		**258**		**167**

1st innings FoW: 65, 65, 126, 189, 247, 250, 250, 251, 252, 258
2nd innings FoW: 55, 81, 101, 136, 136, 152, 157, 167, 167, 167

RGD Willis	13	2	47	0		7	0	21	0
IT Botham	20.1	4	68	3		15	4	41	3
M Hendrick	23	3	50	3		14	4	25	1
JE Emburey	14	1	44	0		21.2	12	30	3
G Miller	19	6	35	3		14	5	39	2

ENGLAND	1st innings		2nd innings	
G Boycott	b Hogg	1	lbw b Hurst	38
JM Brearley*	lbw b Hogg	1	c Maclean b Dymock	0
DW Randall	lbw b Hurst	13	lbw b Hogg	2
GA Gooch	c Border b Dymock	25	lbw b Hogg	40
DI Gower	lbw b Dymock	29	b Dymock	49
IT Botham	c Darling b Higgs	22	c Maclean b Higgs	10
G Miller	b Hogg	7	c Hughes b Higgs	1
RW Taylor+	b Hogg	1	c Maclean b Hogg	5
JE Emburey	b Hogg	0	not out	7
RGD Willis	c Darling b Dymock	19	c Yallop b Hogg	3
M Hendrick	not out	6	b Hogg	0
Extras	(6b, 4lb, 0w, 9nb)	19	(10b, 7lb, 1w, 6nb)	24
	63.6 overs		67 overs	
Total		**143**		**179**

1st innings FoW: 2, 3, 40, 52, 81, 100, 101, 101, 120, 143
2nd innings FoW: 1, 6, 71, 122, 163, 163, 167, 171, 179, 179

RM Hogg	17	7	30	5		17	5	36	5
AG Hurst	12	2	24	1		11	1	39	1
G Dymock	15.6	4	38	3		18	4	37	2
JD Higgs	19	9	32	1		16	2	29	2
AR Border						5	0	14	0

Australia

Australia

No. 546: 4th Test
VENUE: Sydney (SCG)
DATE: 6th-11th January 1979
TOSS WON BY: England
RESULT: England won by 93 runs

ENGLAND	1st innings		2nd innings	
G Boycott	c Border b Hurst	8	lbw b Hogg	0
JM Brearley*	b Hogg	17	b Border	53
DW Randall	c Wood b Hurst	0	lbw b Hogg	150
GA Gooch	c Toohey b Higgs	18	c Wood b Higgs	22
DI Gower	c Maclean b Hurst	7	c Maclean b Hogg	34
IT Botham	c Yallop b Hogg	59	c Wood b Higgs	6
G Miller	c Maclean b Hurst	4	lbw b Hogg	17
RW Taylor+	c Border b Higgs	10	not out	21
JE Embury	c Wood b Higgs	0	c Darling b Higgs	14
RGD Willis	not out	7	c Toohey b Higgs	0
M Hendrick	b Hurst	10	c Toohey b Higgs	7
Extras	(1b, 1lb, 2w, 8nb)	12	(5b, 3lb, 0w, 14nb)	22
	52.6 overs		146.6 overs	
Total		**152**		**346**

1st innings FoW: 18, 18, 35, 51, 66, 70, 94, 98, 141, 152
2nd innings FoW: 0, 111, 169, 237, 267, 292, 307, 334, 334, 346

RM Hogg	11	3	36	2	28	10	67	4
G Dymock	13	1	34	0	17	4	35	0
AG Hurst	10.6	2	28	5	19	3	43	0
JD Higgs	18	4	42	3	59.6	15	148	5
AR Border					23	11	31	1

AUSTRALIA	1st innings		2nd innings	
GM Wood	b Willis	0	run out	27
WM Darling	c Botham b Miller	91	c Gooch b Hendrick	13
KJ Hughes	c Embury b Willis	48	c Embury b Miller	15
GN Yallop*	c Botham b Hendrick	44	c & b Hendrick	1
PM Toohey	c Gooch b Botham	1	b Miller	5
AR Border	not out	60	not out	45
JA Maclean+	lbw b Embury	12	c Botham b Miller	0
RM Hogg	run out	6	b Embury	0
G Dymock	b Botham	5	c Botham b Embury	0
JD Higgs	c Botham b Hendrick	11	lbw b Embury	3
AG Hurst	run out	0	b Embury	0
Extras	(2b, 3lb, 0w, 11nb)	16	(0b, 1lb, 0w, 1nb)	2
	108 overs		49.2 overs	
Total		**294**		**111**

1st innings FoW: 1, 126, 178, 179, 210, 235, 245, 276, 290, 294
2nd innings FoW: 38, 44, 45, 59, 74, 76, 85, 85, 105, 111

RGD Willis	9	2	33	2	2	0	8	0
IT Botham	28	3	87	2				
M Hendrick	24	4	50	2	10	3	17	2
G Miller	13	2	37	1	20	7	38	3
JE Embury	29	10	57	1	17.2	7	46	4
GA Gooch	5	1	14	0				

No. 547: 5th Test
VENUE: Adelaide
DATE: 27th January to 1st Feb 1979
TOSS WON BY: Australia
RESULT: England won by 205 runs

ENGLAND	1st innings		2nd innings	
G Boycott	c Wright b Hurst	6	c Hughes b Hurst	49
JM Brearley*	c Wright b Hogg	2	lbw b Carlson	9
DW Randall	c Carlson b Hurst	4	c Yardley b Hurst	15
GA Gooch	c Hughes b Hogg	1	b Carlson	18
DI Gower	lbw b Hurst	9	lbw b Higgs	21
IT Botham	c Wright b Higgs	74	c Yardley b Hurst	7
G Miller	lbw b Hogg	31	c Wright b Hurst	64
RW Taylor+	run out	4	c Wright b Hogg	97
JE Embury	b Higgs	4	b Hogg	42
RGD Willis	c Darling b Hogg	24	c Wright b Hogg	12
M Hendrick	not out	0	not out	3
Extras	(1b, 4lb, 3w, 2nb)	10	(1b, 16lb, 2w, 4nb)	23
	40.4 overs		142.6 overs	
Total		**169**		**360**

1st innings FoW: 10, 12, 16, 18, 27, 80, 113, 136, 147, 169
2nd innings FoW: 31, 57, 97, 106, 130, 132, 267, 336, 347, 360

RM Hogg	10.4	1	26	4	27.6	7	59	3
AG Hurst	14	1	65	3	37	9	97	4
PH Carlson	9	1	34	0	27	8	41	2
B Yardley	4	0	25	0	20	6	60	0
JD Higgs	3	1	9	2	28	4	75	1
AR Border					3	2	5	0

AUSTRALIA	1st innings		2nd innings	
WM Darling	c Willis b Botham	15	b Botham	18
GM Wood	c Randall b Embury	35	run out	9
KJ Hughes	c Embury b Hendrick	4	c Gower b Hendrick	46
GN Yallop*	b Hendrick	0	b Hendrick	36
AR Border	c Taylor b Botham	11	b Willis	1
PH Carlson	c Taylor b Botham	0	c Gower b Hendrick	21
B Yardley	b Botham	28	c Brearley b Willis	0
KJ Wright+	lbw b Embury	29	c Embury b Miller	0
RM Hogg	b Willis	0	b Miller	2
JD Higgs	run out	16	not out	3
AG Hurst	not out	17	b Willis	13
Extras	(1b, 3lb, 0w, 5nb)	9	(0b, 1lb, 0w, 10nb)	11
	53.4 overs		67 overs	
Total		**164**		**160**

1st innings FoW: 5, 10, 22, 24, 72, 94, 114, 116, 133, 164
2nd innings FoW: 31, 36, 115, 120, 121, 121, 124, 130, 147, 160

RGD Willis	11	1	55	1	12	3	41	3
M Hendrick	19	1	45	2	14	6	19	3
IT Botham	11.4	0	42	4	14	4	37	1
JE Embury	12	7	13	2	9	5	16	0
G Miller					18	3	36	2

Australia | India

	Australia		India
	No. 548: 6th Test		No. 549: 1st Test
	VENUE: Sydney (SCG)		VENUE: Edgbaston
	DATE: 10th–14th February 1979		DATE: 12th–16th July 1979
	TOSS WON BY: Australia		TOSS WON BY: England
	RESULT: England won by 9 wickets		RESULT: Eng won by an innings and 83 runs

AUSTRALIA 1st innings

		1st innings		2nd innings	
GM Wood	c Botham b Hendrick	15	c Willis b Miller	29
AMJ Hilditch	run out	3	c Taylor b Hendrick	1
KJ Hughes	c Botham b Willis	16	c Gooch b Emburey	7
GN Yallop*	c Gower b Botham	121	c Taylor b Miller	17
PM Toohey	c Taylor b Botham	8	c Gooch b Emburey	0
PH Carlson	c Gooch b Botham	2	c Botham b Emburey	0
B Yardley	b Emburey	7	not out	61
KJ Wright+	st Taylor b Emburey	3	c Boycott b Miller	5
RM Hogg	c Emburey b Miller	9	b Miller	7
JD Higgs	not out	9	c Botham b Emburey	2
AG Hurst	b Botham	0	c & b Miller	4
Extras	(0b, 3lb, 0w, 2nb)	5	(3b, 6lb, 0w, 1nb)	10
	60.7 overs		61.1 overs	
Total		**198**		**143**

1st innings FoW: 18, 19, 67, 101, 109, 116, 124, 159, 198, 198
2nd innings FoW: 8, 28, 48, 48, 48, 82, 114, 130, 136, 143

RGD Willis	11	4	48	1	3	0	15	0
M Hendrick	12	2	21	1	7	3	22	1
IT Botham	9.7	1	57	4	24	4	52	4
JE Emburey	18	3	48	2	27.1	6	44	5
G Miller	9	3	13	1				
G Boycott	1	0	6	0				

ENGLAND 1st innings

		1st innings		2nd innings	
G Boycott	c Hilditch b Hurst	19	c Hughes b Higgs	13
JM Brearley*	c Toohey b Higgs	46	not out	20
DW Randall	lbw b Hogg	7	not out	0
GA Gooch	st Wright b Higgs	74		
DI Gower	c Wright b Higgs	65		
IT Botham	c Carlson b Yardley	23		
G Miller	lbw b Hurst	18		
RW Taylor+	not out	36		
JE Emburey	c Hilditch b Hurst	0		
RGD Willis	b Higgs	10		
M Hendrick	c & b Yardley	0		
Extras	(3b, 5lb, 0w, 2nb)	10	(0b, 0lb, 0w, 2nb)	2
	103 overs		10.2 overs	
Total		**308**		**35**

1st innings FoW: 37, 46, 115, 182, 233, 247, 270, 280, 306, 308
2nd innings FoW: 31

RM Hogg	18	6	42	1				
AG Hurst	20	4	58	3				
B Yardley	25	2	105	2	5.2	0	21	0
PH Carlson	10	1	24	0				
JD Higgs	30	8	69	4	5	1	12	1

ENGLAND 1st innings

		1st innings		2nd innings	
JM Brearley*	c Reddy b Kapil Dev	24		
G Boycott	lbw b Kapil Dev	155		
DW Randall	c Reddy b Kapil Dev	15		
GA Gooch	c Reddy b Kapil Dev	83		
DI Gower	not out	200		
IT Botham	b Kapil Dev	33		
G Miller	not out	63		
PH Edmonds				
RW Taylor+				
RGD Willis				
M Hendrick				
Extras	(4b, 27lb, 11w, 18nb)	60		
	165.2 overs			
Total		**633**		

1st innings FoW: 66, 90, 235, 426, 468

N Kapil Dev	48	15	146	5
KD Ghavri	38	5	129	0
M Amarnath	13.2	2	47	0
BS Chan'har	29	1	113	0
S Venk'van	31	4	107	0
AD Gaekwad	3	0	12	0
CPS Chauhan	3	0	19	0

INDIA 1st innings

		1st innings		2nd innings	
SM Gavaskar	run out	61	c Gooch b Hendrick	68
CPS Chauhan	c Gooch b Botham	4	c Randall b Willis	56
DB Vengsarkar	c Gooch b Edmonds	22	c Edmonds b Hendrick	7
GR Viswanath	c Botham b Edmonds	78	c Taylor b Botham	51
AD Gaekwad	c Botham b Willis	25	c Gooch b Botham	15
M Amarnath	b Willis	31	lbw b Botham	10
N Kapil Dev	lbw b Botham	1	c Hendrick b Botham	21
KD Ghavri	c Brearley b Willis	6	c Randall b Hendrick	4
B Reddy+	b Hendrick	21	lbw b Hendrick	0
S Venk'an*	c Botham b Hendrick	28	lbw b Botham	0
BS Chan'har	not out	0	not out	0
Extras	(1b, 4lb, 3w, 12nb)	20	(7b, 12lb, 0w, 2nb)	21
	116.1 overs		95.4 overs	
Total		**297**		**253**

1st innings FoW: 15, 59, 129, 205, 209, 210, 229, 251, 294, 297
2nd innings FoW: 124, 136, 136, 182, 227, 240, 249, 250, 251, 253

RGD Willis	24	9	69	3	14	3	45	1
IT Botham	26	4	86	2	29	8	70	5
M Hendrick	24.1	9	36	2	20.4	8	45	4
PH Edmonds	26	11	60	2	17	6	37	0
G Boycott	5	1	8	0				
G Miller	11	3	18	0	9	1	27	0
GA Gooch					6	3	8	0

No. 550: 2nd Test	No. 551: 3rd Test
VENUE: Lord's	VENUE: Headingley
DATE: 2nd-7th August 1979	DATE: 16th-21st August 1979
TOSS WON BY: India	TOSS WON BY: England
RESULT: Match drawn	RESULT: Match drawn

INDIA 1st innings / 2nd innings

	1st innings		2nd innings	
SM Gavaskar	c Taylor b Gooch	42	c Brearley b Botham	59
CPS Chauhan	c Randall b Botham	2	c Randall b Edmonds	31
DB Vengsarkar	c Botham b Hendrick	0	c Boycott b Edmonds	103
GR Viswanath	c Brearley b Hendrick	21	c Gower b Lever	113
AD Gaekwad	c Taylor b Botham	13	not out	1
Y'pal Sharma	c Taylor b Botham	11	not out	5
N Kapil Dev	c Miller b Botham	4		
KD Ghavri	not out	3		
B Reddy+	lbw b Botham	0		
S Venk'van*	run out	0		
BS Bedi	b Lever	0		
Extras	(0b, 0lb, 0w, 0nb)	0	(2b, 2lb, 1w, 1nb)	6
	55.5 overs		148 overs	
Total		**96**		**318**

1st innings FoW: 12, 23, 51, 75, 79, 89, 96, 96, 96, 96
2nd innings FoW: 79, 99, 309, 312

JK Lever	9.5	3	29	1	24	7	69	1
IT Botham	19	9	35	5	35	13	80	1
M Hendrick	15	7	15	2	25	12	56	0
PH Edmonds	2	1	1	0	45	18	62	2
GA Gooch	10	5	16	1	2	0	8	0
G Miller					17	6	37	0

ENGLAND 1st innings / 2nd innings

	1st innings		2nd innings
JM Brearley*	c Reddy b Kapil Dev	12	
G Boycott	c Gavaskar b Ghavri	32	
GA Gooch	b Kapil Dev	10	
DI Gower	b Ghavri	82	
DW Randall	run out	57	
IT Botham	b Venkataraghavan	36	
G Miller	st Reddy b Bedi	62	
PH Edmonds	c Reddy b Kapil Dev	20	
RW Taylor+	c Vengsarkar b Bedi	64	
JK Lever	not out	6	
M Hendrick			
Extras	(11b, 21lb, 2w, 4nb)	38	
	129.5 overs		
Total		**419**	

1st innings FoW: 21, 60, 71, 185, 226, 253, 291, 394, 419

N Kapil Dev	38	11	93	3
KD Ghavri	31	2	122	2
BS Bedi	38.5	13	87	2
S Venk'van	22	2	79	1

ENGLAND 1st innings / 2nd innings

	1st innings		2nd innings
G Boycott	c Viswanath b Kapil Dev	31	
JM Brearley*	c Viswanath b Amarnath	15	
GA Gooch	c Vengsarkar b Kapil Dev	4	
DI Gower	lbw b Kapil Dev	0	
DW Randall	b Ghavri	11	
IT Botham	c Ghavri b Venkatag'n	137	
G Miller	c Reddy b Amarnath	27	
PH Edmonds	run out	18	
RW Taylor+	c Chauhan b Bedi	1	
RGD Willis	not out	4	
M Hendrick	c (sub) b Bedi	0	
Extras	(4b, 6lb, 4w, 8nb)	22	
	80.5 overs		
Total		**270**	

1st innings FoW: 53, 57, 57, 58, 89, 176, 264, 264, 266, 270

N Kapil Dev	27	7	84	3
KD Ghavri	18	4	60	1
M Amarnath	20	7	53	2
S Venkataraghavan	7	2	25	1
BS Bedi	8.5	2	26	2

INDIA 1st innings / 2nd innings

	1st innings		2nd innings
SM Gavaskar	b Edmonds	78	
CPS Chauhan	c Botham b Willis	0	
M Amarnath	c Taylor b Willis	0	
GR Viswanath	c Brearley b Hendrick	1	
Y'pal Sharma	c Botham b Miller	40	
DB Vengsarkar	not out	65	
N Kapil Dev	c Gooch b Miller	3	
KD Ghavri	not out	20	
S Venk'van*			
B Reddy+			
BS Bedi			
Extras	(11b, 4lb, 1w, 0nb)	16	
	110 overs		
Total		**223**	

1st innings FoW: 1, 9, 12, 106, 156, 160

RGD Willis	18	5	42	2
M Hendrick	14	6	13	1
IT Botham	13	3	39	0
PH Edmonds	28	8	59	1
G Miller	32	13	52	2
GA Gooch	3	1	2	0
G Boycott	2	2	0	0

India | Australia '79

<table>
<tr><td>

No. 552: 4th Test
VENUE: The Oval
DATE: 30th August to 4th Sep 1979
TOSS WON BY: England
RESULT: Match drawn

</td><td>

No. 553: 1st Test
VENUE: Perth (WACA)
DATE: 14th-19th December 1979
TOSS WON BY: England
RESULT: Australia won by 138 runs

</td></tr>
</table>

ENGLAND

	1st innings		2nd innings	
G Boycott	lbw b Kapil Dev	35	b Ghavri	125
AR Butcher	c Yajurvindra b Venkat	14	c Venkatarag'n b Ghavri	20
GA Gooch	c Viswanath b Ghavri	79	lbw b Kapil Dev	31
DI Gower	lbw b Kapil Dev	0	c Reddy b Bedi	7
P Willey	c Yajurvindra b Bedi	52	c Reddy b Ghavri	31
IT Botham	st Reddy b Venk'van	38	run out	0
JM Brearley*	b Ghavri	34	b Venkataraghavan	11
DL Bairstow+	c Reddy b Kapil Dev	9	c Gavaskar b Kapil Dev	59
PH Edmonds	c Kapil Dev b Venkat	16	not out	27
RGD Willis	not out	10		
M Hendrick	c Gavaskar b Bedi	0		
Extras	(0b, 9lb, 4w, 5nb)	18	(0b, 14lb, 2w, 7nb)	23
Total	124.5 overs	**305**	116.5 overs	**334**

1st innings FoW: 45, 51, 51, 148, 203, 245, 272, 275, 304, 305
2nd innings FoW: 43, 107, 125, 192, 194, 215, 291, 334

N Kapil Dev	32	12	83	3	28.5	4	89	2
KD Ghavri	26	8	61	2	34	11	76	3
BS Bedi	29.5	4	69	2	26	4	67	1
Yaj' Singh	8	2	15	0	2	0	4	0
S Venk'van	29	9	59	3	26	4	75	1

INDIA

	1st innings		2nd innings	
SM Gavaskar	c Bairstow b Botham	13	c Gower b Botham	221
CPS Chauhan	c Botham b Willis	6	c Botham b Willis	80
DB Vengsarkar	c Botham b Willis	0	c Botham b Edmonds	52
GR Viswanath	c Brearley b Botham	62	c Gooch b Willey	0
Y'pal Sharma	lbw b Willis	27	lbw b Botham	19
Yaj' Singh	not out	43	c Brearley b Willey	15
N Kapil Dev	b Hendrick	16	lbw b Botham	1
KD Ghavri	c Bairstow b Botham	7	run out	6
B Reddy+	c Bairstow b Botham	12	not out	3
S Venk'van*	c & b Hendrick	2	not out	5
BS Bedi	c Brearley b Hendrick	1		
Extras	(2b, 3lb, 5w, 3nb)	13	(11b, 15lb, 1w, 0nb)	27
Total	79.3 overs	**202**	150.5 overs	**429**

1st innings FoW: 9, 9, 47, 91, 130, 161, 172, 192, 200, 202
2nd innings FoW: 213, 366, 367, 389, 410, 411, 419, 423

RGD Willis	18	2	53	3	28	4	89	1
IT Botham	28	7	65	4	29	5	97	3
M Hendrick	22.3	7	38	3	8	2	15	0
P Willey	4	1	10	0	43.5	15	96	2
GA Gooch	2	0	6	0	2	0	9	0
PH Edmonds	5	1	17	0	38	11	87	1
AR Butcher					2	0	9	0

AUSTRALIA

	1st innings		2nd innings	
JM Wiener	run out	11	c Randall b Underwood	58
BM Laird	lbw b Botham	0	c Taylor b Underwood	33
AR Border	lbw b Botham	4	c Taylor b Willis	115
GS Chappell*	c Boycott b Botham	19	st Taylor b Underwood	43
KJ Hughes	c Brearley b Underw'd	99	c Miller b Underwood	4
PM Toohey	c Underwood b Dilley	19	c Taylor b Botham	3
RW Marsh+	c Taylor b Dilley	42	c Gower b Botham	4
RJ Bright	c Taylor b Botham	17	lbw b Botham	12
DK Lillee	c Taylor b Botham	18	c Willey b Dilley	19
G Dymock	b Botham	5	not out	20
JR Thomson	not out	1	b Botham	8
Extras	(4b, 3lb, 0w, 2nb)	9	(4b, 5lb, 2w, 7nb)	18
Total	100 overs	**244**	141.5 overs	**337**

1st innings FoW: 2, 17, 20, 88, 127, 186, 219, 219, 243, 244
2nd innings FoW: 91, 100, 168, 183, 191, 204, 225, 303, 323, 337

GR Dilley	18	1	47	2	18	3	50	1
IT Botham	35	9	78	6	45.5	14	98	5
RGD Willis	23	7	47	0	26	7	52	1
DL Underwood	13	4	33	1	41	14	82	3
G Miller	11	2	30	0	10	0	36	0
P Willey					1	0	1	0

ENGLAND

	1st innings		2nd innings	
DW Randall	c Hughes b Lillee	0	lbw b Dymock	1
G Boycott	lbw b Lillee	0	not out	99
P Willey	c Chappell b Dymock	9	lbw b Dymock	12
DI Gower	c Marsh b Lillee	17	c Thomson b Dymock	23
G Miller	c Hughes b Thomson	25	c Chappell b Thomson	8
JM Brearley*	c Marsh b Lillee	64	c Marsh b Lillee	18
IT Botham	c Toohey b Thomson	15	c Marsh b Bright	11
RW Taylor+	b Chappell	14	b Lillee	15
GR Dilley	not out	38	c Marsh b Dymock	16
DL Underw'd	lbw b Dymock	13	c Wiener b Dymock	0
RGD Willis	b Dymock	11	c Chappell b Dymock	0
Extras	(0b, 7lb, 0w, 15nb)	22	(0b, 3lb, 1w, 8nb)	12
Total	91.1 overs	**228**	90.2 overs	**215**

1st innings FoW: 1, 12, 14, 41, 74, 90, 123, 185, 203, 228
2nd innings FoW: 8, 26, 64, 75, 115, 141, 182, 211, 211, 215

DK Lillee	28	11	73	4	23	5	74	2
G Dymock	29.1	14	52	3	17.2	4	34	6
GS Chappell	11	6	5	1	6	4	6	0
JR Thomson	21	3	70	2	11	3	30	1
RJ Bright	2	0	6	0	23	11	30	1
JM Wiener					8	3	22	0
AR Border					2	0	7	0

Australia

No. 554: 2nd Test	
VENUE:	Sydney (SCG)
DATE:	4th-8th January 1980
TOSS WON BY:	Australia
RESULT:	Australia won by 6 wickets

ENGLAND	1st innings		2nd innings	
GA Gooch	b Lillee	18	c G Chappell b Dymock	4
G Boycott	b Dymock	8	c McCosker b Pascoe	18
DW Randall	c GS Chappell b Lillee	0	b Pascoe	3
P Willey	c Wiener b Dymock	8	c Marsh b Pascoe	19
JM Brearley*	c Pascoe b Dymock	7	c Border b Dymock	43
DI Gower	b GS Chappell	8	c Marsh b G Chappell	25
IT Botham	c GS Chappell b Pascoe	27	not out	98
RW Taylor+	c Marsh b Lillee	10	c Wiener b GS Chappell	0
GR Dilley	not out	22	b Lillee	8
RGD Willis	c Wiener b Dymock	3	b Dymock	8
DL Underw'd	c Border b Lillee	12	c GS Chappell b Lillee	1
Extras	(0b, 0lb, 0w, 5nb)	5	(1b, 10lb, 1w, 2nb)	14
	44.3 overs		96.3 overs	
Total		**123**		**237**

1st innings FoW: 10, 13, 31, 38, 41, 74, 75, 90, 98, 123
2nd innings FoW: 6, 21, 29, 77, 105, 156, 174, 211, 218, 237

DK Lillee	13.3	4	40	4	24.3	6	63	2
G Dymock	17	6	42	4	28	8	48	3
LS Pascoe	9	4	14	1	23	3	76	3
GS Chappell	4	1	19	1	21	10	36	2
JD Higgs	1	0	3	0				

AUSTRALIA	1st innings		2nd innings	
RB McCosker	c Gower b Willis	1	c Taylor b Underwood	41
JM Wiener	run out	22	b Underwood	13
IM Chappell	c Brearley b Gooch	42	c Botham b Underwood	9
GS Chappell*	c Taylor b Underwood	3	not out	98
KJ Hughes	c Taylor b Botham	18	c Dilley b Willis	47
AR Border	c Gooch b Botham	15	not out	2
RW Marsh+	c Underwood b Gooch	7		
DK Lillee	c Brearley b Botham	5		
G Dymock	c Taylor b Botham	4		
LS Pascoe	not out	10		
JD Higgs	b Underwood	2		
Extras	(2b, 12lb, 2w, 0nb)	16	(0b, 8lb, 1w, 0nb)	9
	58.2 overs		85.3 overs	
Total		**145**		**219**

1st innings FoW: 18, 52, 71, 92, 100, 114, 121, 129, 132, 145
2nd innings FoW: 31, 51, 98, 203

IT Botham	17	7	29	4	23.3	12	43	0
RGD Willis	11	3	30	1	12	2	26	1
DL Underwood	13.2	3	39	2	26	6	71	3
GR Dilley	5	1	13	0	12	0	33	0
P Willey	1	0	2	0	4	0	17	0
GA Gooch	11	4	16	2	8	2	20	0

Australia

No. 555: 3rd Test	
VENUE:	Melbourne (MCG)
DATE:	1st-6th February 1980
TOSS WON BY:	England
RESULT:	Australia won by 8 wickets

ENGLAND	1st innings		2nd innings	
GA Gooch	run out	99	b Mallett	51
G Boycott	c Mallett b Dymock	44	b Lillee	7
W Larkins	c GS Chappell b Pascoe	25	lbw b Pascoe	3
DI Gower	lbw b Lillee	0	b Lillee	11
P Willey	lbw b Pascoe	1	c Marsh b Lillee	2
IT Botham	c Marsh b Lillee	8	c Border b Pascoe	10
JM Brearley*	not out	60	not out	119
RW Taylor+	b Lillee	23	c Border b Lillee	32
DL Underw'd	c IM Chappell b Lillee	3	b Pascoe	0
JK Lever	b Lillee	22	c Marsh b Lillee	12
RGD Willis	c GS Chappell b Lillee	4	c G Chappell b Pascoe	2
Extras	(1b, 2lb, 0w, 14nb)	17	(2b, 12lb, 0w, 10nb)	24
	128.1 overs		91.5 overs	
Total		**306**		**273**

1st innings FoW: 116, 170, 175, 177, 177, 192, 238, 242, 296, 306
2nd innings FoW: 25, 46, 64, 67, 88, 92, 178, 179, 268, 273

DK Lillee	33.1	9	60	6	33	6	78	5
G Dymock	28	6	54	1	11	2	30	0
AA Mallett	35	9	104	0	14	1	45	1
LS Pascoe	32	7	71	2	29.5	3	80	4
AR Border					4	0	16	0

AUSTRALIA	1st innings		2nd innings	
RB McCosker	c Botham b Underwood	33	lbw b Botham	2
BM Laird	c Gower b Underwood	74	c Boycott b Underwood	25
IM Chappell	c & b Underwood	75	not out	26
KJ Hughes	c Underwood b Botham	15	not out	40
AR Border	c & b Lever	63		
GS Chappell*	c Larkins b Lever	114		
RW Marsh+	c Botham b Lever	17		
DK Lillee	c Willey b Lever	8		
G Dymock	b Botham	19		
AA Mallett	lbw b Botham	25		
LS Pascoe	not out	1		
Extras	(13b, 12lb, 1w, 7nb)	33	(0b, 8lb, 0w, 2nb)	10
	179.5 overs		38.4 overs	
Total		**477**		**103**

1st innings FoW: 52, 179, 196, 219, 345, 411, 421, 432, 465, 477
2nd innings FoW: 20, 42

JK Lever	53	15	111	4	7.4	3	18	0
IT Botham	39.5	15	105	3	12	5	18	1
RGD Willis	21	4	61	0	5	3	8	0
DL Underwood	53	19	131	3	14	2	49	1
P Willey	13	2	36	0				

India

No. 556: 1st Test
VENUE: Bombay (Wankhede)
DATE: 15th-19th February 1980
TOSS WON BY: India
RESULT: England won by 10 wickets

INDIA

Batsman	1st innings		2nd innings	
SM Gavaskar	c Taylor b Botham	49	c Taylor b Botham	24
RMH Binny	run out	15	lbw b Botham	0
DB Vengsarkar	c Taylor b Stevenson	34	lbw b Lever	10
GR Viswanath*	b Lever	11	c Taylor b Lever	5
SM Patil	c Taylor b Botham	30	lbw b Botham	0
Y'pal Sharma	lbw b Botham	21	lbw b Botham	27
N Kapil Dev	c Taylor b Botham	0	c Gooch b Botham	0
SMH Kirmani+	not out	40	not out	45
KD Ghavri	c Taylor b Stevenson	11	c Brearley b Lever	5
NS Yadav	c Taylor b Botham	8	c Taylor b Botham	15
DR Doshi	c Taylor b Botham	6	c & b Lever	0
Extras	(5b, 3lb, 0w, 9nb)	17	(4b, 8lb, 1w, 5nb)	18
	69.5 overs		52.1 overs	
Total		**242**		**149**

1st innings FoW: 56, 102, 108, 135, 160, 160, 181, 197, 223, 242

Bowler	O	M	R	W	O	M	R	W
JK Lever	23	3	82	1	20.1	2	65	3
IT Botham	22.5	7	58	6	26	7	48	7
GB Stevenson	14	1	59	2	5	1	13	0
DL Underwood	6	1	23	0	1	0	5	0
GA Gooch	4	2	3	0				

ENGLAND

Batsman	1st innings		2nd innings	
GA Gooch	c Kirmani b Ghavri	8	not out	49
G Boycott	c Kirmani b Binny	22	not out	43
W Larkins	lbw b Ghavri	0		
DI Gower	lbw b Kapil Dev	16		
JM Brearley*	lbw b Kapil Dev	5		
IT Botham	lbw b Ghavri	114		
RW Taylor+	lbw b Kapil Dev	43		
JE Emburey	c Binny b Ghavri	8		
JK Lever	b Doshi	21		
GB Stevenson	not out	27		
DL Underw'd	b Ghavri	1		
Extras	(8b, 9lb, 0w, 14nb)	31	(3b, 1lb, 0w, 2nb)	6
	97.1 overs		29.3 overs	
Total		**296**		**98**

1st innings FoW: 21, 21, 45, 57, 58, 229, 245, 262, 283, 296
2nd innings FoW: 4, 22, 31, 31, 56, 58, 102, 115, 148, 149

Bowler	O	M	R	W	O	M	R	W
N Kapil Dev	29	8	64	3	8	2	21	0
KD Ghavri	20.1	5	52	5	5	0	12	0
RMH Binny	19	3	70	1				
DR Doshi	23	6	57	1	6	1	12	0
NS Yadav	6	2	22	0	6	0	31	0
SM Patil					3	0	8	0
SM Gavaskar					1	0	4	0
GR Viswanath					0.3	0	4	0

West Indies

No. 557: 1st Test
VENUE: Trent Bridge
DATE: 5th-10th June 1980
TOSS WON BY: England
RESULT: West Indies won by 2 wickets

ENGLAND

Batsman	1st innings		2nd innings	
GA Gooch	c Murray b Roberts	17	run out	27
G Boycott	c Murray b Garner	36	b Roberts	75
CJ Tavare	b Garner	13	c Richards b Garner	4
RA Woolmer	c Murray b Roberts	46	c Murray b Roberts	29
DI Gower	c Greenidge b Roberts	20	lbw b Garner	1
IT Botham*	c Richards b Garner	57	c Richards b Roberts	4
P Willey	b Marshall	13	b Marshall	38
APE Knott+	lbw b Roberts	6	lbw b Marshall	7
JK Lever	c Richards b Holding	15	c Murray b Garner	4
RGD Willis	b Roberts	8	b Garner	9
M Hendrick	not out	7	not out	2
Extras	(7b, 11lb, 3w, 4nb)	25	(19b, 13lb, 10w, 10nb)	52
	91.5 overs		111.1 overs	
Total		**263**		**252**

1st innings FoW: 27, 72, 74, 114, 204, 208, 228, 246, 254, 263
2nd innings FoW: 46, 68, 174, 175, 180, 183, 218, 237, 248, 252

Bowler	O	M	R	W	O	M	R	W
AME Roberts	25	7	72	5	24	6	57	3
MA Holding	23.5	7	61	1	26	5	65	0
MD Marshall	19	3	52	1	24	8	44	2
IVA Richards	1	0	9	0				
J Garner	23	9	44	3	34.1	20	30	4
CG Greenidge					3	2	4	0

WEST INDIES

Batsman	1st innings		2nd innings	
CG Greenidge	c Knott b Hendrick	53	c Knott b Willis	6
DL Haynes	c Gower b Willis	12	run out	62
IVA Richards	c Knott b Willis	64	lbw b Botham	48
SFAF Bacchus	c Botham b Willis	30	c Knott b Hendrick	19
AI Kallicharran	b Botham	17	c Knott b Willis	9
DL Murray+	b Willis	64	lbw b Willis	3
CH Lloyd*	c Knott b Lever	9	c Hendrick b Willis	16
MD Marshall	c Tavare b Gooch	20	b Willis	7
AME Roberts	lbw b Botham	21	not out	22
J Garner	c Lever b Botham	2	not out	0
MA Holding	not out	0		
Extras	(1b, 9lb, 2w, 4nb)	16	(0b, 8lb, 0w, 9nb)	17
	91.1 overs		68.4 overs	
Total		**308**		**209**

1st innings FoW: 19, 107, 151, 165, 208, 227, 265, 306, 308, 308
2nd innings FoW: 11, 69, 109, 125, 129, 165, 180, 205

Bowler	O	M	R	W	O	M	R	W
RGD Willis	20.1	5	82	4	26	4	65	5
JK Lever	20	2	76	1	8	2	25	0
M Hendrick	19	4	69	1	14	5	40	1
P Willey	5	3	4	0	2	0	12	0
IT Botham	20	6	50	3	16.4	6	48	1
GA Gooch	7	2	11	1	2	1	2	0

West Indies | West Indies

Match 558 — Lord's

ENGLAND	1st innings		2nd innings	
GA Gooch	lbw b Holding	123	b Garner	47
G Boycott	c Murray b Holding	8	not out	49
CJ Tavare	c Greenidge b Holding	42	lbw b Garner	6
RA Woolmer	c Kallicharran b Garner	15	not out	19
MW Gatting	b Holding	18		
IT Botham*	lbw b Garner	8		
DL Underw'd	lbw b Garner	3		
P Willey	b Holding	4		
APE Knott+	c Garner b Holding	9		
RGD Willis	b Garner	14		
M Hendrick	not out	10		
Extras	(4b, 1lb, 4w, 6nb)	15	(0b, 1lb, 0w, 11nb)	12
	95.3 overs		52 overs	
Total		**269**		**133**

1st innings FoW: 20, 165, 190, 219, 220, 231, 232, 244, 245, 269
2nd innings FoW: 71, 96

AME Roberts	18	3	50	0	13	3	24	0
MA Holding	28	11	67	6	15	5	51	0
J Garner	24.3	8	36	4	15	6	21	2
CEH Croft	20	3	77	0	8	2	24	0
IVA Richards	5	1	24	0	1	0	1	0

WEST INDIES	1st innings		2nd innings
CG Greenidge	lbw b Botham	25	
DL Haynes	lbw b Botham	184	
IVA Richards	c (sub) b Willey	145	
CEH Croft	run out	0	
AI Kallicharran	c Knott b Willis	15	
SFAF Bacchus	c Gooch b Willis	0	
CH Lloyd*	b Willey	56	
DL Murray+	c Tavare b Botham	34	
AME Roberts	b Underwood	24	
J Garner	c Gooch b Willis	15	
MA Holding	not out	0	
Extras	(1b, 9lb, 1w, 9nb)	20	
	147.2 overs		
Total		**518**	

1st innings FoW: 37, 260, 275, 326, 330, 437, 469, 486, 518, 518

RGD Willis	31	12	103	3
IT Botham	37	7	145	3
DL Underwood	29.2	7	108	1
M Hendrick	11	2	32	0
GA Gooch	7	1	26	0
P Willey	25	8	73	2
G Boycott	7	2	11	0

Match 559 — Old Trafford

ENGLAND	1st innings		2nd innings	
GA Gooch	lbw b Roberts	2	c Murray b Marshall	26
G Boycott	c Garner b Roberts	5	lbw b Holding	86
BC Rose	b Marshall	70	c Kallich'an b Holding	32
W Larkins	lbw b Garner	11	c Murray b Marshall	33
MW Gatting	c Richards b Marshall	33	c Kallicharran b Garner	56
IT Botham*	c Murray b Garner	8	lbw b Holding	35
P Willey	b Marshall	0	not out	62
APE Knott+	run out	2	c & b Garner	6
JE Emburey	c Murray b Roberts	3	not out	28
GR Dilley	b Garner	0		
RGD Willis	not out	5		
Extras	(0b, 4lb, 3w, 4nb)	11	(5b, 8lb, 1w, 13nb)	27
	48.2 overs		143 overs	
Total		**150**		**391**

1st innings FoW: 3, 18, 35, 126, 131, 132, 142, 142, 142, 150
2nd innings FoW: 32, 86, 181, 217, 290, 290, 309

AME Roberts	11.2	3	23	3	14	2	36	0
MA Holding	14	2	46	0	34	8	100	3
J Garner	11	2	34	3	40	11	73	2
MD Marshall	12	5	36	3	35	5	116	2
IVA Richards					16	6	31	0
CH Lloyd					1	0	1	0
SFAF Bacchus					1	0	3	0
DL Haynes					1	0	2	0
AI Kallicharran					1	0	2	0

WEST INDIES	1st innings		2nd innings
CG Greenidge	c Larkins b Dilley	0	
DL Haynes	c Knott b Willis	1	
IVA Richards	b Botham	65	
SFAF Bacchus	c Botham b Dilley	0	
AI Kallicharran	c Knott b Botham	13	
CH Lloyd*	c Gooch b Emburey	101	
DL Murray+	b Botham	17	
MD Marshall	c Gooch b Dilley	18	
AME Roberts	c Knott b Emburey	11	
J Garner	lbw b Emburey	0	
MA Holding	not out	4	
Extras	(2b, 13lb, 3w, 12nb)	30	
	72.3 overs		
Total		**260**	

1st innings FoW: 4, 25, 25, 67, 100, 154, 209, 250, 250, 260

RGD Willis	14	1	99	1
GR Dilley	28	7	47	3
IT Botham	20	6	64	3
JE Emburey	10.3	1	20	3

No. 560: 4th Test	No. 561: 5th Test
VENUE: The Oval	VENUE: Headingley
DATE: 24th-29th July 1980	DATE: 7th-12th August 1980
TOSS WON BY: England	TOSS WON BY: West Indies
RESULT: Match drawn	RESULT: Match drawn

ENGLAND

	1st innings		2nd innings	
GA Gooch	lbw b Holding	83	lbw b Holding	0
G Boycott	run out	53	c Murray b Croft	5
BC Rose	b Croft	50	lbw b Garner	41
W Larkins	lbw b Garner	7	b Holding	0
MW Gatting	b Croft	48	c Bacchus b Croft	2
P Willey	c Lloyd b Holding	34	c Murray b Garner	15
APE Knott+	c Lloyd b Marshall	3	c Greenidge b Garner	4
IT Botham*	lbw b Croft	9	not out	100
JE Emburey	c Holding b Marshall	24	lbw b Holding	3
GR Dilley	b Garner	1	c (sub) b Holding	1
RGD Willis	not out	1	not out	24
Extras	(7b, 21lb, 10w, 19nb)	57	(0b, 6lb, 1w, 7nb)	14
	128.3 overs		94 overs	
Total		**370**		**209**

1st innings FoW: 155, 157, 182, 269, 303, 312, 336, 343, 368, 370
2nd innings FoW: 2, 10, 13, 18, 63, 67, 73, 84, 92

MA Holding	28	5	67	2		29	7	79	4
CEH Croft	35	9	97	3		10	6	8	2
MD Marshall	29.3	6	77	2		23	7	47	0
J Garner	33	8	67	2		17	5	24	3
IVA Richards	3	1	5	0		9	3	15	0
AI Kallicharran						6	1	22	0

WEST INDIES 1st innings   2nd innings

CG Greenidge	lbw b Willis	6
DL Haynes	c Gooch b Dilley	7
IVA Richards	c Willey b Botham	26
SFAF Bacchus	c Knott b Emburey	61
AI Kallicharran	c Rose b Dilley	11
DL Murray+	hit wkt b Dilley	0
MD Marshall	c Rose b Emburey	45
J Garner	c Gatting b Botham	46
MA Holding	lbw b Dilley	22
CEH Croft	not out	0
CH Lloyd*	absent hurt	0
Extras	(0b, 12lb, 1w, 28nb)	41
	95.2 overs	
Total		**265**

1st innings FoW: 15, 34, 72, 99, 105, 187, 197, 261, 265

RGD Willis	19	5	58	1
GR Dilley	23	6	57	4
IT Botham	18.2	8	47	2
JE Emburey	23	12	38	2
GA Gooch	1	0	2	0
P Willey	11	5	22	0

ENGLAND

	1st innings		2nd innings	
GA Gooch	c Marshall b Garner	14	lbw b Marshall	55
G Boycott	c Kallicharran b Holding	4	c Kallicharran b Croft	47
BC Rose	b Croft	7	lbw b Marshall	30
W Larkins	c Kallicharran b Garner	9	lbw b Holding	1
MW Gatting	c Marshall b Croft	1	not out	43
IT Botham*	c Richards b Holding	37	lbw b Marshall	7
P Willey	c Murray b Croft	1	c Murray b Holding	10
DL Bairstow+	lbw b Marshall	40	not out	9
JE Emburey	not out	13		
CM Old	c Garner b Marshall	6		
GR Dilley	b Garner	0		
Extras	(3b, 3lb, 1w, 4nb)	11	(5b, 11lb, 2w, 7nb)	25
	47 overs		75 overs	
Total		**143**		**227**

1st innings FoW: 9, 27, 28, 34, 52, 59, 89, 131, 140, 143
2nd innings FoW: 95, 126, 129, 162, 174, 203

MA Holding	10	4	34	2		23	2	62	2
CEH Croft	12	3	35	3		19	2	65	1
J Garner	14	4	41	3		1	0	1	0
MD Marshall	11	3	22	2		19	5	42	3
CL King						12	3	32	0
IVA Richards						1	1	0	0

WEST INDIES 1st innings   2nd innings

CG Greenidge	lbw b Botham	34
DL Haynes	b Emburey	42
IVA Richards*	b Old	31
SFAF Bacchus	c & b Dilley	11
AI Kallicharran	c Larkins b Dilley	37
CL King	c Bairstow b Gooch	12
DL Murray+	c Emburey b Dilley	14
MD Marshall	c Bairstow b Dilley	0
MA Holding	b Old	35
J Garner	c Emburey b Gooch	0
CEH Croft	not out	1
Extras	(2b, 9lb, 3w, 14nb)	28
	84.5 overs	
Total		**245**

1st innings FoW: 83, 105, 133, 142, 170, 198, 198, 207, 207, 245

CM Old	28.5	9	64	2
IT Botham	19	8	31	1
JE Emburey	6	0	25	1
GA Gooch	8	3	18	2

Australia

No. 562:	1st Test	
VENUE:	Lord's	
DATE:	28th August to 2nd Sep 1980	
TOSS WON BY:	Australia	
RESULT	Match drawn	

West Indies

No. 563:	1st Test	
VENUE:	Port-of-Spain (Trinidad)	
DATE:	13th-18th February 1981	
TOSS WON BY:	England	
RESULT:	W I won by an innings and 79 runs	

AUSTRALIA 1st innings / 2nd innings

Batsman	1st innings		2nd innings	
GM Wood	st Bairstow b Emburey	112	lbw b Old	8
BM Laird	c Bairstow b Old	24	c Bairstow b Old	6
GS Chappell*	c Gatting b Old	47	b Old	59
KJ Hughes	c Athey b Old	117	lbw b Botham	84
GN Yallop	lbw b Hendrick	2	not out	21
AR Border	not out	56		
RW Marsh+	not out	16		
RJ Bright				
DK Lillee				
AA Mallett				
LS Pascoe				
Extras	(1b, 8lb, 0w, 2nb)	11	(1b, 8lb, 0w, 2nb)	11
	134 overs		53.2 overs	
Total		**385**		**189**

1st innings FoW: 64, 150, 260, 267, 320
2nd innings FoW: 15, 28, 139, 189

Bowler								
CM Old	35	9	91	3	20	6	47	3
M Hendrick	30	6	67	1	15	4	53	0
IT Botham	22	2	89	0	9.2	1	43	1
JE Emburey	38	9	104	1	9	2	35	0
GA Gooch	8	3	16	0				
P Willey	1	0	7	0				

WEST INDIES 1st innings / 2nd innings

Batsman	1st innings		2nd innings
CG Greenidge	c Botham b Emburey	84	
DL Haynes	c & b Emburey	96	
IVA Richards	c Gower b Miller	29	
EH Mattis	c Miller b Emburey	0	
HA Gomes	c Downton b Old	5	
CH Lloyd*	b Emburey	64	
DA Murray+	c Botham b Emburey	46	
AME Roberts	not out	50	
MA Holding	lbw b Botham	26	
J Garner	lbw b Botham	4	
CEH Croft	not out	4	
Extras	(0b, 15lb, 0w, 3nb)	18	
	147 overs		
Total		**426**	

1st innings FoW: 168, 203, 203, 215, 257, 332, 348, 383, 393

Bowler				
GR Dilley	28	4	73	0
IT Botham	28	6	113	2
CM Old	16	4	49	1
JE Emburey	52	16	124	5
G Miller	18	4	42	1
GA Gooch	2	0	3	0
P Willey	3	1	4	0

ENGLAND 1st innings / 2nd innings

Batsman	1st innings		2nd innings	
GA Gooch	c Bright b Lillee	8	lbw b Lillee	16
G Boycott	c Marsh b Lillee	62	not out	128
CWJ Athey	b Lillee	9	c Laird b Pascoe	1
DI Gower	b Lillee	45	b Mallett	35
MW Gatting	lbw b Pascoe	12	not out	51
IT Botham*	c Wood b Pascoe	0		
P Willey	lbw b Pascoe	5		
DL Bairstow+	lbw b Pascoe	6		
JE Emburey	lbw b Pascoe	3		
CM Old	not out	24		
M Hendrick	c Border b Mallett	5		
Extras	(6b, 8lb, 0w, 12nb)	26	(3b, 2lb, 0w, 8nb)	13
	63.2 overs		82 overs	
Total		**205**		**244**

1st innings FoW: 10, 41, 137, 151, 158, 163, 164, 173, 200, 205
2nd innings FoW: 19, 43, 124

Bowler								
DK Lillee	15	4	43	4	19	5	53	1
LS Pascoe	18	5	59	5	17	1	73	1
GS Chappell	2	0	2	0				
RJ Bright	21	6	50	0	25	9	44	0
AA Mallett	7.2	3	25	1	21	2	61	1

ENGLAND 1st innings / 2nd innings

Batsman	1st innings		2nd innings	
GA Gooch	b Roberts	41	lbw b Holding	5
G Boycott	c Richards b Croft	30	c Haynes b Holding	70
BC Rose	c Haynes b Garner	10	c Murray b Holding	5
DI Gower	lbw b Croft	48	c Murray b Roberts	27
G Miller	c Murray b Croft	3	c Greenidge b Croft	8
IT Botham*	lbw b Croft	0	c Holding b Richards	16
P Willey	lbw b Garner	13	c Lloyd b Garner	21
PR Downton+	b Gomes	4	c Lloyd b Roberts	5
JE Emburey	not out	17	b Roberts	1
GR Dilley	b Croft	0	not out	1
CM Old	b Roberts	1	c (sub) b Garner	0
Extras	(4b, 4lb, 0w, 3nb)	11	(1b, 3lb, 0w, 6nb)	10
	78 overs		99 overs	
Total		**178**		**169**

1st innings FoW: 45, 63, 110, 121, 127, 143, 151, 163, 167, 178
2nd innings FoW: 19, 25, 86, 103, 134, 142, 163, 167, 169, 169

Bowler								
AME Roberts	13	3	41	2	21	7	41	3
MA Holding	11	3	29	0	18	6	38	3
CEH Croft	22	6	40	5	16	5	26	1
J Garner	23	8	37	2	25	10	31	2
IVA Richards	7	2	16	0	10	6	9	1
HA Gomes	2	1	4	1	9	4	14	0

No. 564:	3rd Test
VENUE:	Bridgetown (Barbados)
DATE:	13th-18th March 1981
TOSS WON BY:	England
RESULT:	West Indies won by 298 runs

No. 565:	4th Test
VENUE:	St. John's (Antigua)
DATE:	27th March to 1st April 1981
TOSS WON BY:	England
RESULT:	Match drawn

WEST INDIES 1st innings / 2nd innings (No. 564)

Batsman	1st innings		2nd innings	
CG Greenidge	c Gooch b Jackman	14		
DL Haynes	c Bairstow b Jackman	25	lbw b Dilley	0
IVA Richards	c Botham b Dilley	0	lbw b Botham	25
EH Mattis	lbw b Botham	16	c Boycott b Jackman	33
CH Lloyd*	c Gooch b Jackman	100	not out	182
HA Gomes	c Botham b Dilley	58	c Butcher b Jackman	24
DA Murray+	c Bairstow b Dilley	9	run out	34
AME Roberts	c Bairstow b Botham	14	lbw b Botham	66
J Garner	c Bairstow b Botham	15	c Bairstow b Botham	0
MA Holding	c Gatting b Botham	4	not out	5
CEH Croft	not out	0		
Extras	(4b, 6lb, 2w, 2nb)	14	(3b, 7lb, 0w, 0nb)	10
	90.1 overs		109 overs	
Total		**265**		**379**

1st innings FoW: 24, 25, 47, 65, 219, 224, 236, 258, 258, 265
2nd innings FoW: 0, 57, 71, 130, 212, 365, 365

Bowler	O	M	R	W	O	M	R	W
GR Dilley	23	7	51	3	25	3	111	1
IT Botham	25.1	5	77	4	29	5	102	3
RD Jackman	22	4	65	3	25	5	76	2
JE Emburey	18	4	45	0	24	7	57	0
GA Gooch	2	0	13	0				
P Willey					6	0	23	0

ENGLAND 1st innings / 2nd innings (No. 564)

Batsman	1st innings		2nd innings	
GA Gooch	b Garner	26	c Garner b Croft	116
G Boycott	b Holding	0	c Garner b Holding	1
MW Gatting	c Greenidge b Roberts	2	b Holding	0
DI Gower	c Mattis b Croft	17	b Richards	54
RO Butcher	c Richards b Croft	17	lbw b Richards	2
IT Botham*	c Murray b Holding	26	c Lloyd b Roberts	1
P Willey	not out	19	lbw b Croft	17
DL Bairstow+	c Mattis b Holding	0	c Murray b Croft	2
JE Emburey	c Lloyd b Roberts	0	b Garner	9
RD Jackman	c Roberts b Croft	7	b Garner	7
GR Dilley	c Gomes b Croft	0	not out	7
Extras	(1b, 1lb, 0w, 6nb)	8	(1b, 3lb, 0w, 4nb)	8
	47.5 overs		91.2 overs	
Total		**122**		**224**

1st innings FoW: 6, 11, 40, 55, 72, 94, 94, 97, 122, 122
2nd innings FoW: 2, 2, 122, 134, 139, 196, 198, 201, 213, 224

Bowler	O	M	R	W	O	M	R	W
AME Roberts	11	3	29	2	20	6	42	1
MA Holding	11	7	16	3	19	6	46	2
CEH Croft	13.5	2	39	4	19	1	65	3
J Garner	12	5	30	1	16.2	6	39	2
IVA Richards					17	6	24	2

ENGLAND 1st innings / 2nd innings (No. 565)

Batsman	1st innings		2nd innings	
GA Gooch	run out	33	c Greenidge b Richards	83
G Boycott	c Murray b Croft	38	not out	104
CWJ Athey	c Lloyd b Croft	2	c Richards b Croft	1
DI Gower	c Mattis b Holding	32	c Murray b Croft	22
RO Butcher	c Greenidge b Croft	20	not out	1
IT Botham*	c Lloyd b Croft	1		
P Willey	not out	102		
PR Downton+	c Murray b Garner	13		
JE Emburey	b Croft	10		
GB Stevenson	b Croft	0		
GR Dilley	c Murray b Holding	2		
Extras	(6b, 7lb, 1w, 3nb)	17	(11b, 3lb, 0w, 9nb)	23
	90.2 overs		93 overs	
Total		**271**		**234**

1st innings FoW: 60, 70, 95, 135, 138, 138, 176, 233, 235, 271
2nd innings FoW: 144, 146, 217

Bowler	O	M	R	W	O	M	R	W
AME Roberts	22	4	59	0	17	5	39	0
MA Holding	18.2	4	51	2	9	2	21	0
J Garner	16	5	44	1	15	3	33	0
CEH Croft	25	5	74	6	16	4	39	2
IVA Richards	9	4	26	0	22	7	54	1
HA Gomes					13	5	21	0
EH Mattis					1	0	4	0

WEST INDIES 1st innings / 2nd innings (No. 565)

Batsman	1st innings		2nd innings	
CG Greenidge	c Athey b Stevenson	63		
DL Haynes	c Downton b Botham	4		
IVA Richards	c Embury b Dilley	114		
EH Mattis	c Butcher b Botham	71		
HA Gomes	c Gower b Botham	12		
CH Lloyd*	c Downton b Stevenson	58		
DA Murray+	c Boycott b Botham	1		
AME Roberts	b Stevenson	13		
J Garner	c Butcher b Dilley	46		
MA Holding	not out	58		
CEH Croft	not out	17		
Extras	(1b, 7lb, 1w, 2nb)	11		
	155 overs			
Total		**468**		

1st innings FoW: 12, 133, 241, 268, 269, 271, 296, 379, 401

Bowler	O	M	R	W
GR Dilley	25	5	99	2
IT Botham	37	6	127	4
GB Stevenson	33	5	111	3
JE Emburey	35	12	85	0
P Willey	20	8	30	0
GA Gooch	2	2	0	0
G Boycott	3	2	5	0

West Indies | ## Australia

	West Indies	Australia
	No. 566: 5th Test	No. 567: 1st Test
VENUE:	Kingston (Jamaica)	Trent Bridge
DATE:	10th-15th April 1981	18th-21st June 1981
TOSS WON BY:	West Indies	Australia
RESULT:	Match drawn	Australia won by 4 wickets

ENGLAND 1st innings / 2nd innings (West Indies match)

Batsman	1st innings		2nd innings	
GA Gooch	c Murray b Holding	153	c Lloyd b Marshall	3
G Boycott	c Murray b Garner	40	c Garner b Croft	12
CWJ Athey	b Holding	3	c Murray b Holding	1
DI Gower	b Croft	22	not out	154
P Willey	c Murray b Marshall	4	c Greenidge b Richards	67
RO Butcher	b Garner	32	lbw b Croft	0
IT Botham*	c Greenidge b Marshall	13	c Garner b Holding	16
PR Downton+	c Croft b Holding	0	not out	26
JE Emburey	b Holding	1		
RD Jackman	c Haynes b Holding	0		
GR Dilley	not out	1		
Extras	(8b, 0lb, 0w, 8nb)	16	(6b, 13lb, 0w, 4nb)	23
	83 overs		128 overs	
Total		**285**		**302**

1st innings FoW: 93, 148, 196, 210, 249, 275, 283, 283, 284, 285
2nd innings FoW: 5, 10, 32, 168, 168, 215

Bowler	O	M	R	W	O	M	R	W
MA Holding	18	3	56	5	28	7	58	2
MD Marshall	16	2	49	2	5	0	15	1
CEH Croft	17	4	92	1	29	7	80	2
J Garner	20	4	43	2	24	7	46	0
IVA Richards	12	2	29	0	23	8	48	1
HA Gomes					13	3	18	0
EH Mattis					5	1	10	0
DL Haynes					1	0	4	0

WEST INDIES 1st innings / 2nd innings

Batsman	1st innings		2nd innings
CG Greenidge	c Botham b Dilley	62	
DL Haynes	b Willey	84	
IVA Richards	c Downton b Dilley	15	
EH Mattis	c (sub) b Dilley	34	
CH Lloyd*	c Downton b Jackman	95	
HA Gomes	not out	90	
DA Murray+	c Gooch b Emburey	14	
MD Marshall	b Emburey	15	
J Garner	c (sub) b Dilley	19	
MA Holding	c Downton b Botham	0	
CEH Croft	c (sub) b Botham	0	
Extras	(0b, 8lb, 1w, 5nb)	14	
	163.1 overs		
Total		**442**	

1st innings FoW: 116, 136, 179, 227, 345, 372, 415, 441, 442, 442

Bowler	O	M	R	W
IT Botham	26.1	9	73	2
RD Jackman	26.2	6	57	1
GA Gooch	8	3	20	0
JE Emburey	56	23	108	2
P Willey	18	3	54	1

ENGLAND 1st innings / 2nd innings (Australia match)

Batsman	1st innings		2nd innings	
GA Gooch	c Wood b Lillee	10	c Yallop b Lillee	6
G Boycott	c Border b Alderman	27	c Marsh b Alderman	4
RA Woolmer	c Wood b Lillee	0	c Marsh b Alderman	0
DI Gower	c Yallop b Lillee	26	c (sub) b Lillee	28
MW Gatting	lbw b Hogg	52	lbw b Alderman	15
P Willey	c Border b Alderman	10	lbw b Lillee	13
IT Botham*	b Alderman	1	c Border b Lillee	33
PR Downton+	c Yallop b Alderman	8	lbw b Alderman	3
GR Dilley	b Hogg	34	c Marsh b Alderman	13
RGD Willis	c Marsh b Hogg	0	c Chappell b Lillee	1
M Hendrick	not out	6	not out	0
Extras	(0b, 6lb, 1w, 4nb)	11	(0b, 8lb, 0w, 1nb)	9
	56.4 overs		38.4 overs	
Total		**185**		**125**

1st innings FoW: 13, 13, 57, 67, 92, 96, 116, 159, 159, 185
2nd innings FoW: 12, 12, 13, 39, 61, 94, 109, 113, 125, 125

Bowler	O	M	R	W	O	M	R	W
DK Lillee	13	3	34	3	16.4	2	46	5
TM Alderman	24	7	68	4	19	3	62	5
RM Hogg	11.4	1	47	3	3	1	8	0
GF Lawson	8	3	25	0				

AUSTRALIA 1st innings / 2nd innings

Batsman	1st innings		2nd innings	
GM Wood	lbw b Dilley	0	c Woolmer b Willis	8
J Dyson	c Woolmer b Willis	5	c Downton b Dilley	38
GN Yallop	b Hendrick	13	c Gatting b Botham	6
KJ Hughes*	lbw b Willis	7	lbw b Dilley	22
TM Chappell	b Hendrick	17	not out	20
AR Border	c & b Botham	63	b Dilley	20
RW Marsh+	c Boycott b Willis	19	lbw b Dilley	0
GF Lawson	c Gower b Botham	14	not out	5
DK Lillee	c Downton b Dilley	12		
RM Hogg	c Boycott b Dilley	0		
TM Alderman	not out	12		
Extras	(4b, 8lb, 1w, 4nb)	17	(1b, 6lb, 0w, 6nb)	13
	86.5 overs		54.1 overs	
Total		**179**		**132**

1st innings FoW: 0, 21, 21, 33, 64, 89, 110, 147, 153, 179
2nd innings FoW: 20, 40, 77, 80, 122, 122

Bowler	O	M	R	W	O	M	R	W
GR Dilley	20	7	38	3	11.1	4	24	4
RGD Willis	30	14	47	3	13	2	28	1
M Hendrick	20	7	43	2	20	7	33	0
IT Botham	16.5	6	34	2	10	1	34	1

No. 568: 2nd Test
VENUE: Lord's
DATE: 2nd-7th July 1981
TOSS WON BY: Australia
RESULT: Match drawn

No. 569: 3rd Test
VENUE: Headingley
DATE: 16th-21st July 1981
TOSS WON BY: Australia
RESULT: England won by 18 runs

ENGLAND 1st innings			2nd innings	
GA Gooch	c Yallop b Lawson	44	lbw b Lawson	20
G Boycott	c Alderman b Lawson	17	c Marsh b Lillee	60
RA Woolmer	c Marsh b Lawson	21	lbw b Alderman	9
DI Gower	c Marsh b Lawson	27	c Alderman b Lillee	89
MW Gatting	lbw b Bright	59	c Wood b Bright	16
P Willey	c Border b Alderman	82	b Bright	0
JE Emburey	run out	31	c Chappell b Bright	12
IT Botham*	lbw b Lawson	0	not out	27
RW Taylor+	c Hughes b Lawson	0	b Lillee	9
GR Dilley	not out	7		
RGD Willis	c Wood b Lawson	5		
Extras	(2b, 3lb, 3w, 10nb)	18	(2b, 8lb, 0w, 13nb)	23
Total	124.1 overs	**311**	98.4 overs	**265**

1st innings FoW: 60, 65, 134, 187, 284, 293, 293, 293, 298, 311
2nd innings FoW: 31, 55, 178, 217, 217, 217, 242, 265

DK Lillee	35.4	7	102	0	26.4	8	82	3
TM Alderman	30.2	7	79	1	17	2	42	1
GF Lawson	43.1	14	81	7	19	6	51	1
RJ Bright	15	7	31	1	36	18	67	3

AUSTRALIA 1st innings			2nd innings	
GM Wood	c Taylor b Willis	44	not out	62
J Dyson	c Gower b Botham	7	lbw b Dilley	1
GN Yallop	b Dilley	1	c Botham b Willis	3
KJ Hughes*	c Willis b Emburey	42	lbw b Dilley	4
TM Chappell	c Taylor b Dilley	2	c Taylor b Botham	5
AR Border	c Gatting b Botham	64	not out	12
RW Marsh+	lbw b Dilley	47		
RJ Bright	lbw b Emburey	33		
GF Lawson	lbw b Willis	5		
DK Lillee	not out	40		
TM Alderman	c Taylor b Willis	5		
Extras	(6b, 11lb, 6w, 32nb)	55	(0b, 0lb, 1w, 2nb)	3
Total	118.4 overs	**345**	48.5 overs	**90**

1st innings FoW: 62, 62, 69, 81, 167, 244, 257, 268, 314, 345
2nd innings FoW: 2, 11, 17, 62

RGD Willis	27.4	9	50	3	12	3	35	1
GR Dilley	30	8	106	3	7.5	1	18	2
IT Botham	26	8	71	2	8	3	10	1
GA Gooch	10	4	28	0				
JE Emburey	25	12	35	2	21	10	24	0

AUSTRALIA 1st innings			2nd innings	
J Dyson	b Dilley	102	c Taylor b Willis	34
GM Wood	lbw b Botham	34	c Taylor b Botham	10
TM Chappell	c Taylor b Willey	27	c Taylor b Willis	8
KJ Hughes*	c & b Botham	89	c Botham b Willis	0
RJ Bright	b Dilley	7	c Gatting b Willis	0
GN Yallop	c Taylor b Botham	58	b Old	0
AR Border	lbw b Botham	8	c Dilley b Willis	4
RW Marsh+	b Botham	28	b Willis	19
GF Lawson	c Taylor b Botham	13	c Taylor b Willis	1
DK Lillee	not out	3	c Gatting b Willis	17
TM Alderman	not out	0	not out	0
Extras	(4b, 13lb, 3w, 12nb)	32	(0b, 3lb, 1w, 14nb)	18
Total	155.2 overs	**401**	36.1 overs	**111**

1st innings FoW: 55, 149, 196, 220, 332, 354, 357, 396, 401
2nd innings FoW: 13, 56, 58, 58, 65, 68, 74, 75, 110, 111

RGD Willis	30	8	72	0	15.1	3	43	8
CM Old	43	14	91	0	9	1	21	1
GR Dilley	27	4	78	2	2	0	11	0
IT Botham	39.2	11	95	6	7	3	14	1
P Willey	13	2	31	1	3	1	4	0
G Boycott	3	2	2	0				

ENGLAND 1st innings			2nd innings	
GA Gooch	lbw b Alderman	2	c Alderman b Lillee	0
G Boycott	b Lawson	12	lbw b Alderman	46
JM Brearley*	c Marsh b Alderman	10	c Alderman b Lillee	14
DI Gower	c Marsh b Lawson	24	c Border b Alderman	9
MW Gatting	lbw b Lillee	15	lbw b Alderman	1
P Willey	lbw b Lawson	8	c Dyson b Lillee	33
IT Botham	c Marsh b Lillee	50	not out	149
RW Taylor+	c Marsh b Lillee	5	c Bright b Alderman	1
GR Dilley	c & b Lillee	13	b Alderman	56
CM Old	c Border b Alderman	0	b Lawson	29
RGD Willis	not out	1	c Border b Alderman	2
Extras	(6b, 11lb, 6w, 11nb)	34	(5b, 3lb, 3w, 5nb)	16
Total	50.5 overs	**174**	87.3 overs	**356**

1st innings FoW: 12, 40, 42, 84, 87, 112, 148, 166, 167, 174
2nd innings FoW: 0, 18, 37, 41, 105, 133, 135, 252, 319, 356

DK Lillee	18.5	7	49	4	25	6	94	3
TM Alderman	19	4	59	3	35.3	6	135	6
GF Lawson	13	3	32	3	23	4	96	1
RJ Bright					4	0	15	0

No. 570: 4th Test
VENUE: Edgbaston
DATE: 30th July to 2nd August 1981
TOSS WON BY: England
RESULT: England won by 29 runs

No. 571: 5th Test
VENUE: Old Trafford
DATE: 13th-17th August 1981
TOSS WON BY: England
RESULT: England won by 103 runs

Match No. 570 — Edgbaston

ENGLAND	1st innings		2nd innings	
G Boycott	c Marsh b Alderman	13	c Marsh b Bright	29
JM Brearley*	c Border b Lillee	48	lbw b Lillee	13
DI Gower	c Hogg b Alderman	0	c Border b Bright	23
GA Gooch	c Marsh b Bright	21	b Bright	21
MW Gatting	c Alderman b Lillee	21	b Bright	39
P Willey	b Bright	16	b Bright	5
IT Botham	b Alderman	26	c Marsh b Lillee	3
JE Emburey	b Hogg	3	c Marsh b Alderman	23
RW Taylor+	b Alderman	0	not out	37
CM Old	not out	11	lbw b Alderman	8
RGD Willis	c Marsh b Alderman	13	c Marsh b Alderman	2
Extras	(1b, 5lb, 1w, 10nb)	17	(0b, 6lb, 1w, 9nb)	16
Total	69.1 overs	**189**	92 overs	**219**

1st innings FoW: 29, 29, 60, 101, 126, 145, 161, 161, 165, 189
2nd innings FoW: 18, 52, 89, 98, 110, 115, 154, 167, 217, 219

DK Lillee	18	4	61	2	26	9	51	2
TM Alderman	23.1	8	42	5	22	5	65	3
RM Hogg	16	3	49	1	10	3	19	0
RJ Bright	12	4	20	2	34	17	68	5

AUSTRALIA	1st innings		2nd innings	
GM Wood	run out	38	lbw b Old	2
J Dyson	b Old	1	lbw b Willis	13
AR Border	c Taylor b Old	2	c Gatting b Emburey	40
RJ Bright	lbw b Botham	27	c Emburey b Willis	5
KJ Hughes*	lbw b Old	47	c Botham b Emburey	30
GN Yallop	b Emburey	30	b Botham	10
MF Kent	c Willis b Emburey	46	b Botham	4
RW Marsh+	b Emburey	2	lbw b Botham	0
DK Lillee	b Emburey	18	c Taylor b Botham	3
RM Hogg	run out	0	not out	0
TM Alderman	not out	3	b Botham	0
Extras	(4b, 19lb, 0w, 21nb)	44	(1b, 2lb, 0w, 11nb)	14
Total	86.5 overs	**258**	67 overs	**121**

1st innings FoW: 5, 14, 62, 115, 166, 203, 220, 253, 253, 258
2nd innings FoW: 2, 19, 29, 87, 105, 114, 114, 120, 121, 121

RGD Willis	19	3	63	0	20	6	37	2
CM Old	21	8	44	3	11	4	19	1
JE Emburey	26.5	12	43	4	22	10	40	2
IT Botham	20	1	64	1	14	9	11	5

Match No. 571 — Old Trafford

ENGLAND	1st innings		2nd innings	
GA Gooch	lbw b Lillee	10	b Alderman	5
G Boycott	c Marsh b Alderman	10	lbw b Alderman	37
CJ Tavare	c Alderman b Whitney	69	c Kent b Alderman	78
DI Gower	c Yallop b Whitney	23	c Bright b Lillee	1
JM Brearley*	lbw b Alderman	2	lbw b Alderman	11
MW Gatting	c Border b Lillee	32	c Marsh b Alderman	3
IT Botham	c Bright b Lillee	0	c Marsh b Whitney	118
APE Knott+	c Border b Alderman	13	c Dyson b Lillee	59
JE Emburey	c Border b Alderman	1	c Kent b Whitney	57
PJW Allott	not out	52	c Hughes b Bright	14
RGD Willis	c Hughes b Lillee	11	not out	5
Extras	(0b, 6lb, 2w, 0nb)	8	(1b, 12lb, 0w, 3nb)	16
Total	86.1 overs	**231**	151.4 overs	**404**

1st innings FoW: 19, 25, 57, 62, 109, 109, 131, 137, 175, 231
2nd innings FoW: 7, 79, 80, 98, 104, 253, 282, 356, 396, 404

DK Lillee	24.1	8	55	4	46	13	137	2
TM Alderman	29	5	88	4	52	19	109	5
MR Whitney	17	3	50	2	27	6	74	2
RJ Bright	16	6	30	0	26.4	12	68	1

AUSTRALIA	1st innings		2nd innings	
GM Wood	lbw b Allott	19	c Knott b Allott	6
J Dyson	c Botham b Willis	0	run out	5
KJ Hughes*	lbw b Willis	4	lbw b Botham	43
GN Yallop	c Botham b Willis	0	b Emburey	114
MF Kent	c Knott b Emburey	52	not out	123
AR Border	c Gower b Botham	11	c Brearley b Emburey	2
RW Marsh+	c Botham b Willis	1	c Knott b Willis	47
RJ Bright	c Knott b Botham	22	c Knott b Willis	5
DK Lillee	c Gooch b Botham	13	c Botham b Allott	28
MR Whitney	b Allott	0	lbw b Botham	0
TM Alderman	not out	2	c Gatting b Willis	0
Extras	(0b, 0lb, 0w, 6nb)	6	(0b, 9lb, 2w, 18nb)	29
Total	30.2 overs	**130**	135.5 overs	**402**

1st innings FoW: 20, 24, 24, 24, 58, 59, 104, 125, 126, 130
2nd innings FoW: 7, 24, 119, 198, 206, 296, 322, 373, 378, 402

RGD Willis	14	0	63	4	30.5	2	96	3
PJW Allott	6	1	17	2	17	3	71	2
IT Botham	6.2	1	28	3	36	16	86	2
JE Emburey	4	0	16	1	49	9	107	2
MW Gatting					3	1	13	0

No. 572:	6th Test
VENUE:	The Oval
DATE:	27th August to 1st Sep 1981
TOSS WON BY:	England
RESULT:	Match drawn

No. 573:	1st Test
VENUE:	Bombay (Wankhede)
DATE:	27th November to 1st Dec 1981
TOSS WON BY:	India
RESULT:	India won by 138 runs

AUSTRALIA 1st innings / 2nd innings

Batsman	1st innings	Runs	2nd innings	Runs
GM Wood	c Brearley b Botham	66	c Knott b Hendrick	21
MF Kent	c Gatting b Botham	54	c Brearley b Botham	7
KJ Hughes*	hit wkt b Botham	31	lbw b Hendrick	6
GN Yallop	c Botham b Willis	0	b Hendrick	35
AR Border	not out	106	c Tavare b Emburey	84
DM Wellham	b Willis	24	lbw b Botham	103
RW Marsh+	c Botham b Willis	12	c Gatting b Botham	52
RJ Bright	c Brearley b Botham	3	b Botham	11
DK Lillee	b Willis	11	not out	8
TM Alderman	b Botham	0	c Botham b Hendrick	0
MR Whitney	b Botham	4		
Extras	(4b, 6lb, 1w, 4nb)	15	(1b, 8lb, 1w, 7nb)	17
Total	132 overs	352	104.2 overs	344

1st innings FoW: 120, 125, 169, 199, 260, 280, 303, 319, 320, 352
2nd innings FoW: 26, 36, 41, 104, 205, 291, 332, 343, 344

Bowler	O	M	R	W	O	M	R	W
RGD Willis	31	6	91	4	10	0	41	0
M Hendrick	31	8	63	0	29.2	6	82	4
IT Botham	47	13	125	6	42	9	128	4
JE Emburey	23	2	58	0	23	3	76	1

INDIA 1st innings / 2nd innings

Batsman	1st innings	Runs	2nd innings	Runs
SM Gavaskar*	c Taylor b Botham	55	c Taylor b Botham	14
K Srikkanth	c Fletcher b Willis	0	run out	13
DB Vengsarkar	c Tavare b Dilley	17	c Tavare b Botham	5
GR Viswanath	c Boycott b Botham	8	c Taylor b Botham	37
SM Patil	lbw b Botham	17	lbw b Botham	13
K Azad	c (sub) b Underwood	14	lbw b Dilley	33
N Kapil Dev	c Taylor b Botham	38	lbw b Emburey	17
SMH Kirmani+	lbw b Dilley	12	lbw b Willis	46
S Madan Lal	c Taylor b Dilley	0	c Taylor b Emburey	0
RJ Shastri	not out	3	not out	17
DR Doshi	c Taylor b Dilley	0	b Botham	7
Extras	(0b, 5lb, 0w, 10nb)	15	(8b, 8lb, 0w, 9nb)	25
Total	57 overs	179	77.3 overs	227

1st innings FoW: 1, 40, 70, 104, 112, 164, 164, 168, 179, 179
2nd innings FoW: 19, 24, 43, 72, 90, 138, 154, 157, 203, 227

Bowler	O	M	R	W	O	M	R	W
RGD Willis	12	5	33	1	13	4	31	1
IT Botham	28	6	72	4	22.3	3	61	5
GR Dilley	13	1	47	4	18	5	61	1
DL Underwood	4	2	12	1	11	4	14	0
JE Emburey					13	2	35	2

ENGLAND 1st innings / 2nd innings

Batsman	1st innings	Runs	2nd innings	Runs
G Boycott	c Yallop b Lillee	137	lbw b Lillee	0
W Larkins	c Alderman b Lillee	34	c Alderman b Lillee	24
CJ Tavare	c Marsh b Lillee	24	c Kent b Whitney	8
MW Gatting	b Lillee	53	c Kent b Lillee	56
JM Brearley*	c Bright b Alderman	0	c Kent b Alderman	13
PWG Parker	c Kent b Alderman	0	c Marsh b Alderman	51
IT Botham	c Yallop b Lillee	3	lbw b Alderman	16
APE Knott+	b Lillee	36	not out	70
JE Emburey	lbw b Lillee	0	not out	5
RGD Willis	b Alderman	3		
M Hendrick	not out	0		
Extras	(0b, 9lb, 3w, 12nb)	24	(2b, 5lb, 2w, 9nb)	18
Total	110.4 overs	314	95 overs	261

1st innings FoW: 61, 131, 246, 248, 248, 256, 293, 293, 302, 314
2nd innings FoW: 0, 18, 88, 101, 127, 144, 237

Bowler	O	M	R	W	O	M	R	W
DK Lillee	31.4	4	89	7	30	10	70	4
TM Alderman	35	4	84	3	19	6	60	2
MR Whitney	23	3	76	0	11	4	46	1
RJ Bright	21	6	41	0	27	12	50	0
GN Yallop					8	2	17	0

ENGLAND 1st innings / 2nd innings

Batsman	1st innings	Runs	2nd innings	Runs
GA Gooch	b Madan Lal	2	c Kirmani b Kapil Dev	1
G Boycott	c Srikkanth b Azad	60	lbw b Madan Lal	3
CJ Tavare	c Shastri b Doshi	56	c Gavaskar b Kapil Dev	0
DI Gower	run out	5	lbw b Kapil Dev	20
KWR Fletcher*	lbw b Doshi	15	lbw b Madan Lal	4
IT Botham	c Gavaskar b Doshi	7	c Azad b Kapil Dev	29
JE Emburey	lbw b Doshi	0	c Gavaskar b Madan Lal	1
GR Dilley	b Shastri	0	b Madan Lal	9
RW Taylor+	not out	9	b Madan Lal	1
DL Underw'd	c Kirmani b Kapil Dev	8	not out	13
RGD Willis	c Gavaskar b Doshi	1	c Kirmani b Kapil Dev	13
Extras	(1b, 2lb, 0w, 0nb)	3	(4b, 3lb, 0w, 2nb)	9
Total	100.1 overs	166	26.2 overs	102

1st innings FoW: 3, 95, 105, 131, 143, 146, 147, 147, 163, 163
2nd innings FoW: 2, 4, 28, 29, 42, 50, 73, 74, 75, 102

Bowler	O	M	R	W	O	M	R	W
N Kapil Dev	22	10	29	1	13.2	0	70	5
S Madan Lal	12	2	24	1	12	6	23	5
DR Doshi	29.1	12	39	5	1	1	0	0
RJ Shastri	19	6	27	1				
SM Patil	3	0	9	0				
K Azad	15	4	35	1				

No. 574: 2nd Test
VENUE: Bangalore
DATE: 9th-14th December 1981
TOSS WON BY: England
RESULT: Match drawn

No. 575: 3rd Test
VENUE: Delhi
DATE: 23rd-28th December 1981
TOSS WON BY: England
RESULT: Match drawn

2nd Test — Bangalore

ENGLAND	1st innings		2nd innings	
GA Gooch	c Gavaskar b Shastri	58	lbw b Kapil Dev	40
G Boycott	c Gavaskar b Kapil Dev	36	b Doshi	50
CJ Tavare	lbw b Madan Lal	22	c Patil b Shastri	31
DI Gower	lbw b Shastri	82	not out	34
JK Lever	lbw b Kapil Dev	1	not out	12
KWR Fletcher*	c Kirmani b Shastri	25		
IT Botham	c Madan Lal b Doshi	55		
MW Gatting	lbw b Kapil Dev	29		
GR Dilley	c Gavaskar b Shastri	52		
RW Taylor+	c Kapil Dev b Doshi	33		
DL Underw'd	not out	2		
Extras	(0b, 2lb, 0w, 3nb)	5	(0b, 6lb, 0w, 1nb)	7
Total	158 overs	400	69 overs	174

1st innings FoW: 88, 96, 180, 181, 223, 230, 278, 324, 393, 400
2nd innings FoW: 59, 105, 152

N Kapil Dev	40	3	136	3		12	2	49	1
S Madan Lal	24	7	46	1		4	2	14	0
DR Doshi	39	15	83	2		21	8	37	1
K Azad	12	1	47	0		12	3	36	0
RJ Shastri	43	14	83	4		20	7	31	1

INDIA	1st innings		2nd innings
SM Gavaskar*	c & b Underwood	172	
K Srikkanth	c Gooch b Botham	65	
DB Vengsarkar	c Taylor b Lever	43	
GR Viswanath	lbw b Lever	3	
RJ Shastri	lbw b Lever	1	
SM Patil	lbw b Lever	17	
K Azad	c Fletcher b Underwood	24	
N Kapil Dev	c Taylor b Lever	59	
SMH Kirmani+	lbw b Botham	9	
S Madan Lal	not out	7	
DR Doshi	c Boycott b Underwood	0	
Extras	(2b, 15lb, 3w, 8nb)	28	
Total	150 overs	428	

1st innings FoW: 102, 195, 208, 214, 242, 284, 376, 412, 428, 428

IT Botham	47	9	137	2
GR Dilley	24	4	75	0
JK Lever	36	9	100	5
DL Underwood	43	21	88	3

3rd Test — Delhi

ENGLAND	1st innings		2nd innings	
GA Gooch	c Kapil Dev b Doshi	71	not out	20
G Boycott	c Madan Lal b Doshi	105	not out	34
CJ Tavare	b Madan Lal	149		
DI Gower	lbw b Madan Lal	0		
KWR Fletcher*	b Patil	51		
IT Botham	c Azad b Madan Lal	66		
MW Gatting	b Madan Lal	5		
RW Taylor+	lbw b Madan Lal	0		
JK Lever	b Kapil Dev	2		
DL Underw'd	not out	2		
RGD Willis				
Extras	(0b, 15lb, 0w, 10nb)	25	(9b, 0lb, 0w, 5nb)	14
Total	156.4 overs	476	19 overs	68

1st innings FoW: 132, 248, 248, 368, 459, 465, 465, 474, 476

N Kapil Dev	40.4	5	126	1		4	1	18	0
S Madan Lal	32	4	85	5		3	1	4	0
DR Doshi	40	15	68	2					
RJ Shastri	27	3	109	0					
K Azad	9	2	35	0					
SM Patil	8	1	28	1		3	1	10	0
K Srikkanth						6	1	10	0
SM Gavaskar						3	0	12	0

INDIA	1st innings		2nd innings
SM Gavaskar*	c Taylor b Lever	46	
K Srikkanth	b Willis	6	
DB Vengsarkar	c Fletcher b Underwood	8	
GR Viswanath	b Botham	107	
SM Patil	b Willis	31	
K Azad	st Taylor b Underwood	16	
N Kapil Dev	c Gooch b Botham	16	
RJ Shastri	lbw b Gooch	93	
SMH Kirmani+	lbw b Lever	67	
S Madan Lal	b Gooch	44	
DR Doshi	not out	0	
Extras	(20b, 8lb, 4w, 21nb)	53	
Total	160.1 overs	487	

1st innings FoW: 11, 41, 89, 174, 213, 237, 254, 382, 486, 487

RGD Willis	26	3	99	2
JK Lever	37	7	104	2
DL Underwood	48	18	97	2
IT Botham	41	6	122	2
GA Gooch	8.1	1	12	2

No. 576: 4th Test
VENUE: Calcutta
DATE: 1st-6th January 1982
TOSS WON BY: England
RESULT: Match drawn

No. 577: 5th Test
VENUE: Madras (Chepauk)
DATE: 13th-18th January 1982
TOSS WON BY: England
RESULT: Match drawn

ENGLAND 1st innings / 2nd innings

Batsman	1st innings		2nd innings	
GA Gooch	c Viswanath b Doshi	47	b Doshi	63
G Boycott	c Kirmani b Kapil Dev	18	lbw b Madan Lal	6
CJ Tavare	c Kirmani b Kapil Dev	7	run out	25
DI Gower	c Kirmani b Shastri	11	run out	74
KWR Fletcher*	lbw b Madan Lal	69	c Yadav b Doshi	31
IT Botham	c Gavaskar b Kapil Dev	58	not out	60
DL Underw'd	c Patil b Kapil Dev	13	not out	2
MW Gatting	c Kirmani b Kapil Dev	0		
JE Emburey	lbw b Kapil Dev	1		
RW Taylor+	c Vengsarkar b Doshi	6		
RGD Willis	not out	11		
Extras	(0b, 3lb, 0w, 4nb)	7	(0b, 4lb, 0w, 0nb)	4
Total	108.2 overs	248	90 overs	265

1st innings FoW: 25, 39, 68, 95, 188, 216, 218, 224, 230, 248
2nd innings FoW: 24, 88, 107, 154, 259

Bowler	O	M	R	W	O	M	R	W
N Kapil Dev	31	6	91	6	21	3	81	0
S Madan Lal	20	4	58	1	19	3	58	1
DR Doshi	19.2	8	28	2	27	5	63	2
NS Yadav	17	7	42	0	3	0	11	0
RJ Shastri	21	10	22	1	17	4	35	0
SM Patil					3	0	13	0

INDIA 1st innings / 2nd innings

Batsman	1st innings		2nd innings	
SM Gavaskar*	b Underwood	42	not out	83
K Srikkanth	b Underwood	10	c Botham b Emburey	25
DB Vengsarkar	c Taylor b Botham	70	c Tavare b Fletcher	32
GR Viswanath	c & b Emburey	15	c Gooch b Emburey	0
SM Patil	c Fletcher b Emburey	0	not out	17
N Kapil Dev	c Tavare b Underwood	22		
RJ Shastri	run out	8		
SMH Kirmani+	b Botham	10		
S Madan Lal	c Gooch b Willis	1		
NS Yadav	c Taylor b Willis	5		
DR Doshi	not out	7		
Extras	(2b, 4lb, 1w, 11nb)	18	(0b, 2lb, 0w, 11nb)	13
Total	100 overs	208	83 overs	170

1st innings FoW: 33, 83, 117, 117, 143, 180, 184, 187, 196, 208
2nd innings FoW: 48, 117, 120

Bowler	O	M	R	W	O	M	R	W
RGD Willis	14	3	28	2	6	0	21	0
IT Botham	27	8	63	2	11	3	26	0
DL Underwood	29	13	45	3	31	18	38	0
JE Emburey	24	11	44	2	30	11	62	2
GA Gooch	6	1	10	0	2	0	4	0
KWR Fletcher					3	1	6	1

INDIA 1st innings / 2nd innings

Batsman	1st innings		2nd innings	
SM Gavaskar*	c Taylor b Willis	25	c Botham b Willis	11
Pran Roy	c Taylor b Dilley	6	not out	60
DB Vengsarkar	retired hurt	71	run out	31
GR Viswanath	b Willis	222	c Botham b Underwood	25
Y'pal Sharma	c Tavare b Botham	140	not out	15
N Kapil Dev	not out	6		
A Malhotra				
SMH Kirmani+				
RJ Shastri				
S Madan Lal				
DR Doshi				
Extras	(0b, 1lb, 1w, 9nb)	11	(12b, 1lb, 0w, 5nb)	18
Total	152.1 overs	481	50 overs	160

1st innings FoW: 19, 51, 466, 481
2nd innings FoW: 19, 69, 122

Bowler	O	M	R	W	O	M	R	W
RGD Willis	28.1	7	79	2	7	2	15	1
IT Botham	31	10	83	1	8	1	29	0
GR Dilley	31	4	87	1	5	1	13	0
PJW Allott	31	4	135	0				
DL Underwood	22	7	59	0	15	8	30	1
GA Gooch	9	2	27	0	8	2	24	0
KWR Fletcher					1	0	9	0
RW Taylor					2	0	6	0
CJ Tavare					2	0	11	0
DI Gower					1	0	1	0
MW Gatting					1	0	4	0

ENGLAND 1st innings / 2nd innings

Batsman	1st innings	
GA Gooch	c & b Shastri	127
CJ Tavare	c Gavaskar b Doshi	35
KWR Fletcher*	b Doshi	3
DI Gower	lbw b Shastri	64
IT Botham	c Kirmani b Shastri	52
MW Gatting	c Viswanath b Doshi	0
GR Dilley	c & b Kapil Dev	8
RW Taylor+	b Doshi	8
DL Underw'd	c Kirmani b Kapil Dev	0
PJW Allott	c Roy b Kapil Dev	6
RGD Willis	not out	1
Extras	(1b, 11lb, 0w, 12nb)	24
Total	155.5 overs	328

1st innings FoW: 155, 164, 195, 279, 283, 307, 307, 311, 320, 328

Bowler	O	M	R	W
N Kapil Dev	25.5	7	88	3
S Madan Lal	9	1	41	0
RJ Shastri	63	23	104	3
DR Doshi	57	31	69	4
SM Gavaskar	1	0	2	0

India | Sri Lanka

ENGLAND 1st innings

Batsman	Dismissal	Runs	2nd innings
GA Gooch	b Doshi	58	
CJ Tavare	b Doshi	24	
KWR Fletcher*	b Kapil Dev	14	
DI Gower	lbw b Kapil Dev	85	
IT Botham	st Kirmani b Doshi	142	
MW Gatting	c Madan Lal b Doshi	32	
GR Dilley	lbw b Shastri	1	
RW Taylor+	b Shastri	0	
JE Emburey	run out	2	
DL Underw'd	not out	0	
RGD Willis			
Extras	(2b, 5lb, 6w, 7nb)	20	
	115.2 overs		
Total		**378**	

1st innings FoW: 82, 89, 121, 248, 349, 354, 354, 360, 378

Bowler	O	M	R	W
N Kapil Dev	34	3	147	2
S Madan Lal	24	4	79	0
DR Doshi	34.2	8	81	4
RJ Shastri	23	6	51	2

INDIA 1st innings

Batsman	Dismissal	Runs	2nd innings
SM Gavaskar*	run out	52	
Pran Roy	b Botham	5	
DB Vengsarkar	c Fletcher b Dilley	46	
GR Viswanath	c Gower b Willis	74	
Y'pal Sharma	not out	55	
A Malhotra	lbw b Willis	0	
RJ Shastri	c Taylor b Willis	2	
N Kapil Dev	c Dilley b Gower	116	
SMH Kirmani+	not out	1	
S Madan Lal			
DR Doshi			
Extras	(1b, 7lb, 2w, 16nb)	26	
	122 overs		
Total		**377**	

1st innings FoW: 12, 79, 166, 197, 197, 207, 376

Bowler	O	M	R	W
RGD Willis	23	5	75	3
IT Botham	25	6	67	1
GR Dilley	14	2	67	1
DL Underwood	25	8	55	0
JE Emburey	32	7	81	0
KWR Fletcher	2	1	5	0
DI Gower	1	0	1	1

SRI LANKA 1st innings

Batsman	Dismissal	Runs	2nd innings		
B Warnapura*	c Gower b Willis	2	c Gooch b Emburey	38	
S Wettimuny	c Taylor b Botham	6	b Willis	9	
RL Dias	c Cook b Willis	0	c Taylor b Underwood	77	
LRD Mendis	lbw b Botham	17	c Willis b Emburey	27	
RS Madugalle	c Gower b Underwood	65	c Cook b Emburey	3	
A Ranatunga	b Underwood	54	c Fletcher b Emburey	2	
DS de Silva	c Gower b Underwood	3	c Fletcher b Underwood	1	
ALF de Mel	c Fletcher b Underwood	19	c Gower b Emburey	2	
L Kaluperuma	c Cook b Underwood	1	c Taylor b Emburey	0	
Goonatillake+	not out	22	not out	2	
GRA de Silva	c Emburey b Botham	12	c Willis b Underwood	0	
Extras	(2b, 4lb, 2w, 9nb)	17	(0b, 6lb, 0w, 8nb)	14	
	81.5 overs		83.5 overs		
Total		**218**		**175**	

1st innings FoW: 9, 11, 29, 34, 133, 149, 181, 183, 190, 218
2nd innings FoW: 30, 113, 140, 167, 169, 170, 172, 173, 174, 175

Bowler	O	M	R	W	O	M	R	W
RGD Willis	19	7	46	2	9	3	24	1
IT Botham	12.5	1	28	3	12	1	37	0
PJW Allott	13	4	44	0				
JE Emburey	19	3	55	0	25	9	33	6
DL Underwood	18	6	28	5	37.5	15	67	3

ENGLAND 1st innings

Batsman	Dismissal	Runs	2nd innings	
GA Gooch	lbw b de Mel	22	b GRA de Silva	31
G Cook	c Kaluperuma b de Mel	11	lbw b de Mel	0
CJ Tavare	b de Mel	0	st Goona'ke b G de Silva	85
DI Gower	c Goona'ke b DS de Silva	89	not out	42
KWR Fletcher*	c Warnapura b G de Silva	44	not out	0
IT Botham	b de Mel	13		
RW Taylor+	not out	31		
JE Emburey	lbw b GRA de Silva	0		
PJW Allott	c Kalup'ma b DS de Silva	3		
DL Underw'd	c Mendis b DS de Silva	0		
RGD Willis	run out	0		
Extras	(0b, 3lb, 0w, 6nb)	9	(7b, 5lb, 0w, 1nb)	13
	86.5 overs		58.1 overs	
Total		**223**		**171**

1st innings FoW: 34, 34, 40, 120, 151, 200, 207, 216, 216, 223
2nd innings FoW: 3, 84, 167

Bowler	O	M	R	W	O	M	R	W
ALF de Mel	17	2	70	4	13.1	4	33	1
B Warnapura	3	1	9	0	1	0	1	0
DS de Silva	27.5	11	54	3	15	5	38	0
LW Kaluperuma	9	1	29	0	12	3	40	0
GRA de Silva	30	12	52	2	17	6	46	2

No. 580: 2nd Test	No. 581: 2nd Test
VENUE: Lord's	VENUE: Old Trafford
DATE: 10th-15th June 1982	DATE: 24th-28th June 1982
TOSS WON BY: England	TOSS WON BY: England
RESULT: England won by 7 wickets	RESULT: Match drawn

ENGLAND 1st innings / 2nd innings (No. 580)

ENGLAND	1st innings		2nd innings	
G Cook	lbw b Kapil Dev	4	lbw b Kapil Dev	10
CJ Tavare	c Viswanath b Kapil Dev	4	b Kapil Dev	3
AJ Lamb	lbw b Kapil Dev	9	c Malhotra b Kapil Dev	1
DI Gower	c Viswanath b Kapil Dev	37	not out	37
IT Botham	c Malhotra b Madan Lal	67	not out	14
DW Randall	c Parkar b Kapil Dev	126		
DR Pringle	c Gavaskar b Doshi	7		
PH Edmonds	c Kirmani b Madan Lal	64		
RW Taylor+	c Viswanath b Doshi	31		
PJW Allott	not out	41		
RGD Willis*	b Madan Lal	28		
Extras	(1b, 5lb, 0w, 9nb)	15	(0b, 2lb, 0w, 0nb)	2
	148.1 overs		19 overs	
Total		**433**		**67**

1st innings FoW: 5, 18, 37, 96, 149, 166, 291, 363, 363, 433
2nd innings FoW: 11, 13, 18

N Kapil Dev	43	8	125	5	10	1	43	3
S Madan Lal	28.1	6	99	3	2	1	2	0
RJ Shastri	34	10	73	0	2	0	9	0
DR Doshi	40	7	120	2	5	3	11	0
Yashpal Sharma	3	2	1	0				

INDIA 1st innings / 2nd innings (No. 580)

INDIA	1st innings		2nd innings	
SM Gavaskar*	b Botham	48	c Cook b Willis	24
GA Parkar	lbw b Botham	6	b Willis	1
DB Vengsarkar	lbw b Willis	2	c Allott b Willis	157
GR Viswanath	b Botham	1	b Allott	23
Y'pal Sharma	lbw b Pringle	4	c Taylor b Pringle	3
A Malhotra	lbw b Pringle	5	b Willis	37
N Kapil Dev	c Cook b Willis	41	c Taylor b Willis	0
RJ Shastri	c Cook b Willis	4	c Cook b Botham	89
SMH Kirmani+	not out	6	c Gower b Willis	3
S Madan Lal	c Tavare b Botham	6	lbw b Pringle	15
DR Doshi	c Taylor b Botham	0	not out	4
Extras	(0b, 1lb, 0w, 4nb)	5	(0b, 2lb, 0w, 11nb)	13
	50.4 overs		111.5 overs	
Total		**128**		**369**

1st innings FoW: 17, 21, 22, 31, 45, 112, 116, 116, 128, 128
2nd innings FoW: 6, 47, 107, 110, 252, 252, 254, 275, 341, 369

IT Botham	19.4	3	46	5	31.5	7	103	1
RGD Willis	16	2	41	3	28	3	101	6
DR Pringle	9	4	16	2	19	4	58	2
PH Edmonds	2	1	5	0	15	6	39	0
PJW Allott	4	1	15	0	17	3	51	1
G Cook					1	0	4	0

ENGLAND 1st innings / 2nd innings (No. 581)

ENGLAND	1st innings		2nd innings	
G Cook	b Doshi	66		
CJ Tavare	b Doshi	57		
AJ Lamb	c Visw'th b Madan Lal	9		
DI Gower	c Shastri b Madan Lal	9		
IT Botham	b Shastri	128		
DW Randall	c Kirmani b Doshi	0		
G Miller	c Vengsarkar b Doshi	98		
DR Pringle	st Kirmani b Doshi	23		
PH Edmonds	c Kirmani b Madan Lal	1		
RW Taylor+	not out	1		
RGD Willis*	c Gavaskar b Doshi	6		
Extras	(2b, 5lb, 0w, 9nb)	16		
	153.1 overs			
Total		**425**		

1st innings FoW: 106, 117, 141, 161, 161, 330, 382, 413, 419, 425

N Kapil Dev	36	5	109	0
S Madan Lal	35	9	104	3
SV Nayak	12	1	50	0
DR Doshi	47.1	17	102	6
RJ Shastri	23	8	44	1

INDIA 1st innings / 2nd innings (No. 581)

INDIA	1st innings		2nd innings	
SM Gavaskar*	c Tavare b Willis	2		
RJ Shastri	c Cook b Willis	0		
DB Vengsarkar	c Randall b Pringle	12		
GR Viswanath	c Taylor b Botham	54		
SMH Kirmani+	b Edmonds	58		
Y'pal Sharma	b Edmonds	10		
SM Patil	not out	129		
N Kapil Dev	c Taylor b Miller	65		
S Madan Lal	b Edmonds	26		
SV Nayak	not out	2		
DR Doshi				
Extras	(6b, 2lb, 3w, 10nb)	21		
	104 overs			
Total		**379**		

1st innings FoW: 5, 8, 25, 112, 136, 173, 269, 366

RGD Willis	17	2	94	2
DR Pringle	15	4	33	1
PH Edmonds	37	12	94	3
IT Botham	19	4	86	1
G Miller	16	4	51	1

'82

India	Pakistan

India

No. 582: 3rd Test	
VENUE: The Oval	
DATE: 8th-13th July 1982	
TOSS WON BY: England	
RESULT: Match drawn	

ENGLAND

1st innings			2nd innings	
G Cook	c Shastri b Patil	50	c Yashpal b Kapil Dev	8
CJ Tavare	b Kapil Dev	39	not out	75
AJ Lamb	run out	107	b Doshi	45
DI Gower	c Kirmani b Shastri	47	c & b Nayak	45
IT Botham	c Viswanath b Doshi	208		
DW Randall	st Kirmani b Shastri	95		
DR Pringle	st Kirmani b Doshi	9		
PH Edmonds	c (sub) b Doshi	14		
RW Taylor+	lbw b Shastri	3		
PJW Allott	c Yashpal b Doshi	3		
RGD Willis*	not out	1		
Extras	(3b, 5lb, 0w, 10nb)	18	(6b, 8lb, 0w, 4nb)	18
Total	173.3 overs	**594**	70.3 overs	**191**

1st innings FoW: 96, 96, 185, 361, 512, 534, 562, 569, 582, 594
2nd innings FoW: 12, 94, 191

N Kapil Dev	25	4	109	1	19	3	53	1
S Madan Lal	26	8	69	0	11	6	17	0
SV Nayak	21	5	66	0	5.3	0	16	1
SM Patil	14	1	48	1				
DR Doshi	46	6	175	4	19	5	47	1
RJ Shastri	41.3	8	109	3	16	3	40	0

INDIA 1st innings

1st innings			2nd innings	
RJ Shastri	c Botham b Willis	66	c Taylor b Willis	0
DB Vengsarkar	c Edmonds b Botham	6	c Taylor b Pringle	6
GR Viswanath	lbw b Willis	56	c Taylor b Pringle	16
Y'pal Sharma	c Gower b Willis	38	not out	75
SM Patil	c (sub) b Botham	62	not out	9
SMH Kirmani+	b Allott	43		
N Kapil Dev	c Allott b Edmonds	97		
S Madan Lal	c Taylor b Edmonds	5		
SV Nayak	b Edmonds	11		
DR Doshi	not out	5		
SM Gavaskar*	absent hurt	0		
Extras	(3b, 5lb, 0w, 13nb)	21	(0b, 3lb, 0w, 2nb)	5
Total	129.2 overs	**410**	36 overs	**111**

1st innings FoW: 21, 134, 135 , 232, 248, 378, 394, 396, 410
2nd innings FoW: 0, 18, 43

RGD Willis	23	4	78	3	4	0	16	1
IT Botham	19	2	73	2	4	0	12	0
PJW Allott	24	4	69	1	4	1	12	0
DR Pringle	28	5	80	0	11	5	32	2
PH Edmonds	35.2	11	89	3	13	5	34	0

Pakistan

No. 583: 1st Test	
VENUE: Edgbaston	
DATE: 29th July to 1st August 1982	
TOSS WON BY: England	
RESULT: England won by 113 runs	

ENGLAND

1st innings			2nd innings	
DW Randall	b Imran Khan	17	b Imran Khan	105
CJ Tavare	c Javed b Abdul	54	c Mohsin b Imran Khan	17
AJ Lamb	c Wasim Bari b Sikander	6	lbw b Tahir	5
DI Gower	c Wasim Bari b Imran	74	c Mudassar b Tahir	13
IT Botham	b Imran Khan	2	c Wasim Bari b Tahir	5
MW Gatting	b Tahir	17	lbw b Tahir	0
G Miller	b Imran Khan	47	b Tahir	5
IA Greig	c (sub) b Imran Khan	14	b Abdul	7
EE Hemmings	lbw b Imran Khan	2	c Mansoor b Abdul	19
RW Taylor+	lbw b Imran Khan	1	c Abdul b Wasim Raja	54
RGD Willis*	not out	0	not out	28
Extras	(4b, 10lb, 6w, 18nb)	38	(10b, 11lb, 7w, 5nb)	33
Total	92.3 overs	**272**	105.3 overs	**291**

1st innings FoW: 29, 37, 164, 172, 179, 228, 263, 265, 271, 272
2nd innings FoW: 62, 98, 127, 137, 137, 146, 170, 188, 212, 291

Imran Khan	25.3	11	52	7	32	5	84	2
Tahir Naqqash	15	4	46	1	18	7	40	5
Sikander Bakht	18	5	58	1	13	5	34	0
Mudassar Nazar	5	2	8	0				
Abdul Qadir	29	7	70	1	40	10	100	2
Wasim Raja					2.3	2	0	1

PAKISTAN 1st innings

1st innings			2nd innings	
M Nazar lbw	b Botham	0	lbw b Botham	0
Mohsin Khan	c Willis b Botham	26	lbw b Botham	35
Tahir Naqqash	c Taylor b Greig	12	c Taylor b Botham	0
Mansoor A'r	c Miller b Hemmings	58	run out	10
Javed M'dad	c Willis b Hemmings	30	c Taylor b Willis	4
Zaheer Abbas	lbw b Greig	40	c Gower b Willis	16
Wasim Raja	c Tavare b Willis	26	b Miller	65
Imran Khan*	c Taylor b Willis	22	c Taylor b Botham	12
Wasim Bari+	not out	16	c & b Hemmings	39
Abdul Qadir	lbw b Greig	7	c Randall b Miller	9
Sik'der Bakht	c Hemmings b Greig	1	not out	1
Extras	(5b, 2lb, 1w, 5nb)	13	(0b, 3lb, 0w, 5nb)	8
Total	79.2 overs	**251**	56.4 overs	**199**

1st innings FoW: 0, 29, 53, 110, 164, 198, 217, 227, 248, 251
2nd innings FoW: 0, 0, 38, 54, 66, 77, 98, 151, 178, 199

IT Botham	24	1	86	2	21	7	70	4
IA Greig	14.2	3	53	4	4	1	19	0
RGD Willis	15	3	42	2	14	2	49	2
EE Hemmings	24	5	56	2	10	4	27	1
G Miller	2	1	1	0	7.4	1	26	2

No. 584: 2nd Test
VENUE: Lord's
DATE: 12th - 16th August 1982
TOSS WON BY: Pakistan
RESULT: Pakistan won by 10 wickets

No. 585: 3rd Test
VENUE: Headingley
DATE: 26th-31st August 1982
TOSS WON BY: Pakistan
RESULT: England won by 3 wickets

PAKISTAN 1st innings / 2nd innings (No. 584)

Batsman	1st innings		2nd innings	
Mohsin Khan	c Tavare b Jackman	200	not out	39
Mudassar Nazar	c Taylor b Jackman	20		
Mansoor Akhtar	c Lamb b Botham	57		
Javed Miandad	run out	6	not out	26
Zaheer Abbas	b Jackman	75		
Haroon Rashid	lbw b Botham	1		
Imran Khan*	c Taylor b Botham	12		
Tahir Naqqash	c Gatting b Jackman	2		
Wasim Bari+	not out	24		
Abdul Qadir	not out	18		
Sarfraz Nawaz				
Extras	(3b, 8lb, 0w, 2nb)	13	(1b, 10lb, 1w, 0nb)	12
Total	139 overs	428	13.1 overs	77

1st innings FoW: 53, 197, 208, 361, 364, 380, 382, 401

Bowler	O	M	R	W	O	M	R	W
IT Botham	44	8	148	3	7	0	30	0
RD Jackman	36	5	110	4	4	0	22	0
DR Pringle	26	9	62	0				
IA Greig	13	2	42	0				
EE Hemmings	20	3	53	0	2.1	0	13	0

ENGLAND 1st innings / 2nd innings (No. 584)

Batsman	1st innings		2nd innings	
DW Randall	b Sarfraz	29	b Mudassar	9
CJ Tavare	b Sarfraz	8	c Javed b Imran Khan	82
AJ Lamb	c Haroon b Tahir	33	lbw b Mudassar	0
DI Gower*	c Mansoor b Imran	29	c Wasim b Mudassar	0
IT Botham	c Mohsin Khan b Abdul	31	c Sarfraz b Mudassar	69
MW Gatting	not out	32	c Wasim b Mudassar	7
DR Pringle	c Haroon b Abdul	5	c Javed b Abdul	14
IA Greig	lbw b Abdul	3	lbw b Mudassar	2
EE Hemmings	b Sarfraz	6	c Wasim b Imran Khan	14
RW Taylor+	lbw b Abdul	5	not out	24
RD Jackman	lbw b Imran Khan	0	c Haroon b Abdul	17
Extras	(11b, 12lb, 13w, 10nb)	46	(10b, 19lb, 5w, 4nb)	38
Total	86 overs	227	119.5 overs	276

1st innings FoW: 16, 69, 89, 157, 173, 187, 197, 217, 226, 227
2nd innings FoW: 9, 9, 9, 121, 132, 171, 180, 224, 235, 276

Bowler	O	M	R	W	O	M	R	W
Imran Khan	23	4	55	2	42	13	84	2
Sarfraz Nawaz	23	4	56	3	14	5	22	0
Tahir Naqqash	12	4	25	1	7	5	6	0
Abdul Qadir	24	9	39	4	37.5	15	94	2
Mudassar Nazar	4	1	6	0	19	7	32	6

PAKISTAN 1st innings / 2nd innings (No. 585)

Batsman	1st innings		2nd innings	
Mohsin Khan	c Taylor b Botham	10	c Taylor b Willis	0
M Nazar	b Botham	65	c Botham b Willis	0
Mansoor Ak'r	c Gatting b Willis	0	c Randall b Botham	39
Javed M'dad	c Fowler b Willis	54	c Taylor b Botham	52
Zaheer Abbas	c Taylor b Jackman	8	lbw b Botham	4
Majid Khan	lbw b Jackman	21	c Gower b Botham	10
Imran Khan*	not out	67	c Randall b Botham	46
Wasim Bari+	b Jackman	23	c Taylor b Willis	7
Abdul Qadir	c Willis b Botham	5	b Jackman	17
Sik'der Bakht	c Tavare b Willis	7	c Gatting b Marks	7
Ehtesh'ddin	b Botham	0	not out	0
Extras	(1b, 7lb, 4w, 3nb)	15	(0b, 6lb, 4w, 7nb)	17
Total	100.5 overs	275	81 overs	199

1st innings FoW: 16, 19, 119, 128, 160, 168, 207, 224, 274, 275
2nd innings FoW: 0, 3, 81, 85, 108, 115, 128, 169, 199, 199

Bowler	O	M	R	W	O	M	R	W
RGD Willis	26	6	76	3	19	3	55	3
IT Botham	24.5	9	70	4	30	8	74	5
RD Jackman	37	14	74	3	28	11	41	1
VJ Marks	5	0	23	0	2	1	8	1
MW Gatting	8	2	17	0	2	1	4	0

ENGLAND 1st innings / 2nd innings (No. 585)

Batsman	1st innings		2nd innings	
CJ Tavare	c (sub) b Imran Khan	22	c Majid b Imran Khan	33
G Fowler	b Ehteshamuddin	9	c Wasim b M Nazar	86
MW Gatting	lbw b Imran Khan	25	lbw b Imran Khan	25
AJ Lamb	c Mohsin b Imran Khan	0	lbw b M Nazar	4
DI Gower	c (sub) b Sikander	74	c Wasim b M Nazar	7
IT Botham	c (sub) b Sikander	57	c Majid b M Nazar	4
DW Randall	run out	8	lbw b Imran Khan	0
VJ Marks	b Abdul	7	not out	12
RW Taylor+	c Javed b Imran Khan	18	not out	6
RD Jackman	c Mohsin Khan b Imran	11		
RGD Willis*	not out	1		
Extras	(4b, 10lb, 2w, 8nb)	24	(19b, 16lb, 1w, 6nb)	42
Total	89.2 overs	256	80.2 overs	219

1st innings FoW: 15, 67, 69, 77, 146, 159, 170, 209, 255, 256
2nd innings FoW: 103, 168, 172, 187, 189, 189, 199

Bowler	O	M	R	W	O	M	R	W
Imran Khan	25.2	7	49	5	30.2	8	66	3
Ehteshamuddin	14	4	46	1				
Sikander Bakht	24	5	47	2	20	4	40	0
Abdul Qadir	22	5	87	1	8	2	16	0
Mudassar Nazar	4	1	3	0	22	7	55	4

Australia (1st Test)

No. 586:	1st Test
VENUE:	Perth (WACA)
DATE:	12th-17th November 1982
TOSS WON BY:	Australia
RESULT:	Match drawn

ENGLAND

	1st innings		2nd innings	
G Cook	c Dyson b Lillee	1	c Border b Lawson	7
CJ Tavare	c Hughes b Yardley	89	c Chappell b Yardley	9
DI Gower	c Dyson b Alderman	72	lbw b Lillee	28
AJ Lamb	c Marsh b Yardley	46	c Marsh b Lawson	56
IT Botham	c Marsh b Lawson	12	b Lawson	0
DW Randall	c Wood b Yardley	78	b Lawson	115
G Miller	c Marsh b Lillee	30	b Yardley	31
DR Pringle	b Lillee	0	c Marsh b Yardley	0
RW Taylor+	not out	29	not out	47
RGD Willis*	c Lillee b Yardley	26	b Lawson	0
NG Cowans	b Yardley	4	lbw b Chappell	36
Extras	(7b, 9lb, 2w, 6nb)	24	(5b, 11lb, 2w, 11nb)	29
Total	155.4 overs	**411**	116.3 overs	**358**

1st innings FoW: 14, 109, 189, 204, 304, 323, 342, 357, 406, 411
2nd innings FoW: 10, 51, 77, 80, 151, 228, 242, 292, 292, 358

DK Lillee	38	13	96	3	33	12	89	1
TM Alderman	43	15	84	1				
GF Lawson	29	6	89	1	32	5	108	5
GS Chappell	3	0	11	0	2.3	1	8	1
B Yardley	42.4	15	107	5	41	10	101	3
AR Border					7	2	21	0
DW Hookes					1	0	2	0

AUSTRALIA

	1st innings		2nd innings	
GM Wood	c & b Willis	29	c Taylor b Willis	0
J Dyson	lbw b Miller	52	c Cowans b Willis	12
AR Border	c Taylor b Botham	8	not out	32
GS Chappell*	c Lamb b Willis	117	not out	22
KJ Hughes	c Willis b Miller	62		
DW Hookes	lbw b Miller	56		
RW Marsh+	c Cook b Botham	0		
GF Lawson	b Miller	50		
B Yardley	c Lamb b Willis	17		
DK Lillee	not out	2		
TM Alderman				
Extras	(4b, 1lb, 1w, 25nb)	31	(0b, 1lb, 0w, 6nb)	7
Total	131.5 overs	**424**	22 overs	**73**

1st innings FoW: 63, 76, 123, 264, 311, 311, 374, 414, 424
2nd innings FoW: 2, 22

RGD Willis	31.5	4	95	3	6	1	23	2
IT Botham	40	10	121	2	6	1	17	0
NG Cowans	13	2	54	0	3	1	15	0
DR Pringle	10	1	37	0	2	0	3	0
G Miller	33	11	70	4	4	3	8	0
G Cook	4	2	16	0				
AJ Lamb					1	1	0	0

Australia (2nd Test)

No. 587:	2nd Test
VENUE:	Brisbane (Gabba)
DATE:	26th November to 1st Dec 1982
TOSS WON BY:	Australia
RESULT:	Australia won by 7 wickets

ENGLAND

	1st innings		2nd innings	
CJ Tavare	c Hughes b Lawson	1	c Marsh b Lawson	13
G Fowler	c Yardley b Lawson	7	c Marsh b Thomson	83
DI Gower	c Wessels b Lawson	18	c Marsh b Thomson	34
AJ Lamb	c Marsh b Lawson	72	c Wessels b Thomson	12
IT Botham	c Rackemann b Yardley	40	c Yardley b Thomson	4
DW Randall	c Lawson b Rackemann	37	c Marsh b Thomson	15
G Miller	c Marsh b Lawson	0	c Marsh b Lawson	60
RW Taylor+	c Lawson b Rackemann	1	c Hookes b Lawson	3
EE Hemmings	not out	15	b Lawson	18
RGD Willis*	c Thomson b Yardley	1	not out	10
NG Cowans	c Marsh b Lawson	10	c Marsh b Lawson	5
Extras	(0b, 2lb, 1w, 14nb)	17	(8b, 8lb, 1w, 35nb)	52
Total	64.3 overs	**219**	127.3 overs	**309**

1st innings FoW: 8, 13, 63, 141, 152, 152, 178, 191, 195, 219
2nd innings FoW: 54, 144, 165, 169, 194, 201, 226, 285, 295, 309

GF Lawson	18.3	4	47	6	35.3	11	87	5
CG Rackemann	21	8	61	2	12.2	3	35	0
JR Thomson	8	0	43	0	31	6	73	5
B Yardley	17	5	51	2	40.4	21	50	0
GS Chappell					6	2	8	0
DW Hookes					2	0	4	0

AUSTRALIA

	1st innings		2nd innings	
KC Wessels	b Willis	162	b Hemmings	46
J Dyson	b Botham	1	retired hurt	4
AR Border	c Randall b Willis	0	c Botham b Hemmings	15
GS Chappell*	run out	53	c Lamb b Cowans	8
KJ Hughes	c Taylor b Botham	0	not out	39
DW Hookes	c Taylor b Miller	28	not out	66
RW Marsh+	c Taylor b Botham	11		
B Yardley	c Tavare b Willis	53		
GF Lawson	c Hemmings b Willis	6		
CG Rackemann	b Willis	4		
JR Thomson	not out	5		
Extras	(2b, 8lb, 0w, 8nb)	18	(2b, 5lb, 0w, 5nb)	12
Total	110.4 overs	**341**	60.5 overs	**190**

1st innings FoW: 4, 11, 94, 99, 130, 171, 271, 310, 332, 341
2nd innings FoW: 60, 77, 83

RGD Willis	29.4	3	66	5	4	1	24	0
IT Botham	22	1	105	3	15.5	1	70	0
NG Cowans	6	0	36	0	9	1	31	1
EE Hemmings	33.3	6	81	0	29	9	43	2
G Miller	19.3	4	35	1	3	0	10	0

No. 588: 3rd Test	No. 589: 4th Test
VENUE: Adelaide	VENUE: Melbourne (MCG)
DATE: 10th-15th December 1982	DATE: 26th-30th December 1982
TOSS WON BY: England	TOSS WON BY: Australia
RESULT: Australia won by 8 wickets	RESULT: England won by 3 runs

Left match (No. 588)

AUSTRALIA 1st innings

Batsman	1st innings		2nd innings	
KC Wessels	c Taylor b Botham	44	c Taylor b Botham	1
J Dyson	c Taylor b Botham	44	not out	37
GS Chappell*	c Gower b Willis	115	c Randall b Willis	14
KJ Hughes	run out	88	not out	26
GF Lawson	c Botham b Willis	2		
AR Border	c Taylor b Pringle	26		
DW Hookes	c Botham b Hemmings	37		
RW Marsh+	c Hemmings b Pringle	3		
B Yardley	c Gower b Botham	38		
RM Hogg	not out	14		
JR Thomson	c & b Botham	3		
Extras	(0b, 6lb, 0w, 18nb)	24	(0b, 0lb, 0w, 5nb)	5
	156.5 overs		23.5 overs	
Total		**438**		**83**

1st innings FoW: 76, 138, 264, 270, 315, 355, 359, 391, 430, 438
2nd innings FoW: 3, 37

Bowler	O	M	R	W	O	M	R	W
RGD Willis	25	8	76	2	8	1	17	1
IT Botham	36.5	5	112	4	10	2	45	1
DR Pringle	33	5	97	2	1.5	0	11	0
G Miller	14	2	33	0				
EE Hemmings	48	17	96	1	4	1	5	0

ENGLAND 1st innings

Batsman	1st innings		2nd innings	
CJ Tavare	c Marsh b Hogg	1	c Wessels b Thomson	0
G Fowler	c Marsh b Lawson	11	c Marsh b Lawson	37
DI Gower	c Marsh b Lawson	60	b Hogg	114
AJ Lamb	c Marsh b Lawson	82	c Chappell b Yardley	8
IT Botham	c Wessels b Thomson	35	c Dyson b Yardley	58
DW Randall	b Lawson	0	c Marsh b Lawson	17
G Miller	c Yardley b Hogg	7	lbw b Lawson	17
RW Taylor+	c Chappell b Yardley	2	c Marsh b Thomson	9
DR Pringle	not out	1	not out	3
EE Hemmings	b Thomson	0	c Wessels b Lawson	0
RGD Willis*	b Thomson	1	c Marsh b Lawson	10
Extras	(0b, 5lb, 0w, 11nb)	16		31
	67.5 overs		104 overs	
Total		**216**		**304**

1st innings FoW: 1, 21, 140, 181, 181, 194, 199, 213, 213, 216
2nd innings FoW: 11, 90, 118, 236, 247, 272, 277, 289, 290, 304

Bowler	O	M	R	W	O	M	R	W
GF Lawson	18	4	56	4	24	6	66	5
RM Hogg	14	2	41	2	19	5	53	1
JR Thomson	14.5	3	51	3	13	3	41	2
B Yardley	21	7	52	1	37	12	90	2
AR Border					8	2	14	0
DW Hookes					3	1	9	0

Right match (No. 589)

ENGLAND 1st innings

Batsman	1st innings		2nd innings	
G Cook	c Chappell b Thomson	10	c Yardley b Thomson	26
G Fowler	c Chappell b Hogg	4	b Hogg	65
CJ Tavare	c Yardley b Thomson	89	b Hogg	0
DI Gower	c Marsh b Hogg	18	c Marsh b Lawson	3
AJ Lamb	c Dyson b Yardley	83	c Marsh b Hogg	26
IT Botham	c Wessels b Yardley	27	c Chappell b Thomson	46
G Miller	c Border b Yardley	10	lbw b Lawson	14
DR Pringle	c Wessels b Hogg	9	c Marsh b Lawson	42
RW Taylor+	c Marsh b Yardley	1	lbw b Thomson	37
RGD Willis*	not out	6	not out	8
NG Cowans	c Lawson b Hogg	3	b Lawson	10
Extras	(3b, 6lb, 3w, 12nb)	24	(2b, 9lb, 0w, 6nb)	17
	81.3 overs		80.4 overs	
Total		**284**		**294**

1st innings FoW: 11, 25, 56, 217, 227, 259, 262, 268, 278, 284
2nd innings FoW: 40, 41, 45, 128, 129, 160, 201, 262, 280, 294

Bowler	O	M	R	W	O	M	R	W
GF Lawson	17	6	48	0	21.4	6	66	4
RM Hogg	23.3	6	69	4	22	5	64	3
B Yardley	27	9	89	4	15	2	67	0
JR Thomson	13	2	49	2	21	3	74	3
GS Chappell	1	0	5	0	1	0	6	0

AUSTRALIA 1st innings

Batsman	1st innings		2nd innings	
KC Wessels	b Willis	47	b Cowans	14
J Dyson	lbw b Cowans	21	c Tavare b Botham	31
GS Chappell*	c Lamb b Cowans	0	c (sub) b Cowans	2
KJ Hughes	b Willis	66	c Taylor b Miller	48
AR Border	b Botham	2	not out	62
DW Hookes	c Taylor b Pringle	53	c Willis b Cowans	68
RW Marsh+	b Willis	53	lbw b Cowans	13
B Yardley	b Miller	9	b Cowans	0
GF Lawson	c Fowler b Miller	0	c Cowans b Pringle	7
RM Hogg	not out	8	lbw b Cowans	4
JR Thomson	b Miller	1	c Miller b Botham	21
Extras	(0b, 8lb, 0w, 19nb)	27	(5b, 9lb, 1w, 3nb)	18
	79 overs		96.1 overs	
Total		**287**		**288**

1st innings FoW: 55, 55, 83, 89, 180, 261, 276, 276, 278, 287
2nd innings FoW: 37, 39, 71, 171, 173, 190, 190, 202, 218, 288

Bowler	O	M	R	W	O	M	R	W
RGD Willis	15	2	38	3	17	0	57	0
IT Botham	18	3	69	1	25.1	4	80	2
NG Cowans	16	0	69	2	26	6	77	6
DR Pringle	15	2	40	1	12	4	26	1
G Miller	15	5	44	3	16	6	30	1

Australia

No. 590: 5th Test
VENUE: Sydney (SCG)
DATE: 2nd-7th January 1983
TOSS WON BY: Australia
RESULT: Match drawn

AUSTRALIA

	1st innings		2nd innings	
KC Wessels	c Willis b Botham	19	lbw b Botham	53
J Dyson	c Taylor b Hemmings	79	c Gower b Willis	2
GS Chappell*	lbw b Willis	35	c Randall b Hemmings	11
KJ Hughes	c Cowans b Botham	29	c Botham b Hemmings	137
DW Hookes	c Botham b Hemmings	17	lbw b Miller	19
AR Border	c Miller b Hemmings	89	c Botham b Cowans	83
RW Marsh+	c & b Miller	3	c Taylor b Miller	41
B Yardley	b Cowans	24	c Botham b Hemmings	0
GF Lawson	c & b Botham	6	not out	13
JR Thomson	c Lamb b Botham	0	c Gower b Miller	12
RM Hogg	not out	0	run out	0
Extras	(3b, 8lb, 2w, 0nb)	13	(0b, 7lb, 0w, 4nb)	11
Total	115 overs	**314**	131.3 overs	**382**

1st innings FoW: 39, 96, 150, 173, 210, 219, 262, 283, 291, 314
2nd innings FoW: 23, 38, 82, 113, 262, 350, 357, 358, 382, 382

	O	M	R	W	O	M	R	W
RGD Willis	20	6	57	1	10	2	33	1
NG Cowans	21	3	67	1	13	1	47	1
IT Botham	30	8	75	4	10	0	35	1
EE Hemmings	27	10	68	3	47	16	116	3
G Miller	17	7	34	1	49.3	12	133	3
G Cook					2	1	7	0

ENGLAND

	1st innings		2nd innings	
G Cook	c Chappell b Hogg	8	lbw b Lawson	2
CJ Tavare	b Lawson	0	lbw b Yardley	16
DI Gower	c Chappell b Lawson	70	c Marsh b Yardley	95
AJ Lamb	b Lawson	24	c Hookes b Yardley	24
DW Randall	b Thomson	70	c & b Yardley	29
IT Botham	c Wessels b Thomson	5	b Thomson	44
G Miller	lbw b Thomson	34	lbw b Thomson	32
RW Taylor+	lbw b Thomson	1	not out	21
EE Hemmings	c Border b Yardley	29	not out	28
RGD Willis*	c Border b Thomson	1		
NG Cowans	not out	0		
Extras	(4b, 4lb, 0w, 12nb)	20	(1b, 10lb, 1w, 11nb)	23
Total	64.5 overs	**237**	96 overs	**314**

1st innings FoW: 8, 23, 24, 146, 163, 169, 170, 220, 232, 237
2nd innings FoW: 3, 55, 104, 155, 196, 260, 261

	O	M	R	W	O	M	R	W
GF Lawson	20	2	70	3	15	1	50	1
RM Hogg	16	2	50	1	13	6	25	0
JR Thomson	14.5	2	50	5	12	3	30	2
B Yardley	14	4	47	1	37	6	139	4
AR Border					16	3	36	0
DW Hookes					2	1	5	0
GS Chappell					1	0	6	0

New Zealand

No. 591: 1st Test
VENUE: The Oval
DATE: 14th-18th July 1983
TOSS WON BY: England
RESULT: England won by 189 runs

ENGLAND

	1st innings		2nd innings	
G Fowler	lbw b Hadlee	1	run out	105
CJ Tavare	run out	45	c Howarth b Bracewell	109
DI Gower	b Hadlee	11	c Howarth b Hadlee	25
AJ Lamb	b Cairns	24	not out	102
IT Botham	b Hadlee	15	run out	26
DW Randall	not out	75	c Coney b Hadlee	3
VJ Marks	c Lees b Hadlee	4	c MD Crowe b Bracewell	2
PH Edmonds	c & b Bracewell	12	not out	43
RW Taylor+	lbw b Hadlee	0		
RGD Willis*	c JJ Crowe b Bracewell	4		
NG Cowans	b Hadlee	3		
Extras	(6b, 6lb, 0w, 3nb)	15	(8b, 23lb, 0w, 0nb)	31
Total	70.4 overs	**209**	189.2 overs	**446**

1st innings FoW: 2, 18, 67, 104, 116, 154, 184, 191, 202, 209
2nd innings FoW: 223, 225, 269, 322, 329, 336

	O	M	R	W	O	M	R	W
RJ Hadlee	23.4	6	53	6	37.2	7	99	2
EJ Chatfield	17	3	48	0	35	9	85	0
BL Cairns	17	3	63	1	30	7	67	0
JG Bracewell	8	4	16	2	54	13	115	2
MD Crowe	5	0	14	0	3	0	9	0
JV Coney					27	11	39	0
GP Howarth					3	2	1	0

NEW ZEALAND

	1st innings		2nd innings	
JG Wright	c Gower b Willis	0	run out	88
BA Edgar	c Taylor b Willis	12	c Taylor b Willis	3
JJ Crowe	c Randall b Willis	0	c Lamb b Willis	9
GP Howarth*	b Cowans	4	c Taylor b Edmonds	67
MD Crowe	b Willis	0	c Taylor b Edmonds	33
JV Coney	run out	44	lbw b Marks	2
RJ Hadlee	c & b Botham	84	c Taylor b Marks	11
JG Bracewell	c & b Botham	7	run out	8
WK Lees+	not out	0	c Gower b Marks	9
BL Cairns	c Lamb b Botham	2	c Willis b Edmonds	32
EJ Chatfield	c Willis b Botham	0	not out	10
Extras	(0b, 6lb, 0w, 6nb)	12	(3b, 1lb, 0w, 3nb)	7
Total	57 overs	**196**	110.1 overs	**270**

1st innings FoW: 0, 1, 10, 17, 41, 125, 149, 182, 188, 196
2nd innings FoW: 10, 26, 146, 197, 202, 210, 228, 228, 228, 270

	O	M	R	W	O	M	R	W
RGD Willis	20	8	43	4	12	3	26	2
NG Cowans	19	3	60	1	11	2	41	0
IT Botham	16	2	62	4	4	0	17	0
PH Edmonds	2	0	19	0	40.1	16	101	3
VJ Marks					43	20	78	3

No. 592: 2nd Test
VENUE: Headingley
DATE: 28th July to 1st August 1983
TOSS WON BY: New Zealand
RESULT: New Zealand won by 5 wickets

No. 593: 3rd Test
VENUE: Lord's
DATE: 11th-15th August 1983
TOSS WON BY: New Zealand
RESULT: England won by 127 runs

ENGLAND 2nd Test (No. 592)

ENGLAND	1st innings		2nd innings	
G Fowler	c Smith b Chatfield	9	c Smith b Chatfield	19
CJ Tavare	c Smith b Coney	69	b Chatfield	23
DI Gower	c Coney b Cairns	9	not out	112
AJ Lamb	c MD Crowe b Cairns	58	c Smith b Chatfield	28
IT Botham	c Howarth b Cairns	38	c Howarth b Coney	4
DW Randall	c Coney b Cairns	4	c Smith b Chatfield	16
PH Edmonds	c Smith b Cairns	8	c Smith b Chatfield	0
GR Dilley	b Cairns	0	c Smith b Chatfield	15
RW Taylor+	not out	10	b Cairns	9
RGD Willis*	c JJ Crowe b Coney	9	c Coney b Cairns	4
NG Cowans	c Bracewell b Cairns	0	c MD Crowe b Cairns	10
Extras	(4b, 7lb, 0w, 0nb)	11	(8b, 3lb, 1w, 0nb)	12
	89.2 overs		87 overs	
Total		**225**		**252**

1st innings FoW: 18, 35, 135, 175, 185, 205, 205, 209, 225, 225
2nd innings FoW: 39, 44, 116, 126, 142, 142, 190, 217, 221, 252

RJ Hadlee	21	9	44	0		26	9	45	0
EJ Chatfield	22	8	67	1		29	5	95	5
BL Cairns	33.2	14	74	7		24	2	70	3
JV Coney	12	3	21	2		8	1	30	2
JG Bracewell	1	0	8	0					

NEW ZEALAND	1st innings		2nd innings	
JG Wright	c Willis b Cowans	93	c Randall b Willis	26
BA Edgar	b Willis	84	c Edmonds b Willis	2
GP Howarth*	run out	13	c Randall b Willis	20
MD Crowe	lbw b Cowans	37	c Lamb b Willis	1
JJ Crowe	run out	0	b Willis	13
JV Coney	c Gower b Willis	19	not out	10
RJ Hadlee	b Cowans	75	not out	6
JG Bracewell	c Dilley b Edmonds	16		
IDS Smith+	c Tavare b Willis	2		
BL Cairns	not out	24		
EJ Chatfield	lbw b Willis	0		
Extras	(1b, 4lb, 1w, 8nb)	14	(8b, 7lb, 0w, 10nb)	25
	139.3 overs		27.1 overs	
Total		**377**		**103**

1st innings FoW: 52, 168, 169, 169, 218, 304, 348, 351, 377, 377
2nd innings FoW: 11, 42, 60, 61, 83

RGD Willis	23.3	6	57	4		14	5	35	5
GR Dilley	17	4	36	0		8	2	16	0
IT Botham	26	9	81	0		0.1	0	4	0
NG Cowans	28	8	88	3		5	0	23	0
PH Edmonds	45	14	101	1					

ENGLAND 3rd Test (No. 593)

ENGLAND	1st innings		2nd innings	
CJ Tavare	b Crowe	51	c Crowe b Hadlee	16
CL Smith	lbw b Hadlee	0	c Coney b Hadlee	43
DI Gower	lbw b Crowe	108	c Crowe b Gray	34
AJ Lamb	c (sub) b Chatfield	17	c Hadlee b Gray	4
MW Gatting	c Wright b Hadlee	81	b Gray	15
IT Botham	lbw b Cairns	8	c Coney b Chatfield	61
RW Taylor+	b Hadlee	16	c & b Coney	7
NA Foster	c Smith b Hadlee	10	c Wright b Hadlee	3
NGB Cook	b Chatfield	16	c Bracewell b Chatfield	4
RGD Willis*	c Smith b Hadlee	7	not out	2
NG Cowans	not out	1	c Smith b Chatfield	1
Extras	(3b, 3lb, 2w, 3nb)	11	(5b, 6lb, 0w, 9nb)	20
	120.3 overs		89.3 overs	
Total		**326**		**211**

1st innings FoW: 3, 152, 174, 191, 218, 288, 290, 303, 318, 326
2nd innings FoW: 26, 79, 87, 119, 147, 195, 199, 208, 210, 211

RJ Hadlee	40	15	93	5		26	7	42	3
BL Cairns	23	8	65	1		3	0	9	0
EJ Chatfield	36.3	8	116	2		13.3	4	29	3
MD Crowe	13	1	35	2					
JV Coney	8	7	6	0		6	4	9	1
JG Bracewell						11	4	29	0
EJ Gray						30	8	73	3

NEW ZEALAND	1st innings		2nd innings	
JG Wright	c Lamb b Willis	11	c Taylor b Botham	12
BA Edgar	c Willis b Cook	70	c Lamb b Cowans	27
GP Howarth*	b Cook	25	c Taylor b Willis	0
MD Crowe	b Botham	46	c Foster b Cowans	12
JV Coney	b Cook	7	c Gatting b Foster	68
EJ Gray	c Lamb b Botham	11	c Lamb b Cook	17
JG Bracewell	c Gower b Cook	0	b Willis	30
RJ Hadlee	c Botham b Cook	0	lbw b Willis	4
BL Cairns	c Lamb b Botham	5	b Cook	16
IDS Smith+	c Lamb b Botham	3	not out	17
EJ Chatfield	not out	5	c & b Cook	2
Extras	(0b, 5lb, 0w, 3nb)	8	(3b, 4lb, 0w, 7nb)	14
	84.4 overs		69.2 overs	
Total		**191**		**219**

1st innings FoW: 18, 49, 147, 159, 176, 176, 176, 183, 184, 191
2nd innings FoW: 15, 17, 57, 61, 108, 154, 158, 190, 206, 219

RGD Willis	13	6	28	1		12	5	24	3
NA Foster	16	5	40	0		12	0	35	1
NG Cowans	9	1	30	0		11	1	36	2
IT Botham	20.4	6	50	4		7	2	20	1
NGB Cook	26	11	35	5		27.2	9	90	3

No. 594: 4th Test
VENUE: Trent Bridge
DATE: 25th - 29th August 1983
TOSS WON BY:
RESULT: England won by 165 runs

No. 595: 1st Test
VENUE: Wellington
DATE: 20th-24th January 1984
TOSS WON BY: New Zealand
RESULT: Match drawn

ENGLAND	1st innings		2nd innings	
CJ Tavare	c Cairns b Snedden	4	c (sub) b Bracewell	13
CL Smith	c Howarth b Bracewell	31	c Howarth b Snedden	4
DI Gower	b Cairns	72	c Cairns b Bracewell	33
AJ Lamb	c Howarth b Bracewell	22	not out	137
MW Gatting	lbw b Bracewell	14	c Lees b Cairns	11
IT Botham	lbw b Snedden	103	c Edgar b Gray	27
DW Randall	c Edgar b Hadlee	83	b Hadlee	13
RW Taylor+	b Bracewell	21	b Hadlee	0
NGB Cook	c Lees b Snedden	4	c Lees b Cairns	26
RGD Willis*	not out	25	b Hadlee	16
NG Cowans	c Bracewell b Cairns	7	b Hadlee	0
Extras	(11b, 14lb, 0w, 9nb)	34	(6b, 10lb, 1w, 0nb)	17
Total	124.4 overs	**420**	92 overs	**297**

1st innings FoW: 5, 94, 136, 156, 169, 355, 356, 379, 407, 420
1st innings FoW: 5, 58, 61, 92, 149, 188, 188, 252, 297, 297

RJ Hadlee	30	7	98	1	28	5	85	4
MC Snedden	28	7	69	3	8	1	40	1
BL Cairns	33.4	9	77	2	20	9	36	2
JG Bracewell	28	5	108	4	21	2	88	2
JV Coney	2	0	10	0				
EJ Gray	3	0	24	0	15	4	31	1

NEW ZEALAND	1st innings		2nd innings	
TJ Franklin	c Smith b Botham	2	b Willis	7
BA Edgar	c Gatting b Cook	62	c Gower b Cook	76
GP Howarth*	c & b Cook	36	c Tavare b Cowans	24
JV Coney	c Gatting b Cook	20	c Taylor b Cowans	0
EJ Gray	run out	7	c Taylor b Cook	68
RJ Hadlee	c Smith b Cowans	3	c Gatting b Smith	3
WK Lees+	lbw b Cook	1	c Lamb b Cowans	7
MD Crowe	c & b Cook	34	not out	92
MC Snedden	b Cowans	9	c Taylor b Cook	12
BL Cairns	c Gower b Cowans	26	b Cook	11
JG Bracewell	not out	1	c Taylor b Smith	28
Extras	(0b, 5lb, 0w, 1nb)	6	(2b, 0lb, 1w, 14nb)	17
Total	82 overs	**207**	129 overs	**345**

1st innings FoW: 4, 80, 124, 127, 131, 135, 135, 157, 201, 207
2nd innings FoW: 16, 67, 71, 156, 161, 184, 228, 264, 290, 345

IT Botham	14	4	33	1	25	4	73	0
RGD Willis	10	2	23	0	19	3	37	1
NG Cowans	21	8	74	3	21	2	95	3
NGB Cook	32	14	63	5	50	22	87	4
MW Gatting	5	2	8	0	2	1	5	0
CL Smith					12	2	31	2

NEW ZEALAND	1st innings		2nd innings	
JG Wright	c Cook b Botham	17	c Foster b Cook	35
BA Edgar	c Taylor b Botham	9	c Taylor b Willis	30
GP Howarth*	c Gower b Botham	15	run out	34
MD Crowe	b Willis	13	c Botham b Gatting	100
JJ Crowe	c Taylor b Foster	52	lbw b Botham	3
JV Coney	c Gower b Cook	27	not out	174
RJ Hadlee	c Gatting b Botham	24	c Lamb b Foster	18
MC Snedden	c Taylor b Willis	11	c Taylor b Foster	16
IDS Smith+	lbw b Botham	24	b Cook	29
BL Cairns	c Gatting b Willis	3	c (sub) b Willis	64
EJ Chatfield	not out	4	b Cook	0
Extras	(4b, 9lb, 0w, 7nb)	20	(4b, 14lb, 2w, 14nb)	34
Total	93.4 overs	**219**	187.3 overs	**537**

1st innings FoW: 34, 39, 56, 71, 114, 160, 174, 200, 208, 219
2nd innings FoW: 62, 79, 153, 165, 279, 302, 334, 402, 520, 537

RGD Willis	19	7	37	3	37	8	102	2
IT Botham	27.4	8	59	5	36	6	137	1
NA Foster	24	9	60	1	37	12	91	2
NGB Cook	23	11	43	1	66.3	26	153	3
MW Gatting					8	4	14	1
CL Smith					3	1	6	0

ENGLAND	1st innings		2nd innings	
CJ Tavare	b Cairns	9	not out	36
CL Smith	c Hadlee b Cairns	27	not out	30
DI Gower	c Hadlee b Cairns	33		
AJ Lamb	c MD Crowe b Cairns	13		
MW Gatting	lbw b Cairns	19		
IT Botham	c JJ Crowe b Cairns	138		
DW Randall	c MD Crowe b Hadlee	164		
RW Taylor+	run out	14		
NGB Cook	c Smith b Cairns	7		
NA Foster	c Howarth b Hadlee	10		
RGD Willis*	not out	5		
Extras	(0b, 8lb, 0w, 16nb)	24	(0b, 0lb, 0w, 3nb)	3
Total	132.5 overs	**463**	22 overs	**69**

1st innings FoW: 41, 51, 84, 92, 115, 347, 372, 386, 426, 463

RJ Hadlee	31.5	6	97	2				
MC Snedden	21	3	101	0	7	2	28	0
BL Cairns	45	10	143	7				
EJ Chatfield	28	6	68	0	5	0	24	0
MD Crowe	3	0	20	0	6	1	11	0
JV Coney	4	1	10	0				
BA Edgar					3	1	3	0
JJ Crowe					1	1	0	0

No. 596: 2nd Test

VENUE:	Christchurch
DATE:	3rd-5th February 1984
TOSS WON BY:	New Zealand
RESULT:	NZ won by an innings and 132 runs

NEW ZEALAND 1st innings   **2nd innings**

JG Wright	c Taylor b Cowans	25
BA Edgar	c Randall b Pigott	1
GP Howarth*	b Cowans	9
MD Crowe	c Tavare b Botham	19
JJ Crowe	lbw b Cowans	47
JV Coney	c Botham b Pigott	41
RJ Hadlee	c Taylor b Willis	99
IDS Smith+	not out	32
BL Cairns	c Taylor b Willis	2
SL Boock	c Taylor b Willis	5
EJ Chatfield	lbw b Willis	0
Extras	(8b, 11lb, 2w, 6nb)	27
	72.1 overs	
Total		**307**

1st innings FoW: 30, 42, 53, 87, 137, 203, 281, 291, 301, 307

RGD Willis	22.1	5	51	4
IT Botham	17	1	88	1
ACS Pigott	17	7	75	2
NG Cowans	14	2	52	3
MW Gatting	2	0	14	0

ENGLAND   1st innings   **2nd innings**

G Fowler	b Boock	4	c Howarth b Boock	10	
CJ Tavare	c JJ Crowe b Hadlee	3	c Smith b Hadlee	6	
DI Gower	lbw b Hadlee	2	c Cairns b Hadlee	8	
AJ Lamb	c Smith b Chatfield	11	c Coney b Chatfield	9	
DW Randall	c Coney b Hadlee	0	c Hadlee b Boock	0	
IT Botham	c Chatfield b Cairns	18	c MD Crowe b Boock	0	
MW Gatting	not out	19	c Cairns b Hadlee	25	
RW Taylor+	c JJ Crowe b Cairns	2	run out	15	
ACS Pigott	lbw b Cairns	4	not out	8	
RGD Willis*	b Chatfield	6	c Howarth b Hadlee	0	
NG Cowans	c Coney b Chatfield	4	c Smith b Hadlee	7	
Extras	(0b, 6lb, 0w, 3nb)	9	(0b, 2lb, 0w, 3nb)	5	
	50.2 overs		51 overs		
Total		**82**		**93**	

1st innings FoW: 7, 9, 10, 10, 41, 41, 47, 58, 72, 82
2nd innings FoW: 15, 23, 25, 31, 31, 33, 72, 76, 80, 93

RJ Hadlee	18	6	28	5		17	9	16	3
BL Cairns	9	3	21	0		19	5	35	3
SL Boock	13	3	25	3		6	3	12	1
EJ Chatfield	11	1	14	1		8.2	3	10	3

No. 597: 3rd Test

VENUE:	Auckland
DATE:	10th-15th February 1984
TOSS WON BY:	New Zealand
RESULT:	Match drawn

NEW ZEALAND 1st innings   **2nd innings**

JG Wright	b Willis	130	not out	11
BA Edgar	lbw b Willis	0	not out	0
GP Howarth*	c Randall b Cowans	35		
MD Crowe	c Botham b Willis	16		
JJ Crowe	b Marks	128		
JV Coney	b Cowans	9		
RJ Hadlee	b Marks	3		
IDS Smith+	not out	113		
BL Cairns	c Cowans b Foster	28		
SL Boock	lbw b Marks	2		
EJ Chatfield	not out	6		
Extras	(0b, 19lb, 0w, 7nb)	26	(0b, 1lb, 0w, 4nb)	5
	169.2 overs		5 overs	
Total		**496**		**16**

1st innings FoW: 3, 74, 111, 265, 293, 302, 385, 451, 461

RGD Willis	34	7	109	3		3	1	7	0
IT Botham	29	10	70	0					
NG Cowans	36	11	98	2		2	1	4	0
NA Foster	30	8	78	1					
VJ Marks	40.2	9	115	3					

ENGLAND   1st innings   **2nd innings**

G Fowler	c Smith b Hadlee	0	
CL Smith	c Smith b Cairns	91	
DI Gower	b Boock	26	
AJ Lamb	lbw b Cairns	49	
DW Randall	c Wright b Chatfield	104	
RW Taylor+	st Smith b Boock	23	
IT Botham	run out	70	
VJ Marks	c Smith b Chatfield	6	
NA Foster	not out	18	
RGD Willis*	c Smith b Hadlee	3	
NG Cowans	c Cairns b Boock	21	
Extras	(7b, 13lb, 0w, 8nb)	28	
	227.3 overs		
Total		**439**	

1st innings FoW: 0, 48, 143, 234, 284, 371, 387, 391, 396, 439

RJ Hadlee	43	12	91	2
BL Cairns	40	19	52	2
SL Boock	61.3	28	103	3
EJ Chatfield	46	23	72	2
MD Crowe	17	5	62	0
JV Coney	13	8	13	0
GP Howarth	7	1	18	0

No. 598: 1st Test
VENUE: Karachi (National Stadium)
DATE: 2nd-6th March 1984
TOSS WON BY: England
RESULT: Pakistan won by 3 wickets

No. 599: 2nd Test
VENUE: Faisalabad
DATE: 12th-17th March 1984
TOSS WON BY: Pakistan
RESULT: Match drawn

1st Test — Karachi

ENGLAND	1st innings		2nd innings	
CL Smith	c Wasim Raja b Sarfraz	28	lbw b Sarfraz	5
MW Gatting	b Tauseef	26	lbw b Sarfraz	4
DI Gower	lbw b Abdul	58	c Mohsin b Tauseef	57
AJ Lamb	c Rameez Raja b Sarfraz	4	c Anil b Abdul	20
DW Randall	b Abdul	8	b Abdul	16
IT Botham	c Rameez Raja b Abdul	22	b Tauseef	10
VJ Marks	c Rameez Raja b Sarfraz	5	b Abdul	1
RW Taylor+	lbw b Abdul	4	c Mohsin b Tauseef	19
NGB Cook	c Salim b Abdul	9	c Mohsin b Wasim Raja	5
RGD Willis*	c Wasim Raja b Sarfraz	6	c Tauseef b Wasim Raja	2
NG Cowans	not out	1	not out	0
Extras	(0b, 6lb, 0w, 5nb)	11	(6b, 6lb, 0w, 8nb)	20
Total	94.5 overs	182	78.3 overs	159

1st innings FoW: 41, 90, 94, 108, 154, 159, 164, 165, 180, 182
2nd innings FoW: 6, 21, 63, 94, 121, 128, 128, 157, 159, 159

Azeem Hafeez	11	3	21	0		8	3	14	0
Sarfraz Nawaz	25.5	8	42	4		15	1	27	2
Tauseef Ahmed	24	11	33	1		21	6	37	3
Wasim Raja	3	2	1	0		3.3	1	2	2
Abdul Qadir	31	12	74	5		31	4	59	3

PAKISTAN	1st innings		2nd innings	
Mohsin Khan	c Botham b Cook	54	b Cook	10
Qasim Omar	lbw b Cook	29	c Botham b Cook	7
Rameez Raja	c Smith b Cook	1	c Botham b Marks	1
Zaheer Abbas*	c Lamb b Botham	0	b Cook	8
Salim Malik	lbw b Willis	74	run out	11
Wasim Raja	c Cowans b Cook	3	c Cowans b Cook	0
Anil Dalpat+	c Taylor b Willis	12	not out	16
Abdul Qadir	c Lamb b Botham	40	b Cook	7
Sarfraz Nawaz	c Botham b Cook	8	not out	4
Tauseef Ahmed	not out	17		
Azeem Hafeez	c Willis b Cook	24		
Extras	(0b, 5lb, 0w, 10nb)	15	(1b, 0lb, 0w, 1nb)	2
Total	102 overs	277	30.3 overs	66

1st innings FoW: 67, 79, 80, 96, 105, 138, 213, 229, 240, 277
2nd innings FoW: 17, 18, 26, 38, 38, 40, 59

RGD Willis	17	6	33	2		2	0	13	0
NG Cowans	12	3	34	0		2.3	1	10	0
IT Botham	30	5	90	2					
NGB Cook	30	12	65	6		14	8	18	5
VJ Marks	13	4	40	0		12	5	23	1

2nd Test — Faisalabad

PAKISTAN	1st innings		2nd innings	
Mohsin Khan	c Lamb b Dilley	20	b Dilley	2
M Nazar	c Gatting b Cook	12	lbw b Foster	4
Qasim Omar	c Gatting b Foster	16	c Taylor b Dilley	17
Salim Malik	c Lamb b Cook	116	c (sub) b Marks	76
Zaheer Abbas*	lbw b Gatting	68	not out	32
Wasim Raja	b Marks	112	not out	5
Abdul Qadir	c Foster b Dilley	50		
Anil Dalpat+	lbw b Dilley	8		
Sarfraz Nawaz	not out	16		
Tauseef Ahmed	not out	1		
Azeem Hafeez				
Extras	(0b, 11lb, 2w, 17nb)	30	(0b, 1lb, 0w, 0nb)	1
Total	142 overs	449	41 overs	137

1st innings FoW: 35, 53, 70, 200, 323, 416, 430, 433
2nd innings FoW: 6, 6, 56, 123

NA Foster	30	7	109	1		5	1	10	1
GR Dilley	28	6	101	3		9	0	41	2
NGB Cook	54	14	133	2		16	6	38	0
VJ Marks	27	9	59	1		8	2	26	1
MW Gatting	3	0	17	1		2	0	18	0
G Fowler						1	0	3	0

ENGLAND	1st innings		2nd innings
CL Smith	b Sarfraz	66	
MW Gatting	c Salim b Tauseef	75	
DW Randall	b Sarfraz	65	
AJ Lamb	c Anil b Azeem	19	
DI Gower*	st Anil b Mudassar	152	
G Fowler	c Qasim b Wasim	57	
RW Taylor+	c Salim b Abdul	0	
VJ Marks	b Sarfraz	83	
GR Dilley	not out	2	
NGB Cook	not out	1	
NA Foster			
Extras	(10b, 4lb, 0w, 12nb)	26	
Total	189 overs	546	

1st innings FoW: 127, 163, 214, 245, 361, 361, 528, 545

Azeem Hafeez	19	3	71	1
Sarfraz Nawaz	50	11	129	3
Wasim Raja	26	6	61	0
Abdul Qadir	51	14	124	1
Tauseef Ahmed	30	8	96	1
Mudassar Nazar	13	1	39	1

No. 600: 3rd Test		
VENUE: Lahore (Gaddafi)		
DATE: 19th-24th March 1984		
TOSS WON BY: Pakistan		
RESULT: Match drawn		

No. 601: 1st Test		
VENUE: Edgbaston		
DATE: 14th-18th June 1984		
TOSS WON BY: England		
RESULT: WI won by an innings and 180 runs		

ENGLAND 1st innings / 2nd innings (Lahore)

Batsman	1st innings		2nd innings	
CL Smith	c Salim b Sarfraz	18	c Anil b Mohsin Kamal	19
MW Gatting	lbw b Sarfraz	0	run out	15
DI Gower*	c Anil b Mohsin Kamal	9	run out	53
AJ Lamb	c Rameez Raja b Abdul	29	not out	173
DW Randall	c Salim b Abdul	14	c & b Abdul	6
G Fowler	c Qasim b Abdul	58	c Salim b Abdul	0
VJ Marks	c Mohsin Khan b Abdul	74	c (sub) b Abdul	55
RW Taylor+	lbw b Sarfraz	1	lbw b Abdul	0
NA Foster	lbw b Abdul	6	st Anil b Abdul	3
NGB Cook	c Anil b Sarfraz	3	b Sarfraz	5
NG Cowans	not out	3		
Extras	(4b, 5lb, 9w, 8nb)	26	(6b, 3lb, 1w, 5nb)	15
	78.5 overs		107.4 overs	
Total		**241**		**344**

1st innings FoW: 5, 20, 47, 77, 83, 203, 205, 222, 237, 241
2nd innings FoW: 35, 38, 175, 189, 189, 308, 309, 327, 344

Bowler	O	M	R	W	O	M	R	W
Mohsin Kamal	15	0	66	1	17	3	59	1
Sarfraz Nawaz	22.5	5	49	4	27.4	1	112	1
Abdul Qadir	30	7	84	5	42	5	110	5
Wasim Raja	11	4	16	0	21	5	48	0

ENGLAND 1st innings / 2nd innings (Edgbaston)

Batsman	1st innings		2nd innings	
G Fowler	c Dujon b Garner	0	lbw b Garner	7
TA Lloyd	retired hurt	10	c Greenidge b Harper	56
DW Randall	b Garner	0	c Lloyd b Garner	1
DI Gower*	c Harper b Holding	10	c Dujon b Garner	12
AJ Lamb	c Lloyd b Baptiste	15	c Richards b Marshall	13
IT Botham	c Garner b Harper	64	lbw b Garner	38
G Miller	c Dujon b Garner	22	c Harper b Marshall	11
DR Pringle	c Dujon b Holding	4	not out	46
PR Downton+	lbw b Garner	33	run out	9
NGB Cook	c Lloyd b Marshall	2	c Dujon b Garner	22
RGD Willis	not out	10		
Extras	(8b, 5lb, 0w, 8nb)	21	(1b, 5lb, 4w, 10nb)	20
	59.3 overs		76.5 overs	
Total		**191**		**235**

1st innings FoW: 1, 5, 45, 49, 89, 103, 168, 173, 191
2nd innings FoW: 17, 21,. 37, 65, 127, 138, 181, 193, 235

Bowler	O	M	R	W	O	M	R	W
MD Marshall	14	4	37	1	23	7	65	2
J Garner	14.3	2	53	4	23.5	7	55	5
MA Holding	16	4	44	2	12	3	29	0
EAE Baptiste	11	3	28	1	5	1	18	0
RA Harper	4	1	8	1	13	3	48	1

PAKISTAN 1st innings / 2nd innings

Batsman	1st innings		2nd innings	
Mohsin Khan	lbw b Foster	1	c Smith b Cowans	104
Shoaib Moh'd	lbw b Cowans	7	c Gatting b Cowans	80
Qasim Omar	c Fowler b Foster	73	run out	0
Salim Malik	b Marks	38	c Gatting b Cowans	7
Rameez Raja	c Smith b Foster	26	c Gatting b Cowans	5
Wasim Raja	c Gower b Cowans	12	lbw b Cowans	0
Zaheer Abbas*	not out	82	not out	10
Abdul Qadir	c Taylor b Foster	3	not out	6
Anil Dalpat+	c Gower b Foster	2		
Sarfraz Nawaz	c Gatting b Smith	90		
Mohsin Kamal	c Gower b Cook	0		
Extras	(0b, 9lb, 0w, 0nb)	9	(0b, 5lb, 0w, 0nb)	5
	128 overs		58.3 overs	
Total		**343**		**217**

1st innings FoW: 9, 13, 99, 138, 151, 166, 175, 181, 342, 343
2nd innings FoW: 173, 175, 187, 197, 199, 199

Bowler	O	M	R	W	O	M	R	W
NG Cowans	29	5	89	2	14	2	42	5
NA Foster	32	8	67	5	15	4	44	0
NGB Cook	46	12	117	1	18.3	2	73	0
VJ Marks	20	4	59	1	10	0	53	0
CL Smith	1	0	2	1	1	1	0	0

WEST INDIES 1st innings / 2nd innings

Batsman	1st innings		2nd innings
CG Greenidge	lbw b Willis	19	
DL Haynes	lbw b Willis	8	
HA Gomes	c Miller b Pringle	143	
IVA Richards	c Randall b Cook	117	
PJL Dujon+	c Gower b Miller	23	
CH Lloyd*	c Pringle b Botham	71	
MD Marshall	lbw b Pringle	2	
RA Harper	b Pringle	14	
EAE Baptiste	not out	87	
MA Holding	c Willis b Pringle	69	
J Garner	c Lamb b Pringle	0	
Extras	(6b, 17lb, 2w, 28nb)	53	
	143 overs		
Total		**606**	

1st innings FoW: 34, 35, 241, 294, 418, 418, 421, 455, 605, 606

Bowler	O	M	R	W
RGD Willis	25	3	108	2
IT Botham	34	7	127	1
DR Pringle	31	5	108	5
NGB Cook	38	6	127	1
G Miller	15	1	83	1

West Indies | West Indies

No. 602: 2nd Test	No. 603: 3rd Test
VENUE: Lord's	VENUE: Headingley
DATE: 28th June to 3rd July 1984	DATE: 12th-16th July 1984
TOSS WON BY: West Indies	TOSS WON BY: England
RESULT: West Indies won by 9 wickets	RESULT: West Indies won by 8 wickets

No. 602

ENGLAND	1st innings		2nd innings	
G Fowler	c Harper b Baptiste	106	lbw b Small	11
BC Broad	c Dujon b Marshall	55	c Harper b Garner	0
DI Gower*	lbw b Marshall	3	c Lloyd b Small	21
AJ Lamb	lbw b Marshall	23	c Dujon b Marshall	110
MW Gatting	lbw b Marshall	1	lbw b Marshall	29
IT Botham	c Richards b Baptiste	30	lbw b Garner	81
PR Downton+	not out	23	lbw b Small	4
G Miller	run out	0	b Harper	9
DR Pringle	lbw b Garner	2	lbw b Garner	8
NA Foster	c Harper b Marshall	6	not out	9
RGD Willis	b Marshall	2		
Extras	(4b, 14lb, 2w, 15nb)	35	(4b, 7lb, 1w, 6nb)	18
	105.5 overs		98.3 overs	
Total		**286**		**300**

1st innings FoW: 101, 106, 183, 185, 243, 248, 251, 255, 264, 286
2nd innings FoW: 5, 33, 36, 88, 216, 230, 273, 290, 300

J Garner	32	10	67	1	30.3	3	91	3
MA Small	9	0	38	0	12	2	40	3
MD Marshall	36.5	10	85	6	22	6	85	2
EAE Baptiste	20	6	36	2	26	8	48	0
RA Harper	8	0	25	0	8	1	18	1

WEST INDIES	1st innings		2nd innings	
CG Greenidge	c Miller b Botham	1	not out	214
DL Haynes	lbw b Botham	12	run out	17
HA Gomes	c Gatting b Botham	10	not out	92
IVA Richards	lbw b Botham	72		
CH Lloyd*	lbw b Botham	39		
PJL Dujon+	c Fowler b Botham	8		
MD Marshall	c Pringle b Willis	29		
EAE Baptiste	c Downton b Willis	44		
RA Harper	c Gatting b Botham	8		
J Garner	c Downton b Botham	6		
MA Small	not out	3		
Extras	(0b, 5lb, 1w, 7nb)	13	(4b, 4lb, 0w, 13nb)	21
	65.4 overs		66.1 overs	
Total		**245**		**344**

1st innings FoW: 1, 18, 35, 138, 147, 173, 213, 231, 241, 245
2nd innings FoW: 57

RGD Willis	19	5	48	2	15	5	48	0
IT Botham	27.4	6	103	8	20.1	2	117	0
DR Pringle	11	0	54	0	8	0	44	0
NA Foster	6	2	13	0	12	0	69	0
G Miller	2	0	14	0	11	0	45	0

No. 603

ENGLAND	1st innings		2nd innings	
G Fowler	lbw b Garner	10	c & b Marshall	50
BC Broad	c Lloyd b Harper	32	c Baptiste b Marshall	2
VP Terry	c Harper b Holding	8	lbw b Garner	1
DI Gower*	lbw b Garner	2	c Dujon b Harper	43
AJ Lamb	b Harper	100	lbw b Marshall	3
IT Botham	c Dujon b Baptiste	45	c Dujon b Garner	14
PR Downton+	c Lloyd b Harper	17	c Dujon b Marshall	27
DR Pringle	c Haynes b Holding	19	lbw b Marshall	2
PJW Allott	b Holding	3	lbw b Marshall	4
NGB Cook	b Holding	1	c Lloyd b Marshall	0
RGD Willis	not out	4	not out	5
Extras	(4b, 7lb, 0w, 18nb)	29	(0b, 6lb, 0w, 2nb)	8
	97.2 overs		65 overs	
Total		**270**		**159**

1st innings FoW: 13, 43, 53, 87, 172, 236, 237, 244, 254, 270
2nd innings FoW: 10, 13, 104, 106, 107, 135, 138, 140, 146, 159

J Garner	30	11	73	2	16	7	37	2
MD Marshall	6	4	6	0	26	9	53	7
MA Holding	29.2	8	70	4	7	1	31	0
EAE Baptiste	13	1	45	1				
RA Harper	19	6	47	3	16	8	30	1

WEST INDIES	1st innings		2nd innings	
CG Greenidge	c Botham b Willis	10	c Terry b Cook	49
DL Haynes	b Allott	18	c Fowler b Cook	43
HA Gomes	not out	104	not out	2
IVA Richards	c Pringle b Allott	15	not out	22
CH Lloyd*	c Gower b Cook	48		
PJL Dujon+	lbw b Allott	26		
EAE Baptiste	c Broad b Allott	0		
RA Harper	c Downton b Allott	0		
MA Holding	c Allott b Willis	59		
J Garner	run out	0		
MD Marshall	c Botham b Allott	4		
Extras	(0b, 3lb, 0w, 15nb)	18	(0b, 2lb, 0w, 13nb)	15
	73.5 overs		32.3 overs	
Total		**302**		**131**

1st innings FoW: 16, 43, 78, 148, 201, 206, 206, 288, 290, 302
2nd innings FoW: 106, 108

RGD Willis	18	1	123	2	8	1	40	0
PJW Allott	26.5	7	61	6	7	2	24	0
IT Botham	7	0	45	0				
DR Pringle	13	3	26	0	8.3	2	25	0
NGB Cook	9	1	29	1	9	2	27	2

	No. 604: 4th Test	
	VENUE: Old Trafford	
	DATE: 26th-31st July 1984	
	TOSS WON BY: West Indies	
	RESULT: WI won by an innings and 64 runs	

	No. 605: 5th Test	
	VENUE: The Oval	
	DATE: 9th-14th August 1984	
	TOSS WON BY: West Indies	
	RESULT: West Indies won by 172 runs	

WEST INDIES 1st innings / 2nd innings (4th Test)

Batsman	Dismissal	Runs	2nd innings
CG Greenidge	c Downton b Pocock	223	
DL Haynes	c Cowans b Botham	2	
HA Gomes	c Botham b Allott	30	
IVA Richards	c Cook b Allott	1	
CH Lloyd*	c Downton b Allott	1	
PJL Dujon+	c Downton b Botham	101	
WW Davis	b Pocock	77	
EAE Baptiste	b Pocock	6	
RA Harper	not out	39	
MA Holding	b Cook	0	
J Garner	c Terry b Pocock	7	
Extras	(4b, 6lb, 2w, 1nb)	13	
	160.3 overs		
Total		**500**	

1st innings FoW: 11, 60, 62, 70, 267, 437, 443, 470, 471, 500

Bowler	O	M	R	W				
IT Botham	29	5	100	2				
NG Cowans	19	2	76	0				
PJW Allott	28	9	76	3				
NGB Cook	39	6	114	1				
PI Pocock	45.3	14	121	4				

ENGLAND 1st innings / 2nd innings (4th Test)

Batsman	1st innings	Runs	2nd innings	Runs
G Fowler	b Baptiste	38	b Holding	0
BC Broad	c Harper b Davis	42	lbw b Harper	21
VP Terry	b Garner	7	b Harper	24
DI Gower*	c Dujon b Baptiste	4	not out	57
AJ Lamb	not out	100	b Harper	9
IT Botham	c Garner b Baptiste	6	c Haynes b Harper	1
PR Downton+	c Harper b Garner	0	b Garner	14
PJW Allott	c Gomes b Davis	26	c Dujon b Garner	0
NGB Cook	b Holding	13	c Garner b Harper	0
PI Pocock	b Garner	0	b Harper	14
NG Cowans	b Garner	0		
Extras	(5b, 21lb, 0w, 18nb)	44	(9b, 3lb, 1w, 3nb)	16
	105.2 overs		66.4 overs	
Total		**280**		**156**

1st innings FoW: 90, 112, 117, 138, 147, 228, 257, 278, 278, 280
2nd innings FoW: 0, 39, 77, 99, 101, 125, 127, 128, 156

Bowler	O	M	R	W	O	M	R	W
J Garner	22.2	7	51	4	12	4	25	2
WW Davis	20	2	71	2	3	1	6	0
RA Harper	23	10	33	0	28.4	12	57	6
MA Holding	21	2	50	1	11	2	21	1
EAE Baptiste	19	8	31	3	11	5	29	0
IVA Richards					1	0	2	0

WEST INDIES 1st innings / 2nd innings (5th Test)

Batsman	1st innings	Runs	2nd innings	Runs
CG Greenidge	lbw b Botham	22	c Botham b Agnew	34
DL Haynes	b Allott	10	b Botham	125
HA Gomes	c Botham b Ellison	18	c Tavare b Ellison	1
IVA Richards	c Allott b Botham	8	lbw b Agnew	15
PJL Dujon+	c Tavare b Botham	3	c Downton b Ellison	36
CH Lloyd*	not out	60	c Lamb b Ellison	49
MD Marshall	c Gower b Ellison	0	c Downton b Allott	5
EAE Baptiste	c Fowler b Allott	32	c Lamb b Botham	12
RA Harper	b Botham	18	c Downton b Allott	17
MA Holding	lbw b Botham	0	lbw b Botham	30
J Garner	c Downton b Allott	6	not out	10
Extras	(1b, 4lb, 7w, 1nb)	13	(0b, 12lb, 0w, 0nb)	12
	70 overs		96.3 overs	
Total		**190**		**346**

1st innings FoW: 19, 45, 64, 64, 67, 70, 124, 154, 154, 190
2nd innings FoW: 51, 52, 69, 132, 214, 237, 264, 293, 329, 346

Bowler	O	M	R	W	O	M	R	W
JP Agnew	12	3	46	0	14	1	51	2
PJW Allott	17	7	25	3	26	1	96	2
IT Botham	23	8	72	5	22.3	2	103	3
RM Ellison	18	3	34	2	26	7	60	3
PI Pocock					8	3	24	0

ENGLAND 1st innings / 2nd innings (5th Test)

Batsman	1st innings	Runs	2nd innings	Runs
G Fowler	c Richards b Baptiste	31	c Richards b Marshall	7
BC Broad	b Garner	4	c Greenidge b Holding	39
PI Pocock	c Greenidge b Marshall	0	c Richards b Garner	49
CJ Tavare	c Dujon b Holding	0	lbw b Holding	7
DI Gower*	c Dujon b Holding	12	c Haynes b Holding	1
AJ Lamb	lbw b Marshall	12	c Marshall b Garner	54
IT Botham	c Dujon b Marshall	14	lbw b Garner	10
PR Downton+	c Lloyd b Garner	16	c Holding b Garner	13
RM Ellison	not out	20	c Lloyd b Holding	4
PJW Allott	b Marshall	16	c & b Holding	0
JP Agnew	b Marshall	5	not out	2
Extras	(2b, 4lb, 0w, 10nb)	16	(0b, 2lb, 1w, 13nb)	16
	61.5 overs		69.4 overs	
Total		**162**		**202**

1st innings FoW: 10, 22, 45, 64, 83, 84, 116, 133, 156, 162
2nd innings FoW: 15, 75, 88, 90, 135, 181, 186, 200, 200, 202

Bowler	O	M	R	W	O	M	R	W
J Garner	18	6	37	2	18.4	3	51	4
MD Marshall	17.5	5	35	5	22	5	71	1
MA Holding	13	2	55	2	13	2	43	5
EAE Baptiste	12	4	19	1	8	3	11	0
RA Harper	1	1	0	0	8	5	10	0

Sri Lanka

No. 606: 1st Test
VENUE: Lord's
DATE: 23rd-28th August 1984
TOSS WON BY: England
RESULT: Match drawn

India

No. 607: 1st Test
VENUE: Bombay (Wankhede)
DATE: 28th November to 3rd Dec 1984
TOSS WON BY: England
RESULT: India won by 8 wickets

SRI LANKA 1st innings / 2nd innings

Batsman	1st innings		2nd innings	
S Wettimuny	c Downton b Allott	190	c Gower b Botham	13
SAR Silva+	lbw b Botham	8	not out	102
RS Madugalle	b Ellison	5	b Botham	3
RL Dias	c Lamb b Pocock	32	lbw b Botham	38
A Ranatunga	b Agnew	84	lbw b Botham	0
LRD Mendis*	c Fowler b Pocock	111	c Downton b Pocock	3
PA de Silva	c Downton b Agnew	16	c Fowler b Botham	94
ALF de Mel	not out	20	c Ellison b Botham	14
JR Ratnayeke	not out	5	not out	7
DS de Silva				
VB John				
Extras	(2b, 8lb, 2w, 8nb)	20	(5b, 4lb, 0w, 11nb)	20
	166 overs		80 overs	
Total		**491**		**294**

1st innings FoW: 17, 43, 144, 292, 442, 456, 464
2nd innings FoW: 19, 27, 111, 115, 118, 256, 276

Bowler	O	M	R	W	O	M	R	W
JP Agnew	32	3	123	2	11	3	54	0
IT Botham	29	6	114	1	27	6	90	6
RM Ellison	28	6	70	1	7	0	36	0
PI Pocock	41	17	75	2	29	10	78	1
PJW Allott	36	7	89	1	1	0	2	0
AJ Lamb					1	0	6	0
CJ Tavare					3	3	0	0
G Fowler					1	0	8	0

ENGLAND 1st innings / 2nd innings

Batsman	1st innings	
G Fowler	c Madugalle b John	25
BC Broad	c Silva b de Mel	86
CJ Tavare	c Ran'ga b D de Silva	14
DI Gower*	c Silva b de Mel	55
AJ Lamb	c Dias b John	107
IT Botham	c (sub) b John	6
RM Ellison	c Rat'eke b DS de Silva	41
PR Downton+	c Dias b de Mel	10
PJW Allott	b de Mel	0
PI Pocock	c Silva b John	2
JP Agnew	not out	1
Extras	(5b, 7lb, 5w, 6nb)	23
	147.1 overs	
Total		**370**

1st innings FoW: 49, 105, 190, 210, 218, 305, 354, 354, 369, 370

Bowler	O	M	R	W
ALF de Mel	37	10	110	4
VB John	39.1	12	98	4
JR Ratnayeke	22	5	50	0
DS de Silva	45	16	85	2
A Ranatunga	1	1	0	0
RS Madugalle	3	0	4	0

ENGLAND 1st innings / 2nd innings

Batsman	1st innings		2nd innings	
G Fowler	c & b Sivaramakrishnan	28	lbw b Sivar'kris'n	55
RT Robinson	c Kirmani b Sivar'kris'n	22	lbw b Kapil Dev	1
MW Gatting	c & b Sivaramakrishnan	15	c Patil b Sivar'kris'n	136
DI Gower*	b Kapil Dev	13	c Vengsarkar b Shastri	2
AJ Lamb	c Shastri b Kapil Dev	9	st Kirmani b Sivar'kris'n	1
CS Cowdrey	c Kirmani b Yadav	13	c Vengsarkar b Yadav	14
RM Ellison	b Sivaramakrishnan	1	lbw b Sivar'krishnan	62
PR Downton+	not out	37	c Vengsarkar b Yadav	0
PH Edmonds	c Gaekwad b Shastri	48	c Kapil Dev b Sivar'kris'n	8
PI Pocock	c Kirmani b Sivar'kris'n	8	not out	22
NG Cowans	c Shastri b Sivar'kris'n	0	c Ven'ar b Sivar'kris'n	0
Extras	(1b, 0lb, 0w, 0nb)	1	(4b, 8lb, 0w, 4nb)	16
	96.2 overs		135 overs	
Total		**195**		**317**

1st innings FoW: 46, 51, 78, 78, 93, 94, 114, 175, 193, 195
2nd innings FoW: 3, 138, 145, 152, 199, 222, 228, 255, 317, 317

Bowler	O	M	R	W	O	M	R	W
N Kapil Dev	22	8	44	2	21	8	34	1
C Sharma	11	4	28	0	9	2	39	0
RJ Shastri	17	8	23	1	29	8	50	1
M Amarnath	3	2	1	0				
L Sivar'kris'n	31.2	10	64	6	46	10	117	6
NS Yadav	12	2	34	1	29	9	64	2
AD Gaekwad					1	0	1	0

INDIA 1st innings / 2nd innings

Batsman	1st innings		2nd innings	
SM Gavaskar*	c Downton b Cowans	27	c Gower b Cowans	5
AD Gaekwad	run out	24	st Downton b Edmonds	1
DB Vengsarkar	c Lamb b Cowans	34	not out	21
M Amarnath	c Cowdrey b Pocock	49	not out	22
SM Patil	c Gower b Edmonds	20		
RJ Shastri	c Lamb b Pocock	142		
N Kapil Dev	b Cowdrey	42		
SMH Kirmani+	c Lamb b Pocock	102		
C Sharma	not out	5		
NS Yadav	not out	7		
L Sivaramakrishnan				
Extras	(4b, 2lb, 0w, 7nb)	13	(2b, 0lb, 0w, 0nb)	2
	137 overs		15.1 overs	
Total		**465**		**51**

1st innings FoW: 47, 59, 116, 156, 156, 218, 453, 453
2nd innings FoW: 5, 7

Bowler	O	M	R	W	O	M	R	W
RM Ellison	18	3	85	0				
NG Cowans	28	6	109	2	5	2	18	1
PH Edmonds	33	6	82	1	8	3	21	1
PI Pocock	46	10	133	3	2.1	0	10	0
CS Cowdrey	5	0	30	1				
MW Gatting	7	0	20	0				

No. 608: 2nd Test

VENUE:	Delhi
DATE:	12th-17th December 1984
TOSS WON BY:	India
RESULT:	England won by 8 wickets

INDIA 1st innings

	1st innings		2nd innings	
SM Gavaskar*	c Downton b Ellison	1	b Pocock	65
AD Gaekwad	b Pocock	28	c Downton b Cowans	5
DB Vengsarkar	st Downton b Edmonds	24	b Cowans	1
M Amarnath	c Gower b Pocock	42	b Edmonds	64
SM Patil	c Pocock b Edmonds	30	c Lamb b Edmonds	41
RJ Shastri	c Fowler b Pocock	2	not out	25
N Kapil Dev	c Downton b Ellison	60	c Lamb b Pocock	7
SMH Kirmani+	c Gatting b Ellison	27	c Downton b Edmonds	0
M Prabhakar	c Downton b Ellison	25	b Pocock	6
NS Yadav	not out	28	c Lamb b Edmonds	1
L Sivar'kris'n	run out	25	c & b Pocock	0
Extras	(1b, 12lb, 0w, 2nb)	15	(6b, 10lb, 1w, 3nb)	20
Total	125.2 overs	**307**	103.4 overs	**235**

1st innings FoW: 3, 56, 68, 129, 131, 140, 208, 235, 258, 307
2nd innings FoW: 12, 15, 136, 172, 207, 214, 216, 225, 234, 235

NG Cowans	20	5	70	0	13	2	43	2
RM Ellison	26	6	66	4	7	1	20	0
PH Edmonds	44.2	16	83	2	44	24	60	4
PI Pocock	33	8	70	3	38.4	9	93	4
MW Gatting	2	0	5	0	1	0	3	0

ENGLAND 1st innings

	1st innings		2nd innings	
G Fowler	c Gaekwad b Prabhakar	5	c Vengs'ar b Sivar'kris'n	29
RT Robinson	c Gavaskar b Kapil Dev	160	run out	18
MW Gatting	b Yadav	26	not out	30
AJ Lamb	c Vengsarkar b Yadav	52	not out	37
DI Gower*	lbw b Sivar'krishnan	5		
CS Cowdrey	c Gavaskar b Sivar'kris'n	38		
PR Downton+	c Kapil Dev b Sivar'kris'n	74		
PH Edmonds	c Shastri b Sivar'kris'n	26		
RM Ellison	b Sivaramakrishnan	10		
PI Pocock	b Sivaramakrishnan	0		
NG Cowans	not out	0		
Extras	(6b, 13lb, 0w, 3nb)	22	(4b, 7lb, 0w, 2nb)	13
Total	169.1 overs	**418**	23.4 overs	**127**

1st innings FoW: 15, 60, 170, 181, 237, 343, 398, 411, 415, 418
2nd innings FoW: 41, 68

N Kapil Dev	32	5	87	1	6	0	20	0
M Prabhakar	21	3	68	1	3	0	18	0
L Sivaramakris'n	49.1	17	99	6	8	0	41	1
NS Yadav	36	6	95	2	2	0	7	0
RJ Shastri	29	4	44	0	4	0	20	0
M Amarnath	2	0	6	0				
SM Gavaskar					0.4	0	10	0

No. 609: 3rd Test

VENUE:	Calcutta
DATE:	31st Dec 1984 to 5th Jan 1985
TOSS WON BY:	India
RESULT:	Match drawn

INDIA 1st innings

	1st innings		2nd innings	
SM Gavaskar*	c Gatting b Edmonds	13		
AD Gaekwad	c Downton b Cowans	18		
DB Vengsarkar	b Edmonds	48		
M Amarnath	c Cowdrey b Edmonds	42		
M Azharuddin	c Gower b Cowans	110		
RJ Shastri	b Cowans	111	not out	7
SMH Kirmani+	c Fowler b Pocock	35		
M Prabhakar	not out	35	lbw b Lamb	21
C Sharma	not out	13		
NS Yadav			not out	0
L Sivar'kris'n				
Extras	(0b, 8lb, 1w, 3nb)	12	(0b, 0lb, 0w, 1nb)	1
Total	200 overs	**437**	18 overs	**29**

1st innings FoW: 28, 35, 126, 127, 341, 356, 407
2nd innings FoW: 29

NG Cowans	41	12	103	3	4	1	6	0
RM Ellison	53	14	117	0	1	0	1	0
PH Edmonds	47	22	72	3	4	3	2	0
PI Pocock	52	14	108	1	2	1	4	0
MW Gatting	2	1	1	0				
CS Cowdrey	2	0	15	0	4	0	10	0
DI Gower	3	0	13	0				
G Fowler					1	1	0	0
RT Robinson					1	1	0	0
AJ Lamb					1	0	6	1

ENGLAND 1st innings

	1st innings		2nd innings
G Fowler	c Vengs'ar b Sivar'kris'n	49	
RT Robinson	b Yadav	36	
DI Gower*	c Shastri b Yadav	19	
PI Pocock	c Azhar'din b Sivar'kris'n	5	
MW Gatting	b Yadav	48	
AJ Lamb	c Kirmani b Sharma	67	
CS Cowdrey	lbw b Yadav	27	
PR Downton+	not out	6	
PH Edmonds	c Gavaskar b Sharma	8	
RM Ellison	c & b Sharma	1	
NG Cowans	b Sharma	1	
Extras	(0b, 2lb, 0w, 7nb)	9	
Total	100.3 overs	**276**	

1st innings FoW: 71, 98, 110, 152, 163, 229, 261, 270, 273, 276

C Sharma	12.3	0	38	4
M Prabhakar	5	1	16	0
L Sivaramakrishnan	28	7	90	2
NS Yadav	32	10	86	4
RJ Shastri	23	6	44	0

No. 610: 4th Test
VENUE: Madras (Chepauk)
DATE: 13th-18th January 1985
TOSS WON BY: India
RESULT: England won by 9 wickets

INDIA 1st innings / 2nd innings

Batsman	1st innings		2nd innings	
SM Gavaskar*	b Foster	17	c Gatting b Foster	3
K Srikkanth	c Downton b Cowans	0	c Cowdrey b Foster	16
DB Vengsarkar	c Lamb b Foster	17	c Downton b Foster	2
M Amarnath	c Downton b Foster	78	c Cowans b Foster	95
M Azharuddin	b Cowdrey	48	c Gower b Pocock	105
RJ Shastri	c Downton b Foster	2	c Cowdrey b Edmonds	33
N Kapil Dev	c Cowans b Cowdrey	53	c Gatting b Cowans	49
SMH Kirmani+	not out	30	c Lamb b Edmonds	75
NS Yadav	b Foster	2	lbw b Foster	5
L Sivar'kris'n	c Cowdrey b Foster	13	c Downton b Cowans	5
C Sharma	c Lamb b Cowans	5	not out	17
Extras	(0b, 3lb, 0w, 4nb)	7	(1b, 4lb, 0w, 2nb)	7
	67.5 overs		122.5 overs	
Total		**272**		**412**

1st innings FoW: 17, 17, 45, 155, 167, 167, 241, 243, 263, 272
2nd innings FoW: 7, 19, 22, 212, 259, 259, 341, 350, 361, 412

Bowler	O	M	R	W		O	M	R	W
NG Cowans	12.5	3	39	2		15	1	73	2
NA Foster	23	2	104	6		28	8	59	5
PH Edmonds	6	1	33	0		41.5	13	119	2
CS Cowdrey	19	1	65	2		5	0	26	0
PI Pocock	7	1	28	0		33	8	130	1

ENGLAND 1st innings / 2nd innings

Batsman	1st innings		2nd innings	
G Fowler	c Kirmani b Kapil Dev	201	c Kirmani b Sivar'kris'n	2
RT Robinson	c Kirmani b Sivar'kris'n	74	not out	21
MW Gatting	c (sub) b Shastri	207	not out	10
AJ Lamb	b Amarnath	62		
PH Edmonds	lbw b Shastri	36		
NA Foster	b Amarnath	5		
DI Gower*	b Kapil Dev	18		
CS Cowdrey	not out	3		
PR Downton+	not out	3		
PI Pocock				
NG Cowans				
Extras	(7b, 19lb, 0w, 17nb)	43	(0b, 1lb, 0w, 1nb)	2
	175 overs		8 overs	
Total		**652**		**35**

1st innings FoW: 178, 419, 563, 599, 604, 640, 646
2nd innings FoW: 7

Bowler	O	M	R	W		O	M	R	W
N Kapil Dev	36	5	131	2		3	0	20	0
C Sharma	18	0	95	0					
L Sivaramakrishnan	44	6	145	1		4	0	12	1
NS Yadav	23	4	76	0					
RJ Shastri	42	7	143	2		1	0	2	0
M Amarnath	12	1	36	2					

No. 611: 5th Test
VENUE: Kanpur
DATE: 31st January to 5th Feb 1985
TOSS WON BY: India
RESULT: Match drawn

INDIA 1st innings / 2nd innings

Batsman	1st innings		2nd innings	
SM Gavaskar*	b Cowans	9		
K Srikkanth	c Downton b Foster	84	not out	41
M Azharuddin	c (sub) b Cowdrey	122	not out	54
M Amarnath	b Cowans	15		
DB Vengsarkar	c Downton b Foster	137		
A Malhotra	lbw b Pocock	27		
RJ Shastri	b Edmonds	59	run out	2
N Kapil Dev	c Gower b Foster	42		
SMH Kirmani+	not out	16		
L Sivar'kris'n	not out	16		
G Sharma				
Extras	(9b, 12lb, 5w, 0nb)	26	(0b, 0lb, 0w, 0nb)	0
	165 overs		13 overs	
Total		**553**		**97**

1st innings FoW: 19, 169, 209, 277, 362, 457, 511, 533
2nd innings FoW: 2

Bowler	O	M	R	W		O	M	R	W
NG Cowans	36	9	115	2		7	0	51	0
NA Foster	36	8	123	3					
PI Pocock	24	2	79	1					
PH Edmonds	48	16	112	1					
CS Cowdrey	21	1	103	1		5	0	39	0
MW Gatting						1	0	7	0

ENGLAND 1st innings / 2nd innings

Batsman	1st innings		2nd innings	
G Fowler	c Kirmani b Shastri	69		
RT Robinson	lbw b Kapil Dev	96	retired hurt	16
MW Gatting	c & b Sharma	62	not out	41
AJ Lamb	c Srikkanth b Shastri	13		
DI Gower*	lbw b Shastri	78	not out	32
CS Cowdrey	c Kirmani b Sharma	1		
PR Downton+	b Sharma	1		
PH Edmonds	lbw b Kapil Dev	49		
NA Foster	c Kirmani b Kapil Dev	8		
PI Pocock	not out	4		
NG Cowans	b Kapil Dev	9		
Extras	(10b, 17lb, 0w, 0nb)	27	(0b, 2lb, 0w, 0nb)	2
	188.5 overs		36 overs	
Total		**417**		**91**

1st innings FoW: 156, 196, 222, 276, 278, 286, 386, 402, 404, 417

Bowler	O	M	R	W		O	M	R	W
N Kapil Dev	36.5	7	81	4		5	0	19	0
M Amarnath	4	1	6	0					
G Sharma	60	16	115	3		11	4	17	0
L Sivaramakrishnan	54	11	133	0		10	2	22	0
RJ Shastri	32	13	52	3		7	2	12	0
A Malhotra	2	0	3	0					
K Srikkanth						2	0	11	0
M Azharuddin						1	0	8	0

No. 612: 1st Test		
VENUE: Headingley		
DATE: 13th-18th June 1985		
TOSS WON BY: Australia		
RESULT: England won by 5 wickets		

AUSTRALIA 1st innings			2nd innings	
GM Wood	lbw b Allott	14	c Lamb b Botham	3
AMJ Hilditch	c Downton b Gooch	119	c Robinson b Emburey	80
KC Wessels	c Botham b Emburey	36	b Emburey	64
AR Border*	c Botham b Cowans	32	c Downton b Botham	8
DC Boon	lbw b Gooch	14	b Cowans	22
GM Ritchie	b Botham	46	b Emburey	1
WB Phillips+	c Gower b Emburey	30	c Lamb b Botham	91
CJ McDermott	b Botham	18	c Downton b Botham	24
SP O'Donnell	lbw b Botham	0	c Downton b Emburey	15
GF Lawson	c Downton b Allott	0	c Gooch b Emburey	6
JR Thomson	not out	4	not out	2
Extras	(0b, 13lb, 4w, 1nb)	18	(4b, 3lb, 1w, 0nb)	8
	98.1 overs		115.4 overs	
Total		**331**		**324**

1st innings FoW: 23, 155, 201, 229, 229, 284, 326, 326, 327, 331
2nd innings FoW: 5, 144, 151, 159, 160, 192, 272, 307, 318, 324

NG Cowans	20	4	78	1	13	2	50	1
PJW Allott	22	3	74	2	17	4	57	0
IT Botham	29.1	8	86	3	33	7	107	4
GA Gooch	21	4	57	2	9	3	21	0
JE Emburey	6	1	23	2	43.4	14	82	5

ENGLAND 1st innings			2nd innings	
GA Gooch	lbw b McDermott	5	lbw b O'Donnell	28
RT Robinson	c Boon b Lawson	175	b Lawson	21
DI Gower*	c Phillips b McDermott	17	c Border b O'Donnell	5
MW Gatting	c Hilditch b McDermott	53	c Phillips b Lawson	12
AJ Lamb	b O'Donnell	38	not out	31
IT Botham	b Thomson	60	b O'Donnell	12
P Willey	c Hilditch b Lawson	36	not out	3
PR Downton+	c Border b McDermott	54		
JE Emburey	b Lawson	21		
PJW Allott	c Boon b Thomson	12		
NG Cowans	not out	22		
Extras	(5b, 16lb, 5w, 14nb)	40	(0b, 7lb, 1w, 3nb)	11
	125 overs		38.4 overs	
Total		**533**		**123**

1st innings FoW: 14, 50, 186, 264, 344, 417, 422, 462, 484, 533
2nd innings FoW: 44, 59, 71, 83, 110

GF Lawson	26	4	117	3	16	4	51	2
CJ McDermott	32	2	134	4	4	0	20	0
JR Thomson	34	3	166	2	3	0	8	0
SP O'Donnell	27	8	77	1	15.4	5	37	3
AR Border	3	0	16	0				
KC Wessels	3	2	2	0				

No. 613: 2nd Test		
VENUE: Lord's		
DATE: 27th June to 2nd July 1985		
TOSS WON BY: Australia		
RESULT: Australia won by 4 wickets		

ENGLAND 1st innings			2nd innings	
GA Gooch	lbw b McDermott	30	c Phillips b McDermott	17
RT Robinson	lbw b McDermott	6	b Holland	12
DI Gower*	c Border b McDermott	86	b Lawson	20
MW Gatting	lbw b Lawson	14	b Lawson	0
AJ Lamb	c Phillips b Lawson	47	c Phillips b McDermott	22
IT Botham	c Ritchie b Lawson	5	not out	75
PR Downton+	c Wessels b McDermott	21	c Holland b Lawson	9
JE Emburey	lbw b O'Donnell	33	c Border b Holland	85
PH Edmonds	c Border b McDermott	21	c Boon b Holland	0
NA Foster	c Wessels b McDermott	3	c Boon b Holland	1
PJW Allott	not out	1	c Border b Holland	0
Extras	(1b, 4lb, 1w, 17nb)	23	(1b, 12lb, 4w, 3nb)	20
	99.2 overs		80 overs	
Total		**290**		**261**

1st innings FoW: 26, 51, 99, 179, 184, 211, 241, 273, 283, 290
2nd innings FoW: 32, 34, 38, 57, 77, 98, 229, 229, 261, 261

GF Lawson	25	2	91	3	23	0	86	3
CJ McDermott	29.2	5	70	6	20	2	84	2
SP O'Donnell	22	3	82	1	5	0	10	0
RG Holland	23	6	42	0	32	12	68	5

AUSTRALIA 1st innings			2nd innings	
GM Wood	c Emburey b Allott	8	c Lamb b Botham	6
AMJ Hilditch	b Foster	14	c Lamb b Botham	0
KC Wessels	lbw b Botham	11	run out	28
AR Border*	c Gooch b Botham	196	b Allott	2
DC Boon	c Downton b Botham	4	not out	41
GM Ritchie	lbw b Botham	94	b Edmonds	1
WB Phillips+	c Edmonds b Botham	21	c Edmonds b Emburey	29
SP O'Donnell	c Lamb b Edmonds	48	not out	9
GF Lawson	not out	5		
CJ McDermott	run out	9		
RG Holland	b Edmonds	0		
Extras	(0b, 10lb, 1w, 4nb)	15	(0b, 11lb, 0w, 0nb)	11
	124.4 overs		46 overs	
Total		**425**		**127**

1st innings FoW: 11, 24, 80, 101, 317, 347, 398, 414, 425, 425
2nd innings FoW: 0, 9, 22, 63, 65, 116

NA Foster	23	1	83	1				
PJW Allott	30	4	70	1	7	4	8	1
IT Botham	24	2	109	5	15	0	49	2
PH Edmonds	25.4	5	85	2	16	5	35	1
GA Gooch	3	1	11	0				
JE Emburey	19	3	57	0	8	4	24	1

No. 614: 3rd Test
VENUE: Trent Bridge
DATE: 11th-16th July 1985
TOSS WON BY: England
RESULT: Match drawn

No. 615: 4th Test
VENUE: Old Trafford
DATE: 1st-6th August 1985
TOSS WON BY: England
RESULT: Match drawn

Test 614

ENGLAND	1st innings		2nd innings	
GA Gooch	c Wessels b Lawson	70	c Ritchie b McDermott	48
RT Robinson	c Border b Lawson	38	not out	77
DI Gower*	c Phillips b O'Donnell	166	c Phillips b McDermott	17
MW Gatting	run out	74	not out	35
AJ Lamb	lbw b Lawson	17		
IT Botham	c O'Donnell b McDermott	38		
PR Downton+	c Ritchie b McDermott	0		
A Sidebottom	c O'Donnell b Lawson	2		
JE Emburey	not out	16		
PH Edmonds	b Holland	12		
PJW Allott	c Border b Lawson	7		
Extras	(0b, 12lb, 1w, 3nb)	16	(1b, 16lb, 0w, 2nb)	19
Total	129.4 overs	**456**	68 overs	**196**

1st innings FoW: 55, 171, 358, 365, 416, 416, 419, 419, 443, 456
2nd innings FoW: 79, 107

GF Lawson	39.4	10	103	5		13	4	32	0
CJ McDermott	35	3	147	2		16	2	42	2
SP O'Donnell	29	4	104	1		10	2	26	0
RG Holland	26	3	90	1		28	9	69	0
GM Ritchie						1	0	10	0

AUSTRALIA	1st innings		2nd innings
GM Wood	c Robinson b Botham	172	
AMJ Hilditch	lbw b Allott	47	
RG Holland	lbw b Sidebottom	10	
KC Wessels	c Downton b Emburey	33	
AR Border*	c Botham b Edmonds	23	
DC Boon	c & b Emburey	15	
GM Ritchie	b Edmonds	146	
WB Phillips+	b Emburey	2	
SP O'Donnell	c Downton b Botham	46	
GF Lawson	c Gooch b Botham	18	
CJ McDermott	not out	0	
Extras	(6b, 7lb, 2w, 12nb)	27	
Total	201.2 overs	**539**	

1st innings FoW: 87, 128, 205, 234, 263, 424, 437, 491, 539, 539

IT Botham	34.2	3	107	3
A Sidebottom	18.4	3	65	1
PJW Allott	18	4	55	1
PH Edmonds	66	18	155	2
JE Emburey	55	15	129	3
GA Gooch	8.2	2	13	0
MW Gatting	1	0	2	0

Test 615

AUSTRALIA	1st innings		2nd innings	
KC Wessels	c Botham b Emburey	34	c & b Emburey	50
AMJ Hilditch	c Gower b Edmonds	49	b Emburey	40
DC Boon	c Lamb b Botham	61	b Emburey	7
AR Border*	st Downton b Edmonds	8	not out	146
GM Ritchie	c & b Edmonds	4	b Emburey	31
WB Phillips+	c Downton b Botham	36	not out	39
GRJ Matthews	b Botham	4	c & b Edmonds	17
SP O'Donnell	b Edmonds	45		
GF Lawson	c Downton b Botham	4		
CJ McDermott	lbw b Emburey	0		
RG Holland	not out	5		
Extras	(0b, 3lb, 1w, 3nb)	7	(1b, 6lb, 0w, 3nb)	10
Total	89.1 overs	**257**	140 overs	**340**

1st innings FoW: 71, 97, 118, 122, 193, 198, 211, 223, 224, 257
2nd innings FoW: 38, 85, 126, 138, 213

IT Botham	23	4	79	4		15	3	50	0
JP Agnew	14	0	65	0		9	2	34	0
PJW Allott	13	1	29	0		6	2	4	0
JE Emburey	24	7	41	2		51	17	99	4
PH Edmonds	15.1	4	40	4		54	12	122	1
MW Gatting						4	0	14	0
AJ Lamb						1	0	10	0

ENGLAND	1st innings		2nd innings
GA Gooch	lbw b McDermott	74	
RT Robinson	c Border b McDermott	10	
DI Gower*	c Hilditch b McDermott	47	
MW Gatting	c Phillips b McDermott	160	
AJ Lamb	run out	67	
IT Botham	c O'Donnell b McDermott	20	
PR Downton+	b McDermott	23	
JE Emburey	not out	31	
PH Edmonds	b McDermott	1	
PJW Allott	b McDermott	7	
JP Agnew	not out	2	
Extras	(7b, 16lb, 0w, 17nb)	40	
Total	141 overs	**482**	

1st innings FoW: 21, 142, 148, 304, 339, 430, 448, 450, 470

GF Lawson	37	7	114	0
CJ McDermott	36	3	141	8
RG Holland	38	7	101	0
SP O'Donnell	21	6	82	0
GRJ Matthews	9	2	21	0

No. 616: 5th Test	No. 617: 6th Test
VENUE: Edgbaston	VENUE: The Oval
DATE: 15th-20th August 1985	DATE: 29th August to 2nd Sep 1985
TOSS WON BY: England	TOSS WON BY: England
RESULT: Eng won by an innings and 118 runs	RESULT: Eng won by an innings and 94 runs

Match No. 616 — Edgbaston

AUSTRALIA 1st innings

Batsman		Runs	2nd innings		Runs
GM Wood	c Edmonds b Botham	19	c Robinson b Ellison		10
AMJ Hilditch	c Downton b Edmonds	39	c Ellison b Botham		10
KC Wessels	c Downton b Ellison	83	c Downton b Ellison		10
AR Border*	c Edmonds b Ellison	45	lbw b Ellison		0
GM Ritchie	c Botham b Ellison	8	b Ellison		2
WB Phillips+	c Robinson b Ellison	15	c Lamb b Emburey		20
SP O'Donnell	c Downton b Taylor	1	c Gower b Edmonds		59
GF Lawson	run out	53	b Botham		11
CJ McDermott	c Gower b Ellison	35	c Gower b Edmonds		3
JR Thomson	not out	28	c Edmonds b Botham		8
RG Holland	c Edmonds b Ellison	0	not out		4
Extras	(0b, 4lb, 1w, 4nb)	9	(1b, 3lb, 0w, 1nb)		5
	113.5 overs		64.1 overs		
Total		**335**			**142**

1st innings FoW: 44, 92, 189, 191, 207, 208, 218, 276, 335, 335
2nd innings FoW: 10, 32, 32, 35, 36, 113, 117, 120, 137, 142

Bowler	O	M	R	W	O	M	R	W
IT Botham	27	1	108	1	14.1	2	52	3
LB Taylor	26	5	78	1	13	4	27	0
RM Ellison	31.5	9	77	6	9	3	27	4
PH Edmonds	20	4	47	1	15	9	13	2
JE Emburey	9	2	21	0	13	5	19	1

ENGLAND 1st innings

Batsman		Runs
GA Gooch	c Phillips b Thomson	19
RT Robinson	b Lawson	148
DI Gower*	c Border b Lawson	215
MW Gatting	not out	100
AJ Lamb	c Wood b McDermott	46
IT Botham	c Thomson b McDermott	18
PR Downton+	not out	0
JE Emburey		
RM Ellison		
PH Edmonds		
LB Taylor		
Extras	(7b, 20lb, 0w, 22nb)	49
	134 overs	
Total		**595**

1st innings FoW: 38, 369, 463, 572, 592

Bowler	O	M	R	W
GF Lawson	37	1	135	2
CJ McDermott	31	2	155	2
JR Thomson	19	1	101	1
RG Holland	25	4	95	0
SP O'Donnell	16	3	69	0
AR Border	6	1	13	0

Match No. 617 — The Oval

ENGLAND 1st innings

Batsman		Runs	2nd innings
GA Gooch	c & b McDermott	196	
RT Robinson	b McDermott	3	
DI Gower*	c Bennett b McDermott	157	
MW Gatting	c Border b Bennett	4	
JE Emburey	c Wellham b Lawson	9	
AJ Lamb	c McDermott b Lawson	1	
IT Botham	c Phillips b Lawson	12	
PR Downton+	b McDermott	16	
RM Ellison	c Phillips b Gilbert	3	
PH Edmonds	lbw b Lawson	12	
LB Taylor	not out	1	
Extras	(13b, 11lb, 0w, 26nb)	50	
	118.2 overs		
Total		**464**	

1st innings FoW: 20, 371, 376, 403, 405, 418, 425, 447, 452, 464

Bowler	O	M	R	W
GF Lawson	29.2	6	101	4
CJ McDermott	31	2	108	4
DR Gilbert	21	2	96	1
MJ Bennett	32	8	111	1
AR Border	2	0	8	0
KC Wessels	3	0	16	0

AUSTRALIA 1st innings

Batsman		Runs	2nd innings		Runs
GM Wood	lbw b Botham	22	b Botham		6
AMJ Hilditch	c Gooch b Botham	17	c Gower b Taylor		9
KC Wessels	b Emburey	12	c Downton b Botham		7
AR Border*	b Edmonds	38	c Botham b Ellison		58
DM Wellham	c Downton b Ellison	13	lbw b Ellison		5
GM Ritchie	not out	64	c Downton b Ellison		6
WB Phillips+	b Edmonds	18	c Downton b Botham		10
MJ Bennett	c Robinson b Ellison	12	c & b Taylor		11
GF Lawson	c Botham b Taylor	14	c Downton b Ellison		7
CJ McDermott	run out	25	c Botham b Ellison		2
DR Gilbert	b Botham	1	not out		0
Extras	(0b, 3lb, 2w, 0nb)	5	(4b, 0lb, 0w, 4nb)		8
	84 overs		46.3 overs		
Total		241			129

1st innings FoW: 35, 52, 56, 101, 109, 144, 171, 192, 235, 241
2nd innings FoW: 13, 16, 37, 51, 71, 96, 114, 127, 127, 129

Bowler	O	M	R	W	O	M	R	W
IT Botham	20	3	64	3	17	3	44	3
LB Taylor	13	1	39	1	11.3	1	34	2
RM Ellison	18	5	35	2	17	3	46	5
JE Emburey	19	7	48	1	1	0	1	0
PH Edmonds	14	2	52	2				

No. 618: 1st Test	No. 619: 2nd Test
VENUE: Kingston (Jamaica)	VENUE: Port-of-Spain (Trinidad)
DATE: 21st-23rd February 1986	DATE: 7th-12th March 1986
TOSS WON BY: England	TOSS WON BY: West Indies
RESULT: West Indies won by 10 wickets	RESULT: West Indies won by 7 wickets

1st Test

ENGLAND	1st innings		2nd innings	
GA Gooch	c Garner b Marshall	51	b Marshall	0
RT Robinson	c Greenidge b Patterson	6	b Garner	0
DI Gower*	lbw b Holding	16	c Best b Patterson	9
DM Smith	c Dujon b Patterson	1	b Garner	71
AJ Lamb	b Garner	49	c (sub) b Patterson	13
IT Botham	c Patterson b Marshall	15	b Marshall	29
P Willey	c Dujon b Holding	0	c Gomes b Marshall	0
PR Downton+	c Dujon b Patterson	2	c Haynes b Holding	3
RM Ellison	c Haynes b Patterson	9	b Garner	11
PH Edmonds	not out	5	lbw b Patterson	7
JG Thomas	b Garner	0	not out	1
Extras	(0b, 0lb, 0w, 5nb)	5	(5b, 0lb, 0w, 3nb)	8
	45.3 overs		42.5 overs	
Total		**159**		**152**

1st innings FoW: 32, 53, 54, 83, 120, 127, 138, 142, 158, 159
2nd innings FoW: 1, 3, 19, 40, 95, 103, 106, 140, 146, 152

MD Marshall	11	1	30	2		11	4	29	3
J Garner	14.3	0	58	2		9	2	22	3
BP Patterson	11	4	30	4		10.5	0	44	3
MA Holding	7	1	36	2		12	1	52	1
IVA Richards	1	1	0	0					
RB Richardson	1	0	5	0					

WEST INDIES	1st innings		2nd innings	
CG Greenidge	lbw b Ellison	58		
DL Haynes	c Downton b Thomas	32	not out	4
J Garner	c Edmonds b Botham	24		
RB Richardson	lbw b Botham	7	not out	0
HA Gomes	lbw b Ellison	56		
CA Best	lbw b Willey	35		
VA Richards*	lbw b Ellison	23		
PJL Dujon+	c Gooch b Thomas	54		
MD Marshall	c (sub) b Ellison	6		
MA Holding	lbw b Ellison	3		
BP Patterson	not out	0		
Extras	(2b, 4lb, 0w, 3nb)	9	(0b, 0lb, 0w, 1nb)	1
	107.5 overs		1.1 overs	
Total		**307**		**5**

1st innings FoW: 92, 112, 115, 183, 222, 241, 247, 299, 303, 307

IT Botham	19	4	67	2					
JG Thomas	28.5	6	82	2		1	0	4	0
RM Ellison	33	12	78	5					
PH Edmonds	21	6	53	0					
P Willey	4	0	15	1					
GA Gooch	2	1	6	0					
AJ Lamb						0.1	0	1	0

2nd Test

ENGLAND	1st innings		2nd innings	
GA Gooch	c Best b Marshall	2	lbw b Walsh	43
WN Slack	c Payne b Marshall	2	run out	0
DI Gower*	lbw b Garner	66	b Walsh	47
P Willey	c Payne b Patterson	5	b Marshall	26
AJ Lamb	c Marshall b Garner	62	lbw b Walsh	40
IT Botham	c Richardson b Marshall	2	c Payne b Marshall	1
JE Emburey	c Payne b Garner	0	c Best b Walsh	14
PR Downton+	c Marshall b Walsh	8	lbw b Marshall	5
RM Ellison	lbw b Marshall	4	lbw b Marshall	36
PH Edmonds	not out	3	c Payne b Garner	13
JG Thomas	b Patterson	4	not out	31
Extras	(0b, 4lb, 0w, 14nb)	18	(20b, 11lb, 1w, 27nb)	59
	44.4 overs		104.2 overs	
Total		**176**		**315**

1st innings FoW: 2, 11, 30, 136, 147, 148, 153, 163, 165, 176
2nd innings FoW: 2, 82, 109, 190, 192, 197, 214, 214, 243, 315

MD Marshall	15	3	38	4		32.2	9	94	4
J Garner	15	4	45	3		21	5	44	1
BP Patterson	8.4	0	60	2		16	0	65	0
CA Walsh	6	2	29	1		27	4	74	4
IVA Richards						7	4	7	0
HA Gomes						1	1	0	0

WEST INDIES	1st innings		2nd innings	
CG Greenidge	c Lamb b Thomas	37	c Lamb b Edmonds	45
DL Haynes	st Downton b Emburey	67	not out	39
RB Richardson	c Downton b Emburey	102	c Gooch b Emburey	9
HA Gomes	st Downton b Emburey	30	b Emburey	0
CA Best	b Edmonds	22	not out	0
IVA Richards*	c Botham b Edmonds	34		
TRO Payne+	c Gower b Emburey	5		
MD Marshall	not out	62		
J Garner	c Gooch b Emburey	12		
CA Walsh	c Edmonds b Thomas	3		
BP Patterson	c Gooch b Botham	9		
Extras	(0b, 11lb, 1w, 4nb)	16	(0b, 2lb, 0w, 0nb)	2
	104.4 overs		30.3 overs	
Total		**399**		**95**

1st innings FoW: 59, 209, 242, 257, 298, 303, 327, 342, 364, 399
2nd innings FoW: 72, 89, 91

IT Botham	9.4	0	68	1					
JG Thomas	20	4	86	2		5	1	21	0
RM Ellison	18	3	58	0		3	1	12	0
PH Edmonds	30	5	98	2		12.3	3	24	1
JE Emburey	27	5	78	5		10	1	36	2

No. 620: 3rd Test
VENUE: Bridgetown (Barbados)
DATE: 21st-25th March 1986
TOSS WON BY: England
RESULT: WI won by an innings and 30 runs

No. 621: 4th Test
VENUE: Port-of-Spain (Trinidad)
DATE: 3rd-5th April 1986
TOSS WON BY: West Indies
RESULT: West Indies won by 10 wickets

WEST INDIES 1st innings / 2nd innings

CG Greenidge	c Botham b Foster	21
DL Haynes	c Botham b Foster	84
RB Richardson	lbw b Emburey	160
HA Gomes	c Gower b Thomas	33
IVA Richards*	c Downton b Thomas	51
CA Best	lbw b Foster	21
PJL Dujon+	c (sub) b Botham	5
MA Holding	b Thomas	23
MD Marshall	run out	4
J Garner	c Gooch b Thomas	0
BP Patterson	not out	0
Extras	(2b, 9lb, 3w, 2nb)	16
Total	126.1 overs	**418**

1st innings FoW: 34, 228, 286, 361, 362, 367, 406, 413, 418, 418

Bowler	O	M	R	W
IT Botham	24	3	80	1
JG Thomas	16.1	2	70	4
NA Foster	19	0	76	3
PH Edmonds	29	2	85	0
JE Emburey	38	7	96	1

ENGLAND 1st innings / 2nd innings

Batsman	1st innings	Runs	2nd innings	Runs
GA Gooch	c Dujon b Garner	53	b Patterson	11
RT Robinson	c Dujon b Marshall	3	b Patterson	43
DI Gower*	c Dujon b Marshall	66	c Marshall b Garner	23
P Willey	c Dujon b Marshall	5	lbw b Garner	17
AJ Lamb	c Richardson b Marshall	5	c & b Holding	6
IT Botham	c Dujon b Patterson	14	lbw b Garner	4
PR Downton+	lbw b Holding	11	c Dujon b Garner	21
JE Emburey	c Best b Patterson	0	c Dujon b Holding	26
PH Edmonds	c Richardson b Patterson	4	not out	35
NA Foster	lbw b Holding	0	c Richardson b Holding	0
JG Thomas	not out	4	b Patterson	0
Extras	(4b, 8lb, 2w, 10nb)	24	(0b, 1lb, 0w, 12nb)	13
Total	59 overs	**189**	52.4 overs	**199**

1st innings FoW: 6, 126, 134, 141, 151, 168, 172, 181, 185, 189
2nd innings FoW: 48, 71, 94, 108, 108, 132, 138, 188, 188, 199

Bowler	O	M	R	W	O	M	R	W
MD Marshall	14	1	42	4	13	1	47	0
J Garner	14	4	35	1	17	2	69	4
BP Patterson	15	5	54	3	8.4	2	28	3
MA Holding	13	4	37	2	10	1	47	3
IVA Richards	3	0	9	0	4	1	7	0

ENGLAND 1st innings / 2nd innings

Batsman	1st innings	Runs	2nd innings	Runs
GA Gooch	c Richards b Garner	14	c Dujon b Marshall	0
RT Robinson	c Marshall b Garner	0	b Garner	5
DI Gower*	c Dujon b Garner	10	lbw b Patterson	22
DM Smith	c Greenidge b Patterson	47	lbw b Holding	32
AJ Lamb	b Holding	36	b Patterson	11
IT Botham	b Holding	38	c Gomes b Marshall	25
P Willey	c Richardson b Garner	10	lbw b Marshall	2
PR Downton+	c Garner b Marshall	7	not out	11
JE Emburey	c Haynes b Marshall	8	b Holding	0
NA Foster	c Richards b Holding	0	b Garner	14
JG Thomas	not out	5	b Garner	0
Extras	(0b, 3lb, 1w, 21nb)	25	(5b, 7lb, 0w, 16nb)	28
Total	65.4 overs	**200**	38 overs	**150**

1st innings FoW: 8, 29, 31, 123, 124, 151, 168, 181, 190, 200
2nd innings FoW: 0, 30, 30, 75, 105, 109, 115, 126, 150, 150

Bowler	O	M	R	W	O	M	R	W
MD Marshall	23	4	71	2	10	2	42	3
J Garner	18	3	43	4	9	3	15	3
BP Patterson	10	2	31	1	9	1	36	2
MA Holding	14.4	3	52	3	10	1	45	2

WEST INDIES 1st innings / 2nd innings

Batsman	1st innings	Runs	2nd innings	Runs
CG Greenidge	lbw b Emburey	42		
DL Haynes	c Botham b Foster	25	not out	17
RB Richardson	b Emburey	32	not out	22
HA Gomes	c Downton b Foster	48		
IVA Richards*	lbw b Botham	87		
PJL Dujon+	c Downton b Botham	5		
MD Marshall	b Emburey	5		
RA Harper	lbw b Botham	21		
MA Holding	b Botham	25		
J Garner	not out	5		
BP Patterson	c Downton b Botham	3		
Extras	(0b, 10lb, 3w, 1nb)	14	(0b, 0lb, 0w, 0nb)	0
Total	90.1 overs	**312**	5.5 overs	**39**

1st innings FoW: 58, 74, 111, 213, 244, 249, 249, 300, 306, 312

Bowler	O	M	R	W	O	M	R	W
IT Botham	24.1	3	71	5	3	0	24	0
JG Thomas	15	0	101	0				
NA Foster	24	3	68	2	2.5	0	15	0
JE Emburey	27	10	62	3				

West Indies

India

No. 622: 5th Test
VENUE: St. John's (Antigua)
DATE: 11th-16th April 1986
TOSS WON BY: England
RESULT: West Indies won by 240 runs

No. 623: 1st Test
VENUE: Lord's
DATE: 5th-10th June 1986
TOSS WON BY: India
RESULT: India won by 5 wickets

WEST INDIES 1st innings / 2nd innings

Batsman	1st innings		2nd innings	
CG Greenidge	b Botham	14		
DL Haynes	c Gatting b Ellison	131	run out	70
RB Richardson	c Slack b Emburey	24	c Robinson b Emburey	31
HA Gomes	b Emburey	24		
IVA Richards*	c Gooch b Botham	26	not out	110
PJL Dujon+	b Foster	21		
MD Marshall	c Gatting b Gooch	76		
RA Harper	c Lamb b Foster	60	not out	19
MA Holding	c Gower b Ellison	73		
J Garner	run out	11		
BP Patterson	not out	0		
Extras	(2b, 11lb, 1w, 0nb)	14	(4b, 9lb, 1w, 2nb)	16
Total	134.3 overs	**474**	43 overs	**246**

1st innings FoW: 23, 63, 137, 178, 232, 281, 351, 401, 450, 474
2nd innings FoW: 100, 161

Bowler	O	M	R	W		O	M	R	W
IT Botham	40	6	147	2		15	0	78	0
NA Foster	28	5	86	2		10	0	40	0
RM Ellison	24.3	3	114	2		4	0	32	0
JE Emburey	37	11	93	2		14	0	83	1
GA Gooch	5	2	21	1					

ENGLAND 1st innings / 2nd innings

Batsman	1st innings		2nd innings	
GA Gooch	lbw b Holding	51	lbw b Holding	51
WN Slack	c Greenidge b Patterson	52	b Garner	8
RT Robinson	b Marshall	12	run out	3
DI Gower*	c Dujon b Marshall	90	c Dujon b Harper	21
AJ Lamb	c & b Harper	1	b Marshall	1
MW Gatting	c Dujon b Garner	15	b Holding	1
IT Botham	c Harper b Garner	10	b Harper	13
PR Downton+	c Holding b Garner	5	lbw b Marshall	13
RM Ellison	c Dujon b Marshall	6	lbw b Garner	16
JE Emburey	not out	7	c Richardson b Harper	0
NA Foster	c Holding b Garner	10	not out	0
Extras	(5b, 6lb, 0w, 40nb)	51	(10b, 10lb, 2w, 21nb)	43
Total	107.4 overs	**310**	79.1 overs	**170**

1st innings FoW: 127, 132, 157, 159, 205, 213, 237, 289, 290, 310
2nd innings FoW: 14, 29, 84, 101, 112, 124, 147, 166, 168, 170

Bowler	O	M	R	W		O	M	R	W
MD Marshall	24	5	64	3		16.1	6	25	2
J Garner	21.4	2	67	4		17	5	38	2
BP Patterson	14	2	49	1		15	3	29	0
MA Holding	20	3	71	1		16	3	45	2
RA Harper	26	7	45	1		12	8	10	3
IVA Richards	2	0	3	0		3	1	3	0

ENGLAND 1st innings / 2nd innings

Batsman	1st innings		2nd innings	
GA Gooch	b Sharma	114	lbw b Kapil Dev	8
RT Robinson	c Azharuddin b Maninder	35	c Amarnath b Kapil Dev	11
DI Gower*	c More b Sharma	18	lbw b Kapil Dev	8
MW Gatting	b Sharma	0	b Sharma	40
AJ Lamb	c Srikkanth b Sharma	6	c More b Shastri	39
DR Pringle	b Binny	63	c More b Kapil Dev	6
JE Emburey	c Amarnath b Kapil Dev	7	c Shastri b Maninder	29
PR Downton+	lbw b Sharma	5	c More b Binny	19
RM Ellison	c Kapil Dev b Binny	12	c & b Maninder	1
GR Dilley	c More b Binny	4	not out	2
PH Edmonds	not out	7	c Binny b Maninder	7
Extras	(0b, 15lb, 1w, 7nb)	23	(0b, 6lb, 1w, 3nb)	10
Total	128.2 overs	**294**	96.4 overs	**180**

1st innings FoW: 66, 92, 92, 98, 245, 264, 269, 271, 287, 294
2nd innings FoW: 18, 23, 35, 108, 113, 121, 164, 170, 170, 180

Bowler	O	M	R	W		O	M	R	W
N Kapil Dev	31	8	67	1		22	7	52	4
RMH Binny	18.2	4	55	3		15	3	44	1
C Sharma	32	10	64	5		17	4	48	1
Maninder Singh	30	15	45	1		20.4	12	9	3
M Amarnath	7	1	18	0		2	2	0	0
RJ Shastri	10	3	30	0		20	8	21	1

INDIA 1st innings / 2nd innings

Batsman	1st innings		2nd innings	
SM Gavaskar	c Emburey b Dilley	34	c Downton b Dilley	22
K Srikkanth	c Gatting b Dilley	20	c Gooch b Dilley	0
M Amarnath	c Pringle b Edmonds	69	lbw b Pringle	8
DB Vengsarkar	not out	126	b Edmonds	33
M Azharuddin	c & b Dilley	33	run out	14
RJ Shastri	c Edmonds b Dilley	1	not out	20
RMH Binny	lbw b Pringle	9	not out	23
N Kapil Dev*	c Lamb b Ellison	1		
C Sharma	b Pringle	2		
KS More+	lbw b Pringle	25		
Maninder S'gh	c Lamb b Emburey	6		
Extras	(0b, 5lb, 1w, 9nb)	15	(1b, 9lb, 1w, 5nb)	16
Total	137 overs	**341**	42 overs	**136**

1st innings FoW: 31, 90, 161, 232, 238, 252, 253, 264, 303, 341
2nd innings FoW: 10, 31, 76, 78, 110

Bowler	O	M	R	W		O	M	R	W
GR Dilley	34	7	146	4		10	3	28	2
RM Ellison	29	11	63	1		6	0	17	0
JE Emburey	27	13	28	1					
PH Edmonds	22	7	41	1		11	2	51	1
DR Pringle	25	7	58	3		15	5	30	1

No. 624: 2nd Test
VENUE: Headingley
DATE: 19th-23rd June 1986
TOSS WON BY: India
RESULT: India won by 279 runs

INDIA 1st innings / 2nd innings

Batsman	1st innings	R	2nd innings	R
SM Gavaskar	c French b Pringle	35	c French b Lever	1
K Srikkanth	c Emburey b Pringle	31	b Dilley	8
RJ Shastri	c Pringle b Dilley	32	lbw b Lever	3
DB Vengsarkar	c French b Lever	61	not out	102
M Azharuddin	lbw b Gooch	15	lbw b Lever	2
CS Pandit	c Emburey b Pringle	23	b Pringle	17
N Kapil Dev*	lbw b Lever	0	c Slack b Pringle	16
RMH Binny	c Slack b Emburey	6	c Gatting b Lever	31
S Madan Lal	c Gooch b Dilley	20	run out	22
KS More+	not out	36	lbw b Pringle	26
Maninder S'gh	c Gooch b Dilley	3	c Gatting b Pringle	1
Extras	(0b, 5lb, 0w, 5nb)	10	(4b, 4lb, 0w, 0nb)	8
Total	104.2 overs	**272**	76.3 overs	**237**

1st innings FoW: 64, 75, 128, 163, 203, 203, 211, 213, 267, 272
2nd innings FoW: 9, 9, 29, 35, 70, 102, 137, 173, 233, 237

Bowler	O	M	R	W		O	M	R	W
GR Dilley	24.2	7	54	3		17	2	71	1
JK Lever	30	4	102	2		23	5	64	4
DR Pringle	27	6	47	3		22.3	6	73	4
JE Emburey	17	4	45	1		7	3	9	0
GA Gooch	6	0	19	1		7	2	12	0

ENGLAND 1st innings / 2nd innings

Batsman	1st innings	R	2nd innings	R
GA Gooch	c Binny b Kapil Dev	8	c Srikkanth b Kapil Dev	5
WN Slack	b Madan Lal	0	c Gavaskar b Binny	19
CL Smith	b Madan Lal	6	c More b Shastri	28
AJ Lamb	c Pandit b Binny	10	c More b Binny	10
MW Gatting*	c More b Binny	13	not out	31
CWJ Athey	c More b Madan Lal	32	c More b Maninder	8
DR Pringle	c Srikkanth b Binny	8	c More b Maninder	8
JE Emburey	c Kapil Dev b Binny	4	lbw b Maninder	8
BN French+	b Binny	8	c Azhar'din b Kapil Dev	1
GR Dilley	b Shastri	10	c Vengs'ar b Maninder	5
JK Lever	not out	0	run out	2
Extras	(1b, 2lb, 0w, 4nb)	7	(0b, 9lb, 0w, 2nb)	11
Total	45.1 overs	**102**	63.3 overs	**128**

1st innings FoW: 4, 14, 14, 38, 41, 63, 63, 71, 100, 102
2nd innings FoW: 12, 66, 63, 77, 90, 90, 101, 104, 109, 128

Bowler	O	M	R	W		O	M	R	W
N Kapil Dev	18	7	36	1		19.2	7	24	2
S Madan Lal	11.1	3	18	3		9.4	2	30	0
RMH Binny	13	1	40	5		8	1	18	2
RJ Shastri	3	1	5	1		10	3	21	1
Maninder Singh						16.3	6	26	4

No. 625: 3rd Test
VENUE: Edgbaston
DATE: 3rd-8th July 1986
TOSS WON BY: England
RESULT: Match drawn

ENGLAND 1st innings / 2nd innings

Batsman	1st innings	R	2nd innings	R
GA Gooch	c More b Kapil Dev	0	lbw b Sharma	40
MR Benson	b Maninder	21	b Shastri	30
CWJ Athey	c More b Kapil Dev	0	c More b Sharma	38
DI Gower	lbw b Sharma	49	c Gavaskar b Sharma	26
MW Gatting*	not out	183	lbw b Sharma	26
DR Pringle	c Amarnath b Shastri	44	c More b Maninder	7
JE Emburey	c Shastri b Maninder	38	not out	27
NA Foster	b Binny	17	run out	0
PH Edmonds	b Sharma	18	c Binny b Maninder	10
BN French+	b Sharma	8	c More b Sharma	1
NV Radford	c Gavaskar b Sharma	0	c Azharuddin b Sharma	1
Extras	(0b, 7lb, 0w, 5nb)	12	(10b, 6lb, 2w, 11nb)	29
Total	116.3 overs	**390**	94 overs	**235**

1st innings FoW: 0, 0, 61, 88, 184, 278, 327, 367, 384, 390
2nd innings FoW: 49, 102, 152, 163, 190, 190, 190, 217, 229, 235

Bowler	O	M	R	W		O	M	R	W
N Kapil Dev	31	6	89	2		7	1	38	0
RMH Binny	17	1	53	1		16	1	41	0
C Sharma	29.3	2	130	4		24	4	58	6
Maninder Singh	25	3	66	2		22	5	41	2
RJ Shastri	14	1	45	1		23	8	39	1
M Amarnath						2	1	2	0

INDIA 1st innings / 2nd innings

Batsman	1st innings	R	2nd innings	R
SM Gavaskar	b Pringle	29	c French b Foster	54
K Srikkanth	c Pringle b Radford	23	c Pringle b Edmonds	23
M Amarnath	b Edmonds	79	c French b Edmonds	16
DB Vengsarkar	c Gooch b Radford	38	c French b Edmonds	0
M Azharuddin	c French b Foster	64	not out	29
RJ Shastri	c Gooch b Foster	18	c Emburey b Edmonds	0
N Kapil Dev*	c French b Foster	26	not out	31
KS More+	c French b Emburey	48		
RMH Binny	c Gower b Emburey	40		
C Sharma	c Gower b Pringle	9		
Maninder S'gh	not out	0		
Extras	(3b, 7lb, 1w, 5nb)	16	(1b, 15lb, 1w, 4nb)	21
Total	139.5 overs	**390**	78 overs	**174**

1st innings FoW: 53, 58, 139, 228, 266, 275, 302, 370, 385, 390
2nd innings FoW: 58, 101, 101, 104, 105

Bowler	O	M	R	W		O	M	R	W
NV Radford	35	3	131	2		3	0	17	0
NA Foster	41	9	93	3		22	9	48	1
DR Pringle	21	2	61	2		16	5	33	0
PH Edmonds	24	7	55	1		28	11	31	4
JE Emburey	18.5	7	40	2		7	1	19	0
MW Gatting						2	0	10	0

No. 626: 1st Test
VENUE: Lord's
DATE: 24th-29th July 1986
TOSS WON BY: England
RESULT: Match drawn

No. 627: 2nd Test
VENUE: Trent Bridge
DATE: 7th-12th August 1986
TOSS WON BY: New Zealand
RESULT: New Zealand won by 8 wickets

ENGLAND	1st innings		2nd innings	
GA Gooch	c Smith b Hadlee	18	c Watson b Bracewell	183
MD Moxon	lbw b Hadlee	74	lbw b Hadlee	5
CWJ Athey	c JJ Crowe b Hadlee	44	b Gray	16
DI Gower	c MD Crowe b Bracewell	62	b Gray	3
MW Gatting*	b Hadlee	2	c MD Crowe b Gray	26
P Willey	lbw b Watson	44	b Bracewell	42
PH Edmonds	c MD Crowe b Hadlee	6	not out	9
BN French+	retired hurt	0		
GR Dilley	c Smith b Hadlee	17		
NA Foster	b Watson	8		
NV Radford	not out	12		
Extras	(6b, 7lb, 0w, 7nb)	20	(0b, 6lb, 1w, 4nb)	11
Total	118.5 overs	**307**	120.4 overs	**295**

1st innings FoW: 27, 102, 196, 198, 237, 258, 271, 285, 307
2nd innings FoW: 9, 68, 72, 136, 262, 295

RJ Hadlee	37.5	11	80	6	27	3	78	1
W Watson	30	7	70	2	17	2	50	0
MD Crowe	8	1	38	0	4	0	13	0
JV Coney	4	0	12	0				
JG Bracewell	26	8	65	1	23.4	7	57	2
EJ Gray	13	9	29	0	46	14	83	3
KR Rutherford					3	0	8	0

NEW ZEALAND	1st innings		2nd innings	
JG Wright	b Dilley	0	c Gower b Dilley	0
BA Edgar	c Gatting b Gooch	83	c Gower b Foster	0
KR Rutherford	c Gooch b Dilley	0	not out	24
MD Crowe	c & b Edmonds	106	not out	11
JJ Crowe	c Gatting b Edmonds	18		
JV Coney*	c Gooch b Radford	51		
EJ Gray	c Gower b Edmonds	11		
RJ Hadlee	b Edmonds	19		
IDS Smith+	c Edmonds b Dilley	18		
JG Bracewell	not out	1		
W Watson	lbw b Dilley	1		
Extras	(4b, 9lb, 6w, 15nb)	34	(0b, 4lb, 0w, 2nb)	6
Total	140.1 overs	**342**	15 overs	**41**

1st innings FoW: 2, 5, 215, 218, 274, 292, 310, 340, 340, 342
2nd innings FoW: 0, 8

GR Dilley	35.1	9	82	4	6	3	5	1
NA Foster	25	6	56	0	3	1	13	1
NV Radford	25	4	71	1				
PH Edmonds	42	10	97	4	5	0	18	0
GA Gooch	13	6	23	1				
DI Gower					1	0	1	0

ENGLAND	1st innings		2nd innings	
GA Gooch	lbw b Hadlee	18	c Coney b Bracewell	17
MD Moxon	b Hadlee	9	c Smith b Hadlee	23
CWJ Athey	lbw b Watson	55	lbw b Hadlee	20
DI Gower	lbw b Gray	71	c Smith b Bracewell	6
MW Gatting*	b Hadlee	17	c JJ Crowe b Bracewell	26
DR Pringle	c Watson b Stirling	21	c Smith b Gray	4
JE Emburey	c Smith b Hadlee	8	c Gray b Stirling	9
PH Edmonds	c Smith b Hadlee	0	c MD Crowe b Hadlee	75
JG Thomas	b Hadlee	28	c Gray b Stirling	10
BN French+	c Coney b Watson	21	not out	12
GC Small	not out	2	lbw b Hadlee	12
Extras	(1b, 3lb, 0w, 2nb)	6	16	
Total	89.5 overs	**256**	95.1 overs	**230**

1st innings FoW: 18, 43, 126, 170, 176, 191, 191, 205, 240, 256
2nd innings FoW: 23, 47, 63, 87, 98, 104, 178, 203, 203, 230

RJ Hadlee	32	7	80	6	33.1	15	60	4
DA Stirling	17	3	62	1	18	5	48	2
EJ Gray	13	4	30	1	24	9	55	1
W Watson	16.5	6	51	2	9	3	25	0
JV Coney	7	1	18	0				
JG Bracewell	4	1	11	0	11	5	29	3

NEW ZEALAND	1st innings		2nd innings	
JG Wright	c Athey b Small	58	b Emburey	7
BA Edgar	lbw b Thomas	8		
JJ Crowe	c French b Small	23	lbw b Small	2
MD Crowe	c Edmonds b Emburey	28	not out	48
JV Coney*	run out	24	not out	20
EJ Gray	c Athey b Edmonds	50		
RJ Hadlee	c Gooch b Thomas	68		
JG Bracewell	c Moxon b Emburey	110		
IDS Smith+	lbw b Edmonds	2		
DA Stirling	b Small	26		
W Watson	not out	8		
Extras	(0b, 4lb, 2w, 2nb)	8	(0b, 0lb, 0w, 0nb)	0
Total	169.5 overs	**413**	24 overs	**77**

1st innings FoW: 39, 85, 92, 142, 144, 239, 318, 326, 391, 413
2nd innings FoW: 5, 19

GC Small	38	12	88	3	8	3	10	1
JG Thomas	39	5	124	2	4	0	16	0
DR Pringle	20	1	58	0	2	0	16	0
PH Edmonds	28	11	52	2	4	1	16	0
JE Emburey	42.5	17	87	2	6	1	15	1
GA Gooch	2	2	0	0				
DI Gower					0	0	4	0

	New Zealand	Australia
No.	628: 3rd Test	629: 1st Test
VENUE	The Oval	Brisbane (Gabba)
DATE	21st-26th August 1986	14th-19th November 1986
TOSS WON BY	England	Australia
RESULT	Match drawn	England won by 7 wickets

NEW ZEALAND

NEW ZEALAND	1st innings			2nd innings	
JG Wright	b Edmonds	119		not out	7
BA Edgar	c Gooch b Botham	1		not out	0
JJ Crowe	lbw b Botham	8			
MD Crowe	lbw b Dilley	13			
JV Coney*	c Gooch b Botham	38			
EJ Gray	b Dilley	30			
RJ Hadlee	c French b Edmonds	6			
JG Bracewell	c Athey b Emburey	3			
TE Blain+	c Gooch b Dilley	37			
DA Stirling	not out	18			
EJ Chatfield	c French b Dilley	5			
Extras	(1b, 0lb, 1w, 7nb)	9		(0b, 0lb, 0w, 0nb)	0
	128.2 overs			1 over	
Total		**287**			**7**

1st innings FoW: 17, 31, 59, 106, 175, 192, 197, 251, 280, 287

GR Dilley	28.2	4	92	4				
GC Small	18	5	36	0				
IT Botham	25	4	75	3	1	0	7	0
JE Emburey	31	15	39	1				
PH Edmonds	22	10	29	2				
GA Gooch	4	1	15	0				

ENGLAND	1st innings			2nd innings	
GA Gooch	c Stirling b Hadlee	32			
CWJ Athey	lbw b Hadlee	17			
DI Gower	b Chatfield	131			
AJ Lamb	b Chatfield	0			
MW Gatting*	b Chatfield	121			
IT Botham	not out	59			
JE Emburey	not out	9			
BN French+					
PH Edmonds					
GR Dilley					
GC Small					
Extras	(0b, 9lb, 5w, 5nb)	19			
	90.5 overs				
Total		**388**			

1st innings FoW: 38, 62, 62, 285, 326

RJ Hadlee	23.5	6	92	2
DA Stirling	9	0	71	0
EJ Chatfield	21	7	73	3
EJ Gray	21	4	74	0
JG Bracewell	11	1	51	0
JV Coney	5	0	18	0

AUSTRALIA

ENGLAND	1st innings			2nd innings	
BC Broad	c Zoehrer b Reid	8		not out	35
CWJ Athey	c Zoehrer b C Matthews	76		c Waugh b Hughes	1
MW Gatting*	b Hughes	61		c G Matthews b Hughes	12
AJ Lamb	lbw b Hughes	40		lbw b Reid	9
DI Gower	c Ritchie b CD Matthews	51		not out	15
IT Botham	c Hughes b Waugh	138			
CJ Richards+	b CD Matthews	0			
JE Emburey	c Waugh b Hughes	8			
P De Freitas	c CD Matthews b Waugh	40			
PH Edmonds	not out	9			
GR Dilley	c Boon b Waugh	0			
Extras	(3b, 19lb, 0w, 3nb)	25		(2b, 0lb, 0w, 3nb)	5
	134 overs			22.3 overs	
Total		**456**			**77**

1st innings FoW: 15, 116, 198, 198, 316, 324, 351, 443, 451, 456
2nd innings FoW: 6, 25, 40

BA Reid	31	4	86	1	6	1	20	1
MG Hughes	36	7	134	3	5.3	0	28	2
CD Matthews	35	10	95	3	4	0	11	0
SR Waugh	21	3	76	3				
GRJ Matthews	11	2	43	0	7	1	16	0

AUSTRALIA	1st innings			2nd innings	
GR Marsh	c Richards b Dilley	56		b De Freitas	110
DC Boon	c Broad b De Freitas	10		lbw b Botham	14
TJ Zoehrer+	lbw b Dilley	38		not out	16
DM Jones	lbw b De Freitas	8		st Richards b Emburey	18
AR Border*	c De Freitas b Edmonds	7		c Lamb b Emburey	23
GM Ritchie	c Edmonds b Dilley	41		lbw b De Freitas	45
GRJ Matthews	not out	56		c & b Dilley	13
SR Waugh	c Richards b Dilley	0		b Emburey	28
CD Matthews	c Gatting b Botham	11		lbw b Emburey	0
MG Hughes	b Botham	0		b De Freitas	0
BA Reid	c Richards b Dilley	3		c Broad b Emburey	2
Extras	(2b, 8lb, 2w, 6nb)	18		(5b, 6lb, 0w, 2nb)	13
	104.4 overs			116.5 overs	
Total		**248**			**282**

1st innings FoW: 27, 97, 114, 126, 159, 198, 204, 239, 239, 248
2nd innings FoW: 24, 44, 92, 205, 224, 262, 266, 266, 275, 282

PAJ De Freitas	16	5	32	2	17	2	62	3
GR Dilley	25.4	7	68	5	19	6	47	1
JE Emburey	34	11	66	0	42.5	14	80	5
PH Edmonds	12	6	12	1	24	8	46	0
IT Botham	16	1	58	2	12	0	34	1
MW Gatting	1	0	2	0	2	0	2	0

No. 630: 2nd Test

VENUE:	Perth (WACA)
DATE:	28th Nov to 3rd December 1986
TOSS WON BY:	England
RESULT:	Match drawn

ENGLAND	1st innings		2nd innings	
BC Broad	c Zoehrer b Reid	162	lbw b Waugh	16
CWJ Athey	b Reid	96	c Border b Reid	6
AJ Lamb	c Zoehrer b Reid	0	b Waugh	70
MW Gatting*	c Waugh b C Matthews	14	lbw b Reid	2
DI Gower	c Waugh b G Matthews	136	c Zoehrer b Waugh	48
IT Botham	c Border b Reid	0	c GRJ Matthews b Reid	6
CJ Richards+	c Waugh b D Matthews	133	c Lawson b Waugh	15
PAJ De Freitas	lbw b CD Matthews	11	b Waugh	15
JE Emburey	not out	5	not out	4
PH Edmonds				
GR Dilley				
Extras	(4b, 15lb, 3w, 13nb)	35	(4b, 9lb, 0w, 4nb)	17
	170.1 overs		53.3 overs	
Total		**592**		**199**

1st innings FoW: 223, 227, 275, 333, 339, 546, 585, 592
2nd innings FoW: 8, 47, 50, 123, 140, 172, 190, 199

GF Lawson	41	8	126	0		9	1	44	0
CD Matthews	29.1	4	112	3		2	0	15	0
BA Reid	40	8	115	4		21	3	58	3
SR Waugh	24	4	90	0		21.3	4	69	5
GRJ Matthews	34	3	124	1					
AR Border	2	0	6	0					

AUSTRALIA	1st innings		2nd innings	
GR Marsh	c Broad b Botham	15	lbw b Emburey	49
DC Boon	b Dilley	2	c Botham b Dilley	0
SR Waugh	c Botham b Emburey	71	run out	69
DM Jones	c Athey b Edmonds	27	c Lamb b Edmonds	16
AR Border*	c Richards b Dilley	125	not out	24
GM Ritchie	c Botham b Edmonds	33	not out	14
GRJ Matthews	c Botham b Dilley	45		
TJ Zoehrer+	lbw b Dilley	29		
GF Lawson	b De Freitas	13		
CD Matthews	c Broad b Emburey	10		
BA Reid	not out	2		
Extras	(9b, 9lb, 0w, 11nb)	29	(9b, 6lb, 0w, 10nb)	25
	134.4 overs		97 overs	
Total		**401**		**197**

1st innings FoW: 4, 64, 114, 128, 198, 279, 334, 360, 385, 401
2nd innings FoW: 0, 126, 142, 152

IT Botham	22	4	72	1		7.2	4	13	0
GR Dilley	24.4	4	79	4		15	1	53	1
JE Emburey	43	9	110	2		28	11	41	1
PAJ De Freitas	24	4	67	1		13.4	2	47	0
PH Edmonds	21	4	55	2		27	13	25	1
MW Gatting						5	3	3	0
AJ Lamb						1	1	0	0

No. 631: 3rd Test

VENUE:	Adelaide
DATE:	12th-16th December 1986
TOSS WON BY:	Australia
RESULT:	Match drawn

AUSTRALIA	1st innings		2nd innings	
GR Marsh	b Edmonds	43	c & b Edmonds	41
DC Boon	c Whitaker b Emburey	103	lbw b De Freitas	0
DM Jones	c Richards b Dilley	93	c Lamb b Dilley	2
AR Border*	c Richards b Edmonds	70	not out	100
GM Ritchie	c Broad b De Freitas	36	not out	46
GRJ Matthews	not out	73		
SR Waugh	not out	79		
PR Sleep				
GC Dyer+				
MG Hughes				
BA Reid				
Extras	(0b, 2lb, 0w, 15nb)	17	(4b, 6lb, 0w, 2nb)	12
	171 overs		90 overs	
Total		**514**		**201**

1st innings FoW: 113, 185, 311, 333, 368
2nd innings FoW: 1, 8, 77

GR Dilley	32	3	111	1		21	8	38	1
PAJ De Freitas	32	4	128	1		16	5	36	1
JE Emburey	46	11	117	1		22	6	50	0
PH Edmonds	52	14	134	2		29	7	63	1
MW Gatting	9	1	22	0		2	1	4	0

ENGLAND	1st innings		2nd innings	
BC Broad	c Marsh b Waugh	116	not out	15
CWJ Athey	b Sleep	55	c Dyer b Hughes	12
MW Gatting*	c Waugh b Sleep	100	b Matthews	0
AJ Lamb	c Matthews b Hughes	14	not out	9
DI Gower	lbw b Reid	38		
JE Emburey	c Dyer b Reid	49		
JJ Whitaker	c Matthews b Reid	11		
CJ Richards+	c Jones b Sleep	29		
PAJ De Freitas	not out	4		
PH Edmonds	c Border b Sleep	13		
GR Dilley	b Reid	0		
Extras	(4b, 14lb, 4w, 4nb)	26	(2b, 1lb, 0w, 0nb)	3
	148.4 overs		23 overs	
Total		**455**		**39**

1st innings FoW: 112, 273, 283, 341, 341, 361, 422, 439, 454, 455
2nd innings FoW: 21, 22

MG Hughes	30	8	82	1		7	2	16	1
BA Reid	28.4	8	64	4					
PR Sleep	47	14	132	4		5	5	0	0
GRJ Matthews	23	1	102	0		8	4	10	1
AR Border	1	0	1	0					
SR Waugh	19	4	56	1		3	1	10	0

No. 632:	4th Test
VENUE:	Melbourne (MCG)
DATE:	26th-28th December 1986
TOSS WON BY:	England
RESULT:	Eng won by an innings and 14 runs

No. 633:	5th Test
VENUE:	Sydney (SCG)
DATE:	10th-15th January 1987
TOSS WON BY:	Australia
RESULT:	Australia won by 55 runs

AUSTRALIA 1st innings / 2nd innings

	1st innings		2nd innings	
GR Marsh	c Richards b Botham	17	run out	60
DC Boon	c Botham b Small	7	c Gatting b Small	8
DM Jones	c Gower b Small	59	c Gatting b De Freitas	21
AR Border*	c Richards b Botham	15	c Emburey b Small	34
SR Waugh	c Botham b Small	10	b Edmonds	49
GRJ Matthews	c Botham b Small	14	b Emburey	0
PR Sleep	c Richards b Small	0	run out	6
TJ Zoehrer+	b Botham	5	c Athey b Edmonds	1
CJ McDermott	c Richards b Botham	0	b Emburey	1
MG Hughes	c Richards b Botham	2	c Small b Edmonds	8
BA Reid	not out	2	not out	0
Extras	(1b, 1lb, 1w, 7nb)	10	(0b, 3lb, 1w, 2nb)	6
Total	54.4 overs	**141**	73.4 overs	**194**

1st innings FoW: 16, 44, 80, 108, 118, 118, 129, 133, 137, 141
2nd innings FoW: 13, 48, 113, 153, 153, 175, 180, 185, 189, 194

GC Small	22.4	7	48	5	15	3	40	2
PAJ De Freitas	11	1	30	0	12	1	44	1
JE Emburey	4	0	16	0	20	5	43	2
IT Botham	16	4	41	5	7	1	19	0
MW Gatting	1	0	4	0				
PH Edmonds					19.4	5	45	3

ENGLAND 1st innings / 2nd innings

	1st innings		2nd innings
BC Broad	c Zoehrer b Hughes	112	
CWJ Athey	lbw b Reid	21	
MW Gatting*	b Hughes b Reid	40	
AJ Lamb	c Zoehrer b Reid	43	
DI Gower	c Matthews b Sleep	7	
IT Botham	c Zoehrer b McDermott	29	
CJ Richards+	c Marsh b Reid	3	
PAJ De Freitas	c Matthews b McDermott	7	
JE Emburey	c & b McDermott	22	
PH Edmonds	lbw b McDermott	19	
GC Small	not out	21	
Extras	(6b, 7lb, 1w, 11nb)	25	
Total	120.5 overs	**349**	

1st innings FoW: 58, 163, 198, 219, 251, 273, 277, 289, 319, 349

CJ McDermott	26.5	4	83	4	
MG Hughes	30	3	94	1	
BA Reid	28	5	78	4	
SR Waugh	8	4	16	0	
PR Sleep	28	4	65	1	

AUSTRALIA 1st innings / 2nd innings (5th Test)

	1st innings		2nd innings	
GR Marsh	c Gatting b Small	24	c Emburey b Dilley	14
GM Ritchie	lbw b Dilley	6	c Botham b Edmonds	13
DM Jones	not out	184	c Richards b Emburey	30
AR Border*	c Botham b Edmonds	34	b Edmonds	49
DM Wellham	c Richards b Small	17	c Lamb b Emburey	0
SR Waugh	c Richards b Small	0	c Athey b Emburey	73
PR Sleep	c Richards b Small	9	c Lamb b Emburey	10
TJ Zoehrer+	c Gatting b Small	12	lbw b Emburey	1
PL Taylor	c Emburey b Edmonds	11	c Lamb b Emburey	42
MG Hughes	c Botham b Edmonds	16	b Emburey	5
BA Reid	b Dilley	4	not out	1
Extras	(12b, 4lb, 2w, 8nb)	26	(5b, 7lb, 0w, 0nb)	12
Total	144.5 overs	**343**	117 overs	**251**

1st innings FoW: 8, 58, 149, 184, 184, 200, 232, 271, 338, 343
2nd innings FoW: 29, 31, 106, 110, 115, 141, 145, 243, 248, 251

GR Dilley	23.5	5	67	2	15	4	48	1
GC Small	33	11	75	5	8	2	17	0
IT Botham	23	10	42	0	3	0	17	0
JE Emburey	30	4	62	0	46	15	78	7
PH Edmonds	34	5	79	3	43	16	79	2
MW Gatting	1	0	2	0	2	2	0	0

ENGLAND 1st innings / 2nd innings (5th Test)

	1st innings		2nd innings	
BC Broad	lbw b Hughes	6	c & b Sleep	17
CWJ Athey	c Zoehrer b Hughes	5	b Sleep	31
MW Gatting*	lbw b Reid	0	c & b Waugh	96
AJ Lamb	c Zoehrer b Taylor	24	c Waugh b Taylor	3
DI Gower	c Wellham b Taylor	72	c Marsh b Border	37
IT Botham	c Marsh b Taylor	16	c Wellham b Taylor	0
CJ Richards+	c Wellham b Reid	46	b Sleep	38
JE Emburey	b Taylor	69	b Sleep	22
PH Edmonds	c Marsh b Taylor	3	lbw b Sleep	0
GC Small	b Taylor	14	c Border b Reid	0
GR Dilley	not out	4	not out	2
Extras	(9b, 3lb, 2w, 2nb)	16	(8b, 6lb, 1w, 3nb)	18
Total	94 overs	**275**	114 overs	**264**

1st innings FoW: 16, 17, 17, 89, 119, 142, 213, 219, 270, 275
2nd innings FoW: 24, 91, 91, 102, 102, 233, 257, 257, 262, 264

MG Hughes	16	3	58	2	12	3	32	0
BA Reid	25	7	74	2	19	8	32	1
SR Waugh	6	4	6	0	6	2	13	1
PL Taylor	26	7	78	6	29	10	76	2
PR Sleep	21	6	47	0	35	14	72	5
AR Border					13	6	25	1

No. 634: 1st Test
VENUE: Old Trafford
DATE: 4th-9th June 1987
TOSS WON BY: Pakistan
RESULT: Match drawn

No. 635: 2nd Test
VENUE: Lord's
DATE: 18th-23rd June 1987
TOSS WON BY: England
RESULT: Match drawn

ENGLAND	1st innings		2nd innings
CWJ Athey	b Wasim	19	
RT Robinson	c Yousuf b Mohsin	166	
MW Gatting*	b Mohsin	42	
NH Fairbro'	lbw b Mohsin	0	
BN French+	c Imran b Wasim	59	
DI Gower	c Yousuf b Wasim	22	
IT Botham	c Wasim b Tauseef	48	
JE Emburey	c Shoaib b Mohsin	19	
PAJ De Freitas	b Wasim	11	
NA Foster	b Tauseef	8	
PH Edmonds	not out	23	
Extras	(9b, 15lb, 1w, 5nb)	30	
	143.4 overs		
Total		**447**	

1st innings FoW: 50, 133, 133, 246, 284, 373, 397, 413, 413, 447

Wasim Akram	46	11	111	4
Mohsin Kamal	39	4	127	4
Tauseef Ahmed	21.4	4	52	2
Mudassar Nazar	37	8	133	0

ENGLAND	1st innings		2nd innings
BC Broad	b M Nazar	55	
RT Robinson	c Yousuf b Mohsin	7	
CWJ Athey	b Imran	123	
DI Gower	c Yousuf b M Nazar	8	
MW Gatting*	run out	43	
BN French+	b Wasim	42	
IT Botham	c Javed b Wasim	6	
JE Emburey	run out	12	
NA Foster	b Abdul	21	
PH Edmonds	not out	17	
GR Dilley	c Salim Yousuf b Imran	17	
Extras	(0b, 12lb, 1w, 4nb)	17	
	112.5 overs		
Total		**368**	

1st innings FoW: 29, 118, 128, 230, 272, 294, 305, 329, 340, 368

Imran Khan	34.5	7	90	2
Wasim Akram	28	1	98	2
Mohsin Kamal	9	2	42	1
Abdul Qadir	25	1	100	1
Mudassar Nazar	16	6	26	2

PAKISTAN 1st innings			2nd innings
Rameez Raja	c Emburey b De Freitas	15	
Shoaib Moh'd	c French b Foster	0	
Mansoor	c Fairbro' b Edmonds	75	
Javed M'dad	c French b Botham	21	
Salim Malik	run out	6	
Imran Khan*	not out	10	
M Nazar	not out	0	
Salim Yousuf+			
Wasim Akram			
Tauseef Ahmed			
Mohsin Kamal			
Extras	(9b, 2lb, 1w, 1nb)	13	
	64 overs		
Total		**140**	

1st innings FoW: 9, 21, 74, 100, 139

NA Foster	15	3	34	1
PAJ De Freitas	12	4	36	1
IT Botham	14	7	29	1
JE Emburey	16	3	28	0
PH Edmonds	7	5	2	1

PAKISTAN 1st innings	2nd innings
Mudassar Nazar	
Shoaib Mohammad	
Mansoor Akhtar	
Javed Miandad	
Salim Malik	
Ijaz Ahmed	
Imran Khan*	
Salim Yousuf+	
Wasim Akram	
Abdul Qadir	
Mohsin Kamal	

Pakistan — No. 636: 3rd Test

VENUE:	Headingley
DATE:	2nd-6th July 1987
TOSS WON BY:	England
RESULT:	Pak won by an innings and 18 runs

ENGLAND

1st innings			2nd innings	
BC Broad	c S Yousuf b Wasim	8	c Salim Yousuf b Imran	4
RT Robinson	lbw b Imran	0	c Salim Malik b Imran	2
CWJ Athey	c Salim Yousuf b Imran	4	lbw b Imran	26
DI Gower	b Imran	10	b Imran	55
MW Gatting*	lbw b Wasim	8	c Javed b Wasim	9
IT Botham	c Yousuf b M Nazar	26	c Ijaz b Imran	28
DJ Capel	c & b Mohsin	53	c Ijaz b Imran	2
CJ Richards+	lbw b Wasim	6	c Mudassar b Mohsin	24
NA Foster	c Salim Malik b Mohsin	9	b Wasim	22
PH Edmonds	c S Yousuf b Mohsin	0	not out	0
GR Dilley	not out	1	b Imran	0
Extras	(1b, 8lb, 1w, 1nb)	11	(5b, 12lb, 7w, 3nb)	27
	60.4 overs		78.1 overs	
Total		**136**		**199**

1st innings FoW: 1, 13, 13, 31, 85, 113, 133, 133, 136
2nd innings FoW: 4, 9, 60, 94, 120, 122, 160, 197, 197, 199

Imran Khan	19	3	37	3		19.1	5	40	7
Wasim Akram	14	4	36	3		21	5	55	2
Abdul Qadir	5	0	14	0		27	5	60	0
Mudassar Nazar	14	5	18	1		2	0	8	0
Mohsin Kamal	8.4	2	22	3		9	4	19	1

PAKISTAN

1st innings			2nd innings
M Nazar	lbw b Foster	24	
Shoaib Moh'd	c Richards b Foster	16	
Mansoor Ak'ar	lbw b Foster	29	
Salim Yousuf+	c Athey b Foster	37	
Javed Miandad	c Gatting b Foster	0	
Salim Malik	c Gower b Edmonds	99	
Imran Khan*	c Richards b Foster	26	
Ijaz Ahmed	c Athey b Foster	50	
Wasim Akram	c Edmonds b Foster	43	
Abdul Qadir	b Dilley	2	
Mohsin Kamal	not out	3	
Extras	(5b, 13lb, 1w, 5nb)	24	
	131.2 overs		
Total		**353**	

1st innings FoW: 22, 60 , 86, 86, 152, 208, 280, 318, 328, 353

GR Dilley	33	7	89	1	
NA Foster	46.2	15	107	8	
DJ Capel	18	1	64	0	
PH Edmonds	25	10	59	1	
MW Gatting	9	3	16	0	

Pakistan — No. 637: 4th Test

VENUE:	Edgbaston
DATE:	23rd-28th July 1987
TOSS WON BY:	England
RESULT:	Match drawn

PAKISTAN

1st innings			2nd innings	
M Nazar	lbw b Dilley	124	b Dilley	10
Shoaib	c Foster b Edmonds	18	lbw b Foster	50
Mansoor Ak't	b Foster	26	lbw b Foster	17
Javed M'dad	lbw b Dilley	75	c Emburey b Foster	4
Salim Malik	c French b Dilley	24	c & b Botham	17
Ijaz Ahmed	lbw b Botham	20	b Botham	11
Imran Khan*	c Emburey b Dilley	0	lbw b Foster	37
Salim Yousuf+	not out	91	c Gatting b Edmonds	17
Wasim Akram	c Botham b Foster	26	c Edmonds b Dilley	6
Abdul Qadir	c Edmonds b Dilley	4	run out	20
Mohsin Kamal	run out	10	not out	0
Extras	(4b, 11lb, 1w, 3nb)	19	(0b, 13lb, 1w, 2nb)	16
	173.3 overs		73.3 overs	
Total		**439**		**205**

1st innings FoW: 44, 83, 218, 284, 289, 289, 317, 360, 384, 439
2nd innings FoW: 47, 80, 85, 104, 104, 116, 156, 165, 204, 205

GR Dilley	35	6	92	5		18	3	53	2
NA Foster	37	8	107	2		27	7	59	4
JE Emburey	26	7	48	0		4	1	3	0
PH Edmonds	24.3	12	50	1		4	1	11	1
IT Botham	48	13	121	1		20.3	3	66	2
MW Gatting	3	0	6	0					

ENGLAND

1st innings			2nd innings	
BC Broad	c Salim Yousuf b Imran	54	c Mudassar b Imran	30
RT Robinson	c Salim Yousuf b Wasim	80	c Imran b Wasim	4
CWJ Athey	b Imran	0	not out	14
DI Gower	c Salim Yousuf b Imran	61	b Imran	18
MW Gatting*	c Wasim b Imran	124	run out	8
BN French+	b Imran	0		
IT Botham	c & b Wasim	37	c Mohsin b Wasim	6
JE Emburey	lbw b Wasim	58	run out	20
NA Foster	run out	29	run out	0
PH Edmonds	not out	24	not out	1
GR Dilley	b Imran	2		
Extras	(1b, 24lb, 11w, 16nb)	52	(0b, 7lb, 1w, 0nb)	8
	169.5 overs		17.4 overs	
Total		**521**		**109**

1st innings FoW: 119, 132, 157, 251, 251, 300, 443, 484, 512, 521
2nd innings FoW: 37, 39, 53, 72, 73, 108, 108

Imran Khan	41.5	8	129	6		9	0	61	2
Wasim Akram	43	12	83	3		8.4	0	41	2
Abdul Qadir	21	4	65	0					
Mudassar Nazar	35	7	97	0					
Mohsin Kamal	29	2	122	0					

No. 638: 5th Test		No. 639: 1st Test
VENUE: The Oval		VENUE: Lahore (Gaddafi)
DATE: 6th-11th August 1987		DATE: 25th-28th November 1987
TOSS WON BY: Pakistan		TOSS WON BY: England
RESULT: Match drawn		RESULT: Pak won by an innings and 87 runs

PAKISTAN 1st innings　　　　**2nd innings**

M Nazar	c Moxon b Botham	73
Rameez Raja	b Botham	14
Mansoor Ak'r	c French b Dilley	5
Javed M'dad	c & b Dilley	260
Salim Malik	c Gower b Botham	102
Imran Khan*	run out	118
Ijaz Ahmed	c Moxon b Dilley	69
Salim Yousuf+	c & b Dilley	42
Wasim Akram	c Botham b Dilley	5
Abdul Qadir	c Moxon b Dilley	0
Tauseef Ahmed	not out	0
Extras	(2b, 18lb, 0w, 0nb)	20
	220.3 overs	
Total		**708**

1st innings FoW: 40, 45, 148, 382, 573, 601, 690, 707, 707, 708

GR Dilley	47.3	10	154	6
NA Foster	12	3	32	0
IT Botham	52	7	217	3
JE Emburey	61	10	143	0
PH Edmonds	32	8	97	0
MW Gatting	10	2	18	0
MD Moxon	6	2	27	0

ENGLAND 1st innings　　　　**2nd innings**

BC Broad	c Salim Yousuf b Imran	0	c Ijaz Ahmed b Abdul	42
MD Moxon	c Javed b Abdul	8	c Yousuf b Tauseef	15
RT Robinson	b Abdul	30	c Wasim b Abdul	10
DI Gower	b Tauseef Ahmed	28	c M Nazar b Abdul	34
MW Gatting*	c Imran b Abdul	61	not out	150
IT Botham	b Abdul	34	not out	51
JE Emburey	c Salim Malik b Abdul	53		
BN French+	c Salim Malik b Abdul	1		
NA Foster	c Ijaz b Tauseef Ahmed	4		
PH Edmonds	lbw b Abdul	2		
GR Dilley	not out	0		
Extras	(4b, 3lb, 1w, 3nb)	11	(4b, 5lb, 1w, 3nb)	13
	99.4 overs		142 overs	
Total		**232**		**315**

1st innings FoW: 0, 32, 54, 78, 165, 166, 184, 198, 223, 232
2nd innings FoW: 22, 40, 89, 139

Imran Khan	18	2	39	1	26.3	8	59	0
Wasim Akram	14	2	37	0	6	3	3	0
Abdul Qadir	44.4	15	96	7	53	21	115	3
Tauseef Ahmed	23	9	53	2	46.3	15	98	1
Mudassar Nazar					6	0	21	0
Javed Miandad					4	2	10	0

ENGLAND 1st innings　　　　**2nd innings**

GA Gooch	b Abdul	12	c Ashraf b Iqbal	15
BC Broad	c Asif b Abdul	41	c Ashraf b Iqbal	13
RT Robinson	c Ashraf b Abdul	6	lbw b Abdul	1
MW Gatting*	lbw b Abdul	0	lbw b Abdul	23
CWJ Athey	lbw b Abdul	5	c Ashraf b Tauseef	2
DJ Capel	c Asif b Tauseef Ahmed	0	lbw b Abdul	9
PAJ De Freitas	lbw b Abdul	5	c Javed b Abdul	0
JE Emburey	b Abdul	0	c Tauseef b Iqbal	15
NA Foster	lbw b Abdul	39	not out	38
BN French+	not out	38	c (sub) b Tauseef	1
NGB Cook	c Javed b Abdul	10	b Tauseef Ahmed	5
Extras	(4b, 14lb, 0w, 1nb)	19	(4b, 4lb, 0w, 0nb)	8
	83 overs		79.2 overs	
Total		**175**		**130**

1st innings FoW: 22, 36, 36, 44, 55, 70, 81, 94, 151, 175
2nd innings FoW: 23, 24, 38, 43, 66, 70, 73, 105, 116, 130

Wasim Akram	14	4	32	0	2	0	6	0
Mudassar Nazar	5	3	9	0	1	0	4	0
Abdul Qadir	37	13	56	9	36	14	45	4
Tauseef Ahmed	23	9	38	1	20.2	7	28	3
Iqbal Qasim	4	0	22	0	20	10	39	3

PAKISTAN 1st innings　　　　**2nd innings**

M Nazar	lbw b Foster	120
Rameez Raja	b Emburey	35
Salim Malik	b Emburey	0
Javed M'dad*	c Gooch b Cook	65
Ijaz Ahmed	b De Freitas	44
Asif Mujtaba	b Foster	7
Ashraf Ali+	b Emburey	7
Wasim Akram	c Broad b Cook	40
Abdul Qadir	st French b Cook	38
Iqbal Qasim	run out	1
Tauseef Ah'd	not out	5
Extras	(18b, 8lb, 0w, 4nb)	30
	134 overs	
Total		**392**

1st innings FoW: 71, 71, 213, 272, 290, 301, 328, 360, 370, 392

PAJ De Freitas	29	7	84	1
NA Foster	23	6	58	2
JE Emburey	48	16	109	3
NGB Cook	31	10	87	3
DJ Capel	3	0	28	0

No. 640: 2nd Test

VENUE:	Faisalabad
DATE:	7th-12th December 1987
TOSS WON BY:	England
RESULT:	Match drawn

ENGLAND 1st innings / 2nd innings

Batsman	1st innings		2nd innings	
GA Gooch	c Aamer Malik b Iqbal	28	lbw b Abdul	65
BC Broad	b Tauseef Ahmed	116	st Ashraf b Abdul	14
CWJ Athey	c Aamer Malik b Abdul	27	b M Nazar	20
MW Gatting*	b Abdul	79	c Abdul b Iqbal	8
RT Robinson	c Ashraf b Abdul	2	not out	7
NGB Cook	c Ashraf b Iqbal	2		
DJ Capel	c Aamer Malik b Abdul	1	lbw b Iqbal	2
JE Emburey	st Ashraf b Iqbal	15	not out	10
NA Foster	c Aamer Malik b Abdul	0	c Javed b Abdul	0
BN French+	st Ashraf b Iqbal	2		
EE Hemmings	not out	1		
Extras	(10b, 5lb, 1w, 3nb)	19	(1b, 9lb, 0w, 1nb)	11
	114.2 overs		40 overs	
Total		**292**		**137**

1st innings FoW: 73, 124, 241, 249, 258, 259, 288, 288, 288, 292
2nd innings FoW: 47, 102, 107, 115, 115, 120

Bowler	O	M	R	W	O	M	R	W
Aamer Malik	5	0	19	0	3	0	20	0
Mudassar Nazar	3	0	8	0	12	1	33	1
Abdul Qadir	42	7	105	4	15	3	45	3
Tauseef Ahmed	28	9	62	1				
Iqbal Qasim	35.2	7	83	5	10	2	29	2
Shoaib	1	1	0	0				

PAKISTAN 1st innings / 2nd innings

Batsman	1st innings		2nd innings	
M Nazar	c French b Foster	1	b Cook	4
Rameez Raja	c Gooch b Foster	12	not out	13
Salim Malik	b Cook	60	not out	28
Javed M'dad*	b Emburey	19		
Ijaz Ahmed	c Robinson b Emburey	11		
Shoaib Moh'd	b Emburey	0		
Aamer Malik	c French b Foster	5		
Ashraf Ali+	c French b Foster	4		
Abdul Qadir	c Gooch b Cook	38		
Iqbal Qasim	lbw b Hemmings	24		
Tauseef Ah'd	not out	5		
Extras	(0b, 5lb, 0w, 7nb)	12	(4b, 1lb, 0w, 1nb)	6
	84.3 overs		24 overs	
Total		**191**		**51**

1st innings FoW: 11, 22, 58, 77, 77, 115, 122, 123, 175, 191
2nd innings FoW: 15

Bowler	O	M	R	W	O	M	R	W
NA Foster	18	4	42	4	3	0	4	0
DJ Capel	7	1	23	0				
EE Hemmings	18	5	35	1	7	3	16	0
JE Emburey	21	8	49	3	2	0	3	0
NGB Cook	20.3	10	37	2	9	3	15	1
GA Gooch					2	1	4	0
BC Broad					1	0	4	0

No. 641: 3rd Test

VENUE:	Karachi (National Stadium)
DATE:	16th-21st December 1987
TOSS WON BY:	England
RESULT:	Match drawn

ENGLAND 1st innings / 2nd innings

Batsman	1st innings		2nd innings	
GA Gooch	c Ashraf b Wasim	12	b M Nazar	93
BC Broad	lbw b Wasim	7	lbw b Abdul	13
CWJ Athey	b Abdul	26	c Ashraf b Salim Jaffer	12
MW Gatting*	b Abdul	18	lbw b Salim Jaffer	0
NH Fairbro'	c (sub) b Salim Jaffer	3	c (sub) b Abdul	1
DJ Capel	b Abdul	98	c Iqbal b Abdul	24
PAJ De Freitas	b Abdul	12	not out	74
JE Emburey	c Abdul b Salim Jaffer	70	lbw b Salim Jaffer	0
BN French+	c Javed b Salim Malik	31	lbw b Abdul	6
NGB Cook	lbw b Abdul	2	b Abdul	14
GR Dilley	not out	0	not out	0
Extras	(0b, 8lb, 1w, 6nb)	15	(9b, 5lb, 1w, 6nb)	21
	121.4 overs		137 overs	
Total		**294**		**258**

1st innings FoW: 20, 41, 55, 72, 72, 85, 199, 274, 291, 294
2nd innings FoW: 34, 54, 54, 61, 115, 175, 176, 187, 246

Bowler	O	M	R	W	O	M	R	W
Wasim Akram	24.1	3	64	2				
Salim Jaffer	23.5	6	74	2	42	9	79	3
Abdul Qadir	49.4	15	88	5	55	16	98	5
Iqbal Qasim	18	4	51	0	27	10	44	0
Mudassar Nazar	1	1	0	0	4	3	2	1
Salim Malik	5	2	9	1	7	2	14	0
Aamer Malik					2	0	7	0

PAKISTAN 1st innings / 2nd innings

Batsman	1st innings		2nd innings
M Nazar	lbw b De Freitas	6	
Rameez Raja	c French b Cook	50	
Salim Malik	c Gatting b De Freitas	55	
Javed M'dad*	lbw b Emburey	4	
Ijaz Ahmed	run out	0	
Aamer Malik	not out	98	
Ashraf Ali+	c French b Dilley	12	
Wasim Akram	c French b De Freitas	37	
Abdul Qadir	b Capel	61	
Iqbal Qasim	c French b De Freitas	11	
Salim Jaffer	lbw b De Freitas	0	
Extras	(0b, 11lb, 0w, 8nb)	19	
	133.5 overs		
Total		**353**	

1st innings FoW: 18, 105, 110, 110, 122, 146, 222, 316, 349, 353

Bowler	O	M	R	W
GR Dilley	21	2	102	1
PAJ De Freitas	23.5	3	86	5
JE Emburey	53	24	90	1
NGB Cook	33	12	56	1
DJ Capel	3	0	8	1

Australia

No. 642: 1st Test
VENUE: Sydney (SCG)
DATE: 29th January to 2nd Feb 1988
TOSS WON BY: England
RESULT: Match drawn

ENGLAND	1st innings		2nd innings	
BC Broad	b Waugh	139		
MD Moxon	b Sleep	40		
RT Robinson	c Veletta b Dodemaide	43		
MW Gatting*	c Dyer b Waugh	13		
CWJ Athey	c & b Taylor	37		
DJ Capel	c Sleep b Taylor	21		
JE Emburey	st Dyer b Sleep	23		
BN French+	st Dyer b Taylor	47		
NA Foster	c Border b Taylor	19		
EE Hemmings	not out	8		
GR Dilley	b Waugh	13		
Extras	(4b, 9lb, 1w, 8nb)	22		
Total	172.5 overs	**425**		

1st innings FoW: 93, 192, 245, 262, 313, 314, 346, 387, 410, 425

CJ McDermott	35	8	65	0
AIC Dodemaide	36	10	98	1
PL Taylor	34	10	84	4
SR Waugh	22.5	5	51	3
PR Sleep	45	8	114	2

AUSTRALIA	1st innings		2nd innings	
DC Boon	c French b Foster	12	not out	184
GR Marsh	c French b Capel	5	c Athey b Emburey	56
DM Jones	c Emburey b Hemmings	56	c Moxon b Capel	24
AR Border*	c Broad b Capel	2	not out	48
MRJ Veletta	c Emburey b Hemmings	22		
SR Waugh	c French b Dilley	27		
PR Sleep	c Athey b Foster	41		
GC Dyer+	lbw b Dilley	0		
PL Taylor	c French b Hemmings	20		
A Dodemaide	not out	12		
CJ McDermott	c Foster b Dilley	1		
Extras	(0b, 10lb, 1w, 5nb)	16	(3b, 7lb, 0w, 6nb)	16
Total	96.1 overs	**214**	135 overs	**328**

1st innings FoW: 18, 25, 34, 82, 116, 147, 153, 183, 209, 214
2nd innings FoW: 162, 218

GR Dilley	19.1	4	54	3	13	1	48	0
NA Foster	19	6	27	2	15	6	27	0
JE Emburey	30	10	57	0	38	5	98	1
DJ Capel	6	3	13	2	17	4	38	1
EE Hemmings	22	3	53	3	52	15	107	0

New Zealand

No. 643: 1st Test
VENUE: Christchurch
DATE: 12th-17th February 1988
TOSS WON BY: New Zealand
RESULT: Match drawn

ENGLAND	1st innings		2nd innings	
BC Broad	c Smith b Snedden	114	c (sub) b Chatfield	20
MD Moxon	c Jones b Morrison	1	c Jones b Chatfield	27
RT Robinson	c Smith b Morrison	70	c Wright b Chatfield	2
MW Gatting*	c (sub) b Morrison	8	b Snedden	23
CWJ Athey	c (sub) b Morrison	22	c Smith b Snedden	19
DJ Capel	c Bracewell b Chatfield	11	c MD Crowe b Chatfield	0
JE Emburey	c Jones b Morrison	42	run out	19
BN French+	c Smith b Chatfield	7	c JJ Crowe b Snedden	3
PAJ De Freitas	c Morrison b Chatfield	4	lbw b Snedden	16
PW Jarvis	c Smith b Chatfield	14	not out	10
GR Dilley	not out	7	c Jones b Morrison	2
Extras	(0b, 11lb, 1w, 7nb)	19	(0b, 7lb, 0w, 4nb)	11
Total	120.1 overs	**319**	74.1 overs	**152**

1st innings FoW: 7, 175, 186, 219, 237, 241, 248, 260, 285, 319
2nd innings FoW: 32, 38, 55, 95, 96, 99, 118, 125, 147, 152

RJ Hadlee	18	3	50	0				
DK Morrison	21.1	3	69	5	21.1	4	64	1
EJ Chatfield	42	13	87	4	30	13	36	4
MC Snedden	33	9	86	1	23	8	45	4
JG Bracewell	6	1	16	0				

NEW ZEALAND	1st innings		2nd innings	
JG Wright	c Moxon b Dilley	10	lbw b Dilley	23
TJ Franklin	c Athey b Dilley	10	lbw b Dilley	12
AH Jones	c French b Dilley	8	not out	54
MD Crowe	c Moxon b Dilley	5	c French b Jarvis	6
JJ Crowe*	c French b De Freitas	28	lbw b De Freitas	0
JG Bracewell	c French b Dilley	31	not out	20
RJ Hadlee	c French b Dilley	37		
IDS Smith+	c Capel b Jarvis	13		
MC Snedden	lbw b De Freitas	0		
DK Morrison	b Jarvis	0		
EJ Chatfield	not out	0		
Extras	(2b, 12lb, 0w, 12nb)	26	(6b, 4lb, 0w, 5nb)	15
Total	81.5 overs	**168**	77 overs	**130**

1st innings FoW: 20, 25, 32, 40, 96, 131, 151, 155, 156, 168
2nd innings FoW: 37, 43, 61, 78

PAJ De Freitas	22	6	39	2	19	6	26	1
GR Dilley	24.5	9	38	6	18	5	32	2
DJ Capel	10	2	32	0	13	5	16	0
PW Jarvis	21	8	43	2	17	7	30	1
JE Emburey	4	3	2	0	10	4	16	0

No. 644: 2nd Test
VENUE: Auckland
DATE: 25th-29th February 1988
TOSS WON BY: England
RESULT: Match drawn

No. 645: 3rd Test
VENUE: Wellington
DATE: 3rd-7th March 1988
TOSS WON BY: New Zealand
RESULT: Match drawn

NEW ZEALAND 1st innings / 2nd innings (No. 644)

Batsman	1st innings		2nd innings	
JG Wright	c French b Dilley	103	c French b Radford	49
TJ Franklin	b Jarvis	27	b Dilley	62
JJ Crowe*	c Capel b Dilley	11	lbw b Dilley	1
MD Crowe	c Capel b Emburey	36	lbw b Jarvis	26
MJ Greatbatch	c French b Dilley	11	not out	107
KR Rutherford	b Capel	29	b Emburey	2
JG Bracewell	c Moxon b Dilley	9	c French b Capel	20
IDS Smith+	c French b Jarvis	23	lbw b Gatting	38
MC Snedden	c Moxon b Dilley	14	not out	23
DK Morrison	not out	14		
EJ Chatfield	c French b Capel	10		
Extras	(1b, 2lb, 2w, 9nb)	14	(8b, 8lb, 0w, 6nb)	22
	134.2 overs		169 overs	
Total		**301**		**350**

1st innings FoW: 77, 98, 169, 191, 207, 219, 254, 262, 279, 301
2nd innings FoW: 117, 119, 119, 150, 153, 232, 296

Bowler	O	M	R	W	O	M	R	W
GR Dilley	28	9	60	5	23	9	44	2
PW Jarvis	33	9	74	2	27	7	54	1
NV Radford	30	4	79	0	20	4	53	1
DJ Capel	26.2	4	57	2	21	4	40	1
JE Emburey	17	7	28	1	57	24	91	1
MW Gatting					17	4	40	1
NH Fairbrother					2	0	9	0
MD Moxon					2	0	3	0

ENGLAND 1st innings / 2nd innings (No. 644)

Batsman	1st innings		2nd innings
BC Broad	c MD Crowe b Bracewell	9	
MD Moxon	c JJ Crowe b Chatfield	99	
RT Robinson	c Morrison b Bracewell	54	
MW Gatting*	c Smith b Morrison	42	
NH Fairbro'	c Smith b Chatfield	1	
DJ Capel	c Bracewell b Morrison	5	
JE Emburey	c Smith b Chatfield	45	
BN French+	c Franklin b Bracewell	13	
PW Jarvis	c Smith b Snedden	10	
NV Radford	b Chatfield	8	
GR Dilley	not out	8	
Extras	(12b, 12lb, 0w, 5nb)	29	
Total	141.1 overs	**323**	

1st innings FoW: 27, 135, 211, 220, 222, 234, 267, 282, 308, 323

Bowler	O	M	R	W
DK Morrison	32	7	95	2
EJ Chatfield	31.1	15	37	4
JG Bracewell	39	8	88	3
MC Snedden	34	14	71	1
KR Rutherford	5	1	8	0

NEW ZEALAND 1st innings / 2nd innings (No. 645)

Batsman	1st innings		2nd innings
JG Wright*	c Fairbrother b Capel	36	
TJ Franklin	lbw b De Freitas	14	
RH Vance	run out	47	
MD Crowe	lbw b Gatting	143	
MJ Greatbatch	c De Freitas b Emburey	68	
KR Rutherford	not out	107	
JG Bracewell	c Fairbrother b Capel	54	
IDS Smith+	not out	33	
SL Boock			
DK Morrison			
EJ Chatfield			
Extras	(0b, 10lb, 0w, 0nb)	10	
Total	197 overs	**512**	

1st innings FoW: 33, 70, 132, 287, 336, 470

Bowler	O	M	R	W
GR Dilley	11	1	36	0
PAJ De Freitas	50.1	21	110	1
DJ Capel	39	7	129	2
JE Emburey	45.5	10	99	1
EE Hemmings	45	15	107	0
MW Gatting	6	1	21	1

ENGLAND 1st innings / 2nd innings (No. 645)

Batsman	1st innings		2nd innings
BC Broad	b Boock	61	
MD Moxon	not out	81	
RT Robinson	c Smith b Chatfield	0	
MW Gatting*	not out	33	
DJ Capel			
NH Fairbrother			
JE Emburey			
PAJ De Freitas			
BN French+			
GR Dilley			
EE Hemmings			
Extras	(0b, 6lb, 0w, 2nb)	8	
Total	79 overs	**183**	

1st innings FoW: 129, 132

Bowler	O	M	R	W
DK Morrison	6	0	41	0
EJ Chatfield	23	10	38	1
JG Bracewell	23	9	44	0
SL Boock	26	9	53	1
KR Rutherford	1	0	1	0

No. 646: 1st Test
VENUE: Trent Bridge
DATE: 2nd-7th June 1988
TOSS WON BY: England
RESULT: Match drawn

No. 647: 2nd Test
VENUE: Lord's
DATE: 16th-21st June 1988
TOSS WON BY: West Indies
RESULT: West Indies won by 134 runs

ENGLAND 1st innings / 2nd innings

Batsman	1st innings		2nd innings	
GA Gooch	b Marshall	73	c Dujon b Patterson	146
BC Broad	b Marshall	54	c Dujon b Ambrose	16
MW Gatting*	c Logie b Marshall	5	b Marshall	29
DI Gower	c Dujon b Ambrose	18	not out	88
AJ Lamb	lbw b Marshall	0	not out	6
DR Pringle	b Marshall	39		
PR Downton+	not out	16		
JE Emburey	c Dujon b Marshall	0		
PAJ De Freitas	b Ambrose	3		
PW Jarvis	b Ambrose	6		
GR Dilley	b Ambrose	2		
Extras	(0b, 13lb, 5w, 11nb)	29	(0b, 10lb, 0w, 6nb)	16
Total	101 overs	**245**	108 overs	**301**

1st innings FoW: 125, 141, 161, 161, 186, 223, 223, 235, 243, 245
2nd innings FoW: 39, 116, 277

Bowler	O	M	R	W	O	M	R	W
MD Marshall	30	4	69	6	13	4	23	1
BP Patterson	16	2	49	0	24	6	69	1
CEL Ambrose	26	10	53	4	23	4	56	1
CA Walsh	20	4	39	0	25	5	84	0
CL Hooper	8	1	20	0	14	1	33	0
IVA Richards	1	0	2	0	9	1	26	0

WEST INDIES 1st innings / 2nd innings

Batsman	1st innings		2nd innings
CG Greenidge	c Downton b Jarvis	25	
DL Haynes	c Downton b Jarvis	60	
RB Richardson	c Gatting b Emburey	17	
IVA Richards*	c Gooch b De Freitas	80	
CL Hooper	c Downton b De Freitas	84	
AL Logie	c Gooch b Pringle	20	
PJL Dujon+	c & b Dilley	16	
MD Marshall	b Emburey	72	
CEL Ambrose	run out	43	
CA Walsh	not out	3	
BP Patterson			
Extras	(6b, 8lb, 0w, 14nb)	28	
Total	129.1 overs	**448**	

1st innings FoW: 54, 84, 159, 231, 271, 309, 334, 425, 448

Bowler	O	M	R	W
GR Dilley	34	5	101	1
PAJ De Freitas	27	5	93	2
PW Jarvis	18.1	1	63	2
DR Pringle	34	11	82	1
JE Emburey	16	4	95	2

WEST INDIES 1st innings / 2nd innings

Batsman	1st innings		2nd innings	
CG Greenidge	c Downton b Dilley	22	c Emburey b Dilley	103
DL Haynes	c Moxon b Dilley	12	c Downton b Dilley	5
RB Richardson	c Emburey b Dilley	5	lbw b Pringle	26
IVA Richards*	c Downton b Dilley	6	b Pringle	72
CL Hooper	c Downton b Small	3	c Downton b Jarvis	11
AL Logie	c Emburey b Small	81	not out	95
PJL Dujon+	b Emburey	53	b Jarvis	52
MD Marshall	c Gooch b Dilley	11	b Jarvis	6
CEL Ambrose	c Gower b Small	0	b Dilley	0
CA Walsh	not out	9	b Dilley	0
BP Patterson	b Small	0	c Downton b Jarvis	2
Extras	(0b, 6lb, 0w, 1nb)	7	(0b, 19lb, 1w, 5nb)	25
Total	67.5 overs	**209**	108 overs	**397**

1st innings FoW: 21, 40, 47, 50, 54, 184, 199, 199, 199, 209
2nd innings FoW: 32, 115, 198, 226, 240, 371, 379, 380, 384, 397

Bowler	O	M	R	W	O	M	R	W
GR Dilley	23	6	55	5	27	6	73	4
PW Jarvis	13	2	47	0	26	3	107	4
GC Small	18.5	5	64	4	19	1	76	0
DR Pringle	7	3	20	0	21	4	60	2
JE Emburey	6	2	17	1	15	1	62	0

ENGLAND 1st innings / 2nd innings

Batsman	1st innings		2nd innings	
GA Gooch	b Marshall	44	lbw b Marshall	16
BC Broad	lbw b Marshall	0	c Dujon b Marshall	1
MD Moxon	c Richards b Ambrose	26	run out	14
DI Gower	c (sub) b Walsh	46	c Rich'son b Patterson	1
AJ Lamb	lbw b Marshall	10	run out	113
DR Pringle	c Dujon b Walsh	1	lbw b Walsh	0
PR Downton+	lbw b Marshall	11	lbw b Marshall	27
JE Emburey*	b Patterson	7	b Ambrose	30
GC Small	not out	5	c Richards b Marshall	7
PW Jarvis	c Haynes b Marshall	7	not out	29
GR Dilley	b Marshall	0	c Rich'son b Patterson	28
Extras	(0b, 6lb, 0w, 2nb)	8	(5b, 20lb, 2w, 14nb)	41
Total	59 overs	**165**	86.5 overs	**307**

1st innings FoW: 13, 58, 112, 129, 134, 140, 153, 157, 165, 165
2nd innings FoW: 27, 29, 31, 104, 105, 161, 212, 232, 254, 307

Bowler	O	M	R	W	O	M	R	W
MD Marshall	18	5	32	6	25	5	60	4
BP Patterson	13	3	52	1	21.5	2	100	2
CEL Ambrose	12	1	39	1	20	4	47	1
CA Walsh	16	6	36	2	20	1	75	1

No. 648: 3rd Test
VENUE: Old Trafford
DATE: 30th June to 5th July 1988
TOSS WON BY: England
RESULT: WI won by an innings and 156 runs

ENGLAND	1st innings		2nd innings	
GA Gooch	c Dujon b Benjamin	27	lbw b Marshall	1
MD Moxon	b Marshall	0	c Richards b Benjamin	15
MW Gatting	lbw b Marshall	0	c Richardson b Marshall	4
DI Gower	c Harper b Walsh	9	c Richardson b Marshall	34
AJ Lamb	c Greenidge b Ambrose	33	c Logie b Ambrose	9
DJ Capel	b Benjamin	1	c (sub) b Marshall	0
PR Downton+	c Greenidge b Walsh	24	c Harper b Marshall	6
JE Emburey*	c Dujon b Walsh	1	c Logie b Ambrose	8
PAJ De Freitas	c Greenidge b Ambrose	15	c Harper b Marshall	0
GR Dilley	c Harper b Walsh	14	b Marshall	4
JH Childs	not out	2	not out	0
Extras	(0b, 4lb, 0w, 5nb)	9	(1b, 10lb, 0w, 1nb)	12
	60.2 overs		42.4 overs	
Total		**135**		**93**

1st innings FoW: 12, 14, 33, 55, 61, 94, 98, 113, 123, 135
2nd innings FoW: 6, 22, 36, 73, 73, 73, 87, 87, 93, 93

MD Marshall	12	5	19	2	15.4	5	22	7
CEL Ambrose	17	5	35	2	16	4	36	2
CA Walsh	18.2	4	46	4	4	1	10	0
WKM Benjamin	13	4	31	2	4	1	6	1
RA Harper					2	1	4	0
CL Hooper					1	0	4	0

WEST INDIES 1st innings   2nd innings

CG Greenidge	lbw b De Freitas	45
RB Richardson	b Dilley	23
CL Hooper	lbw b Childs	15
IVA Richards*	b Capel	47
AL Logie	lbw b Dilley	39
PJL Dujon+	c Capel b Dilley	67
RA Harper	b Dilley	74
MD Marshall	not out	43
CEL Ambrose	not out	7
WKM Benjamin		
CA Walsh		
Extras	(0b, 21lb, 0w, 3nb)	24
	140.1 overs	
Total		**384**

1st innings FoW: 35, 77, 101, 175, 187, 281, 373

GR Dilley	28.1	4	99	4
JE Emburey	25	7	54	0
PAJ De Freitas	35	5	81	1
DJ Capel	12	2	38	1
JH Childs	40	12	91	1

No. 649: 4th Test
VENUE: Headingley
DATE: 21st-26th July 1988
TOSS WON BY: West Indies
RESULT: West Indies won by 10 wickets

ENGLAND	1st innings		2nd innings	
GA Gooch	c Dujon b Marshall	9	c Hooper b Walsh	50
TS Curtis	lbw b Benjamin	12	b Ambrose	12
CWJ Athey	lbw b Ambrose	16	c Dujon b Walsh	11
DI Gower	c Dujon b Benjamin	13	c Dujon b Marshall	2
AJ Lamb	retired hurt	64	lbw b Marshall	11
RA Smith	c Dujon b Ambrose	38	b Walsh	5
CS Cowdrey*	lbw b Marshall	0	b Ambrose	8
CJ Richards+	b Ambrose	2	c Dujon b Ambrose	19
DR Pringle	c Dujon b Marshall	0	b Benjamin	3
NA Foster	not out	8	c Hooper b Benjamin	0
GR Dilley	c Hooper b Ambrose	8	not out	2
Extras	(1b, 18lb, 6w, 6nb)	31	(3b, 8lb, 0w, 4nb)	15
	69.1 overs		61.5 overs	
Total		**201**		**138**

1st innings FoW: 14, 43, 58, 80, 183, 183, 185, 185, 201
2nd innings FoW: 56, 80, 85, 85, 105, 105, 127, 132, 132, 138

MD Marshall	23	8	55	3	17	4	47	2
CEL Ambrose	25.1	8	58	4	19.5	4	40	3
WKM Benjamin	9	2	27	2	5	4	2	2
CA Walsh	12	4	42	0	20	9	38	3

WEST INDIES 1st innings   2nd innings

DL Haynes	lbw b Pringle	54	not out	25
PJL Dujon+	c Smith b Dilley	13	not out	40
CL Hooper	lbw b Foster	19		
IVA Richards*	c Curtis b Foster	18		
AL Logie	c Foster b Pringle	44		
KLT Arthurton	c Richards b Pringle	27		
RA Harper	c Gower b Foster	56		
MD Marshall	c Gooch b Pringle	3		
CEL Ambrose	lbw b Pringle	8		
W Benjamin	run out	9		
CA Walsh	not out	9		
Extras	(0b, 15lb, 0w, 0nb)	15	(0b, 2lb, 0w, 0nb)	2
	81.2 overs		14.3 overs	
Total		**275**		**67**

1st innings FoW: 15, 61, 97, 137, 156, 194, 210, 222, 245, 275

GR Dilley	20	5	59	1	4	0	16	0
NA Foster	32.2	6	98	3	7	1	36	0
DR Pringle	27	7	95	5				
CS Cowdrey	2	0	8	0	3.3	0	13	0

West Indies

No. 650: 5th Test
VENUE: The Oval
DATE: 4th-8th August 1988
TOSS WON BY: England
RESULT: West Indies won by 8 wickets

ENGLAND

1st innings			2nd innings	
GA Gooch*	c Logie b Ambrose	9	c Greenidge b Ambrose	84
TS Curtis	c Dujon b Benjamin	30	lbw b Marshall	15
RJ Bailey	c Dujon b Ambrose	43	b Benjamin	3
RA Smith	c Harper b Marshall	57	lbw b Benjamin	0
MP Maynard	c Dujon b Ambrose	3	c Logie b Benjamin	34
DJ Capel	c Marshall b Harper	16	c & b Benjamin	10
CJ Richards+	c Logie b Harper	0	lbw b Walsh	12
DR Pringle	c Dujon b Marshall	1	c Dujon b Walsh	3
PAJ De Freitas	c Haynes b Harper	18	b Harper	8
NA Foster	c (sub) b Marshall	7	c Haynes b Harper	0
JH Childs	not out	0	not out	0
Extras	(0b, 6lb, 0w, 15nb)	21	(3b, 15lb, 0w, 15nb)	33
Total	90.3 overs	**205**	89.1 overs	**202**

1st innings FoW: 12, 77, 116, 121, 160, 160, 165, 196, 198, 205
2nd innings FoW: 50, 55, 55, 108, 125, 139, 157, 175, 177, 202

MD Marshall	24.3	3	64	3		25	6	52	1
CEL Ambrose	20	6	31	3		24.1	10	50	1
CA Walsh	10	1	21	0		12	5	21	2
WKM Benjamin	14	2	33	1		22	4	52	4
RA Harper	21	7	50	3		6	3	9	2
CL Hooper	1	1	0	0					

WEST INDIES

1st innings			2nd innings	
CG Greenidge	c De Freitas b Foster	10	c Richards b Childs	77
DL Haynes	c Richards b Foster	2	not out	77
CL Hooper	c Gooch b Foster	11	b Foster	23
IVA Richards*	c Curtis b Foster	0	not out	38
AL Logie	c Gooch b Foster	47		
PJL Dujon+	lbw b Pringle	64		
RA Harper	run out	17		
MD Marshall	c & b Childs	0		
CEL Ambrose	not out	17		
W Benjamin	b Pringle	0		
CA Walsh	c De Freitas b Pringle	5		
Extras	(0b, 7lb, 1w, 2nb)	10	(2b, 3lb, 0w, 6nb)	11
Total	59 overs	**183**	91 overs	**226**

1st innings FoW: 9, 16, 16, 57, 126, 155, 156, 167, 168, 183
2nd innings FoW: 131, 162

NA Foster	16	2	64	5		18	3	52	1
PAJ De Freitas	13	4	33	0		17	2	46	0
DR Pringle	17	4	45	3		13	4	24	0
DJ Capel	7	0	21	0		3	0	20	0
JH Childs	6	1	13	1		40	16	79	1

Sri Lanka

No. 651: 1st Test
VENUE: Lord's
DATE: 25th-30th August 1988
TOSS WON BY: England
RESULT: England won by 7 wickets

SRI LANKA

1st innings			2nd innings	
D Kuruppu	c Gooch b Newport	46	c Barnett b Foster	25
SAR Silva+	c Russell b Foster	1	c Russell b Newport	16
MAR Sam'ra	c Russell b Foster	0	lbw b Emburey	57
PA de Silva	c Gooch b Newport	3	lbw b Lawrence	18
R Madugalle*	lbw b Foster	3	b Foster	20
A Ranatunga	lbw b Newport	5	b Newport	78
LRD Mendis	c Smith b Lawrence	21	lbw b Pringle	56
JR Ratnayeke	not out	59	c Lamb b Lawrence	32
M Madur'ghe	run out	4	b Newport	2
C Raman'ke	lbw b Pringle	0	not out	9
GF Labrooy	lbw b Pringle	42	c Gooch b Newport	2
Extras	(1b, 7lb, 0w, 2nb)	10	(0b, 8lb, 0w, 8nb)	16
Total	65.5 overs	**194**	109.3 overs	**331**

1st innings FoW: 7, 44, 52, 53, 61, 63, 122, 127, 130, 194
2nd innings FoW: 43, 51, 96, 145, 147, 251, 309, 311, 323, 331

NA Foster	21	5	51	3		33	10	98	2
DV Lawrence	15	4	37	1		21	5	74	2
PJ Newport	21	4	77	3		26.3	7	87	4
DR Pringle	6.5	1	17	2		11	2	30	1
JE Emburey	2	1	4	0		18	9	34	1

ENGLAND

1st innings			2nd innings	
GA Gooch*	lbw b Ratnayeke	75	c Silva b Samarasekera	36
RT Robinson	c Sama'kera b Ratnayeke	19	not out	34
RC Russell+	c Sama'kera b Labrooy	94		
KJ Barnett	c Ranatunga b Labrooy	66	c Silva b Samarasekera	0
AJ Lamb	b Labrooy	63	c de Silva b Ranatunga	8
RA Smith	b Ranatunga	31	not out	8
DR Pringle	c Silva b Labrooy	14		
JE Emburey	c de Silva b Sama'kera	0		
PJ Newport	c de Silva b Ramanayake	26		
NA Foster	not out	14		
DV Lawrence	c Mendis b Ramanayake	4		
Extras	(1b, 3lb, 2w, 17nb)	23	(0b, 8lb, 2w, 4nb)	14
Total	143.2 overs	**429**	34.4 overs	**100**

1st innings FoW: 40, 171, 233, 320, 358, 373, 378, 383, 420, 429
2nd innings FoW: 73, 73, 82

JR Ratnayeke	32	3	107	2		7	1	16	0
GF Labrooy	40	7	119	4		9	0	24	0
CPH Ramanayake	27.2	3	86	2					
MA Madurasinghe	16	4	41	0					
MAR Samarasekera	22	5	66	1		10	0	38	2
A Ranatunga	6	3	6	1		8.4	4	14	1

No. 652: 1st Test
VENUE: Headingley
DATE: 8th-13th June 1989
TOSS WON BY: England
RESULT: Australia won by 210 runs

No. 653: 2nd Test
VENUE: Lord's
DATE: 22nd-28th June 1989
TOSS WON BY: England
RESULT: Australia won by 6 wickets

AUSTRALIA 1st innings / 2nd innings

Batsman	1st innings		2nd innings	
GR Marsh	lbw b De Freitas	16	c Broad b Pringle	60
MA Taylor	lbw b Foster	136	c Russell b Foster	6
DC Boon	c Russell b Foster	9	lbw b De Freitas	43
AR Border*	c Foster b De Freitas	66	not out	60
DM Jones	c Russell b Newport	79	not out	40
SR Waugh	not out	177		
IA Healy+	c & b Newport	16		
MG Hughes	c Russell b Foster	71		
GF Lawson	not out	10		
GD Campbell				
TM Alderman				
Extras	(0b, 13lb, 1w, 7nb)	21	(2b, 5lb, 9w, 5nb)	21
Total	178.3 overs	**601**	54.5 overs	**230**

1st innings FoW: 44, 57, 174, 273, 411, 441, 588
2nd innings FoW: 14, 97, 129

Bowler	O	M	R	W		O	M	R	W
PAJ De Freitas	45.3	8	140	2		18	2	76	1
NA Foster	46	14	109	3		19	4	65	1
PJ Newport	39	5	153	2		5	2	22	0
DR Pringle	33	5	123	0		12.5	1	60	1
GA Gooch	9	1	31	0					
KJ Barnett	6	0	32	0					

ENGLAND 1st innings / 2nd innings

Batsman	1st innings		2nd innings	
GA Gooch	lbw b Alderman	13	lbw b Hughes	68
BC Broad	b Hughes	37	lbw b Alderman	7
KJ Barnett	lbw b Alderman	80	c Taylor b Alderman	34
AJ Lamb	c Boon b Alderman	125	c Boon b Alderman	4
DI Gower*	c Healy b Lawson	26	c Healy b Lawson	34
RA Smith	lbw b Alderman	66	c Border b Lawson	0
DR Pringle	lbw b Campbell	6	c Border b Alderman	0
PJ Newport	c Boon b Lawson	36	c Marsh b Alderman	8
RC Russell+	c Marsh b Lawson	15	c Healy b Hughes	2
PAJ De Freitas	lbw b Alderman	1	b Hughes	21
NA Foster	not out	2	not out	1
Extras	(5b, 7lb, 1w, 10nb)	23	(4b, 3lb, 0w, 5nb)	12
Total	121.5 overs	**430**	55.2 overs	**191**

1st innings FoW: 35, 81, 195, 243, 323, 338, 392, 421, 424, 430
2nd innings FoW: 17, 67, 77, 134, 134, 153, 153, 166, 170, 191

Bowler	O	M	R	W		O	M	R	W
TM Alderman	37	7	107	5		20	7	44	5
GF Lawson	34.5	6	105	3		11	2	58	2
GD Campbell	14	0	82	1		10	0	42	0
MG Hughes	28	7	92	1		9.2	2	36	3
SR Waugh	6	2	27	0					
AR Border	2	1	5	0		5	3	4	0

ENGLAND 1st innings / 2nd innings (No. 653)

Batsman	1st innings		2nd innings	
GA Gooch	c Healy b Waugh	60	lbw b Alderman	0
BC Broad	lbw b Alderman	18	b Lawson	20
KJ Barnett	c Boon b Hughes	14	c Jones b Alderman	3
MW Gatting	c Boon b Hughes	0	lbw b Alderman	22
DI Gower*	b Lawson	57	c Border b Hughes	106
RA Smith	c Hohns b Lawson	32	b Alderman	96
JE Emburey	b Alderman	0	c Boon b Lawson	29
RC Russell+	not out	64	not out	36
NA Foster	c Jones b Hughes	16	lbw b Alderman	4
PW Jarvis	c Marsh b Hughes	6	lbw b Alderman	5
GR Dilley	c Border b Alderman	7	c Boon b Hughes	24
Extras	(0b, 9lb, 0w, 3nb)	12	(6b, 6lb, 0w, 2nb)	14
Total	86.5 overs	**286**	130 overs	**359**

1st innings FoW: 31, 52, 58, 131, 180, 185, 191, 237, 253, 286
2nd innings FoW: 0, 18, 28, 84, 223, 274, 300, 304, 314, 359

Bowler	O	M	R	W		O	M	R	W
TM Alderman	20.5	4	60	3		38	6	128	6
GF Lawson	27	8	88	2		39	10	99	2
MG Hughes	23	6	71	4		24	8	44	2
SR Waugh	9	3	49	1		7	2	20	0
TV Hohns	7	3	9	0		13	6	33	0
AR Border						9	3	23	0

AUSTRALIA 1st innings / 2nd innings (No. 653)

Batsman	1st innings		2nd innings	
GR Marsh	c Russell b Dilley	3	b Dilley	1
MA Taylor	lbw b Foster	62	c Gooch b Foster	27
DC Boon	c Gooch b Dilley	94	not out	58
AR Border*	c Smith b Emburey	35	c (sub) b Foster	1
DM Jones	lbw b Foster	27	c Russell b Foster	0
SR Waugh	not out	152	not out	21
IA Healy+	c Russell b Jarvis	3		
MG Hughes	c Gooch b Foster	30		
TV Hohns	b Emburey	21		
GF Lawson	c Broad b Emburey	74		
TM Alderman	lbw b Emburey	8		
Extras	(0b, 11lb, 0w, 8nb)	19	(3b, 4lb, 0w, 4nb)	11
Total	158 overs	**528**	40.2 overs	**119**

1st innings FoW: 6, 151, 192, 221, 235, 265, 331, 381, 511, 528
2nd innings FoW: 9, 51, 61, 67

Bowler	O	M	R	W		O	M	R	W
GR Dilley	34	3	141	2		10	2	27	1
NA Foster	45	7	129	3		18	3	39	3
PW Jarvis	31	3	150	1		9.2	0	38	0
JE Emburey	42	12	88	4		3	0	8	0
GA Gooch	6	2	9	0					

	No. 654: 3rd Test		No. 655: 4th Test
	VENUE: Edgbaston		VENUE: Old Trafford
	DATE: 6th-11th July 1989		DATE: 27th July to 1st August 1989
	TOSS WON BY: Australia		TOSS WON BY: England
	RESULT: Match drawn		RESULT: Australia won by 9 wickets

AUSTRALIA 1st innings / 2nd innings

Batsman	1st innings		2nd innings	
GR Marsh	lbw b Botham	42	b Jarvis	42
MA Taylor	st Russell b Emburey	43	c Botham b Gooch	51
DC Boon	run out	38	not out	22
AR Border*	b Emburey	8	not out	33
DM Jones	c (sub) b Fraser	157		
SR Waugh	b Fraser	43		
IA Healy+	b Fraser	2		
MG Hughes	c Botham b Dilley	2		
TV Hohns	c Gooch b Dilley	40		
GF Lawson	b Fraser	12		
TM Alderman	not out	0		
Extras	(0b, 20lb, 0w, 17nb)	37	(4b, 4lb, 0w, 2nb)	10
	142 overs		65 overs	
Total		**424**		**158**

1st innings FoW: 88, 94, 105, 201, 272, 289, 299, 391, 421, 424
2nd innings FoW: 81, 109

Bowler	O	M	R	W		O	M	R	W
GR Dilley	31	3	123	2		10	4	27	0
PW Jarvis	23	4	82	0		6	1	20	1
ARC Fraser	33	8	63	4		12	0	29	0
IT Botham	26	5	75	1					
JE Emburey	29	5	61	2		20	8	37	0
GA Gooch						14	5	30	1
TS Curtis						3	0	7	0

ENGLAND 1st innings / 2nd innings

Batsman	1st innings		2nd innings
GA Gooch	lbw b Lawson	8	
TS Curtis	lbw b Hughes	41	
DI Gower*	lbw b Alderman	8	
CJ Tavare	c Taylor b Alderman	2	
KJ Barnett	c Healy b Waugh	10	
IT Botham	b Hughes	46	
RC Russell+	c Taylor b Hohns	42	
JE Emburey	c Boon b Lawson	26	
ARC Fraser	run out	12	
GR Dilley	not out	11	
PW Jarvis	lbw b Alderman	22	
Extras	(1b, 2lb, 0w, 11nb)	14	
	96.3 overs		
Total		**242**	

1st innings FoW: 17, 42, 47, 75, 75, 171, 171, 185, 215, 242

Bowler	O	M	R	W
TM Alderman	26.3	6	61	3
GF Lawson	21	4	54	2
MG Hughes	22	4	68	2
SR Waugh	11	3	38	1
TV Hohns	16	8	18	1

ENGLAND 1st innings / 2nd innings

Batsman	1st innings		2nd innings	
GA Gooch	b Lawson	11	c Alderman b Lawson	13
TS Curtis	b Lawson	22	c Boon b Alderman	0
RT Robinson	lbw b Lawson	0	lbw b Lawson	12
RA Smith	c Hohns b Hughes	143	c Healy b Alderman	1
DI Gower*	lbw b Hohns	35	c Marsh b Lawson	15
IT Botham	b Hohns	0	lbw b Alderman	4
RC Russell+	lbw b Lawson	1	not out	128
JE Emburey	lbw b Hohns	5	b Alderman	64
NA Foster	c Border b Lawson	39	b Alderman	6
ARC Fraser	b Lawson	2	c Marsh b Hohns	3
NGB Cook	not out	0	c Healy b Hughes	5
Extras	(0b, 2lb, 0w, 0nb)	2	(0b, 6lb, 2w, 5nb)	13
	103 overs		110.4 overs	
Total		**260**		**264**

1st innings FoW: 23, 23, 57, 132, 140, 147, 158, 232, 252, 260
2nd innings FoW: 10, 25, 27, 28, 38, 59, 201, 223, 255, 264

Bowler	O	M	R	W		O	M	R	W
TM Alderman	25	13	49	0		27	7	66	5
GF Lawson	33	11	72	6		31	8	81	3
MG Hughes	17	6	55	1		14.4	2	45	1
TV Hohns	22	7	59	3		26	15	37	1
SR Waugh	6	1	23	0		4	0	17	0
AR Border						8	2	12	0

AUSTRALIA 1st innings / 2nd innings

Batsman	1st innings		2nd innings	
MA Taylor	st Russell b Emburey	85	not out	37
GR Marsh	c Russell b Botham	47	c Robinson b Emburey	31
DC Boon	b Fraser	12	not out	10
AR Border*	c Russell b Foster	80		
DM Jones	b Botham	69		
SR Waugh	c Curtis b Fraser	92		
IA Healy+	lbw b Foster	0		
TV Hohns	c Gower b Cook	17		
MG Hughes	b Cook	3		
GF Lawson	b Fraser	17		
TM Alderman	not out	6		
Extras	(5b, 7lb, 1w, 6nb)	19	(0b, 0lb, 0w, 3nb)	3
	167.5 overs		32.5 overs	
Total		**447**		**81**

1st innings FoW: 135, 143, 154, 274, 362, 362, 413, 423, 423, 447
2nd innings FoW: 62

Bowler	O	M	R	W		O	M	R	W
NA Foster	34	12	74	2		5	2	5	0
ARC Fraser	36.5	4	95	3		10	0	28	0
JE Emburey	45	9	118	1		13	3	30	1
NGB Cook	28	6	85	2		4.5	0	18	0
IT Botham	24	6	63	2					

Australia

No. 656: 5th Test
VENUE: Trent Bridge
DATE: 10th-14th August 1989
TOSS WON BY: Australia
RESULT: Aus won by an innings and 180 runs

AUSTRALIA 1st innings

	1st innings		2nd innings
GR Marsh	c Botham b Cook	138	
MA Taylor	st Russell b Cook	219	
DC Boon	st Russell b Cook	73	
AR Border*	not out	65	
DM Jones	c Gower b Fraser	22	
SR Waugh	c Gower b Malcolm	0	
IA Healy+	b Fraser	5	
TV Hohns	not out	19	
MG Hughes			
GF Lawson			
TM Alderman			
Extras	(6b, 23lb, 3w, 29nb)	61	
	206.3 overs		
Total		**602**	

1st innings FoW: 329, 430, 502, 543, 553, 560

ARC Fraser	52.3	18	108	2
DE Malcolm	44	2	166	1
IT Botham	30	4	103	0
NGB Cook	40	10	91	3
EE Hemmings	33	9	81	0
MA Atherton	7	0	24	0

ENGLAND 1st innings

	1st innings		2nd innings	
TS Curtis	lbw b Alderman	2	lbw b Alderman	6
MD Moxon	c Waugh b Alderman	0	b Alderman	18
MA Atherton	lbw b Alderman	0	c & b Hohns	47
RA Smith	c Healy b Alderman	101	b Hughes	26
DI Gower*	c Healy b Lawson	11	b Lawson	5
RC Russell+	c Healy b Lawson	20	b Lawson	1
EE Hemmings	b Alderman	38	lbw b Hughes	35
ARC Fraser	b Hohns	29	b Hohns	1
IT Botham	c Waugh b Hohns	12		
NGB Cook	not out	2	b Hughes	5
DE Malcolm	c Healy b Hughes	9		
Extras	(0b, 18lb, 0w, 13nb)	31	(3b, 6lb, 1w, 6nb)	16
	76.5 overs		55.3 overs	
Total		**255**		**167**

1st innings FoW: 1, 1, 14, 37, 119, 172, 214, 243, 244, 255
2nd innings FoW: 5, 13, 67, 106, 114, 120, 134, 160, 167

TM Alderman	19	2	69	5		16	6	32	2
GF Lawson	21	5	57	2		15	3	51	2
TV Hohns	18	8	48	2		12	3	29	2
MG Hughes	7.5	0	40	1		12.3	1	46	3
SR Waugh	11	4	23	0					

Australia

No. 657: 6th Test
VENUE: The Oval
DATE: 24th-29th August 1989
TOSS WON BY: Australia
RESULT: Match drawn

AUSTRALIA 1st innings

	1st innings		2nd innings	
GR Marsh	c Igglesden b Small	17	lbw b Igglesden	4
MA Taylor	c Russell b Igglesden	71	c Russell b Small	48
DC Boon	c Atherton b Small	46	run out	37
AR Border*	c Russell b Capel	76	not out	51
DM Jones	c Gower b Small	122	b Capel	50
SR Waugh	b Igglesden	14	not out	7
IA Healy+	c Russell b Pringle	44		
TV Hohns	c Russell b Pringle	30		
MG Hughes	lbw b Pringle	21		
GF Lawson	b Pringle	2		
TM Alderman	not out	6		
Extras	(1b, 9lb, 0w, 9nb)	19	(2b, 7lb, 0w, 13nb)	22
	132.3 overs		63 overs	
Total		**468**		**219**

1st innings FoW: 48, 130, 149, 345, 347, 386, 409, 447, 453, 468
2nd innings FoW: 7, 100, 101, 189

GC Small	40	8	141	3		20	4	57	1
AP Igglesden	24	2	91	2		13	1	55	1
DR Pringle	24.3	6	70	4		16	0	53	0
NGB Cook	25	5	78	0		6	2	10	0
DJ Capel	16	2	66	1		8	0	35	1
MA Atherton	1	0	10	0					
GA Gooch	2	1	2	0					

ENGLAND 1st innings

	1st innings		2nd innings	
GA Gooch	lbw b Alderman	0	c & b Alderman	10
J Stephenson	c Waugh b Alderman	25	lbw b Alderman	11
MA Atherton	c Healy b Hughes	12	b Lawson	14
RA Smith	b Lawson	11	not out	77
DI Gower*	c Healy b Alderman	79	c Waugh b Lawson	7
DJ Capel	lbw b Alderman	4	c Taylor b Hohns	17
RC Russell+	c Healy b Alderman	12	not out	0
DR Pringle	c Taylor b Hohns	27		
GC Small	c Jones b Lawson	59		
NGB Cook	c Jones b Lawson	31		
AP Igglesden	not out	2		
Extras	(2b, 7lb, 1w, 13nb)	23	(0b, 1lb, 1w, 5nb)	7
	92.1 overs		46.1 overs	
Total		**285**		**143**

1st innings FoW: 1, 28, 47, 80, 84, 98, 169, 201, 274, 285
2nd innings FoW: 20, 27, 51, 67, 138

TM Alderman	27	7	66	5		13	3	30	2
GF Lawson	29.1	9	85	3		15.1	2	41	2
MG Hughes	23	3	84	1		8	2	34	0
TV Hohns	10	1	30	1		10	2	37	1
SR Waugh	3	0	11	0					

West Indies | West Indies

No. 658: 1st Test	No. 659: 3rd Test
VENUE: Kingston (Jamaica)	VENUE: Port-of-Spain (Trinidad)
DATE: 24th–29th February 1990	DATE: 23rd–28th March 1990
TOSS WON BY: West Indies	TOSS WON BY: England
RESULT: England won by 9 wickets	RESULT: Match drawn

WEST INDIES 1st innings / 2nd innings (No. 658)

Batsman	1st innings		2nd innings	
CG Greenidge	run out	32	c Hussain b Malcolm	36
DL Haynes	c & b Small	36	b Malcolm	14
RB Richardson	c Small b Capel	10	lbw b Fraser	25
CA Best	c Russell b Capel	4	c Gooch b Small	64
CL Hooper	c Capel b Fraser	20	c Larkins b Small	8
IVA Richards*	lbw b Malcolm	21	b Malcolm	37
PJL Dujon+	not out	19	b Malcolm	15
MD Marshall	b Fraser	0	not out	8
IR Bishop	c Larkins b Fraser	0	c Larkins b Small	3
CA Walsh	b Fraser	6	b Small	2
BP Patterson	b Fraser	0	run out	2
Extras	(9b, 3lb, 0w, 4nb)	16	(14b, 10lb, 1w, 1nb)	26
	64 overs		72.3 overs	
Total		**164**		**240**

1st innings FoW: 62, 81, 92, 92, 124, 144, 144, 150, 164, 164
2nd innings FoW: 26, 69, 87, 112, 192, 222, 222, 227, 237, 240

Bowler	O	M	R	W	O	M	R	W
GC Small	15	6	44	1	22	6	58	4
DE Malcolm	16	4	49	1	21.3	2	77	4
ARC Fraser	20	8	28	5	14	5	31	1
DJ Capel	13	4	31	2	15	1	50	0

ENGLAND 1st innings / 2nd innings (No. 658)

Batsman	1st innings		2nd innings	
GA Gooch*	c Dujon b Patterson	18	c Greenidge b Bishop	8
W Larkins	lbw b Walsh	46	not out	29
AJ Stewart	c Best b Bishop	13	not out	0
AJ Lamb	c Hooper b Walsh	132		
RA Smith	c Best b Bishop	57		
N Hussain	c Dujon b Bishop	13		
DJ Capel	c Richardson b Walsh	5		
RC Russell+	c Patterson b Walsh	26		
GC Small	lbw b Marshall	4		
ARC Fraser	not out	2		
DE Malcolm	lbw b Walsh	0		
Extras	(23b, 12lb, 1w, 12nb)	48	(0b, 1lb, 0w, 3nb)	4
	109.2 overs		16.3 overs	
Total		**364**		**41**

1st innings FoW: 40, 40, 116, 288, 315, 315, 325, 339, 364, 364
2nd innings FoW: 35

Bowler	O	M	R	W	O	M	R	W
BP Patterson	18	2	74	1	3	1	11	0
IR Bishop	27	5	72	3	7.3	2	17	1
MD Marshall	18	3	46	1				
CA Walsh	27.2	4	68	5	6	0	12	0
CL Hooper	6	0	28	0				
IVA Richards	9	1	22	0				
CA Best	4	0	19	0				

WEST INDIES 1st innings / 2nd innings (No. 659)

Batsman	1st innings		2nd innings	
CG Greenidge	c Stewart b Malcolm	5	lbw b Fraser	42
DL Haynes*	c Lamb b Small	0	c Lamb b Malcolm	45
RB Richardson	c Russell b Fraser	8	c Gooch b Small	34
CA Best	c Lamb b Fraser	10	lbw b Malcolm	0
PJL Dujon+	lbw b Small	4	b Malcolm	0
AL Logie	c Lamb b Fraser	98	c Larkins b Malcolm	20
CL Hooper	c Russell b Capel	32	run out	10
EA Moseley	c Russell b Malcolm	0	c Lamb b Malcolm	26
CEL Ambrose	c Russell b Malcolm	7	c Russell b Fraser	18
IR Bishop	b Malcolm	16	not out	15
CA Walsh	not out	8	lbw b Malcolm	1
Extras	(0b, 4lb, 0w, 7nb)	11	(2b, 13lb, 1w, 12nb)	28
	65.1 overs		84.2 overs	
Total		**199**		**239**

1st innings FoW: 5, 5, 22, 27, 29, 92, 93, 103, 177, 199
2nd innings FoW: 96, 100, 100, 100, 142, 167, 200, 200, 234, 239

Bowler	O	M	R	W	O	M	R	W
GC Small	17	4	41	2	21	8	56	1
DE Malcolm	20	2	60	4	26.2	4	77	6
ARC Fraser	13.1	2	41	3	24	4	61	2
DJ Capel	15	2	53	1	13	3	30	0

ENGLAND 1st innings / 2nd innings (No. 659)

Batsman	1st innings		2nd innings	
GA Gooch*	c Dujon b Bishop	84	retired hurt	18
W Larkins	c Dujon b Ambrose	54	c Dujon b Moseley	7
AJ Stewart	c Dujon b Ambrose	9	c Bishop b Walsh	31
AJ Lamb	b Bishop	32	lbw b Bishop	25
RA Smith	c Dujon b Moseley	5	lbw b Walsh	2
RJ Bailey	c Logie b Moseley	0	b Walsh	0
DJ Capel	c Moseley b Ambrose	40	not out	17
RC Russell+	c Best b Walsh	15	not out	5
GC Small	lbw b Bishop	0		
ARC Fraser	c Hooper b Ambrose	11		
DE Malcolm	not out	0		
Extras	(6b, 13lb, 3w, 16nb)	38	(2b, 7lb, 0w, 6nb)	15
	137.2 overs		33 overs	
Total		**288**		**120**

1st innings FoW: 112, 152, 195, 214, 214, 214, 243, 244, 284, 288
2nd innings FoW: 27, 74, 79, 85, 106

Bowler	O	M	R	W	O	M	R	W
CEL Ambrose	36.2	8	59	4	6	0	20	0
IR Bishop	31	6	69	3	10	1	31	1
CA Walsh	22	5	45	1	7	0	27	3
CL Hooper	18	5	26	0				
EA Moseley	30	5	70	2	10	2	33	1

No. 660:	4th Test
VENUE:	Bridgetown (Barbados)
DATE:	5th-10th April 1990
TOSS WON BY:	England
RESULT:	West Indies won by 164 runs

No. 661:	5th Test
VENUE:	St. John's (Antigua)
DATE:	12th-16th April 1990
TOSS WON BY:	England
RESULT:	WI won by an innings and 32 runs

WEST INDIES 1st innings / 2nd innings

	1st innings		2nd innings	
CG Greenidge	c Russell b De Freitas	41	lbw b Small	3
DL Haynes	c Stewart b Small	0	c Malcolm b Small	109
RB Richardson	c Russell b Small	45	lbw b De Freitas	39
CA Best	c Russell b Small	164	c Small b Capel	12
IVA Richards*	c Russell b Capel	70	lbw b De Freitas	48
AL Logie	c Russell b Capel	31	b Small	5
PJL Dujon+	b Capel	31	c Smith b Small	7
MD Marshall	c Lamb b Small	4	not out	15
CEL Ambrose	not out	20	c Capel b De Freitas	1
IR Bishop	run out	10	not out	11
EA Moseley	b De Freitas	4	absent hurt	0
Extras	(0b, 8lb, 0w, 18nb)	26	(0b, 12lb, 1w, 4nb)	17
Total	121.5 overs	**446**	68 overs	**267**

1st innings FoW: 6, 67, 108, 227, 291, 395, 406, 411, 431, 446
2nd innings FoW: 13, 80, 109, 223, 228, 238, 238, 239

DE Malcolm	33	6	142	0	10	0	46	0
GC Small	35	5	109	4	20	1	74	4
PAJ De Freitas	29.5	5	99	2	22	2	69	3
DJ Capel	24	5	88	3	16	1	66	1

ENGLAND 1st innings / 2nd innings

	1st innings		2nd innings	
AJ Stewart	c Richards b Moseley	45	c Richards b Ambrose	37
W Larkins	c Richardson b Bishop	0	c Dujon b Bishop	0
RJ Bailey	b Bishop	17	c Dujon b Ambrose	6
AJ Lamb*	lbw b Ambrose	119	lbw b Ambrose	0
RA Smith	b Moseley	62	b Ambrose	55
N Hussain	lbw b Marshall	18	c Dujon b Moseley	10
DJ Capel	c Greenidge b Marshall	2	not out	40
RC Russell+	lbw b Bishop	7	lbw b Ambrose	0
PAJ De Freitas	c & b Ambrose	24	lbw b Ambrose	6
GC Small	not out	1	lbw b Ambrose	0
DE Malcolm	b Bishop	12	lbw b Ambrose	4
Extras	(14b, 9lb, 3w, 25nb)	51	(8b, 9lb, 1w, 15nb)	33
Total	109.3 overs	**358**	91.4 overs	**191**

1st innings FoW: 1, 46, 75, 268, 297, 301, 308, 340, 340, 358
2nd innings FoW: 1, 10, 10, 71, 97, 166, 173, 181, 181, 191

IR Bishop	24.3	8	70	4	20	7	40	1
CEL Ambrose	25	2	82	2	22.4	10	45	8
EA Moseley	28	3	114	2	19	3	44	1
MD Marshall	23	6	55	2	18	8	31	0
IVA Richards	9	4	14	0	10	5	11	0
RB Richardson					2	1	3	0

ENGLAND 1st innings / 2nd innings

	1st innings		2nd innings	
AJ Stewart	c Richards b Walsh	27	c Richardson b Bishop	8
W Larkins	c Hooper b Ambrose	30	b Ambrose	10
RJ Bailey	c Dujon b Bishop	42	c Dujon b Bishop	8
AJ Lamb*	c Richards b Ambrose	37	b Baptiste	35
RA Smith	lbw b Walsh	12	retired hurt	8
N Hussain	c Dujon b Bishop	35	c Dujon b Bishop	34
DJ Capel	c Haynes b Bishop	10	run out	1
RC Russell+	c Dujon b Bishop	7	c Richardson b Ambrose	24
PAJ De Freitas	lbw b Bishop	21	c Greenidge b Ambrose	0
GC Small	lbw b Walsh	8	b Ambrose	1
DE Malcolm	not out	0	not out	1
Extras	(5b, 11lb, 0w, 15nb)	31	(1b, 8lb, 1w, 11nb)	21
Total	91.1 overs	**260**	47 overs	**154**

1st innings FoW: 42, 101, 143, 167, 167, 195, 212, 242, 259, 260
2nd innings FoW: 16, 20, 33, 47, 86, 94, 148, 148, 154

IR Bishop	28.1	6	84	5	14	2	36	3
CEL Ambrose	29	5	79	2	13	7	22	4
CA Walsh	21	4	51	3	10	1	40	0
EAE Baptiste	13	4	30	0	10	1	47	1

WEST INDIES 1st innings / 2nd innings

	1st innings		2nd innings
CG Greenidge	run out	149	
DL Haynes	c Russell b Small	167	
RB Richardson	c Russell b Malcolm	34	
CL Hooper	b Capel	1	
IVA Richards*	c Smith b Malcolm	1	
AL Logie	c Lamb b De Freitas	15	
PJL Dujon+	run out	25	
EAE Baptiste	c Russell b Malcolm	9	
CEL Ambrose	c De Freitas b Capel	5	
IR Bishop	not out	14	
CA Walsh	b Malcolm	8	
Extras	(0b, 5lb, 0w, 13nb)	18	
Total	120.5 overs	**446**	

1st innings FoW: 298, 357, 358, 359, 382, 384, 415, 417, 433, 446

GC Small	31	3	123	1
DE Malcolm	34.5	3	126	4
DJ Capel	28	1	118	2
PAJ De Freitas	27	4	74	1

No. 662: 1st Test	No. 663: 2nd Test
VENUE: Trent Bridge	VENUE: Lord's
DATE: 7th-12th June 1990	DATE: 21st-26th June 1990
TOSS WON BY: New Zealand	TOSS WON BY: New Zealand
RESULT: Match drawn	RESULT: Match drawn

NEW ZEALAND 1st innings / 2nd innings

Batsman	1st innings		2nd innings	
TJ Franklin	b Malcolm	33	not out	22
JG Wright*	c Stewart b Small	8	c Russell b Small	1
AH Jones	c Stewart b Malcolm	39	c Russell b De Freitas	13
MD Crowe	b De Freitas	59		
MJ Greatbatch	b Hemmings	1		
MW Priest	c Russell b De Freitas	26		
MC Snedden	c Gooch b De Freitas	0		
JG Bracewell	c Gooch b Small	28		
RJ Hadlee	b De Freitas	0		
IDS Smith+	not out	2		
DK Morrison	lbw b De Freitas	0	not out	0
Extras	(1b, 10lb, 1w, 0nb)	12	(0b, 0lb, 0w, 0nb)	0
	89 overs		17 overs	
Total		**208**		**36**

1st innings FoW: 16, 75, 110, 121, 170, 174, 191, 191, 203, 208
2nd innings FoW: 8, 36

Bowler	O	M	R	W	O	M	R	W
GC Small	29	9	49	2	6	2	14	1
DE Malcolm	19	7	48	2	7	2	22	0
EE Hemmings	19	6	47	1	2	2	0	0
PAJ De Freitas	22	6	53	5	2	2	0	1

ENGLAND 1st innings / 2nd innings

Batsman	1st innings		2nd innings
GA Gooch*	lbw b Hadlee	0	
MA Atherton	c Snedden b Priest	151	
AJ Stewart	c Smith b Hadlee	27	
AJ Lamb	b Hadlee	0	
RA Smith	c Smith b Bracewell	55	
NH Fairbro'	c Franklin b Snedden	19	
RC Russell+	c Snedden b Morrison	28	
PAJ De Freitas	lbw b Bracewell	14	
GC Small	c Crowe b Hadlee	26	
EE Hemmings	not out	13	
DE Malcolm	not out	4	
Extras	(2b, 3lb, 0w, 3nb)	8	
	138 overs		
Total		**345**	

1st innings FoW: 0, 43, 45, 141, 168, 260, 302, 306, 340

Bowler	O	M	R	W
RJ Hadlee	33	6	89	4
DK Morrison	22	3	96	1
MC Snedden	36	17	54	1
JG Bracewell	35	8	75	2
MW Priest	12	4	26	1

ENGLAND 1st innings / 2nd innings

Batsman	1st innings		2nd innings	
GA Gooch*	c & b Bracewell	85	b Hadlee	37
MA Atherton	b Morrison	0	c Bracewell b Jones	54
AJ Stewart	lbw b Hadlee	54	c (sub) b Bracewell	42
AJ Lamb	lbw b Snedden	39	not out	84
RA Smith	c Bracewell b Morrison	64	hit wkt b Bracewell	0
NH Fairbro'	c Morrison b Bracewell	2	not out	33
RC Russell+	b Hadlee	13		
PAJ De Freitas	c Franklin b Morrison	38		
GC Small	b Morrison	3		
EE Hemmings	b Hadlee	0		
DE Malcolm	not out	0		
Extras	(0b, 13lb, 1w, 22nb)	36	(8b, 8lb, 0w, 6nb)	22
	89.4 overs		78 overs	
Total		**334**		**272**

1st innings FoW: 3, 151, 178, 216, 226, 255, 319, 322, 332, 334
2nd innings FoW: 68, 135, 171, 175

Bowler	O	M	R	W	O	M	R	W
RJ Hadlee	29	5	113	3	13	2	32	1
DK Morrison	18.4	4	64	4	16	0	81	0
MC Snedden	21	4	72	1				
JG Bracewell	21	3	72	2	34	13	85	2
AH Jones					12	3	40	1
KR Rutherford					3	0	18	0

NEW ZEALAND 1st innings / 2nd innings

Batsman	1st innings		2nd innings
TJ Franklin	c Russell b Malcolm	101	
JG Wright*	c Stewart b Small	98	
AH Jones	c Stewart b Malcolm	49	
MD Crowe	c Russell b Hemmings	1	
MJ Greatbatch	b Malcolm	47	
KR Rutherford	c Fairbrother b Malcolm	0	
RJ Hadlee	b Hemmings	86	
JG Bracewell	run out	4	
IDS Smith+	c Small b Malcolm	27	
MC Snedden	not out	13	
DK Morrison	not out	2	
Extras	(12b, 15lb, 2w, 5nb)	34	
	157.4 overs		
Total		**462**	

1st innings FoW: 185, 278, 281, 284, 285, 408, 415, 425, 448

Bowler	O	M	R	W
DE Malcolm	43	14	94	5
GC Small	35	4	127	1
PAJ De Freitas	35.4	1	122	0
EE Hemmings	30	13	67	2
GA Gooch	13	7	25	0
MA Atherton	1	1	0	0

No. 664: 3rd Test	No. 665: 1st Test
VENUE: Edgbaston	VENUE: Lord's
DATE: 5th-10th July 1990	DATE: 26th-31st July 1990
TOSS WON BY: New Zealand	TOSS WON BY: India
RESULT: England won by 114 runs	RESULT: England won by 247 runs

ENGLAND — Edgbaston

ENGLAND	1st innings		2nd innings	
GA Gooch*	c Hadlee b Morrison	154	b Snedden	30
MA Atherton	lbw b Snedden	82	c Rutherford b Bracewell	70
AJ Stewart	c Parore b Morrison	9	lbw b Bracewell	15
AJ Lamb	c Parore b Hadlee	2	st Parore b Bracewell	4
RA Smith	c Jones b Bracewell	19	c & b Hadlee	14
NH Fairbro'	lbw b Snedden	2	lbw b Bracewell	3
RC Russell+	b Snedden	43	c (sub) b Hadlee	0
CC Lewis	c Rutherford b Bracewell	32	c Parore b Hadlee	1
GC Small	not out	44	not out	11
EE Hemmings	c Parore b Hadlee	20	b Hadlee	0
DE Malcolm	b Hadlee	0	b Hadlee	0
Extras	(4b, 15lb, 0w, 9nb)	28	(0b, 6lb, 0w, 4nb)	10
Total	141.5 overs	**435**	49 overs	**158**

1st innings FoW: 170, 193, 198, 245, 254, 316, 351, 381, 435, 435
2nd innings FoW: 50, 87, 99, 129, 136, 141, 146, 157, 158, 158

RJ Hadlee	37.5	8	97	3	21	3	53	5
DK Morrison	26	7	81	2	3	1	29	0
MC Snedden	35	9	106	3	9	0	32	1
JG Bracewell	42	12	130	2	16	5	38	4
AH Jones	1	0	2	0				

NEW ZEALAND	1st innings		2nd innings	
TJ Franklin	c Smith b Hemmings	66	lbw b Malcolm	5
JG Wright*	c Russell b Malcolm	24	c Smith b Lewis	46
AH Jones	c Russell b Malcolm	2	c Gooch b Small	40
MD Crowe	lbw b Lewis	11	lbw b Malcolm	25
MJ Greatbatch	b Malcolm	45	c Atherton b Hemmings	22
KR Rutherford	c Stewart b Hemmings	29	c Lamb b Lewis	18
RJ Hadlee	c Atherton b Hemmings	8	b Malcolm	13
JG Bracewell	b Hemmings	25	c Lamb b Lewis	20
AC Parore+	not out	12	c Atherton b Malcolm	0
MC Snedden	lbw b Hemmings	2	not out	21
DK Morrison	b Hemmings	1	b Malcolm	6
Extras	(9b, 11lb, 2w, 2nb)	24	(0b, 9lb, 1w, 4nb)	14
Total	98.3 overs	**249**	91.4 overs	**230**

1st innings FoW: 45, 67, 90, 161, 163, 185, 223, 230, 243, 249
2nd innings FoW: 25, 85, 111, 125, 155, 163, 180, 180, 203, 230

GC Small	18	7	44	0	16	5	56	1
DE Malcolm	25	7	59	3	24.4	8	46	5
CC Lewis	19	5	51	1	22	3	76	3
EE Hemmings	27.3	10	58	6	29	13	43	1
MA Atherton	9	5	17	0				

ENGLAND — Lord's

ENGLAND	1st innings		2nd innings	
GA Gooch*	b Prabhakar	333	c Azharuddin b Sharma	123
MA Atherton	b Kapil Dev	8	c Vengsarkar b Sharma	72
DI Gower	c Manjrekar b Hirwani	40	not out	32
AJ Lamb	c Manjrekar b Sharma	139	c Tendulkar b Hirwani	19
RA Smith	not out	100	b Prabhakar	15
JE Morris	not out	4		
RC Russell+				
CC Lewis				
EE Hemmings				
ARC Fraser				
DE Malcolm				
Extras	(2b, 21lb, 2w, 4nb)	29	(0b, 11lb, 0w, 0nb)	11
Total	162 overs	**653**	54.2 overs	**272**

1st innings FoW: 14, 141, 449, 641
2nd innings FoW: 204, 207, 250, 272

N Kapil Dev	34	5	120	1	10	0	53	0
M Prabhakar	43	6	187	1	11.2	2	45	1
SK Sharma	33	5	122	1	15	0	75	2
RJ Shastri	22	0	99	0	7	0	38	0
ND Hirwani	30	1	102	1	11	0	50	1

INDIA	1st innings		2nd innings	
RJ Shastri	c Gooch b Hemmings	100	c Russell b Malcolm	12
NS Sidhu	c Morris b Fraser	30	c Morris b Fraser	1
SV Manjrekar	c Russell b Gooch	18	c Russell b Malcolm	33
DB Vengsarkar	c Russell b Fraser	52	c Russell b Hemmings	35
M Azhar'din*	b Hemmings	121	c Atherton b Lewis	37
SR Tendulkar	b Lewis	10	c Gooch b Fraser	27
M Prabhakar	c Lewis b Malcolm	25	lbw b Lewis	8
N Kapil Dev	not out	77	c Lewis b Hemmings	7
KS More+	c Morris b Fraser	8	lbw b Fraser	16
SK Sharma	c Russell b Fraser	0	run out	38
ND Hirwani	lbw b Fraser	0	not out	0
Extras	(0b, 1lb, 4w, 8nb)	13	(3b, 1lb, 0w, 6nb)	10
Total	114.1 overs	**454**	62 overs	**224**

1st innings FoW: 63, 102, 191, 241, 288, 348, 393, 430, 430, 454
2nd innings FoW: 9, 23, 63, 114, 127, 140, 158, 181, 206, 224

DE Malcolm	25	1	106	1	10	0	65	2
ARC Fraser	39.1	9	104	5	22	7	39	3
CC Lewis	24	3	108	1	8	1	26	2
GA Gooch	6	3	26	1				
EE Hemmings	20	3	109	2	21	2	79	2
MA Atherton					1	0	11	0

No. 666: 2nd Test
VENUE: Old Trafford
DATE: 9th-14th August 1990
TOSS WON BY: England
RESULT: Match drawn

No. 667: 3rd Test
VENUE: The Oval
DATE: 23rd-28th August 1990
TOSS WON BY: India
RESULT: Match drawn

ENGLAND 1st innings / 2nd innings

Batsman	1st innings		2nd innings	
GA Gooch*	c More b Prabhakar	116	c More b Prabhakar	7
MA Atherton	c More b Hirwani	131	lbw b Kapil Dev	74
DI Gower	c Tendulkar b Kapil Dev	38	b Hirwani	16
AJ Lamb	c Manjrekar b Kumble	38	b Kapil Dev	109
RC Russell+	c More b Hirwani	8	not out	16
RA Smith	not out	121	not out	61
JE Morris	b Kumble	13	retired hurt	15
CC Lewis	b Hirwani	3		
EE Hemmings	lbw b Hirwani	19		
ARC Fraser	c Tendulkar b Kumble	1		
DE Malcolm	b Shastri	13		
Extras	(2b, 9lb, 1w, 6nb)	18	(15b, 0lb, 0w, 7nb)	22
	160.5 overs		81 overs	
Total		**519**		**320**

1st innings FoW: 225, 292, 312, 324, 366, 392, 404, 434, 459, 519
2nd innings FoW: 15, 46, 180, 246

	O	M	R	W		O	M	R	W
N Kapil Dev	13	2	67	1		22	4	69	2
M Prabhakar	25	2	112	1		18	1	80	1
A Kumble	43	7	105	3		17	3	65	0
ND Hirwani	62	10	174	4		15	0	52	1
RJ Shastri	17.5	2	50	1		9	0	39	0

INDIA 1st innings / 2nd innings

Batsman	1st innings		2nd innings	
RJ Shastri	c Gooch b Fraser	25	b Malcolm	12
NS Sidhu	c Gooch b Fraser	13	c (sub) b Fraser	0
SV Manjrekar	c Smith b Hemmings	93	c (sub) b Hemmings	50
DB Vengsarkar	c Russell b Fraser	6	b Lewis	32
M Azhar'din*	c Atherton b Fraser	179	c Lewis b Hemmings	11
SR Tendulkar	c Lewis b Hemmings	68	not out	119
M Prabhakar	c Russell b Malcolm	4	b Hemmings	26
N Kapil Dev	lbw b Lewis	0	not out	67
KS More+	b Fraser	6		
A Kumble	run out	2		
ND Hirwani	not out	15		
Extras	(5b, 4lb, 0w, 12nb)	21	(17b, 3lb, 0w, 6nb)	26
	119.2 overs		90 overs	
Total		**432**		**343**

1st innings FoW: 26, 48, 57, 246, 358, 364, 365, 396, 401, 432
2nd innings FoW: 4, 35, 109, 109, 127, 183

	O	M	R	W		O	M	R	W
DE Malcolm	26	3	96	1		14	5	59	1
ARC Fraser	35	5	124	5		21	3	81	1
EE Hemmings	29.2	8	74	2		31	10	75	3
CC Lewis	13	1	61	1		20	3	86	1
MA Atherton	16	3	68	0		4	0	22	0

INDIA 1st innings / 2nd innings

Batsman	1st innings		2nd innings	
RJ Shastri	c Lamb b Malcolm	187		
NS Sidhu	c Russell b Fraser	12		
SV Manjrekar	c Russell b Malcolm	22		
DB Vengsarkar	c & b Atherton	33		
M Azhar'din*	c Russell b Williams	78		
M Prabhakar	lbw b Fraser	28		
SR Tendulkar	c Lamb b Williams	21		
N Kapil Dev	st Russell b Hemmings	110		
KS More+	not out	61		
AS Wassan	b Hemmings	15		
ND Hirwani	not out	2		
Extras	(7b, 8lb, 6w, 16nb)	37		
	173 overs			
Total		**606**		

1st innings FoW: 16, 61, 150, 289, 335, 368, 478, 552, 576

	O	M	R	W
DE Malcolm	35	7	110	2
ARC Fraser	42	17	112	2
NF Williams	41	5	148	2
GA Gooch	12	1	44	0
EE Hemmings	36	3	117	2
MA Atherton	7	0	60	1

ENGLAND 1st innings / 2nd innings

Batsman	1st innings		2nd innings	
GA Gooch*	c Shastri b Hirwani	85	c Vengsarkar b Hirwani	88
MA Atherton	c More b Prabhakar	7	lbw b Kapil Dev	86
NF Williams	lbw b Prabhakar	38		
DI Gower	lbw b Wassan	8	not out	157
JE Morris	c More b Wassan	7	c More b Wassan	32
AJ Lamb	b Kapil Dev	7	c Shastri b Kapil Dev	52
RA Smith	c Manjrekar b Shastri	57	not out	7
RC Russell+	run out	35		
EE Hemmings	c Vengsarkar b Prabhakar	51		
ARC Fraser	c More b Prabhakar	0		
DE Malcolm	not out	15		
Extras	(8b, 9lb, 4w, 9nb)	30	(16b, 22lb, 6w, 11nb)	55
	123.4 overs		154 overs	
Total		**340**		**477**

1st innings FoW: 18, 92, 111, 120, 139, 231, 233, 295, 299, 340
2nd innings FoW: 176, 251, 334, 463

	O	M	R	W		O	M	R	W
N Kapil Dev	25	7	70	1		24	5	66	2
M Prabhakar	32.4	9	74	4		25	8	56	0
AS Wassan	19	3	79	2		18	2	94	1
ND Hirwani	35	12	71	1		59	18	137	1
RJ Shastri	12	2	29	1		28	2	86	0

No. 668: 1st Test	
VENUE: Brisbane (Gabba)	
DATE: 23rd - 25th November 1990	
TOSS WON BY: Australia	
RESULT: Australia won by 10 wickets	

ENGLAND 1st innings

Batsman	Dismissal	R	Dismissal (2nd)	R
MA Atherton	lbw b Reid	13	b Alderman	15
W Larkins	c Healy b Hughes	12	lbw b Reid	0
DI Gower	c Healy b Reid	61	b Hughes	27
AJ Lamb*	c Hughes b Matthews	32	lbw b Alderman	14
RA Smith	b Reid	7	c Taylor b Alderman	1
AJ Stewart	lbw b Reid	4	c (sub) b Alderman	6
RC Russell+	c & b Alderman	16	lbw b Waugh	15
CC Lewis	c Border b Hughes	20	lbw b Alderman	14
GC Small	not out	12	c Alderman b Hughes	15
ARC Fraser	c Healy b Alderman	1	c (sub) b Alderman	15
DE Malcolm	c Waugh b Hughes	5	not out	0
Extras	(1b, 7lb, 0w, 3nb)	11	(0b, 3lb, 0w, 4nb)	7
	78 overs		53.1 overs	
Total		**194**		**114**

1st innings FoW: 23, 43, 117, 123, 134, 135, 167, 181, 187, 194
2nd innings FoW: 0, 42, 46, 60, 78, 84, 93, 112, 114, 114

Bowler	O	M	R	W	O	M	R	W
TM Alderman	18	5	44	2	22	7	47	6
BA Reid	18	3	53	4	14	3	40	1
MG Hughes	19	5	39	3	12.1	5	17	2
GRJ Matthews	16	8	30	1	1	1	0	0
SR Waugh	7	2	20	0	4	2	7	1

AUSTRALIA 1st innings

Batsman	Dismissal	R	Dismissal (2nd)	R
GR Marsh	lbw b Fraser	9	not out	72
MA Taylor	c Lewis b Fraser	10	not out	67
DC Boon	lbw b Small	18		
AR Border*	c Atherton b Small	9		
DM Jones	c Small b Lewis	17		
SR Waugh	c Smith b Small	1		
GRJ Matthews	c Small b Malcolm	35		
IA Healy+	c Atherton b Lewis	22		
MG Hughes	c Russell b Fraser	9		
BA Reid	b Lewis	0		
TM Alderman	not out	0		
Extras	(1b, 10lb, 0w, 11nb)	22	(3b, 2lb, 3w, 10nb)	18
	63 overs		46 overs	
Total		**152**		**157**

1st innings FoW: 22, 35, 49, 60, 64, 89, 135, 150, 150, 152

Bowler	O	M	R	W	O	M	R	W
DE Malcolm	17	2	45	1	9	5	22	0
ARC Fraser	21	6	33	3	14	2	49	0
GC Small	16	4	34	3	15	2	36	0
CC Lewis	9	0	29	3	6	0	29	0
MA Atherton					2	0	16	0

No. 669: 2nd Test	
VENUE: Melbourne (MCG)	
DATE: 26th-30th December 1990	
TOSS WON BY: England	
RESULT: Australia won by 8 wickets	

ENGLAND 1st innings

Batsman	Dismissal	R	Dismissal (2nd)	R
GA Gooch*	lbw b Alderman	20	c Alderman b Reid	58
MA Atherton	c Boon b Reid	0	c Healy b Reid	4
W Larkins	c Healy b Reid	64	c Healy b Reid	54
RA Smith	c Healy b Hughes	30	c Taylor b Reid	8
DI Gower	c & b Reid	100	c Border b Matthews	8
AJ Stewart	c Healy b Reid	79	c Marsh b Reid	8
RC Russell+	c Healy b Hughes	15	c Jones b Matthews	1
PAJ De Freitas	c Healy b Reid	3	lbw b Reid	0
ARC Fraser	c Jones b Alderman	24	c Taylor b Reid	0
DE Malcolm	c Taylor b Reid	6	lbw b Matthews	1
PCR Tufnell	not out	0	not out	0
Extras	(0b, 2lb, 0w, 9nb)	11	(7b, 3lb, 0w, 6nb)	16
	131.4 overs		73 overs	
Total		**352**		**150**

1st innings FoW: 11, 30, 109, 152, 274, 303, 307, 324, 344, 352
2nd innings FoW: 17, 103, 115, 122, 147, 148, 148, 148, 150, 150

Bowler	O	M	R	W	O	M	R	W
TM Alderman	30.4	7	86	2	10	2	19	0
BA Reid	39	8	97	6	22	12	51	7
MG Hughes	29	7	83	2	9	4	26	0
GRJ Matthews	27	8	65	0	25	9	40	3
SR Waugh	6	2	19	0	7	6	4	0

AUSTRALIA 1st innings

Batsman	Dismissal	R	Dismissal (2nd)	R
GR Marsh	c Russell b De Freitas	36	not out	79
MA Taylor	c Russell b De Freitas	61	c Atherton b Malcolm	5
DC Boon	c Russell b Malcolm	28		
AR Border*	c Russell b Fraser	62		
DM Jones	c Russell b Fraser	44		
SR Waugh	b Fraser	19		
GRJ Matthews	lbw b Fraser	12		
IA Healy+	c Russell b Fraser	5	c Atherton b Fraser	1
MG Hughes	lbw b Malcolm	4	not out	94
TM Alderman	b Fraser	0		
BA Reid	not out	3		
Extras	(4b, 12lb, 0w, 16nb)	32	(4b, 12lb, 0w, 2nb)	18
	112.5 overs		86 overs	
Total		**306**		**197**

1st innings FoW: 63, 133, 149, 224, 264, 281, 289, 298, 302, 306
2nd innings FoW: 9, 10

Bowler	O	M	R	W	O	M	R	W
DE Malcolm	25.5	4	74	2	23	7	52	1
ARC Fraser	39	10	82	6	20	4	33	1
PCR Tufnell	21	5	62	0	24	12	36	0
PAJ De Freitas	25	5	69	2	16	3	46	0
MA Atherton	2	1	3	0	3	0	14	0

No. 670: 3rd Test
VENUE: Sydney (SCG)
DATE: 4th-8th January 1991
TOSS WON BY: Australia
RESULT: Match drawn

No. 671: 4th Test
VENUE: Adelaide
DATE: 25th-29th January 1991
TOSS WON BY: Australia
RESULT: Match drawn

AUSTRALIA 1st innings / 2nd innings (No. 670)

Batsman	1st innings		2nd innings	
GR Marsh	c Larkins b Malcolm	13	c Stewart b Malcolm	4
MA Taylor	c Russell b Malcolm	11	lbw b Hemmings	19
DC Boon	c Atherton b Gooch	97	c Gooch b Tufnell	29
AR Border*	b Hemmings	78	c Gooch b Tufnell	20
DM Jones	st Russell b Small	60	c & b Tufnell	0
SR Waugh	c Stewart b Malcolm	48	c Russell b Hemmings	14
GRJ Matthews	c Hemmings b Tufnell	128	b Hemmings	19
IA Healy+	c Small b Hemmings	35	c Smith b Tufnell	69
CG Rackemann	b Hemmings	1	b Malcolm	9
TM Alderman	not out	26	c Gower b Tufnell	1
BA Reid	c Smith b Malcolm	0	not out	5
Extras	(5b, 8lb, 0w, 8nb)	21	(0b, 16lb, 0w, 0nb)	16
Total	157 overs	518	89 overs	205

1st innings FoW: 21, 38, 185, 226, 292, 347, 442, 457, 512, 518
2nd innings FoW: 21, 29, 81, 129, 129, 166, 166, 189, 192, 205

Bowler	O	M	R	W	O	M	R	W
DE Malcolm	45	12	128	4	6	1	19	2
GC Small	31	5	103	1	2	1	6	0
EE Hemmings	32	7	105	3	41	9	94	3
PCR Tufnell	30	6	95	1	37	18	61	5
GA Gooch	14	3	46	1				
MA Atherton	5	0	28	0	3	1	9	0

ENGLAND 1st innings / 2nd innings (No. 670)

Batsman	1st innings		2nd innings	
GA Gooch*	c Healy b Reid	59	c Border b Matthews	54
MA Atherton	c Boon b Matthews	105	not out	3
W Larkins	run out	11	lbw b Border	0
RA Smith	c Healy b Reid	18	not out	10
DI Gower	c Marsh b Reid	123	c Taylor b Matthews	36
AJ Stewart	lbw b Alderman	91	run out	7
RC Russell+	not out	30		
GC Small	lbw b Alderman	10		
EE Hemmings	b Alderman	0		
PCR Tufnell	not out	5		
DE Malcolm				
Extras	(1b, 8lb, 0w, 8nb)	17	(0b, 1lb, 0w, 2nb)	3
Total	172.1 overs	469	25 overs	113

1st innings FoW: 95, 116, 156, 295, 394, 426, 444, 444
2nd innings FoW: 84, 84, 100, 100

Bowler	O	M	R	W	O	M	R	W
TM Alderman	20.1	4	62	3	4	0	29	0
BA Reid	35.1	9	79	3	3	0	20	0
CG Rackemann	25.5	5	89	0	9	2	26	2
GRJ Matthews	58	16	145	1	9	1	37	1
AR Border	19	5	45	0				
SR Waugh	14	3	40	0				

AUSTRALIA 1st innings / 2nd innings (No. 671)

Batsman	1st innings		2nd innings	
GR Marsh	c Gooch b Small	37	c Gooch b Small	0
MA Taylor	run out	5	run out	4
DC Boon	c Fraser b Malcolm	49	b Tufnell	121
AR Border*	b De Freitas	12	not out	83
DM Jones	lbw b De Freitas	0	lbw b De Freitas	8
ME Waugh	b Malcolm	138	b Malcolm	23
GRJ Matthews	c Stewart b Gooch	65	not out	34
IA Healy+	c Stewart b De Freitas	1		
CJ McDermott	not out	42		
MG Hughes	lbw b Small	1	c Gooch b Fraser	30
BA Reid	c Lamb b De Freitas	5		
Extras	(2b, 23lb, 2w, 4nb)	31	(1b, 7lb, 1w, 2nb)	11
Total	135.2 overs	386	104 overs	314

1st innings FoW: 11, 62, 104, 104, 124, 295, 298, 358, 373, 386
2nd innings FoW: 1, 8, 25, 64, 130, 240

Bowler	O	M	R	W	O	M	R	W
DE Malcolm	38	7	104	2	21	0	87	1
ARC Fraser	23	6	48	0	26	3	66	1
GC Small	34	10	92	2	18	3	64	1
PAJ De Freitas	26.2	6	56	4	23	6	61	1
PCR Tufnell	5	0	38	0	16	3	28	1
GA Gooch	9	2	23	1				

ENGLAND 1st innings / 2nd innings (No. 671)

Batsman	1st innings		2nd innings	
GA Gooch*	c Healy b Reid	87	c Marsh b Reid	117
MA Atherton	lbw b McDermott	0	c Waugh b Reid	87
AJ Lamb	c Healy b McDermott	0	b McDermott	53
RA Smith	c & b Hughes	53	not out	10
DI Gower	c Hughes b McDermott	11	c Jones b McDermott	9
AJ Stewart+	c Healy b Reid	11	not out	19
PAJ De Freitas	c Matthews b McDermott	45		
GC Small	b McDermott	1		
ARC Fraser	c Healy b Reid	2		
DE Malcolm	c Healy b Reid	2		
PCR Tufnell	not out	0		
Extras	(1b, 3lb, 0w, 13nb)	17	(5b, 9lb, 1w, 9nb)	24
Total	81.3 overs	229	96 overs	335

1st innings FoW: 10, 11, 137, 160, 176, 179, 198, 215, 219, 229
2nd innings FoW: 203, 246, 287, 287, 297

Bowler	O	M	R	W	O	M	R	W
BA Reid	29	9	53	4	23	5	59	2
CJ McDermott	26.3	3	97	5	27	5	106	2
MG Hughes	22	4	62	1	14	3	52	1
ME Waugh	4	1	13	0	1	0	4	0
GRJ Matthews					31	7	100	0

Australia

No. 672: 5th Test	
VENUE: Perth (WACA)	
DATE: 1st-5th February 1991	
TOSS WON BY: England	
RESULT: Australia won by 9 wickets	

ENGLAND	1st innings			2nd innings	
GA Gooch*	c Healy b McDermott		13	c Alderman b Hughes	18
MA Atherton	c Healy b McDermott		27	c Boon b Hughes	25
AJ Lamb	c Border b McDermott		91	lbw b McDermott	5
RA Smith	c Taylor b McDermott		58	lbw b Alderman	43
DI Gower	not out		28	c Taylor b Alderman	5
AJ Stewart+	lbw b McDermott		2	c Healy b McDermott	7
PAJ De Freitas	c Marsh b McDermott		5	c Healy b Alderman	5
PJ Newport	c Healy b McDermott		0	not out	40
GC Small	c Boon b Hughes		0	c Taylor b Hughes	4
PCR Tufnell	c Healy b Hughes		0	c Healy b Hughes	8
DE Malcolm	c Marsh b McDermott		7	c Jones b McDermott	6
Extras	(1b, 6lb, 1w, 5nb)		13	(5b, 5lb, 0w, 6nb)	16
Total	66.4 overs		**244**	61.3 overs	**182**

1st innings FoW: 27, 50, 191, 212, 220, 226, 226, 227, 227, 244
2nd innings FoW: 41, 49, 75, 80, 114, 118, 125, 134, 144, 182

TM Alderman	22	5	66	0	22	3	75	3
CJ McDermott	24.4	2	97	8	19.3	2	60	3
MG Hughes	17	3	49	2	20	7	37	4
ME Waugh	1	0	9	0				
GRJ Matthews	2	0	16	0				

AUSTRALIA	1st innings			2nd innings	
GR Marsh	c Stewart b Small		1	not out	63
MA Taylor	c Stewart b Malcolm		12	c Stewart b De Freitas	19
DC Boon	c Stewart b Small		64	not out	30
AR Border*	lbw b De Freitas		17		
DM Jones	b Newport		34		
ME Waugh	c Small b Malcolm		26		
GRJ Matthews	not out		60		
IA Healy+	c Lamb b Small		42		
CJ McDermott	b Tufnell		25		
MG Hughes	c Gooch b Tufnell		0		
TM Alderman	lbw b De Freitas		7		
Extras	(2b, 8lb, 1w, 8nb)		19	(0b, 5lb, 2w, 1nb)	8
Total	90.5 overs		**307**	31.2 overs	**120**

1st innings FoW: 1, 44, 90, 113, 161, 168, 230, 281, 283, 307
2nd innings FoW: 39

DE Malcolm	30	4	94	3	9	0	40	0
GC Small	23	3	65	2	10	5	24	0
PAJ De Freitas	16.5	2	57	2	6.2	0	29	1
PJ Newport	14	0	56	1	6	0	22	0
PCR Tufnell	7	1	25	2				

West Indies '91

No. 673: 1st Test	
VENUE: Headingley	
DATE: 6th-10th June 1991	
TOSS WON BY: West Indies	
RESULT: England won by 115 runs	

ENGLAND	1st innings			2nd innings	
GA Gooch*	c Dujon b Marshall		34	not out	154
MA Atherton	b Patterson		2	c Dujon b Ambrose	6
GA Hick	c Dujon b Walsh		6	b Ambrose	6
AJ Lamb	c Hooper b Marshall		11	c Hooper b Ambrose	0
MR Rampr'sh	c Hooper b Marshall		27	c Dujon b Ambrose	27
RA Smith	run out		54	lbw b Ambrose	0
RC Russell+	lbw b Patterson		5	c Dujon b Ambrose	4
DR Pringle	c Logie b Patterson		16	c Dujon b Marshall	27
PAJ De Freitas	c Simmons b Ambrose		15	lbw b Walsh	3
SL Watkin	b Ambrose		0	c Hooper b Marshall	0
DE Malcolm	not out		5	b Marshall	4
Extras	(0b, 5lb, 2w, 14nb)		21	(4b, 9lb, 1w, 7nb)	21
Total	79.2 overs		**198**	106 overs	**252**

1st innings FoW: 13, 45, 45, 64, 129, 149, 154, 177, 181, 198
2nd innings FoW: 22, 38, 38, 116, 116, 124, 222, 236, 238, 252

CEL Ambrose	26	8	49	2	28	6	52	6
BP Patterson	26.2	8	67	3	15	1	52	0
CA Walsh	14	7	31	1	30	5	61	1
MD Marshall	13	4	46	3	25	4	58	3
CL Hooper					4	1	11	0
IVA Richards					4	1	5	0

WEST INDIES	1st innings			2nd innings	
PV Simmons	c Rampr'sh b De Freitas		38	b De Freitas	0
DL Haynes	c Russell b Watkin		7	c Smith b Pringle	19
RB Richardson	run out		29	c Lamb b De Freitas	68
CL Hooper	run out		0	c Lamb b Watkin	5
IVA Richards*	c Lamb b Pringle		73	c Gooch b Watkin	3
AL Logie	c Lamb b De Freitas		6	c Gooch b Watkin	3
PJL Dujon+	c Ramprakash b Watkin		6	lbw b De Freitas	33
MD Marshall	c Hick b Pringle		0	lbw b Pringle	0
CEL Ambrose	c Hick b De Freitas		0	c Pringle b De Freitas	14
CA Walsh	c Gooch b De Freitas		3	c Atherton b Malcolm	9
BP Patterson	not out		5	not out	0
Extras	(0b, 1lb, 0w, 5nb)		6	(0b, 1lb, 0w, 6nb)	7
Total	54.1 overs		**173**	56.4 overs	**162**

1st innings FoW: 36, 54, 58, 102, 139, 156, 160, 165, 167, 173
2nd innings FoW: 0, 61, 77, 85, 88 , 136, 137, 139, 162, 162

DE Malcolm	14	0	69	0	6.4	0	26	1
PAJ De Freitas	17.1	5	34	4	21	4	59	4
SL Watkin	14	2	55	2	7	0	38	3
DR Pringle	9	3	14	2	22	6	38	2

West Indies

West Indies

No. 674: 2nd Test
VENUE: Lord's
DATE: 20th-24th June 1991
TOSS WON BY: West Indies
RESULT: Match drawn

No. 675: 3rd Test
VENUE: Trent Bridge
DATE: 4th-9th July 1991
TOSS WON BY: England
RESULT: West Indies won by 9 wickets

WEST INDIES 1st innings / 2nd innings

Batsman	1st innings		2nd innings	
PV Simmons	c Lamb b Hick	33	lbw b De Freitas	2
DL Haynes	c Russell b Pringle	60	not out	4
RB Richardson	c De Freitas b Hick	57	c Hick b Malcolm	1
CL Hooper	c Lamb b Pringle	111	not out	1
IVA Richards*	lbw b De Freitas	63		
AL Logie	b De Freitas	5		
PJL Dujon+	c Lamb b Pringle	20		
MD Marshall	lbw b Pringle	25		
CEL Ambrose	c & b Malcolm	5		
CA Walsh	c Atherton b Pringle	10		
IBA Allen	not out	1		
Extras	(3b, 7lb, 0w, 19nb)	29	(0b, 2lb, 0w, 2nb)	4
	120.1 overs		5.5 overs	
Total		**419**		**12**

1st innings FoW: 90, 102 , 198, 322, 332, 366, 382, 402, 410, 419
2nd innings FoW: 9, 10

Bowler	O	M	R	W		O	M	R	W
PAJ De Freitas	31	6	93	2		3	2	1	1
DE Malcolm	19	3	76	1		2.5	0	9	1
SL Watkin	15	2	60	0					
DR Pringle	35.1	6	100	5					
GA Hick	18	4	77	2					
GA Gooch	2	0	3	0					

ENGLAND 1st innings / 2nd innings

Batsman	1st innings		2nd innings
GA Gooch*	b Walsh	37	
MA Atherton	b Ambrose	5	
GA Hick	c Richardson b Ambrose	0	
AJ Lamb	c Haynes b Marshall	1	
MR Ramprakash	c Richards b Allen	24	
RA Smith	not out	148	
RC Russell+	c Dujon b Hooper	46	
DR Pringle	c Simmons b Allen	35	
PAJ De Freitas	c Dujon b Marshall	29	
SL Watkin	b Ambrose	6	
DE Malcolm	b Ambrose	0	
Extras	(0b, 1lb, 0w, 22nb)	23	
	118 overs		
Total		**354**	

1st innings FoW: 5, 6, 16, 60, 84, 180, 269, 316, 353, 354

Bowler	O	M	R	W
CEL Ambrose	34	10	87	4
MD Marshall	30	4	78	2
CA Walsh	26	4	90	1
IBA Allen	23	2	88	2
CL Hooper	5	2	10	1

ENGLAND 1st innings / 2nd innings

Batsman	1st innings		2nd innings	
GA Gooch*	lbw b Marshall	68	b Ambrose	13
MA Atherton	lbw b Ambrose	32	b Marshall	4
GA Hick	c Dujon b Ambrose	43	c Dujon b Ambrose	0
AJ Lamb	lbw b Ambrose	13	lbw b Marshall	29
MR Ramprakash	b Ambrose	13	c Dujon b Ambrose	21
RA Smith	not out	64	c Richards b Walsh	15
RC Russell+	c Logie b Allen	3	b Walsh	3
DR Pringle	c (sub) b Allen	0	c Simmons b Walsh	3
PAJ De Freitas	b Walsh	8	not out	55
RK Illingworth	c Hooper b Ambrose	13	c Simmons b Walsh	13
DV Lawrence	c Allen b Marshall	4	c Hooper b Allen	34
Extras	(0b, 17lb, 1w, 21nb)	39	(0b, 14lb, 3w, 4nb)	21
	103.5 overs		79 overs	
Total		**300**		**211**

1st innings FoW: 108, 113, 138, 186, 192, 212, 217, 228, 270, 300
2nd innings FoW: 4, 8, 25, 67, 100, 106, 106, 115, 153, 211

Bowler	O	M	R	W		O	M	R	W
CEL Ambrose	34	7	74	5		27	7	61	3
MD Marshall	21.5	6	54	2		21	6	49	2
CA Walsh	24	4	75	1		24	7	64	4
IBA Allen	17	0	69	2		7	2	23	1
CL Hooper	6	4	10	0					
IVA Richards	1	0	1	0					

WEST INDIES 1st innings / 2nd innings

Batsman	1st innings		2nd innings	
PV Simmons	b Illingworth	12	c Russell b Lawrence	1
DL Haynes	c Smith b Lawrence	18	not out	57
RB Richardson	b Lawrence	43	not out	52
CL Hooper	c Russell b De Freitas	11		
IVA Richards*	b Illingworth	80		
AL Logie	c Rampr'sh b De Freitas	78		
PJL Dujon+	c Hick b Pringle	19		
MD Marshall	c Illing'rth b De Freitas	67		
CEL Ambrose	b Illingworth	17		
CA Walsh	lbw b Pringle	12		
IBA Allen	not out	4		
Extras	(2b, 13lb, 1w, 20nb)	36	(0b, 0lb, 0w, 5nb)	5
	118.1 overs		32.2 overs	
Total		**397**		**115**

1st innings FoW: 32, 32, 45, 118, 239, 272, 324, 358, 392, 397
2nd innings FoW: 1

Bowler	O	M	R	W		O	M	R	W
PAJ De Freitas	31.1	9	67	3		11	3	29	0
DV Lawrence	24	2	116	2		12.2	0	61	1
RK Illingworth	33	8	110	3		2	0	5	0
DR Pringle	25	6	71	2		7	2	20	0
GA Hick	5	0	18	0					

No. 676: 4th Test
VENUE: Edgbaston
DATE: 25th-28th July 1991
TOSS WON BY: West Indies
RESULT: West Indies won by 7 wickets

ENGLAND	1st innings		2nd innings	
GA Gooch*	b Marshall	45	b Patterson	40
H Morris	c Dujon b Patterson	3	lbw b Patterson	1
MA Atherton	lbw b Walsh	16	c Hooper b Patterson	1
GA Hick	c Richards b Ambrose	19	b Ambrose	1
AJ Lamb	lbw b Marshall	9	c Dujon b Walsh	25
MR Rampr'sh	c Logie b Walsh	29	c Dujon b Marshall	25
RC Russell+	c Richardson b Ambrose	12	c Dujon b Patterson	0
DR Pringle	b Ambrose	2	c Logie b Marshall	45
PAJ De Freitas	c Richardson b Marshall	10	b Patterson	7
CC Lewis	lbw b Marshall	13	c (sub) b Ambrose	65
RK Illingworth	not out	0	not out	5
Extras	(4b, 3lb, 0w, 23nb)	30	(5b, 21lb, 0w, 14nb)	40
Total	70.4 overs	188	105.4 overs	255

1st innings FoW: 6 , 53, 88, 108, 129, 159, 163, 163, 184, 188
2nd innings FoW: 2, 4, 5, 71, 94, 96, 127, 144, 236, 255

CEL Ambrose	23	6	64	3		33	16	42	2
CL Hooper	3	2	2	0		12	3	26	0
BP Patterson	11	2	39	1		31	6	81	5
CA Walsh	21	6	43	2		7	1	20	1
MD Marshall	12.4	1	33	4		19.4	3	53	2
PV Simmons						3	0	7	0

WEST INDIES 1st innings			2nd innings	
PV Simmons	c Hick b Lewis	28	lbw b De Freitas	16
DL Haynes	c Russell b De Freitas	32	c Hick b De Freitas	8
RB Richardson	lbw b Lewis	104	c Hick b De Freitas	0
CL Hooper	b Illingworth	31	not out	55
IVA Richards*	c Lewis b Pringle	22	not out	73
AL Logie	c Atherton b Lewis	28		
PJL Dujon+	lbw b De Freitas	6		
MD Marshall	not out	6		
CEL Ambrose	c Hick b Lewis	1		
CA Walsh	c & b Lewis	18		
BP Patterson	b Lewis	3		
Extras	(0b, 7lb, 0w, 6nb)	13	(0b, 4lb, 0w, 1nb)	5
Total	107.3 overs	292	40.4 overs	157

1st innings FoW: 52, 93, 148, 194, 257, 258, 266, 267, 285, 292
2nd innings FoW: 23, 23, 24

PAJ De Freitas	25.3	9	40	2		13	2	54	3
CC Lewis	35	10	111	6		16	7	45	0
DR Pringle	23	9	48	1		7	1	31	0
RK Illingworth	17	2	75	1		4.4	0	23	0
GA Gooch	6	1	11	0					
GA Hick	1	1	0	0					

No. 677: 5th Test
VENUE: The Oval
DATE: 8th-12th August 1991
TOSS WON BY: England
RESULT: England won by 5 wickets

ENGLAND	1st innings		2nd innings	
GA Gooch*	lbw b Ambrose	60	lbw b Marshall	29
H Morris	c Lambert b Ambrose	44	c Dujon b Patterson	2
MA Atherton	c Hooper b Walsh	0	c Hooper b Patterson	13
RA Smith	lbw b Marshall	109	c Patterson b Walsh	26
MR Rampr'sh	c Lambert b Hooper	25	lbw b Lambert	19
AJ Stewart+	c Richardson b Patterson	31	not out	38
IT Botham	hit wkt b Ambrose	31	not out	4
CC Lewis	not out	47		
PAJ De Freitas	c Dujon b Walsh	7		
DV Lawrence	c Richards b Walsh	9		
PCR Tufnell	c Haynes b Patterson	2		
Extras	(8b, 10lb, 1w, 35nb)	54	(4b, 0lb, 1w, 10nb)	15
Total	151.1 overs	419	31.4 overs	146

1st innings FoW: 112, 114, 120, 188, 263, 336, 351, 386, 411, 419
2nd innings FoW: 3, 40, 80, 80, 142

CEL Ambrose	36	8	83	3		8	0	48	0
BP Patterson	25.1	3	87	2		9	0	63	2
CA Walsh	32	5	91	3		9	3	18	1
MD Marshall	24	5	62	1		5	3	9	1
CL Hooper	34	1	78	1					
CB Lambert						0.4	0	4	1

WEST INDIES 1st innings			2nd innings	
PV Simmons	lbw b Lawrence	15	c Lewis b Botham	36
DL Haynes	not out	75	lbw b Lawrence	43
RB Richardson	c Stewart b Botham	20	c Gooch b Lawrence	121
CL Hooper	c Stewart b De Freitas	3	c Gooch b Tufnell	54
CB Lambert	c Ramprakash b Tufnell	39	lbw b Botham	14
PJL Dujon+	lbw b Lawrence	0	c Stewart b Lawrence	5
MD Marshall	c Botham b Tufnell	0	b De Freitas	17
IVA Richards*	c Stewart b Tufnell	2	c Morris b Lawrence	60
CEL Ambrose	c Botham b Tufnell	0	lbw b De Freitas	0
CA Walsh	c Gooch b Tufnell	0	lbw b Lawrence	14
BP Patterson	c Botham b Tufnell	2	not out	1
Extras	(0b, 9lb, 0w, 11nb)	20	(7b, 5lb, 2w, 6nb)	20
Total	57.3 overs	176	132.5 overs	385

1st innings FoW: 52, 95, 98, 158, 160, 161, 172, 172, 172, 176
2nd innings FoW: 53, 71, 125, 208, 305, 311, 356, 356, 378, 383

PAJ De Freitas	13	6	38	1		20	9	42	2
DV Lawrence	16	1	67	2		25.5	4	106	5
PCR Tufnell	14.3	3	25	6		46	6	150	1
IT Botham	11	4	27	1		16	4	40	2
CC Lewis	3	1	10	0		25	12	35	0

| Sri Lanka | New Zealand |

No. 678: 2nd Test
VENUE: Lord's
DATE: 22nd-27th August 1991
TOSS WON BY: England
RESULT: England won by 137 runs

No. 679: 1st Test
VENUE: Christchurch
DATE: 18th-22nd January 1992
TOSS WON BY: New Zealand
RESULT: Eng won by an innings and 4 runs

ENGLAND — Lord's

ENGLAND	1st innings		2nd innings	
GA Gooch*	c & b Ramanayake	38	b Anurasiri	174
H Morris	lbw b Ratnayake	42	c Mah'ma b Anurasiri	23
AJ Stewart	not out	113	c de Silva b Anurasiri	43
RA Smith	c Tillak'ne b Ratnayake	4	not out	63
MR Rampr'sh	c Mah'ma b Mah'ingha	0	not out	12
IT Botham	c Mah'ma b Raman'ke	22		
CC Lewis	c de Silva b Anurasiri	11		
RC Russell+	b Anurasiri	17		
PAJ De Freitas	b Ratnayake	1		
DV Lawrence	c & b Ratnayake	3		
PCR Tufnell	lbw b Ratnayake	0		
Extras	(9b, 8lb, 0w, 14nb)	31	(15b, 23lb, 1w, 10nb)	49
	95 overs		85.1 overs	
Total		**282**		**364**

1st innings FoW: 70, 114, 119, 120, 160, 183, 246, 258, 276, 282
2nd innings FoW: 78, 217, 322

RJ Ratnayake	27	4	69	5	26	4	91	0	
CPH Ramanayake	24	5	75	2	20	2	86	0	
KIW Wijegunawardene	10	1	36	0	2	0	13	0	
UC Hathurusingha	17	6	40	1					
SD Anurasiri	17	4	45	2	36.1	8	135	3	
ST Jayasuriya					1	0	1	0	

SRI LANKA	1st innings		2nd innings	
DS Kuruppu	b De Freitas	5	lbw b Lewis	21
UC Hath'gha	c Tufnell b De Freitas	66	c Morris b Tufnell	25
AP Gurusinha	lbw b De Freitas	4	b Tufnell	34
PA de Silva*	c Lewis b De Freitas	42	c Russell b Lawrence	18
RS Mahanama	c Russell b Botham	2	c Botham b Tufnell	15
ST Jayasuriya	c Smith b De Freitas	11	c Russell b Lewis	66
HP Tillak'ne+	c Morris b Lawrence	20	b Tufnell	16
RJ Ratnayake	c Smith b De Freitas	52	c (sub) b Lawrence	17
C Raman'ke	lbw b De Freitas	0	not out	34
K Wijeg'dene	not out	6	c Botham b De Freitas	4
SD Anurasiri	b Lawrence	1	lbw b Tufnell	16
Extras	(0b, 15lb, 0w, 0nb)	15	(1b, 16lb, 0w, 2nb)	19
	68.1 overs		103.3 overs	
Total		**224**		**285**

1st innings FoW: 12, 22, 75, 86, 105, 139, 213, 213, 220, 224
2nd innings FoW: 50, 50, 111, 119, 159, 212, 212, 241, 253, 285

PAJ De Freitas	26	8	70	7	22	8	45	1	
DV Lawrence	15.1	3	61	2	23	7	83	2	
CC Lewis	10	5	29	0	18	4	31	2	
IT Botham	10	3	26	1	6	2	15	0	
PCR Tufnell	7	2	23	0	34.3	14	94	5	

ENGLAND — Christchurch

ENGLAND	1st innings		2nd innings	
GA Gooch*	c Smith b Morrison	2		
AJ Stewart	c Crowe b Morrison	148		
GA Hick	lbw b Cairns	35		
RA Smith	c Greatbatch b Pringle	96		
AJ Lamb	b Patel	93		
RC Russell+	run out	36		
DA Reeve	c Jones b Pringle	59		
CC Lewis	b Pringle	70		
DR Pringle	c Greatbatch b Patel	10		
PAJ De Freitas	not out	7		
PCR Tufnell				
Extras	(5b, 10lb, 1w, 8nb)	24		
	163 overs			
Total		**580**		

1st innings FoW: 6, 95, 274, 310, 390, 466, 544, 571, 580

DK Morrison	33	5	133	2	
CL Cairns	30	3	118	1	
C Pringle	36	4	127	3	
SA Thomson	15	3	47	0	
DN Patel	46	5	132	2	
AH Jones	3	0	8	0	

NEW ZEALAND	1st innings		2nd innings	
BR Hartland	c Smith b Tufnell	22	c Smith b Tufnell	45
JG Wright	c Lamb b Tufnell	28	st Russell b Tufnell	99
AH Jones	lbw b Lewis	16	c Russell b Pringle	39
MJ Greatbatch	c Stewart b Tufnell	11	c Smith b Tufnell	0
SA Thomson	b Tufnell	5	lbw b Tufnell	0
DN Patel	run out	99	c Pringle b Tufnell	6
MD Crowe*	c Stewart b Pringle	20	c Pringle b Tufnell	48
CL Cairns	c Hick b Reeve	61	c Smith b Tufnell	0
IDS Smith+	lbw b De Freitas	20	c Russell b Lewis	1
DK Morrison	not out	8	c Russell b Lewis	0
C Pringle	c Hick b De Freitas	6	not out	5
Extras	(1b, 7lb, 0w, 8nb)	16	(1b, 7lb, 0w, 13nb)	21
	127.4 overs		132.1 overs	
Total		**312**		**264**

1st innings FoW: 51, 52, 73, 87, 91, 139, 256, 279, 306, 312
2nd innings FoW: 81, 81, 182, 211, 222, 222, 236, 241, 250, 264

PAJ De Freitas	32.4	16	54	2	23	6	54	0	
CC Lewis	30	9	69	1	22	3	66	2	
DR Pringle	15	2	54	1	21	5	64	1	
PCR Tufnell	39	10	100	4	46.1	25	47	7	
GA Hick	3	0	11	0	14	8	11	0	
DA Reeve	8	4	16	1	2	0	8	0	
RA Smith					4	2	6	0	

No. 676: 4th Test
VENUE: Edgbaston
DATE: 25th-28th July 1991
TOSS WON BY: West Indies
RESULT: West Indies won by 7 wickets

No. 677: 5th Test
VENUE: The Oval
DATE: 8th-12th August 1991
TOSS WON BY: England
RESULT: England won by 5 wickets

ENGLAND 4th Test

ENGLAND	1st innings		2nd innings	
GA Gooch*	b Marshall	45	b Patterson	40
H Morris	c Dujon b Patterson	3	lbw b Patterson	1
MA Atherton	lbw b Walsh	16	c Hooper b Patterson	1
GA Hick	c Richards b Ambrose	19	b Ambrose	1
AJ Lamb	lbw b Marshall	9	c Dujon b Walsh	25
MR Rampr'sh	c Logie b Walsh	29	c Dujon b Marshall	25
RC Russell+	c Richardson b Ambrose	12	c Dujon b Patterson	0
DR Pringle	b Ambrose	2	c Logie b Marshall	45
PAJ De Freitas	c Richardson b Marshall	10	b Patterson	7
CC Lewis	lbw b Marshall	13	c (sub) b Ambrose	65
RK Illingworth	not out	0	not out	5
Extras	(4b, 3lb, 0w, 23nb)	30	(5b, 21lb, 0w, 14nb)	40
	70.4 overs		105.4 overs	
Total		**188**		**255**

1st innings FoW: 6 , 53, 88, 108, 129, 159, 163, 163, 184, 188
2nd innings FoW: 2, 4, 5, 71, 94, 96, 127, 144, 236, 255

CEL Ambrose	23	6	64	3		33	16	42	2
BP Patterson	11	2	39	1		31	6	81	5
CA Walsh	21	6	43	2		7	1	20	1
MD Marshall	12.4	1	33	4		19.4	3	53	2
CL Hooper	3	2	2	0		12	3	26	0
PV Simmons						3	0	7	0

WEST INDIES 4th Test

WEST INDIES 1st innings			2nd innings	
PV Simmons	c Hick b Lewis	28	lbw b De Freitas	16
DL Haynes	c Russell b De Freitas	32	c Hick b De Freitas	8
RB Richardson	lbw b Lewis	104	c Hick b De Freitas	0
CL Hooper	b Illingworth	31	not out	55
IVA Richards*	c Lewis b Pringle	22	not out	73
AL Logie	c Atherton b Lewis	28		
PJL Dujon+	lbw b De Freitas	6		
MD Marshall	not out	6		
CEL Ambrose	c Hick b Lewis	1		
CA Walsh	c & b Lewis	18		
BP Patterson	b Lewis	3		
Extras	(0b, 7lb, 0w, 6nb)	13	(0b, 4lb, 0w, 1nb)	5
	107.3 overs		40.4 overs	
Total		**292**		**157**

1st innings FoW: 52, 93, 148, 194, 257, 258, 266, 267, 285, 292
2nd innings FoW: 23, 23, 24

PAJ De Freitas	25.3	9	40	2		13	2	54	3
CC Lewis	35	10	111	6		16	7	45	0
DR Pringle	23	9	48	1		7	1	31	0
RK Illingworth	17	2	75	1		4.4	0	23	0
GA Gooch	6	1	11	0					
GA Hick	1	1	0	0					

ENGLAND 5th Test

ENGLAND	1st innings		2nd innings	
GA Gooch*	lbw b Ambrose	60	lbw b Marshall	29
H Morris	c Lambert b Ambrose	44	c Dujon b Patterson	2
MA Atherton	c Hooper b Walsh	0	c Hooper b Patterson	13
RA Smith	lbw b Marshall	109	c Patterson b Walsh	26
MR Rampr'sh	c Lambert b Hooper	25	lbw b Lambert	19
AJ Stewart+	c Richardson b Patterson	31	not out	38
IT Botham	hit wkt b Ambrose	31	not out	4
CC Lewis	not out	47		
PAJ De Freitas	c Dujon b Walsh	7		
DV Lawrence	c Richards b Walsh	9		
PCR Tufnell	c Haynes b Patterson	2		
Extras	(8b, 10lb, 1w, 35nb)	54	(4b, 0lb, 1w, 10nb)	15
	151.1 overs		31.4 overs	
Total		**419**		**146**

1st innings FoW: 112, 114, 120, 188, 263, 336, 351, 386, 411, 419
2nd innings FoW: 3, 40, 80, 80, 142

CEL Ambrose	36	8	83	3		8	0	48	0
BP Patterson	25.1	3	87	2		9	0	63	2
CA Walsh	32	5	91	3		9	3	18	1
MD Marshall	24	5	62	1		5	3	9	1
CL Hooper	34	1	78	1					
CB Lambert						0.4	0	4	1

WEST INDIES 5th Test

WEST INDIES 1st innings			2nd innings	
PV Simmons	lbw b Lawrence	15	c Lewis b Botham	36
DL Haynes	not out	75	lbw b Lawrence	43
RB Richardson	c Stewart b Botham	20	c Gooch b Lawrence	121
CL Hooper	c Stewart b De Freitas	3	c Gooch b Tufnell	54
CB Lambert	c Ramprakash b Tufnell	39	lbw b Botham	14
PJL Dujon+	lbw b Lawrence	0	c Stewart b Lawrence	5
MD Marshall	c Botham b Tufnell	0	b De Freitas	17
IVA Richards*	c Stewart b Tufnell	2	c Morris b Lawrence	60
CEL Ambrose	c Botham b Tufnell	0	lbw b De Freitas	0
CA Walsh	c Gooch b Tufnell	0	lbw b Lawrence	14
BP Patterson	c Botham b Tufnell	2	not out	1
Extras	(0b, 9lb, 0w, 11nb)	20	(7b, 5lb, 2w, 6nb)	20
	57.3 overs		132.5 overs	
Total		**176**		**385**

1st innings FoW: 52, 95, 98, 158, 160, 161, 172, 172, 172, 176
2nd innings FoW: 53, 71, 125, 208, 305, 311, 356, 356, 378, 383

PAJ De Freitas	13	6	38	1		20	9	42	2
DV Lawrence	16	1	67	2		25.5	4	106	5
PCR Tufnell	14.3	3	25	6		46	6	150	1
IT Botham	11	4	27	1		16	4	40	2
CC Lewis	3	1	10	0		25	12	35	0

Sri Lanka

No. 678: 2nd Test
VENUE: Lord's
DATE: 22nd-27th August 1991
TOSS WON BY: England
RESULT: England won by 137 runs

ENGLAND	1st innings		2nd innings	
GA Gooch*	c & b Ramanayake	38	b Anurasiri	174
H Morris	lbw b Ratnayake	42	c Mahanama b Anurasiri	23
AJ Stewart	not out	113	c de Silva b Anurasiri	43
RA Smith	c Til'ratne b Ratnayake	4	not out	63
MR Rampr'sh	c Mahanama b Hathur'ha	0	not out	12
IT Botham	c Mahanama b Raman'ke	22		
CC Lewis	c de Silva b Anurasiri	11		
RC Russell+	b Anurasiri	17		
PAJ De Freitas	b Ratnayake	1		
DV Lawrence	c & b Ratnayake	3		
PCR Tufnell	lbw b Ratnayake	0		
Extras	(9b, 8lb, 0w, 14nb)	31	(15b, 23lb, 1w, 10nb)	49
	95 overs		85.1 overs	
Total		**282**		**364**

1st innings FoW: 70, 114, 119, 120, 160, 183, 246, 258, 276, 282
2nd innings FoW: 78, 217, 322

RJ Ratnayake	27	4	69	5	26	4	91	0
CPH Ramanayake	24	5	75	2	20	2	86	0
KIW Wijegunawardene	10	1	36	0	2	0	13	0
UC Hathurusingha	17	6	40	1				
SD Anurasiri	17	4	45	2	36.1	8	135	3
ST Jayasuriya					1	0	1	0

SRI LANKA 1st innings			2nd innings	
DSBP Kuruppu	b De Freitas	5	lbw b Lewis	21
UC Hathu'gha	c Tufnell b De Freitas	66	c Morris b Tufnell	25
AP Gurusinha	lbw b De Freitas	4	b Tufnell	34
PA de Silva*	c Lewis b De Freitas	42	c Russell b Lawrence	18
RS Mahanama	c Russell b Botham	2	c Botham b Tufnell	15
ST Jayasuriya	c Smith b De Freitas	11	c Russell b Lewis	66
HP Til'ratne +	c Morris b Lawrence	20	b Tufnell	16
RJ Ratnayake	b De Freitas	52	c (sub) b Lawrence	17
CPH Ramanayake	lbw b De Freitas	0	not out	34
KIW Wijegunawardene	not out	6	c Botham b De Freitas	4
SD Anurasiri	b Lawrence	1	lbw b Tufnell	16
Extras	(0b, 15lb, 0w, 0nb)	15	(1b, 16lb, 0w, 2nb)	19
	68.1 overs		103.3 overs	
Total		**224**		**285**

1st innings FoW: 12, 22, 75, 86, 105, 139, 213, 213, 220, 224
2nd innings FoW: 50, 50, 111, 119, 159, 212, 212, 241, 253, 285

PAJ De Freitas	26	8	70	7	22	8	45	1
DV Lawrence	15.1	3	61	2	23	7	83	2
CC Lewis	10	5	29	0	18	4	31	2
IT Botham	10	3	26	1	6	2	15	0
PCR Tufnell	7	2	23	0	34.3	14	94	5

New Zealand

No. 679: 1st Test
VENUE: Christchurch
DATE: 18th-22nd January 1992
TOSS WON BY: New Zealand
RESULT: Eng won by an innings and 4 runs

ENGLAND	1st innings		2nd innings	
GA Gooch*	c Smith b Morrison	2		
AJ Stewart	c Crowe b Morrison	148		
GA Hick	lbw b Cairns	35		
RA Smith	c Greatbatch b Pringle	96		
AJ Lamb	b Patel	93		
RC Russell+	run out	36		
DA Reeve	c Jones b Pringle	59		
CC Lewis	b Pringle	70		
DR Pringle	c Greatbatch b Patel	10		
PAJ De Freitas	not out	7		
PCR Tufnell				
Extras	(5b, 10lb, 1w, 8nb)	24		
	163 overs			
Total		**580**		

1st innings FoW: 6, 95, 274, 310, 390, 466, 544, 571, 580

DK Morrison	33	5	133	2
CL Cairns	30	3	118	1
C Pringle	36	4	127	3
SA Thomson	15	3	47	0
DN Patel	46	5	132	2
AH Jones	3	0	8	0

NEW ZEALAND 1st innings			2nd innings	
BR Hartland	c Smith b Tufnell	22	c Smith b Tufnell	45
JG Wright	c Lamb b Tufnell	28	st Russell b Tufnell	99
AH Jones	lbw b Lewis	16	c Russell b Pringle	39
MJ Greatbatch	c Stewart b Tufnell	11	c Smith b Tufnell	0
SA Thomson	b Tufnell	5	lbw b Tufnell	0
DN Patel	run out	99	c Pringle b Tufnell	6
MD Crowe*	c Stewart b Pringle	20	c Pringle b Tufnell	48
CL Cairns	c Hick b Reeve	61	c Smith b Tufnell	0
IDS Smith+	lbw b De Freitas	20	c Russell b Lewis	1
DK Morrison	not out	8	c Russell b Lewis	0
C Pringle	c Hick b De Freitas	6	not out	5
Extras	(1b, 7lb, 0w, 8nb)	16	(1b, 7lb, 0w, 13nb)	21
	127.4 overs		132.1 overs	
Total		**312**		**264**

1st innings FoW: 51, 52, 73, 87, 91, 139, 256, 279, 306, 312
2nd innings FoW: 81, 81, 182, 211, 222, 222, 236, 241, 250, 264

PAJ De Freitas	32.4	16	54	2	23	6	54	0
CC Lewis	30	9	69	1	22	3	66	2
DR Pringle	15	2	54	1	21	5	64	1
PCR Tufnell	39	10	100	4	46.1	25	47	7
GA Hick	3	0	11	0	14	8	11	0
DA Reeve	8	4	16	1	2	0	8	0
RA Smith					4	2	6	0

No. 680: 2nd Test	
VENUE: Auckland	
DATE: 30th January to 3rd Feb 1992	
TOSS WON BY: New Zealand	
RESULT: England won by 168 runs	

ENGLAND	**1st innings**		**2nd innings**	
GA Gooch*	c Parore b Morrison	4	run out	114
AJ Stewart	c Parore b Cairns	4	c Parore b Su'a	8
GA Hick	lbw b Cairns	30	lbw b Su'a	4
RA Smith	c Parore b Cairns	0	b Morrison	35
AJ Lamb	b Su'a	13	c Watson b Patel	60
DA Reeve	c Parore b Watson	22	lbw b Watson	25
CC Lewis	c Cairns b Watson	33	run out	23
RC Russell+	c Parore b Cairns	33	c Hartland b Cairns	24
DR Pringle	lbw b Cairns	41	lbw b Cairns	2
PAJ De Freitas	c Crowe b Cairns	1	c Wright b Morrison	0
PCR Tufnell	not out	6	not out	0
Extras	(0b, 11lb, 0w, 5nb)	16	(8b, 16lb, 0w, 2nb)	26
Total	83 overs	**203**	98.4 overs	**321**

1st innings FoW: 9, 9, 9, 31, 72, 91, 128, 165, 171, 203
2nd innings FoW: 29, 33, 93, 182, 263, 269, 319, 321, 321, 321

DK Morrison	17	2	55	1		21.4	6	66	2
CL Cairns	21	4	52	6		19	6	86	2
W Watson	24	13	41	2		26	10	59	1
ML Su'a	21	8	44	1		10	3	43	2
DN Patel						22	7	43	1

NEW ZEALAND	**1st innings**		**2nd innings**	
BR Hartland	lbw b Lewis	0	c Russell b De Freitas	0
JG Wright	b Pringle	15	lbw b Lewis	0
AH Jones	c Smith b De Freitas	14	lbw b De Freitas	5
MD Crowe*	c Hick b Lewis	45	c Lamb b De Freitas	56
KR Rutherford	c Russell b De Freitas	26	c Stewart b Pringle	32
DN Patel	lbw b Lewis	24	c & b Tufnell	17
CL Cairns	c Hick b Tufnell	1	c Russell b Tufnell	24
AC Parore+	lbw b Pringle	0	lbw b Lewis	15
ML Su'a	not out	0	lbw b De Freitas	36
DK Morrison	lbw b Lewis	0	run out	12
W Watson	b Lewis	2	not out	5
Extras	(0b, 0lb, 0w, 15nb)	15	(0b, 1lb, 0w, 11nb)	12
Total	63 overs	**142**	79 overs	**214**

1st innings FoW: 2, 35, 91, 102, 123, 124, 139, 139, 139, 142
2nd innings FoW: 0, 0, 7, 77, 104, 118, 153, 173, 203, 214

PAJ De Freitas	16	2	53	2		27	11	62	4
CC Lewis	21	5	31	5		27	4	83	2
DR Pringle	15	7	21	2		7	2	23	1
DA Reeve	7	1	21	0					
PCR Tufnell	4	2	16	1		17	5	45	2
GA Hick						1	1	0	0

No. 681: 3rd Test	
VENUE: Wellington	
DATE: 6th-10th February 1992	
TOSS WON BY: England	
RESULT: Match drawn	

ENGLAND	**1st innings**		**2nd innings**	
GA Gooch*	b Patel	30	c Rutherford b Cairns	11
AJ Stewart	b Morrison	107	c Smith b Patel	63
GA Hick	b Patel	43	c Smith b Su'a	22
RA Smith	c Rutherford b Patel	6	c & b Su'a	76
AJ Lamb	c Smith b Patel	30	c Latham b Patel	142
DA Reeve	c Latham b Su'a	18	b Su'a	0
DV Lawrence	c Rutherford b Cairns	6		
IT Botham	c Cairns b Su'a	15	lbw b Patel	1
RC Russell+	lbw b Morrison	18	not out	24
PAJ De Freitas	lbw b Morrison	3		
PCR Tufnell	not out	2		
Extras	(4b, 12lb, 0w, 11nb)	27	(0b, 13lb, 0w, 7nb)	20
Total	118.1 overs	**305**	119.3 overs	**359**

1st innings FoW: 83, 159, 169, 215, 235, 248, 277, 286, 298, 305
2nd innings FoW: 17, 52, 127, 249, 249, 254, 359

DK Morrison	22.1	6	44	3		23	5	63	0
CL Cairns	25	3	89	1		22	4	84	1
ML Su'a	36	10	62	2		33	10	87	3
DN Patel	34	10	87	4		41.3	12	112	2
AH Jones	1	0	7	0					

NEW ZEALAND	**1st innings**		**2nd innings**	
BR Hartland	c Botham b Lawrence	2	lbw b Botham	19
JG Wright	c Reeve b Tufnell	116	c Russell b Botham	0
AH Jones	b Hick	143	lbw b Reeve	9
MD Crowe*	b Tufnell	30	not out	13
KR Rutherford	run out	8	not out	2
RT Latham	b Hick	25		
DN Patel	lbw b Hick	9		
CL Cairns	c Russell b Botham	33		
IDS Smith+	b Hick	21		
ML Su'a	not out	20		
DK Morrison	not out	0		
Extras	(1b, 15lb, 1w, 8nb)	25	(0b, 0lb, 0w, 0nb)	0
Total	192 overs	**432**	24 overs	**43**

1st innings FoW: 3, 244, 308, 312, 327, 340, 369, 404, 430
2nd innings FoW: 4, 24, 41

PAJ De Freitas	8	4	12	0					
DV Lawrence	27	7	67	1		2.1	1	4	0
PCR Tufnell	71	22	147	2		9	5	12	0
GA Hick	69	27	126	4					
IT Botham	14	4	53	1		8	1	23	2
DA Reeve	3	1	11	0		4.5	2	4	1

No. 682: 1st Test
VENUE: Edgbaston
DATE: 4th-8th June 1992
TOSS WON BY: England
RESULT: Match drawn

No. 683: 2nd Test
VENUE: Lord's
DATE: 18th-21st June 1992
TOSS WON BY: England
RESULT: Pakistan won by 2 wickets

PAKISTAN 1st innings / 2nd innings

			2nd innings
Aamir Sohail	c Stewart b De Freitas	18	
Rameez Raja	lbw b De Freitas	47	
Asif Mujtaba	c Russell b De Freitas	29	
Javed M'dad*	not out	153	
Salim Malik	lbw b De Freitas	165	
Inzamam	not out	8	
Moin Khan+			
Mushtaq Ahmed			
Waqar Younis			
Aaqib Javed			
Ata-Ur-Rehman			
Extras	(2b, 5lb, 0w, 19nb)	26	
Total	137 overs	**446**	

1st innings FoW: 33, 96, 110, 432

PAJ De Freitas	33	6	121	4
CC Lewis	33	3	116	0
DR Pringle	28	2	92	0
IT Botham	19	6	52	0
GA Hick	13	1	46	0
GA Gooch	10	5	9	0
MR Ramprakash	1	0	3	0

ENGLAND 1st innings / 2nd innings

			2nd innings
GA Gooch*	c Asif b Aaqib Javed	8	
AJ Stewart	c Salim b Ur-Rehman	190	
GA Hick	c Javed M'dad b Waqar	51	
RA Smith	lbw b Mushtaq	127	
MR Rampr'sh	c Moin b Ur-Rehman	0	
AJ Lamb	c M'dad b Ur-Rehman	12	
CC Lewis	b Mushtaq	24	
RC Russell+	not out	29	
DR Pringle	not out	0	
IT Botham			
PAJ De Freitas			
Extras	(5b, 5lb, 1w, 7nb)	18	
Total	119 overs	**459**	

1st innings FoW: 28, 121, 348, 348, 378, 415, 446

Waqar Younis	24	2	96	1
Aaqib Javed	16	3	86	1
Mushtaq Ahmed	50	8	156	2
Ata-Ur-Rehman	18	5	69	3
Asif Mujtaba	8	1	29	0
Aamir Sohail	2	0	8	0
Salim Malik	1	0	5	0

ENGLAND 1st innings / 2nd innings

	1st innings		**2nd innings**	
GA Gooch*	b Wasim	69	lbw b Aaqib Javed	13
AJ Stewart	c Javed Miandad b Asif	74	not out	69
GA Hick	c Javed b Waqar	13	c Moin b Mushtaq	11
RA Smith	c (sub) b Wasim	9	b Mushtaq	8
AJ Lamb	b Waqar	30	lbw b Mushtaq	12
IT Botham	b Waqar	2	lbw b Waqar	6
CC Lewis	lbw b Waqar	2	b Waqar	15
RC Russell+	not out	22	b Wasim	1
PAJ De Freitas	c Inzamam b Waqar	3	c Inzamam b Wasim	0
IDK Salisbury	hit wkt b Mushtaq	4	lbw b Wasim	12
DE Malcolm	lbw b Mushtaq	0	b Wasim	0
Extras	(6b, 12lb, 0w, 9nb)	27	(5b, 8lb, 0w, 15nb)	28
Total	76.1 overs	**255**	52.4 overs	**175**

1st innings FoW: 123, 153, 172, 197, 213, 221, 232, 242, 247, 255
2nd innings FoW: 40, 73, 108, 120, 137, 148, 174, 175, 175, 175

Wasim Akram	19	5	49	2		17.4	2	66	4
Aaqib Javed	14	3	40	0		12	3	23	1
Waqar Younis	21	4	91	5		13	3	40	2
Mushtaq Ahmed	19.1	5	57	2		9	1	32	3
Asif Mujtaba	3	3	0	1		1	0	1	0

PAKISTAN 1st innings / 2nd innings

	1st innings		**2nd innings**	
Aamir Sohail	c Russell b De Freitas	73	b Salisbury	39
Rameez Raja	b Lewis	24	c Hick b Lewis	0
Asif Mujtaba	c Smith b Malcolm	59	c Russell b Lewis	0
Javed M'dad*	c Botham b Salisbury	9	c Russell b Lewis	0
Salim Malik	c Smith b Malcolm	55	c Lewis b Salisbury	12
Inzamam	c & b Malcolm	0	run out	8
Wasim Akram	b Salisbury	24	not out	45
Moin Khan+	c Botham b De Freitas	12	c Smith b Salisbury	3
M Ahmed	c Russell b De Freitas	4	c Hick b Malcolm	5
Waqar Younis	b Malcolm	14	not out	20
Aaqib Javed	not out	5		
Extras	(4b, 3lb, 0w, 7nb)	14	(2b, 5lb, 1w, 1nb)	9
Total	98.5 overs	**293**	45.1 overs	**141**

1st innings FoW: 43, 123, 143, 228, 228, 235, 263, 271, 276, 293
2nd innings FoW: 6, 10, 18, 41, 62, 68, 81, 95

PAJ De Freitas	26	8	58	3		15	2	42	1
DE Malcolm	15.5	1	70	4		16	3	43	3
CC Lewis	29	7	76	1		14.1	0	49	3
IDK Salisbury	23	3	73	2					
IT Botham	5	2	9	0					

No. 684: 3rd Test			No. 685: 4th Test	
VENUE: Old Trafford			VENUE: Headingley	
DATE: 2nd-7th July 1992			DATE: 23rd-26th July 1992	
TOSS WON BY: Pakistan			TOSS WON BY: Pakistan	
RESULT: Match drawn			RESULT: England won by 6 wickets	

Left: 3rd Test — Old Trafford

PAKISTAN 1st innings

			2nd innings	
Aamir Sohail	b Lewis	205	c Smith b Lewis	1
Rameez Raja	c Russell b Malcolm	54	c Hick b Lewis	88
Asif Mujtaba	c Atherton b Lewis	57	c Atherton b Lewis	40
Javed M'dad*	c Hick b Munton	88	not out	45
Moin Khan+	c Gower b Malcolm	15	b Gooch	16
Salim Malik	b Gooch	34	c Atherton b Gooch	13
Inzamam	c Gooch b Malcolm	26	not out	11
Wasim Akram	st Russell b Gooch	0		
Waqar Younis	not out	2		
M Ahmed	c Lewis b Gooch	6		
Aaqib Javed				
Extras	(9b, 4lb, 2w, 3nb)	18	(8b, 5lb, 5w, 7nb)	25
	126 overs		77 overs	
Total		**505**		**239**

1st innings FoW: 115, 241, 378, 428, 432, 492, 497, 497, 505
2nd innings FoW: 1, 143, 148, 195, 217

DE Malcolm					12	2	57	0
CC Lewis	24	5	90	2	17	5	46	3
TA Munton	30	6	112	1	17	6	26	0
IDK Salisbury	20	0	117	0	13	0	67	0
GA Gooch	18	2	39	3	16	5	30	2
GA Hick	3	0	17	0	2	2	0	0

ENGLAND 1st innings

			2nd innings
GA Gooch*	c Moin b Waqar	78	
AJ Stewart	c Inzamam b Wasim	15	
MA Atherton	c Moin b Wasim	0	
RA Smith	lbw b Aaqib Javed	11	
DI Gower	c Moin b Wasim	73	
GA Hick	b Aaqib Javed	22	
CC Lewis	c Moin b Wasim	55	
RC Russell+	c Aamir b Aaqib Javed	4	
IDK Salisbury	c Aamir b Wasim	50	
TA Munton	not out	25	
DE Malcolm	b Aaqib Javed	4	
Extras	(8b, 8lb, 2w, 35nb)	53	
	100.4 overs		
Total		**390**	

1st innings FoW: 41, 42, 93, 186, 200, 252, 256, 315, 379, 390

Wasim Akram	36	4	128	5
Waqar Younis	32	6	96	1
Aaqib Javed	21.4	1	100	4
Asif Mujtaba	1	1	0	0
Mushtaq Ahmed	10	1	50	0

Right: 4th Test — Headingley

PAKISTAN 1st innings

			2nd innings	
Aamir Sohail	c Atherton b Mallender	23	c Stewart b Mallender	1
Rameez Raja	b Pringle	17	c Atherton b Munton	63
Asif Mujtaba	b Mallender	7	c Hick b Mallender	11
Javed M'dad*	c Smith b Pringle	6	c Stewart b Mallender	4
Salim Malik	not out	82	not out	84
Inzamam	c Hick b Munton	5	c Smith b Pringle	19
Wasim Akram	run out	12	c Ramprakash b Pringle	17
Moin Khan+	c Hick b Lewis	2	c Hick b Mallender	3
Waqar Younis	c Hick b Mallender	6	lbw b Pringle	0
M Ahmed	b Lewis	11	b Mallender	3
Aaqib Javed	c Hick b Munton	0	run out	0
Extras	(1b, 2lb, 7w, 16nb)	26	(4b, 1lb, 2w, 9nb)	16
	79.3 overs		69 overs	
Total		**197**		**221**

1st innings FoW: 34, 54, 60, 68, 80, 111, 117, 128, 192, 197
2nd innings FoW: 11, 53, 64, 96, 147, 177, 205, 206, 213, 221

CC Lewis	23	6	48	2	16	3	55	0
NA Mallender	23	7	72	3	23	7	50	5
DR Pringle	17	6	41	2	19	2	66	3
TA Munton	10.3	3	22	2	10	0	40	1
GA Gooch	6	3	11	0	1	0	5	0

ENGLAND 1st innings

			2nd innings	
GA Gooch*	b Mushtaq	135	c Asif b Mushtaq	37
MA Atherton	b Wasim	76	lbw b Waqar	5
RA Smith	c Miandad b Aaqib	42	c (sub) b Waqar	0
AJ Stewart+	lbw b Waqar	8	not out	31
DI Gower	not out	18	c Moin b Mushtaq	2
MR Ramp'ash	lbw b Mushtaq	0	not out	12
GA Hick	b Waqar	1		
CC Lewis	lbw b Waqar	0		
DR Pringle	b Waqar	0		
NA Mallender	b Waqar	1		
TA Munton	c Inzamam b Mushtaq	0		
Extras	(1b, 14lb, 1w, 23nb)	39	(5b, 3lb, 0w, 4nb)	12
	113.5 overs		42.4 overs	
Total		**320**		**99**

1st innings FoW: 168, 270, 292, 298, 298, 303, 305, 305, 313, 320
2nd innings FoW: 27, 27, 61, 65

Wasim Akram	36	12	80	1	17	4	36	0
Aaqib Javed	16	3	48	1				
Waqar Younis	30	3	117	5	12	2	28	2
Mushtaq Ahmed	29.5	6	60	3	13.4	3	27	2
Aamir Sohail	2	2	0	0				

Pakistan

No. 686: 5th Test
VENUE: The Oval
DATE: 6th-9th August 1992
TOSS WON BY: England
RESULT: Pakistan won by 10 wickets

ENGLAND	1st innings		2nd innings	
GA Gooch*	c Asif b Aaqib Javed	20	c Aamir b Waqar	24
AJ Stewart+	c Rameez b Wasim	31	lbw b Waqar	8
MA Atherton	c Rashid b Waqar	60	c Rashid b Waqar	4
RA Smith	b Mushtaq	33	not out	84
DI Gower	b Aaqib Javed	27	b Waqar	1
MR Rampr'sh	lbw b Wasim	2	c Asif b Mushtaq	17
CC Lewis	lbw b Wasim	4	st Rashid b Mushtaq	14
DR Pringle	b Wasim	1	b Wasim	1
NA Mallender	b Wasim	4	c Mushtaq b Wasim	3
PCR Tufnell	not out	0	b Wasim	0
DE Malcolm	b Wasim	2	b Waqar	0
Extras	(4b, 8lb, 1w, 10nb)	23	(1b, 8lb, 0w, 9nb)	18
	78.1 overs		72 overs	
Total		**207**		**174**

1st innings FoW: 39, 57, 138, 182, 190, 196, 199, 203, 205, 207
2nd innings FoW: 29, 47, 55, 59, 92, 153, 159, 173, 173, 174

Wasim Akram	22.1	3	67	6		21	6	36	3
Waqar Younis	16	4	37	1		18	5	52	5
Aaqib Javed	16	6	44	2		9	2	25	0
Mushtaq Ahmed	24	7	47	1		23	6	46	2
Aamir Sohail						1	0	6	0

PAKISTAN	1st innings		2nd innings	
Aamir Sohail	c Stewart b Malcolm	49	not out	4
Rameez Raja	b Malcolm	19	not out	0
Shoaib Moh'd	c & b Tufnell	55		
Javed M'dad*	c & b Lewis	59		
Salim Malik	b Malcolm	40		
Asif Mujtaba	run out	50		
Wasim Akram	c Stewart b Malcolm	7		
Rashid Latif+	c Smith b Mallender	50		
Waqar Younis	c Gooch b Malcolm	6		
M Ahmed	c Lewis b Mallender	9		
Aaqib Javed	not out	0		
Extras	(2b, 6lb, 4w, 24nb)	36	(0b, 0lb, 1w, 0nb)	1
	127.5 overs		0.1 overs	
Total		**380**		**5**

1st innings FoW: 64, 86, 197, 214, 278, 292, 332, 342, 359, 380

NA Mallender	28.5	6	93	2	
DE Malcolm	29	6	94	5	
CC Lewis	30	8	70	1	
PCR Tufnell	34	9	87	1	
DR Pringle	6	0	28	0	
MR Ramprakash	0.1	0	5	0	

India

No. 687: 1st Test
VENUE: Calcutta
DATE: 29th January to 2nd Feb 1993
TOSS WON BY: India
RESULT: India won by 8 wickets

INDIA	1st innings		2nd innings	
M Prabhakar	c Lewis b Salisbury	46	b Hick	13
NS Sidhu	c Hick b Taylor	13	st Stewart b Hick	37
VG Kambli	c Hick b Jarvis	16	not out	18
SR Tendulkar	c Hick b Malcolm	50	not out	9
M Azhar'din*	c Gooch b Hick	182		
PK Amre	c Hick b Jarvis	12		
N Kapil Dev	c Lewis b Hick	13		
KS More+	not out	4		
A Kumble	b Malcolm	0		
RK Chauhan	b Malcolm	2		
SLV Raju	c Salisbury b Hick	1		
Extras	(6b, 6lb, 10w, 10nb)	32	(0b, 4lb, 0w, 1nb)	5
	122.5 overs		29.2 overs	
Total		**371**		**82**

1st innings FoW: 49, 78, 93, 216, 278, 346, 362, 368, 370, 371

DE Malcolm	24	3	67	3		6	1	16	0
PW Jarvis	27	5	72	2		5.2	1	23	0
CC Lewis	23	5	64	0		3	1	5	0
JP Taylor	19	2	65	1		3	1	9	0
IDK Salisbury	17	2	72	1		6	3	16	0
GA Hick	12.5	5	19	3		6	1	9	2

ENGLAND	1st innings		2nd innings	
GA Gooch*	c Azharuddin b Raju	17	st More b Kumble	18
AJ Stewart+	b Prabhakar	0	c Tendulkar b Kumble	49
MW Gatting	b Chauhan	33	b Chauhan	81
RA Smith	c Amre b Kumble	1	c More b Chauhan	8
GA Hick	b Kumble	1	lbw b Raju	25
NH Fairbro'	c More b Kumble	17	c (sub) b Kumble	25
IDK Salisbury	c More b Chauhan	28	c Amre b Raju	16
CC Lewis	b Raju	21	lbw b Raju	6
PW Jarvis	c Prabhakar b Raju	4	c More b Kapil Dev	26
JP Taylor	st More b Chauhan	17	not out	17
DE Malcolm	not out	4	lbw b Kapil Dev	0
Extras	(8b, 8lb, 4w, 0nb)	20	(0b, 13lb, 0w, 2nb)	15
	100.1 overs		137.2 overs	
Total		**163**		**286**

1st innings FoW: 8, 37, 38, 40, 87, 89, 111, 119, 149, 163
2nd innings FoW: 48, 111, 145, 192, 192, 216, 234, 254, 286, 286

N Kapil Dev	6	1	18	0		8.2	5	12	2
M Prabhakar	9	3	10	1		9	4	26	0
A Kumble	29	8	50	3		40	16	76	3
SLV Raju	27	14	39	3		35	9	80	3
RK Chauhan	29.1	15	30	3		45	17	79	2

No. 688: 2nd Test
VENUE: Madras (Chepauk)
DATE: 11th-15th February 1993
TOSS WON BY: India
RESULT: India won by an innings and 22 runs

INDIA 1st innings			2nd innings
M Prabhakar	c Blakey b Lewis	27	
NS Sidhu	c Hick b Jarvis	106	
VG Kambli	lbw b Hick	59	
SR Tendulkar	c & b Salisbury	165	
M Azhar'din*	c Smith b Jarvis	6	
PK Amre	c Jarvis b Salisbury	78	
N Kapil Dev	not out	66	
KS More+	not out	26	
A Kumble			
RK Chauhan			
SLV Raju			
Extras	(0b, 10lb, 2w, 15nb)	27	
	165 overs		
Total		**560**	

1st innings FoW: 41, 149, 296, 324, 442, 499

DE Malcolm	27	7	87	0	
PW Jarvis	28	7	72	2	
CC Lewis	11	1	40	1	
PCR Tufnell	41	3	132	0	
GA Hick	29	2	77	1	
IDK Salisbury	29	1	142	2	

ENGLAND 1st innings			2nd innings	
RA Smith	lbw b Kumble	17	c Amre b Kumble	56
AJ Stewart*	c (sub) b Raju	74	lbw b Kapil Dev	0
GA Hick	lbw b Chauhan	64	c Tendulkar b Kapil Dev	0
MW Gatting	run out	2	lbw b Raju	19
NH Fairbro'	c Kapil Dev b Chauhan	83	c Prabhakar b Kumble	9
RJ Blakey+	b Raju	0	b Kumble	6
CC Lewis	c Azharuddin b Raju	0	c & b Kumble	117
IDK Salisbury	lbw b Kumble	4	b Kumble	12
PW Jarvis	c (sub) b Raju	8	c Tendulkar b Kumble	2
PCR Tufnell	c Azharuddin b Chauhan	2	not out	22
DE Malcolm	not out	0	c (sub) b Raju	0
Extras	(14b, 16lb, 0w, 2nb)	32	(4b, 5lb, 0w, 0nb)	9
	127.3 overs		81.1 overs	
Total		**286**		**252**

1st innings FoW: 46, 157, 166, 175, 179, 179, 220, 277, 279, 286
2nd innings FoW: 10, 12, 71, 82, 88, 99, 172, 186, 241, 252

M Prabhakar	3	2	7	0		3	2	4	0
A Kumble	25	9	61	2		21	7	64	6
RK Chauhan	39.3	16	69	3		21	4	59	0
SLV Raju	54	21	103	4		23.1	3	76	2
N Kapil Dev	4	0	11	0		11	5	36	2
SR Tendulkar	2	1	5	0		2	1	4	0

No. 689: 3rd Test
VENUE: Bombay (Wankhede)
DATE: 19th-23rd February 1993
TOSS WON BY: England
RESULT: India won by an innings and 15 runs

ENGLAND 1st innings			2nd innings	
GA Gooch*	c More b Kapil Dev	4	b Prabhakar	8
AJ Stewart	run out	13	lbw b Prabhakar	10
MA Atherton	c Prabhakar b Kumble	37	c More b Prabhakar	11
RA Smith	c More b Raju	2	b Kumble	62
MW Gatting	c Kapil Dev b Raju	23	st More b Chauhan	61
GA Hick	c Kapil Dev b Prabhakar	178	c Amre b Kumble	47
RJ Blakey+	lbw b Kumble	1	b Kumble	0
CC Lewis	lbw b Kumble	49	c More b Raju	3
JE Emburey	c More b Kapil Dev	12	c Tendulkar b Kumble	1
PAJ De Freitas	lbw b Kapil Dev	11	st More b Raju	12
PCR Tufnell	not out	2	not out	2
Extras	(4b, 5lb, 2w, 4nb)	15	(4b, 6lb, 1w, 1nb)	12
	135 overs		82.5 overs	
Total		**347**		**229**

1st innings FoW: 11, 25, 30, 58, 116, 118, 211, 262, 279, 347
2nd innings FoW: 17, 26, 34, 155, 181, 181, 206, 214, 215, 229

N Kapil Dev	15	3	35	3		7	1	21	0
M Prabhakar	13	2	52	1		11	4	28	3
SLV Raju	44	8	102	2		26.5	7	68	2
A Kumble	40	11	95	3		26	9	70	4
RK Chauhan	23	7	54	0		12	5	32	1

INDIA 1st innings			2nd innings
NS Sidhu	c Smith b Tufnell	79	
M Prabhakar	c Blakey b Hick	44	
VG Kambli	c Gatting b Lewis	224	
SR Tendulkar	lbw b Tufnell	78	
M Azhar'din*	lbw b Lewis	26	
PK Amre	c De Freitas b Hick	57	
N Kapil Dev	c De Freitas b Emburey	22	
KS More+	c Lewis b Emburey	0	
A Kumble	c Atherton b Tufnell	16	
RK Chauhan	c Atherton b Tufnell	15	
SLV Raju	not out	0	
Extras	(5b, 14lb, 5w, 6nb)	30	
	189.3 overs		
Total		**591**	

1st innings FoW: 109, 174, 368, 418, 519, 560, 560, 563, 591, 591

PAJ De Freitas	20	4	75	0	
CC Lewis	42	9	114	2	
JE Emburey	59	14	144	2	
PCR Tufnell	39.3	6	142	4	
GA Hick	29	3	97	2	

Sri Lanka

No. 690: 1st Test
VENUE: Colombo (SSC)
DATE: 13th-18th March 1993
TOSS WON BY: England
RESULT: Sri Lanka won by 5 wickets

ENGLAND

1st innings			2nd innings	
RA Smith	b Muralidharan	128	b Jayasuriya	35
MA Atherton	lbw b Ramanayake	13	c Tillakaratne b Gurusinha	2
MW Gatting	c Jayasuriya b Mura'ran	29	c Tillakaratne b War'era	18
GA Hick	c Tillakaratne b Mura'ran	68	c Ramanayake b War'era	26
AJ Stewart*+	c Tillakaratne b War'era	63	c Mahanama b War'era	3
NH Fairbro'	b Warnaweera	18	run out	3
CC Lewis	run out	22	c Jayasuriya b Mura'ran	45
JE Emburey	not out	1	b Gurusinha	59
PW Jarvis	lbw b Warnaweera	0	st A de Silva b Jayasuriya	3
PCR Tufnell	lbw b Muralidharan	1	c AM de Silva b War'era	1
DE Malcolm	c Gurusinha b Warnaw'ra	13	not out	8
Extras	(5b, 3lb, 1w, 15nb)	24	(4b, 2lb, 1w, 18nb)	25
	130.1 overs		66 overs	
Total		**380**		**228**

2nd innings FoW:40, 82 , 194, 316, 323, 358, 366, 366, 367, 380
2nd innings FoW: 16, 38, 83, 91, 96, 130, 153, 173, 188, 228

CPH Ramanayake	17	2	66	1	3	0	16	0	
AP Gurusinha	5	1	12	0	6	3	7	2	
KPJ Warnaweera	40.1	11	90	4	25	4	98	4	
UC Hathurusingha	8	2	22	0	16	3	55	1	
M Muralidharan	45	12	118	4	16	3	46	2	
ST Jayasuriya	12	1	53	0					
A Ranatunga	3	0	11	0					

SRI LANKA 1st innings

1st innings			2nd innings	
RS Mahanama	c Smith b Emburey	64	c Stewart b Lewis	6
UC Hathur'ha	c Stewart b Lewis	59	c Stewart b Tufnell	14
AP Gurusinha	st Stewart b Tufnell	43	b Emburey	29
PA de Silva	c Stewart b Jarvis	80	c Jarvis b Emburey	1
A Ranatunga*	c Stewart b Lewis	64	c Gatting b Tufnell	35
HP Tillak'tne	not out	93	not out	36
ST Jayasuriya	c Atherton b Lewis	4	not out	6
AM de Silva+	c Gatting b Emburey	9		
C Raman'ke	c Lewis b Jarvis	1		
M Mura'ran	b Lewis	19		
KPJ War'era	b Jarvis	1		
Extras	(2b, 13lb, 2w, 15nb)	32	(1b, 2lb, 0w, 6nb)	9
	156.5 overs		42.4 overs	
Total		**469**		**142**

1st innings FoW: 99, 153, 203, 330, 339, 349, 371, 376, 459, 469
2nd innings FoW: 8, 48, 61, 61, 136

DE Malcolm	25	7	60	0	3	1	11	0
PW Jarvis	25.5	1	76	3	8	2	14	0
CC Lewis	31	5	66	4	8	1	21	1
PCR Tufnell	33	5	108	1	7.4	1	34	2
JE Emburey	34	6	117	2	14	2	48	2
GA Hick	8	0	27	0	2	0	11	0

Australia

No. 691: 1st Test
VENUE: Old Trafford
DATE: 3rd-7th June 1993
TOSS WON BY: England
RESULT: Australia won by 179 runs

AUSTRALIA 1st innings

1st innings			2nd innings	
MJ Slater	c Stewart b De Freitas	58	lbw b Such	9
MA Taylor	c & b Such	124	c Caddick b Such	27
DC Boon	c Lewis b Such	21	c Gatting b De Freitas	93
ME Waugh	c & b Tufnell	6	b Tufnell	64
AR Border*	st Stewart b Such	17	c & b Caddick	31
SR Waugh	b Such	3	not out	78
IA Healy+	c Such b Tufnell	12	not out	102
BP Julian	c Gatting b Such	0		
MG Hughes	c De Freitas b Such	2		
SK Warne	not out	15		
CJ McDermott	run out	8		
Extras	(8b, 8lb, 0w, 7nb)	23	(6b, 14lb, 0w, 8nb)	28
	112.3 overs		130 overs	
Total		**289**		**432**

1st innings FoW: 128, 183, 221, 225, 232, 260, 264, 266, 267, 289
2nd innings FoW: 23, 46, 155, 234 , 252

AR Caddick	15	4	38	0	20	3	79	1
PAJ De Freitas	23	8	46	1	24	1	80	1
PM Such	33.3	9	67	6	31	6	78	2
PCR Tufnell	28	5	78	2	37	4	112	1
CC Lewis	13	2	44	0	9	0	43	0
GA Hick					9	1	20	0

ENGLAND 1st innings

1st innings			2nd innings	
GA Gooch*	c Julian b Warne	65	handled ball	133
MA Atherton	c Healy b Hughes	19	c Taylor b Warne	25
MW Gatting	b Warne	4	b Hughes	23
RA Smith	c Taylor b Warne	4	b Warne	18
GA Hick	c Border b Hughes	34	c Healy b Hughes	22
AJ Stewart+	b Julian	27	c Healy b Warne	11
CC Lewis	c Boon b Hughes	9	c Taylor b Warne	43
PAJ De Freitas	lbw b Julian	5	lbw b Julian	7
AR Caddick	c Healy b Warne	7	c Warne b Hughes	25
PM Such	not out	14	c Border b Hughes	9
PCR Tufnell	c Healy b Hughes	1	not out	0
Extras	(6b, 10lb, 0w, 5nb)	21	(0b, 11lb, 1w, 4nb)	16
	74.5 overs		120.2 overs	
Total		**210**		**332**

1st innings FoW: 71, 80, 84, 123, 148, 168, 178, 183, 203, 210
2nd innings FoW: 73, 133, 171, 223, 230, 238, 260, 299, 331, 332

CJ McDermott	18	2	50	0	30	9	76	0
MG Hughes	20.5	5	59	4	27.2	4	92	4
SK Warne	24	10	51	4	49	26	86	4
BP Julian	11	2	30	2	14	1	67	1
AR Border	1	0	4	0				

No. 692: 2nd Test		No. 693: 3rd Test	
VENUE: Lord's		VENUE: Trent Bridge	
DATE: 17th-21st June 1993		DATE: 1st-6th July 1993	
TOSS WON BY: Australia		TOSS WON BY: England	
RESULT: Aus won by an innings and 62 runs		RESULT: Match drawn	

AUSTRALIA 1st innings / 2nd innings

	1st innings		2nd innings
MA Taylor	st Stewart b Tufnell	111	
MJ Slater	c (sub) b Lewis	152	
DC Boon	not out	164	
ME Waugh	b Tufnell	99	
AR Border*	b Lewis	77	
SR Waugh	not out	13	
IA Healy+			
TBA May			
MG Hughes			
SK Warne			
CJ McDermott			
Extras	(0b, 1lb, 1w, 14nb)	16	
	196 overs		
Total		**632**	

1st innings FoW: 260, 277, 452, 591

AR Caddick	38	5	120	0				
NA Foster	30	4	94	0				
PM Such	36	6	90	0				
PCR Tufnell	39	3	129	2				
CC Lewis	36	5	151	2				
GA Gooch	9	1	26	0				
GA Hick	8	3	21	0				

ENGLAND 1st innings / 2nd innings

	1st innings		2nd innings	
GA Gooch*	c May b Hughes	12	c Healy b Warne	29
MA Atherton	b Warne	80	run out	99
MW Gatting	b May	5	lbw b Warne	59
RA Smith	st Healy b May	22	c (sub) b May	5
GA Hick	c Healy b Hughes	20	c Taylor b May	64
AJ Stewart+	lbw b Hughes	3	lbw b May	62
CC Lewis	lbw b Warne	0	st Healy b May	0
NA Foster	c Border b Warne	16	c ME Waugh b Border	20
AR Caddick	c Healy b Hughes	21	not out	0
PM Such	c Taylor b Warne	7	b Warne	4
PCR Tufnell	not out	2	b Warne	0
Extras	(0b, 8lb, 0w, 9nb)	17	(10b, 13lb, 0w, 0nb)	23
	99 overs		165.5 overs	
Total		**205**		**365**

1st innings FoW: 33, 50, 84, 123, 131, 132, 167, 174, 189, 205
2nd innings FoW: 71, 175, 180, 244, 304, 312, 361, 361, 365, 365

MG Hughes	20	5	52	4		31	9	75	0
ME Waugh	6	1	16	0		17	4	55	0
SR Waugh	4	1	5	0		2	0	13	0
TBA May	31	12	64	2		51	23	81	4
SK Warne	35	12	57	4		48.5	17	102	4
AR Border	3	1	3	0		16	9	16	1

ENGLAND 1st innings / 2nd innings (3rd Test)

	1st innings		2nd innings	
MN Lathwell	c Healy b Hughes	20	lbw b Warne	33
MA Atherton	c Boon b Warne	11	c Healy b Hughes	9
RA Smith	c & b Julian	86	c Healy b Warne	50
AJ Stewart+	c ME Waugh b Warne	25	lbw b Hughes	6
GA Gooch*	c Border b Hughes	38	c Taylor b Warne	120
GP Thorpe	c SR Waugh b Hughes	6	c Boon b Julian	12
N Hussain	c Boon b Warne	71	not out	114
AR Caddick	lbw b Hughes	15	not out	47
MJ McCague	c ME Waugh b Hughes	9		
MC Ilott	c Taylor b May	6		
PM Such	not out	0		
Extras	(5b, 23lb, 4w, 2nb)	34	(11b, 11lb, 0w, 9nb)	31
	118.4 overs		155 overs	
Total		**321**		**422**

1st innings FoW: 28, 63, 153, 159, 174, 220, 290, 304, 321, 321
2nd innings FoW: 11, 100, 109, 117, 159, 309

MG Hughes	31	7	92	5		22	8	41	2
BP Julian	24	3	84	1		33	10	110	1
SK Warne	40	17	74	3		50	21	108	3
TBA May	14.4	7	31	1		38	6	112	0
SR Waugh	8	4	12	0		1	0	3	0
ME Waugh	1	1	0	0		6	3	15	0
AR Border						5	0	11	0

AUSTRALIA 1st innings / 2nd innings (3rd Test)

	1st innings		2nd innings	
MJ Slater	lbw b Caddick	40	b Such	26
MA Taylor	c Stewart b McCague	28	c Atherton b Such	28
DC Boon	b McCague	101	c Stewart b Caddick	18
ME Waugh	c McCague b Such	70	b Caddick	1
SR Waugh	c Stewart b McCague	13	not out	47
IA Healy+	c Thorpe b Ilott	9	lbw b Ilott	5
BP Julian	c Stewart b Ilott	5	not out	56
AR Border*	c Smith b Such	38	c Thorpe b Caddick	2
MG Hughes	b Ilott	17		
SK Warne	not out	35		
TBA May	lbw b McCague	1		
Extras	(4b, 8lb, 4w, 0nb)	16	(5b, 5lb, 4w, 5nb)	19
	108.3 overs		76 overs	
Total		**373**		**202**

1st innings FoW: 55, 74, 197, 239, 250, 262, 284, 311, 356, 373
2nd innings FoW: 46, 74, 75, 81, 93, 115

MJ McCague	32.3	5	121	4		19	6	58	0
MC Ilott	34	8	108	3		18	5	44	1
PM Such	20	7	51	2		23	6	58	2
AR Caddick	22	5	81	1		16	6	32	3

Australia

No. 694:	4th Test
VENUE:	Headingley
DATE:	22nd-26th July 1993
TOSS WON BY:	Australia
RESULT:	Aus won by an innings and 148 runs

AUSTRALIA 1st innings

Batsman	Dismissal		2nd innings
MJ Slater	b Ilott	67	
MA Taylor	lbw b Bicknell	27	
DC Boon	lbw b Ilott	107	
ME Waugh	b Ilott	52	
AR Border*	not out	200	
SR Waugh	not out	157	
IA Healy+			
MG Hughes			
SK Warne			
PR Reiffel			
TBA May			
Extras	(8b, 22lb, 4w, 9nb)	43	
	193 overs		
Total		**653**	

1st innings FoW: 86, 110 , 216, 321

Bowler	O	M	R	W				
MJ McCague	28	2	115	0				
MC Ilott	51	11	161	3				
AR Caddick	42	5	138	0				
MP Bicknell	50	8	155	1				
GA Gooch	16	5	40	0				
GP Thorpe	6	1	14	0				

ENGLAND 1st innings

Batsman	Dismissal		2nd innings	
MN Lathwell	c Healy b Hughes	0	b May	25
MA Atherton	b Reiffel	55	st Healy b May	63
RA Smith	c & b May	23	lbw b Reiffel	35
AJ Stewart+	c Slater b Reiffel	5	c ME Waugh b Reiffel	78
GA Gooch*	lbw b Reiffel	59	st Healy b May	26
GP Thorpe	c Healy b Reiffel	0	c Taylor b Reiffel	13
N Hussain	b Reiffel	15	not out	18
AR Caddick	c ME Waugh b Hughes	9	lbw b Hughes	12
MP Bicknell	c Border b Hughes	12	lbw b Hughes	0
MJ McCague	c Taylor b Warne	0	b Hughes	11
MC Ilott	not out	0	c Border b May	4
Extras	(2b, 3lb, 0w, 17nb)	22	(5b, 3lb, 1w, 11nb)	20
	82.5 overs		127 overs	
Total		**200**		**305**

1st innings FoW: 0, 43, 50, 158 , 158, 169, 184, 195, 200, 200
2nd innings FoW: 60, 131, 149, 202, 256, 263, 279, 279, 295, 305

Bowler	O	M	R	W		O	M	R	W
MG Hughes	15.5	3	47	3		30	10	79	3
PR Reiffel	26	6	65	5		28	8	87	3
TBA May	15	3	33	1		27	6	65	4
SK Warne	23	9	43	1		40	16	63	0
ME Waugh	3	0	7	0		2	1	3	0

Australia

No. 695:	5th Test
VENUE:	Edgbaston
DATE:	5th-9th August 1993
TOSS WON BY:	England
RESULT:	Australia won by 8 wickets

ENGLAND 1st innings

Batsman	Dismissal		2nd innings	
GA Gooch	c Taylor b Reiffel	8	b Warne	48
MA Atherton*	b Reiffel	72	c Border b Warne	28
RA Smith	b ME Waugh	21	lbw b Warne	19
MP Maynard	c SR Waugh b May	0	c Healy b Warne	10
AJ Stewart+	c & b Warne	45	lbw b Warne	5
GP Thorpe	c Healy b May	37	st Healy b Warne	60
N Hussain	b Reiffel	3	c SR Waugh b May	0
JE Emburey	not out	55	c Healy b May	37
MP Bicknell	c ME Waugh b Reiffel	14	c SR Waugh b May	0
PM Such	b Reiffel	1	not out	7
MC Ilott	c Healy b Reiffel	3	b May	15
Extras	(4b, 6lb, 0w, 7nb)	17	(11b, 9lb, 0w, 2nb)	22
	101.5 overs		133.2 overs	
Total		**276**		**251**

1st innings FoW: 17, 71, 76, 156, 156, 160, 215, 262, 264, 276
2nd innings FoW: 60, 104, 115, 115, 124, 125, 229, 229, 229, 251

Bowler	O	M	R	W		O	M	R	W
MG Hughes	19	4	53	0		18	7	24	0
PR Reiffel	22.5	3	71	6		11	2	30	0
ME Waugh	15	5	43	1		5	2	5	0
SR Waugh	5	2	4	0					
TBA May	19	9	32	2		48.2	15	89	5
SK Warne	21	7	63	1		49	23	82	5
AR Border						2	1	1	0

AUSTRALIA 1st innings

Batsman	Dismissal		2nd innings	
MA Taylor	run out	19	c Thorpe b Such	4
MJ Slater	c Smith b Such	22	c Thorpe b Emburey	8
DC Boon	lbw b Emburey	0	not out	38
ME Waugh	c Thorpe b Ilott	137	not out	62
AR Border*	c Hussain b Such	3		
SR Waugh	c Stewart b Bicknell	59		
IA Healy+	c Stewart b Bicknell	80		
MG Hughes	b Bicknell	38		
PR Reiffel	b Such	20		
SK Warne	c Stewart b Emburey	10		
TBA May	not out	3		
Extras	(7b, 8lb, 0w, 2nb)	17	(3b, 5lb, 0w, 0nb)	8
	149.5 overs		43.3 overs	
Total		**408**		**120**

1st innings FoW: 34, 39, 69, 80, 233, 263, 370, 379, 398, 408
2nd innings FoW: 12, 12

Bowler	O	M	R	W		O	M	R	W
MP Bicknell	34	9	99	3		3	0	9	0
MC Ilott	24	4	85	1		2	0	14	0
PM Such	52.5	18	90	3		20.3	4	58	1
JE Emburey	39	9	119	2		18	4	31	1

No. 696: 6th Test

VENUE:	The Oval
DATE:	19th-23rd August 1993
TOSS WON BY:	England
RESULT:	England won by 161 runs

No. 697: 1st Test

VENUE:	Kingston (Jamaica)
DATE:	19th-24th February 1994
TOSS WON BY:	England
RESULT:	West Indies won by 8 wickets

ENGLAND 1st innings / 2nd innings (Oval)

Batsman	1st innings		2nd innings	
GA Gooch	c Border b SR Waugh	56	c Healy b Warne	79
MA Atherton*	lbw b SR Waugh	50	c Warne b Reiffel	42
GA Hick	c Warne b May	80	c Boon b May	36
MP Maynard	b Warne	20	c Reiffel b Hughes	9
N Hussain	c Taylor b Warne	30	c ME Waugh b Hughes	0
AJ Stewart+	c Healy b Hughes	76	c ME Waugh b Reiffel	35
MR Ramp'sh	c Healy b Hughes	6	c Slater b Hughes	64
ARC Fraser	b Reiffel	28	c Healy b Reiffel	13
SL Watkin	c SR Waugh b Reiffel	13	lbw b Warne	4
PM Such	c ME Waugh b Hughes	4	lbw b Warne	10
DE Malcolm	not out	0	not out	0
Extras	(0b, 7lb, 1w, 9nb)	17	(5b, 12lb, 1w, 3nb)	21
Total	101.5 overs	**380**	119.2 overs	**313**

1st innings FoW: 88, 139, 177, 231, 253, 272, 339, 363, 374, 380
2nd innings FoW: 77, 157, 180, 180, 186, 254, 276, 283, 313, 313

Bowler	O	M	R	W	O	M	R	W
MG Hughes	30	7	121	3	31.2	9	110	3
PR Reiffel	28.5	4	88	2	24	8	55	3
SR Waugh	12	2	45	2				
SK Warne	20	5	70	2	40	15	78	3
ME Waugh	1	0	17	0				
TBA May	10	3	32	1	24	6	53	1

AUSTRALIA 1st innings / 2nd innings

Batsman	1st innings		2nd innings	
MA Taylor	c Hussain b Malcolm	70	b Watkin	8
MJ Slater	c Gooch b Malcolm	4	c Stewart b Watkin	12
DC Boon	c Gooch b Malcolm	13	lbw b Watkin	0
ME Waugh	c Stewart b Fraser	10	c Ramp'sh b Malcolm	49
AR Border*	c Stewart b Fraser	48	c Stewart b Malcolm	17
SR Waugh	b Fraser	20	lbw b Malcolm	26
IA Healy+	not out	83	c Maynard b Watkin	5
MG Hughes	c Ramprakash b Watkin	7	c Watkin b Fraser	12
PR Reiffel	c Maynard b Watkin	0	c & b Fraser	42
SK Warne	c Stewart b Fraser	16	lbw b Fraser	37
TBA May	c Stewart b Fraser	15	not out	4
Extras	(5b, 6lb, 2w, 4nb)	17	(2b, 6lb, 2w, 7nb)	17
Total	94.4 overs	**303**	81.1 overs	**229**

1st innings FoW: 9, 30, 53, 132, 164, 181, 196, 196, 248, 303
2nd innings FoW: 23, 23, 30, 92, 95, 106, 142, 143, 217, 229

Bowler	O	M	R	W	O	M	R	W
DE Malcolm	26	5	86	3	20	3	84	3
SL Watkin	28	4	87	2	25	9	65	4
ARC Fraser	26.4	4	87	5	19.1	5	44	3
PM Such	14	4	32	0	9	4	17	0
GA Hick					8	3	11	0

ENGLAND 1st innings / 2nd innings (Kingston)

Batsman	1st innings		2nd innings	
MA Atherton*	c Murray b K Benjamin	55	c Adams b Walsh	28
AJ Stewart	c Murray b K Benjamin	70	run out	19
GP Thorpe	b KCG Benjamin	16	b WK Benjamin	14
RA Smith	b Walsh	0	c Adams b Walsh	2
GA Hick	b Adams	23	c (sub) b KC Benjamin	96
MP Maynard	lbw b KCG Benjamin	35	c Murray b W Benjamin	0
RC Russell+	lbw b KCG Benjamin	0	c Adams b W Benjamin	32
CC Lewis	c Adams b Ambrose	8	lbw b Ambrose	21
AR Caddick	c Adams b KCG Benjamin	3	not out	29
AP Igglesden	not out	0	c Adams b KC Benjamin	2
DE Malcolm	run out	6	b Walsh	18
Extras	(2b, 5lb, 4w, 4nb)	15	(1b, 3lb, 2w, 2nb)	8
Total	98.1 overs	**234**	91.5 overs	**267**

1st innings FoW: 121, 133, 134, 172, 172, 172, 194, 209, 227, 234
2nd innings FoW: 34, 39, 58, 63, 126, 155, 213, 226, 228, 267

Bowler	O	M	R	W	O	M	R	W
CEL Ambrose	22	8	46	1	24	4	67	1
CA Walsh	23	6	41	1	24.5	6	67	3
KCG Benjamin	24	7	66	6	18	2	60	2
WKM Benjamin	19.1	7	43	0	20	3	56	3
JC Adams	10	1	31	1	2	0	9	0
PV Simmons					3	1	4	0

WEST INDIES 1st innings / 2nd innings

Batsman	1st innings		2nd innings	
DL Haynes	c Thorpe b Malcolm	4	not out	43
PV Simmons	c Russell b Caddick	8	lbw b Igglesden	12
RB Richardson*	c Maynard b Malcolm	5	not out	4
BC Lara	b Hick	83	b Caddick	28
KLT Arthurton	c Lewis b Malcolm	126		
JC Adams	not out	95		
JR Murray+	lbw b Igglesden	34		
WKM Benjamin	b Caddick	38		
CEL Ambrose	c Caddick	0		
KCG Benjamin	b Lewis	0		
CA Walsh	lbw b Lewis	0		
Extras	(0b, 10lb, 1w, 3nb)	14	(5b, 3lb, 0w, 0nb)	8
Total	123 overs	**407**	26.2 overs	**95**

1st innings FoW: 12, 12, 23, 167, 256, 319, 389, 389, 390, 407
2nd innings FoW: 38, 87

Bowler	O	M	R	W	O	M	R	W
DE Malcolm	23	3	113	3	5	1	19	0
AR Caddick	29	5	94	3	6	1	19	1
CC Lewis	26	4	82	2	3	0	6	0
AP Igglesden	24	5	53	1	7	0	36	1
GA Hick	21	4	55	1	3	1	2	0
AJ Stewart					2.2	0	5	0

	No. 698: 2nd Test		No. 699: 3rd Test
	VENUE: Georgetown (Guyana)		VENUE: Port-of-Spain (Trinidad)
	DATE: 17th-22nd March 1994		DATE: 25th-30th March 1994
	TOSS WON BY: West Indies		TOSS WON BY: West Indies
	RESULT: WI won by an innings and 44 runs		RESULT: West Indies won by 147 runs

ENGLAND 1st innings / 2nd innings

Batsman	1st innings		2nd innings	
MA Atherton*	c Murray b Ambrose	144	b Ambrose	0
AJ Stewart	b Walsh	0	b KCG Benjamin	79
MR Rampr'sh	lbw b Walsh	2	b Ambrose	5
RA Smith	c Lara b KCG Benjamin	84	c Richardson b Ambrose	24
GA Hick	c Richardson b Ambrose	33	b KCG Benjamin	5
GP Thorpe	b Ambrose	0	b Walsh	20
IDK Salisbury	lbw b WKM Benjamin	8	c Murray b Ambrose	6
RC Russell+	c Richardson b Ambrose	13	c Adams b K Benjamin	24
CC Lewis	c Richardson b K Benjamin	17	b Walsh	19
ARC Fraser	not out	0	b KCG Benjamin	0
AP Igglesden	b KCG Benjamin	0	not out	1
Extras	(0b, 14lb, 0w, 7nb)	21	(2b, 2lb, 1w, 2nb)	7
Total	124.5 overs	**322**	85 overs	**190**

1st innings FoW: 0, 2, 173, 245, 253, 276, 281, 322, 322, 322
2nd innings FoW: 0, 30, 91, 96, 129, 140, 150, 185, 186, 190

Bowler	O	M	R	W		O	M	R	W
CEL Ambrose	30	8	58	4		23	5	37	4
CA Walsh	26	7	69	2		25	4	71	2
KCG Benjamin	23.5	5	60	3		19	6	34	4
WKM Benjamin	26	9	62	1		16	4	44	0
JC Adams	3	1	10	0		2	2	0	0
S Chanderpaul	16	2	49	0					

WEST INDIES 1st innings / 2nd innings

Batsman	1st innings		2nd innings
DL Haynes	c Russell b Salisbury	63	
RB Richardson*	c Lewis b Fraser	35	
BC Lara	c Atherton b Lewis	167	
KLT Arthurton	c Thorpe b Salisbury	5	
JC Adams	lbw b Igglesden	137	
S Chanderpaul	b Salisbury	62	
JR Murray+	lbw b Salisbury	0	
WKM Benjamin	b Fraser	44	
CEL Ambrose	c Russell b Lewis	10	
KCG Benjamin	c Russell b Lewis	1	
CA Walsh	not out	10	
Extras	(2b, 6lb, 1w, 13nb)	22	
Total	153.3 overs	**556**	

1st innings FoW: 63, 177, 203, 315, 441, 441, 505, 520, 532, 556

Bowler	O	M	R	W
CC Lewis	28	1	110	3
AP Igglesden	24.3	3	94	1
ARC Fraser	29	5	85	2
IDK Salisbury	37	4	163	4
GA Hick	20	1	61	0
MR Ramprakash	15	1	35	0

WEST INDIES 1st innings / 2nd innings

Batsman	1st innings		2nd innings	
DL Haynes	b Salisbury	38	b Lewis	19
RB Richardson*	lbw b Salisbury	63	c & b Caddick	3
BC Lara	lbw b Lewis	43	c Salisbury b Caddick	12
KLT Arthurton	lbw b Lewis	1	c Stewart b Caddick	42
JC Adams	c Smith b Lewis	2	c Russell b Salisbury	43
S Chanderpaul	b Fraser	19	c Fraser b Caddick	50
JR Murray+	not out	27	c Russell b Caddick	14
WKM Benjamin	b Fraser	10	c Fraser b Lewis	35
CEL Ambrose	c Thorpe b Fraser	13	b Caddick	12
KCG Benjamin	b Fraser	9	not out	5
CA Walsh	lbw b Lewis	0	lbw b Lewis	1
Extras	(1b, 13lb, 1w, 12nb)	27	(8b, 13lb, 0w, 12nb)	33
Total	95.2 overs	**252**	87.5 overs	**269**

1st innings FoW: 66, 158, 158, 163, 164 , 201, 212, 241, 251, 252
2nd innings FoW: 15, 37, 51, 131, 143, 167, 227, 247, 267, 269

Bowler	O	M	R	W		O	M	R	W
ARC Fraser	24	9	49	4		25	6	71	0
AR Caddick	19	5	43	0		26	5	65	6
CC Lewis	25.2	5	61	4		27.5	6	71	3
IDK Salisbury	22	4	72	2		9	1	41	1
MR Ramprakash	2	1	8	0					
GA Hick	3	1	5	0					

ENGLAND 1st innings / 2nd innings

Batsman	1st innings		2nd innings	
MA Atherton*	c Murray b W Benjamin	48	lbw b Ambrose	0
AJ Stewart	b Ambrose	6	b Ambrose	18
MR Rampr'sh	c & b W Benjamin	23	run out	1
RA Smith	lbw b Ambrose	12	b Ambrose	0
GA Hick	lbw b Walsh	40	c Murray b Ambrose	6
GP Thorpe	c Lara b Ambrose	86	b Ambrose	3
RC Russell+	b Ambrose	23	c Lara b Walsh	0
CC Lewis	b Ambrose	9	c (sub) b Ambrose	4
IDK Salisbury	c Lara b Walsh	36	c W Benjamin b Walsh	6
AR Caddick	c Lara b WKM Benjamin	6	c Lara b Walsh	1
ARC Fraser	not out	8	not out	0
Extras	(10b, 9lb, 1w, 11nb)	31	(0b, 6lb, 0w, 1nb)	7
Total	112.2 overs	**328**	19.1 overs	**46**

1st innings FoW: 16, 82, 87, 115, 167, 249, 273, 281, 294, 328
2nd innings FoW: 0, 1, 5, 21, 26, 27, 37, 40, 45, 46

Bowler	O	M	R	W		O	M	R	W
CEL Ambrose	29	6	60	5		10	1	24	6
CA Walsh	27.2	3	77	2		9.1	1	16	3
KCG Benjamin	20	5	70	0					
WKM Benjamin	24	3	66	3					
JC Adams	4	0	18	0					
S Chanderpaul	5	0	13	0					
KLT Arthurton	3	0	5	0					

No. 700: 4th Test
VENUE: Bridgetown (Barbados)
DATE: 8th-13th April 1994
TOSS WON BY: West Indies
RESULT: England won by 208 runs

ENGLAND	1st innings		2nd innings	
MA Atherton*	c Lara b KCG Benjamin	85	c Lara b Walsh	15
AJ Stewart	b WKM Benjamin	118	b Walsh	143
MR Rampr'sh	c Murray b W Benjamin	20	c Chanderpaul b Walsh	3
RA Smith	c Murray b W Benjamin	10	lbw b KCG Benjamin	13
GA Hick	c Murray b Ambrose	34	c Lara b Walsh	59
GP Thorpe	c (sub) b KCG Benjamin	7	c Arthurton b Walsh	84
RC Russell+	c Chanderpaul b Ambrose	38	not out	17
CC Lewis	c Murray b Ambrose	0	c Walsh b Adams	10
AR Caddick	b Ambrose	8		
ARC Fraser	c Chanderpaul b Walsh	3		
PCR Tufnell	not out	0		
Extras	(0b, 8lb, 0w, 24nb)	32	(8b, 6lb, 0w, 36nb)	50
	100.2 overs		108.5 overs	
Total		**355**		**394**

1st innings FoW: 171, 223, 242, 265, 290, 307, 307, 327, 351, 355
2nd innings FoW: 33, 43, 79, 194, 344, 382, 394

CEL Ambrose	24.2	5	86	4		22	4	75	0
CA Walsh	24	3	88	1		28	5	94	5
WKM Benjamin	22	4	76	3		22	3	58	0
KCG Benjamin	20	5	74	2		20	1	92	1
S Chanderpaul	10	4	23	0		10	3	30	0
JC Adams						6.5	0	31	1

WEST INDIES	1st innings		2nd innings	
DL Haynes	c Atherton b Fraser	35	c Thorpe b Tufnell	15
RB Richardson*	c Atherton b Fraser	20	c Ramprakash b Caddick	33
BC Lara	c (sub) b Lewis	26	c Tufnell b Caddick	64
KLT Arthurton	c Russell b Fraser	0	b Tufnell	52
JC Adams	c Thorpe b Fraser	26	c Russell b Caddick	12
S Chanderpaul	c Ramprakash b Tufnell	77	c (sub) b Hick	5
JR Murray+	c Thorpe b Fraser	0	c Thorpe b Caddick	5
WKM Benjamin	c Hick b Fraser	8	c Stewart b Tufnell	1
CEL Ambrose	c Hick b Fraser	44	b Lewis	12
KCG Benjamin	not out	43	c Hick b Caddick	0
CA Walsh	c Tufnell b Fraser	13	not out	18
Extras	(0b, 1lb, 0w, 11nb)	12	(1b, 7lb, 0w, 10nb)	18
	101.5 overs		82.2 overs	
Total		**304**		**237**

1st innings FoW: 55, 55, 95, 126, 126, 126, 134, 205, 263, 304
2nd innings FoWL43, 43, 128, 150, 164, 179, 195, 199, 216, 237

ARC Fraser	28.5	7	75	8		17	7	40	0
AR Caddick	24	2	92	0		17	3	63	5
CC Lewis	17	2	60	1		8.2	1	23	1
PCR Tufnell	32	12	76	1		36	12	100	3
GA Hick						4	2	3	1

No. 701: 5th Test
VENUE: St. John's (Antigua)
DATE: 16th-21st April 1994
TOSS WON BY: West Indies
RESULT: Match drawn

WEST INDIES	1st innings		2nd innings	
PV Simmons	lbw b Caddick	8	not out	22
SC Williams	c Caddick b Fraser	3	not out	21
BC Lara	c Russell b Caddick	375		
JC Adams	c (sub) b Fraser	59		
KLT Arthurton	c Russell b Caddick	47		
S Chanderpaul	not out	75		
JR Murray+				
CEL Ambrose				
CA Walsh*				
WKM Benjamin				
KCG Benjamin				
Extras	(0b, 3lb, 0w, 23nb)	26	(0b, 0lb, 0w, 0nb)	0
	180.2 overs		24 overs	
Total		**593**		**43**

1st innings FoW: 11, 12, 191, 374, 593

ARC Fraser	43	4	121	2		2	1	2	0
AR Caddick	47.2	8	158	3		2	1	11	0
PCR Tufnell	39	8	110	0		6	4	5	0
CC Lewis	33	1	140	0					
GA Hick	18	3	61	0		8	2	11	0
MR Ramprakash						3	1	5	0
GP Thorpe						2	1	1	0
AJ Stewart						1	0	8	0

ENGLAND	1st innings		2nd innings	
MA Atherton*	c Murray b Ambrose	135		
AJ Stewart	c Ambrose b K Benj'n	24		
MR Ramp'sh	lbw b KCG Benjamin	19		
RA Smith	lbw b KCG Benjamin	175		
GA Hick	b KCG Benjamin	20		
GP Thorpe	c Adams b Chanderpaul	9		
RC Russell+	c Murray b K Benj'n	62		
CC Lewis	not out	75		
AR Caddick	c W K Benj'n b Adams	22		
ARC Fraser	b Adams	0		
PCR Tufnell	lbw b WKM Benjamin	0		
Extras	(9b, 20lb, 0w, 23nb)	52		
	206.1 overs			
Total		**593**		

1st innings FoW: 40, 70, 373, 393, 401, 417, 535, 585, 589, 593

CEL Ambrose	40	18	66	1
CA Walsh	40	9	123	0
WKM Benjamin	41.1	15	93	2
KCG Benjamin	37	7	110	4
S Chanderpaul	24	1	94	1
JC Adams	22	4	74	2
KLT Arthurton	2	1	4	0

New Zealand

No. 702:	1st Test
VENUE:	Trent Bridge
DATE:	2nd-6th June 1994
TOSS WON BY:	New Zealand
RESULT:	Eng won by an innings and 90 runs

NEW ZEALAND 1st innings

Batsman	Dismissal	Runs	2nd innings	Runs
BA Young	c Hick b De Freitas	15	c Rhodes b Fraser	53
BR Hartland	c Hick b De Freitas	6	lbw b De Freitas	22
KR Rutherford*	lbw b De Freitas	25	c Atherton b Such	14
MD Crowe	c Rhodes b White	8	lbw b De Freitas	28
SP Fleming	c White b De Freitas	54	c White b Hick	11
SA Thomson	c Hick b Fraser	14	c White b Such	6
AC Parore+	c Rhodes b Malcolm	38	c Rhodes b De Freitas	42
GR Larsen	c Fraser b Such	8	c Stewart b De Freitas	2
MN Hart	c Hick b Fraser	36	lbw b Fraser	22
DJ Nash	c Rhodes b Malcolm	19	c Rhodes b De Freitas	5
HT Davis	not out	0	not out	0
Extras	(0b, 6lb, 0w, 14nb)	20	(0b, 1lb, 0w, 20nb)	21
Total	93.4 overs	**251**	106.3 overs	**226**

1st innings FoW: 13, 37, 66, 78, 108, 168, 188, 194, 249, 251

Bowler	O	M	R	W	O	M	R	W
DE Malcolm	17.4	5	45	2	10	2	39	0
ARC Fraser	21	10	40	2	23	8	53	2
PAJ De Freitas	23	4	94	4	22.3	4	71	5
PM Such	19	7	28	1	34	12	50	2
C White	13	3	38	1	3	3	0	0
GA Hick					14	6	12	1

ENGLAND 1st innings

Batsman	Dismissal	Runs	2nd innings
MA Atherton*	c Parore b Larsen	101	
AJ Stewart	c Larsen b Davis	8	
GA Gooch	c Crowe b Thomson	210	
GA Hick	b Nash	18	
RA Smith	run out	78	
C White	c Larsen b Hart	19	
SJ Rhodes+	c Thomson b Nash	49	
PAJ De Freitas	not out	51	
ARC Fraser	c Fleming b Larsen	8	
PM Such			
DE Malcolm			
Extras	(0b, 9lb, 6w, 10nb)	25	
Total	174.4 overs	**567**	

1st innings FoW: 16, 279, 314, 375, 414, 482, 528, 567
2nd innings FoW: 59, 95, 95, 122, 141, 141, 147, 201, 224, 226

Bowler	O	M	R	W
HT Davis	21	0	93	1
DJ Nash	36	5	153	2
GR Larsen	44.4	11	116	2
MN Hart	35	7	123	1
SA Thomson	38	6	73	1

New Zealand

No. 703:	2nd Test
VENUE:	Lord's
DATE:	16th-20th June 1994
TOSS WON BY:	New Zealand
RESULT:	Match drawn

NEW ZEALAND 1st innings

Batsman	Dismissal	Runs	2nd innings	Runs
BA Young	lbw b Fraser	0	c Hick b Such	94
BA Pocock	c Smith b Such	10	lbw b De Freitas	2
KR Rutherford*	c Stewart b De Freitas	37	lbw b De Freitas	0
MD Crowe	c Smith b De Freitas	142	b De Freitas	9
SP Fleming	lbw b Fraser	41	lbw b Taylor	39
SA Thomson	run out	69	not out	38
AC Parore+	c Rhodes b Taylor	40	not out	15
MN Hart	b Such	25		
DJ Nash	b White	56		
C Pringle	c Hick b De Freitas	14		
MB Owens	not out	2		
Extras	(3b, 15lb, 1w, 21nb)	40	(0b, 4lb, 0w, 10nb)	14
Total	149.1 overs	**476**	68 overs	**211**

1st innings FoW: 0, 39, 67, 138, 318, 350, 391, 397, 434, 476
2nd innings FoW: 9, 9, 29, 144, 170

Bowler	O	M	R	W	O	M	R	W
ARC Fraser	36	9	102	2	15	0	50	0
PAJ De Freitas	35	8	102	3	16	0	63	3
JP Taylor	20	4	64	1	6	2	18	1
PM Such	30	8	84	2	25	5	55	1
C White	21.1	4	84	1	4	1	21	0
GA Gooch	5	1	13	0				
GA Hick	2	0	9	0	2	2	0	0

ENGLAND 1st innings

Batsman	Dismissal	Runs	2nd innings	Runs
MA Atherton*	lbw b Hart	28	c Young b Nash	33
AJ Stewart	c Parore b Nash	45	c Crowe b Nash	119
GA Gooch	lbw b Nash	13	lbw b Nash	0
RA Smith	c & b Nash	6	c Parore b Nash	23
GA Hick	c Young b Pringle	58	lbw b Pringle	37
C White	run out	51	c Thomson b Nash	9
SJ Rhodes+	not out	32	not out	24
PAJ De Freitas	c Parore b Thomson	11	lbw b Owens	3
ARC Fraser	c & b Nash	10	lbw b Hart	2
JP Taylor	c Parore b Nash	0	not out	0
PM Such	c Parore b Nash	4		
Extras	(4b, 12lb, 0w, 7nb)	23	(2b, 1lb, 0w, 1nb)	4
Total	121 overs	**281**	108 overs	**254**

1st innings FoW: 65, 95, 95, 101, 193, 225, 241, 265, 271, 281
2nd innings FoW: 60, 60, 136, 210, 217, 240, 244, 250

Bowler	O	M	R	W	O	M	R	W
MB Owens	7	0	34	0	10	3	35	1
DJ Nash	25	6	76	6	29	8	93	5
C Pringle	23	5	65	1	16	5	41	1
MN Hart	44	21	50	1	41	23	55	1
SA Thomson	22	8	40	1	12	4	27	0

No. 704: 3rd Test
VENUE: Old Trafford
DATE: 30th June to 5th July 1994
TOSS WON BY: England
RESULT: Match drawn

No. 705: 1st Test
VENUE: Lord's
DATE: 21st-24th July 1994
TOSS WON BY: South Africa
RESULT: South Africa won by 356 runs

ENGLAND 1st innings / 2nd innings

Batsman	1st innings		2nd innings
MA Atherton*	lbw b Nash	111	
AJ Stewart	c Pringle b Nash	24	
GA Gooch	c Young b Nash	0	
RA Smith	b Owens	13	
GA Hick	c Nash b Owens	20	
C White	c Hart b Owens	42	
SJ Rhodes+	c Parore b Nash	12	
PAJ De Freitas	b Owens	69	
D Gough	c (sub) b Pringle	65	
ARC Fraser	c Thomson b Hart	10	
PM Such	not out	5	
Extras	(0b, 8lb, 1w, 2nb)	11	
	146.3 overs		
Total		**382**	

1st innings FoW: 37, 37, 68, 104, 203, 224, 235, 365, 372, 382

Bowler	O	M	R	W
DJ Nash	39	9	107	4
MB Owens	34	12	99	4
C Pringle	39	12	95	1
MN Hart	27.3	9	50	1
SA Thomson	7	1	23	0

NEW ZEALAND 1st innings / 2nd innings

Batsman	1st innings		2nd innings	
BA Young	c Rhodes b De Freitas	25	lbw b De Freitas	8
MJ Greatbatch	c Hick b Gough	0	c De Freitas b White	21
KR Rutherford	c Gooch b De Freitas	7	c Rhodes b Gough	13
SP Fleming	c Rhodes b Gough	14	c Hick b Fraser	11
MD Crowe*	c Gooch b White	70	c Hick b De Freitas	115
MN Hart	c Atherton b Gough	0	c Smith b Gough	21
SA Thomson	c Rhodes b De Freitas	9	c Gooch b De Freitas	71
AC Parore+	c Rhodes b White	7	not out	16
DJ Nash	not out	8	not out	6
C Pringle	b White	0		
MB Owens	c Stewart b Gough	4		
Extras	(0b, 0lb, 0w, 7nb)	7	(8b, 13lb, 0w, 5nb)	26
	57.3 overs		106.2 overs	
Total		**151**		**308**

1st innings FoW: 2, 12, 47, 82, 93, 113, 125, 140, 140, 151
2nd innings FoW: 8, 34, 48, 73, 132, 273, 287

Bowler	O	M	R	W	O	M	R	W
ARC Fraser	12	3	17	0	19	7	34	1
D Gough	16.3	2	47	4	31.2	5	105	2
PAJ De Freitas	17	2	61	3	30	6	60	3
PM Such	5	2	8	0	10	2	39	0
C White	7	1	18	3	14	3	36	1
GA Gooch					2	0	13	0

SOUTH AFRICA 1st innings / 2nd innings

Batsman	1st innings		2nd innings	
AC Hudson	c Gooch b Gough	6	lbw b Fraser	3
G Kirsten	c De Freitas b Hick	72	st Rhodes b Hick	44
WJ Cronje	c Crawley b Fraser	7	c Fraser b Gough	32
KC Wessels*	c Rhodes b Gough	105	c Crawley b Salisbury	28
PN Kirsten	c Rhodes b Gough	8	b Gough	42
JN Rhodes	b White	32	b Gough	32
BM McMillan	c Rhodes b Fraser	29	not out	39
DJ Richardson+	lbw b Gough	26	c Rhodes b Fraser	3
CR Matthews	b White	41	b Gough	25
PS de Villiers	c Rhodes b Fraser	8		
AA Donald	not out	5		
Extras	(0b, 9lb, 0w, 9nb)	18	(8b, 10lb, 0w, 12nb)	30
	118.5 overs		102.3 overs	
Total		**357**		**278**

1st innings FoW: 18, 35, 141, 164, 239, 241, 281, 334, 348, 357
2nd innings FoW: 14, 73, 101, 141, 208, 209, 220, 278

Bowler	O	M	R	W	O	M	R	W
PAJ De Freitas	18	5	67	0	14	3	43	0
D Gough	28	6	76	4	19.3	5	46	4
IDK Salisbury	25	2	68	0	19	4	53	1
ARC Fraser	24.5	7	72	3	23	5	62	2
GA Hick	10	5	22	1	24	14	38	1
C White	13	2	43	2	3	0	18	0

ENGLAND 1st innings / 2nd innings

Batsman	1st innings		2nd innings	
MA Atherton*	c Wessels b Donald	20	c McMillan b de Villiers	8
AJ Stewart	b Donald	12	c Richardson b Matthews	27
JP Crawley	c Hudson b de Villiers	9	c Hudson b McMillan	7
GA Hick	c Richardson b de Villiers	38	lbw b McMillan	11
GA Gooch	lbw b de Villiers	20	lbw b Donald	28
C White	c Richardson b Donald	10	c Wessels b Matthews	0
SJ Rhodes+	b McMillan	15	not out	14
IDK Salisbury	not out	6	c G Kirsten b Matthews	1
PAJ De Freitas	c Wessels b Donald	20	retired hurt	1
D Gough	c & b Donald	12	lbw b Donald	0
ARC Fraser	run out	3	lbw b McMillan	1
Extras	(2b, 5lb, 0w, 8nb)	15	(1b, 1lb, 0w, 0nb)	2
	61.3 overs		45.5 overs	
Total		**180**		**99**

1st innings FoW: 19, 41, 68, 107, 119, 136, 141, 161, 176, 180
2nd innings FoW: 16, 29, 45, 74, 74, 82, 85, 88, 99

Bowler	O	M	R	W	O	M	R	W
AA Donald	19.3	5	74	5	12	5	29	2
PS de Villiers	16	5	28	3	12	4	26	1
CR Matthews	16	6	46	0	14	6	25	3
BM McMillan	10	1	25	1	6.5	2	16	3
WJ Cronje					1	0	1	0

South Africa | South Africa

ENGLAND 1st innings / 2nd innings

Batsman	1st innings		2nd innings	
GA Gooch	c McMillan b de Villiers	23	c Richardson b Matthews	27
MA Atherton*	c & b McMillan	99	c (sub) b de Villiers	17
GA Hick	c McMillan b de Villiers	25	lbw b McMillan	110
GP Thorpe	c Rhodes b McMillan	72	run out	73
AJ Stewart	b McMillan	89	not out	36
JP Crawley	lbw b Matthews	38	c Cronje b McMillan	0
SJ Rhodes+	not out	65		
PAJ De Freitas	b Donald	15		
D Gough	run out	27		
ARC Fraser	c Cronje b de Villiers	6		
PCR Tufnell				
Extras	(1b, 5lb, 0w, 12nb)	18	(0b, 1lb, 0w, 3nb)	4
Total	160.3 overs	**477**	78.3 overs	**267**

1st innings FoW: 34, 84, 226, 235, 350, 367, 394, 447, 477
2nd innings FoW: 39, 57, 190, 267, 267

Bowler	O	M	R	W	O	M	R	W
AA Donald	29	2	135	1				
PS de Villiers	39.3	12	108	3	25	3	98	1
CR Matthews	39	7	97	1	24	8	53	1
BM McMillan	37	12	93	3	15.3	0	66	2
WJ Cronje	16	3	38	0	12	3	39	0
G Kirsten					2	1	10	0

SOUTH AFRICA 1st innings / 2nd innings

Batsman	1st innings		2nd innings	
AC Hudson	c Atherton b Gough	9	c & b Tufnell	12
G Kirsten	c Rhodes b De Freitas	7	c Rhodes b De Freitas	65
DJ Richardson+	b Fraser	48		
WJ Cronje	b De Freitas	0	not out	13
KC Wessels*	c Crawley b Fraser	25	b Tufnell	7
PN Kirsten	c Stewart b De Freitas	104	not out	8
JN Rhodes	c Rhodes b Gough	46		
BM McMillan	b Tufnell	78		
CR Matthews	not out	62		
PS de Villiers	st Rhodes b Tufnell	13		
AA Donald	c Crawley b De Freitas	27		
Extras	(8b, 7lb, 0w, 13nb)	28	(2b, 2lb, 0w, 7nb)	11
Total	133.1 overs	**447**	60 overs	**116**

1st innings FoW: 13, 31, 31, 91, 105, 199, 314, 391, 410, 447
2nd innings FoW: 43, 93, 104

Bowler	O	M	R	W	O	M	R	W
D Gough	37	3	153	2	10	5	15	0
PAJ De Freitas	29.1	6	89	4	14	3	41	1
ARC Fraser	31	5	92	2	7	2	19	0
PCR Tufnell	32	13	81	2	23	8	31	2
GA Gooch	3	0	9	0				
GA Hick	1	0	8	0	6	3	6	0

SOUTH AFRICA 1st innings / 2nd innings

Batsman	1st innings		2nd innings	
G Kirsten	c Rhodes b De Freitas	2	c & b Malcolm	0
PN Kirsten	b Malcolm	16	c De Freitas b Malcolm	1
WJ Cronje	lbw b Benjamin	38	b Malcolm	0
KC Wessels*	lbw b Benjamin	45	c Rhodes b Malcolm	28
DJ Cullinan	c Rhodes b De Freitas	7	c Thorpe b Gough	94
JN Rhodes	retired hurt	8	c Thorpe b Malcolm	25
BM McMillan	c Hick b De Freitas	93	lbw b Malcolm	3
DJ Richardson+	c Rhodes b Benjamin	58	c Rhodes b Malcolm	0
CR Matthews	c Hick b Benjamin	0	c Rhodes b Malcolm	10
PS de Villiers	c Stewart b De Freitas	14	not out	0
AA Donald	not out	14	b Malcolm	0
Extras	(8b, 10lb, 1w, 18nb)	37	(0b, 5lb, 0w, 9nb)	14
Total	92.2 overs	**332**	50.3 overs	**175**

1st innings FoW: 2, 43, 73, 85, 136, 260, 266, 301, 332
2nd innings FoW: 0, 1, 1, 73, 137, 143, 143, 175, 175, 175

Bowler	O	M	R	W	O	M	R	W
PAJ De Freitas	26.2	5	93	4	12	3	25	0
DE Malcolm	25	5	81	1	16.3	2	57	9
D Gough	19	1	85	0	9	1	39	1
JE Benjamin	17	2	42	4	11	1	38	0
GA Hick	5	1	13	0	2	0	11	0

ENGLAND 1st innings / 2nd innings

Batsman	1st innings		2nd innings	
GA Gooch	c Richardson b Donald	8	b Matthews	33
MA Atherton*	lbw b de Villiers	0	c Richardson b Donald	63
GA Hick	b Donald	39	not out	81
GP Thorpe	b Matthews	79	not out	15
AJ Stewart	b de Villiers	62		
JP Crawley	c Richardson b Donald	5		
SJ Rhodes+	lbw b de Villiers	11		
PAJ De Freitas	run out	37		
D Gough	not out	42		
JE Benjamin	lbw b de Villiers	0		
DE Malcolm	c (sub) b Matthews	4		
Extras	(1b, 0lb, 1w, 15nb)	17	(0b, 6lb, 0w, 7nb)	13
Total	77 overs	**304**	35.3 overs	**205**

1st innings FoW: 1, 33, 93, 145, 165, 219, 222, 292, 293, 304
2nd innings FoW: 56, 180

Bowler	O	M	R	W	O	M	R	W
AA Donald	17	2	76	3	12	1	96	1
PS de Villiers	19	3	62	4	12	0	66	0
CR Matthews	21	4	82	2	11.3	4	37	1
BM McMillan	12	1	67	0				
WJ Cronje	8	3	16	0				

No. 708: 1st Test
VENUE: Brisbane (Gabba)
DATE: 25th-29th November 1994
TOSS WON BY: Australia
RESULT: Australia won by 184 runs

No. 709: 2nd Test
VENUE: Melbourne (MCG)
DATE: 24th-29th December 1994
TOSS WON BY: England
RESULT: Australia won by 295 runs

AUSTRALIA 1st innings / 2nd innings

Batsman	1st innings		2nd innings	
MJ Slater	c Gatting b Gooch	176	lbw b Gough	45
MA Taylor*	run out	59	c Stewart b Tufnell	58
DC Boon	b Gough	3	b Tufnell	28
ME Waugh	c Stewart b Gough	140	b Tufnell	15
MG Bevan	c Hick b Gough	7	c Rhodes b De Freitas	21
SK Warne	c Rhodes b Gough	2	c (sub) b Tufnell	7
SR Waugh	c Hick b Gough	19	not out	45
IA Healy+	c Hick b De Freitas	7	c (sub) b De Freitas	0
C McDermott	c Gough b McCague	2	c Rhodes b Gough	6
TBA May	not out	3	not out	9
GD McGrath	c Gough b McCague	0		
Extras	(5b, 2lb, 0w, 1nb)	8	(2b, 9lb, 2w, 1nb)	14
	120.2 overs		88 overs	
Total		**426**		**248**

1st innings FoW: 99, 126, 308, 326, 352, 379, 407, 419, 425, 426
2nd innings FoW: 109, 117, 139, 174, 183, 190, 191, 201

Bowler	O	M	R	W	O	M	R	W
PAJ De Freitas	31	8	102	2	22	1	74	2
MJ McCague	19.2	4	96	2				
D Gough	32	7	107	4	23	3	78	2
PCR Tufnell	25	3	72	0	38	10	79	4
GA Hick	4	0	22	0	2	1	1	0
GA Gooch	9	2	20	1	3	2	5	0

ENGLAND 1st innings / 2nd innings

Batsman	1st innings		2nd innings	
MA Atherton*	c Healy b McDermott	54	lbw b Warne	23
AJ Stewart	c Healy b McDermott	16	b Warne	33
GA Hick	c Healy b McDermott	3	c Healy b Warne	80
GP Thorpe	c & b Warne	28	b Warne	67
GA Gooch	c Healy b May	20	c Healy b Warne	56
MW Gatting	lbw b McDermott	10	c Healy b McDermott	13
MJ McCague	b McDermott	1	c Healy b McDermott	2
SJ Rhodes+	lbw b McDermott	4	b Warne	11
PAJ De Freitas	c Healy b Warne	7	c ME Waugh b Warne	10
D Gough	not out	17	lbw b Warne	0
PCR Tufnell	c Taylor b Warne	0	not out	2
Extras	(0b, 1lb, 0w, 6nb)	7	(9b, 5lb, 0w, 12nb)	26
	67.2 overs		137.2 overs	
Total		**167**		**323**

1st innings FoW: 22, 35, 82, 105, 131, 133, 140, 147, 151, 167
2nd innings FoW: 50, 59, 219, 220, 250, 280, 309, 310, 310, 323

Bowler	O	M	R	W	O	M	R	W
CJ McDermott	19	3	53	6	23	4	90	2
GD McGrath	10	2	40	0	19	4	61	0
TBA May	17	3	34	1	35	16	59	0
SK Warne	21.2	7	39	3	50.2	22	71	8
ME Waugh					7	1	17	0
MG Bevan					3	0	11	0

AUSTRALIA 1st innings / 2nd innings

Batsman	1st innings		2nd innings	
MJ Slater	run out	3	st Rhodes b Tufnell	44
MA Taylor*	lbw b De Freitas	9	lbw b Gough	19
DC Boon	c Hick b Tufnell	41	lbw b De Freitas	131
ME Waugh	c Thorpe b De Freitas	71	c & b Gough	29
MG Bevan	c Atherton b Gough	3	c (sub) b Tufnell	35
SR Waugh	not out	94	not out	26
IA Healy+	c Rhodes b Tufnell	17	c Thorpe b Tufnell	17
SK Warne	c Hick b Gough	6	c De Freitas b Gough	0
TBA May	lbw b Gough	9	not out	2
CJ McDermott	b Gough	0	(1b, 9lb, 1w, 6nb)	17
DW Fleming	c Hick b Malcolm	16	124 overs	
Extras	(0b, 7lb, 0w, 3nb)	10		
	107.3 overs			
Total		**279**		**320**

1st innings FoW: 10, 39, 91, 100, 171, 208, 220, 242, 242, 279
2nd innings FoW: 61, 81, 157, 269, 275, 316, 317

Bowler	O	M	R	W	O	M	R	W
DE Malcolm	28.3	4	78	1	22	3	86	0
PAJ De Freitas	23	4	66	2	26	2	70	1
D Gough	26	9	60	4	25	6	59	3
PCR Tufnell	28	7	59	2	48	8	90	3
GA Hick	2	0	9	0	3	2	5	0

ENGLAND 1st innings / 2nd innings

Batsman	1st innings		2nd innings	
MA Atherton*	lbw b Warne	44	c Healy b McDermott	25
AJ Stewart	c & b Warne	16	not out	8
GA Hick	c Healy b McDermott	23	b Fleming	2
GP Thorpe	c ME Waugh b Warne	51	c Healy b McDermott	9
GA Gooch	c & b McDermott	15	c Healy b Fleming	2
MW Gatting	c SR Waugh b Warne	9	c Taylor b McDermott	25
D Gough	c Healy b McDermott	20	c Healy b Warne	0
SJ Rhodes+	c ME Waugh b Warne	0	c M Waugh b McDer'tt	16
PAJ De Freitas	st Healy b Warne	14	lbw b Warne	0
DE Malcolm	not out	11	c Boon b Warne	0
PCR Tufnell	run out	0	c Healy b McDermott	0
Extras	(0b, 7lb, 0w, 2nb)	9	(0b, 2lb, 0w, 3nb)	5
	83.4 overs		42.5 overs	
Total		**212**		**92**

1st innings FoW: 40, 119, 124, 140, 148, 151, 185, 189, 207, 212
2nd innings FoW: 3, 10, 23, 43, 81, 88, 91, 91, 91, 92

Bowler	O	M	R	W	O	M	R	W
CJ McDermott	24	6	72	3	16.5	5	42	5
DW Fleming	11	5	30	0	9	1	24	2
ME Waugh	3	1	11	0				
SK Warne	27.4	8	64	6	13	6	16	3
TBA May	18	5	28	0	4	1	8	0

Australia | Australia

No. 710: 3rd Test		No. 711: 4th Test
VENUE: Sydney (SCG)		VENUE: Adelaide
DATE: 1st-5th January 1995		DATE: 26th-30th January 1995
TOSS WON BY: England		TOSS WON BY: England
RESULT: Match drawn		RESULT: England won by 106 runs

Left: 3rd Test — Sydney

ENGLAND 1st innings

Batsman		Runs	2nd innings	Runs
GA Gooch	c Healy b Fleming	1	lbw b Fleming	29
MA Atherton*	b McDermott	88	c Taylor b Fleming	67
GA Hick	b McDermott	2	not out	98
GP Thorpe	lbw b McDermott	10	not out	47
JP Crawley	c ME Waugh b Fleming	72		
MW Gatting	c Healy b McDermott	0		
ARC Fraser	c Healy b Fleming	27		
SJ Rhodes+	run out	1		
D Gough	c Fleming b McDermott	51		
DE Malcolm	b Warne	29		
PCR Tufnell	not out	4		
Extras	(8b, 7lb, 0w, 9nb)	24	(0b, 6lb, 1w, 7nb)	14
Total	119.2 overs	**309**	72 overs	**255**

1st innings FoW: 1, 10, 20, 194 , 194, 196, 197, 255, 295, 309
2nd innings FoW: 54, 158

DW Fleming	26.2	12	52	3	20	3	66	2
SK Warne	36	10	88	1	16	2	48	0
TBA May	17	4	35	0	10	1	55	0
ME Waugh	6	1	10	0	2	1	4	0
MG Bevan	4	1	8	0				

AUSTRALIA 1st innings

Batsman		Runs	2nd innings	Runs
MJ Slater	b Malcolm	11	c Tufnell b Fraser	103
MA Taylor*	c & b Gough	49	b Malcolm	113
DC Boon	b Gough	3	c Hick b Gough	17
ME Waugh	c Rhodes b Malcolm	3	lbw b Fraser	25
MG Bevan	c Thorpe b Fraser	8	c Rhodes b Fraser	7
SR Waugh	b Gough	1	c Rhodes b Fraser	0
IA Healy+	c Hick b Gough	10	c Rhodes b Fraser	5
SK Warne	c Gatting b Fraser	1	not out	36
TBA May	c Hick b Gough	0	not out	10
C McDermott	not out	21		
DW Fleming	b Gough	0		
Extras	(6b, 1lb, 0w, 3nb)	10	(12b, 3lb, 1w, 12nb)	28
Total	42.5 overs	**116**	121.4 overs	**344**

1st innings FoW: 12, 15, 18, 38, 39, 57, 62, 65, 116, 116
2nd innings FoW: 208, 239, 265, 282, 286, 289, 292

DE Malcolm	13	4	34	2	21	4	75	1
D Gough	18.5	4	49	6	28	4	72	1
ARC Fraser	11	1	26	2	25	3	73	5
PCR Tufnell					35.4	9	61	0
GA Hick					5	0	21	0
GA Gooch					7	1	27	0

Right: 4th Test — Adelaide

ENGLAND 1st innings

Batsman		Runs	2nd innings	Runs
GA Gooch	c ME Waugh b Fleming	47	c Healy b McDermott	34
MA Atherton*	c Boon b Fleming	80	lbw b ME Waugh	14
MW Gatting	c SR Waugh b McIntyre	117	b ME Waugh	0
GP Thorpe	c Taylor b Warne	26	c Warne b McDermott	83
JP Crawley	b Warne	28	c & b ME Waugh	71
SJ Rhodes+	c Taylor b McDermott	6	c Fleming b Warne	2
CC Lewis	c Blewett b McDermott	10	b Fleming	7
PAJ De Freitas	c Blewett b McIntyre	21	c Healy b ME Waugh	88
ARC Fraser	run out	7	c McDermott b M Waugh	5
DE Malcolm	b McDermott	0	not out	10
PCR Tufnell	not out	0	lbw b Warne	0
Extras	(2b, 5lb, 2w, 2nb)	11	(6b, 8lb, 0w, 0nb)	14
Total	141.3 overs	**353**	94.5 overs	**328**

1st innings FoW: 93, 175, 211, 286, 293, 307, 334, 353, 353, 353
2nd innings FoW: 26, 30, 83, 154, 169, 181, 270, 317, 317, 328

CJ McDermott	41	15	66	3	27	5	96	2
DW Fleming	25	6	65	2	11	3	37	1
GS Blewett	16	4	59	0	4	0	23	0
SK Warne	31	9	72	2	30.5	9	82	2
PE McIntyre	19.3	3	51	2	8	0	36	0
ME Waugh	9	1	33	0	14	4	40	5

AUSTRALIA 1st innings

Batsman		Runs	2nd innings	Runs
MJ Slater	c Atherton b De Freitas	67	c Tufnell b Malcolm	5
MA Taylor*	lbw b Lewis	90	c Thorpe b Malcolm	13
DC Boon	c Rhodes b De Freitas	4	c Rhodes b Fraser	4
ME Waugh	c Rhodes b Fraser	39	c Gatting b Tufnell	24
SR Waugh	c Atherton b Lewis	19	b Malcolm	0
GS Blewett	not out	102	c Rhodes b Lewis	12
IA Healy+	c Rhodes b Malcolm	74	not out	51
SK Warne	c Thorpe b Fraser	7	lbw b Lewis	2
DW Fleming	c Rhodes b Malcolm	0	c Rhodes b Lewis	0
PE McIntyre	b Malcolm	0	lbw b Lewis	24
C McDermott	c Crawley b Fraser	5	lbw b Malcolm	0
Extras	(2b, 7lb, 0w, 7nb)	16	(3b, 5lb, 0w, 13nb)	21
Total	121.5 overs	**419**	61.1 overs	**156**

1st innings FoW: 128, 130, 202, 207, 232, 396, 405, 406, 414, 419
2nd innings FoW: 17, 22, 22, 23, 64, 75, 83, 83, 152, 156

DE Malcolm	26	5	78	3	16.1	3	39	4
ARC Fraser	28.5	6	95	3	12	1	37	1
PCR Tufnell	24	5	64	0	9	3	17	1
PAJ De Freitas	20	3	70	2	11	3	31	0
CC Lewis	18	1	81	2	13	4	24	4
GA Gooch	5	0	22	0				

No. 712: 5th Test	No. 713: 1st Test
VENUE: Perth (WACA)	VENUE: Headingley
DATE: 3rd-7th February 1995	DATE: 8th-11th June 1995
TOSS WON BY: Australia	TOSS WON BY: West Indies
RESULT: Australia won by 329 runs	RESULT: West Indies won by 9 wickets

AUSTRALIA 1st innings / 2nd innings

Batsman	1st innings		2nd innings	
MJ Slater	c Lewis b De Freitas	124	c Atherton b Fraser	45
MA Taylor*	c Rhodes b Lewis	9	b Fraser	52
DC Boon	c Ramprakash b Lewis	1	c Rhodes b Malcolm	18
ME Waugh	c De Freitas b Lewis	88	c Rhodes b De Freitas	1
SR Waugh	not out	99	c Ramprakash b Lewis	80
GS Blewett	c Rhodes b Fraser	20	c Malcolm b Lewis	115
IA Healy+	c Lewis b De Freitas	12	not out	11
SK Warne	c Rhodes b De Freitas	1	c Lewis b Malcolm	6
J Angel	run out	11	run out	0
GD McGrath	run out	0		
CJ McDermott	run out	6		
Extras	(14b, 4lb, 4w, 9nb)	31	(1b, 9lb, 0w, 7nb)	17
Total	135.5 overs	402	90.3 overs	345

1st innings FoW: 47, 55, 238, 247, 287, 320, 328, 386, 388, 402
2nd innings FoW: 75, 79, 102, 115, 123, 326, 333, 345

Bowler	O	M	R	W		O	M	R	W
DE Malcolm	31	6	93	0		23.3	3	105	2
PAJ De Freitas	29	8	91	3		22	10	54	1
ARC Fraser	32	11	84	1		21	3	74	2
CC Lewis	31.5	8	73	3		16	1	71	2
GA Gooch	1	1	0	0					
MR Ramprakash	11	0	43	0		8	1	31	0

ENGLAND 1st innings / 2nd innings

Batsman	1st innings		2nd innings	
GA Gooch	lbw b ME Waugh	37	c & b McDermott	4
MA Atherton*	c Healy b McGrath	4	c Healy b McGrath	8
MW Gatting	b McGrath	0	b McDermott	8
GP Thorpe	st Healy b Warne	123	c Taylor b McGrath	0
JP Crawley	c Warne b ME Waugh	0	c M Waugh b McDermott	0
MR Rampr'sh	b Warne	72	c S Waugh b M Waugh	42
SJ Rhodes+	b Angel	2	not out	39
CC Lewis	c Blewett b McGrath	40	lbw b McDermott	11
PAJ De Freitas	b Angel	0	c Taylor b McDermott	2
ARC Fraser	c Warne b Angel	9	lbw b McGrath	5
DE Malcolm	not out	0	b McDermott	0
Extras	(4b, 1lb, 0w, 3nb)	8	(0b, 1lb, 1w, 4nb)	6
Total	96.3 overs	295	41 overs	123

1st innings FoW: 5, 5, 77, 77, 235, 246, 246, 247, 293, 295
2nd innings FoW: 4, 17, 26, 26, 27, 27, 95, 121, 123, 123

Bowler	O	M	R	W		O	M	R	W
J Angel	22.3	7	65	3		3	0	20	0
GD McGrath	25	6	88	3		13	4	40	3
GS Blewett	4	1	9	0					
ME Waugh	9	2	29	2		3	0	13	1
SK Warne	23	8	58	2		7	3	11	0
CJ McDermott	13	5	41	0		15	4	38	6

ENGLAND 1st innings / 2nd innings

Batsman	1st innings		2nd innings	
RA Smith	c Richardson b Benjamin	16	c Arthurton b Ambrose	6
MA Atherton*	c Murray b Bishop	81	c Murray b Walsh	17
GA Hick	c Campbell b Benjamin	18	c Walsh b Bishop	27
GP Thorpe	lbw b Bishop	20	c Campbell b Walsh	61
AJ Stewart+	c Hooper b Bishop	2	c Murray b Benjamin	4
MR Rampr'sh	c Campbell b Bishop	4	b Walsh	18
PAJ De Freitas	c Murray b Benjamin	23	c (sub) b Walsh	1
D Gough	c Ambrose b Bishop	0	c (sub) b Ambrose	29
PJ Martin	c Murray b Ambrose	2	c Lara b Bishop	19
RK Illingworth	not out	17	not out	10
DE Malcolm	b Benjamin	0	b Ambrose	5
Extras	(1b, 0lb, 0w, 15nb)	16	(1b, 3lb, 0w, 7nb)	11
Total	59.5 overs	199	67.2 overs	208

1st innings FoW: 52, 91, 142, 148, 153, 154, 154, 157, 199, 199
2nd innings FoW: 6, 55, 55, 82, 130, 136, 152, 193, 193, 208

Bowler	O	M	R	W		O	M	R	W
CEL Ambrose	17	4	56	1		20.2	6	44	3
CA Walsh	13	2	50	0		22	4	60	4
IR Bishop	16	2	32	5		19	3	81	2
KCG Benjamin	13.5	2	60	4		6	1	19	1

WEST INDIES 1st innings / 2nd innings

Batsman	1st innings		2nd innings	
CL Hooper	c Thorpe b Malcolm	0	not out	73
SL Campbell	run out	69	c Atherton b Martin	2
BC Lara	c Hick b Illingworth	53	not out	48
JC Adams	c Martin b Hick	58		
KLT Arthurton	c Stewart b De Freitas	42		
RB Rich'son*	lbw b Martin	0		
JR Murray+	c Illingworth b De Freitas	20		
IR Bishop	run out	5		
CEL Ambrose	c Gough b Malcolm	15		
CA Walsh	c Stewart b Gough	4		
KC Benjamin	not out	0		
Extras	(4b, 11lb, 0w, 1nb)	16	(1b, 3lb, 0w, 2nb)	6
Total	90.3 overs	282	19 overs	129

1st innings FoW: 0, 95, 141, 216, 219, 243, 254, 254, 275, 282
2nd innings FoW: 11

Bowler	O	M	R	W		O	M	R	W
DE Malcolm	7.3	0	48	2		4	0	12	0
D Gough	5	1	24	1					
PAJ De Freitas	23	3	82	2		4	0	33	0
PJ Martin	27	9	48	1		8	2	49	1
RK Illingworth	24	9	50	1		3	0	31	0
GA Hick	4	0	15	1					

No. 714: 2nd Test

VENUE: Lord's

DATE: 22nd-26th June 1995

TOSS WON BY: England

RESULT: England won by 72 runs

ENGLAND	1st innings		2nd innings	
MA Atherton*	b Ambrose	21	c Murray b Walsh	9
AJ Stewart+	c Arthurton b Gibson	34	c Murray b Walsh	36
GA Hick	c Lara b Bishop	13	b Bishop	67
GP Thorpe	c Lara b Ambrose	52	c Richardson b Ambrose	42
RA Smith	b Hooper	61	lbw b Ambrose	90
MR Rampr'sh	c Campbell b Hooper	0	c (sub) b Bishop	0
DG Cork	b Walsh	30	c Murray b Bishop	23
D Gough	c Campbell b Gibson	11	b Ambrose	20
PJ Martin	b Walsh	29	c Arthurton b Ambrose	1
RK Illingworth	not out	16	lbw b Walsh	4
ARC Fraser	lbw b Walsh	1	not out	2
Extras	(1b, 10lb, 0w, 4nb)	15	(6b, 27lb, 2w, 7nb)	42
	99.4 overs		99.1 overs	
Total		**283**		**336**

1st innings FoW: 29, 70, 74, 185, 187, 191, 205, 255, 281, 283
2nd innings FoW: 32, 51, 150, 155, 240, 290, 320, 329, 334, 336

CEL Ambrose	26	6	72	2		24	5	70	4
CA Walsh	22.4	6	50	3		28.1	10	91	3
OD Gibson	20	2	81	2		14	1	51	0
IR Bishop	17	4	33	1		22	5	56	3
CL Hooper	14	3	36	2		9	1	31	0
JC Adams						2	0	4	0

WEST INDIES	1st innings		2nd innings	
SL Campbell	c Stewart b Gough	5	c Stewart b Cork	93
CL Hooper	b Martin	40	c Martin b Gough	14
BC Lara	lbw b Fraser	6	c Stewart b Gough	54
JC Adams	lbw b Fraser	54	c Hick b Cork	13
RB Rich'son*	c Stewart b Fraser	49	lbw b Cork	0
KLT Arthurton	c Gough b Fraser	75	c (sub) b Cork	0
JR Murray+	c & b Martin	16	c (sub) b Gough	9
OD Gibson	lbw b Gough	29	lbw b Cork	14
IR Bishop	b Cork	8	not out	10
CEL Ambrose	c Ramprakash b Fraser	12	c Illingworth b Cork	11
CA Walsh	not out	11	c Stewart b Cork	0
Extras	(8b, 11lb, 0w, 0nb)	19	(0b, 5lb, 0w, 0nb)	5
	112 overs		78.3 overs	
Total		**324**		**223**

1st innings FoW: 6, 23, 88, 166 , 169, 197, 246, 272, 305, 324
2nd innings FoW: 15, 99, 124, 130, 138, 177, 198, 201, 223, 223

D Gough	27	2	84	2		20	0	79	3
ARC Fraser	33	13	66	5		25	9	57	0
DG Cork	22	4	72	1		19.3	5	43	7
PJ Martin	23	5	65	2		7	0	30	0
RK Illingworth	7	2	18	0		7	4	9	0

No. 715: 3rd Test

VENUE: Edgbaston

DATE: 6th-8th July 1995

TOSS WON BY: England

RESULT: WI won by an innings and 64 runs

ENGLAND	1st innings		2nd innings	
MA Atherton*	c Murray b Ambrose	0	b Walsh	4
AJ Stewart+	lbw b Benjamin	37	absent hurt	0
GA Hick	c Richardson b Walsh	3	c Hooper b Bishop	3
GP Thorpe	c Campbell b Ambrose	30	c Murray b Bishop	0
RA Smith	c Arthurton b Bishop	46	b Bishop	41
JER Gallian	b Benjamin	7	c Murray b Walsh	0
DG Cork	lbw b Walsh	4	c (sub) b Walsh	16
D Gough	c Arthurton b Bishop	1	c Campbell b Walsh	12
PJ Martin	c (sub) b Walsh	1	lbw b Walsh	0
RK Illingworth	b Bishop	0	c Hooper b Bishop	0
ARC Fraser	not out	0	not out	1
Extras	(0b, 4lb, 4w, 10nb)	18	(0b, 0lb, 0w, 12nb)	12
	44.2 overs		30 overs	
Total		**147**		**89**

1st innings FoW: 4, 9, 53, 84, 100, 109, 124, 141, 147, 147
2nd innings FoW: 17, 20, 26, 61, 62, 63, 88, 88, 89

CEL Ambrose	7.5	1	26	2					
CA Walsh	17.1	4	54	3		15	2	45	5
IR Bishop	6.2	0	18	3		13	3	29	4
KCG Benjamin	13	4	45	2		2	0	15	0

WEST INDIES	1st innings		2nd innings
CL Hooper	c Stewart b Cork	40	
SL Campbell	b Cork	79	
BC Lara	lbw b Cork	21	
JC Adams	lbw b Cork	10	
RB Rich'son*	b Fraser	69	
KLT Arthurton	lbw b Fraser	8	
JR Murray+	c Stewart b Martin	26	
IR Bishop	c Martin b Illingworth	16	
K Benjamin	run out	11	
CA Walsh	run out	0	
CEL Ambrose	not out	4	
Extras	(5b, 5lb, 0w, 6nb)	16	
	98 overs		
Total		**300**	

1st innings FoW: 73, 105, 141, 156, 171, 198, 260, 292, 292, 300

ARC Fraser	31	7	93	2
D Gough	18	3	68	0
DG Cork	22	5	69	4
PJ Martin	19	5	49	1
RK Illingworth	8	4	11	1

No. 716: 4th Test
VENUE: Old Trafford
DATE: 27th-30th July 1995
TOSS WON BY: West Indies
RESULT: England won by 6 wickets

WEST INDIES

1st innings			2nd innings	
CL Hooper	c Crawley b Cork	16	lbw b Cork	0
SL Campbell	c Russell b Fraser	10	c Russell b Watkinson	44
BC Lara	lbw b Cork	87	c Knight b Fraser	145
JC Adams	c Knight b Fraser	24	c & b Watkinson	1
RB Rich'son*	c Thorpe b Fraser	2	b Cork	22
KLT Arthurton	c Cork b Watkinson	17	run out	17
JR Murray+	c Emburey b Watkinson	13	lbw b Cork	0
IR Bishop	c Russell b Cork	9	c Crawley b Watkinson	9
CEL Ambrose	not out	7	not out	23
KCG Benjamin	b Cork	14	c Knight b Fraser	15
CA Walsh	c Knight b Fraser	11	b Cork	16
Extras	(0b, 1lb, 0w, 5nb)	6	(5b, 9lb, 0w, 8nb)	22
	60.2 overs		91.5 overs	
Total		**216**		**314**

1st innings FoW: 21, 35, 86, 94, 150, 166, 184, 185, 205, 216
2nd innings FoW: 36, 93, 97, 161, 161, 161, 191, 234, 283, 314

ARC Fraser	16.2	5	45	4		19	5	53	2	
DG Cork	20	1	86	4		23.5	2	111	4	
C White	5	0	23	0		6	0	23	0	
JE Emburey	10	2	33	0		20	5	49	0	
M Watkinson	9	2	28	2		23	4	64	3	

ENGLAND

1st innings			2nd innings	
NV Knight	b Walsh	17	c (sub) b Bishop	13
MA Atherton*	c Murray b Ambrose	47	run out	22
JP Crawley	b Walsh	8	not out	15
GP Thorpe	c Murray b Bishop	94	c Ambrose b Benjamin	0
RA Smith	c (sub) b Ambrose	44	retired hurt	1
C White	c Murray b Benjamin	23	c (sub) b Benjamin	1
RC Russell+	run out	35	not out	31
M Watkinson	c (sub) b Walsh	37		
DG Cork	not out	56		
JE Emburey	b Bishop	8		
ARC Fraser	c Adams b Walsh	4		
Extras	(18b, 11lb, 1w, 34nb)	64	(0b, 2lb, 1w, 8nb)	11
	136 overs		35.5 overs	
Total		**437**		**94**

1st innings FoW: 45, 65, 122, 226, 264, 293, 337, 378, 418, 437
2nd innings FoW: 39, 41, 45, 48

CEL Ambrose	24	2	91	2		5	1	16	0	
CA Walsh	38	5	92	4		5	0	17	0	
IR Bishop	29	3	103	2		12	6	18	1	
KCG Benjamin	28	4	83	1		9	1	29	2	
JC Adams	8	1	21	0		2	0	7	0	
KLT Arthurton	9	2	18	0		2.5	1	5	0	

No. 717: 5th Test
VENUE: Trent Bridge
DATE: 10th-14th August 1995
TOSS WON BY: England
RESULT: Match drawn

ENGLAND

1st innings			2nd innings	
NV Knight	lbw b Benjamin	57	c Browne b Benjamin	2
MA Atherton*	run out	113	c Browne b Bishop	43
JP Crawley	c Williams b Benjamin	14	b Walsh	11
GP Thorpe	c Browne b Bishop	19	c Browne b Walsh	76
RK Illingworth	retired hurt	8	not out	14
GA Hick	not out	118	b Benjamin	7
C White	c Browne b Bishop	1	c Campbell b Bishop	1
RC Russell+	c Browne b Bishop	35	c Browne b Benjamin	7
M Watkinson	lbw b Benjamin	24	not out	82
DG Cork	c Browne b Benjamin	31	c Browne b Benjamin	4
ARC Fraser	b Benjamin	0	c Arthurton b Benjamin	4
Extras	(4b, 8lb, 0w, 8nb)	20	(0b, 4lb, 0w, 14nb)	18
	152.4 overs		104 overs	
Total		**440**		**269**

1st innings FoW: 148, 179, 206, 211, 239, 323, 380, 440, 440
2nd innings FoW: 17, 36, 117, 125, 140, 149, 172, 177, 190

CA Walsh	39	5	93	0		30	6	70	2	
IR Bishop	30.1	6	62	3		21	8	50	2	
KCG Benjamin	34.3	7	105	5		25	8	69	5	
R Dhanraj	40	7	137	0		15	1	54	0	
KLT Arthurton	9	0	31	0		13	3	22	0	

WEST INDIES

1st innings			2nd innings	
SC Williams	c Atherton b Illingworth	62		
SL Campbell	c Crawley b Watkinson	47	c Russell b Cork	16
BC Lara	c Russell b Cork	152	c Russell b Fraser	20
RB Rich'son*	c Hick b Illingworth	40		
KLT Arthurton	b Illingworth	13		
R Dhanraj	c Knight b Cork	3		
S Chanderpaul	c Crawley b Watkinson	18	not out	5
CO Browne+	st Russell b Illingworth	34	not out	1
IR Bishop	c Hick b Watkinson	4		
KCG Benjamin	not out	14		
CA Walsh	b Fraser	19		
Extras	(2b, 7lb, 0w, 2nb)	11	(0b, 0lb, 0w, 0nb)	0
	148.3 overs		11 overs	
Total		**417**		**42**

1st innings FoW: 77, 217, 273, 319, 323, 338, 366, 374, 384, 417
2nd innings FoW: 36, 36

ARC Fraser	17.3	6	77	1		6	1	17	1	
DG Cork	36	9	110	2		5	1	25	1	
M Watkinson	35	12	84	3						
RK Illingworth	51	21	96	4						
GA Hick	4	1	11	0						
C White	5	0	30	0						

West Indies | South Africa

No. 718: 6th Test
VENUE: The Oval
DATE: 24th-28th August 1995
TOSS WON BY: England
RESULT: Match drawn

No. 719: 1st Test
VENUE: Centurion (Centurion Park)
DATE: 16th-20th November 1995
TOSS WON BY: South Africa
RESULT: Match drawn

ENGLAND	1st innings		2nd innings	
MA Atherton*	c Williams b Benjamin	36	c Browne b Bishop	95
JER Gallian	c Hooper b Ambrose	0	c Williams b Ambrose	25
JP Crawley	c Richardson b Hooper	50	c Browne b Ambrose	2
GP Thorpe	c Browne b Ambrose	74	c Williams b Walsh	38
GA Hick	c Williams b Benjamin	96	not out	51
AP Wells	c Campbell b Ambrose	0	not out	3
RC Russell+	b Ambrose	91		
M Watkinson	c Browne b Walsh	13		
DG Cork	b Ambrose	33		
ARC Fraser	not out	10		
DE Malcolm	c Lara b Benjamin	10		
Extras	(15b, 11lb, 0w, 15nb)	41	(0b, 4lb, 0w, 5nb)	9
	159 overs		98 overs	
Total		**454**		**223**

1st innings FoW: 9, 60, 149, 192, 192, 336, 372, 419, 443, 454
2nd innings FoW: 60, 64, 132, 212

CEL Ambrose	42	10	96	5		19	8	35	2
CA Walsh	32	6	84	1		28	7	80	1
KCG Benjamin	27	6	81	3					
IR Bishop	35	5	111	0		22	4	56	1
CL Hooper	23	7	56	1		22	11	26	0
S Chanderpaul						6	0	22	0
BC Lara						1	1	0	0

WEST INDIES	1st innings		2nd innings
SC Williams	c Russell b Malcolm	30	
SL Campbell	c Russell b Fraser	89	
KCG Benjamin	c Atherton b Cork	20	
BC Lara	c Fraser b Malcolm	179	
RB Rich'son*	c Hick b Cork	93	
CL Hooper	c Russell b Malcolm	127	
S Chanderpaul	c Gallian b Cork	80	
CO Browne+	not out	27	
IR Bishop	run out	10	
CEL Ambrose	not out	5	
CA Walsh			
Extras	(5b, 20lb, 5w, 2nb)	32	
	163 overs		
Total		**692**	

1st innings FoW: 40, 94, 202, 390, 435, 631, 653, 686

DE Malcolm	39	7	160	3
ARC Fraser	40	6	155	1
M Watkinson	26	3	113	0
DG Cork	36	3	145	3
JER Gallian	12	1	56	0
GA Hick	10	3	38	0

ENGLAND	1st innings		2nd innings
MA Atherton*	c Donald b Pollock	78	
AJ Stewart	c Matthews b Schultz	6	
MR Ramp'sh	c Richardson b Donald	9	
GP Thorpe	c Richardson b Pollock	13	
GA Hick	lbw b Pollock	141	
RA Smith	b McMillan	43	
RC Russell+	not out	50	
DG Cork	c Matthews b McMillan	13	
D Gough	b McMillan	0	
RK Illingworth	b Donald	0	
ARC Fraser	not out	4	
Extras	(0b, 16lb, 1w, 7nb)	24	
	143 overs		
Total		**381**	

1st innings FoW: 14, 36, 64, 206, 290, 320, 350, 358, 359

AA Donald	33	10	92	2
BN Schultz	16	5	47	1
CR Matthews	30	13	63	0
SM Pollock	29	7	98	3
BM McMillan	25	10	50	3
WJ Cronje	8	5	14	0
G Kirsten	2	1	1	0

SOUTH AFRICA	1st innings	2nd innings
AC Hudson		
G Kirsten		
WJ Cronje*		
DJ Cullinan		
JN Rhodes		
BM McMillan		
DJ Richardson+		
CR Matthews		
BN Schultz		
SM Pollock		
AA Donald		

No. 720: 2nd Test
VENUE: Johannesburg (Wanderers)
DATE: 30th November to 4th Dec 1995
TOSS WON BY: England
RESULT: Match drawn

No. 721: 3rd Test
VENUE: Durban (Kingsmead)
DATE: 14th-18th December 1995
TOSS WON BY: South Africa
RESULT: Match drawn

SOUTH AFRICA 1st innings / 2nd innings

Batsman	1st innings		2nd innings	
AC Hudson	c Stewart b Cork	0	c Russell b Fraser	17
G Kirsten	c Russell b Malcolm	110	c Russell b Malcolm	1
WJ Cronje*	c Russell b Cork	35	c Russell b Cork	48
DJ Cullinan	c Russell b Hick	69	c Gough b Cork	61
JN Rhodes	c Russell b Cork	5	c Russell b Fraser	57
BM McMillan	lbw b Cork	35	not out	100
DJ Rich'son+	c Russell b Malcolm	0	c Ramp'sh b Malcolm	23
SM Pollock	c Smith b Malcolm	33	lbw b Cork	5
CE Eksteen	c Russell b Cork	13	c Russell b Cork	2
MW Pringle	not out	10	c Hick b Fraser	2
AA Donald	b Malcolm	0	not out	9
Extras	(1b, 14lb, 2w, 5nb)	22	(5b, 12lb, 1w, 3nb)	21
Total	104 overs	**332**	104.3 overs	**346**

1st innings FoW: 3, 74, 211, 221, 260, 260, 278, 314, 331, 332
2nd innings FoW: 7, 29, 116, 145, 244, 296, 304, 311, 314

Bowler	O	M	R	W	O	M	R	W
DG Cork	32	7	84	5	31.3	6	78	4
DE Malcolm	22	5	62	4	13	2	65	2
ARC Fraser	20	5	69	0	29	6	84	3
D Gough	15	2	64	0	12	2	48	0
GA Hick	15	1	38	1	15	3	35	0
MR Ramprakash					4	0	19	0

SOUTH AFRICA 1st innings / 2nd innings

Batsman	1st innings		2nd innings
G Kirsten	c Hick b Martin	8	
AC Hudson	c Crawley b Illingworth	45	
WJ Cronje*	c Martin b Illingworth	4	
DJ Cullinan	c Smith b Martin	10	
JN Rhodes	lbw b Ilott	38	
JH Kallis	c Russell b Martin	1	
BM McMillan	c Russell b Martin	28	
DJ Rich'son+	c Russell b Ilott	7	
SM Pollock	not out	36	
CR Matthews	lbw b Ilott	0	
AA Donald	b Illingworth	32	
Extras	(0b, 11lb, 0w, 1nb)	12	
Total	100 overs	**225**	

1st innings FoW: 54, 56, 73, 84, 89, 141, 152, 153, 153, 225

Bowler	O	M	R	W
DG Cork	27	12	64	0
MC Ilott	15	3	48	3
PJ Martin	27	9	60	4
RK Illingworth	29	12	37	3
GA Hick	2	0	5	0

ENGLAND 1st innings / 2nd innings

Batsman	1st innings		2nd innings	
MA Atherton*	b Donald	9	not out	185
AJ Stewart	c Kirsten b Pringle	45	b McMillan	38
MR Rampr'sh	b Donald	4	b McMillan	0
GP Thorpe	c Kirsten b Eksteen	34	lbw b Pringle	17
GA Hick	c & b Eksteen	6	c Richardson b Donald	4
RA Smith	c & b McMillan	52	c Pollock b Donald	44
RC Russell+	c Rhodes b Eksteen	12	not out	29
DG Cork	c Cullinan b Pollock	8		
D Gough	c & b Pollock	2		
ARC Fraser	lbw b Pollock	0		
DE Malcolm	not out	0		
Extras	(6b, 1lb, 0w, 21nb)	28	(4b, 7lb, 0w, 23nb)	34
Total	68.3 overs	**200**	165 overs	**351**

1st innings FoW: 10, 45, 109, 116, 125, 147, 178, 191, 200, 200
2nd innings FoW: 75, 75, 134, 145, 232

Bowler	O	M	R	W	O	M	R	W
AA Donald	15	3	49	2	35	9	95	2
MW Pringle	17	4	46	1	23	5	52	1
SM Pollock	15	2	44	3	29	11	65	0
BM McMillan	10.3	0	42	1	21	0	50	2
CE Eksteen	11	5	12	3	52	20	76	0
WJ Cronje					3	1	2	0
G Kirsten					2	2	0	0

ENGLAND 1st innings / 2nd innings

Batsman	1st innings		2nd innings
MA Atherton*	c Hudson b Donald	2	
AJ Stewart	c Hudson b Matthews	41	
GP Thorpe	c Cullinan b Donald	2	
RA Smith	c McMillan b Matthews	34	
GA Hick	not out	31	
RC Russell+	c Rhodes b Matthews	8	
DG Cork	not out	23	
JP Crawley			
RK Illingworth			
PJ Martin			
MC Ilott			
Extras	(0b, 4lb, 0w, 7nb)	11	
Total	48.1 overs	**152**	

1st innings FoW: 2, 13, 83, 93, 109

Bowler	O	M	R	W
AA Donald	12.1	1	57	2
SM Pollock	15	2	39	0
CR Matthews	12	5	31	3
BM McMillan	9	3	21	0

South Africa | South Africa

No. 722: 4th Test	No. 723: 5th Test
VENUE: Port Elizabeth	VENUE: Cape Town
DATE: 26th-30th December 1995	DATE: 2nd-4th January 1996
TOSS WON BY: South Africa	TOSS WON BY: England
RESULT: Match drawn	RESULT: South Africa won by 10 wickets

SOUTH AFRICA 1st innings / 2nd innings

Batsman	1st innings		2nd innings	
AC Hudson	c Russell b Cork	31	c Russell b Martin	4
G Kirsten	c Thorpe b Ilott	51	c Illingworth b Martin	69
WJ Cronje*	c Atherton b Martin	4	c Russell b Martin	6
DJ Cullinan	c Russell b Cork	91	st Russell b Illingworth	14
JN Rhodes	c Smith b Cork	49	lbw b Cork	0
BM McMillan	c Russell b Illingworth	49	c Hick b Cork	1
D Rich'son+	c Russell b Illingworth	84	c Russell b Cork	0
SM Pollock	lbw b Cork	23	c Cork b Illingworth	32
CR Matthews	st Russell b Illingworth	15	c & b Illingworth	5
AA Donald	not out	12	not out	12
PR Adams	run out	0	not out	0
Extras	(0b, 11lb, 0w, 8nb)	19	(8b, 7lb, 1w, 3nb)	19
Total	159.5 overs	**428**	65.3 overs	**162**

1st innings FoW: 57, 85, 89, 207, 251, 326, 377, 408, 426, 428
2nd innings FoW: 6, 18, 60, 64, 69, 69, 135, 145, 160

Bowler	O	M	R	W		O	M	R	W
DG Cork	43.2	12	113	4		26.3	5	63	3
MC Ilott	29.4	7	82	1					
PJ Martin	33	9	79	1		17	8	39	3
RK Illingworth	39.5	8	105	3		22	7	45	3
GA Hick	12	2	32	0					
JER Gallian	2	0	6	0					

ENGLAND 1st innings / 2nd innings

Batsman	1st innings		2nd innings	
MA Atherton*	c Richardson b Adams	72	lbw b Matthews	34
AJ Stewart	c Richardson b Pollock	4	c Hudson b Donald	81
JER Gallian	c Cullinan b Pollock	14	lbw b Adams	28
GP Thorpe	c Rhodes b Adams	27	not out	12
GA Hick	lbw b Donald	62	not out	11
RA Smith	lbw b McMillan	2		
RC Russell+	c Cullinan b Donald	30		
DG Cork	c Richardson b Pollock	1		
RK Illingworth	c Hudson b Donald	28		
PJ Martin	b Adams	4		
MC Ilott	not out	0		
Extras	(0b, 9lb, 1w, 9nb)	19	(9b, 8lb, 1w, 5nb)	23
Total	120.4 overs	**263**	92 overs	**189**

1st innings FoW: 7, 50, 88, 163, 168, 199, 200, 257, 263, 263
2nd innings FoW: 84, 157, 167

Bowler	O	M	R	W		O	M	R	W
AA Donald	25.4	7	49	3		19	4	60	1
SM Pollock	22	8	58	3		10	4	15	0
PR Adams	37	13	75	3		28	13	51	1
CR Matthews	20	7	42	0		19	10	29	1
BM McMillan	15	6	30	1		14	6	16	0
WJ Cronje	1	1	0	0					
G Kirsten						2	1	1	0

ENGLAND 1st innings / 2nd innings

Batsman	1st innings		2nd innings	
MA Atherton*	c Hudson b Donald	0	c Richardson b Donald	10
AJ Stewart	b McMillan	13	c Cullinan b Pollock	7
RA Smith	b Adams	66	c Adams b Donald	1
GP Thorpe	c McMillan b Donald	20	c Richardson b Adams	13
GA Hick	c McMillan b Donald	2	run out	59
RC Russell+	c McMillan b Pollock	9	lbw b Pollock	36
M Watkinson	lbw b Pollock	11	c Hudson b Pollock	2
DG Cork	b Donald	16	lbw b Adams	0
PJ Martin	c Hudson b Donald	0	c Kallis b Pollock	8
ARC Fraser	not out	5	c Adams b Pollock	9
DE Malcolm	b Adams	1	not out	0
Extras	(4b, 1lb, 1w, 4nb)	10	(2b, 5lb, 0w, 5nb)	12
Total	68.1 overs	**153**	62.5 overs	**157**

1st innings FoW: 0, 24, 58, 60, 103, 115, 141, 147, 151, 153
2nd innings FoW: 16, 22, 22, 66, 138, 140, 140, 140, 150, 157

Bowler	O	M	R	W		O	M	R	W
AA Donald	16	5	46	5		18	6	49	2
SM Pollock	14	6	26	2		15.5	4	32	5
BM McMillan	10	2	22	1		7	3	16	0
PR Adams	20.1	5	52	2		22	6	53	2
JH Kallis	4	2	2	0					
WJ Cronje	4	4	0	0					

SOUTH AFRICA 1st innings / 2nd innings

Batsman	1st innings		2nd innings	
G Kirsten	c Atherton b Watkinson	23	not out	41
AC Hudson	lbw b Cork	0	not out	27
WJ Cronje*	c Russell b Cork	12	(0b, 1lb, 0w, 1nb)	2
DJ Cullinan	c Russell b Martin	62	15.4 overs	
JN Rhodes	c Russell b Fraser	16		
BM McMillan	run out	11		
JH Kallis	lbw b Martin	7		
DJ Rich'son+	not out	54		
SM Pollock	c Smith b Watkinson	4		
AA Donald	c Russell b Cork	3		
PR Adams	c Hick b Martin	29		
Extras	(0b, 22lb, 0w, 1nb)	23		
Total	101 overs	**244**		**70**

1st innings FoW: 1, 19, 79, 125, 125, 144, 154, 163, 171, 244

Bowler	O	M	R	W		O	M	R	W
DG Cork	25	6	60	3		4	0	23	0
DE Malcolm	20	6	56	0		2	0	12	0
PJ Martin	24	9	37	3		4	2	3	0
ARC Fraser	17	10	34	1					
M Watkinson	15	3	35	2		4	0	24	0
GA Hick						1.4	0	7	0

No. 724: 1st Test

VENUE:	Edgbaston
DATE:	6th-9th June 1996
TOSS WON BY:	India
RESULT:	England won by 8 wickets

INDIA

1st innings			2nd innings	
V Rathore	c Knight b Cork	20	c Hick b Cork	7
AD Jadeja	c Atherton b Lewis	0	c Russell b Lewis	6
SV Manjrekar	c Atherton b Lewis	23	c Hussain b Cork	9
SR Tendulkar	b Cork	24	c Thorpe b Lewis	122
M Azhar'din*	c Knight b Irani	13	b Mullally	0
NR Mongia+	b Mullally	20	c Russell b Mullally	12
SB Joshi	c Thorpe b Mullally	12	c Knight b Lewis	18
A Kumble	c Knight b Cork	5	run out	15
J Srinath	c Russell b Mullally	52	lbw b Lewis	1
PL Mhambrey	c Thorpe b Cork	28	b Lewis	15
BKV Prasad	not out	0	not out	0
Extras	(3b, 10lb, 0w, 4nb)	17	(4b, 9lb, 0w, 1nb)	14
	69.1 overs		70.4 overs	
Total		**214**		**219**

1st innings FoW: 8, 40, 64, 93, 103, 118, 127, 150, 202, 214
2nd innings FoW: 15, 17, 35, 36, 68, 127, 185, 193, 208, 219

CC Lewis	18	2	44	2	22.4	6	72	5
DG Cork	20.1	5	61	4	19	5	40	2
AD Mullally	22	7	60	3	15	4	43	2
RC Irani	7	4	22	1	2	0	21	0
MM Patel	2	0	14	0	8	3	18	0
GA Hick					4	1	12	0

ENGLAND

1st innings			2nd innings	
NV Knight	c Mongia b Srinath	27	lbw b Prasad	14
MA Atherton*	c Rathore b Mhambrey	33	not out	53
N Hussain	c (sub) b Srinath	128	c Srinath b Prasad	19
GP Thorpe	b Srinath	21	not out	17
GA Hick	c Mhambrey b Prasad	8		
RC Irani	c Mongia b Srinath	34		
RC Russell+	b Prasad	0		
CC Lewis	c Rathore b Prasad	0		
DG Cork	c Jadeja b Prasad	4		
MM Patel	lbw b Kumble	18		
AD Mullally	not out	14		
Extras	(16b, 3lb, 0w, 7nb)	26	(8b, 7lb, 1w, 2nb)	18
	90.2 overs		33.5 overs	
Total		**313**		**121**

1st innings FoW: 60, 72, 109, 149, 195, 205, 215, 215, 265, 313
2nd innings FoW: 37, 77

J Srinath	28.2	5	103	4	14.5	3	47	0
BKV Prasad	28	9	71	4	14	0	50	2
A Kumble	24	4	77	1	5	3	9	0
PL Mhambrey	10	0	43	1				

No. 725: 2nd Test

VENUE:	Lord's
DATE:	20th-24th June 1996
TOSS WON BY:	India
RESULT:	Match drawn

ENGLAND

1st innings			2nd innings	
MA Atherton*	lbw b Srinath	0	b Kumble	17
AJ Stewart	b Srinath	20	b Srinath	66
N Hussain	c Rathore b Ganguly	36	c Dravid b Srinath	28
GP Thorpe	b Srinath	89	c Rathore b Kumble	21
GA Hick	c Srinath b Ganguly	1	c Mongia b Prasad	6
RC Irani	b Prasad	1	b Mhambrey	41
RC Russell+	c Tendulkar b Prasad	124	lbw b Ganguly	38
CC Lewis	c Mongia b Prasad	31	not out	26
DG Cork	c Mongia b Prasad	0	c Azharuddin b Kumble	1
PJ Martin	c Tendulkar b Prasad	4	c Rathore b Prasad	23
AD Mullally	not out	0	not out	0
Extras	(13b, 11lb, 0w, 14nb)	38	(1b, 5lb, 0w, 5nb)	11
	130.3 overs		121 overs	
Total		**344**		**278**

1st innings FoW: 0, 67, 98, 102 , 107, 243, 326, 337, 343, 344
2nd innings FoW: 49, 109, 114, 154, 167, 168, 228, 274, 275

J Srinath	33	9	76	3	29	8	76	2
BKV Prasad	33.3	10	76	5	24	8	54	2
PL Mhambrey	19	3	58	0	14	3	47	1
A Kumble	28	9	60	0	51	14	90	3
SC Ganguly	15	2	49	2	3	0	5	1
SR Tendulkar	2	1	1	0				

INDIA

1st innings			2nd innings
V Rathore	c Hussain b Cork	15	
NR Mongia+	lbw b Lewis	24	
SC Ganguly	b Mullally	131	
SR Tendulkar	b Lewis	8	
M Azhar'din*	c Russell b Mullally	16	
AD Jadeja	b Irani	10	
RS Dravid	c Russell b Lewis	95	
A Kumble	lbw b Martin	14	
J Srinath	b Mullally	19	
PL Mhambrey	not out	15	
BKV Prasad	c Stewart b Cork	4	
Extras	(11b, 25lb, 10w, 9nb)	55	
	169.3 overs		
Total		**429**	

1st innings FoW: 25, 59, 123, 154, 202, 296, 351, 388, 419, 429

CC Lewis	40	11	101	3
DG Cork	42.3	10	112	2
AD Mullally	39	14	71	3
PJ Martin	34	10	70	1
RC Irani	12	3	31	1
GA Hick	2	0	8	0

India

No. 726:	3rd Test
VENUE:	Trent Bridge
DATE:	4th-9th July 1996
TOSS WON BY:	India
RESULT:	Match drawn

INDIA 1st innings / 2nd innings

Batsman	1st innings		2nd innings	
V Rathore	c Russell b Cork	4		
NR Mongia+	c Russell b Lewis	9	c Lewis b Mullally	45
SC Ganguly	c Hussain b Mullally	136	b Cork	48
SR Tendulkar	c Patel b Ealham	177	c Stewart b Lewis	74
SV Manjrekar	c Hick b Patel	53	c Stewart b Lewis	11
M Azhar'din*	c Patel b Lewis	5	c Cork b Ealham	8
RS Dravid	c Russell b Ealham	84	c Thorpe b Mullally	8
A Kumble	lbw b Mullally	0	lbw b Ealham	2
J Srinath	c Cork b Lewis	1	c Thorpe b Ealham	3
BKV Prasad	run out	13	not out	0
SLV Raju	not out	1	c (sub) b Ealham	0
Extras	(6b, 12lb, 7w, 13nb)	38	(1b, 1lb, 1w, 9nb)	12
	167 overs		69 overs	
Total		**521**		**211**

1st innings FoW: 7, 33, 288, 377, 385, 446, 447, 453, 513, 521
2nd innings FoW: 17, 103, 140, 160, 204, 208, 208, 211, 211

Bowler	O	M	R	W		O	M	R	W
CC Lewis	37	10	89	3		14	4	50	2
DG Cork	32	6	124	1		7	0	32	1
AD Mullally	40	12	88	2		13	3	36	2
MA Ealham	29	9	90	2		14	5	21	4
MM Patel	24	2	101	1		12	3	47	0
GA Hick	4	1	8	0		9	4	23	0
GP Thorpe	1	0	3	0					

ENGLAND 1st innings / 2nd innings

Batsman	1st innings		2nd innings
MA Atherton*	c Manjrekar b Prasad	160	
AJ Stewart	c Mongia b Srinath	50	
N Hussain	retired hurt	107	
GP Thorpe	lbw b Ganguly	45	
GA Hick	c Srinath b Raju	20	
MA Ealham	c (sub) b Srinath	51	
RC Russell+	c Mongia b Prasad	0	
CC Lewis	lbw b Kumble	21	
DG Cork	not out	32	
MM Patel	c Manjrekar b Ganguly	27	
AD Mullally	c Mongia b Ganguly	1	
Extras	(18b, 18lb, 0w, 14nb)	50	
	198.5 overs		
Total		**564**	

1st innings FoW: 130, 360, 396, 444, 444, 491, 497, 558, 564

Bowler	O	M	R	W
J Srinath	47	12	131	2
BKV Prasad	43	12	124	2
A Kumble	39	6	98	1
SLV Raju	43	12	76	1
SC Ganguly	19.5	2	71	3
SR Tendulkar	7	0	28	0

Pakistan

No. 727:	1st Test
VENUE:	Lord's
DATE:	25th-29th July 1996
TOSS WON BY:	Pakistan
RESULT:	Pakistan won by 164 runs

PAKISTAN 1st innings / 2nd innings

Batsman	1st innings		2nd innings	
Aamir Sohail	lbw b Brown	2		
Saeed Anwar	c Russell b Hick	74	c Russell b Mullally	88
Ijaz Ahmed	b Cork	1	lbw b Cork	76
Inzamam	b Mullally	148	c Ealham b Cork	70
Salim Malik	run out	7	not out	27
Shadab Kabir	lbw b Cork	17	c Russell b Cork	33
Wasim Akram*	lbw b Ealham	10	not out	34
Rashid Latif+	c Hick b Salisbury	45		
M Ahmed	c Russell b Mullally	11	c Thorpe b Brown	5
Waqar Younis	c Brown b Mullally	4		
Ur-Rehman	not out	10		
Extras	(3b, 5lb, 0w, 3nb)	11	(4b, 14lb, 0w, 1nb)	19
	108.2 overs		113.2 overs	
Total		**340**		**352**

1st innings FoW: 7, 12, 142, 153, 209, 257, 267, 280, 290, 340
2nd innings FoW: 136, 136, 161, 279, 308

Bowler	O	M	R	W		O	M	R	W
DG Cork	28	6	100	2		24	4	86	3
SJE Brown	17	2	78	1		16	2	60	1
AD Mullally	24	8	44	3		30.2	9	70	1
IDK Salisbury	12.2	1	42	1		20	4	63	0
MA Ealham	21	4	42	1		16	4	39	0
GA Hick	6	0	26	1		7	2	16	0

ENGLAND 1st innings / 2nd innings

Batsman	1st innings		2nd innings	
NV Knight	lbw b Waqar	51	lbw b Waqar	1
MA Atherton*	lbw b Wasim	12	c (sub) b Mushtaq	64
AJ Stewart	lbw b Mushtaq Ahmed	39	c (sub) b Mushtaq	89
GP Thorpe	b Ata-Ur-Rehman	77	lbw b Mushtaq Ahmed	9
GA Hick	b Waqar	4	b Waqar	4
MA Ealham	c Rashid b Ur-Rehman	25	b Mushtaq	5
RC Russell+	not out	41	c Rashid b Waqar	1
DG Cork	c Saeed b Ur-Rehman	3	b Waqar	3
IDK Salisbury	lbw b Waqar	5	c Rashid b Wasim	40
AD Mullally	b Waqar	0	c (sub) b Mushtaq	6
SJE Brown	b Ata-Ur-Rehman	1	not out	10
Extras	(9b, 13lb, 1w, 4nb)	27	(6b, 7lb, 0w, 4nb)	17
	102.4 overs		97.1 overs	
Total		**285**		**243**

1st innings FoW: 27, 107, 107, 116, 180, 260, 264, 269, 269, 285
2nd innings FoW: 14, 168, 171, 176, 181, 182, 186, 186, 208, 243

Bowler	O	M	R	W		O	M	R	W
Wasim Akram	22	4	49	1		21.1	5	45	1
Waqar Younis	24	6	69	4		25	3	85	4
Mushtaq Ahmed	38	5	92	1		38	15	57	5
Ata-Ur-Rehman	15.4	3	50	4		11	2	33	0
Aamir Sohail	3	1	3	0					
Salim Malik						1	0	1	0
Shadab Kabir						1	0	9	0

No. 728: 2nd Test
VENUE: Headingley
DATE: 8th-12th August 1996
TOSS WON BY: England
RESULT: Match drawn

No. 729: 3rd Test
VENUE: The Oval
DATE: 22nd-26th August 1996
TOSS WON BY: England
RESULT: Pakistan won by 9 wickets

PAKISTAN 1st innings / 2nd innings

	1st innings		2nd innings	
Saeed Anwar	c Atherton b Mullally	1	c Russell b Cork	22
Shadab Kabir	lbw b Caddick	35	c & b Lewis	2
Ijaz Ahmed	c Russell b Cork	141	c Russell b Caddick	52
Inzamam	c Atherton b Mullally	2	c Stewart b Caddick	65
Salim Malik	b Cork	55	c Cork b Caddick	6
Asif Mujtaba	c Thorpe b Cork	51	run out	26
Wasim Akram*	c Russell b Caddick	7	lbw b Atherton	7
Moin Khan+	c Russell b Cork	105	not out	30
Mushtaq M	c Atherton b Caddick	20	not out	6
Waqar Younis	c & b Cork	7		
Ur-Rehman	not out	0		
Extras	(4b, 10lb, 0w, 10nb)	24	(4b, 12lb, 0w, 10nb)	26
	153.2 overs		81 overs	
Total		448		242

1st innings FoW: 1, 98, 103, 233, 252, 266, 378, 434, 444, 448
2nd innings FoW: 16, 34, 132, 142, 188, 201, 221

AR Caddick	40.2	6	113	3		17	4	52	3
AD Mullally	41	10	99	2		15	2	43	0
CC Lewis	32	4	100	0		16	3	52	1
DG Cork	37	6	113	5		16	2	49	1
GP Thorpe	3	1	9	0		10	3	10	0
MA Atherton						7	1	20	1

ENGLAND 1st innings / 2nd innings

	1st innings		2nd innings
MA Atherton*	c Moin b Wasim	12	
AJ Stewart	c & b Mushtaq Ahmed	170	
N Hussain	c & b Waqar	48	
GP Thorpe	c Shadab b Mushtaq	16	
JP Crawley	c Moin b Ata'Rehman	53	
NV Knight	c Mushtaq b Waqar	113	
RC Russell+	b Wasim	9	
CC Lewis	b Mushtaq Ahmed	9	
DG Cork	c Shadab b Wasim	26	
AR Caddick	b Waqar	4	
AD Mullally	not out	9	
Extras	(7b, 23lb, 0w, 2nb)	32	
	156.5 overs		
Total		501	

1st innings FoW: 14, 121, 168, 257, 365, 402, 441, 465, 471, 501

Wasim Akram	39.5	10	106	3
Waqar Younis	33	7	127	3
Ata-Ur-Rehman	22	1	90	1
Mushtaq Ahmed	55	17	142	3
Asif Mujtaba	7	5	6	0

ENGLAND 1st innings / 2nd innings

	1st innings		2nd innings	
MA Atherton*	b Waqar	31	c Inzamam b M Ahmed	43
AJ Stewart+	b Mushtaq Ahmed	44	c Asif b Mushtaq	54
N Hussain	c Saeed b Waqar	12	lbw b Mushtaq Ahmed	51
GP Thorpe	lbw b Moh'ad Akram	54	c W Akram b M Ahmed	19
JP Crawley	b Waqar	106	c Aamir b W Akram	19
NV Knight	b Mushtaq Ahmed	17	c & b Mushtaq Ahmed	8
CC Lewis	b Wasim Akram	5	lbw b Waqar	4
IDK Salisbury	c Inzamam b W Akram	5	b Mushtaq Ahmed	26
DG Cork	c Moin b Waqar	0	c Ijaz Ahmed b W Akram	6
RDB Croft	not out	5	not out	0
AD Mullally	b Wasim Akram	24	b Wasim Akram	0
Extras	(0b, 12lb, 1w, 10nb)	23	(6b, 2lb, 1w, 13nb)	22
	99.2 overs		82.4 overs	
Total		326		242

1st innings FoW: 64, 85, 116, 205, 248, 273, 283, 284, 295, 326
2nd innings FoW: 96 , 136, 166, 179, 187, 205, 220, 238, 242, 242

Wasim Akram	29.2	9	83	3		15.4	1	67	3
Waqar Younis	25	6	95	4		18	3	55	1
Mo'mad Akram	12	1	41	1		10	3	30	0
Mushtaq Ahmed	27	5	78	2		37	10	78	6
Aamir Sohail	6	1	17	0		2	1	4	0

PAKISTAN 1st innings / 2nd innings

	1st innings		2nd innings	
Saeed Anwar	c Croft b Cork	176	not out	29
Aamir Sohail	c Cork b Croft	46	c Knight b Mullally	1
Ijaz Ahmed	c Stewart b Mullally	61	not out	13
Inzamam	c Hussain b Mullally	35		
Salim Malik	not out	100		
Asif Mujtaba	run out	13		
Wasim Akram*	st Stewart b Croft	40		
Moin Khan+	b Salisbury	23		
Mushtaq	c Crawley b Mullally	2		
Waqar Younis	not out	0		
Mohammad Akram				
Extras	(4b, 5lb, 0w, 16nb)	25	(0b, 0lb, 0w, 5nb)	5
	159.1 overs		6.4 overs	
Total		521		48

1st innings FoW: 106, 239, 334, 334, 365, 440, 502, 519
2nd innings FoW: 7

CC Lewis	23	3	112	0					
AD Mullally	37.1	7	97	3		3	0	24	1
RDB Croft	47	10	116	2		0.4	0	9	0
DG Cork	23	5	71	1		3	0	15	0
IDK Salisbury	29	3	116	1					

Zimbabwe

No. 730: 1st Test
VENUE: Queen's Club, Bulawayo
DATE: 18th-22nd December 1996
TOSS WON BY: Zimbabwe
RESULT: Match drawn

ZIMBABWE 1st innings / 2nd innings

Batsman	1st innings		2nd innings	
GW Flower	c Hussain b Silverwood	43	lbw b Gough	0
SV Carlisle	c Crawley b Gough	0	c Atherton b Mullally	4
A Campbell*	c Silverwood b Croft	84	b Croft	29
DL Houghton	c Stewart b Croft	34	c Croft b Tufnell	37
A Flower+	c Stewart b Tufnell	112	c Crawley b Tufnell	14
AC Waller	c Crawley b Croft	15	c Knight b Gough	50
GJ Whittall	c Atherton b Silverwood	7	c Mullally b Tufnell	3
PA Strang	c Tufnell b Silverwood	38	c Croft b Tufnell	56
HH Streak	b Mullally	19	c Crawley b Croft	19
BC Strang	not out	4	not out	8
HK Olonga	c Knight b Tufnell	0	c Stewart b Silverwood	0
Extras	(0b, 4lb, 3w, 13nb)	20	(4b, 6lb, 2w, 2nb)	14
	137.5 overs		101 overs	
Total		**376**		**234**

1st innings FoW: 3, 130, 135, 205, 235, 252, 331, 372, 376, 376
2nd innings FoW: 6, 6, 57, 82, 103, 111, 178, 209, 233, 234

AD Mullally	23	4	69	1	18	5	49	1
D Gough	26	4	87	1	12	2	44	2
CEW Silverwood	18	5	63	3	7	3	8	1
RDB Croft	44	15	77	3	33	9	62	2
PCR Tufnell	26.5	4	76	2	31	12	61	4

ENGLAND 1st innings / 2nd innings

Batsman	1st innings		2nd innings	
NV Knight	lbw b Olonga	56	run out	96
MA Atherton*	lbw b PA Strang	16	b Olonga	4
AJ Stewart+	lbw b PA Strang	48	c Campbell b PA Strang	73
N Hussain	c BC Strang b Streak	113	c Carlisle b PA Strang	0
GP Thorpe	c Campbell b PA Strang	13	c Campbell b Streak	2
JP Crawley	c A Flower b PA Strang	112	c Carlisle b Whittall	7
RDB Croft	lbw b Olonga	7		
D Gough	c GW Flower b Olonga	2	not out	3
C Silverwood	c Houghton b PA Strang	0		
AD Mullally	c Waller b Streak	4		
PCR Tufnell	not out	2		
Extras	(4b, 4lb, 1w, 24nb)	33	(2b, 13lb, 3w, 1nb)	19
	151.4 overs		37 overs	
Total		**406**		**204**

1st innings FoW: 48, 92, 160, 180, 328, 340, 344, 353, 378, 406
2nd innings FoW: 17, 154, 156, 178, 182, 204

HH Streak	36	8	86	2	11	0	64	1
BC Strang	17	5	54	0				
PA Strang	58.4	14	123	5	14	0	63	2
HK Olonga	23	2	90	3	2	0	16	1
GJ Whittall	10	2	25	0	2	0	10	1
GW Flower	7	3	20	0	8	0	36	0

Zimbabwe

No. 731: 2nd Test
VENUE: Harare
DATE: 26th-30th December 1996
TOSS WON BY: Zimbabwe
RESULT: Match drawn

ENGLAND 1st innings / 2nd innings

Batsman	1st innings		2nd innings	
NV Knight	c A Flower b Olonga	15	c Campbell b Strang	30
MA Atherton*	c Campbell b Whittall	13	c Campbell b Streak	1
AJ Stewart+	c GW Flower b Streak	19	not out	101
N Hussain	c A Flower b Streak	11	c Houghton b Strang	6
GP Thorpe	c Dekker b Streak	5	not out	50
JP Crawley	not out	47		
C White	c Campbell b Whittall	9		
RDB Croft	c GW Flower b Whittall	14		
D Gough	b Strang	2		
AD Mullally	c & b Whittall	0		
PCR Tufnell	b Streak	9		
Extras	(1b, 5lb, 1w, 5nb)	12	(0b, 5lb, 1w, 1nb)	7
	83.1 overs		93 overs	
Total		**156**		**195**

1st innings FoW: 24, 50, 50, 65, 73, 94, 128, 133, 134, 156
2nd innings FoW: 7, 75, 89

HH Streak	24.1	7	43	4	18	5	47	1
EA Brandes	16	6	35	0	21	6	45	0
HK Olonga	9	1	23	1	7	0	31	0
GJ Whittall	16	5	18	4	14	6	16	0
PA Strang	18	7	31	1	26	6	42	2
GW Flower					7	2	9	0

ZIMBABWE 1st innings / 2nd innings

Batsman	1st innings		2nd innings
GW Flower	c Crawley b Gough	73	
MH Dekker	c Stewart b Mullally	2	
ADCampbell*	c Thorpe b White	22	
DL Houghton	c Stewart b Gough	29	
A Flower+	lbw b Gough	6	
AC Waller	lbw b Tufnell	4	
GJ Whittall	b Gough	1	
PA Strang	not out	47	
HH Streak	c Crawley b Croft	7	
EA Brandes	c Gough b Croft	9	
HK Olonga	c Hussain b Croft	0	
Extras	(0b, 8lb, 1w, 6nb)	15	
	105 overs		
Total		**215**	

1st innings FoW: 5, 46, 110, 130, 136, 138, 159, 197, 211, 215

AD Mullally	23	7	32	1
D Gough	26	10	40	4
RDB Croft	15	2	39	3
C White	16	4	41	1
PCR Tufnell	25	3	55	1

No. 732: 1st Test
VENUE: Auckland
DATE: 24th-28th January 1997
TOSS WON BY: England
RESULT: Match drawn

No. 733: 2nd Test
DATE: 6th-10th February 1997
VENUE: Wellington
TOSS WON BY: New Zealand
RESULT: Eng won by an innings and 68 runs

NEW ZEALAND 1st innings / 2nd innings (1st Test)

Batsman	1st innings		2nd innings	
BA Young	lbw b Mullally	44	lbw b Gough	20
BA Pocock	lbw b Gough	70	c Hussain b Cork	3
AC Parore	c Stewart b Cork	6	st Stewart b Tufnell	33
SP Fleming	c & b Cork	129	c Crawley b Tufnell	9
NJ Astle	c Stewart b White	10	run out	13
JTC Vaughan	lbw b Cork	3	not out	102
CL Cairns	c Stewart b White	67	lbw b Tufnell	2
LK Germon*+	c Stewart b Gough	14	b Mullally	7
DN Patel	lbw b Gough	0	lbw b Mullally	0
SB Doull	c Knight b Gough	5	b Gough	26
DK Morrison	not out	6	not out	14
Extras	(5b, 12lb, 2w, 17nb)	36	(0b, 11lb, 0w, 8nb)	19
Total	131.5 overs	**390**	114 overs	**248**

1st innings FoW: 85, 114, 193, 210, 215, 333, 361, 361, 380, 390
2nd innings FoW: 17, 28, 47, 88, 90, 92, 101, 105, 142

Bowler	O	M	R	W		O	M	R	W
DG Cork	32.5	8	96	3		16	3	45	1
AD Mullally	27	11	55	1		26	11	47	2
D Gough	32	5	91	4		22	3	66	2
PCR Tufnell	25	5	80	0		40	18	53	3
C White	15	3	51	2		10	2	26	0

NEW ZEALAND 1st innings / 2nd innings (2nd Test)

Batsman	1st innings		2nd innings	
BA Young	c Stewart b Gough	8	c Stewart b Tufnell	56
BA Pocock	c Cork b Caddick	6	c Knight b Gough	64
AC Parore	c Stewart b Gough	4	lbw b Croft	15
SP Fleming	c & b Caddick	1	c & b Croft	0
NJ Astle	c Croft b Gough	36	c Stewart b Gough	4
CL Cairns	c Hussain b Gough	3	c Knight b Caddick	22
LK Germon*+	c Stewart b Caddick	10	b Gough	11
DN Patel	c Cork b Caddick	45	lbw b Croft	0
SB Doull	c Stewart b Gough	0	c Knight b Gough	0
GI Allott	c Knight b Cork	1	b Caddick	2
DL Vettori	not out	3	not out	2
Extras	(0b, 5lb, 0w, 2nb)	7	(4b, 5lb, 0w, 6nb)	15
Total	48.3 overs	**124**	103.2 overs	**191**

1st innings FoW: 14, 18, 19, 19, 23, 48, 85, 85, 106, 124
2nd innings FoW: 89, 125,125, 125, 161, 164, 175, 175, 182, 191

Bowler	O	M	R	W		O	M	R	W
DG Cork	14	4	34	1		10	1	42	0
AR Caddick	18.3	5	45	4		27.2	11	40	2
D Gough	16	6	40	5		23	9	52	4
RDB Croft						20	9	19	3
PCR Tufnell						23	9	29	1

ENGLAND 1st innings (1st Test)

Batsman	1st innings		2nd innings
NV Knight	lbw b Doull	5	
MA Atherton*	c & b Patel	83	
AJ Stewart+	c & b Doull	173	
N Hussain	c Fleming b Patel	8	
GP Thorpe	hit wkt b Cairns	119	
JP Crawley	run out	14	
C White	lbw b Vaughan	0	
DG Cork	c Young b Morrison	59	
D Gough	c Germon b Morrison	2	
AD Mullally	c Germon b Morrison	21	
PCR Tufnell	not out	19	
Extras	(2b, 12lb, 2w, 2nb)	18	
Total	187.4 overs	**521**	

1st innings FoW: 18, 200, 222, 304, 339, 339, 453, 471, 478, 521

Bowler	O	M	R	W
DK Morrison	24.4	4	104	3
SB Doull	39	10	118	2
CL Cairns	30	3	103	1
NJ Astle	14	3	33	0
JTC Vaughan	36	10	57	1
DN Patel	44	10	92	2

ENGLAND 1st innings (2nd Test)

Batsman	1st innings		2nd innings
NV Knight	c Patel b Doull	8	
MA Atherton*	lbw b Doull	30	
AJ Stewart+	c Fleming b Allott	52	
N Hussain	c Young b Vettori	64	
GP Thorpe	st Germon b Patel	108	
JP Crawley	c Germon b Doull	56	
DG Cork	lbw b Astle	7	
RDB Croft	c Fleming b Doull	0	
D Gough	c Fleming b Doull	18	
AR Caddick	c Allott b Vettori	20	
PCR Tufnell	not out	6	
Extras	(3b, 9lb, 0w, 2nb)	14	
Total	137.3 overs	**383**	

1st innings FoW: 10, 80, 106, 213, 331, 331, 331, 357, 357, 383

Bowler	O	M	R	W
SB Doull	28	10	75	5
GI Allott	31	6	91	1
DL Vettori	34.3	10	98	2
CL Cairns	4	2	8	0
NJ Astle	14	5	30	1
DN Patel	24	5	59	1
BA Pocock	2	0	10	0

New Zealand

No. 734: 3rd Test			
VENUE: Christchurch			
DATE: 14th-18th February 1997			
TOSS WON BY: England			
RESULT: England won by 4 wickets			

NEW ZEALAND 1st innings / 2nd innings

Batsman	1st innings		2nd innings	
BA Young	b Cork	11	c Knight b Tufnell	49
BA Pocock	c Atherton b Croft	22	b Cork	0
MJ Horne	c Thorpe b Gough	42	c Stewart b Caddick	13
SP Fleming*	st Stewart b Croft	62	c Knight b Tufnell	11
NJ Astle	c Hussain b Croft	15	c Hussain b Croft	5
AC Parore+	c Hussain b Croft	59	c Stewart b Gough	8
CL Cairns	c Stewart b Caddick	57	c Knight b Tufnell	52
SB Doull	run out	1	c Knight b Croft	5
DL Vettori	run out	25	not out	29
HT Davis	c Hussain b Croft	8	b Gough	1
GI Allott	not out	8	c Stewart b Gough	1
Extras	(1b, 16lb, 0w, 19nb)	36	(0b, 8lb, 0w, 4nb)	12
Total	129.1 overs	**346**	88.3 overs	**186**

1st innings FoW: 14, 78, 106, 137, 201, 283, 289, 310, 337, 346
2nd innings FoW: 0, 42, 61, 76, 80, 89, 107, 178, 184, 186

Bowler	O	M	R	W		O	M	R	W
DG Cork	20	3	78	1		6	2	5	1
AR Caddick	32	8	64	1		10	1	25	1
D Gough	21	3	70	1		13.3	5	42	3
RDB Croft	39.1	5	95	5		31	13	48	2
PCR Tufnell	16	6	22	0		28	9	58	3
GP Thorpe	1	1	0	0					

ENGLAND 1st innings / 2nd innings

Batsman	1st innings		2nd innings	
NV Knight	c Fleming b Allott	14	c Davis b Vettori	29
MA Atherton*	not out	94	c Parore b Astle	118
AJ Stewart+	c (sub) b Allott	15	c Pocock b Vettori	17
N Hussain	c Parore b Cairns	12	c Fleming b Doull	15
GP Thorpe	b Astle	18	c Fleming b Vettori	33
JP Crawley	c Parore b Allott	1	c & b Vettori	2
DG Cork	c Parore b Davis	16	not out	40
RDB Croft	c Davis b Astle	31	not out	39
D Gough	b Vettori	0		
AR Caddick	c (sub) b Allott	4		
PCR Tufnell	c Young b Doull	13		
Extras	(0b, 4lb, 1w, 5nb)	10	(2b, 10lb, 0w, 2nb)	14
Total	84.4 overs	**228**	146.4 overs	**307**

1st innings FoW: 20, 40, 70, 103, 104, 145, 198, 199, 210, 228
2nd innings FoW: 64, 116., 146, 226, 226, 231

Bowler	O	M	R	W		O	M	R	W
GI Allott	18	3	74	4		12.4	2	32	0
SB Doull	17.4	3	49	1		21	8	57	1
HT Davis	18	2	50	1		18	6	43	0
DL Vettori	12	4	13	1		57	18	97	4
CL Cairns	8	5	12	1		10	1	23	0
NJ Astle	11	2	26	2		28	10	45	1

Australia

No. 735: 1st Test			
VENUE: Edgbaston			
DATE: 5th-8th June 1997			
TOSS WON BY: Australia			
RESULT: England won by 9 wickets			

AUSTRALIA 1st innings / 2nd innings

Batsman	1st innings		2nd innings	
MA Taylor*	c Butcher b Malcolm	7	c & b Croft	129
MTG Elliott	b Gough	6	b Croft	66
GS Blewett	c Hussain b Gough	7	c Butcher b Croft	125
ME Waugh	b Gough	5	c Stewart b Gough	1
SR Waugh	c Stewart b Caddick	12	lbw b Gough	33
MG Bevan	c Ealham b Malcolm	8	c Hussain b Gough	24
IA Healy+	c Stewart b Caddick	0	c Atherton b Ealham	30
JN Gillespie	lbw b Caddick	4	run out	0
SK Warne	c Malcolm b Caddick	47	c & b Ealham	32
M Kasprowicz	c Butcher b Caddick	17	c Butcher b Ealham	0
GD McGrath	not out	1	not out	0
Extras	(0b, 0lb, 2w, 2nb)	4	(18b, 12lb, 2w, 5nb)	37
Total	31.5 overs	**118**	144.4 overs	**477**

1st innings FoW: 11, 15, 26, 28, 48, 48, 48, 54, 110, 118
2nd innings FoW: 133, 327, 354, 393, 399, 431, 465, 465, 477, 477

Bowler	O	M	R	W		O	M	R	W
D Gough	10	1	43	3		35	7	123	3
DE Malcolm	10	2	25	2		21	6	52	0
AR Caddick	11.5	1	50	5		30	6	87	0
RDB Croft						43	10	125	3
MA Ealham						15.4	3	60	3

ENGLAND 1st innings / 2nd innings

Batsman	1st innings		2nd innings	
MA Butcher	c Healy b Kasprowicz	8	lbw b Kasprowicz	14
MA Atherton*	c Healy b McGrath	2	not out	57
AJ Stewart+	c Elliott b Gillespie	18	not out	40
N Hussain	c Healy b Warne	207		
GP Thorpe	c Bevan b McGrath	138		
JP Crawley	c Healy b Kasprowicz	1		
MA Ealham	not out	53		
RDB Croft	c Healy b Kasprowicz	24		
D Gough	c Healy b Kasprowicz	0		
AR Caddick	lbw b Bevan	0		
DE Malcolm				
Extras	(4b, 7lb, 1w, 15nb)	27	(4b, 4lb, 0w, 0nb)	8
Total	138.4 overs	**478**	21.3 overs	**119**

1st innings FoW: 8, 16, 50, 338, 345, 416, 460, 463, 478
2nd innings FoW: 29

Bowler	O	M	R	W		O	M	R	W
GD McGrath	32	8	107	2		7	1	42	0
MS Kasprowicz	39	8	113	4		7	0	42	1
JN Gillespie	10	1	48	1					
SK Warne	35	8	110	1		7.3	0	27	0
MG Bevan	10.4	0	44	1					
SR Waugh	12	2	45	0					

	No. 736: 2nd Test			No. 737: 3rd Test
	VENUE: Lord's			VENUE: Old Trafford
	DATE: 19th-23rd June 1997			DATE: 3rd-7th July 1997
	TOSS WON BY: Australia			TOSS WON BY: Australia
	RESULT: Match drawn			RESULT: Australia won by 268 runs

ENGLAND 1st innings / **2nd innings**

		1st		2nd
MA Butcher	c Blewett b McGrath	5	b Warne	87
MA Atherton*	c Taylor b McGrath	1	hit wkt b Kasprowicz	77
AJ Stewart+	b McGrath	1	c Kasprowicz b McGrath	13
N Hussain	lbw b McGrath	19	c & b Warne	0
GP Thorpe	c Blewett b Reiffel	21	not out	30
JP Crawley	c Healy b McGrath	1	not out	29
MA Ealham	c Elliott b Reiffel	7		
RDB Croft	c Healy b McGrath	2		
D Gough	c Healy b McGrath	10		
AR Caddick	lbw b McGrath	1		
DE Malcolm	not out	0		
Extras	(4b, 0lb, 0w, 5nb)	9	(8b, 14lb, 1w, 7nb)	30
Total	42.3 overs	**77**	79 overs	**266**

1st innings FoW: 11, 12, 13, 47, 56, 62, 66, 76, 77, 77
2nd innings FoW: 162, 189, 197, 202

GD McGrath	20.3	8	38	8	20	5	65	1
PR Reiffel	15	9	17	2	13	5	29	0
MS Kasprowicz	5	1	9	0	15	3	54	1
SK Warne	2	0	9	0	19	4	47	2
MG Bevan					8	1	29	0
SR Waugh					4	0	20	0

AUSTRALIA 1st innings / **2nd innings**

		1st
MA Taylor*	b Gough	1
MTG Elliott	c Crawley b Caddick	112
GS Blewett	c Hussain b Croft	45
ME Waugh	c Malcolm b Caddick	33
SK Warne	c Hussain b Gough	0
SR Waugh	lbw b Caddick	0
MG Bevan	c Stewart b Caddick	4
IA Healy+	not out	13
PR Reiffel	not out	1
MS Kasprowicz		
GD McGrath		
Extras	(1b, 3lb, 0w, 0nb)	4
Total	61 overs	**213**

1st innings FoW: 4, 73, 147, 147, 147, 159, 212

D Gough	20	4	82	2
AR Caddick	22	6	71	4
DE Malcolm	7	1	26	0
RDB Croft	12	5	30	1

AUSTRALIA 1st innings / **2nd innings**

		1st		2nd
MA Taylor*	c Thorpe b Headley	2	c Butcher b Headley	1
MTG Elliott	c Stewart b Headley	40	c Butcher b Headley	11
GS Blewett	b Gough	8	c Hussain b Croft	19
ME Waugh	c Stewart b Ealham	12	b Ealham	55
SR Waugh	b Gough	108	c Stewart b Headley	116
MG Bevan	c Stewart b Headley	7	c Atherton b Headley	0
IA Healy+	c Stewart b Caddick	9	c Butcher b Croft	47
SK Warne	c Stewart b Ealham	3	c Stewart b Caddick	53
PR Reiffel	b Gough	31	not out	45
JN Gillespie	c Stewart b Headley	0	not out	28
GD McGrath	not out	0		
Extras	(8b, 4lb, 0w, 3nb)	15	(1b, 13lb, 0w, 6nb)	20
Total	77.3 overs	**235**	122 overs	**395**

1st innings FoW: 9, 22, 42, 85, 113, 150, 160, 230, 235, 235
2nd innings FoW: 5, 33, 39, 131, 132, 210, 298, 333

D Gough	21	7	52	3	20	3	62	0
DW Headley	27.3	4	72	4	29	4	104	4
AR Caddick	14	2	52	1	21	0	69	1
MA Ealham	11	2	34	2	13	3	41	1
RDB Croft	4	0	13	0	39	12	105	2

ENGLAND 1st innings / **2nd innings**

		1st		2nd
MA Butcher	st Healy b Bevan	51	c McGrath b Gillespie	28
MA Atherton*	c Healy b McGrath	5	lbw b Gillespie	21
AJ Stewart+	c Taylor b Warne	30	b Warne	1
N Hussain	c Healy b Warne	13	lbw b Gillespie	1
GP Thorpe	c Taylor b Warne	3	c Healy b Warne	7
JP Crawley	c Healy b Warne	4	hit wkt b McGrath	83
MA Ealham	not out	24	c Healy b McGrath	9
RDB Croft	c SR Waugh b McGrath	7	c Reiffel b McGrath	4
D Gough	lbw b Warne	1	b McGrath	6
AR Caddick	c ME Waugh b Warne	15	c Gillespie b Warne	17
DW Headley	b McGrath	0	not out	0
Extras	(4b, 3lb, 0w, 2nb)	9	(14b, 4lb, 1w, 1nb)	20
Total	84.4 overs	**162**	73.4 overs	**200**

1st innings FoW: 8, 74, 94 , 101, 110, 111, 122, 123, 161, 162
2nd innings FoW: 44, 45, 50, 55, 84, 158, 170, 177, 188, 200

GD McGrath	23.4	9	40	3	21	4	46	4
PR Reiffel	9	3	14	0	2	0	8	0
SK Warne	30	14	48	6	30.4	8	63	3
JN Gillespie	14	3	39	0	12	4	31	3
MG Bevan	8	3	14	1	8	2	34	0

Australia	Australia

No. 738: 4th Test	No. 739: 5th Test
VENUE: Headingley	VENUE: Trent Bridge
DATE: 24th-28th July 1997	DATE: 7th-10th August 1997
TOSS WON BY: Australia	TOSS WON BY: Australia
RESULT: Aus won by an innings and 61 runs	RESULT: Australia won by 264 runs

No. 738: 4th Test — Headingley

ENGLAND	1st innings		2nd innings	
MA Butcher	c Blewett b Reiffel	24	c Healy b McGrath	19
MA Atherton*	c Gillespie b McGrath	41	c Warne b McGrath	2
AJ Stewart+	c Blewett b Gillespie	7	b Reiffel	16
N Hussain	c Taylor b McGrath	26	c Gillespie b Warne	105
DW Headley	c SR Waugh b Gillespie	22	lbw b Reiffel	3
GP Thorpe	b Gillespie	15	c ME Waugh b Gillespie	15
JP Crawley	c Blewett b Gillespie	2	b Reiffel	72
MA Ealham	not out	8	c ME Waugh b Reiffel	4
RDB Croft	c Ponting b Gillespie	6	c Healy b Reiffel	5
D Gough	b Gillespie	0	c ME Waugh b Gillespie	0
AM Smith	b Gillespie	0	not out	4
Extras	(4b, 4lb, 1w, 12nb)	21	(6b, 4lb, 0w, 13nb)	23
Total	59.4 overs	172	91.1 overs	268

1st innings FoW: 43, 58, 103, 138, 154, 154, 163, 172, 172, 172
2nd innings FoW: 23, 28, 57, 89, 222, 252, 256, 263, 264, 268

GD McGrath	22	5	67	2	22	5	80	2
PR Reiffel	20	4	41	1	21.1	2	49	5
JN Gillespie	13.4	1	37	7	23	8	65	2
GS Blewett	3	0	17	0				
SK Warne	1	0	2	0	21	6	53	1
SR Waugh					4	1	11	0

AUSTRALIA	1st innings		2nd innings
MA Taylor*	c Stewart b Gough	0	
MTG Elliott	b Gough	199	
GS Blewett	c Stewart b Gough	1	
ME Waugh	c & b Headley	8	
SR Waugh	c Crawley b Headley	4	
RT Ponting	c Ealham b Gough	127	
IA Healy+	b Ealham	31	
SK Warne	c Thorpe b Ealham	0	
PR Reiffel	not out	54	
JN Gillespie	b Gough	3	
GD McGrath	not out	20	
Extras	(9b, 10lb, 0w, 35nb)	54	
Total	123 overs	501	

1st innings FoW: 0, 16, 43, 50, 318, 382, 383, 444, 461

D Gough	36	5	149	5
DW Headley	25	2	125	2
AM Smith	23	2	89	0
MA Ealham	19	3	56	2
RDB Croft	18	1	49	0
MA Butcher	2	0	14	0

No. 739: 5th Test — Trent Bridge

AUSTRALIA	1st innings		2nd innings	
MTG Elliott	c Stewart b Headley	69	c Crawley b Caddick	37
MA Taylor*	b Caddick	76	c Hussain b B Hollioake	45
GS Blewett	c Stewart b B Hollioake	50	c Stewart b Caddick	60
ME Waugh	lbw b Caddick	68	lbw b Headley	7
SR Waugh	b Malcolm	75	c A Hollioake b Caddick	14
RT Ponting	b Headley	9	c Stewart b A Hollioake	45
IA Healy+	c A Hollioake b Malcolm	16	c Stewart b A Hollioake	63
SK Warne	c Thorpe b Malcolm	0	c Thorpe b Croft	20
PR Reiffel	c Thorpe b Headley	26	c BC Hollioake b Croft	22
JN Gillespie	not out	18	c Thorpe b Headley	4
GD McGrath	b Headley	1	not out	1
Extras	(4b, 10lb, 1w, 4nb)	19	(1b, 11lb, 0w, 6nb)	18
Total	121.5 overs	427	98.5 overs	336

1st innings FoW: 117, 160, 225, 311, 325, 355, 363, 386, 419, 427
2nd innings FoW: 51, 105, 134, 156, 171, 276, 292, 314, 326, 336

DE Malcolm	25	4	100	3	16	4	52	0
DW Headley	30.5	7	87	4	19	3	56	2
AR Caddick	30	4	102	2	20	2	85	3
BC Hollioake	10	1	57	1	5	1	26	1
RDB Croft	19	7	43	0	26.5	6	74	2
AJ Hollioake	7	0	24	0	12	2	31	2

ENGLAND	1st innings		2nd innings	
MA Atherton*	c Healy b Warne	27	c Healy b McGrath	8
AJ Stewart+	c Healy b Warne	87	c SR Waugh b Reiffel	16
JP Crawley	c Healy b McGrath	18	c Healy b Gillespie	33
N Hussain	b Warne	2	b Gillespie	21
GP Thorpe	c Blewett b Warne	53	not out	82
AJ Hollioake	c Taylor b Reiffel	45	lbw b Gillespie	2
BC Hollioake	c ME Waugh b Reiffel	28	lbw b Warne	2
RDB Croft	c Blewett b McGrath	18	c McGrath b Warne	6
AR Caddick	c Healy b McGrath	0	lbw b Warne	0
DW Headley	not out	10	c Healy b McGrath	4
DE Malcolm	b McGrath	12	c ME Waugh b McGrath	0
Extras	(2b, 6lb, 0w, 5nb)	13	(6b, 2lb, 0w, 4nb)	12
Total	93.5 overs	313	48.5 overs	186

1st innings FoW: 106, 129, 135, 141 , 243, 243, 272, 290, 290, 313
2nd innings FoW: 25, 25, 78, 99, 121, 144, 150, 166, 186, 186

GD McGrath	29.5	9	71	4	13.5	4	36	3
PR Reiffel	21	2	101	2	11	3	34	1
JN Gillespie	11	3	47	0	8	0	65	3
SK Warne	32	8	86	4	16	4	43	3

No. 740:	6th Test	
VENUE:	The Oval	
DATE:	21st-23rd August 1997	
TOSS WON BY:	England	
RESULT:	England won by 19 runs	

No. 741:	1st Test	
VENUE:	Kingston (Jamaica)	
DATE:	29th January 1998	
TOSS WON BY:	England	
RESULT:	Match drawn	

ENGLAND — Australia Test

ENGLAND	1st innings		2nd innings	
MA Butcher	b McGrath	5	lbw b ME Waugh	13
MA Atherton*	c Healy b McGrath	8	c S Waugh b Kasprowicz	8
AJ Stewart+	lbw b McGrath	36	lbw b Kasprowicz	3
N Hussain	c Elliott b McGrath	35	c Elliott b Warne	2
GP Thorpe	b McGrath	27	c Taylor b Kasprowicz	62
MR Ramp'sh	c Blewett b McGrath	4	st Healy b Warne	48
AJ Hollioake	b Warne	0	lbw b Kasprowicz	4
AR Caddick	not out	26	not out	0
PJ Martin	b McGrath	20	c & b Kasprowicz	3
PCR Tufnell	c Blewett b Warne	1	c Healy b Kasprowicz	0
DE Malcolm	lbw b Kasprowicz	0	b Kasprowicz	0
Extras	(2b, 6lb, 0w, 10nb)	18	(6b, 10lb, 0w, 4nb)	20
	56.4 overs		66.5 overs	
Total		**180**		**163**

1st innings FoW: 18, 24, 97, 128, 131, 132, 132, 158, 175, 18
2nd innings FoW: 20, 24, 26, 52, 131, 138, 160, 163, 163, 163

GD McGrath	21	4	76	7	17	5	33	0
MS Kasprowicz	11.4	2	56	1	15.5	5	36	7
SK Warne	17	8	32	2	26	9	57	2
S Young	7	3	8	0	1	0	5	0
ME Waugh					7	3	16	1

ENGLAND — West Indies Test

ENGLAND	1st innings		2nd innings
MA Atherton*	c Campbell b Walsh	2	
AJ Stewart+	not out	9	
MA Butcher	c SC Williams b Walsh	0	
N Hussain	c Hooper b Ambrose	1	
GP Thorpe	not out	0	
JP Crawley			
AJ Hollioake			
AR Caddick			
DW Headley			
ARC Fraser			
PCR Tufnell			
Extras	(4b, 0lb, 0w, 1nb)	5	
	10.1 overs		
Total		**17**	

1st innings FoW: 4, 4, 9

CA Walsh	5.1	1	10	2
CEL Ambrose	5	3	3	1

AUSTRALIA

AUSTRALIA	1st innings		2nd innings	
MTG Elliott	b Tufnell	12	lbw b Malcolm	4
MA Taylor*	c Hollioake b Tufnell	38	lbw b Caddick	18
GS Blewett	c Stewart b Tufnell	47	c Stewart b Caddick	19
ME Waugh	c Butcher b Tufnell	19	c Hussain b Tufnell	1
SR Waugh	lbw b Caddick	22	c Thorpe b Caddick	6
RT Ponting	c Hussain b Tufnell	40	lbw b Tufnell	20
IA Healy+	c Stewart b Tufnell	2	c & b Caddick	14
S Young	c Stewart b Tufnell	0	not out	4
SK Warne	b Caddick	30	c Martin b Tufnell	3
M Kasprowicz	lbw b Caddick	0	c Hollioake b Caddick	4
GD McGrath	not out	1	c Thorpe b Tufnell	1
Extras	(0b, 3lb, 1w, 5nb)	9	(3b, 4lb, 1w, 2nb)	10
	79.3 overs		32.1 overs	
Total		**220**		**104**

1st innings FoW: 49, 54, 94, 140, 150, 164, 164, 205, 205, 220
2nd innings FoW: 5, 36, 42, 49, 54, 88, 92, 95, 99, 104

DE Malcolm	11	2	37	0	3	0	15	1
PJ Martin	15	5	38	0	4	0	13	0
AR Caddick	19	4	76	3	12	2	42	5
PCR Tufnell	34.3	16	66	7	13.1	6	27	4

WEST INDIES

WEST INDIES	1st innings	2nd innings
SC Williams		
SL Campbell		
BC Lara*		
S Chanderpaul		
CL Hooper		
JC Adams		
D Williams+		
NAM McLean		
IR Bishop		
CEL Ambrose		
CA Walsh		

West Indies | West Indies

No. 742: 2nd Test	No. 743: 3rd Test
VENUE: Port-of-Spain (Trinidad)	VENUE: Port-of-Spain (Trinidad)
DATE: 5th-9th February 1998	DATE: 13th-17th February 1998
TOSS WON BY: England	TOSS WON BY: England
RESULT: West Indies won by 3 wickets	RESULT: England won by 3 wickets

ENGLAND 1st innings

Batsman	1st innings		2nd innings	
MA Atherton*	c Lara b Ambrose	11	b Walsh	31
AJ Stewart	lbw b Benjamin	50	c Hooper b McLean	73
JP Crawley	c S Williams b Ambrose	17	lbw b McLean	22
N Hussain	not out	61	c & b Walsh	23
GP Thorpe	c D Williams b Hooper	8	c Lara b Walsh	39
AJ Hollioake	run out	2	c Lara b Ambrose	12
RC Russell+	c S Williams b McLean	0	lbw b Ambrose	8
AR Caddick	lbw b Walsh	8	c D Williams b Ambrose	0
DW Headley	c D Williams b Ambrose	11	not out	0
ARC Fraser	c D Williams b Benjamin	17	c Hooper b Ambrose	4
PCR Tufnell	c Lara b Benjamin	0	c D Williams b Ambrose	6
Extras	(6b, 10lb, 0w, 13nb)	29	(5b, 15lb, 1w, 11nb)	32
Total	109 overs	**214**	94.5 overs	**258**

1st innings FoW: 26, 87, 105, 114, 124, 126, 143, 172, 214, 214
2nd innings FoW: 91, 143, 148, 202, 228, 238, 239, 239, 246, 258

Bowler	O	M	R	W	O	M	R	W
CA Walsh	27	7	55	1	29	5	67	3
CEL Ambrose	26	16	23	3	19.5	3	52	5
NAM McLean	19	7	28	1	12	1	46	2
KCG Benjamin	24	5	68	3	15	3	40	0
CL Hooper	9	3	14	1	19	8	33	0
JC Adams	3	0	8	0				
S Chanderpaul	1	0	2	0				

WEST INDIES 1st innings

Batsman	1st innings		2nd innings	
SL Campbell	c Russell b Headley	1	c Stewart b Headley	10
SC Williams	c Atherton b Fraser	19	c Crawley b Fraser	62
BC Lara*	c Atherton b Fraser	55	c Russell b Fraser	17
CL Hooper	b Fraser	1	not out	94
S Chanderpaul	c Thorpe b Fraser	34	c Thorpe b Tufnell	0
JC Adams	lbw b Fraser	1	c Stewart b Fraser	2
D Williams+	lbw b Tufnell	16	c Thorpe b Headley	65
CEL Ambrose	c & b Fraser	31	c Russell b Headley	1
KCG Benjamin	b Fraser	0	not out	6
NAM McLean	c Caddick b Fraser	2		
CA Walsh	not out	0		
Extras	(12b, 5lb, 0w, 14nb)	31	(10b, 8lb, 0w, 7nb)	25
Total	73.1 overs	**191**	98.2 overs	**282**

1st innings FoW: 16, 42, 48, 126, 134, 135, 167, 177, 190, 191
2nd innings FoW: 10, 68, 120, 121, 124, 253, 259

Bowler	O	M	R	W	O	M	R	W
DW Headley	22	6	47	1	16	2	68	3
AR Caddick	14	4	41	0	16	2	58	0
ARC Fraser	16.1	2	53	8	27	8	57	3
PCR Tufnell	21	8	33	1	34.2	9	69	1
					5	0	12	0

WEST INDIES 1st innings

Batsman	1st innings		2nd innings	
SL Campbell	c Thorpe b Fraser	28	lbw b Fraser	13
SC Williams	c Thorpe b Caddick	24	c Atherton b Caddick	23
BC Lara*	c Russell b Fraser	42	lbw b Fraser	47
CL Hooper	c Butcher b Fraser	1	lbw b Headley	5
S Chanderpaul	lbw b Fraser	28	c Russell b Headley	39
JC Adams	c Atherton b Caddick	11	c Atherton b Fraser	53
D Williams+	b Caddick	0	lbw b Headley	0
CEL Ambrose	b Caddick	4	b Headley	0
KCG Benjamin	lbw b Caddick	0	c Russell b Fraser	1
NAM McLean	c Headley b Fraser	11	c Stewart b Caddick	2
CA Walsh	not out	5	not out	1
Extras	(0b, 0lb, 0w, 5nb)	5	(0b, 16lb, 0w, 10nb)	26
Total	67.4 overs	**159**	84.3 overs	**210**

1st innings FoW: 36, 93, 95, 100, 131, 131, 140, 140, 150, 159
2nd innings FoW: 27, 66, 82, 92, 102, 158, 159, 159, 189, 210

Bowler	O	M	R	W	O	M	R	W
DW Headley	14	0	40	0	26	3	77	4
AR Caddick	22	7	67	5	19	6	64	2
ARC Fraser	20.4	8	40	5	25.3	11	40	4
PCR Tufnell	9	5	11	0	14	6	13	0
MA Butcher	2	1	1	0				

ENGLAND 1st innings

Batsman	1st innings		2nd innings	
MA Atherton*	lbw b Ambrose	2	c D Williams b Walsh	49
AJ Stewart	c D Williams b Hooper	44	c D Williams b Walsh	83
JP Crawley	b Ambrose	1	run out	5
DW Headley	b Ambrose	1	not out	7
N Hussain	c D Williams b Walsh	0	lbw b Hooper	5
GP Thorpe	c D Williams b Hooper	32	c D Williams b Ambrose	19
MA Butcher	c & b Adams	28	not out	24
RC Russell+	not out	20	c Hooper b Ambrose	4
AR Caddick	run out	0	c D Williams b Ambrose	0
ARC Fraser	c & b Ambrose	5		
PCR Tufnell	lbw b Ambrose	0		
Extras	(1b, 4lb, 0w, 7nb)	12	(2b, 15lb, 0w, 12nb)	29
Total	71.4 overs	**145**	108 overs	**225**

1st innings FoW: 5, 15, 22, 27, 71, 101, 134, 135, 145, 145
2nd innings FoW: 129, 145, 152, 167, 201, 213, 213

Bowler	O	M	R	W	O	M	R	W
CA Walsh	17	5	35	1	38	11	69	2
CEL Ambrose	15.4	5	25	5	33	6	62	3
NAM McLean	9	2	23	0	4	0	17	0
KCG Benjamin	13	3	34	0	11	3	24	0
CL Hooper	15	3	23	2	16	3	31	1
JC Adams	2	2	0	1	6	3	5	0

No. 744: 4th Test

VENUE:	Georgetown (Guyana)
DATE:	27th February to 2nd March 1998
TOSS WON BY:	West Indies
RESULT:	West Indies won by 242 runs

WEST INDIES 1st innings

Batsman	Dismissal	Runs	2nd innings	Runs
SL Campbell	c Russell b Headley	10	c Ramprakash b Fraser	17
SC Williams	c Thorpe b Fraser	13	c Stewart b Headley	0
BC Lara*	c Thorpe b Croft	93	c Butcher b Tufnell	30
S Chanderpaul	c Thorpe b Fraser	118	run out	0
CL Hooper	c Hussain b Headley	43	lbw b Headley	34
JC Adams	lbw b Tufnell	28	lbw b Croft	18
D Williams+	c Croft b Headley	0	c Tufnell b Ramprakash	15
IR Bishop	c Butcher b Croft	14	not out	44
CEL Ambrose	c Headley b Tufnell	0	lbw b Croft	2
CA Walsh	not out	3	c Russell b Croft	0
D Ramnarine	c Russell b Croft	0	c Russell b Headley	19
Extras	(4b, 14lb, 0w, 12nb)	30	(1b, 11lb, 0w, 6nb)	18
Total	128.1 overs	**352**	72 overs	**197**

1st innings FoW: 16, 38, 197, 295, 316, 320, 347, 349, 352, 352
2nd innings FoW: 4, 32, 32, 75, 93, 123, 123, 127, 127, 197

Bowler	O	M	R	W	O	M	R	W
DW Headley	31	7	90	3	13	5	37	3
ARC Fraser	33	8	77	2	11	2	24	1
MA Butcher	3	0	15	0				
RDB Croft	36.1	9	89	3	22	9	50	3
PCR Tufnell	25	10	63	2	24	5	72	1
MR Ramprakash					2	1	2	1

ENGLAND 1st innings

Batsman	Dismissal	Runs	2nd innings	Runs
MA Atherton*	c Lara b Ambrose	0	lbw b Ambrose	1
AJ Stewart	c D Williams b Walsh	20	lbw b Walsh	12
MA Butcher	lbw b Bishop	11	lbw b Hooper	17
N Hussain	lbw b Walsh	11	c Adams b Walsh	0
GP Thorpe	c D Williams b Ram'ine	10	c Ramnarine b Ambrose	3
MR Rampr'sh	not out	64	c D Williams b Walsh	34
RC Russell+	lbw b Ramnarine	0	c Lara b Ambrose	21
RDB Croft	c Lara b Hooper	26	c D Williams b Hooper	14
DW Headley	c D Williams b Hooper	0	c Chanderpaul b Ambrose	9
ARC Fraser	c Lara b Ramnarine	0	c Walsh b Hooper	2
PCR Tufnell	c Bishop b Ambrose	2	not out	0
Extras	(10b, 2lb, 0w, 14nb)	26	(9b, 2lb, 1w, 12nb)	24
Total	87.1 overs	**170**	62.1 overs	**137**

1st innings FoW: 1, 37, 41, 65, 73, 75, 139, 139, 140, 170
2nd innings FoW: 6, 22, 22, 28, 58, 90, 118, 125, 135, 137

Bowler	O	M	R	W	O	M	R	W
CA Walsh	27	7	47	2	15	4	25	3
CEL Ambrose	12.1	5	21	2	14.1	3	38	4
D Ramnarine	17	8	26	3	11	5	23	0
IR Bishop	13	4	34	1	3	1	4	0
JC Adams	3	2	1	0	1	0	5	0
CL Hooper	15	5	29	2	18	8	31	3

No. 745: 5th Test

VENUE:	Bridgetown (Barbados)
DATE:	12th-16th March 1998
TOSS WON BY:	West Indies
RESULT:	Match drawn

ENGLAND 1st innings

Batsman	Dismissal	Runs	2nd innings	Runs
MA Atherton*	c Ambrose b Walsh	11	c Williams b Bishop	64
AJ Stewart	c Williams b Walsh	12	c Lara b Bishop	48
MA Butcher	c Hooper b Ambrose	19	c Lambert b Ambrose	26
N Hussain	c Lara b McLean	5	not out	46
GP Thorpe	c Lara b Hooper	103	not out	36
MR Ram'ash	c & b McLean	154		
RC Russell+	c Wallace b Hooper	32		
DW Headley	c Holder b Hooper	31		
AR Caddick	c Chanderpaul b Hooper	3		
ARC Fraser	c Walsh b Hooper	3		
PCR Tufnell	not out	1		
Extras	(0b, 10lb, 2w, 17nb)	29	(1b, 6lb, 0w, 6nb)	13
Total	153.5 overs	**403**	71 overs	**233**

1st innings FoW: 23, 24, 33, 53, 131, 336, 382, 392, 402, 403
2nd innings FoW: 101, 128, 173

Bowler	O	M	R	W	O	M	R	W
CA Walsh	34	8	84	2	12	1	40	0
CEL Ambrose	31	6	62	1	12	4	48	1
NAM McLean	27	5	73	2	7	0	16	0
CL Hooper	37.5	7	80	5	21	5	58	0
IR Bishop	20	1	74	0	14	1	51	2
S Chanderpaul	4	0	20	0	5	3	13	0

WEST INDIES 1st innings

Batsman	Dismissal	Runs	2nd innings	Runs
CB Lambert	c Russell b Caddick	55	c Headley b Fraser	29
PA Wallace	lbw b Headley	45	lbw b Caddick	61
IR Bishop	c Russell b Tufnell	4		
BC Lara*	c Butcher b Headley	31	not out	13
S Chanderpaul	c Stewart b Fraser	45	not out	3
RIC Holder	b Ramprakash	10		
CL Hooper	lbw b Fraser	9		
D Williams+	c Ramprakash b Caddick	2		
NAM McLean	not out	7		
CEL Ambrose	st Russell b Tufnell	26		
CA Walsh	c & b Headley	6		
Extras	(13b, 2lb, 0w, 7nb)	22	(0b, 5lb, 0w, 1nb)	6
Total	107.3 overs	**262**	37.3 overs	**112**

1st innings FoW: 82, 91, 134, 164, 190, 214, 221, 221, 256, 262
2nd innings FoW: 72, 108

Bowler	O	M	R	W	O	M	R	W
DW Headley	17.3	2	64	3	2	0	14	0
ARC Fraser	22	5	80	2	11	3	33	1
AR Caddick	17	8	28	2	6	1	19	1
PCR Tufnell	33	15	43	2	16.3	3	38	0
MR Ramprakash	18	7	32	1	2	1	3	0

West Indies

No. 746: 6th Test
VENUE: St. John's (Antigua)
DATE: 20th-24th March 1998
TOSS WON BY: West Indies
RESULT: WI won by an innings and 52 runs

South Africa

No. 747: 1st Test
VENUE: Edgbaston
DATE: 4th-8th June 1998
TOSS WON BY: South Africa
RESULT: Match drawn

ENGLAND

	1st innings		2nd innings	
MA Atherton*	c Ramnarine b Ambrose	15	lbw b Ambrose	13
AJ Stewart	b Rose	22	c Wallace b Hooper	79
MA Butcher	c Lara b Ambrose	0	c Murray b Ambrose	0
DW Headley	c Lara b Ambrose	1	c Murray b Ramnarine	1
N Hussain	c Holder b Ramnarine	37	run out	106
GP Thorpe	lbw b Ramnarine	5	not out	84
MR Ramp'sh	c Chanderpaul b Walsh	14	b Ramnarine	0
RC Russell+	c Lambert b Ramnarine	0	lbw b Walsh	9
AR Caddick	c Walsh b Ramnarine	8	c Murray b Walsh	0
ARC Fraser	b Walsh	9	c Chanderpaul b Walsh	4
PCR Tufnell	not out	2	c Lambert b Walsh	0
Extras	(1b, 2lb, 0w, 11nb)	14	(6b, 4lb, 1w, 14nb)	25
Total	70.5 overs	**127**	147.2 overs	**321**

1st innings FoW: 27, 27, 38, 57, 66, 105, 105, 105, 117, 127
2nd innings FoW: 45, 49, 127, 295, 300, 312, 313, 316, 320, 321

CA Walsh	25.5	8	52	2	31.2	8	80	4
CEL Ambrose	17	5	28	3	20	5	66	2
D Ramnarine	17	5	29	4	46	19	70	2
CL Hooper	1	1	0	0	39	18	56	1
FA Rose	9	4	14	1	11	2	39	0
CB Lambert	1	0	1	0				

WEST INDIES 1st innings

			2nd innings
CB Lambert	c Thorpe b Ramprakash	104	
PA Wallace	b Headley	92	
BC Lara*	c Stewart b Caddick	89	
S Chanderpaul	lbw b Fraser	5	
CL Hooper	not out	108	
RIC Holder	c & b Caddick	45	
JR Murray+	c Hussain b Headley	4	
FA Rose	lbw b Caddick	2	
CEL Ambrose	not out	19	
D Ramnarine			
CA Walsh			
Extras	(0b, 14lb, 0w, 18nb)	32	
Total	131 overs	**500**	

1st innings FoW: 167, 300, 317, 324, 451, 458, 465

AR Caddick	26	3	111	3
ARC Fraser	21	3	88	1
DW Headley	30	3	109	2
PCR Tufnell	35	6	97	0
MR Ramprakash	19	0	81	1

ENGLAND

	1st innings		2nd innings	
MA Butcher	c Kallis b Adams	77	lbw b Pollock	11
MA Atherton	c Boucher b Donald	103	b Klusener	43
AJ Stewart*+	c Cullinan b Klusener	49	b Donald	28
N Hussain	lbw b Adams	35	lbw b Donald	0
GP Thorpe	b Pollock	10	b Klusener	43
MR Rampr'sh	b Donald	49	c Kallis b Adams	11
MA Ealham	b Adams	5	c Pollock b Klusener	7
DG Cork	c Pollock b Donald	36	st Boucher b Adams	2
RDB Croft	c Boucher b Donald	19	not out	1
D Gough	not out	16		
ARC Fraser	c Cronje b Pollock	9		
Extras	(18b, 26lb, 8w, 2nb)	54	(10b, 6lb, 8w, 0nb)	24
Total	181 overs	**462**	45.1 overs	**170**

1st innings FoW: 179, 249, 309, 309, 329, 356, 411, 430, 437, 462
2nd innings FoW: 24, 31, 80, 148, 153, 167, 167, 170

AA Donald	35	9	95	4	10	1	48	2
SM Pollock	42	12	92	2	12	2	43	1
L Klusener	31	7	74	1	11	4	27	3
WJ Cronje	11	3	28	0				
PR Adams	42	10	83	3	12.1	3	36	2
JH Kallis	20	7	46	0				

SOUTH AFRICA 1st innings

			2nd innings
G Kirsten	c Butcher b Cork	12	
G Liebenberg	c (sub) b Cork	3	
JH Kallis	c Stewart b Cork	61	
DJ Cullinan	b Fraser	78	
WJ Cronje*	c (sub) b Cork	1	
JN Rhodes	c Stewart b Fraser	95	
SM Pollock	c Croft b Fraser	16	
MV Boucher+	c Stewart b Fraser	0	
L Klusener	c Stewart b Ealham	57	
AA Donald	c & b Cork	7	
PR Adams	not out	6	
Extras	(0b, 5lb, 0w, 2nb)	7	
Total	117.3 overs	**343**	

1st innings FoW: 6, 38, 119, 125, 191, 211, 224, 328, 328, 343

ARC Fraser	34	6	103	4
DG Cork	32.3	7	93	5
MA Ealham	23	8	55	1
RDB Croft	27	3	85	0
MA Butcher	1	0	2	0

No. 748: 2nd Test

VENUE:	Lord's
DATE:	18th-22nd June 1998
TOSS WON BY:	England
RESULT:	South Africa won by 10 wickets

No. 749: 3rd Test

VENUE:	Old Trafford
DATE:	2nd-6th July 1998
TOSS WON BY:	South Africa
RESULT:	Match drawn

SOUTH AFRICA 1st innings / 2nd innings

Batsman	1st innings		2nd innings	
AM Bacher	c Stewart b Cork	22		
G Kirsten	b Cork	4	not out	9
JH Kallis	b Cork	0		
DJ Cullinan	c Stewart b Cork	16	not out	5
WJ Cronje*	c Rampr'sh b Ealham	81		
JN Rhodes	c Stewart b Fraser	117		
SM Pollock	c Hussain b Cork	14		
MV Boucher+	c Stewart b Headley	35		
L Klusener	b Headley	34		
AA Donald	not out	7		
PR Adams	c Stewart b Cork	3		
Extras	(1b, 20lb, 0w, 6nb)	27	(0b, 0lb, 0w, 1nb)	1
Total	108.1 overs	360	1.1 overs	15

1st innings FoW: 8, 16, 43, 46, 230, 273, 283, 340, 353, 360

Bowler	O	M	R	W		O	M	R	W
ARC Fraser	31	8	78	1		1	0	10	0
DG Cork	31.1	5	119	6		0.1	0	5	0
DW Headley	22	2	69	2					
MA Ealham	15	2	50	1					
RDB Croft	9	3	23	0					

ENGLAND 1st innings / 2nd innings

Batsman	1st innings		2nd innings	
SP James	c Boucher b Donald	10	c Kallis b Pollock	0
MA Atherton	c Kirsten b Pollock	0	c Kallis b Adams	44
N Hussain	c Boucher b Donald	15	lbw b Klusener	105
AJ Stewart*+	lbw b Pollock	14	c Boucher b Kallis	56
DW Headley	c Boucher b Donald	2	c Cronje b Adams	1
GP Thorpe	c Bacher b Kallis	10	lbw b Kallis	0
MR Rampr'sh	c Boucher b Donald	12	b Klusener	0
MA Ealham	run out	8	b Kallis	4
DG Cork	c Klusener b Pollock	12	c Boucher b Kallis	2
RDB Croft	not out	6	not out	16
ARC Fraser	c Boucher b Donald	1	c Pollock b Adams	17
Extras	(8b, 10lb, 0w, 2nb)	20	(1b, 6lb, 5w, 7nb)	19
Total	46.3 overs	110	120 overs	264

1st innings FoW: 15, 15, 40, 48, 49, 64, 74, 97, 109, 110
2nd innings FoW: 8, 102, 106, 222, 224, 224, 225, 228, 233, 264

Bowler	O	M	R	W		O	M	R	W
AA Donald	15.3	5	32	5		24	6	82	0
SM Pollock	18	5	42	3		27	16	29	1
L Klusener	8	5	10	0		23	5	54	2
JH Kallis	5	3	8	1		19	9	24	4
PR Adams						23	7	62	3
WJ Cronje						4	2	6	0

SOUTH AFRICA 1st innings / 2nd innings

Batsman	1st innings		2nd innings
G Kirsten	c Stewart b Fraser	210	
G Liebenberg	b Gough	16	
JH Kallis	b Gough	132	
DJ Cullinan	b Giles	75	
WJ Cronje*	not out	69	
JN Rhodes	c Cork b Gough	12	
L Klusener	not out	17	
MV Boucher+			
AA Donald			
PR Adams			
M Ntini			
Extras	(4b, 10lb, 1w, 6nb)	21	
Total	199.5 overs	552	

1st innings FoW: 25, 263, 439, 457, 490

Bowler	O	M	R	W
D Gough	37	5	116	3
DG Cork	35.5	7	109	0
ARC Fraser	35	11	87	1
RDB Croft	51	14	103	0
AF Giles	36	7	106	1
MR Rampr'sh	5	0	17	0

ENGLAND 1st innings / 2nd innings

Batsman	1st innings		2nd innings	
NV Knight	c Boucher b Donald	11	c Boucher b Donald	1
MA Atherton	c Boucher b Ntini	41	c Ntini b Kallis	89
N Hussain	c Boucher b Donald	4	b Kallis	5
AJ Stewart*+	b Kallis	40	c Klusener b Donald	164
MR Rampr'sh	c Boucher b Adams	30	lbw b Donald	34
DG Cork	c Cronje b Adams	6	b Adams	1
RDB Croft	b Ntini	11	not out	37
GP Thorpe	lbw b Adams	0	b Donald	0
AF Giles	not out	16	c (sub) b Donald	1
D Gough	c Donald b Adams	6	c Kirsten b Donald	12
ARC Fraser	b Kallis	0	not out	0
Extras	(5b, 12lb, 0w, 1nb)	18	(20b, 2lb, 1w, 2nb)	25
Total	82.1 overs	183	171 overs	369

1st innings FoW: 26, 34, 94, 108, 136, 155, 156, 161, 179, 183
2nd innings FoW: 4, 11, 237, 293, 293, 296, 323, 329, 367

Bowler	O	M	R	W		O	M	R	W
AA Donald	13	3	28	2		40	14	88	6
L Klusener	14	4	37	0		3	0	15	0
M Ntini	16	7	28	2		29	11	67	0
PR Adams	31	10	63	4		51	22	90	1
JH Kallis	8.1	3	10	2		41	19	71	2
WJ Cronje						6	3	15	0
DJ Cullinan						1	0	1	0

South Africa | South Africa

	No. 750: 4th Test	No. 751: 5th Test
VENUE:	Trent Bridge	Headingley
DATE:	23rd-27th July 1998	6th-10th August 1998
TOSS WON BY:	England	England
RESULT:	England won by 8 wickets	England won by 23 runs

SOUTH AFRICA 1st innings / 2nd innings

Batsman	1st innings		2nd innings	
G Kirsten	b Gough	7	lbw b Fraser	6
G Liebenberg	c Stewart b Gough	13	lbw b Gough	0
JH Kallis	c Stewart b Flintoff	47	c Stewart b Cork	11
DJ Cullinan	c Ramprakash b Fraser	30	c Ramprakash b Fraser	56
WJ Cronje*	c Hick b Fraser	126	c Stewart b Cork	67
JN Rhodes	lbw b Fraser	24	c Stewart b Cork	2
SM Pollock	c Stewart b Fraser	50	c Stewart b Cork	7
MV Boucher+	lbw b Fraser	4	c Hussain b Fraser	35
S Elworthy	c Ramprakash b Gough	48	lbw b Fraser	10
AA Donald	not out	4	not out	7
PR Adams	c Hick b Gough	0	c Stewart b Fraser	1
Extras	(9b, 3lb, 0w, 9nb)	21	(1b, 4lb, 1w, 0nb)	6
	103.2 overs		75.3 overs	
Total		**374**		**208**

1st innings FoW: 21, 26, 68, 147, 196, 292, 302, 325, 374, 374
2nd innings FoW: 3, 17, 21, 119, 122, 136, 189, 193, 200, 208

Bowler	O	M	R	W	O	M	R	W
D Gough	30.2	4	116	4	16	4	56	1
DG Cork	17	2	65	0	20	4	60	4
ARC Fraser	26	7	60	5	28.3	6	62	5
A Flintoff	17	2	52	1	6	1	16	0
IDK Salisbury	9	1	57	0	5	2	9	0
MA Butcher	4	1	12	0				

ENGLAND 1st innings / 2nd innings

Batsman	1st innings		2nd innings	
MA Butcher	lbw b Donald	75	c Boucher b Pollock	22
MA Atherton	c Boucher b Donald	58	not out	98
N Hussain	lbw b Elworthy	22	c Kallis b Donald	58
AJ Stewart*+	c Kirsten b Kallis	19	not out	45
MR Rampr'sh	not out	67		
IDK Salisbury	b Donald	23		
GA Hick	b Donald	6		
A Flintoff	c Boucher b Kallis	17		
DG Cork	c Boucher b Pollock	6		
D Gough	c Boucher b Donald	2		
ARC Fraser	lbw b Pollock	7		
Extras	(7b, 13lb, 1w, 13nb)	34	(2b, 11lb, 2w, 9nb)	24
	127.5 overs		87 overs	
Total		**336**		**247**

1st innings FoW: 145, 150, 191, 199, 244, 254, 285, 302, 307, 336
2nd innings FoW: 40, 192

Bowler	O	M	R	W	O	M	R	W
AA Donald	33	8	109	5	23	8	56	1
SM Pollock	35.5	12	75	2	26	3	79	1
S Elworthy	22	8	41	1	9	1	38	0
JH Kallis	28	9	60	2	13	5	26	0
PR Adams	9	2	31	0	12	4	23	0
WJ Cronje					4	1	12	0

ENGLAND 1st innings / 2nd innings

Batsman	1st innings		2nd innings	
MA Butcher	b Pollock	116	c McMillan b Pollock	37
MA Atherton	c Kallis b Ntini	16	lbw b Donald	1
N Hussain	c Boucher b Pollock	9	c Cronje b Pollock	94
AJ Stewart*+	c Kallis b Donald	15	c Boucher b Pollock	35
MR Rampr'sh	c Boucher b Donald	21	lbw b Pollock	25
GA Hick	c Rhodes b Ntini	2	c Kirsten b Donald	1
A Flintoff	c Liebenberg b Pollock	0	c Boucher b Donald	0
DG Cork	not out	24	c Boucher b Donald	10
IDK Salisbury	b Ntini	0	c Boucher b Pollock	4
D Gough	c McMillan b Ntini	2	c Cullinan b Donald	5
ARC Fraser	c Cullinan b Donald	4	not out	1
Extras	(4b, 5lb, 2w, 10nb)	21	(14b, 1lb, 2w, 10nb)	27
	83.3 overs		110.2 overs	
Total		**230**		**240**

1st innings FoW: 45, 83, 110, 181, 196, 196, 198, 200, 213, 230
2nd innings FoW: 2, 81, 143, 200, 206, 207, 207, 229, 235, 240

Bowler	O	M	R	W	O	M	R	W
AA Donald	20.3	6	44	3	29.2	9	71	5
SM Pollock	24	8	51	3	35	14	53	5
M Ntini	21	5	72	4	15	4	43	0
JH Kallis	9	4	30	0	15	6	31	0
BM McMillan	9	0	24	0	11	0	22	0
DJ Cullinan					1	0	1	0
WJ Cronje					4	1	4	0

SOUTH AFRICA 1st innings / 2nd innings

Batsman	1st innings		2nd innings	
G Kirsten	lbw b Fraser	6	c Atherton b Gough	3
GFJ Liebenberg	c Hick b Fraser	21	lbw b Gough	6
JH Kallis	c Ramprakash b Cork	40	lbw b Fraser	3
DJ Cullinan	c Stewart b Gough	27	lbw b Gough	0
WJ Cronje*	lbw b Fraser	57	c Stewart b Fraser	0
JN Rhodes	c Stewart b Gough	32	c Flintoff b Gough	85
BM McMillan	c Salisbury b Cork	7	c Stewart b Cork	54
SM Pollock	c Salisbury b Fraser	31	not out	28
MV Boucher+	c Atherton b Gough	6	lbw b Gough	4
AA Donald	lbw b Fraser	0	c Stewart b Fraser	4
M Ntini	not out	4	lbw b Gough	0
Extras	(0b, 20lb, 0w, 1nb)	21	(0b, 6lb, 0w, 2nb)	8
	90.3 overs		75 overs	
Total		**252**		**195**

1st innings FoW: 17, 36, 83, 120, 163, 184, 237, 242, 242, 252
2nd innings FoW: 9, 12, 12, 12, 27, 144, 167, 175, 194, 195

Bowler	O	M	R	W	O	M	R	W
D Gough	24.3	7	58	3	23	6	42	6
ARC Fraser	25	9	42	5	23	8	50	3
DG Cork	21	3	72	2	17	1	50	1
A Flintoff	8	1	31	0	4	0	13	0
IDK Salisbury	3	0	6	0	8	0	34	0
MA Butcher	9	4	23	0				

Sri Lanka

No. 752: 1st Test
VENUE: The Oval
DATE: 27th-31st August 1998
TOSS WON BY: Sri Lanka
RESULT: Sri Lanka won by 10 wickets

ENGLAND	1st innings		2nd innings	
MA Butcher	c Jayasuriya b Wick'he	10	st Kaluwith'na b Murali'n	15
SP James	c & b Murali'n	36	c Jaya'ene b Murali'n	25
GA Hick	c Kaluwith'na b Wick'he	107	lbw b Murali'n	0
AJ Stewart*+	c Tillakaratne b Perera	2	run out	32
MR Rampr'sh	c Jaya'ene b Murali'n	53	c Tilla'tne b Murali'n	42
JP Crawley	not out	156	b Muralidharan	14
BC Hollioake	c Atapattu b Murali'n	14	lbw b Muralidharan	0
DG Cork	b Muralidharan	6	c Kaluwith'na b Murali'n	8
IDK Salisbury	b Muralidharan	2	lbw b Muralidharan	0
D Gough	c Kaluwith'na b Murali'n	4	b Muralidharan	15
ARC Fraser	b Muralidharan	32	not out	0
Extras	(1b, 11lb, 2w, 9nb)	23	(7b, 8lb, 1w, 14nb)	30
	158.3 overs		129.2 overs	
Total		**445**		**181**

1st innings FoW: 16, 78, 81, 209, 230, 277, 333, 343, 356, 445
2nd innings FoW: 25, 78, 78, 93, 116, 116, 127, 127, 180, 181

GP Wickramasinghe	30	4	81	2	4	0	16	0
SA Perera	40	10	104	1	11	2	22	0
HDPK Dharmasena	18	3	55	0	19.3	13	12	0
M Muralidharan	59.3	14	155	7	54.2	27	65	9
ST Jayasuriya	11	0	38	0	28	14	30	0
PA de Silva					10.3	3	16	0
DPM Jayawardene					2	0	5	0

SRI LANKA	1st innings		2nd innings	
ST Jayasuriya	c Stewart b Hollioake	213	not out	24
MS Atapattu	lbw b Cork	15	not out	9
DPM Jayaw'ne	c Hollioake b Fraser	9		
PA de Silva	c Stewart b Hollioake	152		
A Ranatunga*	lbw b Gough	51		
H Tillakaratne	lbw b Gough	0		
R Kaluwith'na+	c Crawley b Cork	25		
H Dharmasena	lbw b Fraser	13		
SA Perera	not out	43		
GP Wickr'he	b Fraser	0		
M Murali'n	c Stewart b Salisbury	30		
Extras	(15b, 20lb, 1w, 4nb)	40	(0b, 4lb, 0w, 0nb)	4
	156.5 overs		5 overs	
Total		**591**		**37**

1st innings FoW: 53, 85, 328, 450, 450, 488, 504, 526, 532, 591

D Gough	30	5	102	2				
ARC Fraser	23	3	95	3	2	0	19	0
BC Hollioake	26	2	105	2	1	0	11	0
DG Cork	36	5	128	2	2	0	3	0
IDK Salisbury	25.5	7	86	1				
MR Ramprakash	5	0	24	0				
MA Butcher	11	2	16	0				

Australia

No. 753: 1st Test
VENUE: Brisbane (Gabba)
DATE: 20th-24th November 1998
TOSS WON BY: Australia
RESULT: Match drawn

AUSTRALIA	1st innings		2nd innings	
MA Taylor*	c Hussain b Cork	46	b Cork	0
MJ Slater	c Butcher b Mullally	16	c & b Fraser	113
JL Langer	lbw b Gough	8	c Mullally b Croft	74
ME Waugh	c Stewart b Mullally	31	not out	27
SR Waugh	c Stewart b Mullally	112	not out	16
RT Ponting	c Butcher b Cork	21		
IA Healy*+	c Mullally b Fraser	134		
M Kasprowicz	c Stewart b Mullally	0		
DW Fleming	not out	71		
SCG MacGill	c Stewart b Mullally	20		
GD McGrath	c Atherton b Croft	5		
Extras	(0b, 14lb, 1w, 6nb)	21	(1b, 1lb, 0w, 5nb)	7
	158 overs		62 overs	
Total		**485**		**237**

1st innings FoW: 30, 59, 106, 106, 178, 365, 365, 420, 445, 485
2nd innings FoW: 20, 182, 199

D Gough	34	4	135	1	6	0	50	0
DG Cork	31	6	98	2	5	0	18	1
AD Mullally	40	10	105	5	14	4	38	0
RDB Croft	23	6	55	1	20	2	71	1
ARC Fraser	28	7	76	1	15	1	52	1
MR Ramprakash	2	1	2	0	2	0	6	0

ENGLAND	1st innings		2nd innings	
MA Butcher	c & b ME Waugh	116	lbw b MacGill	40
MA Atherton	c ME Waugh b McGrath	0	c Fleming b McGrath	28
N Hussain	c Healy b Kasprowicz	59	b MacGill	47
AJ Stewart*+	c Kasprowicz b MacGill	8	c Ponting b ME Waugh	3
GP Thorpe	c Langer b McGrath	77	c Langer b ME Waugh	9
MR Rampr'sh	not out	69	st Healy b MacGill	14
DG Cork	c MacGill b McGrath	0	not out	21
RDB Croft	b Kasprowicz	23	not out	4
D Gough	lbw b McGrath	0		
AD Mullally	c Kasprowicz b McGrath	0		
ARC Fraser	c ME Waugh b McGrath	1		
Extras	(1b, 9lb, 0w, 12nb)	22	(0b, 3lb, 1w, 9nb)	13
	128.2 overs		68 overs	
Total		**375**		**179**

1st innings FoW: 11, 145, 168, 240, 315, 319, 360, 372, 372, 375
2nd innings FoW: 46, 96, 103, 133, 148, 161

GD McGrath	34.2	11	85	6	16	6	30	1
DW Fleming	27	5	83	0	7	2	12	0
MS Kasprowicz	29	6	82	2	8	3	28	0
SCG MacGill	24	5	70	1	22	3	51	3
SR Waugh	3	0	17	0				
RT Ponting	3	0	10	0	1	1	0	0
ME Waugh	8	1	18	1	14	0	55	2

Australia

ENGLAND	1st innings		2nd innings	
MA Butcher	c Healy b Fleming	0	c Ponting b Fleming	1
MA Atherton	c Healy b McGrath	1	c Taylor b Fleming	35
N Hussain	c Healy b McGrath	6	lbw b Fleming	1
AJ Stewart*+	b McGrath	38	c Taylor b Fleming	0
MR Ramp'sh	c Taylor b Fleming	26	not out	47
JP Crawley	c ME Waugh b Gillespie	4	c Langer b Miller	15
GA Hick	c Healy b Gillespie	0	c Ponting b Gillespie	68
DG Cork	c Taylor b Fleming	2	lbw b Gillespie	16
AJ Tudor	not out	18	c Healy b Gillespie	0
D Gough	c ME Waugh b Fleming	11	lbw b Gillespie	0
AD Mullally	c Healy b Fleming	0	b Gillespie	0
Extras	(0b, 2lb, 2w, 2nb)	6	(0b, 0lb, 0w, 8nb)	8
Total	39 overs	**112**	70.2 overs	**191**

1st innings FoW: 2, 4, 19, 62, 74, 74, 81, 90, 108, 112
2nd innings FoW: 5, 11, 15, 40, 67, 158, 189, 189, 189, 191

GD McGrath	16	4	37	3	26	10	47	0
DW Fleming	14	3	46	5	19	7	45	4
JN Gillespie	7	0	23	2	15.2	2	88	5
CR Miller	2	0	4	0	10	4	11	1

AUSTRALIA	1st innings		2nd innings	
MA Taylor*	c Stewart b Cork	61	c Hick b Mullally	3
MJ Slater	c Butcher b Gough	34	c & b Gough	17
JL Langer	c Crawley b Ramprakash	15	c Atherton b Tudor	7
ME Waugh	c Butcher b Tudor	36	not out	17
JN Gillespie	c Stewart b Mullally	11		
SR Waugh	b Tudor	33	not out	15
RT Ponting	c Stewart b Tudor	11		
IA Healy+	lbw b Gough	12		
DW Fleming	c Hick b Gough	0		
CR Miller	not out	3		
GD McGrath	c Cork b Tudor	0		
Extras	(1b, 10lb, 0w, 13nb)	24	(0b, 3lb, 0w, 2nb)	5
Total	89.2 overs	**240**	23 overs	**64**

1st innings FoW: 81, 115, 138, 165, 208, 214, 228, 228, 239, 239
2nd innings FoW: 16, 24, 36

D Gough	25	10	43	3	9	5	18	1
DG Cork	21	5	49	1				
AJ Tudor	20.2	5	89	4	5	0	19	1
AD Mullally	21	10	36	1	9	0	24	1
MR Ramprakash	2	0	12	1				

Australia

AUSTRALIA	1st innings		2nd innings	
MJ Slater	c Stewart b Headley	17	lbw b Gough	103
MA Taylor*	c Hussain b Such	59	lbw b Such	29
JL Langer	not out	179	c (sub) b Such	52
ME Waugh	c & b Such	7	not out	51
SR Waugh	c Hick b Gough	59	c Hick b Headley	7
RT Ponting	c Hick b Gough	5	b Gough	10
IA Healy+	c Ramprakash b Headley	13	not out	7
DW Fleming	lbw b Headley	12		
SCG MacGill	b Such	0		
CR Miller	lbw b Headley	11		
GD McGrath	c Stewart b Gough	10		
Extras	(0b, 6lb, 0w, 13nb)	19	(0b, 12lb, 1w, 6nb)	19
Total	125.5 overs	**391**	98 overs	**278**

1st innings FoW: 28, 140, 156, 264, 274, 311, 338, 339, 354, 391
2nd innings FoW: 54., 188, 216, 230, 268

D Gough	29.5	4	103	3	22	2	76	2
AD Mullally	26	5	59	0	16	6	18	0
DW Headley	23	1	97	4	18	1	78	1
PM Such	38	8	99	3	29	5	66	2
MR Ramprakash	9	1	27	0	12	1	27	0
GA Hick					1	0	1	0

ENGLAND	1st innings		2nd innings	
MA Butcher	lbw b Miller	6	c Healy b Fleming	19
MA Atherton	c Taylor b MacGill	41	c ME Waugh b Miller	5
N Hussain	not out	89	lbw b Miller	41
AJ Stewart*+	c Slater b Miller	0	not out	63
MR Rampr'sh	c M Waugh b McGrath	61	b Fleming	57
JP Crawley	b McGrath	5	c M Waugh b McGrath	13
GA Hick	c Taylor b MacGill	8	c Ponting b McGrath	0
DW Headley	lbw b MacGill	0	c ME Waugh b Miller	2
D Gough	c Healy b MacGill	7	c Healy b McGrath	3
AD Mullally	b Fleming	0	c Healy b Fleming	4
PM Such	lbw b Fleming	0	lbw b McGrath	0
Extras	(1b, 3lb, 1w, 5nb)	10	(7b, 9lb, 0w, 14nb)	30
Total	82.5 overs	**227**	89 overs	**237**

1st innings FoW: 18, 83, 84, 187, 195, 210, 210, 226, 227, 227
2nd innings FoW: 27, 31, 120, 122, 163, 221, 221, 231, 236, 237

GD McGrath	18	4	48	2	17	0	50	4
DW Fleming	10.5	2	34	2	21	3	56	3
CR Miller	23	6	71	2	24	1	57	3
SCG MacGill	28	6	53	4	25	8	55	0
ME Waugh	3	0	17	0	2	1	3	0

No. 756: 4th Test

VENUE:	Melbourne (MCG)
DATE:	26th-29th December 1998
TOSS WON BY:	Australia
RESULT:	England won by 12 runs

ENGLAND

Batsman	1st innings		2nd innings	
MA Atherton	c Healy b McGrath	0	b Fleming	0
AJ Stewart*	b MacGill	107	c Slater b MacGill	52
MA Butcher	c Langer b McGrath	0	c Slater b MacGill	14
N Hussain	c Healy b Nicholson	19	b McGrath	1
MR Rampr'sh	c McGrath b SR Waugh	63	c Slater b Nicholson	50
GA Hick	c Fleming b MacGill	39	b Nicholson	14
WK Hegg+	c Healy b SR Waugh	3	b Fleming	60
DW Headley	c Taylor b McGrath	14	c MacGill b Nicholson	9
D Gough	b MacGill	11	c Slater b MacGill	4
ARC Fraser	not out	0	not out	7
AD Mullally	lbw b MacGill	0	c & b McGrath	16
Extras	(0b, 7lb, 1w, 6nb)	14	(2b, 4lb, 0w, 11nb)	17
	76 overs		80.2 overs	
Total		**270**		**244**

1st innings FoW: 0, 4, 81, 200, 202, 206, 244, 266, 270, 270
2nd innings FoW: 5, 61, 66, 78, 127, 178, 202, 221, 221, 244

Bowler	O	M	R	W	O	M	R	W
GD McGrath	22	5	64	3	20.2	5	56	2
DW Fleming	19	3	71	0	17	4	45	2
MJ Nicholson	10	0	59	1	15	4	56	3
SCG MacGill	19	2	61	4	27	3	81	3
SR Waugh	6	2	8	2	1	1	0	0

AUSTRALIA

Batsman	1st innings		2nd innings	
MA Taylor*	c Hick b Gough	7	c Headley b Mullally	19
MJ Slater	lbw b Gough	1	lbw b Headley	18
JL Langer	c Hussain b Gough	44	c Rampr'sh b Mullally	30
ME Waugh	lbw b Fraser	36	c Hick b Headley	43
SR Waugh	not out	122	not out	30
DS Lehmann	c Hegg b Gough	13	c Hegg b Headley	4
IA Healy+	c Headley b Fraser	36	c Hick b Headley	0
DW Headley	c Hick b Mullally	12	lbw b Headley	0
MJ Nicholson	b Gough	5	c Hegg b Headley	9
SCG MacGill	c Hegg b Mullally	43	b Gough	0
GD McGrath	b Mullally	0	lbw b Gough	0
Extras	(4b, 6lb, 0w, 11nb)	21	(4b, 1lb, 0w, 4nb)	9
	98.3 overs		46.4 overs	
Total		**340**		**162**

1st innings FoW: 13, 26, 98, 127, 151, 209, 235, 252, 340, 340
2nd innings FoW: 31, 41, 103, 130, 140, 140, 140, 161, 162, 162

Bowler	O	M	R	W	O	M	R	W
D Gough	28	7	96	5	15.4	2	54	2
DW Headley	25	3	86	0	17	5	60	6
AD Mullally	21.3	5	64	3	10	4	20	2
MR Ramprakash	2	0	6	0				
ARC Fraser	22	0	78	2	4	0	23	0

No. 757: 5th Test

VENUE:	Sydney (SCG)
DATE:	2nd-5th January 1999
TOSS WON BY:	Australia
RESULT:	Australia won by 98 runs

AUSTRALIA

Batsman	1st innings		2nd innings	
MA Taylor*	c Hick b Headley	2	c Stewart b Gough	2
MJ Slater	c Hegg b Headley	18	c Hegg b Headley	123
JL Langer	c Ramprakash b Tudor	26	lbw b Headley	1
ME Waugh	c Hegg b Headley	121	c Rampr'sh b Headley	24
SR Waugh	b Such	96	b Headley	8
DS Lehmann	c Hussain b Tudor	32	c Crawley b Such	0
IA Healy+	c Hegg b Gough	14	c Crawley b Such	5
SK Warne	not out	2	c Ramprakash b Such	8
SCG MacGill	b Gough	0	c Butcher b Such	6
CR Miller	b Gough	0	not out	3
GD McGrath	c Hick b Headley	0	c Stewart b Such	0
Extras	(0b, 2lb, 0w, 9nb)	11	(3b, 1lb, 0w, 0nb)	4
	87.3 overs		64.5 overs	
Total		**322**		**184**

1st innings FoW: 4, 52, 52, 242, 284, 319, 321, 321, 321, 322
2nd innings FoW: 16, 25, 64, 73, 91, 110, 141, 180, 184, 184

Bowler	O	M	R	W	O	M	R	W
D Gough	17	4	61	3	15	3	51	1
DW Headley	19.3	4	62	4	19	7	40	4
AJ Tudor	12	1	64	2	5	2	8	0
PM Such	24	6	77	1	25.5	5	81	5
MR Ramprakash	15	0	56	0				

ENGLAND

Batsman	1st innings		2nd innings	
MA Butcher	lbw b Warne	36	st Healy b Warne	27
AJ Stewart*	c Warne b McGrath	3	st Healy b MacGill	42
N Hussain	c ME Waugh b Miller	42	c & b MacGill	53
MR Rampr'sh	c MacGill b McGrath	14	c Taylor b McGrath	14
GA Hick	c Warne b MacGill	23	b MacGill	7
JP Crawley	c Taylor b MacGill	44	lbw b Miller	5
WK Hegg+	b Miller	15	c Healy b MacGill	3
AJ Tudor	b MacGill	14	b MacGill	3
DW Headley	c McGrath b MacGill	8	c Healy b MacGill	16
D Gough	lbw b MacGill	0	not out	7
PM Such	not out	0	c & b MacGill	2
Extras	(8b, 8lb, 1w, 4nb)	21	(0b, 5lb, 1w, 3nb)	9
	80.1 overs		66.1 overs	
Total		**220**		**188**

1st innings FoW: 18, 56, 88, 137, 139, 171, 204, 213, 213, 220
2nd innings FoW: 57, 77, 110, 131, 150, 157, 162, 175, 180, 188

Bowler	O	M	R	W	O	M	R	W
GD McGrath	17	7	35	2	10	1	40	1
CR Miller	23	6	45	2	17	1	50	1
SCG MacGill	20.1	2	57	5	20.1	4	50	7
SK Warne	20	4	67	1	19	3	43	1

No. 758: 1st Test

VENUE:	Edgbaston
DATE:	1st-3rd July 1999
TOSS WON BY:	New Zealand
RESULT:	England won by 7 wickets

NEW ZEALAND

Batsman	1st innings		2nd innings	
RG Twose	c Thorpe b Mullally	0	lbw b Caddick	0
MJ Horne	lbw b Caddick	12	c Read b Mullally	1
SP Fleming*	c Thorpe b Tudor	27	c Read b Tufnell	25
NJ Astle	c Read b Butcher	26	c Read b Mullally	9
CD McMillan	c Thorpe b Caddick	18	c Butcher b Mullally	15
CL Cairns	c & b Caddick	17	c Read b Caddick	3
AC Parore+	c Read b Mullally	73	c Stewart b Caddick	0
DJ Nash	c Hussain b Tufnell	21	c Read b Caddick	0
DL Vettori	c Hussain b Tufnell	1	b Caddick	0
SB Doull	c Butcher b Tufnell	11	st Read b Tufnell	46
GI Allott	not out	7	not out	0
Extras	(1b, 5lb, 1w, 6nb)	13	(1b, 4lb, 1w, 2nb)	8
	88.4 overs		37.1 overs	
Total		**226**		**107**

1st innings FoW: 0, 19, 55, 73, 103, 104, 189, 191, 211, 226
2nd innings FoW: 0, 5, 17, 39, 46, 46, 52, 52, 106, 107

Bowler	O	M	R	W	O	M	R	W
AD Mullally	26.4	5	72	2	16	3	48	3
AR Caddick	27	12	57	3	14	3	32	5
AJ Tudor	11	2	44	1	5	2	15	0
MA Butcher	7	2	25	1				
PCR Tufnell	17	9	22	3	2.1	0	7	2

ENGLAND

Batsman	1st innings		2nd innings	
MA Butcher	run out	11	c Parore b Nash	32
AJ Stewart	lbw b Allott	1	b Allott	0
N Hussain*	b Doull	10	b Allott	44
GP Thorpe	c Astle b Allott	6	not out	21
MR Rampr'sh	c Parore b Cairns	0		
A Habib	b Cairns	1		
CMW Read+	c (sub) b Nash	1		
AR Caddick	c Parore b Nash	33		
AJ Tudor	not out	32	not out	99
AD Mullally	c Parore b Nash	0		
PCR Tufnell	c Fleming b Cairns	6		
Extras	(8b, 11lb, 0w, 6nb)	25	(7b, 2lb, 0w, 5nb)	14
	46.4 overs		43.4 overs	
Total		**126**		**210**

1st innings FoW: 5, 26, 28, 33, 38, 40, 45, 115, 115, 126
2nd innings FoW: 3, 76, 174

Bowler	O	M	R	W	O	M	R	W
GI Allott	14	3	38	2	15	0	71	2
SB Doull	12	6	17	1	7	0	48	0
CL Cairns	9.4	3	35	3	4	0	18	0
DJ Nash	11	7	17	3	7	0	29	1
DL Vettori					6	1	22	0
NJ Astle					1	1	0	0
CD McMillan					3.4	0	14	0

No. 759: 2nd Test

VENUE:	Lord's
DATE:	22nd-27th July 1999
TOSS WON BY:	England
RESULT:	New Zealand won by 9 wickets

ENGLAND

Batsman	1st innings		2nd innings	
MA Butcher	c Parore b Cairns	8	c Astle b Vettori	20
AJ Stewart	c Fleming b Nash	50	b Vettori	35
*N Hussain	c Parore b Cairns	61	absent hurt	
GP Thorpe	c Astle b Cairns	7	b Cairns	7
MR Rampr'sh	lbw b Nash	4	c Parore b Astle	24
A Habib	b Nash	6	c Astle b Allott	19
C Read	b Cairns	0	lbw b Nash	37
AR Caddick	run out (Horne/Astle)	18	c Fleming b Allott	45
DW Headley	lbw b Cairns	4	c Fleming b Allott	12
AD Mullally	c Astle b Cairns	0	c Twose b Cairns	10
PCR Tufnell	not out	1	not out	5
Extras	(5b, 8lb, 14nb)	27	(5b, 3lb, 7nb)	15
Total		**186**		**229**

1st innings FoW: 35, 79, 102, 112, 123, 125, 150, 165, 170, 186
2nd innings FoW: 55, 71, 78, 97, 123, 127, 205, 216, 229

Bowler	O	M	R	W	O	M	R	W
Allott	10	1	37	0	16.4	6	36	3
Cairns	21.1	1	77	6	25	6	67	2
Nash	23	11	50	3	25	9	50	1
Astle	7	3	9	0	4	2	6	1
Vettori	31	12	62	2				

NEW ZEALAND

Batsman	1st innings		2nd innings	
MJ Horne	c Hussain b Headley	100	lbw b Caddick	26
MD Bell	lbw b Headley	15	not out	26
*SP Fleming	c Read b Mullally	1	not out	5
NJ Astle	c Read b Mullally	43		
RG Twose	c Caddick b Headley	52		
CD McMillan	c Read b Caddick	3		
DL Vettori	c Thorpe b Tufnell	54		
A Parore	b Caddick	12	27	
CL Cairns	b Caddick	31	42	
DJ Nash	c Mullally b Tufnell	6		
GI Allott	not out	1		
Extras	(1b, 24lb, w2, 13nb)	40	(2b, 1nb)	3
Total		**358**		**60**

1st innings FoW: 43, 45, 112, 232, 239, 242, 275, 345, 351, 358
2nd innings FoW: 37

Bowler	O	M	R	W	O	M	R	W
Mullally	27	7	98	2	5	0	21	0
Caddick	34	11	92	3	10	4	18	1
Headley	27	7	74	3				
Tufnell	27.1	7	61	2	8	2	19	0
Butcher	3	0	7	0				
Ramprakash	1	0	1	0				

No. 760: 3rd Test	No. 761: 4th Test
VENUE: Old Trafford	VENUE: Oval
DATE: 3rd-9th August 1999	DATE: 19th-23rd August 1999
TOSS WON BY: England	TOSS WON BY: England
RESULT: Match drawn	RESULT: New Zealand won by 83 runs

England 1st innings / 2nd innings

Batsman	1st innings		2nd innings	
*MA Butcher	c Fleming b Cairns	5	lbw b Nash	9
MA Atherton	c Parore b Cairns	11	c Astle b Vettori	48
AJ Stewart	c Parore b Nash	23	not out	83
GP Thorpe	c Bell b Vettori	27	not out	25
GA Hick	lbw b Nash	12		
MR Rampr'sh	not out	69		
DW Headley	c Fleming b Harris	18		
+C Read	b Harris	0		
AR Caddick	run out	12		
PM Such	c Bell b Vettori	0		
PCR Tufnell	c Astle b Nash	1		
Extras	(6b, 10lb, 5w)	21	(9b, 7lb)	16
Total		**199**		**181**

1st innings FoW: 13, 54, 60, 83, 104, 133, 133, 152, 183, 199
2nd innings FoW: 19, 118

Cairns	34	12	72	2	11	1	54	0
Nash	31.1	15	46	3	10	3	26	1
Astle	11	5	14	0	3	1	7	0
Vettori	25	7	35	2	26	12	48	1
Harris	8	4	16	2	18	6	30	0

New Zealand 1st innings / 2nd innings

Batsman	1st innings	
MJ Horne	b Caddick	39
MD Bell	c Atherton b Headley	83
*SP Fleming	lbw b Such	38
NJ Astle	c Such b Caddick	101
RG Twose	lbw b Such	20
CD McMillan	not out	107
+A Parore	c Butcher b Such	10
CL Cairns	c Caddick b Tufnell	41
DJ Nash	c Caddick b Such	26
CZ Harris	b Tufnell	3
DL Vettori	not out	2
Extras	(6b, 17lb, 3nb)	26
Total		**496**

1st innings FoW: 46, 110, 263, 280, 321, 331, 425, 476, 487

Caddick	39	11	112	2
Headley	31	4	115	1
Tufnell	46	12	111	2
Such	41	11	114	4
Hick	1	0	8	0
Butcher	2	0	13	0

New Zealand 1st innings / 2nd innings

Batsman	1st innings		2nd innings	
MJ Horne	c Caddick b Irani	15	lbw b Giddins	10
MD Bell	c Stewart b Mullally	23	c Irani b Caddick	4
*SP Fleming	not out	66	c Thorpe b Caddick	4
NJ Astle	c Stewart b Caddick	9	c Irani b Giddins	5
RG Twose	c Maddy b Giddins	1	c Stewart b Giddins	0
CD McMillan	b Tufnell	19	lbw b Mullally	26
+A Parore	c Ramprakash b Tufnell	0	b Caddick	1
CL Cairns	b Mullally	11	c & b Mullally	80
DJ Nash	c Ramprakash b Caddick	18	not out	10
DL Vettori	lbw b Tufnell	51	c Ramprakash b Tufnell	6
SB O'Connor	lbw b Caddick	1	b Tufnell	6
Extras	(9b, 9lb, 2w, 2)	22	(4lb, 1w, 5)	10
Total		**236**		**162**

1st innings FoW: 39, 45, 54, 62, 87, 87, 104, 157, 235, 236
2nd innings FoW: 15, 15, 22, 22, 37, 39, 79, 149, 156, 162

Caddick	33.1	17	66	3	17	4	35	3
Mullally	26	12	34	2	11	1	27	2
Giddins	16	4	41	1	10	3	38	3
Tufnell	16	3	39	3	16	3	58	2
Irani	11	3	38	1				

England 1st innings / 2nd innings

Batsman	1st innings		2nd innings	
MA Atherton	c Fleming b Nash	10	c Parore b Nash	64
DL Maddy	b Vettori	14	c Fleming b Nash	5
*N Hussain	c Bell b Cairns	40	c Parore b O'Connor	9
GP Thorpe	c Fleming b Cairns	10	c Fleming b O'Connor	44
+AJ Stewart	b Vettori	11	c Bell b Nash	12
MR Rampr'sh	c Parore b Cairns	30	c Parore b Nash	0
RC Irani	lbw b Cairns	1	c Parore b Vettori	9
AR Caddick	b O'Connor	15	c Bell b Vettori	3
AD Mullally	c Bell b Vettori	5	c Twose b Cairns	3
PCR Tufnell	not out	0	run out (Nash)	1
ESH Giddins	lbw b Cairns	0	not out	0
Extras	(1b, 5lb, 5w, 6nb)	17	(2b, 3lb, 7nb)	12
Total		**153**		**162**

1st innings FoW: 25, 29, 46, 87, 91, 94, 141, 153, 153, 153
2nd innings FoW: 23, 45, 123, 143, 143, 148, 157, 160, 161, 162

Cairns	19	8	31	5	15.1	4	50	1
Nash	14	5	40	1	14	3	39	4
O'Connor	13	3	30	1				
Vettori	33	12	46	3	16	6	36	2
Astle	1	1	0	0				
O'Connor	11	2	32	2				

South Africa

No. 762: 1st Test
VENUE: Johannesburg
DATE: 25th-29th November 1999
TOSS WON BY: South Africa
RESULT: SA won by an innings and 21 runs

South Africa

No. 763: 2nd Test
VENUE: Crusaders Ground
DATE: 9th-13th December 1999
TOSS WON BY: England
RESULT: Match drawn

England 1st innings / 2nd innings

England 1st innings		2nd innings	
MA Butcher	c Boucher b Donald	1	lbw b Donald	32
MA Atherton	b Donald	0	c Boucher b Pollock	0
*N Hussain	c Klusener b Pollock	0	b Pollock	16
MP Vaughan	c Boucher b Pollock	33	lbw b Donald	5
+AJ Stewart	lbw b Donald	0	c Rhodes b Donald	86
CJ Adams	c Boucher b Donald	16	c Boucher b Donald	1
A Flintoff	c Boucher b Pollock	38	c & b Adams	36
GM Hamilton	c Pollock b Donald	0	c Pollock b Donald	0
AR Caddick	c Boucher b Donald	4	b Pollock	48
D Gough	not out	15	not out	16
AD Mullally	lbw b Pollock	10	c Kallis b Pollock	0
Extras	(3lb, 2w)	5	(4b, 10lb, 6w)	20
Total		122		260

1st innings FoW: 1, 2, 2, 2, 34, 90, 91, 91, 103, 122
2nd innings FoW: 0, 31, 41, 145, 147, 166, 166, 218, 260, 260

Donald	15	3	53	6		23	7	74	5
Pollock	14.4	6	16	4		24.4	11	64	4
Cronje	5	2	15	0		6	3	22	0
Klusener	6	1	30	0		19	4	55	0
Adams	1	0	5	0		11	0	31	1

South Africa 1st innings / 2nd innings

South Africa 1st innings		2nd innings	
G Kirsten	c Hussain b Caddick	15	c Vaughan b Gough	2
HH Gibbs	run out (Flintoff)	48	c Flintoff b Caddick	10
JH Kallis	c Caddick b Silverwood	58	not out	85
DJ Cullinan	st Stewart b Tufnell	58	b Caddick	18
*WJ Cronje	c Flintoff b Tufnell	2	c Vaughan b Flintoff	27
JN Rhodes	c Atherton b Flintoff	50	not out	57
L Klusener	c Adams b Gough	174		
SM Pollock	c Vaughan b Flintoff	7		
+C Boucher	c Stewart b Tufnell	42		
AA Donald	c Hussain b Tufnell	9		
M Hayward	not out	10		
Extras	(10b, 5lb, 1w, 18)	34	(4b, 11lb, 1w, 9)	25
Total		450		224

1st innings FoW: 28, 57, 87, 91, 146, 252, 268, 387, 401, 450
2nd innings FoW: 5, 17, 50, 98

Gough	21.1	1	107	1		19	6	52	1
Caddick	31	5	100	1		18	4	29	2
Silverwood	24	4	57	1		10	1	24	0
Tufnell	42	9	124	4		35	9	71	0
Vaughan	3	0	16	0		2	0	9	0
Flintoff	7	0	31	2		8.5	2	24	1

South Africa 1st innings / 2nd innings

South Africa 1st innings		2nd innings
G Kirsten	lbw b Mullally	13	
HH Gibbs	b Mullally	85	
JH Kallis	c Stewart b Gough	12	
DJ Cullinan	b Caddick	108	
*WJ Cronje	b Gough	44	
JN Rhodes	lbw b Mullally	26	
L Klusener	b Gough	72	
SM Pollock	c Stewart b Gough	2	
+C Boucher	not out	4	
AA Donald	b Gough	0	
PR Adams	not out	0	
Extras	(7b, 18lb, w 2w, 10)	37	
Total		403	

1st innings FoW: 37, 79, 175, 284, 299, 378, 398, 403, 403

Gough	30	8	70	5
Caddick	34	12	81	1
Mullally	34	7	80	3
Flintoff	14	5	45	0
Hamilton	15	1	63	0
Vaughan	11	2	39	0

England 1st innings / 2nd innings

England 1st innings		2nd innings	
MA Butcher	b Pollock	4	lbw b Hayward	1
MA Atherton	b Hayward	108	b Pollock	3
*N Hussain	c Boucher b Donald	82	not out	70
MP Vaughan	b Hayward	21	c Boucher b Kallis	29
+AJ Stewart	b Donald	15	lbw b Pollock	28
CJ Adams	c Kallis b Pollock	25	c Rhodes b Cronje	1
A Flintoff	b Pollock	42	c Boucher b Kallis	12
AR Caddick	b Hayward	35	not out	4
D Gough	b Donald	6		
CEW Silverwood	c Klusener b Hayward	6		
PCR Tufnell	not out	7		
Extras	(1b, 8lb, 13)	22	(2lb, 3)	5
Total		373		153

1st innings FoW: 5, 160, 228, 229, 264, 281, 336, 349, 364, 373
2nd innings FoW: 5, 5, 80, 125, 137, 149

Donald	34	9	109	3		13	4	37	0
Pollock	34	7	112	3		17	8	18	2
Hayward	28.1	7	75	4		20	8	55	1
Klusener	25	9	48	0		14	9	17	0
Cronje	16	5	20	0		6	4	2	1
Kallis	7	1	22	2					

No. 764: 3rd Test
VENUE: Durban (Kingsmead)
DATE: 26th-30th December 1999
TOSS WON BY: England
RESULT: Match drawn

No. 765: 4th Test
VENUE: Cape Town
DATE: 2nd-6th January 2000
TOSS WON BY: England
RESULT: SA won by an innings and 37 runs

England 1st innings / 2nd innings

MA Butcher	c Klusener b Adams	48
MA Atherton	b Hayward	1
*N Hussain	not out	146
DL Maddy	c Adams b Donald	24
+AJ Stewart	lbw b Hayward	95
CJ Adams	b Adams	19
A Flintoff	lbw b Cronje	5
AR Caddick	lbw b Cronje	0
D Gough	c Klusener b Donald	9
CEW Silverwood	c Boucher b Pollock	0
PCR Tufnell	not out	0
Extras	(1b, 14lb, 3w, 1nb)	19
Total		**366**

1st innings FoW: 7, 82, 138, 294, 336, 345, 345, 362, 362

Bowler	O	M	R	W
Donald	23.4	3	67	2
Pollock	33	14	55	1
Hayward	20	3	74	2
Kallis	23	9	38	0
Klusener	17	5	38	0
Adams	43	17	74	2
Cronje	7	5	5	2

England 1st innings / 2nd innings

Batsman	Dismissal	Runs	Dismissal	Runs
MA Butcher	c Kirsten b Donald	40	c Boucher b Pollock	4
MA Atherton	c Kirsten b Donald	71	c Cullinan b Pollock	35
*N Hussain	c Boucher b Adams	15	lbw b Klusener	16
MP Vaughan	c Kirsten b Donald	42	c Boucher b Klusener	5
+AJ Stewart	c Kirsten b Donald	40	b Adams	5
AR Caddick	c Cullinan b Donald	0	b Adams	31
CJ Adams	c Pollock b Kallis	10	c Gibbs b Donald	14
A Flintoff	c Rhodes b Klusener	22	c Donald b Kallis	8
D Gough	c Boucher b Klusener	4	not out	5
CEW Silverwood	not out	1	c Cullinan b Adams	0
PCR Tufnell	b Kallis	2	absent hurt	-
Extras	(6lb, 2w, 3nb)	11	(3lb)	3
Total		**258**		**126**

1st innings FoW: 115, 125, 141, 213, 213, 218, 231, 253, 255, 258
2nd innings FoW: 4, 40, 59, 62, 66, 105, 113, 125, 126

Bowler	O	M	R	W	O	M	R	W
Donald	26	13	47	5	10.4	2	35	1
Pollock	27	8	59	0	14	8	19	2
Kallis	20	4	61	2	9.2	2	19	1
Klusener	16	5	42	2	7	4	8	2
Cronje	3	2	5	0				
Adams	21	9	38	1	19.3	5	42	3

South Africa 1st innings / 2nd innings

Batsman	Dismissal	Runs	Dismissal	Runs
G Kirsten	c Stewart b Caddick	11	b Butcher	275
HH Gibbs	c Stewart b Caddick	2	c Maddy b Caddick	26
JH Kallis	c Stewart b Caddick	0	c Stewart b Gough	69
DJ Cullinan	b Gough	20	c Stewart b Flintoff	16
*WJ Cronje	c Stewart b Caddick	28	c Stewart b Flintoff	1
L Klusener	c Maddy b Tufnell	15	c Stewart b Adams	108
SM Pollock	b Caddick	64	b Butcher	45
+C Boucher	c Caddick	0	not out	7
AA Donald	c Atherton b Caddick	0		
PR Adams	c Silverwood b Gough	9		
M Hayward	not out	0		
Extras	(4b, 1lb, 1w, 1nb)	7	(5b, 13lb, 2w, 5nb)	25
Total		**156**		**572**

1st innings FoW: 11, 11, 24, 57, 74, 84, 84, 84, 154, 156
2nd innings FoW: 41, 193, 242, 244, 436, 537, 572

Bowler	O	M	R	W	O	M	R	W
Gough	15.3	6	36	2	28	5	82	1
Caddick	16	5	46	7	36	12	70	1
Silverwood	6	1	38	0	30	6	89	0
Tufnell	10	1	24	1	45	6	117	0
Flintoff	3	0	7	0	30	9	67	2
Adams	13	3	42	1				
Maddy	14	1	40	0				
Butcher	8.2	0	32	2				
Hussain	5	0	15	0				

South Africa 1st innings / 2nd innings

G Kirsten	c Stewart b Silverwood	80
HH Gibbs	c Vaughan b Silverwood	29
JH Kallis	c Atherton b Gough	105
DJ Cullinan	c Vaughan b Tufnell	120
*WJ Cronje	c Vaughan b Caddick	0
JN Rhodes	c Adams b Silverwood	16
L Klusener	b Gough	3
SM Pollock	c Adams b Caddick	4
+C Boucher	lbw b Silverwood	36
AA Donald	c Adams b Silverwood	7
PR Adams	not out	3
Extras	(1b, 7lb, 10nb)	18
Total		**421**

1st innings FoW: 43, 201, 246, 247, 279, 290, 307, 397, 405, 421

Bowler	O	M	R	W
Gough	37	6	88	2
Caddick	31	6	95	2
Silverwood	32	6	91	5
Flintoff	4	0	16	0
Tufnell	39.4	10	97	1
Butcher	3	0	9	0
Adams	7	2	17	0

South Africa

No. 766: 5th Test
VENUE: Centurion (Supersport Park)
DATE: 14th-18th January 2000
RESULT: England won by 2 wickets

South Africa 1st innings / 2nd innings

G Kirsten	c Adams b Gough	0	forfeited
HH Gibbs	c Adams b Caddick	3	
JH Kallis	b Caddick	25	
DJ Cullinan	c & b Mullally	46	
*WJ Cronje	c Maddy b Gough	0	
PC Strydom	c Stewart b Silverwood	30	
L Klusener	not out	61	
SM Pollock	run out (Hussain)	30	
+C Boucher	b Mullally	22	
PR Adams	not out	4	
M Hayward			
Extras	(2b, 11lb, 3w, 11)	27	
Total		**248**	

1st innings FoW: 1, 15, 50, 55, 102, 136, 196, 243

Bowler	O	M	R	W
Gough	20	2	92	2
Caddick	19	7	47	2
Mullally	24	10	42	2
Silverwood	7	1	45	1
Vaughan	2	0	9	0

England 1st innings / 2nd innings

Batsman	1st innings	2nd innings	Runs
MA Butcher	forfeited	lbw b Klusener	36
MA Atherton		c Boucher b Pollock	7
*N Hussain		c Gibbs b Pollock	25
+AJ Stewart		c Boucher b Hayward	73
CJ Adams		c Boucher b Hayward	1
MP Vaughan		b Hayward	69
DL Maddy		run out (Kirsten/Boucher)	3
AR Caddick		c Boucher b Pollock	0
D Gough		not out	6
CEW Silverwood		not out	7
AD Mullally			
Extras		(4b, 9lb, 4w, 7)	24
Total			**251**

1st innings FoW: 28, 67, 90, 102, 228, 236, 236, 240

Bowler	O	M	R	W
Pollock	20	7	53	3
Hayward	17.1	3	61	3
Klusener	14	4	38	1
Kallis	13	2	44	0
Cronje	5	3	15	0
Strydom	6	0	27	0

SUMMARY

PERIOD	V	PRIZE	ENGLAND CAPTAIN	P	W	L	T	NR
January 1971	A	One-off	R Illingworth	1	–	1	–	–
August 1972	E	Prudential Trophy vs Australia	DB Close	3	2	1	–	–
July 1973	E	Prudential Trophy vs New Zealand	R Illingworth	2	1	–	–	1
September 1973	E	Prudential Trophy vs West Indies	MH Denness	2	1	1	–	–
July 1974	E	Prudential Trophy vs India	MH Denness	2	2	–	–	–
Aug/Sept 1974	E	Prudential Trophy vs Pakistan	MH Denness	2	–	2	–	–
January 1975	A	One-off	MH Denness	1	1	–	–	–
March 1975	NZ	One-Day Series	JH Edrich (1) MH Denness (1)	2	–	–	–	2
June 1975	E	Prudential World Cup	MH Denness	4	3	1	–	–
August 1976	E	Prudential Trophy vs West Indies	APE Knott (1) AW Greig (2)	3	–	3	–	–
June 1977	E	Prudential Trophy vs Australia	JM Brearley	3	2	1	–	–
Dec/Jan 1977-78	P	Wills Series	JM Brearley (2) G Boycott (1)	3	2	1	–	–
May 1978	E	Prudential Trophy vs Pakistan	G Boycott (1) RGD Willis (1)	2	2	–	–	–
July 1978	E	Prudential Trophy vs New Zealand	JM Brearley	2	2	–	–	–
January 1979	A	Benson and Hedges Cup	JM Brearley	4	1	2	–	1
June 1979	E	Prudential World Cup	JM Brearley	5	4	1	–	–
Nov-Jan 1979-80	A	Benson and Hedges WSC	JM Brearley	9	5	4	–	–
May 1980	E	Prudential Trophy vs West Indies	IT Botham	2	1	1	–	–
August 1980	E	Prudential Trophy vs Australia	IT Botham	2	2	–	–	–
February 1981	WI	One-Day Series	IT Botham	2	–	2	–	–
June 1981	E	Prudential Trophy vs Australia	IT Botham	3	1	2	–	–
Nov-Jan 1981-82	I	Wills Series	KWR Fletcher	3	1	2	–	–
February 1982	SL	One-Day Series	KWR Fletcher	2	1	1	–	–
June 1982	E	Prudential Trophy vs India	RGD Willis	2	2	–	–	–
July 1982	E	Prudential Trophy vs Pakistan	RGD Willis	2	2	–	–	–
Jan/Feb 1983	A	Benson and Hedges WSC	RGD Willis	10	4	6	–	–
February 1983	NZ	Rothmans Cup	RGD Willis	3	–	3	–	–
June 1983	E	Prudential World Cup	RGD Willis	7	5	2	–	–
February 1984	NZ	Rothmans Cup	RGD Willis	3	2	1	–	–
March 1984	P	Wills Series	RGD Willis (1) DI Gower (1)	2	1	1	–	–
May/June 1984	E	Texaco Trophy vs West Indies	DI Gower	3	1	2	–	–
Dec/Jan 1984-85	I	One-Day Series	DI Gower	5	4	1	–	–
Feb/March 1985	A	B&H World Ch'ship	DI Gower	3	–	3	–	–
March 1985	SJ	Rothmans Four Nations Trophy	N Gifford	2	–	2	–	–
May/June 1985	E	Texaco Trophy	DI Gower (1) AR Border (1)	3	1	2	–	–
Feb/March 1986	WI	One-Day Series	DI Gower	4	1	3	–	–
May 1986	E	Texaco Trophy vs India	DI Gower	2	1	1	–	–
July 1986	E	Texaco Trophy vs New Zealand	MW Gatting	2	1	1	–	–
Dec/Jan 1986-87	A	Perth Challenge Cup	MW Gatting	4	4	–	–	–
Jan/Feb 1987	A	Benson and Hedges WSC	MW Gatting	10	6	4	–	–
April 1987	SJ	Sharjah Cup	JE Emburey	3	2	1	–	–
May 1987	E	Texaco Trophy vs Pakistan	MW Gatting (2) JE Emburey (1)	3	2	1	–	–
Oct/Nov 1987	P/I	Reliance World Cup	MW Gatting	8	5	3	–	–
November 1987	P	Wills Series	MW Gatting	3	3	–	–	–

SUMMARY

PERIOD	V	PRIZE	ENGLAND CAPTAIN	P	W	L	T	NR
February 1988	A	Bicentennial One-dayer	MW Gatting	1	–	1	–	–
March 1988	NZ	One-Day Series	MW Gatting	4	2	2	–	–
May 1988	E	Texaco Trophy vs West Indies	MW Gatting	3	3	–	–	–
September 1988	E	Texaco Trophy vs Sri Lanka	GA Gooch	1	1	–	–	–
May 1989	E	Texaco Trophy vs Australia	DI Gower	3	1	1	1	–
October 1989	I	Nehru Cup	GA Gooch	6	3	3	–	–
Feb-April 1990	WI	One-Day Series	GA Gooch (5)	6	–	4	–	2
			AJ Lamb (1)					
May 1990	E	Texaco Trophy vs New Zealand	GA Gooch	2	1	1	–	–
July 1990	E	Texaco Trophy vs India	GA Gooch	2	–	2	–	–
Dec/Jan 1990-91	A	Benson and Hedges WSC	AJ Lamb (3)	8	2	6	–	–
			GA Gooch (5)					
February 1991	NZ	One-Day Series	GA Gooch	3	1	2	–	–
May 1991	E	Texaco Trophy vs West Indies	GA Gooch	3	3	–	–	–
Jan/Feb 1992	NZ	One-Day Series	GA Gooch (2)	3	3	–	–	–
			AJ Stewart (1)					
Feb/March 1992	A/NZ	Benson and Hedges World Cup	GA Gooch (8)	10	6	3	–	1
			AJ Stewart (2)					
May/August 1992	E	Texaco Trophy vs Pakistan	GA Gooch	5	4	1	–	–
Jan/March 1993	I	One-Day Series	GA Gooch	6	3	3	–	–
March 1993	SL	One-Day Series	AJ Stewart	2	–	2	–	–
May 1993	E	Texaco Trophy vs Australia	GA Gooch	3	–	3	–	–
Feb/March 1994	WI	One-Day Series	MA Atherton	5	2	3	–	–
May 1994	E	Texaco Trophy vs New Zealand	MA Atherton	1	1	–	–	–
August 1994	E	Texaco Trophy vs South Africa	MA Atherton	2	2	–	–	–
Dec/Jan 1994-95	A	Benson and Hedges WSC	MA Atherton	4	2	2	–	–
May 1995	E	Texaco Trophy vs West Indies	MA Atherton	3	2	1	–	–
January 1996	SA	One-Day Series	MA Atherton (6)	7	1	6	–	–
			AJ Stewart (1)					
Feb/March 1996	I/P	Wills World Cup	MA Atherton	6	2	4	–	–
May 1996	E	Texaco Trophy vs India	MA Atherton	3	2	–	–	1
Aug/Sep 1996	E	Texaco Trophy vs Pakistan	MA Atherton	3	2	1	–	–
Dec/Jan 1996-97	Z	One-Day Series	MA Atherton	3	–	3	–	–
Feb/March 1997	NZ	One-Day Series	MA Atherton (4)	5	2	2	1	–
			N Hussain (1)					
May 1997	E	Texaco Trophy vs Australia	MA Atherton	3	3	–	–	–
December 1997	SJ	Champions' Trophy	AJ Hollioake	4	4	–	–	–
March/April 1998	WI	One-Day Series	AJ Hollioake	5	1	4	–	–
May 1998	E	Texaco Trophy vs South Africa	AJ Hollioake	3	1	2	–	–
August 1998	E	Emirates Triangular	AJ Stewart	3	1	2	–	–
October 1998	BD	Wills Mini World Cup	AJHollioake	1	–	1	–	–
Jan/Feb 1999	A	Carlton and United WSC	AJ Stewart	10	5	7	–	–
April 1999	SJ	Coca-Cola Cup	AJ Stewart	4	1	3	–	–
May 1999	E	World Cup	AJ Stewart	5	3	2	–	–
Jan/Feb 2000	SA	Standard Bank Series	N Hussain	9	5	4	-	-
		Grand Total	**51.65%**	**310**	**156**	**144**	**2**	**8**

Percentage figure = success rate excluding no-result matches
i.e. (310-8) = 302
(156/302) x 100 = 51.65%

MAJOR ONE-DAY SUCCESSES

DATE	VENUE	PRIZE	CAPTAIN
1/1/87	Australia	Perth Challenge Cup	MW Gatting
2/2/87	Australia	World Series Cricket	MW Gatting
3/4/87	Sharjah	Sharjah Cup	JE Emburey
4/12/97	Sharjah	Champions' Trophy	AJ Hollioake

OTHER SUCCESSES IN ONE-TO-ONE SERIES (HOME)

DATE	VS	PRIZE	RESULT	CAPTAIN
1/8/72	Australia	PT	2-0	DB Close
2/7/73	New Zealand	PT	1-0	MH Denness
3/7/74	India	PT	2-0	MH Denness
4/6/77	Australia	PT	2-1	JM Brearley
5/5/78	Pakistan	PT	2-0	G Boycott (1), RGD Willis (1)
6/7/78	New Zealand	PT	2-0	JM Brearley
7/8/80	Australia	PT	2-0	IT Botham
8/6/82	India	PT	2-0	RGD Willis
9/7/82	Pakistan	PT	2-0	RGD Willis
10/5/87	Pakistan	TT	2-1	MW Gatting (2), JE Emburey (1)
11/5/88	West Indies	TT	3-0	MW Gatting
12/9/88	Sri Lanka	TT	1-0	GA Gooch
13/5/89	Australia	TT	1-1*	DI Gower
14/5/90	New Zealand	TT	1-1*	GA Gooch
15/5/91	West Indies	TT	3-0	GA Gooch
16/8/92	Pakistan	TT	4-1	GA Gooch
17/5/94	New Zealand	TT	1-0	MA Atherton
18/8/94	South Africa	TT	2-0	MA Atherton
19/5/95	West Indies	TT	2-1	MA Atherton
20/5/96	India	TT	2-0	MA Atherton
21/9/96	Pakistan	TT	2-1	MA Atherton
22/5/97	Australia	TT	3-0	MA Atherton
6/22000	Zimbabwe	OS	3-0	N Hussain

England declared winner on the basis of superior run rate.
PT = Prudential Trophy. TT = Texaco Trophy.

OTHER SUCCESSES IN ONE-TO-ONE (AWAY)

DATE	VS	PRIZE	RESULT	CAPTAIN
1/1/78	Pakistan	WS	2-1	JM Brearley (2), G Boycott (1)
2/2/84	New Zealand	RT	2-1	RGD Willis
3/1/85	India	OS	4-1	DI Gower
4/11/87	Pakistan	WS	3-0	MW Gatting
5/2/92	New Zealand	OS	3-0	GA Gooch (2), AJ Stewart (1)

SUCCESSFUL CAPTAINS (MINIMUM MATCHES: 10)

	P	W	L	T	NR	SR%
MW Gatting	37	26	11	-	-	70.27
MH Denness	12	7	4	-	1	63.63
JM Brearley	25	15	9	-	1	62.50
N Hussain	10	6	4	-	-	60.00

RGD Willis	29	16	13	-	-	55.17
GA Gooch	51	24	24	-	3	50.00
MA Atherton	43	20	21	1	1	47.61
AJ Hollioake	13	6	7	-	-	46.15
DI Gower	24	10	13	1	-	41.66
AJ Stewart	30	12	18	-	-	40.00

TOTAL SUMMARY OF THE MATCHES

	FROM	TO	P	W	L	T	NR	SR%
Home	1972	1999	109	68	38	1	2	63.20
Away	1970-71	1999-00	132	51	75	1	5	40.15
Neutral	1979-80	2000	69	37	31	-	1	54.41
Total			310	156	144	2	8	51.65

SIX FIVE-YEAR CALENDAR SPANS

PERIOD	P	W	L	T	NR	SR%
71-75	19	10	6	-	3	62.50
76-80	35	21	13	-	1	61.76
81-85	55	25	30	-	-	45.45
86-90	73	38	32	1	2	53.52
91-95	52	29	22	-	1	56.86
96-2000	76	33	41	1	1	44.00
Total	310	156	144	2	8	51.65

BREAKDOWN OF HOME MATCHES (1972-1999)

VS	FROM	TO	P	W	L	T	NR	SR%
Australia	1972	1997	25	13	11	1	-	52.00
New Zealand	1973	1994	13	9	3	-	1	75.00
West Indies	1973	1995	20	11	9	-	-	55.00
India	1974	1999	14	8	5	-	1	69.23
Pakistan	1974	1996	20	15	5	-	-	75.00
East Africa	1975		1	1	-	-	-	100.00
Canada	1979		1	1	-	-	-	100.00
Sri Lanka	1983	1999	6	5	1	-	-	83.33
South Africa	1994	1999	7	3	4	-	-	75.00
Kenya	1999		1	1	-	-	-	100.00
Zimbabwe	1999		1	1	-	-	-	100.00
Total	1972	1999	109	68	38	1	2	63.55

BREAKDOWN OF AWAY AND NEUTRAL MATCHES (1970-71 – 1999-2000)

VENUE	FROM	TO	P	W	L	T	NR	SR%
Australia	70-71	98-99	76	36	38	-	2	48.64
New Zealand	74-75	96-97	24	10	11	1	2	45.45
Pakistan	77-78	95-96	17	10	7	-	-	58.82
West Indies	80-81	97-98	22	4	16	-	2	20.00
India	81-82	95-96	25	14	11	-	-	56.00
Sri Lanka	81-82	92-93	4	1	3	-	-	25.00
Sharjah	84-85	98-99	13	7	6	-	-	53.84
South Africa	95-96	99-00	13	3	10	-	-	23.07
Zimbabwe	96-97	99-00	6	3	3	-	-	50.00
Bangladesh	98-99		1	-	1	-	-	
Total			201	88	106	1	6	45.12

BETWEEN WORLD CUPS

FROM	TO	P	W	L	T	NR	SR%
1976	1978-79	17	9	7	-	1	56.25
1979-80	1982-83	40	19	21	-	-	47.50
1983-84	1987	49	26	23	-	-	53.06
1987-88	1991-92	48	22	23	1	2	47.82
1992	1995-96	38	17	21	-	-	44.73
1996	1998-99	49	22	25	1	1	45.83
1999	2000	9	5	4	-	-	55.55

PATTERNS OF BATTING AGGREGATES
FIVE CALENDAR YEAR SPANS

FROM	TO	M	RUNS	WKTS	BALLS	R/100B	W/B
1971	1975	19	3637	126	5529	65.78	43.88
1976	1980	35	6573	255	9925	66.22	38.92
1981	1985	55	11094	399	15270	72.65	38.27
1986	1990	73	15152	500	20673	73.92	41.34
1991	1995	52	11250	369	14747	76.28	39.96
1996	2000	76	15722	566	20896	75.23	36.91
Total		310	63428	2215	87040	72.87	39.29

PATTERNS OF BOWLING AGGREGATES
FIVE CALENDAR YEAR SPANS

FROM	TO	M	RUNS	WKTS	BALLS	R/100B	W/B
1971	1975	19	3025	123	4909	61.62	39.91
1976	1980	35	6283	268	9941	63.20	37.09
1981	1985	55	11137	388	15693	70.96	40.44
1986	1990	73	15099	481	20835	72.46	43.31
1991	1995	52	10984	389	15110	72.69	38.84
1996	2000	76	16196	575	21586	75.03	37.54
Total		310	62724	2224	88074	71.21	39.60

TEAM RECORDS
HIGHEST INNINGS TOTALS – FOR ENGLAND

TOTAL	OVERS	R/O	VS	VENUE	YEAR
363-7	55	6.60	Pakistan	Nottingham	1992
334-4	60	5.56	India	Lord's	1975
333-9	60	5.55	Sri Lanka	Taunton	1983
322-6	60	5.36	New Zealand	The Oval	1983
320-8	55	5.81	Australia	Birmingham	1980
306-5	55	5.56	West Indies	The Oval	1995
302-5	55	5.49	Pakistan	The Oval	1992
302-3	50	6.04	Sri Lanka	Adelaide	1998-99
296-4	50	5.92	Sri Lanka	Peshawar	1987-88
296-5	50	5.92	New Zealand	Adelaide	1982-83
295-6	55	5.36	New Zealand	Leeds	1990
295-8	55	5.36	Pakistan	Manchester	1982
293-5	50	5.86	West Indies	Bridgetown	1997-98
292-8	50	5.84	Pakistan	Birmingham	1996
291-8	50	5.82	India	The Oval	1996
290-5	60	4.83	East Africa	Birmingham	1975
286-4	53.4	5.32	New Zealand	Manchester	1986
282-4	50	5.64	Australia	Sydney	1998-99
281-7	50	5.62	South Africa	Dhaka	1998-99
281	55	5.10	India	Nottingham	1990

HIGHEST INNINGS TOTAL – AGAINST ENGLAND

TOTAL	OVERS	R/O	FOR	VENUE	YEAR
323-5	50	6.46	Pakistan	Sharjah	1998-99
313-6	50	6.26	West Indies	Arnos Vale	1993-94
303-9	49.4	6.10	Sri Lanka	Adelaide	1998-99
302-5	50	6.04	West Indies	Port-of-Spain	1997-98
298-6	54.5	5.43	New Zealand	The Oval	1990
297-6	48.5	6.08	New Zealand	Adelaide	1982-83
295-6	50	5.90	New Zealand	Wellington	1982-83
286-9	60	4.76	West Indies	Lord's	1979
286	58	4.93	Sri Lanka	Taunton	1983
284-5	55	5.16	New Zealand	Manchester	1986
283-5	50	5.66	Australia	Brisbane	1990-91
283-4	46.4	6.06	South Africa	Dhaka	1998-99
282-5	53	5.32	India	Nottingham	1990
281	53	5.30	West Indies	The Oval	1995
280-4	53.3	5.23	Australia	Birmingham	1993
280-6	50	5.60	Sri Lanka	Ballarat	1991-92

HIGHEST MATCH AGGREGATES

TOTAL	OVERS	R/O	VS	VENUE	YEAR
619-19	119	5.20	Sri Lanka	Taunton	1983
605-12	99.4	6.07	Sri Lanka	Adelaide	1998-99
593-13	110	5.39	Australia	Birmingham	1980
593-11	98.5	6.00	New Zealand	Adelaide	1982-83
593-12	109.5	5.39	New Zealand	Leeds	1990
587-15	10	5.43	West Indies	The Oval	1995
570-9	108.4	5.24	New Zealand	Manchester	1986
570-15	96.5	5.88	West Indies	Bridgetown	1997-98
567-9	108.3	5.22	Australia	Birmingham	1993
565-15	105.5	5.33	Pakistan	The Oval	1992
564-11	96.4	5.83	South Africa	Dhaka	1998-99
563-17	108	5.21	India	Nottingham	1990
557-11	109.3	5.08	Australia	Lord's	1989
557-10	100	5.57	Australia	Sydney	1998-99
556-15	95.5	5.80	Pakistan	Sharjah	1998-99

LOWEST INNINGS TOTAL – FOR

TOTAL	OVERS	R/O	VS	VENUE	YEAR
93	36.2	2.55	Australia	Leeds	1975
94	31.7	2.94	Australia	Melbourne	1978-79
103	41	2.51	South Africa	The Oval	1999
107	34.2	3.11	Zimbabwe	Cape Town	1999-00
110	31.5	3.45	Australia	Melbourne	1998-99
111	38	2.92	South Africa	Johannesburg	1999-00
114	39	2.92	West Indies	Bridgetown	1985-86
115	43.4	2.63	South Africa	East London	1995-96
118	30	3.93	Zimbabwe	Harare	1996-97

LOWEST INNINGS TOTAL – AGAINST

TOTAL	OVERS	R/O	VS	VENUE	YEAR
45	40.3	1.11	Canada	Manchester	1979
70	25.2	2.76	Australia	Birmingham	1977
74	40.2	1.83	Pakistan	Adelaide	1991-92
85	47	1.80	Pakistan	Manchester	1978
94	52.3	1.79	East Africa	Birmingham	1975
99	33.3	2.95	Sri Lanka	Perth	1998-99
101	33.5	3.00	Australia	Melbourne	1978-79
109	27.3	3.96	Australia	Sydney	1982-83

SUCCESSFUL RUN-CHASE – FOR

TOTAL	OVERS	BR	VS	VENUE	YEAR
286-4	53.4	8	New Zealand	Manchester	1986
270-4	49	6	Australia	Lord's	1997
266-6	51.1	23	India	Leeds	1974
265-3	46.1	53	West Indies	Lord's	1991
265-5	48.2	10	South Africa	Bloemfontein	1995-96
257-2	49	36	Australia	Lord's	1985
256-5	53.5	7	India	Manchester	1986
255-4	43.4	68	Pakistan	The Oval	1992
253-4	48.2	10	Australia	The Oval	1997
252-3	47.1	47	Pakistan	Nottingham	1982

BR = Balls Remaining

SUCCESSFUL RUN CHASE – AGAINST

TOTAL	OVERS	BR	VS	VENUE	YEAR
303-9	49.4	2	Sri Lanka	Adelaide	1998-99
298-6	54.5	1	New Zealand	Leeds	1990
297-6	48.5	7	New Zealand	Adelaide	1982-83
282-5	53	12	India	Nottingham	1990
280-4	53.3	9	Australia	Birmingham	1993
279-4	54.3	3	Australia	Lord's	1989
276-3	48	12	South Africa	Centurion	1995-96
267-6	46.4	22	India	Gwalior	1992-93
267-9	49.5	1	West Indies	Bridgetown	1997-98
260-5	47.1	17	Sri Lanka	Lord's	1998
260-2	46.1	23	Australia	Sydney	1998-99
259-4	48.1	11	India	Kanpur	1989-90
257-7	48	12	India	Gwalior	1992-93
250-3	47.4	14	Pakistan	Karachi	1995-96

LARGEST MARGIN OF VICTORY

RUNS	TOTAL	OVERS	VS	VENUE	YEAR
202	334-4	60	India	Lord's	1975
198	363-7	55	Pakistan	Nottingham	1992
196	290-5	60	East Africa	Birmingham	1975
132	217-7	55	Pakistan	Manchester	1978
128	227-7	50	Sri Lanka	Perth	1998-99
126	278-5	55	New Zealand	Manchester	1978
114	276-9	55	India	The Oval	1982
107	292-8	50	Pakistan	Birmingham	1996
106	322-6	60	New Zealand	The Oval	1983
106	280-6	50	Sri Lanka	Ballarat	1991-92
101	171	53.5	Australia	Birmingham	1977

WKTS	TOTAL	OVERS	VS	VENUE	YEAR
9	194-1	50.1	India	Leeds	1982
9	137-1	24.1	Sri Lanka	Leeds	1983
9	204-1	39	Kenya	Canterbury	1999
9	185-1	39.3	South Africa	Bloemfontein	99-00

SMALLEST MARGIN OF VICTORY

RUNS	TOTAL	OVERS	VS	VENUE	YEAR
2	211-8	50	West Indies	Sydney	1979-80
5	211	44.4	Sri Lanka	SSC.Colom.	1981-82
7	121-6	15	India	Chandrigarh	1984-85
7	250	49.5	India	Sharjah	1997-98
7	178-8	50	Australia	Brisbane	1998-99
7	282-4	50	Australia	Sydney	1998-99
8	187-9	50	Australia	Sydney	1986-87
8	215-9	50	Pakistan	Sharjah	1997-98
9	221-8	60	New Zealand	Manchester	1979
9	270-4	55	West Indies	Manchester	1991
9	236-9	50	India	Perth	1991-92

WICKETS

TOTAL	OVERS	BR	VS	VENUE	YEAR
One					
182-9	54.3	3	West Indies	Leeds	1973
217-9	54.3	3	Pakistan	Birmingham	1987
175-9	49.4	32	West Indies	Birmingham	1991
Two					
180-8	51.3	21	Australia	Birmingham	1972
173-8	45.2	58	Australia	Manchester	1977
164-8	48.5	7	Australia	Sydney	1979-80
246-8	49.3	3	West Indies	Gujranwala	1987-88
167-8	44.3	3	Pakistan	Lahore	1987-88
134-9	44.2	22	Zimbabwe	Bulawayo	1999-00

LARGEST MARGIN OF DEFEAT

RUNS	TOTAL	OVERS	VS	VENUE	YEAR
165	148-9	50	West Indies	Arnos Vale	1993-94
162	110	31.5	Australia	Melbourne	1998-99
135	114	39	West Indies	Bridgetown	1985-86
131	118	30	Zimbabwe	Harare	1996-97
109	139	47.3	Australia	Melbourne	1986-87
107	139	42.5	West Indies	Adelaide	1979-80
104	168	50	West Indies	Manchester	1984
103	192	44.5	New Zealand	Wellington	1982-83
104	107	24.2	Zimbabwe	Cape Town	1999-00

WKTS	TOTAL	OVERS	VS	VENUE	YEAR
9	217-8	50	West Indies	Brisbane	1979-80
9	162	55	India	The Oval	1986
9	178	43.2	Australia	Melbourne	1998-99

SMALLEST MARGIN OF DEFEAT

RUNS	TOTAL	OVERS	VS	VENUE	YEAR
1	203-9	50	South Africa	Cape Town	1999-00
2	213-7	50	West Indies	Melbourne	1979-80
2	125	48.2	West Indies	Arnos Vale	1980-81
2	247	54.5	Australia	Birmingham	1981
2	239-8	50	New Zealand	Melbourne	1982-83
3	212	44.5	Sri Lanka	SSC.Colom.	1981-82
3	219-9	50	Australia	Melbourne	1990-91
3	201	49.2	Pakistan	Lord's	1992
4	254	54.5	Australia	Manchester	1993
6	205	49.5	South Africa	Cape Town	1995-96
7	246-8	50	Australia	Calcutta	1987-88
7	192-9	40	New Zealand	Adelaide	1990-91
7	217	49.5	New Zealand	Auckland	1990-91
9	187	48	New Zealand	Wellington	1990-91
9	125	49.1	Zimbabwe	Albury	1991-92
9	144	41.3	New Zealand	Auckland	1996-97

WICKETS

One	266	50	West Indies	Bridgetown	1997-98
	302-3	50	Sri Lanka	Adelaide	1998-99
Two	177-8	50	Australia	Sharjah	1984-85
	246	50	Pakistan	Nottingham	1996
	234	55.2	New Zealand	Birmingham	1983
	246-8	53.2	Australia	The Oval	1977
	233-8	49.4	South Africa	East London	1999-00

BATTING RECORDS
ENGLISH BATSMEN WITH 1000+ RUNS IN A CAREER

	M	I	NO	RUNS	HS	AVE.	100	50
GA Gooch	125	122	6	4290	142	36.98	8	23
AJ Lamb	122	118	16	4010	118	39.31	4	26
GA Hick	105	104	13	3513	*126	38.60	5	24
AJ Stewart	125	120	8	3378	116	30.16	2	19
DI Gower	114	111	8	3171	158	30.77	7	12
RA Smith	71	70	8	2419	*167	39.01	4	15
IT Botham	116	106	15	2113	79	23.22	-	9
MW Gatting	92	88	17	2095	*115	29.50	1	9
NH Fairbrother	75	71	18	2092	113	39.47	1	16
MA Atherton	54	54	3	1791	127	35.11	2	12
GP Thorpe	53	52	8	1786	89	40.59	-	17
NV Knight	43	43	5	1587	*125	41.76	3	9
G Boycott	36	34	4	1082	105	36.06	1	9
DW Randall	49	45	5	1067	88	26.67	-	5

INDIVIDUAL HUNDREDS
AGAINST NEW ZEALAND (12)

158	DI Gower	Brisbane	1982-83
142*	CWJ Athey	Manchester	1986
131	KWR Fletcher	Lord's	1975
128	RA Smith	Leeds	1990
122	DI Gower	Melbourne	1982-83
117*	CT Radley	Manchester	1978
112*	GA Gooch	The Oval	1990
109	DI Gower	Adelaide	1982-83
108*	AJ Lamb	Sydney	1982-83
106	BC Broad	Napier	1987-88
102	AJ Lamb	The Oval	1983
100	DL Amiss	Swansea	1973

AGAINST INDIA (7)

137	DL Amiss	Lord's	1975
129	RA Smith	Gwalior	1992-93
118	AD Brown	Manchester	1996
116	AJ Stewart	Sharjah	1997-98
115*	MW Gatting	Poona	1984-85
115	GA Gooch	Bombay	1987-88
105*	GA Hick	Gwalior	1992-93

AGAINST WEST INDIES (5)

129*	GA Gooch	Port-of-Spain	1985-86
127	MA Atherton	Lord's	1995
122	NV Knight	Bridgetown	1997-98
113	NH Fairbrother	Lord's	1991

AGAINST SRI LANKA (2)

130	DI Gower	Taunton	1983
126*	GA Hick	Adelaide	1998-99

AGAINST PAKISTAN (7)

142	GA Gooch	Karachi	1987-88
125*	NV Knight	Nottingham	1996
118	AJ Lamb	Nottingham	1982
116*	D Lloyd	Nottingham	1974
114*	DI Gower	The Oval	1978
113	NV Knight	Birmingham	1996
103	AJ Stewart	The Oval	1992

AGAINST AUSTRALIA (15)

167*	RA Smith	Birmingham	1993
136	GA Gooch	Lord's	1989
124	W Larkins	Hyderabad (India)	1989-90
117*	GA Gooch	Lord's	1985
115	GA Gooch	Birmingham	1985
113*	MA Atherton	The Oval	1997
109	GA Hick	Adelaide	1998-99
108	DL Amiss	The Oval	1977
108	GA Gooch	Birmingham	1980
108	GA Hick	Sydney	1998-99
105	G Boycott	Sydney	1979-80
103	DL Amiss	Manchester	1972
102	DI Gower	Lord's	1985
101*	DI Gower	Melbourne	1978-79
100*	AJ Lamb	Nottingham	1989

AGAINST ASSOCIATES

104*	GA Hick	Holland	Peshawar	1995-96

INDIVIDUAL HUNDREDS – AGAINST ENGLAND
FOR WEST INDIES (11)

189*	IVA Richards	Manchester	1984
138*	IVA Richards	Lord's	1979
138*	DL Haynes	Gawalior	1989-90
119*	IVA Richards	Scarborough	1976
119	CB Lambert	Port-of-Spain	1997-98
115	DL Haynes	Port-of-Spain	1993-94
110	BC Lara	Bridgetown	1997-98
108*	RB Richardson	Kingston	1989-90
105	RC Fredricks	The Oval	1973
100*	CL Hooper	Sharjah	1997-98
100	CA Best	Georgetown	1989-90

FOR AUSTRALIA (9)

145	DM Jones	Brisbane	1990-91
125*	GS Chappell	The Oval	1977
114*	GM Wood	Lord's	1985
113	ME Waugh	Birmingham	1993
111*	GR Marsh	Lord's	1989
108*	MG Bevan	The Oval	1997
108	GM Wood	Leeds	1981
104	DM Jones	Perth	1986-87
101	DM Jones	Brisbane	1986-87

FOR PAKISTAN (4)

137	Ijaz Ahmed Sr.	Sharjah	1998-99
113	Javed Minadad	The Oval	1987
113	Rameez Raja	Karachi	1987-88
109	Majid Khan	Nottingham	1974

FOR NEW ZEALAND (6)

111	MJ Greatbatch	The Oval	1990
105*	MD Crowe	Auckland	1983-84
102*	MJ Greatbatch	Leeds	1990
101	BE Congdon	Wellington	1974-75
101	JG Wright	Napier	1987-88
101	NJ Astle	Ahmedabad	1995-96

FOR INDIA (5)

134*	BS Sidhu	Gwalior	1992-93
105	DB Vengsarkar	Poona	1984-85
102	RJ Shastri	Cuttack	1984-85
101*	C Sharma	Kanpur	1989-90
100*	VG Kambli	Jaipur	1992-93

FOR SOUTH AFRICA (1)

116	G Kirsten	Centurion	1995-96

FOR SRI LANKA (2)

132*	MS Atapattu	Lord's	1998
120	DPM Jayawardene	Adelaide	1998-99

100-RUNS PARTNERSHIPS FOR EACH WICKET
FIRST WICKET

193	GA Gooch (91), CWJ Athey(142)	NZ	Manchester	1986
185	GA Gooch (56), W Larkins (124)	A	Huderabad (I)	89-90
165	NV Knight (122), AJ Stewart (74)	WI	Bridgetown	1997-98
161	DL Amiss (108), JM Brearley (78)	A	The Oval	1977
158	B Wood (77), DL Amiss (88)	EA	Birmingham	1975
156	GA Gooch (54), MA Atherton (74)	WI	Manchester	1991
154	GA Gooch (108), G Boycott (78)	A	Birmingham	1980
147	RA Smith (75), MA Atherton (66)	P	Karachi	1995-96
135	P Willey (56), G Boycott (70)	WI	Lord's	1980
133	B Wood (78*), CJ Tavare (66)	I	Leeds	1982
132	NV Knight (94), MA Atherton (64)	SL	Lord's	1998
129	JM Brearley (64), G Boycott (57)	E	Lord's	1979

128	N Hussain (64), NV Knight (72*)	Z	Kimberley	1999-00
123	GA Gooch (61), RT Robinson (55)	SL	Pune	1987-88
123	GA Gooch (136), DI Gower (61)	A	Lord's	1989
121	BC Broad (55), CWJ Athey (64)	WI	Adelaide	1986-87
118	GA Gooch (86), BC Broad (44)	A	Sharjah	1986-87
115	G Fowler (69), CJ Tavare (58)	P	Manchester	1983
114	NV Knight (51), AD Brown (59)	SA	Leeds	1998
112	MA Atherton (46), AJ Stewart (66)	WI	Kingston	1993-94
109	GA Gooch (74), G Cook (32)	SL	SSC Colombo	
				1981-82
108	GA Gooch (54), G Boycott (99)	A	The Oval	1980
107	GA Gooch (58), IT Botham (53)	A	Sydney	1991-92
104	BC Broad (97), CWJ Athey (42)	P	Perth	1986-87
103	AJ Stewart (64), RA Smith (63)	SA	Centurion	1995-96
103	NV Knight (113), AJ Stewart (46)	P	Birmingham	1996
101	GA Gooch (57), BC Broad (66)	P	Peshawar	1987-88
101	RA Smith (129), AJ Stewart (33)	I	Gwalior	1992-93
100	MA Atherton (60), AJ Stewart (48)	A	Sydney	1994-95

SECOND WICKET

202	GA Gooch (117*), DI Gower (102)	A	Lord's	1985
176	DL Amiss(137), KWR Fletcher (68)	I	Lord's	1975
159*	N Hussain (88*), GA Hick (61*)	K	Canterbury	1999
144	MA Atherton (92), GA Hick (66)	WI	The Oval	1995
140	BC Broad (65), RT Robonson (83)	P	Sharjah	1986-87
125	DL Amiss (103), KWR Fletcher (60)	A	Manchester	1972
125	AJ Stewart (88), GA Hick (73*)	SL	Lord's	1999
118	G Boycott (105), P Willey (64)	A	Sydney	1979-80
116	BC Broad (99), AJ Lamb (61)	P	The Oval	1987
116	RA Smith (72), GA Hick (105*)	I	Gwalior	1992-93
113	GA Gooch (55), RA Smith (128)	NZ	Leeds	1990
111	GA Gooch (94), CT Radley (41)	NZ	Scarborough	1978
111	G Boycott (86), P Willey (51)	A	Sydney	1979-80
107	CJ Tavare (48), AJ Lamb (118)	P	Nottingham	1982

THIRD WICKET

213	GA Hick (86*), NH Fairbrother(113)	WI	Lord's	1991
190*	CJ Tavare (83*), AJ Lamb (108*)	NZ	Sydney	1982-83
190	GA Hick (108), N Hussain (93)	A	Sydney	1998-99
170	AJ Stewart (81), GP Thorpe (82)	NZ	Christchurch	96-97
159	AJ Lamb (99), DI Gower (76)	I	The Oval	1982
143	GA Hick (104*), GP Thorpe (89)	H	Peshawar	1995-96
135	CWJ Athey (86), MW Gatting (60)	P	Karachi	1987-88
129	RA Smith (77), NH Fairbrother (62)	P	Nottingham	1992
123	N Hussain (57*), GP Thorpe (62)	Z	Nottingham	1999
118	KJ Barnett (84), AJ Lamb (66)	SL	The Oval	1988
117	GA Gooch (115), MW Gatting (56)	I	Bombay	1987-88
115	DI Gower (81), AJ Lamb (45)	I	Manchester	1986
113	NV Knight (74), GA Hick (64)	SA	Birmingham	1998
110	GA Gooch (51), RA Smith (91)	I	Perth	1991-92
108	JM Brearley (44), GA Gooch (53)	A	Lord's	1979
106*	G Fowler (78*), AJ Lamb (48*)	P	Lord's	1983
105	CT Radley (117*), DI Gower (50)	NZ	Manchester	1978

103	D Lloyd (116), MH Denness (32)	P	Nottingham	1974
103	RA Smith (81*), AJ Lamb (52)	SL	Delhi	1989-90
102	AJ Lamb (118), MW Gatting (37*)	P	Nottingham	1982
102	GA Hick (29), AJ Lamb (62)	WI	Manchester	1991

FOURTH WICKET

154*	GA Hick (126*), NH Fairbrother (78*)	SL	Adelaide	1998-99
139	AJ Lamb (94), DW Randall (51*)	A	Melbourne	1982-83
130	AJ Lamb (91), AJ Stewart (61)	I	Kanpur	1989-90
127	GA Hick (85), NH Fairbrother (59)	A	Manchester	1993
116	GA Gooch (57), IT Botham (72)	A	Manchester	1985
115	AJ Lamb (102), MW Gatting (43)	NZ	The Oval	1983
111	MA Atherton (59), RA Smith (103)	I	Nottingham	1990
109	GA Gooch (142), DJ Capel (50*)	P	Karachi	1987-88
106	DI Gower (109), DW Randall (31)	A	Adelaide	1982-83
106	AJ Lamb (66), IT Botham (68)	A	Perth	1986-87
105	DI Gower (114*), GRJ Roope (35)	P	The Oval	1978

FIFTH WICKET

142	RA Smith (167*), GP Thorpe (36)	A	Birmingham	1993
135*	GP Thorpe (75*), AJ Hollioake (66*)	A	Leeds	1997
113	DI Gower (158), DW Randall (34)	NZ	Brisbane	1982-83
110	DI Gower (53), MW Gatting (71*)	I	Jullundur	1981-82
109*	GA Gooch (112*), RC Russell (47*)	NZ	The Oval	1990

TOP FIVE FOR REST OF THE WICKETS
SIXTH WICKET

98	DI Gower (130), IJ Gould (35)	SL	Taunton	1983
90*	GA Hick (87*), MA Ealham (36*)	Z	Bulawayo	1999-00
88*	AJ Lamb (100*), DR Pringle (25*)	A	Nottingham	1989
84	GA Hick (63), IT Botham (24)	P	Nottingham	1992
74	MW Alleyne (53), MA Ealham (29*)	SA	East London	99-00
68	DW Randall (70), VJ Marks (28)	NZ	Christchurch	83-84
66	KWR Fletcher (131), CM Old (20*)	NZ	Nottingham	1975

SEVENTH WICKET

86*	MW Gatting (115*), PR Downton (27*)	I	Pune	1984-85
77	AW Greig (31), APE Knott (50)	A	Lord's	1972
76	GA Hick (91), MA Ealham (40)	I	The Oval	1996
74	GA Hick (91), D Gough (45)	A	Melbourne	1994-95
70	GP Thorpe (66*), MV Fleming (33)	WI	Sharjah	1997-98

EIGHTH WICKET

62	DA Reeve (35), D Gough (26*)	SL	Faisalabad	1995-96
55	DW Randall (88), RD Jackman (14)	WI	Lord's	1976
55	CM Old (35), JK Lever (27*)	A	Birmingham	1977
53	DI Gower (84), VJ Marks (23*)	NZ	Auckland	1982-83
47	AJ Lamb (67*), PAJ DeFreitas (23)	WI	Gujranwala	1987-88

NINTH WICKET

47	AJ Lamb (75), NA Foster (24)	WI	Manchester	1984
43	RW Taylor (20*), RGD Willis (24)	P	Leeds	1979
42*	RDB Croft (26*), D Gough (23*)	A	Brisbane	1998-99

| 42 | NA Foster (14*), PAJ DeFreitas (33) | P | Birmingham | 1987 |
| 41 | RDB Croft (30*), AD Mullally (20) | Z | Harare | 1996-97 |

TENTH WICKET

44	RDB Croft (13*), ARC Fraser (30)	WI	Port-of-Spain	97-98
43*	ARC Fraser (38*), PCR Tufnell (5*)	A	Melbourne	1990-91
30	DL Bairstow (23*), JK Lever (11)	WI	Adelaide	1979-80
27	D Gough (16), AR Caddick (12*)	NZ	Wellington	1996-97
24	CJ Tavare (82*), JK Lever (6)	WI	Leeds	1980
24	CMW Read (9), AD Mullally (14*)	SA	Johannesburg	99-00

BOWLING RECORDS
ENGLISH BOWLERS WITH 50+ WICKETS

	M	BALLS	RUNS	WKTS	AVE.	BB	4WI	R/O
IT Botham	116	6271	4139	145	28.54	4-31	3	3.96
PAJ DeFreitas	103	5712	3775	115	32.82	4-35	1	3.96
D Gough	65	3636	2580	108	23.88	5-44	6	4.25
RGD Willis	64	3595	1968	80	24.60	4-11	4	3.28
JE Emburey	61	3425	2346	76	30.86	4-37	2	4.10
CC Lewis	53	2625	1942	66	29.42	4-30	3	4.43
GC Small	53	2793	1942	58	33.48	4-31	1	4.17
MA Ealham	48	2439	1671	56	29.83	5-15	4	4.11

STRIKE RATE

	BALLS	WKTS	B/W
D Gough	3636	108	33.66
CC Lewis	2625	66	39.77
IT Botham	6271	145	43.24
MA Ealham	2439	56	43.55
RGD Willis	3595	80	44.93
JE Emburey	3425	76	45.06
GC Small	2793	58	48.15
PAJ DeFreitas	5712	115	49.66

FOUR WICKETS IN AN INNINGS – FOR ENGLAND
AGAINST NEW ZEALAND (10)

5-20	VJ Marks	Wellington	1983-84
4-22	PCR Tufnell	Christchurch	1996-97
4-23	RGD Willis	Sydney	1982-83
4-32	JA Snow	Swansea	1973
4-33	PW Jarvis	Auckland	1987-88
4-35	P Lever	Wellington	1974-75
4-35	CC Lewis	Sydney	1990-91
4-37	C White	Napier	1996-97
4-39	JE Emburey	Dunedin	1987-88
4-45	AW Greig	Nottingham	1975

AGAINST AUSTRALIA (11)

5-31	M Hendrick	The Oval	1980
5-44	D Gough	Lord's	1997
4-18	AD Mullally	Brisbane	1998-99
4-22	ARC Fraser	Melbourne	1994-95
4-25	CM Old	Melbourne	1978-79

4-27	GG Arnold		Birmingham	1972
4-29	JK Lever		Birmingham	1977
4-31	IT Botham		Sydney	1991-92
4-33	GB Stevenson		Sydney	1979-80
4-35	PAJ DeFrieitas		Adelaide	1986-87
4-57	CM Old		Melbourne	1974-75

AGAINST SRI LANKA (5)

5-32	MA Ealham	Perth	1998-99
5-39	VJ Marks	Taunton	1983
4-28	D Gough	Melbourne	1998-99
4-30	CC Lewis	Ballart	1991-92
4-37	MA Ealham	Lord's	1999

AGAINST WEST INDIES (10)

4-23	GR Dilley	Brisbane	1986-87
4-31	GC Small	Birmingham	1988
4-35	CC Lewis	Port-of-Spain	1993-94
4-37	JE Emburey	Adelaide	1986-87
4-44	DL Underwood	Sydney	1979-80
4-44	PJ Martin	The Oval	1995
4-45	IT Botham	Birmingham	1991
4-46	GR Dilley	Perth	1986-87
4-49	SL Watkin	Kingston	1993-94
4-67	DV Lawrence	Lord's	1991

AGAINST INDIA (5)

5-35	PW Jarvis	Bangalore	1992-93
4-40	CC Lewis	The Oval	1996
4-45	MV Fleming	Sharjah	1997-98
4-52	EE Hemmings	Bombay	1987-88
4-56	IT Botham	Leeds	1982

AGAINST PAKISTAN (4)

4-23	AJ Hollioke	Birmingham	1996
4-30	MA Ealham	Sharjah	1998-99
4-42	DR Pringle	Lord's	1992
4-45	AJ Hollioke	Nottingham	1996

AGAINST ZIMBABWE (5)

5-15	MA Ealham	Kimberley	1999-00
5-21	C White	Bulawayo	1999-00
5-33	GA Hick	Harare	1999-00
5-44	D Gough	Sydney	1994-95
4-43	D Gough	Harare	1996-97

AGAINST SOUTH AFRICA (4)

4-19	AR Caddick	Johannesburg	1999-00
4-29	D Gough	Bloemfontein	1999-00
4-33	D Gough	Port Elizabeth	1995-96
4-35	D Gough	Manchester	1998

AGAINST ASSOCIATE COUNTRIES (3)

4-8	CM Old	C	Manchester	1979

4-11	JA Snow	EA	Birmingham	1975
4-11	RGD Willis	C	Manchester	1979

FOUR WICKETS IN AN INNINGS – AGAINST ENGLAND
FOR AUSTRALIA (14)

6-14	GJ Gilmour	Leeds	1975
5-18	GJ Cosier	Birmingham	1977
5-20	GS Chappell	Birmingham	1977
4-12	DK Lillee	Sydney	1979-80
4-25	GD McGrath	Melbourne	1994-95
4-29	RM Hogg	Leeds	1981
4-35	DK Lillee	The Oval	1980
4-37	ME Waugh	Melbourne	1990-91
4-45	SP O'Donnell	Perth	1990-91
4-45	GD McGrath	Sydney	1998-99
4-46	RM Hogg	Sydney	1979-80
4-54	GD McGrath	Melbourne	1998-99
4-56	DK Lillee	Sydney	1979-80
4-69	LS Pascoe	Birmingham	1980

FOR NEW ZEALAND (6)

5-28	BL Cairns	Scarborough	1978
5-32	RJ Hadlee	Christchurch	1983-84
5-45	C Pringle	Birmingham	1994
4-34	MC Snedden	Napier	1987-88
4-35	C Pringle	Sydney	1990-91
4-55	CL Cairns	Auckland	1990-91

FOR SRI LANKA (3)

6-29	ST Jayasuriya	Moratuwa	1992-93
5-34	M Muralitharan	Lord's	1998
4-34	ALF DeMel	S.S.C.Colombo	1981-82

FOR WEST INDIES (13)

6-15	CEH Croft	St Vincent	1980-81
5-22	AME Roberts	Adelaide	1979-80
5-38	J Garner	Lord's	1979
5-47	J Garner	Perth	1986-87
5-50	VA Holder	Birmingham	1976
4-18	CEL Ambrose	Georgetown	1989-90
4-23	CL King	Adelaide	1979-80
4-23	MD Marshall	Kingston	1985-86
4-27	AME Roberts	Lord's	1976
4-28	IR Bishop	Kingston	1989-90
4-32	AME Roberts	Scarborough	1976
4-33	MD Marshall	Gwalior	1989-90
4-37	MD Marshall	Port-of-Spain	1985-86
4-40	RA Harper	Port-of-Spain	1993-94

FOR INDIA (2)

5-41	J Srinath	Bangalore	1992-93
4-54	NM Prabhakar	Gwalior	1992-93

FOR PAKISTAN (6)

4-26	Saqlain Mushtaq	Sharjah	1997-98
4-31	Abdul Qadir	Rawalpindi	1987-88
4-37	Imran Khan	Karachi	1987-88
4-37	Shoaib Akhtar	Sharjah	1998-99
4-50	Manzoor Akhtar	Sharjah	1997-98
4-73	Waqar Younis	Nottingham	1992

FOR ZIMBABWE (3)

6-19	HK Olonga	Cape Town	1999-00
5-28	EA Brandes	Harare	1996-97
4-31	EA Brandes	Albury	1991-92

FOR SOUTH AFRICA (5)

5-20	SM Pollock	Johannesburg	1999-00
4-17	AA Donald	The Oval	1999
4-32	PS de Villiers	Port Elizabeth	1995-96
4-34	SM Pollock	Cape Town	1995-96
4-41	AA Donald	Durban	1995-96

EXPENSIVE BOWLING ANALYSIS – FOR
MINIMUM 8 OVERS

ANALYSIS	R/O	BOWLER	VS	VENUE	YEAR
10.0.83.0	8.30	DR Pringle	WI	Gujranwala	1987-88
8.0.61.2	7.62	IT Botham	NZ	Adelaide	1982-83
9.0.67.0	7.44	CC Lewis	WI	St.Vincent	1993-94
8.4.0.64.0	7.38	DA Reeve	I	Gawalior	1992-93
8.0.59.0	7.37	JP Agnew	A	Melbourne	1984-85
8.1.59.1	7.37	IT Botham	WI	Port-of-Spain	1985-86
9.0.66.0	7.33	AD Mullally	P	Nottingham	1996
10.0.73.1	7.30	GC Small	I	Nottingham	1990
10.0.73.1	7.30	PAJ DeFreitas	WI	The Oval	1995
9.0.65.2	7.22	JE Emburey	P	Karachi	1987-88
9.0.65.1	7.22	RK Illingworth	SA	Centurion	1995-96
10.1.72.1	7.20	RK Illingworth	SL	Faisalabad	1995-96
8.0.57.4	7.12	CM Old	A	Melbourne	1974-75
9.0.63.0	7.00	G.C Small	P	Karachi	1987-88
8.0.56.1	7.00	DE Malcolm	NZ	Birmingham	1990-91
8.0.56.0	7.00	DE Malcolm	I	Gawalior	1992-93

EXPENSIVE BOWLING ANALYSIS – AGAINST ENGLAND
MINIMUM 8 OVERS

ANALYSIS	R/O	BOWLER	FOR	VENUE	YEAR
8.0.76.1	9.50	Iqbal Qasim	P	Manchester	1982
12.1.105.2	8.75	MC Snedden	NZ	The Oval	1983
8.1.64.2	8.00	WW Watson	NZ	Christchurch	1991-92
9.0.72.3	8.00	AA Donald	SA	Centurion	1995-96
9.0.71.1	7.88	GP Wickrem.	SL	Adelaide	1998-99
8.0.63.1	7.87	TJ Laughlin	A	Melbourne	1978-79
10.0.78.2	7.80	C Sharma	I	Kanpur	1989-90
8.0.62.0*	7.75	AN Connolly	A	Melbourne	1970-71
9.0.69.2	7.66	PL Mhambrey	I	The Oval	1996
11.0.84.0	7.63	BL Cairns	NZ	Manchester	1978
10.0.76.1	7.60	MC Snedden	NZ	Brisbane	1982-83
10.0.76.1	7.60	GB Troup	NZ	Adelaide	1982-83
10.0.76.1	7.60	WPUJC Vaas	SL	Adelaide	1998-99
11.1.83.0	7.54	KD Ghavri	I	Lord's	1975
8.0.58.0	7.25	CZ Harris	NZ	Adelaide	1990-91
8.0.58.2	7.25	Waqar Younis	P	Manchester	1992
8.0.58.2	7.25	PV Simmons	WI	Bridgetown	1997-98
10.0.72.1	7.20	MC Snedden	NZ	Adelaide	1982-83
10.0.70.1	7.00	Aaqib Javed	P	The Oval	1992

MOST ECONOMICAL ANALYSIS – FOR ENGLAND
MINIMUM 10 OVERS

ANALYSIS	R/O	BOWLER	VS	VENUE	YEAR
10.5.8.4	0.80	CM Old	C	Manchester	1979
12.6.11.4	0.91	JA Snow	EA	Birmingham	1975
10.3.3.11.4	1.04	RGD Willis	C	Manchester	1979
11.4.12.2	1.09	CM Old	WI	Leeds	1980
11.4.12.2	1.09	PAJ DeFreitas	SA	Manchester	1994
10.5.11.0	1.10	DL Underwood	EA	Birmingham	1975
10.5.12.2	1.20	IT Botham	P	Adelaide	1991-92
12.6.15.4	1.25	M Hendrick	P	Leeds	1979
11.5.11.4	1.36	RGD Willis	P	Manchester	1978
11.2.15.0	1.36	JE Emburey	I	The Oval	1986
10.2.15.1	1.50	PAJ DeFreitas	WI	Melbourne	1986-87
10.3.15.0	1.50	ARC Fraser	P	Cuttack	1989-90
10.3.15.5	1.50	MA Ealham	Z	Kimberley	1999-00
11.2.17.1	1.54	RK Illingworth	SA	Manchester	1994
10.0.16.1	1.60	P Lever	I	Lord's	1975
10.1.16.0	1.60	RDB Croft	A	Leeds	1997
10.4.17.0	1.70	PH Edmonds	P	Manchester	1978
10.3.17.0	1.70	PCR Tufnell	NZ	Auckland	1991-92
11.5.19.2	1.72	DE Malcolm	NZ	The Oval	1990
10.1.18.2	1.80	AW Greig	EA	Birmingham	1975
10.3.18.2	1.80	DL Underwood	I	Ahmedabad	1981-82
10.3.18.1	1.80	RDB Croft	WI	St Vincent	1997-98
11.5.20.1	1.81	PAJ DeFreitas	WI	Lord's	1988
11.2.21.1	1.90	DL Underwood	A	The Oval	1977
11.2.21.1	1.90	M Hendrick	A	Birmingham	1981
11.4.21.2	1.90	PJW Allott	I	Leeds	1982
10.4.19.2	1.90	NL Foster	NZ	Christchurch	1983-84
10.4.19.3	1.90	GA Gooch	P	Cuttack	1989-90

MOST ECONOMICAL BOWLING AGAINST ENGLAND
MINIMUM 10 OVERS

ANALYSIS	R/O	BOWLER	FOR	VENUE	YEAR
11.4.12.1	1.09	LR Gibbs	WI	The Oval	1973
12.6.14.6	1.16	GJ Gilmour	A	Leeds	1975
11.6.13.1	1.18	Sarfraz Nawaz	P	Manchester	1978
10.6.12.4	1.20	DK Lillee	A	Sydney	1979-80
10.2.17.0	1.70	J Garner	WI	St Vincent	1980-81
11.2.19.0	1.72	G Dymock	A	Lord's	1979
11.3.20.1	1.81	GS Chappell	A	Birmingham	1972
11.5.20.5	1.81	GS Chappell	A	Birmingham	1977
11.3.20.0	1.81	Liaqat Ali	P	Manchester	1978
11.3.21.1	1.90	S Abid Ali	I	Oval	1974

WICKET-KEEPING RECORDS
MOST DISMISSALS IN A MATCH

4 (all ct)	APE Knott	NZ	Swansea	1972
4 (all ct)	RW Taylor	I	Leeds	1982
4 (all ct)	PR Downton	WI	Leeds	1988
4 (all ct)	AJ Stewart	Z	Sydney	1994-95
4 (3c,1s)	SJ Rhodes	Z	Brisbane	1994-95
4 (all ct)	AJ Stewart	SA	Cape Town	1995-96
4 (3c.1s)	AJ Stewart	NZ	Napier	1996-97

MOST DISMISSALS IN A CAREER

	M	CT	ST	TOTAL
AJ Stewart	93	99	11	110
RW Taylor	27	26	6	32

FIELDING RECORDS
MOST CATCHES IN A MATCH

3	AW Greig	WI	Leeds	1973
3	G Boycott	P	Lahore	1977-78
3	DI Gower	P	Perth	1986-87
3	CWJ Athey	A	Sydney	1986-87
3	DA Reeve	P	Adelaide	1991-92
3	GA Hick	I	Bangalore	1992-93
3	NH Fairbrother	A	Manchester	1993
3	GP Thorpe	WI	Bridgetown	1993-94
3	AJ Hollioake	WI	Bridgetown	1997-98
3	NH Fairbrother	SL	Adelaide	1998-99
3	VJ Wells	P	Sharjah	1998-99
3	GP Thorpe	SL	Lord's	1999
3	GA Hick	Z	Bulawayo	1999-00

MOST CATCHES IN A CAREER

	M	CT
GA Hick	105	58
GA Gooch	125	45
DI Gower	114	44
IT Botham	116	36
NH Fairbrother	75	33
GP Thorpe	53	32
AJ Lamb	122	31
PAJ DeFreitas	103	26
DW Randall	49	25
RA Smith	71	25

ALL-ROUND RECORDS
(500 RUNS AND 50 WICKETS)

	M	R	W
IT Botham	116	2113	145
PAJ DeFreitas	103	690	115
JE Emburey	61	501	76
MA Ealham	48	573	56

MOST ONE-DAY APPEARANCES (50 OR MORE)

	TOTAL	A	SA	WI	NZ	I	P	SL	Z	AS
GA Gooch	125	32	1	32	16	18	16	6	3	1
AJ Stewart	125	20	14	22	19	14	15	12	6	3
AJ Lamb	122	23	1	26	28	15	22	6	1	-
IT Botham	116	33	2	25	19	7	23	5	1	1
DI Gower	114	32	-	22	24	16	15	4	-	1
GA Hick	105	13	19	19	6	14	11	12	9	2
PAJ DeFreitas	103	21	8	19	11	12	19	8	3	2
MW Gatting	92	21	-	15	11	18	19	8	-	-
NH Fairbrother	75	13	12	6	6	11	14	7	3	3
RA Smith	71	12	6	13	14	10	9	6	1	-
D Gough	74	12	18	3	7	5	6	9	11	3
RGD Willis	64	18	-	10	16	6	9	4	-	1
JE Emburey	61	15	-	19	6	5	11	5		
MA Atherton	54	6	9	11	10	5	4	2	5	2
GC Small	53	10	2	17	7	3	9	4	1	-
CC Lewis	53	4	6	11	11	12	6	3	-	-
GP Thorpe	53	8	10	7	6	7	6	2	4	3

ONE-DAY CAREER RECORDS OF 157 ENGLISH PLAYERS

	M	I	NO	R	HS	AVE	100	50	C/S	BALLS	RUNS	WK	AVE	BB	4WI
CJ Adams	5	4	-	71	42	17.75	-	-	3						
JP Agnew	3	1	1	2	*2	-	-	-	1	126	120	3	40.00	3-38	-
MW Alleyne	9	9	1	151	53	18.87	-	1	2	348	254	10	25.40	3-27	-
PJW Allott	13	6	1	15	8	3.00	-	-	2	819	552	15	36.80	3-41	-
DL Amiss	18	18	-	859	137	47.72	4	1	2						
GG Arnold	14	6	3	48	*18	16.00	-	-	2	714	339	19	17.84	4-27	1
MA Atherton	54	54	3	1791	127	35.11	2	12	15						
CWJ Athey	31	30	3	848	*142	31.40	2	4	16	6	10	0	-	-	-
ID Austin	9	6	1	34	*11	6.80	-	-	-	475	360	6	60.00	2-25	-
RJ Bailey	4	4	2	137	*43	68.50	-	-	1	36	25	0	-	-	-
DL Bairstow	21	20	6	206	*23	14.71	-	-	17/4						
GD Barlow	6	6	1	149	*80	29.80	-	1	4						
KJ Barnett	1	1	-	84	84	84.00	-	1	-						
JE Benjamin	2	1	-	0	0	-	-	-	-	72	47	1	47.00	1-22	-
MR Benson	1	1	-	24	24	24.00	-	-	-						
MP Bicknell	7	6	2	96	*31	24.00	-	-	2	413	347	13	26.69	3-55	-
RJ Blakey	3	2	-	25	25	12.50	-	-	2/1						
IT Botham	116	106	15	2113	79	23.22	-	9	36	6271	4139	145	28.54	4-31	2
G Boycott	36	34	4	1082	105	36.06	1	9	5	168	105	5	21.00	2-14	-
JM Brearley	25	24	3	510	78	24.28	-	3	12						
BC Broad	34	34	-	1361	106	40.02	1	11	10	6	6	0	-	-	-
AD Brown	13	13	-	333	118	25.61	1	1	6	6	5	0	-	-	-
DR Brown	9	8	4	99	21	24.75	-	-	1	324	305	7	43.57	2-28	-
AR Butcher	1	1	-	14	14	14.00	-	-	-						
RO Butcher	3	3	-	58	52	19.33	-	1	-						
AR Caddick	18	10	6	67	*21	16.75	-	-	5	1044	637	26	24.50	4-19	1
DJ Capel	23	19	2	327	*50	19.23	-	1	6	1038	806	17	47.71	3-38	-
DB Close	3	3	-	49	43	16.33	-	-	1	18	21	0	-	-	-
G Cook	6	6	-	106	32	17.66	-	-	2						
NGB Cook	3	-	-	-	-	-	-	-	2	144	95	5	19.00	2-18	-
DG Cork	25	15	2	132	*31	10.15	-	-	6	1440	1071	35	30.60	3-27	-
GA Cope	2	1	1	1	*1	-	-	-	-	112	35	2	17.50	1-16	-
NG Cowans	23	8	3	13	*4	2.60	-	-	5	1282	913	23	39.66	3-44	-
CS Cowdrey	3	3	1	51	*46	25.50	-	-	-	52	55	2	27.50	1-3	-
MC Cowdrey	1	1	-	1	1	1.00	-	-	-						
JP Crawley	13	12	-	236	73	19.66	-	2	1/1						
RDB Croft	44	31	11	299	32	14.95	-	-	9	2244	1245	41	30.36	3-51	-
MH Denness	12	11	2	264	66	29.33	-	1	1						
GR Dilley	36	18	8	114	*31	11.40	-	-	4	2043	1291	48	26.89	4-23	3
PAJ DeFreitas	103	66	23	690	67	16.04	-	1	26	5712	3775	115	32.82	4-35	1
BL D'Oliveira	4	4	1	30	17	10.00	-	-	1	204	140	3	46.66	1-19	-
PR Downton	28	20	5	242	*44	16.13	-	-	26/3						
MA Ealham	48	35	3	573	45	17.90	-	-	7	2439	1671	56	29.83	5-15	3
PH Edmonds	27	18	7	116	20	10.54	-	-	4	1414	869	22	39.50	3-39	-
JH Edrich	7	6	-	223	90	37.16	-	2	-						
RM Ellison	14	12	4	86	24	10.75	-	-	2	696	510	12	42.50	3-42	-

Player															
JE Embury	61	45	10	501	34	14.31	-	-	19	3425	2346	76	30.86	4-37	2
NH Fairbrother	75	71	18	2093	113	39.49	1	16	33	6	9	0	-	-	-
MV Fleming	11	10	1	139	33	15.44	-	-	1	523	434	17	25.52	4-45	1
KWR Fletcher	24	22	3	757	131	39.84	1	5	4						
A Flintoff	9	6	-	100	50	16.66	-	1	-	242	228	7	32.57	2-3	-
NE Foster	48	25	12	150	24	11.53	-	-	12	2627	1836	59	31.11	3-20	-
G Fowler	26	26	2	744	*81	31.00	-	4	4/2						
ARC Fraser	42	20	9	141	*38	12.81	-	-	5	2392	1412	47	30.04	4-22	1
MW Gatting	92	88	17	2095	*115	29.50	1	9	22	392	336	10	33.60	3-32	-
N Gifford	2	1	-	0	0	0.00	-	-	1	120	50	4	12.50	4-23	1
AF Giles	5	3	2	19	*10	19.00	-	-	2	228	197	5	39.40	2-37	-
GA Gooch	125	122	6	4290	142	36.98	8	23	45	2066	1516	36	42.11	3-19	-
D Gough	73	47	16	343	45	11.06	-	-	12	4140	2870	124	23.14	5-44	8
IJ Gould	18	14	2	155	42	12.91	-	-	15/3						
DI Gower	114	111	8	3171	158	30.77	7	12	44	5	14	0	-	-	-
AW Greig	22	19	3	269	48	16.81	-	-	7	916	619	19	32.57	4-45	1
JH Hampshire	3	3	1	48	*25	24.00	-	-	-						
FC Hayes	6	6	1	128	52	25.60	-	1	-						
DW Headley	13	6	4	22	*10	11.00	-	-	2	594	520	11	47.27	2-38	-
EE Hemmings	5	2	-	4	3	2.00	-	-	1	249	175	5	35.00	3-11	-
M Hendrick	22	10	5	6	*2	1.20	-	-	5	1248	681	35	19.45	5-31	3
GA Hick	105	104	13	3513	*126	38.60	5	24	58	1117	919	28	32.82	5-33	1
AJ Hollioake	35	30	6	597	*83	24.87	-	3	13	1208	1019	32	31.84	4-23	1
BC Hollioake	7	6	-	122	63	20.33	-	1	1	150	122	2	61.00	2-43	-
GW Humpage	3	2	-	11	6	5.50	-	-	2						
N Hussain	42	42	7	932	*88	26.62	-	5	23						
AP Igglesden	4	3	1	20	18	10.00	-	-	1	168	122	2	61.00	2-12	-
R Illingworth	3	2	-	4	3	2.00	-	-	1	130	84	4	21.00	3-50	-
RK Illingworth	25	11	5	68	14	11.33	-	-	8	1501	1059	30	35.30	3-33	-
RC Irani	10	10	2	78	*45	9.75	-	-	2	329	246	4	61.50	1-23	-
RD Jackman	15	9	1	54	14	6.75	-	-	4	873	598	19	31.47	3-41	-
JA Jameson	3	3	-	60	28	20.00	-	-	-	12	3	0	-	-	-
PW Jarvis	13	6	2	26	*16	6.0	-	-	1	687	515	22	23.40	5-35	2
TE Jesty	10	10	4	127	*52	21.16	-	1	5	108	93	1	93.00	1-23	-
NV Knight	53	53	5	1924	*125	40.08	3	12	20						
APE Knott	20	14	4	200	50	20.00	-	1	15/1						
AJ Lamb	122	118	16	4010	118	39.31	4	26	31	6	3	0	-	-	-
W Larkins	25	24	-	591	124	24.62	1	-	8	15	22	0	-	-	-
JK Lever	22	11	4	56	*27	8.00	-	-	6	1152	713	24	29.70	4-29	1
P Lever	10	3	2	17	*8	17.00	-	-	2	440	261	11	23.72	4-35	1
CC Lewis	53	40	14	378	33	14.53	-	-	20	2625	1942	66	29.42	4-30	4
D Lloyd	8	8	1	285	*116	40.71	1	-	3	12	3	1	3.00	1-3	-
GD Lloyd	6	5	1	39	22	9.75	-	-	2						

TA Lloyd	3	3	-	101	49	33.66	-	-	-						
JD Love	3	3	-	61	43	20.33	-	-	1						
BW Luckhurst	3	3	-	15	14	5.00	-	-	-						
MA Lynch	3	3	-	8	6	2.66	-	-	1						
DL Maddy	8	6	-	113	53	18.83	-	1	1						
DE Malcolm	10	5	2	9	4	3.00	-	-	1	526	404	16	25.25	3-40	-
VJ Marks	33	24	3	285	44	13.57	-	-	8	1772	1076	44	24.45	5-20	2
PJ Martin	20	13	7	38	6	6.33	-	-	1	1048	806	27	29.85	4-44	1
MP Maynard	10	10	1	153	41	17.00	-	-	3						
G Miller	25	18	2	136	46	8.50	-	-	4	1268	813	25	32.52	3-27	-
JE Morris	8	8	1	167	*63	23.85	-	1	2						
MD Moxon	8	8	-	174	70	21.75	-	1	5						
AD Mullally	34	25	7	65	20	3.61	-	-	7	1881	1198	45	26.62	4-18	2
CM Old	32	25	7	338	*51	18.77	-	1	8	1755	999	45	22.20	4-8	2
PI Pocock	1	1	-	4	4	4.00	-	-	-	60	20	0	-	-	-
DR Pringle	44	30	12	425	*49	23.61	-	-	11	2379	1677	44	38.11	4-42	1
NV Radford	6	3	2	0	*0	-	-	-	2	348	230	2	115.00	1-32	-
CT Radley	4	4	1	250	*117	83.33	1	1	-						
MR Ramprakash	13	13	3	265	51	26.50	-	1	6	12	14	0	-	-	-
DW Randall	49	45	5	1067	88	26.67	-	5	25	2	2	1	2.00	1-2	-
CMW Read	9	6	2	70	*26	17.50	-	-	11/2						
DA Reeve	29	21	9	291	35	24.25	-	-	12	1147	820	20	41.00	3-20	-
SJ Rhodes	9	8	2	107	56	17.83	-	1	9/2						
CJ Richards	22	16	3	154	50	11.84	-	1	16/1						
RT Robinson	26	26	-	597	83	22.96	-	3	6						
GRJ Roope	8	8	-	173	44	21.62	-	-	2						
BC Rose	2	2	-	99	54	49.50	-	1	1						
RC Russell	40	31	7	423	50	17.62	-	1	41/6						
IDK Salisbury	4	2	1	7	5	7.00	-	-	1	186	177	5	35.40	3-41	-
K Shuttleworth	1	1	-	7	7	7.00	-	-	1	56	29	1	29.00	1-29	-
CEW Silverwood	6	4	-	17	12	4.25	-	-	-	252	201	3	67.00	2-27	-
WN Slack	2	2	-	43	34	21.50	-	-	-						
GC Small	53	24	9	98	*18	6.53	-	-	7	2793	1942	58	33.48	4-31	1
CL Smith	4	4	-	109	70	27.25	-	1	-	36	28	2	14.00	2-8	-
DM Smith	2	2	1	15	*10	15.00	-	-	-						
MJ Smith	5	5	-	70	31	14.00	-	-	1						
NMK Smith	7	6	1	100	31	20.00	-	-	1	261	190	6	31.66	3-29	-
RA Smith	71	70	8	2419	*167	39.01	4	15	26						
JA Snow	9	4	2	9	*5	4.50	-	-	1	538	232	14	16.57	4-11	2
VS Solanki	8	7	1	96	24	16.00	-	-	2						
DA Steele	1	1	-	8	8	8.00	-	-	-	6	9	0	-	-	-
AJ Stewart	125	120	8	3378	116	30.16	2	19	111/11						
GB Stevenson	4	4	3	43	*28	43.00	-	-	2	192	125	7	17.85	4-33	1
GP Swann	1	-	-	-	-	-	-	-	-	30	24	0	-	-	-
CJ Tavare	29	28	2	720	*83	27.69	-	4	7	12	3	0	-	-	-

JP Taylor	1	1	-	1	1	1.00	-	-	-	-					
LB Taylor	2	1	1	1	*1	-	-	-	-	84	47	0	-	-	-
RW Taylor	27	17	7	130	*26	13.00	-	-	26/6						
JG Thomas	3	3	2	1	*1	1.00	-	-	-	156	144	3	48.00	2-59	-
GP Thorpe	53	52	8	1786	89	40.59	-	17	32	120	97	2	48.50	2-15	-
FJ Titmus	2	1	-	11	11	11.00	-	-	-						
RW Tolchard	1	-	-	-	-	-	-	-	1						
PCR Tufnell	20	10	9	15	*5	15.00	-	-	4	1020	699	19	36.78	4-22	1
SD Udal	10	6	4	35	*11	17.50	-	-	1	570	371	8	46.37	2-37	-
SL Watkin	4	2	-	4	4	2.00	-	-	-	221	193	7	27.57	4-49	1
M Watkinson	1	-	-	-	-	-	-	-	-	54	43	0	-	-	-
AP Wells	1	1	-	15	15	15.00	-	-	-						
CM Wells	2	2	-	22	17	11.00	-	-	-						
VJ Wells	9	7	-	141	39	20.14	-	-	6	220	189	8	23.62	3-30	-
JJ Whitaker	2	2	1	48	*44	48.00	-	-	1						
C White	23	19	1	280	38	15.55	-	-	4	1032	739	29	25.48	5-21	2
P Willey	22	20	1	487	64	25.63	-	5	4	936	594	12	49.50	3-33	-
RGD Willis	64	22	14	83	24	10.37	-	-	22	3595	1968	80	24.60	4-11	4
B Wood	13	12	2	314	*78	31.40	-	2	6	420	224	9	24.88	2-14	-
RA Woolmer	6	4	-	21	9	5.25	-	-	3	321	260	9	28.88	3-33	-

ONE-DAY INTERNATIONALS

No	Date	Match	Competition	Venue	Winner	Result
1	5th Jan 1971	Aus v Eng		MCG	Aus	5 wickets
2	24th Aug 1972	Eng v Aus	Prudential Trophy	Old Trafford	Eng	6 wickets
3	26th Aug 1972	Eng v Aus	Prudential Trophy	Lord's	Aus	5 wickets
4	28th Aug 1972	Eng v Aus	Prudential Trophy	Edgbaston	Eng	2 wickets
5	18th Jul 1973	Eng v NZ	Prudential Trophy	Swansea	Eng	7 wickets
6	20th Jul 1973	Eng v NZ	Prudential Trophy	Old Trafford	–	no result
7	5th Sep 1973	Eng v WI	Prudential Trophy	Headingley	Eng	1 wicket
8	7th Sep 1973	Eng v WI	Prudential Trophy	The Oval	WI	8 wickets
9	13th Jul 1974	Eng v Ind	Prudential Trophy	Headingley	Eng	4 wickets
10	15th Jul 1974	Eng v Ind	Prudential Trophy	The Oval	Eng	6 wickets
11	31st Aug 1974	Eng v Pak	Prudential Trophy	Trent Bridge	Pak	7 wickets
12	3rd Sep 1974	Eng v Pak	Prudential Trophy	Edgbaston	Pak	8 wickets
13	1st Jan 1975	Aus v Eng		MCG	Eng	3 wickets
14	8th Mar 1975	NZ v Eng		Dunedin	–	no result
15	9th Mar 1975	NZ v Eng		Wellington	–	no result
16	7th Jun 1975	Eng v Ind	World Cup	Lord's	Eng	202 runs
17	11th Jun 1975	Eng v NZ	World Cup	Trent Bridge	Eng	80 runs
18	14th Jun 1975	Eng v EA	World Cup	Edgbaston	Eng	196 runs
19	18th Jun 1975	Eng v Aus	World Cup (SF)	Headingley	Aus	4 wickets
20	26th Aug 1976	Eng v WI	Prudential Trophy	Scarborough	WI	6 wickets
21	28th Aug 1976	Eng v WI	Prudential Trophy	Lord's	WI	36 runs
22	31st Aug 1976	Eng v WI	Prudential Trophy	Edgbaston	WI	50 runs
23	2nd Jun 1977	Eng v Aus	Prudential Trophy	Old Trafford	Eng	2 wickets
24	4th Jun 1977	Eng v Aus	Prudential Trophy	Edgbaston	Eng	101 runs
25	6th Jun 1977	Eng v Aus	Prudential Trophy	The Oval	Aus	2 wickets
26	23rd Dec 1977	Pak v Eng		Sahiwal	Eng	3 wickets
27	30th Dec 1977	Pak v Eng		Sialkot	Eng	6 wickets
28	13th Jan 1978	Pak v Eng		Lahore (Gd.)	Pak	36 runs
29	24th May 1978	Eng v Pak	Prudential Trophy	Old Trafford	Eng	132 runs
30	26th May 1978	Eng v Pak	Prudential Trophy	The Oval	Eng	94 runs
31	15th Jul 1978	Eng v NZ	Prudential Trophy	Scarborough	Eng	19 runs
32	17th Jul 1978	Eng v NZ	Prudential Trophy	Old Trafford	Eng	126 runs
33	13th Jan 1979	Aus v Eng	B & H Cup	Sydney (SCG)	–	no result
34	24th Jan 1979	Aus v Eng	B & H Cup	MCG	Eng	7 wickets
35	4th Feb 1979	Aus v Eng	B & H Cup	MCG	Aus	4 wickets
36	7th Feb 1979	Aus v Eng	B & H Cup	MCG	Aus	6 wickets
37	9th Jun 1979	Eng v Aus	World Cup	Lord's	Eng	6 wickets
38	14th Jun 1979	Eng v Can	World Cup	Old Trafford	Eng	8 wickets
39	16th Jun 1979	Eng v Pak	World Cup	Headingley	Eng	14 runs
40	20th Jun 1979	Eng v NZ	World Cup (SF)	Old Trafford	Eng	9 runs
41	23rd Jun 1979	Eng v WI	World Cup (F)	Lord's	WI	92 runs
42	28th Nov 1979	Eng v WI	B&H World Series	Sydney (SCG)	Eng	2 runs
43	8th Dec 1979	Aus v Eng	B&H World Series	MCG	Eng	3 wickets
44	11th Dec 1979	Aus v Eng	B&H World Series	Sydney (SCG)	Eng	72 runs
45	23rd Dec 1979	Eng v WI	B&H World Series	The Gabba	WI	9 wickets
46	26th Dec 1979	Aus v Eng	B&H World Series	Sydney (SCG)	Eng	4 wickets
47	14th Jan 1980	Aus v Eng	B&H World Series	Sydney (SCG)	Eng	2 wickets
48	16th Jan 1980	Eng v WI	B&H World Series	Adelaide	WI	107 runs

No	Date	Match	Competition	Venue	Winner	Result
49	20th Jan 1980	Eng v WI	B&H World Series (F)	MCG	WI	2 runs
50	22nd Jan 1980	Eng v WI	B&H World Series (F)	Sydney (SCG)	WI	8 wickets
51	28th May 1980	Eng v WI	Prudential Trophy	Headingley	WI	24 runs
52	30th May 1980	Eng v WI	Prudential Trophy	Lord's	Eng	3 wickets
53	20th Aug 1980	Eng v Aus	Prudential Trophy	The Oval	Eng	23 runs
54	22nd Aug 1980	Eng v Aus	Prudential Trophy	Edgbaston	Eng	47 runs
55	4th Feb 1981	WI v Eng		Arnos Vale	WI	2 runs
56	26th Feb 1981	WI v Eng		Berbice	WI	6 wickets
57	4th Jun 1981	Eng v Aus	Prudential Trophy	Lord's	Eng	6 wickets
58	6th Jun 1981	Eng v Aus	Prudential Trophy	Edgbaston	Aus	2 runs
59	8th Jun 1981	Eng v Aus	Prudential Trophy	Headingley	Aus	71 runs
60	25th Nov 1981	Ind v Eng	Wills Series	Ahmedabad (SP)	Eng	5 wickets
61	20th Dec 1981	Ind v Eng	Wills Series	Jullundur	Ind	6 wickets
62	27th Jan 1982	Ind v Eng	Wills Series	Cuttack	Ind	5 wickets
63	13th Feb 1982	SL v Eng		Colombo (SSC)	Eng	5 runs
64	14th Feb 1982	SL v Eng		Colombo (SSC)	SL	3 runs
65	2nd Jun 1982	Eng v Ind	Prudential Trophy	Headingley	Eng	9 wickets
66	4th Jun 1982	Eng v Ind	Prudential Trophy	The Oval	Eng	114 runs
67	17th Jul 1982	Eng v Pak	Prudential Trophy	Trent Bridge	Eng	7 wickets
68	19th Jul 1982	Eng v Pak	Prudential Trophy	Old Trafford	Eng	73 runs
69	11th Jan 1983	Aus v Eng	B&H World Series	Sydney (SCG)	Aus	31 runs
70	13th Jan 1983	Eng v NZ	B&H World Series	MCG	NZ	2 runs
71	15th Jan 1983	Eng v NZ	B&H World Series	The Gabba	Eng	54 runs
72	16th Jan 1983	Aus v Eng	B&H World Series	The Gabba	Aus	7 wickets
73	20th Jan 1983	Eng v NZ	B&H World Series	Sydney (SCG)	Eng	8 wickets
74	23rd Jan 1983	Aus v Eng	B&H World Series	MCG	Aus	5 wickets
75	26th Jan 1983	Aus v Eng	B&H World Series	Sydney (SCG)	Eng	98 runs
76	29th Jan 1983	Eng v NZ	B&H World Series	Adelaide	NZ	4 wickets
77	30th Jan 1983	Aus v Eng	B&H World Series	Adelaide	Eng	14 runs
78	5th Feb 1983	Eng v NZ	B&H World Series	Perth (WACA)	NZ	7 wickets
79	19th Feb 1983	NZ v Eng	Rothman's Cup	Auckland	NZ	6 wickets
80	23rd Feb 1983	NZ v Eng	Rothman's Cup	Wellington	NZ	103 runs
81	26th Feb 1983	NZ v Eng	Rothman's Cup	Christchurch	NZ	84 runs
82	9th Jun 1983	Eng v NZ	World Cup	The Oval	Eng	106 runs
83	11th Jun 1983	Eng v SL	World Cup	Taunton	Eng	47 runs
84	13th Jun 1983	Eng v Pak	World Cup	Lord's	Eng	8 wickets
85	15th Jun 1983	Eng v NZ	World Cup	Edgbaston	NZ	2 wickets
86	18th Jun 1983	Eng v Pak	World Cup	Old Trafford	Eng	7 wickets
87	20th Jun 1983	Eng v SL	World Cup	Headingley	Eng	9 wickets
88	22nd Jun 1983	Eng v Ind	World Cup (SF)	Old Trafford	Ind	6 wickets
89	18th Feb 1984	NZ v Eng	Rothman's Cup	Christchurch	Eng	54 runs
90	22nd Feb 1984	NZ v Eng	Rothman's Cup	Wellington	Eng	6 wickets
91	25th Feb 1984	NZ v Eng	Rothman's Cup	Auckland	NZ	7 wickets
92	9th Mar 1984	Pak v Eng	Wills Series	Lahore (Gd.)	Pak	6 wickets
93	26th Mar 1984	Pak v Eng	Wills Series	Karachi (NS)	Eng	6 wickets
94	31st May 1984	Eng v WI	Texaco Trophy	Old Trafford	WI	104 runs
95	2nd Jun 1984	Eng v WI	Texaco Trophy	Trent Bridge	Eng	3 wickets
96	4th Jun 1984	Eng v WI	Texaco Trophy	Lord's	WI	8 wickets

ODI MATCH SUMMARY

No	Date	Match	Competition	Venue	Winner	Result
97	5th Dec 1984	Ind v Eng		Poona	Eng	4 wickets
98	27th Dec 1984	Ind v Eng		Cuttack	Eng	run rate
99	20th Jan 1985	Ind v Eng		Bangalore	Eng	3 wickets
100	23rd Jan 1985	Ind v Eng		Nagpur	Ind	3 wickets
101	27th Jan 1985	Ind v Eng		Chandigarh	Eng	7 runs
102	17th Feb 1985	Aus v Eng	B&H World Ch	MCG	Aus	7 wickets
103	26th Feb 1985	Eng v Ind	B&H World Ch	Sydney (SCG)	Ind	86 runs
104	2nd Mar 1985	Eng v Pak	B&H World Ch	MCG	Pak	67 runs
105	24th Mar 1985	Aus v Eng	Rothmans Trophy (SF)	Sharjah	Aus	2 wickets
106	26th Mar 1985	Eng v Pak	Rothmans Trophy (PF)	Sharjah	Pak	43 runs
107	30th May 1985	Eng v Aus	Texaco Trophy	Old Trafford	Aus	3 wickets
108	1st Jun 1985	Eng v Aus	Texaco Trophy	Edgbaston	Aus	4 wickets
109	3rd Jun 1985	Eng v Aus	Texaco Trophy	Lord's	Eng	8 wickets
110	18th Feb 1986	WI v Eng		Kingston	WI	6 wickets
111	4th Mar 1986	WI v Eng		Port-of-Spain	Eng	5 wickets
112	19th Mar 1986	WI v Eng		Bridgetown	WI	135 runs
113	31st Mar 1986	WI v Eng		Port-of-Spain	WI	8 wickets
114	24th May 1986	Eng v Ind	Texaco Trophy	The Oval	Ind	9 wickets
115	26th May 1986	Eng v Ind	Texaco Trophy	Old Trafford	Eng	5 wickets
116	16th Jul 1986	Eng v NZ	Texaco Trophy	Headingley	NZ	47 runs
117	18th Jul 1986	Eng v NZ	Texaco Trophy	Old Trafford	Eng	6 wickets
118	1st Jan 1987	Aus v Eng	B&H Challenge	Perth (WACA)	Eng	37 runs
119	3rd Jan 1987	Eng v WI	B&H Challenge	Perth (WACA)	Eng	19 runs
120	5th Jan 1987	Eng v Pak	B&H Challenge	Perth (WACA)	Eng	3 wickets
121	7th Jan 1987	Eng v Pak	B&H Challenge (F)	Perth (WACA)	Eng	5 wickets
122	17th Jan 1987	Eng v WI	B&H World Series	The Gabba	Eng	6 wickets
123	18th Jan 1987	Aus v Eng	B&H World Series	The Gabba	Aus	11 runs
124	22nd Jan 1987	Aus v Eng	B&H World Series	Sydney (SCG)	Eng	3 wickets
125	24th Jan 1987	Eng v WI	B&H World Series	Adelaide	Eng	89 runs
126	26th Jan 1987	Aus v Eng	B&H World Series	Adelaide	Aus	33 runs
127	30th Jan 1987	Eng v WI	B&H World Series	MCG	WI	6 wickets
128	1st Feb 1987	Aus v Eng	B&H World Series	MCG	Aus	109 runs
129	3rd Feb 1987	Eng v WI	B&H World Series	Devonport	Eng	29 runs
130	8th Feb 1987	Aus v Eng	B&H World Series (F)	MCG	Eng	6 wickets
131	11th Feb 1987	Aus v Eng	B&H World Series (F)	Sydney (SCG)	Eng	8 runs
132	2nd Apr 1987	Eng v Ind	Sharjah Cup	Sharjah	Ind	3 wickets
133	7th Apr 1987	Eng v Pak	Sharjah Cup	Sharjah	Eng	5 wickets
134	9th Apr 1987	Aus v Eng	Sharjah Cup	Sharjah	Eng	11 runs
135	21st May 1987	Eng v Pak	Texaco Trophy	The Oval	Eng	7 wickets
136	23rd May 1987	Eng v Pak	Texaco Trophy	Trent Bridge	Pak	6 wickets
137	25th May 1987	Eng v Pak	Texaco Trophy	Edgbaston	Eng	1 wicket
138	9th Oct 1987	Eng v WI	World Cup	Gujranwala	Eng	2 wickets
139	13th Oct 1987	Pak v Eng	World Cup	Pindi CC	Pak	18 runs
140	17th Oct 1987	Eng v SL	World Cup	Peshawar (AN)	Eng	run rate
141	20th Oct 1987	Pak v Eng	World Cup	Karachi (NS)	Pak	7 wickets
142	26th Oct 1987	Eng v WI	World Cup	Jaipur	Eng	34 runs
143	30th Oct 1987	Eng v SL	World Cup	Poona	Eng	8 wickets
144	5th Nov 1987	Ind v Eng	World Cup (SF)	Wankhede	Eng	35 runs

ODI MATCH SUMMARY

No	Date	Match	Competition	Venue	Winner	Result
145	8th Nov 1987	Aus v Eng	World Cup (F)	Calcutta	Aus	7 runs
146	18th Nov 1987	Pak v Eng		Lahore (Gd.)	Eng	2 wickets
147	20th Nov 1987	Pak v Eng		Karachi (NS)	Eng	23 runs
148	22nd Nov 1987	Pak v Eng		Peshawar (AN)	Eng	98 runs
149	4th Feb 1988	Aus v Eng		MCG	Aus	22 runs
150	9th Mar 1988	NZ v Eng	Rothman's Cup	Dunedin	Eng	5 wickets
151	12nd Mar 1988	NZ v Eng	Rothman's Cup	Christchurch	Eng	6 wickets
152	16th Mar 1988	NZ v Eng	Rothman's Cup	Napier	NZ	7 wickets
153	19th Mar 1988	NZ v Eng	Rothman's Cup	Auckland	NZ	4 wickets
154	19th May 1988	Eng v WI	Texaco Trophy	Edgbaston	Eng	6 wickets
155	21st May 1988	Eng v WI	Texaco Trophy	Headingley	Eng	47 runs
156	23rd May 1988	Eng v WI	Texaco Trophy	Lord's	Eng	7 wickets
157	4th Sep 1988	Eng v SL	Texaco Trophy	The Oval	Eng	5 wickets
158	25th May 1989	Eng v Aus	Texaco Trophy	Old Trafford	Eng	95 runs
159	27th May 1989	Eng v Aus	Texaco Trophy	Trent Bridge	tied	
160	29th May 1989	Eng v Aus	Texaco Trophy	Lord's	Aus	6 wickets
161	15th Oct 1989	Eng v SL	Nehru Cup	Delhi (FSK)	Eng	5 wickets
162	19th Oct 1989	Aus v Eng	Nehru Cup	Hyderabad (I)	Eng	7 wickets
163	22nd Oct 1989	Eng v Pak	Nehru Cup	Cuttack	Eng	4 wickets
164	25th Oct 1989	Ind v Eng	Nehru Cup	Kanpur	Ind	6 wickets
165	27th Oct 1989	Eng v WI	Nehru Cup	Gwalior	WI	26 runs
166	30th Oct 1989	Eng v Pak	Nehru Cup (SF)	Nagpur	Pak	6 wickets
167	14th Feb 1990	WI v Eng	Cable & Wireless	Port-of-Spain	–	no result
168	17th Feb 1990	WI v Eng	Cable & Wireless	Port-of-Spain	–	no result
169	3rd Mar 1990	WI v Eng	Cable & Wireless	Kingston	WI	3 wickets
170	7th Mar 1990	WI v Eng	Cable & Wireless	Georgetown	WI	6 wickets
171	15th Mar 1990	WI v Eng		Georgetown	WI	7 wickets
172	3rd Apr 1990	WI v Eng	Cable & Wireless	Bridgetown	WI	4 wickets
173	23rd May 1990	Eng v NZ	Texaco Trophy	Headingley	NZ	4 wickets
174	25th May 1990	Eng v NZ	Texaco Trophy	The Oval	Eng	6 wickets
175	18th Jul 1990	Eng v Ind	Texaco Trophy	Headingley	Ind	6 wickets
176	20th Jul 1990	Eng v Ind	Texaco Trophy	Trent Bridge	Ind	5 wickets
177	1st Dec 1990	Eng v NZ	B&H World Series	Adelaide	NZ	7 runs
178	7th Dec 1990	Eng v NZ	B&H World Series	Perth (WACA)	Eng	4 wickets
179	9th Dec 1990	Aus v Eng	B&H World Series	Perth (WACA)	Aus	6 wickets
180	13th Dec 1990	Eng v NZ	B&H World Series	Sydney (SCG)	Eng	33 runs
181	15th Dec 1990	Eng v NZ	B&H World Series	The Gabba	NZ	8 wickets
182	16th Dec 1990	Aus v Eng	B&H World Series	The Gabba	Aus	37 runs
183	1st Jan 1991	Aus v Eng	B&H World Series	Sydney (SCG)	Aus	68 runs
184	10th Jan 1991	Aus v Eng	B&H World Series	MCG	Aus	3 runs
185	9th Feb 1991	NZ v Eng		Christchurch	Eng	14 runs
186	13th Feb 1991	NZ v Eng		Wellington	NZ	9 runs
187	16th Feb 1991	NZ v Eng		Auckland	NZ	7 runs
188	23rd May 1991	Eng v WI	Texaco Trophy	Edgbaston	Eng	1 wicket
189	25th May 1991	Eng v WI	Texaco Trophy	Old Trafford	Eng	9 runs
190	27th May 1991	Eng v WI	Texaco Trophy	Lord's	Eng	7 wickets
191	11th Jan 1992	NZ v Eng		Auckland	Eng	7 wickets
192	12nd Feb 1992	NZ v Eng		Dunedin	Eng	3 wickets

ODI MATCH SUMMARY

No	Date	Match	Competition	Venue	Winner	Result
193	15th Feb 1992	NZ v Eng		Christchurch	Eng	71 runs
194	22nd Feb 1992	Eng v Ind	World Cup	Perth (WACA)	Eng	9 runs
195	27th Feb 1992	Eng v WI	World Cup	MCG	Eng	6 wickets
196	1st Mar 1992	Eng v Pak	World Cup	Adelaide		no result
197	5th Mar 1992	Aus v Eng	World Cup	Sydney (SCG)	Eng	8 wickets
198	9th Mar 1992	Eng v SL	World Cup	Ballarat	Eng	106 runs
199	12nd Mar 1992	Eng v SA	World Cup	MCG	Eng	run rate
200	15th Mar 1992	NZ v Eng	World Cup	Wellington	NZ	7 wickets
201	18th Mar 1992	Eng v Zim	World Cup	Albury	Zim	9 runs
202	22nd Mar 1992	Eng v SA	World Cup (SF)	Sydney (SCG)	Eng	19 runs
203	25th Mar 1992	Eng v Pak	World Cup (F)	MCG	Pak	22 runs
204	20th May 1992	Eng v Pak	Texaco Trophy	Lord's	Eng	79 runs
205	22nd May 1992	Eng v Pak	Texaco Trophy	The Oval	Eng	39 runs
206	20th Aug 1992	Eng v Pak	Texaco Trophy	Trent Bridge	Eng	198 runs
207	22nd Aug 1992	Eng v Pak	Texaco Trophy	Lord's	Pak	3 runs
208	24th Aug 1992	Eng v Pak	Texaco Trophy	Old Trafford	Eng	6 wickets
209	18th Jan 1993	Ind v Eng		Jaipur	Eng	4 wickets
210	21st Jan 1993	Ind v Eng		Chandigarh	Ind	5 wickets
211	26th Feb 1993	Ind v Eng		Bangalore	Eng	48 runs
212	1st Mar 1993	Ind v Eng		Jamshedpur	Eng	6 wickets
213	4th Mar 1993	Ind v Eng		Gwalior	Ind	3 wickets
214	5th Mar 1993	Ind v Eng		Gwalior	Ind	4 wickets
215	10th Mar 1993	SL v Eng		Khettarama	SL	run rate
216	20th Mar 1993	SL v Eng		Moratuwa	SL	8 wickets
217	19th May 1993	Eng v Aus	Texaco Trophy	Old Trafford	Aus	4 runs
218	21st May 1993	Eng v Aus	Texaco Trophy	Edgbaston	Aus	6 wickets
219	23rd May 1993	Eng v Aus	Texaco Trophy	Lord's	Aus	19 runs
220	16th Feb 1994	WI v Eng		Bridgetown	Eng	61 runs
221	26th Feb 1994	WI v Eng		Kingston	WI	run rate
222	2nd Mar 1994	WI v Eng		Arnos Vale	WI	165 runs
223	5th Mar 1994	WI v Eng		Port-of-Spain	WI	run rate
224	6th Mar 1994	WI v Eng		Port-of-Spain	Eng	run rate
225	19th May 1994	Eng v NZ	Texaco Trophy	Edgbaston	Eng	42 runs
226	25th Aug 1994	Eng v SA	Texaco Trophy	Edgbaston	Eng	6 wickets
227	27th Aug 1994	Eng v SA	Texaco Trophy	Old Trafford	Eng	4 wickets
228	6th Dec 1994	Aus v Eng	B&H World Series	Sydney (SCG)	Aus	28 runs
229	15th Dec 1994	Eng v Zim	B&H World Series	Sydney (SCG)	Zim	13 runs
230	7th Jan 1995	Eng v Zim	B&H World Series	The Gabba	Eng	26 runs
231	10th Jan 1995	Aus v Eng	B&H World Series	MCG	Eng	37 runs
232	24th May 1995	Eng v WI	Texaco Trophy	Trent Bridge	WI	5 wickets
233	26th May 1995	Eng v WI	Texaco Trophy	The Oval	Eng	25 runs
234	28th May 1995	Eng v WI	Texaco Trophy	Lord's	Eng	73 runs
235	9th Jan 1996	SA v Eng		Cape Town	SA	6 runs
236	11th Jan 1996	SA v Eng		Bloemfontein	Eng	5 wickets
237	13th Jan 1996	SA v Eng		Wanderers	SA	3 wickets
238	14th Jan 1996	SA v Eng		Centurion	SA	7 wickets
239	17th Jan 1996	SA v Eng		Kingsmead	SA	5 wickets
240	19th Jan 1996	SA v Eng		East London	SA	14 runs

No	Date	Match	Competition	Venue	Winner	Result
241	21st Jan 1996	SA v Eng		Port Elizabeth	SA	64 runs
242	14th Feb 1996	Eng v NZ	World Cup	Ahmedabad (GS)	NZ	11 runs
243	18th Feb 1996	Eng v UAE	World Cup	Peshawar (AN)	Eng	8 wickets
244	22nd Feb 1996	Eng v Net	World Cup	Peshawar (AN)	Eng	49 runs
245	25th Feb 1996	Eng v SA	World Cup	Rawalpindi CS	SA	78 runs
246	3rd Mar 1996	Pak v Eng	World Cup	Karachi (NS)	Pak	7 wickets
247	9th Mar 1996	Eng v SL	World Cup (QF)	Faisalabad	SL	5 wickets
248	23rd May 1996	Eng v Ind	Texaco Trophy	The Oval	–	no result
249	25th May 1996	Eng v Ind	Texaco Trophy	Headingley	Eng	6 wickets
250	26th May 1996	Eng v Ind	Texaco Trophy	Old Trafford	Eng	4 wickets
251	29th Aug 1996	Eng v Pak	Texaco Trophy	Old Trafford	Eng	5 wickets
252	31st Aug 1996	Eng v Pak	Texaco Trophy	Edgbaston	Eng	107 runs
253	1st Sep 1996	Eng v Pak	Texaco Trophy	Trent Bridge	Pak	2 wickets
254	15th Dec 1996	Zim v Eng		Bulawayo Q.C.	Zim	2 wickets
255	1st Jan 1997	Zim v Eng		Harare	Zim	run rate
256	3rd Jan 1997	Zim v Eng		Harare	Zim	131 runs
257	20th Feb 1997	NZ v Eng		Christchurch	Eng	4 wickets
258	23rd Feb 1997	NZ v Eng		Auckland	Eng	run rate
259	26th Feb 1997	NZ v Eng		Napier	tied	
260	2nd Mar 1997	NZ v Eng		Auckland	NZ	9 runs
261	4th Mar 1997	NZ v Eng		Wellington	NZ	28 runs
262	22nd May 1997	Eng v Aus	Texaco Trophy	Headingley	Eng	6 wickets
263	24th May 1997	Eng v Aus	Texaco Trophy	The Oval	Eng	6 wickets
264	25th May 1997	Eng v Aus	Texaco Trophy	Lord's	Eng	6 wickets
265	11th Dec 1997	Eng v Ind	Singer-Akai Cup	Sharjah	Eng	7 runs
266	13th Dec 1997	Eng v WI	Singer-Akai Cup	Sharjah	Eng	4 wickets
267	15th Dec 1997	Eng v Pak	Singer-Akai Cup	Sharjah	Eng	8 runs
268	19th Dec 1997	Eng v WI	Singer-Akai Cup (F)	Sharjah	Eng	3 wickets
269	29th Mar 1998	WI v Eng		Bridgetown	Eng	16 runs
270	1st Apr 1998	WI v Eng		Bridgetown	WI	1 wicket
271	4th Apr 1998	WI v Eng		Arnos Vale	WI	5 wickets
272	5th Apr 1998	WI v Eng		Arnos Vale	WI	4 wickets
273	8th Apr 1998	WI v Eng		Port-of-Spain	WI	57 runs
274	21st May 1998	Eng v SA	Texaco Trophy	The Oval	SA	3 wickets
275	23rd May 1998	Eng v SA	Texaco Trophy	Old Trafford	SA	32 runs
276	24th May 1998	Eng v SA	Texaco Trophy	Headingley	Eng	7 wickets
277	16th Aug 1998	Eng v SL	Emirates Tri	Lord's	Eng	36 runs
278	18th Aug 1998	Eng v SA	Emirates Tri	Edgbaston	SA	14 runs
279	20th Aug 1998	Eng v SL	Emirates Tri (F)	Lord's	SL	5 wickets
280	25th Oct 1998	Eng v SA	Wills Int Cup (QF)	Dhaka	SA	6 wickets
281	10th Jan 1999	Aus v Eng	Carlton & United	The Gabba	Eng	run rate
282	11th Jan 1999	Eng v SL	Carlton & United	The Gabba	Eng	6 wickets
283	15th Jan 1999	Aus v Eng	Carlton & United	MCG	Aus	9 wickets
284	17th Jan 1999	Aus v Eng	Carlton & United	Sydney (SCG)	Eng	7 runs
285	19th Jan 1999	Eng v SL	Carlton & United	MCG	Eng	7 wickets
286	23rd Jan 1999	Eng v SL	Carlton & United	Adelaide	SL	1 wicket
287	26th Jan 1999	Aus v Eng	Carlton & United	Adelaide	Aus	16 runs
288	29th Jan 1999	Eng v SL	Carlton & United	Perth (WACA)	Eng	128 runs

No	Date	Match	Competition	Venue	Winner	Result
289	3rd Feb 1999	Eng v SL	Carlton & United	Sydney (SCG)	SL	11 runs
290	5th Feb 1999	Aus v Eng	Carlton & United	Sydney (SCG)	Aus	4 wickets
291	10th Feb 1999	Aus v Eng	Carlton & United (F)	Sydney (SCG)	Aus	10 runs
292	13th Feb 1999	Aus v Eng	Carlton & United (F)	MCG	Aus	162 runs
293	7th Apr 1999	Eng v Pak	Coca Cola Cup	Sharjah	Pak	90 runs
294	9th Apr 1999	Eng v Ind	Coca Cola Cup	Sharjah	Ind	20 runs
295	11th Apr 1999	Eng v Ind	Coca Cola Cup	Sharjah	Ind	9 runs
296	12nd Apr 1999	Eng v Pak	Coca Cola Cup	Sharjah	Eng	62 runs
297	14th May 1999	Eng v SL	World Cup	Lord's	Eng	8 wickets
298	18th May 1999	Eng v Ken	World Cup	Canterbury	Eng	9 wickets
299	22nd May 1999	Eng v SA	World Cup	The Oval	SA	122 runs
300	25th May 1999	Eng v Zim	World Cup	Trent Bridge	Eng	7 wickets
301	29th May 1999	Eng v Ind	World Cup	Edgbaston	Ind	63 runs
302	23rd Jan 2000	SA v Eng	Standard Bank Tri	Bloemfontein	Eng	9 wickets
303	26th Jan 2000	SA v Eng	Standard Bank Tri	Newlands	SA	1 run
304	28th Jan 2000	Zim v Eng	Standard Bank Tri	Newlands	Zim	104 runs
305	30th Jan 2000	Zim v Eng	Standard Bank Tri	Diamond Oval	Eng	8 wickets
306	4th Feb 2000	SA v Eng	Standard Bank Tri	East London	SA	2 wickets
307	13th Feb 2000	SA v Eng	Standard Bank Tri	Johannesburg	SA	38 runs
308	16th Feb 2000	Zim v Eng		Bulawayo	Eng	5 wickets
309	18th Feb 2000	Zim v Eng		Bulawayo	Eng	1 wicket
310	20th Feb 2000	Zim v Eng		Harare	Eng	85 runs

No. 1: One-Day International
VENUE: Melbourne (MCG)
DATE: 5th January 1971
TOSS WON BY: Australia
RESULT: Australia won by 5 wickets

ENGLAND

G Boycott	c Lawry b Thomson	8
JH Edrich	c Walters b Mallett	82
KWR Fletcher	c GS Chappell b Mallett	24
BL D'Oliveira	run out	17
JH Hampshire	c McKenzie b Mallett	10
MC Cowdrey	c Marsh b Stackpole	1
R Illingworth*	b Stackpole	1
APE Knott+	b McKenzie	24
JA Snow	b Stackpole	2
K Shuttleworth	c Redpath b McKenzie	7
P Lever	not out	4
Extras	(1b, 9lb, 0w, 0nb)	10
	39.4 overs	
Total		**190**

FoW: 21,87,124, 144,148,152,156,171,183,190

GD McKenzie	7.4	0	22	2
AL Thomson	8	2	22	1
AN Connolly	8	0	62	0
AA Mallett	8	1	34	3
KR Stackpole	8	0	40	3

AUSTRALIA

WM Lawry*	c Knott b Illingworth	27
KR Stackpole	c & b Shuttleworth	13
IM Chappell	st Knott b Illingworth	60
KD Walters	c Knott b D'Oliveira	41
IR Redpath	b Illingworth	12
GS Chappell	not out	22
RW Marsh+	not out	10
AA Mallett		
GD McKenzie		
AN Connolly		
AL Thomson		
Extras	(0b, 4lb, 1w, 1nb)	6
	34.6 overs	
Total		**191**

FoW: 19,51,117,158,165

JA Snow	8	0	38	0
K Shuttleworth	7	0	29	1
P Lever	5.6	0	30	0
R Illingworth	8	1	50	3
BL D'Oliveira	6	1	38	1

No. 2: Prudential Trophy
VENUE: Old Trafford
DATE: 24th August 1972
TOSS WON BY: Australia
RESULT: England won by 6 wickets

AUSTRALIA

KR Stackpole	c D'Oliveira b Greig	37
GD Watson	b Arnold	0
IM Chappell*	b Woolmer	53
GS Chappell	b Woolmer	40
R Edwards	run out	57
AP Sheahan	b Arnold	6
KD Walters	lbw b Woolmer	2
RW Marsh+	c Close b Snow	11
AA Mallett	not out	6
DK Lillee		
RAL Massie		
Extras	(2b, 3lb, 0w, 5nb)	10
	55 overs	
Total		**222**

FoW: 4, 66, 125, 156, 167, 170, 205, 222

JA Snow	11	1	33	1
GG Arnold	11	0	38	2
AW Greig	11	0	50	1
RA Woolmer	10	1	33	3
BL D'Oliveira	9	1	37	0
DB Close	3	0	21	0

ENGLAND

G Boycott	c Marsh b Watson	25
DL Amiss	b Watson	103
KWR Fletcher	b Massie	60
DB Close*	run out	1
JH Hampshire	not out	25
BL D'Oliveira	not out	5
AW Greig		
APE Knott+		
RA Woolmer		
JA Snow		
GG Arnold		
Extras	(1b, 6lb, 0w, 0nb)	7
	49.1 overs	
Total		**226**

FoW: 48, 173, 174, 215

DK Lillee	11	2	49	0
RAL Massie	11	1	49	1
GD Watson	8	1	28	2
AA Mallett	11	1	43	0
GS Chappell	3	0	20	0
KD Walters	3	1	16	0
KR Stackpole	2.1	0	14	0

Australia

No. 3: Prudential Trophy
VENUE: Lord's
DATE: 26th August 1972
TOSS WON BY: Australia
RESULT: Australia won by 5 wickets

ENGLAND

G Boycott	b Lillee	8
DL Amiss	b Mallett	25
DB Close*	run out	43
KWR Fletcher	c Stackpole b GS Chappell	20
JH Hampshire	st Marsh b Mallett	13
BL D'Oliveira	c IM Chappell b Lillee	6
AW Greig	b Massie	31
APE Knott+	c Mallett b Massie	50
RA Woolmer	run out	9
JA Snow	not out	5
GG Arnold	not out	11
Extras	(1b, 10lb, 1w, 3nb)	15
	55 overs	
Total		**236**

FoW: 11, 65, 87, 114, 121, 121, 198, 217, 218

DK Lillee	11	0	56	2
RAL Massie	11	1	35	2
DJ Colley	11	1	72	0
AA Mallett	11	2	24	2
GS Chappell	11	0	34	1

AUSTRALIA

KR Stackpole	lbw b D'Oliveira	52
R Edwards	c Knott b Snow	6
IM Chappell*	c Knott b Woolmer	31
GS Chappell	lbw b Snow	48
AP Sheahan	c Knott b Snow	50
GD Watson	not out	11
RW Marsh+	not out	6
DJ Colley		
AA Mallett		
DK Lillee		
RAL Massie		
Extras	(6b, 14lb, 12w, 4nb)	36
	51.3 overs	
Total		**240**

FoW: 44, 112, 116, 219, 224

JA Snow	11	2	35	3
GG Arnold	11	0	47	0
BL D'Oliveira	11	0	46	1
AW Greig	9	1	29	0
RA Woolmer	9.3	1	47	1

Australia

No. 4: Prudential Trophy
VENUE: Edgbaston
DATE: 28th August 1972
TOSS WON BY: England
RESULT: England won by 2 wickets

AUSTRALIA

KR Stackpole	b Woolmer	61
R Edwards	b Arnold	6
IM Chappell*	run out	3
GS Chappell	c Wood b D'Oliveira	13
AP Sheahan	c Woolmer b Wood	19
KD Walters	b Wood	15
RW Marsh+	lbw b Arnold	0
AA Mallett	b Arnold	8
JR Hammond	not out	15
DK Lillee	c Wood b Arnold	13
RAL Massie	not out	16
Extras	(0b, 6lb, 0w, 4nb)	10
	55 overs	
Total		**179**

FoW: 8, 15, 40, 87, 111, 112, 127, 136, 158

JA Snow	11	0	29	0
GG Arnold	11	3	27	4
AW Greig	10	3	24	0
BL D'Oliveira	6	1	19	1
RA Woolmer	11	1	50	1
B Wood	6	0	20	2

ENGLAND

G Boycott	c Massie b Lillee	41
DL Amiss	c Marsh b GS Chappell	40
DB Close*	c Marsh b Lillee	5
KWR Fletcher	c Marsh b Hammond	34
BL D'Oliveira	run out	2
B Wood	lbw b Lillee	19
AW Greig	not out	24
APE Knott+	c Mallett b Walters	6
RA Woolmer	c Marsh b Walters	0
JA Snow	not out	0
GG Arnold		
Extras	(0b, 5lb, 4w, 0nb)	9
	51.3 overs	
Total		**180**

FoW: 76, 89, 94, 104, 143, 154, 172, 172

DK Lillee	11	2	25	3
RAL Massie	8.3	3	45	0
AA Mallett	4	0	16	0
JR Hammond	9	1	41	1
GS Chappell	11	3	20	1
KD Walters	8	1	24	2

No. 5: Prudential Trophy
VENUE: Swansea
DATE: 18th July 1973
TOSS WON BY: New Zealand
RESULT: England won by 7 wickets

No. 6: Prudential Trophy
VENUE: Old Trafford
DATE: 20th July 1973
TOSS WON BY: New Zealand
RESULT: No result

NEW ZEALAND

RE Redmond	lbw b Arnold	3
GM Turner	c & b Illingworth	26
BE Congdon*	c Knott b Snow	2
BF Hastings	c Roope b Snow	0
MG Burgess	c Knott b Arnold	1
V Pollard	c Knott b Arnold	55
KJ Wadsworth+	lbw b Underwood	3
BR Taylor	c Fletcher b Snow	22
RJ Hadlee	c Snow b Greig	28
RO Collinge	c Knott b Snow	4
HJ Howarth	not out	5
Extras	(0b, 2lb, 7w, 0nb)	9
	52.5 overs	
Total		**158**

FoW: 4, 9, 14, 15, 70, 81, 108, 133, 144, 158

JA Snow	10	0	32	4
GG Arnold	11	2	28	3
AW Greig	9.5	2	26	1
DL Underwood	11	3	29	1
R Illingworth	11	1	34	1

ENGLAND

G Boycott	c Turner b Congdon	20
DL Amiss	c Pollard b Taylor	100
GRJ Roope	b Howarth	0
FC Hayes	not out	20
KWR Fletcher	not out	16
AW Greig		
R Illingworth*		
APE Knott+		
JA Snow		
GG Arnold		
DL Underwood		
Extras	(1b, 1lb, 1w, 0nb)	3
	45.3 overs	
Total		**159**

FoW: 96, 97, 135

RO Collinge	6	2	18	0
RJ Hadlee	11	1	35	0
BR Taylor	8.3	1	37	1
HJ Howarth	11	3	34	1
BE Congdon	9	2	32	1

ENGLAND

G Boycott	lbw b Taylor	15
DL Amiss	c Wadsworth b Congdon	34
GRJ Roope	c Wadsworth b Hadlee	44
FC Hayes	b Congdon	9
KWR Fletcher	c Hadlee b Taylor	25
AW Greig	c Taylor b Collinge	14
R Illingworth*	c Turner b Hadlee	4
APE Knott+	c Wadsworth b Taylor	12
GG Arnold	not out	0
JA Snow		
P Lever		
Extras	(0b, 6lb, 4w, 0nb)	10
	48.3 overs	
Total		**167**

FoW: 23, 57, 75, 112, 150, 153, 160, 167

RO Collinge	11	0	52	1
BR Taylor	10.3	3	25	3
RJ Hadlee	8	1	23	2
BE Congdon	8	1	24	2
HJ Howarth	11	1	33	0

NEW ZEALAND

GM Turner
RE Redmond
BE Congdon*
BF Hastings
MG Burgess
V Pollard
KJ Wadsworth+
BR Taylor
RJ Hadlee
RO Collinge
HJ Howarth
Extras

No. 7: Prudential Trophy (2)
VENUE: Headingley
DATE: 5th September 1973
TOSS WON BY: West Indies
RESULT: England won by 1 wicket

No. 8: Prudential Trophy (2)
VENUE: The Oval
DATE: 7th September 1973
TOSS WON BY: England
RESULT: West Indies won by 8 wickets

WEST INDIES

RC Fredericks	c Greig b Willis	4
MLC Foster	c Greig b Old	25
RB Kanhai*	c Greig b Underwood	55
CH Lloyd	b Willis	31
AI Kallicharran	st Taylor b Underwood	26
GStA Sobers	c Taylor b Old	0
BD Julien	c Taylor b Old	0
KD Boyce	b Underwood	7
DL Murray+	run out	11
VA Holder	c Old b Hendrick	10
LR Gibbs	not out	0
Extras	(0b, 12lb, 0w, 0nb)	12
Total	54 overs	**181**

FoW: 4, 65, 115, 132, 133, 133, 158, 159, 181, 181

RGD Willis	10	2	29	2
M Hendrick	11	4	27	1
CM Old	11	1	43	3
DL Underwood	11	2	30	3
AW Greig	11	0	40	0

ENGLAND

G Boycott	c Kanhai b Holder	0
MJ Smith	lbw b Julien	31
MH Denness*	b Gibbs	66
FC Hayes	c Murray b Julien	9
KWR Fletcher	lbw b Holder	2
AW Greig	c Sobers b Boyce	48
CM Old	b Sobers	4
RW Taylor+	run out	8
M Hendrick	b Boyce	1
RGD Willis	not out	5
DL Underwood	not out	1
Extras	(1b, 3lb, 0w, 3nb)	7
Total	54.3 overs	**182**

FoW: 3, 74, 93, 95, 143, 157, 171, 176, 176

GStA Sobers	10.3	3	31	1
VA Holder	11	1	34	2
KD Boyce	11	1	40	2
BD Julien	11	1	40	2
LR Gibbs	11	0	30	1

ENGLAND

MJ Smith	b Lloyd	19
JA Jameson	c Holder b Gibbs	28
MH Denness*	lbw b Lloyd	0
D Lloyd	run out	8
KWR Fletcher	b Julien	63
AW Greig	c Lloyd b Foster	17
CM Old	c Murray b Holder	21
RW Taylor+	run out	3
GG Arnold	c Julien b Foster	17
RGD Willis	not out	4
DL Underwood	not out	1
Extras	(2b, 3lb, 0w, 3nb)	8
Total	55 overs	**189**

FoW: 38, 39, 59, 59, 100, 135, 142, 177, 184

VA Holder	11	0	40	1
BD Julien	11	2	35	1
CH Lloyd	11	2	25	2
LR Gibbs	11	4	12	1
KD Boyce	6	0	47	0
MLC Foster	5	0	22	2

WEST INDIES

RC Fredericks	b Arnold	105
RGA Headley	c Taylor b Arnold	19
AI Kallicharran	not out	53
DA Murray+	not out	1
RB Kanhai*		
CH Lloyd		
MLC Foster		
BD Julien		
KD Boyce		
VA Holder		
LR Gibbs		
Extras	(1b, 6lb, 0w, 5nb)	12
Total	42.2 overs	**190**

FoW: 43, 186

RGD Willis	10.2	0	55	0
GG Arnold	9	1	24	2
CM Old	10	0	52	0
DL Underwood	7	0	26	0
AW Greig	6	2	21	0

No. 9: Prudential Trophy
VENUE: Headingley
DATE: 13th July 1974
TOSS WON BY: England
RESULT: England won by 4 wickets

No. 10: Prudential Trophy
VENUE: The Oval
DATE: 15th July 1974
TOSS WON BY: India
RESULT: England won by 6 wickets

INDIA

SM Gavaskar	b Arnold	28
SS Naik	lbw b Jackman	18
AL Wadekar*	b Jackman	67
GR Viswanath	b Woolmer	4
FM Engineer+	lbw b Old	32
BP Patel	c Fletcher b Greig	82
ED Solkar	lbw b Arnold	3
S Abid Ali	c & b Woolmer	17
S Madan Lal	b Old	2
S Venkat'van	not out	1
BS Bedi	c Lloyd b Old	0
Extras	(8b, 0lb, 0w, 3nb)	11
	53.5 overs	
Total		**265**

FoW: 44, 50, 60, 130, 181, 194, 246, 264 , 265, 265

GG Arnold	10	1	42	2
CM Old	10.5	0	43	3
RD Jackman	11	0	44	2
RA Woolmer	11	0	62	2
AW Greig	11	0	63	1

ENGLAND

DL Amiss	lbw b Solkar	20
D Lloyd	st Engineer b Solkar	34
JH Edrich	c Bedi b Venkat'van	90
MH Denness*	c Venkat'van b Madan Lal	8
KWR Fletcher	c & b Bedi	39
AW Greig	c & b Bedi	40
APE Knott+	not out	15
CM Old	not out	5
RA Woolmer		
RD Jackman		
GG Arnold		
Extras	(0b, 12lb, 0w, 3nb)	15
	51.1 overs	
Total		**266**

FoW: 37, 84, 96, 179, 212, 254

S Abid Ali	9	0	51	0
ED Solkar	11	1	31	2
S Madan Lal	9.1	1	43	1
S Venkat'van	11	0	58	1
BS Bedi	11	0	68	2

INDIA

SM Gavaskar	c Arnold b Jackman	20
SS Naik	c Greig b Old	20
G Bose	c Denness b Jackman	13
AL Wadekar*	c Lloyd b Underwood	6
GR Viswanath	c Knott b Old	32
FM Engineer+	lbw b Jackman	4
BP Patel	run out	12
AV Mankad	b Old	44
ED Solkar	c Knott b Greig	0
S Abid Ali	c Smith b Greig	6
S Madan Lal	not out	3
Extras	(0b, 9lb, 1w, 1nb)	11
	47.3 overs	
Total		**171**

FoW: 40, 48, 60, 64, 75, 94, 139, 142, 156, 171

GG Arnold	7	0	20	0
CM Old	9.3	0	36	3
RD Jackman	11	1	41	3
DL Underwood	11	0	36	1
AW Greig	9	0	27	2

ENGLAND

MJ Smith	c Engineer b Abid Ali	6
D Lloyd	c (sub) b Bose	39
JH Edrich	c Patel b Madan Lal	19
MH Denness*	c Wadekar b Mankad	24
KWR Fletcher	not out	55
AW Greig	not out	24
APE Knott+		
CM Old		
RD Jackman		
GG Arnold		
DL Underwood		
Extras	(0b, 4lb, 1w, 0nb)	5
	48.5 overs	
Total		**172**

FoW: 19, 65, 71, 113

S Abid Ali	11	3	21	1
ED Solkar	11	3	37	0
S Madan Lal	10	0	23	1
G Bose	11	2	39	1
AV Mankad	5.5	0	47	1

Pakistan

No. 11: Prudential Trophy (2)
VENUE: Trent Bridge
DATE: 31st August 1974
TOSS WON BY: England
RESULT: Pakistan won by 7 wickets

ENGLAND

D Lloyd	not out		116
MJ Smith	c Sadiq b Sarfraz		14
JH Edrich	c Wasim Bari b Asif Iqbal		18
MH Denness*	st Wasim Bari b Intikhab		32
CM Old	st Wasim Bari b Majid Khan		39
AW Greig	not out		7
KWR Fletcher			
APE Knott+			
P Lever			
DL Underwood			
RGD Willis			
Extras	(5b, 11lb, 0w, 2nb)		18
	50 overs		
Total			**244**

FoW: 17, 59, 162, 226

Asif Masood	10	2	31	0
Sarfraz Nawaz	10	0	46	1
Asif Iqbal	10	1	40	1
Imran Khan	10	0	36	0
Intikhab Alam	7	0	58	1
Majid Khan	3	0	15	1

PAKISTAN

Sadiq Moh'd	b Lever		41
Majid Khan	c Old b Underwood		109
Zaheer Abbas	c & b Willis		31
Asif Iqbal	not out		24
Mushtaq Moh'd	not out		24
Wasim Raja			
Intikhab Alam*			
Imran Khan			
Sarfraz Nawaz			
Wasim Bari+			
Asif Masood			
Extras	(1b, 11lb, 0w, 5nb)		17
	42.5 overs		
Total			**246**

FoW: 113, 187, 199

RGD Willis	10	2	34	1
P Lever	10	0	58	1
CM Old	10	0	65	0
DL Underwood	8	1	32	1
AW Greig	4.5	0	40	0

Pakistan

No. 12: Prudential Trophy (2)
VENUE: Edgbaston
DATE: 3rd September 1974
TOSS WON BY: Pakistan
RESULT: Pakistan won by 8 wickets

ENGLAND

D Lloyd	b Sarfraz		4
MJ Smith	lbw b Asif Masood		0
JH Edrich	b Sarfraz		6
MH Denness*	b Imran Khan		9
KWR Fletcher	c Wasim Bari b Asif Masood		2
AW Greig	run out		1
CM Old	c Wasim Raja b Asif Iqbal		0
RW Taylor+	not out		26
GG Arnold	b Imran Khan		2
DL Underwood	b Asif Iqbal		17
P Lever	not out		8
Extras	(0b, 6lb, 0w, 0nb)		6
	35 overs		
Total			**81**

FoW: 1, 12, 13, 20, 24, 25, 25, 28, 68

Asif Masood	7	2	9	2
Sarfraz Nawaz	7	0	15	2
Imran Khan	7	2	16	2
Asif Iqbal	7	1	17	2
Intikhab Alam	6	1	12	0
Majid Khan	1	0	6	0

PAKISTAN

Sadiq Moh'd	c Lloyd b Underwood		12
Majid Khan	lbw b Arnold		0
Zaheer Abbas	not out		57
Mushtaq Moh'd	not out		1
Asif Iqbal			
Wasim Raja			
Intikhab Alam*			
Sarfraz Nawaz			
Wasim Bari+			
Imran Khan			
Asif Masood			
Extras	(1b, 7lb, 0w, 6nb)		14
	18 overs		
Total			**84**

FoW: 1, 60

GG Arnold	6	3	7	1
P Lever	4	0	22	0
CM Old	5	0	25	0
DL Underwood	3	0	16	1

No. 13: One-Day Series	No. 14: One-Day Series
VENUE: Melbourne (MCG)	VENUE: Dunedin
DATE: 1st January 1975	DATE: 8th March 1975
TOSS WON BY: England	TOSS WON BY: New Zealand
RESULT: England won by 3 wickets	RESULT: No result

AUSTRALIA

IR Redpath	c Greig b Lever	2
WJ Edwards	b Arnold	2
IM Chappell*	c Lever b Old	42
GS Chappell	b Old	44
R Edwards	b Old	20
KD Walters	b Old	18
RW Marsh+	run out	14
TJ Jenner	c Fletcher b Greig	12
MHN Walker	b Greig	20
JR Thomson	b Arnold	4
AG Hurst	not out	1
Extras	(7b, 0lb, 1w, 3nb)	11
	34.5 overs	
Total		**190**

FoW: 5, 11, 65, 105, 122, 139, 159, 173, 183, 190

P Lever	5	0	24	1
GG Arnold	8	2	30	2
AW Greig	7.5	0	48	2
CM Old	8	0	57	4
DL Underwood	6	0	20	0

ENGLAND

DL Amiss	b Walker	47
D Lloyd	run out	49
BW Luckhurst	run out	14
KWR Fletcher	c Redpath b Thomson	31
CM Old	b Hurst	12
AW Greig	run out	3
MH Denness*	c Walker b Hurst	12
APE Knott+	not out	2
DL Underwood	not out	1
GG Arnold		
P Lever		
Extras	(5b, 11lb, 0w, 4nb)	20
	37.1 overs	
Total		**191**

FoW: 70, 117, 124, 154, 157, 182, 182

JR Thomson	7	1	33	1
AG Hurst	8	0	27	2
TJ Jenner	8	1	28	0
KD Walters	3	0	32	0
MHN Walker	8	0	27	1
GS Chappell	3	0	24	0
WJ Edwards	0.1	0	0	0

ENGLAND

DL Amiss	c Wadsworth b RJ Hadlee	3
B Wood	b HJ Howarth	33
BW Luckhurst	c GP Howarth b Collinge	0
KWR Fletcher	c Turner b Congdon	11
JH Edrich*	c RJ Hadlee b HJ Howarth	8
CM Old	c Parker b HJ Howarth	27
RW Taylor+	not out	23
FJ Titmus	b DR Hadlee	11
GG Arnold	b DR Hadlee	0
DL Underwood	c Parker b RJ Hadlee	2
M Hendrick	b Collinge	1
Extras	(0b, 12lb, 0w, 5nb)	17
	34.1 overs	
Total		**136**

FoW: 14, 17, 36, 51, 90, 90, 122, 122, 132, 136

RO Collinge	6.1	0	17	2
RJ Hadlee	7	0	21	2
HJ Howarth	7	0	35	3
BE Congdon	7	0	25	1
DR Hadlee	7	1	21	2

NEW ZEALAND

GM Turner	not out	8
BG Hadlee	not out	7
JM Parker		
GP Howarth		
BE Congdon*		
KJ Wadsworth+		
BF Hastings		
RJ Hadlee		
DR Hadlee		
RO Collinge		
HJ Howarth		
Extras	(0b, 0lb, 0w, 0nb)	0
	4 overs	
Total		**15**

GG Arnold	2	0	6	0
M Hendrick	2	0	9	0

New Zealand

No. 15:	One-Day Series
VENUE:	Wellington
DATE:	9th March 1975
TOSS WON BY:	New Zealand
RESULT:	No result

India

No. 16:	World Cup
VENUE:	Lord's
DATE:	7th June 1975
TOSS WON BY:	England
RESULT:	England won by 202 runs

NEW ZEALAND

GM Turner	b Hendrick	18
JFM Morrison	c Taylor b Lever	5
BE Congdon*	lbw b Lever	101
BF Hastings	c Greig b Titmus	37
KJ Wadsworth+	lbw b Titmus	0
JM Parker	c Wood b Titmus	25
GP Howarth	c (sub Amiss) b Old	13
RJ Hadlee	not out	6
DR Hadlee	run out	0
RO Collinge	c Titmus b Lever	0
HJ Howarth	b Lever	11
Extras	(6b, 2lb, 0w, 3nb)	11
	34.6 overs	
Total		**227**

FoW: 13, 46, 130, 130, 178, 206, 209, 209, 210, 227

P Lever	6.6	0	35	4
CM Old	6	0	32	1
M Hendrick	4	0	21	1
AW Greig	5	0	34	0
FJ Titmus	7	0	53	3
B Wood	6	0	41	0

ENGLAND

B Wood	not out	14
BW Luckhurst	c Wadsworth b Collinge	1
KWR Fletcher	not out	18
JH Edrich		
MH Denness*		
AW Greig		
CM Old		
RW Taylor+		
FJ Titmus		
P Lever		
M Hendrick		
Extras	(1b, 1lb, 0w, 0nb)	2
	10 overs	
Total		**35**

FoW: 3

RO Collinge	4	1	9	1
DR Hadlee	3	0	6	0
BE Congdon	2	0	14	0
RJ Hadlee	1	0	4	0

ENGLAND

JA Jameson	c Venkat'van b Amarnath	21
DL Amiss	b Madan Lal	137
KWR Fletcher	b Abid Ali	68
AW Greig	lbw b Abid Ali	4
MH Denness*	not out	37
CM Old	not out	51
B Wood		
APE Knott+		
JA Snow		
P Lever		
GG Arnold		
Extras	(0b, 12lb, 2w, 2nb)	16
	60 overs	
Total		**334**

FoW: 54, 230, 237, 245

S Madan Lal	12	1	64	1
M Amarnath	12	2	60	1
S Abid Ali	12	0	58	2
KD Ghavri	11	1	83	0
S Venkat'van	12	0	41	0
ED Solkar	1	0	12	0

INDIA

SM Gavaskar	not out	36
ED Solkar	c Lever b Arnold	8
AD Gaekwad	c Knott b Lever	22
GR Viswanath	c Fletcher b Old	37
BP Patel	not out	16
M Amarnath		
FM Engineer+		
S Abid Ali		
S Madan Lal		
S Venkat'van*		
KD Ghavri		
Extras	(0b, 3lb, 1w, 9nb)	13
	60 overs	
Total		**132**

FoW: 21, 50, 108

JA Snow	12	2	24	0
GG Arnold	10	2	20	1
CM Old	12	4	26	1
AW Greig	9	1	26	0
B Wood	5	2	4	0
P Lever	10	0	16	1
JA Jameson	2	1	3	0

New Zealand

	No. 17: World Cup
	VENUE: Trent Bridge
	DATE: 11th June 1975
TOSS WON BY:	New Zealand
RESULT:	England won by 80 runs

ENGLAND

JA Jameson	c Wadsworth b Collinge	11
DL Amiss	b Collinge	16
KWR Fletcher	run out	131
FC Hayes	lbw b RJ Hadlee	34
MH Denness*	c Morrison b DR Hadlee	37
AW Greig	b DR Hadlee	9
CM Old	not out	20
APE Knott+		
DL Underwood		
GG Arnold		
P Lever		
Extras	(0b, 6lb, 1w, 1nb)	8
	60 overs	
Total		**266**

FoW: 27, 28, 111, 177, 200, 266

RO Collinge	12	2	43	2
RJ Hadlee	12	2	66	1
DR Hadlee	12	1	55	2
BJ McKechnie	12	2	38	0
HJ Howarth	12	2	56	0

NEW ZEALAND

JFM Morrison	c Old b Underwood	55
GM Turner*	b Lever	12
BG Hadlee	b Greig	19
JM Parker	b Greig	1
BF Hastings	c Underwood b Old	10
KJ Wadsworth+	b Arnold	25
RJ Hadlee	b Old	0
BJ McKechnie	c Underwood b Greig	27
DR Hadlee	c Arnold b Greig	20
HJ Howarth	not out	1
RO Collinge	b Underwood	6
Extras	(1b, 4lb, 1w, 4nb)	10
	60 overs	
Total		**186**

FoW: 30, 83, 91, 95, 129, 129, 129, 177, 180, 186

GG Arnold	12	3	35	1
P Lever	12	0	37	1
CM Old	12	2	29	2
AW Greig	12	0	45	4
DL Underwood	12	2	30	2

East Africa

	No. 18: World Cup
	VENUE: Edgbaston
	DATE: 14th June 1975
TOSS WON BY:	East Africa
RESULT:	England won by 196 runs

ENGLAND

B Wood	b Mehmood	77
DL Amiss	c Nana b Zulfiqar Ali	88
FC Hayes	b Zulfiqar Ali	52
AW Greig	lbw b Zulfiqar Ali	9
APE Knott+	not out	18
CM Old	b Mehmood	18
MH Denness*	not out	12
KWR Fletcher		
JA Snow		
P Lever		
DL Underwood		
Extras	(7b, 7lb, 1w, 1nb)	16
	60 overs	
Total		**290**

FoW: 158, 192, 234, 244, 277

Frasat Ali	9	0	40	0
D Pringle	12	0	41	0
PG Nana	12	2	46	0
Ramesh Sethi	5	0	29	0
Zulfiqar Ali	12	0	63	3
Mehmood Q'shy	10	0	55	2

EAST AFRICA

Frasat Ali	b Snow	0
S Walusimba	lbw b Snow	7
Yunus Badat	b Snow	0
Jawahir Shah	lbw b Snow	4
Ramesh Sethi	b Lever	30
Harilal R Shah*	b Greig	6
Mehmood Q'shy	c Amiss b Greig	19
Zulfiqar Ali	b Lever	7
H McLeod+	b Lever	0
PG Nana	not out	8
D Pringle	b Old	3
Extras	(0b, 6lb, 1w, 3nb)	10
	52.3 overs	
Total		**94**

FoW: 7, 7, 15, 21, 42, 72, 76, 79, 88, 94

JA Snow	12	6	11	4
P Lever	12	3	32	3
DL Underwood	10	5	11	0
B Wood	7	3	10	0
AW Greig	10	1	18	2
CM Old	1.3	0	2	1

Australia

No. 19: World Cup Semi-Final		
VENUE: Headingley		
DATE: 18th June 1975		
TOSS WON BY: Australia		
RESULT: Australia won by 4 wickets		

ENGLAND

DL Amiss	lbw b Gilmour	2
B Wood	b Gilmour	6
KWR Fletcher	lbw b Gilmour	8
AW Greig	c Marsh b Gilmour	7
FC Hayes	lbw b Gilmour	4
MH Denness*	b Walker	27
APE Knott+	lbw b Gilmour	0
CM Old	c GS Chappell b Walker	0
JA Snow	c Marsh b Lillee	2
GG Arnold	not out	18
P Lever	lbw b Walker	5
Extras	(0b, 5lb, 7w, 2nb)	14
	36.2 overs	
Total		**93**

FoW: 2, 11, 26, 33, 35, 36, 37, 52, 73, 93

DK Lillee	9	3	26	1
GJ Gilmour	12	6	14	6
MHN Walker	9.2	3	22	3
JR Thomson	6	0	17	0

AUSTRALIA

A Turner	lbw b Arnold	7
RB McCosker	b Old	15
IM Chappell*	lbw b Snow	2
GS Chappell	lbw b Snow	4
KD Walters	not out	20
R Edwards	b Old	0
RW Marsh+	b Old	5
GJ Gilmour	not out	28
MHN Walker		
DK Lillee		
JR Thomson		
Extras	(1b, 6lb, 0w, 6nb)	13
	28.4 overs	
Total		**94**

FoW: 17, 24, 32, 32, 32, 39

GG Arnold	7.4	2	15	1
JA Snow	12	0	30	2
CM Old	7	2	29	3
P Lever	2	0	7	0

West Indies

No. 20: Prudential Trophy		
VENUE: Scarborough		
DATE: 26th August 1976		
TOSS WON BY: West Indies		
RESULT: West Indies won by 6 wickets		

ENGLAND

B Wood	b Roberts	0
DL Amiss	b Julien	34
DS Steele	c King b Roberts	8
RA Woolmer	c Murray b Holding	3
GD Barlow	not out	80
GA Gooch	c Holder b Roberts	32
IT Botham	c Fredericks b Holding	1
APE Knott*+	run out	16
DL Underwood	c Julien b Roberts	14
JK Lever		
M Hendrick		
Extras	(0b, 11lb, 1w, 2nb)	14
	55 overs	
Total		**202**

FoW: 0, 18, 23, 72, 136, 145, 181, 202

AME Roberts	11	0	32	4
MA Holding	11	1	38	2
VA Holder	11	3	30	0
BD Julien	11	2	37	1
CL King	6	0	25	0
CH Lloyd	5	1	26	0

WEST INDIES

RC Fredericks	b Hendrick	1
CG Greenidge	b Wood	27
IVA Richards	not out	119
CH Lloyd*	b Underwood	20
LG Rowe	c Hendrick b Botham	10
CL King	not out	14
DL Murray+		
BD Julien		
VA Holder		
MA Holding		
AME Roberts		
Extras	(8b, 8lb, 0w, 0nb)	16
	41 overs	
Total		**207**

FoW: 3, 77, 116, 176

JK Lever	9	1	38	0
M Hendrick	9	3	38	1
B Wood	8	2	29	1
DL Underwood	9	1	35	1
IT Botham	3	0	26	1
RA Woolmer	2	0	16	0
DS Steele	1	0	9	0

No. 21: Prudential Trophy		
VENUE: Lord's		
DATE: 28th August 1976		
TOSS WON BY: England		
RESULT: West Indies won by 36 runs		

WEST INDIES

RC Fredericks	c Randall b Hendrick	19
CG Greenidge	b Hendrick	29
IVA Richards	c Woolmer b Greig	97
CH Lloyd*	c Barlow b Woolmer	27
CL King	c Wood b Woolmer	1
LG Rowe	b Underwood	4
DL Murray+	c & b Underwood	1
BD Julien	c Randall b Underwood	4
MA Holding	c Barlow b Wood	16
VA Holder	b Greig	2
AME Roberts	not out	7
Extras	(5b, 5lb, 1w, 3nb)	14
	47.5 overs	
Total		**221**

FoW: 51, 23, 121, 124, 135, 143, 154, 193, 201, 221

M Hendrick	9	2	34	2
RD Jackman	10	1	50	0
RA Woolmer	10	0	52	2
DL Underwood	10	0	27	3
AW Greig	5.5	0	31	2
B Wood	3	0	13	1

ENGLAND

B Wood	c & b Roberts	4
DL Amiss	c Murray b Roberts	12
RA Woolmer	b Roberts	9
GD Barlow	c Holder b Roberts	0
GA Gooch	c Murray b Holder	5
DW Randall	c King b Lloyd	88
AW Greig*	c Richards b Julien	3
APE Knott+	run out	22
RD Jackman	b Holder	14
DL Underwood	c Greenidge b Lloyd	2
M Hendrick	not out	0
Extras	(0b, 14lb, 4w, 8nb)	26
	45.3 overs	
Total		**185**

FoW: 4, 25, 30, 31, 48, 62, 125, 180, 185, 185

AME Roberts	8	1	27	4
MA Holding	8	0	26	0
BD Julien	10	4	22	1
VA Holder	10	0	35	2
CL King	8	0	45	0
CH Lloyd	1.3	0	4	2

No. 22: Prudential Trophy		
VENUE: Edgbaston		
DATE: 31st August 1976		
TOSS WON BY: England		
RESULT: West Indies won by 50 runs		

WEST INDIES

RC Fredericks	c Barlow b Lever	1
CG Greenidge	c Hendrick b Underwood	42
IVA Richards	c Wood b Lever	0
CH Lloyd*	b Greig	79
LG Rowe	run out	45
CL King	lbw b Hendrick	7
BD Julien	b Hendrick	5
DL Murray+	run out	27
MA Holding	b Botham	3
AME Roberts	not out	0
VA Holder		
Extras	(0b, 12lb, 0w, 2nb)	14
	32 overs	
Total		**223**

FoW: 7, 7, 95, 145, 162, 174, 209, 223, 223

M Hendrick	10	0	45	2
JK Lever	10	1	57	2
IT Botham	3	0	31	1
DL Underwood	3	0	28	1
AW Greig	6	0	48	1

ENGLAND

B Wood	b Julien	34
DL Amiss	b Julien	47
GD Barlow	lbw b Holder	0
GA Gooch	c Murray b Holder	3
DW Randall	c Murray b Holder	39
AW Greig*	b Holder	2
IT Botham	c Julien b Fredericks	20
APE Knott+	c Greenidge b Holder	10
DL Underwood	st Murray b Richards	6
JK Lever	b Fredericks	1
M Hendrick	not out	1
Extras	(2b, 6lb, 0w, 2nb)	10
	31.4 overs	
Total		**173**

FoW: 54, 59, 73, 89, 111, 138, 151, 171, 171, 173

AME Roberts	5	1	9	0
MA Holding	7	1	34	0
VA Holder	10	0	50	5
BD Julien	7	0	56	2
RC Fredericks	1.4	0	10	2
IVA Richards	1	0	4	1

Australia

No. 23: Prudential Trophy
VENUE: Old Trafford
DATE: 2nd June 1977
TOSS WON BY: Australia
RESULT: England won by 2 wickets

AUSTRALIA

RB McCosker	c Knott b Willis	1
IC Davis	c Greig b Lever	1
GS Chappell*	lbw b Underwood	30
CS Serjeant	c Randall b Greig	46
KD Walters	c Amiss b Old	0
DW Hookes	c Knott b Greig	11
RW Marsh+	b Lever	42
KJ O'Keeffe	not out	16
MHN Walker	c Barlow b Underwood	5
MF Malone	c Brearley b Underwood	4
LS Pascoe	not out	4
Extras	(4b, 4lb, 0w, 1nb)	9
	55 overs	
Total		**169**

FoW: 2, 2, 55, 62, 93, 94, 145, 152, 156

RGD Willis	8	2	16	1
JK Lever	10	1	45	2
DL Underwood	11	1	29	3
CM Old	11	3	30	1
P Willey	11	1	29	0
AW Greig	4	0	11	2

ENGLAND

DL Amiss	c Serjeant b Walker	8
JM Brearley*	lbw b Malone	29
DW Randall	c McCosker b Malone	19
GD Barlow	run out	42
P Willey	c Walker b O'Keeffe	1
AW Greig	run out	22
APE Knott+	not out	21
CM Old	c Hookes b Walker	25
JK Lever	c Walters b Walker	1
DL Underwood	not out	0
RGD Willis		
Extras	(1b, 3lb, 1w, 0nb)	5
	45.2 overs	
Total		**173**

FoW: 17, 51, 70, 71, 123, 125, 160, 168

LS Pascoe	10.2	1	44	0
MHN Walker	7	3	20	3
MF Malone	11	1	37	2
KJ O'Keeffe	11	3	36	1
GS Chappell	6	1	31	0

Australia

No. 24: Prudential Trophy
VENUE: Edgbaston
DATE: 4th June 1977
TOSS WON BY: Australia
RESULT: England won by 101 runs

ENGLAND

DL Amiss	c Marsh b Chappell	35
JM Brearley*	lbw b Chappell	10
DW Randall	c Marsh b Chappell	0
GD Barlow	c Hughes b Chappell	25
P Willey	c Marsh b Cosier	6
AW Greig	c Chappell b Cosier	0
APE Knott+	lbw b Cosier	0
CM Old	c Hughes b Chappell	35
JK Lever	not out	27
DL Underwood	b Cosier	0
RGD Willis	c Marsh b Cosier	7
Extras	(0b, 15lb, 4w, 7nb)	26
	53.5 overs	
Total		**171**

FoW: 19, 19, 67, 84, 84, 84, 90, 145, 160, 171

JR Thomson	9	0	46	0
MF Malone	11	2	27	0
GS Chappell	11	5	20	5
MHN Walker	11	3	29	0
GJ Cosier	8.5	3	18	5
RJ Bright	3	0	5	0

AUSTRALIA

IC Davis	c Old b Willis	0
CS Serjeant	b Willis	2
GS Chappell*	b Lever	19
GJ Cosier	lbw b Lever	3
KJ Hughes	c Knott b Lever	2
RD Robinson	b Old	12
RW Marsh+	c Old b Lever	1
RJ Bright	not out	17
MHN Walker	run out	0
MF Malone	run out	1
JR Thomson	b Greig	3
Extras	(4b, 5lb, 0w, 1nb)	10
	25.2 overs	
Total		**70**

FoW: 0, 27, 31, 34, 35, 38, 58, 58, 60, 70

RGD Willis	6	1	14	2
JK Lever	11	2	29	4
CM Old	7	2	15	1
AW Greig	1.2	0	2	1

No. 25: Prudential Trophy	No. 26: One-Day Series
VENUE: The Oval	VENUE: Sahiwal
DATE: 6th June 1977	DATE: 23rd December 1977
TOSS WON BY: Australia	TOSS WON BY: Pakistan
RESULT: Australia won by 2 wickets	RESULT: England won by 3 wickets

ENGLAND

DL Amiss	b Pascoe	108
JM Brearley*	st Robinson b O'Keeffe	78
DW Randall	c & b Bright	6
GD Barlow	run out	2
AW Greig	c Robinson b Thomson	4
APE Knott+	c Robinson b Pascoe	4
G Miller	c Robinson b Pascoe	4
CM Old	c Thomson b Chappell	20
JK Lever	b Thomson	2
DL Underwood	c Pascoe b Dymock	5
RGD Willis	not out	0
Extras	(0b, 1lb, 2w, 6nb)	9
	54.2 overs	
Total		**242**

FoW: 161, 168, 179, 196, 208, 207, 217, 227, 241, 242

JR Thomson	11	2	51	2
G Dymock	10	0	39	1
LS Pascoe	11	0	44	3
KJ O'Keeffe	11	0	43	1
RJ Bright	11	1	56	1
GS Chappell	0.2	0	0	1

AUSTRALIA

RD Robinson+	c Brearley b Willis	70
RB McCosker	lbw b Old	11
GS Chappell*	not out	125
KJ Hughes	lbw b Willis	3
KD Walters	c Brearley b Underwood	12
DW Hookes	b Lever	3
RJ Bright	c Randall b Old	0
KJ O'Keeffe	run out	0
JR Thomson	run out	3
G Dymock	not out	2
LS Pascoe		
Extras	(1b, 14lb, 1w, 1nb)	17
	53.2 overs	
Total		**246**

FoW: 33, 181, 186, 209, 225, 228, 228, 237

RGD Willis	11	0	49	2
JK Lever	10	0	43	1
CM Old	10.2	0	56	2
DL Underwood	11	2	21	1
G Miller	5	0	24	0
AW Greig	6	0	36	0

PAKISTAN

Mudassar Nazar	run out	20
Sadiq Moh'd	b Botham	2
Shafiq Ahmed	b Miller	29
Javed Miandad	not out	77
Wasim Raja	c Randall b Botham	36
Parvez Mir	lbw b Hendrick	18
Hasan Jamil	c Downton b Botham	20
Wasim Bari*+	not out	1
Salim Altaf		
Aamer Hameed		
Liaquat Ali		
Extras	(0b, 3lb, 0w, 2nb)	5
	35 overs	
Total		**208**

FoW: 4, 46, 63, 114, 167, 201

M Hendrick	7	0	50	1
IT Botham	7	0	39	3
CM Old	7	0	49	0
PH Edmonds	7	0	19	0
G Miller	7	0	46	1

ENGLAND

JM Brearley*	c Parvez b Aamer	30
BC Rose	c & b Wasim Raja	54
MW Gatting	run out	17
DW Randall	c Wasim Bari b Salim	35
CM Old	lbw b Parvez	1
GRJ Roope	b Liaquat	29
IT Botham	not out	15
PH Edmonds	run out	5
G Miller	not out	0
PR Downton+		
M Hendrick		
Extras	(5b, 14lb, 0w, 7nb)	26
	35 overs	
Total		**212**

FoW: 66, 111, 127, 134, 181, 198, 205

Salim Altaf	7	0	34	1
Liaquat Ali	7	0	50	1
Aamer Hameed	7	1	32	1
Parvez Mir	4	0	18	1
Javed Miandad	7	1	29	0
Wasim Raja	2	0	11	1
Mudassar Nazar	1	0	12	0

Pakistan

Pakistan

No. 27: One-Day Series
VENUE: Sialkot (Jinnah Stadium)
DATE: 30th December 1977
TOSS WON BY: England
RESULT: England won by 6 wickets

No. 28: One-Day Series
VENUE: Lahore (Gaddafi)
DATE: 13th January 1978
TOSS WON BY: England
RESULT: Pakistan won by 36 runs

PAKISTAN

Sadiq Moh'd	c Taylor b Lever	13
Mudassar Nazar	c Randall b Cope	33
Shafiq Ahmed	c & b Edmonds	9
Haroon Rashid	c Rose b Miller	5
Javed Miandad	run out	8
Wasim Raja	b Botham	43
Wasim Bari*+	b Edmonds	1
Hasan Jamil	c Taylor b Lever	28
Salim Altaf	not out	4
Iqbal Qasim	c & b Lever	0
Sikander Bakht	run out	0
Extras	(4b, 2lb, 0w, 1nb)	7
	33.7 overs	
Total		**151**

FoW: 20, 55, 57, 65, 74, 76, 140, 150, 150, 151

JK Lever	6	1	18	3
IT Botham	6.7	0	21	1
GA Cope	7	0	19	1
G Miller	6	1	43	1
PH Edmonds	7	0	28	2
MW Gatting	1	0	15	0

ENGLAND

BC Rose	b Qasim	45
GRJ Roope	c Haroon b Sikander	7
G Miller	c Sikander b Qasim	16
DW Randall	not out	51
MW Gatting	run out	5
IT Botham	not out	17
G Boycott*		
RW Taylor+		
PH Edmonds		
JK Lever		
GA Cope		
Extras	(0b, 4lb, 1w, 6nb)	11
	32.7 overs	
Total		**152**

FoW: 17, 43, 104, 112

Salim Altaf	5.7	0	20	0
Sikander Bakht	6	0	25	1
Javed Miandad	7	0	32	0
Iqbal Qasim	7	2	16	2
Hasan Jamil	6	0	39	0
Wasim Raja	1	0	9	0

PAKISTAN

Mudassar Nazar	b Edmonds	30
Arshad Pervez	b Lever	8
Shafiq Ahmed	st Taylor b Edmonds	3
Javed Miandad	c Boycott b Lever	31
Wasim Raja	c Boycott b Cope	0
Mohsin Khan	not out	51
Hasan Jamil	c Boycott b Old	21
Sarfraz Nawaz	not out	1
Wasim Bari*+		
Aamer Hameed		
Iqbal Qasim		
Extras	(0b, 11lb, 0w, 2nb)	13
	35 overs	
Total		**158**

FoW: 22, 41, 52, 53, 112, 148

CM Old	7	0	35	1
JK Lever	7	1	25	2
IT Botham	7	0	41	0
PH Edmonds	7	1	28	2
GA Cope	7	0	16	1

ENGLAND

G Boycott	lbw b Sarfraz	6
JM Brearley*	c Shafiq b Sarfraz	1
DW Randall	c Mudassar b Wasim Raja	32
MW Gatting	c & b Hasan	3
IT Botham	c Wasim Bari b Iqbal	11
CM Old	c Wasim Raja b Hasan	4
GRJ Roope	run out	37
RW Taylor+	b Wasim Raja	12
PH Edmonds	run out	0
JK Lever	c Aamer b Wasim Raja	0
GA Cope	not out	1
Extras	(2b, 6lb, 1w, 6nb)	15
	31.6 overs	
Total		**122**

FoW: 11, 15, 25, 42, 49, 97, 118, 119, 121, 122

Sarfraz Nawaz	5	2	7	2
Aamer Hameed	4	1	6	0
Hasan Jamil	5	0	20	2
Iqbal Qasim	7	2	25	1
Javed Miandad	6	0	26	0
Wasim Raja	4.6	0	23	3

	No. 29: Prudential Trophy
	VENUE: Old Trafford
	DATE: 24th, 25th May 1978
TOSS WON BY: England	
	RESULT: England won by 132 runs

ENGLAND

B Wood	c Javed b Wasim Raja	26
G Boycott*	c Wasim Bari b Sarfraz	3
CT Radley	c & b Mudassar	79
DI Gower	c Javed b Mudassar	33
GRJ Roope	c Wasim Bari b Sikander	10
IT Botham	c Haroon b Sikander	31
G Miller	b Sikander	0
CM Old	not out	6
PH Edmonds	not out	4
RW Taylor+		
RGD Willis		
Extras	(2b, 15lb, 3w, 5nb)	25
	55 overs	
Total		**217**

FoW: 3, 86, 157, 158, 176, 185, 209

Sarfraz Nawaz	11	6	13	1
Liaquat Ali	11	3	20	0
Sikander Bakht	11	0	56	3
Mudassar Nazar	11	1	52	2
Iqbal Qasim	4	1	24	0
Wasim Raja	7	1	27	1

PAKISTAN

Mudassar Nazar	c Wood b Botham	8
Sadiq Moh'd	b Willis	3
Haroon Rashid	b Old	1
Javed Miandad	lbw b Willis	9
Mohsin Khan	c Roope b Willis	1
Wasim Raja	lbw b Willis	0
Sarfraz Nawaz	c Taylor b Botham	7
Wasim Bari*+	b Wood	19
Iqbal Qasim	b Wood	9
Sikander Bakht	not out	16
Liaquat Ali	b Old	7
Extras	(0b, 3lb, 1w, 1nb)	5
	47 overs	
Total		**85**

FoW: 3, 77, 20, 21, 21, 31, 31, 60, 61,85

RGD Willis	11	5	15	4
CM Old	7	4	6	2
IT Botham	8	1	17	2
B Wood	11	3	25	2
PH Edmonds	10	4	17	0

	No. 30: Prudential Trophy
	VENUE: The Oval
	DATE: 26th May 1978
TOSS WON BY: Pakistan	
	RESULT: England won by 94 runs

ENGLAND

D Lloyd	b Wasim Raja	34
B Wood	b Sarfraz	8
CT Radley	b Liaquat	13
DI Gower	not out	114
GRJ Roope	c Naeem b Mudassar	35
IT Botham	b Mudassar	1
G Miller	lbw b Sikander	0
CM Old	not out	25
RW Taylor+		
JK Lever		
RGD Willis*		
Extras	(5b, 9lb, 0w, 4nb)	18
	55 overs	
Total		**248**

FoW: 27, 60, 83, 188, 194, 195

Sarfraz Nawaz	11	2	48	1
Liaquat Ali	11	1	41	1
Sikander Bakht	11	0	53	1
Wasim Raja	6	0	14	1
Naeem Ahmed	10	0	43	0
Mudassar Nazar	6	0	31	2

PAKISTAN

Mudassar Nazar	c Willis b Botham	56
Sadiq Moh'd	c & b Old	9
Arshad Pervez	lbw b Miller	3
Javed Miandad	b Old	0
Haroon Rashid	st Taylor b Miller	20
Wasim Raja	c (sub Edmonds) b Lloyd	44
Wasim Bari*+	c Taylor b Wood	1
Sarfraz Nawaz	c Gower b Wood	12
Naeem Ahmed	not out	0
Sikander Bakht	not out	0
Liaquat Ali		
Extras	(1b, 7lb, 1w, 0nb)	9
	55 overs	
Total		**154**

FoW: 27, 38, 39, 80, 117, 130, 154, 154

RGD Willis	9	1	25	0
CM Old	11	1	26	2
G Miller	11	3	24	2
IT Botham	11	2	36	1
JK Lever	7	1	17	0
B Wood	4	0	14	2
D Lloyd	2	1	3	1

New Zealand

New Zealand

No. 31: Prudential Trophy (2)
VENUE: Scarborough
DATE: 15th July 1978
TOSS WON BY: New Zealand
RESULT: England won by 19 runs

No. 32: Prudential Trophy (2)
VENUE: Old Trafford
DATE: 17th July 1978
TOSS WON BY: England
RESULT: England won by 126 runs

ENGLAND

JM Brearley*	c Burgess b Boock	31
GA Gooch	c Parker b Cairns	94
CT Radley	c Parker b Cairns	41
DI Gower	c Burgess b Cairns	4
IT Botham	c Anderson b Cairns	3
GRJ Roope	b Cairns	11
G Miller	c Edwards b Hadlee	2
RW Taylor+	lbw b Hadlee	0
JK Lever	not out	5
M Hendrick	not out	2
RGD Willis		
Extras	(2b, 10lb, 1w, 0nb)	13
	55 overs	
Total		**206**

FoW: 67, 178, 181, 185, 185, 198, 198, 198

RJ Hadlee	11	3	22	2
RO Collinge	11	0	46	0
BL Cairns	11	3	28	5
BE Congdon	11	2	25	0
SL Boock	9	1	57	1
GP Howarth	2	0	15	0

NEW ZEALAND

JG Wright	run out	18
RW Anderson	c Taylor b Hendrick	12
GP Howarth	c Taylor b Hendrick	42
MG Burgess*	b Botham	1
JM Parker	b Willis	7
GN Edwards+	c Gower b Gooch	12
RJ Hadlee	st Taylor b Gooch	1
BE Congdon	not out	52
BL Cairns	run out	23
RO Collinge	not out	5
SL Boock		
Extras	(0b, 13lb, 1w, 0nb)	14
	55 overs	
Total		**187**

FoW: 28, 43, 51, 62, 91, 98, 105, 173

RGD Willis	11	1	35	1
M Hendrick	11	1	35	2
JK Lever	11	2	25	0
IT Botham	11	1	43	1
G Miller	1	0	6	0
GA Gooch	10	1	29	2

ENGLAND

JM Brearley*	c Edwards b Bracewell	27
GA Gooch	run out	0
CT Radley	not out	117
DI Gower	run out	50
DW Randall	run out	41
IT Botham	c Edgar b Hadlee	34
G Miller		
RW Taylor+		
JK Lever		
PH Edmonds		
RGD Willis		
Extras	(0b, 6lb, 1w, 2nb)	9
	55 overs	
Total		**278**

FoW: 0, 44, 149, 238, 278

RJ Hadlee	11	1	70	1
RO Collinge	11	0	48	0
BP Bracewell	11	0	41	1
BE Congdon	11	2	26	0
BL Cairns	11	0	84	0

NEW ZEALAND

JG Wright	b Botham	30
BA Edgar	run out	31
GP Howarth	st Taylor b Edmonds	12
GN Edwards+	c Randall b Miller	0
MG Burgess*	c Taylor b Willis	0
BE Congdon	c Randall b Edmonds	2
RJ Hadlee	c Gower b Miller	1
BL Cairns	c Botham b Edmonds	60
RO Collinge	c Gooch b Lever	3
BP Bracewell	not out	0
JM Parker	absent hurt	0
Extras	(7b, 6lb, 0w, 0nb)	13
	41.2 overs	
Total		**152**

FoW: 44, 80, 80, ,84, 84, 85, 88, 133, 152

RGD Willis	9	5	21	1
JK Lever	7	0	28	1
G Miller	11	4	27	2
IT Botham	7	0	24	1
PH Edmonds	7.2	1	39	3

No. 33: Benson & Hedges Cup
VENUE: Sydney (SCG)
DATE: 13th January 1979
TOSS WON BY: England
RESULT: No result

AUSTRALIA

GM Wood	c Tolchard b Old	6
WM Darling	not out	7
KJ Hughes	not out	0
GN Yallop*		
GJ Cosier		
PM Toohey		
AR Border		
PH Carlson		
JA Maclean+		
G Dymock		
AG Hurst		
Extras	(0b, 4lb, 0w, 0nb)	4
	7.2 overs	
Total		**17**

FoW: 17

JK Lever	3	0	8	0
CM Old	3.2	1	5	1
M Hendrick	1	1	0	0

ENGLAND

JM Brearley*
G Boycott
DW Randall
DI Gower
GA Gooch
IT Botham
RW Tolchard+
PH Edmonds
CM Old
M Hendrick
JK Lever

No. 34: Benson & Hedges Cup
VENUE: Melbourne (MCG)
DATE: 24th January 1979
TOSS WON BY: Australia
RESULT: England won by 7 wickets

AUSTRALIA

GM Wood	c Gower b Edmonds	28
AMJ Hilditch	c Bairstow b Botham	10
AR Border	c Willis b Hendrick	11
GN Yallop*	run out	9
KJ Hughes	lbw b Hendrick	0
PH Carlson	c Randall b Willis	11
TJ Laughlin	c Willis b Hendrick	6
JA Maclean+	c Edmonds b Botham	11
RM Hogg	c Botham b Hendrick	4
G Dymock	c & b Botham	1
AG Hurst	not out	0
Extras	(4b, 2lb, 0w, 4nb)	10
	33.5 overs	
Total		**101**

FoW: 27, 52, 54, 55, 76, 78, 94, 99, 101, 101

RGD Willis	8	4	15	1
JK Lever	5	2	7	0
M Hendrick	8	1	25	4
IT Botham	4.5	2	16	3
PH Edmonds	7	0	26	1
GA Gooch	1	0	2	0

ENGLAND

G Boycott	not out	39
JM Brearley*	b Hogg	0
DW Randall	c Yallop b Dymock	12
GA Gooch	b Carlson	23
DI Gower	not out	19
IT Botham		
PH Edmonds		
DL Bairstow+		
JK Lever		
RGD Willis		
M Hendrick		
Extras	(0b, 5lb, 0w, 4nb)	9
	28.2 overs	
Total		**102**

FoW: 7, 29, 69

RM Hogg	6	1	20	1
G Dymock	6	1	16	1
TJ Laughlin	5	1	13	0
PH Carlson	5	0	21	1
AG Hurst	5.2	1	14	0
AR Border	1	0	9	0

Australia

No. 35: Benson & Hedges Cup
VENUE: Melbourne (MCG)
DATE: 4th February 1979
TOSS WON BY: Australia
RESULT: Australia won by 4 wickets

Australia

No. 36: Benson & Hedges Cup
VENUE: Melbourne (MCG)
DATE: 7th February 1979
TOSS WON BY: Australia
RESULT: Australia won by 6 wickets

ENGLAND

G Boycott	lbw b Laughlin	33
JM Brearley*	c Wright b Dymock	0
DW Randall	lbw b Dymock	4
GA Gooch	c Hurst b Carlson	19
DI Gower	not out	101
IT Botham	c Wood b Hurst	31
DL Bairstow+	run out	1
CM Old	not out	16
JK Lever		
RGD Willis		
M Hendrick		
Extras	(3b, 3lb, 0w, 1nb)	7
	40 overs	
Total		**212**

FoW: 0, 7, 50, 89, 153, 158

AG Hurst	8	1	36	1
G Dymock	8	1	31	2
PH Carlson	8	1	27	1
GJ Cosier	8	0	48	0
TJ Laughlin	8	0	63	1

AUSTRALIA

GM Wood	b Old	23
WM Darling	c Old b Willis	7
KJ Hughes	c Boycott b Lever	50
GN Yallop*	c Gower b Hendrick	31
PM Toohey	not out	54
GJ Cosier	b Lever	28
PH Carlson	c Boycott b Lever	0
TJ Laughlin	not out	15
KJ Wright+		
G Dymock		
AG Hurst		
Extras	(0b, 6lb, 0w, 1nb)	7
	38.6 overs	
Total		**215**

FoW: 7, 55, 90, 145, 185, 185

RGD Willis	8	1	21	1
JK Lever	7	1	51	3
M Hendrick	8	0	47	1
CM Old	8	1	31	1
IT Botham	7.6	0	58	0

ENGLAND

G Boycott	c Cosier b Dymock	2
JM Brearley*	c Wright b Cosier	46
DW Randall	c Hughes b Dymock	0
GA Gooch	c Hughes b Hurst	4
DI Gower	c Wood b Hurst	3
IT Botham	b Cosier	13
DL Bairstow+	run out	3
PH Edmonds	lbw b Laughlin	15
JK Lever	b Laughlin	1
RGD Willis	c Wright b Cosier	2
M Hendrick	not out	0
Extras	(0b, 2lb, 0w, 3nb)	5
	31.7 overs	
Total		**94**

FoW: 10, 10, 17, 22, 42, 56, 91, 91, 94, 94

AG Hurst	5	3	7	2
G Dymock	6	1	21	2
PH Carlson	8	2	22	0
GJ Cosier	7	1	22	3
TJ Laughlin	5.7	0	17	2

AUSTRALIA

GM Wood	c Bairstow b Botham	30
WM Darling	c Brearley b Willis	14
KJ Hughes	c Brearley b Willis	0
GN Yallop*	b Lever	25
PM Toohey	not out	16
GJ Cosier	not out	8
PH Carlson		
TJ Laughlin		
KJ Wright+		
G Dymock		
AG Hurst		
Extras	(0b, 0lb, 0w, 2nb)	2
	21.5 overs	
Total		**95**

FoW: 29, 37, 54, 87

RGD Willis	5	2	16	2
M Hendrick	6	0	32	0
IT Botham	5.5	0	30	1
JK Lever	5	0	15	1

	No. 37: World Cup
	VENUE: Lord's
	DATE: 9th June 1979
TOSS WON BY:	England
	RESULT: England won by 6 wickets

	No. 38: World Cup
	VENUE: Old Trafford
	DATE: 14th June 1979
TOSS WON BY:	Canada
	RESULT: England won by 8 wickets

AUSTRALIA

AMJ Hilditch	b Boycott	47
WM Darling	lbw b Willis	25
AR Border	c Taylor b Edmonds	34
KJ Hughes*	c Hendrick b Boycott	6
GN Yallop	run out	10
GJ Cosier	run out	6
TJ Laughlin	run out	8
KJ Wright+	lbw b Old	6
RM Hogg	run out	0
AG Hurst	not out	3
G Dymock	not out	4
Extras	(4b, 5lb, 1w, 0nb)	10
	60 overs	
Total		**159**

FoW: 56, 97, 111, 131, 132, 137, 150, 153, 153

RGD Willis	11	2	20	1
M Hendrick	12	2	24	0
CM Old	12	2	33	1
IT Botham	8	0	32	0
PH Edmonds	11	1	25	1
G Boycott	6	0	15	2

ENGLAND

JM Brearley*	c Wright b Laughlin	44
G Boycott	lbw b Hogg	1
DW Randall	c Wright b Hurst	1
GA Gooch	lbw b Laughlin	53
DI Gower	not out	22
IT Botham	not out	18
PH Edmonds		
RW Taylor+		
CM Old		
M Hendrick		
RGD Willis		
Extras	(0b, 10lb, 0w, 11nb)	21
	47.1 overs	
Total		**160**

FoW: 4, 5, 113, 124

RM Hogg	9	1	25	1
AG Hurst	10	3	33	1
G Dymock	11	2	19	0
GJ Cosier	8	1	24	0
TJ Laughlin	9.1	0	38	2

CANADA

GR Sealy	c Botham b Hendrick	3
CJD Chappell	lbw b Botham	5
FA Dennis	hit wkt b Willis	21
Tariq Javed	lbw b Old	4
JCB Vaughan	b Old	1
CA Marshall	b Old	2
BM Mauricette*+	b Willis	0
MP Stead	b Old	0
JM Patel	b Willis	1
RG Callender	b Willis	0
JN Valentine	not out	3
Extras	(0b, 4lb, 0w, 1nb)	5
	40.3 overs	
Total		**45**

FoW: 5, 13, 25, 29, 37, 38, 41, 41, 42, 45

RGD Willis	10.3	3	11	4
M Hendrick	8	4	5	1
IT Botham	9	5	12	1
G Miller	2	1	1	0
G Boycott	1	0	3	0
CM Old	10	5	8	4

ENGLAND

JM Brearley*	lbw b Valentine	0
G Boycott	not out	14
DW Randall	b Callender	5
GA Gooch	not out	21
DI Gower		
IT Botham		
G Miller		
RW Taylor+		
CM Old		
RGD Willis		
M Hendrick		
Extras	(0b, 0lb, 3w, 3nb)	6
	13.5 overs	
Total		**46**

FoW: 3, 11

JN Valentine	7	2	20	1
RG Callender	6	1	14	1
MP Stead	0.5	0	6	0

Pakistan

New Zealand

No. 39: World Cup
VENUE: Headingley
DATE: 16th June 1979
TOSS WON BY: Pakistan
RESULT: England won by 14 runs

No. 40: World Cup Semi-Final
VENUE: Old Trafford
DATE: 20th June 1979
TOSS WON BY: New Zealand
RESULT: England won by 9 runs

ENGLAND

JM Brearley*	c Wasim Bari b Imran Khan	0
G Boycott	lbw b Majid Khan	18
DW Randall	c Wasim Bari b Sikander	1
DI Gower	b Majid Khan	27
GA Gooch	c Sadiq b Sikander	33
IT Botham	b Majid Khan	22
PH Edmonds	c Wasim Raja b Asif	2
RW Taylor+	not out	20
CM Old	c & b Asif	2
RGD Willis	b Sikander	24
M Hendrick	not out	1
Extras	(0b, 3lb, 7w, 5nb)	15
Total	60 overs	**165**

FoW: 0, 4, 51, 70, 99, 115, 115, 118, 161

Imran Khan	12	3	24	1
Sikander Bakht	12	3	32	3
Mudassar Nazar	12	4	30	0
Asif Iqbal	12	3	37	2
Majid Khan	12	2	27	3

PAKISTAN

Majid Khan	c Botham b Hendrick	7
Sadiq Moh'd	b Hendrick	18
Mudassar Nazar	lbw b Hendrick	0
Zaheer Abbas	c Taylor b Botham	3
Haroon Rashid	c Brearley b Hendrick	1
Javed Miandad	lbw b Botham	0
Asif Iqbal*	c Brearley b Willis	51
Wasim Raja	lbw b Old	21
Imran Khan	not out	21
Wasim Bari+	c Taylor b Boycott	17
Sikander Bakht	c Hendrick b Boycott	2
Extras	(0b, 8lb, 1w, 1nb)	10
Total	56 overs	**151**

FoW: 27, 27, 28, 30, 31, 34, 86, 115, 145, 151

RGD Willis	11	2	37	1
M Hendrick	12	6	15	4
IT Botham	12	3	38	2
CM Old	12	2	28	1
PH Edmonds	3	0	8	0
G Boycott	5	0	14	2
GA Gooch	1	0	1	0

ENGLAND

JM Brearley*	c Lees b Coney	53
G Boycott	c Howarth b Hadlee	2
W Larkins	c Coney b McKechnie	7
GA Gooch	b McKechnie	71
DI Gower	run out	1
IT Botham	lbw b Cairns	21
DW Randall	not out	42
CM Old	c Lees b Troup	0
RW Taylor+	run out	12
RGD Willis	not out	1
M Hendrick		
Extras	(0b, 8lb, 3w, 0nb)	11
Total	60 overs	**221**

FoW: 13, 38, 96, 98, 145, 177, 178, 219

RJ Hadlee	12	4	32	1
GB Troup	12	1	38	1
BL Cairns	12	2	47	1
JV Coney	12	0	47	1
BJ McKechnie	12	1	46	2

NEW ZEALAND

JG Wright	run out	69
BA Edgar	lbw b Old	17
GP Howarth	lbw b Boycott	7
JV Coney	lbw b Hendrick	11
GM Turner	lbw b Willis	30
MG Burgess*	run out	10
RJ Hadlee	b Botham	15
WK Lees+	b Hendrick	23
BL Cairns	c Brearley b Hendrick	14
BJ McKechnie	not out	4
GB Troup	not out	3
Extras	(5b, 4lb, 0w, 0nb)	9
Total	60 overs	**212**

FoW: 47, 58, 104, 112, 132, 162, 180, 195, 208

IT Botham	12	3	42	1
M Hendrick	12	0	55	3
CM Old	12	1	33	1
G Boycott	9	1	24	1
GA Gooch	3	1	8	0
RGD Willis	12	1	41	1

	No. 41: World Cup Final
VENUE:	Lord's
DATE:	23rd June 1979
TOSS WON BY:	England
RESULT:	West Indies won by 92 runs

	No. 42: B&H World Series
VENUE:	Sydney (SCG) Day/Night
DATE:	28th November 1979
TOSS WON BY:	West Indies
RESULT:	England won by 2 runs

WEST INDIES

CG Greenidge	run out	9
DL Haynes	c Hendrick b Old	20
IVA Richards	not out	138
AI Kallicharran	b Hendrick	4
CH Lloyd*	c & b Old	13
CL King	c Randall b Edmonds	86
DL Murray+	c Gower b Edmonds	5
AME Roberts	c Brearley b Hendrick	0
J Garner	c Taylor b Botham	0
MA Holding	b Botham	0
CEH Croft	not out	0
Extras	(1b, 10lb, 0w, 0nb)	11
	60 overs	
Total		**286**

FoW: 22, 36, 55, 99, 238, 252, 258, 260, 272

IT Botham	12	2	44	2
M Hendrick	12	2	50	2
CM Old	12	0	55	2
G Boycott	6	0	38	0
PH Edmonds	12	2	40	2
GA Gooch	4	0	27	0
W Larkins	2	0	21	0

ENGLAND

JM Brearley*	c King b Holding	64
G Boycott	c Kallicharran b Holding	57
DW Randall	b Croft	15
GA Gooch	b Garner	32
DI Gower	b Garner	0
IT Botham	c Richards b Croft	4
W Larkins	b Garner	0
PH Edmonds	not out	5
CM Old	b Garner	0
RW Taylor+	c Murray b Garner	0
M Hendrick	b Croft	0
Extras	(0b, 12lb, 2w, 3nb)	17
	51 overs	
Total		**194**

FoW: 129, 135, 183, 183, 186, 186, 192, 192, 194, 194

AME Roberts	9	2	33	0
MA Holding	8	1	16	2
CEH Croft	10	1	42	3
J Garner	11	0	38	5
IVA Richards	10	0	35	0
CL King	3	0	13	0

ENGLAND

DW Randall	c Parry b Garner	49
JM Brearley*	c Greenidge b Parry	25
DI Gower	b Croft	44
GA Gooch	c & b Parry	2
P Willey	not out	58
IT Botham	b Garner	11
DL Bairstow+	c Murray b Garner	0
G Miller	b Roberts	4
GR Dilley	run out	1
DL Underwood		
RGD Willis		
Extras	(4b, 13lb, 0w, 0nb)	17
	50 overs	
Total		**211**

FoW: 79, 88, 91, 160, 195, 195, 210, 211

AME Roberts	9	0	37	1
MA Holding	9	0	47	0
CEH Croft	10	0	34	1
J Garner	10	0	31	3
DR Parry	10	0	35	2
AI Kallicharran	2	0	10	0

WEST INDIES

(Revised target 199 runs in 47 overs)

CG Greenidge	c Willis b Miller	42
DL Haynes	b Dilley	4
LG Rowe	lbw b Willis	60
AI Kallicharran	run out	44
CH Lloyd*	c Brearley b Willis	4
DL Murray+	c Gower b Underwood	3
DR Parry	b Underwood	4
AME Roberts	c Randall b Underwood	16
J Garner	not out	8
MA Holding	c Gower b Underwood	0
CEH Croft	b Botham	3
Extras	(1b, 7lb, 0w, 0nb)	8
	47 overs	
Total		**196**

FoW: 19, 68, 132, 143, 144, 155, 177, 185, 186, 196

GR Dilley	6	2	21	1
IT Botham	7	1	26	1
DL Underwood	10	0	44	4
G Miller	10	0	33	1
P Willey	8	0	29	0
RGD Willis	6	0	35	2

Australia

No. 43: B&H World Series
VENUE: Melbourne (MCG)
DATE: 8th December 1979
TOSS WON BY: England
RESULT: England won by 3 wickets

No. 44: B&H World Series
VENUE: Sydney (SCG) Day/Night
DATE: 11th December 1979
TOSS WON BY: England
RESULT: England won by 72 runs

AUSTRALIA

JM Wiener	b Botham	7
BM Laird	lbw b Dilley	7
AR Border	c Willey b Dilley	29
GS Chappell*	c Gooch b Willey	92
KJ Hughes	st Bairstow b Gooch	23
KD Walters	c Randall b Gooch	12
RW Marsh+	c Bairstow b Willey	14
RJ Bright	c Gooch b Willey	1
DK Lillee	not out	13
RM Hogg	c Brearley b Underwood	1
JR Thomson		
Extras	(1b, 5lb, 0w, 2nb)	8
	50 overs	
Total		**207**

FoW: 15, 15, 73, 114, 145, 184, 193, 193, 207

GR Dilley	10	1	30	2
IT Botham	9	2	27	1
RGD Willis	7	0	28	0
GA Gooch	6	0	32	2
DL Underwood	10	0	49	1
P Willey	8	0	33	3

ENGLAND

DW Randall	lbw b Bright	28
G Boycott	c Lillee b Hogg	68
P Willey	c Marsh b Hogg	37
DI Gower	c Marsh b Lillee	17
GA Gooch	run out	1
IT Botham	c Walters b Hogg	10
JM Brearley*	c Marsh b Lillee	27
DL Bairstow+	not out	15
GR Dilley	not out	0
DL Underwood		
RGD Willis		
Extras	(0b, 3lb, 0w, 3nb)	6
	49 overs	
Total		**209**

FoW: 71, 134, 137, 138, 148, 183, 205

DK Lillee	10	1	36	2
RM Hogg	10	2	26	3
JR Thomson	10	1	49	0
GS Chappell	8	0	40	0
RJ Bright	9	1	40	1
KD Walters	2	0	12	0

ENGLAND

DW Randall	run out	42
G Boycott	b Lillee	105
P Willey	c Walker b Chappell	64
DI Gower	c Wiener b Lillee	7
GA Gooch	b Thomson	11
IT Botham	c Walters b Lillee	5
DL Bairstow+	c (sub Hoores) b Lillee	18
JM Brearley*	not out	2
GR Dilley		
DL Underwood		
RGD Willis		
Extras	(0b, 6lb, 1w, 3nb)	10
	49 overs	
Total		**264**

FoW: 78, 196, 220, 236, 242, 245, 264

DK Lillee	10	0	56	4
JR Thomson	9	0	53	1
MHN Walker	10	1	30	0
TJ Laughlin	8	0	39	0
AR Border	4	0	24	0
GS Chappell	5	0	28	1
KD Walters	3	0	24	0

AUSTRALIA

JM Wiener	st Bairstow b Willey	14
WM Darling	c Randall b Willis	20
AR Border	b Willey	1
GS Chappell*	run out	0
KJ Hughes	c Bairstow b Willis	1
KD Walters	c Bairstow b Botham	34
RW Marsh+	b Dilley	12
TJ Laughlin	c Gooch b Randall	74
DK Lillee	b Botham	14
JR Thomson	run out	0
MHN Walker	not out	9
Extras	(0b, 10lb, 2w, 1nb)	13
	47.2 overs	
Total		**192**

FoW: 33, 36, 36, 38, 39, 63, 115, 146, 147, 192

GR Dilley	9	0	29	1
IT Botham	10	1	36	2
RGD Willis	10	1	32	2
P Willey	5	0	18	2
DL Underwood	6	1	29	0
GA Gooch	7	0	33	0
DW Randall	0.2	0	2	1

No. 45: B&H World Series
VENUE: Brisbane ('Gabba')
DATE: 23rd December 1979
TOSS WON BY: West Indies
RESULT: West Indies won by 9 wickets

No. 46: B&H World Series
VENUE: Sydney (SCG) Day/Night
DATE: 26th December 1979
TOSS WON BY: Australia
RESULT: England won by 4 wickets

ENGLAND

DW Randall	c Lloyd b Roberts	0
G Boycott	c (sub) b Holding	68
P Willey	run out	34
DI Gower	c Holding b Roberts	59
GA Gooch	b Garner	17
IT Botham	lbw b Holding	4
DL Bairstow+	c Lloyd b Roberts	12
JM Brearley*	not out	9
GR Dilley	b Garner	0
DL Underwood		
RGD Willis		
Extras	(0b, 8lb, 5w, 1nb)	14
	50 overs	
Total		**217**

FoW: 0, 70, 167, 174, 191, 205, 209, 217

AME Roberts	10	3	26	3
MA Holding	10	1	44	2
J Garner	10	0	37	2
IVA Richards	10	0	44	0
CL King	10	0	52	0

WEST INDIES

CG Greenidge	not out	85
DL Haynes	c Underwood b Gooch	41
IVA Richards	not out	85
AI Kallicharran		
LG Rowe		
CH Lloyd*		
CL King		
DL Murray+		
AME Roberts		
J Garner		
MA Holding		
Extras	(0b, 4lb, 0w, 3nb)	7
	46.5 overs	
Total		**218**

FoW: 109

IT Botham	10	1	39	0
GR Dilley	8	1	25	0
RGD Willis	10	2	27	0
DL Underwood	9	0	43	0
P Willey	6	0	39	0
GA Gooch	3.5	0	38	1

AUSTRALIA

BM Laird	b Botham	6
JM Wiener	c Bairstow b Botham	2
AR Border	c Gower b Gooch	22
GS Chappell*	run out	52
KJ Hughes	b Willis	23
IM Chappell	not out	60
RW Marsh+	c Bairstow b Dilley	10
DK Lillee	not out	2
RM Hogg		
G Dymock		
LS Pascoe		
Extras	(3b, 10lb, 0w, 4nb)	17
	47 overs	
Total		**194**

FoW: 5, 21, 50, 109, 135, 179

GR Dilley	10	1	32	1
IT Botham	9	1	33	2
RGD Willis	10	1	38	1
DL Underwood	10	2	36	0
GA Gooch	8	0	38	1

ENGLAND

GA Gooch	lbw b Hogg	29
G Boycott	not out	86
P Willey	b Pascoe	51
DI Gower	c Marsh b Hogg	2
DW Randall	c GS Chappell b Pascoe	1
IT Botham	lbw b Hogg	6
JM Brearley*	c Marsh b Hogg	0
DL Bairstow+	not out	7
GR Dilley		
DL Underwood		
RGD Willis		
Extras	(0b, 1lb, 1w, 11nb)	13
	45.1 overs	
Total		**195**

FoW: 41, 152, 157, 170, 179, 179

DK Lillee	10	0	47	0
LS Pascoe	10	2	28	2
RM Hogg	10	0	46	4
G Dymock	10	1	38	0
GS Chappell	5.1	0	23	0

Australia

AUSTRALIA

JM Wiener	st Bairstow b Emburey	33
RB McCosker	c Brearley b Willey	41
IM Chappell	c Randall b Emburey	8
GS Chappell*	c Randall b Stevenson	34
KJ Hughes	c Larkins b Lever	34
AR Border	c Bairstow b Lever	0
RW Marsh+	c Bairstow b Stevenson	0
DK Lillee	lbw b Stevenson	0
G Dymock	run out	0
JR Thomson	not out	3
LS Pascoe	b Stevenson	5
Extras	(0b, 1lb, 3w, 1nb)	5
	48.4 overs	
Total		**163**

FoW: 74, 82, 89, 148, 149, 150, 150, 152, 155, 163

JK Lever	9	1	11	2
IT Botham	7	0	33	0
GA Gooch	3	0	13	0
GB Stevenson	9.4	0	33	4
JE Emburey	10	1	33	2
P Willey	10	0	35	1

ENGLAND

GA Gooch	c McCosker b Pascoe	69
W Larkins	c Thomson b Lillee	5
P Willey	lbw b Lillee	0
DI Gower	c Marsh b Lillee	3
JM Brearley*	b GS Chappell	5
DW Randall	c Pascoe b GS Chappell	0
IT Botham	b Lillee	0
DL Bairstow+	not out	21
JE Emburey	c GS Chappell b Dymock	18
GB Stevenson	not out	28
JK Lever		
Extras	(0b, 5lb, 1w, 9nb)	15
	48.5 overs	
Total		**164**

FoW: 31, 31, 40, 51, 56, 61, 104, 129

JR Thomson	9.5	0	46	0
G Dymock	9	1	30	1
DK Lillee	10	6	12	4
LS Pascoe	10	0	38	1
GS Chappell	10	3	23	2

West Indies

WEST INDIES

CG Greenidge	c Emburey b Willey	50
DL Haynes	c Gooch b Stevenson	26
IVA Richards	b Botham	88
AI Kallicharran	c & b Botham	57
CL King	run out	12
J Garner	not out	7
AME Roberts	not out	0
CH Lloyd*		
LG Rowe		
DL Murray+		
MA Holding		
Extras	(1b, 4lb, 0w, 1nb)	6
	50 overs	
Total		**246**

FoW: 58, 115, 224, 227, 245

JK Lever	10	1	54	0
IT Botham	10	0	35	2
GA Gooch	2	0	22	0
GB Stevenson	8	1	53	1
JE Emburey	10	0	39	0
P Willey	10	1	37	1

ENGLAND

GA Gooch	b King	20
JM Brearley*	c Murray b Roberts	0
P Willey	c Lloyd b King	5
W Larkins	c Lloyd b King	24
DI Gower	c (sub Parry) b King	12
DW Randall	b Roberts	16
IT Botham	c Haynes b Roberts	22
DL Bairstow+	not out	23
GB Stevenson	b Roberts	1
JE Emburey	c Murray b Roberts	1
JK Lever	b Garner	11
Extras	(0b, 2lb, 1w, 1nb)	4
	42.5 overs	
Total		**139**

FoW: 5, 24, 31, 52, 68, 98, 100, 105, 109, 139

AME Roberts	10	5	22	5
MA Holding	7	0	16	0
CL King	9	3	23	4
J Garner	7.5	3	9	1
IVA Richards	7	0	46	0
AI Kallicharran	2	0	19	0

No. 49: B&H World Series Final
VENUE: Melbourne (MCG)
DATE: 20th January 1980
TOSS WON BY: England
RESULT: West Indies won by 2 runs

WEST INDIES

CG Greenidge	c Larkins b Botham	80
DL Haynes	c Bairstow b Willis	9
IVA Richards	c Bairstow b Dilley	23
AI Kallicharran	b Botham	42
CH Lloyd*	b Botham	4
CL King	not out	31
DL Murray+	c Bairstow b Dilley	4
AME Roberts	run out	1
J Garner	run out	3
MA Holding	not out	5
CEH Croft		
Extras	(0b, 11lb, 1w, 1nb)	13
	50 overs	
Total		**215**

FoW: 17, 66, 161, 168, 168, 181, 183, 197

RGD Willis	10	1	51	1
IT Botham	10	2	33	3
JE Emburey	10	0	31	0
GR Dilley	10	0	39	2
P Willey	10	0	48	0

ENGLAND

GA Gooch	c King b Holding	9
G Boycott	c Greenidge b Roberts	35
P Willey	run out	51
DI Gower	c Holding b Roberts	10
W Larkins	run out	34
IT Botham	c Lloyd b Roberts	19
JM Brearley*	not out	25
DL Bairstow+	run out	4
JE Emburey		
GR Dilley		
RGD Willis		
Extras	(12b, 12lb, 1w, 1nb)	26
	50 overs	
Total		**213**

FoW: 13, 74, 96, 152, 164, 190, 213

AME Roberts	10	1	30	3
MA Holding	10	1	43	1
J Garner	10	1	27	0
CEH Croft	10	1	23	0
CL King	4	0	30	0
IVA Richards	6	1	34	0

No. 50: B&H World Series Final
VENUE: Sydney (SCG)
DATE: 22nd January 1980
TOSS WON BY: England
RESULT: West Indies won by 8 wickets

ENGLAND

GA Gooch	lbw b Garner	23
G Boycott	c Greenidge b Roberts	63
P Willey	b Garner	3
DI Gower	c Murray b Holding	27
W Larkins	b Croft	14
IT Botham	c King b Roberts	37
DL Bairstow+	not out	18
JM Brearley*	run out	4
JE Emburey	run out	6
GR Dilley		
RGD Willis		
Extras	(1b, 11lb, 0w, 1nb)	13
	50 overs	
Total		**208**

FoW: 40, 54, 118, 126, 155, 188, 194, 208

AME Roberts	10	3	31	2
MA Holding	10	1	34	1
CEH Croft	10	3	29	1
J Garner	10	0	44	2
IVA Richards	3	0	19	0
CL King	7	1	38	0

WEST INDIES

CG Greenidge	not out	98
DL Haynes	lbw b Botham	17
IVA Richards	c Botham b Willey	65
AI Kallicharran	not out	8
CH Lloyd*		
CL King		
DL Murray+		
AME Roberts		
J Garner		
MA Holding		
CEH Croft		
Extras	(5b, 10lb, 5w, 1nb)	21
	47.3 overs	
Total		**209**

FoW: 61, 180

RGD Willis	10	0	35	0
GR Dilley	7	0	37	0
IT Botham	10	1	28	1
JE Emburey	9.3	0	48	0
P Willey	10	2	35	1
GA Gooch	1	0	5	0

West Indies

WEST INDIES

CG Greenidge	b Botham	78
DL Haynes	c Tavare b Old	19
IVA Richards	c Gower b Gooch	7
SFAF Bacchus	c Lever b Gooch	2
Al Kallicharran	c Botham b Old	10
CH Lloyd*	c & b Lever	21
MD Marshall	b Botham	6
DL Murray+	run out	9
AME Roberts	c Botham b Dilley	10
J Garner	run out	14
MA Holding	not out	0
Extras	(5b, 15lb, 2w, 0nb)	22
	55 overs	
Total		**198**

FOW: 36, 49, 51, 110, 151, 161, 163, 178, 197, 198

GR Dilley	11	3	41	1
JK Lever	11	3	36	1
IT Botham	11	1	45	2
CM Old	11	4	12	2
GA Gooch	7	2	30	2
P Willey	4	0	12	0

ENGLAND

P Willey	c Richards b Marshall	7
G Boycott	c Kallicharran b Garner	5
CJ Tavare	not out	82
GA Gooch	c Murray b Richards	2
DI Gower	c Murray b Holding	12
IT Botham*	c Murray b Marshall	30
D Lloyd	b Greenidge	1
DL Bairstow+	c Garner b Holding	16
CM Old	b Marshall	4
GR Dilley	c Haynes b Roberts	0
JK Lever	run out	6
Extras	(3b, 4lb, 2w, 0nb)	9
	51.2 overs	
Total		**174**

FoW: 11, 15, 23, 38, 81, 86, 130, 149, 150, 174

MA Holding	9	3	16	2
AME Roberts	11	4	30	1
J Garner	9.2	0	20	1
MD Marshall	11	2	28	3
IVA Richards	7	0	50	1
CG Greenidge	4	0	21	1

West Indies

WEST INDIES

CG Greenidge	c Lever b Marks	39
DL Haynes	c Willis b Marks	50
SFAF Bacchus	run out	40
IVA Richards*	c Lever b Botham	26
Al Kallicharran	c Willis b Old	11
CL King	run out	33
AME Roberts	not out	25
J Garner	run out	0
MD Marshall	b Willis	0
MA Holding	b Willis	0
DA Murray+		
Extras	(0b, 9lb, 0w, 2nb)	11
	55 overs	
Total		**235**

FoW: 86, 113, 147, 168, 186, 231, 233, 233, 935

RGD Willis	10	1	25	2
JK Lever	7	1	23	0
IT Botham	11	2	71	1
CM Old	11	1	43	1
VJ Marks	11	4	44	2
P Willey	5	0	18	0

ENGLAND

P Willey	c & b Holding	56
G Boycott	run out	70
CJ Tavare	c Murray b Holding	5
GA Gooch	c Bacchus b Marshall	12
DI Gower	c Bacchus b Roberts	12
IT Botham*	not out	42
VJ Marks	b Holding	9
DL Bairstow+	run out	2
JK Lever	not out	0
CM Old		
RGD Willis		
Extras	(0b, 22lb, 4w, 2nb)	28
	54.3 overs	
Total		**236**

FoW: 135, 143, 156, 160, 176, 212, 231

AME Roberts	11	3	42	1
MA Holding	11	0	28	3
J Garner	10.3	0	41	0
MD Marshall	11	1	45	1
IVA Richards	5	0	28	0
CG Greenidge	6	0	24	0

No. 53: Prudential Trophy (2)
VENUE: The Oval
DATE: 20th August 1980
TOSS WON BY: England
RESULT: England won by 23 runs

No. 54: Prudential Trophy (2)
VENUE: Edgbaston
DATE: 22nd August 1980
TOSS WON BY: Australia
RESULT: England won by 47 runs

Match No. 53 — ENGLAND

ENGLAND		
GA Gooch	b Border	54
G Boycott	c Hughes b Lillee	99
AR Butcher	lbw b Dymock	14
CWJ Athey	c Chappell b Lillee	32
MW Gatting	not out	17
IT Botham*	c Yallop b Lillee	4
P Willey	c Yallop b Lillee	2
DL Bairstow+	not out	9
RD Jackman		
CM Old		
M Hendrick		
Extras	(2b, 8lb, 3w, 4nb)	17
	55 overs	
Total		**248**

FoW: 108, 140, 212, 221, 225, 232

DK Lillee	11	1	35	4
JR Thomson	11	3	25	0
G Dymock	9	0	50	1
LS Pascoe	11	1	50	0
AR Border	11	2	61	1
GS Chappell	2	0	10	0

AUSTRALIA		
BM Laird	lbw b Gooch	15
GM Wood	c Athey b Jackman	4
GS Chappell*	c Bairstow b Hendrick	36
AR Border	b Hendrick	13
KJ Hughes	not out	73
GN Yallop	b Hendrick	0
RW Marsh+	c Bairstow b Hendrick	41
DK Lillee	c Willey b Hendrick	0
JR Thomson	run out	15
G Dymock	not out	14
LS Pascoe		
Extras	(3b, 10lb, 1w, 0nb)	14
	55 overs	
Total		**225**

FoW: 11, 36, 68, 71, 75, 161, 161, 192

CM Old	9	0	43	0
RD Jackman	11	0	46	1
IT Botham	9	1	28	0
GA Gooch	7	0	29	1
M Hendrick	11	3	31	5
P Willey	8	0	34	0

Match No. 54 — ENGLAND

ENGLAND		
GA Gooch	b Thomson	108
G Boycott	c Marsh b Border	78
CWJ Athey	b Pascoe	51
RO Butcher	c Dyson b Pascoe	52
MW Gatting	run out	2
IT Botham*	b Pascoe	2
DL Bairstow+	b Lillee	6
RD Jackman	c Marsh b Pascoe	6
JE Emburey	not out	1
CM Old	not out	2
M Hendrick		
Extras	(4b, 3lb, 1w, 4nb)	12
	55 overs	
Total		**320**

FoW: 154, 215, 292, 298, 302, 311, 313, 318

JR Thomson	11	1	69	1
DK Lillee	11	0	43	1
LS Pascoe	11	0	69	4
RJ Bright	8	0	48	0
GS Chappell	11	0	65	0
AR Border	3	0	14	1

AUSTRALIA		
BM Laird	c Emburey b Hendrick	36
J Dyson	b Hendrick	24
KJ Hughes	c & b Gooch	98
AR Border	run out	26
GN Yallop	not out	52
DK Lillee	b Hendrick	21
RJ Bright	not out	5
GS Chappell*		
RW Marsh+		
JR Thomson		
LS Pascoe		
Extras	(1b, 9lb, 1w, 0nb)	11
	55 overs	
Total		**273**

FoW: 53, 80, 119, 222, 229

CM Old	11	2	44	0
RD Jackman	11	1	45	0
IT Botham	11	1	41	0
M Hendrick	10	0	54	3
JE Emburey	8	0	51	0
GA Gooch	3	0	16	1
G Boycott	1	0	11	0

West Indies	**West Indies**

WEST INDIES

DL Haynes	c Emburey b Stevenson	34
SFAF Bacchus	c Stevenson b Old	1
EH Mattis	run out	62
AI Kallicharran	b Emburey	2
CH Lloyd*	c Willey b Stevenson	2
HA Gomes	b Willey	8
DA Murray+	b Gooch	1
AME Roberts	st Bairstow b Gooch	2
J Garner	run out	4
MA Holding	b Botham	1
CEH Croft	not out	2
Extras	(0b, 4lb, 1w, 3nb)	8
	47.2 overs	
Total		**127**

FoW: 5, 48, 51, 58, 89, 90, 102, 110, 120, 127

CM Old	5	4	8	1
IT Botham	8	1	32	1
GB Stevenson	8.2	2	18	2
JE Emburey	10	4	20	1
P Willey	10	1	29	1
GA Gooch	6	1	12	2

ENGLAND

G Boycott	c Mattis b Croft	2
GA Gooch	c Lloyd b Roberts	11
P Willey	c Murray b Croft	0
DI Gower	c Haynes b Kallicharran	23
RO Butcher	c Murray b Croft	1
IT Botham*	c Murray b Croft	60
MW Gatting	b Croft	3
DL Bairstow+	b Croft	5
JE Emburey	b Holding	5
GB Stevenson	not out	6
CM Old	b Holding	1
Extras	(0b, 8lb, 0w, 0nb)	8
	48.2 overs	
Total		**125**

FoW: 14, 14, 14, 15, 80, 88, 111, 114, 123, 125

AME Roberts	10	1	30	1
MA Holding	9.2	2	30	2
CEH Croft	9	4	15	6
J Garner	10	2	17	0
AI Kallicharran	10	3	25	1

ENGLAND

G Boycott	b Richards	7
GA Gooch	c Murray b Roberts	11
MW Gatting	c Mattis b Gomes	29
DI Gower	b Gomes	3
RO Butcher	c Haynes b Gomes	5
IT Botham*	b Roberts	27
P Willey	b Croft	21
DL Bairstow+	b Croft	16
JE Emburey	c Croft b Holding	0
GB Stevenson	not out	8
GR Dilley	b Croft	3
Extras	(4b, 2lb, 0w, 1nb)	7
	47.2 overs	
Total		**137**

FoW: 16, 27, 34, 59, 62, 108, 112, 119, 132, 137

AME Roberts	7	0	17	2
MA Holding	7	1	13	1
IVA Richards	10	0	26	1
CEH Croft	6.2	1	9	3
HA Gomes	10	2	30	3
J Garner	7	2	35	0

WEST INDIES

CG Greenidge	run out	2
DL Haynes	c Gooch b Emburey	48
IVA Richards	c Stevenson b Dilley	3
EH Mattis	b Emburey	24
HA Gomes	not out	22
CH Lloyd*	not out	25
DA Murray+		
AME Roberts		
MA Holding		
J Garner		
CEH Croft		
Extras	(4b, 8lb, 0w, 2nb)	14
	39.3 overs	
Total		**138**

FoW: 6, 11, 85, 90

GR Dilley	5	0	21	1
IT Botham	7	1	24	0
GB Stevenson	6	0	21	0
JE Emburey	10	4	22	2
GA Gooch	2	0	8	0
P Willey	9	0	23	0
DI Gower	0.3	0	5	0

No. 57:	Prudential Trophy
VENUE:	Lord's
DATE:	4th June 1981
TOSS WON BY:	England
RESULT:	England won by 6 wickets

AUSTRALIA

J Dyson	lbw b Willis	2
GM Wood	run out	22
TM Chappell	run out	16
KJ Hughes*	lbw b Jackman	12
AR Border	not out	73
MF Kent	c Gooch b Botham	28
RW Marsh+	b Botham	18
RJ Bright	b Willis	18
GF Lawson	not out	12
DK Lillee		
RM Hogg		
Extras	(1b, 8lb, 0w, 0nb)	9
	55 overs	
Total		**210**

FoW: 2, 36, 48, 60, 134, 162, 189

RGD Willis	11	0	56	2
IT Botham	11	1	39	2
M Hendrick	11	2	32	0
RD Jackman	11	1	27	1
P Willey	6	1	26	0
GA Gooch	5	1	21	0

ENGLAND

GA Gooch	c Kent b Lillee	53
G Boycott	not out	75
MW Gatting	lbw b Lillee	0
DI Gower	c Kent b Chappell	47
JD Love	c Bright b Lawson	15
IT Botham*	not out	13
P Willey		
GW Humpage+		
RD Jackman		
RGD Willis		
M Hendrick		
Extras	(5b, 4lb, 0w, 0nb)	9
	51.4 overs	
Total		**212**

FoW: 86, 86, 172, 199

RM Hogg	11	1	36	0
DK Lillee	11	3	23	2
GF Lawson	9	0	51	1
TM Chappell	11	1	50	1
RJ Bright	9.4	0	43	0

No. 58:	Prudential Trophy
VENUE:	Edgbaston
DATE:	6th June 1981
TOSS WON BY:	England
RESULT:	Australia won by 2 runs

AUSTRALIA

GM Wood	c Willis b Jackman	55
TM Chappell	c Humpage b Botham	0
GN Yallop	b Hendrick	63
KJ Hughes*	run out	34
AR Border	run out	17
RW Marsh+	c Love b Botham	20
MF Kent	lbw b Willis	1
GF Lawson	not out	29
DK Lillee	run out	8
RM Hogg	not out	0
TM Alderman		
Extras	(1b, 18lb, 1w, 2nb)	22
	55 overs	
Total		**249**

FoW: 10, 96, 160, 171, 183, 193, 213, 248

RGD Willis	11	3	41	1
IT Botham	11	1	44	2
M Hendrick	11	2	21	1
RD Jackman	11	0	47	1
P Willey	6	0	36	0
GA Gooch	5	0	38	0

ENGLAND

GA Gooch	b Hogg	11
G Boycott	b Lawson	14
MW Gatting	c Lawson b Lillee	96
DI Gower	b Alderman	2
JD Love	b Lawson	43
P Willey	c Wood b Chappell	37
IT Botham*	c Hughes b Lawson	24
GW Humpage+	b Lillee	5
RD Jackman	run out	2
RGD Willis	not out	1
M Hendrick	c Marsh b Lillee	0
Extras	(0b, 12lb, 0w, 0nb)	12
	54.5 overs	
Total		**247**

FoW: 20, 27, 36, 111, 177, 224, 23,2, 244, 244, 247

RM Hogg	11	2	42	1
DK Lillee	10.5	2	36	3
TM Alderman	11	1	46	1
GF Lawson	11	2	42	3
TM Chappell	11	0	69	1

Australia

India

AUSTRALIA

GM Wood	run out	108
J Dyson	c Gooch b Hendrick	22
GN Yallop	run out	48
KJ Hughes*	c Gatting b Jackman	0
AR Border	c Jackman b Willis	5
RW Marsh+	c Humpage b Botham	1
TM Chappell	c Gooch b Willis	14
GF Lawson	run out	8
DK Lillee	not out	0
RM Hogg		
TM Alderman		
Extras	(0b, 27lb, 1w, 2nb)	30
	55 overs	
Total		**236**

FoW: 43, 173, 173, 187, 189, 216, 236, 236

RGD Willis	11	1	35	2
IT Botham	11	2	42	1
M Hendrick	11	3	31	1
GA Gooch	11	0	50	0
RD Jackman	11	1	48	1

ENGLAND

GA Gooch	c Marsh b Lawson	37
G Boycott	c Marsh b Hogg	4
MW Gatting	c Marsh b Hogg	32
DI Gower	b Alderman	5
JD Love	b Chappell	3
P Willey	c Marsh b Hogg	42
IT Botham*	c Hughes b Chappell	5
GW Humpage+	c Border b Alderman	6
RD Jackman	b Chappell	14
RGD Willis	not out	2
M Hendrick	c Marsh b Hogg	0
Extras	(10b, 0lb, 1w, 4nb)	15
	46.5 overs	
Total		**165**

FoW: 5, 71, 80, 89, 95, 106, 133, 160, 164, 165

RM Hogg	8.5	1	29	4
DK Lillee	7	0	37	0
GF Lawson	11	3	34	1
TM Alderman	11	3	19	2
TM Chappell	9	0	31	3

INDIA

SM Gavaskar*	c Gooch b Willis	0
K Srikkanth	b Botham	0
DB Vengsarkar	c & b Underwood	46
GR Viswanath	c Cook b Gooch	8
K Azad	b Botham	30
S Madan Lal	c Lever b Underwood	6
SMH Kirmani+	not out	18
RJ Shastri	run out	19
RMH Binny	not out	2
DR Doshi		
Randhir Singh		
Extras	(4b, 13lb, 7w, 3nb)	27
	46 overs	
Total		**156**

FoW: 2, 8, 39, 91, 113, 119, 154

RGD Willis	9	3	17	1
IT Botham	10	4	20	2
JK Lever	10	0	46	0
GA Gooch	7	0	28	1
DL Underwood	10	3	18	2

ENGLAND

GA Gooch	c Kirmani b Binny	23
G Boycott	lbw b Madan Lal	5
G Cook	c Viswanath b Binny	13
DI Gower	c & b Binny	8
KWR Fletcher*	b Doshi	26
MW Gatting	not out	47
IT Botham	not out	25
CJ Richards+		
JK Lever		
DL Underwood		
RGD Willis		
Extras	(0b, 7lb, 2w, 4nb)	13
	43.5 overs	
Total		**160**

FoW: 5, 43, 46, 61, 126

S Madan Lal	10	2	30	1
Randhir Singh	6	0	18	0
RMH Binny	7.5	3	35	3
RJ Shastri	10	1	24	0
DR Doshi	10	1	40	1

No. 61: Wills Series
VENUE: Jullundur
DATE: 20th December 1981
TOSS WON BY: India
RESULT: India won by 6 wickets

ENGLAND

GA Gooch	b Madan Lal	12
G Boycott	run out	6
IT Botham	lbw b Madan Lal	5
KWR Fletcher*	c Azad b Patil	5
DI Gower	run out	53
MW Gatting	not out	71
G Cook	b Kapil Dev	1
CJ Richards+	lbw b Kapil Dev	0
JK Lever		
DL Underwood		
RGD Willis		
Extras	(2b, 4lb, 1w, 1nb)	8
	36 overs	
Total		**161**

FoW: 18, 22, 25, 48, 158, 161, 161

N Kapil Dev	8	1	26	2
S Madan Lal	7	0	33	2
SV Nayak	7	2	25	0
SM Patil	7	0	16	1
RJ Shastri	7	0	53	0

INDIA

K Srikkanth	lbw b Botham	17
DB Vengsarkar	not out	88
K Azad	c Gower b Gooch	14
SM Patil	b Gooch	3
N Kapil Dev	c Willis b Underwood	6
Yashpal Sharma	not out	28
SM Gavaskar*		
SV Nayak		
S Madan Lal		
SMH Kirmani+		
RJ Shastri		
Extras	(3b, 3lb, 0w, 2nb)	8
	35.3 overs	
Total		**164**

FoW: 41, 69, 78, 89

RGD Willis	7.3	2	41	0
JK Lever	7	0	31	0
GA Gooch	7	0	25	2
IT Botham	7	0	33	1
DL Underwood	7	1	26	1

No. 62: Wills Series
VENUE: Cuttack
DATE: 27th January 1982
TOSS WON BY: India
RESULT: India won by 5 wickets

ENGLAND

GA Gooch	c Arun b Madan Lal	3
G Cook	c Nayak b Patil	30
CJ Tavare	c Madan Lal b Shastri	11
DI Gower	c & b Patil	42
IT Botham	b Nayak	52
KWR Fletcher*	b Madan Lal	69
MW Gatting	not out	8
RW Taylor+	not out	2
JK Lever		
DL Underwood		
RGD Willis		
Extras	(0b, 9lb, 1w, 3nb)	13
	46 overs	
Total		**230**

FoW: 13, 33, 86, 101, 181, 228

N Kapil Dev	8	3	23	0
S Madan Lal	8	0	56	2
SV Nayak	10	1	51	1
RJ Shastri	10	1	34	1
SM Patil	10	0	53	2

INDIA

SM Gavaskar*	st Taylor b Underwood	71
Arun Lal	c Gooch b Botham	9
DB Vengsarkar	c Willis b Gooch	13
SM Patil	b Underwood	64
Yashpal Sharma	not out	34
N Kapil Dev	c Gooch b Underwood	0
A Malhotra	not out	28
SMH Kirmani+		
SV Nayak		
S Madan Lal		
RJ Shastri		
Extras	(0b, 7lb, 2w, 3nb)	12
	42 overs	
Total		**231**

FoW: 16, 59, 135, 184, 184

RGD Willis	6	1	29	0
IT Botham	8	0	48	1
JK Lever	10	0	55	0
GA Gooch	8	0	39	1
DL Underwood	10	0	48	3

No. 63: One-Day Series
VENUE: Colombo (SSC)
DATE: 13th February 1982
TOSS WON BY: Sri Lanka
RESULT: England won by 5 runs

No. 64: One-Day Series
VENUE: Colombo (SSC)
DATE: 14th February 1982
TOSS WON BY: England
RESULT: Sri Lanka won by 3 runs

ENGLAND

GA Gooch	b GRA de Silva	64
G Cook	c GRA de Silva b Kaluper'	28
DI Gower	run out	15
IT Botham	b de Mel	60
KWR Fletcher*	b DS de Silva	12
MW Gatting	c Mendis b de Mel	3
CJ Richards+	b GRA de Silva	3
JE Emburey	lbw b de Mel	0
PJW Allott	run out	0
DL Underwood	b de Mel	4
RGD Willis	not out	2
Extras	(6b, 2lb, 2w, 10nb)	20
	44.4 overs	
Total		**211**

FoW: 55, 83, 152, 191, 197, 202, 205, 205, 205, 211

ALF de Mel	8.4	1	34	4
AN Ranasinghe	8	2	20	0
LW Kaluperuma	7	0	35	1
DS de Silva	9	0	31	1
GRA de Silva	9	0	56	2
S Wettimuny	3	0	15	0

SRI LANKA

B Warnapura*	c Gower b Allott	10
S Wettimuny	c Richards b Allott	46
RSA Jayasekera+	c Gooch b Willis	17
RL Dias	c & b Underwood	4
LRD Mendis	c Gower b Underwood	2
RS Madugalle	b Willis	22
AN Ranasinghe	c Cook b Botham	51
DS de Silva	b Botham	8
ALF de Mel	not out	13
LW Kaluperuma	not out	14
GRA de Silva		
Extras	(5b, 10lb, 2w, 2nb)	19
	45 overs	
Total		**206**

FoW: 34, 75 ,84, 92, 92, 160, 175, 187

RGD Willis	9	1	32	2
IT Botham	9	0	45	2
JE Emburey	5	0	18	0
PJW Allott	9	0	40	2
GA Gooch	6	1	18	0
DL Underwood	7	0	34	2

SRI LANKA

B Warnapura*	c Taylor b Botham	4
S Wettimuny	not out	86
LRD Mendis	c & b Botham	0
RL Dias	hit wkt b Lever	26
A Ranatunga	run out	42
AN Ranasinghe	c Gooch b Underwood	0
RS Madugalle	c Taylor b Lever	12
ALF de Mel	run out	14
DS de Silva	not out	9
HM Goonatillake+		
GRA de Silva		
Extras	(2b, 18lb, 1w, 1nb)	22
	45 overs	
Total		**215**

FoW: 5, 5, 43, 130, 130, 138, 186

RGD Willis	9	1	26	0
IT Botham	9	4	29	2
JK Lever	9	0	51	2
GA Gooch	9	0	50	0
DL Underwood	9	0	37	1

ENGLAND

GA Gooch	st Goonatil' b GRA de Silva	74
G Cook	st Goonatil' b GRA de Silva	32
DI Gower	lbw b de Mel	6
IT Botham	c & b Warnapura	13
KWR Fletcher*	run out	38
CJ Tavare	b DS de Silva	5
MW Gatting	run out	18
RW Taylor+	run out	3
JK Lever	not out	2
DL Underwood	not out	0
RGD Willis	c Madugalle b de Mel	0
Extras	(0b, 19lb, 1w, 1nb)	21
	44.5 overs	
Total		**212**

FoW: 109, 122, 122, 147, 170, 203, 206, 211, 211, 212

ALF de Mel	8.5	0	14	2
AN Ranasinghe	9	0	37	0
B Warnapura	9	0	42	1
DS de Silva	9	0	54	1
GRA de Silva	9	1	44	2

India

No. 65: Prudential Trophy
VENUE: Headingley
DATE: 2nd June 1982
TOSS WON BY: England
RESULT: England won by 9 wickets

INDIA

SM Gavaskar*	c Botham b Allott	38
GA Parkar	c Tavare b Willis	10
DB Vengsarkar	c Taylor b Botham	5
GR Viswanath	b Botham	9
SM Patil	c Taylor b Botham	0
Yashpal Sharma	c Taylor b Allott	20
RJ Shastri	run out	18
N Kapil Dev	run out	60
SMH Kirmani+	c Taylor b Botham	11
SV Nayak	c Tavare b Willis	3
S Madan Lal	not out	1
Extras	(4b, 9lb, 1w, 4nb)	18
	54 overs	
Total		**193**

FoW: 30, 54, 58, 59, 68, 113, 114, 154, 192, 193

RGD Willis	10	0	32	2
GR Dilley	5	1	20	0
PJW Allott	11	4	21	2
IT Botham	11	0	56	4
B Wood	7	2	17	0
G Miller	10	0	29	0

ENGLAND

B Wood	not out	78
CJ Tavare	lbw b Madan Lal	66
AJ Lamb	not out	35
DI Gower		
IT Botham		
DW Randall		
G Miller		
GR Dilley		
RW Taylor+		
PJW Allott		
RGD Willis*		
Extras	(1b, 7lb, 3w, 4nb)	15
	50.1 overs	
Total		**194**

FoW: 133

N Kapil Dev	9	2	21	0
S Madan Lal	9	3	21	1
SV Nayak	9	0	37	0
RJ Shastri	11	0	37	0
SM Patil	7	0	29	0
Yashpal Sharma	5.1	0	34	0

India

No. 66: Prudential Trophy
VENUE: The Oval
DATE: 4th June 1982
TOSS WON BY: India
RESULT: England won by 114 runs

ENGLAND

B Wood	b Patil	15
CJ Tavare	b Patil	27
AJ Lamb	c & b Madan Lal	99
DI Gower	c Vengsarkar b Yashpal	76
IT Botham	run out	4
DW Randall	run out	24
G Miller	run out	0
GR Dilley	c Yashpal b Madan Lal	1
RW Taylor+	not out	3
PJW Allott	run out	5
RGD Willis*		
Extras	(3b, 10lb, 6w, 3nb)	22
	55 overs	
Total		**276**

FoW: 43, 53, 212, 218, 260, 260, 267, 268, 276

N Kapil Dev	11	1	39	0
S Madan Lal	11	0	50	2
SV Nayak	11	1	48	0
SM Patil	11	0	37	2
Yashpal Sharma	3	0	27	1
RJ Shastri	8	0	53	0

INDIA

SM Gavaskar*	c Willis b Miller	15
GA Parkar	c Botham b Willis	2
DB Vengsarkar	c Taylor b Dilley	15
Yashpal Sharma	lbw b Allott	2
A Malhotra	b Botham	4
SM Patil	b Miller	1
N Kapil Dev	c Gower b Wood	47
SMH Kirmani+	c Botham b Miller	8
S Madan Lal	not out	53
RJ Shastri	not out	9
SV Nayak		
Extras	(1b, 3lb, 2w, 0nb)	6
	55 overs	
Total		**162**

FoW: 5, 28, 36, 42, 42, 43, 66, 131

RGD Willis	7	2	10	1
GR Dilley	7	1	19	1
IT Botham	9	2	22	1
PJW Allott	8	3	24	1
G Miller	11	3	27	3
B Wood	11	0	51	1
CJ Tavare	2	0	3	0

Pakistan		**Pakistan**	

No. 67: Prudential Trophy (2)
VENUE: Trent Bridge
DATE: 17th July 1982
TOSS WON BY: Pakistan
RESULT: England won by 7 wickets

No. 68: Prudential Trophy (2)
VENUE: Old Trafford
DATE: 19th July 1982
TOSS WON BY: Pakistan
RESULT: England won by 73 runs

PAKISTAN

Mudassar Nazar	run out	51
Mohsin Khan	b Botham	47
Zaheer Abbas	lbw b Pringle	53
Javed Miandad	c Willis b Pringle	28
Majid Khan	c Willis b Botham	23
Wasim Raja	c Hemmings b Botham	14
Imran Khan*	not out	16
Sarfraz Nawaz	not out	2
Wasim Bari+		
Iqbal Qasim		
Sikander Bakht		
Extras	(4b, 4lb, 6w, 2nb)	16
	55 overs	
Total		**250**

FoW: 102, 103, 175, 208, 222, 238

RGD Willis	11	1	46	0
IT Botham	11	0	57	3
DR Pringle	11	1	50	2
G Miller	11	1	36	0
EE Hemmings	11	1	45	0

ENGLAND

DI Gower	c Wasim Bari b Sikander	17
CJ Tavare	b Imran Khan	48
AJ Lamb	c Wasim Bari b Imran Khan	118
MW Gatting	not out	37
IT Botham	not out	10
DW Randall		
G Miller		
DR Pringle		
EE Hemmings		
RW Taylor+		
RGD Willis*		
Extras	(0b, 12lb, 5w, 5nb)	22
	47.1 overs	
Total		**252**

FoW: 25, 132, 234

Imran Khan	11	2	35	2
Sarfraz Nawaz	11	3	43	0
Sikander Bakht	7	0	34	1
Iqbal Qasim	7	0	49	0
Mudassar Nazar	5.1	0	26	0
Majid Khan	4	0	25	0
Wasim Raja	2	0	18	0

ENGLAND

DI Gower	c Wasim Bari b Mudassar	33
CJ Tavare	run out	16
AJ Lamb	c Wasim Bari b Qasim	27
MW Gatting	run out	76
IT Botham	c Wasim Raja b Imran Khan	49
DW Randall	run out	6
G Miller	b Imran Khan	26
DR Pringle	not out	34
EE Hemmings	c Qasim b Tahir	1
RW Taylor+	not out	1
RGD Willis*		
Extras	(0b, 16lb, 10w, 0nb)	26
	55 overs	
Total		**295**

FoW: 32, 54, 101, 185, 217, 226, 280, 284

Imran Khan	11	1	48	2
Tahir Naqqash	10	0	37	1
Sikander Bakht	11	0	42	0
Mudassar Nazar	11	0	50	1
Iqbal Qasim	8	0	76	1
Majid Khan	4	1	16	0

PAKISTAN

Mudassar Nazar	run out	31
Mohsin Khan	b Pringle	17
Zaheer Abbas	c Randall b Pringle	13
Mansoor Akhtar	run out	28
Majid Khan	b Miller	5
Wasim Raja	c Botham b Willis	60
Imran Khan*	c Gower b Miller	31
Tahir Naqqash	run out	1
Wasim Bari+	b Hemmings	4
Iqbal Qasim	lbw b Botham	13
Sikander Bakht	not out	2
Extras	(0b, 14lb, 2w, 1nb)	17
	49.4 overs	
Total		**222**

FoW: 52, 55, 82, 97, 123, 183, 200, 201, 213, 222

RGD Willis	8	0	36	1
IT Botham	8.4	0	40	1
G Miller	11	1	56	2
DR Pringle	11	0	43	2
EE Hemmings	11	3	30	1

No. 69: B&H World Series		
VENUE: Sydney (SCG) Day/Night		
DATE: 11th January 1983		
TOSS WON BY: England		
RESULT: Australia won by 31 runs		

AUSTRALIA

J Dyson	c Randall b Marks	49
KC Wessels	b Cowans	18
GS Chappell	c Marks b Botham	3
KJ Hughes*	c Taylor b Jesty	0
DW Hookes	b Marks	11
AR Border	b Miller	22
RW Marsh+	c Taylor b Miller	7
GF Lawson	not out	33
JR Thomson	b Miller	8
RM Hogg	c & b Cowans	8
CG Rackemann	b Willis	0
Extras	(0b, 13lb, 8w, 0nb)	21
	46.4 overs	
Total		**180**

FoW: 26, 33, 36, 77, 118, 124, 132, 158, 175, 180

RGD Willis	6.4	1	20	1
NG Cowans	7	0	20	2
IT Botham	7	1	41	1
TE Jesty	6	0	23	1
VJ Marks	10	1	27	2
G Miller	10	0	28	3

ENGLAND

DI Gower	c Hookes b Thomson	9
CJ Tavare	c Border b Rackemann	6
AJ Lamb	b Thomson	49
DW Randall	b Rackemann	5
IT Botham	b Rackemann	18
TE Jesty	run out	12
G Miller	lbw b Hogg	2
VJ Marks	not out	7
RW Taylor+	lbw b Chappell	2
RGD Willis*	c Marsh b Chappell	0
NG Cowans	b Chappell	4
Extras	(0b, 12lb, 17w, 6nb)	35
	41.1 overs	
Total		**149**

FoW: 11, 44, 53, 95, 131, 131, 135, 142, 142, 149

GF Lawson	8	1	33	0
JR Thomson	10	4	21	2
RM Hogg	10	1	15	1
CG Rackemann	8	1	28	3
GS Chappell	5.1	0	17	3

No. 70: B&H World Series		
VENUE: Melbourne (MCG)		
DATE: 13th January 1983		
TOSS WON BY: England		
RESULT: New Zealand won by 2 runs		

NEW ZEALAND

JG Wright	run out	55
BA Edgar	c Randall b Marks	30
BL Cairns	c Miller b Botham	36
GM Turner	b Miller	38
GP Howarth*	c Willis b Botham	13
JFM Morrison	c Randall b Botham	11
RJ Hadlee	c Botham b Willis	24
JV Coney	not out	13
WK Lees+	run out	3
MC Snedden		
EJ Chatfield		
Extras	(1b, 10lb, 5w, 0nb)	16
	50 overs	
Total		**239**

FoW: 87, 100, 137, 164, 188, 205, 231, 239

RGD Willis	8	1	29	1
NG Cowans	10	0	50	0
TE Jesty	3	0	11	0
IT Botham	10	0	40	3
VJ Marks	9	0	47	1
G Miller	10	0	46	1

ENGLAND

DI Gower	c Turner b Hadlee	122
CJ Tavare	run out	16
AJ Lamb	st Lees b Coney	15
TE Jesty	c Wright b Coney	5
IT Botham	c Chatfield b Snedden	41
DW Randall	c Snedden b Coney	8
G Miller	c Turner b Chatfield	2
VJ Marks	b Snedden	5
RW Taylor+	not out	5
RGD Willis*		
NG Cowans		
Extras	(0b, 14lb, 3w, 1nb)	18
	50 overs	
Total		**237**

FoW: 42, 80, 92, 190, 205, 221, 223, 237

MC Snedden	10	0	34	2
EJ Chatfield	10	0	38	1
BL Cairns	10	1	64	0
RJ Hadlee	10	1	37	1
JV Coney	10	0	46	3

New Zealand

No. 71: B&H World Series
VENUE: Brisbane ('Gabba')
DATE: 15th January 1983
TOSS WON BY: New Zealand
RESULT: England won by 54 runs

ENGLAND

IJ Gould+	c Howarth b Troup	15
CJ Tavare	b Cairns	24
DI Gower	c (sub Crowe) b Snedden	158
AJ Lamb	c Cairns b Hadlee	13
IT Botham	c Webb b Hadlee	0
DW Randall	run out	34
TE Jesty	not out	4
G Miller		
VJ Marks		
RGD Willis*		
NG Cowans		
Extras	(0b, 9lb, 9w, 1nb)	19
	50 overs	
Total		**267**

FoW: 26, 89, 114, 116, 229, 267

RJ Hadlee	10	1	44	2
EJ Chatfield	10	3	44	0
MC Snedden	10	0	76	1
GB Troup	7	1	38	1
BL Cairns	10	0	29	1
JV Coney	3	0	17	0

NEW ZEALAND

JG Wright	c Randall b Cowans	30
BA Edgar	c Gould b Botham	40
GP Howarth*	c Jesty b Marks	13
BL Cairns	c Gould b Marks	12
GM Turner	c Jesty b Botham	29
JV Coney	st Gould b Marks	13
PN Webb+	c Cowans b Botham	4
RJ Hadlee	b Willis	21
MC Snedden	run out	0
GB Troup	c Botham b Willis	39
EJ Chatfield	not out	0
Extras	(0b, 6lb, 6w, 0nb)	12
	48.2 overs	
Total		**213**

FoW: 43, 75, 100, 100, 148, 148, 150, 150, 213, 213

RGD Willis	9.2	1	30	2
NG Cowans	10	0	52	1
IT Botham	9	2	47	3
VJ Marks	10	2	30	3
G Miller	10	1	42	0

Australia

No. 72: B&H World Series
VENUE: Brisbane ('Gabba')
DATE: 16th January 1983
TOSS WON BY: Australia
RESULT: Australia won by 7 wickets

ENGLAND

G Cook	c Hookes b Lawson	2
IJ Gould+	run out	2
DI Gower	b Hogg	22
AJ Lamb	c Marsh b Thomson	19
IT Botham	c Hookes b Rackemann	29
DW Randall	b Lawson	57
TE Jesty	c Marsh b Rackemann	0
G Miller	run out	4
VJ Marks	b Thomson	3
RGD Willis*	not out	7
NG Cowans	c Lawson b Rackemann	0
Extras	(4b, 12lb, 13w, 8nb)	37
	46.4 overs	
Total		**182**

FoW: 2, 10, 54, 71, 128, 138, 143, 165, 178, 182

GF Lawson	10	2	23	2
JR Thomson	10	0	32	2
RM Hogg	9	1	29	1
CG Rackemann	8.4	1	28	3
GS Chappell	9	1	33	0

AUSTRALIA

KC Wessels	c Gould b Botham	19
J Dyson	c Marks b Botham	40
GS Chappell	c Jesty b Botham	30
DW Hookes	not out	54
AR Border	not out	30
KJ Hughes*		
RW Marsh+		
GF Lawson		
JR Thomson		
RM Hogg		
CG Rackemann		
Extras	(0b, 9lb, 2w, 0nb)	11
	41 overs	
Total		**184**

FoW: 41, 95, 98

RGD Willis	7	1	31	0
NG Cowans	9	1	35	0
IT Botham	8	1	29	3
G Miller	6	0	25	0
VJ Marks	10	0	46	0
TE Jesty	1	0	7	0

No. 73: B&H World Series
VENUE: Sydney (SCG) Day/Night
DATE: 20th January 1983
TOSS WON BY: New Zealand
RESULT: England won by 8 wickets

No. 74: B&H World Series
VENUE: Melbourne (MCG)
DATE: 23rd January 1983
TOSS WON BY: Australia
RESULT: Australia won by 5 wickets

NEW ZEALAND

JG Wright	c Randall b Willis	9
BA Edgar	c Willis b Cowans	74
GP Howarth*	c Miller b Willis	1
GM Turner	c Gower b Marks	37
BL Cairns	c Gower b Miller	11
WK Lees+	b Botham	12
JJ Crowe	run out	12
RJ Hadlee	c Lamb b Willis	15
JV Coney	c Miller b Willis	6
MC Snedden	not out	2
EJ Chatfield	lbw b Botham	0
Extras	(0b, 17lb, 3w, 0nb)	20
	47.2 overs	
Total		**199**

FoW: 14, 20, 101, 118, 152, 171, 178, 197, 197, 199

RGD Willis	9	0	23	4
NG Cowans	10	1	26	1
IT Botham	8.2	0	30	2
VJ Marks	10	0	49	1
G Miller	10	0	51	1

ENGLAND

CJ Tavare	not out	83
G Fowler	c (sub Webb) b Chatfield	0
DI Gower	b Hadlee	0
AJ Lamb	not out	108
IT Botham		
DW Randall		
G Miller		
IJ Gould+		
VJ Marks		
RGD Willis*		
NG Cowans		
Extras	(1b, 5lb, 3w, 0nb)	9
	42.4 overs	
Total		**200**

FoW: 9, 10

RJ Hadlee	9	2	37	1
EJ Chatfield	10	2	25	1
BL Cairns	8	2	31	0
MC Snedden	8.4	0	61	0
JV Coney	7	0	37	0

ENGLAND

CJ Tavare	c Lillee b Rackemann	20
IT Botham	b Lillee	19
DI Gower	c Marsh b Rackemann	6
AJ Lamb	c (sub) b Lillee	94
DW Randall	not out	51
IJ Gould+	b Hogg	3
TE Jesty	not out	1
DR Pringle		
G Miller		
RGD Willis*		
NG Cowans		
Extras	(0b, 10lb, 4w, 5nb)	19
	37 overs	
Total		**213**

FoW: 32, 50, 66, 205, 209

RM Hogg	7	0	36	1
DK Lillee	8	2	50	2
CG Rackemann	8	0	41	2
GS Chappell	7	0	33	0
JN Maguire	7	0	34	0

AUSTRALIA

J Dyson	run out	54
AR Border	run out	54
DW Hookes	c Gower b Cowans	50
KJ Hughes*	c Miller b Cowans	6
GS Chappell	not out	32
RW Marsh+	run out	8
KC Wessels	not out	5
RM Hogg		
DK Lillee		
JN Maguire		
CG Rackemann		
Extras	(0b, 5lb, 2w, 1nb)	8
	34.4 overs	
Total		**217**

FoW: 85, 157, 167, 176, 190

RGD Willis	6.4	1	29	0
NG Cowans	6	0	46	2
IT Botham	7	1	45	0
DR Pringle	7	0	47	0
G Miller	8	0	42	0

Australia

No. 75: B&H World Series		
VENUE: Sydney (SCG) Day/Night		
DATE: 26th January 1983		
TOSS WON BY: England		
RESULT: England won by 98 runs		

ENGLAND

CJ Tavare	c Marsh b Thomson	14
IT Botham	c Wessels b Hogg	0
DI Gower	b Lillee	25
AJ Lamb	lbw b Lillee	0
DW Randall	run out	47
TE Jesty	b Maguire	30
IJ Gould+	c Wessels b Hogg	42
VJ Marks	c & b Lillee	22
EE Hemmings	run out	3
RD Jackman	b Hogg	0
RGD Willis*	not out	5
Extras	(2b, 4lb, 9w, 4nb)	19
	41 overs	
Total		**207**

FoW: 8, 45, 47, 47, 101, 157, 197, 201, 201, 207

RM Hogg	10	1	44	3
JN Maguire	8	0	42	1
DK Lillee	8	0	34	3
JR Thomson	8	0	40	1
GS Chappell	7	0	28	0

AUSTRALIA

J Dyson	c Randall b Botham	23
AR Border	c & b Willis	31
DW Hookes	b Marks	32
KJ Hughes*	c Gould b Jackman	0
GS Chappell	b Jackman	0
KC Wessels	b Jackman	1
RW Marsh+	b Hemmings	1
DK Lillee	b Hemmings	3
JR Thomson	b Marks	7
RM Hogg	not out	0
JN Maguire	c Lamb b Hemmings	2
Extras	(2b, 2lb, 3w, 2nb)	9
	27.3 overs	
Total		**109**

FoW: 40, 72, 73, 73, 77, 96, 99, 106, 106, 109

RGD Willis	6	1	23	1
RD Jackman	10	1	41	3
IT Botham	2	0	13	1
VJ Marks	6	0	12	2
EE Hemmings	3.3	0	11	3

New Zealand

No. 76: B&H World Series		
VENUE: Adelaide		
DATE: 29th January 1983		
TOSS WON BY: England		
RESULT: New Zealand won by 4 wickets		

ENGLAND

CJ Tavare	c Crowe b Chatfield	16
IT Botham	b Chatfield	65
DI Gower	c Chatfield b Troup	109
AJ Lamb	run out	19
DW Randall	c Wright b Snedden	31
TE Jesty	not out	52
IJ Gould+	not out	1
VJ Marks		
EE Hemmings		
RD Jackman		
RGD Willis*		
Extras	(0b, 1lb, 1w, 1nb)	3
	50 overs	
Total		**296**

FoW: 75, 86, 121, 204, 278

RJ Hadlee	10	1	36	0
BL Cairns	10	1	45	0
MC Snedden	10	0	72	1
EJ Chatfield	10	2	64	2
GB Troup	10	0	76	1

NEW ZEALAND

GM Turner	b Willis	23
JG Wright	run out	30
GP Howarth*	b Jackman	3
JJ Crowe	c Willis b Botham	50
BL Cairns	c Gower b Botham	49
JV Coney	not out	47
RJ Hadlee	c Jesty b Jackman	79
WK Lees+	not out	1
MC Snedden		
EJ Chatfield		
GB Troup		
Extras	(2b, 7lb, 0w, 6nb)	15
	48.5 overs	
Total		**297**

FoW: 26, 33, 96, 166, 166, 287

RGD Willis	9.5	2	43	1
RD Jackman	10	1	49	2
TE Jesty	8	0	52	0
EE Hemmings	6	0	49	0
IT Botham	8	0	61	2
VJ Marks	7	1	28	0

No. 77: B&H World Series			
VENUE: Adelaide			
DATE: 30th January 1983			
TOSS WON BY: England			
RESULT: England won by 14 runs			

ENGLAND

CJ Tavare	b Hogg		18
IT Botham	b Lawson		14
DI Gower	c Lillee b Thomson		77
AJ Lamb	b Hogg		2
DW Randall	c & b Lawson		49
TE Jesty	not out		22
IJ Gould+	c Lillee b Lawson		9
VJ Marks	not out		10
EE Hemmings			
RD Jackman			
RGD Willis*			
Extras	(1b, 14lb, 6w, 6nb)		27
	47 overs		
Total			**228**

FoW: 25,62,70,176,178, 200

GF Lawson	10	0	27	3
DK Lillee	10	0	50	0
RM Hogg	9	1	25	2
JR Thomson	9	0	38	1
GS Chappell	7	0	45	0
DW Hookes	2	0	16	0

AUSTRALIA

AR Border	c Randall b Willis		19
J Dyson	c Lamb b Hemmings		17
DW Hookes	c Jesty b Jackman		76
KJ Hughes*	c Gower b Marks		4
GS Chappell	c Gower b Jackman		33
RW Marsh+	c Jackman b Botham		7
KC Wessels	b Botham		7
GF Lawson	not out		28
JR Thomson	not out		12
DK Lillee			
RM Hogg			
Extras	(6b, 5lb, 0w, 0nb)		11
	47 overs		
Total			**214**

FoW: 27,89, 97,149,161,167,189

RGD Willis	10	1	40	1
RD Jackman	10	3	36	2
IT Botham	7	0	49	2
EE Hemmings	10	0	40	1
VJ Marks	10	1	38	1

No. 78: B&H World Series			
VENUE: Perth (WACA)			
DATE: 5th February 1983			
TOSS WON BY: New Zealand			
RESULT: New Zealand won by 7 wickets			

ENGLAND

CJ Tavare	c Lees b Hadlee		0
IT Botham	c Lees b Hadlee		19
DI Gower	not out		35
AJ Lamb	c Crowe b Snedden		7
DW Randall	c Howarth b Snedden		12
TE Jesty	run out		0
IJ Gould+	b Snedden		0
VJ Marks	b Hadlee		2
RD Jackman	not out		0
RGD Willis*			
NG Cowans			
Extras	(3b, 10lb, 0w, 0nb)		13
	23 overs		
Total			**88**

FoW: 18, 23, 37, 66, 66, 82, 87

RJ Hadlee	8	2	15	3
BL Cairns	5	0	21	0
MC Snedden	6	1	25	3
EJ Chatfield	4	1	14	0

NEW ZEALAND

JG Wright	c Tavare b Willis		12
GM Turner	c Jackman b Willis		0
JJ Crowe	c Botham b Cowans		18
JV Coney	not out		29
GP Howarth*	not out		26
JFM Morrison			
WK Lees+			
RJ Hadlee			
BL Cairns			
MC Snedden			
EJ Chatfield			
Extras	(0b, 1lb, 3w, 0nb)		4
	20.3 overs		
Total			**89**

FoW: 5, 20, 47

RGD Willis	8.3	1	28	2
NG Cowans	8	0	32	1
RD Jackman	2	0	16	0
IT Botham	2	0	9	0

New Zealand

New Zealand

ENGLAND

CJ Tavare	b Cairns	11
IT Botham	c Morrison b Chatfield	12
DI Gower	c Morrison b Snedden	84
AJ Lamb	run out	0
DW Randall	b Chatfield	30
TE Jesty	c Coney b Chatfield	1
IJ Gould+	lbw b Cairns	3
G Miller	lbw b Morrison	3
VJ Marks	not out	23
RD Jackman	b Cairns	4
RGD Willis*	not out	1
Extras	(0b, 10lb, 2w, 0nb)	12
	50 overs	
Total		**184**

FoW: 17, 40, 40, 104, 106, 110, 115, 168, 176

RJ Webb	10	0	30	0
BL Cairns	10	2	28	3
MC Snedden	8	1	35	1
EJ Chatfield	10	0	27	3
JV Coney	2	0	17	0
JFM Morrison	10	1	35	1

NEW ZEALAND

GM Turner	c (sub Cowans) b Willis	88
BA Edgar	c Jackman b Miller	35
BL Cairns	c Lamb b Botham	19
JJ Crowe	lbw b Botham	15
JV Coney	not out	9
GP Howarth*	not out	14
JFM Morrison		
WK Lees+		
MC Snedden		
EJ Chatfield		
RJ Webb		
Extras	(1b, 4lb, 0w, 2nb)	7
	46.3 overs	
Total		**187**

FoW: 101, 129, 164, 166

RGD Willis	10	1	39	1
RD Jackman	8.3	0	38	0
IT Botham	8	0	40	2
VJ Marks	10	1	30	0
G Miller	10	0	33	1

NEW ZEALAND

GM Turner	b Willis	94
BA Edgar	run out	60
BL Cairns	b Willis	44
JG Wright	b Miller	30
JV Coney	not out	31
GP Howarth*	c Botham b Jackman	10
JFM Morrison	b Botham	8
WK Lees+	not out	3
MC Snedden		
EJ Chatfield		
RJ Webb		
Extras	(0b, 9lb, 4w, 2nb)	15
	50 overs	
Total		**295**

FoW: 152, 192, 214, 250, 275, 287

RGD Willis	9	0	54	2
RD Jackman	10	2	38	1
DR Pringle	7	0	57	0
G Miller	10	0	51	1
VJ Marks	7	0	34	0
IT Botham	7	0	46	1

ENGLAND

CJ Tavare	c Howarth b Chatfield	32
IT Botham	c Lees b Cairns	15
DI Gower	c & b Chatfield	2
AJ Lamb	b Coney	7
DW Randall	c Howarth b Morrison	16
IJ Gould+	c Wright b Coney	14
G Miller	b Cairns	46
VJ Marks	c Snedden b Webb	27
DR Pringle	b Webb	11
RD Jackman	b Cairns	9
RGD Willis*	not out	2
Extras	(0b, 6lb, 5w, 0nb)	11
	44.5 overs	
Total		**192**

FoW: 20, 37, 52, 60, 80, 106, 162, 170, 182, 192

MC Snedden	10	1	37	0
BL Cairns	10	0	38	3
RJ Webb	7.5	0	27	2
EJ Chatfield	7	1	28	2
JV Coney	5	0	17	2
JFM Morrison	5	0	34	1

No. 81: Rothman's Cup
VENUE: Christchurch
DATE: 26th February 1983
TOSS WON BY: New Zealand
RESULT: New Zealand won by 84 runs

NEW ZEALAND

GM Turner	lbw b Botham	34
BA Edgar	b Marks	32
JG Wright	st Gould b Marks	2
BL Cairns	c Marks b Jackman	21
JJ Crowe	lbw b Jackman	18
JV Coney	run out	30
GP Howarth*	lbw b Miller	8
JFM Morrison	not out	24
WK Lees+	c Botham b Cowans	2
MC Snedden	not out	31
EJ Chatfield		
Extras	(0b, 5lb, 3w, 1nb)	9
Total	50 overs	**211**

FoW: 64, 70, 93, 108, 126, 152, 153, 156

NG Cowans	10	3	55	1
RGD Willis	10	1	35	0
IT Botham	5	1	17	1
VJ Marks	10	2	31	2
G Miller	7	1	32	1
RD Jackman	8	1	32	2

ENGLAND

IJ Gould+	c Turner b Snedden	0
CJ Tavare	b Snedden	4
DI Gower	c Wright b Chatfield	53
AJ Lamb	c Chatfield b Morrison	37
IT Botham	c & b Morrison	3
DW Randall	b Coney	2
G Miller	c & b Chatfield	7
VJ Marks	b Cairns	1
RD Jackman	b Cairns	5
RGD Willis*	c Coney b Morrison	6
NG Cowans	not out	1
Extras	(0b, 6lb, 1w, 1nb)	8
Total	40.1 overs	**127**

FoW: 0, 8, 94, 103, 105, 114, 114, 116, 125, 127

MC Snedden	7	3	14	2
BL Cairns	7	0	13	2
EJ Chatfield	8	2	26	2
JV Coney	10	0	42	1
JFM Morrison	8.1	0	24	3

No. 82: World Cup
VENUE: The Oval
DATE: 9th June 1983
TOSS WON BY: England
RESULT: England won by 106 runs

ENGLAND

G Fowler	c Coney b Cairns	8
CJ Tavare	c Edgar b Chatfield	45
DI Gower	c Edgar b Coney	39
AJ Lamb	b Snedden	102
MW Gatting	b Snedden	43
IT Botham	c Lees b Hadlee	22
IJ Gould+	not out	14
GR Dilley	not out	31
VJ Marks		
PJW Allott		
RGD Willis*		
Extras	(0b, 12lb, 1w, 5nb)	18
Total	60 overs	**322**

FoW: 13, 79, 117, 232, 271, 278

RJ Hadlee	12	4	26	1
BL Cairns	12	4	57	1
MC Snedden	12	1	105	2
EJ Chatfield	12	1	45	1
JV Coney	6	1	20	1
MD Crowe	6	0	51	0

NEW ZEALAND

GM Turner	lbw b Willis	14
BA Edgar	c Gould b Willis	3
JG Wright	c Botham b Dilley	10
GP Howarth*	c Lamb b Marks	18
JV Coney	run out	23
MD Crowe	run out	97
WK Lees+	b Botham	8
RJ Hadlee	c Lamb b Marks	1
BL Cairns	lbw b Botham	1
MC Snedden	c Gould b Gatting	21
EJ Chatfield	not out	9
Extras	(2b, 4lb, 4w, 1nb)	11
Total	59 overs	**216**

FoW: 3, 28, 31, 62, 85, 123, 136, 138, 190, 216

RGD Willis	7	2	9	2
GR Dilley	8	0	33	1
IT Botham	12	0	42	2
PJW Allott	12	1	47	0
VJ Marks	12	1	39	2
MW Gatting	8	1	35	1

Sri Lanka

Pakistan

No. 83: World Cup
VENUE: Taunton
DATE: 11th June 1983
TOSS WON BY: England
RESULT: England won by 47 runs

No. 84: World Cup
VENUE: Lord's
DATE: 13th June 1983
TOSS WON BY: Pakistan
RESULT: England won by 8 wickets

ENGLAND

G Fowler	b John	22
CJ Tavare	c de Alwis b Ranatunga	32
DI Gower	b de Mel	130
AJ Lamb	b Ratnayake	53
MW Gatting	run out	7
IT Botham	run out	0
IJ Gould+	c Ranatunga b Ratnayake	35
GR Dilley	b de Mel	29
VJ Marks	run out	5
PJW Allott	not out	0
RGD Willis*		
Extras	(0b, 11lb, 9w, 0nb)	20
	60 overs	
Total		**333**

FoW: 49, 78, 174, 193, 194, 292, 298, 333, 333

ALF de Mel	12	3	62	2
VB John	12	0	55	1
RJ Ratnayake	12	0	66	2
A Ranatunga	12	0	65	1
DS de Silva	12	0	65	0

SRI LANKA

S Wettimuny	lbw b Marks	33
DSBP Kuruppu	c Gatting b Dilley	4
RL Dias	c Botham b Dilley	2
LRD Mendis*	c Willis b Marks	56
RS Madugalle	c Tavare b Marks	12
A Ranatunga	c Lamb b Marks	34
DS de Silva	st Gould b Marks	28
RG de Alwis+	not out	58
ALF de Mel	c Dilley b Allott	27
RJ Ratnayake	c Lamb b Dilley	15
VB John	b Dilley	0
Extras	(0b, 12lb, 2w, 3nb)	17
	58 overs	
Total		**286**

FoW: 11, 17, 92, 108, 117, 168, 192, 246, 281, 286

RGD Willis	11	3	43	0
GR Dilley	11	0	45	4
PJW Allott	12	1	82	1
IT Botham	12	0	60	0
VJ Marks	12	3	39	5

PAKISTAN

Mohsin Khan	c Tavare b Willis	3
Mudassar Nazar	c Gould b Allott	26
Mansoor Akhtar	c Gould b Willis	3
Javed Miandad	c Gould b Botham	14
Zaheer Abbas	not out	83
Imran Khan*	run out	7
Wasim Raja	c Botham b Marks	9
Abdul Qadir	run out	0
Sarfraz Nawaz	c & b Botham	11
Wasim Bari+	not out	18
Rashid Khan		
Extras	(5b, 8lb, 3w, 3nb)	19
	60 overs	
Total		**193**

FoW: 29, 33, 49, 67, 96, 112, 118, 154

RGD Willis	12	4	24	2
GR Dilley	12	1	33	0
PJW Allott	12	2	48	1
IT Botham	12	3	36	2
VJ Marks	12	1	33	1

ENGLAND

G Fowler	not out	78
CJ Tavare	lbw b Rashid Khan	8
DI Gower	c Sarfraz b Mansoor	48
AJ Lamb	not out	48
MW Gatting		
IT Botham		
IJ Gould+		
VJ Marks		
GR Dilley		
PJW Allott		
RGD Willis*		
Extras	(1b, 12lb, 2w, 2nb)	17
	50.4 overs	
Total		**199**

FoW: 15, 93

Rashid Khan	7	2	19	1
Sarfraz Nawaz	11	5	22	0
Wasim Raja	3	0	14	0
Mudassar Nazar	8	0	30	0
Abdul Qadir	9.4	0	53	0
Mansoor Akhtar	12	2	44	1

No. 85: World Cup	
VENUE: Edgbaston	
DATE: 15th June 1983	
TOSS WON BY: England	
RESULT: New Zealand won by 2 wickets	

No. 86: World Cup	
VENUE: Old Trafford	
DATE: 18th June 1983	
TOSS WON BY: Pakistan	
RESULT: England won by 7 wickets	

ENGLAND

G Fowler	c JJ Crowe b Chatfield	69
CJ Tavare	c Cairns b Coney	18
IT Botham	c & b Bracewell	12
DI Gower	not out	92
AJ Lamb	c JJ Crowe b Cairns	8
MW Gatting	b Cairns	1
IJ Gould+	lbw b Cairns	4
VJ Marks	b Hadlee	5
GR Dilley	b Hadlee	10
PJW Allott	c Smith b Hadlee	0
RGD Willis*	lbw b Chatfield	0
Extras	(4b, 10lb, 1w, 0nb)	15
	55.2 overs	
Total		**234**

FoW: 63, 77, 117, 143, 154, 162, 208, 233, 233, 234

RJ Hadlee	10	3	32	3
BL Cairns	11	0	44	3
JV Coney	12	2	27	1
JG Bracewell	12	0	66	1
EJ Chatfield	10.2	0	50	2

NEW ZEALAND

GM Turner	lbw b Willis	2
BA Edgar	c Gould b Willis	1
GP Howarth*	run out	60
JJ Crowe	b Allott	17
MD Crowe	b Marks	20
JV Coney	not out	66
IDS Smith+	b Botham	4
RJ Hadlee	b Willis	31
BL Cairns	lbw b Willis	5
JG Bracewell	not out	4
EJ Chatfield		
Extras	(2b, 22lb, 1w, 3nb)	28
	59.5 overs	
Total		**238**

FoW: 2, 3, 47, 75, 146, 151, 221, 231

RGD Willis	12	1	42	4
GR Dilley	12	1	43	0
IT Botham	12	1	47	1
PJW Allott	11.5	2	44	1
VJ Marks	12	1	34	1

PAKISTAN

Mohsin Khan	c Marks b Allott	32
Mudassar Nazar	c Gould b Dilley	18
Zaheer Abbas	c Gould b Dilley	0
Javed Miandad	run out	67
Imran Khan*	c Willis b Marks	13
Wasim Raja	c Willis b Marks	15
Ijaz Faqih	not out	42
Sarfraz Nawaz	b Willis	17
Abdul Qadir	run out	6
Wasim Bari+	not out	2
Rashid Khan		
Extras	(3b, 14lb, 2w, 1nb)	20
	60 overs	
Total		**232**

FoW: 33, 34, 87, 116, 144, 168, 204, 221

RGD Willis	12	3	37	1
GR Dilley	12	2	46	2
PJW Allott	12	1	33	1
IT Botham	12	1	51	0
VJ Marks	12	0	45	2

ENGLAND

G Fowler	c Javed b Mudassar	69
CJ Tavare	c Wasim Raja b Zaheer	58
DI Gower	c Zaheer b Mudassar	31
AJ Lamb	not out	38
MW Gatting	not out	14
IT Botham		
IJ Gould+		
VJ Marks		
GR Dilley		
PJW Allott		
RGD Willis*		
Extras	(1b, 15lb, 7w, 0nb)	23
	57.2 overs	
Total		**233**

FoW: 115, 164, 181

Rashid Khan	11	1	58	0
Sarfraz Nawaz	10.2	2	22	0
Abdul Qadir	11	0	51	0
Ijaz Faqih	6	0	19	0
Mudassar Nazar	12	2	34	2
Zaheer Abbas	7	0	26	1

Sri Lanka

India

No. 87: World Cup		
VENUE: Headingley		
DATE: 20th June 1983		
TOSS WON BY: England		
RESULT: England won by 9 wickets		

No. 88: World Cup Semi-Final		
VENUE: Old Trafford		
DATE: 22nd June 1983		
TOSS WON BY: England		
RESULT: India won by 6 wickets		

SRI LANKA

S Wettimuny	lbw b Botham	22
DSBP Kuruppu	c Gatting b Willis	6
A Ranatunga	c Lamb b Botham	0
RL Dias	c Gould b Cowans	7
LRD Mendis*	b Allott	10
RS Madugalle	c Gould b Allott	0
DS de Silva	c Gower b Marks	15
RG de Alwis+	c Marks b Cowans	19
ALF de Mel	c Lamb b Marks	10
RJ Ratnayake	not out	20
VB John	c Cowans b Allott	15
Extras	(5b, 2lb, 3w, 2nb)	12
	50.4 overs	
Total		**136**

FoW: 25, 30, 32, 40, 43, 54, 81, 97, 103, 136

RGD Willis	9	4	9	1
NG Cowans	12	3	31	2
IT Botham	9	4	12	2
PJW Allott	10.4	0	41	3
MW Gatting	4	2	13	0
VJ Marks	6	2	18	2

ENGLAND

G Fowler	not out	81
CJ Tavare	c de Alwis b de Mel	19
DI Gower	not out	27
AJ Lamb		
MW Gatting		
IT Botham		
IJ Gould+		
VJ Marks		
PJW Allott		
RGD Willis*		
NG Cowans		
Extras	(1b, 3lb, 3w, 3nb)	10
	24.1 overs	
Total		**137**

FoW: 68

ALF de Mel	10	1	33	1
RJ Ratnayake	5	0	23	0
VB John	6	0	41	0
DS de Silva	3	0	29	0
A Ranatunga	0.1	0	1	0

ENGLAND

G Fowler	b Binny	33
CJ Tavare	c Kirmani b Binny	32
DI Gower	c Kirmani b Amarnath	17
AJ Lamb	run out	29
MW Gatting	b Amarnath	18
IT Botham	b Azad	6
IJ Gould+	run out	13
VJ Marks	b Kapil Dev	8
GR Dilley	not out	20
PJW Allott	c Patil b Kapil Dev	8
RGD Willis*	b Kapil Dev	0
Extras	(1b, 17lb, 7w, 4nb)	29
	60 overs	
Total		**213**

FoW: 69, 84, 107, 141, 150, 160, 175, 177, 202, 213

N Kapil Dev	11	1	35	3
BS Sandhu	8	1	36	0
RMH Binny	12	1	43	2
S Madan Lal	5	0	15	0
K Azad	12	1	28	1
M Amarnath	12	1	27	2

INDIA

SM Gavaskar	c Gould b Allott	25
K Srikkanth	c Willis b Botham	19
M Amarnath	run out	46
Yashpal Sharma	c Allott b Willis	61
SM Patil	not out	51
N Kapil Dev*	not out	1
K Azad		
RMH Binny		
S Madan Lal		
SMH Kirmani+		
BS Sandhu		
Extras	(5b, 6lb, 1w, 2nb)	14
	54.4 overs	
Total		**217**

FoW: 46, 50, 142, 205

RGD Willis	10.4	2	42	1
GR Dilley	11	0	43	0
PJW Allott	10	3	40	1
IT Botham	11	4	40	1
VJ Marks	12	1	38	0

No. 89: Rothman's Cup	
VENUE: Christchurch	
DATE: 18th February 1984	
TOSS WON BY: New Zealand	
RESULT: England won by 54 runs	

No. 90: Rothman's Cup	
VENUE: Wellington	
DATE: 22nd February 1984	
TOSS WON BY: New Zealand	
RESULT: England won by 6 wickets	

ENGLAND

DI Gower	c JJ Crowe b Hadlee	3
CL Smith	run out	17
AJ Lamb	c Robertson b Hadlee	43
DW Randall	c Cairns b Hadlee	70
IT Botham	c Smith b Hadlee	1
MW Gatting	b Hadlee	0
VJ Marks	lbw b Cairns	28
RW Taylor+	run out	2
NA Foster	c Wright b Cairns	0
NG Cowans	not out	4
RGD Willis*		
Extras	(8b, 4lb, 0w, 8nb)	20
	50 overs	
Total		**188**

FoW: 9, 59, 107, 109, 109, 177, 184, 184, 188

RJ Hadlee	10	2	32	5
EJ Chatfield	10	4	20	0
BL Cairns	10	2	41	2
JV Coney	10	1	30	0
GK Robertson	10	0	45	0

NEW ZEALAND

JG Wright	c Taylor b Willis	4
BA Edgar	c Taylor b Botham	10
GP Howarth*	run out	18
MD Crowe	run out	0
JJ Crowe	b Botham	0
JV Coney	c Botham b Foster	19
BL Cairns	lbw b Marks	23
RJ Hadlee	c Gower b Marks	23
IDS Smith+	c Gower b Foster	7
GK Robertson	lbw b Willis	10
EJ Chatfield	not out	0
Extras	(0b, 9lb, 6w, 5nb)	20
	42.1 overs	
Total		**134**

FoW: 7, 38, 38, 38, 44, 76, 112, 120, 124, 134

RGD Willis	6.1	1	18	2
NG Cowans	10	2	37	0
IT Botham	6	3	7	2
NA Foster	10	4	19	2
VJ Marks	10	1	33	2

NEW ZEALAND

BA Edgar	b Marks	12
TJ Franklin	c & b Marks	6
GP Howarth*	lbw b Marks	21
MD Crowe	c Foster b Marks	8
JJ Crowe	c Foster b Marks	1
JV Coney	b Botham	44
RJ Hadlee	c Randall b Foster	21
BL Cairns	c Gower b Foster	0
IDS Smith+	lbw b Botham	0
GK Robertson	run out	11
EJ Chatfield	not out	0
Extras	(0b, 9lb, 2w, 0nb)	11
	47.1 overs	
Total		**135**

FoW: 23, 34, 50, 52, 63, 104, 104, 104, 135, 135

RGD Willis	9	4	17	0
NG Cowans	10	1	33	0
VJ Marks	10	3	20	5
IT Botham	8.1	1	25	2
NA Foster	10	3	29	2

ENGLAND

DI Gower	c JJ Crowe b Chatfield	21
CL Smith	b Hadlee	70
AJ Lamb	c & b Chatfield	6
DW Randall	not out	25
IT Botham	b Hadlee	15
MW Gatting	not out	0
VJ Marks		
RW Taylor+		
NA Foster		
NG Cowans		
RGD Willis*		
Extras	(0b, 2lb, 0w, 0nb)	2
	45.1 overs	
Total		**139**

FoW: 36, 54, 117, 135

RJ Hadlee	10	2	31	2
GK Robertson	6	0	28	0
JV Coney	10	1	29	0
EJ Chatfield	10	5	16	2
BL Cairns	9.1	1	33	0

New Zealand		Pakistan

No. 91: Rothman's Cup
VENUE: Auckland
DATE: 25th February 1984
TOSS WON BY: England
RESULT: New Zealand won by 7 wickets

No. 92: Wills Series
VENUE: Lahore (Gaddafi)
DATE: 9th March 1984
TOSS WON BY: Pakistan
RESULT: Pakistan won by 6 wickets

ENGLAND

DI Gower	lbw b Chatfield	35
CL Smith	b Hadlee	5
AJ Lamb	not out	97
DW Randall	b Boock	11
IT Botham	c Wright b Coney	18
MW Gatting	c Smith b Chatfield	4
VJ Marks	b Chatfield	3
RW Taylor+	run out	8
NA Foster	run out	1
NG Cowans	run out	0
RGD Willis*	not out	7
Extras	(4b, 11lb, 1w, 4nb)	20
	50 overs	
Total		**209**

FoW: 6, 73, 86, 130, 140, 148, 185, 192, 192

BL Cairns	10	2	31	0
RJ Hadlee	10	2	51	1
SL Boock	10	0	40	1
JV Coney	10	0	38	1
EJ Chatfield	10	2	29	3

NEW ZEALAND

PN Webb	b Willis	8
JG Wright	c & b Marks	14
GP Howarth*	lbw b Botham	72
MD Crowe	not out	105
JV Coney	not out	2
JJ Crowe		
RJ Hadlee		
BL Cairns		
IDS Smith+		
SL Boock		
EJ Chatfield		
Extras	(0b, 7lb, 2w, 0nb)	9
	45.3 overs	
Total		**210**

FoW: 22, 34, 194

RGD Willis	10	1	36	1
NG Cowans	9.3	0	59	0
VJ Marks	10	1	27	1
IT Botham	7	1	22	1
NA Foster	6	0	37	0
CL Smith	3	0	20	0

ENGLAND

G Fowler+	b Sarfraz	43
CJ Tavare	c Ashraf Ali b Rashid Khan	4
DI Gower	c Qasim b Shahid	7
AJ Lamb	run out	57
DW Randall	run out	16
IT Botham	not out	18
MW Gatting	b Sarfraz	9
GR Dilley	lbw b Sarfraz	1
VJ Marks	b Rashid Khan	2
NA Foster	not out	6
RGD Willis*		
Extras	(0b, 13lb, 6w, 2nb)	21
	40 overs	
Total		**184**

FoW: 11, 24, 94, 134, 147, 160, 164, 173

Rashid Khan	8	1	28	2
Shahid Mahboob	8	2	28	1
Mudassar Nazar	8	1	34	0
Sarfraz Nawaz	8	0	33	3
Wasim Raja	8	0	40	0

PAKISTAN

Mohsin Khan	b Dilley	39
Saadat Ali	run out	44
Qasim Omar	c Fowler b Marks	11
Zaheer Abbas*	not out	59
Salim Malik	c Tavare b Willis	11
Mudassar Nazar	not out	8
Wasim Raja		
Shahid Mahboob		
Ashraf Ali+		
Sarfraz Nawaz		
Rashid Khan		
Extras	(1b, 5lb, 1w, 8nb)	15
	38.4 overs	
Total		**187**

FoW: 79, 96, 120, 156

RGD Willis	7.4	1	25	1
GR Dilley	8	0	38	1
IT Botham	7	0	43	0
VJ Marks	8	1	32	1
NA Foster	8	0	34	0

Pakistan

No. 93: Wills Series	
VENUE: Karachi (National Stadium)	
DATE: 26th March 1984	
TOSS WON BY: England	
RESULT: England won by 6 wickets	

PAKISTAN

Mohsin Khan	st Fowler b Cook	37
Saadat Ali	not out	78
Wasim Raja	c Fowler b Gatting	14
Salim Malik	c Foster b Gatting	2
Qasim Omar	c & b Gatting	7
Naved Anjum	st Fowler b Smith	2
Mudassar Nazar	run out	6
Abdul Qadir	c Cook b Smith	3
Sarfraz Nawaz*	c Gower b Cowans	3
Anil Dalpat+	not out	0
Rashid Khan		
Extras	(4b, 4lb, 0w, 3nb)	11
	40 overs	
Total		**163**

FoW: 76, 102, 107, 123, 135, 146, 155, 160

NA Foster	8	0	36	0
NG Cowans	5	0	20	1
MW Gatting	8	1	32	3
VJ Marks	8	1	22	0
NGB Cook	8	0	34	1
CL Smith	3	0	8	2

ENGLAND

G Fowler+	c Anil b Mudassar	25
CL Smith	lbw b Qadir	17
DI Gower*	b Mudassar	31
AJ Lamb	c Salim b Naved	19
MW Gatting	not out	38
DW Randall	not out	19
CJ Tavare		
VJ Marks		
NA Foster		
NGB Cook		
NG Cowans		
Extras	(1b, 8lb, 3w, 3nb)	15
	38.4 overs	
Total		**164**

FoW: 37, 79, 88, 119

Rashid Khan	8	0	31	0
Sarfraz Nawaz	7.4	1	24	0
Mudassar Nazar	8	0	33	2
Abdul Qadir	8	1	22	1
Wasim Raja	5	0	30	0
Naved Anjum	2	0	9	1

No. 94: Texaco Trophy	
VENUE: Old Trafford	
DATE: 31st May 1984	
TOSS WON BY: West Indies	
RESULT: West Indies won by 104 runs	

WEST INDIES

CG Greenidge	c Bairstow b Botham	9
DL Haynes	run out	1
RB Richardson	c & b Willis	6
IVA Richards	not out	189
HA Gomes	b Miller	4
CH Lloyd*	c Pringle b Miller	8
PJL Dujon+	c Gatting b Miller	0
MD Marshall	run out	4
EAE Baptiste	c Bairstow b Botham	26
J Garner	c & b Foster	3
MA Holding	not out	12
Extras	(4b, 2lb, 1w, 3nb)	10
	55 overs	
Total		**272**

FoW: 5, 11, 43, 63, 89, 98, 102, 161, 166

RGD Willis	11	2	38	1
IT Botham	11	0	67	2
NA Foster	11	0	61	1
G Miller	11	1	32	3
DR Pringle	11	0	64	0

ENGLAND

G Fowler	c Lloyd b Garner	1
TA Lloyd	c Dujon b Holding	15
MW Gatting	lbw b Garner	0
DI Gower*	c Greenidge b Marshall	15
AJ Lamb	c Richardson b Gomes	75
IT Botham	c Richardson b Baptiste	2
DL Bairstow+	c Garner b Richards	13
G Miller	b Richards	7
DR Pringle	c Garner b Holding	6
NA Foster	b Garner	24
RGD Willis	not out	1
Extras	(0b, 6lb, 0w, 3nb)	9
	50 overs	
Total		**168**

FoW: 7, 8, 33, 48, 51, 80, 100, 115, 162, 168

J Garner	8	1	18	3
MA Holding	11	2	23	2
EAE Baptiste	11	0	38	1
MD Marshall	6	1	20	1
IVA Richards	11	1	45	2
HA Gomes	3	0	15	1

No. 95: Texaco Trophy
VENUE: Trent Bridge
DATE: 2nd June 1984
TOSS WON BY: England
RESULT: England won by 3 wickets

No. 96: Texaco Trophy
VENUE: Lord's
DATE: 4th June 1984
TOSS WON BY: West Indies
RESULT: West Indies won by 8 wickets

WEST INDIES

CG Greenidge	c Botham b Pringle	20
DL Haynes	lbw b Willis	4
RB Richardson	c Gower b Pringle	10
IVA Richards	c Pringle b Miller	3
HA Gomes	b Pringle	15
CH Lloyd*	c Pringle b Miller	52
PJL Dujon+	run out	21
MD Marshall	run out	20
EAE Baptiste	lbw b Willis	19
MA Holding	b Botham	0
J Garner	not out	6
Extras	(0b, 7lb, 0w, 2nb)	9
	48.3 overs	
Total		**179**

FoW: 24, 38, 39, 43, 75, 128, 148, 160, 161, 179

RGD Willis	9.3	0	26	2
IT Botham	9	1	33	1
DR Pringle	10	3	21	3
G Miller	10	2	44	2
NA Foster	10	0	46	0

ENGLAND

G Fowler	b Baptiste	25
TA Lloyd	c Dujon b Baptiste	49
DI Gower*	lbw b Marshall	36
AJ Lamb	b Gomes	11
IT Botham	c Gomes b Holding	15
MW Gatting	b Garner	6
DL Bairstow+	b Holding	9
G Miller	not out	3
DR Pringle	not out	2
NA Foster		
RGD Willis		
Extras	(4b, 14lb, 0w, 6nb)	24
	47.5 overs	
Total		**180**

FoW: 75, 103, 131, 145, 157, 173, 177

J Garner	9	1	22	1
MA Holding	8.5	1	29	2
MD Marshall	10	1	30	1
EAE Baptiste	10	2	31	2
IVA Richards	5	0	23	0
HA Gomes	5	0	21	1

ENGLAND

G Fowler	b Holding	34
TA Lloyd	b Harper	37
DI Gower*	b Marshall	29
AJ Lamb	run out	0
IT Botham	c Harper b Baptiste	22
DW Randall	c Dujon b Marshall	8
DL Bairstow+	b Marshall	8
G Miller	b Holding	10
DR Pringle	lbw b Garner	8
NA Foster	not out	4
RGD Willis	not out	6
Extras	(1b, 17lb, 4w, 8nb)	30
	55 overs	
Total		**196**

FoW: 60, 91, 91, 128, 144, 151, 167, 177, 182

J Garner	11	4	17	1
MA Holding	11	0	33	2
MD Marshall	11	0	38	3
EAE Baptiste	11	1	40	1
RA Harper	11	0	38	1

WEST INDIES

CG Greenidge	c Bairstow b Pringle	32
DL Haynes	c Randall b Miller	18
HA Gomes	not out	56
IVA Richards	not out	84
CH Lloyd*		
PJL Dujon+		
MD Marshall		
RA Harper		
EAE Baptiste		
MA Holding		
J Garner		
Extras	(1b, 0lb, 1w, 5nb)	7
	46.5 overs	
Total		**197**

FoW: 50, 63

RGD Willis	10.5	2	52	0
IT Botham	8	0	25	0
G Miller	9	1	35	1
DR Pringle	8	0	38	1
NA Foster	11	1	40	0

No. 97: One-Day Series
VENUE: Poona
DATE: 5th December 1984
TOSS WON BY: England
RESULT: England won by 4 wickets

INDIA

K Srikkanth	b Edmonds	50
SM Gavaskar*	b Foster	0
DB Vengsarkar	b Ellison	105
SM Patil	run out	2
Yashpal Sharma	c Ellison b Foster	37
RJ Shastri	c Ellison b Foster	11
RMH Binny	not out	0
KS More+		
M Prabhakar		
C Sharma		
RS Ghai		
Extras	(0b, 2lb, 7w, 0nb)	9
	45 overs	
Total		**214**

FoW: 1, 119, 126, 189, 212, 214

NG Cowans	8	0	32	0
NA Foster	10	0	44	3
RM Ellison	7	0	45	1
VJ Marks	10	0	48	0
PH Edmonds	10	0	43	1

ENGLAND

G Fowler	c Yashpal b Sharma	5
RT Robinson	lbw b Ghai	15
MW Gatting	not out	115
AJ Lamb	c & b Prabhakar	3
VJ Marks	run out	31
DI Gower*	c Shastri b Binny	3
RM Ellison	run out	4
PR Downton+	not out	27
PH Edmonds		
NA Foster		
NG Cowans		
Extras	(0b, 8lb, 0w, 4nb)	12
	43.2 overs	
Total		**215**

FoW: 14, 43, 47, 114, 117, 129

C Sharma	8.2	0	50	1
M Prabhakar	10	1	27	1
RS Ghai	9	0	38	1
RJ Shastri	8	0	49	0
RMH Binny	8	0	43	1

No. 98: One-Day Series
VENUE: Cuttack
DATE: 27th December 1984
TOSS WON BY: England
RESULT: England won by run rate

INDIA

K Srikkanth	lbw b Gatting	99
RJ Shastri	b Gatting	102
DB Vengsarkar	c Gower b Marks	23
Yashpal Sharma	lbw b Marks	4
M Amarnath	not out	1
RMH Binny	b Marks	2
SM Gavaskar*	not out	6
KS More+		
M Prabhakar		
RS Ghai		
A Patel		
Extras	(5b, 5lb, 3w, 2nb)	15
	49 overs	
Total		**252**

FoW: 188, 235, 243 Shastri, 243, 246

NA Foster	5	0	26	0
NG Cowans	10	0	39	0
RM Ellison	6	0	31	0
PH Edmonds	10	0	47	0
VJ Marks	8	0	50	3
MW Gatting	10	0	49	2

ENGLAND

G Fowler	c Shastri b Binny	15
RT Robinson	b Prabhakar	1
MW Gatting	b Patel	59
DI Gower*	c Prabhakar b Binny	21
AJ Lamb	run out	28
VJ Marks	run out	44
PR Downton+	not out	44
RM Ellison	not out	14
PH Edmonds		
NA Foster		
NG Cowans		
Extras	(0b, 9lb, 1w, 5nb)	15
	46 overs	
Total		**241**

FoW: 3, 50, 93, 128,145, 203

RS Ghai	8	0	40	0
M Prabhakar	10	1	34	1
RMH Binny	7	0	48	2
A Patel	10	0	53	1
RJ Shastri	10	0	48	0
M Amarnath	1	0	9	0

No. 99: One-Day Series
VENUE: Bangalore
DATE: 20th January 1985
TOSS WON BY: England
RESULT: England won by 3 wickets

INDIA

SM Gavaskar*	c Gatting b Marks	40
K Srikkanth	b Cowans	29
DB Vengsarkar	st Downton b Marks	23
N Kapil Dev	c Gower b Marks	8
Yashpal Sharma	run out	8
RJ Shastri	b Edmonds	33
M Azharuddin	not out	47
S Viswanath+	not out	6
A Patel		
RS Ghai		
TAP Sekhar		
Extras	(4b, 6lb, 1w, 0nb)	11
	46 overs	
Total		**205**

FoW: 70, 70, 90, 108, 119, 185

NG Cowans	10	1	31	1
NA Foster	6	0	33	0
RM Ellison	6	0	25	0
VJ Marks	10	1	35	3
PH Edmonds	10	0	44	1
MW Gatting	4	0	27	0

ENGLAND

G Fowler	run out	45
RT Robinson	c Viswanath b Kapil Dev	2
MW Gatting	run out	3
DI Gower*	b Shastri	38
AJ Lamb	not out	59
VJ Marks	c Gavaskar b Patel	17
PR Downton+	c Shastri b Kapil Dev	12
PH Edmonds	c Viswanath b Kapil Dev	7
RM Ellison	not out	1
NA Foster		
NG Cowans		
Extras	(0b, 10lb, 7w, 5nb)	22
	45 overs	
Total		**206**

FoW: 15, 21, 91, 103, 144, 186, 204

N Kapil Dev	10	0	38	3
TAP Sekhar	9	0	36	0
A Patel	10	1	42	1
RS Ghai	4	0	37	0
RJ Shastri	10	2	29	1
Yashpal Sharma	2	0	14	0

No. 100: One-Day Series
VENUE: Nagpur
DATE: 23rd January 1985
TOSS WON BY: India
RESULT: India won by 3 wickets

ENGLAND

G Fowler	b Shastri	37
MD Moxon	c Srikkanth b Kapil Dev	70
MW Gatting	b Shastri	1
DI Gower*	c & b Shastri	11
AJ Lamb	st Viswanath b Shastri	30
CS Cowdrey	not out	46
VJ Marks	b Sekhar	4
PR Downton+	c Rajput b Sekhar	13
PH Edmonds	not out	8
JP Agnew		
NG Cowans		
Extras	(3b, 15lb, 1w, 1nb)	20
	50 overs	
Total		**240**

FoW: 70, 78, 100, 154, 176, 199, 221

N Kapil Dev	10	1	42	1
M Prabhakar	10	1	36	0
TAP Sekhar	10	0	50	2
A Patel	10	1	54	0
RJ Shastri	10	1	40	4

INDIA

K Srikkanth	b Cowans	6
LS Rajput	c Downton b Cowans	0
DB Vengsarkar	c Downton b Agnew	11
M Azharuddin	b Cowdrey	47
SM Gavaskar*	b Agnew	52
N Kapil Dev	c Gatting b Cowans	54
RJ Shastri	not out	24
M Prabhakar	b Agnew	4
S Viswanath+	not out	23
TAP Sekhar		
A Patel		
Extras	(3b, 14lb, 1w, 2nb)	20
	47.4 overs	
Total		**241**

FoW: 5, 11, 31, 90 ,166, 197, 204

NG Cowans	10	0	44	3
JP Agnew	10	0	38	3
VJ Marks	6	0	32	0
PH Edmonds	10	0	44	0
CS Cowdrey	7.4	0	52	1
MW Gatting	4	0	14	0

			No. 101: One-Day Series
		VENUE:	Chandigarh
		DATE:	27th January 1985
	TOSS WON BY:	India	
		RESULT:	England won by 7 runs

ENGLAND

G Fowler	run out	17
MW Gatting	c Azharuddin b Sekhar	31
DI Gower*	b Sekhar	19
AJ Lamb	not out	33
CS Cowdrey	c Rajput b Shastri	5
PH Edmonds	c Azharuddin b Sekhar	5
VJ Marks	run out	2
RM Ellison	not out	4
JP Agnew		
BN French+		
NA Foster		
Extras	(0b, 5lb, 0w, 0nb)	5
	15 overs	
Total		**121**

FoW: 31, 71, 74, 86, 93, 104

N Kapil Dev	3	0	17	0
M Prabhakar	3	0	26	0
C Sharma	3	0	20	0
TAP Sekhar	3	0	23	3
RJ Shastri	3	0	30	1

INDIA

RJ Shastri	run out	53
K Srikkanth	run out	9
N Kapil Dev	c Agnew b Edmonds	17
M Azharuddin	c Gatting b Edmonds	10
Yashpal Sharma	b Cowdrey	6
SM Gavaskar*	not out	2
LS Rajput	not out	1
S Viswanath+		
TAP Sekhar		
M Prabhakar		
C Sharma		
Extras	(0b, 4lb, 12w, 0nb)	16
	15 overs	
Total		**114**

FoW: 22, 49, 83, 111, 112

JP Agnew	3	0	23	0
NA Foster	3	0	17	0
RM Ellison	3	0	20	0
PH Edmonds	3	0	20	2
MW Gatting	2	0	27	0
CS Cowdrey	1	0	3	1

			No. 102: B&H World Championship
		VENUE:	Melbourne (MCG)
		DATE:	17th February 1985
	TOSS WON BY:	England	
		RESULT:	Australia won by 7 wickets

ENGLAND

G Fowler	c & b McDermott	26
PR Downton+	c McCurdy b McDermott	27
DI Gower*	c Alderman b McCurdy	6
AJ Lamb	c Kerr b Lawson	53
MW Gatting	c Alderman b O'Donnell	34
CS Cowdrey	lbw b McDermott	0
VJ Marks	b Lawson	24
PH Edmonds	b Lawson	20
RM Ellison	not out	2
JP Agnew	not out	2
NG Cowans		
Extras	(3b, 12lb, 0w, 5nb)	20
	49 overs	
Total		**214**

FoW: 61, 66, 76, 159, 159, 166, 200, 211

GF Lawson	10	3	31	3
TM Alderman	10	0	48	0
CJ McDermott	10	0	39	3
RJ McCurdy	10	1	42	1
SP O'Donnell	9	0	39	1

AUSTRALIA

KC Wessels	c Gatting b Ellison	39
RB Kerr	not out	87
KJ Hughes	run out	0
AR Border*	c Cowans b Marks	1
DM Jones	not out	78
WB Phillips+		
SP O'Donnell		
GF Lawson		
CJ McDermott		
RJ McCurdy		
TM Alderman		
Extras	(1b, 3lb, 0w, 6nb)	10
	45.2 overs	
Total		**215**

FoW: 57, 57, 58

NG Cowans	10	0	52	0
RM Ellison	10	4	34	1
JP Agnew	8	0	59	0
VJ Marks	7.2	0	33	1
PH Edmonds	10	0	33	0

No. 103: B&H World Championship	No. 104: B&H World Championship
VENUE: Sydney (SCG)	VENUE: Melbourne (MCG)
DATE: 26th February 1985	DATE: 2nd March 1985
TOSS WON BY: England	TOSS WON BY: Pakistan
RESULT: India won by 86 runs	RESULT: Pakistan won by 67 runs

INDIA

RJ Shastri	c Fowler b Ellison	13
K Srikkanth	run out	57
M Azharuddin	c & b Cowans	45
DB Vengsarkar	run out	43
N Kapil Dev	c Downton b Cowans	29
SM Gavaskar*	not out	30
M Amarnath	c Lamb b Cowans	6
RMH Binny	c Marks b Foster	2
S Madan Lal	c Downton b Foster	0
S Viswanath+	run out	8
L Sivaramakrishnan		
Extras	(0b, 2lb, 0w, 0nb)	2
	50 overs	
Total		**235**

FoW: 67, 74 , 147, 183, 197, 216 , 220, 220, 235

NG Cowans	10	0	59	3
RM Ellison	10	1	46	1
NA Foster	10	0	33	2
PH Edmonds	10	1	38	0
VJ Marks	10	0	57	0

ENGLAND

G Fowler	c Viswanath b Binny	26
MD Moxon	c & b Sivaramakrishnan	48
DI Gower*	c Veng'kar b Siva'krishnan	25
AJ Lamb	b Sivaramakrishnan	13
MW Gatting	c Viswanath b Shastri	7
PR Downton+	c Shastri b Kapil Dev	9
VJ Marks	st Viswanath b Shastri	2
PH Edmonds	st Viswanath b Shastri	5
RM Ellison	c Viswanath b Madan Lal	1
NA Foster	c Srikkanth b Madan Lal	1
NG Cowans	not out	3
Extras	(3b, 4lb, 1w, 1nb)	9
	41.4 overs	
Total		**149**

FoW: 41, 94, 113, 126, 126, 130, 142, 144, 146, 149

N Kapil Dev	7	0	21	1
RMH Binny	8	0	33	1
S Madan Lal	6.4	0	19	2
L Siva'krishnan	10	0	39	3
RJ Shastri	10	2	30	3

PAKISTAN

Mudassar Nazar	c Foster b Edmonds	77
Mohsin Khan	c Moxon b Ellison	9
Rameez Raja	c Moxon b Marks	21
Javed Miandad*	c Downton b Foster	11
Imran Khan	b Ellison	35
Salim Malik	c Gatting b Foster	8
Qasim Omar	b Cowans	12
Tahir Naqqash	not out	21
Anil Dalpat+	b Ellison	8
Azeem Hafeez	not out	0
Wasim Akram		
Extras	(5b, 4lb, 2w, 0nb)	11
	50 overs	
Total		**213**

FoW: 37, 93, 114, 126, 144, 181, 183, 212

NG Cowans	10	0	52	1
RM Ellison	10	0	42	3
NA Foster	10	0	56	2
VJ Marks	10	2	25	1
PH Edmonds	10	1	29	1

ENGLAND

G Fowler	c Anil b Imran Khan	0
DI Gower*	c Tahir b Imran Khan	27
AJ Lamb	c Wasim b Azeem	81
MW Gatting	c Mudassar b Tahir	11
PR Downton+	run out	6
RM Ellison	c Anil b Tahir	6
VJ Marks	run out	1
MD Moxon	c Imran Khan b Azeem	3
PH Edmonds	not out	0
NA Foster	run out	1
NG Cowans	b Tahir	0
Extras	(1b, 7lb, 1w, 1nb)	10
	24.2 overs	
Total		**146**

FoW: 0, 56, 102, 125, 138, 139, 141, 145, 146, 146

Imran Khan	7	0	33	2
Wasim Akram	10	0	59	0
Azeem Hafeez	3	0	22	2
Tahir Naqqash	4.2	0	24	3

No. 105: Rothmans Trophy Semi-Final
VENUE: Sharjah
DATE: 24th March 1985 (Day game)
TOSS WON BY: Australia
RESULT: Australia won by 2 wickets

No. 106: Rothmans Trophy Plate Final
VENUE: Sharjah
DATE: 26th March 1985
TOSS WON BY: England
RESULT: Pakistan won by 43 runs

ENGLAND

G Fowler	c Hughes b Alderman	26
RT Robinson	c Rixon b Matthews	37
MD Moxon	lbw b O'Donnell	0
DW Randall	st Rixon b Bennett	19
CM Wells	lbw b Bennett	17
DR Pringle	st Rixon b Border	4
PH Edmonds	not out	15
BN French+	c Rixon b Border	4
RM Ellison	c Wessels b Border	24
NA Foster	not out	
N Gifford*		
Extras	(9b, 5lb, 6w, 6nb)	26
	50 overs	
Total		**177**

FoW: 7, 53, 95, 109, 123, 128, 134, 169

TM Alderman	7	1	36	1
RJ McCurdy	5	0	23	0
SP O'Donnell	8	2	26	1
MJ Bennett	10	2	27	2
GRJ Matthews	10	3	15	1
AR Border	7	0	21	3
KC Wessels	3	0	15	0

AUSTRALIA

KC Wessels	b Edmonds	16
GM Wood	c French b Pringle	35
DM Jones	c Moxon b Edmonds	27
AR Border*	c & b Pringle	9
KJ Hughes	c French b Foster	14
GRJ Matthews	c Foster b Ellison	24
SP O'Donnell	c Moxon b Ellison	19
SJ Rixon+	not out	11
MJ Bennett	run out	0
RJ McCurdy	not out	6
TM Alderman		
Extras	(0b, 9lb, 8w, 0nb)	17
	50 overs	
Total		**178**

FoW: 54, 64, 82, 100, 120, 151, 168, 168

NA Foster	10	1	34	1
RM Ellison	10	1	28	2
DR Pringle	10	0	49	2
PH Edmonds	10	2	31	2
N Gifford	10	1	27	0

PAKISTAN

Mudassar Nazar	c French b Gifford	36
Mohsin Khan	c Robinson b Pringle	13
Rameez Raja	c Robinson b Pringle	16
Javed Miandad*	c Gifford b Edmonds	71
Salim Malik	lbw b Gifford	2
Imran Khan	c Pringle b Gifford	0
Shoaib Moh'd	st French b Gifford	3
Ashraf Ali+	not out	19
Tahir Naqqash	not out	2
Tauseef Ahmed		
Wasim Akram		
Extras	(1b, 9lb, 2w, 1nb)	13
	50 overs	
Total		**175**

FoW: 24, 43, 107, 113, 113, 125, 172

RM Ellison	7	1	18	0
DR Pringle	7	1	32	2
PH Edmonds	10	0	47	1
PI Pocock	10	1	20	0
N Gifford	10	0	23	4
RJ Bailey	6	0	25	0

ENGLAND

G Fowler	c Javed b Tauseef	19
RT Robinson	b Tahir	9
MD Moxon	b Shoaib	11
CM Wells	b Shoaib	5
RJ Bailey	not out	41
DR Pringle	b Wasim	13
PH Edmonds	c & b Shoaib	3
RM Ellison	b Wasim	3
BN French+	c Shoaib b Tauseef	7
N Gifford*	c Javed b Imran Khan	0
PI Pocock	run out	4
Extras	(1b, 12lb, 0w, 4nb)	17
	48.2 overs	
Total		**132**

FoW: 19, 35, 48, 49, 76, 89, 98, 117, 132, 132

Imran Khan	9	2	26	1
Wasim Akram	10	0	28	2
Tahir Naqqash	9.2	1	20	2
Tauseef Ahmed	10	1	25	1
Shoaib Moh'd	10	1	20	3

Australia

ENGLAND

GA Gooch	c O'Donnell b Holland	57
G Fowler	c Phillips b McDermott	10
DI Gower*	b Lawson	3
AJ Lamb	c Phillips b Lawson	0
IT Botham	b Matthews	72
MW Gatting	not out	31
P Willey	b Holland	12
PR Downton+	c Matthews b Lawson	11
PH Edmonds	c Border b Lawson	0
PJW Allott	b McDermott	2
NG Cowans	c & b McDermott	1
Extras	(2b, 7lb, 2w, 9nb)	20
	54 overs	
Total		**219**

FoW: 21, 27, 27, 143, 160, 181, 203, 203, 213, 219

GF Lawson	10	1	26	4
CJ McDermott	11	0	46	3
SP O'Donnell	11	0	44	0
GRJ Matthews	11	1	45	1
RG Holland	11	2	49	2

AUSTRALIA

KC Wessels	c Botham b Willey	39
GM Wood	c Downton b Cowans	8
DM Wellham	c & b Edmonds	12
AR Border*	c & b Allott	59
DC Boon	c Botham b Gooch	12
WB Phillips+	c Gatting b Cowans	28
SP O'Donnell	b Botham	1
GRJ Matthews	not out	29
GF Lawson	not out	14
CJ McDermott		
RG Holland		
Extras	(2b, 12lb, 4w, 0nb)	18
	54.1 overs	
Total		**220**

FoW: 15. 52. 74. 118. 126. 157. 186

NG Cowans	10.1	1	44	2
IT Botham	11	2	41	1
PJW Allott	11	0	47	1
PH Edmonds	11	2	33	1
P Willey	9	1	31	1
GA Gooch	2	0	10	1

Australia

ENGLAND

GA Gooch	b McDermott	115
RT Robinson	c & b O'Donnell	26
DI Gower*	c Phillips b O'Donnell	0
AJ Lamb	b Thomson	25
IT Botham	c Wellham b Lawson	29
MW Gatting	c Lawson b McDermott	6
P Willey	c Phillips b Lawson	0
PR Downton+	not out	16
PH Edmonds	not out	6
PJW Allott		
NG Cowans		
Extras	(0b, 2lb, 2w, 4nb)	8
	55 overs	
Total		**231**

FoW: 63, 69, 134, 193, 206, 208, 216

GF Lawson	11	0	53	2
CJ McDermott	11	0	56	2
SP O'Donnell	11	2	32	2
JR Thomson	11	0	47	1
GRJ Matthews	10	0	38	0
AR Border	1	0	3	0

AUSTRALIA

KC Wessels	c & b Willey	57
GM Wood	lbw b Cowans	5
DM Wellham	c & b Botham	7
AR Border*	not out	85
DC Boon	b Allott	13
WB Phillips+	c Gatting b Cowans	14
SP O'Donnell	b Botham	28
GRJ Matthews	not out	8
GF Lawson		
CJ McDermott		
JR Thomson		
Extras	(0b, 13lb, 2w, 1nb)	16
	54 overs	
Total		**233**

FoW: 10, 19, 116, 137, 157, 222

IT Botham	10	2	38	2
NG Cowans	11	2	42	2
PJW Allott	10	1	40	1
P Willey	11	1	38	1
PH Edmonds	10	0	48	0
GA Gooch	2	0	14	0

Australia

West Indies

No. 109: Texaco Trophy
VENUE: Lord's
DATE: 3rd June 1985
TOSS WON BY: England
RESULT: England won by 8 wickets

No. 110: One-Day Series
VENUE: Kingston (Jamaica)
DATE: 18th February 1986
TOSS WON BY: West Indies
RESULT: West Indies won by 6 wickets

AUSTRALIA

GM Wood	not out	114
AMJ Hilditch	lbw b Foster	4
GM Ritchie	c Gooch b Botham	15
AR Border*	b Gooch	44
DC Boon	c Gower b Willey	45
WB Phillips+	run out	10
SP O'Donnell	not out	0
GRJ Matthews		
GF Lawson		
CJ McDermott		
JR Thomson		
Extras	(2b, 13lb, 6w, 1nb)	22
	55 overs	
Total		**254**

FoW: 6, 47, 143, 228, 252

NG Cowans	8	2	22	0
NA Foster	11	0	55	1
IT Botham	8	1	27	1
PJW Allott	7	1	45	0
GA Gooch	11	0	46	1
P Willey	10	1	44	1

ENGLAND

GA Gooch	not out	117
RT Robinson	lbw b McDermott	7
DI Gower*	c Border b McDermott	102
AJ Lamb	not out	9
IT Botham		
MW Gatting		
P Willey		
PR Downton+		
NA Foster		
PJW Allott		
NG Cowans		
Extras	(2b, 9lb, 2w, 9nb)	22
	49 overs	
Total		**257**

FoW: 25, 227

GF Lawson	9	0	37	0
CJ McDermott	10	0	51	2
JR Thomson	8	1	50	0
SP O'Donnell	11	0	54	0
GRJ Matthews	10	0	49	0
AR Border	1	0	5	0

ENGLAND

GA Gooch	b Marshall	36
RT Robinson	b Patterson	0
DI Gower*	c Richards b Patterson	0
MW Gatting	b Marshall	10
AJ Lamb	c Greenidge b Marshall	30
P Willey	c Richardson b Marshall	26
PR Downton+	lbw b Garner	8
JE Emburey	b Garner	5
NA Foster	not out	5
JG Thomas	not out	0
LB Taylor		
Extras	(8b, 2lb, 4w, 11nb)	25
	46 overs	
Total		**145**

FoW: 2, 10, 47, 63, 125, 125, 137, 143

J Garner	10	0	18	2
BP Patterson	7	0	17	2
CA Walsh	9	0	42	0
MD Marshall	10	1	23	4
RA Harper	10	0	35	0

WEST INDIES

CG Greenidge	c Downton b Thomas	45
DL Haynes	c Downton b Foster	35
RB Richardson	lbw b Gooch	32
HA Gomes	st Downton b Willey	19
PJL Dujon+	not out	3
RA Harper	not out	1
IVA Richards*		
MD Marshall		
J Garner		
BP Patterson		
CA Walsh		
Extras	(4b, 2lb, 0w, 5nb)	11
	43.5 overs	
Total		**146**

FoW: 84, 89, 142, 142

LB Taylor	7	2	17	0
JG Thomas	8	1	35	1
NA Foster	10	1	44	1
JE Emburey	10	3	19	0
P Willey	6.5	0	25	1
GA Gooch	2	2	0	1

No. 111: One-Day Series
VENUE: Port-of-Spain (Trinidad)
DATE: 4th March 1986
TOSS WON BY: England
RESULT: England won by 5 wickets

WEST INDIES

DL Haynes	b Foster	53
CA Best	run out	10
RB Richardson	not out	79
IVA Richards*	c Foster b Botham	82
RA Harper	not out	0
HA Gomes		
TRO Payne+		
MD Marshall		
J Garner		
CA Walsh		
BP Patterson		
Extras	(0b, 4lb, 0w, 1nb)	5
	37 overs	
Total		**229**

FoW: 37, 106, 223

IT Botham	8	1	59	1
NA Foster	10	1	42	1
RM Ellison	8	0	57	0
JE Emburey	8	2	48	0
P Willey	3	0	19	0

ENGLAND

GA Gooch	not out	129
IT Botham	c Richards b Garner	8
WN Slack	c Payne b Walsh	34
AJ Lamb	b Garner	16
DI Gower*	run out	9
P Willey	c Richards b Garner	10
DM Smith	not out	10
PR Downton+		
RM Ellison		
JE Emburey		
NA Foster		
Extras	(1b, 7lb, 0w, 6nb)	14
	37 overs	
Total		**230**

FoW: 9, 98, 143, 170, 183

J Garner	9	1	62	3
BP Patterson	6	0	30	0
CA Walsh	9	0	49	1
MD Marshall	10	1	59	0
RA Harper	3	0	22	0

No. 112: One-Day Series
VENUE: Bridgetown (Barbados)
DATE: 19th March 1986
TOSS WON BY: England
RESULT: West Indies won by 135 runs

WEST INDIES

CG Greenidge	c Downton b Foster	31
DL Haynes	b Foster	28
RB Richardson	b Botham	62
IVA Richards*	c Foster b Emburey	62
PJL Dujon+	c Lamb b Emburey	23
RA Harper	not out	24
J Garner	b Emburey	3
MD Marshall	c & b Botham	9
MA Holding	not out	0
HA Gomes		
BP Patterson		
Extras	(4b, 0lb, 2w, 1nb)	7
	46 overs	
Total		**249**

FoW: 61, 64, 181, 195, 225, 239, 248

IT Botham	9	2	39	2
JG Thomas	7	1	50	0
NA Foster	9	0	39	3
P Willey	6	0	21	0
GA Gooch	6	1	41	0
JE Emburey	9	0	55	2

ENGLAND

GA Gooch	c Dujon b Garner	6
RT Robinson	c Richardson b Marshall	23
WN Slack	c Dujon b Holding	9
DI Gower*	lbw b Holding	0
AJ Lamb	c Marshall b Holding	18
IT Botham	c Garner b Marshall	14
P Willey	c Greenidge b Harper	9
PR Downton+	b Harper	0
JE Emburey	c Dujon b Patterson	15
NA Foster	not out	9
JG Thomas	c Richards b Patterson	0
Extras	(0b, 3lb, 3w, 5nb)	11
	39 overs	
Total		**114**

FoW: 18, 42, 42, 46, 69, 81, 82, 85, 113, 114

J Garner	6	2	6	1
BP Patterson	9	1	38	2
MD Marshall	6	2	14	3
MA Holding	10	1	29	2
RA Harper	8	1	24	2

West Indies

No. 113: One-Day Series
VENUE: Port-of-Spain (Trinidad)
DATE: 31st March 1986
TOSS WON BY: West Indies
RESULT: West Indies won by 8 wickets

ENGLAND

GA Gooch	c Richards b Marshall	10
RT Robinson	b Marshall	55
DI Gower*	b Walsh	20
AJ Lamb	c Dujon b Walsh	16
IT Botham	c Harper b Garner	29
P Willey	c Greenidge b Marshall	6
PR Downton+	c Greenidge b Marshall	12
RM Ellison	b Garner	5
JE Emburey	not out	2
PH Edmonds	b Garner	0
NA Foster		
Extras	(1b, 4lb, 2w, 3nb)	10
	47 overs	
Total		**165**

FoW: 15, 49, 88, 126, 138, 154, 161, 165, 165

MD Marshall	9	0	37	4
J Garner	9	1	22	3
MA Holding	9	1	32	0
CA Walsh	10	0	25	2
RA Harper	10	0	44	0

WEST INDIES

CG Greenidge	b Foster	0
DL Haynes	not out	77
RB Richardson	c Gooch b Emburey	31
IVA Richards*	not out	50
HA Gomes		
PJL Dujon+		
RA Harper		
MD Marshall		
MA Holding		
J Garner		
CA Walsh		
Extras	(0b, 7lb, 1w, 0nb)	8
	38.2 overs	
Total		**166**

FoW: 0, 75

NA Foster	6	1	27	1
RM Ellison	7	0	30	0
IT Botham	5	0	24	0
PH Edmonds	10	1	38	0
JE Emburey	10	2	31	1
DI Gower	0.2	0	9	0

India

No. 114: Texaco Trophy
VENUE: The Oval
DATE: 24th May 1986
TOSS WON BY: India
RESULT: India won by 9 wickets

ENGLAND

GA Gooch	c Azharuddin b Sharma	30
G Fowler	run out	20
MW Gatting	c Kapil Dev b Shastri	27
DI Gower*	c Kapil Dev b Shastri	0
AJ Lamb	c Kapil Dev b Maninder	0
DR Pringle	c Azharuddin b Sharma	28
PR Downton+	c Azharuddin b Binny	4
RM Ellison	c & b Binny	10
JE Emburey	run out	20
GR Dilley	c Pandit b Sharma	6
LB Taylor	not out	1
Extras	(1b, 10lb, 3w, 2nb)	16
	55 overs	
Total		**162**

FoW: 54, 67, 67, 70, 102, 115, 131, 138, 151, 162

N Kapil Dev	11	1	32	0
RMH Binny	11	2	38	2
C Sharma	11	2	25	3
Maninder Singh	11	1	31	1
RJ Shastri	11	0	25	2

INDIA

K Srikkanth	c Downton b Dilley	0
SM Gavaskar	not out	65
M Azharuddin	not out	83
DB Vengsarkar		
SM Patil		
RJ Shastri		
N Kapil Dev*		
CS Pandit+		
C Sharma		
RMH Binny		
Maninder Singh		
Extras	(0b, 9lb, 4w, 2nb)	15
	47.2 overs	
Total		**163**

FoW: 0

GR Dilley	11	0	53	1
LB Taylor	7	1	30	0
DR Pringle	8.2	4	20	0
RM Ellison	10	1	36	0
JE Emburey	11	2	15	0

India

No. 115: Texaco Trophy		
VENUE: Old Trafford		
DATE: 26th May 1986		
TOSS WON BY: England		
RESULT: England won by 5 wickets		

INDIA

K Srikkanth	c Fowler b Emburey	67
SM Gavaskar	c Gooch b Ellison	4
M Azharuddin	c Gower b Edmonds	7
DB Vengsarkar	b Emburey	29
SM Patil	b Dilley	12
RJ Shastri	not out	62
N Kapil Dev*	c Downton b Dilley	51
C Sharma	not out	8
CS Pandit+		
RMH Binny		
Maninder Singh		
Extras	(5b, 4lb, 2w, 3nb)	14
	55 overs	
Total		**254**

FoW: 4, 49, 109, 117, 130, 234

GR Dilley	11	2	46	2
RM Ellison	11	0	55	1
DR Pringle	11	0	49	0
PH Edmonds	11	1	49	1
JE Emburey	11	1	46	2

ENGLAND

GA Gooch	lbw b Kapil Dev	10
G Fowler	c & b Binny	10
DI Gower*	b Binny	81
AJ Lamb	run out	45
MW Gatting	run out	39
DR Pringle	not out	49
PR Downton+	not out	4
PH Edmonds		
JE Emburey		
RM Ellison		
GR Dilley		
Extras	(0b, 13lb, 5w, 0nb)	18
	53.5 overs	
Total		**256**

FoW: 18, 27, 142, 157, 242

N Kapil Dev	10	0	41	1
RMH Binny	10	1	47	2
C Sharma	9.5	0	49	0
RJ Shastri	11	0	37	0
Maninder Singh	11	0	55	0
M Azharuddin	2	0	14	0

New Zealand

No. 116: Texaco Trophy (2)		
VENUE: Headingley		
DATE: 16th July 1986		
TOSS WON BY: New Zealand		
RESULT: New Zealand won by 47 runs		

NEW ZEALAND

BA Edgar	lbw b Foster	0
JG Wright	c Richards b Ellison	21
KR Rutherford	b Ellison	11
MD Crowe	b Ellison	9
JV Coney*	run out	27
JJ Crowe	c & b Foster	66
RJ Hadlee	lbw b Dilley	11
EJ Gray	not out	30
IDS Smith+	run out	4
JG Bracewell	not out	10
EJ Chatfield		
Extras	(0b, 18lb, 7w, 3nb)	28
	55 overs	
Total		**217**

FoW: 9, 36, 48, 54, 112, 138, 165, 187

GR Dilley	11	1	37	1
NA Foster	9	1	27	2
DR Pringle	9	0	42	0
RM Ellison	11	1	43	3
JE Emburey	11	0	30	0
GA Gooch	4	0	20	0

ENGLAND

GA Gooch	b Hadlee	18
MR Benson	c Chatfield b Bracewell	24
DI Gower	b Coney	18
AJ Lamb	run out	33
MW Gatting*	b Gray	19
DR Pringle	c Rutherford b Gray	28
CJ Richards+	run out	8
JE Emburey	lbw b Bracewell	0
RM Ellison	run out	12
NA Foster	b Hadlee	5
GR Dilley	not out	2
Extras	(0b, 1lb, 2w, 0nb)	3
	48.2 overs	
Total		**170**

FoW: 38, 48, 83, 103, 131, 143, 144, 162, 165, 170

RJ Hadlee	9.2	0	29	2
EJ Chatfield	8	2	24	0
JG Bracewell	11	2	27	2
MD Crowe	4	0	15	0
EJ Gray	11	1	55	2
JV Coney	5	0	19	1

	No. 117: Texaco Trophy (2)
	VENUE: Old Trafford
	DATE: 18th July 1986
	TOSS WON BY: England
	RESULT: England won by 6 wickets

	No. 118: B&H Challenge
	VENUE: Perth (WACA) Day/Night
	DATE: 1st January 1987
	TOSS WON BY: England
	RESULT: England won by 37 runs

NEW ZEALAND

JG Wright	c Pringle b Emburey	39
BA Edgar	lbw b Dilley	5
KR Rutherford	b Edmonds	63
MD Crowe	not out	93
JV Coney*	run out	1
JJ Crowe	b Pringle	48
RJ Hadlee	not out	18
EJ Gray		
IDS Smith+		
JG Bracewell		
W Watson		
Extras	(0b, 2lb, 14w, 1nb)	17
	55 overs	
Total		**284**

FoW: 16, 89, 133, 136, 249

GR Dilley	9	0	55	1
NA Foster	7	0	40	0
DR Pringle	10	2	63	1
GA Gooch	7	0	48	0
PH Edmonds	11	1	42	1
JE Emburey	11	1	34	1

ENGLAND

GA Gooch	c & b Coney	91
CWJ Athey	not out	142
DI Gower	c Wright b Coney	9
AJ Lamb	b Bracewell	28
MW Gatting*	b MD Crowe	7
DR Pringle	not out	0
CJ Richards+		
JE Emburey		
NA Foster		
PH Edmonds		
GR Dilley		
Extras	(0b, 5lb, 3w, 1nb)	9
	53.4 overs	
Total		**286**

FoW: 193, 219, 265, 274

RJ Hadlee	11	1	34	0
W Watson	11	1	46	0
MD Crowe	6	0	36	1
JG Bracewell	10.4	0	67	1
EJ Gray	4	0	39	0
JV Coney	11	0	59	2

ENGLAND

BC Broad	run out	76
CWJ Athey	c Zoehrer b O'Donnell	34
DI Gower	c Zoehrer b Whitney	6
AJ Lamb	c Zoehrer b Reid	66
IT Botham	c Zoehrer b Waugh	68
MW Gatting*	not out	5
CJ Richards+	c Border b Reid	4
PAJ de Freitas	not out	0
JE Emburey		
GC Small		
GR Dilley		
Extras	(2b, 6lb, 4w, 1nb)	13
	49 overs	
Total		**272**

FoW: 86, 95, 150, 256, 262, 271

SP Davis	8	1	48	0
MR Whitney	10	0	56	1
KH Macleay	9	0	51	0
BA Reid	10	1	46	2
SP O'Donnell	7	0	39	1
SR Waugh	5	0	24	1

AUSTRALIA

GR Marsh	b Botham	28
DC Boon	c Emburey b de Freitas	1
DM Jones	c Gower b Dilley	104
AR Border*	b Emburey	26
SR Waugh	c Richards b Small	16
SP O'Donnell	run out	0
KH Macleay	c Emburey b Dilley	21
TJ Zoehrer+	c Botham b de Freitas	1
MR Whitney	run out	6
BA Reid	b de Freitas	10
SP Davis	not out	1
Extras	(0b, 7lb, 10w, 4nb)	21
	48.2 overs	
Total		**235**

FoW: 7, 50, 125, 149, 158, 210, 214, 217, 233, 235

PAJ de Freitas	9.2	0	42	3
GR Dilley	10	1	31	2
IT Botham	10	0	52	1
GC Small	9	0	62	1
JE Emburey	10	0	41	1

West Indies

	No. 119: B&H Challenge
	VENUE: Perth (WACA)
	DATE: 3rd January 1987
	TOSS WON BY: West Indies
	RESULT: England won by 19 runs

ENGLAND

BC Broad	c Garner b Marshall	0
CWJ Athey	c Richardson b Garner	1
DI Gower	c Dujon b Garner	11
AJ Lamb	c Harper b Marshall	71
MW Gatting*	c Garner b Walsh	15
IT Botham	c Greenidge b Harper	11
CJ Richards+	c Dujon b Garner	50
JE Emburey	c Harper b Garner	18
PH Edmonds	not out	16
GR Dilley	c & b Garner	1
GC Small	not out	8
Extras	(0b, 10lb, 8w, 8nb)	26
	50 overs	
Total		**228**

FoW: 3, 10, 35, 67, 96, 156, 194, 209, 211

MD Marshall	10	1	30	2
J Garner	10	0	47	5
MA Holding	10	0	33	0
CA Walsh	9	0	40	1
RA Harper	10	0	63	1
IVA Richards	1	0	5	0

WEST INDIES

CG Greenidge	b Small	20
DL Haynes	lbw b Small	4
RB Richardson	c Gatting b Botham	12
IVA Richards*	c Broad b Emburey	45
AL Logie	c Richards b Dilley	51
PJL Dujon+	b Dilley	36
RA Harper	run out	4
MD Marshall	b Dilley	7
MA Holding	c Edmonds b Dilley	7
J Garner	not out	4
CA Walsh	lbw b Emburey	0
Extras	(4b, 9lb, 4w, 2nb)	19
	48.2 overs	
Total		**209**

FoW: 9, 39, 51, 104, 178, 187, 187, 201, 208, 209

GR Dilley	10	0	46	4
GC Small	10	1	37	2
IT Botham	10	1	29	1
PH Edmonds	9	1	53	0
JE Emburey	9.2	0	31	2

Pakistan

	No. 120: B&H Challenge
	VENUE: Perth (WACA) Day/Night
	DATE: 5th January 1987
	TOSS WON BY: Pakistan
	RESULT: England won by 3 wickets

PAKISTAN

Qasim Omar	b Botham	32
Shoaib Moh'd	c de Freitas b Emburey	66
Rameez Raja	run out	15
Javed Miandad	c Athey b Emburey	59
Imran Khan*	c Gower b de Freitas	23
Manzoor Elahi	not out	9
Wasim Akram	not out	1
Asif Mujtaba		
Salim Yousuf+		
Mudassar Nazar		
Salim Jaffer		
Extras	(0b, 15lb, 1w, 8nb)	24
	50 overs	
Total		**229**

FoW: 61, 98, 156, 198, 225

PAJ de Freitas	9	1	24	1
GC Small	10	0	41	0
NA Foster	4	0	23	0
IT Botham	10	1	37	1
MW Gatting	7	0	24	0
JE Emburey	10	0	65	2

ENGLAND

BC Broad	c Salim Yousuf b Imran	97
CWJ Athey	b Manzoor	42
DI Gower	c Shoaib b Mudassar	2
AJ Lamb	c Javed b Shoaib	32
IT Botham	c Rameez b Wasim	10
MW Gatting*	run out	7
CJ Richards+	run out	0
PAJ de Freitas	not out	13
JE Emburey	not out	11
NA Foster		
GC Small		
Extras	(1b, 13lb, 3w, 1nb)	18
	49.4 overs	
Total		**232**

FoW: 104, 108, 156, 184, 199, 204, 208

Wasim Akram	9.4	1	28	1
Salim Jaffer	10	2	43	0
Imran Khan	9	0	41	1
Mudassar Nazar	10	0	39	1
Asif Mujtaba	3	0	19	0
Manzoor Elahi	3	0	24	0
Shoaib Moh'd	5	0	24	1

	No. 121: B&H Challenge Grand Final
	VENUE: Perth (WACA)
	DATE: 7th January 1987
	TOSS WON BY: England
	RESULT: England won by 5 wickets

PAKISTAN

Qasim Omar	c Broad b Botham	21
Shoaib Moh'd	b Dilley	0
Rameez Raja	c Athey b Botham	22
Javed Miandad	not out	77
Asif Mujtaba	c Gower b Botham	7
Imran Khan*	c Richards b Gatting	5
Manzoor Elahi	c Gower b Small	20
Salim Yousuf+	c Athey b Small	0
Mudassar Nazar	c Gower b Emburey	0
Wasim Akram	c Gatting b Small	2
Salim Jaffer	not out	3
Extras	(0b, 5lb, 1w, 3nb)	9
	50 overs	
Total		**166**

FoW: 2, 36, 58, 76, 89, 127, 127, 128, 131

PAJ de Freitas	10	1	33	0
GR Dilley	10	0	23	1
IT Botham	10	2	29	3
GC Small	10	0	28	3
JE Emburey	8	0	34	1
MW Gatting	2	0	14	1

ENGLAND

BC Broad	c Salim Yousuf b Wasim	0
CWJ Athey	c Salim Yousuf b Imran	1
DI Gower	c Shoaib b Imran	31
AJ Lamb	c Salim Yousuf b Wasim	47
MW Gatting*	b Wasim	49
IT Botham	not out	23
CJ Richards+	not out	7
PAJ de Freitas		
JE Emburey		
GR Dilley		
GC Small		
Extras	(0b, 8lb, 1w, 0nb)	9
	40.1 overs	
Total		**167**

FoW: 1, 7, 47, 136, 145

Imran Khan	8	2	30	2
Wasim Akram	10	2	27	3
Salim Jaffer	10	1	43	0
Mudassar Nazar	5.1	0	22	0
Shoaib Moh'd	2	0	11	0
Manzoor Elahi	5	0	26	0

	No. 122: B&H World Series
	VENUE: Brisbane ('Gabba')
	DATE: 17th January 1987
	TOSS WON BY: England
	RESULT: England won by 6 wickets

WEST INDIES

CG Greenidge	lbw b de Freitas	0
DL Haynes	c de Freitas b Emburey	48
RB Richardson	c Botham b Dilley	15
IVA Richards*	b Dilley	0
AL Logie	c Lamb b Emburey	46
PJL Dujon+	b de Freitas	22
RA Harper	lbw b Small	2
MD Marshall	b Dilley	13
MA Holding	c Richards b Emburey	0
J Garner	c Richards b Dilley	1
CA Walsh	not out	3
Extras	(0b, 4lb, 0w, 0nb)	4
	46.3 overs	
Total		**154**

FoW: 1, 26, 26, 112, 120, 122, 147, 148, 151, 154

GR Dilley	8.3	1	23	4
PAJ de Freitas	9	2	17	2
IT Botham	10	1	46	0
GC Small	10	1	29	1
JE Emburey	9	0	35	3

ENGLAND

BC Broad	b Richards	49
CWJ Athey	c Dujon b Holding	14
DI Gower	c Garner b Harper	42
AJ Lamb	c (sub) b Harper	22
MW Gatting*	not out	3
IT Botham	not out	14
CJ Richards+		
PAJ de Freitas		
JE Emburey		
GC Small		
GR Dilley		
Extras	(0b, 2lb, 2w, 8nb)	12
	43.1 overs	
Total		**156**

FoW: 30, 91, 134, 140

MD Marshall	5	1	11	0
J Garner	4	0	17	0
MA Holding	6	0	33	1
CA Walsh	7.1	0	19	0
RA Harper	10	0	43	2
IVA Richards	10	1	27	1
RB Richardson	1	0	4	0

Australia

No. 123: B&H World Series
VENUE: Brisbane ('Gabba')
DATE: 18th January 1987
TOSS WON BY: Australia
RESULT: Australia won by 11 runs

AUSTRALIA

GR Marsh	lbw b Dilley	93
DM Wellham	c Emburey b Small	26
DM Jones	b Emburey	101
AR Border*	b Dilley	11
SR Waugh	not out	14
SP O'Donnell	not out	3
GRJ Matthews		
KH Macleay		
TJ Zoehrer+		
PL Taylor		
BA Reid		
Extras	(0b, 9lb, 3w, 1nb)	13
	50 overs	
Total		**261**

FoW: 48, 226, 234, 246

GR Dilley	10	2	40	2
PAJ de Freitas	10	2	41	0
GC Small	10	0	57	1
IT Botham	10	0	54	0
JE Emburey	10	0	60	1

ENGLAND

BC Broad	c Matthews b O'Donnell	15
CWJ Athey	c O'Donnell b Reid	111
DI Gower	b Waugh	15
AJ Lamb	c Marsh b Matthews	6
IT Botham	b O'Donnell	22
MW Gatting*	b Taylor	30
CJ Richards+	c O'Donnell b Reid	7
PAJ de Freitas	c Border b Waugh	6
JE Emburey	not out	24
GC Small	run out	2
GR Dilley	not out	0
Extras	(1b, 10lb, 0w, 1nb)	12
	50 overs	
Total		**250**

FoW: 48, 73, 92, 149, 197, 210, 218, 225, 250

KH Macleay	8	0	39	0
BA Reid	10	1	34	2
SP O'Donnell	10	0	59	2
SR Waugh	9	0	56	2
GRJ Matthews	10	0	34	1
PL Taylor	3	0	17	1

Australia

No. 124: B&H World Series
VENUE: Sydney (SCG) Day/Night
DATE: 22nd January 1987
TOSS WON BY: Australia
RESULT: England won by 3 wickets

AUSTRALIA

GR Marsh	c Richards b Edmonds	47
DM Wellham	c Athey b Emburey	97
DM Jones	c Athey b de Freitas	34
AR Border*	c Dilley b Edmonds	13
SR Waugh	c Athey b Dilley	10
GRJ Matthews	c de Freitas b Emburey	2
KH Macleay	b Dilley	12
TJ Zoehrer+	not out	9
PL Taylor	st Richards b Emburey	0
SP O'Donnell		
BA Reid		
Extras	(2b, 5lb, 0w, 2nb)	9
	50 overs	
Total		**233**

FoW: 109, 156, 189, 205, 208, 208, 230, 233

GR Dilley	9	2	28	2
PAJ de Freitas	10	0	46	1
MW Gatting	2	0	11	0
IT Botham	10	0	51	0
JE Emburey	9	0	42	3
PH Edmonds	10	0	48	2

ENGLAND

BC Broad	c Matthews b Taylor	45
CWJ Athey	c Zoehrer b Reid	2
DI Gower	c Wellham b O'Donnell	50
AJ Lamb	not out	77
MW Gatting*	b O'Donnell	1
IT Botham	b Waugh	27
JE Emburey	run out	4
CJ Richards+	c Waugh b O'Donnell	3
PAJ de Freitas	not out	6
PH Edmonds		
GR Dilley		
Extras	(0b, 16lb, 2w, 1nb)	19
	49.5 overs	
Total		**234**

FoW: 33, 51, 137, 143, 186, 191, 202

KH Macleay	4	0	22	0
BA Reid	9.5	3	44	1
PL Taylor	10	0	42	1
SR Waugh	5	0	22	1
GRJ Matthews	10	1	36	0
AR Border	3	0	13	0
SP O'Donnell	8	0	39	3

No. 125:	B&H World Series	
VENUE:	Adelaide	
DATE:	24th January 1987	
TOSS WON BY:	West Indies	
RESULT:	England won by 89 runs	

ENGLAND

BC Broad	st Dujon b Richards	55
CWJ Athey	c Marshall b Harper	64
DI Gower	c Haynes b Gray	29
IT Botham	c Logie b Walsh	7
AJ Lamb	not out	33
MW Gatting*	c Dujon b Walsh	3
CJ Richards+	b Marshall	18
JE Emburey	not out	16
PAJ de Freitas		
GC Small		
GR Dilley		
Extras	(4b, 13lb, 5w, 5nb)	27
	50 overs	
Total		**252**

FoW: 121, 148, 161, 177, 182, 220

MD Marshall	9	1	39	1
AH Gray	10	0	43	1
J Garner	9	1	31	0
CA Walsh	10	0	55	2
RA Harper	9	1	46	1
IVA Richards	3	0	21	1

WEST INDIES

CG Greenidge	lbw b de Freitas	3
DL Haynes	b Small	22
RB Richardson	c Lamb b de Freitas	3
IVA Richards*	c Broad b Botham	43
AL Logie	c Gower b Dilley	43
PJL Dujon+	c Dilley b Emburey	25
RA Harper	c Dilley b Emburey	4
MD Marshall	c Athey b Emburey	3
J Garner	c de Freitas b Emburey	0
AH Gray	not out	7
CA Walsh	b de Freitas	3
Extras	(0b, 0lb, 2w, 5nb)	7
	45.5 overs	
Total		**163**

FoW: 3, 15, 60, 92, 136, 141, 150, 150, 157, 163

GR Dilley	8	1	19	1
PAJ de Freitas	7.5	1	15	3
IT Botham	10	0	46	1
GC Small	10	1	46	1
JE Emburey	10	0	37	4

No. 126:	B&H World Series	
VENUE:	Adelaide	
DATE:	26th January 1987	
TOSS WON BY:	Australia	
RESULT:	Australia won by 33 runs	

AUSTRALIA

GR Marsh	c Emburey b de Freitas	8
DM Wellham	c Richards b de Freitas	9
DM Jones	c Richards b de Freitas	8
AR Border*	c Broad b de Freitas	91
SR Waugh	not out	83
SP O'Donnell	run out	6
GRJ Matthews	c Lamb b Dilley	0
TJ Zoehrer+	not out	5
KH Macleay		
PL Taylor		
SP Davis		
Extras	(1b, 8lb, 4w, 2nb)	15
	50 overs	
Total		**225**

FoW: 21, 24, 37, 201, 211, 219

GR Dilley	10	1	41	1
PAJ de Freitas	10	1	35	4
IT Botham	10	0	42	0
GC Small	10	0	42	0
JE Emburey	10	0	56	0

ENGLAND

BC Broad	c Border b Waugh	46
CWJ Athey	lbw b Davis	12
DI Gower	c Waugh b O'Donnell	21
MW Gatting*	b Taylor	46
AJ Lamb	run out	8
IT Botham	st Zoehrer b Taylor	18
CJ Richards+	b Waugh	2
JE Emburey	run out	17
PAJ de Freitas	c Jones b Taylor	8
GC Small	b Macleay	2
GR Dilley	not out	3
Extras	(0b, 8lb, 1w, 0nb)	9
	48.1 overs	
Total		**192**

FoW: 23, 55, 125, 138, 144, 152, 168, 184, 188, 192

SP Davis	8	0	18	1
KH Macleay	10	1	43	1
GRJ Matthews	4	0	21	0
SP O'Donnell	9	0	43	1
SR Waugh	10	1	30	2
PL Taylor	7.1	0	29	3

West Indies

No. 127: B&H World Series
VENUE: Melbourne (MCG) Day/Night
DATE: 30th January 1987
TOSS WON BY: England
RESULT: West Indies won by 6 wickets

ENGLAND

BC Broad	c Garner b Holding	33
CWJ Athey	lbw b Garner	2
DI Gower	b Marshall	8
AJ Lamb	run out	0
MW Gatting*	b Harper	13
IT Botham	c & b Holding	15
JE Emburey	c Harper b Garner	34
CJ Richards+	b Marshall	8
PAJ de Freitas	c Haynes b Garner	13
NA Foster	b Marshall	5
GC Small	not out	1
Extras	(0b, 3lb, 4w, 8nb)	15
	48.2 overs	
Total		**147**

FoW: 11, 27, 37, 61, 77, 84, 111, 136, 144, 147

MD Marshall	9.2	2	30	3
J Garner	9	1	37	3
MA Holding	8.3	2	19	2
CA Walsh	5	1	16	0
RA Harper	10	0	26	1
IVA Richards	6.3	1	16	0

WEST INDIES

DL Haynes	lbw b Foster	13
RB Richardson	c Richards b de Freitas	0
HA Gomes	run out	36
IVA Richards*	b Foster	58
AL Logie	not out	19
PJL Dujon+	not out	1
RA Harper		
MD Marshall		
MA Holding		
J Garner		
CA Walsh		
Extras	(0b, 10lb, 8w, 3nb)	21
	48.3 overs	
Total		**148**

FoW: 7, 49, 98, 146

PAJ de Freitas	10	2	15	1
GC Small	10	3	16	0
IT Botham	10	3	28	0
NA Foster	9	1	25	2
JE Emburey	9.3	1	54	0

Australia

No. 128: B&H World Series
VENUE: Melbourne (MCG)
DATE: 1st February 1987
TOSS WON BY: England
RESULT: Australia won by 109 runs

AUSTRALIA

GR Marsh	c Emburey b Foster	28
AR Border*	c Athey b Small	45
DM Jones	c Athey b Gatting	93
GM Ritchie	st French b Gatting	9
DM Wellham	c Lamb b Gatting	3
SR Waugh	not out	49
SP O'Donnell	not out	4
TJ Zoehrer+		
GRJ Matthews		
PL Taylor		
SP Davis		
Extras	(0b, 7lb, 9w, 1nb)	17
	50 overs	
Total		**248**

FoW: 61, 127, 144, 154, 223

PAJ de Freitas	8	2	37	0
GC Small	10	0	49	1
IT Botham	10	0	35	0
NA Foster	7	1	20	1
JE Emburey	6	0	41	0
MW Gatting	9	0	59	3

ENGLAND

BC Broad	b O'Donnell	2
IT Botham	c & b Matthews	45
DI Gower	c Taylor b Davis	11
AJ Lamb	run out	11
MW Gatting*	c Davis b Waugh	6
CWJ Athey	lbw b O'Donnell	29
JE Emburey	b Matthews	1
PAJ de Freitas	b Waugh	11
NA Foster	b Waugh	4
BN French+	not out	5
GC Small	c Matthews b Jones	4
Extras	(2b, 7lb, 1w, 0nb)	10
	47.3 overs	
Total		**139**

FoW: 4, 25, 52, 65, 86, 90, 117, 129, 130, 139

SP Davis	8	1	20	1
SP O'Donnell	9	2	33	2
GRJ Matthews	10	1	24	2
SR Waugh	10	0	26	3
PL Taylor	9	1	23	0
DM Jones	1.3	0	4	1

No. 129: B&H World Series
VENUE: Devonport
DATE: 3rd February 1987
TOSS WON BY: West Indies
RESULT: England won by 29 runs

No. 130: B&H World Series Final
VENUE: Melbourne (MCG)
DATE: 8th February 1987
TOSS WON BY: England
RESULT: England won by 6 wickets

ENGLAND

BC Broad	c Dujon b Walsh	76
IT Botham	c Richardson b Gray	8
DI Gower	c Payne b Marshall	3
AJ Lamb	c Logie b Harper	36
MW Gatting*	c Richardson b Gray	6
CWJ Athey	lbw b Marshall	3
JE Emburey	c Garner b Walsh	2
PAJ de Freitas	not out	15
NA Foster	run out	0
BN French+	b Marshall	0
GC Small	not out	6
Extras	(0b, 14lb, 3w, 5nb)	22
	50 overs	
Total		**177**

FoW: 23, 29, 103, 129, 133, 143, 158, 159, 160

MD Marshall	10	0	31	3
AH Gray	10	2	29	2
J Garner	10	0	30	0
CA Walsh	10	1	31	2
RA Harper	10	0	42	1

WEST INDIES

RB Richardson	c French b de Freitas	2
TRO Payne	c French b Botham	18
AL Logie	b Foster	31
HA Gomes	c Emburey b Botham	19
IVA Richards*	b Botham	1
PJL Dujon+	c Gatting b Emburey	34
RA Harper	c French b Small	4
MD Marshall	c Athey b de Freitas	27
J Garner	b Emburey	4
AH Gray	c & b Emburey	0
CA Walsh	not out	1
Extras	(0b, 5lb, 2w, 0nb)	7
	48 overs	
Total		**148**

FoW: 10, 25, 71, 73, 90, 95, 132, 147, 147, 148

PAJ de Freitas	9	1	20	2
GC Small	10	0	35	1
NA Foster	10	0	29	1
IT Botham	10	1	33	3
JE Emburey	9	0	26	3

AUSTRALIA

GR Marsh	c Gatting b de Freitas	2
TJ Zoehrer+	c Gatting b Dilley	0
DM Jones	b de Freitas	67
AR Border*	c French b Foster	42
GM Ritchie	run out	13
SR Waugh	c de Freitas b Emburey	1
SP O'Donnell	b Dilley	10
GRJ Matthews	b Dilley	8
PL Taylor	not out	3
BA Reid	not out	5
SP Davis		
Extras	(0b, 10lb, 3w, 7nb)	20
	44 overs	
Total		**171**

FoW: 3, 3, 106, 134, 137, 146, 161, 164

GR Dilley	9	2	32	3
PAJ de Freitas	9	0	32	2
IT Botham	9	0	26	0
NA Foster	9	0	42	1
JE Emburey	8	0	29	1

ENGLAND

BC Broad	c Jones b Matthews	12
IT Botham	c Marsh b Matthews	71
CWJ Athey	c & b Matthews	12
DI Gower	c Taylor b Reid	45
AJ Lamb	not out	15
MW Gatting*	not out	3
JE Emburey		
PAJ de Freitas		
NA Foster		
BN French+		
GR Dilley		
Extras	(5b, 3lb, 4w, 2nb)	14
	36 overs	
Total		**172**

FoW: 91, 93, 147, 159

SP Davis	4	0	17	0
SP O'Donnell	4	0	25	0
BA Reid	5	0	31	1
SR Waugh	8	1	36	0
GRJ Matthews	9	1	27	3
PL Taylor	5	0	24	0
DM Jones	1	0	4	0

Australia

India

ENGLAND

BC Broad	c O'Donnell b Matthews	53
IT Botham	c Ritchie b O'Donnell	25
CWJ Athey	b Matthews	16
DI Gower	c Wellham b Taylor	17
MW Gatting*	run out	7
AJ Lamb	c Zoehrer b O'Donnell	35
JE Emburey	c Zoehrer b Waugh	6
PAJ de Freitas	c Jones b Taylor	1
NA Foster	c Taylor b Davis	7
BN French+	not out	9
GR Dilley	not out	6
Extras	(0b, 4lb, 1w, 0nb)	5
	50 overs	
Total		**187**

FoW: 36, 73, 102, 120, 121, 143, 146, 170, 170

SP Davis	10	0	44	1
SP O'Donnell	10	1	37	2
SR Waugh	10	0	42	1
GRJ Matthews	10	1	31	2
PL Taylor	10	2	29	2

AUSTRALIA

GR Marsh	lbw b Botham	28
AR Border*	c French b Botham	27
DM Jones	c & b Emburey	13
GM Ritchie	c de Freitas b Botham	4
DM Wellham	c Gower b de Freitas	30
SR Waugh	run out	22
SP O'Donnell	not out	40
TJ Zoehrer+	lbw b de Freitas	0
GRJ Matthews	run out	3
PL Taylor	not out	3
SP Davis		
Extras	(1b, 6lb, 2w, 0nb)	9
	50 overs	
Total		**179**

FoW: 55, 70, 72, 80, 124, 135, 135, 151

GR Dilley	10	1	34	0
PAJ de Freitas	10	1	34	2
IT Botham	10	1	26	3
NA Foster	10	0	51	0
JE Emburey	10	2	27	1

ENGLAND

GA Gooch	b Maninder	31
BC Broad	st Viswanath b Shastri	57
RT Robinson	c Srikkanth b Shastri	34
NH Fairbrother	c Azharuddin b Shastri	14
JJ Whitaker	b Sharma	4
DJ Capel	run out	8
JE Emburey*	b Kapil Dev	25
PAJ de Freitas	not out	18
CJ Richards+	not out	14
NA Foster		
PH Edmonds		
Extras	(0b, 4lb, 2w, 0nb)	6
	50 overs	
Total		**211**

FoW: 60, 106, 134, 143, 145, 167, 184

N Kapil Dev	8	1	30	1
M Prabhakar	8	2	17	0
B Arun	4	0	32	0
G Sharma	10	0	38	1
RJ Shastri	10	1	47	3
Maninder Singh	10	0	43	1

INDIA

M Prabhakar	c Edmonds b Foster	4
K Srikkanth	c Fairbrother b Capel	56
R Lamba	c Whitaker b Edmonds	4
DB Vengsarkar	c Robinson b Edmonds	40
RJ Shastri	c Edmonds b Emburey	7
N Kapil Dev*	c Capel b Emburey	64
M Azharuddin	not out	24
S Viswanath+	b Emburey	3
B Arun	not out	7
G Sharma		
Maninder Singh		
Extras	(2b, 2lb, 1w, 0nb)	5
	48.5 overs	
Total		**214**

FoW: 22, 33, 86, 97, 146, 194, 200

PAJ de Freitas	10	3	33	0
NA Foster	9	1	46	1
DJ Capel	10	0	45	1
PH Edmonds	10	0	48	2
JE Emburey	9.5	0	38	3

No. 133: Sharjah Cup
VENUE: Sharjah
DATE: 7th April 1987
TOSS WON BY: England
RESULT: England won by 5 wickets

No. 134: Sharjah Cup
VENUE: Sharjah
DATE: 9th April 1987
TOSS WON BY: Australia
RESULT: England won by 11 runs

PAKISTAN

Mudassar Nazar	c Richards b de Freitas	3
Rameez Raja	run out	44
Ijaz Ahmed	run out	1
Javed Miandad	run out	60
Salim Malik	c Richards b Capel	1
Imran Khan*	c Richards b Foster	46
Manzoor Elahi	c & b Capel	3
Wasim Akram	c Fairbrother b Capel	10
Salim Yousuf+	b Emburey	8
Abdul Qadir	not out	13
Tauseef Ahmed	not out	3
Extras	(8b, 8lb, 4w, 5nb)	25
	50 overs	
Total		**217**

FoW: 10, 11, 77, 83, 175, 175, 188, 190, 211

PAJ de Freitas	10	0	47	1
GC Small	10	2	25	0
NA Foster	10	0	47	1
JE Emburey	10	1	44	1
DJ Capel	10	0	38	3

ENGLAND

GA Gooch	c Salim Yousuf b Imran	1
BC Broad	c Ijaz Ahmed b Mudassar	65
RT Robinson	c Manzoor b Qadir	83
JJ Whitaker	not out	44
NH Fairbrother	c Rameez b Qadir	6
DJ Capel	st Salim Yousuf b Qadir	2
JE Emburey*	not out	5
CJ Richards+		
PAJ de Freitas		
NA Foster		
GC Small		
Extras	(2b, 9lb, 3w, 0nb)	14
	47.2 overs	
Total		**220**

FoW: 3, 143, 166, 182, 188

Imran Khan	9	2	24	1
Wasim Akram	9.2	0	38	0
Abdul Qadir	10	0	47	3
Mudassar Nazar	10	0	41	1
Manzoor Elahi	6	0	39	0
Tauseef Ahmed	3	0	20	0

ENGLAND

GA Gooch	lbw b Waugh	86
BC Broad	b Taylor	44
RT Robinson	lbw b O'Donnell	5
NH Fairbrother	run out	32
RJ Bailey	c O'Donnell b Reid	11
DJ Capel	run out	17
JE Emburey*	not out	18
PAJ de Freitas	not out	1
CJ Richards+		
NA Foster		
GC Small		
Extras	(1b, 7lb, 6w, 2nb)	16
	50 overs	
Total		**230**

FoW: 118, 125, 167, 188, 193, 229

BA Reid	10	0	50	1
SP Davis	8	3	24	0
GRJ Matthews	7	0	31	0
SR Waugh	10	1	49	1
PL Taylor	7	0	41	1
SP O'Donnell	8	0	27	1

AUSTRALIA

GR Marsh	lbw b de Freitas	0
DC Boon	c Broad b Emburey	73
DM Wellham	c Robinson b Small	2
AR Border*	c Bailey b Emburey	84
SP O'Donnell	run out	6
SR Waugh	b Foster	14
GRJ Matthews	c Gooch b de Freitas	13
TJ Zoehrer+	run out	1
PL Taylor	not out	14
BA Reid	run out	2
SP Davis	not out	3
Extras	(0b, 6lb, 0w, 1nb)	7
	50 overs	
Total		**219**

FoW: 0, 7, 166, 166, 177, 195, 200, 200, 204

PAJ de Freitas	10	1	40	2
GC Small	9	1	23	1
DJ Capel	5	0	28	0
GA Gooch	6	0	34	0
JE Emburey	10	1	38	2
NA Foster	10	0	50	1

Pakistan | Pakistan

No. 135: Texaco Trophy
VENUE: The Oval
DATE: 21st May 1987
TOSS WON BY: England
RESULT: England won by 7 wickets

No. 136: Texaco Trophy
VENUE: Trent Bridge
DATE: 23rd May 1987
TOSS WON BY: Pakistan
RESULT: Pakistan won by 6 wickets

PAKISTAN

Mudassar Nazar	c de Freitas b Foster	45
Rameez Raja	run out	0
Mansoor Akhtar	c Gatting b Dilley	12
Javed Miandad	c Lamb b Dilley	113
Imran Khan*	c Broad b Foster	7
Wasim Akram	b Emburey	12
Manzoor Elahi	not out	18
Salim Malik	not out	8
Ijaz Ahmed		
Salim Yousuf+		
Tauseef Ahmed		
Extras	(1b, 8lb, 4w, 4nb)	17
	55 overs	
Total		**232**

FoW: 0, 18, 128, 169, 206, 208

GR Dilley	11	1	63	2
PAJ de Freitas	11	3	50	0
IT Botham	11	2	38	0
NA Foster	11	0	36	2
JE Emburey	11	1	36	1

ENGLAND

BC Broad	c (sub) b Wasim	99
CWJ Athey	c Salim Malik b Mudassar	33
MW Gatting*	retired hurt	2
AJ Lamb	c (sub) b Tauseef Ahmed	61
DI Gower	not out	15
IT Botham	not out	6
CJ Richards+		
JE Emburey		
PAJ de Freitas		
NA Foster		
GR Dilley		
Extras	(0b, 9lb, 2w, 6nb)	17
	53.1 overs	
Total		**233**

FoW: 76, 199, 218

Imran Khan	8	0	30	0
Manzoor Elahi	11	1	31	0
Wasim Akram	11	0	60	1
Mudassar Nazar	11	1	41	1
Tauseef Ahmed	10.1	0	47	1
Mansoor Akhtar	2	0	15	0

ENGLAND

BC Broad	c Salim Yousuf b Wasim	52
CWJ Athey	lbw b Imran	1
GA Gooch	lbw b Mohsin	9
AJ Lamb	c Salim Yousuf b Tauseef	26
DI Gower	b Mudassar	24
IT Botham	c Mohsin b Tauseef	0
CJ Richards+	c Manzoor b Mohsin	0
JE Emburey*	b Wasim	25
PAJ de Freitas	c Manzoor b Imran	3
NA Foster	run out	5
GR Dilley	not out	0
Extras	(0b, 8lb, 4w, 0nb)	12
	51.1 overs	
Total		**157**

FoW: 15, 45, 75, 117, 117, 117, 121, 144, 157, 157

Imran Khan	9	1	31	2
Mohsin Kamal	11	1	31	2
Wasim Akram	9.1	1	18	2
Mudassar Nazar	11	1	36	1
Tauseef Ahmed	11	1	33	2

PAKISTAN

Mudassar Nazar	lbw b Foster	12
Rameez Raja	c Gooch b de Freitas	13
Mansoor Akhtar	b Foster	21
Javed Miandad	not out	71
Salim Malik	run out	9
Imran Khan*	not out	21
Manzoor Elahi		
Wasim Akram		
Salim Yousuf+		
Tauseef Ahmed		
Mohsin Kamal		
Extras	(0b, 8lb, 2w, 1nb)	11
	52 overs	
Total		**158**

FoW: 23, 29, 64, 81

GR Dilley	9	4	16	0
PAJ de Freitas	11	2	30	1
NA Foster	11	1	25	2
IT Botham	7	0	34	0
JE Emburey	11	2	33	0
GA Gooch	3	0	12	0

Pakistan

No. 137:	Texaco Trophy
VENUE:	Edgbaston
DATE:	25th May 1987
TOSS WON BY:	England
RESULT:	England won by 1 wicket

PAKISTAN

Mudassar Nazar	lbw b Thomas	0
Rameez Raja	run out	46
Mansoor Akhtar	c Richards b Thomas	0
Javed Miandad	c Gower b Foster	68
Salim Malik	b Emburey	45
Imran Khan*	not out	24
Manzoor Elahi	b Emburey	0
Salim Yousuf+	run out	0
Wasim Akram	c Richards b Foster	0
Tauseef Ahmed	b Foster	0
Mohsin Kamal	not out	11
Extras	(2b, 13lb, 1w, 3nb)	19
	55 overs	
Total		**213**

FoW: 0, 0, 73, 168, 170, 170, 170, 170, 178

JG Thomas	11	0	59	2
PAJ de Freitas	11	1	30	0
IT Botham	11	1	31	0
NA Foster	11	1	29	3
JE Emburey	11	1	49	2

ENGLAND

BC Broad	c Javed b Mohsin	15
CWJ Athey	c Salim Yousuf b Imran	5
DI Gower	b Mudassar	11
AJ Lamb	c Mansoor b Mudassar	14
MW Gatting*	c Javed b Mohsin	41
IT Botham	c (sub) b Tauseef	24
CJ Richards+	run out	16
JE Emburey	run out	16
NA Foster	not out	14
PAJ de Freitas	b Imran	33
JG Thomas	not out	1
Extras	(0b, 14lb, 12w, 1nb)	27
	54.3 overs	
Total		**217**

FoW: 18, 31, 34, 75, 105, 140, 155, 167, 209

Imran Khan	11	0	43	2
Mohsin Kamal	11	0	47	2
Wasim Akram	10.3	2	34	0
Mudassar Nazar	11	2	17	2
Tauseef Ahmed	11	0	62	1

West Indies

No. 138:	World Cup
VENUE:	Gujranwala
DATE:	9th October 1987
TOSS WON BY:	England
RESULT:	England won by 2 wickets

WEST INDIES

DL Haynes	run out	19
CA Best	b de Freitas	5
RB Richardson	b Foster	53
IVA Richards*	b Foster	27
PJL Dujon+	run out	46
AL Logie	b Foster	49
RA Harper	b Small	24
CL Hooper	not out	1
WKM Benjamin	not out	7
CA Walsh		
BP Patterson		
Extras	(0b, 9lb, 0w, 3nb)	12
	50 overs	
Total		**243**

FoW: 8, 53, 105, 122, 205, 235, 235

PAJ de Freitas	10	2	31	1
NA Foster	10	0	53	3
JE Emburey	10	1	22	0
GC Small	10	0	45	1
DR Pringle	10	0	83	0

ENGLAND

GA Gooch	c Dujon b Hooper	47
BC Broad	c Dujon b Walsh	3
RT Robinson	run out	12
MW Gatting*	b Hooper	25
AJ Lamb	not out	67
DR Pringle	c Best b Hooper	12
PR Downton+	run out	3
JE Emburey	b Patterson	22
PAJ de Freitas	b Patterson	23
NA Foster	not out	9
GC Small		
Extras	(0b, 14lb, 6w, 3nb)	23
	49.3 overs	
Total		**246**

FoW: 14, 40, 98, 99, 123, 131, 162, 209

BP Patterson	10	0	49	2
CA Walsh	9.3	0	65	1
RA Harper	10	0	44	0
WKM Benjamin	10	2	32	0
CL Hooper	10	0	42	3

Pakistan

No. 139: World Cup
VENUE: Rawalpindi (Pindi CC)
DATE: 13th October 1987
TOSS WON BY: England
RESULT: Pakistan won by 18 runs

PAKISTAN

Mansoor Akhtar	c Downton b Foster	6
Rameez Raja	run out	15
Salim Malik	c Downton b de Freitas	65
Javed Miandad	lbw b de Freitas	23
Ijaz Ahmed	c Robinson b Small	59
Imran Khan*	b Small	22
Wasim Akram	b de Freitas	5
Salim Yousuf+	not out	16
Abdul Qadir	not out	12
Tauseef Ahmed		
Salim Jaffer		
Extras	(0b, 10lb, 3w, 3nb)	16
	50 overs	
Total		**239**

FoW: 13, 51, 112, 123, 202, 210, 210

PAJ de Freitas	10	1	42	3
NA Foster	10	1	35	1
GC Small	10	1	47	2
DR Pringle	10	0	54	0
JE Emburey	10	0	51	0

ENGLAND

GA Gooch	b Qadir	21
BC Broad	b Tauseef Ahmed	36
RT Robinson	b Qadir	33
MW Gatting*	b Salim Jaffer	43
AJ Lamb	lbw b Qadir	30
DR Pringle	run out	8
JE Emburey	run out	1
PR Downton+	c Salim Yousuf b Qadir	0
PAJ de Freitas	not out	3
NA Foster	run out	6
GC Small	lbw b Salim Jaffer	0
Extras	(6b, 26lb, 8w, 0nb)	40
	48.4 overs	
Total		**221**

FoW: 52, 92, 141, 186, 206, 207, 207, 213, 221, 221

Wasim Akram	9	0	32	0
Salim Jaffer	9.4	0	42	2
Tauseef Ahmed	10	0	39	1
Abdul Qadir	10	0	31	4
Salim Malik	7	0	29	0
Mansoor Akhtar	3	0	16	0

Sri Lanka

No. 140: World Cup
VENUE: Peshawar (Arbab Niaz)
DATE: 17th October 1987
TOSS WON BY: England
RESULT: England won by run rate

ENGLAND

GA Gooch	c & b Anurasiri	84
BC Broad	c de Silva b Ratnayeke	28
MW Gatting*	b Ratnayeke	58
AJ Lamb	c de Silva b Ratnayeke	76
JE Emburey	not out	30
CWJ Athey	not out	2
PR Downton+		
PAJ de Freitas		
DR Pringle		
EE Hemmings		
GC Small		
Extras	(0b, 13lb, 5w, 0nb)	18
	50 overs	
Total		**296**

FoW: 89, 142, 218, 287

JR Ratnayeke	9	0	62	2
VB John	10	0	44	0
PA de Silva	7	0	33	0
RJ Ratnayake	10	0	60	1
SD Anurasiri	8	0	44	1
A Ranatunga	6	0	40	0

SRI LANKA

(Revised Target 267 runs in 45 overs)

RS Mahanama	c Gooch b Pringle	11
DSBP Kuruppu+	c Hemmings b Emburey	13
AP Gurusinha	run out	1
RS Madugalle	b Hemmings	30
A Ranatunga	lbw b de Freitas	40
LRD Mendis*	run out	14
PA de Silva	c Emburey b Hemmings	6
JR Ratnayeke	c Broad b Emburey	1
RJ Ratnayake	not out	14
VB John	not out	8
SD Anurasiri		
Extras	(2b, 9lb, 6w, 3nb)	20
	45 overs	
Total		**158**

FoW: 31, 32, 37, 99, 105, 113, 119, 137

PAJ de Freitas	9	2	24	1
GC Small	7	0	27	0
DR Pringle	4	0	11	1
JE Emburey	10	1	26	2
EE Hemmings	10	1	31	2
GA Gooch	2	0	9	0
CWJ Athey	1	0	10	0
BC Broad	1	0	6	0
AJ Lamb	1	0	3	0

	Pakistan		West Indies
	No. 141: World Cup		No. 142: World Cup
	VENUE: Karachi (National Stadium)		VENUE: Jaipur
	DATE: 20th October 1987		DATE: 26th October 1987
	TOSS WON BY: Pakistan		TOSS WON BY: West Indies
	RESULT: Pakistan won by 7 wickets		RESULT: England won by 34 runs

ENGLAND

GA Gooch	c Wasim b Imran	16
RT Robinson	b Qadir	16
CWJ Athey	b Tauseef Ahmed	86
MW Gatting*	c Salim Yousuf b Qadir	60
AJ Lamb	b Imran	9
JE Emburey	lbw b Qadir	3
PR Downton+	c Salim Yousuf b Imran	6
PAJ de Freitas	c Salim Yousuf b Imran	13
NA Foster	not out	20
GC Small	run out	0
EE Hemmings	not out	4
Extras	(0b, 7lb, 4w, 0nb)	11
	50 overs	
Total		**244**

FoW: 26, 52, 187, 187, 192, 203, 206, 230, 230

Imran Khan	9	0	37	4
Wasim Akram	8	0	44	0
Tauseef Ahmed	10	0	46	1
Abdul Qadir	10	0	31	3
Salim Jaffer	8	0	44	0
Salim Malik	5	0	35	0

PAKISTAN

Rameez Raja	c Gooch b de Freitas	113
Mansoor Akhtar	run out	29
Salim Malik	c Athey b Emburey	88
Javed Miandad	not out	6
Ijaz Ahmed	not out	4
Imran Khan*		
Salim Yousuf+		
Wasim Akram		
Abdul Qadir		
Tauseef Ahmed		
Salim Jaffer		
Extras	(0b, 6lb, 1w, 0nb)	7
	49 overs	
Total		**247**

FoW: 61, 228, 243

PAJ de Freitas	8	2	41	1
NA Foster	10	0	51	0
EE Hemmings	10	1	40	1
JE Emburey	10	0	34	1
GC Small	9	0	63	0
GA Gooch	2	0	12	0

ENGLAND

GA Gooch	c Harper b Patterson	92
RT Robinson	b Patterson	13
CWJ Athey	c Patterson b Harper	21
MW Gatting*	lbw b Richards	25
AJ Lamb	c Richardson b Patterson	40
JE Emburey	not out	24
PAJ de Freitas	not out	16
PR Downton+		
NA Foster		
GC Small		
EE Hemmings		
Extras	(5b, 10lb, 22w, 1nb)	38
	50 overs	
Total		**269**

FoW: 35, 90, 154, 209, 250

BP Patterson	9	0	56	3
CA Walsh	10	0	24	0
WKM Benjamin	10	0	63	0
RA Harper	10	1	52	1
CL Hooper	3	0	27	0
IVA Richards	8	0	32	1

WEST INDIES

DL Haynes	c Athey b de Freitas	9
PV Simmons	b Emburey	25
RB Richardson	c Downton b Small	93
IVA Richards*	b Hemmings	51
AL Logie	c Hemmings b Emburey	22
CL Hooper	c Downton b de Freitas	8
PJL Dujon+	c Downton b Foster	1
RA Harper	run out	3
WKM Benjamin	c Foster b de Freitas	8
CA Walsh	b Hemmings	2
BP Patterson	not out	4
Extras	(0b, 7lb, 1w, 1nb)	9
	48.1 overs	
Total		**235**

FoW: 18, 65, 147, 182, 208, 211, 219, 221, 224, 235

PAJ de Freitas	9.1	2	28	3
NA Foster	10	0	52	1
JE Emburey	9	0	41	2
GC Small	10	0	61	1
EE Hemmings	10	0	46	2

Sri Lanka

No. 143: World Cup
VENUE: Poona
DATE: 30th October 1987
TOSS WON BY: Sri Lanka
RESULT: England won by 8 wickets

SRI LANKA

RS Mahanama	c Emburey b de Freitas	14
JR Ratnayeke	lbw b Small	7
AP Gurusinha+	run out	34
RL Dias	st Downton b Hemmings	80
LRD Mendis*	b de Freitas	7
RS Madugalle	c (sub) b Hemmings	22
PA de Silva	not out	23
ALF de Mel	c Lamb b Hemmings	0
S Jeganathan	not out	20
VB John		
SD Anurasiri		
Extras	(0b, 3lb, 3w, 5nb)	11
	50 overs	
Total		**218**

FoW: 23, 25, 113, 125, 170, 177, 180

PAJ de Freitas	10	2	46	2
GC Small	10	1	33	1
NA Foster	10	0	37	0
JE Emburey	10	1	42	0
EE Hemmings	10	0	57	3

ENGLAND

GA Gooch	c & b Jeganathan	61
RT Robinson	b Jeganathan	55
CWJ Athey	not out	40
MW Gatting*	not out	46
AJ Lamb		
PR Downton+		
JE Emburey		
PAJ de Freitas		
NA Foster		
GC Small		
EE Hemmings		
Extras	(1b, 13lb, 3w, 0nb)	17
	41.2 overs	
Total		**219**

FoW: 123, 132

JR Ratnayeke	8	1	37	0
VB John	6	2	19	0
ALF de Mel	4.2	0	34	0
S Jeganathan	10	0	45	2
SD Anurasiri	10	0	45	0
PA de Silva	3	0	25	0

India

No. 144: World Cup Semi-Final
VENUE: Bombay (Wankhede)
DATE: 5th November 1987
TOSS WON BY: India
RESULT: England won by 35 runs

ENGLAND

GA Gooch	c Srikkanth b Maninder	115
RT Robinson	st More b Maninder	13
CWJ Athey	c More b Sharma	4
MW Gatting*	b Maninder	56
AJ Lamb	not out	32
JE Emburey	lbw b Kapil Dev	6
PAJ de Freitas	b Kapil Dev	7
PR Downton+	not out	1
NA Foster		
GC Small		
EE Hemmings		
Extras	(1b, 18lb, 1w, 0nb)	20
	50 overs	
Total		**254**

FoW: 40, 79, 196, 203, 219, 231

N Kapil Dev	10	1	38	2
M Prabhakar	9	1	40	0
Maninder Singh	10	0	54	3
C Sharma	9	0	41	1
RJ Shastri	10	0	49	0
M Azharuddin	2	0	13	0

INDIA

K Srikkanth	b Foster	31
SM Gavaskar	b de Freitas	4
NS Sidhu	c Athey b Foster	22
M Azharuddin	lbw b Hemmings	64
CS Pandit	lbw b Foster	24
N Kapil Dev*	c Gatting b Hemmings	30
RJ Shastri	c Downton b Hemmings	21
KS More+	c & b Emburey	0
M Prabhakar	c Downton b Small	4
C Sharma	c Lamb b Hemmings	0
Maninder Singh	not out	0
Extras	(1b, 9lb, 6w, 3nb)	19
	45.3 overs	
Total		**219**

FoW: 7, 58, 73, 121, 168, 204, 205, 218, 219, 219

PAJ de Freitas	7	0	37	1
GC Small	6	0	22	1
JE Emburey	10	1	35	1
NA Foster	10	0	47	3
EE Hemmings	9.3	1	52	4
GA Gooch	3	0	16	0

No. 145: World Cup Final	No. 146: One-Day Series
VENUE: Calcutta	VENUE: Lahore (Gaddafi)
DATE: 8th November 1987	DATE: 18th November 1987
TOSS WON BY: Australia	TOSS WON BY: Pakistan
RESULT: Australia won by 7 runs	RESULT: England won by 2 wickets

AUSTRALIA

DC Boon	c Downton b Hemmings	75
GR Marsh	b Foster	24
DM Jones	c Athey b Hemmings	33
CJ McDermott	b Gooch	14
AR Border*	run out	31
MRJ Veletta	not out	45
SR Waugh	not out	5
SP O'Donnell		
GC Dyer+		
TBA May		
BA Reid		
Extras	(1b, 13lb, 5w, 7nb)	26
	50 overs	
Total		253

FoW: 75, 151, 166, 168, 241

PAJ de Freitas	6	1	34	0
GC Small	6	0	33	0
NA Foster	10	0	38	1
EE Hemmings	10	1	48	2
JE Emburey	10	0	44	0
GA Gooch	8	1	42	1

ENGLAND

GA Gooch	lbw b O'Donnell	35
RT Robinson	lbw b McDermott	0
CWJ Athey	run out	58
MW Gatting*	c Dyer b Border	41
AJ Lamb	b Waugh	45
PR Downton+	c O'Donnell b Border	9
JE Emburey	run out	10
PAJ de Freitas	c Reid b Waugh	17
NA Foster	not out	7
GC Small	not out	3
EE Hemmings		
Extras	(1b, 14lb, 2w, 4nb)	21
	50 overs	
Total		**246**

FoW: 1, 66, 135, 170, 188, 218, 220, 235

CJ McDermott	10	1	51	1
BA Reid	10	0	43	0
SR Waugh	9	0	37	2
SP O'Donnell	10	1	35	1
TBA May	4	0	27	0
AR Border	7	0	38	2

PAKISTAN

Rameez Raja	c Gatting b Capel	38
Shoaib Moh'd	c French b Foster	11
Salim Malik	run out	30
Ijaz Ahmed	c Gooch b Hemmings	17
Mudassar Nazar	c Fairbrother b Foster	10
Salim Yousuf+	c French b Hemmings	22
Manzoor Elahi	b Emburey	14
Wasim Akram	b Emburey	5
Abdul Qadir*	run out	7
Zahid Ahmed	c & b Emburey	0
Salim Jaffer	not out	2
Extras	(1b, 5lb, 2w, 2nb)	10
	41.3 overs	
Total		**166**

FoW: 25, 62, 96, 102, 132, 138, 154, 163, 163, 166

PAJ de Freitas	7	1	19	0
NA Foster	8	1	37	2
DJ Capel	9	0	43	1
JE Emburey	8.3	2	17	3
EE Hemmings	9	0	44	2

ENGLAND

GA Gooch	b Qadir	43
BC Broad	c Manzoor b Wasim	1
MW Gatting*	lbw b Qadir	16
CWJ Athey	lbw b Wasim	20
DJ Capel	run out	8
NH Fairbrother	b Zahid Ahmed	25
JE Emburey	c Ijaz Ahmed b Zahid Ahmed	4
PAJ de Freitas	not out	14
NA Foster	lbw b Wasim	0
BN French+	not out	7
EE Hemmings		
Extras	(13b, 10lb, 4w, 2nb)	29
	44.3 overs	
Total		**167**

FoW: 5, 61, 74, 89, 120, 127, 137, 140

Wasim Akram	9	0	25	3
Salim Jaffer	3	0	18	0
Mudassar Nazar	9	1	19	0
Manzoor Elahi	2	0	12	0
Abdul Qadir	8.3	2	32	2
Zahid Ahmed	9	1	24	2
Shoaib Moh'd	4	0	14	0

Pakistan

Pakistan

No. 147: One-Day Series
VENUE: Karachi (National Stadium)
DATE: 20th November 1987
TOSS WON BY: England
RESULT: England won by 23 runs

No. 148: One-Day Series
VENUE: Peshawar (Arbab Niaz)
DATE: 22nd November 1987
TOSS WON BY: England
RESULT: England won by 98 runs

ENGLAND

GA Gooch	st Zulqarnain b Qadir	142
BC Broad	c Manzoor b Qadir	22
MW Gatting*	run out	21
NH Fairbrother	b Zahid Ahmed	2
DJ Capel	not out	50
JE Emburey	c Manzoor b Qadir	1
PAJ de Freitas	b Mohsin	0
NA Foster	not out	5
CWJ Athey		
BN French+		
EE Hemmings		
Extras	(3b, 9lb, 6w, 2nb)	20
	44 overs	
Total		**263**

FoW: 70, 135, 140, 249, 251, 251

Wasim Akram	4	1	9	0
Mohsin Kamal	9	0	57	1
Manzoor Elahi	3	0	19	0
Zahid Ahmed	7	0	37	1
Asif Mujtaba	3	0	25	0
Abdul Qadir	8	0	30	3
Salim Malik	5	0	32	0
Shoaib Moh'd	5	0	42	0

PAKISTAN

Rameez Raja	obstructing field	99
Shoaib Moh'd	run out	37
Salim Malik	c Fairbrother b Foster	35
Manzoor Elahi	run out	17
Abdul Qadir*	c Broad b Foster	0
Ijaz Ahmed	c Athey b Emburey	26
Wasim Akram	c Foster b Emburey	9
Asif Mujtaba	b Capel	0
Zahid Ahmed	not out	3
Zulqarnain+		
Mohsin Kamal		
Extras	(0b, 7lb, 7w, 0nb)	14
	44 overs	
Total		**240**

FoW: 77, 138, 172, 172, 214, 228, 230, 240

PAJ de Freitas	9	1	35	0
NA Foster	9	0	47	2
DJ Capel	8	1	41	1
EE Hemmings	9	0	45	0
JE Emburey	9	0	65	2

ENGLAND

GA Gooch	c Zulqarnain b Mudassar	57
BC Broad	b Shakil	66
MW Gatting*	c Manzoor b Qadir	53
DJ Capel	st Zulqarnain b Tauseef Ahmed	25
JE Emburey	run out	3
PAJ de Freitas	c Shoaib b Qadir	3
CWJ Athey	st Zulqarnain b Qadir	6
NH Fairbrother	run out	1
NA Foster	not out	2
RC Russell+	not out	2
NGB Cook		
Extras	(1b, 7lb, 5w, 5nb)	18
	45 overs	
Total		**236**

FoW: 101, 168, 214, 221, 221, 231, 232, 234

Mohsin Kamal	9	0	37	0
Shakil Khan	9	0	50	1
Mudassar Nazar	9	0	33	1
Tauseef Ahmed	9	0	59	1
Abdul Qadir	9	0	49	3

PAKISTAN

Rameez Raja	lbw b Foster	5
Shoaib Moh'd	retired hurt	6
Salim Malik	b Cook	52
Ijaz Ahmed	c Russell b Cook	15
Mudassar Nazar	b Capel	1
Manzoor Elahi	c Gooch b Emburey	21
Abdul Qadir*	c Russell b de Freitas	21
Zulqarnain+	c Russell b de Freitas	0
Mohsin Kamal	b Foster	5
Tauseef Ahmed	not out	0
Shakil Khan	b Foster	0
Extras	(0b, 3lb, 3w, 6nb)	12
	31.5 overs	
Total		**138**

FoW: 11, 34, 43, 78, 122, 126, 138, 138, 138

PAJ de Freitas	7	0	31	2
NA Foster	6.5	0	20	3
NGB Cook	6	1	18	2
DJ Capel	9	0	44	1
JE Emburey	3	0	22	1

No. 149: One-Day Series		No. 150: Rothman's Cup
VENUE: Melbourne (MCG)		VENUE: Dunedin
DATE: 4th February 1988		DATE: 9th March 1988
TOSS WON BY: Australia		TOSS WON BY: New Zealand
RESULT: Australia won by 22 runs		RESULT: England won by 5 wickets

AUSTRALIA

DC Boon	c & b Capel	33
GR Marsh	run out	87
DM Jones	c (sub) b Emburey	30
MRJ Veletta	c Capel b Emburey	13
SR Waugh	run out	27
AR Border*	c Gatting b de Freitas	19
AIC Dodemaide	not out	7
PL Taylor	not out	1
GC Dyer+		
SP Davis		
MR Whitney		
Extras	(0b, 6lb, 5w, 7nb)	18
	48 overs	
Total		**235**

FoW: 70, 133, 168, 184, 222, 233

PAJ de Freitas	10	1	43	1
NV Radford	10	0	61	0
DJ Capel	8	1	30	1
PW Jarvis	10	0	42	0
JE Emburey	10	0	53	2

ENGLAND

BC Broad	c Dyer b Waugh	25
RT Robinson	c Dodemaide b Whitney	35
PAJ de Freitas	run out	21
CWJ Athey	c Border b Davis	4
NH Fairbrother	st Dyer b Taylor	22
MW Gatting*	c Border b Whitney	37
DJ Capel	c Taylor b Davis	18
JE Emburey	b Dodemaide	26
CJ Richards+	not out	14
NV Radford	not out	0
PW Jarvis		
Extras	(0b, 9lb, 1w, 1nb)	11
	48 overs	
Total		**213**

FoW: 58, 65, 82, 96, 123, 172, 175, 213

MR Whitney	10	1	37	2
AIC Dodemaide	10	1	35	1
SP Davis	10	0	55	2
SR Waugh	10	0	42	1
PL Taylor	8	0	35	1

NEW ZEALAND

RB Reid	c Broad b de Freitas	8
JG Wright*	c Moxon b Radford	70
MD Crowe	b Jarvis	18
MJ Greatbatch	c Capel b Emburey	28
KR Rutherford	c French b Capel	13
CM Kuggeleijn	c Gatting b de Freitas	34
JG Bracewell	run out	7
IDS Smith+	b Emburey	0
MC Snedden	b Emburey	7
W Watson	not out	0
EJ Chatfield	st French b Emburey	0
Extras	(0b, 13lb, 5w, 1nb)	19
	49.4 overs	
Total		**204**

FoW: 24, 50, 127, 140, 157, 188, 190, 204, 204, 204

PAJ de Freitas	10	1	26	2
NV Radford	10	0	47	1
DJ Capel	10	1	45	1
PW Jarvis	10	2	34	1
JE Emburey	9.4	0	39	4

ENGLAND

BC Broad	run out	33
MD Moxon	c Smith b Chatfield	6
RT Robinson	lbw b Snedden	17
MW Gatting*	c Kuggeleijn b Rutherford	42
NH Fairbrother	not out	50
DJ Capel	c Smith b Chatfield	48
JE Emburey	not out	2
PAJ de Freitas		
BN French+		
PW Jarvis		
NV Radford		
Extras	(0b, 6lb, 2w, 1nb)	9
	49.2 overs	
Total		**207**

FoW: 28, 53, 68, 114, 192

W Watson	10	2	46	0
EJ Chatfield	10	2	15	2
CM Kuggeleijn	7	0	31	0
MC Snedden	10	1	46	1
JG Bracewell	7.2	0	42	0
KR Rutherford	5	0	21	1

No. 151: Rothman's Cup
VENUE: Christchurch
DATE: 12nd March 1988
TOSS WON BY: England
RESULT England won by 6 wickets

No. 152: Rothman's Cup
VENUE: Napier
DATE: 16th March 1988
TOSS WON BY: New Zealand
RESULT: New Zealand won by 7 wickets

NEW ZEALAND

RB Reid	c Broad b Capel	8
JG Wright*	c de Freitas b Emburey	43
MD Crowe	c French b de Freitas	2
MJ Greatbatch	run out	15
KR Rutherford	run out	5
CM Kuggeleijn	b Emburey	40
JG Bracewell	run out	43
IDS Smith+	c Fairbrother b Emburey	19
MC Snedden	not out	1
W Watson	not out	2
EJ Chatfield		
Extras	(0b, 5lb, 3w, 0nb)	8
	45 overs	
Total		**186**

FoW: 24, 26, 53, 68, 86, 149, 183, 183

PAJ de Freitas	9	0	53	1
DJ Capel	9	3	27	1
PW Jarvis	9	0	33	0
NV Radford	9	0	30	0
JE Emburey	9	1	38	3

ENGLAND

BC Broad	c Rutherford b Snedden	56
MD Moxon	c Kuggeleijn b Watson	17
RT Robinson	c Chatfield b Rutherford	44
MW Gatting*	b Watson	33
NH Fairbrother	not out	25
DJ Capel	not out	6
JE Emburey		
PAJ de Freitas		
BN French+		
PW Jarvis		
NV Radford		
Extras	(0b, 4lb, 3w, 0nb)	7
	42.5 overs	
Total		**188**

FoW: 37, 112, 151, 167

W Watson	9	1	31	2
EJ Chatfield	7	0	32	0
JG Bracewell	5	0	28	0
MC Snedden	9	0	33	1
CM Kuggeleijn	6	0	31	0
KR Rutherford	6.5	0	29	1

ENGLAND

BC Broad	b Snedden	106
CWJ Athey	run out	0
RT Robinson	c Smith b Snedden	36
PAJ de Freitas	c Kuggeleijn b Rutherford	23
MW Gatting*	b Rutherford	6
NH Fairbrother	c & b Kuggeleijn	1
DJ Capel	c Morrison b Kuggeleijn	14
JE Emburey	c & b Snedden	15
PW Jarvis	not out	5
BN French+	b Chatfield	0
NV Radford	c Rutherford b Snedden	0
Extras	(0b, 10lb, 2w, 1nb)	13
	47.3 overs	
Total		**219**

FoW: 1, 80, 114, 137, 142, 186, 205, 216, 218, 219

DK Morrison	7	0	32	0
W Watson	5	0	24	0
EJ Chatfield	9	0	40	1
MC Snedden	8.3	0	34	4
KR Rutherford	10	0	39	2
CM Kuggeleijn	8	0	40	2

NEW ZEALAND

JG Wright*	c Robinson b Emburey	101
RH Vance	b de Freitas	5
AH Jones	b Jarvis	16
MJ Greatbatch	not out	64
KR Rutherford	not out	27
CM Kuggeleijn		
IDS Smith+		
MC Snedden		
DK Morrison		
W Watson		
EJ Chatfield		
Extras	(0b, 6lb, 4w, 0nb)	10
	46.3 overs	
Total		**223**

FoW: 24, 62, 172

PAJ de Freitas	10	2	30	1
DJ Capel	9	0	50	0
NV Radford	8	0	31	0
PW Jarvis	9.3	1	45	1
JE Emburey	7	0	47	1
MW Gatting	3	0	14	0

No. 153: Rothman's Cup	No. 154: Texaco Trophy
VENUE: Auckland	VENUE: Edgbaston
DATE: 19th March 1988	DATE: 19th May 1988
TOSS WON BY: New Zealand	TOSS WON BY: England
RESULT: New Zealand won by 4 wickets	RESULT: England won by 6 wickets

ENGLAND

BC Broad	b Snedden	12
MD Moxon	b Watson	19
PAJ de Freitas	c Crowe b Watson	6
RT Robinson	c Kuggeleijn b Rutherford	13
MW Gatting*	c Wright b Watson	48
NH Fairbrother	b Kuggeleijn	54
DJ Capel	b Chatfield	25
JE Embury	b Chatfield	11
PW Jarvis	run out	0
BN French+	c Greatbatch b Chatfield	2
NV Radford	not out	0
Extras	(0b, 12lb, 5w, 1nb)	18
	50 overs	
Total		**208**

FoW: 33, 33, 41, 71, 146, 179, 197, 197, 208, 208

RJ Hadlee	10	0	43	0
W Watson	10	0	36	3
MC Snedden	10	2	30	1
EJ Chatfield	10	2	31	3
CM Kuggeleijn	5	0	28	1
KR Rutherford	5	0	28	1

NEW ZEALAND

JG Wright*	b Radford	47
AH Jones	st Radford b Jarvis	90
MD Crowe	c French b Jarvis	13
MJ Greatbatch	c Radford b Jarvis	5
KR Rutherford	lbw b Jarvis	0
CM Kuggeleijn	b Capel	2
RJ Hadlee	not out	33
IDS Smith+	not out	1
MC Snedden		
W Watson		
EJ Chatfield		
Extras	(3b, 12lb, 5w, 0nb)	20
	49.2 overs	
Total		**211**

FoW: 86, 115, 129, 129, 138, 199

PAJ de Freitas	10	0	45	0
DJ Capel	10	0	42	1
NV Radford	10	2	32	1
PW Jarvis	9.2	1	33	4
JE Embury	10	0	44	0

WEST INDIES

CG Greenidge	b Small	18
PV Simmons	c Lamb b Dilley	22
RB Richardson	lbw b Pringle	11
IVA Richards*	c Embury b Small	13
AL Logie	c Downton b Small	51
CL Hooper	c Embury b Small	51
PJL Dujon+	run out	27
RA Harper	b Embury	4
MD Marshall	c Lamb b de Freitas	6
CEL Ambrose	b Embury	1
CA Walsh	not out	2
Extras	(0b, 2lb, 3w, 6nb)	11
	55 overs	
Total		**217**

FoW: 34, 50, 66, 72, 169, 180, 195, 209, 212, 217

PAJ de Freitas	11	2	45	1
GR Dilley	11	0	64	1
GC Small	11	0	31	4
DR Pringle	11	5	26	1
JE Embury	11	1	49	2

ENGLAND

GA Gooch	c Harper b Ambrose	43
BC Broad	c Greenidge b Marshall	35
MW Gatting*	not out	82
MA Lynch	run out	0
AJ Lamb	b Hooper	11
DR Pringle	not out	23
PR Downton+		
JE Embury		
PAJ de Freitas		
GC Small		
GR Dilley		
Extras	(2b, 10lb, 7w, 6nb)	25
	53 overs	
Total		**219**

FoW: 70, 119, 121, 153

CEL Ambrose	11	1	39	1
CA Walsh	11	1	50	0
IVA Richards	7	1	29	0
MD Marshall	11	1	32	1
RA Harper	7	0	33	0
CL Hooper	6	0	24	1

West Indies	**West Indies**

No. 155: Texaco Trophy
VENUE: Headingley
DATE: 21st May 1988
TOSS WON BY: West Indies
RESULT: England won by 47 runs

No. 156: Texaco Trophy
VENUE: Lord's
DATE: 23rd & 24th May 1988
TOSS WON BY: England
RESULT: England won by 7 wickets

ENGLAND

GA Gooch	c Greenidge b Simmons	32
BC Broad	c Dujon b Ambrose	13
MW Gatting*	c Richards b Marshall	18
MA Lynch	lbw b Marshall	2
AJ Lamb	c Dujon b Simmons	2
DR Pringle	c Dujon b Walsh	39
PR Downton+	c Dujon b Bishop	30
JE Emburey	c Ambrose b Bishop	8
PAJ de Freitas	not out	15
GC Small	not out	7
GR Dilley		
Extras	(3b, 1lb, 3w, 13nb)	20
	55 overs	
Total		**186**

FoW: 29, 64, 72, 80, 83, 149, 154, 169

CA Walsh	11	0	39	1
CEL Ambrose	7	2	19	1
MD Marshall	9	1	29	2
IR Bishop	11	1	32	2
PV Simmons	9	2	30	2
IVA Richards	8	0	33	0

WEST INDIES

CG Greenidge	c Downton b Small	21
PV Simmons	b de Freitas	1
RB Richardson	c Downton b Dilley	1
IVA Richards*	b Small	31
AL Logie	c Lynch b Dilley	8
CL Hooper	lbw b Pringle	12
PJL Dujon+	b Pringle	12
MD Marshall	c Downton b Gooch	1
CEL Ambrose	c Downton b Pringle	23
CA Walsh	b Emburey	18
IR Bishop	not out	2
Extras	(0b, 3lb, 3w, 3nb)	9
	46.3 overs	
Total		**139**

FoW: 2, 11, 38, 67, 67, 83, 84, 104, 132, 139

GR Dilley	11	0	45	2
PAJ de Freitas	9	2	29	1
GC Small	9	2	11	2
DR Pringle	11	0	30	3
GA Gooch	3	0	12	1
JE Emburey	3.3	0	9	1

WEST INDIES

CG Greenidge	c de Freitas b Emburey	39
DL Haynes	run out	10
RB Richardson	c Downton b Pringle	13
IVA Richards*	c Emburey b de Freitas	9
AL Logie	run out	0
CL Hooper	run out	12
PJL Dujon+	not out	30
MD Marshall	b Emburey	41
CA Walsh		
WKM Benjamin		
IR Bishop		
Extras	(2b, 10lb, 12w, 0nb)	24
	55 overs	
Total		**178**

FoW: 40, 75, 79, 79, 95, 111, 178

PAJ de Freitas	11	5	20	1
NV Radford	11	2	29	0
GC Small	10	1	34	0
DR Pringle	11	4	27	1
JE Emburey	10	1	53	2
GA Gooch	2	1	3	0

ENGLAND

GA Gooch	st Dujon b Hooper	28
BC Broad	b Bishop	34
MW Gatting*	not out	40
MA Lynch	b Bishop	6
AJ Lamb	not out	30
DR Pringle		
PR Downton+		
JE Emburey		
PAJ de Freitas		
GC Small		
NV Radford		
Extras	(6b, 17lb, 5w, 14nb)	42
	50 overs	
Total		**180**

FoW: 71, 108, 124

MD Marshall	9	2	21	0
CA Walsh	11	5	11	0
IR Bishop	11	1	33	2
WKM Benjamin	9	0	38	0
CL Hooper	10	0	54	1

No. 157: Texaco Trophy (2)
VENUE: The Oval
DATE: 4th September 1988
TOSS WON BY: England
RESULT: England won by 5 wickets

No. 158: Texaco Trophy
VENUE: Old Trafford
DATE: 25th May 1989
TOSS WON BY: England
RESULT: England won by 95 runs

SRI LANKA

DSBP Kuruppu+	lbw b Gooch	38
MAR Sam'sekera	b Small	10
PA de Silva	b Gooch	16
A Ranatunga	run out	37
LRD Mendis	b Small	60
RS Madugalle*	c Foster b Pringle	17
JR Ratnayeke	c Pringle b Small	19
HP Tillakaratne	not out	15
GF Labrooy	not out	10
MAWR Madurasinghe		
SD Anurasiri		
Extras	(1b, 10lb, 8w, 1nb)	20
	55 overs	
Total		**242**

FoW: 21, 54, 75, 144, 190, 193, 224

NA Foster	11	0	47	0
GC Small	11	1	44	3
GA Gooch	11	1	35	2
DR Pringle	11	0	46	1
VJ Marks	11	0	59	0

ENGLAND

GA Gooch*	c de Silva b Labrooy	7
RT Robinson	lbw b Ratnayeke	13
KJ Barnett	run out	84
AJ Lamb	c (sub) b Labrooy	66
RA Smith	c Kuruppu b Labrooy	9
RJ Bailey	not out	43
DR Pringle	not out	19
RC Russell+		
VJ Marks		
NA Foster		
GC Small		
Extras	(0b, 0lb, 3w, 1nb)	4
	52.4 overs	
Total		**245**

FoW: 9, 22, 140, 154, 213

JR Ratnayeke	9.4	3	37	1
GF Labrooy	10	0	40	3
MAR Samarasekera	11	0	52	0
A Ranatunga	11	0	42	0
SD Anurasiri	6	0	31	0
PA de Silva	2	0	19	0
MAWR Madurasinghe	3	0	24	0

ENGLAND

GA Gooch	c Jones b Border	52
DI Gower*	c Healy b Rackemann	36
MW Gatting	c Boon b Waugh	3
AJ Lamb	b Lawson	35
RA Smith	c & b Alderman	35
IT Botham	c Boon b Lawson	4
DR Pringle	lbw b Waugh	9
SJ Rhodes+	b Lawson	8
PAJ de Freitas	not out	17
JE Emburey	b Rackemann	10
NA Foster	not out	5
Extras	(0b, 12lb, 3w, 2nb)	17
	55 overs	
Total		**231**

FoW: 55, 70, 125, 161, 167, 179, 190, 203, 220

TM Alderman	11	2	38	1
GF Lawson	11	1	48	3
CG Rackemann	10	1	33	2
SR Waugh	11	1	45	2
TM Moody	8	0	37	0
AR Border	4	0	18	1

AUSTRALIA

GR Marsh	c Rhodes b Emburey	17
DC Boon	b de Freitas	5
DM Jones	c Rhodes b Foster	4
AR Border*	b Foster	4
SR Waugh	c Smith b de Freitas	35
TM Moody	b Emburey	24
MRJ Veletta	lbw b Pringle	17
IA Healy+	c Emburey b Foster	10
GF Lawson	c de Freitas b Emburey	0
CG Rackemann	b Botham	6
TM Alderman	not out	0
Extras	(1b, 9lb, 4w, 0nb)	14
	47.1 overs	
Total		**136**

FoW: 8, 13, 17, 64, 85, 115, 119, 120, 136, 136

NA Foster	10	3	29	3
PAJ de Freitas	8	3	19	2
DR Pringle	8	2	19	1
IT Botham	10.1	1	28	1
JE Emburey	11	0	31	3

No. 159: Texaco Trophy
VENUE: Nottingham (Trent Bridge)
DATE: 27th May 1989
TOSS WON BY: England
RESULT: Match tied

No. 160: Texaco Trophy
VENUE: Lord's
DATE: 29th May 1989
TOSS WON BY: England
RESULT: Australia won by 6 wickets

ENGLAND

GA Gooch	c Jones b Alderman	10
DI Gower*	b Waugh	28
MW Gatting	b May	37
AJ Lamb	not out	100
RA Smith	st Healy b May	3
IT Botham	run out	8
DR Pringle	not out	25
SJ Rhodes+		
PAJ de Freitas		
JE Emburey		
NA Foster		
Extras	(0b, 14lb, 1w, 0nb)	15
	55 overs	
Total		**226**

FoW: 30, 57, 119, 123, 138

TM Alderman	9	2	38	1
GF Lawson	11	0	47	0
CG Rackemann	11	1	37	0
SR Waugh	11	1	47	1
TBA May	11	1	35	2
TM Moody	2	0	8	0

AUSTRALIA

DC Boon	b Botham	28
GR Marsh	lbw b Emburey	34
DM Jones	b Emburey	29
AR Border*	c Rhodes b Pringle	39
SR Waugh	run out	43
TM Moody	run out	10
IA Healy+	not out	26
GF Lawson	c Gooch b Foster	1
TBA May	b de Freitas	2
CG Rackemann	not out	0
TM Alderman		
Extras	(1b, 6lb, 7w, 0nb)	14
	55 overs	
Total		**226**

FoW: 59, 81, 116, 153, 174, 205, 218, 225

NA Foster	11	2	44	1
PAJ de Freitas	11	0	48	1
DR Pringle	11	1	38	1
IT Botham	11	0	42	1
JE Emburey	11	0	47	2

ENGLAND

GA Gooch	b Alderman	136
DI Gower*	c Veletta b Moody	61
MW Gatting	run out	18
AJ Lamb	lbw b Alderman	0
RA Smith	b Rackemann	21
IT Botham	not out	25
PAJ de Freitas	c Rackemann b Alderman	0
DR Pringle	run out	0
SJ Rhodes+	not out	1
JE Emburey		
NA Foster		
Extras	(0b, 14lb, 2w, 0nb)	16
	55 overs	
Total		**278**

FoW: 123, 180, 182, 239, 266, 266, 268

TM Alderman	11	2	36	3
CG Rackemann	11	0	56	1
GF Lawson	11	0	48	0
SR Waugh	11	0	70	0
TBA May	6	0	33	0
TM Moody	5	0	21	1

AUSTRALIA

GR Marsh	not out	111
DC Boon	lbw b Foster	19
DM Jones	c Gower b Emburey	27
AR Border*	b Pringle	53
SR Waugh	c Gooch b Foster	35
TM Moody	not out	6
MRJ Veletta+		
GF Lawson		
TBA May		
CG Rackemann		
TM Alderman		
Extras	(0b, 18lb, 8w, 2nb)	28
	54.3 overs	
Total		**279**

FoW: 24, 84, 197, 268

PAJ de Freitas	11	1	50	0
NA Foster	11	0	57	2
DR Pringle	10.3	0	50	1
IT Botham	11	0	43	0
JE Emburey	11	0	61	1

Sri Lanka

No. 161: Nehru Cup
VENUE: Delhi (Feroz Shah Kotla)
DATE: 15th October 1989
TOSS WON BY: England
RESULT: England won by 5 wickets

SRI LANKA

RS Mahanama	run out		1
DSBP Kuruppu+	c Russell b Fraser		5
AP Gurusinha	c Lamb b Capel		19
PA de Silva	lbw b Hemmings		80
A Ranatunga*	b Gooch		7
MAR Sam'sekera	c Stewart b Gooch		24
JR Ratnayeke	c Gooch b de Freitas		6
GF Labrooy	lbw b de Freitas		0
EAR de Silva	b de Freitas		2
SD Anurasiri	not out		5
KIW Wij'wardene	b Fraser		3
Extras	(6b, 22lb, 10w, 3nb)		41
	48.3 overs		
Total			**193**

FoW: 1, 17, 42, 82, 154, 174, 180, 180, 186, 193

PAJ de Freitas	10	3	38	3
ARC Fraser	8.3	1	25	2
GC Small	6	0	26	0
DJ Capel	4	0	16	1
GA Gooch	10	2	26	2
EE Hemmings	10	1	34	1

ENGLAND

GA Gooch*	c PA de Silva b Labrooy		5
W Larkins	c PA de Silva b Ranatunga		19
RA Smith	not out		81
AJ Lamb	c de Silva b Wij'wardene		52
AJ Stewart	c Kuruppu b Ranatunga		4
DJ Capel	lbw b Wijegunawardene		4
RC Russell+	not out		10
PAJ de Freitas			
GC Small			
EE Hemmings			
ARC Fraser			
Extras	(1b, 8lb, 10w, 2nb)		21
	48.4 overs		
Total			**196**

FoW: 18, 34, 137, 157, 170

JR Ratnayeke	7	1	10	0
GF Labrooy	7	1	34	1
A Ranatunga	10	0	39	2
EAR de Silva	10	0	29	0
SD Anurasiri	3	0	22	0
PA de Silva	3	0	16	0
KIW Wijegunawardene	8.4	1	37	2

Australia

No. 162: Nehru Cup
VENUE: Hyderabad (I)
DATE: 19th October 1989
TOSS WON BY: Australia
RESULT: England won by 7 wickets

AUSTRALIA

DC Boon	c Gooch b Fraser		0
GR Marsh	c Lamb b Small		54
DM Jones	run out		50
PL Taylor	not out		36
AR Border*	not out		84
SR Waugh			
SP O'Donnell			
IA Healy+			
TBA May			
GF Lawson			
TM Alderman			
Extras	(0b, 6lb, 4w, 8nb)		18
	50 overs		
Total			**242**

FoW: 0, 108, 122

ARC Fraser	10	2	48	1
DR Pringle	10	3	42	0
GC Small	10	0	55	1
DJ Capel	8	0	39	0
GA Gooch	10	3	35	0
EE Hemmings	2	0	17	0

ENGLAND

GA Gooch*	lbw b Border		56
W Larkins	c Border b May		124
RA Smith	not out		24
AJ Lamb	b Lawson		23
AJ Stewart	not out		4
DJ Capel			
RC Russell+			
DR Pringle			
GC Small			
EE Hemmings			
ARC Fraser			
Extras	(1b, 9lb, 0w, 2nb)		12
	47.3 overs		
Total			**243**

FoW: 185, 191, 234

TM Alderman	7	1	28	0
GF Lawson	10	1	51	1
TBA May	10	0	55	1
SP O'Donnell	7.3	0	27	0
AR Border	10	0	43	1
PL Taylor	3	0	29	0

Pakistan | India

PAKISTAN

Shahid Saeed	b Capel	5
Shoaib Moh'd	c Cook b Capel	3
Ijaz Ahmed	b Cook	15
Javed Miandad	b Gooch	14
Salim Malik	b Small	42
Imran Khan*	st Russell b Hemmings	19
Salim Yousuf+	c Lamb b Gooch	6
Abdul Qadir	c Russell b Cook	13
Wasim Akram	lbw b Gooch	0
Mushtaq Ahmed	not out	9
Waqar Younis	not out	4
Extras	(5b, 8lb, 2w, 3nb)	18
	50 overs	
Total		**148**

FoW: 8, 16, 37, 53, 107, 111, 128, 128, 132

ARC Fraser	10	3	15	0
DJ Capel	8	2	16	2
GC Small	8	2	29	1
GA Gooch	10	4	19	3
NGB Cook	10	0	43	2
EE Hemmings	4	0	13	1

ENGLAND

GA Gooch*	b Wasim	7
W Larkins	c Javed b Wasim	0
RA Smith	c Javed b Mushtaq Ahmed	19
AJ Lamb	b Salim Malik	42
AJ Stewart	c Javed b Qadir	31
DJ Capel	run out	23
RC Russell+	not out	7
GC Small	not out	0
EE Hemmings		
ARC Fraser		
NGB Cook		
Extras	(8b, 4lb, 8w, 0nb)	20
	43.2 overs	
Total		**149**

FoW: 1, 21, 68, 92, 139, 148

Wasim Akram	10	1	32	2
Waqar Younis	10	1	30	0
Abdul Qadir	9.2	2	29	1
Mushtaq Ahmed	6	2	25	1
Salim Malik	2	0	9	1
Imran Khan	6	1	12	0

ENGLAND

GA Gooch*	c Azharuddin b C Sharma	21
W Larkins	lbw b AK Sharma	42
RA Smith	c Azharuddin b Prabhakar	0
AJ Lamb	c Srikkanth b C Sharma	91
AJ Stewart	run out	61
DJ Capel	b Kapil Dev	2
PAJ de Freitas	c Azharuddin b Kapil Dev	11
RC Russell+	not out	10
GC Small	not out	0
EE Hemmings		
ARC Fraser		
Extras	(0b, 7lb, 7w, 3nb)	17
	50 overs	
Total		**255**

FoW: 43, 48, 80, 210, 219, 239, 251

N Kapil Dev	10	0	56	2
M Prabhakar	10	0	50	1
C Sharma	10	0	78	2
Arsh Ayub	10	0	27	0
AK Sharma	10	1	37	1

INDIA

K Srikkanth*	st Russell b Hemmings	32
R Lamba	c Russell b Small	16
NS Sidhu	run out	61
C Sharma	not out	101
DB Vengsarkar	c Larkins b de Freitas	31
N Kapil Dev	not out	4
M Azharuddin		
KS More+		
M Prabhakar		
AK Sharma		
Arsh Ayub		
Extras	(0b, 6lb, 6w, 2nb)	14
	48.1 overs	
Total		**259**

FoW: 41, 65, 170, 251

ARC Fraser	10	2	31	0
PAJ de Freitas	10	0	66	1
EE Hemmings	10	0	51	1
GC Small	10	0	44	1
DJ Capel	3	0	24	0
GA Gooch	5.1	0	37	0

	No. 165: Nehru Cup	
	VENUE: Gwalior	
	DATE: 27th October 1989	
TOSS WON BY: West Indies		
	RESULT: West Indies won by 26 runs	

	No. 166: Nehru Cup Semi-Final	
	VENUE: Nagpur	
	DATE: 30th October 1989	
TOSS WON BY: Pakistan		
	RESULT: Pakistan won by 6 wickets	

WEST INDIES

DL Haynes	not out	138
PV Simmons	run out	13
RB Richardson	run out	44
IVA Richards*	c Hemmings b Small	16
AL Logie	c Stewart b Small	17
MD Marshall	c Smith b Small	16
RC Haynes	not out	0
PJL Dujon+		
WKM Benjamin		
CEL Ambrose		
CA Walsh		
Extras	(0b, 10lb, 9w, 2nb)	21
	50 overs	
Total		**265**

FoW: 31, 155, 188, 236, 264

ARC Fraser	10	1	47	0
PAJ de Freitas	10	1	42	0
DJ Capel	8	0	49	0
GC Small	10	0	39	3
EE Hemmings	7	0	44	0
GA Gooch	5	0	34	0

ENGLAND

GA Gooch*	c Dujon b Marshall	59
W Larkins	c (sub) b Marshall	29
RA Smith	c Dujon b Marshall	65
AJ Lamb	b Marshall	0
AJ Stewart	c Logie b Simmons	20
DJ Capel	b Benjamin	21
PAJ de Freitas	c (sub) b Walsh	7
RC Russell+	not out	8
GC Small	b Benjamin	4
EE Hemmings	not out	1
ARC Fraser		
Extras	(1b, 13lb, 11w, 0nb)	25
	50 overs	
Total		**239**

FoW: 58, 150, 150, 189, 191, 209, 229, 238

CEL Ambrose	10	0	33	0
WKM Benjamin	10	1	46	2
CA Walsh	10	0	41	1
MD Marshall	10	0	33	4
RC Haynes	4	0	25	0
IVA Richards	5	0	44	0
PV Simmons	1	0	3	1

ENGLAND

GA Gooch*	c (sub) b Waqar	35
W Larkins	c & b Akram Raza	25
RA Smith	b Qadir	55
AJ Stewart+	b Waqar	0
N Hussain	lbw b Qadir	2
AJ Lamb	c Aamer Malik b Qadir	6
DJ Capel	run out	20
DR Pringle	not out	21
PAJ de Freitas	not out	4
GC Small		
ARC Fraser		
Extras	(3b, 20lb, 3w, 0nb)	26
	30 overs	
Total		**194**

FoW: 44, 102, 103, 136, 144, 145, 184

Imran Khan	4	0	26	0
Wasim Akram	6	0	28	0
Akram Raza	5	0	28	1
Waqar Younis	6	1	40	2
Mushtaq Ahmed	3	0	19	0
Abdul Qadir	6	0	30	3

PAKISTAN

Rameez Raja	not out	85
Javed Miandad	b de Freitas	17
Ijaz Ahmed	c Smith b de Freitas	2
Imran Khan*	lbw b Small	15
Salim Malik	c Lamb b Fraser	66
Wasim Akram	not out	0
Aamer Malik+		
Abdul Qadir		
Akram Raza		
Mushtaq Ahmed		
Waqar Younis		
Extras	(0b, 10lb, 0w, 0nb)	10
	28.3 overs	
Total		**195**

FoW: 26, 32, 69, 191

ARC Fraser	6	0	58	1
PAJ de Freitas	6	0	40	2
DJ Capel	6	0	24	0
DR Pringle	5	0	33	0
GC Small	5.3	0	30	1

West Indies

No. 167: Cable & Wireless Cup
VENUE: Port-of-Spain (Trinidad)
DATE: 14th February 1990
TOSS WON BY: England
RESULT: No result

WEST INDIES

CG Greenidge	c Stewart b Capel	21
DL Haynes	c Russell b Lewis	25
RB Richardson	c Stewart b Fraser	51
CL Hooper	c Smith b Hemmings	17
CA Best	c & b Gooch	6
IVA Richards*	b Small	32
EA Moseley	c Lewis b Fraser	2
MD Marshall	b Small	9
PJL Dujon+	not out	15
IR Bishop	not out	18
CA Walsh		
Extras	(4b, 4lb, 3w, 1nb)	12
	50 overs	
Total		**208**

FoW: 49, 49, 89, 100, 155, 162, 172, 180

GC Small	10	1	41	2
ARC Fraser	10	1	37	2
DJ Capel	6	0	25	1
CC Lewis	7	1	30	1
EE Hemmings	9	0	41	1
GA Gooch	8	0	26	1

ENGLAND

GA Gooch*	not out	13
W Larkins	c Best b Marshall	2
RA Smith	not out	6
AJ Lamb		
AJ Stewart		
DJ Capel		
RC Russell+		
CC Lewis		
GC Small		
EE Hemmings		
ARC Fraser		
Extras	(0b, 1lb, 0w, 4nb)	5
	13 overs	
Total		**26**

FoW: 9

MD Marshall	6	1	12	1
IR Bishop	5	2	6	0
CA Walsh	1	0	1	0
EA Moseley	1	0	6	0

West Indies

No. 168: Cable & Wireless Cup
VENUE: Port-of-Spain (Trinidad)
DATE: 17th February 1990
TOSS WON BY: England
RESULT: No result

WEST INDIES

CG Greenidge	not out	8
DL Haynes	not out	4
RB Richardson		
CL Hooper		
CA Best		
IVA Richards*		
PJL Dujon+		
MD Marshall		
EA Moseley		
IR Bishop		
CA Walsh		
Extras	(0b, 1lb, 0w, 0nb)	1
	5.5 overs	
Total		**13**

GC Small	3	1	7	0
ARC Fraser	2.5	0	5	0

ENGLAND

GA Gooch*
W Larkins
RA Smith
AJ Lamb
AJ Stewart
DJ Capel
RC Russell+
CC Lewis
GC Small
EE Hemmings
ARC Fraser

No. 169: Cable & Wireless Cup
VENUE: Kingston (Jamaica)
DATE: 3rd March 1990
TOSS WON BY: England
RESULT: West Indies won by 3 wickets

No. 170: Cable & Wireless Cup
VENUE: Georgetown (Guyana)
DATE: 7th March 1990
TOSS WON BY: West Indies
RESULT: West Indies won by 6 wickets

ENGLAND

GA Gooch*	b Bishop	2
W Larkins	b Walsh	33
RA Smith	c Marshall b Hooper	43
AJ Lamb	b Bishop	66
AJ Stewart	c Dujon b Hooper	0
DJ Capel	c Dujon b Bishop	28
RC Russell+	b Marshall	2
PAJ de Freitas	not out	3
GC Small	b Bishop	0
EE Hemmings		
ARC Fraser		
Extras	(3b, 25lb, 6w, 3nb)	37
	50 overs	
Total		**214**

FoW: 20, 71, 117, 117, 185, 206, 212, 214

MD Marshall	10	1	39	1
IR Bishop	10	1	28	4
CA Walsh	6	0	38	1
EA Moseley	6	1	15	0
IVA Richards	9	0	32	0
CL Hooper	9	0	34	2

WEST INDIES

DL Haynes	c Smith b de Freitas	8
CA Best	b Small	4
RB Richardson	not out	108
CL Hooper	b Hemmings	20
IVA Richards*	c Small b Hemmings	25
KLT Arthurton	c Russell b Hemmings	0
PJL Dujon+	c Smith b Small	27
EA Moseley	c Gooch b Fraser	0
IR Bishop	not out	6
MD Marshall		
CA Walsh		
Extras	(12b, 4lb, 1w, 1nb)	18
	50 overs	
Total		**216**

FoW: 11, 23, 74, 158, 158, 204, 210

GC Small	9	0	37	2
PAJ de Freitas	10	2	29	1
DJ Capel	9	1	47	0
ARC Fraser	10	0	41	1
EE Hemmings	10	0	31	3
GA Gooch	2	0	15	0

ENGLAND

GA Gooch*	b Moseley	33
W Larkins	c Richards b Moseley	34
RA Smith	c Hooper b Walsh	18
AJ Lamb	c Dujon b Bishop	22
AJ Stewart	c Dujon b Walsh	0
DJ Capel	b Hooper	1
RC Russell+	b Bishop	28
PAJ de Freitas	run out	11
GC Small	not out	18
EE Hemmings	not out	0
ARC Fraser		
Extras	(1b, 8lb, 6w, 8nb)	23
	48 overs	
Total		**188**

FoW: 71, 88, 109, 109, 112, 132, 165, 181

IR Bishop	10	1	41	2
CA Walsh	10	1	33	2
EAE Baptiste	8	3	21	0
EA Moseley	10	0	52	2
CL Hooper	10	0	32	1

WEST INDIES

DL Haynes	c de Freitas b Hemmings	50
CA Best	run out	100
RB Richardson	c Russell b Capel	19
CL Hooper	not out	16
IVA Richards*	c de Freitas b Fraser	2
KLT Arthurton	not out	0
PJL Dujon+		
EAE Baptiste		
EA Moseley		
IR Bishop		
CA Walsh		
Extras	(0b, 2lb, 1w, 1nb)	4
	45.2 overs	
Total		**191**

FoW: 113, 155, 179, 182

PAJ de Freitas	7	1	32	0
GC Small	9.2	1	43	0
DJ Capel	9	2	39	1
ARC Fraser	10	1	42	1
EE Hemmings	10	1	33	1

West Indies

No. 171: Cable & Wireless Cup
VENUE: Georgetown (Guyana)
DATE: 15th March 1990
TOSS WON BY: West Indies
RESULT: West Indies won by 7 wickets

ENGLAND

GA Gooch*	b Hooper	42
W Larkins	c & b Bishop	1
RA Smith	c Dujon b Bishop	1
AJ Lamb	c Best b Moseley	9
AJ Stewart	b Hooper	13
RJ Bailey	c & b Ambrose	42
DJ Capel	c Dujon b Ambrose	7
RC Russell+	c Best b Ambrose	19
GC Small	c Dujon b Ambrose	0
EE Hemmings	not out	3
ARC Fraser	not out	3
Extras	(2b, 9lb, 13w, 2nb)	26
	49 overs	
Total		**166**

FoW: 13, 18, 46, 86, 88, 102, 149, 150, 160

IR Bishop	7	2	22	2
CEL Ambrose	9	1	18	4
EA Moseley	10	1	48	1
EAE Baptiste	10	1	31	0
CL Hooper	10	0	28	2
CA Best	3	0	8	0

WEST INDIES

CG Greenidge	lbw b Fraser	77
CB Lambert	b Hemmings	48
RB Richardson	c Capel b Small	7
CL Hooper	not out	19
CA Best	not out	7
KLT Arthurton		
PJL Dujon*+		
EAE Baptiste		
EA Moseley		
IR Bishop		
CEL Ambrose		
Extras	(0b, 2lb, 4w, 3nb)	9
	40.2 overs	
Total		**167**

FoW: 88, 105, 152

DJ Capel	9	1	41	0
GC Small	7	0	32	1
ARC Fraser	9.2	1	33	1
GA Gooch	5	1	22	0
EE Hemmings	10	1	37	1

West Indies

No. 172: Cable & Wireless Cup
VENUE: Bridgetown (Barbados)
DATE: 3rd April 1990
TOSS WON BY: West Indies
RESULT: West Indies won by 4 wickets

ENGLAND

DM Smith	b Moseley	5
W Larkins	hit wkt b Walsh	34
RA Smith	run out	69
AJ Lamb*	not out	55
N Hussain	not out	15
DJ Capel		
RC Russell+		
PAJ de Freitas		
CC Lewis		
GC Small		
EE Hemmings		
Extras	(2b, 8lb, 14w, 12nb)	36
	38 overs	
Total		**214**

FoW: 47, 98, 161

CEL Ambrose	9	2	31	0
CA Walsh	8	0	49	1
EA Moseley	7	0	43	1
MD Marshall	8	0	50	0
CL Hooper	6	0	31	0

WEST INDIES

CG Greenidge	c Russell b Small	6
DL Haynes*	c Hussain b Hemmings	45
RB Richardson	b Small	80
CA Best	c (sub) b Capel	51
AL Logie	c RA Smith b de Freitas	2
CL Hooper	c Larkins b Small	12
PJL Dujon+	not out	11
EA Moseley	not out	1
MD Marshall		
CEL Ambrose		
CA Walsh		
Extras	(0b, 6lb, 1w, 2nb)	9
	37.3 overs	
Total		**217**

FoW: 39, 78, 190, 193, 199, 212

GC Small	9	0	29	3
PAJ de Freitas	8.3	0	63	1
CC Lewis	5	0	35	0
DJ Capel	6	0	52	1
EE Hemmings	9	0	32	1

No. 173: Texaco Trophy
VENUE: Headingley
DATE: 23rd May 1990
TOSS WON BY: New Zealand
RESULT: New Zealand won by 4 wickets

No. 174: Texaco Trophy
VENUE: The Oval
DATE: 25th May 1990
TOSS WON BY: England
RESULT: England won by 6 wickets

ENGLAND

GA Gooch*	c Millmow b Pringle	55
DI Gower	c Smith b Hadlee	1
RA Smith	c Crowe b Hadlee	128
AJ Lamb	run out	18
AJ Stewart	lbw b Morrison	33
DR Pringle	not out	30
RC Russell+	c Crowe b Pringle	13
PAJ de Freitas	not out	1
CC Lewis		
GC Small		
EE Hemmings		
Extras	(0b, 10lb, 1w, 5nb)	16
	55 overs	
Total		**295**

FoW: 5, 118, 168, 225, 261, 274

RJ Hadlee	11	4	46	2
C Pringle	11	2	45	2
DK Morrison	11	0	70	1
JP Millmow	11	0	65	0
MW Priest	11	0	59	0

NEW ZEALAND

JG Wright*	c Stewart b Gooch	52
AH Jones	st Russell b Gooch	51
MD Crowe	c Russell b Lewis	46
MJ Greatbatch	not out	102
KR Rutherford	lbw b Lewis	0
RJ Hadlee	c Lamb b Lewis	12
MW Priest	c Gower b Small	2
IDS Smith+	not out	17
C Pringle		
DK Morrison		
JP Millmow		
Extras	(5b, 7lb, 3w, 1nb)	16
	54.5 overs	
Total		**298**

FoW: 97, 106, 224, 224, 254, 259

GC Small	11	1	43	1
PAJ de Freitas	10.5	0	70	0
DR Pringle	7	0	45	0
CC Lewis	11	0	54	3
EE Hemmings	11	0	51	0
GA Gooch	4	0	23	2

NEW ZEALAND

JG Wright*	c Small b Malcolm	15
AH Jones	run out	15
MD Crowe	c Russell b Lewis	7
MJ Greatbatch	c Smith b Malcolm	111
KR Rutherford	retired hurt	0
RJ Hadlee	retired hurt	9
MW Priest	c Smith b de Freitas	24
IDS Smith+	not out	25
C Pringle	b Small	1
JP Millmow		
DK Morrison		
Extras	(0b, 2lb, 3w, 0nb)	5
	55 overs	
Total		**212**

FoW: 25, 34, 53, 174, 202, 212

PAJ de Freitas	11	1	47	1
DE Malcolm	11	5	19	2
CC Lewis	11	1	51	1
GC Small	11	0	59	1
EE Hemmings	11	2	34	0

ENGLAND

GA Gooch*	not out	112
DI Gower	b Hadlee	4
RA Smith	c Smith b Hadlee	5
AJ Lamb	lbw b Pringle	4
AJ Stewart	c Morrison b Priest	28
RC Russell+	not out	47
CC Lewis		
PAJ de Freitas		
GC Small		
EE Hemmings		
DE Malcolm		
Extras	(0b, 7lb, 5w, 1nb)	13
	49.3 overs	
Total		**213**

FoW: 5, 15, 29, 104

RJ Hadlee	11	2	34	2
C Pringle	9.3	0	53	1
JP Millmow	9	1	47	0
DK Morrison	9	0	38	0
MW Priest	11	2	34	1

No. 175: Texaco Trophy
VENUE: Headingley
DATE: 18th July 1990
TOSS WON BY: India
RESULT: India won by 6 wickets

ENGLAND

GA Gooch*	c & b Shastri	45
MA Atherton	lbw b Prabhakar	7
DI Gower	b Kumble	50
AJ Lamb	c Prabhakar b Kapil Dev	56
RA Smith	c More b Kumble	6
RC Russell+	c Manjrekar b Kapil Dev	14
PAJ de Freitas	b Sharma	11
CC Lewis	lbw b Prabhakar	6
EE Hemmings	b Sharma	3
ARC Fraser	not out	4
DE Malcolm	c Kapil Dev b Prabhakar	4
Extras	(6b, 8lb, 9w, 0nb)	23
	54.3 overs	
Total		**229**

FoW: 22, 86, 134, 142, 186, 196, 211, 224, 229

N Kapil Dev	11	1	49	2
M Prabhakar	10.3	1	40	3
SK Sharma	11	1	57	2
RJ Shastri	11	0	40	1
A Kumble	11	2	29	2

INDIA

WV Raman	c Atherton b de Freitas	0
NS Sidhu	lbw b Lewis	39
SV Manjrekar	c Gower b Lewis	82
SR Tendulkar	b Malcolm	19
M Azharuddin*	not out	55
RJ Shastri	not out	23
N Kapil Dev		
M Prabhakar		
KS More+		
SK Sharma		
A Kumble		
Extras	(0b, 5lb, 9w, 1nb)	15
	53 overs	
Total		**233**

FoW: 1, 76, 115, 183

PAJ de Freitas	10	1	40	1
DE Malcolm	11	0	57	1
ARC Fraser	11	3	37	0
CC Lewis	10	0	58	2
EE Hemmings	11	0	36	0

No. 176: Texaco Trophy
VENUE: Trent Bridge
DATE: 20th July 1990
TOSS WON BY: India
RESULT: India won by 5 wickets

ENGLAND

GA Gooch*	b Prabhakar	7
MA Atherton	c More b Prabhakar	59
DI Gower	run out	25
AJ Lamb	run out	3
RA Smith	b Shastri	103
RC Russell+	c Azharuddin b Kapil Dev	50
PAJ de Freitas	c Vengsarkar b Sharma	1
CC Lewis	lbw b Prabhakar	7
GC Small	c Azharuddin b Kapil Dev	4
EE Hemmings	run out	0
ARC Fraser	not out	0
Extras	(1b, 12lb, 8w, 1nb)	22
	55 overs	
Total		**281**

FoW: 12, 47, 62, 173, 246, 254, 275, 280, 281, 281

N Kapil Dev	11	2	40	2
M Prabhakar	11	0	58	3
SK Sharma	10	0	50	1
RJ Shastri	11	0	52	1
A Kumble	11	1	58	0
SR Tendulkar	1	0	10	0

INDIA

RJ Shastri	c Atherton b Hemmings	33
NS Sidhu	b Small	23
SV Manjrekar	st Russell b Hemmings	59
DB Vengsarkar	b Lewis	54
M Azharuddin*	not out	63
SR Tendulkar	b Fraser	31
N Kapil Dev	not out	5
M Prabhakar		
KS More+		
SK Sharma		
A Kumble		
Extras	(0b, 5lb, 9w, 0nb)	14
	53 overs	
Total		**282**

FoW: 42, 69, 166, 186, 249

GC Small	10	0	73	1
PAJ de Freitas	11	0	59	0
ARC Fraser	11	1	38	1
EE Hemmings	11	1	53	2
CC Lewis	10	0	54	1

	No. 177: B&H World Series
VENUE:	Adelaide
DATE:	1st December 1990
TOSS WON BY:	England
RESULT:	New Zealand won by 7 runs

	No. 178: B&H World Series
VENUE:	Perth (WACA) Day/Night
DATE:	7th December 1990
TOSS WON BY:	New Zealand
RESULT:	England won by 4 wickets

NEW ZEALAND

JG Wright	c Russell b Malcolm	67
AH Jones	c Russell b Malcolm	6
MD Crowe*	c Gower b Hemmings	16
KR Rutherford	b Small	50
RT Latham	b Small	27
IDS Smith+	not out	10
CZ Harris	b Fraser	4
RG Petrie		
C Pringle		
DK Morrison		
W Watson		
Extras	(0b, 12lb, 5w, 2nb)	19
	40 overs	
Total		**199**

FoW: 16, 62, 114, 185, 188, 199

ARC Fraser	8	1	33	1
DE Malcolm	9	0	39	2
GC Small	7	1	25	2
CC Lewis	8	0	39	0
EE Hemmings	8	0	51	1

ENGLAND

DI Gower	c Crowe b Pringle	6
MA Atherton	c Smith b Morrison	33
RA Smith	c Crowe b Pringle	8
AJ Lamb*	b Watson	49
JE Morris	not out	63
RC Russell+	b Petrie	7
CC Lewis	c Morrison b Petrie	6
GC Small	c Wright b Morrison	5
EE Hemmings	b Pringle	3
ARC Fraser	run out	0
DE Malcolm	not out	3
Extras	(0b, 5lb, 4w, 0nb)	9
	40 overs	
Total		**192**

FoW: 6, 20, 91, 106, 126, 158, 173, 182, 188

C Pringle	8	1	36	3
RG Petrie	8	0	26	2
DK Morrison	8	0	38	2
W Watson	8	1	29	1
CZ Harris	8	0	58	0

NEW ZEALAND

JG Wright	c Lewis b Bicknell	6
AH Jones	run out	26
MD Crowe*	c Russell b Lewis	37
MJ Greatbatch	c Larkins b Small	19
KR Rutherford	b Fraser	11
IDS Smith+	c Lamb b Bicknell	15
CZ Harris	c Russell b Tufnell	0
RG Petrie	not out	14
C Pringle	c & b Small	2
DK Morrison	c Russell b Lewis	7
W Watson	b Lewis	1
Extras	(4b, 8lb, 4w, 4nb)	20
	49.2 overs	
Total		**158**

FoW: 16, 52, 94, 99, 126, 126, 126, 128, 154, 158

ARC Fraser	10	3	23	1
MP Bicknell	10	1	36	2
CC Lewis	9.2	1	26	3
GC Small	10	1	30	2
PCR Tufnell	10	1	31	1

ENGLAND

JE Morris	c Rutherford b Morrison	31
W Larkins	c Crowe b Morrison	44
RA Smith	c (sub) b Watson	0
AJ Lamb*	lbw b Watson	20
AJ Stewart	not out	29
RC Russell+	c Crowe b Pringle	5
CC Lewis	c Greatbatch b Pringle	0
GC Small	not out	9
MP Bicknell		
ARC Fraser		
PCR Tufnell		
Extras	(4b, 8lb, 10w, 1nb)	23
	43.5 overs	
Total		**161**

FoW: 72, 73, 100, 101, 115, 129

C Pringle	10	1	45	2
RG Petrie	10	0	39	0
DK Morrison	10	1	27	2
W Watson	10	1	26	2
CZ Harris	3.5	0	12	0

Australia

No. 179: B&H World Series
VENUE: Perth (WACA)
DATE: 9th December 1990
TOSS WON BY: England
RESULT: Australia won by 6 wickets

ENGLAND

JE Morris	b SR Waugh	7
W Larkins	b O'Donnell	38
RA Smith	c Healy b Rackemann	37
AJ Lamb*	c Alderman b O'Donnell	3
AJ Stewart	c Alderman b Matthews	41
CC Lewis	lbw b Matthews	2
RC Russell+	c O'Donnell b Alderman	13
GC Small	c Border b O'Donnell	5
MP Bicknell	not out	31
ARC Fraser	c ME Waugh b O'Donnell	4
PCR Tufnell		
Extras	(3b, 3lb, 2w, 3nb)	11
	50 overs	
Total		**192**

FoW: 31, 58, 62, 128, 136, 139, 154, 156, 192

TM Alderman	10	0	34	1
CG Rackemann	10	2	19	1
SR Waugh	10	1	52	1
SP O'Donnell	10	0	45	4
GRJ Matthews	10	0	36	2

AUSTRALIA

DC Boon	b Small	38
GR Marsh	c Lewis b Tufnell	37
DM Jones	not out	63
AR Border*	c Russell b Bicknell	24
ME Waugh	c Lewis b Bicknell	0
SR Waugh	not out	12
GRJ Matthews		
SP O'Donnell		
IA Healy+		
CG Rackemann		
TM Alderman		
Extras	(0b, 8lb, 10w, 1nb)	19
	41 overs	
Total		**193**

FoW: 56, 110, 155, 155

ARC Fraser	9	2	30	0
MP Bicknell	9	0	55	2
GC Small	4.3	1	14	1
CC Lewis	8	1	36	0
W Larkins	0.3	0	1	0
PCR Tufnell	10	1	49	1

New Zealand

No. 180: B&H World Series
VENUE: Sydney (SCG)
DATE: 13th December 1990
TOSS WON BY: New Zealand
RESULT: England won by 33 runs

ENGLAND

GA Gooch*	c Young b Petrie	3
W Larkins	c Watson b Pringle	8
RA Smith	c Latham b Petrie	4
AJ Lamb	b Morrison	72
JE Morris	run out	19
AJ Stewart+	run out	42
CC Lewis	c & b Bradburn	4
MP Bicknell	b Pringle	8
EE Hemmings	not out	8
ARC Fraser	lbw b Pringle	5
PCR Tufnell	b Pringle	2
Extras	(0b, 7lb, 10w, 2nb)	19
	46.4 overs	
Total		**194**

FoW: 7, 16, 23, 66, 143, 156, 179, 179, 188, 194

C Pringle	8.4	0	35	4
RG Petrie	8	2	25	2
W Watson	10	0	38	0
DK Morrison	10	0	45	1
GE Bradburn	10	0	44	1

NEW ZEALAND

MD Crowe*	lbw b Fraser	76
JG Wright	c Lamb b Lewis	23
GE Bradburn	b Lewis	2
KR Rutherford	b Hemmings	1
RT Latham	c Smith b Hemmings	10
BA Young+	c Morris b Bicknell	25
CZ Harris	c Stewart b Lewis	12
RG Petrie	c Stewart b Lewis	2
C Pringle	c Hemmings b Fraser	1
DK Morrison	not out	2
W Watson	run out	0
Extras	(0b, 5lb, 2w, 0nb)	7
	48.1 overs	
Total		**161**

FoW: 56, 64, 66, 84, 138, 151, 158, 159, 160, 161

MP Bicknell	10	0	39	1
ARC Fraser	9	1	21	2
CC Lewis	9.1	0	35	4
PCR Tufnell	10	1	27	0
EE Hemmings	10	1	34	2

New Zealand

ENGLAND

GA Gooch*	b Harris	48
W Larkins	c Young b Petrie	15
RA Smith	b Morrison	41
AJ Lamb	run out	10
JE Morris	c Young b Petrie	16
AJ Stewart+	not out	30
CC Lewis	run out	3
PAJ de Freitas	not out	27
ARC Fraser		
DE Malcolm		
PCR Tufnell		
Extras	(0b, 8lb, 5w, 0nb)	13
	50 overs	
Total		**203**

FoW: 27, 99, 115, 122, 143, 149

C Pringle	10	1	36	0
RG Petrie	10	1	32	2
DK Morrison	10	2	41	1
W Watson	10	0	40	0
CZ Harris	8	0	36	1
RT Latham	2	0	10	0

NEW ZEALAND

MD Crowe*	c Gooch b Malcolm	78
JG Wright	c Stewart b Tufnell	54
AH Jones	not out	41
RT Latham	not out	17
KR Rutherford		
BA Young+		
CZ Harris		
RG Petrie		
C Pringle		
DK Morrison		
W Watson		
Extras	(1b, 4lb, 4w, 5nb)	14
	44.3 overs	
Total		**204**

FoW: 109, 178

ARC Fraser	9	2	38	0
DE Malcolm	8	0	56	1
PAJ de Freitas	8	0	31	0
CC Lewis	9.3	1	31	0
PCR Tufnell	10	0	43	1

Australia

AUSTRALIA

DC Boon	lbw b Fraser	10
GR Marsh	c Larkins b Bicknell	82
DM Jones	c Tufnell b de Freitas	145
SR Waugh	not out	14
ME Waugh	c Tufnell b de Freitas	5
SP O'Donnell	c Morris b de Freitas	0
AR Border*	not out	4
GRJ Matthews		
IA Healy+		
CG Rackemann		
BA Reid		
Extras	(3b, 12lb, 7w, 1nb)	23
	50 overs	
Total		**283**

FoW: 24, 209, 261, 272, 272

ARC Fraser	10	1	47	1
MP Bicknell	10	0	64	1
PAJ de Freitas	10	0	57	3
EE Hemmings	10	0	57	0
PCR Tufnell	10	0	43	0

ENGLAND

GA Gooch*	b Matthews	41
W Larkins	b O'Donnell	19
AJ Lamb	c Border b Matthews	35
AJ Stewart+	run out	40
RA Smith	run out	6
JE Morris	c SR Waugh b Matthews	13
PAJ de Freitas	not out	49
MP Bicknell	b Rackemann	25
EE Hemmings	not out	3
ARC Fraser		
PCR Tufnell		
Extras	(1b, 8lb, 5w, 1nb)	15
	50 overs	
Total		**246**

FoW: 26, 104, 121, 141, 151, 174, 213

BA Reid	10	1	41	0
SP O'Donnell	10	2	43	1
CG Rackemann	10	0	41	1
SR Waugh	4	0	20	0
GRJ Matthews	10	0	54	3
ME Waugh	4	0	23	0
AR Border	1	0	9	0
DM Jones	1	0	6	0

Australia

No. 183: B&H World Series
VENUE: Sydney (SCG) Day/Night
DATE: 1st January 1991
TOSS WON BY: England
RESULT: Australia won by 68 runs

AUSTRALIA

GR Marsh	lbw b Tufnell	29
DC Boon	lbw b Fraser	4
DM Jones	c Small b Tufnell	25
AR Border*	c Small b Hemmings	4
ME Waugh	c Larkins b Fraser	62
SR Waugh	c Stewart b Tufnell	3
SP O'Donnell	not out	71
IA Healy+	c Atherton b Fraser	4
PL Taylor	not out	2
CG Rackemann		
TM Alderman		
Extras	(0b, 5lb, 11w, 1nb)	17
	50 overs	
Total		**221**

FoW: 15, 55, 72, 82, 93, 205, 218

ARC Fraser	10	2	28	3
GC Small	10	1	43	0
PAJ de Freitas	10	0	48	0
PCR Tufnell	10	2	40	3
EE Hemmings	10	0	57	1

ENGLAND

GA Gooch*	b O'Donnell	37
W Larkins	b Taylor	40
MA Atherton	c Healy b SR Waugh	8
AJ Stewart+	c SR Waugh b Border	18
RA Smith	b Taylor	1
JE Morris	c ME Waugh b Taylor	8
PAJ de Freitas	st Healy b Border	9
GC Small	st Healy b Border	15
EE Hemmings	run out	1
ARC Fraser	c Boon b Rackemann	4
PCR Tufnell	not out	0
Extras	(2b, 7lb, 1w, 2nb)	12
	45.5 overs	
Total		**153**

FoW: 65, 81, 103, 109, 117, 125, 135, 136, 153

TM Alderman	8	0	28	0
CG Rackemann	7.5	1	25	1
SP O'Donnell	5	0	15	1
SR Waugh	6	0	25	1
PL Taylor	10	2	27	3
AR Border	9	1	24	3

Australia

No. 184: B&H World Series
VENUE: Melbourne (MCG)
DATE: 10th January 1991
TOSS WON BY: Australia
RESULT: Australia won by 3 runs

AUSTRALIA

DC Boon	c Small b de Freitas	42
GR Marsh	c Stewart b Bicknell	7
DM Jones	c Stewart b Bicknell	2
AR Border*	c Larkins b Small	10
ME Waugh	run out	36
SR Waugh	not out	65
SP O'Donnell	c Bicknell b Gooch	7
IA Healy+	not out	50
PL Taylor		
CG Rackemann		
TM Alderman		
Extras	(0b, 1lb, 1w, 1nb)	3
	50 overs	
Total		**222**

FoW: 14, 16, 40, 81, 112, 127

ARC Fraser	10	2	39	0
MP Bicknell	9.5	0	33	2
GC Small	10	2	50	1
PCR Tufnell	3	0	23	0
PAJ de Freitas	7.1	0	37	1
GA Gooch	10	0	39	1

ENGLAND

GA Gooch*	c Healy b ME Waugh	37
DI Gower	lbw b Alderman	26
W Larkins	b Alderman	0
AJ Stewart+	b Taylor	55
RA Smith	b ME Waugh	7
JE Morris	c Healy b ME Waugh	10
PAJ de Freitas	c Border b ME Waugh	6
GC Small	b Taylor	0
MP Bicknell	c Alderman b SR Waugh	23
ARC Fraser	not out	38
PCR Tufnell	not out	5
Extras	(0b, 6lb, 5w, 1nb)	12
	50 overs	
Total		**219**

FoW: 39, 39, 93, 119, 139, 142, 146, 176

TM Alderman	9	2	31	2
CG Rackemann	7	0	52	0
SP O'Donnell	7	0	28	0
SR Waugh	7	1	25	1
ME Waugh	10	0	37	4
PL Taylor	10	1	40	2

New Zealand

No. 185: One-Day Series
VENUE: Christchurch
DATE: 9th February 1991
TOSS WON BY: England
RESULT: England won by 14 runs

ENGLAND

GA Gooch*	b Pringle	17
DI Gower	b Petrie	4
MA Atherton	b Watson	0
AJ Lamb	run out	61
RA Smith	c Jones b Pringle	65
AJ Stewart	c Wright b Pringle	40
RC Russell+	c (sub) b Petrie	10
PAJ de Freitas	not out	10
MP Bicknell	not out	0
EE Hemmings		
ARC Fraser		
Extras	(0b, 8lb, 12w, 3nb)	23
	50 overs	
Total		**230**

FoW: 6, 9, 46, 129, 192, 217, 220

RG Petrie	10	0	51	2
W Watson	10	2	15	1
C Pringle	10	0	54	3
GR Larsen	10	0	47	0
CZ Harris	8	0	46	0
KR Rutherford	2	0	9	0

NEW ZEALAND

MD Crowe*	c & b Bicknell	13
JG Wright	c Smith b de Freitas	27
AH Jones	run out	17
KR Rutherford	c Gooch b Bicknell	77
MJ Greatbatch	c Russell b Hemmings	0
IDS Smith+	run out	4
CZ Harris	c Russell b Bicknell	56
GR Larsen	not out	1
RG Petrie	c Gower b Fraser	0
C Pringle	not out	0
W Watson		
Extras	(2b, 14lb, 5w, 0nb)	21
	50 overs	
Total		**216**

FoW: 38, 50, 82, 86, 90, 212, 213, 215

ARC Fraser	10	0	28	1
MP Bicknell	10	2	55	3
PAJ de Freitas	10	3	36	1
GA Gooch	10	0	31	0
EE Hemmings	10	0	50	1

New Zealand

No. 186: One-Day Series
VENUE: Wellington
DATE: 13th February 1991
TOSS WON BY: England
RESULT: New Zealand won by 9 runs

NEW ZEALAND

RB Reid	c Russell b Fraser	9
JG Wright	b Fraser	9
MD Crowe*	c Russell b Bicknell	5
AH Jones	b Fraser	64
KR Rutherford	c & b Tufnell	19
CZ Harris	st Russell b Tufnell	9
IDS Smith+	b Bicknell	28
CL Cairns	c Smith b de Freitas	5
GR Larsen	not out	10
C Pringle	not out	18
W Watson		
Extras	(0b, 9lb, 11w, 0nb)	20
	49 overs	
Total		**196**

FoW: 20, 25, 43, 91, 109, 150, 158, 171

ARC Fraser	9	1	22	3
MP Bicknell	10	0	65	2
PAJ de Freitas	10	2	22	1
GA Gooch	10	2	33	0
PCR Tufnell	10	0	45	2

ENGLAND

GA Gooch*	c Wright b Cairns	41
MA Atherton	c Cairns b Harris	26
DI Gower	run out	11
AJ Lamb	b Cairns	33
RA Smith	b Pringle	38
AJ Stewart	c Watson b Harris	5
RC Russell+	c Cairns b Harris	2
PAJ de Freitas	run out	2
MP Bicknell	c Jones b Pringle	9
ARC Fraser	c Crowe b Pringle	5
PCR Tufnell	not out	0
Extras	(0b, 8lb, 7w, 0nb)	15
	48 overs	
Total		**187**

FoW: 73, 81, 93, 147, 160, 170, 173, 174, 179, 187

C Pringle	10	1	43	3
W Watson	10	1	34	0
CL Cairns	9	1	41	2
GR Larsen	9	1	28	0
CZ Harris	10	0	33	3

New Zealand

No. 187: One-Day Series
VENUE: Auckland
DATE: 16th February 1991
TOSS WON BY: England
RESULT: New Zealand won by 7 runs

NEW ZEALAND

MD Crowe*	b de Freitas	6
RB Reid	c Lamb b Tufnell	26
AH Jones	run out	64
KR Rutherford	lbw b Gooch	12
MJ Greatbatch	c Lamb b de Freitas	12
CZ Harris	b Fraser	39
IDS Smith+	not out	51
CL Cairns	run out	6
C Pringle	not out	0
GR Larsen		
W Watson		
Extras	(0b, 5lb, 3w, 0nb)	8
	50 overs	
Total		**224**

FoW: 7, 66, 98, 120, 135, 209, 215

ARC Fraser	10	3	31	1
PAJ de Freitas	10	0	51	2
GC Small	10	2	51	0
GA Gooch	10	0	40	1
PCR Tufnell	10	1	46	1

ENGLAND

GA Gooch*	b Larsen	47
MA Atherton	c Crowe b Harris	34
DI Gower	c Jones b Harris	13
AJ Lamb	c Smith b Cairns	42
RA Smith	b Cairns	35
AJ Stewart	c Smith b Cairns	3
PAJ de Freitas	c Crowe b Pringle	7
RC Russell+	b Cairns	13
GC Small	b Pringle	0
ARC Fraser	b Pringle	6
PCR Tufnell	not out	3
Extras	(0b, 10lb, 4w, 0nb)	14
	49.5 overs	
Total		**217**

FoW: 83, 91, 118, 171, 185, 194, 200, 203, 209, 217

C Pringle	9.5	0	43	3
W Watson	10	1	38	0
CL Cairns	10	0	55	4
GR Larsen	10	0	35	1
CZ Harris	10	1	36	2

West Indies

No. 188: Texaco Trophy
VENUE: Edgbaston
DATE: 23rd May 1991
TOSS WON BY: England
RESULT: England won by 1 wicket

WEST INDIES

CG Greenidge	c Russell b Botham	23
PV Simmons	c Gooch b Lewis	4
RB Richardson	c Illingworth b Botham	3
IVA Richards*	c Fairbrother b Gooch	30
CL Hooper	c Russell b Botham	10
AL Logie	c de Freitas b Botham	18
PJL Dujon+	c Lewis b Illingworth	5
MD Marshall	c Lewis b de Freitas	17
CEL Ambrose	not out	21
CA Walsh	not out	29
BP Patterson		
Extras	(1b, 5lb, 6w, 1nb)	13
	55 overs	
Total		**173**

FoW: 8, 16, 48, 78, 84, 98, 103, 121

PAJ de Freitas	11	3	22	1
CC Lewis	11	3	41	1
DR Pringle	7	0	22	0
IT Botham	11	2	45	4
GA Gooch	5	0	17	1
RK Illingworth	10	1	20	1

ENGLAND

GA Gooch*	lbw b Ambrose	0
MA Atherton	not out	69
GA Hick	c Richardson b Marshall	14
AJ Lamb	b Hooper	18
NH Fairbrother	c Dujon b Hooper	4
IT Botham	lbw b Walsh	8
DR Pringle	c Richardson b Walsh	1
RC Russell+	c Dujon b Patterson	1
PAJ de Freitas	c Richardson b Marshall	8
CC Lewis	c Richardson b Patterson	0
RK Illingworth	not out	9
Extras	(0b, 9lb, 18w, 16nb)	43
	49.4 overs	
Total		**175**

FoW: 1, 41, 80, 87, 123, 126, 134, 147, 152

CEL Ambrose	11	2	34	1
BP Patterson	11	2	38	2
MD Marshall	11	1	32	2
CA Walsh	11	0	34	2
PV Simmons	3	0	10	0
CL Hooper	2.4	0	18	2

West Indies

No. 189: Texaco Trophy
VENUE: Old Trafford
DATE: 25th May 1991
TOSS WON BY: West Indies
RESULT: England won by 9 runs

No. 190: Texaco Trophy
VENUE: Lord's
DATE: 27th May 1991
TOSS WON BY: England
RESULT: England won by 7 wickets

ENGLAND

GA Gooch*	b Hooper	54
MA Atherton	c (sub) b Ambrose	74
GA Hick	b Ambrose	29
AJ Lamb	c Dujon b Patterson	62
NH Fairbrother	not out	5
MR Ramprakash	not out	6
DR Pringle		
RC Russell+		
CC Lewis		
PAJ de Freitas		
RK Illingworth		
Extras	(4b, 16lb, 14w, 6nb)	40
	55 overs	
Total		**270**

FoW: 156, 156, 258, 260

CEL Ambrose	11	3	36	2
BP Patterson	10	1	39	1
CA Walsh	11	0	56	0
MD Marshall	10	0	45	0
PV Simmons	4	0	30	0
CL Hooper	9	0	44	1

WEST INDIES

PV Simmons	run out	28
PJL Dujon+	c de Freitas b Lewis	21
RB Richardson	c Russell b Gooch	13
CL Hooper	c (sub) b Lewis	48
IVA Richards*	lbw b Lewis	78
AL Logie	c Illingworth b Pringle	24
MD Marshall	c & b Pringle	22
CG Greenidge	run out	4
CEL Ambrose	not out	5
CA Walsh	not out	1
BP Patterson		
Extras	(0b, 4lb, 10w, 3nb)	17
	55 overs	
Total		**261**

FoW: 34, 61, 69, 190, 208, 250, 250, 256

PAJ de Freitas	11	3	50	0
CC Lewis	11	0	62	3
DR Pringle	11	2	52	2
RK Illingworth	11	1	42	0
GA Gooch	11	1	51	1

WEST INDIES

PV Simmons	c Russell b de Freitas	5
PJL Dujon+	b Lawrence	0
RB Richardson	c de Freitas b Illingworth	41
BC Lara	c & b Illingworth	23
IVA Richards*	c Illingworth b de Freitas	37
AL Logie	c & b Gooch	82
CL Hooper	c Fairbrother b Lawrence	26
MD Marshall	c de Freitas b Lawrence	13
CEL Ambrose	not out	6
CA Walsh	lbw b Lawrence	0
BP Patterson	not out	2
Extras	(1b, 9lb, 14w, 5nb)	29
	55 overs	
Total		**264**

FoW: 8, 8, 71, 91, 164, 227, 241, 258, 258

DV Lawrence	11	1	67	4
PAJ de Freitas	11	1	26	2
DA Reeve	11	1	43	0
RK Illingworth	11	1	53	2
DR Pringle	9	0	56	0
GA Gooch	2	0	9	1

ENGLAND

GA Gooch*	run out	11
MA Atherton	c Dujon b Marshall	25
GA Hick	not out	86
NH Fairbrother	c Richards b Patterson	113
MR Ramprakash	not out	0
DA Reeve		
DR Pringle		
RC Russell+		
PAJ de Freitas		
RK Illingworth		
DV Lawrence		
Extras	(4b, 12lb, 10w, 4nb)	30
	46.1 overs	
Total		**265**

FoW: 28, 48, 261

CEL Ambrose	8	0	31	0
BP Patterson	10	0	62	1
MD Marshall	11	1	49	1
CA Walsh	11	1	50	0
CL Hooper	4.1	0	36	0
PV Simmons	2	0	21	0

New Zealand

No. 191: One-Day Series
VENUE: Auckland
DATE: 11th January 1992
TOSS WON BY: New Zealand
RESULT: England won by 7 wickets

NEW ZEALAND

JG Wright	c Stewart b Lewis	6
RT Latham	lbw b Pringle	25
MD Crowe*	b Reeve	31
AH Jones	c Stewart b Reeve	1
MJ Greatbatch	c Hick b Reeve	4
CZ Harris	not out	38
CL Cairns	c Hick b Pringle	42
IDS Smith+	c Gooch b Lewis	2
C Pringle	not out	9
GR Larsen		
DK Morrison		
Extras	(0b, 13lb, 4w, 3nb)	20
	50 overs	
Total		**178**

FoW: 21, 45, 54, 61, 81, 165, 167

PAJ de Freitas	10	1	34	0
CC Lewis	8	0	33	2
DR Pringle	6	1	32	2
DA Reeve	10	3	20	3
PCR Tufnell	10	3	17	0
GA Hick	6	0	29	0

ENGLAND

GA Gooch*	c Greatbatch b Harris	47
GA Hick	b Cairns	23
RA Smith	not out	61
AJ Lamb	c Crowe b Harris	12
NH Fairbrother	not out	23
AJ Stewart+		
DA Reeve		
CC Lewis		
DR Pringle		
PAJ de Freitas		
PCR Tufnell		
Extras	(0b, 6lb, 3w, 4nb)	13
	33.5 overs	
Total		**179**

FoW: 64, 109, 123

DK Morrison	5.5	0	35	0
C Pringle	5	0	26	0
CL Cairns	5	0	32	1
GR Larsen	9	3	36	0
CZ Harris	8	0	40	2
RT Latham	1	0	4	0

New Zealand

No. 192: One-Day Series
VENUE: Dunedin
DATE: 12th February 1992
TOSS WON BY: New Zealand
RESULT: England won by 3 wickets

NEW ZEALAND

RT Latham	run out	12
AH Jones	b Botham	20
MJ Greatbatch	c Stewart b Reeve	10
MD Crowe*	c (sub) b Illingworth	29
KR Rutherford	run out	52
CZ Harris	b Pringle	32
CL Cairns	b Lewis	3
IDS Smith+	not out	5
ML Su'a	not out	4
DK Morrison		
GR Larsen		
Extras	(1b, 12lb, 3w, 3nb)	19
	50 overs	
Total		**186**

FoW: 14, 35, 54, 89, 163, 170, 180

DR Pringle	10	2	31	1
CC Lewis	9	0	32	1
DA Reeve	8	1	19	1
IT Botham	6	1	27	1
RK Illingworth	9	1	33	1
PCR Tufnell	8	0	31	0

ENGLAND

GA Gooch*	c Smith b Larsen	24
GA Hick	lbw b Morrison	7
RA Smith	b Larsen	17
AJ Lamb	lbw b Latham	40
IT Botham	c Rutherford b Latham	28
AJ Stewart+	b Latham	0
DA Reeve	not out	31
CC Lewis	c Greatbatch b Morrison	18
DR Pringle	not out	14
RK Illingworth		
PCR Tufnell		
Extras	(0b, 2lb, 7w, 0nb)	9
	49.1 overs	
Total		**188**

FoW: 21, 54, 63, 108, 108, 131, 165

DK Morrison	7	0	27	2
ML Su'a	8	1	35	0
GR Larsen	10	1	24	2
CL Cairns	6.1	0	36	0
CZ Harris	10	1	39	0
RT Latham	8	1	25	3

New Zealand

ENGLAND

IT Botham	c Greatbatch b Latham	79
GA Hick	c Greatbatch b Larsen	18
RA Smith	c Smith b Cairns	85
AJ Stewart*+	c Crowe b Su'a	13
AJ Lamb	c Harris b Watson	25
GA Gooch	not out	22
CC Lewis	c Latham b Watson	0
DR Pringle	c Watson b Cairns	5
DA Reeve	not out	2
RK Illingworth		
GC Small		
Extras	(0b, 2lb, 4w, 0nb)	6
	40 overs	
Total		**255**

FoW: 60, 125, 166, 220, 228, 231, 248

CL Cairns	6	0	37	2
W Watson	8	1	64	2
GR Larsen	6	2	34	1
ML Su'a	5	0	35	1
CZ Harris	8	0	35	0
RT Latham	7	0	48	1

NEW ZEALAND

RT Latham	c Reeve b Lewis	0
JG Wright	c Hick b Reeve	36
MJ Greatbatch	b Pringle	5
MD Crowe*	c Stewart b Pringle	6
KR Rutherford	c (sub) b Botham	37
CZ Harris	run out	37
CL Cairns	c Smith b Illingworth	6
IDS Smith+	c (sub) b Small	27
ML Su'a	not out	12
GR Larsen	not out	3
W Watson		
Extras	(0b, 6lb, 6w, 3nb)	15
	40 overs	
Total		**184**

FoW: 4, 20, 23, 92, 100, 112, 148, 171

CC Lewis	6	1	21	1
DR Pringle	6	2	11	2
GC Small	8	0	46	1
DA Reeve	5	0	26	1
IT Botham	7	1	36	1
RK Illingworth	8	0	38	1

India

ENGLAND

GA Gooch*	c Tendulkar b Shastri	51
IT Botham	c More b Kapil Dev	9
RA Smith	c Azharuddin b Prabhakar	91
GA Hick	c More b Banerjee	5
NH Fairbrother	c Srikkanth b Srinath	24
AJ Stewart+	b Prabhakar	13
CC Lewis	c Banerjee b Kapil Dev	10
DR Pringle	c Srikkanth b Srinath	1
DA Reeve	not out	8
PAJ de Freitas	run out	1
PCR Tufnell	not out	3
Extras	(1b, 6lb, 13w, 0nb)	20
	50 overs	
Total		**236**

FoW: 21, 131, 137, 197, 198, 214, 222, 223, 224

N Kapil Dev	10	0	38	2
M Prabhakar	10	3	34	2
J Srinath	9	1	47	2
ST Banerjee	7	0	45	1
SR Tendulkar	10	0	37	0
RJ Shastri	4	0	28	1

INDIA

RJ Shastri	run out	57
K Srikkanth	c Botham b de Freitas	39
M Azharuddin*	c Stewart b Reeve	0
SR Tendulkar	c Stewart b Botham	35
VG Kambli	c Hick b Botham	3
PK Amre	run out	22
N Kapil Dev	c de Freitas b Reeve	17
ST Banerjee	not out	25
KS More+	run out	1
M Prabhakar	b Reeve	0
J Srinath	run out	11
Extras	(0b, 9lb, 7w, 1nb)	17
	49.2 overs	
Total		**227**

FoW: 63, 63, 126, 140, 149, 187, 194, 200, 201, 227

DR Pringle	10	0	53	0
CC Lewis	9.2	0	36	0
PAJ de Freitas	10	0	39	1
DA Reeve	6	0	38	3
IT Botham	10	0	27	2
PCR Tufnell	4	0	25	0

West Indies

No. 195: World Cup
VENUE: Melbourne (MCG) Day/Night
DATE: 27th February 1992
TOSS WON BY: England
RESULT: England won by 6 wickets

WEST INDIES

DL Haynes	c Fairbrother b de Freitas	38
BC Lara	c Stewart b Lewis	0
RB Richardson*	c Botham b Lewis	5
CL Hooper	c Reeve b Botham	5
KLT Arthurton	c Fairbrother b de Freitas	54
AL Logie	run out	20
RA Harper	c Hick b Reeve	3
MD Marshall	run out	3
D Williams+	c Pringle b de Freitas	6
CEL Ambrose	c de Freitas b Lewis	4
WKM Benjamin	not out	11
Extras	(0b, 4lb, 3w, 1nb)	8
	49.2 overs	
Total		**157**

FoW: 0, 22, 36, 55, 91, 102, 114, 131, 145, 157

DR Pringle	7	3	16	0
CC Lewis	8.2	1	30	3
PAJ de Freitas	9	2	34	3
IT Botham	10	0	30	1
DA Reeve	10	1	23	1
PCR Tufnell	5	0	20	0

ENGLAND

GA Gooch*	st Williams b Hooper	65
IT Botham	c Williams b Benjamin	8
RA Smith	c Logie b Benjamin	8
GA Hick	c & b Harper	54
NH Fairbrother	not out	13
AJ Stewart+	not out	0
DA Reeve		
CC Lewis		
DR Pringle		
PAJ de Freitas		
PCR Tufnell		
Extras	(0b, 7lb, 4w, 1nb)	12
	39.5 overs	
Total		**160**

FoW: 50, 71, 126, 156

CEL Ambrose	8	1	26	0
MD Marshall	8	0	37	0
WKM Benjamin	9.5	2	22	2
CL Hooper	10	1	38	1
RA Harper	4	0	30	1

Pakistan

No. 196: World Cup
VENUE: Adelaide
DATE: 1st March 1992
TOSS WON BY: England
RESULT: No result

PAKISTAN

Rameez Raja	c Reeve b de Freitas	1
Aamir Sohail	c & b Pringle	9
Inzamam-ul-Haq	c Stewart b de Freitas	0
Javed Miandad*	b Pringle	3
Salim Malik	c Reeve b Botham	17
Ijaz Ahmed	c Stewart b Small	0
Wasim Akram	b Botham	1
Moin Khan+	c Hick b Small	2
Wasim Haider	c Stewart b Reeve	13
Mushtaq Ahmed	c Reeve b Pringle	17
Aaqib Javed	not out	1
Extras	(0b, 1lb, 8w, 1nb)	10
	40.2 overs	
Total		**74**

FoW: 5, 5, 14, 20, 32, 35, 42, 47, 62, 74

DR Pringle	8.2	5	8	3
PAJ de Freitas	7	1	22	2
GC Small	10	1	29	2
IT Botham	10	4	12	2
DA Reeve	5	3	2	1

ENGLAND

GA Gooch*	c Moin b Wasim Akram	3
IT Botham	not out	6
RA Smith	not out	5
GA Hick		
NH Fairbrother		
AJ Stewart+		
CC Lewis		
DR Pringle		
DA Reeve		
PAJ de Freitas		
GC Small		
Extras	(1b, 3lb, 5w, 1nb)	10
	8 overs	
Total		**24**

FoW: 14

Wasim Akram	3	0	7	1
Aaqib Javed	3	1	7	0
Wasim Haider	1	0	1	0
Ijaz Ahmed	1	0	5	0

Australia

AUSTRALIA

TM Moody	b Tufnell	51
MA Taylor	lbw b Pringle	0
DC Boon	run out	18
DM Jones	c Lewis b de Freitas	22
SR Waugh	run out	27
AR Border*	b Botham	16
IA Healy+	c Fairbrother b Botham	9
PL Taylor	lbw b Botham	0
CJ McDermott	c de Freitas b Botham	0
MR Whitney	not out	8
BA Reid	b Reeve	1
Extras	(2b, 8lb, 5w, 4nb)	19
	49 overs	
Total		**171**

FoW: 5, 35, 106, 114, 145, 155, 155, 155, 164, 171

DR Pringle	9	1	24	1
CC Lewis	10	2	28	0
PAJ de Freitas	10	3	23	1
IT Botham	10	1	31	4
PCR Tufnell	9	0	52	1
DA Reeve	1	0	3	1

ENGLAND

GA Gooch*	b Waugh	58
IT Botham	c Healy b Whitney	53
RA Smith	not out	30
GA Hick	not out	7
NH Fairbrother		
AJ Stewart+		
CC Lewis		
DR Pringle		
DA Reeve		
PAJ de Freitas		
PCR Tufnell		
Extras	(0b, 13lb, 8w, 4nb)	25
	40.5 overs	
Total		**173**

FoW: 107, 153

CJ McDermott	10	1	29	0
BA Reid	7.5	0	49	0
MR Whitney	10	2	28	1
SR Waugh	6	0	29	1
PL Taylor	3	0	7	0
TM Moody	4	0	18	0

Sri Lanka

ENGLAND

GA Gooch*	b Labrooy	8
IT Botham	b Anurasiri	47
RA Smith	run out	19
GA Hick	b Ramanayake	41
NH Fairbrother	c Ramanayake b Gurusinha	63
AJ Stewart+	c Jayasuriya b Gurusinha	59
CC Lewis	not out	20
DR Pringle	not out	0
DA Reeve		
PAJ de Freitas		
RK Illingworth		
Extras	(1b, 9lb, 9w, 4nb)	23
	50 overs	
Total		**280**

FoW: 44, 80, 105, 164, 244, 268

GP Wickramasinghe	9	0	54	0
CPH Ramanayake	10	1	42	1
GF Labrooy	10	1	68	1
SD Anurasiri	10	1	27	1
AP Gurusinha	10	0	67	2
ST Jayasuriya	1	0	12	0

SRI LANKA

RS Mahanama	c Botham b Lewis	9
MAR Sam'sekera	c Illingworth b Lewis	23
AP Gurusinha	c & b Lewis	7
PA de Silva*	c Fairbrother b Lewis	7
A Ranatunga	c Stewart b Botham	36
HP Tillakaratne+	run out	4
ST Jayasuriya	c de Freitas b Illingworth	19
GF Labrooy	c Smith b Illingworth	19
CPH Ram'ayake	c & b Reeve	12
SD Anurasiri	lbw b Reeve	11
GP Wick'singhe	not out	6
Extras	(0b, 7lb, 8w, 6nb)	21
	44 overs	
Total		**174**

FoW: 33, 46, 56, 60, 91, 119, 123, 156, 158, 174

DR Pringle	7	1	27	0
CC Lewis	8	0	30	4
PAJ de Freitas	5	1	31	0
IT Botham	10	0	33	1
RK Illingworth	10	0	32	2
DA Reeve	4	0	14	2

South Africa

SOUTH AFRICA

KC Wessels*	c Smith b Hick		85
AC Hudson	c & b Hick		79
PN Kirsten	c Smith b de Freitas		11
JN Rhodes	run out		18
AP Kuiper	not out		15
WJ Cronje	not out		13
BM McMillan			
DJ Richardson+			
RP Snell			
MW Pringle			
AA Donald			
Extras	(4b, 4lb, 4w, 3nb)		15
	50 overs		
Total			**236**

FoW: 151, 170, 201, 205

DR Pringle	9	2	34	0
PAJ de Freitas	10	1	41	1
IT Botham	8	0	37	0
GC Small	2	0	14	0
RK Illingworth	10	0	43	0
DA Reeve	2.4	0	15	0
GA Hick	8.2	0	44	2

ENGLAND

(Revised target 226 runs in 41 overs)

AJ Stewart*+	run out		77
IT Botham	b McMillan		22
RA Smith	c Richardson b McMillan		0
GA Hick	c Richardson b Snell		1
NH Fairbrother	not out		75
DA Reeve	c McMillan b Snell		10
CC Lewis	run out		33
DR Pringle	c Kuiper b Snell		1
PAJ de Freitas	not out		1
RK Illingworth			
GC Small			
Extras	(0b, 3lb, 1w, 2nb)		6
	40.5 overs		
Total			**226**

FoW: 63, 63, 64, 132, 166, 216, 225

AA Donald	9	1	43	0
MW Pringle	8	0	44	0
RP Snell	7.5	0	42	3
BM McMillan	8	1	39	2
AP Kuiper	4	0	32	0
WJ Cronje	3	0	14	0
PN Kirsten	1	0	9	0

New Zealand

ENGLAND

AJ Stewart*+	c Harris b Patel		41
IT Botham	b Patel		8
GA Hick	c Greatbatch b Harris		56
RA Smith	c Patel b Jones		38
AJ Lamb	c Cairns b Watson		12
CC Lewis	c & b Watson		0
DA Reeve	not out		21
DR Pringle	c (sub) b Jones		10
PAJ de Freitas	c Cairns b Harris		0
RK Illingworth	not out		2
GC Small			
Extras	(1b, 7lb, 4w, 0nb)		12
	50 overs		
Total			**200**

FoW: 25, 95, 135, 162, 169, 169, 189, 195

DN Patel	10	1	26	2
CZ Harris	8	0	39	2
W Watson	10	0	40	2
CL Cairns	3	0	21	0
GR Larsen	10	3	24	0
AH Jones	9	0	42	2

NEW ZEALAND

MJ Greatbatch	c de Freitas b Botham		35
JG Wright	b de Freitas		1
AH Jones	run out		78
MD Crowe*	not out		73
KR Rutherford	not out		3
CZ Harris			
IDS Smith+			
CL Cairns			
DN Patel			
GR Larsen			
W Watson			
Extras	(0b, 9lb, 1w, 1nb)		11
	40.5 overs		
Total			**201**

FoW: 5, 62, 171

DR Pringle	6.2	1	34	0
PAJ de Freitas	8.3	1	45	1
IT Botham	4	0	19	1
RK Illingworth	9	1	46	0
GA Hick	6	0	26	0
DA Reeve	3	0	9	0
GC Small	4	0	13	0

Zimbabwe

No. 201: World Cup
VENUE: Albury
DATE: 18th March 1992
TOSS WON BY: England
RESULT: Zimbabwe won by 9 runs

ZIMBABWE

WR James	c & b Illingworth	13
A Flower+	b de Freitas	7
AJ Pycroft	c Gooch b Botham	3
KJ Arnott	lbw b Botham	11
DL Houghton*	c Fairbrother b Small	29
AC Waller	b Tufnell	8
AH Shah	c Lamb b Tufnell	3
IP Butchart	c Fairbrother b Botham	24
EA Brandes	st Stewart b Illingworth	14
AJ Traicos	not out	0
MP Jarvis	lbw b Illingworth	6
Extras	(0b, 8lb, 8w, 0nb)	16
	46.1 overs	
Total		**134**

FoW: 12, 19, 30, 52, 65, 77, 96, 127, 127, 134

PAJ de Freitas	8	1	14	1
GC Small	9	1	20	1
IT Botham	10	3	23	3
RK Illingworth	9.1	0	33	3
PCR Tufnell	10	2	36	2

ENGLAND

GA Gooch*	lbw b Brandes	0
IT Botham	c Flower b Shah	18
AJ Lamb	c James b Brandes	17
RA Smith	b Brandes	2
GA Hick	b Brandes	0
NH Fairbrother	c Flower b Butchart	20
AJ Stewart+	c Waller b Shah	29
PAJ de Freitas	c Flower b Butchart	4
RK Illingworth	run out	11
GC Small	c Pycroft b Jarvis	5
PCR Tufnell	not out	0
Extras	(4b, 3lb, 11w, 1nb)	19
	49.1 overs	
Total		**125**

FoW: 0, 32, 42, 42, 43, 95, 101, 108, 124, 125

EA Brandes	10	4	21	4
MP Jarvis	9.1	0	32	1
AH Shah	10	3	17	2
AJ Traicos	10	4	16	0
IP Butchart	10	1	32	2

South Africa

No. 202: World Cup Semi Final
VENUE: Sydney (SCG) Day/Night
DATE: 22nd March 1992
TOSS WON BY: South Africa
RESULT: England won by 19 runs

ENGLAND

GA Gooch*	c Richardson b Donald	2
IT Botham	b Pringle	21
AJ Stewart+	c Richardson b McMillan	33
GA Hick	c Rhodes b Snell	83
NH Fairbrother	b Pringle	28
AJ Lamb	c Richardson b Donald	19
CC Lewis	not out	18
DA Reeve	not out	25
PAJ de Freitas		
RK Illingworth		
GC Small		
Extras	(1b, 7lb, 9w, 6nb)	23
	45 overs	
Total		**252**

FoW: 20, 39, 110, 183, 187, 221

AA Donald	10	0	69	2
MW Pringle	9	2	36	2
RP Snell	8	0	52	1
BM McMillan	9	0	47	1
AP Kuiper	5	0	26	0
WJ Cronje	4	0	14	0

SOUTH AFRICA

(Revised target 252 runs in 43 overs)

KC Wessels*	c Lewis b Botham	17
AC Hudson	lbw b Illingworth	46
PN Kirsten	b de Freitas	11
AP Kuiper	b Illingworth	36
WJ Cronje	c Hick b Small	24
JN Rhodes	c Lewis b Small	43
BM McMillan	not out	21
DJ Richardson+	not out	13
RP Snell		
MW Pringle		
AA Donald		
Extras	(0b, 17lb, 4w, 0nb)	21
	43 overs	
Total		**232**

FoW: 26, 61, 90, 131, 176, 206

IT Botham	10	0	52	1
CC Lewis	5	0	38	0
PAJ de Freitas	8	1	28	1
RK Illingworth	10	1	46	2
GC Small	10	1	51	2

Pakistan

No. 203: World Cup Final
VENUE: Melbourne (MCG) Day/Night
DATE: 25th March 1992
TOSS WON BY: Pakistan
RESULT: Pakistan won by 22 runs

PAKISTAN

Aamir Sohail	c Stewart b Pringle	4
Rameez Raja	lbw b Pringle	8
Imran Khan*	c Illingworth b Botham	72
Javed Miandad	c Botham b Illingworth	58
Inzamam-ul-Haq	b Pringle	42
Wasim Akram	run out	33
Salim Malik	not out	0
Moin Khan+		
Ijaz Ahmed		
Aaqib Javed		
Mushtaq Ahmed		
Extras	(0b, 19lb, 6w, 7nb)	32
	50 overs	
Total		**249**

FoW: 20, 24, 163, 197, 249, 249

DR Pringle	10	2	22	3
CC Lewis	10	2	52	0
IT Botham	7	0	42	1
PAJ de Freitas	10	1	42	0
RK Illingworth	10	0	50	1
DA Reeve	3	0	22	0

ENGLAND

GA Gooch*	c Aaqib Javed b M Ahmed	29
IT Botham	c Moin Khan b Wasim	0
AJ Stewart+	c Moin Khan b Aaqib Javed	7
GA Hick	lbw b Mushtaq Ahmed	17
NH Fairbrother	c Moin Khan b Aaqib Javed	62
AJ Lamb	b Wasim	31
CC Lewis	b Wasim	0
DA Reeve	c Rameez b Mushtaq Ahmed	15
DR Pringle	not out	18
PAJ de Freitas	run out	10
RK Illingworth	c Rameez b Imran Khan	14
Extras	(0b, 5lb, 13w, 6nb)	24
	49.2 overs	
Total		**227**

FoW: 6, 21, 59, 69, 141, 141, 180, 183, 208, 227

Wasim Akram	10	0	49	3
Aaqib Javed	10	2	27	2
Mushtaq Ahmed	10	1	41	3
Ijaz Ahmed	3	0	13	0
Imran Khan	6.2	0	43	1
Aamir Sohail	10	0	49	0

Pakistan

No. 204: Texaco Trophy
VENUE: Lord's
DATE: 20th May 1992
TOSS WON BY: Pakistan
RESULT: England won by 79 runs

ENGLAND

GA Gooch*	c Moin b Aaqib Javed	9
AJ Stewart+	c Asif b Naved	50
RA Smith	c Moin b Aaqib Javed	85
AJ Lamb	c Javed Miandad b Naved	60
NH Fairbrother	c Asif b Aaqib Javed	25
GA Hick	b Wasim	3
IT Botham	not out	10
CC Lewis	not out	6
DR Pringle		
PAJ de Freitas		
RK Illingworth		
Extras	(0b, 14lb, 9w, 7nb)	30
	55 overs	
Total		**278**

FoW: 20, 115, 213, 238, 250, 268

Wasim Akram	11	0	39	1
Aaqib Javed	11	0	54	3
Naved Anjum	11	0	48	2
Mushtaq Ahmed	11	0	56	0
Asif Mujtaba	11	0	67	0

PAKISTAN

Aamir Sohail	run out	36
Rameez Raja	c & b Pringle	0
Salim Malik	c Stewart b Botham	24
Javed Miandad*	c Hick b Pringle	7
Inzamam-ul-Haq	c & b Botham	2
Asif Mujtaba	c Smith b Hick	52
Wasim Akram	st Stewart b Illingworth	34
Naved Anjum	c Hick b Pringle	3
Moin Khan+	c Stewart b Pringle	11
Mushtaq Ahmed	not out	7
Aaqib Javed	b Hick	8
Extras	(0b, 8lb, 5w, 2nb)	15
	54.2 overs	
Total		**199**

FoW: 0, 49, 74, 78, 78, 161, 164, 181, 184, 199

PAJ de Freitas	9	2	17	0
DR Pringle	11	1	42	4
CC Lewis	8	1	35	0
IT Botham	11	0	45	2
RK Illingworth	11	0	36	1
GA Hick	3.2	0	7	2
NH Fairbrother	1	0	9	0

Pakistan

No. 205: Texaco Trophy
VENUE: The Oval
DATE: 22nd May 1992
TOSS WON BY: England
RESULT: England won by 39 runs

ENGLAND

GA Gooch*	run out	25
AJ Stewart+	b Aaqib Javed	103
RA Smith	b Mushtaq	7
AJ Lamb	st Moin b Aamir	11
NH Fairbrother	b Tanvir	63
GA Hick	not out	71
IT Botham	not out	2
CC Lewis		
DR Pringle		
PAJ de Freitas		
RK Illingworth		
Extras	(0b, 8lb, 9w, 3nb)	20
	55 overs	
Total		**302**

FoW: 71, 81, 108, 202, 295

Aaqib Javed	10	0	70	1
Naved Anjum	9	0	37	0
Tanvir Mehdi	11	0	72	1
Mushtaq Ahmed	11	0	47	1
Aamir Sohail	11	0	52	1
Asif Mujtaba	3	0	16	0

PAKISTAN

Aamir Sohail	b Illingworth	32
Rameez Raja	c (sub) b de Freitas	86
Salim Malik	b Pringle	26
Inzamam-ul-Haq	lbw b Pringle	15
Javed Miandad*	lbw b Botham	38
Asif Mujtaba	lbw b Illingworth	29
Naved Anjum	run out	6
Moin Khan+	c & b Lewis	15
Mushtaq Ahmed	c Illingworth b Lewis	8
Tanvir Mehdi	b de Freitas	0
Aaqib Javed	not out	0
Extras	(0b, 4lb, 3w, 1nb)	8
	50.5 overs	
Total		**263**

FoW: 81, 144, 148, 174, 220, 232, 249, 262, 262, 262

PAJ de Freitas	10.5	0	59	2
CC Lewis	8	0	47	2
IT Botham	11	0	52	1
RK Illingworth	11	0	58	2
DR Pringle	9	1	35	2
GA Hick	1	0	8	0

Pakistan

No. 206: Texaco Trophy
VENUE: Trent Bridge
DATE: 20th August 1992
TOSS WON BY: Pakistan
RESULT: England won by 198 runs

ENGLAND

GA Gooch*	b Waqar	42
AJ Stewart+	c Wasim b Waqar	34
RA Smith	c Rameez b Aaqib	77
NH Fairbrother	b Aaqib	62
AJ Lamb	lbw b Waqar	16
GA Hick	b Wasim	63
IT Botham	c Rameez b Waqar	24
CC Lewis	not out	1
PAJ de Freitas	not out	5
RK Illingworth		
GC Small		
Extras	(4b, 12lb, 18w, 5nb)	39
	55 overs	
Total		**363**

FoW: 84, 95, 224, 250, 269, 353, 357

Wasim Akram	11	0	55	1
Aaqib Javed	11	0	55	2
Waqar Younis	11	0	73	4
Mushtaq Ahmed	11	1	58	0
Ijaz Ahmed	4	0	29	0
Aamir Sohail	3	0	34	0
Asif Mujtaba	4	0	43	0

PAKISTAN

Aamir Sohail	c Botham b Lewis	17
Rameez Raja	c Gooch b de Freitas	0
Salim Malik*	c Small b Illingworth	45
Asif Mujtaba	c Lewis b de Freitas	1
Inzamam-ul-Haq	run out	10
Ijaz Ahmed	c Gooch b Botham	23
Wasim Akram	lbw b Illingworth	1
Rashid Latif+	st Stewart b Illingworth	29
Waqar Younis	c Hick b de Freitas	13
Mushtaq Ahmed	not out	14
Aaqib Javed	c Stewart b Small	2
Extras	(0b, 5lb, 5w, 0nb)	10
	46.1 overs	
Total		**165**

FoW: 2, 22, 27, 60, 87, 98, 103, 129, 153, 165

PAJ de Freitas	11	1	33	3
CC Lewis	8	2	24	1
IT Botham	11	1	41	1
GC Small	5.1	0	28	1
RK Illingworth	11	1	34	3

No. 207: Texaco Trophy			No. 208: Texaco Trophy		
VENUE: Lord's			VENUE: Old Trafford		
DATE: 22nd & 23rd August 1992			DATE: 24th August 1992		
TOSS WON BY: Pakistan			TOSS WON BY: Pakistan		
RESULT: Pakistan won by 3 runs			RESULT: England won by 6 wickets		

PAKISTAN

Aamir Sohail	c Stewart b de Freitas	20	Aamir Sohail	run out	87
Rameez Raja	c Stewart b Botham	23	Rameez Raja*	run out	37
Salim Malik	st Blakey b Illingworth	48	Shoaib Mohd	b Reeve	9
Javed Miandad*	not out	50	Inzamam-ul-Haq	lbw b Cork	75
Inzamam-ul-Haq	c Blakey b Reeve	16	Asif Mujtaba	c Smith b de Freitas	10
Wasim Akram	b de Freitas	23	Wasim Akram	not out	15
Naved Anjum	not out	4	Naved Anjum	not out	12
Moin Khan+			Moin Khan+		
Waqar Younis			Waqar Younis		
Mushtaq Ahmed			Mushtaq Ahmed		
Aaqib Javed			Aaqib Javed		
Extras	(2b, 7lb, 11w, 0nb)	20	Extras	(0b, 6lb, 2w, 1nb)	9
	50 overs			55 overs	
Total		**204**	**Total**		**254**

FoW: 32, 91, 102, 137, 189

FoW: 69, 90, 189, 210, 240

PAJ de Freitas	10	2	39	2	PAJ de Freitas	11	1	52	1
CC Lewis	10	0	49	0	DG Cork	11	1	37	1
IT Botham	10	1	33	1	IT Botham	11	0	43	0
DA Reeve	10	1	31	1	DA Reeve	11	1	57	1
RK Illingworth	10	0	43	1	RK Illingworth	11	0	59	0

ENGLAND

IT Botham	st Moin b Aamir	40	GA Gooch*	b Aamir	45
AJ Stewart*	lbw b Waqar	0	AJ Stewart+	st Moin b Aamir	51
RA Smith	c Moin b Aaqib Javed	4	RA Smith	not out	85
NH Fairbrother	b Aaqib Javed	33	NH Fairbrother	b Waqar	15
AJ Lamb	c Moin b Mushtaq	55	AJ Lamb	c Moin b Waqar	2
GA Hick	b Aamir	8	GA Hick	not out	42
RJ Blakey+	b Waqar	25	IT Botham		
DA Reeve	not out	6	DA Reeve		
CC Lewis	c (sub) b Wasim	1	DG Cork		
PAJ de Freitas	c Mushtaq b Wasim	0	PAJ de Freitas		
RK Illingworth	b Waqar	4	RK Illingworth		
Extras	(0b, 8lb, 11w, 6nb)	25	Extras	(0b, 7lb, 3w, 5nb)	15
	49.2 overs			43.4 overs	
Total		**201**	**Total**		**255**

FoW: 15, 30, 72, 111, 139, 172, 191, 193, 193, 201

FoW: 98, 101, 149, 159

Wasim Akram	10	2	41	2	Wasim Akram	9.4	1	45	0
Waqar Younis	9.2	0	36	3	Waqar Younis	8	0	58	2
Mushtaq Ahmed	10	1	34	1	Aaqib Javed	6	0	42	0
Aaqib Javed	9	0	39	2	Mushtaq Ahmed	9	0	48	0
Aamir Sohail	5	0	22	2	Aamir Sohail	7	0	29	2
Naved Anjum	6	0	21	0	Naved Anjum	4	0	26	0

India

No. 209: One-Day Series
VENUE: Jaipur
DATE: 18th January 1993
TOSS WON BY: England
RESULT: England won by 4 wickets

INDIA

M Prabhakar	b Jarvis	25
NS Sidhu	b Jarvis	0
VG Kambli	not out	100
M Azharuddin*	lbw b Lewis	6
SR Tendulkar	not out	82
PK Amre		
N Kapil Dev		
VS Yadav+		
A Kumble		
SLV Raju		
J Srinath		
Extras	(2b, 7lb, 1w, 0nb)	10
	48 overs	
Total		**223**

FoW: 0, 31, 59

PAJ de Freitas	9	3	40	0
PW Jarvis	10	0	49	2
DA Reeve	10	0	37	0
CC Lewis	9	0	26	1
JE Emburey	8	0	49	0
GA Gooch	2	0	13	0

ENGLAND

GA Gooch*	lbw b Kapil Dev	4
AJ Stewart+	c Yadav b Kapil Dev	91
RA Smith	c & b Prabhakar	16
MW Gatting	b Kumble	30
NH Fairbrother	not out	46
GA Hick	run out	13
DA Reeve	lbw b Prabhakar	2
CC Lewis	not out	8
JE Emburey		
PAJ de Freitas		
PW Jarvis		
Extras	(1b, 8lb, 3w, 2nb)	14
	48 overs	
Total		**224**

FoW: 29, 85, 145, 161, 200, 203

N Kapil Dev	10	1	36	2
M Prabhakar	10	0	43	2
J Srinath	10	0	47	0
SLV Raju	8	1	35	0
A Kumble	10	0	54	1

India

No. 210: One-Day Series
VENUE: Chandigarh
DATE: 21st January 1993
TOSS WON BY: India
RESULT: India won by 5 wickets

ENGLAND

GA Gooch*	c Tendulkar b Srinath	7
AJ Stewart+	c Azharuddin b Kapil Dev	7
RA Smith	lbw b Kumble	42
MW Gatting	c & b Srinath	0
NH Fairbrother	lbw b Raju	7
GA Hick	b Kapil Dev	56
DA Reeve	not out	33
CC Lewis	not out	16
PAJ de Freitas		
PW Jarvis		
IDK Salisbury		
Extras	(0b, 13lb, 13w, 4nb)	30
	50 overs	
Total		**198**

FoW: 19, 20, 22, 49, 132, 153

N Kapil Dev	10	2	40	2
M Prabhakar	8	0	30	0
J Srinath	10	2	34	2
SR Tendulkar	3	0	16	0
SLV Raju	9	0	28	1
A Kumble	10	0	37	1

INDIA

NS Sidhu	c Reeve b de Freitas	76
M Prabhakar	c Reeve b Lewis	36
VG Kambli	c & b Jarvis	9
M Azharuddin*	lbw b Reeve	36
SR Tendulkar	lbw b de Freitas	1
PK Amre	not out	24
N Kapil Dev	not out	5
VS Yadav+		
A Kumble		
SLV Raju		
J Srinath		
Extras	(0b, 3lb, 5w, 6nb)	14
	45.1 overs	
Total		**201**

FoW: 79, 99, 148, 161, 195

PAJ de Freitas	10	1	31	2
PW Jarvis	10	1	43	1
DA Reeve	6.1	0	33	1
CC Lewis	10	0	47	1
IDK Salisbury	8	1	42	0
MW Gatting	1	0	2	0

'93

India

No. 211: One-Day Series
VENUE: Bangalore
DATE: 26th February 1993
TOSS WON BY: India
RESULT: England won by 48 runs

ENGLAND

RA Smith	c More b Srinath	29
AJ Stewart+	lbw b Srinath	14
GA Hick	c Amre b Prabhakar	56
MW Gatting	b Srinath	7
NH Fairbrother	run out	5
GA Gooch*	b Prabhakar	45
CC Lewis	c Tendulkar b Srinath	19
DA Reeve	not out	13
PAJ de Freitas	c Prabhakar b Srinath	2
PW Jarvis	c Azharuddin b Kapil Dev	1
DE Malcolm	not out	0
Extras	(0b, 15lb, 4w, 8nb)	27
	47 overs	
Total		**218**

FoW: 42, 65, 79, 102, 157, 185, 210, 213, 218

N Kapil Dev	8	1	27	1
M Prabhakar	10	0	50	2
J Srinath	9	1	41	5
SLV Raju	10	0	46	0
A Kumble	10	1	39	0

INDIA

M Prabhakar	run out	0
NS Sidhu	c Gooch b de Freitas	40
VG Kambli	c Stewart b Jarvis	33
SR Tendulkar	c Hick b Lewis	3
M Azharuddin*	lbw b Jarvis	1
PK Amre	c Hick b Jarvis	16
N Kapil Dev	c Gooch b Malcolm	32
KS More+	lbw b Jarvis	0
A Kumble	b Jarvis	24
J Srinath	c Hick b Malcolm	2
SLV Raju	not out	1
Extras	(0b, 4lb, 11w, 3nb)	18
	41.4 overs	
Total		**170**

FoW: 3, 61, 66, 67, 100, 114, 115, 160, 166, 170

DE Malcolm	9	1	47	2
PAJ de Freitas	8	0	27	1
CC Lewis	10	0	32	1
PW Jarvis	8.4	1	35	5
DA Reeve	6	0	25	0

India

No. 212: One-Day Series
VENUE: Jamshedpur
DATE: 1st March 1993
TOSS WON BY: England
RESULT: England won by 6 wickets

INDIA

NS Sidhu	c de Freitas b Malcolm	18
M Prabhakar	c Blakey b de Freitas	2
VG Kambli	run out	23
SR Tendulkar	b Jarvis	24
M Azharuddin*	c Fairbrother b Lewis	23
N Kapil Dev	not out	15
PK Amre	c Gooch b Jarvis	19
SA Ankola	run out	2
KS More+	not out	1
A Kumble		
J Srinath		
Extras	(0b, 6lb, 3w, 1nb)	10
	26 overs	
Total		**137**

FoW: 11, 46, 51, 96, 99, 122, 127

PAJ de Freitas	4	0	17	1
DE Malcolm	6	0	17	1
CC Lewis	5	0	25	1
DA Reeve	6	0	32	0
PW Jarvis	5	0	40	2

ENGLAND

GA Gooch*	c More b Kapil Dev	15
RA Smith	run out	17
GA Hick	c Azharuddin b Ankola	1
NH Fairbrother	not out	53
CC Lewis	lbw b Prabhakar	25
DA Reeve	not out	17
MW Gatting		
RJ Blakey+		
PAJ de Freitas		
PW Jarvis		
DE Malcolm		
Extras	(0b, 8lb, 5w, 0nb)	13
	25.4 overs	
Total		**141**

FoW: 27, 33, 43, 93

N Kapil Dev	4	1	10	1
M Prabhakar	5.4	0	34	1
J Srinath	6	0	38	0
SA Ankola	6	0	28	1
A Kumble	4	0	23	0

No. 213: One-Day Series		
VENUE: Gwalior		
DATE: 4th March 1993		
TOSS WON BY: India		
RESULT: India won by 3 wickets		

ENGLAND

RA Smith	lbw b Srinath	129
AJ Stewart	b Kumble	33
GA Hick	c More b Prabhakar	18
NH Fairbrother	c Maninder b Srinath	37
CC Lewis	lbw b Prabhakar	4
GA Gooch*	run out	1
DA Reeve	run out	3
RJ Blakey+	lbw b Srinath	0
PAJ de Freitas	not out	2
PW Jarvis	b Prabhakar	0
DE Malcolm	b Prabhakar	0
Extras	(1b, 16lb, 8w, 4nb)	29
	50 overs	
Total		**256**

FoW: 101, 154, 227, 246, 251, 251, 256, 256, 256, 256

N Kapil Dev	9	0	39	0
M Prabhakar	10	0	54	4
J Srinath	10	0	41	3
A Kumble	10	0	41	1
Maninder Singh	8	0	46	0
AK Sharma	3	0	18	0

INDIA

NS Sidhu	not out	134
M Prabhakar	lbw b de Freitas	0
VG Kambli	c Gooch b Malcolm	2
M Azharuddin*	c Stewart b Malcolm	74
SR Tendulkar	b Jarvis	5
AK Sharma	run out	0
N Kapil Dev	c Hick b Jarvis	2
KS More+	c Hick b Malcolm	1
A Kumble	not out	19
Maninder Singh		
J Srinath		
Extras	(2b, 9lb, 8w, 1nb)	20
	48 overs	
Total		**257**

FoW: 1, 4, 179, 189, 190, 202, 205

PAJ de Freitas	10	0	52	1
DE Malcolm	10	0	40	3
CC Lewis	10	0	56	0
PW Jarvis	10	0	43	2
DA Reeve	6	0	37	0
GA Hick	2	0	18	0

No. 214: One-Day Series		
VENUE: Gwalior		
DATE: 5th March 1993		
TOSS WON BY: India		
RESULT: India won by 4 wickets		

ENGLAND

RA Smith	c Sharma b Maninder	72
AJ Stewart+	c More b Srinath	11
GA Hick	not out	105
NH Fairbrother	c Kapil Dev b Srinath	41
MW Gatting	c Sidhu b Srinath	6
CC Lewis	not out	3
GA Gooch*		
DA Reeve		
PAJ de Freitas		
PW Jarvis		
DE Malcolm		
Extras	(0b, 8lb, 17w, 2nb)	27
	48 overs	
Total		**265**

FoW: 42, 158, 246, 258

N Kapil Dev	10	2	48	0
M Prabhakar	9	0	52	0
J Srinath	9	0	37	3
Maninder Singh	10	0	62	1
A Kumble	10	0	58	0

INDIA

M Prabhakar	b Jarvis	73
NS Sidhu	c Hick b Lewis	19
VG Kambli	c Reeve b de Freitas	22
M Azharuddin*	not out	95
SR Tendulkar	c (sub) b Lewis	34
N Kapil Dev	c Reeve b Jarvis	2
AK Sharma	c Gooch b Jarvis	2
KS More+	not out	10
A Kumble		
Maninder Singh		
J Srinath		
Extras	(0b, 1lb, 7w, 2nb)	10
	46.4 overs	
Total		**267**

FoW: 41, 99, 166, 245, 251, 253

DE Malcolm	8	0	56	0
CC Lewis	10	1	51	2
PW Jarvis	10	0	39	3
DA Reeve	8.4	0	64	0
PAJ de Freitas	10	0	56	1

Sri Lanka

Sri Lanka

No. 215: One-Day Series
VENUE: Colombo (Khettarama)
DATE: 10th March 1993 Day/Night
TOSS WON BY: Sri Lanka
RESULT: Sri Lanka won by run rate

No. 216: One-Day Series
VENUE: Moratuwa
DATE: 20th March 1993
TOSS WON BY: Sri Lanka
RESULT: Sri Lanka won by 8 wickets

SRI LANKA

UC Hath'usingha	lbw b Emburey	43
RS Mahanama	c Hick b Malcolm	7
AP Gurusinha	c de Freitas b Jarvis	5
PA de Silva	c & b Reeve	34
A Ranatunga*	c Stewart b Lewis	36
HP Tillakaratne	not out	66
ST Jayasuriya	not out	34
AM de Silva+		
RS Kalpage		
CPH Ram'ayake		
GP Wick'singhe		
Extras	(3b, 4lb, 10w, 8nb)	25
	47 overs	
Total		**250**

FoW: 16, 33, 101, 109, 180

DE Malcolm	7	1	32	1
CC Lewis	9	0	40	1
PW Jarvis	9	0	57	1
PAJ de Freitas	3	0	25	0
JE Emburey	10	1	42	1
DA Reeve	9	1	47	1

ENGLAND

(Revised target 203 runs in 38 overs)

RA Smith	c & b Wickramasingha	3
AJ Stewart*+	lbw b Ramanayake	5
GA Hick	c Mahanama b Hath'usingha	31
NH Fairbrother	lbw b Jayasuriya	34
MW Gatting	b Kalpage	1
CC Lewis	b Kalpage	16
DA Reeve	c Ranatunga b Kalpage	16
PAJ de Freitas	c Ranatunga b Wick'asinghe	21
JE Emburey	st AM de Silva b Jayasuriya	10
PW Jarvis	not out	16
DE Malcolm	run out	2
Extras	(0b, 10lb, 4w, 1nb)	15
	36.1 overs	
Total		**170**

FoW: 7, 9, 67, 70, 99, 103, 120, 137, 152, 170

CPH Ramanayake	7	0	25	1
GP Wickramasinghe	6.1	1	21	2
UC Hathurusingha	6	0	28	1
AP Gurusinha	2	0	7	0
RS Kalpage	8	0	34	3
ST Jayasuriya	7	0	45	2

ENGLAND

CC Lewis	c Ramanayake b Wickram	8
RA Smith	st AM de Silva b Jayasuriya	31
GA Hick	lbw b Kalpage	36
NH Fairbrother	c AM de Silva b Jayasuriya	21
AJ Stewart*+	lbw b Tillakaratne	14
MW Gatting	lbw b PA de Silva	2
DA Reeve	b Jayasuriya	20
JE Emburey	c Ramanayake b Jayasuriya	21
IDK Salisbury	not out	2
PW Jarvis	c AM de Silva b Jayasuriya	4
JP Taylor	b Jayasuriya	1
Extras	(2b, 9lb, 3w, 6nb)	20
	48.5 overs	
Total		**180**

FoW: 23, 77, 85, 111, 114, 125, 168, 172, 177, 180

CPH Ramanayake	4	0	20	0
GP Wickramasinghe	8	0	23	1
AP Gurusinha	4	0	21	0
UC Hathurusingha	2	0	13	0
RS Kalpage	10	0	27	1
ST Jayasuriya	9.5	0	29	6
PA de Silva	7	1	22	1
HP Tillakaratne	4	0	14	1

SRI LANKA

RS Mahanama	c Stewart b Salisbury	29
UC Hath'usingha	c & b Salisbury	33
AP Gurusinha	not out	35
PA de Silva	not out	75
A Ranatunga*		
HP Tillakaratne		
ST Jayasuriya		
AM de Silva+		
RS Kalpage		
CPH Ramanayake		
GP Wickramasinghe		
Extras	(1b, 2lb, 2w, 6nb)	11
	35.2 overs	
Total		**183**

FoW: 66, 68

CC Lewis	7	1	13	0
PW Jarvis	4	0	22	0
JP Taylor	3	0	20	0
JE Emburey	6	0	29	0
IDK Salisbury	4	0	36	2
GA Hick	6.2	1	36	0
DA Reeve	5	0	24	0

Australia

No. 217: Texaco Trophy
VENUE: Old Trafford
DATE: 19th May 1993
TOSS WON BY: England
RESULT: Australia won by 4 runs

AUSTRALIA

ML Hayden	c Stewart b Lewis	29
MA Taylor	c Fairbrother b Illingworth	79
ME Waugh	c Fairbrother b Jarvis	56
DC Boon	c Fairbrother b Illingworth	2
AR Border*	c Lewis b Illingworth	4
SR Waugh	c & b Lewis	27
IA Healy+	c Thorpe b Caddick	20
MG Hughes	b Lewis	20
PR Reiffel	run out	2
CJ McDermott	not out	3
TBA May	not out	1
Extras	(1b, 8lb, 2w, 4nb)	15
	55 overs	
Total		**258**

FoW: 60, 168, 171, 178, 186, 219, 237, 254, 255

AR Caddick	11	1	50	1
DR Pringle	10	3	36	0
CC Lewis	11	1	54	3
PW Jarvis	11	0	55	1
RK Illingworth	11	0	48	3
GA Hick	1	0	6	0

ENGLAND

GA Gooch*	c ME Waugh b McDermott	4
AJ Stewart+	b Hughes	22
RA Smith	c & b McDermott	9
GA Hick	b Reiffel	85
NH Fairbrother	c Reiffel b SR Waugh	59
GP Thorpe	c Taylor b McDermott	31
CC Lewis	run out	4
DR Pringle	c Taylor b SR Waugh	6
RK Illingworth	run out	12
PW Jarvis	c Reiffel b SR Waugh	2
AR Caddick	not out	1
Extras	(0b, 8lb, 9w, 2nb)	19
	54.5 overs	
Total		**254**

FoW: 11, 38, 44, 171, 194, 211, 227, 240, 247,254

CJ McDermott	11	2	38	3
MG Hughes	9.5	1	40	1
TBA May	11	2	40	0
PR Reiffel	11	0	63	1
ME Waugh	2	0	12	0
SR Waugh	10	0	53	3

Australia

No. 218: Texaco Trophy
VENUE: Edgbaston
DATE: 21st May 1993
TOSS WON BY: Australia
RESULT: Australia won by 6 wickets

ENGLAND

GA Gooch*	c Healy b McDermott	17
AJ Stewart+	b McDermott	0
RA Smith	not out	167
GA Hick	c Healy b Reiffel	2
NH Fairbrother	c Taylor b SR Waugh	23
GP Thorpe	c Border b McDermott	36
CC Lewis	not out	13
DR Pringle		
DG Cork		
PW Jarvis		
AR Caddick		
Extras	(2b, 4lb, 2w, 11nb)	19
	55 overs	
Total		**277**

FoW: 3, 40, 55, 105, 247

CJ McDermott	11	1	29	3
MG Hughes	11	2	51	0
PR Reiffel	11	1	70	1
TBA May	11	0	45	0
SR Waugh	8	0	55	1
ME Waugh	3	0	21	0

AUSTRALIA

MA Taylor	b Lewis	26
ML Hayden	b Jarvis	14
ME Waugh	c Fairbrother b Lewis	113
DC Boon	c Stewart b Pringle	21
AR Border*	not out	86
SR Waugh	not out	6
IA Healy+		
MG Hughes		
PR Reiffel		
CJ McDermott		
TBA May		
Extras	(0b, 5lb, 3w, 6nb)	14
	53.3 overs	
Total		**280**

FoW: 28, 55, 95, 263

AR Caddick	11	1	43	0
PW Jarvis	10	1	51	1
CC Lewis	10.3	0	61	2
DR Pringle	11	0	63	1
DG Cork	11	1	57	0

Australia

AUSTRALIA

ML Hayden	c Stewart b Caddick	4
MA Taylor*	c Stewart b Reeve	57
ME Waugh	c Stewart b Caddick	14
DC Boon	b Illingworth	73
DR Martyn	not out	51
SR Waugh	c Gooch b Caddick	8
IA Healy+	not out	12
MG Hughes		
BP Julian		
CJ McDermott		
TBA May		
Extras	(0b, 3lb, 6w, 2nb)	11
	55 overs	
Total		**230**

FoW: 12, 31, 139, 193, 208

PW Jarvis	11	1	51	0
AR Caddick	11	3	39	3
DG Cork	9	2	24	0
RK Illingworth	10	0	46	1
DA Reeve	11	1	50	1
GA Hick	3	0	17	0

ENGLAND

GA Gooch*	c Hughes b May	42
AJ Stewart+	c ME Waugh b Julian	74
RA Smith	st Healy b May	6
GA Hick	b Julian	7
NH Fairbrother	c Boon b Julian	18
GP Thorpe	c Healy b SR Waugh	22
DA Reeve	run out	2
DG Cork	b Hughes	11
RK Illingworth	c Healy b Hughes	9
PW Jarvis	c Hayden b McDermott	3
AR Caddick	not out	2
Extras	(0b, 6lb, 8w, 1nb)	15
	53.1 overs	
Total		**211**

FoW: 96, 115, 129, 159, 160, 169, 195, 201, 208, 211

CJ McDermott	10	1	35	1
MG Hughes	10.1	0	41	2
BP Julian	11	1	50	3
TBA May	11	1	36	2
SR Waugh	11	0	43	1

West Indies

ENGLAND

MA Atherton*	c Richardson b Cummins	86
AJ Stewart+	c Lara b Benjamin	11
GP Thorpe	c Adams b Benjamin	4
RA Smith	c & b Harper	12
GA Hick	c Simmons b Cummins	47
MP Maynard	not out	22
CC Lewis	not out	6
SL Watkin		
AP Igglesden		
PCR Tufnell		
DE Malcolm		
Extras	(4b, 7lb, 0w, 3nb)	14
	50 overs	
Total		**202**

FoW: 35, 45, 73, 166, 176

CEL Ambrose	10	2	35	0
CA Walsh	10	0	42	0
WKM Benjamin	10	2	38	2
AC Cummins	10	1	28	2
RA Harper	10	0	48	1

WEST INDIES

DL Haynes	c Malcolm b Igglesden	17
BC Lara	c Igglesden b Malcolm	9
RB Richardson*	c Maynard b Lewis	12
KLT Arthurton	b Lewis	6
PV Simmons	b Lewis	0
JC Adams+	c Thorpe b Igglesden	29
RA Harper	lbw b Watkin	11
AC Cummins	c Thorpe b Malcolm	24
WKM Benjamin	c Thorpe b Tufnell	0
CEL Ambrose	c Smith b Malcolm	10
CA Walsh	not out	1
Extras	(1b, 10lb, 11w, 0nb)	22
	40.4 overs	
Total		**141**

FoW: 17, 43,48, 48, 55, 82,1 21, 122, 136, 141

DE Malcolm	8.4	1	41	3
SL Watkin	8	1	27	1
CC Lewis	8	2	18	3
AP Igglesden	8	2	12	2
PCR Tufnell	8	0	32	1

	No. 221: One-Day Series
VENUE:	Kingston (Jamaica)
DATE:	26th February 1994
TOSS WON BY:	West Indies
RESULT:	West Indies won by 3 wkts

ENGLAND

MA Atherton*	c Arthurton b Harper	46
AJ Stewart+	run out	66
RA Smith	c Harper b KCG Benjamin	56
GA Hick	c Cummins b Arthurton	31
MP Maynard	b Cummins	22
N Hussain	c Richardson b Cummins	10
CC Lewis	b KCG Benjamin	0
SL Watkin	b KCG Benjamin	0
AP Igglesden	not out	2
PCR Tufnell	not out	2
ARC Fraser		
Extras	(0b, 9lb, 7w, 2nb)	18
	50 overs	
Total		**253**

FoW: 112, 128, 209, 214, 247, 248, 248, 249

CA Walsh	5	1	26	0
KCG Benjamin	10	1	44	3
AC Cummins	8	1	42	2
WKM Benjamin	8	0	33	0
RA Harper	8	0	45	1
PV Simmons	7	0	32	0
KLT Arthurton	4	0	22	1

WEST INDIES

(Revised target 238 runs in 47 overs)

DL Haynes	c & b Hick	53
BC Lara	lbw b Watkin	8
PV Simmons	b Fraser	39
KLT Arthurton	st Stewart b Hick	12
RB Richardson*	c Fraser b Watkin	32
JC Adams+	not out	52
RA Harper	lbw b Watkin	0
AC Cummins	c Smith b Watkin	16
WKM Benjamin	not out	9
KCG Benjamin		
CA Walsh		
Extras	(3b, 7lb, 6w, 3nb)	19
	45.5 overs	
Total		**240**

FoW: 13, 111, 128, 130, 186, 186, 223

AP Igglesden	7	1	29	0
SL Watkin	9.5	1	49	4
ARC Fraser	9	0	50	1
CC Lewis	9	0	48	0
PCR Tufnell	4	0	22	0
GA Hick	7	0	32	2

	No. 222: One-Day Series
VENUE:	Arnos Vale (St. Vincent)
DATE:	2nd March 1994
TOSS WON BY:	England
RESULT:	West Indies won by 165 runs

WEST INDIES

DL Haynes	c Lewis b Tufnell	83
PV Simmons	c Hussain b Tufnell	63
BC Lara	c Stewart b Fraser	60
KLT Arthurton	c Smith b Watkin	28
RB Richardson*	not out	52
JC Adams+	c Atherton b Watkin	6
RA Harper	run out	15
AC Cummins	not out	0
WKM Benjamin		
CEL Ambrose		
KCG Benjamin		
Extras	(0b, 4lb, 2w, 0nb)	6
	50 overs	
Total		**313**

FoW: 145, 156, 230, 242, 256, 300

AP Igglesden	10	1	65	0
SL Watkin	9	0	61	2
CC Lewis	9	0	67	0
ARC Fraser	10	1	46	1
GA Hick	3	0	18	0
PCR Tufnell	9	0	52	2

ENGLAND

CC Lewis	lbw b Cummins	2
AJ Stewart+	c Adams b KCG Benjamin	13
RA Smith	b Ambrose	18
GA Hick	c Cummins b Harper	32
MP Maynard	c Simmons b Cummins	6
N Hussain	c & b Harper	16
MA Atherton*	not out	19
SL Watkin	c Lara b Arthurton	4
AP Igglesden	c Ambrose b Lara	18
ARC Fraser	st Adams b Lara	1
PCR Tufnell	not out	0
Extras	(1b, 12lb, 6w, 0nb)	19
	50 overs	
Total		**148**

FoW: 7, 24, 41, 64, 98, 105, 119, 144, 148

KCG Benjamin	6	0	21	1
AC Cummins	8	1	22	2
WKM Benjamin	5	1	15	0
CEL Ambrose	6	2	13	1
PV Simmons	7	1	18	0
RA Harper	10	0	29	2
KLT Arthurton	6	1	12	1
BC Lara	2	0	5	2

West Indies

No. 223: One-Day Series
VENUE: Port-of-Spain (Trinidad)
DATE: 5th March 1994
TOSS WON BY: England
RESULT: West Indies won by 15 runs

WEST INDIES

DL Haynes	b Lewis	115
PV Simmons	c Hick b Lewis	16
BC Lara	lbw b Fraser	19
KLT Arthurton	c Stewart b Fraser	0
RB Richardson*	c Ramprakash b Caddick	13
JC Adams+	c Caddick b Fraser	40
RA Harper	b Lewis	23
AC Cummins	not out	13
WKM Benjamin	not out	0
CEL Ambrose		
KCG Benjamin		
Extras	(4b, 4lb, 13w, 5nb)	26
	45.4 overs	
Total		**265**

FoW: 4, 5, 75, 75, 98, 222, 238, 265

AP Igglesden	3	0	16	0
AR Caddick	10	0	60	1
ARC Fraser	10	0	31	3
CC Lewis	9.4	1	59	3
IDK Salisbury	9	0	58	0
GA Hick	4	0	33	0

ENGLAND

(Revised target 209 runs in 36 overs)

MA Atherton*	b KCG Benjamin	41
AJ Stewart+	b KCG Benjamin	2
RA Smith	b Harper	45
GA Hick	c & b Harper	10
MP Maynard	b Harper	8
MR Ramprakash	b Ambrose	31
CC Lewis	c Lara b Harper	4
AR Caddick	not out	20
IDK Salisbury	b Cummins	5
AP Igglesden	run out	0
ARC Fraser	not out	4
Extras	(1b, 9lb, 11w, 2nb)	23
	36 overs	
Total		**193**

FoW: 23, 86, 110, 121, 130, 145, 177, 184, 184

KCG Benjamin	8	0	37	2
AC Cummins	6	0	34	1
CEL Ambrose	8	0	34	1
WKM Benjamin	7	0	38	0
RA Harper	7	0	40	4

West Indies

No. 224: One-Day Series
VENUE: Port-of-Spain (Trinidad)
DATE: 6th March 1994
TOSS WON BY: West Indies
RESULT: England won by 5 wkts

WEST INDIES

PV Simmons	b Salisbury	84
JC Adams+	c Atherton b Salisbury	23
BC Lara	c Stewart b Caddick	16
KLT Arthurton	c Ramprakash b Lewis	17
RB Richardson*	c Stewart b Salisbury	15
RIC Holder	run out	26
RA Harper	c & b Lewis	37
AC Cummins	c Smith b Lewis	11
WKM Benjamin	c Ramprakash b Lewis	8
KCG Benjamin	not out	0
CA Walsh		
Extras	(1b, 10lb, 1w, 1nb)	13
	50 overs	
Total		**250**

FoW: 89, 126, 135, 164, 164, 230, 232, 248, 250

ARC Fraser	10	2	41	0
SL Watkin	10	0	56	0
CC Lewis	10	0	35	4
AR Caddick	10	2	66	1
IDK Salisbury	10	0	41	3

ENGLAND

(Revised target 201 runs in 40 overs)

MA Atherton*	b KCG Benjamin	51
AJ Stewart+	b Cummins	53
RA Smith	lbw b Cummins	4
GA Hick	not out	47
MP Maynard	c Adams b KCG Benjamin	1
MR Ramprakash	c Adams b Walsh	10
CC Lewis	not out	16
AR Caddick		
IDK Salisbury		
SL Watkin		
ARC Fraser		
Extras	(2b, 9lb, 4w, 4nb)	19
	36.4 overs	
Total		**201**

FoW: 62, 83, 151, 156, 174

WKM Benjamin	8	1	33	0
CA Walsh	10	0	58	1
AC Cummins	7.4	0	36	2
KCG Benjamin	9	0	55	2
RA Harper	2	0	8	0

New Zealand

ENGLAND

MA Atherton*	run out	81
AJ Stewart	c Nash b Pringle	24
RA Smith	c Parore b Thomson	15
GA Gooch	b Thomson	23
GA Hick	b Pringle	18
DA Reeve	c Fleming b Pringle	16
SJ Rhodes+	c Thomson b Pringle	12
CC Lewis	b Pringle	19
SD Udal	not out	3
D Gough		
ARC Fraser		
Extras	(1b, 5lb, 7w, 0nb)	13
	55 overs	
Total		**224**

FoW: 33, 84, 140, 161, 180, 199, 199, 224

DK Morrison	6	0	31	0
C Pringle	11	1	45	5
DJ Nash	6	1	20	0
GR Larsen	10	1	43	0
MN Hart	11	0	45	0
SA Thomson	11	0	34	2

NEW ZEALAND

BA Young	b Gough	65
MD Crowe	c Stewart b Gough	0
AC Parore+	b Udal	42
KR Rutherford*	lbw b Udal	0
SP Fleming	c & b Hick	17
SA Thomson	c Lewis b Hick	7
GR Larsen	c & b Lewis	13
DJ Nash	b Lewis	0
MN Hart	c Stewart b Lewis	13
C Pringle	c Hick b Fraser	3
DK Morrison	not out	17
Extras	(0b, 4lb, 1w, 0nb)	5
	52.5 overs	
Total		**182**

FoW: 2, 78, 81, 110, 134, 136, 136, 149, 152, 182

ARC Fraser	10	0	37	1
D Gough	11	1	36	2
SD Udal	11	0	39	2
DA Reeve	4	0	15	0
CC Lewis	9.5	2	20	3
GA Hick	7	0	31	2

South Africa

SOUTH AFRICA

KC Wessels*	b de Freitas	4
G Kirsten	c de Freitas b Lewis	30
PN Kirsten	c Rhodes b de Freitas	8
JN Rhodes	c Thorpe b Cork	35
DJ Cullinan	b de Freitas	45
WJ Cronje	b Lewis	36
DJ Richardson+	not out	20
RP Snell	c Gough b Lewis	2
TG Shaw	not out	17
CR Matthews		
PS de Villiers		
Extras	(0b, 6lb, 10w, 2nb)	18
	55 overs	
Total		**215**

FoW: 5, 30, 58, 103, 174, 176, 182

PAJ de Freitas	9	1	38	3
D Gough	11	2	40	0
CC Lewis	8	0	32	3
SD Udal	11	0	34	0
DG Cork	11	0	46	1
GA Hick	5	1	19	0

ENGLAND

MA Atherton*	run out	49
AJ Stewart	c de Villiers b Shaw	32
GA Hick	c Shaw b Snell	81
GP Thorpe	run out	26
NH Fairbrother	not out	19
SJ Rhodes+	not out	0
CC Lewis		
PAJ de Freitas		
DG Cork		
D Gough		
SD Udal		
Extras	(0b, 9lb, 2w, 1nb)	12
	54 overs	
Total		**219**

FoW: 57, 126, 181, 215

PS de Villiers	11	2	27	0
CR Matthews	11	1	42	0
TG Shaw	11	0	34	1
WJ Cronje	9	0	50	0
RP Snell	11	0	49	1
G Kirsten	1	0	8	0

South Africa

No. 227: Texaco Trophy (2)		
VENUE: Old Trafford		
DATE: 27th & 28th August 1994		
TOSS WON BY: England		
RESULT: England won by 4 wickets		

SOUTH AFRICA

G Kirsten	c Lewis b Cork	30
KC Wessels*	lbw b de Freitas	21
WJ Cronje	run out	0
JN Rhodes	lbw b Cork	0
DJ Cullinan	run out	54
BM McMillan	st Rhodes b Udal	0
DJ Richardson+	c Lewis b Gough	14
TG Shaw	b Gough	6
CR Matthews	b Cork	26
PS de Villiers	not out	14
AA Donald	not out	2
Extras	(0b, 6lb, 4w, 4nb)	14
Total	55 overs	**181**

FoW: 43, 47, 47, 64, 68, 113, 121, 163, 163

PAJ de Freitas	11	4	12	1
D Gough	10	1	39	2
CC Lewis	9	0	44	0
SD Udal	11	2	17	1
DG Cork	11	1	49	3
GA Hick	3	0	14	0

ENGLAND

MA Atherton*	c Wessels b Matthews	19
AJ Stewart	c Cullinan b Donald	11
GA Hick	lbw b Donald	0
GP Thorpe	c Cullinan b Shaw	55
NH Fairbrother	run out	3
SJ Rhodes+	run out	56
CC Lewis	not out	17
PAJ de Freitas	not out	7
DG Cork		
D Gough		
SD Udal		
Extras	(0b, 0lb, 4w, 10nb)	14
Total	48.2 overs	**182**

FoW: 27, 28, 42, 60, 130, 171

AA Donald	10.2	1	47	2
PS de Villiers	8	1	29	0
BM McMillan	10	1	53	0
CR Matthews	9	2	20	1
TG Shaw	11	0	33	1

Australia

No. 228: B&H World Series		
VENUE: Sydney (SCG) Day/Night		
DATE: 6th December 1994		
TOSS WON BY: Australia		
RESULT: Australia won by 28 runs		

AUSTRALIA

MA Taylor*	c & b Hick	57
MJ Slater	c Hick b Udal	50
ME Waugh	b Udal	4
DC Boon	not out	64
MG Bevan	c Gooch b Gough	46
SG Law	not out	0
IA Healy+		
CJ McDermott		
SK Warne		
TBA May		
GD.McGrath		
Extras	(0b, 2lb, 1w, 0nb)	3
Total	50 overs	**224**

FoW: 96, 106, 126, 218

JE Benjamin	6	0	25	0
PAJ de Freitas	9	1	43	0
D Gough	10	0	51	1
C White	5	0	22	0
SD Udal	10	1	37	2
GA Hick	10	0	44	1

ENGLAND

MA Atherton*	lbw b Law	60
AJ Stewart	c Law b May	48
GA Hick	c Boon b May	6
GP Thorpe	c Bevan b McDermott	21
GA Gooch	c McDermott b Warne	21
C White	b McDermott	0
SJ Rhodes+	c Warne b Law	8
PAJ de Freitas	run out	6
D Gough	not out	8
SD Udal	b McGrath	4
JE Benjamin	b McDermott	0
Extras	(0b, 7lb, 6w, 1nb)	14
Total	48.3 overs	**196**

FoW: 100, 112, 133, 147, 148, 164, 180, 187, 195, 196

CJ McDermott	9.3	0	34	3
GD McGrath	9	4	22	1
SK Warne	10	0	46	1
SG Law	10	0	52	2
TBA May	10	1	35	2

Zimbabwe

No. 229:	B&H World Series
VENUE:	Sydney (SCG) Day/Night
DATE:	15th December 1994
TOSS WON BY:	Zimbabwe
RESULT:	Zimbabwe won by 13 runs

ZIMBABWE

A Flower*+	c Stewart b Fraser	12
GW Flower	not out	84
ADR Campbell	b Gough	23
GJ Whittall	c Stewart b Gough	0
DL Houghton	c Stewart b Gough	57
MH Dekker	c de Freitas b Fraser	5
GC Martin	b de Freitas	7
PA Strang	run out	0
HH Streak	run out	1
SG Peall	c Stewart b Gough	0
DH Brain	b Gough	7
Extras	(0b, 7lb, 1w, 1nb)	9
	49.3 overs	
Total		**205**

FoW: 24, 61, 61, 171, 179, 192, 192, 198, 198, 205

PAJ de Freitas	10	2	27	1
ARC Fraser	10	0	45	2
D Gough	9.3	0	44	5
PCR Tufnell	10	0	43	0
SD Udal	8	0	31	0
GA Hick	2	0	8	0

ENGLAND

GA Gooch	c & b Strang	38
MA Atherton*	c A Flower b Whittall	14
GA Hick	run out	64
GP Thorpe	lbw b Strang	0
JP Crawley	lbw b Dekker	18
AJ Stewart+	b Streak	29
PAJ de Freitas	run out	5
D Gough	b Streak	2
SD Udal	run out	10
ARC Fraser	b Dekker	2
PCR Tufnell	not out	0
Extras	(0b, 5lb, 5w, 0nb)	10
	49.1 overs	
Total		**192**

FoW: 49, 60, 60, 105, 169, 178, 179, 181, 192, 192

DH Brain	8	1	27	0
HH Streak	8.1	1	36	2
GJ Whittall	4	1	21	1
PA Strang	10	2	30	2
SG Peall	10	2	29	0
MH Dekker	9	0	44	2

No. 230:	B&H World Series
VENUE:	Brisbane ('Gabba')
DATE:	7th January 1995
TOSS WON BY:	England
RESULT:	England won by 26 runs

ENGLAND

GA Gooch	b Brain	0
MA Atherton*	lbw b Martin	26
GA Hick	c A Flower b Streak	8
GP Thorpe	c Brain b Strang	89
NH Fairbrother	run out	7
JP Crawley	lbw b GW Flower	14
SJ Rhodes+	st A Flower b Dekker	20
D Gough	c Campbell b Dekker	4
PAJ de Freitas	not out	12
SD Udal	not out	11
JE Benjamin		
Extras	(4b, 2lb, 3w, 0nb)	9
	50 overs	
Total		**200**

FoW: 0, 20, 72, 82, 107, 164, 170, 182

DH Brain	8	0	27	1
HH Streak	7	1	26	1
GJ Whittall	5	0	19	0
GC Martin	5	1	15	1
SG Peall	5	0	19	0
PA Strang	10	0	42	1
GW Flower	3	0	16	1
MH Dekker	7	0	30	2

ZIMBABWE

GW Flower	c Rhodes b Udal	19
ADR Campbell	c Fairbrother b de Freitas	3
MH Dekker	b Benjamin	5
A Flower*+	c Rhodes b Gough	52
GJ Whittall	c Rhodes b de Freitas	53
IP Butchart	run out	2
GC Martin	st Rhodes b Hick	1
PA Strang	b Gough	16
DH Brain	c Hick b Udal	2
HH Streak	not out	9
SG Peall	run out	3
Extras	(0b, 7lb, 2w, 0nb)	9
	48.1 overs	
Total		**174**

FoW: 8, 16, 56, 103, 123, 124, 149, 156, 169, 174

D Gough	9.1	3	17	2
PAJ de Freitas	10	0	28	2
JE Benjamin	6	0	22	1
SD Udal	8	0	41	2
GA Hick	7	1	29	1
GA Gooch	8	0	30	0

Australia

No. 231:	B&H World Series	
VENUE:	Melbourne (MCG) Day/Night	
DATE:	10th January 1995	
TOSS WON BY:	England	
RESULT:	England won by 37 runs	

ENGLAND

GA Gooch	c Taylor b McGrath	2
MA Atherton*	c SR Waugh b ME Waugh	14
GA Hick	c Fleming b Warne	91
GP Thorpe	c Healy b ME Waugh	8
NH Fairbrother	c Healy b Warne	35
JP Crawley	c Healy b McGrath	2
SJ Rhodes+	lbw b McGrath	2
D Gough	b McGrath	45
PAJ de Freitas	not out	2
SD Udal	not out	2
ARC Fraser		
Extras	(4b, 10lb, 6w, 2nb)	22
	50 overs	
Total		**225**

FoW: 11, 31, 44, 133, 136, 142, 216, 223

DW Fleming	10	1	36	0
GD McGrath	10	1	25	4
ME Waugh	10	1	43	2
SK Warne	10	0	37	2
GR Robertson	5	0	38	0
SG Law	5	0	32	0

AUSTRALIA

MA Taylor*	c Rhodes b Fraser	6
MJ Slater	b Fraser	2
ME Waugh	b Hick	41
SR Waugh	c Rhodes b Fraser	0
SG Law	c & b Udal	17
DC Boon	b Hick	26
IA Healy+	c Atherton b Hick	56
GR Robertson	run out	1
SK Warne	b Fraser	21
DW Fleming	not out	5
GD McGrath	b de Freitas	10
Extras	(0b, 0lb, 3w, 0nb)	3
	48 overs	
Total		**188**

FoW: 3, 16, 19, 62, 76, 125, 131, 173, 173, 188

ARC Fraser	10	2	22	4
PAJ de Freitas	9	0	32	1
GA Gooch	10	0	50	0
SD Udal	9	1	43	1
GA Hick	10	1	41	3

West Indies

No. 232:	Texaco Trophy	
VENUE:	Trent Bridge	
DATE:	24th & 25th May 1995	
TOSS WON BY:	West Indies	
RESULT:	West Indies won by 5 wickets	

ENGLAND

MA Atherton*	c Lara b Walsh	8
AJ Stewart+	b Hooper	74
GA Hick	c Murray b Benjamin	8
GP Thorpe	c Murray b Walsh	7
NH Fairbrother	b Bishop	12
MR Ramprakash	b Walsh	32
PAJ de Freitas	run out	15
DG Cork	b Arthurton	14
D Gough	run out	3
SD Udal	not out	5
ARC Fraser	not out	4
Extras	(0b, 11lb, 5w, 1nb)	17
	55 overs	
Total		**199**

FoW: 25, 60, 85,121, 125, 157, 186, 190, 191

CEL Ambrose	8	1	33	0
CA Walsh	10	1	28	3
IR Bishop	11	2	30	1
WKM Benjamin	8	1	22	1
CL Hooper	10	0	45	1
KLT Arthurton	8	0	30	1

WEST INDIES

CL Hooper	b Cork	34
SL Campbell	run out	80
BC Lara	c Atherton b Gough	70
RB Richardson*	c de Freitas b Gough	1
JC Adams	lbw b Cork	2
KLT Arthurton	not out	1
JR Murray+	not out	7
CEL Ambrose		
CA Walsh		
WKM Benjamin		
IR Bishop		
Extras	(0b, 1lb, 4w, 1nb)	6
	52.4 overs	
Total		**201**

FoW: 66, 180, 183, 191, 194

PAJ de Freitas	10.4	1	44	0
ARC Fraser	10	2	29	0
D Gough	11	1	30	2
DG Cork	11	0	48	2
SD Udal	8	0	37	0
GA Hick	2	0	12	0

West Indies

No. 233: Texaco Trophy
VENUE: The Oval
DATE: 26th May 1995
TOSS WON BY: West Indies
RESULT: England won by 25 runs

ENGLAND

MA Atherton*	b Benjamin	92
AJ Stewart+	c Murray b Bishop	16
GA Hick	run out	66
GP Thorpe	run out	26
NH Fairbrother	not out	61
MR Ramprakash	c Adams b Hooper	16
D Gough	not out	8
PAJ de Freitas		
DG Cork		
SD Udal		
PJ Martin		
Extras	(6b, 5lb, 7w, 3nb)	21
	55 overs	
Total		**306**

FoW: 33, 177, 188, 243, 296

CEL Ambrose	10	1	47	0
CA Walsh	5.2	0	17	0
IR Bishop	11	0	60	1
WKM Benjamin	10.4	0	55	1
KLT Arthurton	8	0	48	0
CL Hooper	10	0	68	1

WEST INDIES

CL Hooper	c Atherton b Gough	17
SL Campbell	c Thorpe b Martin	20
BC Lara	b Martin	39
JC Adams	lbw b Martin	2
RB Richardson*	c & b Cork	15
KLT Arthurton	run out	39
JR Murray+	run out	86
WKM Benjamin	c Ramprakash b de Freitas	17
IR Bishop	run out	18
CEL Ambrose	b Martin	10
CA Walsh	not out	5
Extras	(0b, 6lb, 7w, 0nb)	13
	53 overs	
Total		**281**

FoW: 25, 69, 77, 88, 114, 166, 213, 261, 275, 281

D Gough	11	0	62	1
PAJ de Freitas	10	0	73	1
DG Cork	11	0	56	1
SD Udal	11	0	40	0
PJ Martin	10	1	44	4

West Indies

No. 234: Texaco Trophy
VENUE: Lord's
DATE: 28th May 1995
TOSS WON BY: West Indies
RESULT: England won by 73 runs

ENGLAND

MA Atherton*	c Adams b Gibson	127
AJ Stewart+	c Lara b Bishop	8
GA Hick	b Hooper	24
GP Thorpe	c Hooper b Gibson	28
MR Ramprakash	not out	29
AP Wells	b Gibson	15
D Gough	b Benjamin	8
DG Cork	lbw b Benjamin	0
PJ Martin	not out	4
ARC Fraser		
SD Udal		
Extras	(4b, 13lb, 9w, 7nb)	33
	55 overs	
Total		**276**

FoW: 12, 79, 152, 244, 263, 272, 272

CEL Ambrose	11	1	45	0
IR Bishop	11	2	53	1
WKM Benjamin	10	0	61	2
OD Gibson	11	0	51	3
CL Hooper	11	0	38	1
KLT Arthurton	1	0	11	0

WEST INDIES

SC Williams	c Atherton b Cork	21
CL Hooper	c Gough b Cork	40
BC Lara	c Stewart b Cork	11
JC Adams	c Stewart b Martin	29
KLT Arthurton	c Stewart b Gough	35
RB Richardson*	lbw b Gough	23
JR Murray+	b Fraser	5
OD Gibson	c Atherton b Fraser	7
WKM Benjamin	b Fraser	6
IR Bishop	not out	1
CEL Ambrose	b Martin	1
Extras	(0b, 13lb, 11w, 0nb)	24
	48.2 overs	
Total		**203**

FoW: 29, 44, 94, 128, 171, 184, 190, 198, 201, 203

ARC Fraser	11	3	34	3
PJ Martin	9.2	1	36	2
DG Cork	9	2	27	3
D Gough	10	0	31	2
SD Udal	8	0	52	0
GA Hick	1	0	10	0

South Africa

No. 235: One-Day Series	
VENUE: Cape Town Day/Night	
DATE: 9th January 1996	
TOSS WON BY: South Africa	
RESULT: South Africa won by 6 runs	

SOUTH AFRICA

G Kirsten	lbw b Cork	8
DJ Richardson+	c Stewart b Martin	11
BM McMillan	c Stewart b Martin	4
DJ Cullinan	c Stewart b Reeve	17
JN Rhodes	c Stewart b White	16
WJ Cronje*	run out	24
JH Kallis	c Thorpe b White	38
SM Pollock	not out	66
CR Matthews	c Reeve b Cork	10
AA Donald		
PR Adams		
Extras	(1b, 6lb, 4w, 6nb)	17
	50 overs	
Total		**211**

FoW: 12, 20, 44, 57, 77, 107, 152, 211

DG Cork	10	0	51	2
PJ Martin	10	1	34	2
D Gough	9	0	39	0
DA Reeve	9	1	40	1
C White	10	1	31	2
NMK Smith	2	0	9	0

ENGLAND

MA Atherton*	b Donald	35
AJ Stewart+	lbw b Donald	23
GA Hick	lbw b Donald	21
GP Thorpe	c Matthews b McMillan	62
NH Fairbrother	c Adams b Pollock	28
C White	c & b Pollock	5
DA Reeve	c Richardson b Matthews	2
DG Cork	run out	7
NMK Smith	c McMillan b Pollock	3
D Gough	b Pollock	3
PJ Martin	not out	4
Extras	(0b, 6lb, 4w, 2nb)	12
	42.5 overs	
Total		**205**

FoW: 59, 64, 94, 155, 161, 166, 177,189, 199, 205

CR Matthews	10	1	39	1
SM Pollock	9.5	0	34	4
AA Donald	10	0	38	3
BM McMillan	10	0	38	1
PR Adams	2	0	18	0
WJ Cronje	5	0	18	0
JH Kallis	3	0	14	0

South Africa

No. 236: One-Day Series	
VENUE: Bloemfontein Day/Night	
DATE: 11th January 1996	
TOSS WON BY: South Africa	
RESULT: England won by 5 wickets	

SOUTH AFRICA

AC Hudson	c Stewart b Hick	64
RP Snell	c Fairbrother b Hick	63
BM McMillan	b Martin	44
JH Kallis	c Hick b Smith	29
WJ Cronje*	b Cork	19
JN Rhodes	b Cork	4
G Kirsten	c Fairbrother b Cork	2
SM Pollock	c Ramprakash b Smith	5
DJ Richardson+	not out	13
N Boje	not out	2
AA Donald		
Extras	(4b, 6lb, 7w, 0nb)	17
	50 overs	
Total		**262**

FoW: 116, 164, 197, 226, 228, 236, 237, 248

DG Cork	10	0	44	3
PAJ de Freitas	6	0	30	0
C White	6	0	37	0
PJ Martin	6	0	43	1
NMK Smith	10	0	46	2
GA Hick	10	0	38	2
MR Ramprakash	2	0	14	0

ENGLAND

PAJ de Freitas	c Rhodes b Pollock	17
MA Atherton*	c Cronje b Pollock	85
GA Hick	lbw b Cronje	55
GP Thorpe	not out	72
MR Ramprakash	run out	1
NH Fairbrother	c Rhodes b McMillan	12
AJ Stewart+	not out	13
C White		
NMK Smith		
DG Cork		
PJ Martin		
Extras	(0b, 4lb, 5w, 1nb)	10
	48.2 overs	
Total		**265**

FoW: 37, 108, 198, 201, 223

SM Pollock	9.2	0	48	2
RP Snell	6	0	39	0
BM McMillan	7	0	46	1
AA Donald	10	1	44	0
WJ Cronje	7	0	32	1
JH Kallis	5	0	27	0
N Boje	4	0	25	0

South Africa

No. 237: One-Day Series
VENUE: Johannesburg (Wanderers)
DATE: 13th January 1996
TOSS WON BY: England
RESULT: South Africa won by 3 wickets

ENGLAND

PAJ de Freitas	c Donald b Pollock	13
MA Atherton*	c McMillan b Pollock	0
RA Smith	lbw b Pollock	9
GA Hick	b Donald	14
MR Ramprakash	c Richardson b Cronje	27
NH Fairbrother	not out	57
C White	c Cronje b McMillan	34
DA Reeve	c Richardson b Donald	10
RC Russell+	c Cronje b Snell	18
M Watkinson		
D Gough		
Extras	(0b, 7lb, 7w, 2nb)	16
	50 overs	
Total		**198**

FoW: 1, 23, 25, 53, 88, 139, 168, 198

SM Pollock	10	2	31	3
CR Matthews	8	0	34	0
AA Donald	10	0	53	2
BM McMillan	10	0	27	1
RP Snell	6	1	29	1
WJ Cronje	6	0	17	1

SOUTH AFRICA

AC Hudson	b Gough	17
RP Snell	c Fairbrother b de Freitas	8
WJ Cronje*	c Russell b de Freitas	7
DJ Cullinan	c Russell b Gough	25
JH Kallis	run out	16
JN Rhodes	c Russell b Gough	44
BM McMillan	c Smith b White	35
SM Pollock	not out	18
DJ Richardson+	not out	10
CR Matthews		
AA Donald		
Extras	(1b, 7lb, 8w, 3nb)	19
	48.1 overs	
Total		**199**

FoW: 19, 29, 63, 73, 114, 157, 180

D Gough	10	2	31	3
PAJ de Freitas	8	0	35	2
DA Reeve	10	1	43	0
GA Hick	3	0	13	0
M Watkinson	9	0	43	0
C White	8.1	1	26	1

South Africa

No. 238: One-Day Series
VENUE: Centurion (Centurion Park)
DATE: 14th January 1996
TOSS WON BY: England
RESULT: South Africa won by 7 wickets

ENGLAND

AJ Stewart*	c Cullinan b Symcox	64
RA Smith	c Symcox b Donald	63
GA Hick	b Cronje	21
GP Thorpe	c Pollock b Symcox	15
MR Ramprakash	c Kallis b Donald	32
C White	c Donald b Cronje	19
RC Russell+	not out	39
DG Cork	c Richardson b Matthews	0
PAJ de Freitas	c Cullinan b Donald	2
D Gough	not out	1
RK Illingworth		
Extras	(0b, 5lb, 10w, 1nb)	16
	50 overs	
Total		**272**

FoW: 103, 139, 168, 174, 216, 245, 249, 260

CR Matthews	10	0	48	1
SM Pollock	10	1	36	0
WJ Cronje	10	0	57	2
AA Donald	9	0	72	3
PL Symcox	10	1	48	2
G Kirsten	1	0	6	0

SOUTH AFRICA

AC Hudson	lbw b Gough	72
G Kirsten	b Cork	116
WJ Cronje*	c Thorpe b Illingworth	47
DJ Cullinan	not out	25
JH Kallis	not out	14
JN Rhodes		
DJ Richardson+		
SM Pollock		
CR Matthews		
PL Symcox		
AA Donald		
Extras	(0b, 0lb, 2w, 0nb)	2
	48 overs	
Total		**276**

FoW: 156, 223, 247

DG Cork	10	0	65	1
PAJ de Freitas	10	0	46	0
D Gough	10	1	41	1
GA Hick	3	0	17	0
RK Illingworth	9	0	65	1
C White	6	0	42	0

South Africa

No. 239: One-Day Series
VENUE: Durban (Kingsmead) Day/Night
DATE: 17th January 1996
TOSS WON BY: South Africa
RESULT: South Africa won by 5 wickets

ENGLAND

MA Atherton*	c Richardson b Donald	17
AJ Stewart	b Donald	31
RA Smith	c Richardson b Donald	8
GA Hick	c Richardson b Donald	6
GP Thorpe	b Matthews	63
C White	b Pollock	16
RC Russell+	run out	21
DG Cork	b Matthews	1
PAJ de Freitas	b Pollock	3
D Gough	b de Villiers	3
PJ Martin	not out	2
Extras	(1b, 6lb, 6w, 0nb)	13
	49.5 overs	
Total		**184**

FoW: 51, 52, 61, 78, 132, 164, 170, 177, 178, 184

SM Pollock	10	1	31	2
CR Matthews	10	1	37	2
PS de Villiers	9.5	0	35	1
AA Donald	10	0	41	4
BM McMillan	8	0	25	0
WJ Cronje	2	0	8	0

SOUTH AFRICA

AC Hudson	lbw b Cork	5
G Kirsten	c Russell b Cork	0
WJ Cronje*	b White	78
JH Kallis	c Hick b de Freitas	67
BM McMillan	c Hick b de Freitas	14
JN Rhodes	not out	12
SM Pollock	not out	1
DJ Richardson+		
PS de Villiers		
CR Matthews		
AA Donald		
Extras	(0b, 1lb, 3w, 4nb)	8
	48.2 overs	
Total		**185**

FoW: 1, 9, 127, 150, 183

PJ Martin	10	2	34	0
DG Cork	9.2	3	29	2
PAJ de Freitas	9	0	41	2
D Gough	10	0	32	0
C White	8	1	40	1
GA Hick	2	0	8	0

South Africa

No. 240: One-Day Series
VENUE: East London Day/Night
DATE: 19th January 1996
TOSS WON BY: South Africa
RESULT: South Africa won by 14 runs

SOUTH AFRICA

G Kirsten	c Smith b Cork	17
RP Snell	c Atherton b Martin	8
WJ Cronje*	b White	13
JH Kallis	lbw b Martin	0
BM McMillan	not out	45
JN Rhodes	c Gough b Illingworth	10
L Klusener	lbw b Gough	0
SM Pollock	b Gough	6
DJ Richardson+	lbw b Gough	0
PS de Villiers	b White	15
PR Adams	b Cork	0
Extras	(1b, 11lb, 1w, 2nb)	15
	41.4 overs	
Total		**129**

FoW: 25, 29, 29, 54, 89, 89, 98, 98, 128, 129

DG Cork	8.4	1	22	2
PJ Martin	7	0	23	2
D Gough	10	1	25	3
C White	7	1	18	2
RK Illingworth	9	1	29	1

ENGLAND

MA Atherton*	c Richardson b de Villiers	6
C White	c Richardson b de Villiers	6
RA Smith	b Pollock	0
GA Hick	c Kirsten b Adams	39
RC Russell+	run out	12
GP Thorpe	b Adams	0
NH Fairbrother	b Snell	13
DG Cork	b Adams	2
RK Illingworth	run out	1
D Gough	lbw b Snell	4
PJ Martin	not out	5
Extras	(1b, 13lb, 12w, 1nb)	27
Total		**115**

FoW: 10, 11, 19, 75, 76, 78, 88, 95, 104, 115

SM Pollock	10	3	15	1
PS de Villiers	8	1	10	2
L Klusener	4	0	19	0
RP Snell	9.4	2	22	2
JH Kallis	3	0	9	0
PR Adams	9	0	26	3

South Africa

No. 241: One-Day Series		
VENUE: Port Elizabeth		
DATE: 21st January 1996		
TOSS WON BY: South Africa		
RESULT: South Africa won by 64 runs		

SOUTH AFRICA

AC Hudson	c Thorpe b White	44
SJ Palframan+	c Russell b Martin	10
G Kirsten	c Russell b Gough	17
WJ Cronje*	c Hick b Martin	60
AP Kuiper	not out	61
JH Kallis	run out	2
BM McMillan	b White	4
SM Pollock	c Thorpe b Gough	0
PL Symcox	b Gough	7
PS de Villiers	b Gough	0
PR Adams	not out	0
Extras	(1b, 7lb, 5w, 0nb)	13
	50 overs	
Total		**218**

FoW: 30, 61, 123, 167, 172, 195, 196, 206, 206

DG Cork	10	0	53	0
PJ Martin	9	0	47	2
D Gough	10	0	33	4
RK Illingworth	10	1	31	0
GA Hick	4	0	19	0
C White	7	0	27	2

ENGLAND

MA Atherton*	c McMillan b Pollock	3
C White	c (sub) b de Villiers	20
RA Smith	c Palframan b McMillan	21
GA Hick	b Symcox	43
NH Fairbrother	b McMillan	0
GP Thorpe	b Adams	21
RC Russell+	c McMillan b Symcox	3
DG Cork	lbw b de Villiers	21
PJ Martin	c Symcox b de Villiers	6
D Gough	b de Villiers	4
RK Illingworth	not out	2
Extras	(1b, 5lb, 2w, 2nb)	10
	46.1 overs	
Total		**154**

FoW: 5, 35, 70, 70, 113, 118, 124, 147, 151, 154

PS de Villiers	9.1	1	32	4
SM Pollock	6	1	17	1
WJ Cronje	4	0	17	0
BM McMillan	8	0	29	2
PL Symcox	10	0	31	2
PR Adams	9	1	22	1

New Zealand

No. 242: World Cup		
VENUE: Ahmedabad (Gujarat Stadium)		
DATE: 14th February 1996		
TOSS WON BY: England		
RESULT: New Zealand won by 11 runs		

NEW ZEALAND

CM Spearman	c & b Cork	5
NJ Astle	c Hick b Martin	101
SP Fleming	c Thorpe b Hick	28
RG Twose	c Thorpe b Hick	17
CL Cairns	c Cork b Illingworth	36
CZ Harris	run out	10
SA Thomson	not out	17
LK Germon*+	not out	13
GR Larsen		
DJ Nash		
DK Morrison		
Extras	(4b, 2lb, 4w, 2nb)	12
	50 overs	
Total		**239**

FoW: 12, 108, 141, 196, 204, 212

DG Cork	10	1	36	1
PJ Martin	6	0	37	1
D Gough	10	0	63	0
RK Illingworth	10	1	31	1
GA Hick	9	0	45	2
C White	5	0	21	0

ENGLAND

MA Atherton*	b Nash	1
AJ Stewart	c & b Harris	34
GA Hick	run out	85
GP Thorpe	b Larsen	9
NH Fairbrother	b Morrison	36
RC Russell+	c Morrison b Larsen	2
C White	c Cairns b Thomson	13
DG Cork	c Germon b Nash	19
D Gough	not out	15
PJ Martin	c Cairns b Nash	3
RK Illingworth	not out	3
Extras	(1b, 4lb, 1w, 2nb)	8
	50 overs	
Total		**228**

FoW: 1, 100, 123, 144, 151, 180, 185, 210, 222

DK Morrison	8	0	38	1
DJ Nash	7	1	26	3
CL Cairns	4	0	24	0
GR Larsen	10	1	33	2
SA Thomson	10	0	51	1
CZ Harris	9	0	45	1
NJ Astle	2	0	6	0

UAE

No. 243: World Cup
VENUE: Peshawar (Arbab Niaz)
DATE: 18th February 1996
TOSS WON BY: United Arab Emirates
RESULT: England won by 8 wickets

UNITED ARAB EMIRATES

Azhar Saeed	lbw b de Freitas	9
G Mylvaganam	c Fairbrother b de Freitas	0
Mazhar Hussain	b Smith	33
V Mehra	c Russell b Smith	1
Moh'mad Aslam	b Gough	23
Arshad Laiq	b Smith	0
Salim Raza	b Cork	10
JA Samarasekera	run out	29
Sultan Zarawani*	b Cork	2
Sh'kat Duk'wala	lbw b Illingworth	15
Imtiaz Abbasi+	not out	1
Extras	(4b, 4lb, 4w, 1nb)	13
	48.3 overs	
Total		**136**

FoW: 3, 32, 48, 49, 49, 80, 88, 100, 135, 136

DG Cork	10	1	33	2
PAJ de Freitas	9.3	3	16	2
D Gough	8	3	23	1
C White	1.3	1	2	0
NMK Smith	9.3	2	29	3
RK Illingworth	10	2	25	1

ENGLAND

AJ Stewart	c Mylvaganam b Arshad	23
NMK Smith	retired hurt	27
GP Thorpe	not out	44
MA Atherton*	b Azhar	20
NH Fairbrother	not out	12
RC Russell+		
C White		
DG Cork		
PAJ de Freitas		
D Gough		
RK Illingworth		
Extras	(4b, 2lb, 2w, 6nb)	14
	35 overs	
Total		**140**

FoW: 52, 109

JA Samarasekera	7	1	35	0
Arshad Laiq	7	0	25	1
Salim Raza	5	1	20	0
Azhar Saeed	10	1	26	1
Sultan Zarawani	6	0	28	0

Netherlands

No. 244: World Cup
VENUE: Peshawar (Arbab Niaz)
DATE: 22nd February 1996
TOSS WON BY: England
RESULT: England won by 49 runs

ENGLAND

AJ Stewart	b Bakker	5
NMK Smith	c Clarke b Jansen	31
GA Hick	not out	104
GP Thorpe	lbw b Lefebvre	89
MA Atherton*	b Lubbers	10
NH Fairbrother	not out	24
RC Russell+		
DG Cork		
PAJ de Freitas		
D Gough		
PJ Martin		
Extras	(0b, 12lb, 4w, 0nb)	16
	50 overs	
Total		**279**

FoW: 11, 42, 185, 212

RP Lefebvre	10	1	40	1
PJ Bakker	8	0	46	1
F Jansen	7	0	40	1
GJAF Aponso	8	0	55	0
SW Lubbers	10	0	51	1
TBM Deleede	2	0	9	0
PE Cantrell	5	0	26	0

NETHERLANDS

NE Clarke	lbw b Cork	0
PE Cantrell	lbw b de Freitas	28
TBM Deleede	lbw b de Freitas	41
SW Lubbers*	c Russell b de Freitas	9
KJ van Noortwijk	c Gough b Martin	64
B Zuiderent	c Thorpe b Martin	54
RP Lefebvre	not out	11
M Schewe+	not out	11
GJAF Aponso		
F Jansen		
PJ Bakker		
Extras	(0b, 4lb, 6w, 2nb)	12
	50 overs	
Total		**230**

FoW: 1, 46, 70, 81, 195, 210

DG Cork	8	0	52	1
PAJ de Freitas	10	3	31	3
NMK Smith	8	0	27	0
D Gough	3	0	23	0
PJ Martin	10	1	42	2
GA Hick	5	0	23	0
GP Thorpe	6	0	28	0

South Africa

No. 245: World Cup
VENUE: Rawalpindi (Cricket Stadium)
DATE: 25th February 1996
TOSS WON BY: South Africa
RESULT: South Africa won by 78 runs

SOUTH AFRICA

G Kirsten	run out	38
SJ Palframan+	c Russell b Martin	28
WJ Cronje*	c Russell b Gough	15
DJ Cullinan	b de Freitas	34
JH Kallis	c Russell b Cork	26
JN Rhodes	b Martin	37
BM McMillan	b Smith	11
SM Pollock	c Fairbrother b Cork	12
PL Symcox	c Thorpe b Martin	1
CR Matthews	not out	9
PS de Villiers	c Smith b Gough	12
Extras	(0b, 1lb, 5w, 1nb)	7
	50 overs	
Total		**230**

FoW: 56, 85, 88, 137, 163, 195, 199, 202, 213, 230

DG Cork	10	0	36	2
PAJ de Freitas	10	0	55	1
D Gough	10	0	48	2
PJ Martin	10	0	33	3
NMK Smith	8	0	40	1
GP Thorpe	2	0	17	0

ENGLAND

MA Atherton*	c Palframan b Pollock	0
NMK Smith	b de Villiers	11
GA Hick	c McMillan b de Villiers	14
GP Thorpe	c Palframan b Symcox	46
AJ Stewart	run out	7
NH Fairbrother	c Palframan b Symcox	3
RC Russell+	c Rhodes b Pollock	12
DG Cork	b Matthews	17
PAJ de Freitas	run out	22
D Gough	b Matthews	11
PJ Martin	not out	1
Extras	(0b, 7lb, 1w, 0nb)	8
	44.3 overs	
Total		**152**

FoW: 0, 22, 33, 52, 62, 97, 97, 139, 141, 152

SM Pollock	8	1	16	2
PS de Villiers	7	1	27	2
CR Matthews	9.3	0	30	2
BM McMillan	6	0	17	0
PL Symcox	10	0	38	2
WJ Cronje	4	0	17	0

Pakistan

No. 246: World Cup
VENUE: Karachi (National Stadium)
DATE: 3rd March 1996
TOSS WON BY: England
RESULT: Pakistan won by 7 wickets

ENGLAND

RA Smith	c Waqar b Salim	75
MA Atherton*	b Aamir	66
GA Hick	st Rashid b Aamir	1
GP Thorpe	not out	52
NH Fairbrother	c Wasim b Mushtaq Ahmed	13
RC Russell+	c & b Mushtaq Ahmed	4
DA Reeve	b Mushtaq Ahmed	3
DG Cork	lbw b Waqar	0
D Gough	b Wasim	14
PJ Martin	run out	2
RK Illingworth	not out	1
Extras	(0b, 11lb, 4w, 3nb)	18
	50 overs	
Total		**249**

FoW: 147, 151, 156, 194, 204, 212, 217, 241, 247

Wasim Akram	7	1	31	1
Waqar Younis	10	1	45	1
Aaqib Javed	7	0	34	0
Mushtaq Ahmed	10	0	53	3
Aamir Sohail	10	0	48	2
Salim Malik	6	1	27	1

PAKISTAN

Aamir Sohail	c Thorpe b Illingworth	42
Saeed Anwar	c Russell b Cork	71
Ijaz Ahmed	c Russell b Cork	70
Inzamam-ul-Haq	not out	53
Javed Miandad	not out	11
Salim Malik		
Rashid Latif+		
Wasim Akram*		
Mushtaq Ahmed		
Waqar Younis		
Aaqib Javed		
Extras	(0b, 1lb, 2w, 0nb)	3
	47.4 overs	
Total		**250**

FoW: 81, 139, 214

RK Illingworth	10	0	46	1
DG Cork	10	0	59	2
D Gough	10	0	45	0
PJ Martin	9	0	45	0
DA Reeve	6.4	0	37	0
GA Hick	2	0	17	0

'96

Sri Lanka

ENGLAND

RA Smith	run out	25
MA Atherton*	c Kaluwitharana b Vaas	22
GA Hick	c Ranatunga b Muralidharan	8
GP Thorpe	b Dharmasena	14
PAJ de Freitas	lbw b Jayasuriya	67
AJ Stewart	b Muralidharan	17
RC Russell+	b Dharmasena	9
DA Reeve	b Jayasuriya	35
D Gough	not out	26
PJ Martin	not out	0
RK Illingworth		
Extras	(0b, 8lb, 4w, 0nb)	12
	50 overs	
Total		**235**

FoW: 31, 58, 66, 94, 145, 171, 173, 235

GP Wickramasinghe	7	0	43	0
WPUJ Vaas	8	1	29	1
M Muralidharan	10	1	37	2
HDPK Dharmasena	10	0	30	2
ST Jayasuriya	9	0	46	2
PA de Silva	6	0	42	0

SRI LANKA

ST Jayasuriya	st Russell b Reeve	82
RS Kaluwit'rana+	b Illingworth	8
AP Gurusinha	run out	45
PA de Silva	c Smith b Hick	31
A Ranatunga*	lbw b Gough	25
HP Tillakaratne	not out	19
RS Mahanama	not out	22
HDPK Dharmasena		
WPUJ Vaas		
M Muralidharan		
GP Wickramasinghe		
Extras	(0b, 1lb, 2w, 1nb)	4
	40.4 overs	
Total		**236**

FoW: 12, 113, 165, 194, 198

PJ Martin	9	1	41	0
D Gough	10	1	36	1
RK Illingworth	10	1	72	1
PAJ de Freitas	3.4	0	38	0
DA Reeve	4	1	14	1
GA Hick	4	0	34	1

India

ENGLAND

MA Atherton*	c Mongia b Prasad	13
AD Brown	b Mhambrey	37
NMK Smith	c Tendulkar b Mhambrey	17
GA Hick	c Manjrekar b Srinath	91
GP Thorpe	c Mongia b Jadeja	26
AJ Stewart+	run out	3
RC Irani	c Prasad b Kumble	11
MA Ealham	b Kumble	40
CC Lewis	not out	29
DG Cork	not out	0
PJ Martin		
Extras	(1b, 11lb, 11w, 1nb)	24
	50 overs	
Total		**291**

FoW: 31, 57, 85, 141, 147, 176, 252, 276

J Srinath	10	1	45	1
BKV Prasad	10	1	63	1
PL Mhambrey	9	0	69	2
A Kumble	10	1	29	2
SR Tendulkar	6	0	44	0
AD Jadeja	5	0	29	1

INDIA

V Rathore	lbw b Lewis	23
SR Tendulkar	lbw b Martin	30
A Kumble	c Hick b Lewis	0
NS Sidhu	b Lewis	3
M Azharuddin*	not out	15
SV Manjrekar	b Lewis	3
AD Jadeja	not out	11
NR Mongia+		
J Srinath		
PL Mhambrey		
BKV Prasad		
Extras	(4b, 2lb, 4w, 1nb)	11
	17.1 overs	
Total		**96**

FoW: 54, 54, 56, 62, 68

DG Cork	3	0	21	0
CC Lewis	8.1	0	40	4
PJ Martin	6	0	29	1

India

No. 249: Texaco Trophy
VENUE: Headingley
DATE: 25th May 1996
TOSS WON BY: England
RESULT: England won by 6 wickets

INDIA

V Rathore	c Thorpe b Cork	7
SR Tendulkar	run out	6
NS Sidhu	run out	20
M Azharuddin*	c Brown b Martin	40
SV Manjrekar	run out	24
AD Jadeja	c Martin b Cork	33
NR Mongia+	c Atherton b Cork	9
A Kumble	c Stewart b Martin	0
J Srinath	c Cork b Gough	5
PL Mhambrey	not out	7
BKV Prasad	c Stewart b Martin	1
Extras	(0b, 1lb, 5w, 0nb)	6
	40.2 overs	
Total		**158**

FoW: 16, 17, 58, 94, 113, 145, 145, 149, 155, 158

DG Cork	9	1	46	3
CC Lewis	9	1	30	0
PJ Martin	8.2	1	34	3
D Gough	8	1	24	1
MA Ealham	6	0	23	0

ENGLAND

MA Atherton*	c Tendulkar b Prasad	7
AD Brown	lbw b Srinath	0
GA Hick	lbw b Prasad	0
GP Thorpe	not out	79
MP Maynard	run out	14
AJ Stewart+	not out	47
MA Ealham		
CC Lewis		
D Gough		
DG Cork		
PJ Martin		
Extras	(0b, 5lb, 8w, 2nb)	15
	39.3 overs	
Total		**162**

FoW: 1, 2, 23, 68

J Srinath	9	4	18	1
BKV Prasad	9	2	33	2
A Kumble	9	0	36	0
PL Mhambrey	6	0	29	0
SR Tendulkar	3	0	15	0
AD Jadeja	3	0	22	0
SV Manjrekar	0.3	0	4	0

India

No. 250: Texaco Trophy
VENUE: Old Trafford
DATE: 26th & 27th May 1996
TOSS WON BY: India
RESULT: England won by 4 wickets

INDIA

V Rathore	c Cork b Thorpe	54
SR Tendulkar	c Hick b Cork	1
SC Ganguly	st Stewart b Thorpe	46
M Azharuddin*	not out	73
AD Jadeja	c Stewart b Cork	29
RS Dravid	not out	22
A Kumble		
NR Mongia+		
J Srinath		
SLV Raju		
BKV Prasad		
Extras	(1b, 4lb, 6w, 0nb)	11
	50 overs	
Total		**236**

FoW: 11, 103, 118, 190

DG Cork	10	3	35	2
CC Lewis	10	1	49	0
D Gough	10	1	43	0
PJ Martin	10	0	50	0
NMK Smith	6	0	39	0
GP Thorpe	4	0	15	2

ENGLAND

MA Atherton*	lbw b Srinath	0
AD Brown	c Dravid b Srinath	118
NMK Smith	c & b Prasad	11
GA Hick	c Ganguly b Prasad	32
GP Thorpe	run out	29
MP Maynard	lbw b Kumble	14
AJ Stewart+	not out	13
CC Lewis	not out	4
D Gough		
DG Cork		
PJ Martin		
Extras	(0b, 10lb, 8w, 0nb)	18
	48.5 overs	
Total		**239**

FoW: 2, 32, 117, 186, 217, 226

J Srinath	10	0	35	2
BKV Prasad	10	1	26	2
A Kumble	10	0	52	1
SLV Raju	9.5	1	50	0
SC Ganguly	2	0	14	0
SR Tendulkar	2	0	22	0
AD Jadeja	5	0	30	0

Pakistan

No. 251: Texaco Trophy (2)
VENUE: Old Trafford
DATE: 29th August 1996
TOSS WON BY: Pakistan
RESULT: England won by 5 wickets

PAKISTAN

Saeed Anwar	c Mullally b Irani	57
Aamir Sohail	b Croft	48
Ijaz Ahmed	c Irani b Mullally	48
Wasim Akram*	b Croft	6
Inzamam-ul-Haq	not out	37
Moin Khan+	b Gough	10
Salim Malik	not out	6
Waqar Younis		
Saqlain Mushtaq		
Mushtaq Ahmed		
Ata-Ur-Rehman		
Extras	(2b, 4lb, 7w, 0nb)	13
	50 overs	
Total		**225**

FoW: 82, 141, 160, 174, 203

D Gough	10	0	44	1
AD Mullally	10	3	31	1
DW Headley	10	0	52	0
RC Irani	10	0	56	1
RDB Croft	10	1	36	2

ENGLAND

NV Knight	c Moin b Wasim	26
AJ Stewart+	lbw b Waqar	48
MA Atherton*	b Wasim	65
GP Thorpe	st Moin b Aamir	23
MP Maynard	b Wasim	41
GD Lloyd	not out	2
RC Irani	not out	6
D Gough		
DW Headley		
RDB Croft		
AD Mullally		
Extras	(0b, 4lb, 7w, 4nb)	15
	46.4 overs	
Total		**226**

FoW: 57, 98, 146, 200, 220

Wasim Akram	9.4	1	45	3
Waqar Younis	7	0	28	1
Saqlain Mushtaq	10	1	54	0
Ata-Ur-Rehman	3	0	14	0
Mushtaq Ahmed	10	0	52	0
Aamir Sohail	7	1	29	1

Pakistan

No. 252: Texaco Trophy (2)
VENUE: Edgbaston
DATE: 31st August 1996
TOSS WON BY: Pakistan
RESULT: England won by 107 runs

ENGLAND

NV Knight	st Moin b Saqlain Mushtaq	113
AJ Stewart+	b Mushtaq Ahmed	46
MA Atherton*	lbw b Mushtaq Ahmed	1
GP Thorpe	lbw b Ata-Ur-Rehman	21
MP Maynard	run out	1
RC Irani	not out	45
AJ Hollioake	run out	15
D Gough	run out	0
RDB Croft	b Waqar	15
DW Headley	not out	3
AD Mullally		
Extras	(0b, 25lb, 4w, 3nb)	32
	50 overs	
Total		**292**

FoW: 103, 105, 163, 168, 221, 257, 257, 286

Wasim Akram	10	0	50	0
Waqar Younis	9	0	54	1
Ata-Ur-Rehman	6	0	40	1
Saqlain Mushtaq	10	0	59	1
Mushtaq Ahmed	10	0	33	2
Aamir Sohail	5	0	31	0

PAKISTAN

Saeed Anwar	c Stewart b Gough	33
Aamir Sohail	c Croft b Gough	0
Moin Khan+	lbw b Mullally	0
Ijaz Ahmed	b Croft	79
Inzamam-ul-Haq	c Thorpe b Croft	6
Salim Malik	c Stewart b Hollioake	23
Wasim Akram*	c Knight b Hollioake	21
Mushtaq Ahmed	not out	14
Saqlain Mushtaq	b Hollioake	0
Waqar Younis	lbw b Gough	4
Ata-Ur-Rehman	c Knight b Hollioake	2
Extras	(0b, 2lb, 0w, 1nb)	3
	37.5 overs	
Total		**185**

FoW: 1, 6, 54, 104, 137, 164, 164, 168, 177, 185

D Gough	8	0	39	3
AD Mullally	6	0	30	1
DW Headley	7	0	32	0
RC Irani	2	0	22	0
RDB Croft	8	0	37	2
AJ Hollioake	6.5	1	23	4

Pakistan

No. 253: Texaco Trophy (2)
VENUE: Trent Bridge
DATE: 1st September 1996
TOSS WON BY: England
RESULT: Pakistan won by 2 wickets

ENGLAND

NV Knight	not out	125
AJ Stewart+	c & b Wasim	3
MA Atherton*	c Shahid Nazir b Wasim	30
MP Maynard	b Shahid Nazir	24
GD Lloyd	c Shadab b Saqlain	15
RC Irani	b Shahid Nazir	0
AJ Hollioake	c Ijaz b Saqlain	13
D Gough	b Wasim	5
RDB Croft	b Waqar	0
PJ Martin	run out	6
AD Mullally	b Waqar	2
Extras	(2b, 8lb, 9w, 4nb)	23
	50 overs	
Total		**246**

FoW: 10, 108, 137, 139, 176, 216, 226, 231, 240, 246

Wasim Akram	10	1	45	3
Waqar Younis	10	1	49	2
Shahid Nazir	10	0	47	2
Asif Mujtaba	5	0	27	0
Saqlain Mushtaq	10	0	35	2
Aamir Sohail	5	0	33	0

PAKISTAN

Saeed Anwar	b Martin	61
Shahid Anwar	lbw b Martin	37
Ijaz Ahmed	c Lloyd b Gough	59
Aamir Sohail	b Croft	29
Shadab Kabir	c Irani b Hollioake	0
Asif Mujtaba	b Hollioake	2
Wasim Akram*	lbw b Hollioake	5
Rashid Latif+	not out	31
Saqlain Mushtaq	c Maynard b Hollioake	12
Waqar Younis	not out	0
Shahid Nazir		
Extras	(0b, 5lb, 6w, 0nb)	11
	49.4 overs	
Total		**247**

FoW: 93, 114, 177, 182, 187, 199, 219, 240

D Gough	10	1	43	1
AD Mullally	9	0	66	0
PJ Martin	10	0	38	2
RDB Croft	10	0	38	1
RC Irani	2	0	12	0
AJ Hollioake	8.4	0	45	4

Zimbabwe

No. 254: One-Day Series
VENUE: Bulawayo (Queen's Club)
DATE: 15th December 1996
TOSS WON BY: Zimbabwe
RESULT: Zimbabwe won by 2 wickets

ENGLAND

NV Knight	lbw b Streak	13
AJ Stewart+	c A Flower b Streak	26
MA Atherton*	c (sub) b GW Flower	23
GP Thorpe	b Brandes	1
N Hussain	not out	49
JP Crawley	c Campbell b Rennie	10
RC Irani	c & b Rennie	7
AD Mullally	c & b Rennie	0
RDB Croft	c GW Flower b Streak	0
D Gough	run out	9
CEW Silverwood	c Houghton b Strang	1
Extras	(0b, 6lb, 3w, 4nb)	13
	45.5 overs	
Total		**152**

FoW: 28, 41, 47, 96, 124, 134, 134, 135, 150, 152

EA Brandes	8	2	28	1
JA Rennie	8	1	27	3
HH Streak	9	1	30	3
GJ Whittall	5	1	17	0
PA Strang	9.5	1	27	1
GW Flower	6	0	17	1

ZIMBABWE

GW Flower	b Silverwood	14
AC Waller	run out	48
A Flower+	c Knight b Silverwood	10
DL Houghton	c Crawley b Gough	2
CN Evans	c Stewart b Gough	1
GJ Whittall	c Stewart b Mullally	13
ADR Campbell*	not out	32
PA Strang	c Stewart b Mullally	0
HH Streak	c & b Croft	11
EA Brandes	not out	8
JA Rennie		
Extras	(0b, 9lb, 4w, 1nb)	14
	43.5 overs	
Total		**153**

FoW: 33, 58, 73, 87, 97, 106, 106, 137

AD Mullally	10	2	24	2
D Gough	10	2	31	2
CEW Silverwood	10	0	27	2
RDB Croft	5	0	32	1
RC Irani	6.5	1	25	0
GP Thorpe	2	1	5	0

Zimbabwe

Zimbabwe

No. 255: One–Day Series
VENUE: Harare
DATE: 1st January 1997
TOSS WON BY: England
RESULT: Zimbabwe won by 6 runs

No. 256: One–Day Series
VENUE: Harare
DATE: 3rd January 1997
TOSS WON BY: England
RESULT: Zimbabwe won by 131 runs

ZIMBABWE

GW Flower	c Hussain b Gough	4
AC Waller	b Mullally	0
ADR Campbell*	c Stewart b Gough	14
DL Houghton	c Croft b Mullally	5
A Flower+	c Stewart b Mullally	63
CN Evans	lbw b Croft	32
GJ Whittall	run out	14
PA Strang	c Atherton b Croft	1
HH Streak	not out	43
EA Brandes	c Atherton b Gough	0
JA Rennie	b Gough	0
Extras	(0b, 11lb, 10w, 3nb)	24
	48.5 overs	
Total		**200**

FoW: 2, 14, 26, 38, 97, 125, 126, 200, 200, 200

AD Mullally	9	1	29	3
D Gough	8.5	1	43	4
CEW Silverwood	6	0	30	0
C White	10	1	39	0
RDB Croft	10	2	33	2
RC Irani	5	0	15	0

ENGLAND

(Revised target 185 runs in 42 overs)

NV Knight	c Houghton b Brandes	0
AJ Stewart+	c A Flower b Whittall	41
JP Crawley	st A Flower b Strang	73
N Hussain	lbw b Whittall	7
MA Atherton*	c Whittall b Strang	25
RC Irani	st A Flower b Strang	5
C White	lbw b Streak	4
RDB Croft	not out	10
D Gough	not out	2
CEW Silverwood		
AD Mullally		
Extras	(2b, 5lb, 5w, 0nb)	12
	42 overs	
Total		**179**

FoW: 1, 67, 95, 137, 157, 165, 169

EA Brandes	6	2	25	1
JA Rennie	5	0	26	0
HH Streak	8	0	41	1
GJ Whittall	8	0	30	2
CN Evans	2	0	6	0
PA Strang	9	0	24	3
GW Flower	4	0	20	0

ZIMBABWE

GW Flower	c Mullally b White	62
AC Waller	run out	19
ADR Campbell*	not out	80
A Flower+	c Stewart b Irani	35
CN Evans	c Stewart b Gough	1
GJ Whittall	b Croft	1
DL Houghton	c Stewart b Mullally	19
PA Strang	run out	13
HH Streak		
EA Brandes		
JA Rennie		
Extras	(4b, 5lb, 8w, 2nb)	19
	50 overs	
Total		**249**

FoW: 58, 131, 181, 183, 190, 220, 249

AD Mullally	10	3	39	1
D Gough	10	1	42	1
CEW Silverwood	5	0	27	0
C White	7	0	39	1
RC Irani	10	0	39	1
RDB Croft	8	0	54	1

ENGLAND

NV Knight	c A Flower b Brandes	3
AJ Stewart+	c A Flower b Brandes	29
JP Crawley	lbw b Brandes	0
N Hussain	c A Flower b Brandes	0
MA Atherton*	c A Flower b Brandes	18
RC Irani	c Whittall b Streak	0
C White	c A Flower b Streak	0
RDB Croft	not out	30
D Gough	c Streak b Strang	7
AD Mullally	b Whittall	20
CEW Silverwood	c Evans b Whittall	0
Extras	(0b, 0lb, 8w, 3nb)	11
	30 overs	
Total		**118**

FoW: 9, 13, 13, 45, 54, 55, 63, 77, 118, 118

EA Brandes	10	0	28	5
JA Rennie	3	0	11	0
HH Streak	10	0	50	2
PA Strang	5	0	18	1
GJ Whittall	2	0	11	2

No. 257: One-Day Series
VENUE: Christchurch Day/Night
DATE: 20th February 1997
TOSS WON BY: New Zealand
RESULT: England won by 4 wickets

NEW ZEALAND

BA Young	c Thorpe b Mullally	14
NJ Astle	c Thorpe b Tufnell	50
AC Parore	c & b Tufnell	26
SP Fleming	st Stewart b Tufnell	34
CL Cairns	c Mullally b Tufnell	15
CZ Harris	not out	48
LK Germon*+	b Cork	19
DN Patel	not out	1
GR Larsen		
SB Doull		
HT Davis		
Extras	(2b, 7lb, 4w, 2nb)	15
	50 overs	
Total		**222**

FoW: 24, 87, 100, 134, 148, 203

DG Cork	9	0	52	1
AD Mullally	5	2	21	1
RDB Croft	10	1	41	0
D Gough	10	0	45	0
PCR Tufnell	10	1	22	4
GP Thorpe	6	0	32	0

ENGLAND

NV Knight	c Germon b Doull	8
MA Atherton*	b Patel	19
AJ Stewart	c Astle b Davis	81
GP Thorpe	b Davis	82
N Hussain	not out	11
JP Crawley	b Doull	0
DG Cork	c Young b Davis	5
RDB Croft	not out	8
D Gough		
AD Mullally		
PCR Tufnell		
Extras	(0b, 6lb, 6w, 0nb)	12
	48.5 overs	
Total		**226**

FoW: 28, 28, 198, 205, 207, 218

SB Doull	10	0	33	2
DN Patel	7	0	43	1
NJ Astle	4	0	26	0
CL Cairns	4	0	25	0
HT Davis	8.5	0	44	3
GR Larsen	8	0	23	0
CZ Harris	7	0	26	0

No. 258: One-Day Series
VENUE: Auckland
DATE: 23rd February 1997
TOSS WON BY: New Zealand
RESULT: England won by 6 wkts

NEW ZEALAND

BA Young	c Stewart b Irani	46
NJ Astle	c Stewart b Mullally	4
AC Parore	run out	2
SP Fleming	c Caddick b Gough	42
CL Cairns	run out	79
CZ Harris	c (sub) b Caddick	14
LK Germon*+	b Caddick	1
DN Patel	run out	24
GR Larsen	not out	12
HT Davis		
SB Doull		
Extras	(0b, 9lb, 16w, 4nb)	29
	50 overs	
Total		**253**

FoW: 24, 44, 94, 137, 189, 202, 219, 253

DG Cork	10	0	51	0
AD Mullally	7	0	36	1
AR Caddick	6	0	33	2
D Gough	10	0	65	1
RC Irani	7	0	26	1
RDB Croft	10	1	33	0

ENGLAND

(Revised target 132 runs in 26 overs)

NV Knight	not out	84
AJ Stewart+	lbw b Davis	30
DG Cork	c Young b Larsen	4
RC Irani	c Astle b Doull	0
GP Thorpe	c & b Doull	4
N Hussain*	not out	9
RDB Croft		
JP Crawley		
AD Mullally		
AR Caddick		
D Gough		
Extras	(0b, 0lb, 3w, 0nb)	3
	19.3 overs	
Total		**134**

FoW: 86, 91, 92, 100

HT Davis	6	1	39	1
SB Doull	5	0	39	2
GR Larsen	5	0	31	1
CZ Harris	2	0	8	0
NJ Astle	1.3	0	17	0

New Zealand

No. 259: One-Day Series
VENUE: Napier Day/Night
DATE: 26th February 1997
TOSS WON BY: New Zealand
RESULT: Match tied

NEW ZEALAND

BA Young	b Caddick	53
NJ Astle	c Stewart b Gough	34
LK Germon*+	st Stewart b Croft	22
SP Fleming	run out	12
CL Cairns	c Cork b Caddick	11
AC Parore	c & b White	24
CZ Harris	c Stewart b White	19
GR Larsen	c Stewart b Gough	19
SB Doull	b White	22
HT Davis	b White	1
GI Allott	not out	1
Extras	(0b, 11lb, 4w, 4nb)	19
	49.4 overs	
Total		**237**

FoW: 50, 103, 125, 140, 145, 178, 191, 233, 234, 237

DG Cork	9	1	42	0
AR Caddick	10	2	43	2
D Gough	10	0	34	2
RC Irani	5	0	28	0
RDB Croft	10	0	42	1
C White	5.4	0	37	4

ENGLAND

NV Knight	c & b Allott	39
MA Atherton*	b Harris	23
AJ Stewart+	b Harris	17
GP Thorpe	c Germon b Doull	55
N Hussain	b Harris	13
RC Irani	c Doull b Larsen	4
C White	run out	38
DG Cork	not out	31
RDB Croft	b Allott	4
D Gough	not out	0
AR Caddick		
Extras	(2b, 4lb, 5w, 2nb)	13
	50 overs	
Total		**237**

FoW: 67, 82, 87, 114, 127, 174, 232, 236

SB Doull	9	0	53	1
GI Allott	9	2	49	2
HT Davis	10	0	40	0
CZ Harris	10	3	20	3
GR Larsen	10	0	50	1
NJ Astle	2	0	19	0

New Zealand

No. 260: One-Day Series
VENUE: Auckland
DATE: 2nd March 1997
TOSS WON BY: England
RESULT: New Zealand won by 9 runs

NEW ZEALAND

BA Young	c & b White	16
NJ Astle	c Stewart b Irani	51
LK Germon*+	lbw b Gough	0
SP Fleming	c Hussain b Croft	37
CL Cairns	run out	2
AC Parore	c Croft b Caddick	13
CZ Harris	c Hussain b Croft	0
GR Larsen	run out	2
SB Doull	not out	13
HT Davis	b Caddick	0
GI Allott	b Gough	3
Extras	(2b, 3lb, 11w, 0nb)	16
	39.5 overs	
Total		**153**

FoW: 53, 54, 113, 116, 120, 120, 129, 136, 141, 153

AR Caddick	8	1	29	2
CEW Silverwood	5	0	20	0
D Gough	5.5	0	29	2
C White	5	0	21	1
RDB Croft	9	1	26	2
RC Irani	7	0	23	1

ENGLAND

NV Knight	not out	1
MA Atherton*	c Harris b Allott	9
AJ Stewart+	b Astle	42
GP Thorpe	c Parore b Allott	7
N Hussain	b Davis	3
RC Irani	c Fleming b Davis	0
C White	c Parore b Harris	32
RDB Croft	run out	20
D Gough	c & b Larsen	5
AR Caddick	b Larsen	0
CEW Silverwood	c Allott b Larsen	12
Extras	(0b, 6lb, 7w, 0nb)	13
	41.3 overs	
Total		**144**

FoW: 22, 32, 41, 41, 91, 113, 132, 132, 133, 144

HT Davis	6	0	32	2
GI Allott	5	1	21	2
SB Doull	6	1	15	0
GR Larsen	8.3	0	20	3
CZ Harris	9	0	26	1
NJ Astle	7	1	24	1

New Zealand

No. 261: One-Day Series	
VENUE: Wellington	
DATE: 4th March 1997	
TOSS WON BY: New Zealand	
RESULT: New Zealand won by 28 runs	

NEW ZEALAND

BA Young	c Russell b Caddick	11
NJ Astle	c Atherton b Caddick	94
SP Fleming	lbw b Croft	17
CL Cairns	c Russell b White	1
AC Parore	lbw b Caddick	18
CZ Harris	c Stewart b Gough	36
LK Germon*+	lbw b Silverwood	2
DN Patel	not out	16
GR Larsen	run out	0
HT Davis	not out	7
GI Allott		
Extras	(0b, 10lb, 14w, 2nb)	26
	50 overs	
Total		**228**

FoW: 28, 84, 87, 122, 197, 200, 206, 208

AR Caddick	10	1	35	3
D Gough	10	1	48	1
CEW Silverwood	10	0	53	1
C White	10	0	44	1
RDB Croft	10	1	38	1

ENGLAND

MA Atherton*	run out	43
AJ Stewart	c Patel b Allott	18
N Hussain	st Germon b Harris	20
GP Thorpe	st Germon b Larsen	55
CEW Silverwood	b Patel	4
JP Crawley	lbw b Larsen	11
RC Russell+	c Germon b Astle	2
C White	c Germon b Astle	0
RDB Croft	run out	2
D Gough	c Fleming b Davis	16
AR Caddick	not out	12
Extras	(0b, 8lb, 8w, 1nb)	17
	47.5 overs	
Total		**200**

FoW: 43, 77, 107, 119, 136, 139, 139, 158, 173, 200

GI Allott	8	0	40	1
HT Davis	7.5	0	44	1
GR Larsen	10	0	31	2
CZ Harris	10	2	22	1
DN Patel	7	0	29	1
NJ Astle	5	0	26	2

Australia

No. 262: Texaco Trophy	
VENUE: Headingley	
DATE: 22nd May 1997	
TOSS WON BY: England	
RESULT: England won by 6 wickets	

AUSTRALIA

MA Taylor*	c Stewart b Gough	7
ME Waugh	b Headley	11
SR Waugh	lbw b Ealham	19
MG Bevan	run out	30
GS Blewett	b Gough	28
MJ Slater	c & b Ealham	17
IA Healy+	c Atherton b Hollioake	17
SK Warne	c Thorpe b Hollioake	4
MS Kasprowicz	not out	17
JN Gillespie	not out	3
GD McGrath		
Extras	(0b, 7lb, 9w, 1nb)	17
	50 overs	
Total		**170**

FoW: 8, 39, 43, 106, 106, 140, 140, 157

PAJ de Freitas	9	1	35	0
D Gough	10	2	33	2
MA Ealham	8	3	21	2
DW Headley	8	0	36	1
RDB Croft	10	1	16	0
AJ Hollioake	5	0	22	2

ENGLAND

NV Knight	lbw b McGrath	12
MA Atherton*	c Healy b Kasprowicz	4
AJ Stewart+	lbw b McGrath	7
GP Thorpe	not out	75
GD Lloyd	run out	0
AJ Hollioake	not out	66
MA Ealham		
PAJ de Freitas		
D Gough		
RDB Croft		
DW Headley		
Extras	(1b, 0lb, 6w, 4nb)	11
	40.1 overs	
Total		**175**

FoW: 18, 20, 32, 40

GD McGrath	10	2	34	2
MS Kasprowicz	7	0	27	1
JN Gillespie	8.1	1	39	0
SK Warne	10	0	46	0
ME Waugh	2	0	16	0
GS Blewett	3	0	12	0

Australia

No. 263: Texaco Trophy
VENUE: The Oval
DATE: 24th May 1997
TOSS WON BY: England
RESULT: England won by 6 wickets

AUSTRALIA

ME Waugh	run out		25
MA Taylor*	run out		11
SR Waugh	b Croft		24
MG Bevan	not out		108
MJ Slater	run out		1
AC Gilchrist	lbw b Hollioake		53
IA Healy+	run out		7
SK Warne	not out		11
JN Gillespie			
MS Kasprowicz			
GD McGrath			
Extras	(0b, 8lb, 1w, 0nb)		9
	50 overs		
Total			**249**

FoW: 35, 37, 94, 98, 211, 226

PAJ de Freitas	8	0	47	0
D Gough	10	3	42	0
MA Ealham	9	2	40	0
AF Giles	9	0	48	0
RDB Croft	10	2	39	1
AJ Hollioake	4	0	25	1

ENGLAND

NV Knight	lbw b Kasprowicz		4
MA Atherton*	not out		113
AJ Stewart+	b Warne		40
GP Thorpe	c SR Waugh b Bevan		7
GD Lloyd	c Warne b McGrath		22
AJ Hollioake	not out		53
MA Ealham			
PAJ de Freitas			
D Gough			
RDB Croft			
AF Giles			
Extras	(0b, 5lb, 8w, 1nb)		14
	48.2 overs		
Total			**253**

FoW: 6, 77, 104, 158

GD McGrath	9	1	46	1
MS Kasprowicz	9.2	0	58	1
JN Gillespie	8	1	42	0
SK Warne	10	0	39	1
MG Bevan	9	0	43	1
SR Waugh	3	0	20	0

Australia

No. 264: Texaco Trophy
VENUE: Lord's
DATE: 25th May 1997
TOSS WON BY: England
RESULT: England won by 6 wickets

AUSTRALIA

MTG Elliott	c AJ Hollioake b Gough		1
ME Waugh	lbw b Gough		95
SR Waugh*	c Thorpe b Gough		17
MG Bevan	c (sub) b Gough		8
JL Langer	run out		29
AC Gilchrist	lbw b Ealham		33
IA Healy+	c Lloyd b Croft		27
SK Warne	c Stewart b Ealham		5
MS Kasprowicz	not out		28
JN Gillespie	c Thorpe b Gough		6
GD McGrath	st Stewart b AJ Hollioake		1
Extras	(2b, 10lb, 5w, 2nb)		19
	49.2 overs		
Total			**269**

FoW: 2, 52, 63, 142, 184, 218, 228, 242, 268, 269

D Gough	10	0	44	5
CEW Silverwood	6	0	44	0
MA Ealham	10	0	47	2
RDB Croft	10	0	51	1
BC Hollioake	7	0	36	0
AJ Hollioake	6.2	0	35	1

ENGLAND

MA Atherton*	lbw b Kasprowicz		1
AJ Stewart+	c Langer b ME Waugh		79
BC Hollioake	c SR Waugh b Gillespie		63
JP Crawley	run out		52
GP Thorpe	not out		45
AJ Hollioake	not out		4
GD Lloyd			
MA Ealham			
RDB Croft			
CEW Silverwood			
D Gough			
Extras	(0b, 9lb, 13w, 4nb)		26
	49 overs		
Total			**270**

FoW: 22, 113, 193, 253

GD McGrath	9	2	45	0
MS Kasprowicz	8	1	40	1
SK Warne	9	0	44	0
JN Gillespie	10	0	55	1
MG Bevan	3	0	27	0
SR Waugh	4	0	22	0
ME Waugh	6	0	28	1

India

ENGLAND

AD Brown	c Ganguly b Kuruvilla	18
AJ Stewart+	c Azharuddin b Kumble	116
NV Knight	c Kumble b Chauhan	42
GA Hick	b Kuruvilla	32
AJ Hollioake*	b Kuruvilla	4
MA Ealham	run out	9
GP Thorpe	run out	3
MV Fleming	c Karim b Srinath	9
DR Brown	c Tendulkar b Srinath	6
RDB Croft	c Kuruvilla b Srinath	5
DW Headley	not out	1
Extras	(0b, 4lb, 1w, 0nb)	5
	49.5 overs	
Total		**250**

FoW: 42, 131, 209, 211, 215, 218, 232, 237, 248, 250

J Srinath	8.5	0	37	3
A Kuruvilla	10	0	50	3
A Kumble	10	0	53	1
RR Singh	6	0	34	0
SC Ganguly	2	0	14	0
RK Chauhan	9	0	34	1
SR Tendulkar	4	0	24	0

INDIA

SS Karim+	c Croft b Headley	29
SC Ganguly	b Ealham	29
NS Sidhu	c Hollioake b Ealham	3
SR Tendulkar*	st Stewart b Fleming	91
M Azharuddin	c Headley b Hollioake	3
AD Jadeja	c Thorpe b Fleming	50
RR Singh	lbw b Fleming	12
A Kumble	run out	2
RK Chauhan	b Fleming	12
J Srinath	b Headley	3
A Kuruvilla	not out	1
Extras	(0b, 3lb, 3w, 2nb)	8
	49.3 overs	
Total		**243**

FoW: 60, 64, 65, 74, 182, 207, 221, 232, 237, 243

DR Brown	7	0	44	0
DW Headley	9	0	38	2
MA Ealham	10	0	43	2
AJ Hollioake	9	1	38	1
RDB Croft	5	0	32	0
MV Fleming	9.3	0	45	4

West Indies

WEST INDIES

PA Wallace	b DR Brown	0
SC Williams	c Thorpe b Headley	22
BC Lara	lbw b DR Brown	0
CL Hooper	not out	100
S Chanderpaul	lbw b Ealham	16
PV Simmons	c Croft b Hollioake	29
D Williams+	run out	4
RN Lewis	b Fleming	13
FA Rose	not out	11
M Dillon		
CA Walsh*		
Extras	(0b, 0lb, 0w, 2nb)	2
	50 overs	
Total		**197**

FoW: 0, 0, 50, 77, 143, 151, 181

DR Brown	7	1	28	2
DW Headley	7	1	24	1
MA Ealham	10	1	28	1
RDB Croft	10	0	40	0
AJ Hollioake	8	0	41	1
MV Fleming	8	1	36	1

ENGLAND

AD Brown	c Lewis b Walsh	10
AJ Stewart+	c Walsh b Rose	23
NV Knight	c D Williams b Dillon	10
GA Hick	run out	28
GP Thorpe	c D Williams b Hooper	57
AJ Hollioake*	c Chanderpaul b Dillon	9
MA Ealham	not out	28
DR Brown	not out	16
MV Fleming		
RDB Croft		
DW Headley		
Extras	(0b, 7lb, 4w, 6nb)	17
	45.5 overs	
Total		**198**

FoW: 21, 45, 53, 100, 123, 173

CA Walsh	9.5	0	51	1
FA Rose	10	0	38	1
M Dillon	10	0	38	2
RN Lewis	6	0	34	0
PV Simmons	2	0	8	0
CL Hooper	8	1	22	1

Pakistan

No. 267: Singer-Akai Cup		
VENUE: Sharjah		
DATE: 15th December 1997		
TOSS WON BY: England		
RESULT: England won by 8 runs		

ENGLAND

AD Brown	c Moin b Saqlain Mushtaq	41
AJ Stewart+	b Manzoor Akhtar	47
NV Knight	b Manzoor Akhtar	18
GA Hick	b Manzoor Akhtar	40
GP Thorpe	run out	3
AJ Hollioake*	c Shahid b Manzoor Akhtar	17
MA Ealham	c & b Saqlain Mushtaq	6
DR Brown	not out	18
MV Fleming	c & b Saqlain Mushtaq	0
RDB Croft	c Ahmed b Saqlain Mushtaq	6
DW Headley	not out	6
Extras	(1b, 4lb, 7w, 1nb)	13
	50 overs	
Total		**215**

FoW: 71, 108, 121, 126, 168, 180, 185, 185, 203

Wasim Akram	6	1	34	0
Azhar Mahmood	7	1	31	0
Saqlain Mushtaq	10	1	26	4
Mushtaq Ahmed	10	0	43	0
Manzoor Akhtar	10	0	50	4
Shahid Afridi	7	0	26	0

PAKISTAN

Aamir Sohail	b Headley	1
Shahid Afridi	b DR Brown	0
Saeed Anwar	b Croft	54
Ijaz Ahmed	c Croft b Ealham	41
Akhtar Sarfraz	b Croft	20
Manzoor Akhtar	run out	44
Moin Khan+	c Knight b Fleming	10
Wasim Akram*	c DR Brown b Hollioake	4
Azhar Mahmood	c Stewart b Hollioake	12
Saqlain Mushtaq	run out	9
Mushtaq Ahmed	not out	0
Extras	(0b, 5lb, 5w, 2nb)	12
	49 overs	
Total		**207**

FoW: 1, 5, 99, 99, 134, 152, 177, 185, 207, 207

DR Brown	5	0	29	1
DW Headley	8	0	33	1
MA Ealham	10	1	39	1
RDB Croft	10	1	39	2
AJ Hollioake	10	0	35	2
MV Fleming	6	0	27	1

West Indies

No. 268: Singer-Akai Cup Final		
VENUE: Sharjah		
DATE: 19th December 1997		
TOSS WON BY: West Indies		
RESULT: England won by 3 wickets		

WEST INDIES

SC Williams	c AD Brown b Croft	55
S Chanderpaul	run out	76
BC Lara	st Stewart b Ealham	2
CL Hooper	lbw b Fleming	34
PV Simmons	not out	39
RIC Holder	lbw b Fleming	0
RN Lewis	b Fleming	16
FA Rose	run out	0
D Williams+	not out	9
CA Walsh*		
M Dillon		
Extras	(0b, 3lb, 1w, 0nb)	4
	50 overs	
Total		**235**

FoW: 97, 101, 164, 174, 174, 200, 200

DR Brown	5	0	35	0
DW Headley	7	0	39	0
MA Ealham	10	1	26	1
AJ Hollioake	10	0	50	0
RDB Croft	10	0	40	1
MV Fleming	8	0	42	3

ENGLAND

AD Brown	c Chanderpaul b Rose	1
AJ Stewart+	b Hooper	51
NV Knight	run out	24
GA Hick	c Hooper b Lewis	9
GP Thorpe	not out	66
AJ Hollioake*	st D Williams b Hooper	16
MA Ealham	b Walsh	4
MV Fleming	run out	33
DR Brown	not out	4
RDB Croft		
DW Headley		
Extras	(1b, 16lb, 5w, 9nb)	31
	48.1 overs	
Total		**239**

FoW: 14, 89, 107, 107, 152, 165, 235

CA Walsh	9.1	1	39	1
FA Rose	10	0	36	1
M Dillon	6	0	36	0
PV Simmons	4	0	25	0
RN Lewis	9	0	51	1
CL Hooper	10	0	35	2

West Indies

No. 269: One–Day Series			
VENUE: Bridgetown (Barbados)			
DATE: 29th March 1998			
TOSS WON BY: West Indies			
RESULT: England won by 16 runs			

ENGLAND

NV Knight	run out		122
AJ Stewart+	b Walsh		74
GA Hick	b Lewis		29
GP Thorpe	b Simmons		4
AJ Hollioake*	not out		18
MA Ealham	b Simmons		20
MV Fleming	not out		22
DR Brown			
BC Hollioake			
RDB Croft			
DW Headley			
Extras	(0b, 4lb, 0w, 0nb)		4
	50 overs		
Total			**293**

FoW: 165, 227, 228, 249, 271

FA Rose	6	0	31	0
CA Walsh	10	0	57	1
CEL Ambrose	8	0	42	0
CL Hooper	10	0	46	0
RN Lewis	8	0	55	1
PV Simmons	8	0	58	2

WEST INDIES

CB Lambert	c Stewart b Headley		11
PA Wallace	c Hick b Brown		13
BC Lara*	run out		110
CL Hooper	c Headley b Fleming		45
S Chanderpaul	c Knight b Croft		8
PV Simmons	b AJ Hollioake		18
JR Murray+	c Stewart b Headley		7
RN Lewis	st Stewart b Ealham		27
FA Rose	c AJ Hollioake b Fleming		24
CEL Ambrose	not out		3
CA Walsh	b Ealham		0
Extras	(0b, 7lb, 1w, 3nb)		11
	46.5 overs		
Total			**277**

FoW: 25, 27, 115, 145, 187, 219, 222, 266, 274, 277

DR Brown	5	1	32	1
DW Headley	10	0	63	2
MA Ealham	7.5	0	37	2
MV Fleming	7	0	54	2
RDB Croft	10	0	37	1
AJ Hollioake	7	1	47	1

West Indies

No. 270: One–Day Series			
VENUE: Bridgetown (Barbados)			
DATE: 1st April 1998			
TOSS WON BY: West Indies			
RESULT: West Indies won by 1 wicket			

ENGLAND

NV Knight	lbw b Simmons		90
AJ Stewart+	c Lara b Walsh		3
BC Hollioake	c & b Rose		16
GA Hick	b Lewis		0
MR Ramprakash	c Ambrose b Lewis		29
AJ Hollioake*	run out		11
MA Ealham	c Ambrose b Simmons		45
DR Brown	b Simmons		21
MV Fleming	c Williams b Ambrose		28
RDB Croft	not out		11
DW Headley	b Ambrose		0
Extras	(0b, 2lb, 9w, 1nb)		12
	50 overs		
Total			**266**

FoW: 21, 71, 72, 131, 154, 158, 206, 238, 257, 266

CEL Ambrose	10	0	44	2
CA Walsh	10	1	51	1
FA Rose	8	0	50	1
RN Lewis	10	0	40	2
PV Simmons	8	0	46	3
CL Hooper	4	0	33	0

WEST INDIES

CB Lambert	run out		25
PA Wallace	c AJ Hollioake b Headley		22
BC Lara*	c Ramprakash b Headley		24
SC Williams	c Fleming b AJ Hollioake		68
CL Hooper	c Croft b Fleming		66
PV Simmons	lbw b Fleming		5
RD Jacobs+	not out		28
RN Lewis	run out		4
FA Rose	c AJ Hollioake b Fleming		3
CEL Ambrose	c & b AJ Hollioake		14
CA Walsh	not out		1
Extras	(0b, 4lb, 1w, 2nb)		7
	49.5 overs		
Total			**267**

FoW: 41, 54, 79, 211, 221, 226, 236, 265

DR Brown	8	1	36	1
DW Headley	7	0	68	1
RDB Croft	10	0	46	0
MA Ealham	8	0	29	0
MV Fleming	9	0	41	3
AJ Hollioake	7.5	0	43	2

West Indies

ENGLAND

NV Knight	c Wallace b Ambrose	15
AJ Stewart+	c Arthurton b Simmons	33
BC Hollioake	c Wallace b Simmons	35
GA Hick	c Williams b Arthurton	45
MR Ramprakash	b Hooper	1
AJ Hollioake*	b Lewis	31
MA Ealham	st Jacobs b Lewis	23
MV Fleming	c Williams b Arthurton	7
DR Brown	not out	2
RDB Croft	not out	1
ARC Fraser		
Extras	(0b, 7lb, 6w, 3nb)	16
	50 overs	
Total		**209**

FoW: 26, 84, 90, 91, 166, 184, 195, 208

CEL Ambrose	5	0	12	1
NAM McLean	7	0	33	0
RN Lewis	10	0	51	2
PV Simmons	10	0	45	2
CL Hooper	10	2	30	1
KLT Arthurton	8	0	31	2

WEST INDIES

CB Lambert	c Stewart b Fraser	22
PA Wallace	b Fleming	33
BC Lara*	c AJ Hollioake b Ealham	21
CL Hooper	run out	50
SC Williams	c Knight b Croft	4
KLT Arthurton	not out	35
PV Simmons	not out	23
RD Jacobs+		
RN Lewis		
CEL Ambrose		
NAM McLean		
Extras	(1b, 16lb, 7w, 1nb)	25
	48.1 overs	
Total		**213**

FoW: 33, 71, 112, 125, 173

DR Brown	5	0	32	0
ARC Fraser	10	2	35	1
MA Ealham	7.1	0	41	1
RDB Croft	10	3	18	1
MV Fleming	9	0	30	1
AJ Hollioake	5	0	27	0
GA Hick	2	0	13	0

West Indies

ENGLAND

NV Knight	c Jacobs b Dillon	3
AJ Stewart	c Lara b McLean	1
BC Hollioake	c Jacobs b McLean	2
GA Hick	b McLean	22
AJ Hollioake*	c Hooper b Dillon	23
RC Russell+	b Dillon	21
MA Ealham	st Jacobs b Hooper	17
DR Brown	c Jacobs b Lewis	19
MV Fleming	b Simmons	7
RDB Croft	c Jacobs b Simmons	12
ARC Fraser	not out	12
Extras	(0b, 2lb, 8w, 0nb)	10
	48.5 overs	
Total		**149**

FoW: 7, 9, 17, 33, 79, 83, 115, 120, 126, 149

NAM McLean	10	1	44	3
M Dillon	10	0	32	3
CL Hooper	10	1	24	1
PV Simmons	9.5	0	26	2
RN Lewis	9	1	21	1

WEST INDIES

CB Lambert	c Ealham b Croft	52
PA Wallace	b Fraser	4
SC Williams	c Knight b Ealham	19
PV Simmons	lbw b Croft	1
BC Lara*	b AJ Hollioake	51
CL Hooper	c Fraser b Fleming	15
RD Jacobs+	not out	0
KLT Arthurton	not out	3
RN Lewis		
M Dillon		
NAM McLean		
Extras	(0b, 2lb, 1w, 2nb)	5
	37.4 overs	
Total		**150**

FoW: 18, 66, 67, 104, 137, 145

ARC Fraser	6	0	27	1
DR Brown	4	0	20	0
RDB Croft	9	2	41	2
BC Hollioake	4	0	18	0
MA Ealham	4	0	19	1
MV Fleming	5.4	1	11	1
AJ Hollioake	5	0	12	1

West Indies

No. 273: One-Day Series		
VENUE: Port-of-Spain (Trinidad)		
DATE: 8th April 1998		
TOSS WON BY: West Indies		
RESULT: West Indies won by 57 runs		

WEST INDIES

CB Lambert	c Stewart b BC Hollioake	119
PA Wallace	run out	0
SC Williams	c Stewart b BC Hollioake	27
BC Lara*	b Brown	93
CL Hooper	not out	35
LR Williams	lbw b Brown	1
RD Jacobs+	not out	5
S Chanderpaul		
CM Tuckett		
NC McGarrell		
M Dillon		
Extras	(4b, 15lb, 3w, 0nb)	22
	50 overs	
Total		**302**

FoW: 13, 67, 252, 266, 270

ARC Fraser	10	3	28	0
DR Brown	8	0	49	2
BC Hollioake	10	0	43	2
RDB Croft	8	1	33	0
MA Ealham	5	0	41	0
MV Fleming	7	0	56	0
AJ Hollioake	2	0	33	0

ENGLAND

NV Knight	run out	65
AJ Stewart+	c Hooper b Tuckett	12
BC Hollioake	run out	2
GA Hick	c Chanderpaul b Tuckett	1
MR Ramprakash	c McGarrell b Hooper	51
AJ Hollioake*	b McGarrell	2
MA Ealham	c LR Williams b Chand'paul	26
DR Brown	st Jacobs b Hooper	13
MV Fleming	c L Williams b S Williams	10
RDB Croft	not out	13
ARC Fraser	run out	30
Extras	(0b, 6lb, 13w, 1nb)	20
	45.5 overs	
Total		**245**

FoW: 41, 60, 71, 109, 115, 161, 186, 196, 201, 245

M Dillon	5.5	0	41	0
CM Tuckett	8	0	41	2
LR Williams	8	0	32	0
NC McGarrell	10	0	46	1
S Chanderpaul	5	0	23	1
SC Williams	4	0	30	1
CL Hooper	2	0	6	2
CB Lambert	2	0	8	0
BC Lara	1	0	13	0

South Africa

No. 274: Texaco Trophy		
VENUE: The Oval		
DATE: 21st May 1998		
TOSS WON BY: South Africa		
RESULT: South Africa won by 3 wickets		

ENGLAND

NV Knight	run out	64
AJ Stewart+	b Donald	27
CJ Adams	c Boucher b Kallis	25
N Hussain	c Boucher b Donald	27
DL Maddy	lbw b Symcox	1
AJ Hollioake*	c Symcox b Klusener	32
MA Ealham	run out	1
CC Lewis	run out	16
AF Giles	c Boucher b Cronje	2
RDB Croft	not out	7
D Gough	not out	0
Extras	(0b, 7lb, 12w, 2nb)	21
	50 overs	
Total		**223**

FoW: 58, 109, 155, 158, 160, 161, 201, 209, 220

SM Pollock	10	1	45	0
L Klusener	8	1	33	1
AA Donald	10	2	45	2
WJ Cronje	8	1	26	1
JH Kallis	4	0	24	1
PL Symcox	10	0	43	1

SOUTH AFRICA

G Kirsten	c Adams b Gough	4
GFJ Liebenberg	b Giles	30
JH Kallis	c Hollioake b Croft	62
DJ Cullinan	run out	16
WJ Cronje*	c Hussain b Croft	40
JN Rhodes	not out	39
SM Pollock	b Croft	0
L Klusener	lbw b Giles	22
MV Boucher+	not out	2
PL Symcox		
AA Donald		
Extras	(4b, 2lb, 2w, 1nb)	9
	48.4 overs	
Total		**224**

FoW: 4, 76, 105, 134, 175, 175, 214

D Gough	10	1	38	1
CC Lewis	8.4	1	46	0
MA Ealham	10	0	38	0
AF Giles	9	0	37	2
RDB Croft	10	0	51	3
AJ Hollioake	1	0	8	0

South Africa

No. 275: Texaco Trophy
VENUE: Old Trafford
DATE: 23rd May 1998
TOSS WON BY: England
RESULT: South Africa won by 32 runs

No. 276: Texaco Trophy
VENUE: Headingley
DATE: 24th May 1998
TOSS WON BY: South Africa
RESULT: England won by 7 wickets

SOUTH AFRICA

GFJ Liebenberg	lbw b Ealham	39
G Kirsten	c Adams b Gough	2
JH Kallis	c Stewart b Gough	9
DJ Cullinan	lbw b Ealham	14
WJ Cronje*	c Stewart b Lewis	35
JN Rhodes	lbw b Croft	41
SM Pollock	lbw b Croft	3
L Klusener	not out	55
MV Boucher+	b Gough	6
PL Symcox	b Gough	2
AA Donald	not out	6
Extras	(2b, 6lb, 3w, 3nb)	14
	50 overs	
Total		**226**

FoW: 6, 24, 42, 103, 130, 143, 166, 189, 200

D Gough	10	0	35	4
CC Lewis	10	1	42	1
MA Ealham	10	0	34	2
MV Fleming	8	0	51	0
RDB Croft	10	0	43	2
AJ Hollioake	2	0	13	0

ENGLAND

NV Knight	c Boucher b Donald	34
AD Brown	c Rhodes b Klusener	13
AJ Stewart+	run out	52
N Hussain	c Boucher b Donald	1
CJ Adams	lbw b Symcox	3
AJ Hollioake*	lbw b Pollock	46
MA Ealham	b Cullinan	12
MV Fleming	c Kallis b Cullinan	5
CC Lewis	not out	10
RDB Croft	run out	7
D Gough	c Rhodes b Donald	2
Extras	(0b, 2lb, 7w, 0nb)	9
	46.4 overs	
Total		**194**

FoW: 30, 77, 83, 90, 143, 169, 169, 182, 190, 194

SM Pollock	8	0	28	1
L Klusener	9	0	58	1
PL Symcox	10	0	34	1
AA Donald	8.4	0	32	3
DJ Cullinan	9	0	30	2
JH Kallis	2	0	10	0

SOUTH AFRICA

G Kirsten	b Fraser	19
GFJ Liebenberg	lbw b Ealham	13
JH Kallis	run out	1
DJ Cullinan	run out	13
WJ Cronje*	c Stewart b Ealham	35
JN Rhodes	c Stewart b Ealham	6
SM Pollock	b Fleming	60
L Klusener	c Stewart b Fraser	14
MV Boucher+	not out	26
PL Symcox	not out	1
AA Donald		
Extras	(0b, 9lb, 5w, 3nb)	17
	50 overs	
Total		**205**

FoW: 26, 28, 57, 68, 78, 118, 146, 198

D Gough	10	2	57	0
ARC Fraser	10	1	23	2
MV Fleming	10	1	41	1
MA Ealham	10	0	44	3
RDB Croft	10	0	31	0

ENGLAND

NV Knight	c Rhodes b Donald	51
AD Brown	run out	59
MV Fleming	b Donald	18
AJ Stewart+	not out	26
N Hussain	not out	33
DL Maddy		
AJ Hollioake*		
MA Ealham		
RDB Croft		
D Gough		
ARC Fraser		
Extras	(4b, 2lb, 3w, 10nb)	19
	35 overs	
Total		**206**

FoW: 114, 139, 148

SM Pollock	7	1	34	0
L Klusener	6	0	45	0
AA Donald	7	0	35	2
PL Symcox	9	1	51	0
WJ Cronje	6	0	35	0

Sri Lanka

No. 277: Emirates Triangular Tournament
VENUE: Lord's
DATE: 16th August 1998
TOSS WON BY: England
RESULT: England won by 36 runs

ENGLAND

NV Knight	c Atapattu b Wickramasinghe	17
AD Brown	c Atapattu b Wickramasinghe	12
AJ Stewart*+	b Jayasuriya	51
GA Hick	run out	86
N Hussain	b Dharmasena	39
AJ Hollioake	b Jayasuriya	3
RDB Croft	c Kaluwitharana b Perera	3
ID Austin	b Jayasuriya	8
PJ Martin	run out	3
D Gough	not out	1
AD Mullally	b Perera	1
Extras	(0b, 11lb, 12w, 0nb)	23
Total	49.3 overs	**247**

FoW: 14, 56, 132, 223, 224, 228, 233, 241, 244, 247

GP Wickramasinghe	7	0	33	2
SA Perera	9.3	0	48	2
UC Hathurusingha	3	0	23	0
HDPK Dharmasena	10	0	54	1
M Muralidharan	10	0	42	0
ST Jayasuriya	10	0	36	3

SRI LANKA

ST Jayasuriya	c Knight b Gough	11
R Kaluwit'ana+	c Stewart b Martin	2
MS Atapattu	lbw b Gough	6
PA de Silva	lbw b Austin	33
RP Arnold	b Mullally	3
A Ranatunga*	b Croft	33
U Hathu'singha	c Stewart b Mullally	7
H Dharmasena	not out	33
SA Perera	c Brown b Hollioake	17
GP Wick'singhe	b Gough	18
M Muralidharan	b Austin	18
Extras	(1b, 13lb, 10w, 6nb)	30
Total	49.3 overs	**211**

FoW: 13, 17, 28, 49, 83, 97, 126, 159, 189, 211

D Gough	10	0	51	3
PJ Martin	8	0	34	1
AD Mullally	8	1	20	2
ID Austin	8.3	0	37	2
RDB Croft	10	0	37	1
AJ Hollioake	5	0	18	1

South Africa

No. 278: Emirates Triangular Tournament
VENUE: Edgbaston
DATE: 18th August 1998
TOSS WON BY: South Africa
RESULT: South Africa won by 14 runs

SOUTH AFRICA

G Kirsten	c Stewart b Gough	7
MJR Rindel	lbw b Gough	10
DJ Cullinan	b Gough	70
JN Rhodes	c Stewart b Mullally	15
WJ Cronje*	lbw b Croft	31
JH Kallis	b Austin	19
SM Pollock	not out	22
PL Symcox	b Mullally	51
MV Boucher+	not out	3
M Hayward		
AA Donald		
Extras	(0b, 9lb, 5w, 2nb)	16
Total	50 overs	**244**

FoW: 20, 25, 73, 140, 160, 172, 240

D Gough	10	1	43	3
PJ Martin	9	0	47	0
ID Austin	10	0	41	1
AD Mullally	9	0	33	2
AJ Hollioake	2	0	22	0
RDB Croft	10	0	49	1

ENGLAND

NV Knight	b Symcox	74
AD Brown	run out	0
AJ Stewart*+	c Rhodes b Pollock	27
GA Hick	c Symcox b Cronje	64
N Hussain	c & b Cronje	1
AJ Hollioake	b Symcox	10
RDB Croft	c Rhodes b Rindel	8
ID Austin	b Donald	10
D Gough	lbw b Pollock	15
PJ Martin	c Cronje b Donald	1
AD Mullally	not out	1
Extras	(0b, 7lb, 11w, 1nb)	19
Total	48.5 overs	**230**

FoW: 7, 48, 161, 170, 186, 193, 208, 213, 217, 230

AA Donald	9	1	41	2
SM Pollock	8.5	0	36	2
JH Kallis	4	0	24	0
M Hayward	4	0	35	0
PL Symcox	10	0	36	2
WJ Cronje	10	0	43	2
MJR Rindel	3	0	8	1

Sri Lanka

	No. 279: Emirates Triangular	
	Tournament Final	
VENUE:	Lord's	
DATE:	20th August 1998	
TOSS WON BY:	England	
RESULT:	Sri Lanka won by 5 wickets	

ENGLAND

NV Knight	c & b Muralidharan	94
MA Atherton	c Ranatunga b Muralidharan	64
AJ Stewart*+	c Kaluwitharana	
	b Muralidharan	18
GA Hick	b Chandana	14
AD Brown	b Muralidharan	18
N Hussain	lbw b Muralidharan	0
RDB Croft	c Kaluwitharana b Perera	17
ID Austin	not out	11
D Gough	b Perera	0
PJ Martin	not out	1
AD Mullally		
Extras	(4b, 5lb, 10w, 0nb)	19
	50 overs	
Total		**256**

FoW: 132, 170, 191, 218, 218, 223, 246, 246

GP Wickramasinghe	5	0	29	0
SA Perera	9	0	44	2
HDPK Dharmasena	9	0	47	0
M Muralidharan	10	0	34	5
PA de Silva	2	0	10	0
ST Jayasuriya	8	0	45	0
UDU Chandana	7	0	38	1

SRI LANKA

ST Jayasuriya	b Gough	0
R Kaluwitt'ana+	c Hick b Croft	68
MS Atapattu	not out	132
PA de Silva	c Brown b Gough	34
A Ranatunga*	c Knight b Martin	1
UDU Chandana	c Knight b Croft	2
HP Tillakaratne	not out	10
HDPK Dharmasena		
GP Wickramasinghe		
SA Perera		
M Muralidharan		
Extras	(0b, 7lb, 6w, 0nb)	13
	47.1 overs	
Total		**260**

FoW: 2, 140, 210, 224, 233

D Gough	10	0	50	2
PJ Martin	10	1	60	1
AD Mullally	10	0	37	0
ID Austin	10	1	48	0
RDB Croft	7	0	54	2
GA Hick	0.1	0	4	0

South Africa

	No. 280: Wills International Cup	
	Quarter Final	
VENUE:	Dhaka	
DATE:	25th October 1998	
TOSS WON BY:	England	
RESULT:	South Africa won by 6 wickets	

ENGLAND

NV Knight	c Boucher b Kallis	32
AD Brown	c Kallis b Symcox	6
MA Ealham	c Rhodes b Kallis	44
GA Hick	lbw b Kallis	2
NH Fairbrother	b Rindel	56
GD Lloyd	lbw b Boje	0
AJ Hollioake*	not out	83
RC Russell+	c Benkenstein b Dawson	19
AF Giles	not out	5
ID Austin		
PJ Martin		
Extras	(3b, 19lb, 9w, 3nb)	34
	50 overs	
Total		**281**

FoW: 14, 80, 93, 94, 95, 207, 256

AC Dawson	9	0	51	1
PL Symcox	10	0	45	1
JH Kallis	10	0	48	3
WJ Cronje	3	0	19	0
N Boje	10	0	39	1
DN Crookes	3	0	20	0
MJR Rindel	5	0	37	1

SOUTH AFRICA

DJ Cullinan	c Fairbrother b Hick	69
MJR Rindel	c Brown b Giles	41
JH Kallis	run out	14
WJ Cronje*	c Brown b Hollioake	67
JN Rhodes	not out	61
DM Benkenstein	not out	13
DN Crookes		
PL Symcox		
MV Boucher+		
N Boje		
AC Dawson		
Extras	(1b, 8lb, 7w, 2nb)	18
	46.4 overs	
Total		**283**

FoW: 113, 124, 135, 252

PJ Martin	8	0	55	0
ID Austin	9	0	53	0
MA Ealham	7	0	51	0
AF Giles	10	1	41	1
GA Hick	7	0	28	1
AJ Hollioake	4.4	0	41	1
AD Brown	1	0	5	0

Australia

No. 281: Carlton & United Series
VENUE: Brisbane ('Gabba')
DATE: 10th January 1999
TOSS WON BY: England
RESULT: England won by 7 runs

ENGLAND

NV Knight	c Gilchrist b McGrath	30
AJ Stewart*+	lbw b Dale	0
VJ Wells	b Dale	10
GA Hick	c Gilchrist b Fleming	8
NH Fairbrother	b McGrath	47
AJ Hollioake	c Gilchrist b Fleming	5
MW Alleyne	run out	2
MA Ealham	c Ponting b Julian	14
RDB Croft	not out	26
D Gough	not out	23
AD Mullally		
Extras	(0b, 4lb, 8w, 1nb)	13
	50 overs	
Total		**178**

FoW: 0, 29, 42, 72, 87, 93, 122, 136

GD McGrath	10	1	24	2
AC Dale	10	3	25	2
DW Fleming	10	0	33	2
BP Julian	5	0	29	1
SK Warne	10	0	42	0
GS Blewett	5	0	21	0

AUSTRALIA

(Revised target 153 runs in 36 overs)

ME Waugh	c Stewart b Mullally	23
AC Gilchrist+	b Mullally	13
RT Ponting	c Hollioake b Mullally	8
DR Martyn	b Mullally	0
GS Blewett	c Stewart b Ealham	0
MG Bevan	not out	56
BP Julian	b Croft	23
SK Warne*	run out	8
DW Fleming	c Mullally b Croft	2
AC Dale	b Gough	4
GD McGrath	not out	1
Extras	(0b, 2lb, 5w, 0nb)	7
	36 overs	
Total		**145**

FoW: 24, 46, 47, 48, 48, 94, 117, 129, 142

D Gough	6	0	47	1
AD Mullally	8	1	18	4
MA Ealham	7	1	16	1
AJ Hollioake	7	1	31	0
RDB Croft	7	0	24	2
MW Alleyne	1	0	7	0

Sri Lanka

No. 282: Carlton & United Series
VENUE: Brisbane ('Gabba')
DATE: 11th January 1999
TOSS WON BY: Sri Lanka
RESULT: England won by 4 wickets

SRI LANKA

ST Jayasuriya	c Hick b Gough	1
RS Kaluwit'na+	c Headley b Croft	58
MS Atapattu	b Hollioake	51
A Ranatunga*	c & b Hollioake	0
HP Tillakaratne	not out	50
RS Mahanama	c Knight b Hollioake	2
UDU Chandana	c Fairbrother b Ealham	23
WPUJ Vaas	b Mullally	5
GP Wicksinghe	not out	7
M Muralidharan		
DNT Zoysa		
Extras	(1b, 3lb, 6w, 0nb)	10
	50 overs	
Total		**207**

FoW: 2, 99, 102, 128, 135, 185, 200

D Gough	9	0	37	1
AD Mullally	10	2	35	1
DW Headley	5	1	22	0
MA Ealham	6	0	33	1
RDB Croft	10	0	44	1
AJ Hollioake	10	0	32	3

ENGLAND

NV Knight	st Kaluwit'rana b Chandana	40
AJ Stewart*+	run out	24
GA Hick	c Kaluwitharana b Muralidharan	37
NH Fairbrother	not out	67
AJ Hollioake	b Muralidharan	1
MW Alleyne	st Kaluwitharana b Muralidharan	18
MA Ealham	lbw b Tillakaratne	1
RDB Croft	not out	10
DW Headley		
D Gough		
AD Mullally		
Extras	(0b, 3lb, 1w, 6nb)	10
	49.3 overs	
Total		**208**

FoW: 59, 87, 128, 130, 187, 190

WPUJ Vaas	7.3	0	40	0
DNT Zoysa	6	0	31	0
GP Wickramasinghe	4	0	16	0
M Muralidharan	10	0	34	3
UDU Chandana	10	1	41	1
ST Jayasuriya	10	1	35	0
HP Tillakaratne	2	0	8	1

Australia

No. 283: Carlton & United Series
VENUE: Melbourne (MCG)
DATE: 15th January 1999
TOSS WON BY: England
RESULT: Australia won by 9 wickets

ENGLAND

NV Knight	c Waugh b Warne	27
AJ Stewart*+	c Gilchrist b McGrath	8
MA Ealham	b McGrath	21
N Hussain	c Warne b McGrath	47
GA Hick	c Gilchrist b Fleming	3
NH Fairbrother	c Bevan b Dale	15
AJ Hollioake	c Gilchrist b McGrath	13
RDB Croft	run out	2
D Gough	c Waugh b Bevan	15
DW Headley	not out	10
AD Mullally	c Ponting b Bevan	2
Extras	(0b, 3lb, 8w, 4nb)	15
	43.2 overs	
Total		**178**

FoW: 15, 44, 77, 85, 112, 139, 143, 145, 173, 178

GD McGrath	10	0	54	4
AC Dale	8	2	27	1
BP Julian	5	0	28	0
SK Warne	10	0	44	1
DW Fleming	7	1	13	1
MG Bevan	3.2	0	9	2

AUSTRALIA

ME Waugh	not out	83
AC Gilchrist+	b Mullally	21
RT Ponting	not out	75
DR Martyn		
DS Lehmann		
MG Bevan		
BP Julian		
SK Warne*		
DW Fleming		
AC Dale		
GD McGrath		
Extras	(0b, 2lb, 1w, 0nb)	3
	39.2 overs	
Total		**182**

FoW: 44

D Gough	10	0	48	0
AD Mullally	10	2	42	1
DW Headley	3	0	21	0
MA Ealham	6.2	0	25	0
AJ Hollioake	4	0	14	0
RDB Croft	6	0	30	0

Australia

No. 284: Carlton & United Series
VENUE: Sydney (SCG)
DATE: 17th January 1999
TOSS WON BY: England
RESULT: England won by 7 runs

ENGLAND

NV Knight	c Gilchrist b McGrath	0
AJ Stewart*+	c Gilchrist b Fleming	17
GA Hick	lbw b Fleming	108
N Hussain	b Fleming	93
NH Fairbrother	not out	17
AJ Hollioake	not out	22
MA Ealham		
RDB Croft		
D Gough		
AF Giles		
AD Mullally		
Extras	(4b, 5lb, 9w, 7nb)	25
	50 overs	
Total		**282**

FoW: 1, 39, 229, 245

GD McGrath	10	0	56	1
AC Dale	10	0	26	0
DW Fleming	10	0	64	3
DS Lehmann	4	0	20	0
SK Warne	10	0	57	0
MG Bevan	3	0	26	0
GS Blewett	3	0	24	0

AUSTRALIA

AC Gilchrist+	c Hussain b Gough	6
ME Waugh	c Croft b Hollioake	85
RT Ponting	c Hick b Gough	6
DS Lehmann	b Mullally	76
SR Waugh*	c Gough b Hollioake	0
MG Bevan	not out	45
GS Blewett	b Giles	32
SK Warne	not out	6
DW Fleming		
AC Dale		
GD McGrath		
Extras	(4b, 9lb, 5w, 1nb)	19
	50 overs	
Total		**275**

FoW: 9, 36, 151, 152, 203, 263

D Gough	10	2	40	2
AD Mullally	10	0	45	1
MA Ealham	10	0	52	0
AF Giles	5	0	40	1
AJ Hollioake	10	0	48	2
RDB Croft	5	0	37	0

Sri Lanka

No. 285: Carlton & United Series		
VENUE: Melbourne (MCG)		
DATE: 19th January 1999		
TOSS WON BY: Sri Lanka		
RESULT: England won by 7 wickets		

SRI LANKA

ST Jayasuriya	c Hussain b Gough	1
RS Kaluwit'rana+	b Gough	15
MS Atapattu	c Hick b Gough	1
HP Tillakaratne	b Gough	0
DPM Jayaw'dene	c Stewart b Hollioake	12
A Ranatunga*	run out	76
UDU Chandana	c Wells b Croft	50
GP Wick'singhe	b Hollioake	8
WPUJ Vaas	not out	11
M Muralidharan	c Hussain b Mullally	1
DNT Zoysa	run out	0
Extras	(0b, 8lb, 3w, 0nb)	11
	50 overs	
Total		**186**

FoW: 10, 19, 20, 21, 48, 140, 158, 180, 184, 186

D Gough	10	3	28	4
AD Mullally	10	2	23	1
AJ Hollioake	9	0	46	2
MA Ealham	10	0	32	0
RDB Croft	8	0	29	1
VJ Wells	3	0	20	0

ENGLAND

NV Knight	c Jayasuriya b Zoysa	31
AJ Stewart*+	c Ranatunga b Zoysa	20
GA Hick	not out	66
N Hussain	st Kaluwitharana b Muralidharan	29
JP Crawley	not out	32
AJ Hollioake		
MA Ealham		
D Gough		
AD Mullally		
RDB Croft		
VJ Wells		
Extras	(0b, 2lb, 6w, 3nb)	11
	45.2 overs	
Total		**189**

FoW: 52, 53, 115

WPUJ Vaas	10	0	39	0
GP Wickramasinghe	10	0	35	0
DNT Zoysa	6	1	22	2
M Muralidharan	10	0	40	1
UDU Chandana	7.2	0	38	0
ST Jayasuriya	2	0	13	0

Sri Lanka

No. 286: Carlton & United Series		
VENUE: Adelaide		
DATE: 23rd January 1999		
TOSS WON BY: Sri Lanka		
RESULT: Sri Lanka won by 1 wicket		

ENGLAND

NV Knight	run out	45
AJ Stewart*+	c Ranatunga b Vaas	39
GA Hick	not out	126
N Hussain	c Tillakaratne b Jayasuriya	5
NH Fairbrother	not out	78
AJ Hollioake		
VJ Wells		
MA Ealham		
RDB Croft		
D Gough		
AD Mullally		
Extras	(0b, 2lb, 4w, 3nb)	9
	50 overs	
Total		**302**

FoW: 64, 139, 148

WPUJ Vaas	10	0	76	1
GP Wickramasinghe	9	0	71	0
DPM Jayawardene	4	0	24	0
M Muralidharan	7	0	46	0
ST Jayasuriya	10	0	42	1
UDU Chandana	10	0	41	0

SRI LANKA

ST Jayasuriya	c Fairbrother b Gough	51
R Kaluwitra'na+	run out	0
MS Atapattu	c Fairbrother b Mullally	3
HP Tillakaratne	b Croft	28
DPM Jayawdene	lbw b Wells	120
A Ranatunga*	c Wells b Gough	41
WPUJ Vaas	run out	5
UDU Chandana	c Fairbrother b Wells	25
RS Mahanama	run out	13
M Muralidharan	not out	2
GP Wick'singhe	not out	2
Extras	(0b, 9lb, 4w, 0nb)	13
	49.4 overs	
Total		**303**

FoW: 3, 8, 68, 137, 223, 235, 269, 288, 298

D Gough	10	1	68	2
AD Mullally	10	0	61	1
AJ Hollioake	5	0	45	0
MA Ealham	10	1	48	0
RDB Croft	10	0	42	1
VJ Wells	4.4	0	30	2

'99

Australia

No. 287: Carlton & United Series
VENUE: Adelaide
DATE: 26th January 1999
TOSS WON BY: Australia
RESULT: Australia won by 16 runs

AUSTRALIA

ME Waugh	c Hussain b Croft	65
AC Gilchrist+	b Gough	0
GS Blewett	b Gough	4
DS Lehmann	b Croft	51
DR Martyn	not out	59
SG Law	c Stewart b Ealham	3
S Lee	c Fairbrother b Headley	41
BP Julian	b Headley	0
SK Warne*	run out	11
AC Dale		
GD McGrath		
Extras	(0b, 4lb, 0w, 1nb)	5
	50 overs	
Total		**239**

FoW: 1, 25, 118, 131, 134, 224, 224, 239

D Gough	10	0	51	2
AD Mullally	10	0	39	0
DW Headley	10	0	59	2
MA Ealham	10	1	46	1
RDB Croft	10	0	40	2

ENGLAND

NV Knight	c & b Warne	42
AJ Stewart*+	c Gilchrist b Dale	6
GA Hick	run out	109
N Hussain	lbw b McGrath	21
NH Fairbrother	b McGrath	10
JP Crawley	c & b Julian	11
MA Ealham	c & b Warne	4
RDB Croft	c & b Julian	0
D Gough	c Dale b Warne	2
DW Headley	b McGrath	2
AD Mullally	not out	0
Extras	(0b, 7lb, 2w, 7nb)	16
	48.3 overs	
Total		**223**

FoW: 18, 100, 162, 176, 193, 202, 204, 210, 223, 223

GD McGrath	9.3	0	40	3
AC Dale	10	1	35	1
S Lee	3	0	23	0
BP Julian	10	0	44	2
SK Warne	10	0	39	3
DR Martyn	3	0	15	0
SG Law	2	0	8	0
DS Lehmann	1	0	12	0

Sri Lanka

No. 288: Carlton & United Series
VENUE: Perth (WACA)
DATE: 29th January 1999
TOSS WON BY: Sri Lanka
RESULT: England won by 128 runs

ENGLAND

NV Knight	c de Silva b Perera	13
AJ Stewart*+	b Perera	0
GA Hick	lbw b Vaas	10
N Hussain	c Kaluwitharana b Perera	0
NH Fairbrother	not out	81
AJ Hollioake	run out	46
MA Ealham	c Mahanama b Muralidharan	16
RDB Croft	c Chandana b Vaas	32
D Gough	not out	0
DW Headley		
AD Mullally		
Extras	(0b, 6lb, 8w, 15nb)	29
	50 overs	
Total		**227**

FoW: 6, 30, 37, 38, 127, 166, 221

WPUJ Vaas	10	2	38	2
RL Perera	10	0	55	3
M Muralidharan	10	1	26	1
UDU Chandana	8	0	39	0
ST Jayasuriya	9	0	47	0
PA de Silva	3	0	16	0

SRI LANKA

ST Jayasuriya	c Hollioake b Ealham	40
RS Kaluwit'rana+	c Hollioake b Gough	5
MS Atapattu	c Knight b Ealham	17
PA de Silva	c Stewart b Ealham	1
DPM Jayaw'dene	c Hussain b Gough	3
A Ranatunga*	c Knight b Ealham	11
RS Mahanama	c Hussain b Ealham	6
UDU Chandana	c Gough b Headley	9
WPUJ Vaas	not out	0
M Muralidharan	b Mullally	1
RL Perera	c Hick b Mullally	0
Extras	(0b, 2lb, 1w, 3nb)	6
	33.3 overs	
Total		**99**

FoW: 15, 65, 65, 67, 71, 85, 98, 98, 99, 99

D Gough	8	2	15	2
AD Mullally	6.3	0	17	2
DW Headley	8	0	33	1
MA Ealham	10	2	32	5
RDB Croft	1	1	0	0

Sri Lanka

No. 289: Carlton & United Series
VENUE: Sydney (SCG)
DATE: 3rd February 1999
TOSS WON BY: England
RESULT: Sri Lanka won by 11 runs

SRI LANKA

A Gunawardene	st Crawley b Giles	24
R Kaluwit'rana+	c Gough b Alleyne	54
WPUJ Vaas	run out	14
PA de Silva	not out	52
A Ranatunga*	c Hussain b Gough	0
DP Jayaw'dene	c BC Hollioake b Alleyne	2
MS Atapattu	lbw b Alleyne	4
UDU Chandana	c Giles b Wells	0
HP Tillakaratne	not out	13
TT Samaraweera		
GP Wickramasinghe		
Extras	(0b, 4lb, 12w, 2nb)	18
	44 overs	
Total		**181**

FoW: 71, 99, 109, 111, 122, 133, 134

D Gough	9	2	35	1
BC Hollioake	4	0	25	0
MA Ealham	9	2	30	0
AF Giles	5	0	31	1
MW Alleyne	9	1	27	3
VJ Wells	8	1	29	1

ENGLAND

NV Knight	b Chandana	58
VJ Wells	b Samaraweera	26
GA Hick	b Samaraweera	0
N Hussain	st Kaluwit'rana b Chandana	9
JP Crawley+	c Ranatunga b Samaraweera	13
MA Ealham	c (sub) b Jayawardene	0
MW Alleyne	c Jayawardene b Chandana	18
AJ Hollioake*	st Kaluwit'rana b Chandana	13
BC Hollioake	run out	4
AF Giles	not out	10
D Gough	not out	1
Extras	(1b, 5lb, 11w, 1nb)	18
	44 overs	
Total		**170**

FoW: 53, 53, 74, 118, 119, 122, 150, 155, 162

WPUJ Vaas	6	0	24	0
PA de Silva	9	0	25	0
TT Samaraweera	9	0	34	3
UDU Chandana	9	0	35	3
HP Tillakaratne	5	0	22	1
DPM Jayawardene	6	0	24	1

Australia

No. 290: Carlton & United Series
VENUE: Sydney (SCG)
DATE: 5th February 1999
TOSS WON BY: England
RESULT: Australia won by 4 wickets

ENGLAND

NV Knight	b Dale	3
AJ Stewart*+	c Lee b Julian	25
GA Hick	c Gilchrist b Dale	4
N Hussain	c Lehmann b Waugh	31
VJ Wells	run out	39
AJ Hollioake	c Gilchrist b Bevan	19
MW Alleyne	not out	38
MA Ealham	c Bevan b Warne	33
RDB Croft	c Gilchrist b Kasprowicz	0
D Gough	not out	1
AD Mullally		
Extras	(2b, 6lb, 5w, 4nb)	17
	50 overs	
Total		**210**

FoW: 11, 26, 57, 90, 124, 143, 201, 205

MS Kasprowicz	8	0	39	1
AC Dale	10	1	28	2
BP Julian	10	0	39	1
S Lee	5	0	22	0
SK Warne	10	0	48	1
ME Waugh	3	0	11	1
MG Bevan	4	0	15	1

AUSTRALIA

ME Waugh	c Stewart b Mullally	27
AC Gilchrist+	b Mullally	19
RT Ponting	c Wells b Ealham	43
DS Lehmann	lbw b Hollioake	41
BP Julian	c Hick b Wells	25
DR Martyn	not out	38
MG Bevan	c Ealham b Croft	0
S Lee	not out	8
SK Warne*		
MS Kasprowicz		
AC Dale		
Extras	(0b, 5lb, 2w, 3nb)	10
	47 overs	
Total		**211**

FoW: 50, 51, 130, 158, 180, 181

D Gough	5	0	24	0
AD Mullally	10	1	31	2
MA Ealham	9	0	46	1
MW Alleyne	5	0	24	0
RDB Croft	10	2	43	1
AJ Hollioake	6	0	28	1
VJ Wells	2	0	10	1

Australia

AUSTRALIA

ME Waugh	c Stewart b Wells	42
AC Gilchrist+	b Gough	29
RT Ponting	c Stewart b Wells	10
DS Lehmann	c Mullally b Wells	19
DR Martyn	c Stewart b Ealham	21
MG Bevan	not out	69
S Lee	c Fairbrother b Ealham	12
BP Julian	c (sub) b Ealham	12
SK Warne*	b Gough	9
AC Dale	not out	1
GD McGrath		
Extras	(0b, 6lb, 1w, 1nb)	8
	50 overs	
Total		**232**

FoW: 40, 67, 98, 115, 139, 176, 199, 222

D Gough	10	0	43	2
AD Mullally	7	0	42	0
VJ Wells	10	2	30	3
MA Ealham	10	0	45	3
RDB Croft	5	1	28	0
AJ Hollioake	8	0	38	0

ENGLAND

NV Knight	b Dale	22
AJ Stewart*+	c Waugh b Dale	27
GA Hick	run out	42
N Hussain	st Gilchrist b Warne	58
NH Fairbrother	c Gilchrist b McGrath	8
VJ Wells	c Julian b Lee	33
AJ Hollioake	lbw b Warne	0
MA Ealham	c Gilchrist b McGrath	4
RDB Croft	not out	12
D Gough	b McGrath	0
AD Mullally	b McGrath	7
Extras	(0b, 3lb, 2w, 4nb)	9
	49.2 overs	
Total		**222**

FoW: 34, 67, 114, 131, 198, 198, 198, 204, 204, 222

GD McGrath	9.2	1	45	4
AC Dale	10	0	33	2
S Lee	7	1	29	1
SK Warne	10	0	40	2
BP Julian	4	0	28	0
DR Martyn	6	0	27	0
DS Lehmann	3	0	17	0

Australia

AUSTRALIA

AC Gilchrist+	c Knight b Croft	52
ME Waugh	c Hick b Gough	1
RT Ponting	c Fairbrother b Hollioake	37
DS Lehmann	c Hussain b Wells	71
DR Martyn	b Mullally	57
SG Law	not out	20
S Lee	not out	20
BP Julian		
SK Warne*		
AC Dale		
GD McGrath		
Extras	(0b, 10lb, 3w, 1nb)	14
	50 overs	
Total		**272**

FoW: 11, 92, 104, 216, 244

D Gough	9	1	55	1
AD Mullally	10	1	53	1
MA Ealham	6	0	41	0
VJ Wells	5	0	34	1
RDB Croft	10	0	40	1
AJ Hollioake	10	0	39	1

ENGLAND

NV Knight	run out	4
AJ Stewart*+	c Lee b Julian	32
GA Hick	c Dale b McGrath	0
N Hussain	c Gilchrist b McGrath	0
NH Fairbrother	c Gilchrist b Dale	0
VJ Wells	b Warne	23
AJ Hollioake	c Gilchrist b Dale	7
MA Ealham	b Warne	12
RDB Croft	not out	13
D Gough	c Gilchrist b Julian	6
AD Mullally	lbw b Warne	9
Extras	(0b, 0lb, 1w, 3nb)	4
	31.5 overs	
Total		**110**

FoW: 9, 10, 10, 13, 43, 50, 72, 88, 100, 110

GD McGrath	6	0	26	2
AC Dale	10	1	27	2
BP Julian	6	2	18	2
ME Waugh	4	0	23	0
SK Warne	5.5	0	16	3

Pakistan

No. 293: Coca-Cola Cup		
VENUE: Sharjah		
DATE: 7th April 1999		
TOSS WON BY: Pakistan		
RESULT: Pakistan won by 90 runs		

PAKISTAN

Saeed Anwar	c Stewart b Gough	17
Shahid Afridi	c Gough b Ealham	41
Ijaz Ahmed	c Hick b Gough	137
Inzamam-ul-Haq	c Hick b Gough	59
Wasim Akram*	c Hollioake b Flintoff	22
Moin Khan+	not out	29
Azhar Mahmood	not out	0
Yousuf Youhana		
Salim Malik		
Saqlain Mushtaq		
Shoaib Akhtar		
Extras	(1b, 10lb, 3w, 4nb)	18
	50 overs	
Total		**323**

FoW: 30, 116, 261, 280, 311

D Gough	10	1	55	3
AD Mullally	10	0	64	0
MA Ealham	10	0	52	1
RDB Croft	6	0	36	0
AJ Hollioake	5	0	30	0
GA Hick	2	0	13	0
A Flintoff	7	0	62	1

ENGLAND

NV Knight	b Shoaib	1
AJ Stewart*+	c Inzamam-ul-Haq b Shoaib	18
GA Hick	c Shoaib b Saqlain	65
GP Thorpe	c Azhar b Shoaib	18
NH Fairbrother	b Azhar	19
A Flintoff	c Shoaib b Saqlain	50
AJ Hollioake	b Shahid	18
MA Ealham	st Moin b Shahid	11
RDB Croft	c Yousuf b Shahid	4
D Gough	c (sub) b Saqlain	4
AD Mullally	not out	2
Extras	(0b, 10lb, 10w, 3nb)	23
	45.5 overs	
Total		**233**

FoW: 12, 29, 53, 91, 185, 186, 208, 221, 224, 233

Wasim Akram	7	0	33	0
Shoaib Akhtar	10	2	42	3
Saqlain Mushtaq	7.5	0	23	3
Azhar Mahmood	10	1	55	1
Shahid Afridi	9	0	53	3
Salim Malik	2	0	17	0

India

No. 294: Coca-Cola Cup		
VENUE: Sharjah		
DATE: 9th April 1999		
TOSS WON BY: India		
RESULT: India won by 20 runs		

INDIA

S Ramesh	c Stewart b Gough	60
SC Ganguly	c Stewart b Gough	7
RS Dravid	c & b Hick	16
M Azharuddin*	not out	74
AD Jadeja	c Thorpe b Flintoff	21
RR Singh	c Gough b Flintoff	11
NR Mongia+	not out	20
SB Joshi		
A Kumble		
J Srinath		
BKV Prasad		
Extras	(0b, 3lb, 3w, 7nb)	13
	50 overs	
Total		**222**

FoW: 24, 61, 120, 159, 175

D Gough	10	0	42	2
AD Mullally	10	1	32	0
ID Austin	8	0	45	0
MA Ealham	7	0	36	0
RDB Croft	5	0	22	0
GA Hick	5	0	18	1
A Flintoff	5	0	24	2

ENGLAND

NV Knight	b Prasad	11
AJ Stewart*+	b Srinath	11
GA Hick	st Dravid b Joshi	32
GP Thorpe	c (sub) b Joshi	20
NH Fairbrother	c Dravid b Jadeja	57
A Flintoff	b Prasad	32
MA Ealham	b Prasad	7
RDB Croft	c (sub) b Jadeja	9
ID Austin	run out	2
D Gough	b Jadeja	2
AD Mullally	not out	1
Extras	(3b, 8lb, 6w, 1nb)	18
	47.5 overs	
Total		**202**

FoW: 25, 25, 80, 83, 155, 169, 196, 197, 199, 202

J Srinath	9.5	1	36	1
BKV Prasad	10	2	28	3
A Kumble	9	0	31	0
SB Joshi	10	1	36	2
RR Singh	7	0	43	0
SC Ganguly	1	0	14	0
AD Jadeja	1	0	3	3

India

No. 295: Coca-Cola Cup
VENUE: Sharjah
DATE: 11th April 1999
TOSS WON BY: India
RESULT: India won by 9 runs

INDIA

S Ramesh	c Wells b Fraser	12
SC Ganguly	b Gough	2
RS Dravid	run out	63
VG Kambli	c Hick b Ealham	23
J Srinath	c & b Hick	28
AD Jadeja*	not out	74
RR Singh	c Fairbrother b Gough	18
NR Mongia+	not out	11
A Kumble		
SB Joshi		
BKV Prasad		
Extras	(0b, 2lb, 2w, 4nb)	8
	50 overs	
Total		**239**

FoW: 16, 16, 61, 120, 149, 207

D Gough	10	2	49	2
ARC Fraser	10	3	24	1
ID Austin	7	0	49	0
A Flintoff	8	0	43	0
MA Ealham	10	0	41	1
GA Hick	3	0	13	1
VJ Wells	2	0	18	0

ENGLAND

NV Knight	b Kumble	84
AJ Stewart*+	lbw b Srinath	2
VJ Wells	c & b Prasad	7
MA Ealham	run out	7
GA Hick	st Mongia b Kumble	1
GP Thorpe	st Mongia b Joshi	79
A Flintoff	run out	3
NH Fairbrother	b Prasad	16
ID Austin	b Prasad	2
D Gough	not out	20
ARC Fraser	run out	1
Extras	(1b, 4lb, 0w, 3nb)	8
	48.5 overs	
Total		**230**

FoW: 26, 41, 55, 66, 125, 131, 184, 188, 219, 230

J Srinath	9.5	0	64	1
BKV Prasad	10	2	35	3
A Kumble	10	2	28	2
RR Singh	5	0	25	0
SB Joshi	9	0	54	1
SC Ganguly	4	0	17	0
AD Jadeja	1	0	2	0

Pakistan

No. 296: Coca-Cola Cup
VENUE: Sharjah
DATE: 12th April 1999
TOSS WON BY: England
RESULT: England won by 62 runs

ENGLAND

NV Knight	c Wasim b Shoaib	26
AJ Stewart*+	c Ijaz b Shoaib	11
VJ Wells	run out	3
GA Hick	b Azhar	24
GP Thorpe	b Shoaib	62
A Flintoff	b Azhar	0
NH Fairbrother	c Wajahatullah b Ars'd Khan	25
MA Ealham	b Shoaib	36
ID Austin	run out	1
D Gough	c Shahid b Saqlain	5
ARC Fraser	not out	0
Extras	(0b, 6lb, 5w, 2nb)	13
	49.1 overs	
Total		**206**

FoW: 42, 43, 60, 86, 86, 129, 192, 193, 206, 206

Wasim Akram	7	0	25	0
Shoaib Akhtar	10	1	37	4
Saqlain Mushtaq	9.1	0	41	1
Azhar Mahmood	10	1	37	2
Arshad Khan	9	0	40	1
Shahid Afridi	4	0	20	0

PAKISTAN

Wajahatullah	c Thorpe b Fraser	31
Shahid Afridi	c Wells b Gough	3
Ijaz Ahmed	c Knight b Fraser	16
Inzamam-ul-Haq	lbw b Fraser	5
Salim Malik	not out	47
Azhar Mahmood	c Wells b Ealham	13
Moin Khan+	b Flintoff	23
Wasim Akram*	lbw b Ealham	2
Saqlain Mushtaq	b Ealham	0
Arshad Khan	lbw b Ealham	0
Shoaib Akhtar	c Wells b Flintoff	0
Extras	(0b, 1lb, 2w, 1nb)	4
	40.2 overs	
Total		**144**

FoW: 12, 34, 55, 72, 91, 138, 141, 143, 143, 144

D Gough	8	1	39	1
ARC Fraser	10	2	32	3
ID Austin	8	0	21	0
MA Ealham	10	0	30	4
VJ Wells	2	0	18	0
A Flintoff	2.2	0	3	2

Sri Lanka

SRI LANKA

ST Jayasuriya	c Hick b Mullally	29
RS Mahanama	c Hick b Mullally	16
MS Atapattu	c Thorpe b Austin	3
HP Tillakaratne	c Stewart b Ealham	0
PA de Silva	c Thorpe b Mullally	0
A Ranatunga*	c Hussain b Ealham	32
R Kaluwit'rana+	c Stewart b Mullally	57
WPUJ Vaas	not out	12
KEA Upashantha	c Thorpe b Hollioake	11
GP Wick'singhe	c Stewart b Austin	11
M Muralidharan	b Gough	12
Extras	(0b, 9lb, 9w, 3nb)	21
	48.4 overs	
Total		**204**

FoW: 42, 50, 63, 63, 65, 149, 155, 174, 190, 204

D Gough	8.4	0	50	1
ID Austin	9	1	25	2
AD Mullally	10	1	37	4
MA Ealham	10	0	31	2
A Flintoff	2	0	12	0
GA Hick	3	0	19	0
AJ Hollioake	6	1	21	1

ENGLAND

N Hussain	st Kaluwitharana b Muralidharan	14
AJ Stewart*+	c Kaluwitharana b Vaas	88
GA Hick	not out	73
GP Thorpe	not out	13
NH Fairbrother		
A Flintoff		
AJ Hollioake		
MA Ealham		
ID Austin		
D Gough		
AD Mullally		
Extras	(0b, 6lb, 12w, 1nb)	19
	46.5 overs	
Total		**207**

FoW: 50, 175

WPUJ Vaas	10	2	27	1
GP Wickramasinghe	10	0	41	0
KEA Upashantha	8	0	38	0
M Muralidharan	10	0	33	1
ST Jayasuriya	7.5	0	55	0
PA de Silva	1	0	7	0

Kenya

KENYA

K Otieno+	c Thorpe b Austin	0
Ravindu Shah	c Stewart b Gough	46
S Tikolo	c Gough b Ealham	71
M Odumbe	b Gough	6
H Modi	run out	5
A Vader	b Croft	6
T Odoyo	not out	34
Asif Karim*	b Ealham	9
A Suji	b Gough	4
M Sheikh	b Gough	7
M Suji	run out	0
Extras	(1b, 5lb, 6w, 3nb)	15
	49.4 overs	
Total		**203**

FoW: 7, 107, 115, 130, 142, 150, 181, 186, 202, 203

D Gough	10	1	34	4
ID Austin	9.4	0	41	1
AD Mullally	10	0	41	0
MA Ealham	10	0	49	2
RDB Croft	10	1	32	1

ENGLAND

N Hussain	not out	88
AJ Stewart*+	b Odoyo	23
GA Hick	not out	61
GP Thorpe		
NH Fairbrother		
A Flintoff		
MA Ealham		
RDB Croft		
ID Austin		
D Gough		
AD Mullally		
Extras	(5b, 6lb, 13w, 8nb)	32
	39 overs	
Total		**204**

FoW: 45

M Suji	9	0	46	0
A Suji	3	0	6	0
T Odoyo	10	0	65	1
Asif Karim	8	0	39	0
M Odumbe	6	1	23	0
M Sheikh	3	0	14	0

South Africa

No. 299: World Cup
VENUE: The Oval
DATE: 22nd May 1999
TOSS WON BY: England
RESULT: South Africa won by 122 runs

Zimbabwe

No. 300: World Cup
VENUE: Trent Bridge
DATE: 25th May 1999
TOSS WON BY: England
RESULT: England won by 7 wickets

SOUTH AFRICA

G Kirsten	c Stewart b Ealham	45
HH Gibbs	c Hick b Ealham	60
JH Kallis	b Mullally	0
DJ Cullinan	c Fraser b Mullally	10
WJ Cronje*	c Stewart b Flintoff	16
JN Rhodes	c (sub) b Gough	18
L Klusener	not out	48
SM Pollock	b Gough	0
MV Boucher+	not out	16
S Elworthy		
AA Donald		
Extras	(0b, 7lb, 5w, 0nb)	12
	50 overs	
Total		**225**

FoW: 111, 112, 112, 127, 146, 168, 168

D Gough	10	1	33	2
ARC Fraser	10	0	54	0
AD Mullally	10	1	28	2
RDB Croft	2	0	13	0
MA Ealham	10	2	48	2
A Flintoff	8	0	42	1

ENGLAND

N Hussain	c Boucher b Kallis	2
AJ Stewart*+	lbw b Kallis	0
GA Hick	c Gibbs b Elworthy	21
GP Thorpe	lbw b Donald	14
NH Fairbrother	lbw b Donald	21
A Flintoff	c Rhodes b Donald	0
MA Ealham	c Cullinan b Donald	5
RDB Croft	c Rhodes b Klusener	12
D Gough	c Cronje b Elworthy	10
ARC Fraser	c Kirsten b Pollock	3
AD Mullally	not out	1
Extras	(0b, 4lb, 9w, 1nb)	14
	41 overs	
Total		**103**

FoW: 2, 6, 39, 44, 45, 60, 78, 97, 99, 103

JH Kallis	8	0	29	2
SM Pollock	9	3	13	1
S Elworthy	10	3	24	2
AA Donald	8	1	17	4
L Klusener	6	0	16	1

ZIMBABWE

NC Johnson	b Gough	6
GW Flower	c Thorpe b Ealham	35
PA Strang	c Hick b Mullally	0
MW Goodwin	c Thorpe b Mullally	4
A Flower+	run out	10
ADR Campbell*	c Stewart b Fraser	24
GJ Whittall	lbw b Ealham	28
SV Carlisle	c Fraser b Gough	14
HH Streak	not out	11
HK Olonga	not out	1
M Mbangwa		
Extras	(0b, 16lb, 17w, 1nb)	34
	50 overs	
Total		**167**

FoW: 21, 29, 47, 79, 86, 124, 141, 159

D Gough	10	2	24	2
ARC Fraser	10	0	27	1
AD Mullally	10	4	16	2
MA Ealham	10	1	35	2
A Flintoff	3	0	14	0
AJ Hollioake	7	0	35	0

ENGLAND

N Hussain	not out	57
AJ Stewart*+	c Goodwin b Johnson	12
GA Hick	c A Flower b Mbangwa	4
GP Thorpe	c Campbell b Mbangwa	62
NH Fairbrother	not out	7
A Flintoff		
AJ Hollioake		
MA Ealham		
D Gough		
ARC Fraser		
AD Mullally		
Extras	(0b, 3lb, 16w, 7nb)	26
	38.3 overs	
Total		**168**

FoW: 21, 36, 159

NC Johnson	7	2	20	1
HH Streak	8	0	37	0
M Mbangwa	7	1	28	2
GJ Whittall	4	0	23	0
HK Olonga	3	0	27	0
PA Strang	9.3	1	30	0

India

No. 301:	World Cup	
VENUE:	Edgbaston	
DATE:	29th May 1999	
TOSS WON BY:	England	
RESULT:	India won by 63 runs	

INDIA

SC Ganguly	run out	40
S Ramesh	c Hick b Mullally	20
RS Dravid	c Ealham b Flintoff	53
SR Tendulkar	c Hick b Ealham	22
M Azharuddin*	c Hussain b Ealham	26
AD Jadeja	c Fraser b Gough	39
NR Mongia+	b Mullally	2
J Srinath	b Gough	1
A Kumble	not out	6
BKV Prasad	not out	2
DS Mohanty		
Extras	(0b, 7lb, 10w, 4nb)	21
	50 overs	
Total		**232**

FoW: 49, 93, 139, 174, 188, 209, 210, 228

D Gough	10	0	51	2
ARC Fraser	10	2	30	0
AD Mullally	10	0	54	2
MA Ealham	10	2	28	2
A Flintoff	5	0	28	1
AJ Hollioake	5	0	34	0

ENGLAND

N Hussain	b Ganguly	33
AJ Stewart*+	c Azharuddin b Mohanty	2
GA Hick	b Mohanty	0
GP Thorpe	lbw b Srinath	36
NH Fairbrother	c Mongia b Ganguly	30
A Flintoff	lbw b Kumble	15
AJ Hollioake	lbw b Kumble	6
MA Ealham	c Azharuddin b Ganguly	0
D Gough	c Kumble b Prasad	19
ARC Fraser	not out	15
AD Mullally	b Srinath	0
Extras	(4b, 3lb, 5w, 1nb)	13
	45.2 overs	
Total		**169**

FoW: 12, 13, 72, 81, 118, 130, 131, 132, 161, 169

J Srinath	8.2	3	25	2
DS Mohanty	10	0	54	2
BKV Prasad	9	1	25	1
SC Ganguly	8	0	27	3
A Kumble	10	1	30	2

South Africa

No. 302:	Standard Bank Triangular (2)	
VENUE:	Bloemfontein (Goodyear Park)	
DATE:	23 January 2000	
TOSS WON BY:	South Africa	
RESULT:	England won by 9 wickets	

SOUTH AFRICA

G Kirsten	c Read b Gough	1
HH Gibbs	lbw b Caddick	9
JH Kallis	b Gough	57
DM Benkenstein	b Gough	2
WJ Cronje*	c Read b Gough	2
MV Boucher+	c Gough b White	11
PC Strydom	c Caddick b Ealham	34
L Klusener	c Caddick b Hick	27
SM Pollock	not out	19
N Boje	c Adams b White	2
DJ Terbrugge	b White	5
Extras	(4b, 5lb, 4w, 2nb)	15
	50 overs	
Total		**184**

FoW: 3, 18, 21, 23, 53, 122, 137, 172, 176, 184

Gough	10	1	29	4
Caddick	10	1	23	1
White	8.5	0	45	3
Swann	5	0	24	0
Ealham	10	1	22	1
Hick	6	0	32	1

ENGLAND

N Hussain*	c Gibbs b Boje	85
NV Knight	not out	71
GA Hick	not out	12
Extras	(10lb, 6w, 1nb)	17
	39.3 overs	
Total		**185**

FoW: 1-165

Pollock	8	2	22	0
Terbrugge	6	1	23	0
Kallis	4	0	34	0
Boje	10	1	47	1
Strydom	2	0	7	0
Klusener	5	0	25	0
Cronje	4.3	0	17	0

South Africa

No. 302: Standard Bank Triangular (3)
VENUE: Cape Town (Newlands) Day/Night
DATE: 26 January 2000
TOSS WON BY: South Africa
RESULT: South Africa won by 1 run

SOUTH AFRICA

G Kirsten	lbw b Gough	13
HH Gibbs	c & b Gough	13
JH Kallis	run out (Ealham)	43
JN Rhodes	c Caddick b White	14
WJ Cronje*	c Read b Gough	39
L Klusener	not out	42
PC Strydom	b Caddick	2
MV Boucher+	c Ealham b Alleyne	15
SM Pollock	not out	13
Extras	(0b, 3lb, 7w, 0nb)	10
	50 overs	
Total		**204**

FoW: 26, 32, 71, 109, 147, 153, 182

Gough	10	0	36	3
Caddick	10	0	29	1
White	10	0	36	1
Ealham	6	0	33	0
Alleyne	10	0	42	1
Hick	4	0	25	0

ENGLAND

N Hussain*	c Boucher b Hayward	1
NV Knight	c Boucher b Williams	36
GA Hick	lbw b Kallis	25
VS Solanki	c Kallis b Klusener	7
CJ Adams	c Pollock b Klusener	42
MW Alleyne	c Boucher b Hayward	12
C White	c Rhodes b Williams	6
MA Ealham	c Rhodes b Pollock	25
CMW Read+	not out	26
AR Caddick	b Kallis	0
D Gough	not out	3
Extras	(0b, 5lb, 9w, 6nb)	20
	50 overs	
Total		**203**

FoW: 4, 72, 72, 86, 121, 138, 15, 191, 197

Pollock	10	0	48	1
Hayward	10	0	39	2
Williams	10	0	36	2
Kallis	10	0	41	2
Klusener	10	0	34	2

Zimbabwe

No. 304: Standard Bank Triangular (4)
VENUE: Cape Town (Newlands) Day/Night
DATE: 28 January 2000 (day/night)
TOSS WON BY: Zimbabwe
RESULT: Zimbabwe won by 104 runs

ZIMBABWE

NC Johnson	c Hick b Ealham	97
GW Flower	c Hick b Alleyne	23
ADR Campbell	run out (Alleyne)	0
MW Goodwin	c Read b Hick	21
A Flower*+	c Solanki b Caddick	20
SV Carlisle	c Alleyne b Gough	2
GJ Whittall	not out	21
HH Streak	b White	18
JA Rennie	not out	1
Extras	(0b, 4lb, 3w, 1nb)	8
	50 overs	
Total		**211**

FoW: 56, 56, 111, 151, 163, 181, 210

Gough	10	1	42	1
Caddick	10	1	30	1
Ealham	9	0	35	1
Alleyne	7	0	30	1
Hick	4	0	25	1
White	10	0	45	1

ENGLAND

N Hussain*	b Olonga	15
NV Knight	lbw b Olonga	5
GA Hick	c A Flower b Olonga	0
VS Solanki	c Goodwin b Olonga	14
CJ Adams	c Johnson b Olonga	1
MW Alleyne	c A Flower b Rennie	4
C White	c Campbell b Johnson	18
MA Ealham	run out (Streak)	2
CMW Read+	c GJ Whittall b Olonga	23
D Gough	c Carlisle b AR Whittall	3
AR Caddick	not out	4
Extras	(4b, 1lb, 13w, 0nb)	18
	34.2 overs	
Total		**107**

FoW: 11, 1, 37, 42, 47, 47, 63, 73, 91, 107

Olonga	8.2	3	19	6
Rennie	8	1	22	1
Streak	6	0	24	0
Johnson	4	0	12	1
GJ Whittall	5	0	17	0
AR Whittall	3	0	8	1

Zimbabwe

ZIMBABWE

NC Johnson	c Hussain b Caddick	11
GW Flower	lbw b Ealham	28
ADR Campbell	c Solanki b Alleyne	28
MW Goodwin	lbw b Ealham	15
A Flower*+	lbw b Ealham	8
SV Carlisle	lbw b Ealham	2
GJ Whittall	lbw b Ealham	0
HH Streak	not out	35
JA Rennie	c Hussain b Gough	23
HK Olonga	b Gough	0
Extras	(0b, 4lb, 6w, 1nb)	11
	50 overs	
Total		**161**

FoW: 115, 71, 73, 92, 96, 97, 98, 160, 161

Gough	10	2	31	2
Caddick	10	2	21	1
White	10	1	44	0
Alleyne	10	0	46	1
Ealham	10	3	15	5

ENGLAND

N Hussain*	c Rennie b Olonga	64
NV Knight	not out	72
GA Hick	b Streak	2
VS Solanki	not out	16
Extras	(4b, 1lb, 2w, 1nb)	8
	32.1 overs	
Total		**162**

FoW: 128, 140

Olonga	9	0	52	1
Rennie	7	0	27	0
Streak	7.1	0	26	1
AR Whittall	4	1	25	0
GJ Whittall	5	0	27	0

South Africa

ENGLAND

N Hussain*	c Boucher b Pollock	10
NV Knight	c & b Strydom	64
GA Hick	c Koen b Hayward	11
VS Solanki	c Pollock b Kallis	10
DL Maddy	c Strydom b Cronje	22
MW Alleyne	c Kallis b Pollock	53
MA Ealham	not out	29
CMW Read+	not out	10
Extras	(0b, 4lb, 13w, 5nb)	22
	50 overs	
Total		**231**

FoW: 22, 35, 61, 105, 144, 218

Pollock	10	0	36	2
Hayward	8	0	46	1
Cronje	10	0	25	1
Kallis	8	0	51	1
Klusener	9	0	51	0
Strydom	5	0	18	1

SOUTH AFRICA

HH Gibbs	c Read b Mullally	14
LJ Koen	c Read b Ealham	28
MV Boucher+	c Knight b Caddick	5
JH Kallis	c Read b Alleyne	36
ND McKenzie	run out (Solanki)	37
WJ Cronje*	c Ealham b Alleyne	10
JN Rhodes	c Alleyne b Gough	42
L Klusener	b Alleyne	26
PC Strydom	not out	7
SM Pollock	not out	9
Extras	(0b, 5lb, 7w, 7nb)	19
	49.4 overs	
Total		**233**

FoW: 36, 46, 79, 110, 126, 163, 201, 221

Gough	10	0	46	1
Caddick	10	0	50	1
Mullally	10	1	24	1
Ealham	9.4	0	53	1
Alleyne	10	0	55	3

Zimbabwe

No. 307: Standard Bank Triangular (9)
VENUE: Centurion (Supersport Park)
DATE: 9 February 2000 Day/Night
TOSS WON BY: No Toss
RESULT: Match abandoned without a ball
bowled

South Africa

No. 308: Standard Bank Triangular Final
VENUE Johannesburg (New Wanderers)
DATE: 13 February 2000 Day/Night
TOSS WON BY: England
RESULT: South Africa won by 38 runs

South Africa

HH Gibbs	c Knight b Gough	8
ND McKenzie	b Caddick	4
JH Kallis	b Gough	0
WJ Cronje*	c Knight b Mullally	56
JN Rhodes	c Hick b Caddick	5
SM Pollock	c White b Caddick	0
MV Boucher+	c Hick b Alleyne	36
L Klusener	c Hussain b Gough	10
PC Strydom	c Maddy b Caddick	3
S Elworthy	not out	8
HS Williams	run out (Gough)	7
Extras	(0b, 5lb, 6w, 1nb)	12
	45 overs	
Total		**149**

FoW: 14, 14, 14, 21, 21, 95, 129, 132, 134, 149

Caddick	9	1	19	4
Gough	9	2	18	3
Mullally	9	3	22	1
White	7	0	38	0
Ealham	5	0	24	0
Alleyne	6	0	23	1

England

N Hussain*	c Boucher b Pollock	8
NV Knight	c Boucher b Pollock	10
GA Hick	c Kallis b Pollock	12
DL Maddy	c Kallis b Pollock	0
MW Alleyne	c Cronje b Pollock	6
C White	b Klusener	16
MA Ealham	c Boucher b Klusener	4
CMW Read+	lbw b Williams	9
AR Caddick	c Boucher b Kallis	7
D Gough	c Boucher b Kallis	1
AD Mullally	not out	14
Extras	(0b, 1lb, 21w , 2nb)	24
	38 overs	
Total		**111**

FoW: 16, 22, 23, 41, 45, 64, 72, 83,87, 111

Pollock	9	1	20	5
Kallis	8	0	25	2
Elworthy	6	0	19	0
Williams	6	0	18	1
Klusener	9	1	28	2

No. 309: 1st One-Day International
VENUE Bulawayo (Queens Sports Club)
DATE: 16 February 2000
TOSS WON BY: Zimbabwe
RESULT: England won by 5 wickets
(D/L method)

ZIMBABWE

(48 overs maximum)

NC Johnson	b Mullally	21
ADR Campbell	run out (White)	29
SV Carlisle	c Hussain b White	30
MW Goodwin	lbw b White	2
A Flower*+	c Knight b Mullally	19
GW Flower	not out	55
CB Wishart	c Read b Mullally	6
HH Streak	c Hussain b White	16
DP Viljoen	not out	0
Extras	(0b, 8lb, 5w, 3nb)	16
	48 overs	
Total		**194**

FoW: 43, 82, 87, 93, 124, 160, 192

Caddick	10	0	36	0
Gough	10	2	47	0
Mullally	10	1	37	3
Ealham	9	0	37	0
White	9	1	29	3

ENGLAND

(48 overs maximum)

N Hussain*	b Olonga	3
NV Knight	b Streak	20
GA Hick	not out	87
DL Maddy	c Streak b GW Flower	24
VS Solanki	b GW Flower	11
C White	c Olonga b GW Flower	0
MA Ealham	not out	36
Extras	(0b, 1b, 6lb, 11w)	18
	46.3 overs	
Total		**199**

FoW: 13, 37, 90, 107, 109

Olonga	8.3	1	47	1
Johnson	6	0	25	0
Streak	9	2	39	1
Brent	8	0	30	0
GW Flower	10	1	27	3
Viljoen	5	0	24	0

No. 310: 2nd One-Day International
VENUE Bulawayo (Queens Sports Club)
DATE: 18 February 2000
TOSS WON BY: England
RESULT: England won by 1 wicket

ZIMBABWE

(48 overs maximum)

NC Johnson	c Hussain b White	30
ADR Campbell	c Hick b Caddick	6
SV Carlisle	c Read b White	31
MW Goodwin	c Hick b Mullally	21
A Flower*+	c Read b White	3
GW Flower	b White	2
DP Viljoen	c Read b White	2
HH Streak	c Hick b Caddick	1
JA Rennie	not out	18
GB Brent	b Ealham	10
HK Olonga	b Ealham	0
Extras	(0b, 0lb, 1w, 6nb)	7
	47.3 overs	
Total		**131**

FoW: 16, 60, 76, 80, 84, 98, 98, 102, 131, 131

Caddick	10	4	24	2
Gough	9	1	31	0
Mullally	10	0	28	1
White	10	1	21	5
Ealham	8.3	0	27	2

ENGLAND

(48 overs maximum)

N Hussain*	lbw b Streak	2
NV Knight	c A Flower b Streak	0
GA Hick	c A Flower b Streak	13
DL Maddy	c Olonga b Brent	13
VS Solanki	c Streak b GW Flower	24
C White	c Goodwin b Olonga	26
MA Ealham	lbw b Brent	32
CMW Read+	c sub (CB Wishart) b Brent	0
AR Caddick	b Viljoen	0
D Gough	not out	4
AD Mullally	not out	5
Extras	(0b, 5lb, 9w, 1nb)	15
	44.2 overs	
Total		**134**

FoW: 2, 6, 30, 58, 73, 120, 124, 125, 125

Streak	10	1	26	3
Rennie	5	0	17	0
Olonga	10	1	29	1
Brent	5.2	0	29	3
GW Flower	10	2	18	1
Viljoen	4	1	10	1

Zimbabwe

No. 311: 3rd One-Day International	
VENUE: Harare Sports Club	
DATE: 20 February 2000	
TOSS WON BY: Zimbabwe	
RESULT: England won by 85 runs	

No. 312: 4th One-Day International	
VENUE: Harare Sports Club	
DATE: 23 February 2000	
TOSS WON BY: No Toss	
RESULT: Match abandoned without a ball bowled	

ENGLAND

N Hussain*	c Campbell b Strang	1
NV Knight	c Strang b Olonga	26
GA Hick	run out (Goodwin)	80
DL Maddy	c Brent b Viljoen	53
VS Solanki	c Carlisle b Brent	14
C White	not out	27
MA Ealham	b Viljoen	0
CMW Read+	c & b Viljoen	2
AR Caddick	not out	21
Extras	(0b, 4lb, 17w, 3nb)	24
	50 overs	
Total		**248**

FoW: 4, 85 149, 171, 198, 198, 208

Streak	8	0	44	0
Strang	10	0	34	1
Johnson	2	0	16	0
Olonga	6	1	44	1
GW Flower	10	0	37	0
Brent	7	0	42	1
Viljoen	6	0	20	3
Campbell	1	0	7	0

ZIMBABWE

NC Johnson	b Gough	7
ADR Campbell	c White b Gough	2
SV Carlisle	run out (Knight)	41
MW Goodwin	c Mullally b Hick	28
A Flower*+	st Read b Hick	21
GW Flower	st Read b Hick	5
DP Viljoen	c Ealham b Hick	4
HH Streak	c Hussain b Mullally	7
BC Strang	c Mullally b Hick	13
GB Brent	not out	13
HK Olonga	c Knight b White	11
Extras	(0b, 7lb, 3w, 1nb)	11
	46.5 overs	
Total		**163**

FoW: 5, 16, 83, 91, 104, 112, 124, 126, 146, 163

Caddick	8	4	7	0
Gough	6	2	10	2
Mullally	10	1	43	1
White	5.5	0	35	1
Ealham	7	0	28	0
Hick	10	2	33	5

ALSO AVAILABLE . . .

Virgin

THE DON

THE DEFINITIVE BIOGRAPHY OF SIR DONALD BRADMAN

£16.99 PAPERBACK
ISBN 0 7535 0408 1

'An unsurpassed record
of a phenomenal figure'
E.W. Swanton